REGIMENTALLY CLASSIFIED LIST
OF THE OFFICERS INCLUDED IN VOLUME I.

(The biographies of Officers with composite surnames will be found under the initial letter of the last name.)

COMMANDS AND STAFF

Major-General Hamilton, H. I. W., *late* Royal West Surrey Regiment, Divisional Commander.

Brigadier-General Findlay, N. D., Royal Artillery, R.A. Divisional Commander.

Brigadier-General Fitzclarence, C., *late* Irish Guards, Commanding 1st Guards Brigade.

Colonel Boileau, F. R. F., *late* Royal Engineers, G.S.O. 1st Grade.

,, Kerr, F. W., *late* Gordon Highlanders, G.S.O. 1st Grade.

,, Marker, R. J., *late* Coldstream Guards, A.A. and Q.M.G.

Major Cawley, J. S., 20th Hussars, Brigade-Major 1st Cavalry Brigade.

,, Chenevix-Trench, F. M., Royal Field Artillery, Brigade-Major R.A.

,, Green, A. D., Worcestershire Regiment, Brigade-Major.

,, Paley, G., Rifle Brigade, G.S.O. 2nd Grade.

,, *(temp.* Lieutenant-Colonel) Percival A. J.-B., Northumberland Fusiliers, G.S.O. 2nd Grade.

,, Young, A., 1st Gurkha Rifles, Brigade-Major.

Captain Barker, R. V., Royal Welsh Fusiliers, Staff Captain 22nd Brigade, VIIth Division.

,, Giffard, R., Royal Field Artillery, Aide-de-Camp.

,, Hawley, C. F., King's Royal Rifle Corps, G.S.O. 3rd Grade.

,, James, G. M., East Kent Regiment, Brigade-Major, 22nd Infantry Brigade, VIIth Division.

,, Jenkinson, J. B., Rifle Brigade, Brigade-Major, 3rd Infantry Brigade, Ist Division.

,, Neill, N., 13th Hussars, Brigade-Major, 6th Cavalry Brigade.

,, Stevens, R. W. M., Royal Irish Rifles, Brigade-Major, 9th Infantry Brigade.

,, Stewart, B., West Kent Yeomanry, attd. Intelligence Corps.

2nd Lt. Sang, A., *(temp.)* Intelligence Corps.

,, Seabrook, J. H., *(temp.)* Intelligence Corps, attd. Royal Engineers.

,, Smith, J. H. M., *(temp.)* Intelligence Corps, attd. 9th (Queen's Royal) Lancers.

ROYAL FLYING CORPS

Captain Crean, T., Northants. Regt.

,, Picton-Warlow, W., Welsh Regiment.

Lieut. Bayly, C. G. G., R.E.

2nd Lt. Perry, E. W. C.

,, Waterfall, V., East Yorkshire Regt.

CAVALRY
1st Life Guards

Lt.-Col. Cook, E. B.

Major Cavendish, Lord J. S.

Lieut. Levinge, Sir R. W., Bart.

2nd Lt. St. George, H. A. B.

2nd Life Guards

Major Dawnay, Hon. H.

Captain O'Neill, Hon. A. E. B.

,, Pemberton, F. P. C.

Lieut. Duff, Sir R. G. V., Bart., (attd.), Reserve of Officers.

,, Smith, A. G. M.

2nd Lt. Petersen, W. S.

Royal Horse Guards

Lt.-Col. Wilson, G. C.

Lieut. Heath, V. P.

,, Naylor-Leyland, G. V.

,, Worsley, C. S. P. Lord

2nd Lt. Lambton, Hon. F.

1st (King's) Dragoon Guards

Lieut. Hawkins, L. H.

,, White, L. W.

2nd Dragoon Guards (Queen's Bays)

Major Browning, J. A.

Captain Springfield, P. O.

Lieut. de Crespigny, C. N. C.

,, McGrath, N. G. S.

2nd Lt. Paul, G.

3rd (Prince of Wales's) Dragoon Guards

Captain Hodgkinson, J. F., Special Reserve.
,, Sadler, G. G.
,, Wright, E.
Lieut. Chapman, E. W.
,, Talbot, H. R.

4th (Royal Irish) Dragoon Guards

Captain Fitzgerald, G. H.
,, Oldrey, R. J. B., Adjutant.
Lieut. Elmslie, K. W., Special Reserve.
,, Holman, J.
,, Ramsay, N. (attd.), Reserve of Officers.
2nd Lt. Powell, H. O., Special Reserve.

5th (Princess Charlotte of Wales's) Dragoon Guards

Lt.-Col. Ansell, G. K.
Captain Crawshay, M.
,, Partridge, R. C.
2nd Lt. Patteson, J. D.

6th Dragoon Guards (Carabiniers)

Major Home, W. G.
,, Watson, W. E.
Captain Gwyer, A. G.

7th (Princess Royal's) Dragoon Guards

Lt.-Col. Lemprière, H. A.

1st (Royal) Dragoons

Major Dorington, T. P. G.
,, Mercer-Nairne, Lord C. G. F.
Captain Charrington, A. C.
2nd Lt. Burn, A. H. R.

2nd Dragoons (Royal Scots Greys)

Major Swetenham, F.
2nd Lt. Baillie, Sir G. G. S., Bart.

3rd (King's Own) Hussars

Captain Sherlock, G. L., (empl. Nigeria Regiment, West African Frontier Force).
Lieut. Leechman, C. B.
2nd Lt. Gath, C. H.

4th (Queen's Own) Hussars

Lt.-Col. Hogg, I. G.
Major Gatacre, J. K.
Lieut. Levita, F. E.
,, Lonsdale, J. R. Mc.
,, North, K. C.
,, Schuster, A. F., Special Reserve.
,, Sword, J. H.

5th (Royal Irish) Lancers

Lieut. Juler, G. C.
,, Robinson, E. W.
,, Wordsworth, J. L.

6th (Inniskilling) Dragoons

Captain Herringham, G. W.

9th (Queen's Royal) Lancers

Major Abadie, E. H. E.
,, Brooke, V. R.
Captain Lucas-Tooth, D. K. L.
Lieut. Allfrey F. de V. B.
2nd Lt. Garstin, C. W. N.
,, Harvey, D. L.
,, Taylor-Whitehead, G. E.

Xth (Prince of Wales's Own Royal) Hussars

Major Cadogan, Hon. W. G. S.
Captain Annesley, Hon. A.
,, Peto, C. H.
,, Rose, Sir, F. S., Bart.
Lieut. Drake, R. F.
,, Turnor, C. R.

11th (Prince Albert's Own) Hussars

Captain Halliday, J. A.
Lieut. Ainsworth, J. S.
,, Marshall, G. G.
2nd Lt. de Gunzburg, Baron A.
,, Lumley, R. J.

12th (Prince of Wales's Royal) Lancers

Major Crawley, E.
Captain Michell, J. C.
,, Murray, F. W. S.
Lieut. Eden, J.
,, Leatham, E. H.
2nd Lt. Wroughton, M. C.

13th Hussars

Captain Neill, N., Staff.
Lieut. Lawson-Smith, T. E.

15th (The King's) Hussars

Captain Walker, O. B.
Lieut. Hardinge, Hon. E. C.
,, Hoare, C. M.
,, Osborne, B.
,, Tylee, J. M.
,, Whittle, C. H. S.

16th (The Queen's) Lancers

Captain Dixon, C. M., Special Reserve.
,, Macarthur-Onslow, A. W.
2nd Lt. Macneill W. M., Special Reserve.

18th (Queen Mary's Own) Hussars

Lieut. Denroche-Smith, A. J.
2nd Lt. Nicholson, A. K.

19th (Queen Alexandra's Own Royal) Hussars

Major McClure, C. R.
2nd Lt. Murray, E. D.

20th Hussars

Major Cawley, J. S., Staff.
Captain Christy, S. H., Reserve of Officers.
Lieut. Soames, H. M.
2nd Lt. Carew, F. L.

21st (Empress of India's) Lancers

Lieut.   Payne Gallwey, P. F.

Special Reserve
North Irish Horse

Lieut.   Combe, S. B.

YEOMANRY
(Territorial Force)
Buckinghamshire

Captain   Grenfell, R. N., attd. 9th Lancers.

West Kent

Captain   Stewart, B., attd. Intelligence Corps.

Leicestershire

Captain   Blackett, W. S. B.

Lincolnshire

Captain   Wyndham, Hon. W. R., attd. 1st Life
          Guards.

2nd County of London

Captain   Norwood, J., attd. 5th Dragoon Guards.

1st Lovat's Scouts

Captain   Maxwell, A. E., (temp.) Lieut.-Col. Royal
          Marines.

Oxfordshire

Captain   Molloy, B. C. B.

North Somerset

Lieut.   Davey, J. S.
  ,,   Liebert, F. A. C.

Warwickshire

Captain   Guernsey, H. G., Lord, Reserve of Officers,
          attd. Irish Guards.

ROYAL REGIMENT OF ARTILLERY
Royal Horse and Royal Field Artillery

Major   Baillie, G.
  ,,   Bolster, G. E.
  ,,   Chenevix-Trench, F. M., Staff.
  ,,   England, R.
  ,,   Holland, C. S.
  ,,   Johnstone, J. H. W.
  ,,   Mackworth, F. J. A.
  ,,   Maidlow, J. S.
  ,,   Phillips, E. H.
  ,,   Smith-Rewse, H. B. W.
  ,,   Stapylton, G. J. C.
  ,,   Wynter, H. T.
Captain   Barber-Starkey, W. H. J.
  ,,   Battersby, C. F. P.
  ,,   Blathwayt, G. W.
  ,,   Blount, G. H. R., Adjutant XXVth Brigade.

Captain   Bradbury, E. K.
  ,,   Browning, C. H.
  ,,   Buckle, H.
  ,,   Charles, A. A. MacG.
  ,,   Cree, W. C. H.
  ,,   Fitze, G. G.
  ,,   Furse, G. A.
  ,,   Giffard, R., Staff.
  ,,   Grayson, A.D.H. (attd., Reserve of Officers.)
  ,,   Jones, R. A.
  ,,   Kerr, W. C. R.
  ,,   O'Brien, A. U. M.
  ,,   Woodhouse, A. J.
Lieut.   Bowles, J. A., Adjutant XXVIIIth Brigade.
  ,,   Campbell, J. D.
  ,,   Clarke, J. E. L.
  ,,   Davies, H. L.
  ,,   Dennis, J. O. C.
  ,,   Edwards, F. G. de B.
  ,,   Forsyth, J. C.
  ,,   Gough, J. B.
  ,,   Hosking, C. G.
  ,,   Mundy, L. F. H.
  ,,   Nixon, G. F.
  ,,   Parker, R. E.
  ,,   Pollard, G. B.
  ,,   Simson, R. F.
  ,,   Talbot, E. L.
  ,,   Welch, W. G. F.
  ,,   Wissmann, J. R.
2nd Lt.   Brown, J. W.
  ,,   Coghlan, W. H.
  ,,   Coxe, A. N.
  ,,   Farmer, J. D. H.
  ,,   Fletcher, R. W.
  ,,   Gosset, W. B.
  ,,   Harman, J. B.
  ,,   Morse, G. S.
  ,,   Owen, N. M.
  ,,   Pilliner, R. C. L.
  ,,   Rogers, C. H.
  ,,   Tucker, J. A.
  ,,   Wright, N. J. R.

Royal Garrison Artillery

Major   Chrystie, J.
  ,,   Massie, J. H.
Captain   Dodgson, D. S.
  ,,   Pierson, C. F. L.
  ,,   Shedden, G. P.
  ,,   Smyth, R. A. N.
Lieut.   Caldecott, J. L.
2nd Lt.   Scott, E. C.
  ,,   Williamson, R. H.

Royal Field Artillery, (Territorial Force)

Lieut.   Chalmers, J. B.

CORPS OF ROYAL ENGINEERS
Royal Engineers

Major   Barstow, J. B.
  ,,   Corry, J. B.
  ,,   Douglas, W. S.
  ,,   Gardiner, A.

Major	Molesworth, E. K.
,,	Moore, J. O'H.
,,	Neville, L. J. N.
,,	North, C. N.
,,	Ommanney, R.
,,	Rose, L. St. V.
,,	Tyler, A. H.
Captain	Bamberger, C. D. W., attd. Indian Army.
,,	Carr-Harris, E. D.
,,	Collins, A. E. J.
,,	Cumine-Robson, R. G. G., attd. Indian Army.
,,	Dawson-Scott, J. K.
,,	Kelly, H. H.
,,	McEnery, J. A.
,,	McKay, H. M.
,,	Moores, C. G.
,,	Twiss, A. M., attd. Indian Army.
,,	Wright, T.
Lieut.	Bayly, C. G. G., attd. Royal Flying Corps.
,,	Dewar, A., Special Reserve.
,,	Egerton, R. R.
,,	Hayes Sadler, E. J. B.
,,	Hutton, G. A.
,,	Schneider, H. H.
,,	Smeathman, J. M.
,,	Smith, A. G.
,,	Tyler, A.
,,	Wynne-Jones, M.
2nd Lt.	Holl, H. N., Special Reserve.
,,	Manley, J. D.
,,	Miller, G. L.
,,	Renny-Tailyour, H. F. T.

Royal Engineers, (Territorial Force)

East Lancashire Division

2nd Lt.	Woods, B. H.

FOOT GUARDS

Grenadier Guards

Major	Colby, L. R. V.
,,	Gordon-Lennox, Lord B. C.
,,	Stucley, H. St. L.
,,	Weld Forester, Hon. A. O. W. C.
Captain	Cecil, Hon. W. A.
,,	Cholmeley, Sir M. A. R.
,,	MacDougall, I.
,,	Stephen, D. C. L.
,,	Symes-Thompson, C.
,,	Wellesley, Lord R.
Lieut.	Antrobus, E.
,,	Congleton, Lord H. B. F.
,,	des Voeux, F. W.
,,	Douglas-Pennant, Hon. A. G. S.
,,	Lee Steere, J. H. G.
,,	Manners, Hon. J. N.
,,	Miller, F. W. J. M.
,,	Stocks, M. G.
,,	Tudway, H. R. C.
,,	Tufnell, C. W.
,,	Van Neck, P.
,,	Welby, R. W. G.
2nd Lt.	Cecil, G. E.
,,	Pickersgill-Cunliffe, J. R.

2nd Lt.	Somerset, N. A. H.
,,	Vereker, R. H. M.
,,	Walter S.

Special Reserve

2nd Lt.	Nevill, J. H. G., attd. 3rd Battn.

Coldstream Guards

Major	Hamilton, Hon. L. d'H.
,,	Markham, R. A.
Captain	Banbury, C. W.
,,	Campbell, G. A.
,,	Dawson, R. L., Reserve of Officers.
,,	Fuller-Maitland, W. A.
,,	Monck, Hon. C. H. S.
,,	Stewart, G., Reserve of Officers.
,,	Tritton, A. G.
Lieut.	Bingham, D. C:
,,	Douglas-Pennant, Hon. C.
,,	Gordon-Ives, V. M. G.
,,	Graves-Sawle, R. C.
,,	Hawarden, Viscount (Sir R. C. Maude)
,,	Lambton, G.
,,	Legge-Bourke, N. W. H.
,,	Pollock, F. R.
,,	Smith, G. K.-F.
,,	Trotter, A.
,,	Windsor-Clive, Hon. A.
,,	Wyndham, P. L.
2nd Lt.	de Winton, W.
,,	Freeman-Thomas, Hon. G. F.
,,	Lockwood, R. W. M.
,,	Tollemache, B. D.
.,	Williams-Wynn, C. W.

Special Reserve

Lieut.	Campbell, A. W. G., attd. 1st Battn.
,,	Wallis, H. D., attd. 3rd Battn.
2nd Lt.	Boscawen, Hon. V. D., attd. 1st Battn.

4th (Reserve) Battalion

Captain	Adeane, H. R. A., Reserve of Officers.
Lieut.	Murray, C. J.
2nd Lt.	Beauchamp, E. A.

Scots Guards

Major	Carpenter-Garnier, J. T.
,,	Fraser, Hon. H. J.
Captain	Balfour, R. F.
,,	Bulkeley, T. H. R.
,,	Campbell, C. F. F.
,,	de la Pasture, C. E. M.
,,	Hamilton, C. F. P.
,,	Kinnaird, Hon. D. A.
,,	Smith, B. R. W.
,,	Stephen, A. A. L., Adjutant.
,,	Taylor, H.
,,	Wickham, W. J.
Lieut.	Compton-Thornhill, R. A.
,,	Cottrell-Dormer, C.
,,	Drummond, D. R.
,,	Gipps, R. N.
,,	Hanbury-Tracy, Hon. F. C. H.
,,	Hill-Trevor, H. G. E.
,,	Holbech, W. H., Reserve of Officers.
,,	Jones, H. R. I.
,,	Lawson, W. B. W.

Lieut.	Loyd, G. A.
,,	Macdonald, Hon. G. E. H.
,,	Monckton, F. A.
,,	Nugent, R. F. R., Reserve of Officers
,,	Ogilvy, Sir G. N., Bart.
,,	Ottley. G. C. L.
,,	Stirling-Stuart, J.
2nd Lt.	Gibbs, R. C. M.
,,	Houldsworth, W. G.

Special Reserve

| Lieut. | Gladwin, R. H. F., attd. 1st Battn. |

Irish Guards

Lt.-Col.	Morris, Hon. G. H.
Major	Crichton, H. F.
,,	Herbert-Stepney, H. A.
,,	Tisdall, C. A.
Captain	Berners, H. H.
,,	Gough, E. J. F.
,,	Hay, Lord A. V.
,,	Mulholland, Hon. A. E. S.
,,	Stafford-King-Harman, E. C.
Lieut.	Brooke G., Reserve of Officers.
,,	Coke, L. S., Reserve of Officers.
,,	Hope, W. E.
,,	Woodroffe, N. L.

Special Reserve

| Captain | Hamilton, Lord A. J., attd. 1st Battn. |
| Lieut. | Mathieson, K. R., attd. 1st Battn. |

INFANTRY

The Royal Scots (Lothian Regiment)

Captain	Hewat, A. M. C.
,,	Price, C. L.
,,	Shafto, A. Duncombe
Lieut.	Thompson, G. M.,(empl. Gold Coast Regt.)

3rd Battalion

Captain	Bruce, Hon. H. L., attd. 2nd Battn.
Lieut.	Trotter, A. N., attd. 2nd Battn.
2nd Lt.	Cowan, R. C., attd. 2nd Battn.
,,	Hewitt, W. G.
,,	Kerr, D. A., attd. 2nd Battn.
,,	Snead-Cox, R. M., attd. 2nd Battn.

8th Battalion (T.F.)

| Captain | Todrick, T. |
| Lieut. | Burt, A. |

The Queen's (Royal West Surrey Regiment)

Lt.-Col.	Pell, B. T.
,,	Pilleau, H. C.
,,	Warren, D.
Captain	Foy, M. V.
,,	Wilson, C. E.
Lieut.	Bird, J. G. H.
,,	Eastwood, F. M.
,,	Haigh, C. R., Adjutant.
,,	Henriques, R. L. Q.
,,	Ingram, G. S.
,,	Oldfield, G. C. O., (empl. King's African Rifles).

Lieut.	Strong, H. B.
,,	Thomas, A. C.
,,	Wilson, D. R.
2nd Lt.	Ive, D.
,,	Schunck, R. H.

Special Reserve

| 2nd Lt. | Holmes, T. S., attd. 1st Battn. East Kent Regiment. |
| ,, | Pound, M. S., attd. 1st Battn. |

The Buffs (East Kent Regiment)

Captain	James, G. M., Staff.
Lieut.	McDougall, R.
,,	Philips, J. D.
2nd Lt.	Noott, M.
,,	Stock, H. R.

3rd Battalion

Captain	Chichester, E. B.
,,	Wells, W. N., attd. 1st Battn.
Lieut.	Glyn, R. S., attd. 1st Battn.
2nd Lt.	Cronk, W. G., attd. 1st Battn. King's Royal Rifle Corps.
,,	Ley, M. A., attd. 3rd Battn.

The King's Own (Royal Lancaster Regt.)

Lt.-Col.	Dykes, A. McN.
Major	Lysons, N. L. S.
,,	Morrah, J. H.
Captain	Clutterbuck, H.
,,	Sparenborg, H. R.
,,	Theobald, F. G.
Lieut.	Aitchison, R. A. C.
,,	Morris, A. G. A.
,,	Steele-Perkins, C. S.
,,	Thornycroft, E. G. M., empl. King's African Rifles).
,,	Woodgate, L. S.
2nd Lt.	Heaney, P. O.

3rd Battalion

Captain	Lendon, P. B., attd. 1st Battn.
Lieut.	Brockelbank, L. S.
2nd Lt.	Waterhouse, A., attd. 1st Battn.

The Northumberland Fusiliers

Major	(*temp.* Lieut. Col.) Percival, A. J.-B., Staff.
Captain	Fletcher, R. S.
,,	Matthews, J. H.
,,	Selby, B. H.
,,	Toppin, H. S.
2nd Lt.	Boyd, E. F.
,,	Laws, A. V.
,,	Tottie, E. H.

3rd Battalion

Captain	Lamb, E. J., attd. 2nd Battn. King's Own Yorkshire Light Infantry.
,,	Lambert, J. M., attd. 1st Battn.
Lieut.	Coles, D. M., attd. 1st Battn.
,,	Leather, C., attd. 1st Battn.
,,	Nunneley, C. F., attd. 1st Battn.
,,	Van Neck, C. H., attd. 1st Battn.
,,	Willans, R. St. J., attd. 1st Battn.

The Royal Warwickshire Regiment

Lt.-Col. (*temp.*) Brewis, R. H. W.
,, Loring, W. L.
Major Christie, W. C.
Captain Bentley, C. A. C.
,, Brownfield, R. J.
,, Gilliat, C. G. P.
,, Methuen, C. O'B. H.
,, Taylour, G. R.
Lieut. Bernard, B. F. P.
,, Knapton, O. A.
,, Ratcliff, J. E.
,, Stainforth, R. T.
2nd Lt. Deane, D.
,, Monk, G. B. F.
,, Pearce, G. V.
,, Standring, B. A. .

3rd Battalion

Captain Crowe, W. M. C., attd. 1st Battn.
,, Hodgson, C. A. R.

4th Battalion

Captain McCormick, J. H. G., attd. 2nd Battn.
2nd Lt. Campbell, B., attd. 2nd Battn.
,, Vacher, G. H., attd. 2nd Battn.

The Royal Fusiliers (City of London Regt.)

Lt.-Col. McMahon, N. R.
Captain Attwood. A. F.
,, Bowden-Smith, W. A. C.
,, Brand, E. S. (empl. West African Regt.).
,, Byng, A. M.
,, Carey, L. W. le M.
,, Docker, G. A. M.
,, Forster, F.
,, Puzey, A. K.
,, Steele, F. W. A.
Lieut. Dease, M. J.
,, Longman, F.
2nd Lt. Gorst. E. W.
,, Hodges, S. H., Reserve of Officers, attd.
,, Mead, J. F.
,, Undery, J. A.

Special Reserve

Lieut. Johnstone, W. G. T. H., attd. 4th Battn.
2nd Lt. Hardman, F. McM., attd. 4th Battn.

5th Battalion

Captain Shaw, H. J., attd. 1st Battn.
2nd Lt. Rennie. D. W., attd. 1st Battn.
,, Stables, H. R., attd. 1st Battn. Cheshire Regiment.

6th Battalion

Captain Waller, Sir F. E., attd. 4th Battn.
Lieut. Combe, B. A., attd. 4th Battn.

7th Battalion

Lieut. Ferrier, G. C. C., attd. 4th Battn.

The King's (Liverpool Regiment)

Lt.-Col. Bannatyne, W. S.
Captain Batten, J. H. S.
,, Kyrke-Smith, A.
,, Marshall, F.
,, Tanner, R. E.

Lieut. Doll, P. W. R.
,, Furneaux, P. T.
2nd Lt. Denny, B. M. R., Reserve of Officers.
,, Wallace, H. B.
,, Ward. A.

3rd Battalion

Lieut. Baker, E. B., attd. 1st Battn.
,, Sweet-Escott, M. R., attd. 1st Battn.

4th Battalion

Lieut. Andrews, F. G., attd. 2nd Battn, South Lancashire Regiment.

10th (Scottish) Battalion, T.F.

Captain Twentyman, A.

The Norfolk Regiment

Major Orr, J. B.
Captain Cresswell, F. J.
Lieut. Foley, T. A. F.
,, Openshaw, H. M.

3rd Battalion

Lieut. Teeling, A. M. A. I. de L.

The Lincolnshire Regiment

Captain Dawson, H. E.
,, Drake, R. E.
,, King, R. N., Reserve of Officers.
,, Lyall, C. G., Reserve of Officers.
Lieut. (*temp*. Capt.) Holmes, C. C.
,, Huntington, J. N. S.
,, Welchman, E. L.
2nd Lt. Barnes, E.
,, Wade, S. S. A.
,, Willis, R.

3rd Battalion

Lieut. Bransbury, V. D. B., attd. 1st Battn.
,, Owen, E. H., attd. 1st Battn. South Wales Borderers.

The Devonshire Regiment

Captain Besly, B. H.
,, Elliot, H. G.
,, Featherstone, R. B.
,, Spencer, C. J.
,, Whipple, H. C.
Lieut. Dunsterville, G. E.
,, Hancock, R. E.
2nd Lt. Ainslie, D. A. L.

3rd Battalion

Captain Chichester, H. A.
,, Quicke, E. O. St. C. G., attd. 1st Battn.
Lieut. Toms, A. W., attd. 2nd Scottish Rifles.

The Suffolk Regiment

Lt.-Col. Brett, C. A. H.
Captain Reid, E. H.
,, Temple, A. H. W., Reserve of Officers.
Lieut. Payne, G. H.

3rd Battalion

Captain Pollock-Hodsoll, G. B., attd. 1st Battn. Cheshire Regt.
,, Winn, A.
Lieut. Myddelton, E. G., attd. 2nd Battn.
2nd Lt. Wilder, R. C. P., attd. 2nd Battn.

Prince Albert's (Somerset Light Infantry)

Major   Thoyts, F. G. G.
Captain Bradshaw, F. S.
,,   Maud, C. C.
Lieut.   Moore, R. L.
,,   Parr, G. R.
2nd Lt. Read, A. B.

Special Reserve

2nd Lt. Filleul, L. A., attd. 1st Battn.
,,   Henson, S. B., attd. 1st Battn.

3rd Battalion

Captain Orr, R. C., attd. 1st Battn.

The Prince of Wales's Own (West Yorkshire Regiment)

Major   Cooper-King, R. G.
,,   Ingles, A. W.
Captain Clothier, J. K.
,,   Fisher, M.
,,   Welchman, E. T.
Lieut.   Costin, B. D.
,,   Eliot, W. L.
,,   Lawson-Smith, J.
,,   (*temp.* Capt.) Loveband, A. R.
,,   Meautys, T. G.
,,   Shaw, B. H. G.
,,   Thompson, O. C. W.
2nd Lt. Carew, J.
,,   Wilson, E. W.

3rd Battalion

Major   Cliff, H. T., attd. 1st Battn.
Captain I'Anson, J. F., attd. 1st Battn.

4th Battalion

Major   Slade, C. G. M., attd. North Lancs. Regt.
Captain Smart, G. H., attd. 1st Battn.

The East Yorkshire Regiment

Lt.-Col. Benson, R. E.
Major   Campion, W. E.
Captain Edwards, E. L. P.
,,   Hind, F.
,,   Lawrence, B.
,,   Maxwell, P. B.
,,   Wilson, A. H.
Lieut.   Cosens, H. S. F.
2nd Lt. Bottomley, T. R.
,,   Elrington, G. G. C.
,,   Studley, L.

Special Reserve

2nd Lt. Pease, M. R., attd. 1st Battn.

3rd Battalion

Captain Walker, E. W., attd. 1st Battn.
,,   Wood, C. S., Res. of Off., attd. 1st Battn.
2nd Lt. Waterfall, V., attd. Royal Flying Corps.

The Bedfordshire Regiment

Major   Stares, R. P.
,,   Traill, J. M.
Captain Garnett-Botfield, C. S.
,,   Hall, A. G.
,,   Ker, C. H.
,,   McCloughlin, R. J.

Lieut.   Bastard, W.
,,   Punchard, E. E.
2nd Lt. Bell, C. O.
,,   Fernandes, D. L. de T.
,,   Paterson, J. A.
,,   Rendell, L. W.
,,   Stafford, C. C., Reserve of Officers.
,,   Wright, G. D. C.

3rd Battalion

Lieut.   Downes, V. C., attd. 1st Battn.
,,   Edwards, E. A. J., attd. 1st Battn.
,,   Graves, W. F., attd. 1st Battn.
,,   Shippey, J. R., attd. 1st Battn.

4th Battalion

Captain Baird, W. F. G., attd. 1st Linc. Regt.
Lieut.   Charlton, St. J. A., attd. 1st Battn.
,,   Harding, R. D. S., attd. 1st Battn.

The Leicestershire Regiment

Captain Grant, H. A.
,,   Gruchy, F. le M.
,,   Hawes, R. F.
,,   Puckle, T. N., (empl. West African Frontier Force).
,,   Tristram, L. B. C.
,,   Viney, P. E.
Lieut.   Dods, W. H. G.
,,   Prain, T.
,,   Seton-Browne, M. W.
,,   Smeathman, C.
,,   Wateridge, E. L.
2nd Lt. Bowley, T. H., attd. Border Regiment.

3rd Battalion

Lieut.   Vandeleur, J. B., attd. 3rd Battn. Worc. Regiment.
2nd Lt. Farrar, H. R., attd. 2nd Battn. Man. Regt.
,,   Hutton, R., attd. Royal Warwick. Regt.

The Royal Irish Regiment

Major   Daniell, E. H. E.
Capt. (Bt. Maj.) Panter-Downes, E. M., (empl. West African Frontier Force).
,,   Mellor, W.
Lieut.   Brown, H. W.
,,   Rushton, F. H. L.
,,   Tandy, A. M. S.
2nd Lt. Howard, P. E. N.
,,   Shine, J. D.

3rd Battalion

2nd Lt. Anderson, A. J. R., attd. 2nd Battn.
,,   Smyth, J. R., attd. 2nd Battn.

Alexandra, Princess of Wales's Own (Yorkshire Regiment)

Colonel King, C. A. C.
Major   Walker, W. B.
Captain Broun, E. S.
,,   Jeffery, C. G.
Lieut.   Brooksbank, H. G.
,,   Ledgard, F. C.
,,   Phayre, R. H.
,,   Walmesley, R.
2nd Lt. Hatton, F. C.

The Lancashire Fusiliers

Captain Moody, R. H. M.
,, Sidebottom, R Y.
,, Ward, A. C.
Lieut. Boyle, D. E.
,, Stuart, C. E.
2nd Lt. Humfrey, W. K.
,, Paulson, J. S.

3rd Battalion

Captain Bass, C. H., attd. 2nd Battn.
,, Lucas-Tooth, S. L., attd. 2nd Battn.

4th Battalion

Captain Barnsley, A., attd. 1st Northumb. Fus.
,, Sneyd, T. H., attd. 2nd Battn.

The Royal Scots Fusiliers

Captain Barrett, C. J. C.
,, Boyle, The Hon. J.
,, Briggs, G. C.
,, Fairlie, F.
,, Hurt, S. F. A. A.
,, Tullis, J. D.
,, Young, J. E.
Lieut. Alston, C. McC.
,, Henderson, N. W. A.
,, Kennedy, N.
,, Lyon, C. J.
,, Mackenzie, C. G. G.
,, Thomson, K. C.
2nd Lt. Anderson, E. L. L.
,, Barton, H. W. F.

3rd Battalion

Lieut. Ness, G. S., attd. 1st Battn.
2nd Lt. Cozens-Brooke, J. G. S., attd. 1st Battn.

The Cheshire Regiment

Captain Forster, L. A., Reserve of Officers.
,, Hartford, H. I. St. J.
,, Jones, E. R.
,, Mahony, F. H.
,, Nicholson, H. W.
,, Rich, W. S.
Lieut. Campbell, C. A.
,, Maitland-Addison, A. C.
2nd Lt. Downes, A. C.

3rd Battalion

Lieut. Frost, K. T.
2nd Lt. Anderson, G. R. L., attd. 1st Battn.

The Royal Welsh Fusiliers

Lt.-Col. Cadogan, H. O. S.
Captain Barker, R. V., Staff.
,, Jones-Vaughan, E. N.
,, Kington, W. M.
,, Lloyd, M. E.
,, Philips, R. N.
,, Stable, L. L.
,, Vyvyan, W. G.
Lieut. Ackland-Allen, H. T.
,, Chance, G. O. de P.
,, Dooner, A. E. C. T., Adjutant.
,, Egerton, R. le B.
,, Hoskyns, E. C. L.

2nd Lt. Collingwood-Thompson, E. J. V.
,, Gore, G. R.
,, Snead-Cox, G. P. J.
,, Stone, E. R. C.

3rd Battalion

Captain Brennan, J. H., attd. 1st Battn.
,, Prichard, T. L., attd. 2nd Battn.

The South Wales Borderers

Major Lawrence, W. L.
,, Welby, G. E. E.
Captain Curgenven, W. C.
,, Paterson, C. J.
,, Peel, A. R. (empl. Nigeria Regiment).
,, Yeatman, M. E.
Lieut. Blackall-Simonds, G. P., Reserve of Officers, attd.
,, Coker, J. C.
,, Homfray, J. R.
,, Johnson, M. T.
2nd Lt. Farrier, A. M.
,, Pryce-Jenkin, R. D.
,, Sills, C. C.

3rd Battalion

Captain Maxwell, I. B., attd. 1st Battn.
Lieut. Sparrow, L. G., attd. 2nd Battn. K.O.S.B.
2nd Lt. Watkins, H. H., attd. 1st Battn.

The King's Own Scottish Borderers

Major Leigh, C.
Captain Turnbull, H. V. C.
Lieut. Holme, R. H. P.
2nd Lt. Amos, G. S.
,, Bayley, G. B., attd. 2nd Battn. Royal Scots Fusiliers.
,, Gillespie, T. C.
,, Hammond, G. P.
,, Woollcombe, C. S.
Hon. Capt. and Quartermaster Murray, A.

3rd Battalion

Major Allan, W. L. C., attd. 2nd Battn.
Lieut. Cox, G. H., attd. 2nd Battn.
2nd Lt. MacRae, I. A., attd. 2nd Battn.

The Cameronians (Scottish Rifles)

Captain Gilkison, D. S.
,, Gordon, J. F. S., attd. Royal Scots Fusiliers
,, Ritchie, A. G.
,, Rose, R. H. W.
Lieut. Dunn, T. E. D.
,, Hewitt, J. F.
,, Hopkins, C. R. I.

4th Battalion

Lieut. Miller, C. R. E., attd. King's Own Scottish Borderers.

The Royal Inniskilling Fusiliers

Captain Auchinleck, D. G. H.
,, Geoghegan, J. R.
,, Lloyd, E. R.
,, Ponsonby, G. M.
,, Roe, S. G.

Lieut. Dunlop, C.
2nd Lt. Boyd, H. A.
,, Miller, I. F. R.
,, Thomas, J. G. B.

Special Reserve

2nd Lt. Aplin, K. S., attd. 2nd Battn.
,, Roberts, A. G. M., attd. 2nd Battn.

The Gloucestershire Regiment

Major Gardner, R. M. S.
,, Rising, R. E.
Captain McLeod, A. A.
,, Pritchett, W. P.
,, Shipway, G. M.
,, Temple, W. A. M.
Lieut. Danckwerts, R. W.
,, Holme, A. C.
,, Stewart, A. H., empl. West African Frontier Force.
,, Yalland, W. S.
2nd Lt. Foster, H. K.
,, (temp. Lieut.) Wiggin, D. H.

Special Reserve

2nd Lt. Hippisley, H. E., attd. 1st Battn.

3rd Battalion

Captain Duncan, S., Reserve of Officers.
Lieut. Hickling, E. R. E., attd. 1st Battn. Loyal North Lancashire Regiment.
,, Swanwick, R. K., attd. 1st Battn.
2nd Lt. Walters, E. C., attd. 1st Battn.

4th Battalion

Lieut. Harding, A. D., attd. 1st Battn.

The Worcestershire Regiment

Major Bacon, B. K. W.
,, Green, A. D., Staff.
Captain Carr, M. R.
,, Eliott, H. R.
,, Hughes, T. H.
,, Lea, G. E.
,, Nesbitt, A. S.
,, Pepys, R. W.
,, Underhill, W. A.
Lieut. Clarke, M. E. L. H.
,, Gilmour, H. J. G.
,, Goldsmid, S. A.
,, Harrison, C. C.
,, Hartnoll, H. P.
,, Henry, C.
,, Lowe, H. S.
,, Northey, A.
,, Pope, C. M.
,, Slater, R. M.
2nd Lt. Battle, E. C. V.
,, Curtler, F. G. O.
,, Darby, F.
,, Hastings-Medhurst, F. L.
,, Smythe, F. F.

5th Battalion

Lieut. Hudson, A. W.

6th Battalion

Captain Graham, A. G. M., attd. 1st Battn. Loyal North Lancashire Regiment.
2nd Lt. Galton, T. H., attd. 3rd Battn.

The East Lancashire Regiment

Lt.-Col. Le Marchant, L. St. G.
Captain Aubin, A. C.
,, Cane, L. A. F.
,, Clayhills, G.
,, Coventry, E. E.
,, Warner, H. M.
Lieut. Chisholm, W. M.
,, Hughes, F. D. (empl. West African Frontier Force).
,, Mathews, T. H.
,, Waud, L. D.
2nd Lt. Stanley, G. H.

3rd Battalion

Captain Preston, T. H., Lieut. Reserve of Officers.

The East Surrey Regiment

Captain Benson, J. P.
,, Burn, A. G. McC., attd. 1st Battn. Gloucestershire Regiment.
,, Hopkinson, C. R. T. (empl. 1st Battn. Nigeria Regiment).
,, Whish, J. K. T.
2nd Lt. Relton, G. L.
,, Ward, N. L.

Special Reserve

Captain Maclean, A. de V.

3rd Battalion

Lieut. Benning, M. S., attd. 1st Battn.
,, Bridgland, N. L., attd. 1st Battn.
,, Simpson, W. H. M., attd. 1st Battn.

4th Battalion

2nd Lt. Housecroft, H., attd. 1st Battn.

The Duke of Cornwall's Light Infantry

Captain Olivier, R. H.
,, Passy, L. D.
,, Romilly, A. H.
Lieut. Garsia, O. D. M.
2nd Lt. Crane, C. E.
,, Elliott, P. L.

The Duke of Wellington's (West Riding Regiment)

Major Strafford, P. B.
Captain Denman-Jubb, C. O., Adjutant.
Lieut. De Wend, D. F.
,, Russell, L. E.
,, Thompson, J. H. L.

3rd Battalion

Lieut. Williamson, G., attd. 1st Battn.

The Border Regiment

Major Allen, W. L.
Captain Andrews, C. G. W., Adjutant.
,, Askew, H. A.
,, Cholmondeley, C. A. J.
,, Gerrard, H. V.
,, Gordon, R. N.
,, Lamb, C.
,, Lees, E. H. H.
,, Molyneux-Seel, L. E. H.
,, Radcliffe, M.

Lieut.	Cooch, C. R.
,,	Egerton, P. J.
,,	Hodgson, G. W. H.
,,	Warren, J. B. B.
2nd Lt.	Clancey, T. J.
,,	Surtees, C. G. V.

3rd Battalion

Captain Pyman, J., attd. 2nd Battn. Manchester Regiment.

The Royal Sussex Regiment

Lt.-Col.	Crispin, H. T.
,,	Montresor, E. H.
Major	Cookson, M. E.
Captain	Aldridge, R. J. P. D.
,,	Crawley-Boevey, E. M., attd. 4th Battn. Royal Fusiliers.
,,	Jemmett-Browne, A. E.
,,	Slater, L.
Lieut.	Daun, E. C.
,,	Lousada, E. A.
,,	Pelham, The Hon. H. L., Adjutant.
,,	Ramsay, D. G., attd. Royal West Surrey Regiment.
,,	Verrall, C. F.
2nd Lt.	Croft, L. R.
,,	Hughes, W. S.
,,	Marillier, F. C. J.
,,	Moore, G.

Special Reserve

2nd Lt.	Shaw, C. F., attd. 2nd Battn.
,,	Silvester, A. L., attd. 2nd Battn.

3rd Battalion

Lieut. Duke, B. P., attd. 2nd Battn.

The Hampshire Regiment

Major	Parker, G. H.
Captain	(*temp*. Major) Connellan, P. M.
,,	Dolphin, J. E. W.
,,	Harland, R. W. (attd.)
Lieut.	Foster, A. C. H. (empl. King's African Rifles).
,,	Kent, E. M. S.
,,	Trimmer, W. D. M.
2nd Lt.	Cowan, D. H.

3rd Battalion

Lieut.	Griffith, G.
,,	Harington, H. A. B., attd. 1st Battn.

The South Staffordshire Regiment

Major	Loder-Symonds, J. F.
Captain	Dunlop, J. S. S.
,,	Powell, H. M. (empl. West African Regt.).
,,	Ransford, C. G.
,,	Thomas, C. H.
,,	Vallentin, J. F.
Lieut.	Bean, C. R. C.
,,	Bower, H. R. S.
,,	Crousaz, C. F.
,,	Foster, W. A. P.
,,	Holmes, F. L.
,,	Hume, C. G.
,,	Moor-Radford, L. C.
,,	Tomlinson, F. R. J.
2nd Lt.	Scott, B. J. H.

3rd Battalion

Lieut.	Archer-Shee, G., attd. 1st Battn.
,,	Fitzpatrick, D. T. F., attd. 2nd Battn.
,,	Robinson, F. E., attd. 2nd Battn.

4th Battalion

Captain Campbell, D. W. A., attd. 1st Battn. Sherwood Foresters.

The Dorsetshire Regiment

Major	Mercer, A. A.
,,	Roper, R. T.
Captain	Davidson, W. T. C.
,,	George, A. K. D.
,,	Middleton, F.
,,	Moffat, A. L. N. M.
,,	Parkinson, J. A. F.
,,	Priestley, A. B. (empl. West African Frontier Force).
,,	Roe, A. R. M.
Lieut.	Pitt, J. M., Adjutant.
2nd Lt.	Smith, T. S.

3rd Battalion

Lieut.	Bishop, E. M., attd. 2nd Battn. K.O. Yorks. L.I.
,,	Turner, J. R. (Spec. Res.), attd. 1st Battn.

The Prince of Wales's Volunteers
(South Lancashire Regiment)

Lt.-Col.	Green, M. C. A.
Captain	Robson, E.
,,	Wesché, E. B. (empl. West African Frontier Force).
Lieut.	Fulcher, B. V.
,,	Gebbie, J. F. R.
,,	Hadfield, W. J. M.
,,	Hewitt, G. H.
2nd Lt.	Birdwood, G. A. B.
,,	Mitchell, E. A.
,,	Spendlove, G. T.
,,	Waldy, C. T.
,,	Wallace, D. S.
,,	Watson, E. G.

Special Reserve

2nd Lt. Widdowson, A. J. H. R.

3rd Battalion

Lieut. Gibson, A. T., attd. 2nd Battn.

The Welsh Regiment

Lt.-Col.	Morland, C. B.
Major	Kerrich, J. H.
Captain	Davies, H. C., (attd.) Reserve of Officers.
,,	Ferrar, W. H., Adjutant.
,,	Haggard, M.
,,	Moore, W. A. G.
,,	Picton-Warlow, W., attd. Royal Flying Corps.
2nd Lt.	Weeding, J. R. B.

3rd Battalion

Captain	Fitzpatrick, G. R., attd. 2nd Battn.
,,	Herd, H. F., attd. 2nd Battn.
Lieut.	Cornelius, C. V. P., attd. 2nd Battn.
2nd Lt.	Nicholl, J. W. H., attd. 2nd Battn.

The Black Watch (Royal Highlanders)

Lt.-Col. Duff, A. G.
Captain Dalglish, C. A. de G.
,, Strahan, C. E.
,, Urquhart, E. F. M.
Lieut. Cumming, L. R.
,, Polson, G. W.
,, Wilson, E. H. H. J.
2nd Lt. Blair, P. E. A.
,, Boyd, N. J. L.
,, Lawson, A. S.
,, McAndrew, A.
,, Stirling-Smurthwaite, D. S.

3rd Battalion

Captain Boddam-Whetham, C., attd. 1st Battn. Gordon Highlanders.
,, Moubray, P. L., attd. 1st Battn.
,, Parker, A. E., attd. 2nd Battn. Seaforth Highlanders.
,, Stewart-Richardson, Sir E. A., Bart., attd. 1st Battn.
Lieut. Lyon, C. L. C. B., attd. 1st Battn.
,, Nolan, R. P. D., attd. 1st Battn.
2nd Lt. Webster, J. F., attd. 1st Battn. Gordon Highlanders.

The Oxfordshire and Buckinghamshire Light Infantry

Captain Evelegh, R. C.
,, Harden, A. H.
Lieut. Mockler-Ferryman, H.
,, Murphy, C. F.
,, Worthington, R. G.
2nd Lt. Barrington-Kennett, A. H.
,, Girardot, P. C.
,, Jones, J.
,, Marshall, J. S. C.
,, Pepys, F.
,, Ward, J. B. M.

3rd Battalion

Lieut. Turbutt, G. M. R., attd. 2nd Battn.

The Essex Regiment

Captain Vandeleur, W. M. C.
Lieut. Round, A. F. H.
,, Vance, J.

3rd Battalion

Captain Rose, A. H. P., attd 2nd Battn.

The Sherwood Foresters (Nottinghamshire and Derbyshire Regt.)

Captain Frend, W. R., Adjutant.
Lieut. Ash, B. C.
,, Bernard, L. A.
,, Dilworth, M. P.
,, Murray, P. M.
2nd Lt. Browne, A. G.
,, Harris, L. G. H.
,, Milner, R. D. P.
,, Ruegg, K. S.
,, Smalley, W. M.

Special Reserve

2nd Lt. Atkin, J. M., attd. Worcestershire Regt.
,, Smith, H. L. C., attd. 2nd Battn.

The Loyal North Lancashire Regiment

Lt.-Col. Knight, G. C.
,, Lloyd, W. R.
Major Braithwaite, F. J.
,, Carter, A. J.
Captain Allason, L. T.
,, Allen, J. F., Adjutant.
,, Helme, H. L.
,, Prince, A. L.
Lieut. Dickson, C. G.
,, Loomes, H. R.
,, Mason, R. C.
2nd Lt. Calrow, W. R. L.
,, Einem-Hickson, S. V.
,, Kingsley, G. C.
Lieut. and Quartermaster Wilkinson, E.

3rd Battalion

Captain Miller, E. C.. attd. 1st Battn.

The Northamptonshire Regiment

Major Norman, H. H.
Captain Bentley, G. M.
,, Crean, T., attd. Royal Flying Corps.
,, Gordon, R. E.
,, Parker, R. B.
,, Russell, W. R.
,, Savage, J. A.
,, Watts, C. H. R.
,, White, E. E.
Lieut. Paget. G. G. B.
,, Rastrick, U.
,, Vandell, H. I., (attd.), Reserve of Officers.
2nd Lt. Gordon, C. G.
,, Jarvis, A. S. G.
,, Sherriff, A. N.
,, Wainwright. G. C.

Princess Charlotte of Wales's (Royal Berkshire Regiment)

Captain Shott, H. H.
,, Steele, O.
Lieut. Garnett, P. N. (empl. King's African Rifles).
,, Perrott, A. H., Adjutant.
2nd Lt. Knott, T. A.
,, Perkins, R. G. B.

3rd Battalion

Lieut. Nicholson, L. C., attd. 1st Battn.

The Queen's Own (Royal West Kent Regiment)

Major Buckle, M. P.
,, Hastings, P.
,, Pack-Beresford, C.G.
Captain Fisher, F.
,, Keenlyside, G. F. H.
,, Legard, G. B., Adjutant.
,, Phillips, W. C. O.
Lieut. Ames, W. K.
,, Gore, S. K.
,, Pringle, R. S.
,, Vicat, H. J.
2nd Lt. Broadwood, M. F.
,, Harding, J. M.
,, Thompson, M. N.

2nd Lt.   McDonagh, P., attd. Suffolk Regiment

3rd Battalion

Captain Battersby, E. M., attd. 1st Battn.
,,   Beeman, A. C., attd. 1st Battn.
Lieut.   Anderson, C. K., attd. 1st Battn.
,,   Sewell, D. C. C., attd. 1st Battn.
2nd Lt. Waghorn, L. P., attd. Berks. Regiment.
,,   Whitehouse, P. J., attd. Northants. Regt.

The King's Own (Yorkshire Light Infantry)

Major   Yate, C. A. L.
Captain Simpson, J. E.
,,   Smyth, A. B.
2nd Lt. Grubb, L. E. P.
,,   Pepys, J.
,,   Ritchie, A. F.

3rd Battalion

Captain Richmond, T. H., attd. 2nd Battn.
2nd Lt. Carswell, R. N., attd. 2nd Battn.

The King's (Shropshire Light Infantry)

Major   Masefield, R.
Captain Miles, R. P., attd. Royal Irish Rifles.
Lieut.   Herdman, A. W.
,.   Jenings, G. P. C.
,,   Verner, F. C.

3rd Battalion

Captain Mitchell, J. A. S.

The Duke of Cambridge's Own (Middlesex Regiment)

Lt.-Col. Ward, B. E.
Major   Abell, W. H.
,,   Bentley, G. W.
Captain Evatt, G. R. K.
,,   Knowles, J. E.
,,   Roy, K. J.
,,   Skaife, A. F.
,,   Tulloh, C. F.
,,   Wordsworth, A. G.
Lieut.   Harvey, C. M.
,,   Henstock, K. P.
,,   Tagg, H. A.
,,   Trewman, A. B.
,,   Wilkinson, J. R. M.
2nd Lt. Morse, G. T. H.
,,   Sayers, R.

5th Battalion

Major   Corcoran, W. J.
2nd Lt. Bosanquet, S. C., attd. 1st Battn.
,,   Hilton, H. D., attd. 4th Battn.
,,   Hughes, G. W., attd. 4th Battn.
,,   Robinson-Pastfield, J. T., attd. Northants. Regiment.
,,   Shawyer, M. A. P., attd. 1st Battn.

6th Battalion

Lieut.   Sneath, C. D., attd. 4th Battn.
2nd Lt. Coles, S. H., attd. 4th Battn.

The King's Royal Rifle Corps

Major   Foljambe, H. F. F. B.
Captain Cathcart, A. E.
,,   Hawley, C. F., Staff.
Lieut.   Battenberg, H. H. Prince M. V. D. of
,,   Bond, R. H.
,,   Pleydell-Bouverie, J. E.
2nd Lt. Anderson, C. A. K., attd. R. Scots. Fus.
,,   Barclay, R. H. M.
,,   Casey, J.
,,   Crossman, W. R. M.
,,   Davison, S.
,,   Dean, F.
,,   Forster, J.
,,   Lawrence, C. H.
,,   Thompson, G. S. R.
,,   Tindall, E. V.

5th Battalion

2nd Lt. Waring, E. R., attd. 1st Battn.

6th Battalion

Captain Spottiswoode, J., attd. 2nd Battn.
2nd Lt. St. Aubyn, The Hon. P. S., attd. 2nd Battn.

The Duke of Edinburgh's (Wiltshire Regiment)

Major   Roche, T.
Captain Browne, G. S., Adjutant 1st Battn.
,,   Carter, C. G. M.
,,   Dawes, W. R. A. A.
,,   Formby, M. L.
,,   Grimston, H. S.
,,   Stoddart, F. W.
Lieut.   Spencer, E.
2nd Lt. Chandler, C. H.

Special Reserve

2nd Lt. Roseveare, H. W., attd. 1st Battn.

3rd Battalion

Captain Magor, A. C., attd. 2nd Battn.
,,   Reynolds, H. C. C.
,,   Wyld, G. R., attd. R. Berkshire Regiment.
Lieut.   Cruikshank, E. O.
2nd Lt. Burges, E. L. A. H., attd. 2nd Battn.
,,   Campbell, W. P., attd. 2nd Battn.
,,   Gee, R. F. McL., attd. 1st Battn.

The Manchester Regiment

Captain Creagh, L.
,,   Dunlop, F. C. S.
,,   Fisher, H.
,,   Fowke, M. C.
,,   Mansergh, W. G.
,,   Nisbet, F. S.
,,   Trueman, C. F. H.
Lieut.   Caulfield, J. C.
,,   Connell, S. D.
,,   Davidson, R. I. M.
,,   Norman, S. S.
,,   Reade, J. H. L.
,,   (local Capt.) Wickham, T. S., (empl. West African Frontier Force).

2nd Lt. Bentley, C. L.
,, Chittenden, A. G. B.
,, Smith, J. H. M.
,, Walker, R. F.

3rd Battalion

Captain King-Peirce, W. G., attd. 2nd Battn.
,, Tillard, A. G., attd. 2nd Battn.

4th Battalion

Lieut. Horridge, R., attd. 2nd Battn.

The Prince of Wales's
(North Staffordshire Regiment)

Captain Hume-Kelly, G. H.
,, Reid, E. B.
Lieut. Leggett, A. R. A.
,, Royle, A. C. F.

3rd Battalion

Lieut. Hill, W. E., attd. 1st Battn.
2nd Lt. Chester, G. A. B., attd. 1st Battn.
,, Hughes, L. H., attd. 1st Battn.

4th Battalion

Lieut. Meakin, S. A., attd. 1st Battn.

The York and Lancaster Regiment

Captain Sandys, M. K.
Lieut. Hardy, V. H., attd. 1st Battn. Lincolnshire Regiment.

3rd Battalion

Lieut. Peace, H. K.
,, Ripley, C. R., attd. 2nd Battn.

The Durham Light Infantry

Major Blake, E. A. C.
,, Mander, D'A. W.
,, Northey, W.
,, Robb, A. K.
Captain Hare, H. V.
Lieut. Parke, W. E.
,, Swetenham, E.
2nd Lt. Marshall, R.
,, Stanuel, C. M.
,, Storey, H. H.

The Highland Light Infantry

Captain Cameron, W. H. V.
,, Chichester, R. G. I.
,, Pringle, L. G.
Lieut. Cornish, C. L.
,, Dickson, A. J.
,, Fergusson, J. A. H.
,, Gibson-Craig, Sir A. C., Bart.
,, Hall, G. P.
,, Kerr, H. R. G.
,, Mackenzie, C. L.
,, Pitts-Tucker, C. M.
2nd Lt. McBride, A.
,, Macdonald, E. R. H. K.
,, Mears, J. W.
,, Powell, R. C. ff.

3rd Battalion

2nd Lt. Mylles, J. R. J., attd. 1st Battn. Gordon Highlanders.

The Seaforth Highlanders
(Ross-shire Buffs, the Duke of Albany's)

Lt.-Col. Bradford, Sir E. R., Bart.
Major Stockwell, C. I.
Captain Forbes-Robertson, K.
,, Mackenzie, K. B.
,, Methven, D. G.
,, St. Clair, The Hon. C. H. M.
,, Wilson, R. S.
Lieut. Macandrew, I. M.
2nd Lt. Hepburn, M. A.

Special Reserve

2nd Lt. Williamson, A. J. N.

3rd Battalion

2nd Lt. Maitland, W. E., attd. 2nd Battn.

The Gordon Highlanders

Captain Brooke, J. A. O., Ass. Adj. 2nd Battn.
,, Hamilton, M. J., Reserve of Officers.
,, Ker, A. M.
,, Lumsden, C. R.
Lieut. Fraser, J. H.
,, Graham, A. S. B.
,, Latta, C. K.
,, Lyon, A. P. F.
,, MacWilliam, J. J. G.
,, Richmond, L.
,, Sandeman, W. A. F.
,, Trotter, J. K.
2nd Lt. McGrigor, J. N. G.
,, Pirie, A.

3rd Battalion

Major Buckingham, A. W., attd. 1st Battn.
Captain Gordon-Duff, L., attd. 1st Battn.
,, Murray, W. E., attd. Seaforth Highlanders.
2nd Lt. Fraser, The Hon. S., attd. 2nd Battn.

The Queen's Own Cameron Highlanders

Major Maitland, The Hon. A. H.
Captain Brodie, E. J.
,, Cameron, A. G.
,, Cameron, N. C. G.
,, Horne, A.
,, Miers, D. N. C. C.
,, Orr, J. A.
,, Robertson, L.
Lieut. Johnstone, R. F. L.
,, Macdonald, R. M.
,, Meiklejohn, K. F., Adjutant 1st Battn.
,, Sprot, I. B.
2nd Lt. Gearey, E., attd. 1st Battn. Highland Light Infantry.
,, McAuliffe, G. H.

The Royal Irish Rifles

Captain Kennedy, H. A.
,, Master, C. L.
,, Stevens, R. W. M., Staff.
,, Whelan, J. P.
Lieut. Rea, V. T. T.
,, Whitfeld, A. N.
2nd Lt. Swaine, H. P.

3rd Battalion

Captain Allgood, B., attd. 1st Battn.
,, Reynolds, T. J., attd. 2nd Battn.
2nd Lt. Magenis, R. H. C.

5th Battalion

Captain Davis, H. O., attd. 2nd Battn.

Princess Victoria's (Royal Irish Fusiliers)

Major Phibbs, W. G. B.
Captain Carbery, M. B. C.
Lieut. Wakefield, R. O. B.
2nd Lt. Samuels, A. M.

3rd Battalion

Lieut. Crymble, C. R., attd. 1st Battn.

The Connaught Rangers

Major Sarsfield, W. S.
Captain Armstrong-Lushington-Tulloch, G. De M.
,, Hack, C. E.
,, Jackson, F. H.
,, Leader, F. W. M.
Lieut. Abbott, G. D.
,, Blacker, C. F.
,, de Stacpoole, R. A.
,, Fenton, G. R.
,, Fraser, J.
,, George, F. R., Adjutant 1st Battn.
,, Henderson, R. M. H.
,, Ovens, J. R.
,, (*temp.*) Spreckley, R. L.
,, Thomas, R. I.
2nd Lt. Benison, R. B.
,, Lentaigne, V. A.
,, Mallins, C. J. O'C.
,, Vaughan, H. R.
,, Winspear, A.

3rd Battalion

2nd Lt. Montgomery, A., attd. 2nd Battn.

4th Battalion

Captain Saker, F. H.
Lieut. Wickham, A. T. C., attd. 2nd Battn.

Princess Louise's
(Argyll and Sutherland Highlanders)

Major Maclean, A. H.
Captain Bruce, The Hon. R., Master of Burleigh.
,, Fraser, J. A., 2nd Battn.
,, Henderson, W. A.
,, Kennedy, A. E.
Lieut. Aytoun, R. M. G.
,, Burt-Marshall, W. M.
,, Gilkison, J. D.
,, MacLean, A. K.
,, Rose, J. C. R., 2nd Battn.

4th Battalion

Captain Thomas, D. C. W., attd. 1st Battn.
Gordon Highlanders.

The Prince of Wales's Leinster Regiment
(Royal Canadians)

Captain Maffett, H. T.

Captain Montgomerie, W. G.
Lieut. Cormac-Walshe, E. J.
,, Gaitskell, C. E.
,, Lecky, A.
2nd Lt. Eldred, J. S.

The Royal Munster Fusiliers

Major Charrier, P. A.
,, Day, F. I.
,, Thomson, E. P.
Captain Barrett, P. G.
,, O'Brien, H. C. H.
,, Pemberton, O., attd. Royal Dublin Fusiliers.
,, Simms, G. N.
Lieut. Banning, P. S.
,, Chute, C. F. T.
,, O'Brien, J. F.
,, Phayre, C. F.
,, Styles, F. E.
2nd Lt. Awdry, C. E. V.
,, Crozier, J. C. B.
,, Sulivan, P. H.
,, Young, R. A.

3rd Battalion

Captain Durand, F. W., attd. 2nd Battn.
,, Reymes-Cole, W. E., attd. 2nd Battn.

5th Battalion

Captain Travers, H. M., attd. 2nd Battn.

The Royal Dublin Fusiliers

Major (*temp.* Lieut.-Col.) Maclear, P. (empl. West African Frontier Force).
Lieut. Philby, D. D., attd. Royal Munster Fusiliers.
2nd Lt. McGuire, B.

Special Reserve

2nd Lt. Dunlop, J. G. M., attd. 2nd Battn.

The Rifle Brigade
(The Prince Consort's Own)

Lt.-Col. Alexander, R.
Major Harman, G. M. N.
,, Paley, G., Staff.
,, Percival, C. V. N.
,, Rickman, S. H.
Captain Gilliat, O. C. S.
,, Grenville, The Hon. R. G. G. M.
,, Jenkinson, J. B., Staff.
,, Leslie, N. J. B.
,, Toynbee, G. P. R.
,, Whitaker, H.
Lieut. Landale, D. B.

5th Battalion

Captain Prittie, Hon. F. R. D., attd. 1st Battn.
2nd Lt. Daniell, A. S. L., attd. 1st Battn.

6th Battalion

Captain Turner, B. A., attd. King's Royal Rifle Corps.
Lieut. Bradley, G. M., attd. 2nd Battn. Welsh Regiment.

INFANTRY TERRITORIAL FORCE

The Monmouthshire Regiment

2nd Battalion

2nd Lt.   Paton, J. E

The London Regiment

County of London Battalions

14th London Scottish

2nd Lt.   Gulland, R. G. K.

The West India Regiment

2nd Lt.   Williams, A. J. F. de C., attd. 4th
      Battn. Middlesex Regiment.

The Army Service Corps

2nd Lieut.   Walker, W. A. B., attd. 2nd Battn.
      Bedfordshire Regiment.

Royal Army Medical Corps

Lt.-Col.   Dalton, C.
Major   Steel, E. B.
Captain   Conyngham, C. A. T.
,,   Forrest, F.
,,   Glanvill, E. M.
,,   Kinkead, R. C. G. M.
,,   Leckie, M.
,,   Lochrin, M. J.
,,   Macnab, A., Territorial.
,,   Nolan, R. H.
,,   O'Brien-Butler, C. P.
,,   O'Connor, R. D.
,,   Phillips, T. McC.
,,   Ranken, S.
,,   Scatchard, T.
Lieut.   Armstrong, A. K.
,,   Ball, W. O. W.
,,   Chisnall, G. H.
,,   Crocket, J.
,,   Hopkins, H. L.
,,   Huggan, J. L.
,,   Iles, C. C., Special Reserve.
,,   O'Connell, J. F.
,,   Porter, R. E.
,,   Richardson, M. J.
,,   Rintoul, D. W.
,,   Shields, H. S. J.

Army Veterinary Corps

Lieut.   Fox, V.
,,   Jones, S. K., Special Reserve.

West African Regiment

Captain   Brand, E. S., Royal Fusiliers.
,,   Powell, H. M., South Staffordshire Regt.

INDIAN ARMY

INDIAN CAVALRY

14th Murray's Jat Lancers

Captain   Bradshaw, A. E., attd. 15th Hussars.

18th King George's Own Lancers

Lieut.   Railston, S. J. W., attd. 4th Dragoon
      Guards

19th Lancers (Fane's Horse)

Captain   Blane, H. S., attd. 5th Dragoon Guards.
,,   Hunt, F. W.

20th Deccan Horse

Captain   McEuen, J. S.

21st Prince Albert Victor's Own Cavalry (Frontier Force) (Daly's Horse)

Captain   Whitchurch, L. S.

26th King George's Own Light Cavalry

Captain   Chaytor, H. C.

27th Light Cavalry

Major   Henderson, A. F.

34th Prince Albert Victor's Own Poona Horse

Lt.-Col.   Swanston, C. O.
Lieut.   de Pass, F. A.

37th Lancers (Baluch Horse)

Major   Loring, C. B., attd. Poona Horse.

INDIAN INFANTRY

Captain   Birdwood, R. L.

6th Jat Light Infantry

Captain   Anderson, A. C.
,,   Dudley, L. G.
Lieut.   Liptrott, E. C.

9th Bhopal Infantry

Lt.-Col.   Anderson, H. L.

10th Jats

Captain   Mortimer, G. H. W., attd. 9th Bhopal
      Infantry.

13th Rajputs (The Shekhawal Regiment)

Cap'ain   Clothier, R. F.
Lieut.   Day, M. C.

20th Duke of Cambridge's Own Infantry (Brownlow's Punjabis)

Major   Ducat, R.
,,   Rome, H. C.

31st Punjabis
Lieut. Reilly, R. A., attd. 58th Vaughan's Rifles.

34th Sikh Pioneers
Lt.-Col. Kelly, G. H. F.
Captain Mackain, J. F.
,, Masters, A.
,, Vaughan-Sawyer, G. H.

35th Sikhs
Captain Buchanan, C. G., attd. 8th Gurkha Rifles.

36th Sikhs
Captain Padday, W. H., attd. 47th Sikhs.

38th Dogras
Captain Waller, R. H.

39th Garhwal Rifles
Captain Robertson-Glasgow, A. W.

41st Dogras
Captain Marsh, G. H. M.

46th Punjabis
Captain Gilchrist, R. C.

47th Sikhs
Captain McCleverty, R. J.

54th Sikhs (Frontier Force)
Captain Bell, M. A. R., attd. 58th Vaughan's Rifles.

57th Wilde's Rifles (Frontier Force)
Major Barwell, E. E.
Captain Gordon, R. S.
,, Shepherd, G. A. G.
,, Craig, J. M.

58th Vaughan's Rifles (Frontier Force)
Lt.-Col. Venour, W. E.
Captain Baldwin, H. L. C.
,, Black, W. McM., Adjutant.
Lieut. Gaisford, L.

59th Scinde Rifles (Frontier Force)
Lt.-Col. Fenner, C. C.
Captain Lee, H. N.
,, Scott, W. F.
Lieut. Atkinson, J. C.
,, Bruce, W. A. McC.

61st King George's Own Pioneers
Captain Hart, L. G.
,, Manson, B. E. A.

83rd Wallajahbad Light Infantry
Captain Fuller, J. H. M., attd. 63rd Palmacottah
Light Infantry.

97th Deccan Infantry
Captain Cavendish, G. L. J.

98th Infantry
Captain Hall, B. H.

101st Grenadiers
Major Tatum, H.
Captain Brookes, H. R.
,, Brown, F. G.
,, Hogg, I. D. M.
Lieut. Hughes, R. P.

107th Pioneers
Major Bruce, J. M.
Lieut. Burridge, H. G.

108th Infantry
Lieut. Hamer, H. J. T., attd. 101st Grenadiers.

127th Queen Mary's Own Baluch Light Infantry
Major Humphreys, G. G. P.

129th Duke of Connaught's Own Baluchis
Captain Adair, W. F.
,, Hampe-Vincent, P. C.
,, Ussher, S.

1st King George's Own Gurkha Rifles (The Malaun Regiment)
Major Bliss, C.
,, Young, A., Staff
Captain Burke, T. C.
,, Duff, B. O.
,, Money, H. I.
Lieut. Rundall, L. B.

2nd King Edward's Own Gurkha Rifles (The Sirmoor Rifles)
Major Becher, H. S.
,, Macpherson, N.
,, Ross, F. G. C.
Captain Barton, F. H.
Lieut. Innes, I. C.
,, Reid, J. L. I.
2nd Lt. Walcott, J. H. L.

3rd Queen Alexandra's Own Gurkha Rifles
Major Drummond, E. G. (attd.), Res. of Officers.
,, Manners-Smith, F.

4th Gurkha Rifles
Captain Inglis, D.
,, Rundall, A. M.

5th Gurkha Rifles (Frontier Force)
Captain Graham, A. M., attd. King Edward's
Own Gurkha Rifles.

7th Gurkha Rifles

Major   Elliott, R. W. S.
Lieut.   Macpherson, D. S. R.
,,   Rogers, L. C. C.

8th Gurkha Rifles

Major   Wake, H. St. A.
Captain   Davidson, D. B.
,,   Hartwell, H.
,,   Hayes Sadler, E. R.
,,   Stack, E. H. B.
,,   Wright, H. S. N.
Lieut.   Maxwell, C. W.

9th Gurkha Rifles

Lieut.   Baillie, D.
,,   Walton, R. C.

Supply and Transport Corps

Major   Logan, L. S.

Unattached List for Indian Army

2nd Lt.   Mercer, E. C., attd. Royal Dublin Fusiliers.
,,   Tucker, A. R. L., attd. 4th Royal Warwickshire Regiment.

Indian Medical Service

Major   Atal, P. P. L.
Captain   Singh, K. I.

WEST AFRICAN FRONTIER FORCE

Nigeria Regiment

Major   (*temp*. Lieut.-Col.) Maclear, P., R. Dublin Fusiliers.
Captain   Hopkinson, C. R. T., East Surrey Regt.
,,   Peel, A. R., South Wales Borderers.
,,   Priestley, A. B., Dorsetshire Regiment.
,,   (*temp*. Major) Puckle, T. N., Leicestershire Regiment.
,,   Sherlock, G. L. E., 3rd Hussars.
,,   Wesché, E. B., South Lancashire Regt.
Lieut.   (local Capt.) Wickham, T. S., Manchester Regiment.
,,   Hughes, F. D., East Lancashire Regiment.
,,   Stewart, A. H., Gloucestershire Regiment.

Gold Coast Regiment

Bt. Major (*temp*. Lieut.-Col.) Panter-Downes, E.M., Royal Irish Regiment.
Lieut.   Thompson. G. M., Royal Scots.

THE KING'S AFRICAN RIFLES

Lieut.   Bowen, C. E. L. (attd.), late Royal West Surrey Regiment.
,,   Garnett, P. N., 1st (Central Africa) Battn., Royal Berkshire Regiment.
,,   Oldfield, G. C. O., 4th (Uganda) Battn., Royal West Surrey Regiment.
,,   (local Capt.) Thornycroft, E. G. M., 4th (Uganda) Battn. Royal Lancashire Regt.

THE BIOGRAPHIES

MAJOR EUSTACE HENRY AGRE-
MONT ABADIE, D.S.O., p. s. c.,
9th (QUEEN'S ROYAL) LANCERS,

is reported to have
been killed in action
at Messines in Octo-
ber, 1914. He was at
first officially report-
ed to be a prisoner of
war; as no official
confirmation of his
death has been re-
ceived, and as noth-
ing has been heard of
or from him since, it
must be unhappily
assumed that the gallant officer has lost his life.
He was the elder surviving son of the late Major-
General Henry Richard Abadie, C.B., 9th
Lancers, whose death occurred after that of his
son, and was born on the 24th January, 1877.
He joined the 9th Lancers in August, 1897,
becoming Lieutenant in May, 1899. He
served with much distinction in the South
African War, having taken part in the advance
on and relief of Kimberley, including the actions
at Belmont, Enslin, and Magersfontein; he was
present at operations in the Orange Free State,
and at Paardeberg, including actions at Poplar
Grove, Driefontein, Karee Siding, Houtnek
(Thoba Mountain), Vet River and Zand River,
between February and May, 1900; at operations in the Transvaal, East of Pretoria; and
in the Cape Colony between November, 1900,
and May, 1902. He was mentioned in Despatches, "London Gazette," 10th September,
1901, was awarded the D.S.O., and received the
Queen's medal with eight clasps, and the King's
medal with two clasps. It is believed that no
other officer received more than eight clasps with
the Queen's medal, in that campaign.

Major Abadie, who was a Staff College Graduate,
was promoted Captain in March, 1904; from
February, 1906, to August, 1907, he was
Adjutant of his Regiment, and he received his
Majority in March, 1912. For his services in
the Great War he was mentioned in Sir
John French's Despatch of the 14th January,
1915.

It is an interesting fact, illustrating how the
name of the same family recurs in military
history, that the first name in "The Last
Post," a work containing biographies of officers
who lost their lives in the South African War,
which commenced fifteen years before the
present war, was also that of a cavalry
officer named Abadie, viz., Lieutenant H. B.
Abadie, 11th Hussars. That officer was Major
E. H. A. Abadie's eldest brother; and another
brother, Captain G. H. F. Abadie, late 16th
Lancers, died of fever in February, 1904,
at Kam, West Africa, where he was serving
as Resident, after having been awarded the
C.M.G. for his services in the Kam-Sohoto
Campaign.

Major-General Abadie, the late officer's father,
also had a most distinguished military career
of 46 years.

LIEUTENANT GEOFFREY DYETT
ABBOTT, 1st BATTN. CONNAUGHT
RANGERS,

who was born on the
12th October, 1891,
at Srinagar, Kash-
mir, was the son of
the late Colonel
Frank Abbott, late
37th Lancers
(Baluch Horse), and
a grandson of the
late Lieutenant-
General H. D.
Abbott, C.B., and of
Major-General J. C. Berkeley, C.I.E.

He was educated at Cheltenham College and
the R.M.C., Sandhurst. Having been gazetted
to the Connaught Rangers in March, 1911, he
served with the 1st Battalion in India, and
was promoted Lieutenant in June, 1914.

He was a good shot, and played football,
cricket, billiards, and tennis.

Lieut. Abbott was killed in action at Laventie,
France, on the 2nd November, 1914. His
Company Commander sent the following
account of the circumstances :—

" On the 2nd instant (November, 1914) we
went to relieve the 2nd Gurkhas and came
under rather heavy fire crossing an open place.
It was in the above open place he was
killed."

MAJOR WILLIAM HENRY ABELL, 4th BATTN. DUKE OF CAMBRIDGE'S OWN (MIDDLESEX REGIMENT),

who was stated in the Casualty List published by the War Office in the November Army List to have been " reported killed in action," it is believed at Obourg, near Mons, was the second son of the late Martin Abell, of Norton Hall, Worcestershire. He was born on the 20th September, 1873, and joined the Middlesex Regiment from the Militia in December, 1896, becoming Lieutenant in October, 1899. Major Abell served in St. Helena during the South African War from March to May, receiving the Queen's medal. From September, 1907, to March, 1908, he was an Adjutant of Volunteers, and from April, 1908, to March, 1910, an Adjutant of the Territorial Force; he was promoted to his Majority in September, 1912. Major Abell left a widow.

CAPTAIN WILLIAM FINLAY ADAIR, 129th DUKE OF CONNAUGHT'S OWN BALUCHIS,

was born at Mauchline, Ayrshire, Scotland, on the 21st September, 1877, the youngest son of the late Major Wallace Adair, Northumberland Fusiliers (the " Fighting Fifth "). He was educated at the French College at St. Serven, Brittany, and afterwards in Jersey. He obtained his commission as unattached Second Lieutenant in January, 1897, joining the Indian Staff Corps in March, 1898, in which he became Lieutenant in July, 1899, and Captain in January, 1906. He saw most of his service with the 130th King George's Own Baluchis, of which for some years he was Adjutant, being transferred to the 129th, on promotion, as Double Company Commander, and he was also qualified as a First Class Interpreter in French. He served in China in 1900 and received the medal; in the operations in Somaliland, 1902, receiving the medal and clasp, and in operations in the interior, Aden, 1903–04.

He was a member of the Junior Army and Navy Club, and of the Bath and County Club, Bath. Captain Adair was killed on the 30th October, 1914, at Hollebeke, Belgium, having been, at his own request, left mortally wounded in a trench when his men had to retire. The following account of the circumstances was received by his relatives :—" On October 30th, 1914, at Hollebeke, Belgium, Captain Adair had orders from his General to retire, as the Germans were close up ; while giving instructions to his men he was shot high up under the arm. The native Corporal wished to carry him away, but he refused, fearing to delay them, and so insisted on being left in the trench alone. The Germans came up almost immediately, and nothing further has been heard. The Corporal, who said Captain Adair was mortally wounded and could not have lived long, led the men back to a safe position already prepared, without any loss, and so the sacrifice was not in vain."

Captain Adair was mentioned in Sir John French's Despatch of 14th January, 1915.

LIEUTENANT ALEC CRICHTON MAITLAND-ADDISON, 1st BATTN. THE CHESHIRE REGIMENT,

born at Brighton in 1886, was the son of Major A. Maitland-Addison, late 71st Highlanders; he was a great grandson of Charles Bisset, 42nd Highlanders (mentioned in " Lives of Eminent Scotchmen ") and closely connected with the family of the poet Joseph Addison.

He was educated privately, and was gazetted to the Cheshire Regiment in September, 1914, as Second Lieutenant.

Joining the Royal Flying Corps, he landed in France in August, 1914, and served continuously till the time of his death, having been promoted for distinguished service in the Field. He was wounded at Ypres on the 25th October, 1914, and died at Boulogne on the 27th October, 1914. Lieutenant Maitland-Addison was a fine man —6 feet 3 inches in height, and broad in proportion—extremely powerful, and without fear.

CAPTAIN HENRY ROBERT AUGUSTUS ADEANE, COLDSTREAM GUARDS,

son of the late Admiral Edward Adeane and the late Lady Edith Adeane, was born at 28, Eaton Place, London, on the 31st July, 1882. He was educated at Winchester, and the R.M.C., Sandhurst, and was gazetted to the Coldstream Guards in 1902, becoming Lieutenant in 1905, and Captain in 1912, retiring in May, 1913. At the outbreak of the war, he was voluntarily in the Reserve of Officers, and joined his regiment for service at the front. He was killed near Ypres on the 2nd November, 1914.

3

AIN—ALE

Captain Adeane married in 1909, Victoria Eugénie Bigge, daughter of Lieutenant-Colonel Lord Stamfordham, and left one son, Michael Edward, born 30th September, 1910.

2nd LIEUTENANT DENYS ALFRED LAFONE AINSLIE, 1st BATTN. DEVONSHIRE REGT.,

who was killed in action on the 24th October, 1914, in France, was the third son of Mr. and Mrs. W. L. Ainslie, of Hanworth House, Harrow Weald.

He was educated at Wellington, where he was in the Talbot from 1906—1910. He was gazetted to the 3rd Battalion of his regiment in April, 1913, and was granted a commission in the 1st Battalion in August, 1914.

LIEUTENANT JOHN STIRLING AINSWORTH, 11th (PRINCE ALBERT'S OWN) HUSSARS,

who was killed in action on the 14th October, 1914, was the second son of J. S. Ainsworth, Ardanaiseig, Argyllshire, and of 55, Eaton Place, London, S.W.; his mother, Margaret Catherine, being a daughter of R. R. Macredie, D.L.,

J.P. for Argyllshire and Cumberland, and M.P. for the first named County from 1903. He was born on the 9th November, 1889, and joined the 11th Hussars in April, 1909. Lieutenant Ainsworth, who reached that rank in November, 1912, was mentioned in Sir John French's Despatch of the 8th October, 1914.

LIEUTENANT RONALD ANDREW COLQUHOUN AITCHISON, 1st BATTN. THE KING'S OWN ROYAL LANCASTER REGIMENT,

who died on the 14th September, 1914, of wounds received in action, was the son of G. Colquhoun Aitchison, of South Collingham, Newark. He received his commission in September, 1913, and was promoted Lieutenant on the 15th November, 1914.

CAPTAIN REGINALD JOHN PETTY DEVENISH ALDRIDGE, 2nd BATTN. THE ROYAL SUSSEX REGIMENT,

was born on the 7th September, 1877, at Poole, Dorset, and was the son of the late Reginald Aldridge, solicitor, and Mrs. Aldridge, of Parkstone, Dorset. He was educated by a private tutor, and at Worcester College, Oxford, where he took his B.A. degree; won some prizes for Athletics, and was an Oxford Blue for Football. He was also a hockey player. In May, 1900, he received his commission in the Royal Sussex Regiment, in which he became Lieutenant in March, 1903. In 1902 he was Instructor of Signalling at Kasauli, India, and in 1904 he commanded a Company of Mounted Infantry in Malta. He was attached to the West African Regiment from 1905-08, being appointed Assistant-Adjutant and Quartermaster in January, 1906. From January, 1908, to January, 1912, he was Adjutant of the Guernsey Light Infantry, and then rejoined his battalion at Woking, becoming Captain in April, 1910.

At the Battle of the Aisne he was killed by a shell on the 7th October, 1914, and was buried at Troyon.

Captain Aldridge married, in May, 1908, Mabel Dulcibella, daughter of the late Rev. J. Padmore Noble, Vicar of Childs Ercall, Market Drayton, from 1876-96, and left two children, Dulcibella Noble, born 24th December, 1909, and Reginald Charles Petty, born 24th December, 1914.

LIEUTENANT-COLONEL REGINALD ALEXANDER, 3rd BATTN. RIFLE BRIGADE,

died on the 29th December, 1914, from wounds received in action. He was born on the 6th September, 1867, and joined the Royal West Kent Regiment from the Militia in January, 1889. In December, 1891, he was transferred to the Rifle Brigade as Lieutenant, and from 1894-98 was Adjutant of his Battalion.

He was a fair cricketer, very fond of racing and of a most cheery disposition.

He served in the South African War, taking part in operations in Natal, including the action at Laing's Nek ; in the Transvaal east of Pretoria, including action at Belfast, being severely wounded.   Later he was Commandant at Uitkyk, and afterwards at Olifant's River. He was twice mentioned in Despatches ("London Gazette," 10th September, 1901, and 29th July, 1902), and received the Queen's and the King's medals, each with two clasps.

He obtained his Majority in April, 1905, and succeeded to the command of his Battalion in October, 1913.

MAJOR WILLIAM LEWIS CAMPBELL ALLAN, 3rd (attd. 2nd) BATTN. KING'S OWN SCOTTISH BORDERERS,

was killed in action on the 12th October, 1914, near Cuinchy, La Bassée, France.

He was the eldest son of Major-General William Allan, Colonel of the Welsh Regiment, of Hillside, Edinburgh, and Bidborough, Kent, and was born at Dalhousie, India, on the 6th July, 1871.

Major-General Allan, the late officer's father, had himself a very distinguished military career, for he served in the Crimea with the 41st Regiment—now the Welsh Regiment— taking part in the battles of the Alma and Inkerman, both the assaults on the Redan, and was present at the siege and fall of Sebastopol: his services were recognised by the award of the British medal with three clasps, the Turkish medal, and by his being appointed a Knight of the Legion of Honour. Major Allan was educated at Wellington College, where he was in the Hopetown from 1885-1889, and at Brasenose College, Oxford.   He joined the 3rd Battalion King's Own Scottish Borderers in November, 1890, and served in the South African War of 1900-1902, being Station Staff Officer on the Lines of Communication at Modder River (graded as a Staff Captain) from the 21st March, 1900.   He was present at operations in Cape Colony, and for his services received the Queen's medal with two clasps, and the King's medal with two clasps. He was at the School of Musketry and went through the Machine Gun course at Hythe, and received the rank of Hon. Major in June, 1899.

Major Allan was fond of cricket, shooting and fishing, and was a member of the Conservative Club, Edinburgh, and of the Junior Carlton Club, London.

CAPTAIN LIONEL THEOPHILUS ALLASON, 1st BATTN. LOYAL NORTH LANCASHIRE REGIMENT,

fourth son of the late Alfred Allason, Esq., of Randolph Crescent, London, W., was born on the 3rd February, 1877, and was educated at Dulwich College and by private tuition abroad.

He joined the 3rd (Militia) Battalion East Lancashire Regiment, and served with it, when embodied, in the South African War ; he was Station Staff Officer at Vet River, and was present at operations in Cape Colony south of Orange River, in the Orange River Colony in 1900, and again in both Colonies in 1901 and 1902. Before that war was over he was gazetted to the Loyal North Lancashire Regiment in July, 1901.   For his services he received the Queen's and the King's medals, each with two clasps.

Captain Allason, who was promoted Lieutenant in September, 1904, and Captain in November, 1912, was qualified as a first-class Interpreter in German, but above all he was a regimental man who took keen interest in all the sports and doings of his regiment.

He was killed by shrapnel on the 7th October, 1914, at Vendresse, near Troyon, and was buried there.   He was mentioned in Sir John French's Despatch of the 8th October, 1914.

LIEUTENANT HUGH THOMAS ACKLAND-ALLEN, 1st BATTN. ROYAL WELSH FUSILIERS,

who was killed in action on the 23rd October, 1914, was the only son of C. Ackland-Allen, of St. Hilary Manor, Cowbridge, South Wales.   Lieutenant Ackland-Allen was educated at Wellington College, where he was in the Beresford from 1907-1910, proceeding to the R.M.C., Sandhurst, in 1912. He received his commission in the Royal Welsh Fusiliers in September, 1913 ; the battalion went to Malta in January, 1914, returned to England in September, and went out with the VIIth Division on the 4th October.

He was 21 years of age when he was killed near Zonnebeke on the 23rd October, 1914.

CAPTAIN AND ADJUTANT JOHN FRANCIS ALLEN, 1st LOYAL NORTH LANCASHIRE REGIMENT,

son of William Henry Allen, J.P., D.L., of Bromham House, Bromham, near Bedford, was born at 16, Greville Road, Kilburn, N.W., on the 9th October, 1881, and was educated at Repton School.

He obtained his commission in 1899 in the Loyal North Lancashire Regiment from the Militia during the Boer War. He served with the 2nd Battalion in Malta, Gibraltar, South Africa, Mauritius, and India, and was transferred to the 1st Battalion, in which he became Captain, in April, 1912. He received the South African War (Mediterranean) medal; also the Delhi Durbar medal whilst he was A.D.C. to Lord Sydenham, Governor of Bombay.

Captain Allen left Aldershot August, 1914, attached to the 1st Division Staff, and was appointed Adjutant in September, 1914. He took part in all the engagements in Belgium and France, from the commencement of hostilities up to the time of his death, which occurred on the 4th November, 1914, from wounds received near Ypres, while in the act of rescuing two men who had been buried by earth thrown up by a shell.

Captain Allen was a good all-round sportsman, interested in all forms of sport, and also in amateur theatricals. He was not married.

MAJOR WILLIAM LYNN ALLEN, D.S.O., 2nd BATTN. BORDER REGT.,

who was killed in action on the 25th October, 1914, was the son of the late Bulkeley Allen, Esq., J.P., and Mrs. Bulkeley Allen, of West Lynn, Altrincham, Cheshire. He had two soldier brothers: the late Major E. Lynn Allen, Royal Warwickshire Regiment, and Major A. Lynn Allen, A.P.D., formerly in the Suffolk Regiment; and his cousin, Captain J. Derwent Allen, C.B., R.N., is now commanding H.M.S. " Kent "; while another cousin is Major W. A. Frere Jones, R.F.A., also on Active Service.

He was born on the 8th May, 1871, and was educated at Rugby (Rev. C. Elsee's house), to which he went in 1885. He joined the Border Regiment from the Militia in September, 1893, becoming Lieutenant in 1896. From August, 1901, to August, 1904, he was Adjutant of his battalion. He served all through the South African War, being present at operations in Natal in 1899; at the Relief of Ladysmith, including action at Colenso, and the actions at Spion Kop and Vaal Krans; operations in the Tugela Heights and action at Pieters Hill; operations in the Orange Free State, in the Transvaal east and west of Pretoria, in the Orange River Colony, and in Cape Colony north and south of Orange River. During the latter part of the war he was Adjutant of his Battalion. For his services he was twice mentioned in Despatches (" London Gazette," 10th September, 1901, and 29th July, 1902), was awarded the D.S.O., and received the Queen's medal with five clasps and the King's medal with two clasps.

From September, 1905, to September, 1909, Major Lynn Allen was Adjutant of the Discharge Depot, and he received his Majority in October, 1913, in the 2nd Battalion, in which he had commanded a Company.

The circumstances under which Major Lynn Allen met his death were as follows :—

On the evening of the 25th October, about 7.30, he was holding a point between the villages of Kruiseik and America, about 4½ miles from Ypres. For the previous seven days Major Lynn Allen had been occupying with his men a salient point at the extreme left of his regiment, and his Company was badly in need of reinforcements. On that particular night about 100 of the enemy made their way over trenches occupied by a neighbouring battalion, and appeared in the vicinity of a farmhouse in the rear of the Borderers. These men were at first mistaken for Belgians sent in support, but the error having been realised they were fired upon and a considerable number killed. Immediately afterwards the remainder signified their wish to surrender and asked for an English Officer. In response Major Lynn Allen left his trench with two men, and had hardly advanced more than a step or two before the enemy treacherously opened fire, and he fell back mortally wounded.

Colonel Wood, the Commanding Officer, in a letter to Mrs. Lynn Allen, and subsequently at a personal interview with a brother of the deceased officer, paid a high tribute to his value as an officer, to his popularity with the men of the regiment, and to the splendid example he set them by his coolness under fire. Major Lynn Allen married Adeline Miriam, third daughter of the late Isaac Carbutt Dickinson, of Newcastle-on-Tyne, and leaves two sons and one daughter.

LIEUTENANT FREDERIC DE VERE BRUCE ALLFREY, 9th LANCERS,

who was the son of Mr. and Mrs. F. Vere Allfrey. of Wokingham, Reading, was reported unofficially as having been killed in action in September, 1914.

Lieutenant Allfrey was born on the 21st September, 1891, and was educated at Wellington College, his father having been at the same school, and was in Brougham's and Upcott's from 1905–09, going to the R.M.C., Sandhurst, in 1910, from which he passed into the 9th Lancers in February, 1911. He was promoted Lieutenant in January, 1913. Since the unofficial report of his death it has transpired that after a charge of the 9th Lancers on the 6th September, 1914, near Provins, Lieutenant Allfrey dismounted to help a wounded brother officer, and was himself shot and killed by a wounded German.

CAPT. BERTRAM ALLGOOD, ROYAL IRISH RIFLES,

who was killed in action on the 7th December, 1914, was the second son of the late Major-General Allgood, C.B., Indian Army, latterly Chief Constable of Northumberland.

He was born on the 11th February, 1874, was educated at Eton and received his commission in the Royal Irish Rifles from the Militia in May, 1897, becoming Lieutenant in the following year and Captain in February, 1904. At the time of the South African War he was serving with the 1st Battalion at Calcutta, and so did not take part in that campaign. He continued to serve in India till 1905, when he came home for duty at the Depot at Belfast. He returned to India, but again came back to Belfast, and then served for a time in the 2nd Battalion at Dover. In 1912 he was appointed Adjutant of the 4th Battalion, which appointment he gave up on retiring from the Army in February, 1914, when he joined the Reserve of Officers. On the outbreak of the war with Germany he was called up for service with the 3rd Battalion, but later went to the Front with his old battalion, the 1st, on the 7th November, 1914. He was shot through the heart on the 7th December, 1914, while seeing his men into safety on returning

to the trenches near Ypres, and was buried in a cemetery at Estaires.

He was very fond of hunting, polo, and all sport, and was a member of the Naval and Military Club. Captain Allgood married in April, 1913, Isa Cochrane, daughter of the late Arthur Bayley and Mrs. Herbert Lyde, and left a daughter, born August, 1914.

LIEUTENANT CLAUDE McCAUL ALSTON, 2nd BATTN. ROYAL SCOTS FUSILIERS,

who was reported as wounded and missing, no news being subsequently received for many months, is now reported to have been killed near Ypres, in Flanders, while with the VIIth Division about the 27th October, 1914.

He was the only son of C. Ross Alston, Barrister-at-Law, and Mrs. Ross Alston, Allahabad, India, and nephew of Geo. R. Alston, Rosemount, Chislehurst.

Lieutenant Alston was born on the 29th September, 1892, was educated at Charterhouse, and received his commission in the Royal Scots Fusiliers in September, 1912. He was gazetted Lieutenant, to date from the 27th October, 1914, the day on which he was killed.

LIEUTENANT WILLIAM KERR AMES, 1st BATTN. ROYAL WEST KENT REGIMENT,

who died of wounds in hospital at Compiègne on the 17th September, 1914, being then just 23 years of age, was the youngest son of the late Mr. Thomas Ames, Huish House, Kilmersdoon, Somerset, and of Mrs. Ames, 29, Clifton Gardens, Folkestone. He was born at Huish House, Southampton, on the 6th September, 1891.

He was educated at Dover College, and by an Army coach, passing into the R.M.C., Sandhurst, whence he joined the West Kent Regiment in March, 1912.

He was shot through both legs at Crepy, near Compiègne, during the retirement from Mons, on the 1st September, 1914. His Company Officer had been killed, and Lieutenant Ames had then assumed command of the Company, when he too was hit.

2nd LIEUTENANT GILBERT STRATTON AMOS, 2nd BATTN. KING'S OWN SCOTTISH BORDERERS,

who was killed in action at the battle of the Aisne on the 14thSeptember,1914, a few days before he had completed his 19th year, was the only son of Major Amos, D.S.O., late King's Own Scottish Borderers, of St.Ibbs, Hitchin.

Second Lieutenant Amos was educated at Wellington College, where he was in Mr. Upcote's House from 1909-1912, when he went to the R.M.C., Sandhurst, whence he was gazetted to the King's Own Scottish Borderers in February, 1914.

CAPTAIN ALEXANDER CLAIR. MONTE ANDERSON, 6th JAT LIGHT INFANTRY,

son of Lieutenant-Colonel A. Anderson, late R.A.M.C., was born at Muttra, North-West Provinces, India, on the 28th April, 1885.

After his education at Kelly College, Tavistock, Devon, and the R.M.C., Sandhurst, he received his commission as Second Lieutenant in the Royal Sussex Regiment in January, 1895, joining the Indian Army in 1907, and becoming Captain in January, 1914.

He was killed in the trenches at Festubert, near Bethune, France, on the 22nd November, 1914, by the premature explosion of a hand-bomb which he was about to throw.

Captain Anderson was a member of the Junior Army and Navy Club. He was not married.

2nd LIEUTENANT ALAN JAMES RAMSAY ANDERSON, 3rd BATTN. ROYAL IRISH REGIMENT,

was the third son of Robert Andrew Anderson, Secretary of the Irish Agricultural Organisation Society, and was born at Doneraile, Co. Cork, Ireland, on the 15th December,1891. He was educated at Bedford Grammar School, and University College, Oxford. He won the Public Schools Boxing Championship. Feather Weights, in 1909, and was the Oxford University Boxing Club Light Weight in 1912, 1913, and 1914. He was a member of Vincent's Club, Oxford University, and of the Oxford Union ; Secretary of the Oxford University Boxing Club, and President of St. Patrick's Club, Oxford ; he was also a member of the Royal Dublin Golf Club.

Applying through the Oxford University O.T.C. on the outbreak of the war, he was given a commission in the Royal Irish Regiment in August, 1914.

He was killed at Le Pilly, near Aubers, Lille, on the 20th October, 1914, his second day in the firing line. His battalion had carried Le Pilly with the bayonet, when it was cut off and surrounded, and Second Lieutenant Anderson was shot through the head in the front trench.

2nd LIEUT. CHARLES ALEXANDER KENNETH ANDERSON, 1st BATTN. THE KING'S ROYAL RIFLE CORPS,

aged 21, was the only son of A. R. Anderson, Esq., F.R.C.S., of Nottingham.

He was educated at Stanmore Park, and at Harrow (Mr. Moss, 1907 - 1911). After leaving Harrow he went to Pembroke College, Cambridge, and was gazetted to the 1st Battalion

The Royal Scots Fusiliers as a University Candidate on the 4th August, 1914. On the 14th August he was gazetted as Second Lieutenant to the King's Royal Rifle Corps, but having already left England with the Royal Scots Fusiliers, he remained attached to that regiment throughout the campaign.

He took part in the successive engagements at Mons, the Marne, the Aisne, and lastly on the Franco-Belgian frontier in the first battle of Ypres. He was killed in action about 3 a.m. on the 12th November, 1914, while leading his men in a night attack on the German trenches, being at that time in command of half of "C" Company, 1st Battalion Royal Scots Fusiliers. Second Lieutenant Anderson was a member of the University Pitt Club, Cambridge.

LIEUTENANT COLIN KNOX ANDERSON, 3rd BATTN. THE QUEEN'S OWN (ROYAL WEST KENT REGIMENT), whose name appeared in the first list of British losses issued by the War Office on the 1st September, 1914, as killed in action, was the youngest son of G. K. Anderson,

Esq., D.L., of Bridge Hill, near Canterbury. Lieutenant Anderson, who was 26 years of age  at the time of his death, was educated at Malvern College, where he was a school Prefect, in the Cricket XI, and Football XXII. Lieutenant Anderson joined the 3rd Battalion Royal West Kent Regiment, in December, 1908, and was promoted Lieutenant in April, 1911. When war was declared he was employed on civil work in Rochester, but at once offered his services which were accepted. He was then attached to the 1st Battalion of his regiment and proceeded with it to France.

He was good at all games, but chiefly excelled at cricket, being a successful fast bowler. He was well known in regimental cricket and with the Kent Amateurs "The Band of Brothers."

2nd LIEUTENANT ERNEST LIONEL LANE ANDERSON, 1st BATTN. ROYAL SCOTS FUSILIERS, who was killed in action on the 10th-11th November, 1914, aged 20, was the son of Mr. and Mrs. Lane Anderson, of The Drive, Hove.

He was born on the 24th December, 1893, and went to the R.M.C., Sandhurst, in 1912, becoming an under-officer and winning the sword for drill. He joined the Scots Fusiliers in February, 1913, and went to the Continent with them at the beginning of the war, being mentioned in Sir John French's Despatch of the 8th October, 1914.

2nd LIEUT. GERARD RUPERT LAURIE ANDERSON, 3rd BATTN. CHESHIRE REGIMENT,  who was killed in action on the 8th November, 1914, aged 25, was the son of Prebendary and Mrs. Anderson, of 20, Chester Street, London, S.W., and grandson of Sir Emilius Laurie, Bart., of Maxwelton House, Dumfrieshire. He was educated at Eton, where he established a reputation as an athlete, especially in Fives and the Field game. He was captain of the Oppidans, President of the Eton Society, and Keeper of the Field ; he won the School Fives and House Fives each

three times, and the Hurdles also thrice. He won a scholarship at Trinity College, Oxford, where he took first classes in " Mods " and " Greats," and was President of the University Athletic Club, being finally elected a Fellow of All Souls in 1913. He continued his athletic successes at the 'Varsity, where he ran in the quarter and half miles and Hurdles, also competing in 1911 for Oxford and Cambridge against Yale and Harvard. He twice won the English, and once the Scotch, Championship over hurdles, and made his final appearance in the athletic field at Stockholm.

After leaving College he entered the firm of Cammell Laird, at Birkenhead, and on the outbreak of the war with Germany, applied for and was given a commission on probation in the 3rd Battalion Cheshire Regiment on the 14th August, 1914, and was attached for active service to the 1st Battalion of that Regiment, sailing for France on the 21st September.

Mr. Anderson was twice wounded at La Bassée, but remained on duty, and was shot through the heart on the 8th November, 1914, while leading a charge against the German trenches. For his services he was mentioned in Sir John French's Despatch of the 14th January, 1915.

LIEUTENANT-COLONEL HENRY LAWRENCE ANDERSON, SECOND IN COMMAND, 9th BHOPAL INFANTRY, INDIAN ARMY, who died on the 28th-29th October, 1914, of wounds received in action, was the son of the late General R. P. and Mrs. Anderson, Holland Road, Kensington.

He was born in June, 1867, and was gazetted to the Yorkshire Light Infantry in August, 1888. He was promoted Lieutenant in March, 1890, and in the following month was transferred to the Indian Staff Corps. He was promoted Captain in the Indian Army in August, 1899, and in 1903-4 saw active service in Tibet, for which he received the medal.

Lieutenant-Colonel Anderson, who left a widow, obtained his Majority in August, 1906, and was promoted Lieutenant-Colonel in August, 1914.

CAPTAIN CHARLES GEORGE WILLIAM ANDREWS, ADJUTANT 2nd BATTN. BORDER REGIMENT, who was killed in action on the 28th October, 1914, leaving a widow, was the only child of the late G. J. W. Andrews, of Dorchester, and of Mrs. Andrews, of Bedford. He was born on the 16th May, 1878, and joined the Border Regiment from the Militia in May,

1898, becoming Lieutenant in August, 1901. He took part in the South African War, being present at operations in Natal, at the Relief of Ladysmith (wounded on the 21st January, 1900); at operations in the Orange Free State, the Transvaal, Orange River Colony, and Cape Colony, south and north of Orange River. He received the Queen's medal with four clasps and the King's medal with two clasps.

From November, 1905, to November, 1910, he was an Adjutant of Volunteers and of the Territorial Force, having been promoted Captain in his regiment in April, 1909. In December, 1911, he was appointed Adjutant of the 2nd Battalion of his regiment, and held that position when he was killed.

His battalion formed part of the 20th Brigade of the memorable VIIth Division which left Lyndhurst for Belgium on October 4th, and Captain Andrews was with it in all the fighting which took place in the retirement from Bruges and Ghent, to Ypres, and fell in the first battle which took place to the east of that town.

LIEUTENANT FREDERICK GEORGE ANDREWS, 4th BATTN. THE KING'S (LIVERPOOL REGIMENT),

who was killed in action on the 21st October, 1914, at the age of 43, was born in New Zealand, and educated at Christ College, Wellington. When the war with Germany broke out he was living at Hallaton, Market Harborough, Leicestershire, where he had resided for several years.

He received a commission as Lieutenant in the Liverpool Regiment in August, 1914, and was attached to the 2nd Battn. South Lancashire Regiment when he was killed.

CAPTAIN THE HON. ARTHUR ANNESLEY, 10th (PRINCE OF WALES'S OWN ROYAL) HUSSARS,

was the son and heir of Arthur, 11th Viscount Valentia, and was born at Bletchington Park, Oxford, on 24th August, 1880. His next brother,

who is now heir to the title, is a Lieutenant in the Oxfordshire Light Infantry. He was educated at Eton

and received his commission in the 10th Royal Hussars, from the 3rd (Militia) Oxfordshire and Buckinghamshire Light Infantry in April, 1900. He became Lieutenant in November, 1901. With his regiment he served in the South African War from 1900 to 1902, being present at operations in the Transvaal and Cape Colony, for which he received the Queen's medal with three clasps and the King's medal with two clasps. He also received the Coronation medal of King George V.

Having obtained his Captaincy in 1907, he served as Adjutant of his regiment from May, 1907, to December, 1908, and in November, 1912, was appointed A.D.C. to the General Officer Commanding in Egypt, an appointment he was holding when the Great War broke out.

He was killed in action by a sniper at Zillebeke, near Ypres, on the 16th November, 1914.

Captain Annesley was a member of the Cavalry Club, and his recreations were hunting and polo.

LIEUTENANT-COLONEL GEORGE KIRKPATRICK ANSELL, p.s.c., COMMANDING 5th (PRINCESS CHARLOTTE OF WALES'S) DRAGOON GUARDS,

son of the late Colonel R. Ansell, Royal Marine Artillery, was born at Fort Cumberland, near Portsmouth, in 1872.

He was educated at Wellington College, and joined the 6th (Inniskilling) Dragoons from the Militia in April, 1894,

becoming Lieutenant in September, 1895, and Captain in July, 1901. He served with distinction in the South African War as Regimental Adjutant, which appointment he held with the break of a few months from 1897 to 1902, afterwards acting as Brigade-Major to General Rimington. He took part in operations in the Transvaal, east of Pretoria, including actions at Reit Vlei and Belfast, and in operations in Cape Colony, south of Orange River, including the action of Colesberg. For his services he was twice mentioned in Despatches, received his

Brevet Majority, the Queen's medal with three clasps and the King's medal with two clasps. Lieutenant-Colonel Ansell also held the Diamond Jubilee medal, 1897, and the Royal Humane Society's bronze medal for saving a life in South Africa.

Lieutenant-Colonel Ansell was not only qualified for Staff employment in consequence of service on the Staff in the Field, but he was also a graduate of the Staff College, where he passed the final examination in 1903, receiving the appointment of Brigade-Major, 3rd Cavalry Brigade, in 1904, and retaining it till 1907. He held an appointment as General Staff Officer, 2nd Grade, at the War Office from 1910-1911, in August of which year he was selected for the command of the 5th Dragoon Guards. He was a noted polo player and formed one of the regimental teams of the Inniskillings and the 5th Dragoon Guards, being in the winning team of the former when they won the Inter-regimental Cup in 1897, 1898, and 1905 ; he was also in the team when the same regiment won the Army Cup in 1899. He won several point-to-point races with his horses—Glencoe, Absalom, Newboy, and Napper Tandy.

Just before the war with Germany broke out he had been offered the appointment of Commandant at the Cavalry School, but this position, of course, was not taken up. He was killed on the 1st September, 1914, while leading his regiment. For his services in this war he was mentioned in Sir John French's Despatch of 8th October, 1914.

Lieutenant-Colonel Ansell married in 1899, Kathleen, daughter of J. P. Cross, of Catthorpe Towers, Rugby, and leaves a son and a daughter.

LIEUTENANT EDMUND ANTROBUS, 1st BATTN. GRENADIER GUARDS, who was killed in action on the 24th October, 1914, was the only son of Sir Edmund Antrobus, 4th Baronet, of Antrobus, County Chester, and Rutherford, County Roxburgh, at one time commanding 3rd Battalion Grenadier Guards. Lieutenant Antrobus was born on the 23rd December, 1886, and received his commission as Second Lieutenant in the Grenadier Guards from the Militia in May, 1908, being promoted Lieutenant in November, 1908.

The 1st Battn. Grenadier Guards formed part of the 20th Brigade of the VIIth Division which was in the centre of our line at the first Battle of Ypres. On the 24th October the Germans made a determined effort to break through on the left of the Grenadiers near Kruiseik, and No. 4 Company, to which Lieut. Antrobus belonged, made a counter-attack, driving back the enemy. He was killed while gallantly fighting with his platoon, only one officer and forty-five men of the Company returning unhurt.

2nd LIEUTENANT K. S. APLIN attd. 2nd BATTN. ROYAL INNISKILLING FUSILIERS, who was killed in action on the 1st November, 1914, was the son of Mr. and Mrs. J. Shorland Aplin, of Englefield Green, and Yeovil, and was born in 1892. He was educated at Mill Hill School, London, and at Worcester College,

Oxford. He was appointed to the Special Reserve, Royal Inniskilling Fusiliers, on probation, on the 6th August, 1913, his commission being finally dated the 27th June, 1914.

LIEUTENANT (temp.) ARTHUR KEITH ARMSTRONG, ROYAL ARMY MEDICAL CORPS, who was killed in action on the 16th September, 1914, aged 33, leaving a widow, was the only son of Mr. and Mrs. H. Armstrong, 42, Dartmouth Park Road, London, N.W. He was gazetted Temporary Lieutenant in the

R.A.M.C. on the 15th August, 1914.

LIEUTENANT BASIL CLAUDIUS ASH, THE SHERWOOD FORESTERS (NOTTINGHAMSHIRE AND DERBYSHIRE REGIMENT), who was killed in action on the 20th September, 1914, was the son of Claudius James Ash, of Blakeney, Norfolk, and 2, Parkhill Road, Hampstead, and was born on the 25th April, 1886. He joined the Sherwood Foresters from the Militia in March, 1907, and became Lieutenant in June, 1909. From October of that year till the Great War broke out, he was employed with the Nigerian Regiment, West African Frontier Force.

CAPTAIN HENRY ADAM ASKEW, 2nd BATTN. BORDER REGIMENT, was the son of the late Canon Edmund Adam Askew, Rector of Greystoke, Cumberland, where he was born on the 8th September, 1881 ; he was a grandson of Mr. Askew, of Burwood Park, Walton-on-Thames.

Captain Askew was educated at Aysgarth School, Harrow, and the R.M.C., Sandhurst ; he obtained the Gymnastic Certificate at

Aldershot, 1908, and that for the Mounted Infantry previously at Bulford. He joined the Border

Regiment in 1901, and with it served in the South African War, having been present at the operations in the Transvaal, receiving the Queen's medal with five clasps. Among other appointments he held that of Assistant Superintendent of Gymnasia at Devonport for four years.

Captain Askew only obtained promotion a few days before the battalion left for Flanders ; he went out as an Officer in charge of the regimental transport, and was twice mentioned in Despatches, 14th January and 31st May, 1915. He was one of the 44 officers remaining of the VIIth Division after the heavy fighting at Ypres, and one of the five left of the 2nd Battn. Border Regiment ; he then became Adjutant, and also, for about a fortnight, held command of the Borderers and the Gordon Highlanders, which position he occupied at the time of the King's visit.

He was killed on the 19th December, 1914, while leading an attack on a German trench, and was buried by the enemy, who, as a tribute to his bravery, erected a cross inscribed with the words. " To a brave British Officer, Captain Askew."

He was a keen sportsman, horse master, and gymnast. He married in 1908, Winifred Lucy, daughter of the late Colonel and Mrs. Irwin, of Lynehow, Cumberland, and left a daughter, Anne, age 4 years, and two sons, Cuthbert and David, age 5 years and 1 year respectively.

MAJOR PANDIT PIARAY LAL ATAL, INDIAN MEDICAL SERVICE, attd. to the 129th DUKE OF CONNAUGHT'S OWN BALUCHIS,

was born on the 2nd August, 1872. He was the son of Pandit Kishan lal Atal, formerly Private Secretary to the Maharaja of Jodhpore and afterwards to the Maharaja of Jaipur State, and was a grandson of the late Dewan Pandit Motilal Atal, Prime Minister of Jaipur State, Rajputana.

He was educated in the Maharaja's Collegiate School, Jaipur, until matriculating, when he entered the Medical School, Lahore. After studying there for three or four years he came to England, and passing the competitive examination for the I.M.S. in May, 1898, was appointed Lieutenant in February, 1899. After serving in India he returned to England and specialised in diseases of the nose, throat and ear, during the year 1912.

While in the Army he served in China in 1900, receiving the medal for his services. After a few years he left the Military and was employed in the Civil Service, but was again, a few years later, transferred to the military side.

When at school he was fond of cricket, and later was a well-known cricketer in the teams of the States in which he was employed. He was a member of several clubs in the Madras Presidency. Major Atal was killed on the 23rd November, 1914, by the destruction of the Military Hospital from the effects of shell fire while he was attending to a wounded officer. Previously he had escaped unhurt while attending wounded in the field under heavy fire.

He married Mrs. Raj Atal, daughter of the late Pandit Sri Kishan Kichloo, Extra Assistant Commissioner of Ferozepore, Punjab, and only granddaughter of the late Judicial Commissioner, Pandit Bihari Lal Kichloo, Rai Bahadur. Major Atal left five children : three sons, Hiralal born January, 1904, Ram Nath born August, 1908, and Kanahiya Lal born December, 1912, and two daughters, Kamlapati born December, 1910, and Brijpati born December 1911.

He was promoted Captain in 1902 and Major in 1911, and was shortly to be promoted to the rank of Lieut.-Colonel. He was in his 43rd year when he met his death.

2nd LIEUTENANT JESSE MARSON ATKIN, SHERWOOD FORESTERS (NOTTINGHAMSHIRE & DERBYSHIRE REGIMENT), attd. 3rd BATTN. WORCESTERSHIRE REGIMENT,

was the youngest son of Mr. H. Atkin, of New Westwood, Nottingham, where he was born on the 23rd September, 1891.

After a very successful career at the Nottingham Mundella School he studied at the University, obtaining his B.A. at the age of 20. While there he joined the O.T.C. and was offered and accepted a commission, being gazetted to the Special Reserve of his Battalion in May, 1913. On taking up a scholastic position at Bournemouth he took a very prominent part with the O.T.C. in connection with his school.

He joined the Expeditionary Force in France on the 25th October, 1914, and was killed on the 7th November in the same year at Ploegsteert.

LIEUTENANT JOHN CYRIL ATKINSON, 59th SCINDE RIFLES (FRONTIER FORCE),

elder son of Major-General J. R. B. Atkinson, Indian Army (retired) and Mrs. Atkinson, was born on the 30th December, 1888, at Rajanpur, North West Frontier, Trans Indus, India.

He was educated at Clifton College, and the R.M.C., Sandhurst, at which he was a King's Indian Cadet. He joined the Army in November, 1908, being attached at first to the West Yorkshire Regiment in India, and being appointed to the 59th Scinde Rifles Field Force in December, 1909. He was promoted Lieutenant in December, 1910.

Fond of all sports, he spent his leave in India shooting in Kashmir and Ladak. He was a member of the East India United Service Club. Lieutenant Atkinson landed at Marseilles with the Indian Expeditionary Force in September, 1914, and went to the front the following month. He was killed in action on the 19th December, 1914, on the parapet of a German trench near La Bassée, France. The Officer Commanding his regiment thus described his death :—" He had led his platoon right up to the German trench and was shot dead on the parapet. His action could not have been more gallant." The Officer Commanding also referred to him as " a most gallant officer and a very well-loved comrade."

The Officer commanding his Company, who saw him killed, wrote :—" He was such a fine fellow in every way, and we all loved him. He was most hardworking and efficient as Quarter-Master in this war, and he was always keen on any dangerous or difficult job."

Another brother officer wrote :—" Since I have been in the regiment there has never been anyone who was more popular, not only with the officers, but also with the men. We have lost a splendid Officer and a good friend."

CAPTAIN ALGERNON FOULKES ATTWOOD, 4th BATTN. ROYAL FUSILIERS, was the only son of Mr. Llewellyn

C. F. Attwood, J.P., and Mrs. Rachel Edith Attwood (née Corsellis), of Pandy, near Abergavenny, Monmouthshire, and was born on the 17th May, 1880.

He was educated at Haileybury, and Christ Church, Oxford, where he accepted a University commission during the South African War.

He was gazetted Second Lieutenant in the 4th Battalion Royal Fusiliers in May, 1901, became Lieutenant in 1904, and Captain in March, 1912. In the spring of 1914 he underwent a course of instruction in aviation at Upavon, and was recommended for an appointment in the Royal Flying Corps, but rejoined his battalion on mobilisation in August. This was one of the first units of the British Expeditionary Force to arrive on the Belgian frontier in that month.

He fought at the battle of Mons, and took part in the retirement to the Marne and in the subsequent advance to the Aisne, but on the 14th September he was reported severely wounded and missing, and it has since been ascertained that at Vailly, near Soissons, at the battle of the Aisne " while skilfully and gallantly withdrawing his men from an advanced position which could not be held, he was hit twice in rapid succession and fatally wounded."

He was unmarried and was the only male representative of the last generation of the family of Attwood, formerly of Hawne House, Corngreaves Hall, and The Leasowes, Worcestershire.

CAPTAIN ALFRED CHARLES AUBIN, EAST LANCASHIRE REGIMENT,

who was reported in the War Office monthly Casualty List published in November, 1914, as having been killed in action at Garua on the 30th August, 1914, was born on the 16th October, 1878.

He joined the East Lancashire Regiment from the Militia in April, 1900. He served in the South African War, where he was employed with the Mounted Infantry, and acted as Railway Staff Officer for a short time ; he was present at operations in the Transvaal and Orange River Colony, receiving the Queen's medal with three clasps and the King's medal with two clasps.

From July, 1904, to February, 1909, he was employed with the West African Frontier Force, and was again appointed to that Corps in January, 1911.

13   AUC—AWD

CAPTAIN DANIEL GEORGE HAROLD AUCHINLECK, 2nd BATTN. ROYAL INNISKILLING FUSILIERS,

who was killed in action on the 21st October, 1914, while gallantly leading his Company against the enemy, who had broken through our trenches at Ploegsteert, Belgium, was the only son of the late Major Thomas Auchinleck, D.L., of Crevenagh, County Tyrone, and Shannoch Green, County Fermanagh, and succeeded his father in 1893.

He was born on the 18th September, 1877, and was educated at Winchester and Trinity College, Oxford. He joined the Army in September, 1898, and became Lieutenant in March, 1900. In the South African War of 1899–1900 he was present at the Relief of Ladysmith as Divisional Loot Officer, and at the actions at Colenso and Spion Kop ; at operations on the Tugela Heights, in Natal, and the Transvaal east of Pretoria, including the actions at Belfast and Lydenberg ; also at operations in the Transvaal from November, 1900, to February, 1901. He received the Queen's medal with five clasps.

He was promoted Captain in January, 1904, and from October of that year to March, 1908, was an Adjutant of Militia.

Captain Auchinleck married in 1902 Madoline, only daughter of the late Robert Scott, Esq., formerly of Bloomhill, County Tyrone.

2nd LIEUTENANT CAROL EDWARD VERE AWDRY, 2nd BATTN. ROYAL MUNSTER FUSILIERS,

born at Broad Hinton Vicarage, Swindon, Wilts, on the 11th June, 1894, was the son of the Rev. Vere Awdry, Vicar (since 1895) of Ampfield, Hants, and Mary Louisa (née Man), his second wife. He was also related to the late Major-General Webber Desborough Harris, who commanded Second Lieutenant Awdry's battalion when it was the 104th Bengal Fusiliers.

Second Lieutenant Awdry was educated at Marlborough House, Hove (Mrs. Wolsey White and Rev. T. Bullick), from 1903 to 1907 ; he was then a Foundation Scholar at Marlborough College from 1908 to 1912, in June of which

year he entered the R.M.C., Sandhurst, passing out in June, 1913. He was gazetted to the Munster Fusiliers in September and joined the 2nd Battalion at Aldershot in October, 1913. With it he left for the front on the 13th August, 1914. He was killed in action on the 27th August, and Captain Jervis, the senior surviving officer of the battalion, wrote the following account to Second Lieutenant Awdry's father, when he himself was a prisoner in the hands of the Germans :—

"In order to better safeguard the withdrawal of part of our Army, the 2nd Royal Munster Fusiliers were occupying an important position and were attacked on three sides, and when finally ordered to withdraw found themselves cut off from the main body. Faced by odds of six or eight to one they put up the best fight they could, till the fire from all sides compelled a surrender. Second Lieutenant Awdry's Company was chosen to watch the right rear, and that Officer was selected to take his platoon to an exposed position at the far end of a village named Fesmy, through which the line of retreat lay. He performed this duty in a most able manner, and holding on in face of a heavy fire, rejoined the main body with his little force intact. It was a commendable performance, worthy of one of far greater age and experience. Later on C Company (Second Lieutenant Awdry's) was detailed to act as rearguard, and again through their gallantry, the battalion was able to safely withdraw, Second Lieutenant Awdry's party being the last to come in. It was then about 6 p.m., and it was found that the battalion was cut off from the main body. The battalion extended in an endeavour to break through, every officer doing good work. Second Lieutenant Awdry, with drawn sword, led his men in support of the attack that was in progress, and fell, shot through the lungs, as he advanced. His death was painless and practically instantaneous."

His brother Officers and all his Company expressed their deepest sympathy. By Second Lieutenant Awdry's death they lost a cheery companion, an honourable gentleman, and an Officer of distinct promise. He was buried with eight of his brother Officers who fell the same day, in a grave near the railway station of Etreux, a service being read over the grave at the time.

One of Second Lieutenant Awdry's platoon, who saw him actually fall, stated that " at one time during the last stand this platoon of 54 men all told, held 500 Germans back for full three-quarters of an hour. Only 17 of them got away." He states that Second Lieutenant Awdry was kneeling behind a mound with his revolver levelled and actually giving the command " Open fire on the Cavalry," when he was shot through the chest.

LIEUTENANT ROBERT MERLIN GRAHAM AYTOUN, 2nd BATTN. PRINCESS LOUISE'S (ARGYLL AND SUTHERLAND HIGHLANDERS, who had been previously reported unofficially as killed in action, died, as has since been ascertained, in Le Cateau Town Hospital (French Red Cross), on the 27th August, 1914, of wounds received the previous day while leading his platoon.

He was the only child of Lieutenant-Colonel and Mrs. Andrew Aytoun, and was born on the 19th January, 1890.

He was gazetted to the Argyll and Sutherland Highlanders in May, 1910, and was promoted Lieutenant in July, 1912.

MAJOR BASIL KENRICK WING BACON, 1st BATTN. WORCESTER-SHIRE REGT.,

born at Eastbourne, Sussex, on the 28th May, 1872, was the son of Kenrick Verulam Bacon, Esq., J.P. for Surrey, formerly Captain 1st Battalion Worcestershire Regiment, of The Lodge, Hale, Farnham. He was educated at the United Services College, Westward Ho! North Devon. Major Bacon joined the Worcestershire Regiment from the Militia in October 1893, becoming Lieutenant in 1896, Captain in February, 1900, and Major in April, 1909. He served in the South African War from 1899-1902 ; being present at operations in the Transvaal and Orange River Colony, including actions at Bethlehem and Wittebergen, and at operations in Cape Colony, including the action at Colesberg For his services he was mentioned in Despatches, and received the Queen's medal with three clasps, and the King's medal with two clasps. He was serving with his battalion when he was killed in action near Neuve Chapelle, France, on the 13th December, 1914. A Memorial Brass has been erected to his memory in Hale Church by the non-commissioned officers and men of his Company.

Major Bacon was a member of the Junior United Service Club.

LIEUTENANT DUNCAN BAILLIE, 9th GURKHA RIFLES, INDIAN ARMY, who was killed in action on the 4th November, 1914, was the eldest son of Sir Duncan Colvin Baillie, K.C.S.I., lately acting Lieutenant Governor of the United Provinces.

He was born on the 23rd September, 1889, at Muzzaffarnagar, India, and was educated at Charterhouse and the R.M.C., Sandhurst,

at both of which he was distinguished as a ong distance runner, gymnast, and swimmer. He

passed first out of Sandhurst, and received the Sword of Honour. He obtained his first commission in September, 1909, and was selected for the Indian Army. After being attached for a year to the High-land Light Infantry at Lucknow, he was posted in October, 1910, to the 2/9th Gurkha Rifles, in which he became Lieutenant in 1911. He was attached for active service in the war to the 1st Battalion. The following account of the circumstances attending his death and of the remarks upon him, was received from Lieutenant-General Sir James Willcocks, Commanding the Indian Expeditionary Army Corps :—" The evacuation of Neuve Chapelle left the trenches of the 2nd Gurkhas in a very vulnerable salient which was enfiladed by a German mortar at a range of 400 yards. The three right double Companies were in a short time blown out of their trenches. A movement in relief was organised and Duncan Baillie was sent with two platoons of the 9th to help. All his brother officers were unanimous in their praise of the manner in which he took up his men. After he had accomplished this he proceeded to reconnoitre to ascertain the exact situation amongst the 2nd Gurkhas. Whilst running across a road towards the 2nd Gurkha trenches he was hit by a rifle bullet through the temple and killed instantaneously. Although still quite a junior officer in the 9th Gurkhas he had already made his mark as a first-rate soldier, beloved alike by officers and men."

MAJOR GEORGE BAILLIE, 46th BATTERY ROYAL FIELD ARTILLERY, who was killed near Ypres on the 18th November, 1914, was born at Mhow, Central India, on the 23rd November,1870, son of the late Captain George Baillie, Bengal Artillery, and Mrs. Baillie, of Meon-stoke, Hants, and nephew of Major-

General John Baillie, Bengal Staff Corps. Educated at Cheltenham College, and the R.M.A., Woolwich, and joined the Royal Artillery in 1890, becoming Lieutenant in 1893, Captain in 1900, and Major in 1908 He served in the South African War from November, 1899, to May, 1902, at first with "P" Battery, Royal Horse Artillery, and then on promotion to Captain in 1900 in flying columns with Pompom Section F. He was present at the Relief of Kimberley and took part in the following operations : in the Orange Free State from February to May, 1900, including the operations at Paardeberg (17th to 26th February) and the action at Driefontein. He was also present at operations in the Transvaal in May and June, 1900, including the actions near Johannesburg and Diamond Hill (11th and 12th June). He afterwards took part in further operations in the Transvaal, to the west of Pretoria from July to November, 1900, and in operations in the Orange River Colony, including the action at Wittebergen (1st to 29th July). Finally he was present in subsequent operations in the Transvaal and Orange River Colony. For his services in the campaign he received the Queen's medal with six clasps and the King's medal with two clasps.

Colonel Carey, Royal Field Artillery, wrote the following account of Major Baillie's death :— " He was a most gallant soldier, and had always set such a good example to those about him for courage, and kindness, and thoughtfulness for others. I saw him only a few minutes before his death. We had been rather heavily shelled in our cottage, and he came down from his battery to see how we were. While we were talking the shelling began again, and we moved our headquarters to a safer place, while he walked away towards his battery, and was killed about 100 yards from the house. I am glad to think that he suffered no pain, as he was killed instantaneously. His death has caused a gap in the 39th Brigade which it will be impossible to fill. All the Officers of the Brigade and the men in his battery were devoted to him, and his loss is very keenly felt by all. He was always thinking of others, and what he could do to make things pleasant for everybody : to soldier with him was a real pleasure."

A junior Officer wrote :—" He was beloved by everyone, Officers and men, and their grief was pitiable to behold when I returned to the battery, as I had been away at the time of the sad event."

Major Baillie married Louise Isabel (who died 6th December, 1904), daughter of the late Major Phillipp, of Barham, Suffolk, and left one son, born 6th December, 1904.

2nd LIEUTENANT SIR GAWAINE GEORGE STUART BAILLIE, BART., 2nd DRAGOONS (ROYAL SCOTS GREYS),

of Polkemmet, Whitburn, Linlithgowshire, born on the 29th May, 1893, was the elder son of Sir Robert Alexander Baillie, fourth Bart., B.A. (Oxon.), late Major Commanding the Australian Squadron The King's Colonials, Imperial Yeo-

manry, whom he succeeded as fifth Baronet in 1907, and of Lady Isabel Baillie, daughter of David Elliot Wilkie, of Ratho Byres, Midlothian.

Sir Gawaine Baillie was gazetted 2nd Lieutenant in the Royal Scots Greys in September, 1912. That regiment went to Flanders in the early stages of the Great War and was present at the retirement from Mons, and in the subsequent fighting at the Marne and round Ypres. 2nd Lieutenant Sir Gawaine Baillie was killed in action in France on the 7th September, 1914. He was succeeded in the baronetcy by his brother, Sir Adrian William Maxwell Baillie, for whom the property is held in trust until he attains the age of twenty-two years.

CAPT. WILLIAM FRANK GARDINER BAIRD, 4th BATTN. BEDFORDSHIRE REGIMENT, attd. 1st BATTN. THE LINCOLNSHIRE REGIMENT,

was the second son of Sir William James Gardiner Baird, eighth Bart., of Saughton Hall, Midlothian, formerly Lieutenant 7th Hussars, late Lieutenant - Colonel and Honorary Colonel Lothians and Berwickshire Imperial Yeomanry, and of the Honble. Arabella

Rose Evelyn Hozier, eldest daughter of the first Baron Newlands. He was born on the 18th April, 1885, and was educated at Eton and the R.M.C., Sandhurst, and served for a time in the 7th Dragoon Guards and Scots Guards, afterwards retiring from the active list and joining the Reserve of Officers as Second Lieutenant, from which he was gazetted Captain in the 4th Battalion Bedfordshire Regiment on the 11th August, 1914. He went to the front attached to the 1st Lincolnshire Regiment, was wounded in the British attack on Neuve Chapelle on October 27th or 28th, and died on the 5th November, 1914, in hospital at Boulogne. Captain Baird, who was a member of the Cavalry Club and of the New Club, Edinburgh, married in 1910 Violet Mary, daughter of Richard Croft Benyon, D.L., of Fanhams Hall, Ware, Herts, and left three children : James Richard Gardiner, born 1913, Lilias Mary, born 1911, and William Henry Gardiner, born 1914.

LIEUTENANT EDWARD BENJAMIN BAKER, 3rd (attd. 1st) BATTN. THE KING'S (LIVERPOOL REGIMENT),

was born at Campbellpore, Punjab, India, on the 12th July, 1894, the only son of the late Edward Baker, Ex-Engineer, Indian State Railway, and Mrs. E. J. Boyle, now the wife of Joseph Barnes Boyle, Barrister-at-Law.

Lieutenant Baker was educated at Grenville School, Guildford, afterwards joining the Special Reserve King's Liverpool Regiment, from which he was attached to the 1st Battalion for service in the Great War. He was killed on the 26th October, 1914, while leading his platoon in an attack on a village.

The following letter was received from his Commanding Officer :—

" Lieutenant Baker had done so well with the regiment since he joined, and his name had gone up for mention in despatches."

Lieutenant Baker has since been mentioned in Sir John French's Despatch of 31st May, 1915.

CAPT. HUGH LAURENTS CHENEVIX BALDWIN, 58th VAUGHAN'S RIFLES, INDIAN ARMY,

born on the 13th June, 1878, at the Castle, Cape Town, was the son of the late Major F. Chenevix Baldwin, the Connaught Rangers (the old 88th Regiment), and Mrs. Baldwin, of Lancefield, Camberley.

He was educated at Haileybury, and the R.M.C., Sandhurst. He received his commission in July, 1898, being first attached to the Middlesex Regiment, and entered the Indian Army in 1899, joining the 27th Madras Infantry, in which he became Lieutenant in October, 1900. He was transferred to the 58th Rifles in 1901, and obtained the " Distinguished " Musketry certificate in 1906, and the " Special " Signalling and Mounted Infantry certificates in 1903.

In 1901–02 he served in the Waziristan Expedition on the North-West Frontier (operations against Darwesh Khel Waziris) for which he received the medal, with clasp for Waziristan.

On the outbreak of the Great War he was on leave in England, and, having volunteered for active service, was appointed a Company Commander in the 7th Battalion Rifle Brigade of the New Army (Service Battalion). He brought the officers and men under him to a high state of efficiency during the time he was with them. On the 6th November, 1914, he received orders to rejoin his own regiment at the front, where they had arrived a month previously, and left England the next day. On the 23rd of that month he was killed while leading a charge on the German trenches near Festubert, Pas de Calais. He was mentioned for his services in Sir John French's Despatch of 14th January, 1915. Captain Baldwin was a good hockey and football player, having been captain of the regimental team on several occasions. He was the keenest of soldiers, and a general favourite.

CAPTAIN ROBERT FREDERICK BALFOUR, 1st BATTN. SCOTS GUARDS,

was the eldest son of Edward Balfour, J.P., D.L., and Mrs. Balfour, of Balbirnie, Fifeshire, and a grandson of the late Colonel John Balfour and Lady Georgeina Isabella, second daughter of the first Earl of Cawdor. Captain Balfour's uncle, Brevet-Colonel A. G.

Balfour, late Highland Light Infantry, served in the Great War as Assistant Embarkation Commandant, to which position he was appointed in August, 1914.

Captain Balfour was born on the 16th March, 1883, and was gazetted to the Scots Guards as 2nd Lieutenant in January, 1903, becoming Lieutenant in June, 1904. From July, 1907, to August, 1910, he was Adjutant of his battalion, and he was promoted Captain in January, 1913. His Staff Appointments included one as A.D.C. to the General Officer Commanding the VIth Division of the Irish Command from 1st April, 1912, to 17th January, 1913.

In the Great War the 1st Battalion Scots Guards formed part of the 1st Infantry Brigade, 1st Division, which was the first portion of the Expeditionary Force to leave Great Britain, being present at the fighting from the very commencement of the war. Captain Balfour was killed in action at Gheluvelt, near Ypres, on the 28th October, 1914.

LIEUTENANT WILLIAM ORMSBY WYNDHAM BALL, ROYAL ARMY MEDICAL CORPS,

born at 5, Palmerston Park, Dublin, on the 27th September, 1889, was the son of the late Henry Wyndham Ball, Registry of Deeds Office, Dublin, and Mrs. Ball, of the above address. He was a step-brother of Lieutenant-Colonel A. A. Seeds,

R.A.M.C., now serving with the Expeditionary Force in France, and of the late Captain J. T.

Seeds, 5th Battalion Royal Irish Rifles, who died on active service in the South African War.

Lieutenant Ball received the degrees of M.B. and B.A. at Dublin University, having been a resident Student in Sir Patrick Dun's Hospital in 1911–1912, where a tablet has been erected to his memory. He obtained his colours in the University Hockey XI. in 1909 and 1910, and represented Ireland in the six International Hockey matches in 1910 and 1911.

Receiving his commission in the R.A.M.C. in January, 1913, he was stationed in the Aldershot command till the war broke out, when he was attached for active service to the 2nd Battalion South Staffordshire Regiment. He arrived in France on 13th August, was present during the retirement from Mons to the Marne, and was killed by a shell while attending to the wounded under fire, at Soupir, on the Aisne, on the 26th September, 1914.

CAPTAIN CECIL DAVID WOODBURN BAMBERGER, ROYAL ENGINEERS,

who was killed in action on the 20th December, 1914, was the eldest son of Mr. Louis Bamberger, of Lancaster Road, Belsize Park, London, N.W.

He was born on the 22nd December, 1883, and was educated at University College School, whence he passed into the R.M.A., Woolwich, in 1901. He was gazetted to the Royal Engineers in March, 1903, becoming Lieutenant in December, 1905.

He served in India, where he was employed on the Eastern Jumna Canal Works, and with the Mishmi Road Work party, Sadiya, Assam. In 1913 he was in charge of the Jhansi Division Betwa Canal, and was promoted Captain in March, 1914. On the outbreak of the war with Germany he joined the Meerut Division of the Indian Expeditionary Force, and was killed while helping to build a barricade in a trench that had been captured from the Germans.

CAPTAIN CHARLES WILLIAM BANBURY, 3rd BATTN. COLDSTREAM GUARDS,

was the son of Sir Frederick Banbury, Bart., M.P., of Warneford Place, Highworth, Wilts, and was born at 19, Grosvenor Street, London, on the 11th February, 1877.

He was educated at Eton and Oxford, at both of which he

rowed, in the Eton Eight in 1891, and in the University College boat at Oxford in 1896. Joining the Coldstream Guards in August, 1899, he soon saw active service in the South African War, during which he took part in operations in Cape Colony, south of Orange River ; and in the Transvaal, at the end of the year 1900 : also at operations in the Orange River Colony in November, 1900, and at further operations in Cape Colony between November, 1900, and May, 1902 : for his services he received the Queen's medal with three clasps, and the King's medal with two clasps. He was promoted Lieutenant in February, 1901, and Captain in March, 1909. In the latter year he was appointed A.D.C. to the General Commanding in Chief, Eastern Command, and in April, 1912, A.D.C. to the late Lieutenant-General Sir J. M. Grierson, K.C.B., C.V.O., C.M.G., and was with that Officer when he died suddenly in France in August, 1914. He accompanied Lieutenant-General Grierson's body to England, and attended the military funeral at Glasgow.

Captain Banbury returned to France on the 23rd August, and joined the 3rd Battalion of his Regiment, forming part of the 3rd Brigade, on the 30th of that month. He was twice wounded, the second wound received on the 14th September, 1914, while he was in command of the 2nd Company of his battalion, proving fatal ; from the effects of that wound he died on the 16th of the month at Soupir. He was buried, with several other officers of the Brigade of Guards, in the little graveyard at Soupir.

Captain Banbury, who was known to all his friends as " Cakes," was a very successful rider, winning both the Grand Military and the Household Brigade Cup in 1909–1910 on " Sprinkle Me." He was a member of the Guards' and the Turf Clubs.

He married Joséphine Marguerite, daughter of Don José Reixach, and left two children : Mary Heritage, born 28th March, 1914, at Wadley Manor, Faringdon, Berks, and Charles William, born after his father's death, on the 18th May, 1915, at 19, Queen Street, Mayfair, London.

LIEUT.-COLONEL WILLIAM STIRLING BANNATYNE, p.s.c., COMMANDING 1st BATTN. THE KING'S LIVERPOOL REGIMENT,

was the son of Lieutenant - Colonel John Millar Bannatyne, late of the same regiment, who served through the Indian Mutiny, and was born at Farme, Lanarkshire, Scotland, on the 9th December, 1868. He was a nephew of Lieutenant-Colonel William Bannatyne, also of the same regiment.

The subject of this memoir was educated privately in Switzerland, and passed first into the R.M.C., Sandhurst, obtaining his commission in the King's in August, 1888, becoming Lieutenant in May, 1890, and Captain in June, 1896. He served in the South African War, 1899–1902, being present at operations in Natal, including actions at Rietfontein and Lombard's Kop; the defence of Ladysmith, including the sorties of 7th and 10th December, 1899, and the action of 6th January, 1900; operations in Northern Natal, including the action at Laing's Nek; operations in the Transvaal east of Pretoria, including actions at Belfast and Lydenberg, and elsewhere in the Transvaal. From March, 1900, to October, 1902, he was employed as Provost-Marshal, first on General Lyttleton's staff and then at Middelburg. For his South African services he was mentioned in Despatches (8th February, 1901), and received the Queen's medal with three clasps and the King's medal with two clasps.

He was Deputy Assistant Adjutant-General and General Staff Officer (2nd grade) at Gibraltar from 1903 to 1907, having become a Major in February, 1904; served on the General Staff (2nd grade) under the late Sir Charles Douglas from April to November, 1910, and was General Staff Officer (2nd grade) to the 2nd London Division, London District, from January, 1911—February, 1912. He succeeded to the command of his battalion in the latter month and left England with it on the 12th August, 1914. He took part in the Battle of Mons, the retirement towards Paris, the battles of the Marne and the Aisne, and finally in the actions in Flanders. For his services he was mentioned in Field-Marshal Sir John French's Despatch of September, 1914. He was killed in action near Ypres on the 24th October, 1914, being shot through the heart from a loop-holed house in the village of Nord Westhoek, about five miles from Ypres, which village his battalion had received orders to clear of

Germans. He was again mentioned in Despatches of 14th January, 1915.

Lieutenant-Colonel Bannatyne, who was an officer of the highest merit, married in 1889 Ethel Louisa, daughter of the Rev. H. H. Winwood, of Bath, and sister of Lieutenant-Colonel W. Q. Winwood, D.S.O., 5th (Princess Charlotte of Wales's) Dragoon Guards. He left no children.

LIEUTENANT PERCY STUART BANNING, 2nd BATTN. ROYAL MUNSTER FUSILIERS,

who was killed in action on the 4th November, 1914, was born on the 22nd June, 1887. He obtained his first appointment in the Army in September, 1908, when he was gazetted 2nd Lieutenant in the Royal Munster Fusiliers and was posted to the 1st Battalion of that Regiment. His promotion to Lieutenant was gazetted in March, 1910. For active service in the Great War, Lieutenant Banning accompanied his battalion to France, where he took part in operations in October, 1914.

2nd LIEUTENANT RAFE HEDWORTH MYDDELTON BARCLAY, 3rd BATTN. KING'S ROYAL RIFLE CORPS,

was born in London on the 14th November, 1892, and was the only son of Major Hedworth T. Barclay, Leicestershire Yeomanry, of the Turf Club, London, W. He was educated at Rugby, and at the Military College, Farnham (R. C. Welch, Esq.). 2nd Lieutenant Barclay joined the 3rd Battalion, Duke of Edinburgh's (Wiltshire Regiment), in which he became Lieutenant in August, 1913, and was transferred as Second Lieutenant to the King's Royal Rifle Corps in June, 1914, with which he served in the Great War. He was reported "missing" on the 14th September, 1914, the first day of the battle of the Aisne, near Troyon, and was subsequently reported by a Court of Inquiry as killed.

Lieutenant Barclay was a member of White's Club.

CAPTAIN RICHARD VINCENT BARKER, 1st BATTN. ROYAL WELSH FUSILIERS,

born at Middleham, Yorkshire, was the son of the late Rev. Frederick Barker, Rector of Wimborne St. Giles; was a Scholar of Winchester, and subsequently went to New College, Oxford.

Entering the Army through the Militia in January, 1901, he served from that date in  the South African War as Second Lieutenant in the Royal Welsh Fusiliers, being present at operations in the Transvaal and Orange River, for which he received the Queen's medal with four clasps. He was Adjutant of his battalion from July, 1904, to January, 1909, and of the West African Frontier Force from April, 1909.

He was a fine rider to hounds, and was well known in the South of Ireland with the United and other Hunts.

When the Great War broke out, Captain Barker was with his battalion in Malta, and, upon returning to England, was appointed Staff Captain to the 22nd Brigade, VIIth Division, under Brigadier General Lawford. On the 31st October, 1914, at the Battle of Ypres, after very severe fighting for two days—when nearly all the regimental officers were killed and some men were falling back — Captain Barker, who was then attending to wounded men under a heavy fire, asked permission to rally them, and while leading them forward, fell shot through the chest.

His Brigadier reported of him " Quite exceptional, a good friend and splendid officer, no matter how hard the work and discomforts great, he was always cheerful."

Captain Barker was mentioned, after his death, in Sir John French's Despatch of the 14th January, 1915.

2nd LIEUTENANT ERIC BARNES, 1st BATTN. LINCOLNSHIRE REGIMENT,

 was the son of John Barnes, Solicitor, and grandson of the late John Carter Holding, of Kingsclere, Hampshire, and Southsea. He was born at Kingsclere on the 26th October, 1894, and was educated at Bruton (King's School) from 1904–1912. The Headmaster's report of him was " an admirable specimen of the best type of all-round usefulness at athletics and of good intellectual attainments."

He passed through the R.M.C., Sandhurst, and was gazetted to the 1st Lincolnshire Regiment

as Second Lieutenant on the 1st February, 1914. He had been in the fighting line from the commencement of the War till he fell. He was killed on the 1st November, 1914, while leading his men in an attack to take the village of Wytschaete, near Ypres, Belgium, from the enemy. The Commanding Officer of his regiment wrote the following account of the action:—
" He fell whilst gallantly leading his Company in the attack on a village called Wytschaete which the regiment had been ordered to take. He was struck by a bullet and died immediately. He died, as he had lived, upholding the best traditions of the regiment he loved so well, and his loss is deplored by us all."

Another brother officer wrote :—
" Eric was near me in the advance, and when I got up to take a few men forward, he was the next to come, but as he stood up from the ditch where we had been lying, to lead his men under very heavy fire forward, he was shot straight through the head and died immediately. He was so plucky, always eager and active in the firing line."

His friends expressed their appreciation of the young Officer as follows :—
" There are some who possess a certain indefinable charm which makes them general favourites. Barnes was one of these. Strangers took a fancy to him and the longer one knew him, the more one liked him. One of the traits which made him such an attractive character was his cheerfulness ; he was a born optimist, and genuine optimism is infectious. Another was the frankness so clearly expressed in his features. A third was the keenness he displayed in everything he took up. The fact that he enjoyed life immensely heightens the tragedy of his early death."

CAPTAIN ALAN BARNSLEY, 4th BATTN. LANCASHIRE FUSILIERS,

who was killed in action on the 27th October, 1914, aged 37, was the youngest son of the late Mr. Arthur Barnsley, of Southward Road, Liverpool.

He served with the Imperial Yeomanry in the South African War, during 1900 and 1901, being present at operations in the Transvaal and the Orange River and Cape Colonies ; he was twice mentioned in Despatches and was granted the Queen's medal with two clasps. On entering the Lancashire Fusiliers he was given the rank of Honorary Lieutenant in the Army from December, 1902. While serving Captain

Barnsley took the opportunity of becoming proficient in many military subjects : he had passed for the rank of Captain, he was qualified as an officer of Militia in military subjects, and at a School of Musketry, had obtained a certificate in Transport (A.S.C.) duties, and was qualified as an Instructor in Signalling.

On the outbreak of the war with Germany, Captain Barnsley, who attained that rank in May, 1896, was Instructor of Musketry of his battalion. For active service he was attached to the 1st Battn. Northumberland Fusiliers, and was serving with that Corps when he was killed.

CAPTAIN CHARLES JOHN CHARD BARRETT, ROYAL SCOTS FUSILIERS,

who was killed in action at Hooge, near Ypres, on the 14th November, 1914, was born on the 26th August, 1873. He was the youngest son of the late Major Barrett, and of Mrs. Barrett, of Moreton, North Curry, Taunton, Somersetshire, and a nephew of Colonel J. R. M. Chard, V.C., R.E., the hero of Rorke's Drift. He married, in 1904, Lena, daughter of the late Albert Vaucamps, Esq.

He was educated at Eton, and the R.M.C., Sandhurst, where he won the riding prize (the saddle) in July, 1894, and the billiard cue, and whence he passed out third. He was gazetted Second Lieutenant in the Royal Scots Fusiliers in October, 1894, becoming Captain in 1900. Three years later (in 1903) he was appointed Adjutant of the 1st Battalion, which he was leading when he fell.

He served in the South African War, commencing with the operations in Natal in March, 1900 ; also in operations in the Transvaal, the Orange River Colony, and the action of Ruidam. He raised a Company of Mounted Infantry on active service, and gained the Queen's medal with three clasps. He was Adjutant of the 1st Volunteer Battalion the Welsh Regiment from January, 1905—1908. While stationed in Dublin with his regiment in 1909 he won the Irish Grand Military at Punchestown with his horse " Scarlet Runner." He had nearly completed four years as an Officer of Gentlemen Cadets at Sandhurst, and had raised a new Company (L Company), which he was commanding, when he was called on to join the 1st Battalion Royal Scots Fusiliers at the front.

He was killed during the attack of the Prussian Guard, when the Royal Scots Fusiliers held them back so splendidly, and was in temporary command of his battalion at the time he fell. He was mentioned in Sir John French's Despatch of the 14th January, 1915. Capt. Barrett was a good all-round sportsman : played polo, cricket, was a good shot and a very fine rider to hounds. He won several races in India, including his regimental Cup (the St. Andrew's Cup), and was very keen on pig-sticking.

CAPTAIN PHILIP GODFREY BARRETT, 2nd BATTN. ROYAL MUNSTER FUSILIERS,

who is believed to have been killed in action in November, 1914, was born on the 17th April, 1876. He received his commission in the Royal Munster Fusiliers from the Militia in April, 1900. He proceeded almost at once on active service in the South African War, being present at operations in Cape Colony in September, 1900, for which he received the Queen's medal with two clasps.

He was promoted Lieutenant in March, 1902 ; from November, 1907, to September, 1908, he was an Adjutant of Militia and of the Special Reserve, and was promoted Captain in August, 1908.

MAJOR JOHN BAILLIE BARSTOW, ROYAL ENGINEERS,

who was killed in action at Bailly on the 31st August, 1914, was the eldest son of Henry C. Barstow, Hazelbush, York. He was born on the 31st October, 1872, and was educated at Clifton College, and the R.M.A., Woolwich, entering the Royal Engineers in July, 1891. He became Lieutenant in July, 1894, was promoted Captain in July, 1902, and obtained his Majority in July, 1911.

Major Barstow left a widow and four children. He was a member of the Army and Navy Club, and of the Royal and Ancient (St. Andrew's) Golf Club.

CAPT. FRANCIS HEWSON BARTON, 2nd BATTN. 2nd (KING EDWARD'S OWN) GURKHA RIFLES (THE SIR MOOR RIFLES),

who was killed in action, it is believed on the 2nd November, 1914, was born on the 10th June, 1880. After serving with the embodied Militia for a year and three-quarters, he joined the Royal Irish Rifles in October, 1901, entering the Indian Army in November, 1903.

He served in the South African War, being present at operations in the Transvaal, Orange River Colony and the Cape Colony. He was mentioned in Despatches ("London Gazette," 10th September, 1901) and received the Queen's medal with three clasps and the King's medal with two clasps.

He received his promotion to Lieutenant in January, 1904, and to Captain in February, 1909.

2nd LIEUTENANT HAROLD WILLIAM FERGUSON BARTON, 1st BATTN. ROYAL SCOTS FUSILIERS,

who was reported as "missing" in October, 1914, is since reported to have been killed near Lille on the 18th of that month.

He was the younger son of the late Mr. W. S. Barton, and Mrs. Barton, of Woodstock, Camberley, and grandson of the late Dean of Moray and Ross. He was born on the 5th September, 1893, at Morriston, Elgin, Scotland, and received his education at Stratheden House, proceeding to Radley College and the R.M.C., Sandhurst. He received his commission in August, 1914.

Mrs. Barton received a letter from a German officer, saying :—" Dear Mrs. Barton, Your son fell on the field of honour against our regiment. I admired his courage after a very hard struggle against us. Your son will be buried in the near (sic) of Castle Warneton, near Lille." (Signed) Ewald, Lieutenant Feldart., Regiment No. 7.

MAJOR EDWARD EGERTON BARWELL, 57th WILDE'S RIFLES (FRONTIER FORCE),

who was killed in action about the 30th October, 1914, was the youngest son of the late General Charles Arthur Barwell, C.B., who served all through the Indian Mutiny.

Major Barwell was born at Harrow on the 20th May, 1872, and was educated at Harrow, being a Home Boarder from 1886 to 1889, and at the R.M.C., Sandhurst, where he was a Queen's India Cadet.

After receiving his commission in September, 1892, he was attached for a year to the East Lancashire Regiment at Lucknow, and joined the Indian Staff Corps in December, 1893, being attached to the 9th Gurkhas for two months, and then transferred to the 4th Punjab Infantry, Punjab Frontier Force, now the 57th Rifles Frontier Force. He became Lieutenant in that regiment in December, 1895, and served with it for 20 years.

Major Barwell had seen a good deal of war service : he took part in the Waziristan Expedition, 1894-5, receiving the medal and clasp ; was at Tochi, North-West Frontier of India, in 1897-8, again receiving a medal and clasp ; in China in 1900, for which he received the medal, and again in 1908—having been promoted Captain in September, 1901—on the North-West Frontier of India, serving on the Staff during operations in the Zakka Khel country, and at operations in the Mohmand country, including engagements at Matta and Kargha. In the latter expeditions he served as Deputy Assistant Quarter-Master-General of the 1st Brigade, was mentioned in Despatches ("London Gazette," August, 1908) and received the medal with clasp.

Major Barwell, who received his Majority in September, 1910, went to Belgium with his regiment as part of the Indian Expeditionary Force. He was killed at Messines, whilst leading his men into action.

He married in 1902 Mary Cicely, eldest daughter of H. Tunstill, Esq., Thornton Lodge, Aysgarth, Yorkshire, and left three children : James William, born December, 1903, Eric, born June, 1908, and Cicely Egerton, born August, 1909.

CAPTAIN CHARLES HAROLD BASS, 3rd BATTN. LANCASHIRE FUSILIERS,

who was stated in the Casualty List issued by the War Office in May, 1915, to have been "un-officially reported killed or died of wounds," was the only child of the Rev. Charles and Annie Bass, Steeple Claydon Vicarage,

Bucks. Captain Bass, who was 24 years of age at the time of his death, was educated

at Cranleigh School, Surrey, where he was a member of the Officers' Training Corps.

He joined the Special Reserve of Officers in 1908, and received his commission in the Lancashire Fusiliers in May, 1909, becoming Lieutenant in 1911. He was gazetted Captain in January, 1915.

He was wounded on the 26th August, 1914, during the retirement from Mons, four days after his battalion landed in France. No news of him could be obtained until his identity disc was received, in March, 1915, from the American Ambassador in London. It appears that a British Sergeant, who was a prisoner of war at Döberitz, had given it to his Camp Commandant, who in his turn forwarded it to the Ambassador in Berlin. Later, a postcard was received from a Corporal of the Lancashire Fusiliers, a prisoner at Döberitz, saying " Lieutenant Bass is dead." From the same source it has since been ascertained that Captain Bass was wounded in the Battle of Cambrai on August 26th, 1914, died of wounds the same day, and was buried in a churchyard, together with Lieutenant-Colonel Dykes, of the King's Own Regiment, and Lance-Corporal Sturgess, of the Essex Regiment. The writer adds :—" There was also a Captain of our regiment buried there, and I know it was not Captain Sidebottom, because he was buried in the same trench where he fell."

A superior officer wrote to Captain Bass's friends :—" I cannot find words to say all I should like ; but this I can say, that Harold's example, whether in his life or his death, will be to me a great help. Those of us who knew and loved him realise what an example such a life as his can be."

A former schoolfellow and friend writes from Ceylon :—" I always valued Harold's friendship, and I valued it especially because he was, to my mind, a splendid type of a God-fearing man, both mentally and physically."

Another friend in the regiment, when writing after Captain Bass was wounded, said :—" It is very hard luck that he has been wounded before he had time to show what a fine officer he was."

LIEUTENANT WILLIAM BASTARD, 2nd BATTN. BEDFORDSHIRE REGT., born on the 20th April, 1891, at Coltscombe, Slapton, near Kingsbridge, South Devon, was the son of William and Helen Bastard, and a nephew of Dr. Adkins, Medical Officer for the County of Devon.

Educated at Blundell's School, Tiverton, he won the " Spurway " medal, and was one of the cadet winners of the Devon County Shield, 1910. Proceeding to Exeter College, Oxford, he obtained the degree of B.A., and received his commission in the Bedfordshire Regiment in January, 1912, becoming Lieutenant in September, 1914. He served with his battalion in South Africa, and, returning to England in September, joined the Expeditionary Force in Belgium on the 4th October, 1914.

On the 26th October he was in the trenches directing the fire of his platoon to help the advance of another battalion, when a German machine gun opened fire and killed him instantly. This occurred at Gheluvelt, about six miles from Ypres. He was mentioned for his services in Sir John French's Despatch of 14th January, 1915. His Colonel wrote of him :—" From the day he joined I recognised that your son was one of the best types of officers ; very keen on his work, thoroughly sensible, and willing to take responsibility. I always had him in my eye as being well fitted for the Adjutancy later on. He was very popular with both officers and men, and I can assure you his loss to the Battalion is very, very great."

His Company Sergeant-Major and Quartermaster-Sergeant also wrote expressing the regard which not only his platoon, but the whole of his Company had for this young Officer, who died gallantly, rifle in hand, and who was always solicitous for the welfare of his men, whom he led in battle without fear.

CAPTAIN JOHN HENRY STRODE BATTEN, 1st BATTN. THE KING'S (LIVERPOOL REGIMENT), who was killed in action on the 26th October, 1914, was the son of Colonel J. Mount Batten, C.B., Mornington Lodge, West Kensington, and was born on the 23rd December, 1875. He was educated at Rossall, and Trinity Hall, Cambridge, where he took his

B.A. degree, and joined the Liverpool Regiment in May, 1899, becoming Lieutenant in March, 1900. He took part in the South African War, being employed with the Mounted Infantry, and was present at operations in Natal, including actions at Rietfontein and Lombard's Kop, the defence of Ladysmith, including action on 6th January, 1900 ; operations in Natal, the Transvaal, and Cape Colony ; from June to October, 1901, he acted as Supply Officer. He received the Queen's and King's medals each with two clasps. He was promoted Captain in December, 1909.

He was shot through the heart at Zonnebeke, death being instantaneous.

He was a member of the Junior Army and Navy Club, and was married, but left no family.

LIEUTENANT HIS HIGHNESS PRINCE MAURICE VICTOR DONALD OF BATTENBERG, K.C.V.O., 1st BATTN. KING'S ROYAL RIFLE CORPS,

who died of wounds received in action on the 27th October, 1914, was the youngest son of H.R.H. Princess Henry of Battenberg (Princess Beatrice of England), daughter of Her late Majesty Queen Victoria, and was born at Balmoral on the 3rd October, 1891.

His father, Prince Henry of Battenberg, died of fever contracted in the Ashanti War in 1896. Prince Maurice's two elder brothers are in the Army, Prince Alexander in the Grenadier Guards, and Prince Leopold in the King's Royal Rifle Corps.

He was educated at Wellington and the R.M.C., Sandhurst, where he was a Sergeant, from which he was gazetted to the King's Royal Rifle Corps as second Lieutenant in March, 1911, being promoted Lieutenant in February, 1914.

The following account of his death was published in the Wellington Year Book of 1914 :— " He met his death leading his men against a German position. On the advance, they came to a wood which was too thick for them to get through conveniently, and they had to cross an open field. Prince Maurice was leading his men across this open space when a shell fell and burst right by him. He knew that his injuries were mortal. He was carried to a field dressing room, but died before it was reached." He was buried in the cemetery at Ypres.

Prince Maurice was mentioned in Sir John French's Despatch of the 8th October, 1914.

CAPTAIN CHARLES FREMOULT PRESTON BATTERSBY, 113th BATTERY, XXVth BRIGADE, ROYAL FIELD ARTILLERY,

who was killed by a shell at Ypres on the 4th November, 1914, was the only child of Major-General Thomas Preston Battersby, late Royal Artillery, now Principal Ordnance Officer, of "Cromlyn," Westmeath, Ireland. He was born at the Castle Barracks, Enniskillen, on the 11th July, 1887, and was educated first at a preparatory school at Colchester. He gained the Probationers' and Junior Scholarships in Classics at the King's School, Canterbury, and passed direct from the Army Class to the R.M.A. Woolwich. He received his commission in the Royal Artillery in June, 1907, becoming Lieutenant in June, 1910, and obtaining his Company in October, 1914.

He was very keen on all games and sports, and though not distinguished in any, could play a good game of cricket, football, golf, and tennis; was fond of hunting and shooting, and very keen on his profession, in which he won the liking, respect, and confidence of the officers and men with whom he served.

CAPTAIN ERIC MAY BATTERSBY, 3rd (attd. 1st) BATTN. ROYAL WEST KENT REGIMENT.

was the third son of Worsley Battersby, Esq., J.P., for West Somerset, of Knowle Dunster, and of his wife Jessie Battersby.

He was educated at Sherborne, and joined the 3rd (Militia) Battalion of the Regiment in 1903, resigning with the rank of Lieutenant in 1906. When the War broke out he at once volunteered his services in his old battalion, and was sent out to France in command of a draft on the 19th September, being promoted Captain a week later.

He fell in the action at Neuve Chapelle on the 28th October, 1914. Brigadier F. W. N. McCracken, C.B., D.S.O., said to Captain Battersby on that day :—" Your regiment has done splendidly ; you will hear more of it." Captain Battersby was then in command of the battalion, and was killed a few hours afterwards. He was 30 years of age, and was not married.

2nd LIEUTENANT EDWARD CHARLES VULLIAMY BATTLE, 3rd BATTN. WORCESTERSHIRE REGIMENT,

was the eldest son of Lieutenant - Colonel W. H. Battle, R.A.M.C. (T.F.), and was born in London on the 17th November, 1894.

He was educated at Malvern College, where he was a Corporal in the Officers' Training Corps and a member of the College Eight, making the highest possible score in the Public Schools Competition at Bisley in 1912.

In September, 1913, he entered the R.M.C., Sandhurst, where he became Sergeant of his Company, and in August, 1914, was gazetted to the Worcestershire Regiment as Second Lieutenant. He went to France at the beginning of September ; on the 21st October, at Illies, near La Bassée, he was shot through the shoulder, and after getting his men to bandage him, he went on fighting. He got into a trench with another officer and some men, making a gallant attempt to repulse the Germans, who came up in great numbers in front and on the flank, when he was shot through the head.

Much regret was expressed at his death by the officers, non-commissioned officers, and men of his battalion, who had learned to know him, and appreciated his constant cheerfulness and brave endurance during the trying night marches of the Brigade on the way from the Aisne to the North of France.

2nd LIEUTENANT GEORGE BAIRD BAYLEY, 2nd BATTN. KING'S OWN SCOTTISH BORDERERS,

son of I. F. Bayley, Halls, East Lothian, was born there on the 1st July, 1894. After receiving his education at Cheltenham College, and the R.M.C., Sandhurst, he was gazetted to the Scottish Borderers in January, 1914, and went with his battalion to the front at the commencement of the War. He was slightly wounded during the retirement

from Mons on the 26th August at Le Cateau, and after being invalided home for a few weeks returned to the front with the VIIth Division, attached to the 2nd Battalion Royal Scots Fusiliers. It was while serving with this battalion that he met his death at the Battle of Ypres on the 24th October, 1914.

On the morning of that day the Royal Scots Fusiliers were holding a line of trenches running from the Ypres-Menin road northwards towards the village of Reutel, Second-Lieutenant Bayley's Company being in reserve. On the Germans breaking through the line, his company was ordered up in support, and while running forward to the trenches he was shot, death being instantaneous. He was mentioned in Sir John French's Despatches of 17th February, 1915, for gallant and distinguished service in the field.

LIEUTENANT CHARLES GEORGE GORDON BAYLY, 56th FIELD CO. ROYAL ENGINEERS, AND No. 5 SQUADRON ROYAL FLYING CORPS,

was born at Rondebosch, Cape Colony, South Africa, on the 30th May, 1891. He was the only son of the late Brackenbury Bayly, Memb. Inst. Elect. Eng. (died 4th August, 1914), of the Cape Civil Service, who saw service as a civilian under the military authorities

in the Zulu War of 1879, for which he received the War medal and clasp ; he also served in the Tembu Campaign of 1881, for which he received the General Service medal and clasp.

Lieutenant Bayly came of military stock : one grandfather was the late Major Neville Saltren Keats Bayly, R.A., who served in the Crimean War and Indian Mutiny, and was wounded at Aden ; the other is Colonel William Jesser Coope, late Captain 57th Regiment, who also served in the Crimea and Mutiny, for which he received the medals ; and in the Russo-Turkish War of 1878 with the Red Cross, when he was taken prisoner of war at the fall of Plevna, as he was an officer in the Imperial Ottoman Gendarmerie at the time ; for these services he received Turkish orders of two degrees, and afterwards took part in the South African War, 1899–1902, for which he received the King's and the Queen's medals. Lieutenant Bayly was also a great-nephew of General Charles George Gordon of Khartoum, his grandfather (Major Bayly) having married General Gordon's sister. Lieutenant Bayly was educated at the Diocesan

College School, Rondebosch, Cape Colony ; St. Edmund's Preparatory School, Hindhead, Surrey ; St. Paul's School, Hammersmith, and finally at the Royal Military Academy, Woolwich. At all of them he took a prominent place in athletics and sports, as well as on the academic roll : he won the Rifleman's Certificate, and was in the cricket and football teams of his earlier schools ; at St. Paul's he won a senior scholarship, got his football and cricket colours, was Sergeant in the School Cadet Corps, taking certificate A, and gained the School Exhibition for Woolwich : he was proficient at boxing, in which he represented his School House ; and later won his colours in the Rosslyn Park Football Team. At the Royal Military Academy he unfortunately broke his wrist during his first season and was therefore unable to play football for Woolwich, but he won several prizes for other forms of athletics, including the swimming obstacle race in 1910, and he was twice in the leading team of the swimming relay race : he was also one of the twelve selected to compete for the saddle awarded to the best rider of the cadets receiving commissions. He passed seventh out of Woolwich, and was gazetted to the Royal Engineers in August, 1911, as Second Lieutenant. Proceeding to the School of Military Engineering at Chatham, he, while there, passed the test for a Pilot's Certificate at the Hendon Aerodrome in March, 1913, and after attaining what was then considered the good altitude of 400 feet, and making good landings, he received his Aviator's Certificate (No. 441). He obtained his football colours in the Royal Engineers and played cricket for the Corps. Passing out of Chatham he was gazetted Lieutenant on 2nd August, 1913, and was posted to the 56th Field Company stationed at Bulford Camp. He rode in the Royal Artillery Harriers' Point-to-Point Light Weight Hunt Cup, winning second prize, 1914. He joined the Royal Flying School, Upavon, in May, 1914, and on leaving— having been highly reported on as Pilot and Observer—on the outbreak of the War was gazetted to No. 5 Squadron Royal Flying Corps, dating from June, 1914. He was entrusted with various duties prior to his flight to France on the 12th August, reaching Amiens the same day, and flying thence to Maubeuge.

He was killed on the 22nd August, 1914, while on reconnaissance duty, flying over the German lines in the neighbourhood of Enghien-Rassily as Observer, with Second-Lieutenant Waterfall as Pilot. They were fired at by a column of infantry, and finally brought down by anti-aircraft gun fire. They were hastily buried by the Germans under 10 centimetres of soil, and the Belgians covered the grave with flowers. Later, the owner of the park where they were buried, exhumed the bodies and placed them in zinc-lined coffins, in order to give them more decent burial.

LIEUTENANT CHARLES REGINALD CHAMBERLAIN BEAN, 1st BATTN. SOUTH STAFFORDSHIRE REGIMENT,

who was officially reported to be wounded, in the middle of November, 1914, but whose death was unofficially confirmed, and who is now reported to have been killed on the 26th October, 1914, was born in 1892. He was educated at Sherborne School, on the Continent, and at Sandhurst, joining the South Staffordshire Regiment in January, 1913, and becoming Lieutenant in September, 1914. It was stated in " The Times " that, having gone to the front early in October, he was, on the 25th of that month, sent to support a hotly-pressed trench near Ypres, and, after fighting all night, was wounded on the morning of the 26th. Although pressed to leave the trench for medical aid, he refused, and was killed shortly afterwards, his body having been last seen lying on the parapet of the trench.

2nd LIEUTENANT EDWARD ARCHIBALD BEAUCHAMP, attd. 3rd BATTN. COLDSTREAM GUARDS,

was the elder son of Sir Edward Beauchamp, Bart., M.P. for Lowestoft, Suffolk, J.P. for Norfolk, and his second wife Betty Campbell, daughter of Archibald Woods, of Columbus, Ohio, U.S.A.

Born on the 5th April, 1891, he was educated at Eton, and joined the Special Reserve of the Coldstream Guards in February, 1914, being gazetted as Second Lieutenant in that regiment in November, 1914. After being wounded near Ypres in November he came to England, but on his recovery returned to the front and joined the 1st Battalion, when he again received wounds from the effects of which he died on the 22nd December, 1914.

MAJOR HENRY SULLIVAN BECHER, 1/2nd KING EDWARD'S OWN GURKHA RIFLES (THE SIRMOOR RIFLES),
who was killed in Flanders on the 2nd November, 1914, was the only son of the late Colonel Sullivan Becher and Mrs. Becher, of Kingswood House, Wotton - under - Edge, Gloucestershire. The

regiment in which he served was raised by his father in 1884.

He was born on the 9th April, 1876, and was educated at Marlborough from 1888–1892, in Germany, and at the R.M.C., Sandhurst. He received his commission as Second Lieutenant (unattached) in January, 1896, and joined the Indian Staff Corps in April, 1897, becoming Lieutenant in the Indian Army in April, 1898, and Captain in January, 1905.

He served in operations on the Samana, North-West Frontier of India in 1897, receiving the medal with two clasps. He also took part in the Tirah Expedition, 1897–98, and was present at the actions of Chagru Kotal and Dargai, the capture of the Sampagha and Arhanga Passes ; at operations in the Waran and Bara Valleys, and action of the 16th November, 1897 ; operations at and round Dwatoi and action of the 24th November, 1897 ; also operations against the Khani Khel Chamkanis, and in the Bara Valley in December, 1897, receiving a clasp to his medal. He took part in the Waziristan Expedition, North-West Frontier, of 1901–02, receiving an additional clasp.

From November, 1909, to September, 1911, he was A.D.C. to the Commander-in-Chief, East Indies, which appointment he gave up to rejoin his regiment in 1912, to take part in the Expedition to the Abor Country, for which campaign he received the medal and was mentioned in Despatches. He was promoted Major in January, 1914.

" The Times " of the 11th November, 1914, published the following letter from one who knew him well :—

" Sullivan Becher's was a personality widely known and universally beloved. He lived in and for, and has died, as he would have wished, leading the gallant Gurkhas of the regiment which his father, Colonel Sullivan Becher (who was recommended for the Victoria Cross for his gallantry at the Battle of Kandahar), raised in 1884."

CAPTAIN A. C. BEEMAN, 3rd (attd. 1st) BATTN. THE QUEEN'S OWN (ROYAL WEST KENT REGIMENT), who was killed on the 26th October, 1914, joined the 3rd Battalion in September, 1899, as Second Lieutenant, being promoted Lieutenant in June, 1900, and reaching the rank of Captain in his regiment in May, 1902.

He served in the South African War, having been present at operations in Cape Colony in May, 1902, receiving the Queen's medal with two clasps.

2nd LIEUTENANT CHARLES OCKLEY BELL, 2nd BATTN. BEDFORDSHIRE REGIMENT,

was born in 1891 at Grimsby, the son of Alfred Frederick and Sarah Susanna Bell. He was educated at Alford Grammar School, Lincolnshire.

This young officer served in the ranks of the South Staffordshire Regiment for four and a half years, and when he had attained the rank of Corporal his conspicuous ability was rewarded by his being selected for a commission as Second Lieutenant in the Bedfordshire Regiment, which he received on the 20th May, 1914. He was, it is believed, the first officer to gain his commission from the ranks under the new regulations introduced in 1914.

He proceeded to South Africa to join his new regiment, and returned to go to the front with it at the commencement of the War. He was killed on Sunday, the 18th October, 1914, and was buried at Le Touret.

His mother's father was an Indian Mutiny veteran. Mr. and Mrs. Bell had the honour of receiving the following telegram on the occasion of their son's death :—

" The King and Queen deeply regret the loss you and the Army have sustained by the death of your son in the service of his country. Their Majesties truly sympathise with you in your sorrow."—PRIVATE SECRETARY.

Second-Lieutenant Bell was unmarried.

CAPTAIN MALCOLM ARTHUR RUSSELL BELL, OF THE 54th SIKHS, FRONTIER FORCE,

born in Edinburgh in 1880, was the eldest son of the late Russell Bell, Advocate, Sheriff-Substitute of Stirlingshire, and the late Mrs. Russell Bell, of The Close, Salisbury : his brothers are in the Services, Lieutenant-Commander Norman Leven Russell Bell,

R.N., H.M.S. " Vanguard," and Second-Lieutenant Gerald Hallam Russell Bell, 3rd Battalion King's Own Scottish Borderers ; he was a nephew of Mr. H. D. Bell, of Peelwalls, Ayton, Berwickshire.

Captain Bell was educated at St. Salvators, St. Andrews, Fettes College, and the R.M.C., Sandhurst. In 1900 he was appointed to the King's Own Scottish Borderers, and two years later was ransferred to the Indian Army, in which he was promoted Captain in January, 1909. He was on active service on the North-West Frontier in 1902, being present at operations against the Darwesh Khel Waziris, and in 1908 at operations in the Zakka Khel Country, and in the Mohmand Country : for his services he received the medal with clasp.

Captain Bell volunteered for service in the Great War in November, 1914, and was attached to the 58th Rifles, Frontier Force, Meerut Division ; he was killed in action in France on the 26th December, 1914. He had been ordered up to support a part of the line where the enemy had broken through, and was leading his men towards the German trenches when he was shot through the head, dying almost immediately. He was buried by the Divisional Chaplain, the Rev. R. Irwin, close to Le Touret, four miles east of Bethune, on the Bethune-Richebourg Road, at a little burial ground, where some 50 other officers are laid. A cross is erected at the spot.

Captain Bell was a member of the Junior Army and Navy Club, and his recreations were golf and polo.

2nd LIEUTENANT ROBERT BURTON BENISON, 2nd BATTN. THE CONNAUGHT RANGERS,

who was killed in action on the 20th September, 1914, was the youngest son of the late Mr. T. T. Benison, of Slieve Russell, Ballyconnell, Co. Cavan.

He was born in 1891, and entered the R.M.C., Sandhurst, in August, 1910, being gazetted to the Connaught Rangers in September, 1911.

LIEUTENANT MURRAY STUART BENNING, 3rd BATTN. EAST SURREY REGIMENT,

was born at Dunstable, Bedfordshire, on the 23rd August, 1894, the youngest son of Mr. Charles Crichton Stuart Benning, Town Clerk, of The Limes, Dunstable. Among his relatives are Major A. C. S. Benning, Bedfordshire Yeomanry, Lieutenant-Commander C. S. Benning, Submarine E5, and Flight-Lieutenant Brian Stuart Benning, Royal Naval Air Service.

Lieutenant Benning was educated at Dunstable Grammar School, and at Uppingham, where he was in the Officers' Training Corps. He was gazetted to the 3rd Battalion, East Surrey Regiment in December, 1912, being promoted Lieutenant on the 5th August, 1914.

In the Great War he was attached to the 1st Battalion and was wounded at Richebourg L'Avoué on the 28th October, and died at Christol Hospital, Boulogne, on the 1st November, 1914. The following is extracted from an account of the circumstances published in the " Bedfordshire Standard " of 13th November, 1914 :—

" From a letter received from a brother officer, it appears that the Surreys had been subjected to tremendous shell and rifle fire for three days by greatly superior numbers of the enemy, but held their own. On this particular day the Germans poured shot and shell at them in a perfect storm, and men who have been at the front all the time say that it was the hottest fire they ever saw. Lieutenant Benning was on the right of the trench, and was very cool, but a bullet caught him in the head. It was too hot to remove him from the trench, as by that time the Germans had got within about 150 yards, and were actually shelling them with the siege guns they used at Antwerp. Another officer knelt beside him to protect him from injury by shrapnel, and it was lucky he did, as a piece of shell quite six inches in length fell and caught him instead of striking the wounded Lieutenant in the face. At last he was got under cover until a stretcher arrived to take him out of the firing line. He was operated on at Boulogne and seemed to be going on well, until a relapse occurred."

At the time he answered the call to serve his country, Lieutenant Benning was the representative of Messrs. Wright & Co., rubber brokers, and, although a very young man, was already well known among Mincing Lane brokers. His comrades in the field have spoken of him as being wonderfully cool and brave in the firing line. He was one of the earliest of many members to go to the front from Mincing Lane.

CAPTAIN JOHN PENRICE BENSON 1st BATTN. EAST SURREY REGIMENT,

who was born at Kilvrough, Glamorganshire, on the 1st October, 1877, was the son of Judge William Denman Benson and Jane Penrice his wife. He had several relations in the Army and Navy, among them his grandfather, the late General H. R.

Benson, C.B., 17th Lancers; Colonel H. W. Benson, D.S.O.; Colonel S. M. Benson, 17th Lancers; Colonel R. E. Benson, East Yorkshire Regiment, also killed in this war, and Admiral of the Fleet, Sir A. Lyons G.C.B.

Captain Benson was educated at Charterhouse and the R.M.C., Sandhurst, having been at both a cricketer and a footballer. He received his commission in the East Surrey Regiment in 1897, and served with it through the whole of the South African War, having been wounded on Pieter's Hill, at the Relief of Ladysmith. He received the Queen's medal with five clasps and the King's medal with two clasps.

In September, 1902, he was appointed Adjutant of his battalion and subsequently passed to the Reserve of Officers having become a Captain in October, 1904.

On the outbreak of the war he rejoined his old regiment, and went with it to the front. At the Battle of Mons he was wounded by a machine gun while fighting in the first line of trenches on the 23rd August; he was taken down to a convent school hospital at Boussu, left there on the retirement, and died there, probably on the 24th August, 1914.

Captain Benson, who was a member of the Army and Navy Club, married Laura Annette Rideout, daughter of General Rideout and grand-daughter of the late Admiral Montresor. He left two children, William Frank Montresor, born 7th October, 1907, and Jane Penrice, born 2nd January, 1915.

LIEUTENANT - COLONEL RICHARD ERLE BENSON, COMMANDING 1st BATTN. THE EAST YORKSHIRE

REGIMENT, was the son of General H. R. Benson, C.B., 17th Lancers, grandson of Sir William Wightman, one of H.M.'s Judges, and a nephew of Father Richard M. Benson, a Cowley Father. The family residence was in Glamorganshire.

Lieutenant-Colonel Benson was born on the 4th October, 1862, and was educated at Eton, where he was in the College Boats.

He joined the East Yorkshire Regiment in May, 1884, became Captain in 1891, and Major in 1903. He was twice Adjutant of his battalion, from 1885–1886, and again from 1891–1894, and was specially employed with the Bechuanaland Police from July, 1889–May, 1890. He was also Adjutant of the 4th Battalion East Surrey Regiment for five years from 1899. After the embodiment of the Battalion in December,

1899, he accompanied it to South Africa in 1902, for the Boer War; he received the Queen's medal with three clasps, and was recommended for the D.S.O., but it was decided not to give that decoration for services after a certain date, so he was precluded from receiving it.

Major Benson, as he then was, accompanied the 2nd Battalion of the regiment to Burma in 1906, and afterwards to Fyzabad, where he acted as Second in Command; in 1911 he was transferred to the 1st Battalion, and on the 15th of August of that year succeeded to the Command of the Battalion. An appreciative notice of Lieutenant-Colonel Benson appeared in the monthly journal of the regiment, the "Snapper," for October, 1914. Special mention is therein made of the very high state of efficiency to which Lieutenant-Colonel Benson had brought his battalion, and in which it embarked for the front in the Great War. It says:—"His period of command will long be known as one of the brightest chapters in the history of the 1st Battalion . . . wherever he went his popularity with all ranks was soon seen."

While leading his battalion in a charge at the Battle of the Aisne Lieutenant-Colonel Benson was wounded, on Sunday, the 20th September, 1914, and died in the Australian Hospital, St. Nazaire, on the following Sunday, the 27th September.

A brother Officer wrote of him :—" He was so magnificent, so full of energy and courage—always in the front—and the men would have followed him anywhere. Even after he was wounded he would not be brought in till he knew the other wounded were safe, and his one thought was for the safety and welfare of his regiment." Lieutenant-Colonel Benson was keenly interested in all sporting matters connected with his battalion, and was a member of the Naval and Military Club.

He married Florence, daughter of M. W. Armour, Esq., and left three children—two girls, Rita and Molly, and one boy, Jack.

CAPTAIN CHARLES ARTHUR CAMPBELL BENTLEY, 1st BATTN. ROYAL WARWICKSHIRE REGIMENT,

was the eldest son of Dr. George Herbert Bentley, of Kirkliston, Linlithgowshire, and his wife Anna Campbell of Edinburgh, and grandson of Captain C. S. Bentley, 51st Regiment; he was born at Kirkliston, Linlithgowshire, on the 24th March, 1879.

After his school education he matriculated at Edinburgh University, and studied for the Medical Profession. When a medical student at the University he enlisted in the Scots Greys, in 1898, and served with them through the Boer War, having been present at the Relief of Kimberley, operations in the Orange Free State, including actions at Paardeberg and Driefontein ; in the Transvaal, in actions near Johannesburg and Diamond Hill, and in the Transvaal East of Pretoria, including the action at Belfast. He received the Queen's medal with six clasps, and the King's medal with two clasps.

In April, 1902, he received his commission as Second Lieutenant in the Royal Warwickshire Regiment, becoming Lieutenant in October, 1905, and Captain in June, 1914.

In 1910 Captain Bentley was selected as Staff Officer of the Local Forces and Adjutant of Constabulary at Trinidad, with the local rank of Captain, carrying on his duties to the entire satisfaction of the authorities. He returned to England at the expiration of his appointment, early in 1914. It is a remarkable coincidence that his grandfather, Captain Bentley, of the 51st Regiment, also did good service in Trinidad when he was Adjutant of his regiment in 1837, and acted very bravely in helping to suppress a meeting of the Native Troops, as recorded by Charles Kingsley in his book " At Last."

Captain Bentley went with his battalion to the front in August, 1914, and was in the retirement from Mons, and in the subsequent advance, and on the 23rd October, 1914, was killed while gallantly leading his company at the capture of an entrenched village close to Armentières ; he was buried in the cemetery at that place. He was mentioned in Field-Marshal Sir John French's Despatch, January, 14th, 1915, " for gallant and distinguished service in the field."

The following is an abbreviated account of his death, given by a Private of his Battalion:—

" Captain Bentley always went ahead of his men, cheering them on. He did not seem to know what fear was, and that made them all brave, too. The Warwicks were told a little village near Armentières must be taken at any cost, and Captain Bentley's Company had to lead the four Companies sent out. Two hundred and seventy set out to do it, and when they took the place there were only 20 left ; 100 were killed, and 150 wounded. The Captain was at the head of the 20 when he fell, sniped in three places. He never seemed to think of his wounds, but went on cheering the men, and almost the last words he said were : ' Go on, my men ; keep up the good name of the Warwicks ; don't give in.' He lived for a few hours after he was wounded."

Three days after the publication of the article referring to his death, in the " Daily Graphic,"

the " Times " printed a touching poem, " Aftermath," probably inspired by the " Daily Graphic " notice ; at all events, the poem's opening lines were perfectly true as regards Captain Bentley :—

" Slain by a Prussian bullet, leading the men who loved him,
        Dying, cheered them on."

Captain Bentley married Geraldine Sadleir, daughter of Lieutenant-Colonel F. S. Stoney, J.P., late R.A., of The Downs, Delgany, Co. Wicklow, and left three young children : Charles Francis Campbell, born 1907 ; Sybil Moyra, born 1908 ; and Hester Doreen, born 1912.

2nd LIEUTENANT CLARENCE LESLIE BENTLEY, 2nd BATTN. MANCHESTER REGIMENT,

was born at York on the 8th August, 1894, and was the youngest son of Mrs. Bentley, of Fulford Grange, York, and of the late Alderman Bentley, J.P. He was a nephew of the late Colonel J. W. Cameron, of the 4th Durham Artillery, West Hartlepool. Second Lieutenant Bentley's eldest brother is a Captain in the West Riding Heavy Artillery Battery, now on the Humber Defences ; and his second brother is a Lieutenant in the 2nd Battalion A.P.W.O. Yorkshire Regiment (" Green Howards "), and was wounded in the great advance at Neuve Chapelle on the 11th March, 1915, having since recovered from his wounds and returned to the front.

Second Lieutenant Bentley was educated at Bootham School, York, and Mill Hill School, London, N.W. ; afterwards he went to the R.M.C., Sandhurst. At school he took all his colours, and at Sandhurst took his " blue " for hockey. He received his commission on the 8th August, 1914, his twentieth birthday, and was with the 3rd Battalion of his regiment on the Humber Defences for a short time. He then took a draft across to the Continent, and joined his own battalion at the front. He saw a good deal of fighting all along the Yser and Marne, and was killed in action near Ypres on the 29th October, 1914. A sniper shot him through the head when directing his men in a supporting trench, the front trenches having been rushed by the Germans.

2nd Lieut. Bentley was buried in a garden at the back of a farm on the west side of La Quinque Rue. A little cross over the grave marks his resting place. His Company's Captain, in expressing the regret he felt at his loss, spoke of him as being of an exceptional and outstanding character.

CAPTAIN GEOFFREY MALCOLM BENTLEY, 1st BATTN. NORTHAMPTONSHIRE REGIMENT,

who died on the 29th October, 1914, of wounds received in action, was the fifth son of Lieutenant-Colonel A. W. Bentley, V.D., J.P., The Grove, Monken Hadley, Middlesex. He was born on the 3rd May, 1883, and was educated at Wellington College, where he was in the Picton from 1897–1900. After serving with the embodied Militia for a year and a half, he joined the Northamptonshire Regiment in January, 1903. He took part in the South African War, being present at operations in Cape Colony from June, 1901, to January, 1902, and served in St. Helena from January to May, 1902, receiving the Queen's medal with two clasps.

He was promoted Lieutenant in December, 1904, and Captain in May, 1910.

In the Great War he had taken part in the retirement from Mons, and the battle of the Aisne, and was shot by a sniper while handing over the trenches to the French troops at Pilkem. He was mentioned in Sir John French's Despatch of the 14th January, 1915.

His elder brother, Major Gerald W. Bentley, Middlesex Regiment, died of wounds received in this war on the 14th October, 1914.

Captain Geoffrey Bentley married Edith Marie (née Galway), Belgravia, Bangor, Co. Down, and left an only daughter, Maureen Sheila.

MAJOR GERALD WILSON BENTLEY, MIDDLESEX REGIMENT,

who was shown in the monthly War Office Casualty List, published in November, 1914, as having been killed in action between the 12th–14th October, 1914, died on the latter date at Croix Barbee of wounds received in action. He had been at Mons and succeeding engagements until his death.

He was the third son of Lieutenant-Colonel A. W. Bentley, J.P., of The Grove, Monken Hadley, Middlesex, and was born on the 1st August, 1879, and educated at Haileybury. He joined the Middlesex Regiment from the Militia in May, 1899, becoming Lieutenant in

March, 1900, and Captain in October, 1901. His rapid promotion was due to the South African War, in which he served from 1899–1902. He was present at the relief of Ladysmith and the action at Spion Kop, where he was severely wounded ; at operations on the Tugela Heights, and action at Pieter's Hill ; operations in Natal, the Transvaal, East of Pretoria, and in Cape Colony, South of the Orange River in 1899–1900, and again in the Transvaal from 1900–1901. He received the Queen's medal with four clasps, and the King's medal with two clasps. In April, 1912, he was appointed Superintendent of Gymnasia, Northern Command, which appointment he held till the outbreak of the Great War.

His younger brother, Captain Geoffrey M. Bentley, Northamptonshire Regiment, died of wounds on the 29th October, 1914. Major Bentley, who was unmarried, was promoted temporarily to his rank in October, 1914.

He won the light and heavy-weight boxing competitions at the Army and Navy Boxing Championships in 1910.

MAJOR CHARLES GEORGE PACK-BERESFORD, 1st BATTN. THE QUEEN'S OWN (ROYAL WEST KENT REGT.),

was born on the 21st of November, 1869, and was the son of Denis W. Pack-Beresford, Esq., J.P., D.L., M.P., Co. Carlow, of Fenagh House, Bagnalstown, Ireland, and grandson of Major-General Sir Denis Pack, K.C.B.

He was educated at Wellington College and the R.M.C., Sandhurst, joining the Royal West Kent Regiment as Second Lieutenant in November, 1889, becoming Lieutenant in February, 1893. From December, 1896, to March, 1900, he was Adjutant of his Battalion, having become Captain in December, 1899, and Major in March, 1908. Major Pack-Beresford was employed on the North-West Frontier of India, 1897–98, having been in Malakand and the action at Landaki ; at operations in Bajaur and in the Mamund country ; at Buner in the attack and capture of the Tanga Pass. For these services he received the medal with clasp.

He also served in the South African War from 1900–02, and was engaged in operations in the Orange River Colony, in 1900 ; in the Transvaal and Cape Colony in 1900 and 1901. He was mentioned in Despatches (" London Gazette," September, 1901), and received the Queen's medal with four clasps.

From 1905–09 Major Pack-Beresford was Officer of a Company of Gentlemen Cadets at the R.M.C., Sandhurst. He commanded the Depot of his regiment at Maidstone from 1910 to 1914.

He was killed in action at Wasimes, near Mons, on the 24th August, 1914. He was not married.

LIEUTENANT BERNARD FREDERICK PAUL BERNARD, 2nd BATTN. ROYAL WARWICKSHIRE REGIMENT,

who was killed in December, 1914, at the age of 20, was the only son of Colonel E. E. Bernard, C.M.G., Financial Secretary to the Sudan Government.

He only joined the Army in October, 1914, and, on the 20th December, was promoted temporarily to Lieutenant.

LIEUTENANT LAURENCE ARTHUR BERNARD, 2nd BATTN. THE SHERWOOD FORESTERS (NOTTINGHAMSHIRE AND DERBYSHIRE REGIMENT),

was born on the 27th August, 1886, at Copdock, Ipswich, Suffolk, the son of Arthur Montague Bernard, J.P. for Suffolk.

Lieutenant Bernard was educated at Bradfield College, Berkshire, and at the Royal Military College, Sandhurst.

At both Colleges he was in the cricket and football first XIs, and gained the Marksmanship Badge at Sandhurst. He joined the Sherwood Foresters in 1906, and was stationed at Bangalore till 1909. During the following four years he was seconded for service with the S. Nigeria Regiment W.A.F.F., with which he served in the Expeditions at Munshi, Agoni, and Sonkwala.

On the outbreak of the War his battalion joined the Expeditionary Field Force; on Sunday, 20th September, 1914, Lieutenant Bernard was killed near Troyon while leading his men to recapture trenches taken by the Germans in the battle of the Aisne. This action was successful and most important in preserving intact the British Line.

CAPTAIN HAMILTON HUGH BERNERS, 1st BATTN. IRISH GUARDS,

who was killed on the 14th September, 1914, was the son of Charles Hugh Berners, Esq., and his late wife Mary, daughter of Sir Ralph Anstruther. He was born in 1881 at Longcross, Surrey, England, educated at Eton, and, joining the Irish Guards from the Militia in November, 1905, was promoted Lieutenant in

April, 1906, and Captain in December, 1912. At the time of his death Captain Berners was second in command of his battalion, owing to the heavy casualties which had occurred in the battalion at Villiers Cotteret. Five minutes before he was killed he carried into safety, under heavy fire, one of his men badly wounded by a shell. He was in the act of raising his field glasses to locate the source of the enemy's fire, when he was shot through the chest and body, and died in a few minutes.

The following account was given by a Corporal of the Guards :—

" Captain Berners, of the Irish Guards, as at the depôt, was the life and soul of our lot. When shells were bursting over our heads he would buck us up with his humour about Brock's displays at the Palace. But when we got into close quarters it was he who was in the thick of it, and didn't he fight !

" He was one of the best of officers, and there is not a Tommy who would not have gone under for him."

Captain Berners married Edith Mary Georgina, daughter of the late Charles Sandham, Esq., of Rowdell, Pulborough, Sussex, and of Evelyn Sandham, of 13, Egerton Place, London, and grand-daughter of the late Right Hon. Sir Walter Barttelot, Bart., M.P., of Stopham, Pulborough, Sussex.

CAPTAIN BARTON HOPE BESLY, 1st BATTN. DEVONSHIRE REGIMENT,

who was killed in action at Givenchy on the 25th October, 1914, was the only surviving son of the late Rev. W. Blundell Besly and Mrs. Besly, of Ivedon, Honiton.

He was born on the 28th February, 1879, and was educated at Bradfield College, Berks, from 1891 to

1897. He joined the Devonshire Regiment from the Militia in May, 1899, becoming Lieutenant in April, 1900.

He took part in the South African War, being employed with the Mounted Infantry from

October, 1900, to May, 1902, and being present at the relief of Ladysmith, including the action at Colenso ; the actions at Spion Kop and Vaal Krans ; operations on the Tugela Heights and action at Pieter's Hill ; operations in Natal, including the action at Laing's Nek ; operations in the Transvaal, Orange River Colony, on the Zululand frontier of Natal, including the defence of Forts Itala and Prospect. He received the Queen's medal with five clasps, and the King's medal with two clasps.

He was promoted Captain in February, 1906. He was a good rider, fond of hunting and polo, and a keen all-round sportsman.

Captain Besly took part in the battle of the Aisne, and in the operations around La Bassée. He was mentioned for his services in Sir John French's Despatch of the 14th January, 1915.

LIEUTENANT DAVID CECIL BINGHAM, 3rd BATTN. COLDSTREAM GUARDS,

who was killed in action on the 14th September, 1914, during the battle of the Aisne, was the younger son of Major-General the Hon. C. E. Bingham, C.V.O., C.B. (second son of the 4th Earl of Lucan), now Commanding the 1st Cavalry Division, British Expeditionary Force. He was born on the 18th March, 1887, and was educated at Eton, and the R.M.C., Sandhurst, receiving his commission in the Coldstream Guards in August, 1906, and becoming Lieutenant in March, 1909. In July, 1911, he was appointed Adjutant of his battalion.

Lieutenant Bingham married, in 1912, Lady Rosabelle Millicent St. Clair-Erskine, only daughter of the 5th Earl of Rosslyn, and left a daughter, Rose, born 1913.

LIEUTENANT JOHN GREVILLE HOBART BIRD, 2nd BATTN. THE QUEEN'S (ROYAL WEST SURREY REGIMENT),

born at Wolverhampton on the 11th November, 1888, was the only son of Mr. William Hobart Bird, M. Inst. M. E., The Gate House, Coventry, and grandson of Alderman Maycock, J.P., a former Mayor of Coventry.

He was educated at Eversley House, Southwold, and privately, receiving his commission in The Queen's in June, 1913. He came, at the commencement of the war with Germany, with his regiment from South Africa, and proceeding to the front, was shot dead in the desperate fighting near Ypres on the 26th October, 1914: he had been sent with his platoon to defend a trench at a spot where the enemy's firing was particularly severe, and while directing his men's return fire, he was told that one of his best men had been hit, and in trying to go to his aid he was instantaneously killed.

His promotion to Lieutenant, to take effect from the 21st October, 1914, was notified in the "London Gazette," of 22nd May, 1915.

2nd LIEUT. GORDON ALIC BRODRICK BIRDWOOD, 2nd BATTN. THE PRINCE OF WALES'S VOLUNTEERS (SOUTH LANCASHIRE REGIMENT),

born at Mhow, India, on the 22nd December, 1895, was the son of Colonel William S. Birdwood, Indian Army (retired), General Officer Commanding the Baroda State Army, and a grandson of General Christopher Birdwood, Bombay Staff Corps, and of George Frederick Sheppard, Esq., Indian Civil Service ; he was also related to Sir George Birdwood, K.C.I.E., C.S.I., Lieutenant-General Sir William R. Birdwood, K.C.S.I., C.B., C.I.E., D.S.O., and to Colonel S. H. Sheppard, R.E., D.S.O., and was a nephew of Herbert Mills Birdwood, C.S.I., I.C.S., who is the father of the present Lieutenant-General Sir William R. Birdwood, Commanding the Australian and New Zealand Contingents at the front.

Educated at Mr. Bickmore's, Yardley Court, Tonbridge, and at Tonbridge School, Kent, at both of which he won prizes for running and swimming, he proceeded to the R.M.C., Sandhurst, where he was a Prize Cadet, and was gazetted to the 2nd Battalion The Prince of Wales's Volunteers (South Lancashire Regiment), in August, 1914, three months before he would have been in ordinary circumstances. After a short preliminary training at Liverpool, he left England to join his battalion in France on the 8th September, reaching his Corps on the 17th of the month. On Sunday, the 20th September, the battalion was in support, in rear of two other battalions of the brigade, in a thickly-wooded hill side, when at 5 p.m. the Germans broke through the two battalions. The South Lancashires charged and the hill was retaken, but at the cost of seven officers killed (of whom Second Lieutenant Birdwood was one) and wounded, his own company losing three officers and 66 of the rank and file, including the Company Sergeant-Major and three platoon Sergeants. One of the men, who was subsequently wounded and who helped to carry Second Lieutenant Birdwood from the battlefield, described the fight to an Officer, who communicated the account to Second Lieutenant Birdwood's grandfather. He said " the extreme gallantry of your grandson seems to have been the cause of his early death," and then quoted the words of the wounded man : " There was a young Officer who joined us, called Lieutenant Birdwood, he was almost too brave, and as a matter of fact it eventually got him knocked over. . . . Lieutenant Birdwood led a brilliant bayonet charge, and it was mainly due to him that this was successful, and that this part of the position was captured." It appears some of the enemy surrendered, and the Germans turned their machine guns on their surrendering comrades, and, Lieutenant Birdwood being riddled by their bullets, must have died instantaneously ; his body was recovered next day and buried near where he fell, with two other officers.

Second Lieutenant Birdwood was a member of the " Old Tonbridgians' Society."

CAPTAIN RICHARD LOCKINGTON BIRDWOOD, INDIAN ARMY,

who was killed on the 17th November, 1914, in the attack on Basra, in the Persian Gulf, was the youngest son of the late Herbert M. Birdwood, C.S.I., Judge of the High Court, and Member of Council, Bombay. Captain Birdwood was born on the 7th September, 1879, and was educated at Clifton College, and the R.M.C., Sandhurst, receiving his commission as Second Lieutenant, unattached, in July, 1898. In November of the following year he joined the Indian Staff Corps, becoming Lieutenant in January, 1901.

He served in the Tibet Expedition of 1903-04, for which he received the medal, and obtained his Captaincy in July, 1907. His service was chiefly in the Political Department, and before the war he was Assistant Political Agent in the Persian Gulf.

LIEUTENANT E. MAURICE BISHOP, 3rd BATTN. DORSETSHIRE REGIMENT,

was the son of Edwin and Janette Bishop, of The Lawns, Swanwick, near Southampton, and was born on the 19th June, 1891, at Gosport, Alverstoke. He was educated at Bradfield College, Berks, and was gazetted to the 3rd Dorset Regiment as Second Lieutenant in June, 1912, becoming Lieutenant in May, 1913.

In the Great War he was attached to the King's Own Yorkshire Light Infantry from September, 1914, and was serving with the 2nd Battn. of that regiment when he was killed at Illies, France, on 18th October, 1914, while gallantly leading his platoon to the attack.

CAPTAIN WILLIAM McMILLAN BLACK, ADJUTANT 58th VAUGHANS' RIFLES (FRONTIER FORCE) INDIAN ARMY,

who was killed in action on the 31st October, 1914, was the elder son of the late Rev. W. McMillan Black and Mrs. Black. He was born at Anwoth Manse, Gatehouse of Fleet, Kircudbrightshire, on the 12th September, 1883, and was educated at Edinburgh Academy, where he was Captain of the 2nd Football XV., and won prizes for athletics.

He joined the Royal Scots Fusiliers from the Militia in May, 1902. In November of the following year he was transferred to the Indian Army, becoming Lieutenant in August, 1904, and Captain in May, 1911.

He served with the 114th Mahrattas in Hong-Kong, and was transferred to the 58th Vaughans' Rifles in June, 1906.

Captain Black had qualified in Musketry and Transport Work, and could speak many of the Eastern tongues, having passed the Higher Standard in Baluchi, Chinese (Pekingese dialect), Marathi and Phuhtu, and the Lower Standard in Persian.

He was a very keen sportsman, fond of polo, shooting and other sports, and won several Cups in point-to-point races.

The following account of the circumstances of his death was given by a senior brother-officer :—

" We had been ordered to drive the Germans from a position they had captured a day before, and your son and I had crawled forward to reconnoitre the position, which we had difficulty in making out in the dark. We managed to get within some twenty yards, and were then discovered. Your son was shot through the heart and death was instantaneous. We brought back his body, and he is buried in a little village near here. . . . We shall miss your son in the regiment very much. He was always most popular with everyone, and a great loss to us. In my report on the operations, in which we lost some one hundred killed and wounded, I am specially mentioning your son's name for the skill and daring he displayed yesterday : the brilliant success we achieved was mainly due to the excellent manner in which he guided us to the position we had been ordered to attack."

A brother-officer says :—" He was marvellously cool and plucky, and his example all through the night did much to cheer up the men through the trying conditions of their first fight. He worked like a slave all night, and met his death in a very dangerous but necessary piece of work which he undertook as he was going off to mount a guard."

Captain Black was only one night in the firing line and was mentioned in Sir John French's Despatch of the 14th January, 1915.

LIEUTENANT CECIL FRANCIS BLACKER, 2nd BATTN. CONNAUGHT RANGERS,

was the son of Major F. H. Blacker, late 4th Queen's Own Hussars, and Mrs. Blacker, and was born at Scaftworth Hall, Bawtry, Yorkshire, on the 15th May, 1889.

He was educated at Mr. A. E. Tillard's School at May Place, Malvern Wells, at Wellington College, and at the R.M.C., Sandhurst.

Lieutenant Blacker received his commission as Second Lieutenant in the Connaught Rangers in November, 1909, and was promoted Lieutenant in January, 1911.

He was severely wounded at the Battle of Mons on the 23rd August, 1914, and died at Netley Hospital from the effects on the 6th September, 1914. At the time he was wounded he was serving in the Brigade Cycling Corps. Lieutenant Blacker was a good rider, and won several races at Punchestown and other places in 1912-13.

CAPTAIN WILLIAM STEWART BURDETT BLACKETT attd. LEICESTERSHIRE YEOMANRY, formerly 3rd GRENADIER GUARDS,

(of Arbigland, Dumfries), was born in 1873, and was the only son of Commander A. S. Blackett, R.N. Captain Blackett was the nephew and heir of his uncle, Colonel Blackett, of Arbigland, Dumfries.

He was educated at Wellington College, and at the R.M.C., Sandhurst, and joined the Grenadier Guards in May, 1895, being promoted Lieutenant in February, 1898, and Captain in May, 1900.

With the 3rd Battalion he served during the whole of the South African War, for which he received the Queen's medal with three clasps, and the King's medal with two clasps.

In the Great War he was attached for service to the Leicestershire Yeomanry, and died on the 24th November, 1914, from wounds received at Ypres on the 20th November.

Captain Blackett was a keen fisherman and cricketer, and fond of hunting and shooting. He was a member of the Guards', Bachelors', and Army and Navy Clubs.

He married Kathleen Prudence Eirene, youngest daughter of B. F. Bagenal, D.L., of Benekerry, Carlow, and left one son, C. W. S. Blackett, born 1908.

2nd LIEUTENANT PATRICK EDWARD ADAM BLAIR, 2nd BATTN. THE BLACK WATCH (ROYAL HIGHLANDERS),

was the elder son of Mr. A. S. Blair, Writer to the Signet, Edinburgh, who as Lieutenant-Colonel Commanding the 9th Battalion (Highlanders) Royal Scots, is himself taking part in the war with Germany.

Second Lieutenant Blair was born in June, 1893, and was educated at Cargilfield School, Midlothian, and Malvern College. He was gazetted to the Black Watch from the Special Reserve, in June, 1914, and accompanied the 1st Battalion to the front in August. Early in November Second Lieutenant Blair was reported " missing," but is now stated to have been killed near Gheluvelt on the 29th October, 1914.

MAJOR EDWARD ALGERNON CLEADER BLAKE, 2nd BATTN. DURHAM LIGHT INFANTRY,

was the younger son of the late Mr. Samuel Frederick Blake, of Great Budbridge

Manor, and Shanklin, Isle of Wight, and was born on the 27th August, 1871.

He was educated at Rugby (Whitelaw), which he entered in 1886. He received his commission in the Durham Light Infantry from the Militia in April, 1893, being posted to the 1st Battalion, and became Lieutenant in May, 1896, and Captain in February, 1900.

He served in the South African War while Adjutant of his battalion, an appointment he held from April, 1901, to April, 1904, and was present at the relief of Ladysmith, including action at Colenso, the action at Vaal Krans, where he was severely wounded, and at operations in the Transvaal from November, 1900, to May, 1902. For his services he was mentioned in Despatches ("London Gazette," 29th July, 1902), received his Brevet Majority 22nd August, 1902, and the Queen's and King's medals, each with two clasps.

He was Adjutant of the 3rd (Special Reserve) Battalion of his regiment at Newcastle from August, 1912, to July, 1913, when he obtained his substantive Majority.

Major Blake, who was not married, was fond of all kinds of sport, especially hunting, shooting and golf, and extremely popular with all ranks in his regiment. He was killed at Ennetières, France, while gallantly leading his men on the 20th October, 1914, and by his bravery and good leadership drove back a strong attack of the enemy.

CAPTAIN HUGH SEYMOUR BLANE, 19th LANCERS (FANE'S HORSE),

INDIAN ARMY, was the youngest son of Mrs. Rodney Blane, Montpelier Street, London, and of the late Captain Rodney Blane, Commander R.N. Captain Blane's eldest brother is Sir Charles Rodney Blane, who succeeded his uncle as fourth Baronet in 1911.

He was born on the 2nd February, 1885, and was educated at Aldenham, and after receiving his commission in August, 1905, was attached to the Wiltshire Regiment for a year before he joined the 19th Lancers, Indian Army, in November, 1906.

He was promoted Lieutenant in November, 1907, and Captain in August, 1914. In June, 1907, while in India, Captain Blane was shot at and wounded in a train by Pathans, but recovered after being in King Edward VII Hospital in Grosvenor Gardens.

He was a good polo player; in 1913 he was Captain of the Regimental Polo team, and acted as umpire at Hurlingham in the summer of 1914. He was a member of the Cavalry Club. He married in April, 1914, Molly, daughter of Mrs. O'Callaghan.

For active service Captain Blane was attached to the 5th (Princess Charlotte of Wales's) Dragoon Guards. He was wounded on the 31st October and lay in the trenches for sixteen hours before he was moved to the Field Hospital, where he died on the morning of 1st November, 1914. He was buried at Neuve Eglise. The man who carried him out of the trench received the D.C.M. for the action.

CAPTAIN GERALD WYNTER BLATHWAYT, ROYAL FIELD ARTILLERY,

was born at Belvedere, Kent, on the 30th June, 1879, being the son of Arthur P. Blathwayt, Esq., of Northwood Grange, Middlesex. He was educated at Aldenham School, Herts.

In 1896 he received a commission in the Kent Artillery Militia, and having passed the qualifying examination obtained a commission in the Garrison Artillery in 1898, and was transferred to the Royal Field Artillery on the outbreak of the South African War, to which he went in the specially formed Royal African Mounted Rifles. For his services he received the South African medal, with three clasps. On his return to England he was appointed Adjutant of the 49th Brigade Royal Field Artillery, and subsequently Garrison Adjutant at Woolwich, having become Captain in July, 1906. On expiration of his Staff appointment in February, 1914, he joined the 56th Battery, 44th (Howitzer) Brigade, at Brighton.

On the first day of the Battle of the Aisne, 14th September, 1914, he was killed by the bursting of a shell, and his body was buried in the garden of the Château Verneuil, in the village of that name. Major Barker, Commanding the 56th Battery, wrote :—" In him the Army has lost a gallant Officer, and myself and his other companions in the Brigade a beloved comrade and friend."

Captain Blathwayt was for some years Honorary

Secretary of the Garrison Cricket Club, Woolwich; he was a member of the " Band of Brothers," and of the Junior United Service Club. He married Margaret Aline, daughter of the late C. Pickersgill-Cunliffe, of Beacon Hill Park, Hindhead, and of Mrs. Pickersgill-Cunliffe, of Cobb Court, Cootham, Sussex, and left two daughters, Madeleine Margaret, and Elizabeth, aged two years and one year respectively at the time of their father's death.

MAJOR CHARLES BLISS, C.I.E., 1st BATTN. 1st KING GEORGE'S OWN GURKHA RIFLES (THE MALAUN REGIMENT),

who died on the 22nd December, 1914, at Lillers, France, of wounds received on the 20th December, was the second surviving son of Sir Henry William Bliss, K.C.I.E., Indian Civil Service (retired), and was born on the 30th December 1871, at Dindigul, Madura District, Madras Presidency, India.

He was educated at Clifton College, Neuenheim College, and the R.M.C., Sandhurst, and received his first commission in the North Staffordshire Regiment, to which he was gazetted in 1891. Two years later he was transferred to the Derbyshire regiment, in which he became Lieutenant in 1896. In December of the latter year he joined the Indian Staff Corps and was appointed to the 44th Gurkha Rifles. Having been promoted Captain in 1901, he was Deputy Assistant Adjutant-General for Musketry in 1903, an appointment he gave up to rejoin his regiment for service in Tibet; he took part in the action at Niani, the operations at and around Gyantse, and the march to Lhasa, during which he was wounded. He was mentioned in Despatches ("London Gazette," 13th December, 1904), and received the Tibet medal and clasp. From 1907 he was seconded for service with the Assam Military Police, and commanded several small expeditions on the North-East Frontier; he received the C.I.E. and the Police medal and also had the Durbar medal, 1911, and Abor medal.

He was appointed to the 1st Gurkha Rifles in 1908, but only joined his regiment in August, 1914, just before it left India for the front. He was mentioned in Sir John French's Despatch of 31st May, 1915.

Major Bliss married Mabel Emmeline, daughter of Colonel Maxwell, late Derbyshire Regiment, and left one daughter, aged nine years.

CAPTAIN GREVILLE HUBERT ROBINS BLOUNT, ROYAL ARTILLERY,

son of the late Major Hubert Blount, Royal Artillery, who died of fever on service in the South African War, was born at Woolwich on the 23rd February, 1883.

He was educated at Harrow, and the R.M.A., Woolwich, and joined the Royal Field Artillery as Second Lieutenant in August, 1900, becoming Lieutenant in August, 1903, and Captain in November, 1911. He was appointed Adjutant of the 25th Brigade at Farnborough in July, 1913.

Captain Blount died on the 23rd September, 1914, of wounds received in action.

He married Gladys, younger daughter of the Rev. Canon Wilson, of Mitcham, and left an orphan boy four years old.

CAPTAIN EDWARD MARTIN CRAWLEY-BOEVEY, 1st BATTN. ROYAL SUSSEX REGIMENT,

was the second son of Sir Thomas Hyde Crawley-Boevey, 5th Baronet, of Flaxley Abbey, Newnham, Gloucestershire, and was born at Flaxley on the 26th March, 1873.

He was educated at Rugby, and the R.M.C., Sandhurst, joining the Royal Sussex Regiment as Second Lieutenant in March, 1895, becoming Lieutenant in July, 1897, and Captain in December, 1902. He served with his battalion in the South African War, taking part in actions at Houtnek, Vet River, Zand River, Pretoria, Johannesburg, Diamond Hill, Wittebergen, and Ladybrand. He received the Queen's medal with four clasps and the King's medal with two clasps.

As a Lieutenant Captain Crawley-Boevey was sent from South Africa to England with some of the battalion to represent the Royal Sussex Regiment at the Coronation of H.M. King Edward VII.

Captain Crawley-Boevey was killed in the trenches near Bailleul, on 24th December, 1914, while attached for duty with the 4th Battalion Royal Fusiliers (City of London Regiment), when he was trying to shoot a sniper.

Captain Crawley-Boevey was a member of the Junior Army and Navy Club. He was fond of shooting and all sport. He was a particularly gifted draughtsman and good shot with both revolver and rifle. Most of his service was spent in India with the 1st Battalion.

He married Rosalie Winifred, daughter of Colonel Sartorius, C.B., and granddaughter of Sir George Rose Sartorius, K.C.B., late Admiral of the Fleet, and left one son, Richard Martin, born 31st July, 1908.

COLONEL FRANK RIDLEY FARRER BOILEAU, p.s.c., LATE ROYAL ENGINEERS,

died on the 27th August, 1914, of wounds received at Ham, France.

He was the eldest surviving son of Colonel F.W. Boileau, C.B., of Elstowe, Camberley, was born on the 29th November, 1867, and was educated at Cheltenham College. He joined the Royal Engineers in February, 1887, becoming Lieutenant three years later. In 1892 he took part in the Lushai Expedition, for which he received the medal and clasp, and in 1895 was employed with the Relief Force in the Chitral Expedition, receiving the medal and clasp. In July, 1897, he was promoted Captain. From April, 1898, to February, 1900, he was Assistant Commissioner, Anglo-German South-East African Boundary Commission. From June to November, 1900, he was Deputy Assistant Adjutant-General in South Africa, and took part in the Boer War, being present at the advance on Kimberley, including actions at Belmont, Enslin, Modder River and Magersfontein; operations in the Orange Free State, and at Paardeberg; actions at Poplar Grove, Driefontein, Houtnek (Thoba Mountain), Vet and Zand Rivers; in the Transvaal, with actions near Johannesburg, Pretoria, and Diamond Hill; at further operations in the Transvaal west of Pretoria, including action at Zilikats Nek. For his services he was mentioned in Despatches (London Gazette, 8th February, 1901), given his Brevet Majority November, 1900, and received the Queen's medal with six clasps.

From May, 1901, to July, 1905, he was Deputy Assistant Adjutant-General, Royal Engineers, at Head Quarters of the Army. In addition to being a Staff College Graduate, Colonel Boileau was a second-class Interpreter in French. He received his substantive Majority in August,

1905, and in March, 1906, was given a half-pay Lieutenant-Colonelcy, with the appointment of Professor at the Indian Staff College, which he held till January, 1910. He was promoted Brevet-Colonel in March, 1909, and a substantive Colonel on the 21st January, 1910, going on half-pay till July, 1910, when he was appointed a General Staff Officer, First Grade, IIIrd Division, Southern Command. This appointment he was holding when the war broke out, and he then became Chief Staff Officer of the IIIrd Division Expeditionary Force, and was so serving when he received the injuries from which he died.

He married in 1902, Mary, daughter of Prebendary Tudor, Lustleigh, Devon, and leaves three sons.

MAJOR GEORGE ENIL BOLSTER, ROYAL FIELD ARTILLERY,

was born at Dagshai, India, on the 21st July, 1876, the son of Surgeon-Major T. G. Bolster, M.D., F.R.C.S., A.M.S., and Mrs. Bolster, of Twickenham, and grandson of Brevet Lieutenant - Colonel J. F. Nembhard, Bengal Army.

His early years were spent at various places at home and abroad, where his father was stationed. After coming to England in 1888, he was educated at Ipswich Grammar School, whence he passed direct into the Royal Military Academy in 1893, and in the passing out examinations gained the sixth place, and the prize for Artillery.

He was gazetted to the Royal Artillery in November, 1895, became Lieutenant in November, 1898, Captain in September, 1901, and Major in February, 1912. Much of his early service was spent in India. In 1903 he was appointed Adjutant of the 35th Brigade Royal Field Artillery, and held the position for over three years. In 1909 he was appointed Staff Captain, Vth Division, Irish Command, and left that post on being nominated for the Staff College in 1911. On completion of his course there in 1914, he joined the 106th Battery in South Africa, and returning home he embarked for the Front with the 106th Battery, 22nd Brigade, Royal Field Artillery, forming part of the VIIth Division of the Expeditionary Force.

He took part in the heroic stand made by that Division at Ypres, until the 1st Army Corps came up from the Aisne on the 21st

October. On the 23rd October, 1914, while taking up an observation post in advance of his battery, a high explosive shell burst close to him, and he was killed instantaneously by the shock, there being no external wounds. His body was buried in the portion of the Municipal Cemetery, Ypres, set aside for British Officers, a wooden cross with his name being erected over his grave by the Officer who succeeded him in the command of the battery.

A distinguished Officer of Head Quarters wrote to his mother, saying : " I cannot tell you how sorry I was to hear that George had been killed . . . we all mourn his loss. In George not only the regiment but the army has lost a most able Officer and also a most staunch friend . . . loved by all who have had to serve with him."

Shortly before leaving for the front, Major Bolster's engagement to a daughter of Colonel T. J. de Burgh, of Oldtown, Naas, had been publicly announced.

Major Bolster was a keen huntsman, and rode in several point-to-point races. He was well known with the Kildare and Duhallow Hunts. He was also a hockey player and often joined in games with his men.

LIEUTENANT ROBERT HAROLD BOND, 2nd BATTN. KING'S ROYAL RIFLE CORPS,

was born at Aldershot in 1882, only son of Colonel R. J. Bond, R.E., of Moorefield, Co. Kildare, Ireland, and nephew of General Bond, C.B.

He was educated at Wellington College, where he was Head of his House.

He joined the King's Royal Rifle Corps in 1903 from the Leicestershire Militia, and was promoted to his Lieutenancy in 1907, serving in India till 1909, and then at Shorncliffe and Blackdown.

He was killed on the 14th September, 1914, in the Battle of the Aisne. In the early morning of that day Lieutenant Bond's company were in a brilliant action in which they lost all their officers killed or wounded, as well as many riflemen, but held their position most gallantly.

Lieutenant Bond was a keen soldier, fine horseman and athlete, being a very good long distance runner.

2nd LIEUTENANT SIDNEY COURTHOPE BOSANQUET, 5th BATTN. DUKE OF CAMBRIDGE'S OWN (MIDDLESEX REGT.),

who was killed in trench fighting at Houplines, near Armentières, on the 16th December,1914, was the elder son of Charles John Bosanquet, M.S.A., A. M. I. E. E., of " Stokesay," Blackheath, and a nephew of Samuel Courthope Bosanquet, Esq., of Dingestow Court, Monmouth. He was educated at St. Lawrence College, Ramsgate. He was first given a commission in March, 1913, in the 5th Battalion Middlesex Regiment, and went through his training and the manœuvres of that autumn. Later he resigned his commission and went into the Ironworks of David Bridge & Co., Castleton, Lancashire. On the mobilisation for the war he at once offered his services and was gazetted Second Lieutenant on probation in his previous battalion on the 15th August, 1914. He was attached to the 1st Battalion while on active service. He was in his 21st year, having been born at Belvedere on the 15th July, 1894.

2nd LIEUTENANT the Honble. VERE DOUGLAS BOSCAWEN, COLDSTREAM GUARDS (SPECIAL RESERVE),

whose death was notified in the official monthly list published in January, 1915, but who is believed to have been killed on the 29th October, 1914, was the third son of the seventh Viscount Falmouth, K.C.V.O., C.B.

It was stated in the " Times " of the 21st December, 1914, that, on the 29th October four companies of the Coldstream Guards were completely surrounded . . . and that Mr. Boscawen, refusing to surrender, fell fighting against overwhelming odds. Second Lieutenant Boscawen was born on the 3rd August, 1890, and was attached to the 1st Battalion Coldstream Guards in March, 1914.

CAPTAIN CHARLES SIDNEY GARNETT-BOTFIELD, 2nd BATTN. BEDFORDSHIRE REGIMENT,

son of the Rev. C. R. Garnett-Botfield, M.A., Moreton Vicarage, near Oswestry, was born at Rochdale on the 5th October, 1887. He was educated at Rossall School, and the

R.M.C., Sandhurst. He joined the Bedfordshire Regiment as Second Lieutenant in February, 1908, becoming Lieutenant in March, 1910, and Captain in September, 1914.

In the Great War Captain Garnett-Botfield was wounded in the elbow at Ypres on the 30th October, 1914, but continued fighting, till later his right thigh was shattered. He was removed to the Christol Base Hospital, Boulogne, where he died on the 14th December, 1914.

Captain Garnett-Botfield, who was said to be one of the finest Machine Gun Officers, was mentioned in Sir John French's Despatch of 14th January, 1915, for gallant and distinguished service.

2nd LIEUTENANT THOMAS REGINALD BOTTOMLEY, 1st BATTN. THE EAST YORKSHIRE REGIMENT,

was born at Ripponden, Yorkshire, on the 17th October, 1887, the son of Thomas and Ellen Bottomley, now of Thornton Heath, Surrey, formerly of Belle Vue, Barkisland, Halifax, Yorkshire. He was educated at Rishworth Grammar School from 1898 to 1903, at the Halifax Technical College till 1907, and subsequently at St. John's College, Battersea, and Birkbeck College, London, till 1914.

Second Lieutenant Bottomley obtained many academic distinctions, including the degree of B.A., London University (as an Internal student), in 1913, and the Teachers' Diploma of the Board of Education; moreover, after joining the Army he passed successfully examinations for promotion and in Physical drill. In athletics also he won prizes, including the College mile and half mile; was a member of the St. John's College First XV., and of the South London Harriers.

Mr. Bottomley had intended to adopt the Teaching profession as his career, and on leaving St. John's College was appointed Teacher by the Croydon Educational Committee. He was acknowledged by all who knew him to have had an enormous influence for good over boys under him, preferring to teach by example rather than by precept alone. One of his Headmasters said of him: "His life was a pattern—steel true and blade straight."

While at London University, Mr. Bottomley joined the Officers' Training Corps, in which he spent three years, up to April, 1914, when he received his commission as Second Lieutenant in the 1st Battalion East Yorkshire Regiment (Special Reserve), joining in June for his first year's period of training. Previously he had served as cadet and sergeant in the 10th (Territorial) Battalion Duke of Cambridge's Own (Middlesex Regiment) from 1908–11.

On September 7th Second Lieutenant Bottomley accompanied his battalion to the Continent, and three days after arriving in the fighting line, was killed by shell, in a trench, early on the morning of the 23rd September, 1914.

A senior Officer gave his widow the following account of his death :—" The whole company, officers and men, deeply sympathise with you in your loss ; he was our loss too, as we all admired and respected him. He fell in the trenches, hit by the first shell of the day ; he could not have suffered at all. The nearest village to the place is Vendresse, and the trenches were on the ridge north of the village. He was buried near Troyon, a cross marking his grave."

Second Lieutenant Bottomley had married on the 29th August, a few days before leaving for the front, Eveline Mary, only daughter of W. H. Gibson, Esq., of Sowerby Bridge, and sister of Doctor Gibson, Professor of Engineering, St. Andrew's University, now serving as Lieutenant in the 2nd Highland Brigade, Royal Field Artillery (Territorial).

LIEUT. NIGEL WALTER HENRY LEGGE-BOURKE, 2nd BATTN. COLDSTREAM GUARDS,

was the only son of Colonel the Hon. Sir Harry Legge, K.C.V.O., late Coldstream Guards, and Lady Legge, and was born at 45, Grosvenor Square, London, on the 13th November, 1889.

He was educated at "Evelyns" (Mr. G. T. Worsley's) from April, 1899, to August, 1902, and at Eton (Rev. H. T. Bowlby's) from September,

1902—December, 1907, and entered the Royal Military College, Sandhurst, after attaining the age of 18 in January, 1908. From Sandhurst he received his commission in the 1st Coldstream Guards in February, 1909, becoming Lieutenant in the 2nd Battalion in June, 1910. He left with his battalion for the front on the 12th August, 1914. On the 4th October his name was sent in for mention " for his very excellent work and exceptionally good leading of his platoon on all occasions up to the battle of the Aisne."

He was killed in action on the 30th October, 1914, while in command of a platoon of No. 1 Company, holding advanced trenches in Reutal Wood, near Ypres.

Lieutenant Legge-Bourke married on 3rd June, 1913, at the Guards' Chapel, Wellington Barracks, Lady Victoria Carrington, daughter of the Marquis of Lincolnshire, and left one son, Edward Alexander Henry, born 16th May, 1915.

LIEUTENANT JACOB EDWARD PLEYDELL-BOUVERIE, 2nd BATTN. KING'S ROYAL RIFLE CORPS,

who died in hospital at Boulogne on the 1st November, 1914, was the only son of the late Hon. Duncombe Pleydell-Bouverie, second son of the fourth Earl of Radnor, and his wife, Marie Eleanor Pleydell-Bouverie, of Coleshill House, Highworth, Berkshire, daughter of Sir Edward Hulse, 5th Baronet. He was born on the 12th July, 1887, and was educated at Eton and the R.M.C., Sandhurst, from which he was gazetted to the King's Royal Rifle Corps in February, 1908, being posted to the 4th Battalion. In 1909 he went to India with his battalion, and having been promoted Lieutenant in January, 1911, soon after returned to England and was stationed at the Rifle Depot, Winchester, until the war broke out.

Lieutenant Pleydell-Bouverie, who was a member of the Bath Club, was a keen cricketer and played frequently for the Green Jackets and Free Foresters.

At the end of August, 1914, he left Sheerness with a draft, and joined the 2nd Battalion of his regiment on the 20th September, taking command of the 13th and 14th platoons. He was mortally wounded at Gheluvelt on the 31st October during the German attack on Ypres, and died early next morning in No. 13 Stationary Hospital at Boulogne.

LIEUTENANT CUTHBERT EDWARD LATIMER BOWEN, attd. to the KING'S AFRICAN RIFLES,

son of the Rev. Thomas James and Susan Elvina Bowen, was born at All Saints' Vicarage, Swansea, on the 23rd September, 1881.

He received his education first at Mr. Pridden's Preparatory School, Grove House, Boxgrove, Guildford, and afterwards at Rugby (Mr. Stallard's House). In 1902 he entered the Queen's Royal West Surrey Regiment (Militia) and served with it in South Africa. After the Boer War he entered the Regular Army, being gazetted to the Queen's Own Royal West Surrey Regiment, January, 1903, and joined the 1st Battalion at Peshawar, India. Leaving the Army in 1905, he accepted a post under the Colonial Office as Assistant District Inspector of Police in British East Africa. At the time of his death, which occurred 1st December, 1914, he was operating on the border of the Kissi District under Major Ross, with half a company of the King's African Rifles, to which regiment he was then attached, and some thirty European Scouts. A day or two previously he had captured a German, and on the day he was killed news was brought in concerning two more Germans. He obtained permission to go out and endeavour to capture them, and left with an officer of the King's African Rifles, some men of the regiment, and some police. The Germans were located on a stony hill and the Officer of the King's African Rifles went up one way, Lieutenant Bowen another, the latter apparently reaching the top first with his Sergeant, a Corporal, and other police. On meeting the enemy a fight ensued in which Lieutenant Bowen and some of his men were killed, but the Germans were eventually driven out of the position. His body and those of the men killed were recovered next morning and buried at the foot of the hill.

The General Officer Commanding, on hearing of the death of Mr. Bowen and the men of the East African Police, desired to express his regret, adding that Mr. Bowen evidently lost his life in a gallant attempt to take Susuni Hill, and Major Edwards, Inspector-General of Police, added :—" I feel I have lost both a gallant and loyal friend. The Police intend at the end of the war to erect a memorial, either over the spot where he rests, or elsewhere, in memory of a brother officer who died so gallantly, and whose name will always be amongst those most honoured by us."

LIEUTENANT HENRY RAYMOND SYNDERCOMBE BOWER, 1st BATTN. SOUTH STAFFORDSHIRE REGIMENT,

who was killed in action at the age of 20, was the eldest son of Mr. H. G. S. Bower, of Marnhull, Dorset.

He was educated at a preparatory school at Repton, then at Repton School itself, and the R. M. C., Sandhurst. He received his commission in September, 1913, and was promoted Lieutenant in November, 1914.

Lieutenant Bower was killed on the 20th December, 1914, while helping a wounded soldier to shelter, having already brought in several others safely. He had himself been previously wounded on the 26th October at Ypres, where his battalion formed part of the famous VIIth Division.

His recreations were cricket, tennis, hunting and hockey.

LIEUTENANT JAMES ARTHUR BOWLES, ROYAL FIELD ARTILLERY,

was born on March 9th, 1883, and was the son of General F. A. Bowles, C.B., Royal Artillery, and was educated at Boxgrove School, Guildford, Surrey; Clifton College, and the Royal Military Academy.

He obtained his first Commission in the Royal Artillery in July, 1902. From 1909–12 he served on the Staff as A.D.C. to his father, General F. A. Bowles, when commanding at Devonport. In April, 1912, he joined the 28th Brigade Royal Field Artillery, and in the same year was appointed Adjutant of the Brigade. Previous to this he had served with the 132nd Battery at Fermoy, and in the Royal Horse Artillery at the Depot, Woolwich.

He was killed in action at Le Cateau, France, on the 26th August, 1914.

He married Dorothy Emily, youngest daughter of Mrs. Bainbridge and the late Rear-Admiral J. H. Bainbridge, of " Elfordleigh," Plympton, South Devon, and " Frankfield," Cork. Ireland, and left two children, Rose Ella Moïna, born 26th June, 1912, and Ruth Kathleen, born 26th September, 1913.

Lieutenant Bowles was a member of the Junior Army and Navy Club.

2nd LIEUT. THOMAS HENRY BOWLEY, 1st BATTN. LEICESTERSHIRE REGIMENT,

who is presumed to have been killed on 26th October, 1914, was born at Hugglescote, Leicester, on 18th May, 1875, the son of John Welborne Bowley (believed to be from the French name de Boulay) of Ashby de la Zouche.

After receiving the usual elementary education he joined the Border Regiment, and served in its ranks for just twenty-one years, including the South African War, for his services in which he was made King's Sergeant, was mentioned in Despatches for capturing a " Commandant " and taking a Boer position, after his Officer had been killed, and received the King's and Queen's medals with seven clasps; he also held the Good Conduct medal, and almost every certificate, including " D." in Musketry, which it was possible for a soldier in his position to obtain. He was an all-round sportsman and was noted for the remarkable control he exercised over his men.

On the 10th October, 1914, while on active service in the Great War, he was gazetted to a commission in the 1st Battalion Leicestershire Regiment, but never joined his new Battalion, continuing to serve, till his presumed death, in his old regiment. Though endeavours have been made to obtain authentic information about him through the usual official channels, the Red Cross Society and the American Embassy, they have unfortunately been unsuccessful.

More than one account has been received from men of the battalion who professed to be able to give information, but the accounts differ so materially that it is feared little reliance can be placed on them.

Second Lieutenant Bowley married Louisa S., daughter of the late John Thomas Palmer, of Camberwell, and left three children, Violet Lydia, born in Burmah in September, 1903, Ronald Graham, born in India in February, 1905, and Leslie Welborne, born in Carlisle in May, 1908.

2nd LIEUTENANT EDWARD FENWICK BOYD, 1st BATTN. NORTHUMBERLAND FUSILIERS,

killed in action at the battle of the Aisne on the 20th September, 1914, was the only son of the late Robert Fenwick Boyd, of Houghton-le-Spring, Co. Durham, and of Mrs. Boyd, of Hill House, Wadhurst, Sussex.

He was born in 1890, and educated at Rugby, where he was Cadet Officer in the Officers' Training Corps, and won his football colours in 1912; and University College, Oxford, where he was a member of Vincent's Club. He played football for Blackheath for two seasons, and for the Army v. Navy in 1914.

He was gazetted Second Lieutenant in the Northumberland Fusiliers in September, 1912. Second Lieutenant Boyd went out to France with the 1st Battalion on the 13th August, 1914, and was mentioned in Sir John French's Despatch of the 8th October, 1914.

2nd LIEUTENANT HAROLD ALEXANDER BOYD, 2nd BATTN. ROYAL INNISKILLING FUSILIERS,

was the only son of Dr. A. J. Boyd, The Manor House, Ware, Herts, and was born there on the 19th January, 1895. Mrs. Boyd was a daughter of the late B. C. Berkeley, of Collett Hall, Ware. Dr. Boyd had served in the 1st (Herts) Volunteer Battalion Bedfordshire Regiment, retiring as Captain in 1902. Second Lieutenant Boyd was educated at Rugby, and Trinity College, Cambridge, where he was a member of the First Trinity Boat Club. He joined the Army in the Special Reserve in April, 1913, and on the outbreak of the war was first stationed on coast defence duty at Lough Swilly, Co. Donegal, and in August, 1914, proceeded to France with the 2nd Battalion Royal Inniskilling Fusiliers, in which he had been appointed Second Lieutenant.

A corporal of the battalion gave the following account of Second Lieutenant Boyd's death, which occurred on the 7th September, 1914 :—

" In the evening the Inniskillings had to find the outposts at a village to which we had come ; . . . the shelling was terrific and we had no artillery with us. Our officers were trying to find the range, and had no cover from the shells, thus exposing themselves, notably Mr. Boyd, who was standing by an apple tree. He was struck by shrapnel and killed instantly."

2nd LIEUTENANT NIGEL JOHN LAWSON BOYD, OF THE 1st BATTN. THE BLACK WATCH (ROYAL HIGHLANDERS),

was born at Edinburgh on the 14th September, 1894, the son of William Boyd, Esq., Writer to the Signet, Edinburgh, Member of the King's Body Guard for Scotland (R.C.A.), and his wife Laura, daughter of the late John Crerar, Esq., of Halifax, Nova Scotia. He was a grandson of Sir John Boyd, of Maxpoffle, Roxburghshire, and great grandson of John Lawson, Esq., 14th Laird of Cairnmuir, Peebleshire, Scotland. Second Lieutenant Boyd was educated at Cargilfield School, Midlothian ; Winchester College, and the Royal Military College, Sandhurst. In passing into Sandhurst he obtained a Prize Cadetship, and in passing out was fourth on the list. From his earliest childhood it had been his ambition to be in the Black Watch, and he was gazetted to that distinguished regiment in February, 1914. Accompanying it to France at the beginning of August, 1914, he took part with it in all the fighting in which it was engaged, including the memorable retirement from Mons to the Marne, until the Battle of the Aisne. Here, on his birthday, he received the wound which proved fatal. From a description he gave his father, when in hospital at Rouen, it seems that early in the morning of that day the Black Watch, in concert with the Cameron Highlanders, found themselves on the banks of the Aisne, opposed by a strong force of Germans. Second Lieutenant Boyd had been directed to take up a position with his platoon and had been instructed to hold it at all costs. The enemy pressed him in overpowering numbers, till they were within 100 yards. Second Lieutenant Boyd, having fired ten rounds from a rifle, afterwards emptied his revolver at them. He had stood up to give an order to those of his men who were left, and had drawn his claymore, when a bullet struck the scabbard, and, glancing off it, entered the left hip and lodged in the bladder. The position was then rushed by the enemy. The young Officer and his men had unquestionably upheld the best traditions of the grand old regiment to which he was so proud to belong.

While lying wounded, he asked a passing German for assistance, who replied with a threat to shoot him ; after this he pretended to be dead when Germans passed. At last Captain Napier Cameron, of the Cameron

Highlanders, happened to see him, and carried him, under fire, to shelter in the rear. At the time this undoubtedly saved his life. While lying wounded he had most of his belongings stolen, revolver, field glasses, flask, and money. He lay where Captain Napier Cameron had placed him for 16 hours in the rain, and was then found by a stretcher party and carried to the Field Hospital. Subsequently, at the Hospital in Rouen, he was operated on, and throughout behaved with the greatest fortitude, being held up as an example to men less severely hurt than himself. Great hopes were entertained of his recovery, but in the early morning of the 12th October, he suddenly succumbed, the immediate cause of death being a blood clot. Thus ended a young life, not, we may be sure, given in vain for his country. His body was brought to Scotland and interred with military honours in the Dean Cemetery, Edinburgh, on the 19th October, 1914.

From the Head Master, his House Master at Winchester, and other sources, came striking testimony to the respect and affection in which he had been held there.

A Senior Officer of his regiment wrote that " He was very popular with all ranks."

He was keen on all outdoor sports. At Winchester he played in the " Houses Fifteen " matches, was a fair cricketer, and Scratch Golf player ; a good rider, keen fisherman and excellent shot with gun and rifle. He shot for Winchester at Bisley in 1911 for the Cadet Trophy, and was again at Bisley in the Winchester " Eight " in 1912.

LIEUTENANT DAVID ERSKINE BOYLE, 2nd BATTN. LANCASHIRE FUSILIERS,

who was killed in action near Cambrai, on the 26th August, 1914, was the son of the late Rear-Admiral Robert Hornby Boyle.

He was born on the 9th September, 1889, and was educated at Malvern College (Swann, 1903–08), where he was a school prefect, head of his house, in the cricket XXII, the football XI, and in the Officers' Training Corps.

He entered the R.M.C., Sandhurst, in September, 1908, became a Colour-sergeant in 1909, was gazetted Second Lieutenant in September of that year, and promoted Lieutenant in January, 1911. When he was killed he was in the act of summoning aid for a fellow officer who had just been wounded. He was buried by his own men close to where he fell.

CAPTAIN the Honble. JAMES BOYLE, 1st BATTN. ROYAL SCOTS FUSILIERS,

third son of the 7th Earl of Glasgow, was born at Shewalton on the 11th March, 1880. He was educated at Wanganui, New Zealand, and Trinity Hall, Cambridge.

He joined the Ayrshire Militia in 1890, and served with it in the South African War 1901–02, for which he received the Queen's medal with five clasps. In 1903 he was transferred to the Royal Scots Fusiliers ; from October, 1908, to April, 1911, he was extra A.D.C. and A.D.C. to the Governor of Victoria. He became Captain in April, 1912. In that year he was appointed A.D.C. to General Sir H. Smith-Dorrien till April, 1914, when he became Adjutant of his battalion, and proceeded with it to France in August.

He was killed on the 18th October, 1914, at Chateau Warneton, near La Bassée, while charging a trench. Captain Boyle, who was a member of the United Service and Caledonian Clubs, married in 1908 Katherine Isabel Salvin, daughter of the late Edward Salvin Bowlby, of Gilston Park, Herts, and Knoydart, Inverness ; he left three children, Patrick John Salvin, born April, 1910, Edward James, born February, 1912, and Belinda Margaret Graeme, born December, 1913.

CAPTAIN EDWARD KINDER BRADBURY, V.C., ROYAL HORSE ARTILLERY,

who was killed in action at Nery in September, 1914, was born on the 16th August, 1881, and was educated at Marlborough and the R.M.A., Woolwich. He joined the Royal Artillery in May, 1900, and was promoted Lieutenant in April, 1901. From January to October, 1902, he was employed with the Imperial Yeomanry. He served in the South African War, being present at operations in Cape Colony in 1902, and received the Queen's medal with two clasps. From February, 1905, to March, 1907, he was employed with the King's African Rifles, and was promoted Captain in February, 1910. He was a member of the Junior Naval and Military and of the Royal Automobile Clubs, and was a well-known follower of hounds in the South of Ireland, and a keen fisherman.

Captain Bradbury was one of the officers of the famous " L" Battery, Royal Horse Artillery, all the officers and men of which have gained undying fame for their gallantry on the 1st September, 1914. Captain Bradbury was awarded the V.C. for his part in this action, the following being the official record in the "London Gazette" of the 25th November, 1914: —" For gallantry and ability in organising the defence of ' L ' Battery against heavy odds at Nery on 1st September, 1914."

A General Officer referring to the incident wrote :—" Poor Brad was killed yesterday ; he knocked out eight German guns first and we got his gun and the German ones afterwards. . . . I have sent Brad's gun to Paris with three of the ones he knocked out. A foot of the muzzle of his own gun was blown off with melanite, and it shows what work he had done."

Another General, writing of Captain Bradbury, said : " I must tell you how deeply we all in the Artillery of VIth Division sympathise with you in the loss of your son. He was simply beloved by us all, from me, his General, to the last joined subaltern. He was very nearly four years under my command, and I looked upon him as one of the most brilliant officers I had ever come across, one who, had God willed it, had a great career in front of him, and the manner in which he met his death fighting a single gun to the end after the loss of one leg, was worthy of him."

An Officer of the Queen's Bays wrote :—" Your son died the bravest of the brave, he served the last gun himself when all his battery were either killed or wounded."

The following account of " L " Battery's fight at Nery has been published :—

" The battery got into bivouac after dark on the night of August 31st, near the little village of Nery, about twelve miles south-west of Compiègne. A squadron of the Queen's Bays were bivouacked in the same field. In the morning, while the men were having their breakfasts, and before the river mists had yet cleared away, the camp was startled by the sound of guns very close to. Soon the shells began to fall among the teams harnessed up ready to march. In two minutes there was not a horse living in the field, and many men were lying about killed and wounded. Captain Bradbury, Royal Artillery, and Lieutenants John Campbell, Mundy, and Giffard each tried to bring guns into action against the Germans, who had eight guns and were only 500 yards away. Captain Bradbury succeeded in getting his gun into action, and seeing there was no chance of the other guns being brought to bear he called their detachment over to lend a hand to his gun. Lieutenant Giffard was wounded in four places, getting across to the gun. The detachment then consisted of the three officers,

Sergeant-Major Dorell, a sergeant and a gunner and driver, every other on the field being killed or wounded. Unfortunately they could not get an ammunition wagon alongside the gun, so had to carry up each round separately. Captain Bradbury early in the fight had had one leg taken off by a shell, but insisted on still directing the fire of the gun. Lieutenant John Campbell behaved in the most gallant way, bringing up ammunition, and was killed just as he had brought up the last round from the wagon. Lieutenant Mundy had his leg partly taken off by a shell and has since died. He could not see how the fire was going, so he stepped out to have a better look, saying, ' They can't hit me,' and then he stayed observing till a shell wounded him. But still the fight went on. Sergeant-Major Dorell, aided by the sergeant and the gunner and driver, brought up ammunition from another wagon, and then poor Bradbury, who refused to give in, was struck by another shell. This gun did not cease fire till they had used every round of ammunition in the wagon, and alone it succeeded in knocking out four guns of the Germans. ' I ' Battery finally arrived, and with the help of a machine gun of the Bays silenced the other four German guns, the eight being captured. It is an open secret that Captain Bradbury was to have had the V.C. had he lived, and were posthumous V.C.'s given, both he and Lieutenant John Campbell would certainly get them. Lieutenant Mundy was recommended for the V.C., but died from his wounds. Lieutenant Giffard, the sole surviving officer, has been awarded the French Order of Merit.

"Sergeant-Major Dorell and the sergeant have both been recommended for the V.C., and the gunner and driver for the Distinguished Conduct Medal. " Though owing to the German fire the battery's guns are never likely to be of use again, they are at the base for a memorial to the gallant officers and men. No better trophy will ever be shown than these six bullet-riddled guns."

LIEUTENANT-COLONEL SIR EVELYN RIDLEY BRADFORD, BART., p.s.c., COMMANDING 2nd BATTN. SEAFORTH HIGHLANDERS (ROSS-SHIRE BUFFS, THE DUKE OF ALBANY'S), was the second son of the late Colonel Sir Edward R. C. Bradford, Bart., some time Commissioner of Police, and was born on the 16th April, 1869. Educated at Eton and the R.M.C., Sandhurst, he was gazetted to the Seaforth Highlanders in

August, 1888, becoming Lieutenant in June, 1890, and Captain in July, 1895. As an Officer qualified for Staff employment in consequence of service on the Staff in the Field, and as a Staff College Graduate, he had considerable Staff service at home and abroad, in peace and in war. He served with his battalion in the Nile Expedition of 1898, being present at the battles of Atbara and Khartoum. From May, 1899, to January, 1900, he was A.D.C. to the Governor and Commander-in-Chief, Malta. He also went through the South African War, partly with his battalion, and during 1901—1902 as a Staff Officer and as Deputy Assistant Adjutant-General, being present at operations in the Orange Free State from February to May, 1900, including actions at Poplar Grove and Driefontein ; at operations in the Orange River Colony from May to November, 1900, including action at Wittebergen, and again from the latter date to January, 1901 ; at operations in Cape Colony from February to March, 1901. For his services he was twice mentioned in Despatches ("London Gazette," 7th May and 10th September, 1901), was placed on the list of Officers qualified for Staff employment, and received his Brevet Majority June, 1902, the Queen's medal with four clasps and the King's medal with two clasps. After returning to England he held appointments as Brigade-Major at Aldershot, Commander of a Company of Gentlemen Cadets (General Staff Officer second grade), and a General Staff Officer at Head-quarters of the Army, War Office.

He obtained his substantive majority in March, 1905, and reached the rank of Lieutenant-Colonel in May, 1913, succeeding to the command of the 2nd Battalion of his regiment in June, 1913. He took his battalion to the front in August, 1914. For his services in the earlier part of the war he was mentioned in Sir John French's Despatch of 8th October, 1914. He was killed in action by a shell on the 14th September, 1914, at the battle of the Aisne. Lieutenant-Colonel Sir E. Bradford was a cricketer, and played for the county of Hampshire, and for the Army.

He married in 1909, Elsie Clifton, daughter of Colonel J. Clifton Brown, who survives him, and left three sons, Edward Montagu Andrew, born November, 1910—who succeeds to the title— Ridley Lewkenor, born April, 1912, and Donald Clifton, born May, 1914.

LIEUTENANT GEOFFREY MONTA-GUE BRADLEY, 6th BATTN. RIFLE BRIGADE (THE PRINCE CON-SORT'S OWN), born at Dover in February, 1893, was the third son of Edwin Bradley, J.P. for the County of Kent.

He was educated at Dover College and Jesus College, Cambridge, where he gained a classical

scholarship, and graduated B.A., second class, in the Classical Tripos : at Cambridge he was

Captain of the University Shooting VIII. in 1914, was a member of the first Rugby football team of his College, and was a keen Lacrosse player.

On the outbreak of the War he was given a commission in the 6th Battalion Rifle Brigade, and went to France in November, 1914, being attached to the 2nd Battalion Welsh Regiment. He was promoted Lieutenant in December, 1914, and was mentioned in Sir John French's Despatch of the 31st May, 1915, for his gallantry at Festubert on the 21st December, 1914, the date of his death, which occurred during a night attack.

CAPTAIN ARTHUR EDWIN BRAD-SHAW, M.A., 14th MURRAY'S JAT LANCERS, attd. 15th HUSSARS,

who was killed in action on the 13th October, 1914, leaving a widow (Florence Mary, sister of Sir William Price, of Quebec, Canada), was the youngest son of Surgeon Major-General Sir A. Frederick Bradshaw, K.C.B., K.H.P., and Lady Bradshaw, of Oxford.

He was born on the 20th March, 1882, and was educated at Marlborough College, 1896—99, and at the R.M.C., Sandhurst. On his mother's side he came of a family which had seen service at the Battle of Plassey and in almost every Indian campaign since then. His father served in India for thirty-five years from 1857, and in the Mutiny, Afghan, Zhob and Hazara campaigns. Captain Bradshaw entered the Army as Second Lieutenant in the Bedfordshire Regiment in May, 1901 ; in December, 1902, he joined the Indian Army, 14th Jat Lancers, becoming Lieutenant in August, 1903, and Captain in May, 1910. He was Adjutant of his regiment for several years and qualified as a second-class Interpreter in French. While on leave in England he entered Worcester College and obtained the degree of M.A. in June, 1914. In the following September he was sent to France and was killed during a reconnaissance in the village of Bout de Ville, Pas de Calais.

CAPTAIN FRANK SEYMOUR BRADSHAW, 1st BATTN. PRINCE ALBERT'S (SOMERSET LIGHT INFANTRY),

son of Major Frank Boyd Bradshaw, formerly of the Somerset Light Infantry, who died of fever in the Burmese War in July, 1886, and a great grandson of General Lawrence Bradshaw, who commanded the 13th Foot in Egypt in 1800, was born at Weston-super-Mare, Somerset, on the 4th December, 1883.

He was educated at Temple Grove, East Sheen, at Harrow, and the R.M.C., Sandhurst; he was good at all sports, hunting and shooting, and especially polo.

He joined the Somerset Light Infantry in January, 1904, and went to India, where he served till 1908, having been promoted Lieutenant in June, 1906; on returning to England he was stationed at Portland, and in 1911 went to the Depot at Taunton.

In 1914 he rejoined the 1st Battalion at Colchester and accompanied it to France in August; he was promoted Captain (temporarily) in November, 1914.

He took part in the action at Le Cateau during the retirement, in the subsequent advance to the Aisne and in the Battle of the Marne. He was slightly wounded on the 2nd November, 1914, but returned to duty on the 22nd of the month. On the 19th December his battalion attacked some Saxon trenches in front of Ploegsteert; Captain Bradshaw's company was in reserve, but seeing Lieutenant Parr killed at the head of his platoon, Captain Bradshaw at once left his trench and took command of Mr. Parr's men. He was shot almost immediately and died in a few minutes.

MAJOR FRANCIS JOSEPH BRAITHWAITE, 2nd BATTN. LOYAL NORTH LANCASHIRE REGIMENT,

who was killed in action in East Africa at the end of the year 1914, was the eldest son of the late F. J. Braithwaite, R.D., Rector of Great Waldingfield, Sudbury, Suffolk.

He was born on the 5th December, 1872, and joined the North Lancashire Regiment in January, 1893, becoming Lieutenant in February, 1895, and Captain in May, 1901. He served in the South African War, being employed with the Mounted Infantry, and for his services was mentioned in Despatches ("London Gazette," 10th September, 1901), and received the Queen's and King's medals, each with two clasps.

Major Braithwaite afterwards served on the Claims Commission Board of the Orange River Colony, and latterly was stationed in India.

Major Braithwaite, who was promoted to that rank in February, 1911, left a widow and four children.

CAPTAIN ERNEST STANLEY BRAND, ROYAL FUSILIERS (CITY OF LONDON REGIMENT),

who was killed in action while serving with the West African Regiment in the Cameroons, West Africa, was the son of W. B. Brand, Esq., late of The Grange, Finchley, and Boxwood, Herts. He was born on the 3rd December, 1878, at Stoke Newington,

and was educated at Arlington House, Brighton, and Charterhouse, joining the 3rd Battalion Royal Fusiliers from the Militia in January, 1897, becoming Lieutenant in January, 1900. He served in Malta, Gibraltar, and China for five years, and while at the latter obtained his Company in October, 1904, and passed in the Chinese language.

From July, 1906, to December, 1910, he served with the West African Regiment, to which he was transferred in September, 1912, and with which he did useful work until he was killed. He was ordered to the Cameroons on the outbreak of the war and was acting as Second-in-Command, West African Regiment, when he was shot in the neck and killed instantaneously in the attack on Yabassi on the 8th October, 1914.

Captain Brand was a member of the Junior Naval and Military and Sports Clubs, and his recreations were steeplechasing, shooting, hunting, and polo.

LIEUTENANT VERNON DUDLEY BRAMSDON BRANSBURY, 3rd (attd. 1st) BATTN. LINCOLNSHIRE REGIMENT,

born in 1883, at Southsea, Hants, was the son of Mr. and Mrs. Henry Bransbury, of Holme Chase, Putney, and a nephew of Sir Thomas Bramsdon, late M.P. for Portsmouth.

He was educated by private tutors, and

at Clifton College, and received a commission in the Royal Irish Rifles, being subsequently appointed to the 3rd Battalion (Special Reserve) Lincolnshire Regiment, in June, 1913.

He was killed at Neuve Chapelle on the 25th October, 1914 ; while trying to locate a machine gun which had been firing on his trench, he was struck by a bullet in the temple and killed instantaneously.

Lieutenant Bransbury married in February, 1908, Zoila Kathleen Mary, daughter of Dr. Ponsonby Widdup, late Medical Service British Guiana, and left two sons, Stuart Ponsonby Bramsdon, born May, 1910, and John Brian, born June, 1913.

CAPTAIN JOHN HENRY BRENNAN, 3rd BATTN. ROYAL WELSH FUSILIERS,

was born on the 14th May, 1869, only son of the late T. C. Brennan, of Montreal, Canada.

He was a Dublin man, and was educated at St. Columba's, matriculating thence at Dublin University, where he was a prominent member of the Cricket Team, and after leaving, played in matches with the Long Vacation Team.

In 1902 Captain Brennan joined the 4th (Vol.) Battalion Royal Welsh Fusiliers, becoming Captain in the 3rd Battalion in June, 1903, and seriously devoted himself to his military duties ; at the Hythe Musketry Course he obtained special distinction. In civil life he was a prominent member of the Irish Land Commission, a body from which many members have joined the colours for this war, on the outbreak of which Captain Brennan was attached to the 1st Battalion of his regiment, with which he proceeded to the front.

While gallantly leading his men across an open plain at Zonnebeke on the 19th October, 1914, he was shot through the head.

A sergeant in Captain Brennan's company, himself wounded on the same date, gave the following account of his Officer's death : " He fell gallantly cheering on his men, and had just said, ' Come on boys, we will show them the way to Tipperary,' when a shell burst and he was killed instantly."

Captain Brennan was a member of the Hibernian United Service, Yeomanry, and Kingstown Golf Clubs. He married Miss K. C. Murray, daughter of the late T. Murray, of Millmount, Co. Westmeath, and left three children, Gladys Evelyn H., age 16, S. Charlotte, age 14½, and T. Henry L'Estrange, age 11½.

LIEUT.-COLONEL CHARLES ARTHUR HUGH BRETT, D.S.O., COMMANDING 2nd BATTN. SUFFOLK REGIMENT,

was born at Muttra, India, on the 28th March, 1865, the eldest son of Lieutenant-Colonel Arthur Brett, A.P.D., formerly of the 2nd Dragoon Guards (Queen's Bays), and his wife Georgina, daughter of Hugh Hannay, Paymaster, Royal Navy.

Lieutenant-Colonel Brett came of an old Anglo-Irish family, having been a grandson of Mr. Curtis Brett, of Oadby Hall, Leicestershire, whose ancestors came from Ireland ; his mother was a member of an old Wigtownshire family, formerly the Hannays of Sorbie Castle (a baronetcy now in abeyance), many members of which were in the Royal Navy ; his maternal grandfather and great-uncle were in the wars against Napoleon.

After being educated privately, Lieutenant-Colonel Brett proceeded to the R.M.C., Sandhurst, from which he was gazetted to the Suffolk Regiment in 1885, in which he obtained his Company in 1894. From 1895–99 he was Adjutant of the 1st Battalion, and from 1900 was Adjutant of the 4th (Territorial) Battalion at Ely, Cambridge. He served with the Hazara Expedition of 1888, receiving the medal and clasp, and was again on active service in the South African War, taking part in the operations south of the Orange River in 1899–1900, including the action at Colesberg, where he was severely wounded, and taken prisoner by the Boers while unconscious, being afterwards sent to Pretoria. An officer, who was his subaltern on this occasion, said that, though shot through the lungs, he kept command of his company, and actually charged the Boer trenches in this state, till he fell exhausted from loss of blood, adding that " his comrades of that night will always remember him as one of old England's most gallant sons." Later he was present at operations in the Transvaal east of Pretoria, and in the Orange River Colony. He was mentioned in Despatches, awarded the D.S.O. for his gallantry at Colesberg, and received the Queen's medal with three clasps.

Lieutenant-Colonel Brett was fond of travel, and interested in astronomy, and while on leave in 1904, joined Sir W. Christie's party, going to Sfax, Tunisia, to observe the eclipse, and received the thanks of the Admiralty for his assistance to the Astronomer Royal. He also, at other times, visited Mesopotamia, and engaged in explorations in Muscat, Busra, Bagdad and Babylon ; his visits were the more interesting from the fact that he was a good water colour artist, a talent possibly inherited, for his uncle John Brett, A.R.A., was celebrated as a sea painter, and his aunt, Rosa Brett, A.R.A., was also a well-known artist in her time.

Very early in the Great War, Lieutenant-Colonel Brett took his battalion abroad as part of the Expeditionary Force. He was killed at Le Cateau, France, on the 26th August, 1914, after the retirement from Mons.

Lieutenant-Colonel Brett married in January, 1909, Enid Geraldine, daughter of the late Lieutenant-Colonel Harry Hamersley St. George, Senior Ordnance Officer, Scottish District ; he left one daughter, Ione Moncrieff St. George, born October, 1909.

Mrs. Brett received a great number of letters of sympathy and appreciation of her late husband from comrades of all ranks. Lieutenant-Colonel Brett seems to have been the possessor of a peculiar " magnetism" which attracted and endeared him to all who met him. A brother officer wrote : " I don't suppose there was a single Commanding Officer in the service more beloved by the officers and men ; his loss to the regiment is absolutely irreparable." In another letter a brother officer, who has himself since fallen on the field of honour, says :—" If ever there was a commanding officer that I would wish to have gone on service with, it was he whose loss we now mourn. The one consolation is that he fell as a soldier at the head of his regiment for which he did so much, and every man of which looked up to him, admired him and tried to follow his grand example in everything. His life was noble and straight and his death was the same. We of the regiment, or what is left of it, mourn his loss as the best of comrades."

A Private states :—" He was a hero to the last in the way he encouraged the men."

Lieutenant-Colonel Brett was in command of the Depot, Bury St. Edmunds, from 1909 till 1912. At a meeting of the Bury St. Edmunds Town Council, the Mayor referred to the death in action of Lieutenant-Colonel Brett, and said that he knew he was voicing the feelings of all the Council in suggesting that they should pass a vote of condolence with Mrs. Brett in the great loss she had sustained, coupled with an expression of their deep respect and admiration of that gallant soldier. The Council signified their agreement by standing.

Lieutenant-Colonel Brett's name was mentioned in Sir John French's first Despatch, 8th October, 1914.

LIEUTENANT-COLONEL ROBERT HENRY WATKIN BREWIS, 2nd BATTN. ROYAL WARWICKSHIRE REGIMENT,

was born at Howbery Park, Wallingford, on the 29th September, 1873, and was the eldest son of the late S. R. Brewis, of Ibstone, Bucks, and Mrs. Brewis, of 86, Cromwell Road, S.W. On the maternal side, Lieutenant-Colonel Brewis was a great-grandson of the Right Hon. Sir Henry Watkin Williams Wynne, Minister Plenipotentiary to the Court of Denmark, and of Hester, daughter of Robert, 1st Baron Carrington. He was educated at Harrow, and at Jesus College, Cambridge, subsequently joining the 4th Battalion Oxford Light Infantry (Militia) in March, 1892; from it he obtained his commission in the Royal Warwickshire Regiment in 1895, becoming Captain in 1900, and Major in December, 1912.

Lieutenant-Colonel Brewis served in the Nile Expedition of 1898, and was present at the battles of Atbara and Khartoum, receiving the Queen's medal with two clasps, and the Egyptian medal. From 1907—1910 he was Adjutant of his battalion, and in April of the latter year was appointed Adjutant and Quartermaster at the Staff College. On the 19th August, 1914, he was appointed to the Staff of the Expeditionary Force as Deputy Assistant Adjutant-General, and on the 14th October was promoted to Assistant Adjutant-General with the temporary rank of Lieutenant-Colonel. This appointment he resigned in order to rejoin his battalion, which he was commanding when he fell on 18th December, 1914, at Sailly, near Armentières, where he was buried.

Lieutenant-Colonel Brewis was not married.

LIEUTENANT NEVILLE LINTON BRIDGLAND, 3rd BATTN. EAST SURREY REGT.,

was born at Gravesend, Kent, on 9th August, 1894, and was the son of Mr. and Mrs. Loftus Frederick Linton Bridgland, of The Cedars, Gravesend. He was a great grandson of William Alchin, of Court Lodge Farm, Linton, Kent.

Lieutenant Bridgland was educated at King's School, Rochester, Kent, where he attained distinction as a cricketer, having been in the 1st XI. from 1909 to 1912 inclusive. In playing for his school against St. Lawrence's College, Ramsgate, in partnership with his brother, he scored 110 runs, not out, out of 201 for one wicket in an hour-and-a-half. He was also in the first Football XI. Playing for his regiment in June, 1914, at Shorncliffe, he made 300 runs for eight innings, an average of 37 odd.

He was gazetted to the Special Reserve of Officers as Second Lieutenant 3rd East Surrey Regiment in November, 1912, doing his six months' probationary training with the 1st Battalion in Dublin. He was confirmed in his rank in April, 1913, and promoted Lieutenant in March, 1914.

On the 11th September, 1914, he took a draft of the 1st Battalion to France, and was in several engagements; he was killed on the 22nd October, 1914, at Lorgies, near La Bassée, and was buried in the garden of a house in that village. The church and churchyard were under the fire of German guns, thus preventing his being buried in the churchyard.

Possessed of charming manners, he was liked and loved both by his friends in private life and also by his brother officers and men. His Colonel wrote of him very highly at the time of his death, and his soldier servant, writing at the same time, said "he was a brave officer and a gentleman, he led his men into action without any fear, and his heart was in the right place."

CAPTAIN GEORGE CLARK BRIGGS, 1st BATTN. ROYAL SCOTS FUSILIERS,

born at Trinity, Edinburgh, on 4th March, 1878, was the only son of Francis Briggs, of Huntington, Haddington, and a grandson of the late Dr. Munro of Moffat.

He was educated at Edinburgh Academy, Malvern College, and Clare College, Cambridge, and joined the Royal Scots Fusiliers in May, 1899, six months before the outbreak of the Boer War, through which he served; during the latter part of the war he was chosen for duty with the 2nd Mounted Infantry. He was present at the attempt to relieve Ladysmith, being taken prisoner at Colenso. After his release he escorted Boer prisoners to Ceylon. He received the Queen's medal with four clasps and the King's medal with two clasps. Serving with his battalion in the Great War, he was mentioned in Sir John French's Despatch of 8th October, 1914, for his services during the retirement from Mons, and was killed at the battle of the Aisne on 14th September, 1914. His company had to retire and he waited to see all his men away before he left the position; he was hit and fell, and was at first reported missing on 19th September, but subsequently, on the 6th October, as having been killed on the date mentioned.

2nd LIEUTENANT MAXIMILIAN FRANCIS BROADWOOD, 1st BATTN. THE QUEEN'S OWN (ROYAL WEST KENT REGT.),

was the son of Francis and Mary Sylvestre Charlotte (née Dalison) Broadwood, and was born at Hove, Sussex, on the 1st April, 1893. He was a grandson of the late Thomas Broadwood, of Holmbush, Sussex, and of the late M. H. Dalison, of Hamptons, Kent.

Second Lieutenant Broadwood was educated at " Evelyns " (G. T. Worsley, Esq.), 1902–06; Wellington College (T. A. Roger's House), 1906 –11; passing from there into the Royal Military College, Sandhurst, he obtained his commission in the Queen's Own (Royal West Kent Regiment) on the 12th September, 1912, and joined the 1st Battalion in Dublin the following month. He was killed in action at Wasmes, near Mons, on the 24th August, 1914.

Second Lieutenant Broadwood was a member of the Royal Aero Club.

LIEUTENANT LAWRENCE SEYMOUR BROCKELBANK, 3rd BATTN. (RESERVE) THE KING'S OWN (ROYAL LANCASTER REGIMENT),

who is believed to have been killed at the end of the year 1914, though his name has not appeared in the official Casualty Lists, was educated at King's College and entered the Theological Faculty in 1910. He left in 1914, and shortly afterwards received a commission as Second Lieutenant in the Special Reserve.

On the outbreak of the war he was appointed Second Lieutenant on probation to the 3rd Battalion Royal Lancashire Regiment and was promoted Lieutenant in February, 1915, there evidently having been some doubt of his death.

CAPTAIN EWEN JAMES BRODIE (of Lethen), 1st BATTN. THE QUEEN'S OWN CAMERON HIGHLANDERS,

born 17th July, 1878, was the son of the late J. C. J. Brodie, of Lethen, Lord Lieutenant of the County of Nairn.

Captain Brodie succeeded to Lethen on the death of his brother in 1908.

He was educated at Harrow and Cambridge, joining the

2nd Cameron Highlanders in May, 1900, from the Militia, becoming Lieutenant in February, 1902, and Captain in May, 1911. He served in the Mediterranean, Africa, and China. In 1909 he was appointed Adjutant to the Lovat Scouts, an appointment he held for four years when he rejoined his battalion and left with it for the front in August, 1914.

After having been through the Battle of the Aisne and all the subsequent fighting in Belgium he was killed at the Battle of Ypres on the 11th November, 1914, the day of the tremendous assault of the Prussian Guard on our thin line. He fell in the Nonne Bosch Wood, having succeeded in driving back the last survivors of the Guard with a handful of transport drivers, cooks, and other details. Captain Brodie had acted as Adjutant of his battalion since 25th September, 1914, and he and two other officers were at the time of his death the sole survivors of the thirty officers who left Edinburgh Castle in August.

Captain Brodie married in 1911 Miss Stirling, of Fairburn, and left two sons and a daughter.

LIEUTENANT GEORGE BROOKE, RESERVE OF OFFICERS, IRISH GUARDS, was serving with the 1st Battalion of that regiment when he met his death.

He was the eldest son of Sir George Brooke, Bart., and his first wife Anna, daughter of Geoffrey Shakerley, and niece of Sir Charles Shakerley, Bart.; he was also related to Viscount Monck, and Sir Basil Brooke, Bart. He was born on the 10th June, 1877, at Summerton, Co. Dublin, educated at Eton, and last resided at Ballyford, Coolgreaney, Co. Wexford. During the South African War he served with the Hampshire Regiment, and obtained the South African medal with three clasps. He was one of the first group of officers appointed to the Irish Guards when that regiment was raised in 1900.

He was wounded near the trenches at the Battle of the Aisne on the 7th October, 1914, when with the Irish Guards, and died of his wounds on the 9th October, 1914.

At one time he kept hounds in Wexford, and was much interested in the breaking-in of dogs for shooting. He was a member of the Kildare St. Club, Dublin, and the Guards' Club, London. He married, in 1907, Nina, daughter of the Right Hon. Lord Arthur Hill, P.C., and left a daughter, Nancy Myra, the only child who survived him.

CAPTAIN JAMES ANSON OTHO BROOKE, V.C., ASSISTANT ADJUTANT 2nd BATTN. THE GORDON HIGHLANDERS, was born at Fairley, Countesswells, Aberdeenshire, on the 3rd February, 1884, and was the son of Captain

Harry Vesey Brooke, J.P., D.L., of Fairley, and grandson of Sir Arthur Brooke, Bart., M.P. of Colebrooke, Co. Fermanagh, Ireland, and great grandson of General Sir George Anson, G.C.B. Captain Brooke, V.C., was educated at Winton House, Winchester; Wellington College, and the R.M.C., Sandhurst, where he was Senior Under Officer in 1905.

He was also Captain of the Shooting Eight, was in the Football team, won the Obstacle race, tied for the saddle, and on leaving was the cadet selected for the Sword of Honour.

He joined the 1st Battalion of his regiment at Cork in November, 1905, and was transferred to the 2nd Battalion in 1906, serving with it in India and Egypt till the outbreak of the Great War. He was one of the officers to receive the new colours of the regiment from H.M. the King at Delhi, and received the Durbar medal. He was killed on the 29th October, 1914, and was awarded the V.C. after his death "for conspicuous bravery and great ability near Gheluvelt on 29th October, in leading two attacks on the German trenches under heavy fire, regaining a lost trench at a very critical moment, and thus saving the situation."

In the "London Gazette" of the 13th March, 1915, he was promoted temporary Captain, such promotion to take effect from the 11th September, 1914.

Captain Brooke, V.C., was a good shot, rider, and golfer; he procured many head of big game in India and Arabia, including ibex, bison, and samboc.

MAJOR VICTOR REGINALD BROOKE, C.I.E., D.S.O., p.s.c., 9th LANCERS, a notification of whose death on the 29th August, 1914, was included in the monthly Casualty List published by the War Office in September, 1914, was born on the 22nd January, 1873, and was the fifth son of Sir Victor Alexander Brooke, 3rd Bart. He joined the 9th (Queen's Royal) Lancers in December, 1894, becoming Lieutenant in April, 1896, and Captain in May, 1901.

He served in the South African War, taking part in the advance on and relief of Kimberley, including actions at Belmont, Enslin, Modder River and Magersfontein; was present at operations in the Orange Free State and at Paardeberg, and actions at Poplar Grove and Karee Siding. From November, 1901, to September, 1902, he served as A.D.C. to the Chief of the Staff in South Africa; he was then at operations in the Transvaal. He was slightly wounded in the war, and for his services was twice mentioned in Despatches (" London Gazette," 16th April, 1901, and 29th July, 1902), was awarded the D.S.O. and received the Queen's medal with four clasps, and the King's medal with two clasps. From November, 1902, to December, 1905, he was A.D.C., and from 1905 to May, 1907, Assistant Military Secretary and Interpreter to the Commander-in-Chief, East Indies, and from June, 1907, to November, 1910, Military Secretary to the Viceroy of India. He received his Brevet Majority in June, 1905, and his substantive rank in February, 1907.

2nd LIEUTENANT JOHN GILBERT SOMERSET COZENS-BROOKE, 3rd (attd. 1st) BATTN. ROYAL SCOTS FUSILIERS, who was killed in action on the 18th October, 1914, aged 20 years, was the only son of Ernest and Isabel Cozens-Brooke, of 6, Collingham Road, London, S.W.

He joined the Royal Scots Fusiliers as 2nd Lieutenant in April, 1912, becoming Lieutenant in August, 1914.

CAPTAIN HENRY RICHARD BROOKES, 101st GRENADIERS, INDIAN ARMY,

was born at Port Blair, Andamans, on 10th January, 1886, and was the youngest son of Octavius Henry Brookes, of Chaucer Road, Bedford, and a grandson of the late Colonel William Brookes, Gordon Highlanders, formerly the 75th Stirlingshire Regiment

Captain Brookes was educated at Bedford and entered the Bedfordshire Regiment from the Militia in 1905, being transferred two years later to the Indian Army and becoming Lieutenant in 1908. His promotion to Captain, dating from 29th November, 1914, was not gazetted until March, 1915. He was a member of the Sports Club, Bangalore.

In the Great War Captain Brookes was serving in German East Africa when he met his death. After the unsuccessful attack upon Tanga on the 4th November, 1914, he was reported missing, and, as no definite news has been received since, his parents have been reluctantly bound to assume that he was killed on that day and buried by the Germans.

The landing and attack were carried out under great difficulties, after giving notice of the intention to bombard what was believed to be an open and undefended town. Owing to the dense bush it was almost impossible to use artillery, and when the advance began, our troops came under a heavy fire from rifles and machine guns.

The 101st Grenadiers, making a fine effort to fill a gap in the firing line due to the difficulty of advancing in line through the dense bush came under exceedingly heavy cross fire of rifles and machine guns, and were unable to advance, but tenaciously held their own. Darkness coming on brought the action to a conclusion, after which our troops withdrew unmolested to an entrenched position a quarter-of-a-mile in the rear. In view of the extreme difficulty of the country in the vicinity of Tanga it was judged inadvisable to attempt a second attack without adequate reinforcements. Orders for embarkation were accordingly issued, and this was carried out without any interference on the part of the enemy.

LIEUTENANT HUGH GODFREY BROOKSBANK, 2nd BATTN. ALEXANDRA PRINCESS OF WALES'S OWN (YORKSHIRE REGIMENT), known in the Service as the "Green Howards,"

was born on the 24th November, 1893, at Healaugh Old Hall, Tadcaster, and was the son of Edward Clitherow Brooksbank by his wife Katherine Graham, daughter of H. M. Lang, of Broadmeadows, Selkirkshire.

Lieutenant Brooksbank was educated at Radley, and joined the Yorkshire Regiment in February, 1913, becoming Lieutenant in October, 1914. While serving with his battalion in the Great War, he was severely wounded at the Battle of Ypres, on the 1st November, 1914, and died from the effects on the 16th December, at 26, Park Lane, London.

He was mentioned in Sir John French's Despatch of 14th January, 1915, for gallantry in the battle in which he was wounded. His relatives received the following tribute to his memory from a senior officer in the battalion :—" A braver lad never stepped the earth ; he was left in command of " B " Company when all his seniors had been shot. He commanded it like a veteran, and on two occasions he was largely responsible for the regiment being saved."

CAPTAIN ERNEST SCOTT BROUN, 2nd BATTN. ALEXANDRA PRINCESS OF WALES'S OWN (YORKSHIRE REGIMENT),

who was reported in December, 1914, as having been killed in action near Ypres, was the youngest son of the late James Broun, of Orchard, Carluke, Lanarkshire, and only son of Mrs. Broun, of St. Mary Abbot's Terrace, Kensington.

He was born on the 7th December, 1879, was educated privately, and joined the Yorkshire Regiment from the Militia in February, 1899, becoming Lieutenant in December, 1900. He served in the South African War, being present at the relief of Kimberley, at operations in the Orange Free State, and at Paardeberg ; actions at Poplar Grove, Driefontein, Vet and Zand Rivers ; in the Transvaal, including actions near Johannesburg, Pretoria, and Diamond Hill, also east of Pretoria, including action at Belfast ; and Cape Colony, including action at Colesberg; and further operations in the Transvaal in 1900 and 1902. He received the Queen's medal with six clasps, and the King's medal with two clasps. Having been promoted Captain in April, 1906, he was appointed A.D.C. to the Governor and Commander-in-Chief, Barbados, in July, 1911. He was fond of shooting, and was a member of the United Service and Sports Clubs.

Captain Broun was killed instantaneously by a bullet while looking over a parapet on the 30th October, 1914. He was mentioned in Sir John French's Despatch of the 31st May, 1915.

CAPTAIN FREDERICK GEORGE BROWN, 101st GRENADIERS, INDIAN ARMY,

who was killed on the 2nd November, 1914, was born on the 7th December, 1881, and joined the Royal Inniskilling Fusiliers from the 4th Battalion Royal Dublin Fusiliers in October, 1901.

He served in the South African War, being present at operations in the Transvaal, and in the Orange River and Cape Colonies, receiving the Queen's medal with four clasps, and the King's medal with two clasps. He was promoted Lieutenant in January, 1904, joining the Indian Army in June of the same year, and was promoted Captain in October, 1910.

LIEUTENANT HUBERT WILLIAM BROWN, 2nd BATTN. ROYAL IRISH REGIMENT,

who died in September, 1914, of wounds received when fighting in the Cameroons, was the son of the late John Mosse Brown, and was born at Greenville, Waterford, on the 11th January, 1890.

He was educated at Aravon, Bray, St. Faughnans College, Co. Cork, and Cheltenham College, where he was a prefect, and in the cricket XI. He joined the Royal Irish Regiment in November, 1909, becoming Lieutenant in September, 1911.

No details of Lieutenant Brown's death have been procurable.

2nd LIEUT. JAMES WILLIAM BROWN, XXVth BRIGADE ROYAL FIELD ARTILLERY,

was born on the 26th May, 1888, at Upper Dean, Bedfordshire.

He joined the 117th Battery, Royal Field Artillery, as a gunner in 1907. While in the ranks he obtained a First Class Certificate, 1909, and passed through the School of Gunnery at Shoeburyness in the same year. He left Aldershot with the 117th Battery 26th Brigade, on the 16th August, 1914, and while on service was given his commission on 1st October, 1914, being transferred to the 25th Brigade Ammunition Column. He was wounded on the 31st October and died from the effects on the 2nd November, in No. 5 Field Hospital.

The Major of his old battery, the 117th, wrote to his widow : " Before he left the battery he dined with us in our mess (an old barn) as a farewell. I cannot tell you what a help he was to the various Battery Commanders of the 117th Battery during his time in it, as he was such a capable chap at his work ; always willing to do anything for us, and we should all have been pleased indeed if he had been posted to the battery as an officer. I, of course, had known him the longest, and knew what it was to have such a good and capable man at one's elbow.

" The battery had seen a great deal of fighting before your husband left us, and I sent his name in to my Colonel for his good work all the time, especially at the long battle of the Aisne, where he mended a telephone wire for us at a particularly nasty time."

The Officer Commanding the Ammunition Column wrote : " As far as I know, the circumstances are these. The Sussex Regiment had had both their machine guns put out of action in a hot attack, and we were told to get another one through to them as soon as possible, as it might be the means of saving the situation. Your husband went up to try and get into communication with the Sussex Regiment, and I much regret that he was wounded, gallantly doing his duty."

CAPTAIN ANTHONY EDWARD JEMMETT-BROWNE, 2nd BATTN. ROYAL SUSSEX REGIMENT,

younger son of Lieut. Colonel and Mrs. Edward Jemmett-Browne, of 50, Elm Park Gardens, London, S.W., was born on the 26th January, 1882.

He was educated at Wellington, being the younger of two brothers who were in the Anglesey 1895-98. Thence he went to the R.M.C., Sandhurst, and in August, 1900, joined the 1st Battalion Royal Sussex Regiment, in which, when it was the 35th Royal Sussex, his father had served for many years.

He served in the South African War 1901-02, being present at operations in the Cape and Orange River Colonies and in the Transvaal, receiving the Queen's medal with two clasps. He became Lieutenant in July, 1903, and on obtaining his company in April, 1910, was transferred to the 2nd Battalion of his regiment. Captain Jemmett-Browne, who was a member of the United Service Club, was most active in promoting sports in his battalion, and the best men—two of whom were Army Champion runners—belonged to his company.

He was killed on the 10th September, 1914, the last day of the battle of the Marne, at Priez, leading the front platoon of the advance guard of the division into action, and was buried that evening at the spot where he fell.

2nd LIEUTENANT A. G. BROWNE, 2nd BATTN. SHERWOOD FORESTERS (NOTTINGHAMSHIRE AND DERBYSHIRE REGIMENT),

who was unofficially reported to have died of wounds received in action on the 20th October, 1914, was gazetted to his regiment on the 16th September, 1914.

CAPTAIN GORDON STEWART BROWNE, 1st BATTN. THE DUKE OF EDINBURGH'S (WILTSHIRE REGT.),

died on the 27th November, 1914, at the Allied Forces Base Hospital, Boulogne, from the effects of wounds received in action near Ypres on the 17th November, after being previously wounded on the fourth day of the retirement from Mons.

He was the fourth son of Mr. Henry J. Browne, of Grosvenor House, Faversham, and was born on the 15th May, 1890. He was educated at Haileybury College, and Sandhurst, from which he was gazetted to the Wiltshire Regiment in September, 1909, becoming Lieutenant in January, 1911. He was promoted Captain after his death, to date from October, 1914, and was Adjutant of his battalion, having been Assistant Adjutant since April, 1913. He was mentioned in Sir John French's Despatch of 14th January, 1915, for gallant and distinguished service in the field.

He served with his battalion for three and a half years in South Africa, was captain of the regimental rifle team which won the Methuen Cup, and was Assistant Commandant, and then Commandant of the School of Signalling at Roberts Heights, Pretoria, in 1912-13.

Captain Browne was a member of the Junior Army and Navy Club. He was a keen cricketer and golfer, was fond of hunting, and was a good game shot. He was not married.

The following is an extract from the letter of the Commanding Officer of the Gordon Highlanders to Captain Browne's father, which led to his mention in Despatches :—

" When the brigade, of which the Wiltshires and my own regiment formed part, was ordered to take over the trench lines near Ypres, I happened to be, temporarily, in command of it, and was lucky enough to obtain the services of your son as staff officer during the few days that I was in command. Not only did your son do yeoman service during those few days when he was acting as staff officer for me, but throughout the very trying period which followed, it was easy to see what sterling stuff he was made of. . . . Your son's gallant behaviour will live long in the memory of others beside those of his own particular brother officers, and I considered it my duty to bring to the official notice of our Brigadier the very splendid way in which he had performed his duties during those strenuous days near Ypres."

LIEUTENANT MONTAGUE WILLIAM SETON-BROWNE, 2nd BATTN. LEICESTERSHIRE REGIMENT,

who was born at Grenada, British West Indies, on the 17th February, 1893, was the son of G. S. Seton-Browne, Esq., Member of the Executive and Legislative Councils, J.P., Grenada; he was related to Major Seton-Browne, D.S.O., Indian Army.

He was educated at a private school at Crondall, Surrey, and at Berkhampstead School, Herts, being gazetted to the Leicestershire Regiment as Second Lieutenant in September, 1913, and joining it in India two months later. With it he went to France for the Great War, and was killed while leading an attack on German trenches at Richebourg l'Avoué, on the 24th November, 1914. The attack was successful, and Second Lieutenant Seton-Browne's name was mentioned for his gallantry in Sir John French's Despatch of the 14th January, 1915. He was gazetted Lieutenant on the 1st November, 1914. The following account of his death was received from a brother officer :—" I joined our 2nd Battalion on getting home and have the same Company " B " that your son was in and Captain Grant. My Company Sergeant-Major was with your son when he was killed in action. They had got into a German trench at night and your son was getting on to a traverse with Germans on the other side. He was wounded and called out to the men and lay still; before they could get him back he was hit again and killed. They got him back amongst them into the trench. . . . He was very well thought of by all ranks, and the men would have followed him anywhere."

Lieutenant Seton-Browne was a member of the Junior United Service Club.

CAPTAIN REGINALD JOHN BROWNFIELD, 2nd BATTN. ROYAL WARWICKSHIRE REGIMENT,

the son of Douglas Harold Brownfield, was born at Hem-Heath, Trentham, Staffordshire, in April, 1886. Captain Brownfield was a cousin of Major Ed. Etches, many years at the School of Musketry, Hythe, and one of the best shots in the Army.

Captain Brownfield joined the Royal Warwicks in August, 1905, being promoted Lieutenant in January, 1909. With his regiment he served at different places in England, and in Peshawar. In 1913 he retired from the regular Army and joined the 4th Battalion, the old 2nd Warwick Militia. On the outbreak of the war he rejoined the 2nd Battalion of his regiment, and was serving with it when he was killed on the 18th December, 1914.

An Officer of the 1st Battalion sent the following account of his death :—" They had to attack the German trenches, and he, followed by three subalterns and 30 men, went for a machine gun —a plucky thing to do—and every one of them were killed within five yards of the German trenches. The three subalterns were killed, and I believe they all lay in a heap. They tell me that it was a very fine effort to take the maxim, and would have greatly helped the rest of the attack; but unfortunately they were just killed before they got there. They all thought the world of him." He was a splendid athlete.

The action was also described as follows :—
" On December 18th the Warwicks attacked the main German trenches at Rouge Bancs, near Armentières. They were double trenches, and were held in unexpected strength. It was a desperate and bloody business, for there were wire entanglements and the enemy had guns in the trenches. . . . In that action 13 out of 17 officers were killed, and more than half the rank and file of the regiment."

CAPTAIN CHARLES HUNTER BROWNING, 124th BATTERY, XXVIIIth BRIGADE, ROYAL FIELD ARTILLERY,

son of Captain Hugh Edmond Browning, late of the 2nd Dragoons (Royal Scots Greys) of Clapham Park, Bedfordshire, was born at The Woodlands, Clapham, Bedford, on the 9th April, 1878.

He was educated at Eton, where he was captain of the School in 1897, and in the Eton XI (kept wicket) in 1896 and 1897. Proceeding to the Royal Military Academy, Woolwich, he obtained his commission in the Royal Field Artillery in June, 1898, becoming Lieutenant in February, 1901, and Captain in March, 1908. He served in the South African War, taking part in operations in the Orange Free State, including engagements at Poplar Grove and Driefontein, from February to May, 1900, subsequently receiving the Queen's medal with two clasps.

Captain Browning was killed on the 26th August at Le Cateau, while his battery was under very heavy fire.

He was the prospective Liberal candidate for Windsor at the next election.

MAJOR JAMES ALEXANDER BROWNING, 2nd DRAGOON GUARDS (QUEEN'S BAYS),

who was killed in action on the 31st October, 1914, was born on the 25th June, 1878, and joined the 2nd Dragoon Guards in May, 1898, becoming Lieutenant on the 16th August, 1899. From March, 1900, to November, 1901, he was A.D.C. to the Inspector General of Cavalry in Great Britain and Ireland.

He served in the South African War, 1901–02, being present at operations in the Transvaal, Orange River and Cape Colonies, and received the Queen's medal with five clasps. He was promoted Captain in September, 1901. From July, 1906 to July, 1909, he was Adjutant of his regiment, and obtained his Majority in July, 1911.

CAPTAIN THE HON. HENRY LYND-HURST BRUCE, 3rd (attd. 2nd) BATTN. ROYAL SCOTS (LOTHIAN REGIMENT),

was the eldest son of Henry Campbell, 2nd Baron Aberdare of Duffryn, Mountain Ash, Glamorgan, and was born on the 25th May, 1881, at 42, Lowndes Street, London, S.W. Through his mother he was related to the late Lord Lyndhurst, and the great painter, J. S. Copley.

He was educated at Winchester, and New College, Oxford, and was gazetted Lieutenant in the 3rd (Militia) Battalion the Hampshire Regiment in 1903, and in May, 1906, became Captain in the 3rd (Special Reserve) Battalion Royal Scots.

Captain Bruce was very fond of polo, shooting, and motor racing, and was a member of the Royal Automobile Club, Pall Mall. He married in October, 1906, Camilla, daughter of the late Reynold Clifford; their daughter,

Margaret, born in August, 1909, died two days after her birth.

In the middle of December, 1914, the Royal Scots had been for several weeks in the neighbourhood of Ypres, holding back the enemy; all through that time Captain Bruce and his men had been under almost continuous fire, and had taken part in many brilliant bayonet charges. During the greater part of that time Captain Bruce was acting as Second in Command of the battalion.

On the 14th December came the order for the offensive movement that proved successful, and of which Captain Bruce partly planned the attack. He led his men most gallantly against the enemy over the intervening ground, which had become a swamp, ankle deep in mud, in face of a terrible fire. They captured the trench they were attacking, taking 59 prisoners and several guns. Captain Bruce was shot in the forehead by a German concealed in a dug-out while he was climbing out of the captured trench to lead his men on to the next line of trenches. He was buried where he fell. The battalion received the congratulations of Sir John French and Sir H. Smith-Dorrien, and the charge was described as magnificent. General Haldane also wrote saying how much Captain Bruce's services had been appreciated, and what skill and bravery he had displayed.

He was greatly beloved by his men, and his death was a real sorrow to them and to his brother officers. He had written most interesting letters home, always cheerful and never complaining. In one letter he said, "It is the finest life I have ever lived."

Captain Bruce was mentioned in Sir John French's Despatch of the 14th January, 1915. His daring conduct on the night of the 24th October had attracted the attention of the Officer in Command of the battalion, and there is little doubt but that had he lived he would have received some recognition of it, as well as of his gallantry on the 14th December, in addition to being mentioned in Despatches.

MAJOR JONATHAN MAXWELL BRUCE, 107th PIONEERS, INDIAN ARMY,

born at Dharmsala, Punjab, India, on the 22nd June, 1873, was the eldest son of Richard J. Bruce, C.I.E., of Quetta, Teddington, a direct descendant of the Bruces of Miltown Castle, County Cork, Ireland (whose genealogy is given in Burke's Landed Gentry).

Major Bruce was educated at Haileybury and the R.M.C., Sandhurst, receiving his first commission in January, 1895, becoming Lieutenant in the following year, and Captain in 1904, having joined the Indian Army in 1896. In 1908 he was appointed Double Company Commander in the 107th Pioneers. He saw active service on the North-West Frontier of India in 1897–98, and was present at the relief of Malakand, receiving the medal and two clasps.

Having obtained his Majority in 1913, he was serving with his regiment when he was killed on the 24th November, 1914, in the desperate fighting which took place on that day between Ypres and Bethune ; he was buried at Bethune. Major Bruce, who was a very keen sportsman, good at polo and other games, was a member of the East India United Service Club, St. James's Square, S.W.

He married in September, 1905, Mabel Walrond, youngest daughter of Henry Trengrouse, Esq., J.P., of Chesfield, Teddington, and left two girls : Mary Aileen, born May, 1908, and Barbara Maxwell, born March, 1910.

CAPTAIN the Honble. ROBERT BRUCE, MASTER OF BURLEIGH, PRINCESS LOUISE'S (ARGYLL AND SUTHERLAND HIGHLANDERS),

who was killed at Le Cateau on the 26th August, 1914, was the elder son of Lord Balfour of Burleigh. He was born on the 25th September, 1880, in Edinburgh, and was educated at Horris Hill (Mr. A. H. Evans) and at Eton. Captain Bruce joined the 3rd Battalion of the Argyll and Sutherland Highlanders in 1898, and accompanied the 4th Battalion to South Africa in January, 1900 ; in April of the latter year he was transferred to the 1st (Regular) Battalion, and with it served through the South African War. He was present at operations in the Orange Free State, in the Transvaal, in Orange River Colony, and Cape Colony ; he received the Queen's medal with three clasps, and the King's medal with two clasps. Subsequently Captain Bruce joined the 2nd Battalion and served with it in India and South Africa. In March, 1910, he was attached to the Egyptian Army, with the rank of Bimbashi, and in September of that year became Captain in the British Army. In 1912 he took part in an expedition against certain tribes between the sources of the White and the Blue Nile, receiving

a medal for his services. In the following year he was Intelligence Officer to the force which accompanied the Joint Commission sent to delimit the boundary between the Soudan and Uganda, receiving for his services the 4th Class Order of the Medjidie.

Captain Bruce proceeded on active service at the very commencement of the Great War, and was one of the officers killed soon after the British Force entered the field. Only a short time before the outbreak of the war, the engagement had been announced of the Master of Burleigh to Miss Cicely Blair, only daughter of Colonel and Mrs. Blair of Dalry, Ayrshire.

In Clackmannan Church on the 8th November, the Rev. A. Irvine Robertson, D.D., in the course of his address, made sympathetic reference to the loss that parish and the country had suffered through the untimely death of this young officer, representative of a family of whom it can be said " that no name for the last six centuries has stood higher in the esteem of Scotland than the name of Bruce."

In a report received a few days after the arrival of the Argyll and Sutherland Highlanders at the front, reference was made to the Master of Burleigh :—" There the same spirit of brotherly helpfulness that had always marked our friend once more manifested itself. He would not be content with supervision ; he would share the labours of the lads he commanded ; and so doing, with rifle and bayonet in hand, leading on his men against overwhelming odds, Robert Bruce met a hero's fate."

LIEUTENANT WILLIAM ARTHUR McCRAE BRUCE, 59th SCINDE RIFLES, FRONTIER FORCE, INDIAN ARMY,

only son of Colonel Andrew McCrae Bruce, C.B., Indian Army, and Mrs. McCrae Bruce, of Roche d'Or Samares, Jersey, was born in Edinburgh on the 15th June, 1890.

He was educated at Cliff House School, Southbourne, Hampshire, and Victoria

College, St. Helier, Jersey, from which he proceeded to the R.M.C., Sandhurst, where he was a King's Indian Cadet, and a Corporal. Passing out of Sandhurst, he received his commission as Second Lieutenant in January, 1910, and, leaving for India the following month, was attached for a year to the 1st Battalion Northumberland Fusiliers ; in March, 1911, he joined the 59th Scinde Rifles F.F., and became Lieutenant in April, 1912. He was good at golf and cricket, and a keen hockey player.

When the war broke out Lieutenant Bruce was at home on leave, and, being ordered to rejoin his regiment in India, sailed from England on the 11th August. On reaching Egypt he received orders to proceed to Cairo and await the arrival of his regiment there; in September he landed with it in France, being the first part of the Indian Expeditionary Force to arrive.

He was killed in a German trench to the east of Givenchy, near La Bassée, on the 19th December, 1914; he was in command of a bombing party of his regiment in a night attack on a German trench, was wounded on the way up to the trench but continued to lead his men, and was the first man to get into the trench; shortly afterwards he was shot through the chest, being killed instantaneously

CAPTAIN CLAUDE GRAY BUCHANAN, p.s.c., 35th SIKHS, attd. 8th GURKHA RIFLES,

who was killed on the 4th November, 1914, having previously been reported missing, was the eldest son of Lieutenant-Colonel M. R. Gray Buchanan, Ettrickdale, Isle of Bute.

He was born on the 11th February, 1878, and was educated at Harrow (Small Houses and The Park) from 1892–96, afterwards going to the R.M.C., Sandhurst. He passed first out of the latter and was gazetted to an unattached Second Lieutenancy in July, 1898, and served his probationary period with the Hampshire Regiment at Lundi Khotal (Khyber Pass) and on the North-West Frontier of India, joining the Indian Staff Corps in 1899. He served in the Waziristan Campaign, North-West Frontier, of 1901–02, receiving the medal with clasp.

He was promoted Captain in July, 1907, and passed out of the Staff College, Quetta, in December, 1913. In August, 1914, he was appointed to the Headquarters Staff of the Royal Flying Corps, Expeditionary Force, and in November was attached to the 8th Gurkha Rifles.

Captain Buchanan married in July, 1914, Jane Cecilia Hope, only daughter of Mr. Robert Elmsall Findlay, of Boturich, Dumbartonshire. Many of the above details were printed in the " Harrovian War Supplement " for November, 1914.

MAJOR AUBREY WEBSTER BUCKINGHAM, 3rd (attd. 1st) BATTN. GORDON HIGHLANDERS,

of Harrietsham Manor, Kent, who was killed in action on the 17th November, 1914, near Ypres, was the son of the late J. H. Buckingham, of Lancaster Gate, and was born in 1870.

He was educated at Elstree and Harrow (Rendalls 1884—1887), and served in the South African War, being present at operations in Natal in 1899. He was in command of Volunteer details, and afterwards Garrison Adjutant at Green Point Camp, near Capetown. For his services he received the Queen's medal with three clasps, and the King's medal with two clasps. He also had the Coronation medal, 1911.

Major Buckingham was a member of the Junior Athenæum Club, and of the M.C.C. He was promoted honorary Captain in the Army in May, 1901, and honorary Major in January, 1902. He married Mabel Felizarda, daughter of the late Colonel Walter Rudge, R.A., Stede Court, Harrietsham, Kent.

CAPTAIN HENRY BUCKLE, ROYAL FIELD ARTILLERY,

who died in a German Hospital on the 4th October, 1914, from blood poisoning following a wound received at Cambrai on the 26th August, was the elder son of Mr. Henry Buckle, British Burma Commission, retired.

He was born on the 24th August, 1880, and educated at Clifton College and the R.M.A., Woolwich. He was gazetted to the Royal Artillery in June, 1899, becoming Lieutenant in 1901. He took part in the South African War and was present at operations in the Orange Free State in 1900; in the Transvaal, including actions near Johannesburg and Diamond Hill; in the Orange River Colony May to November, 1900, including action at Wittebergen; in Cape Colony, South of Orange River. He was also present at later operations 1900–02, in Orange River and Cape Colonies. For his services he received the Queen's medal with four clasps, and the King's medal with two clasps. Captain Buckle was promoted to that rank in April, 1906.

MAJOR MATTHEW PERCEVAL BUCKLE, D.S.O., p.s.c., 1st BATTN. THE QUEEN'S OWN (ROYAL WEST KENT REGT.),

was the second son of Admiral and Mrs. Buckle, The Red House, Raithby, Spilsbury, Lincolnshire, and was born on the 29th September, 1869, at Wray Cottage, Ambleside. He was educated at Summerfield, Oxford, and was gazetted to the Royal West Kent Regiment in April, 1889, becoming Lieutenant in December, 1892. From June, 1897, to August, 1901, he was Adjutant of his battalion, having been promoted Captain in July, 1898. He took part in the South African War, while Adjutant, and was present at operations in the Orange Free State in 1900, being severely wounded; at operations later in the year in the Orange River Colony, including the action at Wittebergen; operations in Cape Colony and the Transvaal; later operations in the Orange River Colony, and on the Zululand frontier of Natal in 1901. He was mentioned in Despatches ("London Gazette," 10th September, 1901), was awarded the D.S.O., and received the Queen's medal with four clasps and the King's medal with two clasps.

In 1903 he passed out of the Staff College with distinction, and from January, 1904, to January, 1906, he was Staff Captain (Mobilisation) at Headquarters, War Office, and from January, 1906, to January, 1908, Brigade-Major at Aldershot. Major Buckle, being a Staff College Graduate and a qualified Second Class Interpreter in French, was appointed in March, 1909, Professor at the Staff College, India, later General Staff Officer, Second Grade, Staff College, Quetta, with the temporary rank of Lieutenant-Colonel from July, 1909. He obtained his Majority in the Army in March, 1907. On the outbreak of hostilities Major Buckle was about to start for Albania to take up a Staff appointment at Scutari for which he had been specially selected, but his orders were cancelled and he rejoined his regiment as second in command, at Richmond Barracks, Dublin, from which place he sailed on the 13th August, 1914, en route for France. He was present at the retirement from Mons and in the battles of the Marne and the Aisne. He was twice mentioned in Despatches, viz., that of the 8th October, 1914, and 14th January, 1915.

He was killed in action near Neuve Chapelle on the 27th October, 1914, while in command of his battalion. The Royal West Kents held their position at this time for eight days without losing a trench. The following memoir from the pen of Brigadier-General Grove was published in "'The Queen's Own' Gazette":—
" The regiment has sustained a grievous loss in the death of Major Buckle. He was quite the finest type of officer that can be met. Thoroughly knowing his duty and very strict in the performance of it, he was at the same time always gentle and courteous. He was most conscientious, and never spared himself as long as there was work to do. It may well be said of him that he was " sans peur et sans reproche." Major Buckle married in 1909, Marjorie Ethel Grace, elder daughter of Col. C. A. Swan, C.M.G., and left two children, Margaret Elizabeth, born January, 1910, and Peter Claude Matthew, born May, 1914.

He was a member of the Army and Navy Club, and a Freemason, belonging to the following Lodges : Old Wykehamists (London), Shakespeare (Spilsby), and the Baluchistan (Quetta, India).

His recreations were cricket, shooting, polo and racquets.

CAPTAIN THOMAS HENRY RIVERS BULKELEY, C.M.G., M.V.O., SCOTS GUARDS,

born on the 23rd June, 1876, was the son of Colonel C. Rivers Bulkeley, C.B., and was killed in action on the 22nd October, 1914.

He was educated at Eton, and joined the Oxfordshire Militia in 1894, becoming Captain in 1897. In January, 1899, he was transferred to the Scots Guards as Second Lieutenant, becoming Lieutenant in April, 1900 ; from July, 1901–04 he was Adjutant of his battalion, becoming Captain in July of the latter year. He served in the South African War, taking part in the advance on Kimberley, including the action at Belmont, where he was wounded ; operations in the Orange Free State, and at Paardeberg ; actions at Poplar Grove, Driefontein, Vet River and Zand River ; operations in the Transvaal, including actions near Johannesburg, Pretoria and Diamond Hill; operations in the Transvaal, including action at Belfast. For these services he was three times mentioned in Despatches, and received the Queen's medal with six clasps, and the King's medal with two clasps.

From 1904–05 Captain Rivers Bulkeley was A.D.C. and Comptroller of the Household to

Lord Curzon, Viceroy of India ; from 1906–07 he held the same posts under Lord Minto. In the latter year he was appointed A.D.C. to Field Marshal H.R.H. the Duke of Connaught, Inspector General of the Forces, and High Commissioner in the Mediterranean, and more lately Governor General and Commander-in-Chief in Canada. In October, 1909, Captain Bulkeley was appointed Equerry to H.R.H. the Duke of Connaught and was Comptroller of his Household in Canada.

On the outbreak of the Great War, Captain Rivers Bulkeley resigned his appointment on the Staff of His Royal Highness, and rejoined his regiment, being in command of the left flank Company of the 2nd Battalion Scots Guards, forming part of the VIIth Division. He was killed while leading his Company to fill a gap in the fighting line.

Captain Rivers Bulkeley was a member of the Guards', Carlton, Junior Carlton, and Shrewsbury County Clubs. He married in 1913, Evelyn, daughter of Lady Lilian Yorke, Lady-in-Waiting to H.R.H. the Duchess of Connaught, and the late Sir Henry Pelly, 3rd Baronet, and leaves a son, born in January, 1914.

2nd LIEUTENANT ERIC LAURENCE ARTHUR HART BURGES, 3rd (attd. 2nd) BATTN. THE DUKE OF EDINBURGH'S (WILTSHIRE REGT.),

was the younger son of the late Rev. J. Hart Burges, D.D., Rector of Devizes, and of Mrs. Burges, 81, Humber Road, Blackheath, and grandson of the Rev. W. C. Burges, M.A., first cousin and Domestic Chaplain to the Earl of Rosse. He was born at Devizes and educated at St. Edmund's School, Canterbury, and at St. John's College, Oxford, where he graduated B.A. in 1913, with Third Class Honours in Modern History. In August, 1914, he had just completed his studies at the University, taking with distinction the Diploma in Economics and Political Science, and the Certificate in Social Training. He was also a keen member of the Oxford University Officers' Training Corps, holding the rank of Corporal and having qualified for Certificate " B." When war was declared he at once applied for a commission, and was gazetted to the 3rd Wilts. Later he was transferred to the 2nd Battalion, and sailed for Belgium on the 4th October. His battalion was attached to the " Immortal " VIIth Division, and took part in its magnificent

stand near Ypres against overwhelming numbers. He was killed by shell fire near the village of Reutel on the morning of the 23rd October, 1914—his 23rd birthday—the day before the 1st Army Corps came to their relief.

CAPTAIN THOMAS CAMPBELL BURKE, 1/1st KING GEORGE'S OWN GURKHA RIFLES (THE MALAUN REGIMENT),

in which he was a Double Company Commander, was the son of Joseph Francis Burke and Kate Marlow Burke, and was born on the 27th May, 1877, at Stratford-on-Avon. He was educated at Trinity College, Stratford-on-Avon, and at the R.M.C., Sandhurst. After passing out of Sandhurst he was, in August, 1897, attached to the Royal Irish Rifles for a year, receiving his commission in the Indian Staff Corps in October, 1898, when he was gazetted to the 125th Napier's Rifles. In 1900 he served in the Boxer Rebellion in China with the 122nd Rajputana Infantry, receiving the medal. On returning from Hong Kong he was appointed Adjutant of his regiment, the 125th Napier's Rifles, a position he held for three years, earning a reputation as a hard worker and a conscientious and reliable officer. From 1904—1907—being promoted Captain in August, 1906—he was Assistant Inspecting Officer with the Imperial Service troops (Rajputana Infantry), his itinerary of inspection including the native States of Gwalior, Alwar and Bhurtpore, and for some time the Bikaneer Camel Corps. For most of this time, owing to the absence through illness of his senior officer, Captain Burke had to assume full control and responsibilities. He was an excellent Hindustani scholar, and, while being a strict disciplinarian, earned the esteem and regard of the native officers and men by his wisdom, patience, and tactful handling of many a difficult situation.

From April, 1909, to March, 1913, he was Adjutant of the Bangalore Volunteer Rifles, during which time he started the first corps of Boy Scouts in India. He then returned to his own regiment as Double Company Commander, rejoining at Dharmsala.

Captain Burke was a good all-round sportsman ; he was a member of the Junior Naval and Military Club.

On the outbreak of the War, the 1st Gurkhas were ordered to the front, but were detained in Egypt for ten weeks to guard the Suez Canal, arriving eventually in France in

November, 1914, as part of the Sirkind Brigade. On the 18th December, 1914, the Gurkhas were in action at Festubert; on the 19th Captain Burke, with 70 men, was ordered to effect a lodgment in the German fire trench, and, in attempting to carry out the order, was killed within twenty yards of the British trenches. The official report on the incident was as follows :—

" The attack failed, both officers—Captain Burke and Lieutenant Rundall—being killed and more than 50 per cent. other ranks being hit. It should, however, be recorded that all ranks showed the greatest gallantry in resolutely attempting such an operation in daylight."

The Brigade-Major, referring to the occurrence, wrote :—

" As regards Burke I think everyone was absolutely unanimous in rating what he did as one of the most gallant deeds imaginable, and he and Rundall and the men who followed, cannot be thought of except as ranking with the bravest."

The Officer Commanding 1/1st Gurkhas wrote of him :—" The action was most gallant and well worthy of the Victoria Cross."

A Captain of his regiment wrote :—" His loss is greatly felt by us. His sound commonsense, keenness and professional ability were recognised by all of us and I am very sorry we shall see him no more."

And an Officer who was his subaltern, wrote :— " I cannot say how much we liked him and feel his loss. Having worked with him all his time here I found him one of the soundest and best officers I know, and his loss to the regiment is great. His death was a fine example of sacrifice to duty and obedience to orders which he knew could not be carried out."

Captain Burke married in 1906, Ada Mary, daughter of the Rev. Thomas Wall Langshaw, of West Grinstead Rectory, Sussex.

CAPTAIN ARTHUR GEORGE McCAUSLAND BURN, 2nd BATTN. EAST SURREY REGT., attd. 1st GLOUCESTERSHIRE

REGIMENT, born at Dorunda, Chota Nagpore, India, on the 22nd December, 1882, was the only son of Lieutenant - Colonel A. G. Burn, Indian Army, of Mansel Lacy, Hereford. He was descended from a long line of soldiers on both sides : on his father's side he was the fifth soldier in direct succession, his great-great-grandfather having

been Lieutenant-Colonel (afterwards General) William Burn, who in 1804 successfully held Delhi against Holkar.

Captain Burn was educated at Wellington (Mr. Hardinge) from 1897–1900, whence he passed direct into the R.M.C., Sandhurst, at the age of 18. In the first Army examination he did well, taking the 17th place in the Honours list, with the prize for Military Engineering. He was gazetted in January, 1902, to the East Surrey Regiment, joining the 1st Battalion in India shortly afterwards. He was promoted Lieutenant in January, 1904, and Captain in March, 1910.

Captain Burn, who was a member of the Junior Army and Navy Club, was a great shot and a keen sportsman. He did a good deal of big game shooting in India and Burmah, his trophies including elephant, tiger, bison, &c. When war broke out he was at home on leave from India, and being ordered to join the 1st Battalion Gloucestershire Regiment immediately, proceeded with it as part of the Expeditionary Force to France, and took part in the retirement from Mons. A brother officer writing of this time said that Captain Burn was not very well at the beginning of the war, but stuck to it pluckily during the retirement, and was of the greatest help to his Company Commander. He afterwards went through the battles of the Marne and the Aisne, and was killed on the 29th October, 1914, in the first battle of Ypres. At 5.30 a.m. on that morning the enemy began to attack, and the Gloucesters were ordered to advance, the fighting taking place on the Gheluvelt-Menin road, about half a mile from the former village. Captain Burn was shot and killed instantly while leading his men against the enemy, who were only 50 yards from them at that point. An officer to whom he had just before given a message wrote: " He was very cool, and sent to the Major to let him know that there were Germans working round our flank," and continued, " he always showed to advantage under fire, apparently quite indifferent to bullets and shells, and had a wonderfully steadying effect on the men."

His Colonel wrote :—" We all had a very high opinion of Captain Burn's worth as a leader and we all deplored his great loss ; we, indeed, felt we had lost one of us, although he belonged to another regiment and was at first a stranger."

2nd LIEUTENANT ARTHUR HERBERT ROSDEW BURN, 1st (ROYAL DRAGOONS), who was killed in action on the 30th October, 1914, at the age of 22, was the eldest son of Colonel Charles R. Burn, A.D.C. to the King, M.P., and the Hon. Mrs. Burn, of 77, Cadogan Square, S.W., and Stoodley Knowle, Torquay.

He was a grandson of Lord Leith of Fyvie. 2nd Lieutenant Burn was educated at Ludgrove,

Eton, and Christ Church, Oxford, and was a member of Bullingdon and the Bachelors' Clubs.

He obtained his commission as a University candidate on the 16th August, 1914. Colonel Burn is himself serving in the war as a General Staff Officer.

LIEUTENANT HENRY GARDINER BURRIDGE, 107th PIONEERS, INDIAN ARMY,

who was shot through the head near La Bassée on the 16th November, 1914, while examining the damage done by German shells, was the son of the late Lieutenant-Colonel F. J. Burridge, R.A., and was born on the 20th January, 1890, at Bareilly, North-West Provinces, India. He was a grandson of the late William Burridge, Bradford Court, Taunton, Somerset.

Lieutenant Burridge was educated at Winton House, Winchester, and Wellington College, where he was a prefect, was in the first fifteen and first eleven, was a gentleman of the Hunt, and where he won the Challenge Cup in 1906; he also broke the College record in 1908 by winning the half-mile race in two minutes one second. In 1909 he joined the Infantry Company at the R.M.A., Woolwich, and there he won the mile race, was second in the two mile, and third in the half-mile, in the sports between the R.M.A. and the R.M.C.

On joining the Army he was attached to the North Staffordshire Regiment for his year's training, being then posted to the 15th Ludhlana Sikhs, and, two years later, to the 107th Pioneers, in which he ranked as Lieutenant from December, 1911. He was known to all his friends as " Lal."

LIEUTENANT ANDREW BURT, 8th BATTN. THE ROYAL SCOTS, (LOTHIAN REGIMENT),

who was killed in action near Armentières between the 18th and the 20th October, 1914, became Lieutenant in his regiment in May, 1913, and had qualified for the rank of Captain.

CAPTAIN CHARLES PAGET O'BRIEN-BUTLER, ROYAL ARMY MEDICAL CORPS,

born at The Curragh, Ireland, on the 19th July, 1881, was the son of Major Pierce O'Brien-Butler, 60th Rifles, and a great-great-grandson of Edmund Butler, Seventeenth Baron Dunboyne.

He was educated at Belvedere College, Dublin. He was a good footballer, playing in the Monkstown eleven, Ireland, but gave up football for racing, in which he soon became famous as a gentleman rider; he rode for His Majesty the late King Edward VII, was head of the list of winning riders in Ireland in 1907, and won races for many well-known owners in England, Ireland, India, and on the Continent, both on the flat and over country. His brother, Pierce O'Brien-Butler, was an International football player, and lost his life in the Boer War.

After qualifying he entered the Army in July, 1907, becoming Captain in January, 1911. He left for France, attached to the 5th Lancers, in August, 1914, and was mentioned in Sir John French's Despatch of 8th October, 1914. On the 1st November, 1914, he was shot down by maxim gun fire when going across an open space to help some wounded comrades.

Captain O'Brien-Butler married Winifred O'Brien, and left one son, Terence, born at Poona in August, 1911.

CAPTAIN ARTHUR MAITLAND BYNG, 4th ROYAL FUSILIERS (CITY OF LONDON REGIMENT),

was the son of Major A. H. Byng, late of the Prince of Wales's Leinster Regiment, and formerly Lieutenant Royal Navy, and was related to the Viscount Torrington. He was born at Southsea on the 26th October, 1872.

Captain Byng was educated at " The Grange," Cowes, and by an Army Tutor at Caen. In September, 1895, he was gazetted to the West Indian Regiment, and served in it till March, 1901, being promoted Captain in June, 1900; he was transferred to the Royal Fusiliers, as Captain in March, 1901. He served in the South African

War in 1901 and 1902, having been employed with the Mounted Infantry, and being present at operations in the Transvaal, Orange River Colony and Cape Colony. He received the Queen's medal with four clasps.

From 1903–05 he was employed with the Egyptian Army and was Adjutant in the Special Reserve from 1908–1912. At Hounslow he inaugurated a Labour Department for Old Soldiers who were out of work, and set on foot schemes for the social improvement of Army dependents, and amongst other things had such soldiers' wives as wished it, taught to cook properly.

Captain Byng was killed at Vailly, at the battle of the Aisne, on the 14th September, 1914, while looking through his field glasses; he was shot in the throat and killed instantaneously.

Brother officers gave the following account of him and his work during the early part of the war :—" He has done *very well* with his Company ; no man could have done more. . . . He was our great interpreter, being very good at French." Again : " He was always taking risks and leaving the trenches with a rifle to walk about in front."

Captain Byng was a member of the M.C.C. and had played both cricket and football for Hampshire. He was a fine all-round cricketer, being a clean and effective bowler, with very deceptive pitch and pace, and a polished and punishing bat. He had taken many wickets and made hundreds of runs for the Royal Fusiliers.

LIEUTENANT-COLONEL HENRY OSBERT SAMUEL CADOGAN, ROYAL WELSH FUSILIERS,

was serving at Malta in command of the 1st Battalion when war was declared. It was shortly afterwards decided to order this Unit to England, to form part of the VIIth Division, which was to be organised for active service as quickly as possible. The Battalion arrived at Southampton on the 15th September, 1914, and was then sent to Lyndhurst to prepare for embarkation for the Continent, and left for the seat of war on the 4th October. Having disembarked at Zeebrugge, the Division moved in the direction of Ghent, the Royal Welsh Fusiliers taking up a position in front of that town on the 9th October. Here a scene of great confusion was noticeable, as the inhabitants were fleeing in a westerly direction in order to escape from the advancing Germans.

On the night of the 11th the Battalion moved back with the Division through Roulers to Ypres, which was reached on the 14th, and on the 19th was heavily engaged in front of Dadizeele against vastly superior numbers. Severe fighting continued daily until the 30th October, on which date the battalion—owing to casualties—had been reduced to about three hundred officers and men, and formed part of the VIIth Division line in front of Zandvoorde. The long line from near the Menin Canal to Zonnebeke was thinly held, and the enemy in very superior strength was endeavouring to capture Ypres, and thus penetrate to Calais. On the 30th the attack was renewed, and some dismounted cavalry on the right of the Welsh Fusiliers having suffered severe losses were forced back, thus leaving the battalion open to a flank attack. Seeing this danger, the Adjutant (Lieutenant Dooner) rushed across a fire-swept piece of ground—the trenches were not continuous—to give some instructions to the company on the right, and was returning to rejoin his Commanding Officer when he was seen to fall. Survivors of the regiment, now prisoners in Germany, state that Lieutenant-Colonel Cadogan at once ran out of the trench to his Adjutant's assistance, and while stooping over him was shot down and, they believe, killed. Shortly after, the remnant of the battalion, many having been killed or wounded, was surrounded and captured. Only one officer—Captain Parker—and eighty-six men, answered the roll-call that evening.

Lieutenant-Colonel Cadogan was a member of a Welsh family formerly settled for many generations in Monmouthshire, and was the only surviving son of the late Rev. Edward Cadogan, Rector of Wicken, Northamptonshire. He was born in 1868, was educated at the Royal Military Academy, Gosport, and, joining the Royal Welsh Fusiliers from the Militia in 1888, was promoted Captain in 1896, Major in 1907, and succeeded to the command of the 1st Battalion in 1912. He had been Assistant-Commandant, Indian Mounted Infantry School, from 1906 to 1908, and commanded at Kasauli in 1908 and 1909. He served throughout the Hazara Expedition in 1891, being granted the Medal, and in the China Expedition and relief of Pekin in 1900, receiving the Medal and clasp. Lieutenant-Colonel Cadogan was twice mentioned in Sir John French's Despatches (14th January and 31st May, 1915) for his gallant and distinguished conduct during the eleven days' fighting from October 19th to 30th.

He married in 1906 Evelyn, daughter of the late H. T. Ross, and leaves one son born in 1908.

MAJOR THE HON. WILLIAM GEORGE SYDNEY CADOGAN, M.V.O., 10th (PRINCE OF WALES'S OWN ROYAL) HUSSARS,

who was killed in action on the 14th November, 1914, while in command of his regiment, was the fifth son of the fifth Earl Cadogan and Countess Cadogan, fourth daughter of the second Earl of Craven.

He was born on the 31st January, 1879, and was educated at Eton, joining the 10th Hussars as Second Lieutenant in February, 1899, and becoming Lieutenant in January, 1900. He served in the South African War, being present at the relief of Kimberley, operations in the Orange Free State, and at Paardeberg; actions at Driefontein, Poplar Grove, Houtnek (Thoba Mountain), Vet and Zand Rivers; in the Transvaal, 1900 and 1901, and in Cape Colony, 1901 and 1902. He received the Queen's medal with four clasps, and the King's medal with two clasps.

In 1906 he was awarded the M.V.O., and he also received the Cross of Honour of the Order of the Crown of Würtemberg. He was promoted Captain in March, 1904, Major in January, 1911, and in 1912 was appointed Equerry to H.R.H. the Prince of Wales. Prior to this he was A.D.C. to His Royal Highness during his Indian Tour, 1905–06.

Major Cadogan was a member of the Turf and White's Clubs.

LIEUTENANT JOHN LESLIE CALDECOTT, ROYAL GARRISON ARTILLERY,

was reported as killed in action in Nyassaland in September, 1914.

He was born on the 7th August, 1886, and joined the Royal Artillery from the Militia in February, 1908, becoming Lieutenant in February, 1911. In August, 1913, he was appointed A.D.C. to the Governor and Commander-in-Chief of Nyassaland at Zomba.

2nd LIEUTENANT WILLIAM ROBERT LAUNCELOT CALROW, 1st BATTN. LOYAL NORTH LANCASHIRE REGT.,

was born at San Antonio, Texas, U.S.A., on the 12th March, 1895. His parents were both English, Gerald Walton Calrow, and Mabel Calrow, daughter of the late Edmund King. He was a great-grandson of the late William Calrow, Esq., J.P., D.L., of Walton Lodge, Lancashire.

Second-Lieutenant Calrow lost his mother when

he was only a year-and-a-half old, and having come to England with his father was

brought up by his grandmother, Mrs. Calrow, and educated in England. He was first at a preparatory school at Seascale, Cumberland, then at the School House, Rugby, and finally at the R.M.C., Sandhurst. He was gazetted to the Army in September, 1913, and joined at Aldershot, where he remained till the 12th August, 1914, when he accompanied his battalion to France for the Great War. He was present at the battle of Mons, in the retirement thence, and in the battles of the Aisne and the Marne.

He was killed instantaneously by high-explosive shell on the 7th October, 1914. Both officers and men testified in the highest terms to his courage, coolness and efficiency, and to his kindness and consideration for his men. Only on the morning of his death one of the latter said to the Officer commanding his company: "Young Mr. Calrow is a hero, if ever there was one." The same Officer, in writing to his Aunt said: "Calrow behaved perfectly splendidly; he was wonderfully cool and collected." While yet another wrote: "A thoroughly efficient young officer, as brave as you make them, and a great loss to us."

Second-Lieutenant Calrow was very fond of hunting and was a fearless rider from early boyhood. His recreations also included camping out, and walking among the mountains of Wales, Cumberland, and Switzerland, where he enjoyed ski-ing.

CAPTAIN ALLAN GEORGE CAMERON, 1st BATTN. THE QUEEN'S OWN CAMERON HIGHLANDERS,

who was born at Achnacarry on the 27th July, 1880, was the third son of the late Lochiel and Lady Margaret Cameron, daughter of the fifth Duke of Buccleuch.

He was educated at Eton (where he was in the "Field" XI), whence he passed direct into the R.M.C., Sandhurst, having previously been gazetted to the Royal Scots Militia, with which regiment he served during one annual training. Captain Cameron was gazetted Second-Lieutenant in October, 1899, and joined the 2nd Battalion of his regiment at Gibraltar, proceeding with it to Crete, Malta, and South Africa. He was promoted Lieutenant in 1901 and Captain in May, 1910. He was Adjutant of the 1st Lovat's Scouts from 1907—1911, when he joined the 1st Battalion of his regiment at Aldershot and went with it to France in August, 1914.

He was killed on the 25th September, 1914, near Beaulne, north of the river Aisne. Being the senior unwounded officer at the moment, he was sent for to take over command of the battalion ; he walked to Headquarters through heavy shell fire, and as he entered the cave, where the regimental Headquarters were, a high-explosive shell blew it in, and he and thirty others were killed, only one man getting out alive. He was buried at Bourg, on the Aisne. Captain Cameron possessed in a marked degree the qualities of chivalry and courage that have been characteristic of his family ; tall, handsome, and of martial bearing, while modest and genial in manner, he was extremely popular. A hard worker himself, he expected those under him to maintain a high standard of efficiency. He was a good piper, and rifle shot, winning the Officers' aggregate for the highest number of points at the Scottish Command Rifle Meeting in 1913, and being third in the individual aggregate of all ranks. At Sandhurst he was in the revolver team and at Malta rowed stroke in the Officers' boat race. He was fond of stalking, and all kinds of shooting. In 1902 he received the Royal Humane Society's Certificate for jumping into the sea off the embankment at Oban and saving a child's life.

Captain Cameron married in October, 1908, Hester Vere, daughter of Lieutenant-Colonel and the late Mrs. Fraser-Tytler, of Aldourie, and left one son, Angus Ewen, born 20th January, 1914.

CAPTAIN NAPIER CHARLES GORDON CAMERON, 1st BATTN. THE QUEEN'S OWN CAMERON HIGHLANDERS,

was born at Gibraltar on the 14th December, 1876, being the son of the late General Sir William Gordon Cameron, G.C.B., of Nea House, Christchurch, Hants, who served in the Crimea.
Captain Cameron began his military career by joining

Strathcona's Horse in 1900 ; in the following year he received a commission in the Scottish Horse, and served with them during the remainder of the South African war, in which he was wounded. For his services he was mentioned in Despatches and received the Queen's medal with four clasps. In June, 1902, he was gazetted to the Northumberland Fusiliers, and when the battalion was disbanded in 1908, obtained a commission in the 1st Battalion Cameron Highlanders as a Lieutenant.

With this battalion he served in the Great War, being promoted Captain in September, 1914. On the 14th of that month he was reported wounded and missing, but rejoined his regiment after two days. On this occasion he owed his escape from capture by the Germans by feigning death, and lay for some time on the ground while German soldiers cut off his belt and removed his claymore and revolver. Later on, while waiting till darkness to return to the regiment, with some private soldiers, they heard an officer of the Black Watch calling for help, and Captain Cameron with a private in the Camerons went out and brought him in under heavy fire.

He was killed in action at the Battle of the Aisne on the 25th September, 1914.

On the 4th November, 1913, Captain Cameron married Constance Geraldine, eldest daughter of Captain Harry Brooke, D.L., late Gordon Highlanders, of Fairley, Countesswells, Aberdeenshire, and grand-daughter of the late Sir Arthur Brooke, Bart., of Colebrooke, County Fermanagh, Ireland, and left one child, Honor Napier Gordon Cameron, born on the 31st December, 1914, after her father's death.

Captain Cameron was a member of the United Service Club. He took his Flying Certificate at Brooklands in July, 1913.

CAPTAIN WILLIAM HENRY VEITCH CAMERON, 1st BATTN. (attd.) HIGHLAND LIGHT INFANTRY,

is believed to have been killed in action on the 20th December, 1914, near Festubert, though his name had not been included in the monthly official casualty lists up to June, 1915. He was the second son of the late Sir Ewen Cameron, K.C.M.G., and of Lady Cameron, of 39, Hyde Park Gate, London, S.W., and was born on the 4th February, 1883. He joined the Highland Light Infantry in May, 1901, becoming Lieutenant in July, 1906.

He served in the South African War, being present at operations in the Cape Colony from October, 1901, to May, 1902, receiving the Queen's medal with three clasps. From August, 1908, to August, 1911, he was Adjutant of his battalion, and was promoted Captain in September, 1912.

LIEUTENANT ALLAN WILLIAM GEORGE CAMPBELL, SPECIAL RESERVE, COLDSTREAM GUARDS,

who died of wounds received at the battle of the Aisne on the 20th September, 1914, was the only son of Mr. and Mrs. Allan Campbell, of 21, Upper Brook Street, London.

He was born in London on the 20th October, 1884, and was educated at E. P. Arnold's Wixenford Preparatory School, where he was in the school XI. for cricket and football; at Eton, and New College, Oxford. He was gazetted to the Coldstream Guards as Second-Lieutenant in February, 1908, becoming Lieutenant in October, 1910. In August, 1913, he joined the Special Reserve of the 2nd Battalion Coldstream Guards.

When at Eton he was captain of, and played cricket and football for his House, Mr. A. A. Somerville's, was a leading member of the Musical Society, and won a cup for fives; he was a member of the Volunteer Band and was " sent up for good " several times (original Greek and Latin verse), and won the Headmaster's Prize. Later in life he frequently played cricket for the Household Brigade. His recreations were cricket, shooting, fishing, golf, tennis, billiards, racquets and motoring. He was also very fond of music, and was a good musician, being able to play by ear anything he heard, including operas. While at Oxford he conducted a small orchestra of his own.

He was a member of the following clubs: the Guards', Lord's, Travellers', Bath, Junior Carlton, United Empire, Royal Automobile, Prince's, Queen's, Alpine Sports; Worpleston and Harewood Downs Golf Clubs, and of the Free Foresters and Eton Ramblers.

In June, 1914, he was accepted as Unionist Candidate for the Doncaster Division of Yorkshire.

On the outbreak of the war he rejoined his regiment, and was one of three officers to take out the first draft to the front. He was serving with the 1st Battalion when he was mortally wounded at the Aisne on the 19th September, 1914, and succumbed to his wounds next day. He was buried in Troyon Churchyard.

Lieutenant Campbell married on the 15th February, 1912, Lady Moya Melisende Browne, second daughter of the sixth Marquess of Sligo, and Agatha Stewart, daughter of J. Stewart-Hodgson of Lythe Hill, Haslemere, and left a son born October, 1913.

2nd LIEUTENANT BRABAZON CAMPBELL, 4th BATTN. ROYAL WARWICKSHIRE REGT.,

was the only son of Mr. and Mrs. Brabazon Campbell, The Northgate, Warwick, and was 21 years of age at the time of his death, having been born on the 3rd March, 1893, at The Northgate, Warwick. He was educated at Repton and Queen's College, Oxford, where he had nearly completed his second year when war broke out. He was given a commission in the Royal Warwickshire Regiment on the 15th August, 1914, joining it in the Isle of Wight, and on the 26th November was sent out to the 2nd Battalion. He fell on the 18th December, 1914, with three other officers of his battalion. The senior Officer left of this battalion gave the following account of the circumstances :—

" May I be allowed to express on behalf of all ranks our deep sympathy with you in the loss of your son. He died a gallant death when within a few yards of a machine gun in the enemy's trenches, together with four officers and 32 men. It was obvious that the party was trying to capture the gun when they were killed. It may be some consolation for you to know that the General Officer Commanding 4th Army Corps has issued an order praising in the highest terms the effort made to capture the enemy's trench, an effort in which your son took a very prominent and gallant part."

LIEUTENANT CHARLES ARTHUR CAMPBELL, 1st BATTN. CHESHIRE REGIMENT,

was born in London on the 3rd June, 1891, the son of Arthur Campbell, of Wye House, West Worthing, and grandson of the late Robert Campbell, of Buscot Park, Berkshire.

He was educated at Downside School from 1901 to 1909, when he passed into the R.M.C., Sandhurst. He received his commission in October, 1911, and served with his battalion in Ireland until the war broke out, when it was one of the first to go to the front.

He was a keen motor-cyclist, and captain of the regimental hockey team.

Lieutenant Campbell, who was promoted in April, 1914, took part in the fighting at Mons on the 24th August and was shot through the head while leading his men, and killed instantly. He was buried in the cemetery at Andregnies.

CAPTAIN COLIN FREDERICK FITZROY CAMPBELL, 1st BATTN. SCOTS GUARDS,

was killed in action near Ypres on the 29th October, 1914. He was the only son of Major-General F. Lorn Campbell, Highfield House, West Byfleet, Surrey, of the Melfort family, Argyllshire, and was born on the 29th September, 1880.

He joined the Cameron Highlanders from the Militia in January, 1901, becoming Lieutenant in August, 1904. He was transferred to the Scots Guard in March, 1905, and from September, 1911, to September, 1913, was Adjutant of the Guards' Depot. Captain Campbell was gazetted to his rank on the 29th October, the date of his death. He married on the 11th June, 1914, Helen Margaret, eldest daughter of Mr. C. J. and Lady Mary Stewart. He was a member of the Guards' and Caledonian Clubs.

CAPTAIN DONALD WILLIAM AUCHINBRECK CAMPBELL, 4th BATTN. SOUTH STAFFORDSHIRE REGIMENT,

third son of the late Rev. W. P. A. Campbell, Rector of Fladbury Worcestershire, was born on the 20th March, 1872.

Educated at Clifton College he was gazetted to the 1st Battalion South Staffordshire Regiment in June, 1892, serving with it at home and in Egypt until 1899 ; in that year he was appointed Adjutant of the 3rd V.B. South Staffordshire Regiment, retaining the appointment till 1903. He then resigned his commission in the Regular Army and joined the Special Reserve of his regiment, which, however, he left in 1913. On the outbreak of war with Germany he volunteered for service, and rejoined the 4th Battalion in August ; in October he volunteered for active service with the VIIIth Division, and was attached to the 1st Battalion Sherwood Foresters with which he went to France early in November. Captain Campbell was killed at Neuve Chapelle on the 22nd November, 1914, in an attempt to recover the body of the machine-gun officer, which lay a short distance in front of his trench ; he had made an unsuccessful attempt alone the previous night, and at daybreak tried again with two volunteers, one of whom also lost his life. He was mentioned for his gallant conduct in Sir John French's Despatch of 14th January, 1915. Captain Campbell married, Helen Gertrude Philpott, and left two daughters.

CAPTAIN GEOFFREY ARTHUR CAMPBELL, 1st BATTN. COLDSTREAM GUARDS,

killed in action on the 29th October, 1914, at Gheluvelt, Flanders, was the youngest son of Mr. and the Hon. Mrs. George Campbell, 46, Wilton Crescent, London, S.W., and Market House, Brackley, and was born on the 8th January, 1885.

He was educated at Eton and joined his regiment in February, 1907, became Lieutenant in June, 1909, and was appointed Battalion Adjutant in January, 1912. He was a member of the Guards' Club, and was fond of hunting and polo. He was mentioned in Sir John French's Despatch of the 14th October, 1914, and was promoted temporary Captain.

LIEUTENANT JOHN DAVIES CAMPBELL, "L" BATTERY, ROYAL HORSE ARTILLERY,

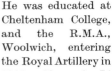

was born at Tacna, Chile, South America, on the 1st March, 1883, the son of J. D. Campbell, Esq., of Howden Court, Tiverton, Devon.

He was educated at Cheltenham College, and the R.M.A., Woolwich, entering the Royal Artillery in 1901, and becoming Lieutenant in December, 1904. He was killed on the 1st September, 1914, at Nery, near Compiegne, France, during " L " Battery's glorious stand at that place (see Captain E. K. Bradbury, V.C.).

2nd LIEUTENANT WILLIAM PERCY CAMPBELL, 3rd (RESERVE) attd. 2nd BATTN. THE DUKE OF EDINBURGH'S (WILTSHIRE REGIMENT),

was the second son of John Edward Campbell, Esq., F.R.S., Fellow and Bursar of Hertford College, Oxford.

He was born on the 2nd May, 1894, and was educated at the Oxford Preparatory School and at Clifton College, of which he was a scholar. He gained a scholarship at Hertford College, where he had been in residence a year, studying medicine, when the war broke out. He at once volunteered and was gazetted in August, 1914, to the Wiltshire Regiment, proceeding to the front with the VIIth Division at the beginning of October.

It is believed that he was killed on the morning of Saturday, the 24th October, 1914, a few miles East of Ypres, in an attempt to bring a wounded comrade to a place of safety.

MAJOR WALTER ERNEST CAMPION, 1st BATTN. EAST YORKSHIRE REGT.,

son of Henry Campion, Esq., Bletsoe Castle, near Bedford, was born at Dean, Bedfordshire, on 9th August, 1871, and was educated at the Modern School, Bedford.

He was gazetted to the 2nd Battalion East Yorkshire Regiment from the Militia in December, 1894, becoming Captain in May, 1900, and Brevet-Major in August, 1902. After serving in Ireland, he went through the South African War, where he was employed with the Mounted Infantry, and was slightly wounded. He was present at operations in the Transvaal, including actions near Johannesburg, Pretoria and Diamond Hill; operations in the Orange River Colony, including actions at Wittebergen, Bothaville, and Caledon River, and the action at Frederickstad. He was twice mentioned in Despatches, "London Gazette," 10th September, 1901, and 29th July, 1902, promoted Brevet-Major and received the Queen's medal with four clasps and the King's medal with two clasps.

Subsequently he served in Burma and India. He was a keen sportsman, hunted with the Oakley and won many races in Ireland, England, South Africa and India, including the Army Cup in 1910.

In the Great War he was wounded on 20th September, 1914, but returned to the front, and was killed in action near Lille on the 28th October, 1914.

CAPTAIN LIONEL ALFRED FRANCIS CANE, 1st BATTN. EAST LANCASHIRE REGIMENT, son of the Reverend A. G. Cane,

Vicar of Great Paxton, formerly Chaplain to the Indian Government, and Mrs. Cane, was born at Poona on the 19th December, 1884. He was first cousin to Lieutenant-General Sir E. Allenby, K.C.B. Captain Cane was edu-

cated at Haileybury, and joined the Sherwood Foresters (Nottinghamshire and Derbyshire Regiment) in Feb-

ruary, 1903, being transferred to the 2nd Battalion East Lancashire Regiment in December, 1904. From 1910 to 1913, when he was promoted Captain, he was Adjutant of his battalion at the Cape, South Africa. On the expiration

of his Adjutancy he returned to England on leave and was, almost at once, posted to the Depot at Preston. While serving there the war broke out, and he applied to join the 1st Battalion in the field.

He was ordered to the front at the end of September. When Major Green was wounded, Captain Cane took charge of his two Companies, "C" and "D," and was in command of them when he fell, on the 7th November, 1914, while leading them to attack a trench, which was captured just after he was killed.

Captain Cane won the Hunt Point-to-Point and the Regimental Steeplechase at Wynberg, South Africa, in 1914, riding his own horse.

CAPTAIN MILES BERTIE CUNNINGHAME CARBERY, 1st BATTN. PRINCESS VICTORIA'S (ROYAL IRISH FUSILIERS).

who was killed in action on the 17th October, 1914, in France, was the son of the late William Carbery, Esq., and Mrs. Carbery, of 17, Hartington Mansions, Eastbourne. He was born on the 6th June, 1877, and joined the Royal Irish Fusiliers from

the Militia in December, 1897, becoming Lieutenant in December, 1899. He served in the South African War, being present at operations in Natal, including the action at Talana, where he was dangerously wounded; he received for his services the Queen's medal with clasp.

He got his Company in February, 1903, and from 1910 to 1913 was an Adjutant of the Territorial Force.

Captain Carbery married a daughter of the late Right Honourable Thomas Sinclair.

2nd LIEUTENANT FRANCIS LUDOVIC CAREW, XXth HUSSARS,

was the son of Charles Carew, Esq., of Collipriest, Tiverton, and was born there on the 4th March, 1895.

He was educated at Winchester College, and the R.M.C., Sandhurst, receiving his commission in the 20th Hussars on the 24th March, 1914.

He was killed in the trenches at Oosttaverne, near Ypres, on the 30th October, 1914.

2nd LIEUTENANT JASPER CAREW, 1st BATTN. PRINCE OF WALES'S OWN (WEST YORKSHIRE REGIMENT),

who was killed in action on the 14th October, 1914, was the younger son of the late Rev. Henry Carew and Mrs. Carew of Airlea, South Brent, Devon. He was born at Rattery Vicarage, Devon, in 1894, and was educated at Blundell's School, Tiverton, and the R.M.C., Sandhurst, joining the West Yorkshire Regiment in January, 1914. He fell while leading his platoon in an advance guard action near Hazebrouck, where he was killed instantaneously by machine gun fire.

CAPTAIN LEICESTER WILLIAM LE MARCHANT CAREY, 4th BATTN. THE ROYAL FUSILIERS (CITY OF LONDON REGIMENT),

who had been reported wounded and missing, is believed to have been killed on the 20th October, 1914, near Kerlies, but his name had not been included in the monthly official casualty lists up to June, 1915.

He was the only son of the late Major-General C. P. Carey, R.E., C.B., and of Mrs. Carey, and was born on the 12th November, 1877. He joined the Royal Fusiliers in February, 1908, becoming Lieutenant in November of the same year, and Captain in July, 1901. He served in the South African War taking part in the relief of Ladysmith, including the action at Colenso; he was present at operations in the Transvaal in 1900 and 1901, in the Cape Colony, north of the Orange River in April and May, 1900, including the action at Ruidam, and again in Cape Colony between January, 1901, and March, 1902; he received the Queen's medal with five clasps and the King's medal with two clasps.

From July, 1903, to October, 1910, he was employed with the Egyptian Army, and from March to August, 1912, was A.D.C. to the General Officer Commanding-in-Chief, Southern Command.

Captain Carey, who was married, was qualified as an interpreter in French, and was entitled to wear a foreign order.

CAPTAIN MARTIN RAYMOND CARR, 2nd BATTN. WORCESTERSHIRE REGIMENT,

who was killed in action at the battle of the Aisne on the 18th September, 1914, was born on the 8th July, 1877, and joined the Worcestershire Regiment from the Militia, in January, 1899, becoming Lieutenant in February, 1900.

Captain Carr served in the South African War, in which he was wounded, being employed with the Mounted Infantry; he was present at operations in the Orange River Colony in 1900, 1901 and 1902, and in Cape Colony, 1901 and 1902, receiving the Queen's medal with four clasps and the King's medal with two clasps. Captain Carr, who reached that rank in December, 1901, after rather less than three years' service with the Regular Army, married Gwen, second daughter of T. Putnam, Esq., of Greylands, Darlington, who survives him.

2nd LIEUTENANT ROBERT NEVIN CARSWELL, 3rd BATTN. THE KING'S OWN (YORKSHIRE LIGHT INFANTRY),

was the eldest son of John George Carswell and his wife Sarah Constance (née Bell) and was born at Shortlands, Kent, on the 31st August, 1889.

He was educated at Blundell's School, Tiverton, and Sheffield University. At the University he was Quarter-Master-Sergeant of the Officers' Training Corps and received his commission in the 3rd (Reserve Battalion) of the King's Own Yorkshire Light Infantry on 15th August, 1914, sailing from Southampton for France on 7th October. He was killed, shot through the head, on 26th October, 1914, when, leading a bayonet charge at La Bassée, he met a body of Germans coming down the road. He was buried by his own men in the orchard of a farm at Richebourg l'Avoué.

MAJOR AUBREY JOHN CARTER, D.S.O., LOYAL NORTH LANCASHIRE REGIMENT,

was the fourth son of the late T. A. Carter, Esq., Shottery Hall, Stratford-on-Avon. He was born on the 18th January, 1872, and was gazetted to the Loyal North Lancashire Regiment in January, 1892, becoming Lieutenant in May, 1893, and Captain in February, 1901.

He served in the South African War as a Railway Staff Officer from December, 1899, to March, 1900, and as a Brigade Signalling Officer from October, 1900, to March, 1901; he was mentioned in Despatches, "London Gazette," 10th September, 1901, was awarded the D.S.O., and received the Queen's medal with five clasps. From December, 1905, to December, 1909, he was an Instructor at the School of Musketry, where with Lieutenant-Colonel Norman McMahon he was largely responsible for the revolution in the musketry training of the Army, and in July, 1911, having obtained his Majority in February, 1910, was appointed Commandant of the School of Musketry, South Africa, with the temporary rank of Lieutenant-Colonel. His services in this post were recognised in the following extract from a letter signed by Lord Gladstone: "In a special measure, Ministers ask me to record their grateful acknowledgement of the services rendered by Lieutenant-Colonel Carter, Commandant School of Musketry, Tempe, and his Staff."

He was subsequently placed in charge of musketry in the Irish Command, and eventually proceeded to France to take command of the 1st Battalion, Loyal North Lancashire Regiment. It fell to him to lead the Battalion in a charge, which is well described by a brother officer :—

" The men meant business this time. I looked into their faces and could see a sort of dull, fierce look. After the many days of being cooped up in the trenches before we ever arrived in this portion of the theatre of war, it was a real joy to them to be on the move and on the attack. They longed to get at them, and gradually, without a word of command being given, you could hear the click of the bayonet as each man fastened it to his rifle. Suddenly the cry arose, ' Come on, my lads, now for the trenches.' The cry went along the line. Everyone started yelling above the din of battle. We charged yelling, shouting, screaming, rushing madly forward at the enemy. How it looked from the German side I do not know, but it was

grand, simply magnificent from our side. We crossed two hundred yards of root field at a steady run under fire. We leapt into the enemy's trenches, bayoneted those who were still living, and then rushed on to another line of trenches in front. The whole of my battalion were in it. It was our show."

He was killed in action near Ypres on November 4th, 1914, and the following tribute to him voices the opinion of all of his many friends :—

" He was a tall soldier-like figure, standing six feet four inches, and straight as the proverbial pine. His was a soldier's end. He went out from the trenches to direct the machine-gun fire, but fell, shot dead, as the enemy retired. He was a gallant commander, and a great leader under whom it is an honour to have served."

Major Carter married in 1906, Edith Mary, daughter of the late Rev. G. H. Rigby, and niece of the late Right Hon. Sir John Rigby.

CAPTAIN CLEARY GEORGE MOLYNEUX CARTER, 2nd BATTN, THE DUKE OF EDINBURGH'S (WILTSHIRE REGIMENT),
who was killed in action on the 23rd October, 1914, was born on the 3rd January, 1882, and was educated at Marlborough College (Star) from 1893–1900.

He was gazetted to the Wiltshire Regiment in May, 1901, and took part in the South African War, where he was employed with the Mounted Infantry, being present at operations in the Transvaal, Cape Colony, and Orange River Colony, receiving the Queen's medal with five clasps.

He was promoted Lieutenant in September, 1903, and from September, 1908, to September, 1911, was Adjutant of his Battalion, obtaining his Company in March, 1910.

2nd LIEUTENANT JAMES CASEY, 1st BATTN. THE KING'S ROYAL RIFLE CORPS,
was born in London on the 30th November, 1879, the son of the late James Casey, formerly a Corporal in the same Corps.

2nd Lieutenant Casey joined the 1st Battalion King's Royal Rifles in 1897, and served through the South African War with the Mounted Infantry. He was promoted Sergeant for conspicuous gallantry on the field at Balkerlaagte, Transvaal, on the 30th October, 1901, and was mentioned in Despatches, in January, 1902, for distinguished gallantry. He received the Queen's medal with four clasps, and the King's medal with two clasps. After the South African War he rejoined his Battalion and went to France with the Expeditionary Force of which it formed part.

On October 1st he was promoted Second-Lieutenant for gallantry, and was killed in action on the 30th October, 1914, and was mentioned in Sir John French's Despatch of 14th January, 1915.

2nd Lieutenant Casey was married in 1912 to Daisy Casey, and left two children, Ronald James Spion, age two years, and Thomas Henry, age one month, at the time of their father's death.

CAPTAIN AUGUSTUS ERNEST CATHCART, 2nd BATTN. KING'S ROYAL RIFLE CORPS,

who was killed in action on the 14th September, 1914, was born on the 4th March, 1875, and joined the K.R.R.C. from the Militia in January, 1897, becoming Lieutenant in February, 1899.

He took part in the South African War as a Special Service Officer (including service as Station Staff Officer from February, 1901), and was also employed with the Mounted Infantry. He was present at operations in the Transvaal and Orange River Colony, receiving for his services the Queen's medal with three clasps, and the King's medal with two clasps. Captain Cathcart obtained his Company in January, 1902.

LIEUTENANT JAMES CROSBIE CAULFEILD, 2nd BATTN. MANCHESTER REGIMENT,

who was killed in action on the 18th November, 1914, was the youngest son of Brigadier-General (Commanding 8th Reserve Infantry Battalion) and Mrs. James E Caulfeild, of Corozal, Jersey. He was born on the 21st February, 1892, and was educated at Bradfield College, where he became a Prefect, from 1905 to 1910. He joined the Army Service Corps as Second Lieutenant in September, 1911, from the R.M.C., Sandhurst, becoming Lieutenant in September, 1914. He was transferred to the Manchester Regiment in October, 1914.

He was struck by a high explosive shell while in command of a company of his battalion in a front trench near Wulverghem, Belgium.

CAPTAIN GODFREY LIONEL JOHN CAVENDISH, 97th DECCAN INFANTRY,

born at Eastbourne on the 30th March, 1884, was the son of Reginald R. F. Cavendish, and grandson of the late Francis W. H. Cavendish, D.L., J.P., of St. Margaret's, Eastbourne. He was a kinsman of the Duke of Devonshire, and a great-grandson of General the Hon. H. F. C. Cavendish, and of the third Earl of Clare.

Captain Cavendish was educated at Framlingham College, Suffolk, where he showed himself a good swimmer and cricketer. He received his commission in April, 1903, being gazetted to the Manchester Regiment, joining the 1st Battalion at Singapore, and later was transferred to the 2nd East Surrey Regiment. After a probationary period with the 83rd Wallajahbad Light Infantry, he was finally appointed to the 97th Deccan Infantry. His own regiment remaining in India, Captain Cavendish was, at his request, attached for active service to the Reserve of Officers for " A " Force ; on arrival at Marseilles he was attached 1/9 Gurkha Rifles, and a few days later again transferred to 9th Bhopals, which had lost very heavily, joining them on the 15th December, 1914. He was wounded on the 20th of that month and died two days later in a Field Hospital, after having been about three weeks at the front.

The following account of the circumstances is taken from a brother officer's letter :—

"On the 17th December the half-battalion which Captain Cavendish was commanding was ordered up to support the trenches at Givenchy. He remained in these trenches in support till the 20th, when he was ordered to take his command up to support a regiment in front which was being attacked. On the way up he received an order to halt in the support trenches, and he went a few yards ahead to find out what was wanted when he was hit by a rifle bullet, which entered his neck. His wound was tied up and his comrades and himself thought the wound was not serious, so he walked back about two miles to hospital. His brother officers were much distressed to hear a few days later that the wound had proved fatal. He was always very cheery under fire, and helpful by his good spirits."

Captain Cavendish married in March, 1911, Cora Grace Graham Cavendish, and left two sons, Godfrey Herbert Richard, born January, 1912, and Hubert Gordon Compton, born February, 1913.

MAJOR LORD JOHN SPENCER CAVENDISH, D.S.O., 1st LIFE GUARDS,

who was killed in action on the 20th October, 1914, was the third son of the late Lord Edward Cavendish and Lady Edward Cavendish, and grandson of the seventh Duke of Devonshire.

He was born on the 27th March, 1872, and joined the 1st Life Guards from the Militia in February, 1897, becoming Lieutenant in April, 1898. He served in the South African War, where he was Divisional and Brigade Signalling Officer from October, 1899, to October, 1900, and was present at the relief of Ladysmith, including action at Colenso ; at the actions of Spion Kop and Vaal Krans ; operations on the Tugela Heights and action at Pieter's Hill ; in the Orange Free State, and action at Zand River ; in the Transvaal, and actions near Johannesburg, Pretoria, and Diamond Hill ; also in the Transvaal, West of Pretoria, including actions at Elands River ; in the Orange River Colony, including actions at Bethlehem and Wittebergen. He was mentioned in Despatches (" London Gazette," 1st February, 1901), was awarded the D.S.O., and received the Queen's medal with six clasps.

He was promoted Captain in August, 1902, and from June, 1907, to September, 1910, was employed with the West African Frontier Force, obtaining his Majority in April, 1911.

MAJOR JOHN STEPHEN CAWLEY, p.s.c., 20th HUSSARS, BRIGADE MAJOR 1st CAVALRY BRIGADE,

qualified as second-class Interpreter in French, was the son of Sir Frederick Cawley, Bart., M.P., of Berrington Hall, Leominster, and was born at Crumpsall, Lancashire, on the 27th October, 1879. He was educated at Lockers Park, at Rugby, and at the R.M.C., Sandhurst, and obtained his commission in the 20th Hussars in 1898, joining them at Mhow, India. He became Lieutenant in January, 1900, and obtained his Troop in October, 1906. He served in the South African War, going to the Cape in 1901, where he was Signalling Officer to General Low's column, being present at operations in Orange River Colony and Cape Colony ; he received the Queen's medal with four clasps. He subsequently served in Egypt, where he became Adjutant of his regiment. Having passed through the Staff College, he became Instructor at the Cavalry School at Netheravon in 1911, and in 1912 was appointed a General Staff Officer at the War Office. In 1913 he was appointed Brigade Major of the 1st Cavalry Brigade at Aldershot, and accompanied it to France for service in the Great War.

Major Cawley was a good all-round sportsman ; he was in the Rugby football team and shooting eight at Sandhurst ; was in the hockey team and was whip to the drag at the Staff College ; played for his regiment at polo when they won the Inter-regimental Cup in India (Meerut), 1901 ; the Clements Polo Cup in South Africa (Pretoria), 1903 ; and the Inter-regimental Cup (Hurlingham), 1906 and 1907. He won the Officers' riding and jumping prize at the Royal Military Tournament in 1905, and was well known with the North Hereford and Whaddon Chase Hunts.

Major Cawley was killed in action in the retirement from Mons on the 1st September, 1914, at Nery, and was buried there. A brother officer gave the following account of his death :—

" Our Brigade was attacked soon after dawn at Nery by a force double our number—a Cavalry Division with 12 guns. Owing to thick mist they managed to get within 600 yards of us ; 350 horses of the Bays stampeded and their men went after them, and the ' L ' Battery was cut to pieces. The occasion was one which called for personal example, and Major Cawley, by permission of the General, went to help to restore order and get the broken remnants in their places. The situation being met and everyone being in his place, he joined the advanced line and was almost immediately killed by a piece of shell. The splendid manner in which he met his death in deliberately facing the awful fire to help others when he really need not have done so, is only what his whole life has led us to expect." General Briggs, commanding the Brigade, wrote of him :—" He has been a true friend and a loyal conscientious Staff Officer to me for nearly two years, and it is needless to say how much I feel his death. He proved himself to be a real fighter in war and was always cool and collected."

2nd LIEUTENANT GEORGE EDWARD CECIL, 2nd BATTN. GRENADIER GUARDS,

who was reported in the monthly Casualty List published in December, 1914, to have died of wounds received in action, was the only son of Lord and Lady Edward Cecil. He was born on the 9th September, 1895, at 20, Arlington Street, the house of his grandfather, the Marquess of Salisbury. He was educated at Winchester, and the R.M.C., Sandhurst, where he took a prize cadetship, and from which he was gazetted to the Grenadier Guards in February, 1914. In that year he qualified as a second-class Interpreter in French.

His battalion was among the first troops of the Expeditionary Force to proceed to the Continent, and at the battle of Landrecies Second-Lieutenant Cecil acted as Orderly Officer to a General Officer.

CAPTAIN the Honble. WILLIAM AMHERST CECIL, 2nd BATTN. GRENADIER GUARDS,

was born in London on the 30th June, 1886, the eldest son of Lord William Cecil, Grenadier Guards, and Lady William Cecil, Baroness Amherst of Hackney, and heir to the Barony.

He was educated at Eton, and joined the Grenadier Guards in August, 1907, becoming Lieutenant in July, 1908.

For his services in the Great War he was mentioned in Sir John French's Despatch of the 8th October, 1914, was awarded the Military Cross, and recommended for the Legion of Honour. He was promoted Captain on the 9th September, 1914. Captain Cecil was at Landrecies in command of the Machine Gun Section of the 2nd Battalion Grenadier Guards, and was killed at the Battle of the Aisne on the 16th September, 1914.

Captain Cecil was very keen about his profession, especially everything in relation to machine guns; he was a clever draughtsman and took a special interest in Egyptology, in which he was an expert. He was very musical, played the piano, and also the bagpipes. He was also fond of all sports, particularly cricket, hunting,

yachting, and shooting. He was a member of the Guards' and the Junior Carlton clubs.

Captain Cecil married in 1910, Evelyn Gladys, only child of Henry Baggallay, Esq., of Heatherhurst Grange, Frimley, Surrey, and left two sons, William Alexander Evering, born May, 1912, and Henry Kerr Auchmutz, born April, 1914, the elder of whom becomes heir to the Barony of Amherst of Hackney.

LIEUTENANT JOHN BINNY CHALMERS, ROYAL FIELD ARTILLERY (T.F.)

of Moor Court, Sidmouth, only son of the late Mr. J. H. Chalmers, C.E., and grandson of the late Mr. John Binny Chalmers, of the Diplomatic Service, and of The Elms, Highgate, and Westmuir, Forfarshire, was born in August, 1889, and

educated at Ovingdean Hall, Sussex.

After completing his period of attachment to the Scots Greys and South Staffords, he resigned his commission and went abroad. He returned immediately on the outbreak of hostilities and received a temporary commission in the Royal Field Artillery.

He was killed by a fall from his horse in October, 1914.

He was a fine horseman and hunted with the East Devon and Cobleigh packs; was also a splendid shot, an ardent angler, and devoted to all outdoor sports.

LIEUTENANT GUY OGDEN DE PEYSTER CHANCE, 1st BATTN. ROYAL WELSH FUSILIERS,

who was killed in action on the 19th October, 1914, was the youngest son of Mr. W. E. Chance, Thurston Grange, Bury St. Edmunds, and was born on the 28th February, 1892. He entered the Army in September, 1911, becoming Lieutenant in April, 1913.

He accompanied his battalion—which formed part of the VIIth Division—from Lyndhurst, disembarking at Zeebrugge, and was killed in the severe fighting near Dadizeele on the date mentioned.

2nd LIEUTENANT CLIVE HEREWARD CHANDLER, 1st BATTN. THE DUKE OF EDINBURGH'S (WILTSHIRE REGT.),

was born at Exeter on the 18th July, 1884.

He was for many years in the Wiltshire Regiment, and when he accompanied it to the front was Sergeant-Drummer of his Battalion. He was a noted athlete and when stationed at Pretoria won the 220 yards, and other events, at the Army Championship Sports in October, 1910. He had a number of civilian as well as military friends in Maritzburg, and has been described as one of the best all-round Army athletes in South Africa.

During the Great War he was given his commission as Second-Lieutenant for service in the field on the 1st October, and was killed in the firing line on the Yser, on the 17th November, 1914.

One of his senior Officers sent the following account of the circumstances to his widow :—
" It is with the deepest regret I have to send you the sad news that your husband was killed in action on the 17th instant (November). Your poor husband was killed by a bullet wound in the head when defending the trenches. I only saw him half an hour before, as I was commanding the trench at the time. He was a brave fellow and was doing so well ; it is sad that his life should have been forfeited so soon."

Second-Lieutenant Chandler, two of whose brothers are now serving in the Army, married Olivia May Court, and left one daughter, Ethel Muriel, born at Maritzburg, Natal, in September, 1912.

LIEUTENANT EDWARD WYNNE CHAPMAN, 3rd (PRINCE OF WALES'S) DRAGOON GUARDS,

was the eldest son of the late Edward Chapman of Springbank, New Zealand. He was born in 1887 and educated at Christ's College. He held commissions as Lieutenant in the College Cadets and later in the Christchurch Mounted Rifles.

He came to England in 1909 and was attached to the 3rd Dragoon Guards at Aldershot during the following year, becoming 2nd Lieutenant in May, and Lieutenant in November, 1911.

In 1912 he married Elvira Maude, second daughter of H. W. Henderson of Serge Hill, King's Langley, Herts, and went to Egypt, where the Regiment was stationed at Abbasiyeh, Cairo, till the war broke out.

Arriving in England on the 20th October, he went straight to the front, and was killed in action on the 17th November, 1914, near Ypres, being mentioned in Sir John French's Despatch of the 14th January, 1915, for conspicuous bravery. He was buried in the cemetery at Ypres.

Lieutenant Chapman leaves a daughter, born in March, 1915.

CAPTAIN ANGUS ALAN MACGREGOR CHARLES, ROYAL FIELD ARTILLERY,

who was killed in action on the 20th December, 1914, while on observation duty near Cuinchy, was the son of Deputy-Surgeon General Thomas Edmondston Charles, Indian Medical Department, M.D., Edin., K.H.P., LL.D. (Edin.), and Ada Henrietta, eldest daughter of General Rundall, C.S.I., Royal Engineers ; he was a grandson of the late Rev. James Charles, D.D., of Kirkcowan, Wigtownshire.

Captain Charles was born on the 8th September, 1887, and was educated at Winchester College, where he obtained a scholarship in 1901, passing thence direct into the R.M.A., Woolwich, in 1906. From Woolwich he was gazetted to the Royal Field Artillery in December, 1908, and was posted to the 97th Battery in which he served for about five years in South Africa and Madras. At the outbreak of war he was transferred to the 73rd Battery then at Lucknow, with which he proceeded to France, and with which he was serving when killed.

An Officer under whom he was serving wrote:
" He was shot at our most dangerous job, i.e., Observation Officer, and had just finished an excellent piece of work, having silenced a German Battery."

The following account of the circumstances was received :—
" Sergeant Harrell was by his side when he was killed. They were observing the fire of the Battery from a position in the advanced infantry trenches. . . . A telephone wire connected him with his battery, which was about three-quarters of a mile further west, and

he was telephoning the results of the firing. He and the Sergeant went to this position at 11.30 a.m. on December 20th; the Sergeant was grazed in the hand by a rifle bullet. He said something about the Sergeant being the first man in the battery to be hit when his sentence was cut short and he fell against the Sergeant . . . who saw he had been hit just above the right eye, by a bullet, killing him on the spot."

The Madras Correspondent of the Calcutta " Statesman " wrote :—" Lieutenant A. A. M. Charles, 97th Battalion, Royal Field Artillery, who has been killed in action, is well remembered as a fearless and dashing rider and bold sportsman."

Captain Charles was gazetted Captain after his death, but to rank from the 18th December, 1914, and was mentioned in Sir John French's Despatch of 31st May, 1915.

LIEUTENANT ST. JOHN A. CHARLTON, 4th (attd. 1st) BATTN. BEDFORDSHIRE REGIMENT,

who was killed in action at the Battle of the Aisne on the 25th—26th October, 1914, was the only son of St. John Charlton and Elisabeth B r o n n e n, daughter of Hugh Robert and Lady Florentia Hughes, of Kinniel Park, North Wales.

He was born on the 17th November, 1889, and was educated at Eton. He became Lieutenant in his Regiment in December, 1911. He was a member of the Junior Carlton Club, and was fond of shooting and hunting.

MAJOR PAUL ALFRED CHARRIER, 2nd BATTN. ROYAL MUNSTER FUSILIERS,

who is believed to have been killed in action near Etreux, France, on the 27th August, 1914, was the only son of the late Mr. Paul Antoine Charrier, of D i n a p o r e, India. He was born on the 3rd December, 1868, and joined the Royal Munster Fusiliers from the Militia in June, 1890, becoming Lieutenant in April, 1892. From April to November, 1899, he was employed with the

Central African Regiment, and from December, 1900, to October, 1901—having been promoted Captain in March, 1900—he was Adjutant of the West African Regiment. While holding this position he saw active service in West Africa, being present at operations in Ashanti, where he was slightly wounded, and for his services was mentioned in Despatches " London Gazette," 8th March, 1901.

He also served in the South African War, being employed with the Imperial Yeomanry, and was present at operations in Cape Colony in May, 1902, for which he received the Queen's medal with two clasps. Major Charrier again saw service in 1903-04 in East Africa, where he was employed on the Staff (Special Service Officer), and on Transport duty from November, 1903, receiving the medal with clasp.

CAPTAIN A. C. CHARRINGTON, 1st (ROYAL) DRAGOONS,

was born on the 17th May, 1882, at Marden Ash, Ongar, Essex, the son of N. Edward Charrington, Esq., of Bures Manor, Reigate.

He was educated at Eton, and entered the King's Royal Rifle Militia in 1902, being transferred to the 1st (Royal) Dragoons in 1903, and obtaining his Troop in April, 1910. In India he served on the Staff of the Viceroy, Lord Minto, and of the Commander-in-Chief, Sir O'Moore Creagh.

Captain Charrington—who was known to his friends as " Kid "—was a fine horseman; he won many races in India, rode the winner of the Army Cup in 1909 and 1910, of the Grand Annual in 1910, and the Indian Grand National 1911. He made a wonderful record at Simla in 1909, where he rode in twenty races in four days, winning thirteen, coming in second in three and third in one.

He was instantaneously killed by bullet or shell on the 20th October, 1914, and was buried in the cemetery at Ypres.

Captain Charrington was not married.

CAPTAIN HUGH CLERVAUX CHAYTOR, 26th KING GEORGE'S OWN LIGHT CAVALRY,

second son of the late Mr. Clervaux Darley Chaytor, of Spennithorne Hall, Yorkshire, was born there on the 28th November, 1883. He was a cousin of Sir Edmund Chaytor, Bart., of Croft.

He was educated at Clifton College, and the R.M.C., Sandhurst. On passing out of the

latter into the Indian Army he was attached for the usual probationary period of a year to the Middlesex Regiment, joining the 26th King George's Own Light Cavalry in April, 1904, and getting his step in 1905. In February, 1911, he became Adjutant of his Regiment, and in January, 1912, became Captain. In 1913–14 he was Commandant of the Bodyguard of the Governor of Madras.

While in India he did much pig-sticking, and was also in his regimental polo team, helping to win many tournaments. When the war with Germany broke out, he was at home on leave and at once applied to be sent on active service, being attached to the 11th Hussars. He was killed in action at Messines on the 31st October, 1914.

2nd LIEUTENANT GREVILLE ARTHUR BAGOT CHESTER, 3rd (attd. 1st) BATTN. NORTH STAFFORDSHIRE REGIMENT,

was born on the 3rd April, 1891, at Pyrton, Oxfordshire, the son of the Rev. John Greville Chester, Vicar of Gilling, and grandson of Colonel C. M. Chester, D.L., J.P., Chicheley Hall, Newport Pagnall, Bucks. He was educated at Rossall School, and St. John's College, Oxford.

He was appointed to the 3rd (Reserve) Battalion North Staffordshire Regiment in February, 1913, and on the outbreak of the war was attached for service to the 1st Battalion of the Regiment.

He was killed in action on the 13th October, 1914, during an attack on a German rear guard at Oultersteen, a small village near Hazebrouck. His company was in front and carried out the chief attack. The Colonel of his battalion and the Captain of his company testify that " he behaved exceedingly well and showed not only courage but common sense in leading his platoon. . . . He had the makings of a first rate officer—willing, keen, and reliable." He was not married.

CAPTAIN EDMUND BASIL CHICHESTER, 3rd BATTN. THE BUFFS (EAST KENT REGIMENT),

who died on the 7th November, 1914, of wounds received in action, was the fifth son of the late Major Newton Charles Chichester and Mrs. Chichester, of Clayton House, Lechdale.

He was born on the 6th February, 1881. and joined the Army in 1900, retiring from the East Kent Regiment with the rank of Lieutenant in September, 1909. He served in the South African War, being present at operations in Cape Colony, the Orange River Colony, and the Transvaal, receiving the Queen's medal with five clasps.

One of Captain Chichester's brothers, Captain C. O. Chichester, is now serving in the Oxfordshire Light Infantry, and one, Lieutenant J. F. Chichester, is in the Royal Navy ; two of his brothers died on active service, one in 1898, and the other killed in action in Somaliland in 1902.

CAPTAIN HENRY ARTHUR CHICHESTER, 3rd BATTN. DEVONSHIRE REGIMENT (SPECIAL RESERVE),

was born on the 17th August, 1882, at Stowford House, Swimbridge, North Devon, son of the late Colonel Chichester, of Kerswell House, Broad Clyst, near Exeter, and of Stowford House, North Devon, and Mrs. Chichester, of Woodhayne, Culmstock, Devon. He was a first cousin of Brigadier-General A. A. Chichester, now serving in the war.

Captain Chichester was educated at Crewkerne Grammar School, and joined the Exeter Volunteers in 1900 ; the following year he joined the Militia, serving for twelve months in Jersey, and then proceeded to South Africa with the 3rd Battalion East Yorkshire Regiment, to take part in the Boer War, for which he received the medal. He afterwards joined the Special Reserve and was called up for duty on the outbreak of the war with Germany, on the 7th August, 1914, and was killed in action at Canteleux, near La Bassée. on the 20th October, 1914.

CAPTAIN ROBERT GUY INCLEDON CHICHESTER, 2nd BATTN. HIGHLAND LIGHT INFANTRY,

who was killed in action near Ypres on the 13th November, 1914, leaving a widow, was the second son of the Rev. Richard Chichester, Rector of Drewsteignton, Devon, and was born on the 28th January, 1873.

He joined the Highland Light Infantry from the Militia in May, 1895, becoming Lieutenant in September, 1898. He was on active service on the North-West Frontier of India in 1897–98 with the Malakand and Buner Field Forces, and was present at the attack and capture of the Tanga Pass, receiving the medal with clasp. In the South African War he was employed with the Mounted Infantry, and was present at operations in Cape Colony, January to March, 1901, Orange River Colony 1901–02, and in the Transvaal in April and May, 1902, receiving the Queen's medal with five clasps. He was promoted Captain in March, 1901.

LIEUTENANT WILLIAM MALCOLM CHISHOLM, 1st BATTN. EAST LANCASHIRE REGT.,

born on the 25th February, 1892, at 139, Macquarie Street, Sydney, New South Wales, Australia, was the son of Dr. William and Isabel Chisholm, and great great-grandson of Gabriel Louis Marie Huon de Keriliau, of St. Pol-de-Léon, Brittany.

He was educated at Sydney Grammar School, and the R.M.C., Sandhurst; at Sydney he was a Lieutenant in the Senior Cadets of the Grammar School, and afterwards a Lieutenant in the Scottish Rifles, Sydney. He entered Sandhurst in 1911, and on passing out was gazetted to the East Lancashire Regiment in September, 1912; he became Lieutenant in December, 1913.

The 1st Battalion East Lancashire Regiment formed part of the 11th Infantry Brigade, IVth Division of the Expeditionary Force, which Lieutenant Chisholm accompanied to France. He was shot through the abdomen on the 26th August, 1914, and died on the following day at Ligny, France, where he was buried. He had only detrained at Le Cateau at about 5 p.m. on Tuesday, the 25th August, was in action at 4 a.m. on the 26th, and was wounded at about 3 p.m. that day.

LIEUTENANT GEORGE HENRY CHISNALL, ROYAL ARMY MEDICAL CORPS, attd. for duty to the 1st BATTN. CAMERON HIGHLANDERS,

was born at Great Bentley, Essex, on the 4th April, 1886, the son of Charles Henry Chisnall, of Frating Abbey, near Colchester. He was educated at Framlingham College, and the London Hospital Medical College; he held the degrees of M.B., B.S. London, and the diploma of F.R.C.S., England.

He volunteered for active service on the 6th August, 1914, immediately on the outbreak of the Great War, and left England on the 14th August. He was wounded by shell fire on the 23rd October, while attending to a wounded man in the open, during an engagement between the villages of Bixschoote and Langemarck, and died the next day. He was buried in Elverdinghe churchyard.

Lieutenant Chisnall was a plucky rider with the Essex and Suffolk foxhounds. He was not married.

2nd LIEUTENANT ARTHUR GRANT BOURNE CHITTENDEN, 2nd BATTN. THE MANCHESTER REGIMENT,

who was reported as having died of wounds received in action, in France, the actual date of his death not being known, was the youngest son of the late Charles Grant Thomas Faithfull Chittenden, and of Mrs. Chittenden, Steyning, Sussex.

Second Lieutenant Chittenden, who was only twenty years old when he died, was gazetted to the Manchester Regiment on the 24th January, 1914.

CAPTAIN SIR MONTAGU AUBREY ROWLEY CHOLMELEY, 4th BARONET, (of Easton Hall, Grantham, and Norton, Place, Lincoln), 3rd BATTN. (RESERVE OF OFFICERS), GRENADIER GUARDS,

who was killed in action near La Bassée on the 24th December, 1914, was born on the 12th June, 1876, in London, and lived at Easton Hall, Grantham. He succeeded his father in 1904. After his education at Eton he joined the South Lincoln Militia, and from that regiment entered the Grenadier Guards in 1896. Two years later he became Lieutenant, and in 1904 obtained his Company. While in the Guards he was Master of the Household Brigade Draghounds at Windsor from 1899 until he went to South Africa. He was particularly fond of hunting, being a fine and fearless rider. He was Master of the Burton Hounds from 1912 to 1914 and won the Burton Hunt Members' Race in 1913 on "Cardinal." He was also fond of shooting and fishing.

He was on active service in the South African War, and also in the Expedition to Khartoum, for which he held the British and Egyptian medals. Retiring from the active list of the Army, he entered the Reserve of Officers as a Captain in 1906, and in civil life took an interest in all local affairs of his county, being a member of the Lincolnshire Territorial Force Association, Chairman of the Grantham and District Agricultural Association in 1906, and had been Vice-President of the Lincolnshire Agricultural Society since 1907, and Chairman of the Lincolnshire Chamber of Agriculture, on the Council of which body he continued to serve after his period of office as Chairman had expired. He entered the Kesteven County Council without opposition in 1907, and was also a member of the Grantham Board of Guardians and Rural District Council, and was a J.P. for the Parts of Kesteven. He was also deeply interested in the Boy Scout Movement, and, as Chief Commissioner of the organisation in Lincolnshire, rendered it highly valuable service. On the eve of his departure for the front he wrote a characteristic letter to the Scouts of Lincolnshire, expressing a sense of his good fortune in being able to go where he knew they would all wish to be, and urging them to respond loyally to their country's call when occasion arose.

On the outbreak of the war with Germany he was called up for service with the 3rd Battalion of his regiment, taking precedence as Captain from the 6th August, 1914. The following account of his death was received from an officer of the Grenadier Guards :—" Captain Cholmeley was in command of No. 1 Company, 2nd Battalion Grenadier Guards, and they were attacked in the trenches on the 24th December. The Germans blew up one of the trenches further along the line, so that they could fire down his line of trench. Captain Cholmeley during an attack rushed forward towards the flank of the company which was threatened, and was shot through the head and killed instantaneously."

He married in 1903, Mabel Janetta, eldest daughter of Montagu Richard Waldo Sibthorp, Canwick Hall, Lincoln, and left two children, Hugh John Francis Sibthorp, born February, 1906, and Rosamund Mary Edith.

CAPTAIN CHARLES ALMERIC JOHN CHOLMONDELEY, 2nd BATTN. BORDER REGIMENT,

who was killed in action on the 28th October, 1914, was the younger son of the late Lord Henry Vere Cholmondeley, and grandson of the third Marquess of Cholmondeley, and was born on the 5th March, 1880. After serving nearly four months with the embodied Militia he joined the Border Regiment in April, 1900, becoming Lieutenant in January, 1902, and Captain in April, 1910.

On war being declared Captain Cholmondeley was serving with his battalion at Dublin. It afterwards formed part of the 20th Brigade, VIIth Division, which embarked for Belgium early in October, and fought in the first battle of Ypres, near which town Captain Cholmondeley was killed.

MAJOR WILLIAM CHARLES CHRISTIE, 1st BATTN. ROYAL WARWICKSHIRE REGIMENT,

was the son of the late Mr. John Robert Christie, Shipowner, of Cardiff. He was born on the 13th December, 1872, and was educated at Rugby, where he was in Elsee House, entering the School in 1887. There he proved himself an all-round athlete, setting up a number of records for the long-distance runs for which the public school is famous, and winning the well-known " Crick " run (12¼ miles) twice in succession, in 1890 and 1891 ; this in addition to obtaining honours at football and gymnastics. From Rugby he entered the R.M.C., Sandhurst, thirty-fifth out of eleven hundred competitors, passing out fourth in the honour list, and again represented his College for football (being Captain of the Rugby football team), and also for athletic sports against Woolwich.

He joined the Royal Warwickshire Regiment in October, 1893, becoming Lieutenant in February 1898. In that year he served in the Nile Expedition, being present at the battles of Atbara and Khartoum, for which he was mentioned in Despatches, "London Gazette," 30th September, 1898, received the Egyptian medal with two clasps, and the fourth class of the Medjidieh. During this campaign he acted as Orderly Officer to the late General Wauchope, and later as Galloper to General Gatacre.

He next saw active service in the South African War, where he was employed with the Mounted Infantry ; he was present at operations in the Orange Free State in the early part of 1900, including the actions at the Vet and Zand Rivers ; at operations in the Transvaal in May and June, 1900, including actions near Johannesburg, Pretoria and Diamond Hill ; operations in the Transvaal, East of Pretoria, including the action at Belfast. For his services he was mentioned in Despatches, "London Gazette," 29th July, 1902, was given his Brevet Majority (August, 1902), and received the Queen's medal with five clasps, and the King's medal with two clasps. From 1904 to 1907 he was an Adjutant of Militia, and in November, 1912, was appointed Adjutant (attached to General Staff) of the Officers' Training Corps, Birmingham University, Bristol University, and the Royal Agricultural College, Cirencester. He was promoted Substantive Major in November, 1912.

Major Christie was the author of a text book on Tactics, which is widely used by Officers' Training Corps, and has reached its fifth edition. His recreations were steeplechase riding, hunting, and polo.

For his services in the Great War he was twice mentioned in Sir John French's Despatches, 8th October, 1914, and 14th January, 1915. He was killed on the 13th October, 1914, while leading an attack to the right of the village of Meteren on the Belgian Frontier, having been shot in six places. The Officer Commanding the 1st Battalion Royal Warwickshire Regiment, wrote :—

" Charles Christie was one of the bravest soldiers in the British Army and his loss to us is irreparable. As my Second in Command during the past two months, he has been simply invaluable."

Major Christie married Florence Violet, daughter of William Vernon Biden, of Gosport, Hants.

MAJOR JOHN CHRYSTIE, ROYAL GARRISON ARTILLERY, 3rd SIEGE BATTERY, 3rd DIVISION, was the second son of Colonel G. Chrystie, Indian Army, who served in the Indian Mutiny, and Helen Anne Thomasine Chrystie, née Myers, and was born at Mangalore, India, on 9th March, 1872.

Major Chrystie's great-uncles, Lieutenant John Chrystie, R.N., and Captain Thomas Chrystie, R.N., served under Nelson ; the former was on the " Victory " immediately before Trafalgar, but was transferred on promotion ; the latter was at Trafalgar in H.M.S. " Defiance." His twin brother, Major George Chrystie, 25th Cavalry, Frontier Force, Indian Army, was killed in a raid on the North-West Frontier of India on the 2nd May, 1913.

Major Chrystie was educated at Surrey County School, and Portsmouth Grammar School, and joined the Royal Artillery from the R.M.A. Woolwich, in 1891, becoming Lieutenant in 1894, Captain in 1899, and Major in 1911. He served in India, and on the West Coast of Africa, and received the Delhi Durbar medal, 1903, being on the Staff for the Durbar. From 1905–07 he served as Adjutant of Volunteers.

He was killed in the Great War on the 17th November, 1914, when evening was closing in, by a shell from a German heavy gun, which exploded close to him and rendered him unconscious, death occurring soon after.

Major Chrystie was a keen soldier and sportsman, enjoying pig-sticking and big game shooting. He married, in January, 1913, Mignonne Muriel Maude, only daughter of Mr. C. L. Bruce Cumming, Indian Civil Service (retired), and left one daughter, Leslie Mignonne Comyn, born 6th June, 1914.

CAPTAIN STEPHEN HENRY CHRISTY, D.S.O., late LIEUTENANT 20th HUSSARS, RESERVE OF OFFICERS, was the youngest son of the late Mr. Stephen Christy, of Highfield, Bramall, Cheshire.

He was born in 1879 and was educated at Harrow (Mr. B. Smith's, 1893–97), and Christ

Church, Oxford. He joined the 20th Hussars in 1899, and took part in the South African

War, being on the Staff as Signalling Officer from March to May, 1902, and was present at operations in the Transvaal and in the Orange River Colony from January to April, 1902. He received the Queen's medal with four clasps. Captain Christy also served in West Africa (Northern Nigeria) in 1903, taking part in the Sokoto-Burmi operations, during which he was slightly wounded. For his services he was mentioned in Despatches ("London Gazette," 24th January, 1905), was awarded the D.S.O., and received the medal with clasp.

At the beginning of the war he rejoined his regiment with the rank of Captain, on the 16th August, 1914, and was killed in action on the 3rd September, 1914, at Ussy-sur-Marne.

He married in 1905 a daughter of the late Mr. W. Chapell-Hodge, of Pounds, South Devon, and retired from the active list of the Army in 1906, voluntarily entering the Reserve of Officers. After retiring he became Master of the South Shropshire Foxhounds.

LIEUTENANT CHALLONER FRANCIS TREVOR CHUTE, 2nd BATTN. ROYAL MUNSTER FUSILIERS,

third son of the late Mr. F. B. Chute, of Chute Hall, Tralee County Kerry, and of Mrs. Chute, 22 Ashburton Road, Southsea, was born on the 2nd April, 1885.

He joined the Royal Munster Fusiliers from the Militia in November, 1905, be-

coming Lieutenant in February, 1908, and became known as " Chuty " among the officers of his battalion.

He was killed in action on the 27th August 1914, the following abbreviated account of the circumstances having been received from Captain Jervis, the senior surviving officer of the battalion, Lieutenant Chute having been in charge of the machine guns :—

" The Regiment was left in a somewhat exposed position, and Lieutenant Chute, with his guns, covered the withdrawal of Captain Jervis's Company at mid-day. It was pouring

with rain, and with entire disregard to personal comfort, he lay down in six inches of water to manipulate his guns the better. The Germans were crossing the front, and he never neglected an opportunity of delaying their advance.

" The withdrawal continued through a village, and on the other side he came into action again firing down the road, on both sides of which a company was withdrawing. Owing to the help of Lieutenant Chute's guns, the company got safely through. The enemy was now on three sides, and their artillery opened fire. Lieutenant Chute brought his machine guns back at the gallop along the road under a positive hail of lead. It was a splendid feat and was successfully accomplished, and once again the guns were placed in position. We were now completely surrounded and Lieutenant Chute crossed the road to try and find a target to aim at. As he crossed he was shot in the right side and thigh and fell dead." Captain Jervis went on :—" Up to the last he was cheery and full of spirits as ever, in fact the life and soul of the mess. He will leave a large gap not only in the regiment but in each and all of his brother officers' hearts.

" On the 28th August, the Germans allowed a burial party to go out, and they found Lieutenant Chute, who was buried in a grave with eight other officers of the battalion."

Lieutenant Chute married, in June, 1911, Maud Emily St. Clare, only child of the late Edward O'B. Hobson, and left two children.

2nd LIEUTENANT TREVOR JOHN CLANCEY, 2nd BATTN. THE BORDER REGIMENT,

who was killed in action on the 24th October, 1914—the War Office Casualty List giving the date as the 28th October —was born in June, 1893.

He was educated at Stoneyhurst, and the R.M.C., Sandhurst, out of which he

passed at the end of 1912, and in February, 1913, he received his commission as Second Lieutenant in the Border Regiment, being posted to the 2nd Battalion, with which he proceeded to France soon after war was declared. In the Great War his Battalion formed part of the VIIth Division, and on it fell the brunt of the fighting in the earlier stages of the first battle of Ypres. Second Lieutenant Clancey was killed by shrapnel a short distance south-east of Ypres.

LIEUTENANT JOHN EDWARD LANGTON CLARKE, ROYAL FIELD ARTILLERY,

was the eldest son of Lieutenant - Colonel Sir Edward H. St. Lawrence Clarke, fourth Baronet, of Rossmore, Co. Cork ; he was born at Barkhill, Aigburth, Liverpool, on the 22nd November, 1889, and was educated at Clifton College, and the Royal Military Academy, Woolwich.

Lieutenant Clarke joined the 50th Battery, XXXIVth Brigade, Royal Field Artillery, as Second Lieutenant, in July, 1909, and was promoted Lieutenant in July, 1912. During the summer of 1914 he acted as Extra A.D.C. to Lieutenant-General Sir Horace Smith-Dorrien commanding Southern Command.

He accompanied his Battery to France in the Great War, and, for his services up to the battle of the Aisne, was mentioned in Sir John French's first Despatch and awarded the distinction of the Military Cross, his name appearing in the list of 1st January, 1915, after his death on the field of battle, which occurred while he was in action at Moussy-sur-Aisne on the 14th September, 1914.

LIEUTENANT MORDAUNT EDWARD LEONARD HANNAM CLARKE, 3rd BATTN, WORCESTERSHIRE REGT.,

son of Colonel F. C. Hannam Clarke, C.M.G., R.A., Surveyor-General of Ceylon, was born at Bath, Somerset, on the 30th October, 1884.

He was educated at Marlborough, and University College, Oxford, and after serving for a year in the Kent Artillery, was gazetted to the Worcestershire Regiment in May, 1907, becoming Lieutenant in October, 1910. He was a keen cricketer, and was very musical indeed : played the violin and sang well, having an excellent baritone voice.

He was shot through the head by a bullet from a shrapnel shell at Caudry, near Cambrai, on the 26th August, 1914, during the retirement from Mons. He was carried to a civil hospital near, where he died without recovering consciousness, and is believed to be buried there.

CAPTAIN GEORGE CLAYHILLS, D.S.O., 1st BATTN. EAST LANCASHIRE REGIMENT,

was born at Darlington, the son of Thomas Clayhills, of Invergowrie, Forfarshire, and a nephew of the late Captain Clayhills-Henderson, R.N., of Invergowrie, and of Colonel Clayhills-Henderson, who served in the Crimean War with the 93rd Highlanders.

Educated at Cheltenham, and Trinity Hall, Cambridge, he received his commission in the East Lancashire Regiment from the Militia in January, 1899. From April, 1906—April, 1909, he was Adjutant of his Battalion.

While serving in the South African war with the 8th Mounted Infantry, he was present at the actions of Poplar Grove, Driefontein, Karee Siding, Paardeberg, Vet River, Zand River, and those near Johannesburg and Pretoria. For his services he was twice mentioned in Despatches, awarded the D.S.O., and received the Queen's medal with four clasps, and the King's medal with two clasps. He obtained his Company in 1908.

In the Great War his Battalion formed part of the 11th Infantry Brigade, IVth Division, and with it Captain Clayhills was present in the retirement from Mons and the subsequent advance, including the battles of the Marne and the Aisne.

He was killed in action at the battle of Ypres, while his battalion was holding the line three miles north of Armentières, in Belgium, on 2nd November, 1914.

MAJOR H. T. CLIFF, 3rd BATTN. THE PRINCE OF WALES'S OWN (WEST YORKSHIRE REGIMENT),

was killed in action on the 13th October 1914.

He entered his regiment as 2nd Lieutenant in October, 1900, becoming Lieutenant in April, 1901, and Captain in August of the same year.

He served in the Mediterranean during the South African War, and received the medal. He became Major in the 3rd Battalion of his regiment in May, 1913, and was attached to the 1st Battalion when he was killed.

LIEUTENANT the Honble. ARCHER WINDSOR-CLIVE, 3rd BATTN. COLDSTREAM GUARDS,

who was killed in action at Landrecies on the night of the 25th August, 1914, was the third son of the Earl of Plymouth and was born on the 6th November, 1890. He was educated at Eton, where he was in the XI for two years, and at Trinity College, Cambridge. His commission as Second Lieutenant in the Coldstream Guards dated from the 8th September, 1911, and he was promoted Lieutenant in November, 1913.

He was a member of the Guards' Club and was a keen sportsman.

On the occasion of his death, the Guards were defending the village of Landrecies, successfully held at bay, and eventually drove off a greatly superior force of Germans, thereby playing an important part in securing the safety of the British Army in the retirement from Mons.

CAPTAIN JOHN KEITH CLOTHIER, 2nd BATTN. THE PRINCE OF WALES'S OWN (WEST YORKSHIRE REGIMENT),

who was killed in action on the 6th December, 1914, was the youngest son of Henry Clothier, M.D. (London), of Inner-wyke Manor, Felp-ham, Sussex, and was born at High-gate, Middlesex, where his father formerly practised, on the 25th September, 1881.

He was educated at Highgate School, and the R.M.C., Sandhurst, from which he passed out twelfth, taking the prize for Tactics, and where he was Corporal of his Company. He joined the West Yorkshire Regiment as Second Lieutenant in March, 1901, becoming Lieutenant in September, 1903. He served in the South African war, being present at operations in the Transvaal from June, 1901, to March, 1902, for which he received the Queen's medal with clasp. In 1907 he was employed with the King's African Rifles, with the local rank of Captain, and acted as Adjutant. In the Somaliland operations 1908–10, he did useful service, and was mentioned in Despatches, receiving the medal and clasp. He obtained

his Company in June, 1911, and, on rejoining at Bombo as second in command of the 4th King's African Rifles, was given the temporary rank of Major.

In the summer of 1914, while holding that appointment, he was invalided home, and on the outbreak of the Great War he rejoined his old regiment and volunteered for active service with the Expeditionary Force. For some time he was engaged with a new battalion of the regiment in Yorkshire, but eventually went to the front. He was looking through a loophole in the trenches when he was struck by a bullet in the head, and died about two hours afterwards without recovering consciousness. He was buried at La Visée, a little village south of Armentières.

CAPTAIN ROBERT FRANK CLOTHIER, 13th RAJPUTS (THE SHEKHAWATL REGT.), INDIAN ARMY,

who was killed in action on the 2nd November, 1914, was born on the 7th September, 1884, and received an un-attached Second-Lieutenancy in January, 1904. In March of the follow-ing year he joined the Indian Army, and became Lieu-

tenant in April, 1906. Captain Clothier, who reached that rank in January, 1913, was Adjutant of his regiment when he was killed.

CAPTAIN HENRY CLUTTERBUCK, 1st BATTN. THE KING'S OWN (ROYAL LANCASTER REGIMENT),

was the son of the late James Jacques Clutterbuck, Esq., and was born at Chacewater, Corn-wall, on the 23rd January, 1874. He was educated chiefly at King Edward's School, Birmingham. Captain Clutterbuck enlisted in the Coldstream Guards

in 1893, and after having served in the ranks of that regiment for rather more than seven years, he received a commission as Second Lieutenant in the King's Own Yorkshire Light Infantry in August, 1900. He was given accelerated promotion to Captain into the King's Own Royal Lancaster Regiment in November, 1907. He served in the South African war, 1899–1902, and fought through all the fierce battles which marked Lord Methuen's advance to the relief of Kimberley, including the actions at Belmont, Enslin, Modder River, and Magersfontein. He was present during the operations in the Orange Free State, February to May, 1900, including those at Paardeberg, February 17th—26th; actions at Poplar Grove, Diamond Hill, Driefontein, Karee Siding, Vet River, and Zand River, also the operations in the Transvaal, May to September, 1900, and from November, 1900, to May, 1902. During the latter stages of the war he was attached to the Army Service Corps. He received the Queen's medal with six clasps and the King's medal with two clasps.

Captain Clutterbuck was Adjutant to the King's Own Malta Regiment of Militia from June, 1904 —July, 1909. He served in India and laboured for the welfare of the soldier, and encouraged temperance and thrift, being commended by the Commander-in-Chief in India for this work. He wrote a book of Musketry Lectures in 1913, which was very well reviewed.

He had been appointed Garrison Adjutant at Bordon, from October 1st, 1914, but as war broke out he left for France with his regiment on August 19th, 1914. Captain Clutterbuck was mentioned in Field-Marshal Sir John French's Despatch, October 8th, 1914, for his conspicuous bravery under heavy shell fire and his gallantry in leading bayonet charges. He was killed on the 26th August, 1914, at Haucourt, France, only seven days after he had arrived in that country, and the following account of the circumstances under which he gave his life were furnished by a brother-officer :—

" On the fateful 26th August Captain Clutterbuck and myself were in a village, and about 8·30 p.m. about 150 Germans made a night attack on us. Just when the attack was starting Captain Clutterbuck came up with about 50 men to help me, as things looked bad. Captain Clutterbuck then performed an act of great gallantry : he personally led 15 men to drive about 50 of the Germans away from a church where our wounded were. They called upon Captain Clutterbuck to surrender, but he would not, and was then instantly killed. This act of Captain Clutterbuck's was most gallant. He would not entertain the idea of anybody doing the noble work which he did, thereby saving the lives of most of us. Nobody could have died a more noble death."

Captain Clutterbuck married Cora Gwendoline Rafaela, youngest daughter of the late Gerard Myburgh, Esq., of Orange Grove, Cape Town, Consul-General of the Netherlands in South Africa.

2nd LIEUTENANT WILLIAM HUMPHREY COGHLAN, ROYAL FIELD ARTILLERY,

born on the 9th July, 1890, was the son of Colonel Charles Coghlan, C.B., D.L., of Ashfield, Headingley Hill, Leeds. He was educated at the Oratory School, Edgbaston, near Birmingham, of which he was Captain for two years, and then went to University College, Oxford. He joined the West Yorkshire Brigade, Royal Field Artillery (Territorial Force), and, after serving a year at Woolwich, received a commission in the Royal Field Artillery and joined the 11th Battery at Kildare.

In the war he fought from Mons to Le Cateau, where, after being wounded many times, he was killed in action on the evening of the 26th August, 1914.

LIEUTENANT LANGTON SACHEVERELL COKE, J.P., 1st BATTN. IRISH GUARDS, RESERVE OF OFFICERS,

owner of Brookhill Hall, Alfreton, Derbyshire. was the eldest son of the late Colonel Coke, J.P., D.L., 4th Light Dragoons, of that place, whom he succeeded in 1913. This property has been in the family direct from father to son for twenty-three generations; one of Lieutenant Coke's ancestors was Sir John Coke, Secretary of State to Charles the First. Lieutenant Coke was born on the 25th January, 1878, and was educated in Germany and France.

He joined the Irish Guards in 1901, after serving for a short time with the Warwickshire Regiment. He was seconded for service with the Egyptian Army for two years, and in 1908 he left his Regiment, joining the Special Reserve. Intending to take up a political career, he obtained the appointment of Private Secretary to Mr. Hobhouse, Postmaster-General in 1913. On the outbreak of the Great War he rejoined his old regiment, and went to France on the 11th September.

He was killed at Klein Zillebeke, near Ypres, on the 31st October, 1914, a critical day on which the Germans nearly broke through our lines.

Lieutenant Coke, who was a member of the Travellers' and Guards' Clubs, was a good big game shot, fisherman, and motorist.

He married in November, 1908, Dorothy Maye,

daughter of Captain George Huntingford, R.N., and left a daughter, Elizabeth Joan, born August, 1909, and a son, Roger Sacheverell, born October, 1912, who succeeds to the Brookhill estate.

LIEUTENANT JOHN CADWALLADER COKER, 2nd BATTN. SOUTH WALES BORDERERS,

who was killed in action at the Battle of the Aisne on the 26th September, 1914, was the youngest son of Colonel L. E. and Mrs. Coker, of Bicester House, Oxfordshire.

He was born on the 20th January, 1887, and joined the South Wales Borderers in August, 1908, becoming Lieutenant in June, 1911.

MAJOR LAWRENCE ROBERT VAUGHAN COLBY, 1st BATTN. GRENADIER GUARDS,

who was killed on the 24th October, 1914, was the only son of Mr. and Mrs. Colby of Ffynone, Pembrokeshire. He was born on the 3rd April, 1880, and educated at Eton, joining the Grenadier Guards in February, 1899, and becoming Lieutenant in January, 1900.

He took part in the South African War, being present at operations in the Orange Free State, April to May, 1900 ; Orange River Colony, May to November, 1900, including actions at Biddulphsberg and Wittebergen, and again in the same Colony from the end of 1900 to May, 1902. He received the Queen's and the King's medals, each with two clasps.

He became Captain in September, 1905, and obtained his Majority in September, 1914. He was a member of the Guards' Club and was unmarried.

In the action in which he lost his life, Major Colby was valiantly leading his men in a charge near Gheluvelt, and he was buried in a soldier's grave on the field of battle close to where he fell. For his services in his last fight he was mentioned in Sir John French's Despatch of the 14th January, 1915.

CAPTAIN WILLIAM ELMER REYMES-COLE, 3rd (attd. 2nd) BATTN. ROYAL MUNSTER FUSILIERS,

who was killed in action on the 11th November, 1914, was the eldest son of the late Thomas Elmer Cole, of Doddington, Cambridge, and Wingland, Norfolk. Captain Reymes-Cole served for some years in various Government posts in British East Africa, among them that of District Commissioner at Gondokoro. On account of ill-health he had to give up tropical service, and he then became Agent to the Hemsted Estate in Kent.

When the war broke out he rejoined his old regiment, in which he had become Captain in April, 1906.

LIEUTENANT DONALD M. COLES, 3rd BATTN. NORTHUMBERLAND FUSILIERS (SPECIAL RESERVE),

who was appointed 2nd Lieutenant on probation in June, 1913, was killed in action the 27th October, 1914. He became Lieutenant in September, 1914, and was attached for active service to the 1st Battalion of his regiment.

2nd LIEUTENANT SIDNEY HARCOURT COLES, 6th (attd. to 4th) BATTN. DUKE OF CAMBRIDGE'S OWN (MIDDLESEX REGIMENT),

who was killed in action on the 12th October, 1914, aged 24, was the fourth son of Major and Mrs. Lewis Harcourt Coles, Windsor Road, Denmark Hill.

Second Lieutenant Coles joined the Middlesex Regiment in September, 1913.

CAPTAIN ARTHUR EDWARD JEUNE COLLINS, ROYAL ENGINEERS,

eldest son of the late Arthur Herbert Collins, Esq., Indian Civil Service, was born on the 18th August, 1885, in India.

He was educated at Clifton College, and while there, astonished the cricket world in 1899, at the age of 14, by scoring 628 not out in a Junior House Match between Clarke's House and North Town. When in the Senior School, he was in the 1st Cricket XI., the 1st Football

XV., the 1st racquet pair, and represented the school in featherweight boxing at the Public

Schools Competition at Aldershot. He was Head of his House, and at the age of 17 passed into Woolwich, taking the fourth place in the list of successful candidates.

He joined the Royal Engineers in December, 1904, and at the age of 21 went to India, where he was stationed till April, 1914, when he came home and was posted to Aldershot.

In India he played polo, racquets, and tennis, but on returning to England took up cricket again, playing for the Royal Engineers at Aldershot and at Lords against the Royal Artillery.

In August, 1914, he went to the front with the 5th Field Company, Royal Engineers.

On the 11th November his Company, of which he was then in command (his Senior Officers having been killed or wounded), was called up to help thrust the enemy back at Polygon Wood, near Ypres. It was whilst signalling for reinforcements during this action that he was killed.

He was mentioned in Sir John French's Despatch of the 14th January, 1915, and was gazetted Captain after his death, to date from the 30th October, 1914.

Captain Collins, who was a member of the Junior Army and Navy Club, married in April, 1914, Ethel, daughter of the late Stanley Slater, and granddaughter of the late Colonel Slater, 82nd Regiment.

LIEUTENANT BOYCE ANTHONY COMBE, 6th (attd. 4th) BATTN. ROYAL FUSILIERS (CITY OF LONDON REGIMENT),

was the second son of Harvey Trewythen Brabazon Combe, late 3rd Battalion, Royal Sussex Regiment, of Oaklands, Sedlescombe, Sussex.

He was born in 1889 and was educated at Cheltenham. He became Lieutenant in his regiment in June, 1913, and was killed in action on the 11th November, 1914.

LIEUTENANT S. B. COMBE, NORTH IRISH HORSE (SPECIAL RESERVE),

who was reported in October, 1914, to have been missing, was since shown in the official lists as having been killed in action on the 1st October, 1914.

He was the third son of Abram Combe, J.P., Donaghcloney House, Donaghcloney, Co. Down, and Master of the Co. Down Staghounds, and was born on the 20th January, 1880. He was educated at Rugby and in France, and became Lieutenant in the North Irish Horse in April, 1913.

He was a member of the Ulster Club, Belfast, and the Royal Ulster Yacht Club, and was fond of polo and hunting.

The following particulars were obtained from his Major, Lord Massereene, and a brother officer :—He received Staff orders to ascertain if the Germans were holding a position near Condé Bridge on the Aisne. Knowing the great danger, he left his men in hiding and proceeded alone on foot. He was discovered and fell fighting, the shots revealing the presence of the enemy.

From the German officer, by whose men he was shot, it was subsequently learned that, admiring his pluck, the Germans gave him ceremonial burial inside their lines at Condé, and marked his grave by a cross bearing his name and the words " Pro Patria."

LIEUTENANT HENRY BLIGH FORTESCUE PARNELL, 5th BARON CONGLETON, AND A BARONET OF IRELAND, 2nd BATTN. GRENADIER GUARDS,

was the first member of the House of Peers to be killed in the Great War; he succeeded his father in 1906.

Lieutenant Lord Congleton was the eldest son of Major-General Lord Congleton, C.B., a distinguished officer, and was born on the 6th September, 1890, at Annerville, Clonmel, when his father was in command of that District ; he was a grandson of a naval officer who had five sons in the Army and Navy. He was also related to the poet Parnell, a friend of Addison, et al., and was a distant cousin of Charles Stewart Parnell, the famous Irish politician.

He was educated at Eton (Somerville's) and New College, Oxford, where he took very good second class Honours for History; and was also Master of the New College and Magdalen Beagles. He joined the Grenadier Guards as a University candidate in 1912, but his having taken honours at the University gave him many months' seniority, and his commission was antedated to July, 1911. He was promoted Lieutenant in March, 1913.

Lord Congleton was mentioned in Sir John French's Despatch of the 14th January, 1915, for gallant conduct and skilful handling of his platoon against terrific odds on the 6th November, 1914, thereby saving the British line at that point. He was killed in action near Ypres on the 10th November, 1914, and was buried in Zillebeke Churchyard.

Lord Congleton was a gifted and many-sided man : a keen sportsman, a good shot (small and big game), and, as a traveller, he had hoped to go with Stackhouse to the Antarctic. He wrote articles in magazines and in " The Field " on sporting subjects over the signature of " Con." He was a polo player, an ardent Tariff Reformer and student of social problems, but had joined no political party, though he was often in the House of Lords as a listener. He also took an active interest in Rural Housing, etc. By his death his family, his regiment, and his country sustained a great loss. Memoirs of his career have been published in " The Field," " The World," " Truth," " Country Life," " British Sports and Sportsmen," " The Tramp," and in several of the daily papers.

Lord Congleton was not married, and his brother, the Hon. J. B. M. Parnell, a Lieutenant in the Navy, succeeds him in the title.

LIEUTENANT SYDNEY DENNIS CONNELL, 1st BATTN. THE MANCHESTER REGIMENT,

born on the 11th June, 1894, at Allahabad, India, was the son of Major Connell, Royal Horse Artillery, and Mrs. Connell. His elder brother, Lieutenant V. J. A. Connell, is in the 13th Lancers of the Indian Army.

He was educated at Queen Elizabeth's School, Cranbrook, from 1908–12, where he won his football and cricket colours, was in the Bisley Team 1910–12, captain of the Gymnasium and of the Cricket XI in 1912, and represented the School at Aldershot 1911–12. He became a Sergeant in the Officers' Training Corps in 1911. He passed into the R.M.C., Sandhurst, in 1912, and received his commission, on passing out, in the Manchester Regiment, in January, 1914, joining his battalion in India in March, and proceeding to France in August, with the Expeditionary Force.

He was killed on the 28th November, 1914, after successfully destroying a German sap-head in a night attack. The following account of the circumstances was received from the Adjutant of his battalion :—

" Lieutenant Connell was killed just north-east of the cross roads at La Quinque Rue (which is about one mile north-east of Festubert), having most gallantly attacked a sap-head. The sap-head was a double one, and came up to 20 to 25 feet from our fire trench. He went out that night with 20 men, he going with 10 men to one head, and a colour-sergeant with 10 men to the other. They all got in and found the Germans at work and killed 10 of them, two or three escaping down the communicating trench. They then went down the communicating trench, and when coming back along it, found that more Germans had been sleeping in dug-outs at the side. These they also killed as they returned, and it is estimated that they accounted for over 40 altogether. When on the way back, the Germans opened a machine gun on the party he was leading. He and five men were killed and three wounded. . . . We were most awfully cut up about it."

He was mentioned in Sir John French's Despatch of the 14th January, 1915, for his services in the Great War.

CAPTAIN (TEMPORARY MAJOR) PETER MARTIN CONNELLAN, 1st BATTN. HAMPSHIRE REGIMENT,

who was killed in action on the 20th October, 1914, was the only son of Major J. H. Connellam, D.L., Coolmore, Co. Kilkenny, Ireland.

He was born at Sale, Cheshire, on the 19th February, 1882, was educated at Newton Abbot College and at Harrow, and he entered the Army, unattached, in January, 1901, joining the Hampshire Regiment as Second Lieutenant in March of that year, becoming Lieutenant in November, 1903. In that and the following year he took part in operations in the interior near Aden, acting as Brigade Signalling Officer to the Aden Boundary Delimitation Column. From 1906 to 1909 he was Adjutant of his battalion, having become Captain in May, 1907, and subsequently was appointed Adjutant, Special Reserve, in January, 1911. He was awarded the Royal Humane Society's medal for saving the life of a drowning soldier in 1909. He was very fond of hunting, salmon fishing, and tennis, and played in his Regimental Polo Team.

He rejoined his battalion in 1914, went to the front with it as part of the IVth Division, and was present all through the retirement from Mons. For some weeks he was in command of his battalion during the Battles of the Marne and the Aisne, being mentioned in Sir John French's Despatches of the 8th October, 1914, and 14th January, 1915. He was recommended by his Brigadier for promotion and reward.

He married in 1911, Winifred, third daughter of the late Arthur Niblett, Esq., of Haresfield Court, Gloucestershire.

CAPTAIN CECIL ALLEN TAYLOUR CONYNGHAM, M.B., ROYAL ARMY MEDICAL CORPS,

who was killed in action on the 4th November, 1914, was the fourth surviving son of Mr. Henry Conyngham, of Dublin, and was born on the 11th May, 1883. He was educated at St. Andrew's College, and at Trinity College, Dublin, where he obtained his degree of M.B., joining the Army in July, 1907. He was a keen athlete, and swam for Trinity, when they won the Senior Water Polo Cup in 1903 ; he was also in the Wanderers Rugby Football Cup Team, when they won the Leinster Senior Cup in 1906.

Promoted Captain in January, 1911, he was stationed at Bangalore when the war broke out, and was sent to British East Africa, acting as Medical Officer to the Loyal North Lancashire Regiment. The Officer Commanding the 2nd Battalion of that regiment gave the following account of his death :—

" Captain C. T. Conyngham, R.A.M.C., was attached to this battalion, and was killed in action at Tanga, German East Africa, on 4th November, 1914, while attending our wounded under fire. He behaved with great courage under very trying and dangerous circumstances, and was mentioned by me for devotion to duty in my Report.

" We were unable to bury any of our killed, as the action was a reverse, and I conclude the Germans buried them all close to Tanga Town, where the fight was. . . . Your son was much liked by all of us, both professionally and socially. Please accept our deep sympathy in your great loss."

Another more detailed account said :—

" With his regiment he advanced from the beach towards the town of Tanga, which was partly occupied. The heavy fire to which the battalion was subjected is evidenced by the casualty list, as the regiment lost, I think 146 men killed and wounded. During the course of the second day we were unable to hold, the town, as the Germans had such a preponderance of machine guns ; the Loyal North Lancashires, therefore, fell back and occupied a position near a railway embankment. There were several men on the railway line who were wounded, and your brother most gallantly climbed down the steep bank and attended to them. It was under such conditions that he was killed. Had he survived . . . he would most certainly have been singled out for distinction, as all ranks spoke in very glowing terms of his coolness and gallantry. I heard from the German Commandant that all the men killed down on the railway line were buried in the ' Shamba,' on the outskirt of the town. I had an opportunity of finding this out, as I was myself taken prisoner with some of our wounded. I am afraid, therefore, I can give you no hope of his having survived. Conyngham was a fine officer and a very gallant gentleman. and he was killed actually at his work."

LIEUTENANT CHARLES ROLLO COOCH, 2nd BATTN. THE BORDER REGIMENT,

was born at Leamington on the 3rd October, 1894, the son of Major C. E. H. Cooch, Reserve of Officers, the Border Regiment, and Mrs. Cooch. He was a grandson of Colonel Charles Cooch, M.V.O., the King's Bodyguard, and late of the 62nd Regiment, and a great-nephew of General Robert Rollo Gillespie, C.B.

Lieutenant Cooch was educated at the Victoria College, Jersey, from 1904—8, when he went to the Imperial Service College, Windsor, till 1913, entering the R.M.C., Sandhurst, in February, 1914. He played hockey for the Imperial Service College in 1913, and was also in the Rugby Football XV and the School Cricket XI in the years 1912—13.

On 1st October, 1914, he received his commission in the Border Regiment, and was promoted Lieutenant on the 14th December, only three days before his death. He was killed in the trenches near Armentières on the 17th December, 1914, when serving with his battalion.

LIEUTENANT-COLONEL EDWIN BERKELEY COOK, M.V.O., COMMANDING 1st LIFE GUARDS,

who died on the 4th November, 1914, at Sussex House, Regent's Park, from wounds received in action near Messines, Belgium, on the 21st October, 1914, was the elder son of the late Major Edwin Adolphus Cook, 11th Hussars, of Roydon Hall, Tonbridge, Kent, and was born on 4th May, 1869, in London. Lieutenant-Colonel Cook, who was educated at Eton, was gazetted to the 1st Life Guards from the Militia in 1890, becoming Captain in 1894, Major in 1903, and Brevet Lieutenant-Colonel in January, 1909. He served as A.D.C. and Acting Military Secretary to General Sir G. Luck in India from 1898 to 1903, and succeeded to the command of his regiment in November, 1910.

Lieutenant-Colonel Cook, who was a member of the Bachelors' and Arthur's Clubs, was unmarried.

MAJOR MOSTYN EDEN COOKSON, 2nd BATTN. ROYAL SUSSEX REGT.,

of which he was the senior Major, was the son of the late Major William Cookson, 80th Foot, and was born on the 1st January, 1868, at Skipton - in - Craven, Yorkshire.

He joined the Royal Sussex Regiment in February, 1887, becoming Lieutenant in August, 1890, and Captain in May, 1895. He was a member of the Naval and Military Club, and of the M.C.C.

He was killed on the 14th September, 1914, by shrapnel at the Battle of the Aisne.

Major Cookson, who obtained his Majority in September, 1904, married Josephine, daughter of W. G. Pinder, and left no issue.

MAJOR WILLIAM JOSEPH CORCORAN, 5th BATTN. THE DUKE OF CAMBRIDGE'S OWN (MIDDLESEX REGT.),

died on the 25th October, 1914, of wounds received in action. He was educated at St. Paul's School for two years, and then at St. Edmund's College, Ware. He became Captain in the Middlesex Regiment in March, 1906, and his promotion to Major was gazetted after his death, to date from the 7th September, 1914.

LIEUTENANT CECIL VICTOR POWELL CORNELIUS, RESERVE OF OFFICERS, 3rd BATTN. THE WELSH REGIMENT,

son of Walter John Cornelius, was born at Dehra Dun, U.P., India, on the 14th April, 1889. He was educated at St. George's College and York House, Mussoorie, India, and at Wren's Coaching Establishment, Bayswater, London.

Lieutenant Cornelius, who was a member of the Athenæum Club, and by profession a barrister, joined the Reserve of Officers in March, 1912, becoming Lieutenant in December of that year. He was attached for active service to the 2nd Battalion of his regiment.

He was killed on the 12th November, 1914, at Klein Zillebeke, near Ypres, being engaged with the enemy at close quarters. Captain Venables, of the Royal Welsh Fusiliers, had been wounded there, and Lieutenant Cornelius was crawling down at the back of the trench to see if he could help him, when he was shot through the heart. The officer commanding the battalion wrote : " He was only with us a short time, but impressed himself on me as a gallant leader and a brave man."

LIEUTENANT CHARLES LAWSON CORNISH, 2nd BATTN. HIGHLAND LIGHT INFANTRY,

son of Henry Cornish and Emily Henrietta Cornish, of Glastonbury, Surbiton, was born at Brighton on the 13th August, 1887.

He was educated at Stoke House, Slough, at Charterhouse, and Trinity College, Cambridge, where he took the

degree of B.A. Gazetted to the 2nd Battalion Highland Light Infantry in 1910, he became Lieutenant in 1912, afterwards resigning his commission, and voluntarily joining the Reserve of Officers in the spring of 1914. On the outbreak of the war he rejoined his battalion, which was one of the first units of the First Army Corps to go to the relief of the VIIth Division near Ypres, and was almost continuously engaged till the enemy's assaults were broken in November. Lieutenant Cornish took part in the retirement from Mons, and the Battles of the Marne and the Aisne, being killed at last by a shell in the Battle of Ypres on the 13th November, 1914, while his company was taking up its position in the trenches. He was buried alongside the Passchendaele-Becelaere Road.

MAJOR JOHN BEAUMONT CORRY, D.S.O., ROYAL ENGINEERS,

who was killed by shell near Sailly-sur-la-Lys, North France on the 4th November, 1 9 1 4, while serving with the 3rd (Bombay) Sappers and Miners, was the son of the late John Corry, Esq., J.P., of Croydon, Surrey, and was born there on the 21st August, 1874. He was educated at St. Paul's School, Kensington, where he held a scholarship, and from there passed second into the R.M.A., Woolwich, and became Pollock medallist. He was gazetted to the R.E. in 1894, joined the Bombay Sappers and Miners, and became Lieutenant in February, 1897. In the latter year and in 1898 he served on the north-west frontier of India, taking part in the operations on the Samana and in the relief of Gulistan, for which he received the medal with two clasps. He took part in the Tirah Campaign of 1897–98, being present at the capture of the Sampagha and Arhanga Passes, and at operations in the Waran Valley, Bazar Valley, and other places. For these services he received the clasp. In 1901 he took part in the Mekran Campaign, led the attack on Nodiz Fort (which was captured), and was severely wounded. For this campaign he was mentioned in Despatches, and was awarded the D.S.O.

Major Corry received the Delhi Durbar medal, 1902–03, having helped to construct the light railway, and became Captain in 1904. He was also sent to Somaliland to strengthen the defences of Berbera, and in 1912–13 was employed in building roads and bridges in the Mishmi country. In 1914, in which year he obtained his Majority, he was appointed to the Military Works, Bannu, North Western Province, receiving his orders for the front in the Great War at the end of August. He was delayed for some time at Karachi and at the base, finally reaching the fighting line only two days before he was killed. Major Corry was a member of the Army and Navy Club and of the Alpine Club, and had climbed in the Alps, in Cashmir, and in the mountains near Quetta ; he was also a member of the Poona Rowing Club.

LIEUTENANT HARROLD STANLEY FREDERICK COSENS, 1st BATTN. EAST YORKSHIRE REGIMENT,

was born on the 2nd December, 1889, at Observatory Avenue, Kensington, W., and was the son of Frederick George Cosens, of Bacton, Norfolk, and late of Airlie Gardens, Kensington, and Mrs. Cosens (née Ambrose), of Copford, Essex. He was a grandson of the late F. W. Cosens, Esq., of " The Shelleys," Lewes, Sussex.

Lieutenant Cosens was educated at St. Paul's School, Kensington, and at the R.M.C., Sandhurst. He was a prominent supporter of the Boy Scout movement, and a year or two ago, during his leave, gave up every evening to go down to different troops in the East End to teach the boys signalling. He was remarkable for his patience and good temper, and the success he had with boys, even those who were not brilliant. Some of those instructed by him are now non-commissioned officers in the Army and Navy, " as a result of his self-sacrificing labour." At the end of his leave he was given a supper, at which nearly seventy boys, who were said almost to worship him, were present. The above particulars are taken from a report of the Vicar of St. Agatha's Church, Finsbury Avenue, E.C., of the Boy Scouts' Association. The Secretary of St. Barnabas Troop also wrote expressing how much they owed to the young officer. Lieutenant Cosens was gazetted to the East Yorks as 2nd Lieutenant in September, 1909, and promoted Lieutenant in February, 1912. He was for a time with the Mounted Infantry at Longmoor and Strensall Camps. He passed with distinction his examinations for promotion, including Army signalling.

He was killed on the 28th October, 1914, during the struggle for Calais, while retaking trenches from the Germans near La Bassée. He had led his men successfully in accomplishing the work, and was actually in the trench when he was shot by a sniper and instantly killed.

LIEUTENANT BRUCE DUFFUS COSTIN, 1st BATTN. PRINCE OF WALES'S OWN (WEST YORKSHIRE REGIMENT),

son of Adele Hobson, Tan-y-Bryn, Bangor, was born in Australia on the 20th June, 1889. He was educated at Bedford, and passing through the R.M.C., Sandhurst, obtained his commission as 2nd Lieutenant in the West Yorkshire Regiment in 1909, joining his battalion in India, where he served two years, being promoted to his Lieutenancy in April, 1910.

When at Bedford, Lieutenant Costin played in the Rugby XV, and also in the Sandhurst XV, where he was in the winning teams for rifle and revolver shooting and riding. He played football occasionally for Rosslyn Park, and was captain of the battalion football team.

While on active service in the Great War, during the Battle of Ypres-Armentières, he was brought in wounded on the 20th October from the West Yorkshires' trenches between the cross roads at Le Paradis and Ennetières. Four days later he died in hospital at Boulogne, and was buried with military honours in the cemetery there on the 25th October, 1914.

His Colonel being wounded, the officer commanding wrote of him as follows to his mother : " You know without my telling you what a favourite he was with all ranks of the regiment, and how we shall all miss him. He had done splendidly throughout the war, and was invaluable to us. He was always cool and cheery under fire, quite fearless, and had done very well on the 20th under an appalling shell fire. He is a great loss in every way to the regiment and the mess, so keen on both work and play, and the Rugby team will be nothing without him."

The Chaplain to the Forces, who saw him when he was brought in wounded, wrote : " I had many opportunities for forming an estimate of his character, for I knew him well, and I know he was a man of highest qualities and ideals, brave and honourable, respected by all who knew him, and loved by his brother officers and men under his command. His loss is a loss to the whole Army, and the cutting off of a keen soldier who had promise of a brilliant career."

CAPTAIN EDGAR ERNEST COVENTRY, 1st BATTN. EAST LANCASHIRE REGT.,

who was killed in action on the 1st November, 1914, was the fifth son of the late Mr. Edward Coventry, of Bolingbroke Grove, Wandsworth Common, and was born on the 14th September, 1876. He joined the East Lancashire Regiment on the 20th February, 1897, becoming Lieutenant in 1899.

He took part in the South African War, being present at operations in the Orange Free State in the early part of 1900, including actions at Karee Siding and the Vet and Zand Rivers ; also at operations in the Transvaal and Orange River Colony, November, 1900, to May, 1902. He received the Queen's medal with three clasps, and the King's medal with two clasps. He obtained his Company in July, 1906.

2nd LIEUTENANT DOUGLAS HENDERSON COWAN, 1st BATTN. THE HAMPSHIRE REGIMENT,

son of David T. Cowan, M.A., Director of Education for Hampshire, of The Castle, Winchester, was born at Beccles, Suffolk, on the 10th October, 1890. He was educated at a private school at Winchester, and at the Grammar School, Bedford.

Joining the 3rd Hampshire Regiment as 2nd Lieutenant in February, 1910, he became Lieutenant in the following year, and in May, 1912, was transferred to the 1st (Regular) Battalion as 2nd Lieutenant. He left England with the Expeditionary Force on the 22nd August, 1914, and was killed at Cambrai on the 26th of that month, only four days after reaching the scene of action. 2nd Lieutenant Cowan was a good all-round athlete, a first class swimmer, played cricket and Rugby football, while his strongest game was hockey, at which he represented his county.

2nd LIEUTENANT ROBERT CRAIG COWAN, 3rd (attd. 2nd) BATTN. THE ROYAL SCOTS (LOTHIAN REGT.),

born on the 5th March, 1894, at Craigiebield, Penicuik, was the eldest son of Mr. R. C. Cowan, of Eskhill, Inveresk, Midlothian, and grandson of Mr. C. W. Cowan, D.L., Dalhousie Castle.

He was educated at Cargilfield, Cheltenham College, and Pembroke College, Cambridge, and, having been in the O.T.C., was gazetted to his regiment at Glencorse early in August, 1914, being sent to France with a draft in September. He was killed on the 24th October, 1914, at La

Plinche, near Neuve Chapelle. His Commanding Officer wrote : " We miss him, not only as a comrade, but as a very gallant boy who has set a noble example of courage and fearless execution of his duty."

Mr. Cowan's recreations were fishing, shooting, and football.

LIEUT. GEORGE HENRY COX, 3rd (attd. 2nd) BATTN. KING'S OWN SCOTTISH BORDERERS,

of Reedham, Norfolk, was killed in action in France on the 30th–31st October, 1914. He became Lieutenant in his regiment in July, 1913, having received his commission as 2nd Lieutenant in May, 1910.

2nd LIEUTENANT GEOFFREY PHILIP JOSEPH SNEAD-COX, 1st BATTN. ROYAL WELSH FUSILIERS,

who was born on the 20th February, 1895, was the second son of John Snead-Cox, of Broxwood Court, and Eaton Bishop, Herefordshire, Lord of the Manor of Broxwood, and late of Souldern Manor, Banbury, also of 38, Egerton Gardens, London, S.W.

He was educated at Downside School, near Bath, and passed into the R.M.C., Sandhurst, in 1912, obtaining his commission in September, 1913. After joining he qualified as an interpreter in French. At the outbreak of the war his battalion was in Malta, but was ordered home, and it formed part of the 22nd Brigade of the " immortal " VIIth Division, which left England on the 4th October, and landed at Zeebrugge.

2nd Lieutenant Snead-Cox was shot through the head on the 21st October, 1914, in the first part of the Battle of Ypres, where his battalion " fought itself to a standstill."

2nd LIEUTENANT RICHARD MARY SNEAD-COX, 3rd BATTN. THE ROYAL SCOTS (LOTHIAN REGIMENT),

born on the 25th November, 1892, was the eldest son of John Snead-Cox, of Broxwood Court, and Eaton Bishop, Herefordshire, Lord of the Manor of Broxwood.

He was educated at Downside School, near Bath, and New College, Oxford, where he was reading for Honours when war was declared. He immediately offered his services, and on the 7th August, 1914, was given a commission in the 3rd Battalion Royal Scots. After seven weeks' training he was sent to St. Nazaire, France, and thence, on the 7th October with seven other officers and a draft of ninety-four men, to reinforce the 2nd Battalion at the front. His battalion was advancing near Neuve Chapelle on the 28th October, 1914, when 2nd Lieutenant Snead-Cox was shot through the heart as he was leading his platoon to take a German trench.

2nd LIEUTENANT ARTHUR NELSON COXE, ROYAL FIELD ARTILLERY,

who died on the 3rd November, 1914, of wounds received in action, aged nineteen years, was the third son of Mr. Justice Coxe, I.C.S., Judge of the High Court, Calcutta, and of Mrs. H. R. H. Coxe, of Therfield, Farnham. He only joined the Army in August, 1914.

LIEUTENANT SIR ARCHIBALD CHARLES GIBSON-CRAIG, 4th BART. (of Riccarton, Midlothian), 2nd, BATTN. HIGHLAND LIGHT INFANTRY,

who is shown in the official monthly casualty list published in October, 1914, as having been killed in action, no date or place being recorded, was the third surviving son of Sir James Henry Gibson-Craig, Bart., and Julia Lady Gibson-Craig, daughter

of Archibald Buchanan of Curriehill, Midlothian. He succeeded his father in 1908. His elder brother, Robert James, Lieutenant 3rd Battalion Royal Scots, died of dysentry in South Africa, in April, 1900, at the age of seventeen.

He was born on the 24th August, 1883, and was educated at Harrow (Head Master's House, 1896 –1901). From there he went to Trinity College, Cambridge, where he took his degree of B.A. in 1905. He joined the Highland Light Infantry in July, 1906, becoming Lieutenant in April, 1909. In August, 1914, Sir Archibald Gibson-Craig was in Colonial employment with the Nigeria Regiment, West African Frontier Force, to which he was appointed in March, 1913.

The following account of the circumstances attending his death was published in "The Harrovian" of November, 1914 :—

"'Gibson-Craig was shot,' says a narrator, whose communication has been forwarded to the "Morning Post," 'while leading his men to the attack on a German machine gun, which was hidden in a wood. He located the gun, and asked our Second-in-Command whether he might take his platoon (about twenty men) and try to capture the gun, which was doing a lot of damage to our troops at the time. The Major gave his consent, and Gibson-Craig went off to get the gun. . . . He and his men crawled to the top of the hill, and found themselves unexpectedly face to face with a large body of Germans. Our men fired a volley, and then the Lieutenant drew his sword and rushed forward in front of the troops, calling to them, "Charge, men ! At them !" He got to within ten yards of the enemy and then fell. The Germans held up their hands, but our men were so mad at their officer being killed (and also suspected treachery, as the Germans had not thrown down their arms) that about fifty Germans were killed on the spot. By his gallant action Gibson-Craig did a great deal to assist the general advance of the regiment, and, indeed, the whole of the troops concerned. The remaining men silenced the gun, and brought their comrades (two killed and three wounded) back to their lines—two miles, under shell fire the whole way, and not one was touched ! One of these, a Private now in hospital in this country, said that if the Germans had kept cool and used their gun they must have wiped out the whole of the little band of Britishers.'"

Sir Archibald Gibson-Craig was unmarried, and is succeeded in the baronetcy by his brother, Henry Thomas, late Lieutenant 3rd Battn. Royal Scots. He was a member of the Carlton and Royal Automobile Clubs, London, and of the New Club, Edinburgh.

LIEUTENANT JOHN MAC-ADAM CRAIG, 57th WILDE'S RIFLES (FRONTIER FORCE), who was killed in action on the 2nd November, 1914, was the youngest son of Dr. and Mrs. James Craig, late of Beckenham, Kent.

He was born on the 11th May, 1886, and was a Queen's scholar of Westminster; he was gazetted to the Seaforth Highlanders in October, 1906, was promoted Lieutenant in January, 1909, and transferred to the Indian Army in September of that year.

He saw active service on the north-western frontier of India in 1908, taking part in operations in the Mohmand country, for which he received the medal with clasp.

2nd LIEUTENANT CHARLES EDWARD CRANE, 1st BATTN. THE DUKE OF CORNWALL'S LIGHT INFANTRY, was born on the 18th February, 1892, at the Manor House, Birlingham, Worcestershire, the son of Charles Arnold and Georgina Crane.

He was educated at Oakfield, R u g b y, from 1902–06, Cheltenham C o l l e g e from 1906–10, and the R.M.C., Sand-hurst, 1911–12. At Cheltenham and Sandhurst he was in the Rugby Football XV, and also in the hockey team at Sandhurst.

2nd Lieutenant Crane received his commission in the D.C.L.I. in September, 1912. The battalion assembled at the Curragh, was employed at Fermoy during the Home Rule excitement in Ulster in March, 1914.

On the 14th September, 1914, at the Battle of the Aisne, while on his way back from successfully locating—while alone and under heavy fire—a maxim gun, he was wounded, and died from the effects on the 18th September, 1914. His body was buried at the Farm, Mont de Soissons, with a very impressive service, during which there happened to be a lull in the fighting. A temporary wooden cross was erected over his grave by his brother officers.

His Commanding Officer, Lieutenant-Colonel M. N. Turner, C.B., D.C.L.I., wrote to his mother of him as follows : " Your boy was absolutely brave and good. We were all so very fond of him, and he was such an excellent officer ; he was absolutely fearless, and one of the best." A young brother officer wrote : " The cause of your son's death was a very valiant piece of work." Several of his non-commissioned officers and men also sent their tribute to 2nd Lieutenant Crane's worth, among them Lance-Corporal J. Horan, who wrote to the following effect : " His kindness will always live in my memory ; he picked me up when I was lying beside the road one night, and put me, with a private, in an ambulance wagon. We both owe our lives to him. He was most kind and considerate, and would never ask his men to go to any place where he would not go himself. I have seen him carrying the men's rifles."

MAJOR EUSTACE CRAWLEY, 12th (PRINCE OF WALES'S ROYAL) LANCERS,

who was killed near Ypres on the 2nd November, 1 9 1 4 , was born on the 16th April, 1868, third son of the late Baden Crawley.

He was educated at Harrow, and joined the 12th Lancers from the Militia in August, 1889, becoming Lieutenant in 1891, and Captain in November, 1897. Major Crawley saw much active service. In 1898–99 he took part in operations at Sierra Leone, West Coast of Africa, for which he received the medal and clasp. Again, in 1899 he was in command of the Bula Expedition in Nigeria, being mentioned in Despatches by General Wilcox, in December, 1899. He commanded the Nigeria Company Constabulary from the latter date.

In 1900–02 he was appointed a Special Service Officer in the South African War ; was D.A.A.G. Ridley's Corps of Mounted Infantry from April to December, 1900 ; took part in General Ian Hamilton's march, being present at the actions of Diamond Hill, Johannesburg, and Wittebergen ; and also at operations in Cape Colony under General French ; he was Intelligence Officer to Capper's Column at the end of 1901, and Staff Officer to Doran's Column from December, 1901, to May, 1902. For his services he was mentioned in Despatches by Lord Roberts, 4th September, 1901, given the Brevet rank of Major from November, 1900, and received the Queen's medal with four clasps, and the King's medal with two clasps. From May to November, 1902, he was D.A.A.G. on the staff of Colonel Hickman, commanding the troops at Middelburg, Cape Colony.

In 1902–03 he again saw service in Nigeria, being in command of a column in the Kano Expedition, for which he received the medal and clasp. In 1903 he commanded Mounted In-

fantry, in India, and obtained the substantive rank of Major in July, 1905. In 1906–07 he was officiating Brigade-Major of the Amballa Cavalry Brigade and to the Inspector-General of Cavalry in India.

Major Crawley married, in December, 1904, Lady Violet Ella Finch, elder daughter of the eighth Earl of Aylesford.

CAPTAIN MERVYN CRAWSHAY, 5th (PRINCESS CHARLOTTE OF WALES'S) DRAGOON GUARDS,

who was killed in action on the 31st October, 1914, was the son of T. Crawshay, Esq., of Dimlands, Glamorganshire.

He was born on the 4th May, 1881, and after serving with the embodied Militia and being attached to the Regulars for a year, received his commission in the Worcestershire Regiment in April, 1902. He became Lieutenant in that regiment in November, 1904, having served with it in the South African War, being present at operations in the Cape Colony, for which he received the Queen's medal with two clasps.

In February, 1908, he was transferred to the 5th Dragoon Guards, in which he became Captain in April, 1911.

Captain Crawshay was noted as a fine horseman, representing England in the Military Tournaments in America in 1913, and winning the Gold Cup in the competition open to the world. He also won the King George Challenge Cup at the International Military Tournament in the same year.

CAPTAIN LEO CREAGH, 1st BATTN. THE MANCHESTER REGIMENT,

who was killed in action on the 20th– 21st December,1914, was the eldest son of Brigade-Surgeon W. Creagh (retired) and of Mrs. Creagh, of Grangewood Lodge, L u l l i n g t o n near Burton-on-Trent.

He was born on the 20th October, 1878, and was educated at Stonyhurst College, Blackburn. He joined the Manchester Regiment from the Militia in January, 1899, becoming Lieutenant in

September of the same year, and Captain in November, 1901. He served in the South African War, being present at operations in Natal, including the action at Lombard's Kop in 1899, and taking part in the defence of Ladysmith, including the sorties of the 7th and 10th December, 1899. He received the Queen's medal with clasp.

The following account of the circumstances attending his death is taken from the "Stonyhurst Magazine," of February, 1915:—

"Captain Creagh fell in the heavy fighting that took place near Givenchy on the 20th and 21st December. His battalion had only left the trenches on the 17th when they were ordered out again on the 20th. They attacked a village and some trenches in the afternoon, during which action Captain Creagh was reported to have done good work. On the morning of the 21st the attack was renewed at daybreak, and Captain Creagh was shot down in front of the enemy's trenches. A sergeant, who was with him at the time, said he was leading his men with conspicuous gallantry. The above details were received from his Colonel, who, writing to Captain Creagh's mother, expressed his deep regret at the loss of so gallant and capable an officer."

Captain Creagh had been at home on short leave a few days before his death.

CAPTAIN THEODORE CREAN, 1st BATTN. NORTHAMPTON-SHIRE REGIMENT, attd. ROYAL FLYING CORPS,

was the son of Mrs. Crean, of Chester, and of the late R. Crean, M.D., and was born at Manchester on he 23rd October, 1880. He was educated at Stonyhurst College, and at Gonville and Caius College, Cambridge.

Captain Crean joined the Lancashire Fusiliers from the Militia in April, 1902, becoming Lieutenant in March, 1906. He served in the South African War, having been present at operations in the Transvaal, Orange River Colony, and Cape Colony, for which he received the Queen's medal with five clasps. He was employed with the West African Regiment and the West African Frontier Force for several years, and transferred to the Northamptonshire Regiment in May, 1908, being gazetted Captain in June, 1913.

In the Great War Captain Crean was attached to the Royal Flying Corps, and was shot down on the 26th October, 1914, while signalling from an aeroplane to the Royal Field Artillery.

CAPTAIN WILLIAM CECIL HOLT CREE, 71st BATTERY, ROYAL FIELD ARTILLERY,

who died of wounds on the 24th October, 1914, in hospital at Boulogne, was the son of the Rev. William Cree, M.A., St. Matthias, Kensington.

He was born on the 4th August, 1882, at Milton Abbott, Tavistock, Devon, and went to Marlborough College in September, 1895, proceeding to the R.M.A., Woolwich, in January, 1900. He joined the Royal Artillery in July, 1901, becoming Lieutenant in July, 1904. In July, 1909, he was appointed an Adjutant of the Territorial Force, and attained the rank of Captain in July 1914.

He married, in 1910, Avis, daughter of the Rev. Canon T. S. Hichens, Guilsborough, Northampton.

CAPTAIN FRANCIS JOSEPH CRESSWELL, ADJUTANT 1st BATTN. NORFOLK REGIMENT,

son of George and Eva Cresswell, was born on the 15th July, 1883, at King's Lynn, Norfolk, and was educated at Radley College.

He served with the 3rd Battalion in the South African War, 1901–02, taking part in operations in the Orange River Colony and in Cape Colony, for which he received the Queen's medal with four clasps. He was given his commission in the Norfolk Regiment from the Militia in October, 1902, serving with the 1st Battalion in India, and with the King's African Rifles in British East Africa. He was promoted Lieutenant in February, 1905, and Captain in March, 1912, and passed the examination for his Majority, gaining also the special Signalling Certificate. In August, 1913, he was appointed Adjutant of his battalion.

Captain Cresswell was killed during the retirement from Mons on the 24th August, 1914, while he was taking a message to a battery of Royal Field Artillery.

He was a member of the Isthmian Club, and a Freemason. His favourite sport was shooting, and he had killed elephant, lion, rhinoceros, and buffalo in Africa.

He married Barbara, niece of Sir W. H. B. Ffolkes, Bart., and left two daughters, Barbara, age three years, and Eve, age eleven weeks, at the time of his death.

MAJOR HUBERT FRANCIS CRICHTON, 1st BATTN. IRISH GUARDS,

son of Lieutenant-Colonel the Hon. Charles Crichton and Lady Madeline Crichton, and a nephew of the Earl of Erne and of the present Marquis of Headfort, was born in London on the 17th December, 1874.

He was educated at Eton, and the R.M.C., Sandhurst, receiving his commission in the Grenadier Guards in 1896. With his battalion he served in the Nile Expedition of 1898, being present at the Battle of Khartoum, receiving the British medal and the Egyptian medal with clasp. When the Irish Guards were formed in 1900 he was transferred to them, and was appointed Adjutant in May, 1900. He went to South Africa for the Boer War with the 29th Battalion Imperial Yeomanry, taking part in the operations in Cape Colony. For his services he received the Queen's South African medal with two clasps. In 1903 he was A.D.C. to the Commander of the 1st Army Corps at Aldershot.

Having obtained his Majority in March, 1908, Major Crichton accompanied his battalion to France in August, 1914, where he was killed, on the 1st September, in the rearguard action of the 12th Infantry Brigade, the Irish Guards forming part of the 4th Guards' Brigade. He was mentioned in Sir John French's Despatch of 8th October, 1914.

Major Crichton, who was a member of the Guards' Club, Bachelors', and Pratt's Clubs, was a keen fisherman, a good shot, and played polo. He married, in July, 1903, Esther, daughter of Captain and Lady Rachel Saunderson, and left two daughters, Doris, born in May, 1904, and Enid, born in February, 1907.

LIEUTENANT - COLONEL HUGH TREVOR CRISPIN, COMMANDING 2nd BATTN. THE ROYAL SUSSEX REGT.,

was the eldest son of the late Trevor Crispin, of His Majesty's Treasury (Legal Department), and was born in London on the 18th September, 1868.

He was educated at Bradfield College; Trinity College, Cambridge, where he obtained the degree of B.A.; and at the R.M.C., Sandhurst.

Lieutenant-Colonel Crispin obtained his first commission in the Prince of Wales's Leinster Regiment (Royal Canadians) in May, 1892, being transferred to the Northumberland Fusiliers, in which nearly all his Army service was spent, in December of the same year. He became Lieutenant in July, 1895; Captain in February, 1900; Brevet-Major for war service in South Africa in November, 1900; and Substantive Major in February, 1911.

Lieutenant-Colonel Crispin served with the Northumberland Fusiliers in the Nile Expedition of 1898, being present at the Battle of Omdurman, afterwards receiving the Queen's medal with clasp and the Khedive's medal. He also served in Crete during the suppression of the disturbances there. In the South African War he served with the Mounted Infantry in 1899–1900, and was present at the advance on Kimberley (severely wounded), and in actions at Belmont, Enslin, and Modder River. He was present at operations in the Orange Free State from February to May, 1900, when he commanded a battalion of Mounted Infantry, including actions at Paardeberg, Poplar Grove, Driefontein, Vet River, and Zand River. He was also present at operations in the Transvaal in May and June, 1900, including actions near Johannesburg, Pretoria, and Diamond Hill, being again severely wounded. For these services he was mentioned in Despatches ("London Gazette," 10th September, 1901), promoted Brevet-Major, and received the Queen's medal with six clasps.

From 1901–02 Lieutenant-Colonel Crispin was A.D.C. to the Major-General Commanding an Infantry Brigade at Aldershot, and from 1902–04 was A.D.C. to the Major-General Commanding a Division of the 1st Army Corps. He commanded the 6th Regiment of Mounted Infantry in South Africa in 1907–08, and was Adjutant at the R.M.C., Sandhurst, from 1910–14.

Lieutenant-Colonel Crispin was selected to command the 2nd Royal Sussex Regiment on the 14th September, 1914, and, while in command, was killed in action, near Ypres, on the 30th October, 1914.

Lieutenant-Colonel Crispin, who was unmarried, was a member of the Army and Navy, and of the Royal Automobile Clubs.

LIEUTENANT JOHN CROCKET, ROYAL ARMY MEDICAL CORPS,

who was born on the 3rd August, 1886, was the son of William Crocket, Head Master Sciennes Public School, Edinburgh. He was a cousin of the late S. R. Crockett, the novelist.

After his education at George Watson's College, Edinburgh, he qualified as a medical man, and held the appointment of resident House Surgeon at the Edinburgh Royal Infirmary, and afterwards at the Royal Hospital for Sick Children and Chalmers Hospital, Edinburgh. At the University he took a prominent part in the Dumfries and Galloway Literary Society, of which he was President for a time, and was one of the Executive Committee of the Students' Representative Council. When at the University he played golf and tennis.

He entered the R.A.M.C. in 1913, and took the degree of M.D. at Edinburgh University in July, 1914. After joining the Army he was attached to the 1st Battalion Cameron Highlanders at Edinburgh Castle, and left there for the front in August, 1914.

During the Battle of the Aisne on the 25th September, 1914, Lieutenant Crocket was in a cave used partly as headquarters and partly as a collecting base for the wounded. Just after he had finished dressing a soldier's wound the roof, having been struck by two shells, fell in, killing him, together with five Staff officers and about thirty men. The officers were buried at Bourg. It was supposed that the exact locality of the cave had been ascertained by spies and communicated to the enemy, who were thus able to find the exact range.

The following extract is from the "Educational News":—"Lieutenant Crocket was a pupil of George Watson's College, and a student of Edinburgh University. As pupil and student his career was most brilliant, and gave promise of a highly successful future in his chosen profession. Add to his academic record the fact of his bright manner, his winning personality, his almost boyish smile, his unfailing good nature, lit up with a touch of ready humour, and readers can conjure up a picture of one who was beloved by all who knew him, one of whom the nation might well be proud."

2nd LIEUTENANT LESLIE ROBERT CROFT, 2nd BATTN. ROYAL SUSSEX REGIMENT),

youngest son of Major G. Croft, late Yorkshire and Royal Sussex Regiments, and of Mrs. Croft, of Manor House, Hale, Farnham, Surrey, was born in 1892, and was educated at the Farnham Grammar School. The Head Master, the Rev. G. Priestley, writing of him says: "All the boys of his time will remember his . . . unfailing cheerfulness . . . and his absolutely sterling character."

He received his commission in the Royal Sussex Regiment from the ranks of the Cheshire Regiment in September, 1912.

The following account of his death was received from a Sergeant who was with him at the time: Lieutenant Croft was in command of No. 10 Platoon, which was leading "C" Company of his battalion on the 30th October, when advancing against the Germans through a pine wood. As the enemy was found to be in force Lieutenant Croft sent for reinforcements, and a few minutes after was wounded in the head. The Sergeant bandaged his head and selected a way for him to get away safely. Lieutenant Croft, however, refused to leave, saying, "I must see this job finished first." These were his last words, for as he raised his head to give some command he was mortally wounded in the neck, death being practically instantaneous. "We all felt," said the Sergeant, "that we had lost, not only an officer and a leader, but a great friend."

2nd LIEUTENANT WILLIAM GUY CRONK, THE BUFFS (EAST KENT REGIMENT),

the son of William Henry and Winifred Ruth Cronk, was born at Suffolk Place, Sevenoaks, Kent, on the 28th April, 1893.

Educated at Eton and the Royal Military Academy, Woolwich, he was gazetted to the Buffs on the 14th March, 1914. He was attached to the 1st Battn. K.R.R.C. in the Great War, and was killed on the 24th October,

1914, about two and a half miles south-east of Zonnebeke, while leading his platoon to take a German trench, when he came under the fire of a machine gun at short range.

His recreations were hunting, polo, cricket, and tennis.

2nd LIEUTENANT WILLIAM RONALD MORLEY CROSSMAN, 2nd BATTN. KING'S ROYAL RIFLE CORPS,

who was killed in action at Veldhoek, in Flanders, on the 2nd November,1914, was born on the 6th September, 1894, at Goswick House, Beal, Northumberland. He was the younger of two sons, both in the Army, of the late Major Lawrence Morley Crossman, J.P., a freeman of Berwick and Lord of the Manor of Holy Island, and Mrs. Morley Crossman, of Cheswick House, Beal. 2nd Lieutenant Crossman was a grandson of the late Major-General Sir William Crossman, K.C.M.G., R.E., sometime member of Parliament for Portsmouth.

2nd Lieutenant Crossman, who was educated at Lyndhurst, Wellington College, and the R.M.C., Sandhurst, only received his commission in the K.R.R.C. in February, 1914.

LIEUTENANT CECIL FRANCIS CROUSAZ, 1st BATTN. THE SOUTH STAFFORDSHIRE REGIMENT,

was the youngest son of W. de P. Crousaz, Jurat of the Royal Court of Guernsey, and was born in that island on the 7th December, 1888.

He was educated at Elizabeth College, Guernsey, and the R.M.C., Sandhurst, entering the South Staffordshire Regiment in November, 1909, and becoming Lieutenant in March, 1912.

He served with his battalion in South Africa and Gibraltar from 1910–14. He won the Featherweight Army Boxing Cup at Aldershot in 1913.

He was killed in a trench at Zonnebeke, near Ypres, by shell on the 31st October, 1914.

CAPTAIN WILLIAM MAYNARD CARLISLE CROWE, RESERVE OF OFFICERS, ROYAL WARWICKSHIRE REGIMENT,

was the son of Major-General Thomas Carlisle Crowe, R.H.A. (retired), and was born at the Curragh Camp, Ireland, on the 11th September, 1870.

He was educated at St. Paul's School, and the R.A.M.C., Sandhurst, obtaining his commission as 2nd Lieutenant in the Royal Warwicks in July, 1891. He became Captain in September, 1898, and retired in August, 1907, joining the Reserve of Officers.

In the Great War Captain Crowe was attached to the 1st Battalion Northamptonshire Regiment, when he was killed near Ypres on the 8th November, 1914.

Captain Crowe was a member of the United Service Club, and of the Swiss Alpine and Swiss Ski Clubs. He married, in 1904, Elizabeth Hannah Stanley, widow of C. Archer, Esq.

2nd LIEUTENANT JAMES CYRIL BAPTIST CROZIER, 2nd BATTN, ROYAL MUNSTER FUSILIERS.

who was born at Bowden, Cheshire, on the 24th October, 1890, was the son of the late Rev. Henry Wilcox Crozier (brother of the Archbishop of Armagh, Primate of All Ireland), and of Susannah M. M. Spence, daughter of the late James

Spence, well known in Liverpool and Birkenhead. He was educated at Loretto School, where he was in the XV, and at Edinburgh University, where he also played for the 'Varsity XV. At the latter he had studied medicine for two years, when he applied for a commission in the 3rd Battalion Royal Scots, Special Reserve. He was gazetted to the Royal Munster Fusiliers in June, 1914.

He was killed on the 27th August, 1914, near Etreux, when the battalion was nearly surrounded, and no fewer than eight of its officers were killed

LIEUTENANT E. O. CRUIKSHANK, 3rd BATTN. THE DUKE OF EDINBURGH'S (WILTSHIRE REGIMENT), was killed in action on the 19th September, 1914. He was appointed 2nd Lieutenant on probation in December, 1912, and promoted Lieutenant in July, 1914.

LIEUTENANT CECIL REGINALD CRYMBLE, D.Sc., 3rd BATTN. PRINCESS VICTORIA'S (ROYAL IRISH FUSILIERS),

was the youngest son of the late Mr. George G. Crymble, of Gordon House, Annadale, and was born at Belfast on the 6th April, 1885. He was a graduate of the Queen's University, Belfast, of which he was one of the most popular and brilliant students. His most marked abilities were shown in chemical work, in which he gained several distinctions. He was the students' representative in the Senate, and a prominent member of the O.T.C. He held the "Andrews" Scholarship and the 1851 Exhibition for research work for three years, and obtained his degree of D.Sc. with the gold medal. For several years he was also demonstrator of chemistry at Queen's College. Besides being a student of conspicuous ability, he took an active part in the social life of the University, and was President of the Students' Union and of the Students' Representative Council. He was also one of the prime movers in the formation of the O.T.C., and from that Corps was one of the first to join the 3rd Battalion Royal Irish Fusiliers, as 2nd Lieutenant in December, 1910, and in which he became Lieutenant in August, 1912. After leaving Belfast in 1910, he proceeded to University College, London, where he worked under Sir William Ramsay, and subsequently obtained an appointment as Lecturer in Biological Chemistry in the physiological department at University College. On the outbreak of the Great War he was attached for active service to the 1st Battalion of his regiment, and was serving with it when he was shot by a sniper while working at a trench near Armentières on the 20th November, 1914.

LIEUTENANT LEWIS ROBERTSON CUMMING, 1st BATTN. THE BLACK WATCH (ROYAL HIGHLANDERS), who was born on the 5th October, 1892, was the eldest son of John Fleetwood Cumming,

J.P., late Captain V.B. Seaforth Highlanders, of "The Dowans," Aberlour, Banffshire.

He was educated at Rugby, where he played for his House XV, and at the R.M.C., Sandhurst, where he rode for the Saddle. He was a member of the Caledonian Club, and was fond of hunting, shooting, and golfing. Having been gazetted to the Black Watch in February, 1912, becoming Lieutenant in May, 1914, he left with the Expeditionary Force in August, 1914, was present in the retirement from Mons and the Battle of the Marne, and was killed at the Battle of the Aisne on the 14th September, 1914. The following account of his death was given by brother officers : " Lewis was, as you know, Scout Officer of the regiment. After the battle started there was no work for the Scouts, and Lewis was at the headquarters of the battalion with Colonel Grant Duff and the Adjutant. All the time he was anxious to go forward, but was kept back. Eventually, when the Colonel went forward himself at a time when things were not going very well, Lewis collected as many men as he could find, formed them into a platoon, and went forward with them, taking what ammunition he could get to those in front. . . . There was a heavy fire from front and flanks, and Lewis and his men were practically annihilated."

Lieutenant Cumming's body was found by the Gloucestershire Regiment, with those of two officers of the Cameron Highlanders, and the three were buried together near the woods to the north of Chivy.

2nd LIEUTENANT JOHN REYNOLDS PICKERSGILL - CUNLIFFE, 2nd BATTN. GRENADIER GUARDS,

who was included as killed in action in the War Office casualty list issued on the 9th October, 1914, but whose death had been announced on the 21st September, was the only son of Harry Pickersgill - Cunliffe, of Haughton Manor, St. Neot's, and 27, Beaufort Gardens, London, S.W.

2nd Lieutenant Pickersgill-Cunliffe, who was only nineteen years of age, was gazetted to the Grenadier Guards on the 17th September, 1913.

2nd LIEUTENANT FREDERICK GWATKIN OLDHAM CURTLER, 2nd BATTN. WORCESTERSHIRE REGT.,

who was killed in action on the 21st October, 1914, was the only son of Mr. Frederick Lewis Curtler, of Bevere House, Worcestershire.

He was educated at Rugby, which he entered in 1907.

2nd Lieutenant Curtler, who was twenty-one years old when killed, first entered the Army in the 5th Battalion Worcestershire Regiment, as 2nd Lieutenant in April, 1912, being promoted Lieutenant in December, 1913, and afterwards transferred as 2nd Lieutenant to the Regular Battalion in October, 1914.

CAPTAIN WILLIAM CHARLES CURGENVEN, 1st BATTN. SOUTH WALES BORDERERS,

the son of Charles James Curgenven, Paymaster-in-Chief, R.N., was born at Great Missenden, Bucks, on the 7th November, 1876.

He was educated at Hazlehurst School, Frant, and Repton, where he was captain of both the cricket and football teams, and was also a member of the "Hampshire Hogs" and Incognito Cricket Clubs.

He joined the South Wales Borderers from the Militia in December, 1897, and became Lieutenant in April, 1899. He served in the South African War, where he was slightly wounded, taking part in operations in the Orange Free State, including actions at Karee Siding, Vet River, and Zand River; in the Transvaal, including action near Johannesburg; in the Transvaal, west of Pretoria; and in Orange River Colony. He received the Queen's medal with three clasps, and the King's medal with two clasps. He was Adjutant of his battalion from February, 1906, to February, 1909, and from 1909–13 was Instructor of Topography at the R.M.C., Sandhurst.

In the Great War he was in command of No. 4 Company South Wales Borderers, when the regiment was attacked by the enemy near the village of Langemark, on the 21st October, 1914; and, while leading the company under a hot fire, was wounded in the arm, and almost immediately after was shot through the head. Captain Curgenven was a first-rate all-round

athlete, and was a member of the Junior Army and Navy Club.

He married the eldest daughter of the late Henry Forrester, Esq., of " Woodfield," Colinton, Midlothian, and left a daughter, Angela Emily Muriel, born at the Royal Military College in August, 1912.

CAPTAIN CHARLES ANTOINE DE GUERRY DALGLISH, 1st BATTN. THE BLACK WATCH (ROYAL HIGHLANDERS),

who died on the 9th September, 1914, of wounds received in action at Sablonnières, was the third son of the late J. C. Dalglish, Wandara, Goulburn, N.S.W., and of Mrs. Dalglish, Bellasis, Sundorne Castle, Shrewsbury.

He was born on the 11th February, 1883, and was educated at the Oratory School, Edgbaston. He joined the Royal Highlanders from the Militia in January, 1901, becoming Lieutenant in October, 1903, and Captain in January, 1910.

Captain Dalglish served in the South African War from 1901–02, being present at operations in the Transvaal and Orange River Colony, and received for his services the Queen's medal with four clasps.

He was a member of the Caledonian Club, and married Carline de Burgh Purves, daughter of George Purdis Purves, Middle Temple, son of James Purves, of Chintin and Glen Isla, Cape Shank, Australia, and late of Mosspennock, Greenlaw, Berwickshire; he left three daughters: Rosemarie Constance Dorothy, born January, 1908; Carline Frances, born November, 1910; and Margaret Veronica de Lauret, born February, 1912.

LIEUTENANT - COLONEL CHARLES DALTON, ROYAL ARMY MEDICAL CORPS,

the second son of John Edward Dalton, J.P., and Katherine Dalton, was born at Golden Hills, County Tipperary, on the 3rd May, 1867. He was a grandson of Edward Dalton, of Ballygriffin, County Tipperary.

Lieutenant-Colonel Dalton was educated at Clongowes Wood College, to which he went in 1879, remaining there four years, where he is remembered as a steady worker, a leading spirit in all games, and as an influence which, for his age, was almost unique and altogether good. In 1883 he began the study of medicine at the Carmichael Medical School, Dublin, where, again, in work and play he made his mark. He rowed for the Pembroke Rowing Club, helping more than one boat to victory; and as a football player is remembered in the Monkstown Football Club, of which he was vice-president at the time of his death. When in India and on the West Coast of Africa he did some big-game shooting, but it was his hunting and racing career which showed the real grit of the man. Charley Dalton was the first member of the R.A.M.C. to win a military steeplechase in Ireland, and he added to the already high sporting status of the corps when he carried off the Irish Grand Military on " Thowl Pin " in 1912. He took the diploma of the Royal Colleges of Physicians and Surgeons, Ireland, in 1888. At the end of that year, wishing to see the world, he took the appointment of Ship's Surgeon on the R.M.S. " Magellan," sailing to Valparaiso, and repeated the trip in March the following year in R.M.S. " Cotopaxi." This vessel sank after a collision with a German steamer in the Straits of Magellan. Though badly damaged, the " Cotopaxi " continued the voyage through a narrow channel instead of the ordinary route, hoping to escape bad weather. After a week she struck an unknown rock in mid-channel and sank in eight minutes, just giving the passengers and crew time to get into the boats. Everything was lost, and the party landed on the shores of Patagonia, living for four days on mussels and some casks of tallow that floated ashore. On the fourth day they were rescued by a German steamer. During the sinking of the ship Lieutenant-Colonel Dalton behaved with great gallantry in rescuing two of the passengers who were paralysed— one completely so—carrying them up on deck and putting them into a boat. The French Government awarded him a silver medal of the 1st class, and the Royal Humane Society conferred on him their gold medal for saving life. He was also awarded the Albert medal.

After his return to Dublin, Lieutenant-Colonel Dalton was appointed Resident Surgeon to Jervis Street Hospital, and in June, 1891, competed successfully for a commission in the R.A.M.C. He proceeded very shortly to India, and while there served in the Kachlin Hills Expedition in Burma, receiving the medal and clasp. Afterwards he saw service on the north-west frontier of India, 1897, receiving a second medal with clasp. In November of the same year he returned from India, and was stationed at Belfast till March, 1898, when he left England for Sierra Leone, and took part in the Karene Expedition. For his services there he was mentioned in Despatches, receiving a medal and clasp. The following was the report made by the Officer Commanding the column:— " I wish to specially mention the following officer: Captain C. Dalton, R.A.M.C., who displayed conspicuous bravery in attending to Lieutenant Craig-Brown, who was dangerously wounded, under an extremely heavy fire from a stockade a few yards away. While he was binding up this officer's wounds four or five carriers who were lying close by at the time were killed. It was entirely owing to Captain Dalton's coolness and courage that Lieutenant Craig-Brown is now alive."

On another occasion Captain Dalton (as he was then) went out and brought back a private under heavy fire. Through some mischance, the original reports of Captain Dalton's conduct on these two occasions, sent in March, 1898, were not forwarded to or received by the proper authorities, and it was not till three years later that the information was furnished.

Lieutenant-Colonel Dalton returned from Sierra Leone in March, 1899, and in November of that year was posted to the 14th Hussars, then under orders for the South African War, in which he took part, being present at operations in Natal, 1899, the Relief of Ladysmith, including operations of 17th–24th January, 1900 (severely wounded on the 23rd January); in the Orange Free State, February-May, 1900, including actions at Houtnek (Thoba Mountain), Vet River, and Zand River; and in Orange River and Cape Colonies. For these services he received the Queen's medal with three clasps, and was mentioned in Despatches. Having obtained special permission to go and attend the wounded under heavy fire, he himself was dangerously wounded in nobly doing his duty as a good soldier surgeon. Soon after he returned home in 1901, he was awarded the Arnott gold medal for distinguished gallantry in the field by the Irish Medical School and Graduates' Association, this being the first award made.

After a year at home he went a second time to Sierra Leone, and in 1905 to India, where he did some valuable plague work in Pindi, and was selected, " for distinguished service in the field, for appointment as Honorary Surgeon to His Excellency the Viceroy " in May, 1908.

During his next period of home service he filled the position of D.A.D.M.S., Irish Command, and on the outbreak of the Great War he embarked on the 18th August, 1914, with the Expeditionary Force in charge of No. 1 General Hospital. On the 8th September he joined the headquarters, IInd Division 1st Army Corps as A.D.M.S., at Moussey. The following account of his fatal injury is from a statement of an eye-witness :— " Dalton and Bostock went up with G.S. of IInd Division to Verneuil hot-shelled. Teams, etc., knocked about, and nobody but Dalton and Bostock to do the carrying. Dalton did all he could in personally carrying wounded into Verneuil Château. In doing this he got hit in the back (shell). As he lay on the ground a stampeding gun limber bruised his left hip. Rescued by Persell, of Signals, who just pulled him out in time. Was paralysed by concussion of spine, only pain round chest (girdle), but thought he was dying. On admission to the temporary hospital, where he was under the care of Colonel Copeland and Captain Carter, it was found that he was paralysed from the waist downwards. There was a wound between his shoulders ; also some small wounds on his head and face. He considered that the paralysis was caused by the shell before the limber passed over him. Was not too hopeful of his chances, but was very calm, and suffered very little pain. He remained two days in the temporary hospital (a château), and while there was visited by Father Dey, the Army Chaplain, who administered to him the last sacraments. Throughout this time Dalton was cheerful, and more anxious as to how others were faring than troubled about himself. He appeared to do fairly well at first, improved as regards sensation and movement, and got more hopeful. Spoke of going to Paris in a motor-car, and then on home. As the château became too dangerous to be continued as a hospital (it was under very heavy shell fire), Major P. Davidson decided to evacuate it, and risk a journey down the hill, back across the Aisne in the dark, to the next temporary hospital at Vieil Arcy. Dalton stood the journey fairly well, and was pleased to leave Verneuil, but was a bit collapsed at the end. Next morning, at 6 a.m., it was found he had developed gangrene of the hip (where he had been bruised only), and he became comatose and died on the 18th September. He had a peaceful death. Although the injury was so grave the hopes raised by his cheerfulness and great powers of endurance gave an unexpectedness to this early termination. He was buried in the churchyard of Vieil Arcy, near Braisne,

by Father Dey, the Roman Catholic Chaplain, 6th Field Ambulance. There was a big attendance of the R.A.M.C., with shells falling about all the time."

Lieutenant-Colonel Dalton was mentioned in Field-Marshal Sir John French's Despatch of the 8th October, 1914.

During his expeditions abroad Lieutenant-Colonel Dalton wrote home interesting letters describing his various experiences, some of which were published in a memoir in the "Journal of the R.A.M.C." for January, 1915, from which many of the details given above have been obtained.

LIEUTENANT RICHARD WILLIAM DANCKWERTS, THE GLOUCESTER-SHIRE REGT.,

born in London on the 16th June, 1893, was the youngest son of the late Mr. W. O. Danckwerts, K.C., and of Mrs. Danckwerts, of 22, Orsett Terrace, Hyde Park, London, W.

He was educated at Winchester and University College, Oxford, and was gazetted to the Gloucestershire Regiment in August, 1914, being promoted temporary Lieutenant on the 15th December. He was mortally wounded in action at Festubert, in Flanders, on the 22nd December, 1914, and died the same day of his wounds.

When at the 'Varsity he rowed for his College in the Torpids in 1913 and 1914, and was a keen cricketer.

2nd LIEUTENANT ARCHIBALD STEUART LINDSEY DANIELL, 5th (attd. 1st) BATTN. RIFLE BRIGADE (THE PRINCE CONSORT'S OWN),

was the only child of Lindsey and Marion Daniell, and grandson of Sir Steuart Colvin Bayley, G.C.S.I. He was born on the 6th June, 1895, and was educated at Winchester. He joined the Special Reserve of Officers in June, 1914, and was gazetted to the 5th Battalion Rifle Brigade, and attached to the 1st Battalion, which he joined at the front at the end of August, 1914. He was killed while leading his platoon into action at Ploegsteert on the 19th December, 1914, and was mentioned in Sir John French's Despatch of the 14th January, 1915.

MAJOR EDWARD HENRY EDWIN DANIELL, D.S.O., p.s.c., 2nd BATTN. ROYAL IRISH REGIMENT, who is believed to have been killed in 1914, was born on the 5th June, 1868, and joined the Royal Irish Regiment from the Militia in April, 1892, becoming Lieutenant in June, 1894, and Captain in October, 1899. He had a long and varied career on the Staff at home and abroad, and on active service.

In 1897–98 he was present at operations on the Samana, north-west frontier of India, for which he received the medal with two clasps.

He took part in the South African War, being Assistant Provost-Marshal (graded as D.A.A.G.) from October, 1900, to May, 1901, and being present, in 1900, at operations in the Orange Free State, the Transvaal east of Pretoria, including a :tions at Belfast and Lydenberg ; at operations in the Orange River Colony, including actions at Bethlehem and Wittebergen ; at operations in Cape Colony, south of the Orange River, including actions at Colesberg. He was afterwards employed with Damant's Horse (formerly Remington's Guides). He was also present at later operations in the Transvaal and Orange River Colony between 1900 and 1902. For his services he was twice mentioned in Despatches—" London Gazette," the 10th September, 1901, and the 29th July, 1902 —was awarded the D.S.O., was placed on the list of officers qualified for Staff employment in consequence of service on the Staff in the Field, and received the Queen's medal with three clasps and the King's medal with two clasps. Subsequently he passed through the Staff College.

From June, 1902, to May, 1903, he was Adjutant of his battalion ; from August, 1903, to August, 1907, he was D.A.A.G., D.A.A. and Q.M.G., North China ; from October, 1909, to November, 1911, he was employed as a General Staff Officer at Headquarters, War Office ; and in November, 1911, was appointed General Staff Officer, 2nd Grade, at Malta, an appointment he held till 1914.

2nd LIEUTENANT FREDERICK DARBY, 1st BATTN. WORCESTERSHIRE REGIMENT, born at Birmingham on the 23rd March, 1880, was the son of Mr. Joseph Darby, of that city.

2nd Lieutenant Darby enlisted in the Worcestershire Regiment in June, 1898, and with it served through the South African War. At the defence of Ladybrand, accompanied by a patrol who volunteered, he went out to mislead the enemy, and carried out the action with conspicuous energy and skill, subsequently distinguishing himself in leading patrols at Bethlehem. For the Ladybrand action he was awarded the D.C.M. on the 10th December, 1900, and for his services in the war generally he was promoted Sergeant in the field, mentioned in Despatches, and received the Queen's and the King's medals with five clasps. In 1908 he was advanced to the rank of Company Sergeant-Major, and was given his commission as 2nd Lieutenant on proceeding to France in November, 1914.

He was killed on the morning of the 29th November, and was buried at Neuve Chapelle. The exact circumstances attending his death have not been ascertained. Both in the ranks and for the very short time he lived to serve as an officer, 2nd Lieutenant Darby enjoyed the esteem and respect of both officers and men, and in the Great War had been noticed for his skill and absolute fearlessness. One of the officers of the battalion spoke of him as " an officer they could ill afford to lose."

The Commander of the Division in which 2nd Lieutenant Darby was serving, in a letter of sympathy to his widow, said : " It may perhaps be some consolation to you to know that he had won golden opinions from his brother officers of all ranks, and that ever since we began to take our part in active operations he had been conspicuous for his gallant conduct."

2nd Lieutenant Darby was a good all-round sportsman, and an especially good hockey player. He married Alice, third daughter of Mr. Joseph Kirkham, of Brookfields, Birmingham, and left four children : Joseph, born April, 1908 ; Alice, born November, 1909 ; Winifred, born March, 1911 ; and Evelyn, born May, 1913.

LIEUTENANT EDWARD CHARLES DAUN, 2nd BATTN. ROYAL SUSSEX REGIMENT, who was born in June, 1885, at Streatham, Surrey, was the only son of Charles James Daun, Esq., and Ada Margaret, his wife, daughter of the late Lieutenant-General E. A. Williams, C.B., Colonel Commandant of the Royal Artillery. He came of military stock, among his immediate relatives

and ancestors being Lieutenant - Colonel E.G.Williams,C.M.G., Commanding the 1st Battalion Devonshire Regiment in the present war; Lieutenant-General Sir H. F. Williams, K.C.B., Colonel Royal Sussex Regiment, and afterwards Colonel Commandant 3rd K.R.R.C.; Colonel Henry Williams, R.A., who was present at Waterloo ; Captain G. B. Williams, R.N., and others more remotely connected.

Lieutenant Daun was educated at Sunningdale School and Harrow, and joined the 3rd Battalion Royal Sussex Regiment in 1904, being gazetted to the 2nd Battalion in 1905, and becoming Lieutenant in November, 1909. He served with his battalion in the Mediterranean and in Ireland (including the Belfast riots). He had been Instructor of Musketry and of Machine Gunnery, and also Assistant Adjutant.

He fell at the Battle of the Aisne on the 14th September, 1914, the following account of the occurrence appearing in the "Sussex Daily News" of the 14th January, 1915 :—

" On reaching the top of the ridge ' A ' Company came under rifle fire from the trenches near the Chemin de Dames. ' B ' Company and the machine gun came up, and a strong firing line was built up. Soon a white flag was seen displayed by the Germans, and large numbers of them came forward to surrender. Shortly a heavy rifle and artillery fire was opened by the Germans upon the assembled mass of friend and foe. Under this fire ' A ' Company suffered heavily, and it was during this time that . . . Lieutenant Daun was killed."

A Captain in his company wrote : " He was a splendid officer, and worked night and day for the good of his regiment and his company, and had a great future before him. He was to have been our next Adjutant, and will be a great loss to the regiment."

Lieutenant Daun was a member of the United Service Club and of the M.C.C. He was a good rifle shot, winning the Officers' Cup at the Aldershot Command Meeting in 1912 and 1913, securing second place in 1914.

LIEUTENANT JOHN STANLEY DAVEY, NORTH SOMERSET YEOMANRY, who was killed in action near Ypres on the 17th November, 1914, was the youngest son of the late Mr. Thomas Davey and Mrs. Davey, of Bannerleigh, Leigh Woods, Bristol.

He was born on the 12th July, 1881, and was educated at the Rev. S. Cornish's School, Walton Lodge, Clevedon, and at Charterhouse (Girdlestonite).

In 1897 he entered the business of Franklyn, Davey & Co., which subsequently became a branch of the Imperial Tobacco Company of Great Britain and Ireland, Ltd. He was fond of shooting, fishing, hunting, and polo.

He joined the Somerset Yeomanry in April, 1909, and became Lieutenant in August, 1914.

CAPTAIN DOUGLAS BYRES DAVIDSON, 8th GURKHA RIFLES, of which he was Ad-

jutant, who was reported as " missing, believed killed," in 1914, was the eldest son of the late Lieutenant-Colonel D. C. Davidson, I. M. S., and Mrs. Davidson, 78, Lexham Gardens, Kensington. He was born on the 15th September, 1895, and was a grandson of the late General John Clarke, formerly Commissioner in Oudh, Sitapur.

He was educated by tutors and at the R.M.C., Sandhurst. After passing out of Sandhurst he was attached for a year to the K.R.R.C., and joined the Indian Army in April, 1906. He was promoted Lieutenant in April, 1907, and Captain in January, 1914.

He was a very good game shot, and played polo and football.

He was last seen on the 30th October, 1914, leading a charge at Festubert to save a picket, with ten volunteers, only one out of the party returning. He is supposed to have fallen, wounded, into the enemy's trench.

His younger brother, Lieutenant R. I. M. Davidson, Manchester Regiment, died on the 24th November, 1914, of wounds received in action at Festubert.

LIEUTENANT RALPH IVAN MEYNELL DAVIDSON, 1st BATTN. MANCHESTER REGIMENT, born at Satara, Bombay, on the 12th June, 1889, was the second son of the late Lieutenant-Colonel D. C. Davidson, I.M.S.,

Bombay Presidency, and Mrs. Davidson, Lexham Gardens, Kensington. He was a grandson of the late General John Clarke, 25th Bengal Native Infantry, formerly Commissioner in Oudh, Sitapur.

He was educated at Temple Grove, East Sheen, at Cheltenham College, and at the R.M.C., Sandhurst. He was gazetted to the Manchester Regiment in September, 1909, and was promoted Lieutenant in July, 1913. While serving in India he passed the Higher Standard in Hindustani, Pushtu, and Punjabi. He was present at the Delhi Dunbar, 1911, for which he received the medal.

He played Rugby football, hockey, and cricket for his regiment.

While giving orders to his men the previous day, at Festubert, about repairing a damaged trench, he was shot through the head, and died of his wounds on the 24th November, 1914. He was buried at Locon, France.

Lieutenant Davidson's elder brother, Captain D. B. Davidson, Indian Army, is believed to have been killed at Festubert on the 30th October, 1914, on which day he was last seen alive, and no news has since been heard of him.

CAPTAIN WILLIAM THOMAS CHORLEY DAVIDSON, 1st BATTN. THE DORSETSHIRE REGIMENT,

born on the 5th January, 1875, was the son of Thomas Davidson, M.B., Oxon., and grandson of Thomas Davidson, M.D., Oxon.

He was educated at Marlborough from 1887 to 1891, and joined the Dorsetshire Regiment as 2nd Lieutenant from the Militia in May, 1897, becoming Lieutenant in October, 1899.

He served in the South African War, 1899–1902, taking part in the relief of Ladysmith, including the action at Spion Kop ; was present at the action at Vaal Krans, and at operations on the Tugela Heights and action at Pieter's

Hill ; operations in the Transvaal, Natal, with actions at Laing's Nek and Orange River Colony in 1900 ; again, at later operations, in the Transvaal and Orange River Colony in 1901 and 1902. He received the Queen's medal with five clasps and the King's medal with two clasps.

He was killed at Givenchy on the 13th October, 1914.

Captain Davidson, who was a member of the United Service and Ranelagh Clubs, attained the rank of Captain in October, 1904.

CAPTAIN HAROLD CASAMAJOR DAVIES (of Warmil Hall, Mildenhall, Suffolk), RESERVE OF OFFICERS,

having volunteered for service, was killed in action on the 26th September, 1914, while attached to the Welsh Regiment. He was the fourth son of the late Major T. H. Davies, of Odiham Close, Hants, and was born on the 27th February, 1879. Joining the Welsh

Regiment from the Militia as 2nd Lieutenant in March, 1900, he became Lieutenant in February, 1902. He served in the South African War, being present at operations in the Transvaal, 1900–02, and receiving the Queen's medal with three clasps.

LIEUTENANT HARRY LLANOVER DAVIES, ROYAL HORSE ARTILLERY,

who died on the 26th October, 1914, from wounds received in action, was the youngest son of the late Theo. H. Davies, of Craigside, Honolulu, and of Tunbridge Wells.

He was born on the 29th January, 1885, and joined the Royal Horse Artillery in July, 1904, becoming Lieutenant in July, 1907.

CAPTAIN HENRY OUSELEY DAVIS, 5th (attd. 2nd) BATTN. ROYAL IRISH RIFLES,

born at Holywood, County Down, Ireland, on the 15th September, 1884, was the eldest son of the late Henry Davis and Mrs. Davis, of Holywood, and a great-grandson of the late Major-General Sir Ralph Ouseley.

He was educated at Portora Royal School, Enniskillen, and Campbell College, Belfast, from which he passed direct into the R.M.C., Sandhurst. He was gazetted to the Royal Dublin Fusiliers in August, 1905, and posted to the 2nd Battalion, becoming Lieutenant in June, 1908. His recreations were cricket and golf.

He resigned his commission in 1910, and on the outbreak of the war was gazetted Captain in the 5th Battalion Royal Irish Rifles at the end of August, 1914, being attached to the 2nd Battalion for active service in September.

He was killed in action by shrapnel on the 27th October, 1914, in the trenches before Neuve Chapelle.

2nd LIEUTENANT STUART DAVISON, 3rd BATTN. THE KING'S ROYAL RIFLE CORPS,

son of Colonel T. Davison, late commanding the 16th Lancers, was born at Lea Park, Godalming, Surrey, on the 2nd July, 1895.

He was educated at Wellington College, and the R.M.C., Sandhurst, where he won the mile and two-mile races, and the Victor Ludorum medal in 1913, for winning the cross-country and two-mile race.

Joining the King's Royal Rifle Corps in February, 1914, he was killed on the 14th September, 1914.

2nd Lieutenant Davison won the regimental point-to-point race (heavy weight) in 1914 on " Nutmeg."

CAPTAIN WALTER RICHARD AUGUSTUS ASTON DAWES, 1st BATTN. THE DUKE OF EDINBURGH'S (WILTSHIRE REGIMENT),

who was killed on the 24th August, 1914, was well known in Salisbury, having been born there on the 26th April, 1878, and being the son of the late Mr. Frederick Aston Dawes, Official Receiver of that town.

He was educated at Salisbury, then spent some years in his father's office, and subsequently had a varied military career. In 1896 he joined the 1st Wilts Rifle Volunteers as a Private, being appointed 2nd Lieutenant in the same corps in July, 1899, a position he resigned in 1900. He then enlisted in the Volunteer Service Company of the Wiltshire Regiment, and proceeded with that unit to South Africa for the Boer War, becoming successively Lance-Corporal, Corporal, and Lance-Sergeant during the year 1900. Then for about five months he served as Sergeant-Major of Mounted Infantry, as well as Quartermaster-Sergeant and Sergeant of Military Police at various times. For that war he received the King's medal with four clasps. Returning from South Africa with the Volunteer Company in 1901, he was, in June of that year, given a commission in the Wiltshire Regiment, serving with it in India from 1901–09.

From 1906–08 he was Station Staff Officer and Cantonment Magistrate at Dagshai, for part of which time he was in charge of the Dagshai Military Prison. In 1909 he was posted to the depot of his regiment at Devizes, remaining there till he obtained his promotion to Captain in January, 1911, when he joined the 1st Battalion in Natal.

He was killed when serving with his battalion in the Great War, one of his Company officers giving the following account of the circumstances to his widow : " I was quite near at the time. . . . Your husband's death occurred near Mons on Monday, August 24th, somewhere between 7 and 8 a.m. ' A ' Company was occupying a line of trenches which we dug the previous afternoon, and from daylight that morning till the time we retired at about 8 o'clock we were under a very heavy shell fire, with no chance of replying, as the enemy's guns were a long way off, and completely hidden from view. Your husband was in Mr. Loder-Symonds's trench, quite close to him, and a shell burst right over them, killing your husband and one other man and wounding several. As far as I could gather, he was lying on his back at the time, chatting to Mr. Loder-Symonds (of course there was nothing to be done at the time), and a fragment of the shell pierced his heart, death being quite instantaneous and painless."

Some men of the Wilts Regiment, who were taken prisoners and kept in the Döberitz Camp, spoke to an officer there, who wrote home in very highest terms of Captain Dawes, saying they owed their lives to his courage and coolness.

A very great number of Captain Dawes's relatives and ancestors have been, and are, in the services, four, if not more, being at present fighting in the Great War in different parts of the world, while others are serving at home.

Captain Dawes married Muriel Gertrude, eldest daughter of Adam Scott Rankin, Esq., and left two children : Isobel Mary, born November, 1912 ; and Richard Arthur Aston, born December, 1914.

MAJOR the Honble. HUGH DAWNAY, D.S.O., p.s.c., 2nd LIFE GUARDS,

who was killed in action on the 6th November, 1914, was the second son of Viscount Downe. He was born on the 19th September, 1875, and received his commission in the Rifle Brigade in October, 1895, becoming Lieutenant in January, 1898 ; from February, 1899, to November, 1900, he was Adjutant of his battalion. He became a Captain in the Rifle Brigade in March, 1901, and in February of that year was appointed A.D.C. to the Commander-in-Chief, retaining the position till February, 1904, and from April, 1904, to January, 1905, was A.D.C. to the G.O.C., North West District.

He took part in the Nile Expedition, being present at the Battle of Khartoum, and being mentioned in Despatches, " London Gazette," 30th September, 1898 ; received the medal, 4th class of the Order of Medjidieh, and the Egyptian medal with clasp.

He next served in the South African War, 1899–1900, while Adjutant of his Battalion, being present at operations in Natal, including actions at Lombard's Kop ; the defence of Ladysmith, including sortie of the 10th December, 1899, and action of the 6th January, 1900. He was twice mentioned in Despatches ("London Gazette," 8th February and 10th September, 1901) ; was awarded the D.S.O., and received the Queen's medal with clasp.

He also served in East Africa, Somaliland Expedition, 1908–10 for which he was mentioned in Despatches (" London Gazette," 17th June, 1910), and received the medal with clasp.

In the Great War, Major Dawnay was serving as General Staff Officer, 2nd grade, and was mentioned in Sir John French's Despatch of the 8th October, 1914.

Major Dawnay married, in 1902, Lady Susan Beresford, daughter of the fifth Marquess of Waterford, and left four sons.

CAPTAIN HERBERT EDWARD DAWSON, 2nd BATTN. THE LINCOLNSHIRE REGIMENT,

who is believed to have been killed in action at the Battle of the Aisne on the 14th September, 1914, was the only child of Colonel and Mrs. H. C. Dawson, and was married.

He was born on the 3rd May, 1881, and joined the Lincolnshire Regiment in January, 1900, becoming Lieutenant in October, 1901. His military career began on active service, for he took part in the South African War, being present at operations in the Orange Free State from February to May, 1900. He was also at operations in the Transvaal from November, 1900, to May, 1902, and received the Queen's medal with three clasps and the King's medal with two clasps.

He became Captain in February, 1906, and from May of that year to May, 1911, was an Adjutant of Volunteers and of the Territorial Force.

CAPTAIN RICHARD LONG DAWSON, 3rd BATTN. COLDSTREAM GUARDS (RESERVE OF OFFICERS),

who was killed in action on the 20th November, 1914, at Zillebeke, was born on the 23rd June, 1879, the only son of the late Honble. Richard M. W. Dawson and Mrs. Dawson, and a grandson of the first Earl of Dartrey.

In 1898 he received his first appointment in the Army when he was gazetted 2nd Lieutenant in the Coldstream Guards. He was advanced to the rank of Lieutenant in 1899 and was promoted Captain in 1907. Four years later, in 1911, he voluntarily joined the Reserve of Officers with the rank of Captain.

While on the active list he served in the South African War, being present at operations in the Orange Free State, 1900, including actions at the Vet and Zand Rivers ; at operations in the Transvaal in May and June of the same year, including actions near Johannesburg, Pretoria, and Diamond Hill ; operations in the Transvaal, east of Pretoria, and in the Orange River Colony between July and November, 1900 ; and operations in Cape Colony from 1900–02. He received the Queen's medal with four clasps and the King's medal with two clasps.

He rejoined the Coldstream Guards, as Captain, in August, 1914, on the outbreak of the war.

MAJOR FRANCIS INNES DAY, 2nd BATTN. ROYAL MUNSTER FUSILIERS,

was born at Fort Gomer on the 21st January, 1870, and was the son of the late Lieutenant-Colonel Henry James Day, 99th Regiment, and grandson of the late Colonel T h o m a s S h a d f o r t h, 59th R e g i m e n t, a n d the late Colonel H. J. Day, 99th Regiment, and great-grandson of Lieutenant and Adjutant John Day, 34th Regiment.

Major Day was educated at a grammar school, and was an example, now becoming more common, of an officer attaining a high position after serving in the ranks, thus introducing a very valuable element into the service.

He was for six years in the ranks of the Middlesex Regiment before obtaining his commission in the South Wales Borderers in February, 1895. He received special extra-regimental promotion to Captain in the Middlesex Regiment in September, 1902 ; and, again, extra-regimental promotion to Major in the Royal Munster Fusiliers in June, 1913.

Major Day served under the Royal Niger Company in West Africa, as a Sub-Commandant, from September, 1896, to June, 1898, and in the course of active service was present at the capture of Bida and of Ilorin, and took part in operations on the Niger in 1898. For these services he received the Royal Niger Company's medal with clasp and the West African medal with clasp. Major Day also served in the Uganda with the punitive expedition against the Wa Nyangori tribe in 1900.

In the South African War he served in Cape Colony in 1902, in command of a squadron of Imperial Yeomanry, and received the Queen's medal with two clasps.

After the conclusion of the war Major Day remained in command of a squadron of Imperial Yeomanry, and afterwards was employed with the Army Service Corps for two years, 1904 to 1906.

He received the Delhi Durbar medal during the visit of Their Majesties the King and Queen to Calcutta in 1913.

In the Great War he was with the Expeditionary Force from the 13th August, 1914, till he was killed in action, while commanding his company in a bayonet charge at Givenchy, on the 22nd December, 1914.

Mrs. Day was the recipient of many sympathetic letters from officers and others. A senior officer of the R.A.M.C. wrote : " So poor Day has gone at last ; died like a gallant soldier. The Munsters behaved magnificently."

Another officer wrote : " I have seen many Munster men who were close by your husband, who was leading the charge which has won the admiration of all. They all speak of his gallantry. He died happy—no suffering."

A later letter from the same officer says : " He was rallying his men for a second attack when he was shot in the face and legs. A Private Wills, who was just behind him, turned him over, and called some men to carry him away, but he said, ' Go on, lads ! Don't waste your time on me ! Here, Wills ! take this revolver and give it to my wife, and tell her I died happy.' Is it not very sad ? Was it not a true soldier's death ? "

Major Day married Florence, daughter of Mr. O. U. D. Stokes, of Tenby, and left two children : Catherine, age ten and a half years ; and Francis, eight and a half years.

LIEUTENANT MAURICE CHARLES DAY, 13th RAJPUTS, INDIAN ARMY,

who was killed in action at Tanga, German East Africa, on the 3rd November, 1914, was the eldest son of the Very Rev. Maurice W. Day, Dean of W a t e r f o r d, and Katherine L. F. Day, and was born at The Palace, Waterford, on the 26th February, 1891.

He was educated first at Aravon, Bray, and subsequently had a brilliant college and university career at Marlborough and Trinity College, Cambridge. At the former he won Foundation, Senior, and Leaving Scholarships, and at the latter an exhibition and scholarship, together with Bell's University Scholarship, and his Wranglership in 1913.

He received a University nomination for the Indian Army, in which he obtained a commission as 2nd Lieutenant, dated 13th August, 1913, but to rank from September, 1911. He served his probation with the Royal West Kent Regiment from November, 1913, to September, 1914, when he was promoted Lieutenant and joined the 13th Rajputs.

The following account of Lieutenant Day's

death was received by his father from the Colonel commanding the 13th Rajputs : " It is with profound regret that I write to inform you of the sad news of the death in action of your son, 2nd Lieutenant M. C. Day, at Tanga, German East Africa, on the 3rd November, 1914. The Commandant, Lieutenant-Colonel H. W. Codrington, and the Adjutant, Captain R. Clothier, and Major R. Corbett were all hit at the same time and place. Your son was buried by the Germans subsequently. Mr. Day joined us just before we came on service, and when we landed was acting as Brigade Transport Officer. During the short time he was with us we realised what a keen and promising officer he was. There can be no doubt that he would have made a name for himself and that soon. Please accept the sincere condolences of all ranks of the regiment."

A second letter from a brother officer gave the following details : " I was with him when he was killed. Colonel Codrington, the Adjutant, your son, and myself had just got on to a small hillock to have a look round when a machine gun opened on us at close range, and the first three named went down instantaneously. Your son was killed outright. I cannot tell you how very deeply we mourn his loss ; for, although he had been with us such a short time, we knew him for a brave, capable, and resourceful boy. Our casualties at Tanga on the 3rd and 4th November were heavy, and the fact of our attack being unsuccessful makes them feel heavier still. Our regiment lost two officers killed and seven wounded, including myself."

2nd LIEUTENANT FRANK DEAN, 2nd BATTN. KING'S ROYAL RIFLE CORPS,

was born at Widnes, Cheshire, on the 28th August, 1876, and enlisted in the K.R.R.C. in October, 1898. He ran through the non-commissioned ranks, becoming Colour-Sergeant in September, 1910, being given his commission during the war on the 1st October, 1914, in his old regiment.

He had served in the Boer War, where he was present at the relief of Ladysmith, at the action on the Tugela Heights and in the Transvaal and Cape Colony.

He was killed in action on the 31st October, 1914, near Gheluvelt in the Battle of Ypres, and was mentioned in Sir John French's Despatch on the Battle of the Aisne, dated the 7th September, 1914.

2nd Lieutenant Dean was a good shot, and took an active interest in the sports of the battalion, especially cross-country running.

2nd LIEUTENANT DENIS DEANE, 2nd BATTN. ROYAL WARWICKSHIRE REGIMENT,

who was killed in action on the 23rd October, 1915, was the son of Major C. L. Deane, "The Lodge," Kent Road, Fleet, Hants. 2nd Lieutenant Deane, who was just eighteen when he was killed, was educated at Wellington (where he was in the Combermere) and at the R.M.C., Sandhurst, at both of which he distinguished himself as a footballer.

He was gazetted to the Royal Warwickshire Regiment on the 15th August, 1914.

LIEUTENANT MAURICE JAMES DEASE, V.C., 4th BATTN. THE ROYAL FUSILIERS (CITY OF LONDON REGT.),

was the son of Edmund FitzLawrence Dease, Esq., and was born on the 28th September, 1889, at Gaulstown, Coole, County Westmeath. He was educated at Stonyhurst College, at Wimbledon College, and at the R.M.C., Sandhurst.

Lieutenant Dease, V.C., joined the Royal Fusiliers at Aldershot in 1910, becoming Lieutenant in April, 1912. In October, 1910, he was selected by his Commanding Officer to attend a class, which was being held in North Wales by an officer of the Indian Army, to instruct officers in the art of mountain warfare, and subsequently he was Scout Officer of the battalion ; also Machine Gun Officer and at different times Acting Adjutant.

On the 23rd August, 1914, as Machine Gun Officer he was defending the Canal Bridge at Nimy, near Mons, and for his gallantry was mentioned in Field Marshal Sir John French's Despatch of the 18th October, 1914 ; he was one of the first ten to be awarded the coveted distinction of the Victoria Cross in the Great War. The following is the official record of the circumstances :—

" *For Valour.*

War Office, November 16th, 1914.

His Majesty the King has been graciously

pleased to approve of the grant of the Victoria Cross to the under-mentioned officer for conspicuous bravery whilst serving with the Expeditionary Force :

Lieutenant Maurice James Dease,
4th Battalion the Royal Fusiliers.

Though two or three times badly wounded, he continued to control the fire of his machine guns at Mons on the 23rd August until all his men were shot. He died of his wounds."

Lieutenant Dease was heir to his uncle, Major Gerald Dease, D.L., of Turbotston, County Westmeath, who had himself served in the Royal Fusiliers.

LIEUTENANT CLAUDE NORMAN CHAMPION DE CRESPIGNY, 2nd DRAGOON GUARDS (QUEEN'S BAYS),

was born at Southsea on the 14th June, 1888, the fifth son of Sir Claude Champion de Crespigny,Bart., and Lady Champion de Crespigny.

He was educated at Hawtrey's, where he was the swimming champion ; Cheltenham College, where he won the quarter-mile under sixteen ; and the R.M.C., Sandhurst. At the latter he won the saddle, and was a representative of the College in Athletics *v.* Woolwich.

Lieutenant Champion de Crespigny entered the 1st Dragoon Guards in February, 1907, becoming Lieutenant in January, 1908, and, after a short period on half-pay, joined the Queen's Bays in November, 1910. He had been awarded the Emperor of Austria's decoration. He was killed at Compiègne on the 1st September, 1914, the following account of the action being given by General Allenby to his parents : " I and the whole Cavalry Division sympathise with you, and we deeply feel Norman's loss, but I must tell you he died a hero's death. The brigade was hotly engaged, and on the ' Bays ' fell the brunt of the fighting on September 1st. Norman, with a few men, was holding an important tactical point, and he held it until every man was killed or wounded. No man could have done more ; few would have done so much."

Letters from others present went to show that his sortie from the right of his regiment saved the " Bays " from being outflanked and wiped out, and enabled them to charge and capture eleven guns.

Lieutenant Champion de Crespigny was men-

tioned posthumously in Sir John French's Despatch of the 8th October, 1914.

His body was exhumed from the cemetery of Nery, a village at the south-western corner of the Forest of Compiègne, and placed, with military honours, in the Mausoleum at Champion Lodge, on the 12th November, 1914.

He married, in September, 1913, Rose, daughter of Captain Gordon, of Roberts' Horse, a son of the late Sir Henry Gordon, K.C.B., and elder brother of General Charles Gordon, C.B., of Khartoum.

BARON ALEXIS DE GUNZBURG, 2nd LIEUTENANT 11th (PRINCE ALBERT'S OWN) HUSSARS,

who was given his commission at the beginning of September, 1914, and was subsequently attached as Galloper and Interpreter to the Royal Horse Guards (7th Cavalry Brigade), was born on the 6th May, 1887, and was the youngest son of the late Baron and of Baroness de Gunzburg, of Paris. He was related to Mrs. Bischoffsheim, to the Dowager Countess of Desart, and to Sir Maurice and Lady Fitzgerald. He was a member of the St. James's and Bath Clubs.

Baron de Gunzburg, who was Russian by birth and was educated at Eton, was naturalised in order to enlist in the British Army on the outbreak of the war with Germany. He left England with his regiment at the beginning of October, 1914, proceeding directly to the firing line in Belgium, where, by his bravery and coolness under fire, he attracted the favourable attention of both officers and men. He was ever ready to undertake dangerous missions, and always cheery. It was related of him how he left the trenches at great risk to fetch a doctor, after he had himself attended to a wound received by Lord Alastair Innes Ker.

He was killed near Ypres on the 6th November, 1914. At the time he was with the Life Guards, and was sent with three other young officers, who had constituted themselves a little band they called " The Fire Brigade," to bring up the Royal Horse Guards to support an attack at Zillebeke. They were all on foot, and safely carried out their mission, having had to run across an open field for some two hundred yards under fire, but on the way back were shot.

2nd Lieutenant de Gunzburg was buried with Colonel Gordon Wilson, Royal Horse Guards,

Major Dawnay and Captain Wyndham, Life Guards, who were killed on the same day, in the churchyard at Zillebeke. During the day he was killed he had been carrying messages under heavy fire to all parts. Several officers who served with him wrote to his aunt, Mrs. Bischoffsheim, most appreciative accounts of the young officer's conduct, and the Baroness de Gunzburg received a telegram from Their Majesties the King and Queen expressing their sympathy, and adding: " His Majesty has learnt how gallantly Baron de Gunzburg fought with his comrades of the Royal Horse Guards, although his duties as interpreter did not necessitate his presence in the firing line."

CAPTAIN CHARLES EDWARD M. DE LA PASTURE, 1st BATTN. SCOTS GUARDS,

who was killed in action near Ypres on the 29th October, 1914, but whose name has not appeared in the official casualty lists, was the eldest son of the Marquis de la Pasture, Cefn, Usk, Monmouthshire.

He was born at Caley Hall, Otley, Yorkshire, on the 15th September, 1879, and was educated at Downside Abbey, Bath. After serving with the embodied Militia for nearly three months he was gazetted from it to the Derbyshire Regiment in April, 1900. Later in the year, being in South Africa, he joined Plumer's Force as a trooper for the relief of Mafeking, and was also present at operations in Rhodesia from October, 1899, to May, 1900 ; he received the Queen's medal with two clasps. In September, 1900, he was gazetted to the Scots Guards, becoming Lieutenant in April, 1903, and Captain in June, 1907. From June, 1907, to August, 1910, he was A.D.C. to the late General Sir Frederick Forestier Walker, Governor and Commander-in-Chief, Gibraltar.

Captain de la Pasture, who was a member of the Guards' and Travellers' Clubs, married, in April, 1914, Agatha, second daughter of Alexander Mosley, Esq., C.M.G., of Gibraltar.

He left early in August, 1914, with the Expeditionary Force for France, and was in command of the right flank Company, 1st Battalion Scots Guards, when he was killed. He was mentioned in Sir John French's Despatch of the 14th January, 1915.

He was officially reported missing on the 29th October, 1914, and has since been unofficially reported killed on that date.

LIEUTENANT JAMES OWEN CUNNINGHAME DENNIS, 12th BATTERY, ROYAL FIELD ARTILLERY, who was killed in action on the 24th October, 1914, was the only son of Mrs. Dennis, Cumberland Mansions, London, W., and of the late Colonel Dennis, 6th Dragoon Guards (Carabiniers).

He was born on the 5th August, 1888, and was educated at Malvern College from 1903 to 1907. There he was a school prefect, head of his house, in the Shooting VIII, 1906-07, and in the House Football XI. He then went to the R.M.A., Woolwich, and entered the Royal Artillery in July, 1909, becoming Lieutenant three years later.

The following account of the circumstances attending his death was published in "The Malvernian " for December, 1914 :—

" Owen Dennis was killed by a shell when he was directing his battery fire from the infantry trenches. His Major states that he considered him to be his smartest officer. Throughout the time that he was at the front he displayed unflinching bravery. This was quite in accordance with what we noted in him at school."

2nd LIEUTENANT BARRY MAYNARD RYND DENNY, 1st BATTN. THE KING'S (LIVERPOOL REGIMENT), SPECIAL RESERVE, who died on the 26th October from wounds received on the 24th October, 1914, was the third surviving son of the Rev. Edward Denny, of Drumlone, Southborne, Bournemouth. At the time of his death he was twenty-nine years old, and was gazetted to the Special Reserve of the King's in April, 1914.

LIEUTENANT FRANK ALEXANDER DE PASS, V.C., 34th (PRINCE ALBERT VICTOR'S OWN), POONA HORSE, son of Eliot Arthur and Beatrice de Pass, was born in London on the 26th April, 1887. He was educated at the Abbey School, Beckenham, and Rugby, from which he passed direct into the R.M.A., Woolwich, being third on the list of successful candidates.

He was gazetted 2nd Lieutenant in the R.F.A. in December, 1906, and Lieutenant in March, 1909. In the latter year he exchanged into the Poona Horse. From November, 1913, till the outbreak of the war he was Orderly Officer, with the local rank of Captain, to Sir Percy Lake, K.C.M.G., C.B., Chief of the Staff in India.

Lieutenant de Pass, V.C., was killed on the 25th November, 1914, near Festubert. On the 24th he had brought in a wounded sepoy, with the assistance of Trooper Cook, of the 7th Dragoon Guards ; next day he was shot by a German sniper while at the head of a sap supervising repairs.

Lieutenant de Pass was awarded the V.C. for his bravery, the following being the official account in the "London Gazette" February 18th, 1915 :—

" For conspicuous bravery near Festubert, on the 24th November, in entering a German sap and destroying a traverse in the face of the enemy's bombs, and for subsequently [*i.e., next day*, Ed.] rescuing, under heavy fire, a wounded man who was lying exposed in the open. Lieutenant de Pass lost his life on this [*i.e., 25th*, Ed.] day in a second attempt to capture the afore-mentioned sap, which had been re-occupied by the enemy."

The whole circumstances, as detailed by the Captain of the squadron, were as follows : The enemy, by means of a sap, had blown in the main parapet of a trench, causing a breach which left the trench exposed to rifle fire from the sap. Sowar Abdullah Khan volunteered to enter the sap : he returned and reported that the enemy had erected a sandbag traverse, about ten yards from the trenches, and that a man with a rifle was at the loophole. At daylight on the 23rd November the enemy commenced throwing bombs into our trenches, which continued all day, causing many casualties. Early on the morning of the 24th, Lieutenant de Pass, accompanied by Sowars Fattle Khan and Firman Shah, entered the enemy's sap, and, proceeding along it, Lieutenant de Pass placed a charge of gun-cotton in the enemy's loophole and fired the charge, completely demolishing the enemy's traverse, and rounding off the bend sufficiently to expose to our rifle fire the sap for some thirty yards. This action of Lieutenant de Pass stopped all bomb throwing during the 24th. The next day Lieutenant de Pass, accompanied by a trooper of the 7th Dragoon Guards (Trooper Cook), went out in broad daylight and brought in a sepoy of the 58th Rifles, who was lying wounded in the rear of our trenches at about 200-ft. distance. Lieutenant de Pass again volunteered to enter the enemy's sap and blow up the traverse, which the enemy had replaced during the night, but permission was refused. About 3 p.m. on the 25th the bomb-throwing by the enemy became worse,

and Lieutenant de Pass went to the head of the sap to supervise repairs to our defences, which had been seriously impaired. He endeavoured to shoot the enemy's sniper through a loophole, and in so doing was himself shot through the head.

Sowars Abdullah Khan, Fattle Khan, and Firman Shah were all awarded the Indian Distinguished Service medal.

Lieutenant de Pass was a member of the Cavalry Club. He played polo, and was a successful rider, winning several flat races and steeple-chases in India.

LIEUTENANT ROBERT ANDREW DE STACPOOLE, 2nd BATTN. THE CONNAUGHT RANGERS,

who was killed at Verneuil, on the Aisne, by rifle fire on the 20th September, 1914, was the fourth son of the Duke de Stacpoole, J.P., County Galway, late Lieutenant 3rd Battalion Yorkshire Regiment.

He was born at Mount Hazel, Co. Galway, on the 24th May, 1892, and was educated at Downside School, Wimbledon College, and the R.M.C., Sandhurst. He was gazetted to the Connaught Rangers in September, 1911, and was promoted Lieutenant on the 22nd August, 1914.

Lieutenant de Stacpoole was a keen rider to hounds, and hunted with the Galway Blazers, and with the Kildare Hounds when quartered at the Curragh.

LIEUTENANT FREDERICK WILLIAM DES VOEUX, 2nd BATTN. GRENADIER GUARDS,

who was killed in action in France at the Battle of the Aisne, was the younger son of the late Sir G. William des Voeux, G.C.M.G., and Lady des Voeux, of 35, Cadogan Square, S.W.

He was born on the 29th November, 1889, and received his commission in the Grenadier Guards from the Special Reserve, in May, 1910, becoming Lieutenant in October, 1911.

LIEUTENANT ALEXANDER DEWAR, ROYAL ENGINEERS (SPECIAL RESERVE),

who died on the 21st December, 1914, aged 29, of wounds received in action, was the elder son of Mr. John Dewar, J.P., Villa Rosa, Trinity, Edinburgh.

He was educated at the Edinburgh Academy from 1894-1904, ending up as Dux of the Upper Modern Class, and head boy of Scott House in 1904. He won the Weir Class Essay Prize, and was a most consistent and earnest worker. Endowed with a fine physique, he trained indefatigably, and besides winning his XV cap, he won the open mile, 100 yards, and quarter-mile races. He took his degree of B.A. at Clare College, Cambridge, and won the Robert Greene Cup, and was captain both of his College XV and Rowing VIII. After gaining extensive experience in civil engineering at Glasgow, he served one year with the Royal Engineers at Chatham, on probation, and obtained his commission in the Special Reserve of Officers. He subsequently received a good Government appointment in Egypt, and was employed in operations connected with the draining and reclamation of waterlogged districts in the Nile Delta. His work had already received recognition from Lord Kitchener, and a bright and useful career had dawned for him, for which he had schooled himself by a wide and thorough training. Shortly after the outbreak of war he was posted to the 15th Field Company Royal Engineers, and crossed to France with the VIIIth Division early in November. On the 21st December, in the afternoon, Lieutenant Dewar was engaged in making a sketch of the ground on the German side of the British trenches. In order to do this, he made use of a periscope, which enabled him to see the desired ground without exposing himself. He was shot in the trenches, and received two bullet wounds, one in the left forearm and one in the abdomen. He was immediately taken to the dressing station, after which he was brought to the hospital, where he died about ten o'clock in the evening, without recovering consciousness.

Lieutenant Dewar was highly spoken of by his brother officers. In the official report by the Brigadier-General in whose lines he was working, reference to his death was made as follows : " The Brigadier wishes to say how very sorry we all are to hear this news. He has done such very excellent work for us."

The Commanding Officer, in a letter to Lieutenant Dewar's father, says : " Your son devoted himself heart and soul to his work, and never spared himself. He was never foolhardy, but brave to excess."

He was mentioned in Sir John French's Despatch of the 14th January, 1915.

LIEUTENANT DOUGLAS FENTON DE WEND, 2nd BATTN. THE DUKE OF WELLINGTON'S (WEST RIDING REGIMENT),

who was killed in action on the 10th–11th November, 1914, aged twenty-four years, was the surviving twin son of the late Colonel Douglas de Wend, 1st Battalion Duke of Wellington's Regiment, and of Mrs. de Wend (née Chester), of Aislaby Hall, Sleights, Yorkshire.

Lieutenant de Wend's grandfather served in the 44th Regiment, and his great-grandfather in the 60th Rifles.

He was educated at Wellington College, where he was in the Wellesley from 1904–08, and where he was a prominent member of the Rifle Club. In 1908 he went to the R.M.C., Sandhurst, from which he obtained his commission in his father's old regiment in December, 1909, becoming Lieutenant in January, 1914.

He was fond of football and hunting, and was a member of the Public Schools Club.

Lieutenant de Wend was killed while fighting the Prussian Guard at the great Battle of Ypres.

2nd LIEUTENANT WALTER DE WINTON, 3rd BATTN. COLDSTREAM GUARDS,

joined the regiment in February, 1913.

He was unofficially reported as having been killed in action on the 6th September, 1914.

LIEUTENANT ALAN JAMES DICKSON, 2nd BATTN. HIGHLAND LIGHT INFANTRY,

who was killed on the 16th November, 1914, was the son of Patrick Dickson, J.P., of Barnhill, Kincardineshire, and Mrs. Dickson, of Sunnyside House, Montrose, and was born at Laurencekirk, Scotland, on the 28th February, 1892.

He was educated at Fettes College, Edinburgh, and Merton College, Oxford, where he obtained the degree of B.A. in 1914. He received his commission as 2nd Lieutenant from the University O.T.C. in July, 1914, was ordered to the front in August, and was promoted Lieutenant in November.

Lieutenant Dickson was killed in the trenches by a sniper, when looking out to try and locate him.

LIEUTENANT CYRIL GARLIES DICKSON, 2nd BATTN. LOYAL NORTH LANCASHIRE REGIMENT, who was killed in action in East Africa at the end of 1914, aged twenty-four, was the son of James F. G. Dickson, Nuthurst, Avondale Road, Croydon. He joined the Loyal North Lancashire Regiment in February, 1912, and became Lieutenant in March, 1914.

LIEUTENANT MACLEAN PROCTOR DILWORTH, 1st BATTN. SHERWOOD FORESTERS (NOTTINGHAMSHIRE AND DERBYSHIRE REGIMENT),

who was killed in action on the 20th November, 1914, was the only son of Mr. and Mrs. Proctor Dilworth, St. Alban's Mansions, Kensington Court, London, W.

He was born on the 26th April, 1888, was educated at Harrow (The Knoll, 1901-05), and joined the Army in May, 1907, becoming Lieutenant in February, 1910.

CAPTAIN CLIVE MACDONNELL DIXON, 16th LANCERS (SPECIAL RESERVE),

of Chapel-Garth, Stokesley, Yorkshire, who was killed in action near Ypres on the 6th November, 1914, was the eldest son of the late Sir Raylton Dixon, D.L., of Gunnergate Hall, Middlesbrough.

Captain Dixon, who was born in February, 1870, was educated at Rugby, which he entered in 1884. He joined the 16th Lancers in October, 1890, was promoted Lieutenant in January, 1893, and Captain six years later; and, from August, 1898, to March, 1900, was Adjutant of his regiment. He served in the Chitral Campaign, and took part in the South African War, being present at the defence of Ladysmith; he was mentioned in Despatches, given the brevet of Major, November, 1900, and received the Queen's and King's medals with seven clasps. He retired from the active list in 1902, joining the Reserve of Officers. On the outbreak of this war he was posted to his old regiment, of which he was in temporary command when he was killed. Captain Dixon was a keen sportsman and a clever artist, having often exhibited in the Royal Academy.

He married a daughter of the late Mr. John Bell, of Rushpool, and left six children.

CAPTAIN GEORGE ARTHUR MURRAY DOCKER, ROYAL FUSILIERS, (CITY OF LONDON REGIMENT), who was born on the

18th November. 1876, was the elder son of Arthur Robert Docker, late of Sydney, New South Wales. He was at Oriel College, Oxford, where he studied Law, and passed the Law Preliminary Examination, but did not take his degree, as he proceeded to South Africa with the 3rd (Militia) Battalion King's Own Royal Lancaster Regiment.

He received his commission in the King's (Liverpool Regiment) in 1900, becoming Lieutenant the same year; he was transferred to the Royal Fusiliers in 1901 as Lieutenant, and was promoted Captain in 1908. Captain Docker served during the South African War, where he raised and commanded a section of Mounted Infantry at Zand River, and fought in the engagement there on the 14th June, 1900. Shortly after this, he was on the Staff of Lieutenant-Colonel White, R.A., for two months, while the latter was in command of a flying column sent in pursuit of De Wet in the Orange Free State, and also took part in the action at Ladybrand, 2nd to 7th September, 1900. In October, 1900, he joined the 1st Battalion King's at Machadodorp, in the Transvaal. From there he went to Balmoral, under Brigadier-General Barker, and was in several engagements, including an attack on Balmoral on the 19th November, 1900. Subsequently he had charge of a Mounted Infantry detachment at Wilge River. He was invalided home in June, 1901, having had a very severe attack of rheumatic fever. For his services he received the Queen's medal with four clasps.

In 1902, after six months' sick leave, he went to Burma to join the 1st Battalion Royal Fusiliers. In March, 1904, he was posted to the Depot at Hounslow. He rejoined the 1st Battalion at Parkhurst, Isle of Wight, in March, 1906. In that year he went through the musketry and Maxim gun courses at the School of Musketry, Hythe, passing out well in both examinations. From the 16th April, 1907, to the 31st July, 1911, he was Instructor of Military Law and Administration to "F" Company at the R.M.C., Sandhurst, which appointment he held three months beyond the usual term. In June, 1910, he passed with honours his examination for promotion. On the expiration of his appointment at Sandhurst, he was sent to the 4th Battalion of his regiment at Aldershot, pending absorption, and was ultimately posted to the 3rd Battalion in India.

He returned home in April, 1912, to take up the appointment of Adjutant of the 10th Battalion (Duke of Cambridge's Own) Middlesex Regiment. While Adjutant of this battalion, Captain Docker did a great deal to enable it to gain the reputation it has earned since its formation by Colonel St. Leger Glyn (late Grenadier Guards) in 1908.

When the 10th Middlesex were mobilised on the outbreak of the war with Germany, they were sent to Sittingbourne, and very shortly after that, as both the Colonel and the Second-in-Command had to go on sick leave, Captain Docker was for some time in temporary command of the battalion, as well as being Adjutant, and his untiring zeal helped to bring it to a high state of efficiency, while his personal influence did much to raise the whole morale of the corps. At the end of October the battalion was ordered to proceed to India. They had actually embarked, and the ship was on the point of leaving, when Captain Docker was recalled by telegram for service with the Expeditionary Force, and was ordered to take out a draft of the 3rd King's Own Royal Lancaster Regiment to the 1st Battalion of that regiment in Flanders.

He left England with the draft on the 8th November, and reached the 1st Battalion on the 15th November, 1914. The following evening he went into the trenches, and he was killed next morning, the 17th November, at Le Touquet, near Armentières. He was buried near the station there, where there were already many graves of officers and men of the King's Own.

Captain Docker married in 1903 Anna Louisa Maud Josephine, daughter of the late Louis Arthur Goodeve, Barrister-at-Law, and left four children : Arthur Guy, born November, 1904 ; Peter Goodeve, born June, 1908 ; Michael Lee, born November, 1911 ; and Alison Everilda Josephine, born February, 1914.

Captain Docker was well known as a cricketer. He was a member of the M.C.C., the Free Foresters, and the Oxford University Authentics, and was one of the M.C.C. team sent to the West Indies in 1913. He represented his college in cricket, football, and athletics, and played polo and cricket for his regiment. He also won many prizes for athletics and golf. He was a member of the Inner Temple, and was called to the Bar in June, 1914.

CAPTAIN DAVID SCOTT DODGSON, ROYAL GARRISON ARTILLERY,

was the son of the late General Sir David Scott Dodgson, K.C.B., who served through the Indian Mutiny, and of Lady Dodgson, of Southsea.

He was born on the 24th November, 1884, and was educated at Summerfields, near Oxford, at Harrow (The Grove, 1898–1901), and the R.M.A., Woolwich, receiving his commission in December, 1904, becoming Lieutenant three years later, and Captain on the 30th October, 1914. He left for the front on the 17th September, 1914, and was in the ammunition column attached to the 1st and 2nd Siege Batteries of the First Siege Brigade.

He was shot by a German sniper at Gorre, near Bethune, on the 14th November, 1914, and killed instantaneously. It was found necessary to lay a telephone cable for his battery, a task which invariably exposes those employed on it to considerable danger from snipers. Captain Dodgson bravely volunteered to do this work, though it was not part of his duties, and was shot while attempting to carry it out. For his gallantry he was mentioned in Sir John French's Despatch of January, 1915.

Captain Dodgson married in 1908 Blanche Mary, youngest daughter of the late Dr. and Mrs. Leacroft, of Derby, and left one son, David Scott, born in January, 1913.

LIEUTENANT WILLIAM HENRY GORDON DODS, 1st BATTN. LEICESTERSHIRE REGIMENT,

who was killed in action on the 22nd October, 1914, was the son of Major William Sandars Dods, formerly in the Norfolk Regiment, of Uvedale, Norfolk.

He was born on the 27th October, 1891, and joined the Leicestershire Regiment as 2nd Lieutenant in September, 1911, getting his step in May, 1913.

LIEUTENANT PHILIP WALTER RUDOLPH DOLL, 1st BATTN. THE KING'S (LIVERPOOL REGIMENT),

was killed in action near Ypres on the 31st October, 1914, having previously been reported as missing.

He was the fourth son of Mr. Charles FitzRoy Doll, J.P., and Emily Frances, his wife, of Hadham Towers, Much Hadham, Herts. He was born on the 28th May, 1890, and was educated at Charterhouse, where he was in the Cricket XI, and at the R.M.C., Sandhurst, where he was in the Football Team ; he played both cricket and football in the Army, and at the Army Rifle Association meeting won Lord Roberts's prize for machine-gun practice with his squad. He entered "The King's" in November, 1909, and was promoted Lieutenant in April, 1910.

CAPTAIN JOHN ERIC WESTERN DOLPHIN, 1st BATTN. THE HAMPSHIRE REGT.,

was the son of Lieutenant-Colonel H. E. Dolphin, Royal Artillery (retired), and was born at Queenstown on the 27th December, 1885. He was educated at Stubbington, and the R.M.C., Sandhurst.

Captain Dolphin received his commission in the Hampshire Regi-

ment in 1906, becoming Lieutenant in March, 1909, and being promoted Captain 21st October, 1914.

He was treacherously shot by the Germans on the 8th November, 1914, after they had called out "Don't shoot," near Ploegsteert, about four miles north of Armentières.

Captain Dolphin was a good shot and rider, and a fair golf player.

LIEUTENANT AND ADJUTANT ALFRED EDWIN CLAUD TOKE DOONER, 1st BATTN. ROYAL WELSH FUSILIERS,

third son of Colonel William Toke Dooner, of Ditton Place, near Maidstone, Kent, was born at Victoria Barracks, Portsmouth, on the 3rd April, 1892. His great-grandfather, Major Lawrence Dundas, served in the Peninsula in the 5th Fusiliers, gaining the medal with clasps for Corunna, Albuhera, Badajos, and Busaco. Lieutenant Dooner was educated at Tonbridge School, having obtained a scholarship there in 1905 from the King's School, Rochester. At Tonbridge he was in the Shooting VIII during 1907–10, and won the Warner Challenge Cup in 1908–09, helping also to win other trophies for his House. In 1910 he represented his school in the contest for the Spencer Cup, and he was also in the School XV. From Tonbridge he passed third into the R.M.C., Sandhurst (Woolwich Company), in 1910, and there gained the prizes for drill and German, and the 1st prize for revolver shooting. He was gazetted to the Royal Welsh Fusiliers in September, 1911. In 1912 he passed as a first class Interpreter in German, having in 1908, when at Tonbridge, gained the first prize in that language in an examination open to all the public schools.

In September, 1912, he was promoted Lieutenant, and in July, 1914, he was appointed Adjutant of his battalion at the early age of twenty-two years and three months. Lieutenant Dooner was mentioned in Sir John French's Despatch of the 14th January, 1915.

Conflicting reports as to the actual circumstances of his death have been received, he having at first been reported as missing on the 30th October, 1914, but since that date a list of dead has been received from the German Government, through the American Embassy, in which Lieutenant Dooner is included as having been killed, about the date mentioned, at Zandvoorde, near Ypres.

It would appear, from reports received from officers, non-commissioned officers, and men, now prisoners of war, who were present at the fighting on the 30th that the Germans were then making a severe struggle to get through to Calais, and on the right of the Royal Welsh Fusiliers, who held part of a very extended line, were some trenches occupied by dismounted cavalry. Nearly all the latter were killed or wounded, and the trenches taken, thus leaving the right flank of the Royal Welsh Fusiliers open to an attack. Lieutenant Dooner, seeing the danger, ran across an open piece of fire-swept ground to the company on the right, and, having given his instructions, was returning to rejoin his Commanding Officer, when he was seen to fall, it was believed, wounded. Lieutenant-Colonel Cadogan, commanding the battalion, ran to his assistance, accompanied, it is stated, by Sergeant Evans, now a prisoner at Münster. They found Lieutenant Dooner had been killed, and as they were returning, Sergeant Evans states, Lieutenant-Colonel Cadogan was himself shot down and killed, and thus lost his life in a brave and noble attempt to assist a brother officer and comrade.

The previous fighting, from October 19th, had been incessant, and the Royal Welsh Fusiliers had suffered very severely. A letter to the Vicar of Carnarvon from a survivor stated that the Colonel and Adjutant appeared " to bear charmed lives, and did splendid work, and were the talk of the Division." On the evening of the 30th only one officer (Captain Parker) and 86 non-commissioned officers and men answered the roll-call out of a total of 31 officers and 1,100 men who had left Lyndhurst on the 4th October.

Lieutenant Dooner was a member of the Junior United Service Club, and his name appears on the Roll of Honour in the entrance hall of that club.

MAJOR THOMAS PHILIP GODMAN DORINGTON, 1st (ROYAL) DRAGOONS,

who was killed in the trenches near Ypres on the 12th November, 1914, was the third son of the late Major-General R. Temple Godman and Mrs. C. M. Godman, of Highden, Pulborough, Sussex, and assumed the surname of Dorington. He was born on the 22nd May, 1877, and was educated at Harrow

(Small Houses and Druries) from 1891 to 1894, joining the 1st Dragoons in April, 1897, and becoming Lieutenant in July, 1899. He served in the South African War, taking part in the relief of Ladysmith, including the actions at Colenso, Spion Kop, Vaal Krans, Tugela Heights, and Pieters Hill ; operations in Natal, 1900 ; in the Transvaal, Orange River Colony, and Cape Colony, from May, 1901, to May, 1902. He received the Queen's medal with five clasps and the King's medal with two clasps.

Major Dorington was gazetted to his Majority on the 31st October, 1914.

LIEUTENANT CLEMENT COTTRELL-DORMER, 2nd BATTN. SCOTS GUARDS,

the elder son of Captain and Mrs. Cottrell-Dormer, of Rousham, came of a family which had been settled in Oxfordshire for over four centuries, and, through his mother, he was a great-grandson of David, eighth Earl of Leven and seventh Earl of Melville. The first of his name to achieve distinction was Sir Michael Dormer, Lord Mayor of London in 1541. Possibly one of the most famous of the family was James Dormer, born in 1679, who served under Marlborough at Blenheim, and was engaged at the sieges of Mons, Liège, and Namur. He also commanded a brigade in the ill-starred Jacobite rising in 1715.

Lieutenant Cottrell-Dormer, who was born in February, 1891, was educated at Mr. Lionel Helbert's Preparatory School, West Downs, near Winchester, from 1901. His Eton life commenced in 1905 at Mr. J. H. M. Hare's House. He rowed in the Junior House Four, and became a member of the boats, rowing in the " Alexandra." He joined the Eton Volunteer Band, and became a member of the Corps itself. He was very keen on beagling, and was an expert carpenter. He also joined the Eton Debating Society. After leaving Eton in 1910 he went for a short time to Mr. William Trevor's, Lathbury Park ; and in May, 1910, he was given a commission in the Queen's Own Oxfordshire Hussars, the Duke of Marlborough being his Colonel, and Major the Hon. Eustace Fiennes his Squadron Commander. The latter wrote of him : " Clement is a first-rate officer, and will make an A1 soldier." He was gazetted to the Scots Guards on probation in 1911. His ever bright and cheerful disposition made him the idol of his brother officers and men ; and, being a 2nd Lieutenant, the honour to carry the Colours fell to him in the Coronation Procession, 1911. He was finally gazetted to the Scots Guards in February, 1913. Previous to the outbreak of hostilities he had undertaken a course of signalling, as a help to his future career, and worked hard all day long. He was very keen, and had been promised the post of Assistant Adjutant at the next vacancy. Lieutenant Cottrell-Dormer, who was promoted to that rank on the 23rd October, 1914, was killed in action three days later at Kruiseik, near Ypres. A member of the regiment wrote that he was defending his trench when struck by a shell and killed, adding : " He was splendid in front of his men." The Commanding Officer of his battalion—now a prisoner of war—wrote : " We were captured the same day that your boy was killed whilst gallantly defending his trenches against repeated and most determined attacks in force. He was one of the very best and bravest of regimental officers I have ever seen on active service, besides being most popular with all his brother officers. His Captain—C. Fox—could not say enough, he told me, to express his thorough confidence in him on all occasions, which confidence was always justified up to the hilt in everything he most cheerfully did so well. It will, I hope, comfort you a little to know this, and how dreadfully we all deplore his loss." A Brigade-Major wrote : " His men loved him ; yet he was strict with them, and always upheld discipline before everything. He was just the bravest boy we had ; and, though little more than a boy, he set every officer an example of what a soldier should be. He died as he had lived— a soldier and a man."

Lieutenant Cottrell-Dormer, who was devoted to hunting and a very good rider, had hunted all his life with the Bicester and Heythrop Hounds. He was a member of White's and of the Guards' Clubs.

MAJOR WILLIAM SHOLTO DOUGLAS, p.s.c., ROYAL ENGINEERS,

who died at Boulogne on the 14th November, 1914, of wounds received in action near Ypres on the 2nd of that month, leaving a widow, was the only son of Colonel and Mrs. Douglas, Lansdowne House, Bath. He was born on the 18th September, 1875, and joined the Royal Engineers in October, 1895, becoming Lieutenant in October, 1898. He saw much Staff service, chiefly with the Intelligence Department, being a Staff College graduate and a first-class interpreter in French. From December, 1890, to September, 1899, he was specially employed with the Egyptian Army, and from December, 1900, to September, 1901, in the Intelligence Department at headquarters of the Army, becoming in October in the latter year Staff Captain (Intelligence) at headquarters, and remaining so employed till May, 1906 having been promoted Captain in October, 1904. In 1910 he was appointed Assistant Director of Army Signals, IInd Division Aldershot Command, and in the Great War he was employed as a General Staff Officer, 3rd grade. He was gazetted to the rank of Major after his death, to date from the 30th October, 1914.

2nd LIEUTENANT ARCHER CHERNOCKE DOWNES, 1st BATTN, CHESHIRE REGT.,

was the son of the late Lieutenant-Colonel C. Villiers Downes and of Mrs. Villiers Downes, of Aspley House, Aspley Guise, Beds, and was born there on the 5th August, 1892. He was educated at Winchester and Trinity College, Oxford, receiving his commission through the

O.T.C. on the 4th of August, 1914. Proceeding to the front early in October, he was himself wounded at Neuve Eglise, near Bailleul, while attending to a wounded man of his regiment, and died in hospital at Poperinghe, West Flanders, on the 20th of November, 1914. His brother, Lieutenant V. C. Downes, 1st Battalion Bedfordshire Regiment, was wounded near Ypres, and died in hospital, at St. Omer, on the 18th October, 1914.

At Trinity College 2nd Lieutenant Downes was Captain of the Hockey Club.

BREVET-MAJOR EDWARD MARTIN PANTER - DOWNES, ROYAL IRISH REGIMENT,

was born at Rushford Rectory, Norfolk, on the 3rd December, 1873, the son of Captain Edward Panter-Downes, R.N. He was educated at Clifton College and the R.M.C., Sandhurst, distinguishing himself at both

places in athletics and football. He won the gold medal for the half-mile against the R.M.A., Woolwich, and many other races.

He served with his regiment through the South African War, and was for some time on the Staff of Sir Horace Smith-Dorrien. He was present at operations in the Orange Free State, in the Transvaal, including operations at Belfast and Lydenberg; in the Orange River Colony, including actions at Bethlehem and Wittebergen; and in Cape Colony, including the action at Colesberg. For his services he was twice mentioned in Despatches ("London Gazette," 10th September, 1901, and 29th July, 1902), promoted Brevet-Major for distinguished conduct in the field, and received the Queen's medal with three clasps, and the King's medal with two clasps. He was also awarded the Royal Humane Society's medal, the official record of which runs as follows :—

"At 7.30 a.m. on the 25th August, 1898, a man, who was bathing in the sea at Kilkee, could not regain the shore, the sea being very rough with a heavy swell on. Lieutenant E. M. Panter-Downes, 1st Battalion Royal Irish Regiment, plunged in, and with difficulty succeeded in bringing him to the ladder, where they were both helped out.

"Bronze medal awarded 17th October, 1898."

From 1903–06 he was an Adjutant of Militia, and from September, 1909, was employed with the West African Frontier Force, with the temporary rank of Lieutenant-Colonel from September, 1911.

In the Great War he was mortally wounded during the retirement from Mons, and died on the field on the 26th August, 1914. The battalion was cut off at Mons, not having received the order to retire, and as nearly all who were with him were killed it has not been possible to procure authentic details of the circumstances. Major Panter-Downes married Kathleen Cowley, and left one daughter.

LIEUTENANT VILLIERS CHERNOCKE DOWNES, 3rd (attd. 1st) BATTN. THE BEDFORDSHIRE REGIMENT,

was the son of the late Lieutenant-Colonel C. Villiers Downes and Mrs. C. Villiers Downes, of Aspley House, Aspley Guise, Bedfordshire, and was born there on the 5th March, 1891. He was educated at Winchester and Trinity College, Oxford.

After leaving Oxford Lieutenant Downes was for a time at the Royal Agricultural College, Cirencester, where he studied farming and agriculture. In September, 1911, he was gazetted to the 3rd Battalion of his regiment as 2nd Lieutenant, and became Lieutenant in July, 1913. Lieutenant Downes joined the 1st Battalion of his regiment from the 3rd Battalion on the 5th August, the day of the public announcement of a state of war between this country and Germany, and proceeded to the front soon after. He was with this battalion in the retirement from Mons.

In the fighting near Ypres he succeeded in saving three Maxim guns, was wounded there later on, and died of his wounds in hospital at St. Omer on the 18th October, 1914.

CAPTAIN ROBERT EDWARD DRAKE, ADJUTANT 1st BATTN. LINCOLN-SHIRE REGT.,

son of the Rev. John Drake, was born at Great Wratting, Suffolk, on the 4th January, 1878. He was educated at Lancing College, Sussex, and was in the 3rd Battalion Suffolk Regiment (Militia) from 1899–1900. In April of the latter year he received a commission as 2nd Lieutenant in the 1st Battalion Lincolnshire Regiment, becoming Lieutenant in May, 1902, and Captain in August, 1912. He was appointed Adjutant of his battalion in November, 1913. He was serving as Adjutant when he was mortally wounded at the Battle of the Marne on the 8th September, 1914, during a successful attempt made by the battalion to capture a German battery, and died the same day.

LIEUTENANT ROBERT FLINT DRAKE, Xth (PRINCE OF WALES'S OWN ROYAL) HUSSARS,

who was killed near Ypres on the 17th November, 1914, aged twenty-two, was the third son of Mr. and Mrs. J. Ramsay Drake, of Batch Wood, near St. Alban's. He was educated at Eton and the R.M.C., Sandhurst. At the former he was in the Field, Oppidan Wall, and President of the Eton Society ; and at the latter he was a Colour-Sergeant.

He was gazetted to the 10th Hussars in September, 1912, and became Lieutenant on the 27th October, 1914, having been gazetted after his death.

LIEUTENANT DAVID ROBERT DRUMMOND, 2nd BATTN. SCOTS GUARDS,

born on the 30th October, 1884, at 14, Belgrave Square, London, S.W., was the second son of George James Drummond, Esq., of Swaylands House, Penshurst.

After being educated at Harrow, he joined the 3rd Battalion Black Watch (Militia), from which he was transferred to the Scots Guards in 1904. He afterwards voluntarily joined the Reserve of Officers and, in July, 1911, the Special Reserve of the Scots Guards. He held that position when the war broke out, and rejoined the 2nd Battalion of his regiment for active service.

He was killed at Ypres on the 3rd November, 1914, having been shot in the head by a German sniper.

Lieutenant Drummond, who was a member of the Carlton, Guards', and Royal Automobile Clubs, was fond of cricket and shooting. He married, in 1907, Hilda Margaret, daughter of Alfred Harris, Esq., of Donnington, Chichester. and left three daughters : Joan Cecile, born 1909 ; Violet Hilda, born 1911 ; and Winifred Pansy, born 1914.

MAJOR ERIC GREY DRUMMOND, LATE 4th (attd. 3rd) GURKHA RIFLES,

who was killed in action on the 14th November, 1914, was the fourth son of the late Major-General Henry Drummond, and a grandson of Colonel John Drummond, of Strageath, Perthshire.

He was born on the 10th September, 1875, and was educated at Bedford College, joining the Prince Albert's (Somerset Light Infantry) in September, 1895. In November, 1898, he was transferred to the Indian Army as Lieutenant, and was promoted Captain in 1904. He saw active service on the north-western frontier of India, in the Mohmand Campaign, 1897–98, including the engagement near Shabkadr on the 9th August, 1897, where he was severely wounded. For that campaign he received the medal with clasp. He retired in

November, 1913, and was appointed a King's Foreign Messenger, but on the outbreak of war with Germany rejoined the Army, being attached for duty to the 5th Battalion King's Royal Rifle Corps as Major.

For active service he was attached to the 3rd Gurkha Rifles, which regiment he joined in the trenches on the 13th November, 1914. The same evening, after one attack by our troops had failed, he was standing by the Commanding Officer, who had kept him near him owing to his being new to the trenches. Major Drummond volunteered to lead a second attack, and permission being granted he fell mortally wounded while gallantly leading his men.

He was a member of the Caledonian Club, St. James's Square, and was unmarried.

MAJOR RICHARD DUCAT, 20th INFANTRY, INDIAN ARMY,

born at Ahmednuggar, India, on 12th July, 1871, was the son of the late Major-General C. M. Ducat, and a grandson of Mr. Hugh Hamersley, J. P., D.L., Pyrton Manor, Oxfordshire.

He was educated at a private school, and at the R. M. C., Sandhurst, joining the Duke of Cornwall's Light Infantry in August, 1892. Four years later, having received his promotion to Lieutenant, he joined the Indian Army, in which he obtained his Company in 1901 and his Majority in 1910.

Major Ducat saw active service on the north-western frontier of India, 1897–98, and was present at actions at Malakand and Utman Khel, and at the capture of the Tanga Pass. For his services he received the Frontier medal with clasp. He also saw service in China and Thibet, receiving the China medal (1900) and the Thibet medal (1903–04).

Major Ducat fell mortally wounded at Fao, in the Persian Gulf, on the 11th November, 1914. He was leading an attack against the enemy, enabling the other regiments to make a flanking movement, which was entirely successful. His Colonel wrote the next day, saying : " You will like to know that in the position which your husband's companies occupied when he fell he was rendering me an invaluable service in protecting the left of the regiment, and leaving me free to operate with entire confidence on the right."

Major Ducat was a member of the Junior United Service Club.

CAPTAIN LEONARD GREY DUDLEY, 6th JAT LIGHT INFANTRY, IN-DIAN ARMY,

Adjutant of his regiment at the time of his death, was born on Easter Day, 25th March, 1883, at Poona, India, the son of Brigade-Surgeon Lieutenant-Colonel W. E. Dudley, A.M.S., of Sion Hill, Bath, and Templemore, Ireland. He was a grandson of General George Prince Sealy, Royal (late Bombay) Artillery, and had two brothers serving in the Army.

He was educated at Bath College, where he was Captain of the Cricket XI for two years, and from which he entered the R.M.C., Sandhurst, in 1901. Passing out in the Honours list in 1902, taking the third place, and the prize for military history, he was appointed to the Indian Army, and on arriving in India was attached for his probation to the Argyll and Sutherland Highlanders (the old 93rd) at Calcutta, moving with the battalion to Poona in 1903. In December, 1903, he was gazetted to the 6th Jat Light Infantry, and joined his regiment at Meerut. After two years they moved to Jhansi, where they remained four years, and then went to Secunderabad, from which they went to France in October, 1914. He had become Lieutenant in 1904, and had been appointed Adjutant of his regiment in 1911.

Captain Dudley died on the 24th November, 1914, from wounds received four hours previously, when in action at Festubert, in Flanders, resisting the German attempt to break through to Calais.

LIEUTENANT-COLONEL ADRIAN GRANT DUFF, C.B., p.s.c., 1st BATTN. THE BLACK WATCH (ROYAL HIGH-LANDERS),

was the son of the Right Hon. Sir Mountstuart Elphinstone Grant Duff, G.C.S.I., and was born on the 29th September, 1869.
He was educated at Wellington College and the R.M.C., Sandhurst, from which he was gazetted to the Black Watch in March, 1889, becoming Lieutenant the following year. In 1897–98 he was in charge of the Base Depot of the Tirah Expedition in Peshawar, and received for his services the thanks of the highest military authorities in India, and the Tirah medal with clasp.

He served in the South African War from January, 1902, till the end, being present at operations in the Transvaal and Orange River Colony, for which he received the Queen's medal with two clasps. In 1904 he graduated at the Staff College, and from 1905–09 was employed at the War Office as Staff Captain, D.A.Q.M.G., and General Staff Officer, 2nd grade, obtaining his Majority in December, 1907. He also qualified as an Interpreter in French.

From 1910–13 he was Assistant Military Secretary to the Committee of Imperial Defence, being awarded the C.B. in the latter year. He succeeded to the command of the 1st Battalion the Black Watch in May, 1914, and took it to the front for the Great War.

He was killed at the Battle of the Aisne on the 14th September, 1914. Some time after the regiment had been deployed and engaged, it became imperative that a certain locality should be held against the German counter-attack. Having none of his battalion now left in reserve, Lieutenant-Colonel Grant Duff, collecting all available men, personally led them forward, and held this important position, but shortly afterwards was mortally wounded. At the Battle of the Marne, on the 8th September, 1914, he had commanded the advanced guard of the 1st Division with great ability.

Lieutenant-Colonel Grant Duff married, in 1906, the Hon. Ursula Lubbock, daughter of the first Lord Avebury, and left four children : Jean, born November, 1907 ; Ursula Fiona, born December, 1908 ; Neill Adrian Mountstuart, born October, 1910 ; and Shiela, born May, 1913.

CAPTAIN BEAUCHAMP OSWALD DUFF, 1st KING GEORGE'S OWN GURKHA RIFLES (THE MALAUN REGIMENT), attd. 2nd KING EDWARD'S OWN GURKHA RIFLES (THE SIRMOOR RIFLES),

who was killed in action on the 7th November, 1914, was the elder son of General Sir Beauchamp Duff, G.C.B., Commander-in-Chief in India, and Lady Duff. He was born on the 8th September, 1880, and was educated at Clifton

College and the R.M.C., Sandhurst. He received an unattached 2nd Lieutenancy in July, 1900, and joined the Indian Staff Corps in October, 1901, becoming Lieutenant in October, 1902.

He served on the north-western frontier of India in the Waziristan Expedition, 1901–02, receiving the medal with clasp. He also saw active service in East Africa in 1903, taking part in operations in Somaliland, where he was a Special Service Officer; was employed under the Director of Supplies and Transport, and was present at the action at Jidballi. He received the medal with two clasps.

Captain Duff was promoted to his rank in the Indian Army in July, 1909.

CAPTAIN LACHLAN GORDON-DUFF, 3rd BATTN. GORDON HIGHLANDERS,

born in Edinburgh on the 17th January, 1880, was the eldest son of Thomas Gordon Duff, D.L., of Drummuir, and Park, Banffshire, by his first wife, Pauline Emma, daughter of Sir Charles Tennant, Bart., of "The Glen," Peblesshire. He was educated at St. David's, Reigate (W. H. Churchill), at Eton (Miss Evans's House), and at the R.M.C., Sandhurst. He joined the 1st Battalion Gordon Highlanders in August, 1899, in Edinburgh, and served with them through the South African War, taking part in actions at Paardeberg, Poplar Grove, Driefontein, Houtnek, Vet and Zand Rivers, Belfast, and Lydenberg. He received the Queen's medal with five clasps and the King's medal with two clasps. He was promoted Lieutenant in January, 1900, and Captain in February, 1904.

In August, 1909, he retired from the Regular Army, and voluntarily entered the Special Reserve, 3rd Battalion Gordon Highlanders, in which his rank of Captain was dated the 12th August, 1909. Captain Gordon-Duff was a good shot and rider to hounds, and won several point-to-point races. In 1907 he won Lord Grenfell's Cup for lightweights, Irish Army Point-to-Point, at Knocklong, on his own mare, "Juanita."

On retiring from the Army he had settled at Park House, Banffshire, and occupied himself with county work, being a J.P. and D.L. of Banffshire, and taking an interest in the Boy Scouts movement.

He left Aberdeen on the 7th October, 1914, for the Great War, for which he was attached to the 1st Battalion, and was killed on the 24th of the same month. The battalion occupied trenches near Neuve Chapelle. Just after dark a German attack temporarily broke through, and Captain Gordon-Duff was shot in the struggle to regain the line.

He married, in 1908, Lydia Dorothy Muriel, daughter of Joseph Pike, D.L., of Dunsland, Co. Cork, and left three children: Frances Pauline, born 1909; Thomas Robert, born 1911; and Lachlan Cecil, born 1914.

LIEUTENANT SIR ROBERT (ROBIN) GEORGE VIVIAN DUFF, BART., RESERVE OF OFFICERS, attd. 2nd LIFE GUARDS,

who was killed in action on the 16th October, 1914, was the only son of Sir Charles Garden Assheton-Smith, first Bart., of Vaynol Park, Bangor, County Carnarvon, but retained the surname of Duff. He was born on the 14th November, 1876; and, having served for two months in the embodied Militia, was appointed to the 2nd Life Guards in July, 1900, being promoted Lieutenant in September, 1901. After serving in the 2nd Life Guards, of which he was for a time Adjutant, he voluntarily joined the Reserve of Officers.

Sir Robert Duff married, in June, 1903, Lady (Gladys Mary) Juliet Lowther, only daughter of the fourth Earl of Lonsdale, and left two children: a daughter, Victoria Maud Veronica, born September, 1904; and a son, Charles Michael Robert Vivian, born May, 1907, who succeeds him in the baronetcy.

LIEUTENANT BARRY PEVENSEY DUKE, 3rd (attd. 2nd) BATTN. ROYAL SUSSEX REGIMENT,

who was killed in action on the 3rd November, 1914, was the eldest son of Lieutenant-Colonel O. T. Duke and Mrs. Duke, Bouverie Road, W., Folkestone. He was born on the 5th September, 1889, and was educated at Wellington College, where he was in the Murray, 1900–04, was captain of the shooting eight, and passed thence into the R.M.C., Sandhurst.

He was gazetted to the Royal Sussex Regiment in October, 1906, and became Lieutenant in December, 1909.

CAPTAIN STUART DUNCAN, GLOUCESTERSHIRE REGIMENT,

killed in action at Hooge on the 13th November, 1914, was born in London in 1865, the youngest son of the late Dr. James Duncan and Mrs. Duncan, of 24, Chester Street, Grosvenor Place, S.W.

He was educated at Marlborough College, and obtained his commission in 1884, becoming Captain in 1891. With his regiment he served in the South African War, taking part in operations in Natal, including actions at Rietfontein and Lombard's Kop, where he was slightly wounded. He was also at operations in the Transvaal and Orange River Colony. He received the Queen's medal with three clasps.

In 1904 Captain Duncan left the Army and joined the Reserve of Officers, Gloucestershire Regiment. He had therefore been retired from the active list for ten years when the Great War broke out, but at once patriotically volunteered for active service, and was posted first to the 3rd Battalion of his old corps, from which he was sent out to the 2nd Battalion South Lancashire Regiment at the front, but when killed was serving with the 4th Battalion Middlesex Regiment. He behaved with great gallantry during the war, particularly on the day of his death, when he had been ten days in the trenches, continually shelled, and was shot down while leading his men, by whom he was specially beloved. Captain Duncan left a large circle of friends to deeply mourn his loss. He was unmarried.

LIEUTENANT CHARLES DUNLOP, 2nd BATTN. ROYAL INNISKILLING FUSILIERS,

who died at Versailles on the 22nd October, 1914, from wounds received at the Battle of the Aisne, was the elder son of Fleet Surgeon James Dunlop, R.N., of Eden Perry House, Ballylesson, Ireland. He joined the Royal Inniskilling Fusiliers in January, 1913, and was promoted Lieutenant in September, 1914.

CAPTAIN FREDERICK CLEAVE STRICKLAND DUNLOP, 1st BATTN. MANCHESTER REGIMENT,

who was killed in action on the 8th November, 1914, was the fourth son of Andrew Dunlop, M.D., of St. Helier, Jersey, and was born there on the 14th December, 1877. His brother, Captain J. S. S. Dunlop, 1st Battalion South Staffordshire Regiment, was killed in action on the 24th October, 1914; while another brother, Lieutenant (now Captain) W. H. S. Dunlop, 3rd East Surrey Regiment, was wounded on the 25th April, 1915. Captain Dunlop was educated at Victoria College, Jersey, afterwards entering the Royal Jersey Militia, from which he became 2nd Lieutenant in the Manchester Regiment in December, 1897; Lieutenant in March, 1899; and in which he obtained his Company in March, 1901. He served in the Boer War, taking part in the defence of Ladysmith, and being present at operations in the Transvaal, February to August, 1901, for which he received the Queen's medal with three clasps. From 1902–05 Captain Dunlop was Adjutant of the 4th Battalion Manchester Regiment, and from 1906–11 of the Malabar Volunteer Rifles.

He married Maud, daughter of the late Surgeon-General Williams, Heathfield, Jersey, and left two children : Mavis, born 1905 ; and Andrew, born 1907.

2nd LIEUTENANT JOHN GUNNING MOORE DUNLOP, SPECIAL RESERVE, 2nd BATTN. ROYAL DUBLIN FUSILIERS,

was the third son of the late Archibald Dunlop, Esq., M.D., and was born on the 14th December, 1885, at Holywood, Co. Down.

He was educated at Summerfields, Charterhouse, and Caius College, Cambridge, where he obtained the degree of M.A., and was a member of the O.T.C. He joined the Special Reserve in September, 1910 ; and, being called up for active service in the Great War, he was killed in action at Clary, France, on the 27th August, 1914, while directing part of the firing line.

CAPTAIN JULIAN SILVER STRICKLAND DUNLOP, 1st BATTN. SOUTH STAFFORDSHIRE REGIMENT,

who was killed while leading a bayonet charge on the 24th October, 1914, was born at St. Helier, Jersey, on the 15th September, 1876, the son of Andrew Dunlop, M.D., of St. Helier. One of his brothers, Captain F. C. S. Dunlop, Manchester Regiment, was killed in action on the 8th November, 1914, and another, Lieutenant W. H. S. Dunlop, 3rd East Surrey Regiment, was wounded on the 25th April, 1915.

Captain Dunlop was educated at Victoria College, Jersey, and entered the South Staffordshire Regiment, from the Royal Jersey Militia, in 1895, becoming a Lieutenant in 1898 and a Captain in 1904.

From 1899 to 1903 he was A.D.C. to the Lieutenant-Governor of Burma, and was Adjutant of the South Staffordshire Militia from 1905-10. He received the Delhi Durbar decoration awarded in 1911.

For his services in the Great War he was mentioned, after his death, in Sir John French's Despatch of the 14th January, 1915.

Captain Dunlop was a polo player, and was for some time Secretary to the Garrison Beagles at Lichfield.

LIEUTENANT THOMAS EDWARD DONCASTER DUNN, 2nd BATTN. THE CAMERONIANS (SCOTTISH RIFLES),

who died on the 21st December, 1914, of wounds received in action, was the eldest son of the late Lieutenant-Colonel Duncan Dunn, Hampshire Regiment, and Mrs. Duncan Dunn, of 34, Hill Street, Knightsbridge.

He was born on the 30th June, 1890, and was educated at Wellington College, where he was in the Wellesley from 1904-06, passing into the R.M.C., Sandhurst, in the latter year. He was gazetted to the Scottish Rifles in April, 1910, and was promoted Lieutenant in February, 1913.

LIEUTENANT GRAHAM EARDLEY DUNSTERVILLE, 1st BATTN. DEVONSHIRE REGIMENT,

was the younger son of Colonel Knightley Dunsterville, late R.A., Guyers House, Corsham, Wiltshire. He was born on the 9th July, 1884, educated at Cheltenham College, and joined the Devonshire Regiment from the Militia in June, 1904, becoming Lieutenant in the Army in September, 1906, and being transferred to the Indian Army in September, 1908. In the same month of the latter year he joined the Indian Army, with which he served till 1910, when he rejoined the Devonshire Regiment as Lieutenant from July, 1910. He was a born fighter and all-round athlete, especially fond of boxing, football, and all military sports and physical exercises. He did well in the fencing tournaments at The Hague, and twice in Paris. At the Naval and Military Tournament at Olympia, in the years 1911-14, he won six challenge cups for officers for all the four dismounted events—bayonet fighting, sabres, épées, and foils—and for two of the mounted events—sword v. sword and sword v. lance. These six wins with six different weapons is quite a record.

He was in command of " A " Company in the trenches at Festubert, when, on the 29th October, 1914, hearing a wounded man crying out for water, he went out to bring him in, and was killed in the attempt by a bullet in the head.

Mr. Dunsterville married Eveline, daughter of F. Hastings Coldney, Esq., J.P., of Corsham, in Wiltshire, and leaves a daughter, Petronilla, born the 7th July, 1913; and a son, Hugh Graham Evelyn, born the 20th December, 1914.

CAPTAIN FRANCIS WILLIAM DURAND, 3rd BATTN. ROYAL MUNSTER FUSILIERS,

was born on the 29th January, 1875, at Earley Vicarage, Berkshire, the son of the Rev. Havilland Durand, M.A., Vicar of Earley. He was educated at Elizabeth College, Guernsey, where he won the quarter-mile, and was second in the one hundred yards race in 1889, winning two cups.

Captain Durand was gazetted to the 3rd Royal Guernsey Light Infantry (Militia) as 2nd Lieutenant in 1891, and in 1895 he joined the Rhodesian Horse. He served in the Matabeleland campaign with the Gwelo Field Force, receiving the Matabeleland medal, 1896 ; and in the Mashonaland campaign with the Mashonaland Field Force, receiving the clasp for Mashonaland, 1897.

From 1899–1901 he was employed in the African Transcontinental Survey through German East Africa, and in 1901-02 with the Tanganyika Concessions Expedition to Katanga, Congo Free State. In 1903 he served in the Zanzibar Protectorate under the Foreign Office, being Secretary and A.D.C. to the First Minister.

In 1906 he was promoted Captain in the 3rd Munster Fusiliers, remaining seconded for duty under the Foreign Office. In 1907 he was Acting Commandant of the Zanzibar Military Police, and Acting Governor, Central Jail. In this year he received the Zanzibar Order of " El Aliyeh."

Returning to England he, in 1908, passed the School of Musketry at Hythe. In 1909 he was again in civil employment in Zanzibar, as 2nd Class Magistrate and Governor of the District Jail, and in 1911 was second in command of the Zanzibar Armed Constabulary. In 1912 he passed in all subjects for promotion to the rank of Field Officer, being one of only five officers specially mentioned in the Examiner's Report (May, 1912) to the Army Council. In 1914 he received the decoration of the 3rd Class Brilliant Star of Zanzibar.

On the mobilisation for the Great War, the 5th August, 1914, he joined the 3rd Battalion Royal Munster Fusiliers, and went to Bere Island. On the 8th September he joined the 2nd Battalion in France, and was present at the Battles of the Aisne and the Marne. He was killed on the 22nd September, 1914, while leading his men in an attempt to retake trenches between Givenchy and Festubert, near La Bassée.

Captain Durand was a member of the Naval and Military and of the Sports Clubs. While in Africa he enjoyed much big-game shooting. He married, in 1903, Geraldine Vesey, daughter of the late Rev. John W. Hawtrey, of Aldin House, Slough, and St. Michael's, Westgate-on-Sea.

LIEUTENANT-COLONEL ALFRED McNAIR DYKES, p.s.c., 1st BATTN. THE KING'S OWN (ROYAL LANCASTER REGIMENT), who was killed in action on the 26th August,

1914, was the son of the late William Alston Dykes and of Mrs. Dykes of the Orchard, Hamilton, Scotland. He was born on the 15th March, 1874, and joined the Royal Lancaster Regiment from the Militia in December, 1894. He became Lieutenant in November, 1896, and from November, 1897, to November, 1899, was Adjutant of

the 2nd Battalion ; became Captain in February, 1900, and, again, Adjutant of his battalion from January, 1900, to July, 1902. He served in the South African War as a Special Service Officer from November, 1899, to January, 1900 ; was present at the relief of Ladysmith and operations in January, including the action at Spion Kop, where he was severely wounded ; operations in Cape Colony, north of Orange River, November, 1899, to January, 1900, and in the Transvaal, September to November, 1900 ; also further operations in the Transvaal and Orange River Colony in 1901.

For his services he was twice mentioned in Despatches ("London Gazette," 10th September, 1901, and 29th July, 1902) ; received the Brevet of Major, the Queen's medal with four clasps and the King's medal with two clasps. Lieutenant-Colonel Dykes, who left a widow, succeeded to the command of his, the 1st Battalion, the King's Own, on 1st August, 1913.

LIEUTENANT FRANK MOLYNEUX EASTWOOD, 1st BATTN. THE QUEEN'S (ROYAL WEST SURREY REGIMENT), who died on the 30th October, 1914, of wounds received at Gheluvelt, near Ypres, on the evening of the same day, was the fourth son of John Edmund and Ethel Eastwood, of Enton, Witley. He was born in November, 1892, and was educated at Mr.

Arthur Dunn's, Ludgrove ; at Eton ; and the R.M.C., Sandhurst. He received his commission in the Queen's Royal West Surrey Regiment in September, 1912, becoming Lieutenant in September, 1914. He was a member of the Conservative Club.

He went out with the regiment on the outbreak of the war, was at the Battle of Mons and through the retirement, and at the Battles of the Marne and the Aisne.

LIEUTENANT JOHN EDEN, 12th (PRINCE OF WALES'S ROYAL) LANCERS,

eldest son of Sir William and Lady Eden, was born on the 9th October, 1888, and was killed while on patrol duty near Wervecq. on the 8th October, 1914. He was buried near the small village of America, in Belgium. Educated at Eton and the R.M.C., Sandhurst, he joined the 12th Lancers in India, in January, 1909, and became Lieutenant in May, 1914. He went to France with his regiment in August, 1914; was at the Battle of Mons, through the retirement; the Battles of the Marne and the Aisne, and the first Battle of Ypres.

LIEUTENANT EDWIN ALLEN JAMES EDWARDS, 3rd BATTN. BEDFORD-SHIRE REGT.,

was born at Brixton on the 13th March, 1895, and was the youngest son of Mr. and Mrs. H. Edwards, of Suva, Glenbuck Road, Surbiton, Surrey. His two brothers are serving their country, one in the Royal Navy and one in a London regiment.

He was educated at St. John's College, Brixton, and Dulwich College, matriculating in June, 1911. At Dulwich he was in the O.T.C., and in the Army qualifying examination passed at the top of the list, being gazetted to the Bedfordshire Regiment in June, 1913, and getting his step in June, 1914. He was a good left-handed tennis player, and was fond of boating.

He went to France with the 1st Battalion in August, 1914, and fought with it at the Battles of the Marne and the Aisne. He was wounded on the 15th October, while gallantly leading his men at Givenchy, and died from his wounds on the 31st December, 1914, in the Fishmongers' Hall Hospital, London Bridge.

CAPTAIN ERIC LEA PRIESTLEY EDWARDS, 1st BATTN. EAST YORKSHIRE REGIMENT,

born at Scarborough on the 2nd March, 1877, was the son of Lea Priestley Edwards, Esq., of Warberry Court, Torquay, Devon, and grandson of the late Sir Henry Edwards, Bart., C.B. Having been educated at Harrow and the Royal Military College, Sandhurst, he joined the East Yorkshire Regiment as 2nd Lieutenant in February, 1897, becoming Lieutenant in July, 1898, and Captain in May, 1903.

Captain Edwards served in the Tirah Campaign of 1897–98, and was present at operations in the Bara Valley, receiving the medal with two clasps.

He was killed in the Battle of the Aisne on the 20th September, 1914.

LIEUTENANT FRANK GLEN-CAIRN DE BURGH EDWARDS ROYAL HORSE ARTILLERY,

was born on the 9th June, 1885, and entered the Royal Artillery from the Militia in May, 1907, being promoted Lieutenant in May, 1910.

He was killed in action on the 12th October, 1914.

LIEUTENANT PHILIP JOHN EGERTON, 1st BATTN. BORDER REGIMENT,

who died of wounds on the 17th October, 1914, was the elder son of Hubert D. and Annie Egerton. St. Michael's Lodge, Chislehurst, and was born on the 10th April, 1882.

He first joined the 3rd (Militia) Battalion West Yorkshire Regiment, in January, 1901, being promoted Lieutenant in the following August, and was given a commission as 2nd Lieutenant in the Border Regiment, on the 29th July, 1903, becoming Lieutenant in June, 1905.

During the South African War, 1901–02 Lieutenant Egerton served in the Mediterranean, receiving the medal. In October, 1910, he was appointed Adjutant of his battalion, which appointment he held till September, 1913.

LIEUTENANT ROWLAND LE BELWARD EGERTON, 2nd (attd. 1st) BATTN. ROYAL WELSH FUSILIERS,

whose name has not yet appeared in the official lists as killed, lost his life on the 30th October, 1914, being killed in action near the village of Zonnebeke on that date.

He was the younger (twin) son of Sir Philip Henry Brian Grey-Egerton, twelfth Bart., of Egerton and Oulton, County Chester, and was born on the 4th April, 1895. He was educated at Wellington, where he was in the Talbot from 1908–12, and went to the R.M.C., Sandhurst, in 1913. He joined the Royal Welsh Fusiliers in August, 1914, and was gazetted Lieutenant on the 24th October. He was fond of cricket and shooting.

LIEUTENANT ROBERT RANDLE EGERTON, ROYAL ENGINEERS,

who was killed in action on the 15th November, 1914, was the only son of Mr. and Mrs. Robert Egerton, of Stansty Lodge, Wrexham. He was born on the 20th March, 1888, and was educated at Clifton College and the R.M.A., Woolwich, from which he passed into the Royal Engineers in December, 1908, becoming Lieutenant in February, 1911. Lieutenant Egerton was a cricketer and hockey player, having twice played cricket for his corps against the R.A., and twice as goalkeeper at hockey for Army v. Navy. He was also a good revolver and rifle shot, having won the Army championship for the former, and having often shot at Bisley in the Army Eight. He also held the Royal Humane Society's certificate for saving a man from drowning.

2nd LIEUTENANT JOHN STURGESS ELDRED, 2nd BATTN. THE PRINCE OF WALES'S LEINSTER REGIMENT (ROYAL CANADIANS),

born at Sheerness-on-Sea on the 19th September, 1894, was the second son of Fleet-Paymaster Edward H. Eldred, R.N., and a grandson of Edgar Eldred, Esq., of Petersfield, and of the late Commander Richard Sturgess.
He was educated at Weymouth College (Junior School), Old Catton, Norwich, and the R.M.C.. Sandhurst. He was gazetted to the Leinster Regiment in August, 1914, and served for a short time at Tipperary and Cork, being then attached to the 2nd Battn. Royal Irish Rifles in the North of France.

He died at Boulogne on the 27th November of wounds received at Ypres on the 8th November, 1914.

LIEUTENANT WILLIAM LAURENCE ELIOT, 1st BATTN. PRINCE OF WALES'S OWN (WEST YORKSHIRE REGIMENT),

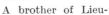

who was killed in action on the 20th September, 1914, in France, was the son of Commander Laurence Eliot, R.N., and Mrs. Laurence Eliot, Mullion, Cornwall, and was born on the 9th July, 1890.

A brother of Lieutenant Eliot's, Laurence Charles Drake Eliot served in the war as a Private in Lord Strathcona's Horse, Royal Canadians, and was killed in action on the 22nd May, 1915. Another brother is in training as a 2nd Lieutenant in the Royal Marines; while another is serving as Second Officer on a transport in the Dardanelles, Mediterranean Station.

Lieutenant W. L. Eliot was educated at Falmouth Grammar School and Exeter School, and joined the West Yorkshire Regiment in October, 1910, becoming Lieutenant in September, 1912.

CAPTAIN HUGH RUSSELL ELIOTT, 3rd BATTN. WORCESTERSHIRE REGT.,

was the son of the late Major-General William Russell Eliott, grandson of the late Sir Daniel Eliott, K.C.S.I., and a descendant of General Eliott Lord Heathfield, defender of Gibraltar, and was born at South Kensington on the 10th February, 1873.

He was educated at Wellington College, and joined the 3rd Battalion Royal Welsh Fusiliers in 1899, being attached to the 2nd Battalion the Buffs (East Kent Regiment) in 1900; he was given a commission as 2nd Lieutenant in the Worcestershire Regiment in April, 1900, and served with it through the South African War. In that year he was present at operations in the Orange Free State, in the Orange River Colony, including the actions at Bethlehem and Wittebergen; and operations in the Transvaal West of Pretoria. In 1901-02 he took part in further operations in the Transvaal and Orange River Colony; he received the Queen's medal with three clasps and the King's medal with two clasps. He was promoted Lieutenant in November, 1900, and attained the rank of Captain in November, 1904.

Captain Eliott served with the Southern Nigerian Force from 1903-05, receiving the medal with two clasps, and subsequently was appointed Adjutant to the 7th Royal Warwickshire Regiment (Territorial) from 1910-13. In the Great War he was in the retirement from Mons, Le Cateau, the Battles of the Rivers Marne and Aisne, and La Couture. He was killed in action, on the 12th October at Richebourg St. Vaast, while leading his Company against the Germans at the beginning of the struggle for Ypres.

He was a member of the Junior Army and Navy Club, and his recreations were fishing and hunting.

Captain Eliott married Constance Mary, daughter of the late A. O. Sedgwick, Esq., North End House, Watford, Herts.

CAPTAIN HENRY GRATTAN ELLIOT, 1st BATTN. DEVONSHIRE REGIMENT,

born on the 21st June, 1881, was the son of the late Colonel G. A. Elliot and Mrs. Elliot, of "The Marches," Leatherhead, Surrey, and a kinsman of the Earl of Minto. He had a very large number of relations in the service, including two brothers, one of whom, Captain G. A. Elliot, of the Royal Irish Regiment, was taken prisoner at Cambrai, and was one of the thirty-nine British officers subjected to reprisals by the German Government on account of our differential treatment of officers of German submarines who sank unarmed vessels. Another brother,

Captain F. B. Elliot, is serving in the Princess Charlotte of Wales's (Royal Berkshire Regiment). Generals William Elliot and W. O. Barnard were his uncles, and an ancestor was General G. A. Elliot, afterwards Lord Heathfield, the defender of Gibraltar in the great siege. Educated at Wellington College and the R.M.C., Sandhurst, he joined the Devonshire Regiment in December, 1899, serving with it through the South African War, and being present at the relief of Ladysmith, action at Vaal Krans, operations on the Tugela Heights, and action at Pieter's Hill; operations in Natal, including actions at Laing's Nek and in the Transvaal. He received the Queen's medal with five and the King's medal with two clasps. On his return he was appointed A.D.C. to General Sir O'Moore Creagh, G.C.B., G.C.S.I., Commander-in-Chief in India, subsequently serving in Crete. On the outbreak of the Great War he was Adjutant at the depot of his regiment at Exeter, and proceeded to the front with his battalion.

Captain Elliot was killed in the trenches at Vailly during the Battle of the Aisne on the 19th September, 1914.

He was a member of the Junior Army and Navy Club, and was unmarried.

2nd LIEUTENANT PHILIP LLOYD ELLIOTT, 1st BATTN. DUKE OF CORNWALL'S LIGHT INFANTRY,

who was killed in action on the 20th October, 1914, in his nineteenth year, was the second son of the late Gilbert Lloyd Elliott, D.C.L.I., and 13th Hussars, of Dolhaidd, Carmarthenshire, and of Mrs. Lloyd Elliott. He was educated at Cheltenham and the R.M.C., Sandhurst, and was gazetted to his regiment in August, 1914.

MAJOR REGINALD WILLIAM SIDNEY ELLIOTT, 1st BATTN. 7th GURKHA RIFLES,

was born at Johnstown House, County Carlow, on the 18th April, 1874, son of Nicholas G. Elliott, Esq., late of the 62nd Regiment, and a grandson of the late Captain Sir Thomas Ross, R.N. Major Elliott went to Cheltenham College in 1887, and gained a classical scholarship there in 1888, and the Schacht German prize in 1891. He was in the College boat, and in the football XV in 1891, in which year he also passed into the R.M.C., Sandhurst, taking the seventh place.

He received an unattached commission in 1893, and in the following year joined the Indian Army, becoming Lieutenant in 1895, Captain in 1902, and Major in 1911.

He fell at Festubert on the 23rd November, 1914, while leading part of the 2nd Battalion of the 8th Gurkha Rifles in an attack to recover lost trenches.

Major Elliott married Mary Emilia, youngest daughter of the late Captain Robert H. Swinton, R.N., and left one son, Robert Allen, born May, 1906.

LIEUTENANT KENWARD WALLACE ELMSLIE, 4th (ROYAL IRISH) DRAGOON GUARDS (SPECIAL RESERVE),

who was killed in action on the 4th November, 1914, aged twenty-seven years, was the second son of Mr. and Mrs. Kenward Wallace Elmslie, of May Place, Hampton Wick, Middlesex. Lieutenant Elmslie, who was an LL.B., Cambridge, joined the Special Reserve in May, 1909, and became Lieutenant in May, 1914. In the war he was in command of a machine-gun section.

2nd LIEUTENANT GERARD GORDON CLEMENT ELRINGTON, 1st BATTN. EAST YORKSHIRE REGIMENT,

who was born on the 28th April, 1894, was the son of the late Captain Gerard Gordon Elrington, Dorsetshire Regiment, and of Mrs. Miles, and stepson of General Miles, Indian Army.

He was educated at Cranleigh School, Surrey, where he was a Corporal in the Cadet Corps. He received his commission in the 3rd Battalion, East Yorkshire Regiment, in October, 1912, and in August, 1914, was transferred to the 1st Battalion.

He went to the front in charge of a draft for the 2nd Battalion Duke of Wellington's Regiment, and on arrival was attached to that regiment. He was killed at Festubert on the 30th to 31st October, the officer commanding the battalion to which he was attached giving the

following account of the circumstances: after saying that this young officer had on previous occasions during the fighting on the Aisne and north of Arras shown conspicuous gallantry, cheerfulness, and disregard of danger, he concluded : " Near Festubert, on the night of the 30th to 31st, a company of this battalion was ordered to co-operate with the Sikhs in recovering a trench captured by the Germans the previous night. 2nd Lieutenant Elrington was leading his platoon in this attack, and was shot through the head within a few feet of the trench. The trench was not taken, but I assured myself later that he was quite dead, and his burial was carried out by the officers of the Sikh (58th Rifles) Company in the trench later on."

MAJOR RAYMOND ENGLAND, ROYAL FIELD ARTILLERY,

who was killed in action, it is stated, on the 26th August, no date being given in the official casualty list issued in October, 1914, was the fourth son of Mr. Nicholas England, The Gables, Colne, Lancashire. He was born on the 31st May, 1871, and joined the R.A. in February, 1891, becoming Lieutenant in February, 1894, and Captain in February, 1900.

He served in the South African War, in which he was slightly wounded, being present at operations in the Orange Free State, including actions at Houtnek (Thoba Mountain), Vet and Zand Rivers ; in the Transvaal, including actions near Johannesburg, Pretoria, and Diamond Hill. He received the Queen's medal with four clasps. From November, 1901, to June, 1905, he was an Adjutant of his regiment, and he obtained his Majority in June, 1908.

LIEUTENANT MURRAY ROBERTSON SWEET-ESCOTT, 3rd (attd. 1st) BATTN. KING'S LIVERPOOL REGIMENT,

who was killed in action near Missy, on the Aisne, on the 20th September, 1914, was the younger son of the Rev. E. H. and Mrs. Sweet-Escott, of Dulwich College, and Hartrow Manor, Taunton, Somerset.

He was born on the 14th December,  1887, and educated at Marlborough. He joined the 3rd Battn. of the King's in November, 1909, became Lieutenant in February, 1911,

and, in January, 1912, was appointed A.D.C. to Sir E. B. Sweet-Escott, Governor and Commander-in-Chief of the Leeward Islands, which position he held till September, 1913.
He was twenty-seven years of age at the time of his death.

CAPTAIN GEORGE RALEIGH KERR EVATT, 1st BATTN. THE DUKE OF CAMBRIDGE'S OWN (MIDDLESEX REGIMENT),

who was killed in action in France on the 13th November, 1914, was the only son of Surgeon-General G. J. H. Evatt, M.D., C.B., Army Medical Staff, retired, and Mrs. Evatt, of Wayside, Camberley, Surrey.
He was born on the 30th September, 1883, and joined the Middlesex Regiment in March, 1904, becoming Lieutenant in May, 1906. From April, 1909, to December, 1913, he was employed with the West African Frontier Force, and was promoted Captain in September, 1914.

CAPTAIN ROSSLYN CURZON EVELEGH, 2nd BATTN. OXFORDSHIRE AND BUCKINGHAMSHIRE LIGHT INFANTRY,

who was killed in action at the Battle of the Aisne on the 19th September, 1914 was the elder son of the late Colonel Frederick Evelegh, formerly in the 52nd (Oxfordshire) Light Infantry, and of Mrs. Evelegh, Elder Wick, Shotover-hill, near Oxford.
Captain Evelegh was born at Eccles, Lancashire, on the 13th May, 1885, and was educated at Hinwick House, near Wellingborough; at Rugby; and the R.M.C., Sandhurst. He joined the Oxfordshire Light Infantry, becoming Lieutenant in the combined Oxfordshire and Buckinghamshire Light Infantry in December, 1905. He played Rugby football, and was good at all sorts of gymnastics.
From November, 1906, to November, 1909, he was A.D.C. to the G.O.C., Mauritius. He was qualified as an interpreter in both French and German.

His fatal wound was caused by a piece of shell striking him over the heart. He had been wounded by shell in five places three days before, but remained on duty and attended to his wounded comrades.

CAPTAIN FRANK FAIRLIE, 2nd BATTN. ROYAL SCOTS FUSILIERS,

who was killed in action on the 23rd October, 1914, at Gheluvelt, while taking a house at the head of his men, was born on the 17th January, 1878, and was educated at St. Paul's School, to which he went in 1893.
He was appointed Lieutenant in the 3rd Battn. Scottish Rifles in February, 1901, and after serving for nearly eight months with that battalion when embodied, was given a commission in the Royal Scots Fusiliers in October, 1901. He served in the South African War, 1899–1901, being present at operations in the Orange Free State; in the Transvaal, west of Pretoria, including actions at Frederickstad; and in Cape Colony, south of the Orange River, receiving the Queen's medal with four clasps. He was promoted Lieutenant in June, 1905, and from 1911 to 1913 was employed with the West African Frontier Force.
Captain Fairlie, who was married, attained his rank in January, 1912.

2nd LIEUTENANT JAMES DOUGLAS HERBERT FARMER, ROYAL FIELD ARTILLERY,

who was killed in action on the 4th November, 1914, at the age of twenty-one, was the second son of James Herbert Farmer, of Fairfield, Mundesley, Norfolk, and a grandson of the late James Farmer, Esq., J.P., and of the late Sir George Harris, J.P., L.C.C.
2nd Lieutenant Farmer was the second of three brothers educated at St. Paul's, all of whom were keenly interested in the school games; he was a member of Mr. Cholmeley's House, and played occasionally for the First XV.
He was gazetted to the Royal Artillery in July, 1913.

2nd LIEUTENANT HERBERT RONALD FARRAR, 3rd BATTN. LEICESTERSHIRE REGIMENT, attd. 2nd BATTN. MANCHESTER REGIMENT,

who was killed on the 24th December, 1914, at the age of twenty-seven, was the elder son of

the Rev. H. W. and Mrs. Farrar, All Saints'
Vicarage, Woolwich.

2nd Lieutenant Farrar, who was a B.A. of
Cambridge (Queens' College), was for some years
in the O.T.C., and received his commission on
probation in the Leicestershire Regiment in
August, 1914.

2nd LIEUTENANT ARCHIBALD MANATON FARRIER, 1st BATTN. SOUTH WALES BORDERERS,

was born at South
Molton, Devonshire,
on the 13th July,
1891, and was the
son of Richard and
Lucy Farrier, and
a grandson of Wil-
liam and Belvedera
Manaton. He was
at an early age
adopted by his aunt,
Mrs. Edwards, of
Dulverton, who
brought him up. His brother is now serving
in the Royal Navy.

2nd Lieutenant Farrier was educated at Devon
County School, where he showed considerable
ability, for he took a silver medal at the age
of ten, and when eleven years old won a
scholarship of £30.

In 1907 he joined the 2nd Battalion Devonshire
Regiment, with which he served in Crete, Malta,
Cyprus, and other places. While in the ranks
he earnestly applied himself to his work and
duties, obtaining a first-class (highest) certificate
of education in October, 1910, and in August,
1911, as a Lance-Corporal, he obtained the
certificate qualifying him to teach, among other
subjects, map-reading, English history, and
physical exercises, and he acted for some time
as Assistant Schoolmaster of his battalion. For
his success he was congratulated by General
Kelly Kenny, then commanding in the district
in which he was serving. He did not neglect
the physical side of his education, for in 1911
he received a regimental certificate for swimming one mile while stationed at Pembroke
Barracks, Malta.

He returned to England in August, 1914,
having received his commission in the South
Wales Borderers, and joined the 1st Battalion
early in November.

He was wounded on the 28th December, 1914,
and died the following day " somewhere in
Flanders." Major Reddie, commanding the
battalion at the front, writing to his relatives to
express his sympathy in a letter dated the 29th
December, gave the following account of

the circumstances attending his death :—
" Last night he was sent out with a party
to dig some trenches, was wounded in three
places, and unfortunately died from his wounds
this morning. . . . During his short stay with
the regiment he made himself very popular
with all ranks, and did not seem to know the
meaning of the word 'fear.' . . . We feel his
loss very much. I am unable to mention places
in letter."

He was buried in the grounds of Château Gorre.
Another comrade wrote saying how cheerful
he always was, and that the men formed a high
opinion of him at once. He was always ready
to undertake little odd jobs that could only
be carried out with danger, whenever an officer
was required. " If Farrier goes on like this
he'll be getting the D.S O.," one of the officers
remarked on the evening before he died. A
Captain of his battalion said : " He was a
fearless officer, and will be missed by us all who
had grown to like him so much."

CAPTAIN REGINALD BENJAMIN FEATHERSTONE, 1st BATTN. DEVONSHIRE REGT.,

born at Anerley,
Surrey, on the 28th
November, 1 8 8 1,
was the son of the
late Benjamin
Featherstone, Esq.,
of Adelaide, South
Australia, and York
House, Blenkarne
Road, Wandsworth
Common, S.W.

He was educated at
Westminster School, and after serving with
the embodied Militia for a year and two months
joined the Devonshire Regiment in December,
1901, becoming Lieutenant in December, 1904.
He took part in the South African War, being
present at operations in the Transvaal, Orange
River Colony, and Cape Colony in 1902. He
received the Queen's medal with four clasps.
Afterwards he served with the 1st Battalion of
his regiment in India, subsequently being posted
to the depot at Exeter, where he did duty with
the 3rd Battalion. In November, 1909, he was
appointed Adjutant of the 5th (Prince of
Wales's) Battalion (Territorial Force) of the
Devonshire Regiment. Later he served in Egypt,
and was promoted Captain in October, 1914.

He went to Flanders with the 2nd Battalion
in November, 1914, and was killed near Neuve
Chapelle on the 18th December, 1914.

Captain Featherstone married Elizabeth, daughter of Ernest Robinson, Esq., and left two
children : Betty, born October, 1910 ; and
Jack, born May, 1912.

LIEUTENANT-COLONEL CLAUDE CAMBRIDGE FENNER, COMMANDING 59th SCINDE RIFLES, FRONTIER FORCE, INDIAN ARMY,

was the only son of Mr. H. A. Shrapnel Fenner, Mem. Inst. C.E., Public Works Department, India (retired), of 6, Eliot Hill, Blackheath, and was killed at Richebourg L'Avoué, France, in the forty-seventh year of his age; he was buried at Le Touret, Rue du Bois.

He was gazetted to the 1st Battalion, Dorsetshire Regiment (the old 39th) from Sandhurst in February, 1888, and served with that regiment for about two and a quarter years, when he was transferred to the Indian Army. He obtained his promotion to Lieutenant in 1889, Captain in 1899, Major in 1906, and Lieutenant-Colonel in August, 1913, when he became Commandant of the 59th. With the exception of a short time spent in the 24th Bombay Infantry (now the 124th Duchess of Connaught's Own Beluchistan Infantry), his entire service in the Indian Army was with the 59th. In 1902 the 59th Rifles (then the 6th Punjab Infantry) gained under his instruction the distinction of being second in all India in Musketry, Colonel Fenner himself being a marksman.

In 1903–04 he was on active service in Somaliland as Second-in-Command of the 52nd Sikhs, F.F., his linked battalion. He commanded the regiment at the Battle of Jidballi, where it formed the front of the square when attacked by the Mullah and his hosts. He was attached, with some four hundred of his men, to a force of Mounted Infantry, the whole under the command of Colonel Kenna, V.C., which force went through incredible hardships from hunger, thirst, and long marches in intense heat. General Sir Charles Egerton, K.C.B.—himself an old frontier officer—mentioned him in his special despatch, and he received the medal and two clasps. In 1908 he took part in the operations against the Zakka Khel tribesmen who inhabit the mountains near Peshawar, and which led to a rising of the Kyber Pass tribes and the great Mohmand tribe. He received a medal and clasp for these services.

Lieutenant-Colonel Fenner spent a month in the trenches in France, with the exception of a few hours, during most of which time his regiment held nearly a mile of the line. He was killed instantaneously by a bullet from the German trenches, while standing up directing operations. He was mentioned in Sir John French's Despatch of 31st May, 1915, the 59th having the sad and unique distinction of having three Commanding Officers mentioned in that one despatch, Colonel Fenner, under whose command they went to France, being the first to fall. The 59th was one of the first Indian Regiments to land in France.

Colonel Fenner was a gallant gentleman, if we may use the term, which denotes so much. Dauntless and brave, his numerous letters home are full of thought for his men and their comfort, and recognition of the services of the splendid European officers in his regiment. Many of his native officers and men he must have known for years, and they were as comrades to him. He was a keen sportsman and an expert rifle shot, much big game having fallen to his gun. He played back for his regiment at polo, and had a handicap at three at golf.

Colonel Fenner married on the 27th March, 1899, Louise Victoria MacMahon, daughter of the late Major G. F. W. MacMahon, I. A., and grand-daughter of the late General W. P. MacMahon.

LIEUTENANT GEOFFREY RUSSELL FENTON, 2nd BATTN. CONNAUGHT RANGERS,

who was killed in action at the Battle of the Aisne on the 20th September, 1914, was the son of William Russell Fenton, of Ardaghowen, Sligo, and was born on the 7th November, 1889, at Sligo.

He was educated at Cheltenham College and the R.M.C., Sandhurst, and joined the Connaught Rangers in September, 1909, becoming Lieutenant in February, 1910.

He was a keen all-round sportsman, a good shot and fisherman, and constantly rode to hounds when stationed in Ireland.

Lieutenant Fenton joined his battalion with a draft in August, 1914, during the early part of the retirement from Mons, in which therefore he took part, and subsequently in the advance to the Aisne, where he was killed within about three hundred yards of the German trenches. The Observation Officer of his platoon was killed by a sniper, and Lieutenant Fenton at once took his place, and was shot through the brain a few minutes later. This occurred before the use of periscopes by our men, who were thus left at a great disadvantage compared with the enemy's snipers, who were using telescopic sights.

Lieutenant Fenton married in October, 1912, Millicent, elder daughter of Lieutenant-Colonel E. H. Montrésor, Royal Sussex Regiment, who also was killed at the Battle of the Aisne on the 14th September, 1914.

LIEUTENANT JAMES ADAM HAMILTON FERGUSSON, 2nd BATTN. HIGHLAND LIGHT INFANTRY,

was the son of Sir James Fergusson, Bart., of Spitalhaugh, West Linton, Peeblesshire, and was born on the 22nd March, 1892, at Curzon Street, Mayfair, London.

He was educated at Ardvreck, Perthshire; Winchester College; and the Royal Military College, Sandhurst. He joined the Highland Light Infantry as 2nd Lieutenant on the 14th February, 1912, and was promoted Lieutenant in August, 1914.

At the Battle of the Aisne on the 20th September, 1914, he had been kneeling while attending to a wounded man, and on rising a bullet struck him in the forehead and killed him instantaneously.

He was a keen sportsman, an excellent shot, and a good golfer.

" He was an affectionate and dutiful son."

2nd LIEUTENANT DUDLEY LUIS DE TAVORA FERNANDES, 2nd BATTN. BEDFORDSHIRE REGIMENT,

who was killed in action on the 23rd October, 1914, aged twenty-one, by the bursting of a shell, was the son of Mr. T. W. L. Fernandes, of Scarborough. He was educated at St. Peter's School, York, and the R.M.C., Sandhurst, from which he was gazetted to the Bedfordshire Regiment in September, 1913. He joined his battalion in South Africa, coming to Europe with it in the autumn of the year 1914 for active service.

CAPTAIN WALTER HUGHES FERRAR, ADJUTANT 2nd BATTN. THE WELSH REGIMENT, who was killed in action on the 31st October, 1914 (according to the official lists), was the youngest son of the late A. M.

Ferrar, Esq., D.L., of Torwood, Belfast. He was born on the 29th June, 1876, and was educated at Marlborough College (Crescent, 1889–93), joining the Welsh Regiment from the Militia in May, 1897, becoming Lieutenant in June, 1899.

He took part in the South African War, during which he served with the Mounted Infantry, and was present at the relief of Kimberley, at operations in the Orange Free State and Paardeberg, actions at Poplar Grove, Karee Siding, Houtnek (Thoba Mountain), Vet and Zand Rivers; operations in the Transvaal, including actions near Johannesburg, Pretoria, and Diamond Hill; operations in the Orange River Colony, including actions at Wittebergen and Witpoort; in Cape Colony, south of the Orange River; again in the Orange River and Cape Colonies in 1901, and in the Transvaal, 1901–02. He received the Queen's medal with five clasps and the King's medal with two clasps.

Captain Ferrar, who reached that rank in March, 1904, was employed with the Egyptian Army from May of that year to July, 1911, during which time he again saw active service, taking part in operations in the Soudan in the Jebel Nyima District of Southern Kordofan, for which he received the medal with clasp, and the 4th class of the Osmanieh.

He was killed whilst leading a charge on the village of Gheluvelt, and was mentioned in Sir John French's first despatch of the 8th October, 1914.

He was a member of the Army and Navy Club, Pall Mall, and was not married.

LIEUTENANT GILBERT COLIN CUNNINGHAME FERRIER, 7th BATTN. ROYAL FUSILIERS (CITY OF LONDON REGIMENT),

about whose fate there was for a long time some uncertainty, was included in the casualty list published by the War Office in May, 1915, as " unofficially reported killed or died of wounds " on the 11th November, 1914.

Lieutenant Ferrier was appointed to his regiment, on probation, from the New Zealand Defence Forces, in August, 1914, and was attached for service to the 4th Battalion of his regiment when he died. While his death was still in doubt, he was promoted Lieutenant, to date from February, 1915.

LIEUTENANT HUGH MOCKLER-FERRYMAN, 2nd BATTN. OXFORDSHIRE AND BUCKINGHAMSHIRE LIGHT INFANTRY,

was the son of Lieutenant - Colonel A. F. Mockler-Ferryman, late Oxfordshire Light Infantry, and of Evelyn L. Mockler - Ferryman, daughter of the late Sir C. Whitehead, and was born at Maidstone on the 3rd May, 1892. Lieutenant Mockler-Ferryman was educated at Wellington College, Berkshire, where he was in the Cricket XI in 1909–10, and at the Royal Military College, Sandhurst. He received his commission as 2nd Lieutenant in September, 1911, and became Lieutenant in April, 1914. Proceeding abroad with the Expeditionary Force in August, 1914, he was present in the retirement from Mons up to the Battle of the Aisne, where he was killed near La Soupir on the 16th September, 1914.

Lieutenant Mockler-Ferryman played cricket for Berkshire, the Aldershot Command, and in other club teams. Among his other recreations were Alpine sports and curling, he having been a member of the Caledonian (Curling) Club.

2nd LIEUTENANT LEONARD AMAURI FILLEUL, B.A., SPECIAL RESERVE, SOMERSET LIGHT INFANTRY,

was the son of the Rev. Philip William Girdlestone Filleul, Rector of Devizes, Wiltshire, and was born at St. James's Lodge, Bath, on the 6th February, 1888. 2nd Lieutenant Filleul was a relative of the late Dr. Valpy, of scholastic fame, whose daughter was his great-grandmother, and to Canon Robert Girdlestone, formerly Principal of Wycliffe Hall, Oxford.

2nd Lieutenant Filleul was educated at the Preparatory School, Cleveland House, Weymouth ; and at Trent College, Derbyshire ; afterwards proceeding to Lincoln College, Oxford. At the University he rowed for four years in his college eight. While he was Secretary and Captain the College boat rose to fifth on the river. In 1910 he rowed in the winning

Trial Eights. He was in his School Cadet Corps, winning the National Service League gold medal for proficiency, and was in the Oxford University Officers' Training Corps. On leaving the 'Varsity he, in January, 1912, received a commission in Prince Albert's Regiment (Somersetshire Light Infantry), with which he trained for three weeks each year during his vacations. He was a master at Monkton Combe School, Bath, until the war broke out. For two years he was Captain of the Football Club at Trent College, and an oarsman at Oxford ; while at Monkton Combe School he greatly developed the School Rowing Club.

He left England at the end of September, 1914, with a draft of the Oxfordshire and Buckinghamshire Light Infantry, to which regiment he was then attached. On the 21st October, 1914 (Trafalgar Day) he was engaged in an attack on German infantry in the great Battle of Ypres, near St. Julien. During a rush forward in the early morning over some open ground he was struck by a bullet near the heart, dying instantly.

BRIGADIER-GENERAL NEIL DOUGLAS FINDLAY, C.B., p.s.c., COMMANDING ROYAL ARTILLERY 1st DIVISION,

was killed in action near Courchamps, France, on the 10th September, 1914, whilst directing the fire of his guns.

He entered the R.M.A., Woolwich, on the 19th January, 1877, and was commissioned into the Royal Artillery as Lieutenant on the

18th December, 1878. He became Captain on the 28th April, 1887 ; Major on the 21st December, 1896 ; Brevet Lieutenant-Colonel on the 29th November, 1900 ; Lieutenant-Colonel R.A. on the 1st September, 1904 ; Brevet-Colonel on the 15th October, 1905 ; Substantive Colonel on the 2nd March, 1908 ; Brigadier-General on the 14th July, 1910. He passed the final examination Staff College, 1897. He held the following Staff appointments : Adjutant R.A., 1st March, 1894, to 14th January, 1896 ; Staff Officer R.A., 1st Army Corps, and Brigade-Major R.A., Aldershot, 5th March, 1901, to 14th April, 1904 ; A.A.G., headquarters of Army and A.A.G., War Office, 2nd March, 1908, to 13th July, 1910 ; Commanding R.A., 1st Division Aldershot Command, 14th July, 1910.

His war services included the Hazara Expedition, 1888, for which he was mentioned in despatches and received the medal with clasp. He also took part in the South African War, 1899–1900, being present at operations in Natal in December, 1899, at the relief of Ladysmith, at further operations in Natal from March to June, 1900, at operations in the Transvaal, east of Pretoria, July to November, 1900. For these services he was mentioned in Despatches " London Gazette," 8th February, 1901; (Sir R. H. Buller, 30th March and 9th November, 1900); and " London Gazette," 22nd February, 1901; and received the Queen's medal with six clasps and the Brevet of Lieutenant-Colonel.

Brigadier-General Findlay was the second son of Thomas Dunlop Findlay, of Easterhill, Lanarkshire, and married, in 1892, Alma, daughter of Thomas Lloyd, of Minard, Argyll-shire.

CAPTAIN FRANK FISHER, 1st BATTN. ROYAL WEST KENT REGIMENT,

who was killed in action on the 13th September, 1 9 1 4, whilst leading his company when advancing to the Aisne, was the younger son of F r e d e r i c k Fisher, of Tulse Hill, London, S.W., and was born in London on the 23rd December, 1883.

He was educated at Charterhouse and the R.M.C., Sandhurst, and joined the Royal West Kent Regiment in October, 1903, becoming Lieutenant in January, 1906. He was promoted Captain on the 5th August, 1914.

Captain Fisher was a member of the Junior Naval and Military and the Royal Automobile Clubs, and was unmarried.

CAPTAIN HAROLD FISHER, D.S.O., 1st BATTN. MANCHESTER REGT.,

was the son of the Rev. Canon F. H. Fisher, Church Croft, Hemel Hempstead, and was born at Fulham on the 3rd March, 1877.

He was educated at Haileybury, and first joined the Suffolk Artillery Militia, in October, 1895, entering the Manchester Regiment in April, 1898, becoming Lieutenant in May, 1899, and Captain in July, 1901.

With his battalion he served in the South

African War, being present at operations in Natal and the Transvaal, including action at Belfast; again at operations in the Transvaal, 1901–02. For his services he was mentioned in Despatches (" London Gazette," 8th February, 1901; Sir G. S. White, 2nd December, 1899, and 23rd March, 1900; and "London Gazette," 10th September, 1901). He was awarded the D.S.O., and received the Queen's medal with three clasps and the King's medal with two clasps.

He was killed in action near La Bassée on the 16th December, 1914.

CAPTAIN MORTIMER FISHER, 1st BATTN. THE PRINCE OF WALES'S OWN (WEST YORKSHIRE REGIMENT),

was the son of Frederick Charles F i s h e r, E s q., F.R.C.S., and was born at King's Langley, Herts, on the 24th March, 1883.

He was educated at Aldenham School, Elstree, Herts, and joined the 3rd (then Militia) Battalion of the West Yorkshire Regiment in April, 1900, and, having passed third in his examination was transferred to the 2nd Battalion in June, 1901. He joined his battalion in South Africa on active service in October, 1901, remaining there over two years, during which he held the position of Acting Adjutant, and, as he held the Hythe certificate, Musketry Instructor. He was present at operations in the Transvaal, November, 1901—May, 1902, receiving the Queen's medal with three clasps.

In 1905 he exchanged into the 1st Battalion and went to India, where he went through the Mohmand Campaign, 1908, receiving the medal with clasp.

On promotion to Captain in July, 1910, he joined the depot of his regiment at York.

Captain Fisher accompanied his battalion to the Continent for active service in the Great War and took part in some of the severe fighting in the early stages of the campaign.

He was killed on the 20th September, 1914, near Troyon, but it has not been possible to obtain particulars of the occurrence, as so many of the battalion were killed, wounded, or missing.

He married Margaret Sarah, daughter of C. H. Bailey, Esq., of Charlcombe, Watford, and left one son, Richard Mortimer, born 3rd February, 1913.

He played football, golf, and polo.

BRIGADIER-GENERAL CHARLES FITZCLARENCE, V.C., p.s.c., IRISH GUARDS, COMMANDING THE 1st GUARDS BRIGADE,

was the son of the late Captain the Hon. George Fitz-Clarence, R.N., third son of the first Earl of Munster, and was born on the 8th May, 1865, at Bishop's Court, County Kildare, Ireland. All four sons of the Earl of Munster served either in the Navy or Army, the youngest dying of wounds received in the attack on the Redan in the Crimea. A twin brother of Brigadier-General FitzClarence served with distinction in the Egyptian Army, and was killed at Abu-Hamed in 1897.

Brigadier-General FitzClarence was educated at Eton, and Wellington College, and joined the Army, in which he had a most distinguished career, by entering the Royal Fusiliers (City of London Regiment) from the Militia in November, 1886, as Lieutenant. He became Captain in that regiment in April, 1898, and was transferred to the Irish Guards on the formation of that regiment in October, 1900.

In the South African War Brigadier-General FitzClarence earned the V.C. for three distinct acts of great bravery, during the siege of Mafeking, on separate dates, he having gone to South Africa on special service in July, 1899. His gallantry and daring throughout the siege had become proverbial, and earned for him the sobriquet of " The Demon " among his men. Three specific acts of valour are officially recorded in connection with the award of the V.C., the first having been at Five Mile Bank. The armoured train had gone out on the 14th October, 1899, and had got into difficulties. Captain FitzClarence took about fifty men of the newly formed Protectorate Regiment—which he had himself helped to raise—to its assistance. It was their first engagement, but starting at one thousand yards FitzClarence advanced them, under a very heavy fire, to a distance of between four and five hundred yards from the train. At one time the squadron was nearly surrounded, but the Captain's perfect coolness and clever handling effected the object in view, with a loss of only two killed and fifteen wounded, they having succeeded in killing fifty of the enemy, besides wounding a large number. They were supported by No. 2 Troop, and a part of " D " Squadron covered their retirement, but the moral effect upon the enemy was very great.

The second occasion was a pitch-dark night, on the 27th October, when he led about sixty men, supported by a handful of police, in a sortie to attack the Boers' main trench to the east of the town. So cautiously did they work that they came on the enemy sleeping, and attacked them with bayonet and butt end of rifles. FitzClarence was the first man in, sword in hand, and is said to have killed four himself. The Boers in the rear fired on the trench indiscriminately, and when the whistle sounded to retire the little party returned, leaving six dead and nine wounded.

The third time was on the 23rd December, when he greatly distinguished himself by his courage and dash in the action at Game Tree, being himself shot through the leg and seriously wounded.

From August, 1900, to February, 1901, having received his Brevet Majority in November, 1900, he was Brigade-Major in South Africa. For his war service she was mentioned in Despatches (" London Gazette," 8th February, 1901), and in addition to being awarded the V.C. and his brevet promotion he received the Queen's South Africa Medal with three clasps. From April, 1903, to March, 1906, he was Brigade-Major of the 5th Brigade at Aldershot. He received his substantive Majority in the Irish Guards in May, 1904, and succeeded to the command of the 1st Battalion in July, 1909. In 1913 he was appointed to the command of the regiment and regimental district, a post he held till the outbreak of the war with Germany, when he took over command of the 29th Brigade, Xth Division, at the Curragh till the 22nd September, and on the 27th of that month he took command of the 1st Guards Brigade of the Expeditionary Force, which he held till his death in action at Ypres on the night of the 11th November or early morning of the 12th November, 1914, leading the 1st Guards' Brigade against the Prussian Guard.

At the time of the fighting near Gheluvelt on the 31st October, 1914, when the Germans had broken the line of the Ist Division and taken the village, Sir John French, in his Despatch published on the 30th November, 1914, referring to this incident, says : " Perhaps the most important and decisive attack (except that of the Prussian Guard on the 10th November) made against the 1st Corps during the whole of its arduous experiences in the neighbourhood of Ypres took place on the 31st October. After several attacks and counter-attacks during the course of the morning along the Menin-Ypres Road, south-east of Gheluvelt, an attack against that place developed in great force, and the line of the Ist Division was broken. Meantime, on the Menin Road, a counter-attack delivered by the left of the Ist Division and the right of the IInd Division against the right flank of the German line was completely successful, and the 2nd Worcester Regiment was to the fore in this. I was present, with Sir Douglas Haig, at Hooge between two and three o'clock on this day when the Ist Division was retiring. I regard it as the most critical moment in the whole of this great battle. The rally of the Ist Division and the recapture of the village of Gheluvelt at such a time was fraught with momentous consequences. If any one unit can be singled out for especial praise it is the Worcesters."

Sir John French, in a speech he made to the Worcesters on the 26th November, 1914, which appeared in "The Times" of the 14th December, 1914, praising the Worcesters for what they had done on the 31st October, said : " I have made repeated enquiries as to what officer was responsible for the conduct of this counter-attack on October 31st, but have never so far been able to find out."

It has since been officially established that it was Brigadier-General FitzClarence, V.C., who was responsible.

In his despatch of the 20th November, 1914, Sir John French made the following reference to the late officer : " Another officer whose name was particularly mentioned to me was that of Brigadier-General FitzClarence, V.C., commanding the 1st Guards' Brigade. He was unfortunately killed in the night attack of the 11th November. His loss will be severely felt."

Brigadier-General FitzClarence was a military member of the London Territorial Force Association, and a member of I Zingari, the Guards', and the Naval and Military Clubs.

He married, in April, 1898, Violet, youngest daughter of the late Lord Alfred Spencer Churchill, son of the sixth Duke of Marlborough, and left a son and a daughter : Edward Charles, born October, 1899 ; and Joan Harriet, born December, 1901.

CAPTAIN GERALD GADSDEN FITZE, "C" BATTERY, ROYAL HORSE ARTILLERY,

who is believed to have been killed whilst reconnoitring on or about the 28th October, 1914, at or near Zandvoorde, Belgium, was the elder son of the late Mr. Samuel Fitze, of Trevanion, Eastbourne, and of Mrs. Fitze, Trehayne, Ashburnham Road, Eastbourne. Born at 56 Kensington Park Road, London, W., on the 11th January, 1886, he was educated at Lambrook, Bracknell, and at Marlborough College, proceeding afterwards to the R.M.A., Woolwich.

He received his first appointment in the Army in July, 1906, when he was gazetted 2nd Lieutenant in the Royal Field Artillery ; and in January, 1907, he joined the 31st Battery at Kilkenny, Ireland. He became Lieutenant two years later, and in 1912 was posted to " C " Battery, Royal Horse Artillery. His promotion to Captain was gazetted to date from the 30th October, 1914, after his presumed death.

Captain Fitze, whose favourite recreation was hunting, was a member of the Junior Army and Navy and Marlborough Clubs.

CAPTAIN GERALD HUGH FITZGERALD, 4th (ROYAL IRISH) DRAGOON GUARDS,

born at Johnstown Castle, Wexford, Ireland, on the 11th April, 1886, was the only son of the late Lord Maurice FitzGerald, second son of the fourth Duke of Leinster, and Lady Adelaide Forbes, eldest daughter of the seventh Earl of Granard, K.P.

He was educated at Eton, and joined the Royal North Devon Hussars (Yeomanry), from which he was gazetted to the (Royal Irish) Dragoon Guards in December, 1907, obtaining his troop in November, 1913.

He was shot through the head while taking machine-gun observations on the 13th September, 1914, at Bourg-et-Comin (Aisne).

Captain FitzGerald belonged to the Cavalry Club, and his recreations were hunting, shooting, polo, and cricket.

He married, on the 6th August, 1914, Dorothy, youngest daughter of Spencer Charrington, Esq., of Winchfield, Hampshire.

LIEUT. D. T. F. FITZPATRICK, 3rd (attd. 2nd) BATTN. SOUTH STAFFORDSHIRE REGT.,

was killed in action on the 27th October, 1914. He was educated at Stonyhurst, and joined the 3rd Battalion South Staffordshire Regiment, on probation, in March, 1913, becoming Lieutenant in February, 1914.

CAPTAIN GABRIEL ROY FITZ-PATRICK, 3rd (attd. 2nd) BATTN. THE WELSH REGIMENT,

was born at Chelsea, London, S.W., on the 20th October, 1883, and was the son of J. F. J. Fitzpatrick, Esq., of Highgate. He was educated at the Jesuit College, Stamford Hill, and Ratcliff College. He served in the City Imperial Yeomanry from 1901–02, in the 3rd Essex Regiment from 1905–09, and became Lieutenant in the 3rd Battalion Welsh Regiment in August, 1909. He also served with the British East African Police from 1909–12.

He was with the 2nd Battalion Welsh Regiment in this war, being present in the retirement from Mons to the Marne, was promoted Captain on the 1st September, 1914, and was killed on the 14th of that month at Beaulne, in the Battle of the Aisne.

Captain Fitzpatrick married May, daughter of the late Rev. W. F. Attenborough, Vicar of Fletching, and adopted daughter of the late Henry North, Earl of Sheffield, of Sheffield Park, Sussex. He left no family.

CAPTAIN ROLAND SACKVILLE FLETCHER, 1st BATTN. NORTHUMBERLAND FUSILIERS,

born in London on the 24th March, 1882, was the second son of Lionel Fletcher and Eleanor Mary, his wife (née Stopford Sackville), of Elmscroft, West Farleigh, Kent, and a nephew of Colonel Stopford Sackville, of Drayton House, Northants.

He was educated at Charterhouse, and entered the Northumberland Fusiliers from the Northamptonshire Militia (with which he served when it was embodied for nearly nine months), in January, 1901, becoming Lieutenant in February, 1902. From November, 1904, to January, 1910, he was seconded for employment with the North Nigeria Regiment, West African Frontier Force, under the Colonial Office, and was promoted Captain in September, 1912.

On arrival at the front on the 29th October he was sent on the 1st November, 1914, with his company to help in holding Wytschaete against an overwhelming force of the enemy. He was seen to fall on the morning of the 1st November, after which he was not seen again, but the news of his death on the following day was obtained from one of the prisoners in a German camp in June, 1915.

Captain Fletcher was of a very literary turn of mind, and several articles by him, chiefly on his experiences in Northern Nigeria, appeared in "Blackwood's Magazine." He made a great study of the language and customs of the natives, and published a book called " Hausa Sayings and Folk-lore." He was qualified as a first-class Interpreter in Hausa, in 1912, as part of his examination for the Staff College.

He was a member of the Wellington Club, and was very fond of sports and games.

2nd LIEUTENANT REGINALD WILLIAM FLETCHER, ROYAL FIELD ARTILLERY,

who was killed in action on the 31st October, 1914, at the age of twenty-two, was the youngest son of C. R. L. Fletcher, Esq., Norham End, Oxford, and was born on the 19th March, 1892. He was educated at Eton, where he was a scholar, and was a commoner of Balliol College, Oxford. At Oxford he was in the Artillery Section of the O.T.C. He rowed in the Leander Four at Henley Regatta, 1913, and in the Oxford University Eight in 1914, and was also for some years stroke of his college boat.

He was gazetted to the R.A. in December, 1912.

LIEUTENANT THOMAS ALGERNON FITZGERALD FOLEY, 1st BATTN. THE NORFOLK REGIMENT,

who was born on the 29th December, 1889, at Egerton Gardens, London, S.W., was the only son of the late Vice-Admiral Francis John Foley, grandson of Admiral the Hon. Fitzgerald A. C. Foley, a grandnephew of Colonel the Hon. Augustus Frederick Foley, Grenadier Guards, and of General the Hon. Sir St. George Gerald Foley, and a cousin of the present Baron Foley.

He was educated at Eton (Mr. F. H. Rawlins' and Mr. H. de Havilland's Houses), to which he went in 1904. There he was in the Army Class, took prizes for history, mathematics, etc., and was in the O.T.C. From Eton he passed direct into the R.M.C., Sandhurst, in 1908, passing first in order of merit in the Junior Trials. He was in the revolver team in 1909, which won many competitions, and he himself made the highest score against Woolwich. He passed sixth out of Sandhurst, and was gazetted 2nd Lieutenant in the Norfolk Regiment in September, 1909, joining his battalion at Brentwood, from which it went to Aldershot. There he shot successfully in several of the Aldershot rifle meetings, and was in his company's team for the Inter-Regimental Grand Challenge Shield, which they retained.

He was promoted Lieutenant in October, 1911, and on the 3rd August, 1914, his battalion being then at Holywood, Belfast, was sent to take charge of Grey Point Fort. On the 6th he was recalled to his battalion for mobilisation, and sailed with it for the front on the 14th August, landing at Havre. Within a few days the battalion was in action at Dour, in Belgium ; and, beginning with the retirement from Mons, Lieutenant Foley was in every action till he fell at Festubert on the 25th October, 1914.

The following account of the circumstances was given by the Colonel and others :—" He had just made a most gallant advance to the trenches with his men under a very heavy fire, and had reached there safely. He was in the very foremost of the British lines when he fell, and he died at the head of his men, driving back a most desperate attack by overwhelming numbers of the enemy. He was buried, like a soldier, where he fell. The actual place where he was laid to rest is close to the most advanced trenches, as our line in that part of the battle-field has not advanced a yard since the day when he fell, gallantly defending it."

Lieutenant Foley was a keen soldier, an excellent shot and horseman, his chief recreation having been hunting.

His mother received several letters from soldiers, showing that they held their late officer in great esteem.

MAJOR HUBERT FRANCIS FITZ-WILLIAM BRABAZON FOLJAMBE, 2nd BATTN. THE KING'S ROYAL RIFLE CORPS, who was born on the 16th November, 1872, was the son of the Right Hon. F. J. S. Foljambe and the Lady Gertrude Foljambe, daughter of the third Earl of Gosford, of Osberton, Nottinghamshire.

He was educated at Eton, and joined the King's Royal Rifle Corps from the Militia in March, 1895, becoming Lieutenant in February, 1898, and Captain in July, 1901. He served in the South African War, being present at operations in Natal in May, 1900, and in the Transvaal from November, 1900, to May, 1902. He was Commandant at Helvetia for some time from December, 1901, and for his services he received the King's and the Queen's medals, each with two clasps.

Major Foljambe was a member of the Army and Navy Club. He was a good rider, a very keen cricketer, a good shot, and fond of racquets. He played cricket for the Eton Ramblers, Free Foresters, and the " Green Jackets."

He was killed on the 14th September, 1914, while leading his company up the heights of the Aisne, near Troyon.

Major Foljambe, who was promoted to that rank in July, 1912, married Gladys, daughter of General and Mrs. Bewicke-Copley, of Sprotborough, Yorkshire, and left one son, John Savile, born October, 1911.

MAJOR the Honble. ARTHUR ORLANDO WOLSTAN CECIL WELD FORESTER, M.V.O., 1st BATTN. GRENADIER GUARDS, COMMANDING THE KING'S COMPANY, died at King Edward VII Hospital, London, from wounds received near Ypres, Belgium, on the 29th October, 1914, having gone out with the VIIth Division. He was the fifth son of Cecil, fifth Baron Forester, and was

born in London on the 13th July, 1877.

He was educated at Harrow, and joined the Grenadier Guards from the 3rd Shropshire Light Infantry (Militia) in December, 1897, becoming Lieutenant in October, 1899. With his battalion he served in Malta, and subsequently, under Sir Leslie Rundle, in the VIIIth Division through the Boer War, receiving the Queen's medal with three clasps and the King's medal with two clasps. He was promoted Captain in the 3rd Battalion in January, 1905, of which he was Adjutant from January, 1907, to 31st December, 1909. From 1910 to 1912 he was A.D.C. to Lord Hardinge, Viceroy of India, and was awarded the M.V.O. for his services in that position during the visit of King George V. In 1912 he obtained his Majority, with the command of the King's Company of his regiment. Major Weld Forester was a member of the Guards' and Turf Clubs, played cricket and golf, and was fond of hunting and shooting.

CAPTAIN MYLES LONSDALL FORMBY, 1st BATTN. THE DUKE OF EDINBURGH'S (WILTSHIRE REGIMENT),

who was killed in action at Neuve Chapelle on the 26th October, 1914, was the son of the late Myles L o n s d a l l Formby, J.P., D.L. for Essex, formerly of the Carabiniers, and Mrs. Formby, Haydown, Goring, Oxfordshire. He was born on the 15th December, 1874, and was educated at Newton College, Newton Abbot, South Devon.

He first served in the Wiltshire Militia, from which he was gazetted to the Wiltshire Regiment in December, 1896, joining the 1st Battalion in Karachi, India. During the South African War he was sent from India to South Africa with a draft ; so, being in the Transvaal while hostilities were proceeding, he received the Queen's medal. He was sent home to the depot, and afterwards to Mullingar as Adjutant of the 13th Provisional Battalion. He was promoted Captain in February, 1902, and from October, 1903, to September, 1908, was Adjutant of the Warminster Volunteers.

He went to the front in August, 1914, and was all through the fighting at, and the retirement from, Mons, gaining the reputation of a brave officer, beloved by his men.

Captain Formby married, in April, 1903, Winifred Powys, daughter of Percy Stone, Esq., Merston, Isle of Wight. She died in June, 1914, leaving two children : a son, Myles Lonsdall ; and a daughter, Winifred Joan.

CAPTAIN FRANK FORREST, ROYAL ARMY MEDICAL CORPS,

born at Blackburn on the 21st May, 1879, was the son of Dr. Forrest.

He was educated at Clitheroe Grammar School, Blackburn, and at Owens College, Manchester. After qualifying in medicine he passed into the R.A.M.C. in January, 1906, becoming Captain in July, 1909. In 1914 he passed the Captain's course, obtaining a "special" in physical training.

He was killed on the 13th September, 1914, by a shell bursting while he was attending to wounded men under heavy shell fire.

Captain Forrest married, in September, 1913, Maud, daughter of John and Amelia Child. He left no family.

He belonged to the Junior Army and Navy Club, was a very keen sportsman, very good at football, cricket, and billiards, and won many cups at lawn tennis.

CAPTAIN FREDERICK FORSTER, 4th BATTN. THE ROYAL FUSILIERS, (CITY OF LONDON REGIMENT),

was the second son of the late Paul Forster, of Malverleys, East Woodhay, Hants, was born on the 24th December, 1879, and educated at Eton and Trinity College, Cambridge.

He joined the Royal Fusiliers in May, 1900, becoming Lieutenant in April, 1902. He was employed with the West African Frontier Force from April, 1904, to January, 1907, during which time he saw active service in Northern Nigeria in 1906, receiving the medal with clasp.

He was promoted Captain in April, 1909, and in October, 1910, was appointed Adjutant of the 1st Battalion, an appointment he held till September, 1913. In April, 1914, he was appointed Adjutant (attending General Staff) of the O.T.C.'s of the Universities of Leeds, Manchester, Sheffield, and Nottingham.

On the outbreak of the war Captain Forster was ordered to join the 4th Battalion of his regiment at Newport, Isle of Wight, and proceeded with it to France on the 13th August, 1914.

At the beginning of the year 1915 it was stated in the casualty lists that Captain Forster had been "unofficially reported killed or died of wounds," but it has since been ascertained that he died on the 23rd August, 1914, two hours after he was wounded. He was wounded three times while defending a bridge on the canal at Nimy, a suburb of Mons, and was buried on the battlefield.

His recreations were hunting and shooting, and he was a member of the United Service Club, London, and of the Kildare Street Club, Dublin.

2nd LIEUTENANT JOHN FORSTER, 2nd BATTN. KING'S ROYAL RIFLE CORPS,

who was killed in action at the Battle of the Aisne on the 14th September, 1914, at the age of twenty-one, was the elder son of Mr. H. M. Forster, M.P., and the Hon. Mrs. Forster, of 41 Hans Place, S.W.

He obtained his commission in the K.R.R.C. in September, 1913.

CAPTAIN LIONEL ARCHIBALD FORSTER, RESERVE OF OFFICERS (attd. 1st BATTN.) CHESHIRE REGIMENT, who died on the 4th November, 1914, at the Lycée Hospital, Douai, of wounds received in action, but whose name has not appeared in the official casualty lists, was the youngest son of the late Right Hon. William Forster, M.P., and of Maud Forster, of Bornhill, Bramford Speke, Devon. (" Times " Obit. Notice.)

He was born on the 16th March, 1879, and joined the Army in August, 1898. He served in the South African War, in the course of which he acted as Station Staff Officer and as Garrison Adjutant. He took part in operations in the Orange Free State, and in the Transvaal between 1900 and 1902, including actions at Karee Siding, Vet and Zand Rivers, and near Johannesburg. He received the Queen's medal with three clasps and the King's medal with two clasps.

Captain Forster, who was married, obtained his Company in October, 1905, and retired from the active list with that rank in January, 1914.

LIEUTENANT JOHN CUSACK FORSYTH, ADJUTANT 23rd BRIGADE, ROYAL FIELD ARTILLERY, was the son of the late Lieutenant-Colonel Frederick Arthur Forsyth, late Northumberland Fusiliers, and of Mrs. Ellen Sanford Forsyth, of Leamington. He was born at Leamington Spa on the 2nd November, 1883, and was educated at Wellington College from 1897–1900, and the Royal Military Academy, Woolwich, from 1900 –1902.

He received his commission in the Royal Field Artillery in 1902, becoming Lieutenant in December, 1905. He was appointed Adjutant of the 23rd Brigade in August, 1912.

In this war he served with the 3rd Division at Mons, Le Cateau, the Battles of the Marne and the Aisne, and was mentioned in Field-Marshal Sir John French's Despatch of the 8th October, 1914.

He was killed in action on the 22nd September, 1914, at Brenelle, during the Battle of the Aisne. Lieutenant Forsyth was a member of the Caledonian Club, and unmarried. His recreations were hunting and racing.

LIEUTENANT ARCHIBALD COURTENAY HAYES FOSTER, HAMPSHIRE REGIMENT, attd. 4th BATTN. THE KING'S AFRICAN RIFLES, of which he was commanding " A " Company when killed, was the fourth son of the late Montagu H. Foster, of Stubbington House, Fareham, and of Mrs. Foster, The Lodge, Stubbington. He was born at Stubbington House on the 19th May, 1886, and was educated at Stubbington and at Cheltenham College. He received his commission in the Hampshire Regiment in January,

1906, becoming Lieutenant in October, 1907. In October, 1913, he was seconded in his regiment for employment with the 4th (Uganda) Battalion King's African Rifles, with whom he was serving at the time of his death. He had only recently returned from an expedition in Jubaland.

He was killed in action on the 19th September, 1914, at Campi ya Marabu, Tsavo, British East Africa, gallantly urging on his men after he was hit. The following account of the action forwarded by the General Officer commanding troops, British East Africa and Uganda Protectorate, to His Excellency the Governor and Commander-in-Chief, East African Protectorate, was published in the " East African Standard " of the 14th October, 1914 :—

" Campi ya Marabu.

" This little action was fought with spirit and determination. Lieutenant Foster died a gallant death, and the British officers and rank and file of the Somali section and ' A ' Company K.A.R. gave him courageous support."

2nd LIEUTENANT HERBERT KNOLLYS FOSTER, 1st BATTN. GLOUCESTERSHIRE REGIMENT, born at All Saints' Vicarage, Gloucester, on the 18th October, 1895, was the son of the Rev. Canon and Edith Susan Foster, St.Thomas'Vicarage, Groombridge, Tunbridge Wells.

He was educated at Marlborough College and the R.M.C., Sandhurst, and was gazetted to the Army in August, 1914.

2nd Lieutenant Foster is believed to have been killed at Gheluvelt, in Flanders, on the 29th October, 1914.

LIEUTENANT WILLIAM AUGUSTUS PORTMAN FOSTER, 1st BATTN. THE SOUTH STAFFORDSHIRE REGIMENT, eldest son of Colonel Sir William Yorke Foster, Bart., and of Lady Foster, daughter of the late Colonel Augustus Berkeley Portman, Bombay Staff Corps, was born on the 2nd June, 1887, at Hardingham, Norfolk.

He was educated at Wellington College, where he was in the Blucher from 1901 to 1905, and at the R.M.C., Sandhurst. Gazetted to the South Staffordshire Regiment in February, 1908,

he became Lieutenant in September of the same year. He served with the 2nd Battalion in South Africa and subsequently in Gibraltar, and again in South Africa ; then with the 1st Battalion, with which, after its return to England to form part of the immortal VIIth Division, he sailed for Belgium in October, 1914.

After many days of continuous fighting, being the last officer left with his company, he was severely wounded on the 31st October, 1914, while holding his position with the remnants of his battalion towards the end of the first great Battle of Ypres. Having lain on the field for two days and nights, he fell into the hands of the Germans and died of his wounds in hospital at Frankfurt-on-Maine on the 11th November, 1914.

Lieutenant Foster was devoted to polo, and a fine racquet player, playing both games for his regiment. With Lieutenant Naylor, of the battalion, he won the Garrison Racquet cup at Gibraltar in 1912.

CAPTAIN MANSERGH CUTHBERT FOWKE, 2nd BATTN. MANCHESTER REGIMENT,

whose name is shown in the monthly casualty list published in June, 1915, as having been killed in action, no date being given, is believed to have died in August, 1914, after having been severely wounded at Le Cateau.

He was the elder son of C. H. F. Fowke, Esq., of Wolverhampton, and was born on the 14th May, 1882, at Codsall, Staffordshire. He was educated at Clifton College, and joined the Manchester Regiment from the Militia in January, 1901, becoming Lieutenant in October of the same year.

He took part in the South African War, being present at operations in the Transvaal in July, 1901, and in the Orange River Colony from July 1901, to May, 1902. He received the Queen's

medal with three clasps and the King's medal with two clasps. From November, 1908, to November, 1913, he was employed with the King's African Rifles, and took part in operations in Somaliland, 1908–10, for which he received the medal with clasp.

He was given the local rank of Captain in January, 1911, and was promoted Captain in his regiment in December, 1912. He was a member of the Sports Club and was not married.

Captain Fowke was reported missing after the engagement at Le Cateau on the 25th August, 1914, and official confirmation was received on the 18th May, 1915, by his name appearing in the German lists, as dead and buried at a place unknown.

LIEUTENANT V. FOX, ARMY VETERINARY CORPS,

was killed in action on the 26th August, 1914.

CAPTAIN MARTIN VICTOR FOY, 1st BATTN. THE QUEEN'S (ROYAL WEST SURREY REGT.),

who was killed in the trenches on the 13th October, 1914, was the son of the late John Foy, and was born at Edith Grove, Chelsea, on the 20th June, 1884. He was educated at Bradfield College, where he was in the Cricket XI, and

at the R.M.C., Sandhurst.

Captain Foy was gazetted to the Queen's in 1903, becoming Lieutenant in May, 1909. He served in India and at home, and was Assistant-Adjutant of his battalion. He played cricket for his regiment, and was good at all games. In 1914 he took part in the final lawn tennis doubles in the Army Championship.

He left Bordon Camp for the front on the 12th August, 1914, and became Captain on the 8th October, 1914, only a few days before he was killed.

The General commanding his Brigade wrote as follows of Captain Foy :—

" To the grief of all, your gallant husband was killed in the trenches last evening by some one of the enemy, who have been picking off anyone whom they could see. The trenches are so close to each other that the risk has been ever present. He was shot through the head and died very soon afterwards. He had done *so* well, always cheerful and ready for anything. His sad death is felt by all to be an irreparable loss. It must in time be a source of pride that your husband has given his life for his country, and that all who knew him loved and respected him as an example of bravery which must be a lasting help in enabling us to bring this war to an end."

The following account was given by a Sergeant of the Queen's, and was published in the "Hindhead Herald":—

"Captain Foy was, as usual, looking after the comfort of his men, and was just asking if No. 4 platoon had had hot tea, when he incautiously stood up in the trench and was picked off by a sniper. He was buried the following day, and I acted as one of the bearers."

A brother officer wrote:—

"I wish you could have seen Martin one day—about the third day on the Aisne. My half-company was in the trenches in support, when the front line was frightfully heavily attacked, and we were wanted badly. Martin came doubling back through an absolute hail of stuff and got us up. It was grand to see him shoving the men on through it."

MAJOR the Honble. HUGH JOSEPH FRASER, M.V.O., 2nd BATTALION SCOTS GUARDS,

who was killed in action at Ypres on the 27th October, 1914, was the third and second surviving son of Simon Fraser, thirteenth Baron Lovat, and the Dowager Lady Lovat (née Alice Weld Blundell), and brother of the present peer.

He was born on the 6th July, 1874, at Phoiness, Beauly, Inverness-shire, was educated at St. Benedict's Abbey School, Fort Augustus, Scotland, and joined the Scots Guards from the Militia in December, 1894, becoming Lieutenant in November, 1897.

He took part in the South African War, being present at operations in the Orange River Colony from May to November, 1900, including actions at Biddulphsberg and Wittebergen, and at operations in the Transvaal and Orange River Colony from November, 1900, to May, 1902. He was mentioned in Despatches ("London Gazette," 10th September, 1901), and received the Queen's medal with three clasps and the King's medal with two clasps.

He was promoted Captain in March, 1901; from April, 1903, to July, 1907, he was an Adjutant of Imperial Yeomanry; and from November, 1910, to 1913 A.D.C. to the Viceroy of India. At the time of his death he was Second in Command of his battalion.

LIEUTENANT JOHN FRASER, 2nd BATTN. THE CONNAUGHT RANGERS,

was the son of John Fraser, Esq., J.P., of Riversdale, Boyle, Ireland, and was born at Tientsin, China, in 1884.

He was educated at Mr. Bookey's School, Bray, County Wicklow, and at the Royal Military College, Sandhurst, whence he obtained his commission in the Connaught Rangers in January, 1905, becoming Lieutenant in April, 1906.

After three years' service in India he was employed with the King's African Rifles in the operations in Somaliland from 1908–10. For his services he received the Somaliland medal. For some time he acted as A.D.C. to the Governor and Commander-in-Chief in Uganda.

At the Battle of the Aisne he was wounded while attempting the rescue of a wounded brother officer, and died from the effect of his wounds on the 14th September, 1914. The notebook of the late Major Sarsfield, who commanded the 2nd Battalion Connaught Rangers, which has been discovered, contains a note, mentioning Lieutenant Fraser, 2nd Connaught Rangers, for his coolness under fire, and his efficient leading of his men at all times, especially at the action of La Cour de Poupière on the 14th of September, where he behaved with conspicuous gallantry, and was very dangerously wounded.

Lieutenant Fraser was a keen soldier, fine sportsman, and a very successful big-game hunter. He was a member of the Junior United Service Club.

CAPTAIN JOHN ALEXANDER FRASER, 2nd BATTN. PRINCESS LOUISE'S (ARGYLL AND SUTHERLAND HIGHLANDERS),

who was killed at Le Cateau on the 26th August, 1914, was born in India on the 28th October, 1872, son of John Alexander Fraser, and a nephew of Sir Thomas Fraser, of Edinburgh.

Captain Fraser served in the ranks with Lumsden's Horse in the early part of the South African War, having joined that corps in

Calcutta when the Boer War broke out. He was present at operations in the Orange Free State, including actions at Karee Siding, Houtnek (Thoba Mountain), Vet River, and Zand River. In the same year—1900—he was in the Transvaal, taking part in actions near Johannesburg and Pretoria. He received the Queen's medal with three clasps. In July, 1900, he was promoted from the ranks of Lumsden's Horse, and given a commission in the West India Regiment, in which he became Lieutenant in February, 1901. Subsequently he was transferred to the Argyll and Sutherland Highlanders, in which he obtained his company in April, 1909. He served as an Adjutant of the Territorial Force for three years from February, 1911. He was a very keen sportsman.

Captain Fraser married Mary Claudine Stirling, daughter of the late Colin Dunlop Donald, and left two daughters : Margaret Stirling, born at Bloemfontein, July, 1909 ; and Alexandra Mary Agnes, born at Nairn, September, 1914.

LIEUTENANT JAMES HOWIE FRASER, 2nd BATTN. GORDON HIGHLANDERS,

son of Edward Cleather F r a s e r, C.M.G., M.L.C. of Mauritius, was born at Blackheath on the 4th April, 1888. He was educated at Rugby, and was gazetted to the Gordon Highlanders in October, 1907. He served with his battalion in India and Egypt, and was promoted Lieutenant in March, 1909.

Lieutenant Fraser was killed on the 30th October, 1914, while advancing on Klein Zillebeke Farmhouse. For his services he was mentioned in Sir John French's Despatch of the 14th January, 1915.

2nd LIEUTENANT the Honble. SIMON FRASER, 3rd (attd. 2nd) BATTN. GORDON HIGHLANDERS,

who was killed in action near Ypres on the 29th October, 1914, was the third son of the eighteenth Lord Saltoun, of Abernethy.

He was born on the 7th September, 1888, and was educated at Winton House, Winchester (preparatory school), and at Charterhouse. He received a commission as 2nd Lieutenant in the 3rd Battalion Gordon Highlanders on the 7th September, 1914, and at the end of that month was attached to the 2nd Battalion, leaving with it for the front on the 4th October, 1914.

2nd Lieutenant Fraser was a member of the Stock Exchange. Two of his brothers are serving in the Gordon Highlanders as Lieutenants : the Master of Saltoun and the Hon. William Fraser.

CAPTAIN WILLIAM REGINALD FREND, ADJUTANT 2nd BATTN. SHERWOOD FORESTERS (NOTTINGHAMSHIRE AND DERBYSHIRE REGIMENT),

was killed in action at the Battle of the Aisne on the 21st September, 1914. He was born at Hambledon, Henley-on-Thames, on the 8th May, 1875, the second son of the late Edwin Frend, Esq., of Brighton, and was educated at Haileybury, and Trinity College, Cambridge. He joined the Derbyshire Regiment in November, 1898, becoming Lieutenant in the amalgamated Nottinghamshire and Derbyshire Regiment in May, 1900.

He took part in the South African War, being present at operations in the Orange Free State, including actions at Houtnek (Thoba Mountain), Vet River, and Zand River ; also at operations in the Transvaal and Cape Colony, and received the Queen's medal with three clasps and the King's medal with two clasps. He also served with the 1st Battalion in China.

Becoming Captain in September, 1904, he was from April, 1906, to December, 1910, Adjutant of a battalion of Volunteers, afterwards the 5th Territorial Battalion of his own regiment ; while in December, 1912, he was appointed Adjutant of the 2nd Battalion.

Captain Frend married, in July, 1907, Phyllis, second daughter of Mr. and Mrs. T. H. Mills, of White Bank House, Stockport, Cheshire, and leaves two children : Richard William, born June, 1909 ; and Dorothea Elizabeth, born November, 1911.

LIEUTENANT K. T. FROST, 3rd BATTN. CHESHIRE REGIMENT,

whose name was included in the monthly casualty list published in October among officers " reported (unofficially) killed, or died of wounds received in action," no date being given, became Lieutenant in the 3rd Battalion Cheshire Regiment in June, 1913, having joined in September of the previous year.

LIEUTENANT BERNARD VINCENT FULCHER, 2nd BATTN. THE PRINCE OF WALES'S VOLUNTEERS (SOUTH LANCASHIRE REGIMENT),

was born at Lorne House, Great Yarmouth, on the 22nd January, 1892, and was the son of William Popplewell Fulcher and Alice, his wife, of "Walton," Wimbledon Hill Road, Wimbledon.

He was educated at Wimbledon College, and was at King's College School from 1906 to 1910, where he was Captain of the VIII (shooting), and was also in the First XV (football) in 1909–10. He was a member of the Officers' Training Corps, and was "efficient" for three years, holding the "A" certificate.

Lieutenant Fulcher went to the R.M.C., Sandhurst, in 1910, and received his commission in 1911, becoming Lieutenant in July, 1913.

He was present with his battalion in the Great War from August till the day he died. He was mentioned in Sir John French's Despatches of the 8th October, 1914, and of 14th January, 1915, and was awarded the Military Cross in the latter month, but he did not live to personally receive the decoration, for he had been killed in a dugout by shell on the 17th November, 1914, at Ypres, being at the time the only surviving officer left of his battalion.

Major Baird, commanding 1st Battalion Gordon Highlanders, who was for fifteen days, between the 5th and 20th November, in command of the line of trenches in which Lieutenant Fulcher was killed, wrote to his mother saying : " I wish to tell you how nobly your boy was doing his duty when he met his death. . . . Your son was quite indefatigable in doing his duty under conditions the difficulties of which can never be fully realised except by those who were there. . . . Often I used to feel that he was destined to go far in our profession. . . . None of us who served together in those fifteen strenuous days will ever forget his splendid work. As officer commanding that particular section of the trenches, I have officially brought to notice the very splendid way in which his conduct was distinguished."

The late Head Master of King's College School also wrote saying : " He was with us just the best kind of English boy, straight and loyal and keen, . . . with a healthy influence with his friends and all the school."

The Adjutant and other officers, and also men in the ranks, wrote most feelingly, saying how all appreciated his courage and capacity.

CAPTAIN JOHN HENRY MIDDLETON FULLER, 83rd WALLAJAHBAD LIGHT INFANTRY (attd. 63rd PALAM-COTTAH LIGHT INFANTRY),

who was killed in action in German East Africa, was the son of Deputy Surgeon - General John Charles Fuller, and was born at Ealing on the 19th November, 1879.

He was educated at Banister Court School, Southampton, and received his commission from the ranks in 1901, being transferred to the Indian Army two years later. He served in the South African War, for which he received the Queen's medal with three clasps. He also had the Durbar medal, 1912, for his services during the Royal visit while fulfilling the appointment of Garrison Quartermaster of Fort William, Calcutta.

Captain Fuller was made an honorary member of Bisley in recognition of his success in shooting, and in training the 88th Carnatic Infantry Rifle Corps, who won the Cubborn Cup on several occasions for their regiment.

He was shot on the 4th November, 1914, at Tanga, German South East Africa, while showing one of his men how to fire to the best advantage.

Captain Fuller married Violet Overton, daughter of Brevet-Colonel Frederick Smith, D.S.O., R.A.M.C., on the 31st October, 1912 ; and left one daughter, Jean Violet Overton, born at Fort William, Calcutta, in March, 1915, after her father's death.

LIEUTENANT PHILIP TEMPLER FURNEAUX, 1st BATTN. THE KING'S (LIVERPOOL REGIMENT),

who was killed in action on the 26th October, 1914, in Belgium, was the only son of the Rev. Walter Furneaux, Vicar of Dean, Bedfordshire, formerly Chaplain to the King's Regiment, Mian Mir, and grandson of the late Colonel Templer, Lyndridge, South Devon.

He was born on the 23rd September, 1889, was educated at Rossall (S.E., 1905–08), and joined the Liverpool Regiment in September, 1909, becoming Lieutenant in May, 1910. At the time of his death he was Assistant Adjutant of his battalion.

CAPTAIN GEORGE ARMAND FURSE, ROYAL FIELD ARTILLERY,

was born on the 21st February, 1881, in the United States of America. He was the son of Edmund Furse, Esq., of Alphington, Frimley, Surrey, and nephew of the late Colonel G. A. Furse, C.B., The Black Watch.

He was educated at Cheltenham and the Royal Military Academy, Woolwich, and received his  first commission in December, 1898, being promoted Captain in April, 1907. He was appointed to the Royal Horse Artillery in 1900, and was again appointed as a Captain to the R.H.A. in 1909. He twice qualified for the Staff College, and had served twelve years in India. Captain Furse had just completed the gunnery course when war broke out, and was posted to the 60th Battery, 40th Brigade, R.F.A. He embarked with the first portion of the British Expeditionary Force, and was killed at the Battle of the Aisne on the 16th September, 1914. Captain Furse married Hazel, daughter of the late Elton Forrest (Conservator of Forests), son of Captain J. H. Forrest, who was for many years Chief Constable of Hampshire, and granddaughter of the late Rev. Frederick Wickham, well known as a Master of Winchester College. He leaves three daughters : Lilian, born 1906 ; Aileen, born 1910 ; and Mélanie, born 1912.

LIEUTENANT LIONEL GAISFORD, 58th VAUGHAN'S RIFLES, FRONTIER FORCE, INDIAN ARMY,

 was born at Quetta, Baluchistan, India, on the 21st June, 1888, the son of the late Colonel Gilbert Gaisford, Indian Army, Political Agent, Baluchistan, who was murdered by a " Ghazi " on the frontier in March, 1898, and a grandson, on the maternal side, of the late General C. W. Hutchinson, R.E. (Bengal).

He was educated at Brighton College and the R.M.C., Sandhurst, and qualified as 1st Class Interpreter in French in June, 1914. He obtained his commission as a King's Indian Cadet in August, 1906, and joined the Royal Irish Regiment at Rawal Pindi in October of that year, being transferred to the 58th Vaughan's Rifles in April, 1907. With this regiment he formed part of the Expeditionary Force to France during the Great War. Previously he had served in the Mohmand Expedition of 1908, for which he received the Indian Frontier medal. He was killed in an attack on German trenches in the La Bassée district, France, on the 24th

November, 1914, and was buried in Bethune Cemetery.

Lieutenant Gaisford was a member of the Junior Army and Navy Club.

LIEUTENANT CYRIL EGREMONT GAITSKELL, 2nd BATTN. PRINCE OF WALES'S LEINSTER REGT. (ROYAL CANADIANS), was born at Cheltenham on the 15th November, 1892, the son of Major Charles Gaitskell, late Lincolnshire Regiment, and a grandson of the late Lieutenant-Colonel Gaitskell, of Waldon House, Cheltenham.

He was educated at Heidelberg, Germany, and at Cheltenham College. He joined the Leinster Regiment from the R.M.C., Sandhurst, in September, 1911, and became Lieutenant in January, 1913.

At Armentières, France, while gallantly leading his men to attack a position, he was mortally wounded on the 19th October, 1914. He was interred on the same day in a temporary cemetery, called " Le Maroc," in the quarter " Cité-Bon-Jean " at Armentières.

Lieutenant Gaitskell was a good all-round athlete, fond of golf and boxing.

LIEUTENANT PHILIP FRANCIS PAYNE GALLWEY, 21st (EMPRESS OF INDIA'S) LANCERS, was born on the 7th March, 1894, at Kirby Knowle Rectory, near Thirsk, Yorkshire, and was the son of the Rev. Francis Henry Payne Gallwey, Rector of Sessay, Thirsk. He was cousin to Sir Ralph Payne Gallwey, Bart., and a nephew of General

A. Lowry Cole, C.B., D.S.O. He was educated at West Downes, Winchester College, and the R.M.C., Sandhurst. Lieutenant Payne Gallwey joined his regiment in September, 1912, becoming Lieutenant in March, 1914.

On the outbreak of the war, being on leave at home from Rawal Pindi, India, where his regiment was stationed, he was attached for service to the 9th (Queen's Royal) Lancers.

He was killed near Messines, in the Battle of Ypres, on the 31st October, 1914.

2nd LIEUTENANT THEODORE HUGH GALTON, 6th (attd. 3rd) BATTN. WORCESTERSHIRE REGIMENT,

who was killed in action on the 21st October, 1914, was the eldest son of Major Galton, late R.A., and Mrs. Galton, of Hadzor, Droitwich, and was born on the 20th October, 1888.

He was educated at the Oratory School, Edgbaston, and Exeter College, Oxford. He offered his services as soon as the war broke out, and was gazetted to the Worcestershire Regiment on probation in August, 1914, joining the 3rd Battalion in October. He had been attached to the Irish Guards for a year in 1911, and was a member of the Windham Club.

When he was killed the German trenches were attacked at 7 a.m.; at about 8 a.m. the enemy began to retire, and Mr. Galton—the foremost of the party that advanced to cut them off— was shot through the heart.

MAJOR ALEC GARDINER, ROYAL ENGINEERS,

was the elder son of Lieutenant - Colonel R. Gardiner, R.E. (retired), 28, Barkston Gardens, London, S.W., and grandson of the late Major-General Irving, C.B., R.A. He was born on the 28th June, 1873, at Ulwar, Rajputana, India, and educated privately, mainly under Dr. Stevenson Jellie, of Clifton.

After passing successfully through the R.M.A., Woolwich, he gained a commission in the Royal Engineers in July, 1891, becoming Lieutenant three years later, Captain in April, 1902, and Major in July, 1911. He took part in the expedition to the Soudan in 1896 as Assistant Field Engineer with the force at Suakin, for which he received the English and Egyptian medals. Major Gardiner proceeded to India in 1893, and after a short period on military works joined the Railway Department of the Government of India, and with some short intervals of military duty continued serving on the survey construction and administration of Indian railways up to the outbreak of the Great War, when he was holding the appointment of Agent (Chief Administrative Officer) of the Oudh

and Rohilkhand South Railway. Previously, in 1909, Major Gardiner had been appointed Lieutenant-Colonel Commandant of the Oudh and Rohilkhand Railway Rifle Volunteers, a corps which he brought to a high pitch of efficiency, devoting special attention to armoured train working and fighting, for which they offered their services on the declaration of war. Major Gardiner's services were placed at the disposal of the Commander-in-Chief of India in October, 1914, and he was ordered to proceed to England, but was intercepted in the Mediterranean, and directed to join the Indian Expeditionary Force in Northern France. He was serving as a Field Engineer with the Lahore Division when he fell in the fighting before Givenchy on the 20th December, 1914.

He was at first reported as missing, and it was hoped that he might be alive as a prisoner of war in Germany, but all enquiries proved fruitless. His fate was not definitely set at rest until the 25th July, 1915, when his body was found during mining operations near Givenchy, it having been exposed by the explosion of a German shell. The body was subsequently buried near the Red House on the Sunken Road, Givenchy, some four hundred yards north-east of the Church.

Letters from the officers under whom Major Gardiner served at the front testify to the high esteem in which he was held, and express admiration of the skill, devotion, and gallantry with which he carried out all the duties entrusted to him. During the short time he was serving in France he was several times specially reported upon, and subsequently to his being killed his name appeared amongst those mentioned in Sir John French's Despatch of the 31st May, 1915. On his death being confirmed his widow received from the King and Queen a telegram expressing their deep regret at the loss the Army had sustained by the death of her husband in the service of his country, and adding Their Majesties' true sympathy in her sorrow. Lord Kitchener also, through the Military Secretary, conveyed his sincere sympathy; and the Railway Board of India, in recording their very great regret at his death, remarked that he was an officer of whom the Board entertained the highest opinion.

Major Gardiner, who was keen on the training of his men in rifle shooting, and captained the regimental team on two occasions, being also successful himself in individual competitions with both the rifle and revolver, was an executive member of the Council of the Bengal Presidency Rifle Association. He was conspicuous in connection with the work of the St. John Ambulance Association in India, especially as regards the instruction of the men under his command. In recognition of his services he was appointed a serving brother of the Order of St. John of Jerusalem, and received the decoration of the Order from the Viceroy of India. He was an Associate of the Institution of Civil Engineers, and also of the Institute of Electrical Engineers, and was known in the English railway world as the inventor of a system of engine cab signals and for the automatic control of moving trains.

Major Gardiner married, in 1897, Edith, daughter of Mr. Campbell Thomson, M.I.C.E., late Chief Engineer of the North West Railway of India, and left two sons and a daughter. He devoted most of his spare time to his Volunteer and Ambulance work. He was a good rifle shot, and won several prizes. His recreations were shooting, rowing—the R.E. crew, under his leadership, being several times successful in local regattas—tennis, etc.

MAJOR ROBERT MACGREGOR STEWART GARDNER, 1st BATTN. GLOUCESTERSHIRE REGIMENT,

who was killed in action on the 31st October, 1914, was the second son of the late Mr. William Gardner and Mrs. Gardner, of Thorpe, S u r r e y, and a nephew of General Sir Robert Stewart, G.C.B. He was born on the 25th August, 1870, and joined the Gloucestershire Regiment from the Militia in February, 1891, becoming Lieutenant in May, 1892, and getting his company in February, 1900.

He served in the South African War, being present at the relief of Kimberley, at operations in the Orange Free State, at Paardeberg, and at the actions of Poplar Grove and Driefontein ; also at operations in Natal and Cape Colony. He was mentioned in Despatches ("London Gazette," 10th September, 1901), and received the Queen's medal with four clasps. He was promoted Major in July, 1914.

He proceeded to France with his regiment at the beginning of the Great War. On the 31st October his company was ordered to retake a trench the Germans had captured at Gheluvelt. He led his men close up to the Germans, and assembled for a further advance in a sunken road. There Major Gardner gave the order to advance and to charge the Germans. He was first up the bank, and was immediately mortally wounded in the arm and side. On the previous day he had led a counter-attack with what was described as " reckless bravery," and those with him said he seemed that day to bear a charmed life.

Major Gardner married May, daughter of Mr. Charles Whitchurch Wasbrough, of Clifton, and left two daughters, the younger of whom was born, after her father's death, on the 11th February, 1915.

LIEUTENANT PHILIP NIGEL GARNETT, PRINCESS CHARLOTTE OF WALES'S (ROYAL BERKSHIRE REGT.),

who died of wounds received in action in Nyassaland, probably in September, 1914, was born on the 4th November, 1886, and joined the Royal Berkshire Regiment in May, 1907, becoming Lieutenant in September, 1911.

In October, 1913, he was seconded in his regiment for service with the 1st (Central Africa) Battalion, the King's African Rifles.

MAJOR JOHN TREFUSIS CARPENTER-GARNIER, 1st BATTN. SCOTS GUARDS,

was the eldest son of John Carpenter-Garnier, Esq., J.P., D.L., M.P. for South Devon, 1873–84, and the Hon. Mary Louisa Carpenter-Garnier, daughter of the n i n e t e e n t h Baron Clinton. He was born in 1874 at R o o k e s b u r y Park, W i c k h a m, Hants, and was educated at Harrow and Christ Church, Oxford.

He first served in the Royal Scots Militia from 1894–96. In August of the latter year he joined the Scots Guards, and served in the South African War for two and a half years in General Rundle's Division, being present at the actions of Biddulphsberg and Wittebergen, receiving the Queen's medal with three clasps and the King's medal with two clasps.

From 1903–06 he was Adjutant of his battalion, and Regimental Adjutant from 1906–1909. In August, 1914, he was appointed second in command of his battalion. In the Battle of the Aisne he was struck by shrapnel on the 14th September, and died of his wounds on the following day. His body was buried in Vendresse Churchyard.

Major Carpenter-Garnier was a member of the Guards' and Bachelors' Clubs, and was a keen cricketer, belonging to the M.C.C. and I Zingari. He also played polo, and was fond of hunting and shooting. He was not married.

LIEUTENANT OLIVER DUNHAM MELVILLE GARSIA, 1st BATTN. DUKE OF CORNWALL'S LIGHT INFANTRY,

born at Riccarton, Christchurch, New Zealand, on 18th November, 1885, was the fourth son of Captain Christopher Garsia, for many years associated with the promotion of Art in

Christchurch as Hon. Secretary of the Canterbury Society of Arts.

He was educated, like his four brothers, at the Christchurch Boys' High School, and all five entered the services. The eldest, Haly, who was in the Durham Light Infantry, was killed in India ten years ago; Clive, in the Hampshire Regiment, is now a General Staff Officer at the front; another, Eric, served in the South African War; Rupert, in the Royal Navy, now in H.M.A.S. "Sydney"; and Oliver, who was in the Duke of Cornwall's Light Infantry—a proud record for their gallant father, himself a veteran of the Mutiny, and for fourteen years A.D.C. to Sir William O'Grady Haly. Lieutenant-Colonel Garsia, C.B., Commissioner of Prisons, Inspector-General of Military Prisons, who initiated in them valuable reforms, was a member of the same family.

The subject of this memoir joined the Duke of Cornwall's Light Infantry as Second-Lieutenant in 1907, being promoted Lieutenant in November, 1908. For a short time he was A.D.C. to Sir Thomas Gibson Carmichael (now Lord Carmichael), and he had been to Russia to study the language, as he was convinced that the two countries would sooner or later be drawn together in a common defence. Lieutenant Garsia was killed at the Battle of the Aisne on the 18th September, 1914. One who knew him well said he was as staunch and sincere as he was brave and fearless, a true soldier, and a very gallant gentleman.

A Private of his battalion, writing some time after, said : " I don't think there are more than sixty or seventy of us left in the battalion that came out first. . . . My section had to advance up a slope or hill, and my Lieutenant, Mr. Garsia, got shot through the neck."

2nd LIEUTENANT C. W. N. GARSTIN, 9th (QUEEN'S ROYAL) LANCERS,

whose name is included in the monthly official list published in October, 1914, as having been killed, no place, date, or circumstances being given, joined the 9th Lancers in February, 1913.

He was qualified as a 2nd Class Interpreter in German.

MAJOR JOHN KIRWAN GATACRE, 4th (QUEEN'S OWN) HUSSARS,

younger son of the late Major-General Sir William Gatacre, K.C.B., D.S.O., was born in Dublin on the 6th September, 1883.

He was educated at Rugby and the R.M.C., Sandhurst, from which, after being attached for a time to the 2nd Battalion The Black Watch, he was posted to the 11th (K.E.O.) Lancers, Indian Army.

He was a member of the Junior Army and Navy Club. When in India he was known as a sportsman, winning the Kadir Cup (pigsticking), 1912, and as one of the best polo players in India. He was also a gifted watercolour artist.

Being on leave in Europe on the outbreak of the war with Germany, he was attached to the 4th (Queen's Own) Hussars, and in September, 1914, was promoted Major in that regiment. He was killed at the attack on the Mont des Cats on the 12th October, 1914. He had been previously awarded the French decoration of the " Croix de Chevalier " of the Legion of Honour.

2nd LIEUTENANT CHARLES HENRY GATH, 3rd HUSSARS,

who was killed in action on the 30th October, 1914, at Klein Zillebeke, Belgium, was born in London in September, 1882. In 1899 he joined the ranks of the 18th Hussars, with whom he served in the South African War for two years, re-

ceiving the Queen's and King's medals with clasps.

He was afterwards transferred to the 3rd Hussars, accompanying them to India, where he remained four years, and then returned to Pretoria, South Africa, for a further three years. In 1911 he returned to England for a course of instruction at the Cavalry School, Netheravon. At the outbreak of the war he went to the front with the Expeditionary Force, and was given his commission on the 1st October, 1914.

Mr. Gath was not married.

2nd LIEUTENANT EDWARD GEAREY, 1st BATTN. QUEEN'S OWN CAMERON HIGHLANDERS, attd. 1st BATTN. HIGHLAND LIGHT INFANTRY,

who had previously been reported missing, was afterwards reported to have been killed on the 20th December,1914, near Festubert. He was the eldest son of the late James Gearey, Sergeant-Major,HighlandLight Infantry, (Blythswood), and was born at Maryhill Barracks on the 26th April, 1881. Educated at Meadowpark School, Dennistown, Glasgow, Mr. Gearey joined the ranks of the Highland Light Infantry in 1895, and served until 1899 with the 2nd battalion in India. After serving for a few years at home, he returned to India in 1907 to join the 1st battalion of his regiment, and at the outbreak of the war with Germany he was stationed at Ambala, and had risen to the rank of Company Sergeant-Major. His battalion formed part of the Lahore Division, and proceeded with it to France. In December, 1914, Mr. Gearey received his commission as 2nd Lieutenant in the Cameron Highlanders, but was attached to his old battalion. He was reported missing on the 20th December, 1914, and hopes were entertained of his safety, until, in September, 1915, a returned prisoner of war brought evidence of his death, and it was concluded he had been killed on that date.

2nd Lieutenant Gearey, who held the Long Service medal and the Delhi Durbar Decoration, married Helen, daughter of Thomas Drawbell, Edinburgh, and left two sons, James and Thomas Drawbell, age respectively seven and four years.

LIEUTENANT JAMES FRANCIS ROY GEBBIE, 2nd BATTN. THE PRINCE OF WALES'S VOLUNTEERS (SOUTH LANCASHIRE REGT.)

was the son of Mr. James Gebbie, of Netherfield, Strathaven, Lanarkshire, Scotland, and was born there on the 27th June, 1888. He was educated at Bath College, and at the R.M.C., Sandhurst, where he was in the revolver team. Lieutenant Gebbie was gazetted to the South Lancashire Regiment in September, 1908, becoming Lieutenant in January, 1910.

While serving with the 2nd Battalion he was wounded on the 19th September when leading a bayonet charge on the heights of Vailly, and died of his wounds on the 4th October, 1914, at St. Nazaire, France.

Lieutenant Gebbie was a member of the Junior United Service Club.

2nd LIEUTENANT ROBERT FRANCIS McLEAN GEE, 3rd (attd. 1st) BATTN. THE DUKE OF EDINBURGH'S (WILTSHIRE REGIMENT),

who died at Netley Hospital on the 27th October, 1914, from wounds received in action, aged twenty, was the eldest son of Mr. and Mrs. G. F. Gee, of Wellington, New Zealand, and of Te Whare, Eastbourne. He was a great-great-grandson, on his mother's side, of Captain William Buckley, Royal Scots Regiment, who was killed at Quatre Bras; a great-grandson of Captain William Henry Buckley, 82nd Regiment; and a grandson of the late Hon. George Buckley, of Christchurch, New Zealand. His younger brother is a Lieutenant in the Royal Horse Artillery. He was educated at Wellington, New Zealand, and at Eastbourne College, and had entered at Trinity College, Cambridge. He was in the O.T.C.; and, having volunteered his services at the outbreak of the war, was given a commission in the 3rd Wiltshire Regiment. He joined on the 3rd September, and after four weeks' training at Weymouth was transferred to the 1st Battalion and sent to France.

He received his fatal wounds—a sniper's bullet in the head—a few days after his arrival at the firing line, during an attempt to capture the village of Ilies. His body is buried in the Ocklynge Cemetery, Eastbourne.

CAPTAIN JAMES RANDOLPH GEOGHEGAN, 2nd BATTN. ROYAL INNISKILLING FUSILIERS,

who was killed in action on the 7th November, 1914, was the son of Samuel Geoghegan, Esq., C.E., and was born in Dublin on the 27th March, 1886.

He was educated at Cheltenham College, and joined the Royal Inniskilling Fusiliers from the Wicklow Militia in May, 1906. In January, 1910, he was detached for employment with the West African Frontier Force, with the local rank of Lieutenant, being promoted to that rank in his regiment in February, 1910.

He returned from Northern Nigeria in April, 1914, and rejoined his regiment. He was promoted Captain on the 22nd October, 1914.

LIEUTENANT ATHELSTANE KEY DURANCE GEORGE, 1st BATTN. DORSETSHIRE REGIMENT,

was born at Beverstone House, Brixton, Surrey, on the 25th of March, 1887, and was the son of Arthur Durance and Charlotte Ada George, of Alderholt, Bournemouth (West), grandson of Jonathan Muckleston Key, D.L. of City of London, Middlesex, great-nephew of Sir John Key, Bart., and direct descendant, through the female line, of Sir William Bloet, who came over with William the Conqueror in 1066.

Lieutenant George commenced his education at Hailey, Bournemouth, going afterwards to Tonbridge School; thence to Caius College, Cambridge.

He began his military career in the King's (Liverpool Regiment), joining subsequently the 2nd Battalion Dorsetshire Regiment at Madras. While in India he served on the Staff as A.D.C. to Lord Sydenham, Governor of Bombay, and Sir Maurice Hammick, K.C.M.G., Governor of Madras. He returned to England in March, 1913, and joined the 1st Battalion of his regiment at Belfast, from which station he proceeded with it to the front.

He was shot through the head at Bezu-le-Query on the 11th September, 1914, while in the trenches, urging his men not to expose their heads. He was carried to the Hospice at Coulommiers, where he died on the 14th September, never having regained consciousness, and was buried, with military honours, in the cemetery of that town.

Under date 10th March, 1915, Brigadier-General Bols, D.S.O., then commanding the battalion, wrote:—

" I am glad that you have written to me, as I have often wished to tell his friends and relatives how deeply every officer and man of the Dorsets grieved with you at the loss of your dear son.

" During the period which followed our fights on the Marne there was little time to write, or even to think. Then came the rush northwards, and the great fight of the battalion at Givenchy, where we lost three-quarters of our men, and all but four of our original corps of officers, and then I had to spend ten weeks in England recovering from wounds.

" I first met your son about last May when he returned to Belfast after going through a course of flying, and I think that a month later he returned to England to begin a course of signalling, from which he returned just before mobilisation, so that I did not get to know him well till the beginning of the war. During those first six weeks he was—I think there is only one word to describe him—magnificent. Always cheerful; always caring for others; watching over his men, no matter how weary; never sparing himself. To my mind he was the ideal of a British officer, gallant and brave, of course, but in addition tireless in helping others who did not possess his powers of mind and body.

" That fight near Bezu, on the Marne, cost us dear, for with your dear son fell Captain Roe and Captain Priestley. The next morning all were seen, and hopes were given that all would survive, but in each case our hopes were dashed. I fear this is a poor sketch to give you of one who earned our love and esteem to so great a degree. I know his memory will live long in the Dorsets."

Captain and Adjutant Ransome, under date January 18th, 1915, wrote:—

" May I, even at this late date, offer my sympathy to you in the loss you have sustained? I knew your son well, and am only too conscious of what a loss he is to the battalion. He was an exceptionally good officer—one of those whose influence did much towards bringing the Dorsets to the standard which this war has, I think, proved them to have reached."

Lieutenant George was a member of the Junior Naval and Military Club, and was unmarried.

LIEUTENANT FREDERICK RALPH GEORGE, ADJUTANT 1st BATTN. THE CONNAUGHT RANGERS,

who was killed on the 5th November, 1914, son of the late Barry George, 13th Foot, was born at Mountshannon House, County Clare, the residence of his uncle, on the 9th September, 1883. He was educated at Abbey School, Tipperary, and Trinity

College, Dublin, where he was presented with Professor John Wardell's sword.

He joined the Connaught Rangers in January, 1906, became Lieutenant in January, 1909, and was appointed Adjutant of his battalion in June, 1914.

He was very fond of all kinds of sport, polo, hunting, shooting, fishing, and football. He played Rugby football for Trinity. He was also fond of sailing.

Lieutenant George volunteered to take part in a bayonet attack on the night of the 5th November, and was shot during the charge.

CAPTAIN HARRY VERNON GERRARD, 2nd BATTN. THE BORDER REGT., born in Dublin on the 18th April, 1878, was the son of Thomas Gerrard, of Dublin, Crown Solicitor for Queen's County and Carlow. Captain Percy N. Gerrard, M.D., Malay States Volunteers, killed in the Indian Riots at Singapore on the 15th February, 1915, was his brother, and other brothers are John D. Gerrard, Resident Magistrate, Ireland, now a temporary Lieutenant in the A.S.C., Wing Commander E. L. Gerrard, R.N.A.S., while another relative is Flight Sub-Lieutenant T. F. N. Gerrard, R.N.A.S. Captain Gerrard was educated at King's School, Warwick, and Tipperary Grammar School, at both of which he took part in athletics. He joined the 4th Battalion Royal Dublin Fusiliers (Militia) in April, 1900, and was attached to the A.S.C. In August, 1902, he was gazetted to the 2nd Battalion Royal Garrison Regiment (formed during the South African War), of which he was Adjutant from May, 1904, till July, 1905, when he was transferred to the 2nd Border Regiment as Lieutenant. He served three tours with the West African Frontier Field Force, Southern Nigeria, and was promoted Captain in October, 1914.

Captain Gerrard was killed in action on the 2nd November, 1914, by a shell while commanding his company at or near Ypres. His battalion was complimented by the Commander-in-Chief for their behaviour at this battle. For his services Captain Gerrard was mentioned in Sir John French's Despatch of the 14th January, 1915, referring to his Despatch of the 20th November, 1914.

2nd LIEUTENANT RONALD CHARLES MELBOURNE GIBBS, 2nd BATTN. SCOTS GUARDS, born at "Salisbury," Melbourne, Australia, was the son of the late Hon. Henry Lloyd Gibbs and Alice Mary, daughter of the late General Charles Crutchley, of Sunninghill Park, Ascot, and nephew of the second

Lord Aldenham, Aldenham House, Elstree.

He was educated at Wellington House, Westgate-on-Sea (Rev. Herbert Bull), and at Eton (P. V. Broke's House). At the latter he was in the O.T.C., and obtained his "A" certificate. He rowed in the boats on the 4th June, 1913, and was in the procession of boats when Their Majesties King  George and Queen Mary visited Eton.

He received a commission in the Special Reserve of Officers in September, 1913, and joined the 1st Battalion Scots Guards at Aldershot in October. He passed the Army examination in June, 1914, joining the 3rd Battalion of his regiment on the 5th August, and exchanged into the 2nd Battalion at Lyndhurst in September, proceeding with it to the front on the 4th October.

He was killed in action at Ypres on the 28th October, 1914, his battalion forming part of the 20th Infantry Brigade, VIIth Division, and was buried at the Château, Gheluvelt.

2nd Lieutenant Gibbs was a member of the Guards' Club.

LIEUTENANT ATHOL THOMAS GIBSON, 3rd (attd. 2nd) BATTN. THE PRINCE OF WALES'S VOLUNTEERS (SOUTH LANCASHIRE REGT.), who was killed in action on the 21st October, 1914, was the son of the late Thomas Gibson, of Penarth, South Wales, son-in-law of J. W. Pyman, Penarth. He was only appointed to his regiment after the outbreak of the war, and was promoted Lieutenant in September, 1914.

CAPTAIN ROBERT GIFFARD, ROYAL FIELD ARTILLERY, A.D.C. TO MAJOR GENERAL LOMAX, COMMANDING THE 1st DIVISION, BRITISH EXPEDITIONARY FORCE, son of Henry Rycroft Giffard, of Lockeridge House, Wilts, was born at Wilton Street, London, S.W., on the 27th June, 1884.

He was educated at Marlborough College and the R.M.A., Woolwich, where in his second year he was in the Cricket and Hockey XI's. Joining the R.A. as 2nd Lieutenant in December, 1903, he became Lieutenant in December, 1906, and Captain in October, 1914. He served at Bulford,

Horfield, and Aldershot, being in August, 1910, appointed A.D.C. to Major-General Lomax,

then commanding the 1st Division of the Field Troops at Aldershot, and accompanied him when the Expeditionary Force proceeded to the Continent for the war.

He was wounded at Hooge, near Ypres, by the bursting of a shell in Divisional Head Quarters on the 31st October, and died November 1st, 1914. Many of the Staff of the 1st Division were killed or wounded on the same occasion. Lieutenant-General Lomax, who had received his promotion in October, was among the wounded, and, as in the case of his A.D.C., his wounds proved fatal, although he lingered until the spring of the following year. Captain Giffard, who was a member of the I Zingari and Free Foresters' Cricket Clubs, married Janet Haig Boyd, of Moor House, County Durham, and left one daughter, Robina, in her third year when her father was killed.

CAPTAIN ROBERT CROOKS GILCHRIST, 46th PUNJABIS, INDIAN ARMY,

son of Brigadier-General R. A. Gilchrist, Indian Army, was born at Aurungabad, Deccan, India, on the 24th June, 1878.

Educated at Dover College and the R.M.C., Sandhurst, he was appointed to the Indian Army from the latter in August, 1896, and reached the rank of Captain in August, 1906. Lieutenant-Colonel G. Mockler, Commandant 46th Punjabis, mentioned that he was a most exceptionally fine officer, and thoroughly deserved the esteem in which he was held by all ranks—British and Indian— of the regiment. He served for five years in the Burmah Military Police on the frontier, for which he was awarded the Police medal. The D.I. General of Military Police, Burmah, Colonel J. ffrench-Mullens, wrote : " He served under me for five years, and on two expeditions, so I had occasion to know of his sterling qualities and character."

He was killed in the Great War on the 19th December, 1914, the official report from the officer commanding 59th Rifles, Frontier Force, stating : " Captain Gilchrist, attached to us, was killed yesterday morning, the 19th December, 1914, in a night attack on the German trenches. He was most gallantly leading a storming party up a German sap under heavy fire when he was hit in the head by a rifle bullet." The engagement was at La Bassée, France.

Captain Gilchrist played polo, hockey, and other games with his regiment, and when he had opportunities in India and Cashmere he went in for shooting. He was not married.

CAPTAIN DUGALD STEWART GILKISON, p.s.c., THE CAMERONIANS (SCOTTISH RIFLES),

who was killed in action at the Battle of the Aisne on the 20th September, 1914, was the elder son of Mr. D. S. and Mrs. Gilkison, of Wimbledon and Dalquharran, Ayrshire. He was born on the 5th March, 1880, and was educated at Rugby, which he entered in 1894, and from which he went to the R.M.C., Sandhurst, in 1897. He joined the Scottish Rifles in February, 1899, becoming Lieutenant in December of the same year. He took part in the South African War, 1899–1902, being present at the relief of Ladysmith, including the action at Colenso, at the operations of 17th to 24th January, including the action at Spion Kop. He also took part in the operations of 5th to 7th February, 1900, and the action at Vaal Krans, in the operations on Tugela Heights, 16th to 27th February, 1900, and the action at Pieter's Hill ; at operations in Natal and the Transvaal, east of Pretoria, in 1900; again in the Transvaal, and in the Orange River Colony from November, 1900–02. He received the Queen's medal with five clasps and the King's medal with two clasps.

He was promoted Captain in January, 1905, and from July, 1906, to July, 1909, was Adjutant of his battalion. Captain Gilkison was a Staff College Graduate, and was appointed Staff Officer at York in 1911, and Brigade-Major, 5th Infantry Brigade, IInd Division, Aldershot Command, in April, 1912.

His younger brother, Lieutenant J. D. Gilkison, Argyll and Sutherland Highlanders, was killed in action on the 26th August, 1914, at Le Cateau. Captain Gilkison married, in 1905, Kate, daughter of the Rev. I. Harcourt-Vernon, of Cocaban, Orange River Colony, South Africa.

LIEUTENANT JAMES DAVID GILKISON, 1st BATTN. PRINCESS LOUISE'S (ARGYLL AND SUTHERLAND HIGHLANDERS), who was reported missing after the Battle of Le Cateau on the 26th August, 1914, and since stated by an officer, who is a prisoner of war, to have been killed on that date, was the younger and only surviving son of D. S. and Mrs. Gilkinson, of Wimbledon, and Dalquharran, Ayrshire. He was born on the 1st August, 1884, and was educated at Rugby (Donkin House) and Trinity College, Oxford, which he entered in 1903. He was called to the Bar (Inner Temple) in January, 1906. He joined the Argyll and Sutherland Highlanders from the Militia in December, 1907, becoming Lieutenant in March, 1910.

Lieutenant Gilkison's elder brother, Captain D. S. Gilkison, p.s.c., the Cameronians (Scottish Rifles), was killed in action on the 20th September, 1914.

2nd LIEUTENANT THOMAS CUNNINGHAM GILLESPIE, 2nd BATTN. KING'S OWN SCOTTISH BORDERERS,

was the son of T. P. Gillespie, Longcroft, Linlithgow, and a grandson of the late Alexander Gillespie, of Biggar Park, Lanarkshire, and of the late Thomas Chalmers, of Longcroft. He was born at Clanna Cottage, Alvington, Gloucestershire, on the 14th December, 1892.

2nd Lieutenant Gillespie was educated at Cargilfield School, Cramond Bridge, at Winchester College, and at New College, Oxford, which he entered in 1911, and where he took his degree in June, 1914. He was a fine athlete, and rowed three years in the New College eight, twice keeping his boat the head of the river. He also was one of the New College Olympian crew at Stockholm in 1912.

At Winchester and at the University he was a member of the Officers' Training Corps, and intended to make the Army his career. He obtained a University commission, and on the outbreak of the war was gazetted to the King's Own Scottish Borderers, joining his regiment in France in time to take part in the advance from the Marne. He was in the trenches at Missy-sur-Aisne, took part in the movement towards the Belgian frontier, and was killed in action near Quinchy on the 18th October, 1914.

CAPTAIN CECIL GLENDOWER PERCIVAL GILLIAT, 1st BATTN. ROYAL WARWICKSHIRE REGIMENT,

who died on the 14th October, 1914, of wounds received in action, was the eldest son of Cecil and Mrs. Gilliat, of Arch Hall, County Meath, Ireland. He was born at Arch Hall on the 6th December, 1884, was educated at Cheltenham, and joined the Royal Worcestershire Regiment from the Militia in November, 1905.

He served in operations in the Zekka Khel country, north-western frontier of India, in 1908, receiving the medal with clasp. He became Lieutenant in April, 1909, and was gazetted Captain, after his death, on the 29th October, 1914, to date from the 12th September, 1914.

A brother officer wrote : " We were attacking a village called Meteren. My company was next to ' Glennie's ' when I fell. He saw at once, and ran to me with two of his men, and started bandaging my wound. It was a very plucky thing to do, as I was lying in a very exposed place, and the Germans were firing at me all the time. Glennie left me after he had put the dressing on, and said he would send some men to carry me back, but he was killed himself—shot through the forehead—when he got back to the trench."

CAPTAIN OTHO CLAUDE SKIPWITH GILLIAT, 1st BATTN. RIFLE BRIGADE, (THE PRINCE CONSORT'S OWN),

born on the 7th December, 1881, at Buckingham Gate, London, S.W., was the son of the late Howard Gilliat, of Abbot's Ripton Hall. Huntingdon, and of Mrs. Howard Gilliat. He was educated at Golden Parsonage, Cheam ; and at Eton, where he was in the Cricket XI in 1899, and in the Field XI in 1898 and 1899. He was also a member of the Free Foresters, I Zingari, Eton Ramblers, and Green Jackets Cricket Clubs.

Proceeding to the R.M.C., Sandhurst, he joined the 4th Battalion Rifle Brigade in January, 1901. He served in the South African War, being present during operations in the Orange River and Cape Colonies, receiving the Queen's medal with three clasps. From 1908–09 he was A.D.C. to Admiral Sir F. Bedford, in Western Australia, and to Earl Dudley, Governor-General from 1909–11, in which year he became Captain. He retired from the Regular battalion, and joined the 5th Battalion; but on the outbreak of the Great War he rejoined the Regular Army, proceeding to France with the 1st Battalion. He was shot through the heart by shrapnel bullet on the 30th October, 1914.

Captain Gilliat, who was a member of the Army and Navy Club, was a golf player, handicap "scratch." He was unmarried.

LIEUTENANT HERBERT JAMES GRAHAM GILMOUR, 3rd BATTN. WORCESTERSHIRE REGIMENT,

was the son of Mrs. Price Hughes, of Redhill, near Worcester, and her first husband, the late James Graham Gilmour, of Whittington Lodge, near Worcester; grandson of the Rev. J. Cook, Peopleton Pershore. He was born on the 2nd August, 1883, at Southport, Lancashire, and was educated at Hartford House, Winchfield, and Radley College, Oxford.

He was gazetted to the Worcestershire Militia in December, 1900, and served in the South African War from January to May, 1902, for which he received the Queen's medal with two clasps. After the war he, in January, 1903, received a commission in the 3rd Battalion of the regiment.

On the outbreak of the Great War he was at home on leave from the 4th Battalion, then stationed at Bareilly, India. He joined the 3rd Battalion, and accompanied it to the front, being present with it in all engagements up to the time of his death. This occurred on the 19th September, 1914, when he was killed in action at Vailly, in France, while trying to save his men who were under heavy fire.

He was a member of the Junior Naval and Military and of the Worcestershire County Clubs. He was also a member of the Worcestershire County Cricket Club and St. John's, Worcester, playing frequently for both. In his regiment he was chosen as one of the twelve shots for England, and was in the regimental Cricket XI. He was a keen sportsman and fine rider, having won many races in India, and in 1912 was third in the Army Cup on "Exchange."

LIEUTENANT REGINALD NIGEL GIPPS, 1st BATTN. SCOTS GUARDS,

son of the late General Sir Reginald Gipps, G.C.B., of Sycamore House, Farnborough, Hants, who served in the Crimea, was born in London on the 22nd November, 1891.

Educated at Wellington College and the R.M.C., Sandhurst, he joined his father's old regiment, the Scots Guards in February, 1911, becoming Lieutenant in January, 1913. In that year he went with his battalion to Egypt, and accompanied it to France, as part of the Expeditionary Force, in August, 1914. He was killed in action near Ypres on the 7th November, 1914. Lieutenant Gipps was a member of the Guards' and Boodle's Clubs. He played polo for his battalion in 1913.

2nd LIEUTENANT PAUL CHANCOURT GIRARDOT, 1st BATTN. OXFORDSHIRE AND BUCKINGHAMSHIRE LIGHT INFANTRY,

only child of the late Lieutenant-Colonel J. F. Girardot, 43rd Light Infantry, Colston Hall, Nottinghamshire, was born on the 17th November, 1895.

He was educated at Ashampstead School, Eastbourne, and Cheltenham College, and was gazetted to the Army in February, 1914. He was an all-round sportsman, and shot three years running in the Bisley Eight.

He was killed in action on the 16th September, 1914, near Soupir-sur-Aisne, by the bursting of a shell while resting in a quarry with his company. The same shell killed three subalterns of his battalion, wounded several others, and killed and wounded forty of the rank and file, and fifty of a company of the Coldstream Guards, whom they were relieving.

LIEUTENANT RALPH HAMILTON FANE GLADWIN, 1st BATTN. SCOTS GUARDS, LATE LIEUTENANT SCOTS GUARDS, SPECIAL RESERVE,

was officially reported as missing in November, 1914, but has since been stated to have been killed near Ypres on the 26th October, 1914. He was the youngest son of the late Mr. Hamilton Fane Gladwin, of Seven Springs, Gloucestershire, and was born on the 4th October, 1885. He joined the Scots Guards in February, 1907, becoming Lieutenant in November, 1909. Subsequently he retired from the Army, but on the outbreak of the war with Germany was gazetted to the Special Reserve of the regiment in August, 1914, joining the 1st Battalion for active service.

CAPTAIN ERNEST MURE GLANVILL, M.B., ROYAL ARMY MEDICAL CORPS,

who was killed in action on the 2nd November, 1914, was the only son of Henry Glanvill, late Registrar of the Inland Revenue, Estate Duty Department, and was born in Edinburgh on the 14th November, 1877.

He qualified in medicine at Edinburgh University in 1901, and joined the R.A.M.C. in August, 1903, being promoted Captain in February, 1907. He passed through the Army Medical College, Milbank, in August, 1911, with six months' acceleration for promotion to Major, and would have attained that rank in February, 1915, had he not been killed.

He went to France in August, 1914, as Medical Officer in charge of the Scots Greys, and was mentioned in Sir John French's Despatch of the 14th January, 1915, having shown great coolness and conspicuous bravery on many occasions. Captain Glanvill left a widow and two children, a boy and a girl.

CAPTAIN ARCHIBALD WILLIAM ROBERTSON-GLASGOW, 2/39th GARHWAL RIFLES, INDIAN ARMY,

who was born on the 24th May, 1880, at Montgreenan, Kilwinning, Ayrshire, was the fourth and youngest son of the late R. B. Robertson-Glasgow, Esq., D.L., of Montgreenan, formerly in the 7th Highland Light Infantry. The late Colonel J. C. Robertson-Glasgow, of the Suffolk Regiment, was his uncle.

He was educated at Wellington House School, Westgate-on-Sea, from 1889 to 1894, and at Marlborough College from 1894 to 1897. In the latter year he passed the entrance examination for the R.M.A., Woolwich; and later in the same year that for the R.M.C., Sandhurst, which he entered in January, 1898. He was gazetted 2nd Lieutenant in January, 1899; and, having passed for the Indian Army, was attached for a year to the Royal Scots in India. He joined the Indian Staff Corps in April, 1900, becoming Lieutenant in the 16th Bombay Infantry in April, 1901.

He took part in the operations against the Ogaden Somalis in Jubaland, British East Africa, 1901, receiving the medal with clasp. After the return of the expedition he was transferred to the 2/39th Garhwal Rifles, in which he became Captain in January, 1908.

Captain Robertson-Glasgow, who was a member of the Junior Naval and Military Club, was a keen sportsman, a fine fisherman, and good shot with both gun and rifle. During two years when serving in Chitral he made some successful shooting trips into the hills, securing a number of fine heads of various sorts. He commanded the machine-gun section of his battalion, and in 1913–14 was Captain of the " Empire Day " Battalion Shooting Team.

He left India for France in September, 1914, with his regiment, which formed part of the VIIth (Meerut) Division, detailed for service with the Indian Expeditionary Force.

Captain Robertson-Glasgow was officially reported as " missing " after a local attack upon the enemy's trenches, some miles east of Bethune, on the 13th November, 1914. From that date till the 25th December, 1914, his actual fate was unknown, but on that day, during a short informal truce, the intervening ground between the lines was searched, and his body was found under the parapet of a German trench, which he alone of the party he was leading seemed to have reached. He was buried in a graveyard reserved for British officers near the village of Le Touret, a short distance east of Bethune.

The letters of brother officers all bear witness to the cool and cheerful daring displayed by the late officer during the period of trench fighting which preceded his death. On one occasion he went to the rescue, under shrapnel fire, of some of his men who had been buried by the explosion of a shell which destroyed part of their trench, his work being done in full view of the enemy. His example in such peculiarly trying circumstances as these was of inestimable value in encouraging his men to face the inevitable dangers to which they were exposed. He was exceedingly popular with all ranks, and his influence on those who came in contact with him was of the very best.

Captain Robertson-Glasgow married, in January,

1911, Philadelphia Constance Violet Flora Macdonald, daughter of Major F. Fraser, of Tornaveen, Aberdeenshire, and niece to the late Lady Robertson, of Forteviot, and left one son, Archibald Francis Colin, born July, 1914.

LIEUTENANT RICHARD SPENCER GLYN, 3rd BATTN. THE BUFFS (EAST KENT REGIMENT),

who was killed in action on the 20th October, aged twenty-two, was the son of Lewis Edmund Glyn, K.C., of Bexley, Kent, and Thistlewood, Carlisle.

He was educated at King's School, Canterbury, where he was in the O.T.C., and entered the Army in 1910, being promoted Lieutenant in January, 1913.

Lieutenant Glyn, who was fond of shooting and fishing, afterwards entered at the Middle Temple, London, for the study of law.

For active service he was attached to the 1st Battalion of his regiment, and was with it when he was shot through the heart at Radingham while directing the fire of his men.

LIEUTENANT SYDNEY ALEXANDER GOLDSMID, 3rd BATTN. WORCESTERSHIRE REGT.,

was born at Southsea, Hampshire, on the 6th May, 1893, the only surviving son of the late Sydney Goldsmid, and step-son of Colonel Annesley-Smith, late Worcestershire Regiment and A.P.D. He was second cousin to the late Sir Julian Goldsmid, Bart., and was related to the late Sir Isaac Lyon Goldsmid, Bart., and the late Sir Francis Goldsmid, Bart. Lieutenant Goldsmid was the last of the male line of the Goldsmid family. According to a family legend, there was never to be a direct heir to the baronetcy, which is now in abeyance, and the family in the direct male line has now become extinct.

Lieutenant Goldsmid was educated at the United Services Colleges, now called the Imperial Services College, Windsor, and entered Sandhurst in 1911, obtaining his commission in the 3rd Battalion Worcestershire Regiment, then at Tidworth, in 1912. He became Lieutenant

in September, 1914. He was spoken of by his Colonel as a most efficient and promising young officer.

During the Great War he was mentioned in Field-Marshal Sir John French's Despatch of the 8th October, 1914, for important reconnaissance work. He was shot near Ypres on the 7th November, 1914, while holding a trench which the Germans rushed during a fog.

Lieutenant Goldsmid was a keen soldier and a good shot; his favourite pastime was riding, and he was fond of sport.

2nd LIEUTENANT COSMO GEORGE GORDON, 1st BATTN. NORTHAMPTONSHIRE REGT.,

born on the 7th May, 1894, at the Royal Marine Barracks, Walmer, Kent, was the son of Major-General and Mrs. Gordon, of Culdrain, Gartly, Aberdeenshire; a grandson of General Gordon, R.A., and great-grandson of Colonel Gordon, 92nd (Gordon) Highlanders.

He received his education at Warden House, Deal, and Cheltenham College. After passing through the R.M.C., Sandhurst, where he was known as a good football and hockey player (which latter game he also played for his regiment), he joined the 1st Battalion Northamptonshire Regiment six months before he left with the Expeditionary Force for the Continent on the 12th August, 1914. He had already passed his examination for promotion. On the 17th September, 1914, while holding some trenches which the Northamptons had attacked and taken against great odds, he was mortally wounded, and died in a few hours.

2nd Lieutenant Gordon was a keen sportsman. a marksman with the rifle, and a good game shot.

CAPTAIN JOHN FR'EDERICK STRATHEARN GORDON, THE CAMERONIANS (SCOTTISH RIFLES),

who was killed in action, near Ypres, on the 13th November, 1914, was the younger son of the late General Sir John Gordon, G.C.B., and a grandson of the late Lord Gordon, of Drumearn.

He was born on the 19th May, 1882, and joined the Royal

Scots in August, 1900. He served in the South African War, being present at operations in the Transvaal, Orange River Colony, and Cape Colony, between March, 1901, and May, 1902, receiving the Queen's medal with five clasps. He was promoted Lieutenant in December, 1902, and from November, 1904, to July, 1910, was employed with the King's African Rifles, being promoted Captain in the Royal Scots in April, 1910, and in September of the same year was transferred to the Scottish Rifles.

Captain Gordon was qualified as an Interpreter in French and in Swahili. In April, 1913, he was appointed Assistant District Officer in Nigeria, Northern Provinces.

CAPTAIN ROBERT EDDING-TON GORDON, 1st BATTN. NORTHAMPTONSHIRE REGIMENT,

the son of George Gordon, M.Inst.C.E., was born at Ellerslie, Toorak, Melbourne, Australia, on the 8th February, 1877.

He was educated at Toorak College, Melbourne, and by private tutors at Edinburgh, returning afterwards to Australia, where he was appointed 2nd Lieutenant in the Military Forces, Victoria. In December, 1897, he was gazetted 2nd Lieutenant in the Northamptonshire Regiment, and joined the 1st Battalion at Peshawar. He was promoted Lieutenant in January, 1900, and Captain in August, 1905. In that year he left India to join the 2nd Battalion of his regiment, then in England. Captain Gordon applied for foreign service, and from November, 1907, to December, 1911, he was employed with the West African Frontier Force, afterwards rejoining his own regiment in England.

Captain Gordon went to France with the 1st Expeditionary Force in August, 1914, and was with the 1st Battalion Northamptonshire Regiment in the retirement from Mons, and in subsequent fighting until the Battle of the Aisne. He was killed on the 15th September, 1914, as he was advancing, trying to get his company into a more advanced position during an attack by the enemy. He was shot in the head and body, death being instantaneous.

CAPTAIN ROBERT NORMAN GORDON, 1st BATTN. BORDER REGIMENT,

son of John and Harriet Gordon, now residing at Didmarton, Tunbridge Wells, was born at Rio de Janeiro, Brazil, South America, on the 18th June, 1875, and was educated at the

Preparatory School of Captain Lewin, Frant, Sussex, afterwards going to Repton.

He was gazetted to the Border Regiment in September, 1895, becoming Lieutenant in April, 1898, and obtaining his company in April, 1904. He served with his regiment in India, Burma, and the Cape.

He was killed by the explosion of a shell at Ypres, on the 26th October, 1914, when leaving the trenches.

Captain Gordon married Miss Rhoda Jefferson, and left one boy, born the 5th May, 1912.

CAPTAIN RONALD STEUART GORDON, 57th WILDE'S RIFLES (FRONTIER FORCE),

fifth son of the late John Lewis Gordon, of West Park, Elgin, Scotland, was born there on the 24th November, 1876.

He was educated at Trinity College, Glenalmond, Perthshire, and passed into Sandhurst in July, 1895, receiving an unattached 2nd Lieutenancy for the Indian Army in January, 1897. He joined the latter in March, 1898, serving for a short time in the 61st Pioneers, and being transferred later to the 57th Wilde's Rifles. He served as Adjutant of his regiment, and was promoted Captain in January, 1906.

He was on active service in China in 1900, receiving the medal with clasp, and again on the north-western frontier of India in 1908, taking part in operations in the Mohmand country, and the engagements of Kargha and Matta. For these services he was mentioned in Despatches ("London Gazette," 14th August, 1908), and received the medal with clasp.

When at Sandhurst he won the bronze medals for cricket and Rugby and Association football. He was a very fine shot and keen fisherman. In India he helped to win many cups for polo, football, golf, and cricket, being a good all-round athlete and sportsman. He was a member of the Caledonian Club, London.

Captain Gordon married on the 6th August, 1914, at St. Peter's, Melbourne, Ruby Mary, eldest daughter of Henry Byron Moore, Melbourne, Australia, and sailed the following day for India to rejoin his regiment.

He was killed in action at Messines on the 31st October, 1914, the following account of the circumstances being received from an officer of a British regiment who was present: " He did the most gallant thing I have ever seen: he took a platoon and went forward to check the advance of the Germans to cover the retirement of the rest of his company, though he must have known it was certain death. While advancing he was shot through the head and died instantaneously."

Another officer wrote: " He was the best officer I have ever known. He was extraordinarily popular with the men, and I have never seen them so cut up about anything as they were when they came in."

2nd LIEUTENANT GERARD RIBTON GORE, 1st BATTN. ROYAL WELSH FUSILIERS,

who died on the 20th December, 1914, from wounds received in action on the previous day, was the only son of Lieutenant - Colonel Ribton Gore, late 1st Royal Sussex Regiment Thornfields, C o u n t y Limerick.

He was born on the 2nd May, 1893, and was educated at Cheltenham College.

He was appointed to the 3rd Battalion of his regiment in March, 1914, and was attached to and accompanied the 2nd Battalion to France at the commencement of the war, being wounded during the retirement from Mons.

He afterwards served with the 1st Battalion in Flanders, where he was fatally wounded, having been gazetted to the R.W.F. and posted to the 1st Battalion, in December, 1914; and was especially recommended for transfer to the Regular Battalion by his Commanding Officer and the General commanding the Division.

LIEUTENANT SYDNEY KINGSTON GORE, 1st BATTN. THE QUEEN'S OWN (ROYAL WEST KENT REGIMENT),

who was killed in action on the 28th October, 1914, was the son of Dr. A. J. Gore, of Kingston, Cherry Garden Avenue, Folkestone, and was born at Barry, Glamorganshire, on the 12th July, 1889. He was educated at the Folkestone Grammar School

and by private tuition, and entered the Army from the Special Reserve in December, 1912, becoming Lieutenant in September, 1914. He was a member of the United Service Club; played cricket for the Kent 2nd XI and Band of Brothers, and was wicket-keeper of his regimental team. He was also Captain of the

Irish Army football team, 1913-14, and played centre-forward for Army officers against Dutch officers at Aldershot in 1914.

He went out with the British Expeditionary Force in August, 1914, and was present at the Battles of Mons, the Aisne, and Neuve Chapelle. The following details of his death were furnished by a sergeant of the Royal West Kent Regiment in his evidence in relation to another officer of the same regiment:—" It was the same action where we lost Lieutenant Gore. He was shot right through the brain. We were surrounded. The right front was held by the K.O.Y.L.I., the left by the Wilts. One platoon advanced and took up flank fire. Others went off, and I did not see them till nightfall. Lieutenant Gore went on with Sergeant-Major Penney. Their bodies were found on the road. I saw them the same night when I was guiding a Major of the Bedfords across to defend our left flank. I don't know about Mr. Gore's burial, but would like to say how pluckily we thought he died."

2nd LIEUTENANT ERIC WILLIAM GORST, 4th BATTN. THE ROYAL FUSILIERS (CITY OF LONDON REGIMENT,

who was killed in action at Neuve Chapelle on the 26th October, 1914, aged twenty-one, but whose name has not appeared in the official casualty lists, was the eldest surviving son of the late T. W. Gorst.

He was gazetted to the Royal Fusiliers on the 14th August, 1914.

2nd LIEUTENANT WILLIAM BERESFORD GOSSET, 115th BATTERY ROYAL FIELD ARTILLERY,

born at Farm Hill, in the Blue Mountains of Jamaica, on the 17th November, 1893, was the son of the Hon. Beresford Smyly Gosset, Custos Rotulorum of St. Andrew, Jamaica, and his wife, Mary Jean Gosset. He was educated at Ascham House

School, Eastbourne, where he was captain of games, and at Clifton College, where he was in the Second XI. He then proceeded to the R.M.A., Woolwich, in 1911, from which he obtained his commission in the R.F.A. in December, 1912, going to the front with his battery in August, 1914.

He was killed in action near Ypres on the 1st November, 1914, when he had gone out of his trench to see what was wrong with a telephone, messages having ceased to come in. He was buried, with Lieutenant Tucker, the officer who had been working the telephone, and who was killed just before him, in Ypres Churchyard, the service being conducted by Army Chaplain George. The Captain of the 115th Battery wrote to his parents : " Your brave boy was killed on the 1st November. He had gone forward into the trenches to observe fire, and was killed by a shell close to the trenches while returning to the battery. One of our gunners was with him at the time, and death was quite instantaneous. His friend, Lieutenant Tucker, was killed on the same day. I brought back his body that evening, and we buried him with Lieutenant Tucker in the cemetery at Ypres the following day. We put up two crosses over their graves. . . . Your son was a most valuable and useful officer, always ready and eager for every kind of work, and always too much inclined to run into danger. We all were devoted to him, and the loss of two such young and brave lives in one day was a great blow to us."

Another account said that when Lieutenant Tucker's telephone messages stopped, Gosset went to see why, and found the telephone cut. Under a terrible shell fire he calmly went down to it, and was hit by a shell and killed instantaneously.

CAPTAIN ERIC JOHN FLETCHER GOUGH, 1st BATTN. IRISH GUARDS,

was born on the 20th November, 1888, the only son of the late Major Thomas Armstrong Gough, and of Mrs. Claude Langley, of 9, Onslow Crescent, S.W. He was a member of the Irish family of Gough, which has contributed so many distinguished soldiers to the Army.

Captain Gough was educated at Mr. Hawtrey's School at Westgate and at Eton. He joined the (then) 7th Battalion Rifle Brigade (Special Reserve) in 1906, and was gazetted to the Irish Guards in 1909, becoming Lieutenant in November, 1911, and Captain in September, 1914.

He went to France with his battalion on the 12th August, 1914, and was present at the retirement from Mons, the actions at Villers Cotterets, the Marne (where he acted as Adjutant), the Aisne, and the fighting at Ypres in the early days of November. He was killed in the trenches between Bethune and La Bassée on the 30th December, 1914, when a life full of promise was cut short. He was mentioned in Sir John French's Despatch of the 31st May, 1915.

Captain Gough was a member of the Guards'

and Pratt's Clubs. His recreations were racing, shooting, fishing, and golf.

LIEUTENANT JOHN BLOOMFIELD GOUGH, ROYAL HORSE ARTILLERY,

who was killed in action on the 8th September, 1914, was the eldest son of Colonel Bloomfield Gough, formerly of the 9th Lancers, and of Mrs. Gough, of Belchester, Berwickshire. His grandfather, General Sir John Bloomfield Gough, was a distinguished officer of the Indian Army, who fought at Sobraon and in the Gwalior campaign, member of a family which has given so many officers to the Army.

Lieutenant Gough, who was born on the 24th July, 1886, was educated at Haileybury, and received his commission in the Royal Artillery in December, 1906, becoming Lieutenant in December, 1909.

He was an all-round sportsman, very good rider in races, first-class man to hounds, and a most successful pig-sticker.

The following account of the circumstances attending his death was given by the Major of his battery :—

" When I was hit he ran up to take my place and command the battery, and was hit by the very next shell as he reached me. What his loss means to me and to the old troop I cannot at all express, nor can I ever forget. He has been magnificent all through our very trying rearguard ordeals. As Battery Leader he was quite invaluable, and so very clever at using ground, which probably saved us heavier losses on numerous occasions."

CAPTAIN ALEC G. M. GRAHAM, 6th BATTN. WORCESTERSHIRE REGIMENT, attd. 1st BATTN. LOYAL NORTH LANCASHIRE REGIMENT,

was killed in action on the 22nd December, 1914.

Captain Graham was promoted to that rank in the Worcestershire Regiment in August, 1914, having first entered the 6th Battalion in December, 1901; with it he served in the South African War, being present at operations in Cape Colony from January to May, 1902.

CAPTAIN ALAN MOIR GRAHAM, 5th GURKHA RIFLES (FRONTIER FORCE), attd. 2nd KING EDWARD'S OWN GURKHA RIFLES (SIRMOOR RIFLES),

who was killed on the 21st December, 1914, was the younger son of Major-General Sir Thomas Graham, K.C.B., of Heatherdale Lodge, Camberley. Born on the 25th June, 1878, he was educated at Haileybury and the R.M.C., Sandhurst, on passing out of which he received an unattached 2nd Lieutenancy in August, 1897, and served his probationary period with the Devonshire Regiment.

In November, 1898, he was gazetted to the Indian Staff Corps, became Lieutenant in the Indian Army in July, 1900, and was promoted Captain in August, 1906. He was in command of the Military Police Escort to a Surveying Party in the Miri country in 1912, and was granted the King's Police medal for conspicuous gallantry in repelling an attack. Captain Graham also commanded the Military Police during the Akha Expedition in the early part of 1914, and obtained the medal.

He was killed on the 21st December, 1914, while covering the retreat of his company from an attack which had taken it in flank at Festubert. Captain Graham, who was a member of the Junior Naval and Military Club, married Edith Margaret, second daughter of Stafford F. Still.

LIEUTENANT ARCHIBALD STUART BULLOCH GRAHAM, 2nd BATTN. GORDON HIGHLANDERS,

born on the 28th April, 1891, was the son of Archibald Bulloch Graham, 3, Park Gardens, Glasgow, W., formerly Captain in the Glasgow Highlanders, T.F.

He was educated at Glasgow Academy, Rossall School, and the R.M.C., Sandhurst, from which he was gazetted to the Gordon Highlanders in March, 1911, joining the 1st Battalion at Colchester. In October, 1911, he was transferred to the 2nd Battalion at Cawnpore, India, from which place the battalion went to Cairo in December, 1912. He was promoted Lieutenant in July, 1914.

He left Cairo with his battalion for Southampton in September, 1914, and after a few days at Lyndhurst they left for Zeebrugge as part of the VIIth Division. During the latter days of October, Lieutenant Graham frequently attracted attention by his bravery and cheeriness under trying conditions, and especially in the charge after which he was treacherously killed. Several officers wrote saying how well he had done, and in 1915 his father received a parchment certificate to the effect that Lieutenant Graham's conduct on the 29th–31st October, 1914, had been brought to the notice of the Commanding Officer, who had had much pleasure in bringing it to the notice of higher authority.

He was killed on the afternoon of the 31st October, 1914, the following account having been received from his soldier servant : " At the time of his death he was one of three officers left with the remains of the battalion, which after the recent severe fighting had been largely reduced in numbers. They were ordered to take a wood, and this they did in such a manner that the enemy thought they were overpowered by numbers, and threw up their hands to surrender. While the officers were seeing that the enemy's arms were given up a wounded German officer, pretending to be dead, waited till Lieutenant Graham was close in front of him, and then shot him in the back of the head with his revolver. Our men were so enraged that they gave the Germans no quarter."

His Commanding Officer, writing on the 12th November, 1914, said : " The Gordons had charged through the Germans, and had them in full retreat when your boy (Stuart) was hit from behind, and has not been heard of from that time. I can tell you that he was a splendid officer and a great loss to his country, the Army, and his regiment. When he had to do a thing I knew it would be well done, and it always was well done. I cannot tell you how much I regret his loss." And writing again on the 15th he said : " His popularity with the men was very great, and he proved himself a born leader of men. He is a great loss to us and the Army at large."

CAPTAIN HUBERT ANTHONY GRANT, 2nd BATTN. LEICESTERSHIRE REGIMENT,

son of the Reverend Canon Grant, and grandson of Archdeacon Grant, both formerly of Aylesford, Kent, was born there on the 16th January, 1878.

He was educated at Marlborough College, and joined the Leicestershire

Regiment from the R.M.C., Sandhurst, in May, 1898, becoming Lieutenant in 1900. He served in the South African War, 1900–02, being present at operations in Natal, including the action at Laings Nek; in the Transvaal, including actions at Belfast and Lydenburg; in the Orange River Colony; and on the Zululand frontier of Natal. For his services he received the Queen's medal and the King's medal, each with two clasps. Captain Grant was serving with his battalion when he was killed on the 24th November, 1914. The Lieutenant-Colonel commanding his battalion gives the following account of the circumstances :—

" We had been out of our trenches for some days to have a rest, and on the night of the 23rd-24th November we were ordered to go in support of another brigade on our right. The enemy had taken, early on the 23rd, a part of the trench belonging to this brigade, and the order came that this trench was to be retaken at any cost. It was a most important and urgent task, and half of our battalion was told off to attack a certain point in the line. ' B ' Company, commanded by Captain Grant, was leading, and he led his men with great dash right into the enemy's trench, and as he got there was shot through the head. The men followed and took the trench, with the result that the Germans were routed, and over one hundred prisoners and other things, such as machine guns, rifles, etc., were captured, and a good many of the enemy were killed. The Army Corps Commander and the Commander-in-Chief both congratulated the troops concerned in the action, and Captain Grant's name was brought to notice for gallantry. He died a fine death for a soldier at the head of his men, leading them to the enemy. His death was instantaneous. " He was buried by Rev. Irwin, our Chaplain, in consecrated ground, which we have bought for the burial of officers and men of our regiment, in the presence of the officers and as many men as could be spared from the regiment. He will be long remembered in the regiment, for all loved him, and will feel his loss very much.

" He will be remembered as one of the best of comrades and kindest of men. He was loved by his men, and, as you know, all of us officers mourn his loss deeply."

Captain Grant was mentioned in Sir John French's Despatch of the 18th February, 1915, for his gallantry.

He married in January, 1906, Cara Gillespie, daughter of the late Major-General Robert Rollo Gillespie, C.B., and grand-daughter of the late Admiral John Townsend Coffin.

LIEUTENANT WALTER FRANCIS GRAVES, 3rd (attd. 1st) BATTN. BEDFORDSHIRE REGIMENT, who was killed in action on the 9th November,

1914, at the age of twenty-nine, was the eldest son of Mrs. W. Graves, Sandye Place, Sandy, Bedfordshire.

He was appointed Lieutenant in the 3rd Battalion of his regiment in September, 1914, having previously been a 2nd Lieutenant in the same battalion.

Lieutenant Graves was a member of the Cardiff City Council and of the Coal Exchange, and was interested in educational work.

CAPT. AMBROSE DIXON HALDREGE GRAYSON, RESERVE OF OFFICERS, attd. ROYAL FIELD ARTILLERY,

who was killed in action near Festubert on the 13th October, 1914, was the third son of the late Henry H. and Mrs. Grayson, 12, Bolton Gardens, London, S.W., and was born on the 14th May, 1874. He was educated at Wellington College and the R.M.A., Woolwich, from which he was appointed 2nd Lieutenant in the R.A. in 1894, Lieutenant in 1897, and Captain in November, 1900. He served with both horse and field batteries, and in 1901–02 took part in the Aro Expedition, Southern Nigeria. He was a member of the Naval and Military Club, and played polo, tennis, and golf. In March, 1903, he retired from the Army for family reasons, but at the outbreak of the war Captain Grayson was again employed with the Royal Field Artillery, ranking as Captain from the 30th August, 1914.

MAJOR ARTHUR DAWSON GREEN, D.S.O., p.s.c., THE WORCESTER-SHIRE REGT.,

son of the late Henry Green, Esq., of Blackwall, Old Charlton, was born on the 13th April, 1874, at Belvedere, Kent, and was educated at Haileybury College, where he had a reputation as a good athlete. He joined the 1st Essex Regiment as 2nd Lieutenant in 1894, and in the course of his military career obtained many decorations and distinctions. He became Lieutenant in 1897, and served with the West African Regiment in the Sierra Leone Hut Tax

Rebellion and in the Sierra Leone Hinterland Expedition, under the late General Sir E. R. P. Woodgate, from April, 1898, to June, 1899.

For these services he received the West African medal and two clasps. He was promoted to a Captaincy in the Worcestershire Regiment on the 20th June, 1900. From January, 1903, to February, 1907, he was employed with the West African Frontier Force. For his Nigerian service in 1906 he was mentioned in Despatches (Major Goodwin, 15th March ; and Colonel Cole, 20th May, 1906 ; recorded in " London Gazette " of the 2nd July, 1907) and received the medal with clasp.

From 1899–1902 he served in the Boer War with Thorneycroft's Mounted Infantry ; was present at the relief of Ladysmith ; at operations on the Tugela Heights, and also in Natal, including the action at Laing's Nek. He also took part in operations in Cape Colony, Orange River Colony, and the Transvaal. For these services he was mentioned in Despatches by General Sir Redvers Buller on the 19th June and the 9th November, 1900 ("London Gazette" of the 29th July, 1902) ; was decorated with the D.S.O., and received the Queen's medal with six clasps and the King's medal with two clasps. He was appointed Brigade-Major of the 17th Infantry Brigade in the Irish Command in June, 1911.

When he met his death he was reconnoitring with his General in the trenches at Soupir, and was shot through the heart by a sniper on the 28th September, 1914.

He was fond of hunting, was Master of the Staff College Drag Hounds in 1909–10, and was a member of the Army and Navy Club.

He married Isabella Margaret, second daughter of the late William Lindsay Stewart, Esq., of Stanmore, Lanarkshire, N.B., and left a son, Henry James Lindsay, born 24th September, 1911.

LIEUTENANT-COLONEL MALCOLM CHARLES ANDREW GREEN, PRINCE OF WALES'S VOLUNTEERS (SOUTH LANCASHIRE REGIMENT),

who was killed in the trenches near Ypres on the 17th November, 1 9 1 4, was born at St. George's Road, London, S.W., on the 2nd July, 1871, the son of the late Colonel Malcolm S. Green, C.B., of 3rd Scinde Horse, and a grandson of Admiral Sir Andrew Pellet Green, who commanded H.M.S. " Collingwood " at Trafalgar.

Lieutenant-Colonel Green was educated at the Oxford Military College and at the R.M.C., Sandhurst, receiving his commission in the South Lancashire Regiment (the old 82nd) in 1891, becoming Lieutenant in 1894, Captain in 1900, and obtaining his Majority in May, 1909. He served in India and in the South African War, being present at operations in Natal, including the action at Laing's Nek and operations in Cape Colony. He received the Queen's medal with four clasps.

On the outbreak of the Great War Lieutenant-Colonel Green was serving at Tidworth, having just previously been in command of the depot of his regiment at Warrington with the newly formed Army, but received his orders to proceed on service to take command of his battalion.

Lieutenant-Colonel Green, who was a member of the United Service Club, Pall Mall, married Miss Elsie Bisdee, and left three sons, age five, three, and two years respectively, at the time of their father's death.

CAPTAIN RIVERSDALE NONUS GRENFELL, BUCKINGHAMSHIRE YEOMANRY (ROYAL BUCKS HUSSARS), attd. 9th LANCERS,

was killed in action on the 14th September, 1914, at the beginning of the Battle of the Aisne. He was the ninth son of Mr. Pascoe Dupré Grenfell, of Wilton Park, Beaconsfield, Bucks, and a nephew of Field-Marshal Lord Grenfell. He was born on the 4th September, 1880, was educated at Eton, and joined the Royal Bucks Hussars in September, 1908, becoming Captain in August, 1914. He was well known as a fine polo player, and was a member of the " Old Etonian " team that won the Champion Cup in 1907. While on a visit to his twin brother in India he won the Kadir Cup. Captain Grenfell was a member of the Turf and Bath Clubs, was very interested in philanthropy, and organised a branch of the Invalid Children's Aid Association at Islington. One of his brothers, Lieutenant R. S. Grenfell, 12th Lancers, was killed in action at Omdurman, and his twin brother, Captain Francis Octavius Grenfell, V.C., 9th Lancers, after being twice wounded, fell in action at Ypres on the 24th May, 1915.

CAPTAIN the Honble. RICHARD GEORGE GRENVILLE MORGAN GRENVILLE, Master of Kinloss, 1st BATTN. RIFLE BRIGADE,

was the son of Major Morgan Grenville, late of the York and Lancaster Militia, and the Baroness Kinloss. He was a grandson of the late Duke of Buckingham and Chandos.

Captain Morgan Grenville was born on the 25th September, 1887, and was educated at

Eton and the R.M.C., Sandhurst, obtaining his commission in the Rifle Brigade in 1906, becoming Lieutenant in January, 1910, and Captain in August, 1914.

He was killed in action at Ploegsteert, near Armentières, when serving with his battalion on the 19th December, 1914, having been twice previously wounded, his name having appeared in the casualty lists published on September 10th and November 16th. He was mentioned in Sir John French's Despatch of the 8th October, 1914.

He was a member of the Bath Club, London. Captain the Hon. Richard G. G. Morgan Grenville having been the eldest son, his brother, the Hon. Luis Chandos Francis Temple, becomes heir to the barony. Another brother, Lieutenant the Hon. T. G. B. Morgan Grenville, is also serving in the Rifle Brigade.

LIEUTENANT GERALD GRIFFITH, 3rd BATTN. HAMPSHIRE REGIMENT,

younger son of Dr. and Mrs. P. G. Griffith, St. Colomb, Walton-on-Thames, was born at Furneaux Pelham, Hertfordshire, on the 14th July, 1893. He was educated at Pinewood, Farnborough, Hants, and at Blundell's School, Tiverton. He was gazetted to the Hampshire Regiment in September, 1911, and was promoted Lieutenant in January, 1914.

Lieutenant Griffith went to the front on the 21st August, 1914, and was unofficially reported as having been killed in action soon afterwards, no definite news being obtained for some time. At last it was ascertained that he was wounded and left behind in the trenches on the 26th August, 1914, and it must unhappily be assumed that he died on or about that date.

A brother officer wrote of him : " He was killed and left behind in the trenches he had helped to hold so gallantly. He was a gallant, cheery lad, and we can ill spare such boys. He was much liked by his brother officers and men."

CAPTAIN HORACE SYLVESTER GRIMSTON, 2nd BATTN. THE DUKE OF EDINBURGH'S (WILTSHIRE REGT.),

was born on the 27th October, 1891, at Newera Eliya, Ceylon. He was the son of Edward John Grimston, of Rambodde, Ramboda, Ceylon, and his second wife, Toonie Clara (née Woodhouse), and was a grandson of the Hon. and Rev. Francis

Sylvester Grimston, and great-grandson of the second Earl Verulam.

Captain Grimston was educated at St. Edward's School, Newera Eliya, Ceylon, at Clifton College and the R.M.C., Sandhurst.

He joined the 2nd Battalion Wiltshire Regiment as 2nd Lieutenant in April, 1911 ; became Lieutenant in March, 1914, and was promoted Captain on the battlefield in October, 1914.

Captain Grimston was shot through the temple in the trenches at Reutel, near Ypres, on the 23rd October, 1914. His battalion formed part of the VIIth Division, which has since been named " The Immortal Division," because of the glorious stand it made in front of Ypres.

He was a keen polo player and gentleman jockey, and was a member of the United Service Club.

2nd LIEUT. LAWRENCE ERNEST PELHAM GRUBB, THE KING'S OWN (YORKSHIRE LIGHT INFANTRY),

was killed in action on the 15th November, 1914.

He was born in 1892 at Wembley, Middlesex, the only son of Ernest Pelham Grubb, gentleman, and Emily Mary Grubb. He was a great-grandson of Mr. Richard Grubb, of Cahir Abbey,

County Tipperary. He was educated at Rugby (Town House), which he entered in 1906, and proceeded with an exhibition to Brasenose College, Oxford, in 1911. There he obtained his degree with honours in 1914. When war was declared he threw up an excellent post abroad, and, having belonged to the O.T.C., went out as a despatch rider. He received his commission a few weeks before his death, which he met while leading a charge against a château near Hooge on the night of the 15th November, 1914.

CAPTAIN FRANK LE MAISTRE GRUCHY, 1st BATTN. LEICESTER-SHIRE REGT.,

was the son of the late George Gruchy, Esq., and Mrs. Gruchy, of Rouce-ville, St. Saviour's, Jersey, and was born there on the 23rd January, 1876.

He was educated at Victoria College, Jersey, and also studied with tutors in Jersey and England. For two years he was in the Jersey Militia, and joined the 2nd Battalion Leicestershire Regiment in 1898, being subsequently transferred to the 1st Battalion, in which he became Captain on the 3rd March, 1903, being at the time of his death the senior Captain with the battalion.

He served at various stations in Ireland, and went to South Africa in February, 1900, with the 2nd Mounted Infantry, remaining there till the end of the Boer War, during which he was, in December, 1901, wounded in the knee. For his services he was mentioned in Despatches, and received the Queen's and the King's medals, with five clasps. Afterwards he served in India, and later at the depot at Leicester and other English stations.

While leading his men towards the enemy he was shot through the heart, and died instantane-ously, on the 23rd October, 1914. His body was buried near La Houssaie, close to the Armen-tières-Ecquinghem Railway, west of Lille. His battalion formed part of the 16th Brigade, VIth Division, of the Expeditionary Force.

Captain Gruchy rode well and hunted. He was also a very good ski runner and fond of all athletic sports. He was unmarried.

CAPTAIN HENEAGE GREVILLE, LORD GUERNSEY, IRISH GUARDS,

was the eldest son of the eighth Earl of Aylesford and Lady Aylesford, daughter of the third Lord Bagot, and was born in London on the 2nd June, 1883.

He was educated at Eton, and first joined the 3rd Battalion Wiltshire Regiment in August, 1901, with which he served in the South African War, receiving the South African medal. He was then for a short time in the 7th Hussars, and in June, 1902, was gazetted to the Irish Guards. He was on the Staff as A.D.C. to the Governor of Gibraltar in 1905. In 1911 he was on duty at the Coronation of Their Majesties King George and Queen Mary, and received the Coronation medal. He also served in the Warwickshire Yeomanry, in which his com-mission as Captain was dated the 17th August, 1910, and subsequently passed into the Reserve of Officers on April, 15th, 1914.

In the Great War Lord Guernsey was leading his men to an attack at Soupir on the 14th September, 1914, when he was shot.

Lord Guernsey, who was a member of the Turf Club and of White's Club, married on the 11th June, 1907, the Hon. Gladys C. G. Fellowes, second daughter of the second Baron de Ramsey, and left a son, Michael Charles Heneage Finch, born 1908, who succeeds as next heir to his grandfather, and four other children — two daughters and two sons.

2nd LIEUTENANT REGINALD GLOVER KER GULLAND, 14th (COUNTY OF LONDON) BATTN. THE LONDON REGIMENT (LONDON SCOTTISH),

was born in London on the 2nd Decem-ber, 1885, and was the son of James Ker Gulland, M.I.M.E., F.G.S., and F.S.A.

He was educated at Clifton College and the Central Techni-cal College, London, becoming afterwards a civil and mecha-nical engineer. At Clifton he was in the Cadet Corps, and joined the " electrical engineers " while at college in 1904, was transferred to the London Scottish in 1908, and received his commission in July, 1910.

He passed through musketry and machine-gun courses at Hythe, and was appointed Instructor of Musketry and Machine Gun Officer to his battalion.

His chief hobby was rifle shooting. He was a member of the National Rifle Association and the North London Rifle Club. In 1910 he was in the " King's Hundred," and shot for Scotland in the National Challenge Trophy Competition in 1911 ; was again in the " King's Hundred," and also in the final stage for the St. George's Vase in 1914. He was also in the Old Cliftonian team for the Public Schools' Veterans' Challenge Trophy on many occasions.

He was hit by a sniper on the 11th November, 1914, while in command of his machine-gun section near Ypres, and died early next morning. Lieutenant Ker Gulland married, in June, 1914, Miss Beatrice E. Welch.

164

CAPTAIN ALEXANDER GRANT GWYER, 6th DRAGOON GUARDS (CARABINIERS),
killed in action on the 22nd October, 1914, was the younger son of the late Cecil F. Gwyer and Mrs. Gwyer, of Croftinloan, Pitlochrie.

He was born on the 10th May, 1883, and joined the 6th Dragoon Guards in January, 1902, becoming Lieutenant in September, 1903, and Captain in May, 1908.

He had retired from the active list, and had voluntarily entered the Reserve of Officers, rejoining his old regiment on the outbreak of the war.

CAPTAIN CHARLES EDWARD HACK, 1st BATTN. CONNAUGHT RANGERS,

was the second son of the late William Lionel Frederick Hack, Esq., of Silk-Willoughby, Lincolnshire, and of Mrs. Hack, Thruxton, Hampshire, and was born at Silk-Willoughby on the 29th August, 1877.

He was educated at Bedford Grammar School, and joined the Connaught Rangers from the Sligo Militia in December, 1897, being posted to the 1st Battalion, with which he remained for all his service. He was promoted Lieutenant in April, 1900, and Captain in May, 1904.

He had a fine record in South Africa, where he put in over two and a half years of active service, being present at a large number of important actions, including those of Colenso, Spion Kop, Vaal Krans, Pieter's Hill, and Riet Vlei. He was with Hart's Irish Brigade in Natal, in the forcing of Fourteen Streams and the relief of Mafeking. He was also present at operations on the Tugela Heights, including the assault on Hart's Hill, where six hundred of his battalion fell, and at other operations in the Orange Free State, the Transvaal, Cape Colony, and Orange River Colony. For his services he was mentioned in Despatches ("London Gazette," 10th September, 1901), received the Queen's medal with five clasps and the King's medal with two clasps. He also received the Durbar medal, 1911.

In June, 1911, he was appointed Adjutant of his battalion, holding the appointment till June, 1914. In July he came home on a year's leave, but on the outbreak of the war he rejoined his regiment. He was at first reported as wounded and missing after an action on the 4th-5th November, 1914, and as his body was not recovered hopes were entertained that

he might be alive. A Court of Enquiry subsequently found that he had been killed in an attack on the enemy's trenches that night.

It seems that a trench which had been vacated by our troops had been occupied by the Germans, and Captain Hack's company was ordered to retake it and fill it in. The attack was delivered soon after midnight on the 4th November, and the company was filling in the trench when the enemy returned in overwhelming numbers, and the company was forced to retire, having lost its three officers. Captain Hack was using his revolver and giving orders when he fell.

Captain Hack was an excellent sportsman, especially fond of polo and hunting, and always took a great interest in his men's games.

A good horseman, a keen soldier, and a staunch friend, he will be missed by a large number of friends, as well as in his regiment.

In announcing his death a brother officer wrote : " To all of us he represented, as it were, the battalion."

LIEUTENANT WILFRID JOHN MACKENZIE HADFIELD, 2nd BATTN. THE PRINCE OF WALES'S VOLUNTEERS (SOUTH LANCASHIRE REGIMENT),
was the son of Major-General C. A. Hadfield, and was born at Southsea on the 11th January, 1889.

He was educated first at Mr. Norman's Preparatory School, Sevenoaks ; then at Repton ; and at "The Army School," Stratford-on-Avon, whence he proceeded to the R.M.C., Sandhurst. He joined the 2nd Battalion South Lancashire Regiment on the 6th November, 1909, becoming Lieutenant on the 17th April, 1912.

He was Assistant Adjutant of his battalion, and embarked with it for the Continent as Regimental Transport Officer.

On the 6th September, 1914, he was severely wounded at the Battle of the Marne, having been ambushed whilst accompanying his battalion at dusk on outpost duty. He was sent to the base in a hospital train, but on the journey he was taken from the train, on the 10th September, 1914, to a civil hospital for an operation, and died there the same day. He was buried at Angers, with full military honours, by the French garrison.

Lieutenant Hadfield was a member of the Junior Army and Navy Club. He was a keen rifle shot and winner of the first prize at the Officers' Competition, Salisbury Plain Rifle Meeting, in 1914.

CAPTAIN MARK HAGGARD, 2nd BATTN. THE WELSH REGIMENT,

born in 1876, was the son of the late Bazett Michael Haggard, of Kirby Cane, Norfolk, and of Mrs. Lofthouse, of Shipdham and Hemsby, Norfolk. He was a nephew of Sir W. D. Haggard and of Sir Rider Haggard, and was educated at Trinity Hall, Cambridge, where he obtained the degree of B.A. He served with the Cyclist Section, Inns of Court, R.V., C.I.V., and in the South African War with that Corps in 1900, receiving the Queen's medal with four clasps. Subsequently he served with the Welsh Regiment in India and South Africa. For the latter services he received the South African medal with four clasps.

In May, 1910, he was appointed Adjutant of the Welsh Regiment (Territorial) at Cardiff, and became Captain in the Welsh Regiment on the 1st January, 1911.

He was wounded when leading a charge at Chivy in the Battle of the Aisne, and died of his wounds on the 15th September, 1914.

Captain Haggard was fond of football, polo, and boxing, having been a lightweight boxer at Cambridge and in the Army. He married, on the 15th October, 1913, Elizabeth, elder daughter of Colonel Edwards Vaughan, of Rheola, South Wales.

LIEUTENANT CHARLES RODERICK HAIGH, ADJUTANT 2nd BATTN. THE QUEEN'S (ROYAL WEST SURREY REGIMENT),

who was born on the 3rd September, 1888, was the elder son of the late Mr. Arthur Elam Haigh, M.A., Fellow and Tutor of Corpus Christi College, Oxford, and a nephew of Mr. and Mrs. G. T. Pilcher, Godalming.

He was educated at the Oxford Preparatory School, at Winchester College, where he won an exhibition; and at Corpus Christi College, Oxford, where he took the B.A. degree.

He was given a commission as a University candidate in the Queen's (Royal West Surrey Regiment) in February, 1911, becoming Lieutenant in April, 1912, and was gazetted Adjutant of his battalion in January, 1914. He was killed near Ypres on the 7th November, 1914, while " gallantly leading a charge against overwhelming odds."

CAPTAIN ARTHUR GORDON HALL, 2nd BATTN. BEDFORDSHIRE REGT.,

eldest son of Edward Hall, Esq., coffee planter, of Santaveri, Mysore, and Mrs. Edward Hall, both now residing at 17, Southfields Road, Eastbourne, was born on the 20th November, 1879, at " Shimogah," in the Province of Mysore, a Native State of India.

Educated at Bradfield College, Berks, where he was good at school games, he first joined the Militia, and through it the Bedfordshire Regiment in 1899, becoming Lieutenant in 1900, and obtaining his company in December, 1906. In 1909 he was appointed Adjutant of his battalion. After serving at the depot of his regiment he was with his battalion in Gibraltar, Bermuda, and South Africa during the Boer War from 1899–1902, being employed with the Mounted Infantry. He was present at operations in the Orange Free State and in the Orange River Colony, including action at Colesberg. For his services he was mentioned in Despatches ("London Gazette," 10th September, 1901), and received the Queen's and the King's medals, each with two clasps.

In the Great War he was shot by a stray bullet at Gheluvelt, Flanders, in the Battle of Ypres, on the 26th October, 1914. The following account of his death was furnished to his relatives : " He was waiting with his company, in support at the time, having just come down from a château close by, and had sent a junior officer to the rear to ask for the orders of the day. While looking through his glasses to locate snipers he was himself shot by one in the neck, and fell at once without any pain. The officer who had gone for orders found Captain Hall dead on his return and had him buried, with great reverence, in the trench in which he fell at Gheluvelt. He was much beloved by his brother officers and men. An officer of much ability was lost to the Army by his death."

Captain Hall was a member of the Junior Naval and Military Club, fond of sport, especially polo (in which he excelled), shooting, and fishing. He played football for his regiment, taking part in the final for the Army Football Cup in 1907. When in the Mounted Infantry at Bordon he was in the winning polo team in the Inter-Company Tournament of 1905, and in 1909 was in the winning team of the Gibraltar Polo Club Open Tournament. In South Africa he captained the team which won the Polo Cup presented by Lord Gladstone in a handicap tournament at Johannesburg.

CAPTAIN BURTON HOWARD HALL, 98th INFANTRY, INDIAN ARMY,

who was killed in action in East Africa on the 2nd November, 1914, was the younger son of the Rev. S. Howard Hall, M.A., Rector of Sproatley and Chaplain, 1st class (T.F.) 5th Battalion Duke of Wellington's West Riding Regiment.

He was educated at Haileybury and the R.M.C., Sandhurst, and passed for the Indian Army, being gazetted as unattached 2nd Lieutenant in January, 1901, and becoming 2nd Lieutenant in the Yorkshire Regiment in March of the same year. He was promoted Lieutenant in the Yorkshire Regiment in February, 1904, and in the following May was transferred to the Indian Army, in which he became Captain in January, 1910.

LIEUTENANT GERALD PERCY HALL, 2nd BATTN. HIGHLAND LIGHT INFANTRY,

son of Mr. and Mrs. Hall, of Glenmervyn, Glanmire, County Cork, was born there on the 11th February, 1894, and was educated at Clifton College.

He received his commission in August, 1914, and was killed near Ypres on the 13th November, 1914.

Lieutenant Hall was fond of all sport, especially hunting, shooting, and fishing.

CAPTAIN JOHN ALEXANDER HALLIDAY, 11th HUSSARS,

son of the late John Halliday, of Chicklade House, Salisbury, was born in London on the 10th April, 1875. He was educated at Harrow, where, in 1893, he was in the School Cricket XI, in 1892–93 in the Football XI, won the second prize for heavy-weight boxing in the Public Schools' Competition in 1893, and the first prize for the same in 1894. He then went to Trinity College, Cambridge,

where he won the hammer-throwing prize at the Inter-'Varsity Sports in 1897.

Captain Halliday joined the 11th Hussars in March, 1898, becoming Lieutenant in March, 1900, and obtaining his troop in March, 1905. He took part in the South African War in 1901 on special service, and afterwards on the Staff, as signalling officer. He was present at operations in the Transvaal, Orange River and Cape Colonies, receiving the Queen's medal with five clasps. From April, 1908, to February, 1911, he was Adjutant of his regiment, and from March, 1911, to February, 1914, Adjutant of the Leicestershire Yeomanry.

In the Great War he was with his regiment during the retirement from Mons, and was fatally wounded at Messines on the 31st October, dying from the effects in the Duchess of Westminster's Hospital at Le Touquet on the 13th November, 1914.

Captain Halliday, who was a member of the Cavalry Club and of the M.C.C. and I Zingari, was well known in the hunting field in Ireland, where he hunted for twelve consecutive seasons.

LIEUTENANT HUBERT JAMES TUDOR HAMER, 108th INFANTRY, INDIAN ARMY, attd. 101st GRENADIERS,

born at Glan-yr-afon Hall, Oswestry, Shropshire, on the 12th February, 1883, was the son of the late John Parry Hamer, J.P., formerly of the 8th (the King's) Regiment, and of Mrs. Hamer. Two of his brothers are serving:
Captain J. L. P.
Hamer, M.A. Oxon, J.P., in the 9th King's Shropshire Light Infantry: and Flag-Lieutenant-Commander R. L. Hamer, R.N.

He was educated privately, and in September, 1902, he received a commission as 2nd Lieutenant in the 4th Battalion Royal Welsh Fusiliers, and in 1904 enlisted in a Regular battalion of that regiment, serving in the ranks for three years.

In August, 1907, he received a commission in the King's Liverpool Regiment, and was transferred to the Indian Army in February, 1909, becoming Lieutenant in November of that year. In 1911 he was shooting in Somaliland and Abyssinia, and procured many fine heads, some of which are on loan to the Junior Army and Navy Club, of which he was a member, and were noticed and much admired by the late Field-Marshal Earl Roberts shortly before the latter's death. He was also a hockey and polo player.

He was killed in action at Tanga, German East Africa, the following account having been received from the India Office :—

" As an important German railway terminus was reported to be weakly held, a force was sent from British East Africa to seize it.   On the evening of the 2nd November one-and-a-half battalions were landed within two miles of the place, and at once advanced.   This small force became heavily engaged just outside the town, but as the enemy were in much superior strength it was compelled to fall back and await reinforcements.

" At 11 a.m. on the 4th the attack was renewed. When within eight hundred yards of the position the troops engaged came under very heavy fire.   On the left flank, in spite of heavy casualties, the 101st Grenadiers actually entered the town and crossed bayonets with the enemy. The North Lancashire Regiment and Kashmir Rifles on the right pushed on in support under very heavy fire, and also reached the town, but found themselves opposed by tiers of fire from the houses, and were eventually compelled to fall back to cover, five hundred yards from the enemy's position.

" The losses were so heavy and the position so strong that it was considered useless to renew the attack, and the force re-embarked and returned to its base to prepare for future operations.   From recent reports just received the total casualties in this unsuccessful operation were seven hundred and ninety-five, including one hundred and forty-one British officers and men.   The wounded are mostly doing well, and many are convalescent.   The above casualties were included in the statement recently made by Lord Crewe in the House of Lords.

" There is no information available other than that contained in the above statement."

An officer of his regiment gave the following additional details, writing from Mombassa on the 10th November, 1914 :—

" The regiment was widely extended, and we were on opposite flanks, so that I can only give you hearsay news about your son ; and, as after the engagement—which was extremely heavy—we had to retire, we were unable to recover our dead, who were buried by the Germans (who treated our wounded with the greatest courtesy and kindness).   I could not see his body.

" We lost seven British and six native officers killed, but one of the native officers who was with your son escaped, wounded.   He tells me your son was leading his men on when he was shot in the throat and died instantaneously.

" We all feel his loss exceedingly, as a more perfect gentleman and better soldier one could not find, and everyone who knew him liked him. I never met anyone who had not always the highest praise for him.

" Keen in his work and keen in his play, he was the very ideal of the best type of British officer, and his loss to us is indeed irreparable.

" In these few lines I am not giving only my opinion, but that of all his brother officers, both in this regiment and in our own."

The Lieutenant-Colonel of his own regiment— the 108th Infantry—also wrote saying :—" He was not only popular with all ranks, but a very able and zealous officer, and it is only a few weeks ago that the good work done by him in the training of the regimental signallers was the subject of favourable comment in regimental orders.   As his Commanding Officer, I always found him keen on his work and honest and straightforward in all his actions ; in fact, a true officer and a true gentleman, whose loss will be deeply felt by the regiment."

CAPTAIN LORD ARTHUR JOHN HAMILTON, attd. 1st BATTN. IRISH GUARDS (SPECIAL RESERVE), DEPUTY MASTER OF HIS MAJESTY'S HOUSEHOLD,

was included in the War Office monthly casualty list published in February, 1915, as " unofficially reported killed," no date being given.   He had been officially reported as missing, but later in the same year it was heard from a German officer that he had been killed early in September, 1914.

Lord Arthur Hamilton was the second son of the second Duke of Abercorn, and was born on the 20th August, 1883, and educated at Wellington, where he was in the Benson from 1898–1900.

After serving with the embodied Militia for seven or eight months, he received a commission as 2nd Lieutenant in the Irish Guards in December, 1901, becoming Lieutenant in August, 1904, and Captain in December, 1909.   Retiring from active service, he joined the Special Reserve as Captain in March, 1913, and was appointed Deputy Master of the Household in that year.

CAPTAIN CECIL FIFE PRYCE HAMILTON, 1st BATTN. SCOTS GUARDS,

who died at Ypres on the 27th October, 1914, of wounds received in action, was the only child of Mr. and Mrs. Pryce Hamilton, of Seaford, Ryde, and Villa Valetta, Nice.   He was born on the 9th October, 1879, and, after serving with the embodied Militia for nearly a year, he was gazetted to the Scots Guards in May, 1901.

He served in the South African War, being present at operations in Cape Colony and the Orange River Colony in 1900, receiving the Queen's medal with three clasps. He became Lieutenant in June, 1903, and from October, 1907, to November, 1910, he was Adjutant at the School of Instruction for Volunteer Infantry (later Territorial Force) Officers at Chelsea Barracks.

In February, 1911, he was appointed Regimental Adjutant Scots Guards, and was promoted Captain in January, 1912.

MAJOR-GENERAL HUBERT ION WETHERALL HAMILTON, C.V.O., C.B., D.S.O., p.s.c.,

who was killed in action on the 14th October, 1914, and who, when the Great War broke out, was commanding the IIIrd Division Field Troops (Regular) at Bulford, was the third son of Major-General Henry Meade Hamilton, and a brother of General Sir Bruce Hamilton, K.C.B., K.C.V.O.

He was born on the 27th June, 1861, and entered the 2nd Foot (now the Royal West Surrey Regiment) in 1880, and was Adjutant of his battalion from 1886 to 1890. Major-General Hamilton, who was a Staff College graduate, had seen much active service, and held several Staff appointments. He served in the Burmese Expedition, 1886–88, receiving the medal with two clasps. He was A.D.C. from 1896–97 to the Major-General, 3rd Infantry Brigade, Aldershot, and to the Lieutenant-General, Infantry Division, South Africa, from 1899–1900. He was with the Nile Expeditions of 1897 and 1898, including the Battles of Atbara and Khartoum, for the first of which he received the Egyptian medal with clasp, and for the second was mentioned twice in Despatches, and had two additional clasps.

From 1897–9 he was employed with the Egyptian Army, in the latter year as D.A.G. in operations in the first advance against the Khalifa, receiving the D.S.O. and an additional clasp to his Egyptian medal. He was on the Staff as D.A.A.G., A.A.G., and Military Secretary to the General Officer Commanding-in-Chief the Forces in South Africa from January, 1900, to June 1902, during the South African War, being present at operations in the Orange Free State, including operations at Paardeberg, in the Transvaal, including actions near Johannesburg and Pretoria ; at further operations in the Transvaal, Orange River Colony, Cape Colony,

and on the Zululand frontier of Natal. He was mentioned three times in Despatches and promoted to a half-pay Lieutenant-Colonelcy. He also received the Queen's medal with four clasps and the King's medal with two clasps. During the year 1902 he was employed specially at the headquarters of the Army, and as Military Secretary to the Commander-in-Chief, East Indies. In June of the same year he was appointed A.D.C. to the King.

From 1906–09 he served as Brigadier-General 7th Brigade, Southern Command, and Major-General on the General Staff in the Mediterranean. In January, 1911, he was appointed G.O.C., North Midland Division, Northern Command, and in June, 1914, to the command at Bulford.

In the Great War Major-General Hamilton commanded a Division. The following account of his death was published in "The Times" as given by a distinguished officer and personal friend :—

" General Hamilton was standing with a group of others in a covered place when a shell burst about one hundred yards off, and he was hit on the temple by a bullet and killed on the spot. No one else was touched. It was a fine death," adds the writer, " but I know how he would feel that he was taken before his work was done. All day we could not get near the place where he was lying owing to heavy shell fire, but at dusk we went out and carried him to a little church near by. Just as we got there the attack began violently, so that we could not hear the Chaplain's voice for musketry and pom-pom fire close by. Flashes from the guns lit us up now and then, but no other light than a tiny torch for the parson to see to read by. He was doing so splendidly that it was cruel luck that he should have been the one taken out of the group."
Major-General Hamilton was mentioned in Sir John French's Despatch of the 14th January, 1915.

A brass tablet to his memory is placed in the chancel of St. Peter's Church, Marchington, Uttoxeter.

MAJOR the Honble. LESLIE D'HENIN HAMILTON, M.V.O., 1st BATTN. COLDSTREAM GUARDS,

was killed in action on the 29th October, 1914.

He was the third son of the first Baron Hamilton of Dalzell, County Lanark, and was heir-presumptive to the title.

He obtained his commission in March, 1893, and

became Lieutenant in April, 1897. He took part in the South African War, being present at the advance on Kimberley, including actions at Belmont, Enslin, Modder River, and Magersfontein, and at operations in Cape Colony, receiving the Queen's medal with four clasps.
He was promoted Captain in February, 1901, and Major in January, 1910.

CAPTAIN MERVYN JAMES HAMILTON, 1st BATTN. GORDON HIGHLANDERS (RESERVE OF OFFICERS),

of Cornacassa, County Monaghan, who died of wounds on the 28th November, 1914, was the only son of the late Mr. Dacre Hamilton, of Cornacassa.

He was born on the 12th December, 1879, and was educated at Winchester College. While there he saved a boy from drowning, and was awarded the Royal Humane Society's certificate.
He joined the Lancashire Fusiliers from the Militia in May, 1899, being promoted Lieutenant in February, 1900, and served in the South African War, during which he was Adjutant of a Mounted Infantry Battalion from April to December, 1901. He was present at operations in the Orange River Colony, July to November, 1900, including actions at Bethlehem, Wittebergen, and Witpoort, and at operations in the Orange River Colony till May, 1902. For his services he was mentioned in Despatches ("London Gazette," 10th September, 1901), and received the Queen's medal with two clasps and the King's medal with two clasps.
He was promoted Captain in November, 1903, and from August, 1905, to October, 1907, was employed with the Egyptian Army. He was transferred to the Gordon Highlanders in May, 1908, and retired from the active list in May, 1914, passing to the Reserve of Officers, from which he was called up on the outbreak of the war. He was at first appointed Assistant Provost-Marshal at Plymouth, but in response to repeated applications to be sent to his old regiment received his orders to proceed to the front in October, 1914, joining his battalion on the 25th of that month.
He was wounded in the head and hand by shell on the 17th November in a dug-out, and was moved to a convent at Popperinghe, where an operation was performed in the hope of saving his life, but he gradually lost consciousness and died on the 28th November, 1914.
He made himself very popular with his men, always showing keen personal interest in their circumstances and welfare, though at the same time requiring strict attention to duty.
The following account of the manner in which he received his wounds was given by a Sergeant of his company : " On the morning of the 17th November the enemy started to shell a wood in which the company was resting about a mile and a half behind the main trenches. Captain Hamilton and another officer were in a dug-out, when after the burst of a shell someone said, ' The Captain is struck!' On going to him it was found that, while his companion had got off with a bruising and temporary suffocation, Captain Hamilton was wounded in the head. The company stretcher-bearers were called up, and he talked sensibly while being put on the stretcher. On the Sergeant shaking hands with him his last words were, ' Stick it, " C " Company!'"
He was a keen sportsman and shot big game, once securing by himself at fifty yards a very fine lion. Captain Hamilton married, in 1909, Hildred Laura, daughter of General the Hon. B. Ward, C.B., of Staplecross, Christchurch, Hants, and left a daughter, Phœbe Maxwell, born 1911.

2nd LIEUTENANT GILBERT PHILIP HAMMOND, 2nd BATTN. KING'S OWN SCOTTISH BORDERERS,

eldest son of the late Frederick Hammond, Esq., of " The Bank," Newmarket, and Florence Amy Holland, " The Cottage," Finborough Stowmarket, whose name appeared in the first list of British losses issued by the War Office on the 1st
September, 1914, was killed in action at the age of twenty-two.
He obtained his commission in his regiment in December, 1912, from the Special Reserve.

LIEUTENANT RALPH ESCOTT HANCOCK, D.S.O., 2nd BATTN. DEVONSHIRE REGT.,

was born at Llandaff, South Wales, on the 20th December, 1887, the son of Mr. and Mrs. Frank Hancock, of Ford, Wiveliscombe, Somerset.
He was educated at Connaught House Preparatory School, Portmore, Wey-

mouth, and at Rugby, where he played for the 1st Cricket XI in 1905 and 1906, and from which he passed direct into the R.M.C., Sandhurst, in August, 1906. He was gazetted to the 2nd Battalion Devonshire Regiment, then stationed at Devonport, in January, 1908, becoming Lieutenant in February, 1911, and served with it at Crete, Malta, and Alexandria from 1909–12. He was then at the depot, Exeter, for two years, and on the 30th August, 1914, left with a draft to reinforce the 1st Battalion in France.

During the war he was awarded the D.S.O., the following being the official record from the " London Gazette " of 1st December, 1914 :—
" Lieutenant Ralph Escott Hancock, 1st Battalion Devonshire Regiment, on October 23rd displayed conspicuous gallantry in leaving his trench under very heavy fire, and going back some sixty yards over absolutely bare ground to pick up Corporal Warwick, who had fallen whilst coming up with a party of reinforcements. Lieutenant Hancock conveyed this non-commissioned officer to the cover of a haystack, and then returned to his trench. (Since killed in action.)"
He was killed on the 29th October, 1914, and was subsequently mentioned in Sir John French's Despatch of the 14th January, 1915.

Lieutenant Hancock was a good athlete and rider. At Malta he played in the polo team that won the regimental cup, and captained the Army- polo team v. the Navy. He also won several prizes for shooting. He played cricket and football for the County of Somerset ; won the East Devon Hunt heavyweight Point-to-Point in 1913 and 1914 on horses taught and trained by himself ; and was a well-known follower of the West Somerset and East Devon Foxhounds.

Lieutenant Hancock married Mary Hamilton, younger daughter of the Rev. P. P. Broadmead, of Olands, Milverton, Somerset, in September, 1913, and left one son, Patrick Frank, born June, 1914.

CAPTAIN ALLAN HUMPHREY HARDEN, 2nd BATTN. OXFORDSHIRE AND BUCKINGHAMSHIRE LIGHT

INFANTRY, was born at Ealing, Middlesex, on the 23rd March, 1881, and was the son of the late Lieutenant-Colonel J. E. Harden, 101st and 109th Regiments (since named Royal Munster Fusiliers and Leinster Regiment), being a grandson of the late Judge Harden, of Cheshire, and, on his mother's side, of the late General Atkinson, Madras Army.

He was educated at Dulwich College, and joined the Oxford and Bucks Light Infantry from the Militia on the 5th January, 1901, becoming Lieutenant in September, 1903, and Captain in January, 1910. From 1908 to 1912 Captain Harden was Adjutant to the 6th (Territorial) Battalion South Staffordshire Regiment. He served throughout the South African War, being present at operations in the Orange River Colony and Cape Colony, receiving the Queen's medal and King's medal, each with two clasps.

In the Great War, during the operations round Ypres, Captain Harden was, on the 21st October, 1914, in command of his company in extended position in close contact with the enemy. He was taking orders from his Colonel when he was shot through the head by a rifle bullet. His body was carried to a farm building close by, which, being shortly afterwards set on fire by the enemy's shells, was totally consumed, and so formed a funeral pyre for a brave soldier. Captain Harden, for his gallantry in this war, was mentioned in Field-Marshal Sir John French's Despatch of the 14th January, 1915.

His widow received several highly appreciative letters of sympathy, showing the high esteem in which her late husband was held.

Lieutenant-Colonel Davies, commanding the battalion, wrote : " Your husband's death is a great loss to the regiment. He was one of the best company commanders we had. . . . I liked him so much personally. His death was quite instantaneous. I was talking to him at the moment that he was shot, and I feel sure that he felt nothing. We have lost a very good soldier, and all of us feel much for you in your sorrow."

Lieutenant-Colonel Waterhouse, commanding the Territorial Regiment, with which he had served, wrote : " His great example will be before us to try and follow. He was one of the finest men I ever knew."

A junior officer of the battalion, who had been with him throughout the war, wrote : " He was never downhearted in the depressing days of that retirement from Mons, and was so brave and capable. . . . I shall always be proud to have served under him."

A Major of his battalion said : " Your husband's death is a very real loss to all ranks of the regiment."

Captain Harden married, in July, 1905, Daisy, only daughter of the late Captain George Thomas Scott (Scots Greys) and Mrs. G. T. Scott, 67, Egerton Gardens, London, S.W., and grand-daughter of the late John Howe, Esq., J.P., D.L., Ballycross House, County Wexford, and a cousin of the Right Honourable the Lord Muskerry, Springfield Castle, Drumcollogher, County Limerick, and left a son and a daughter.

LIEUTENANT ARTHUR DENNIS HARDING, 4th (attd. 1st) BATTN. GLOUCESTERSHIRE REGIMENT,

who died on the 30th October, 1914, at the age of twenty-two, of wounds received on the previous day, was the only son of the late Major A. Harding, R.A.M.C., and of Mrs. Harding, and a grandson of Major - General Worthy Bennett, R.M.L.I. He joined the Gloucestershire Regiment in September, 1912, and was promoted Lieutenant in August, 1914.

2nd LIEUTENANT JACK MAYNARD HARDING, 1st BATTN. QUEEN'S OWN (ROYAL WEST KENT REGIMENT),

son of Lieutenant-Colonel Maynard Ffolliott Harding, commanding 69th Punjabis, was born at Berhampore, India, on the 4th October, 1894.

Educated at Felsted School, he represented his school for gymnastics at Aldershot, and for musketry at Bisley. He proceeded to the R.M.C., Sandhurst, where he was in the gymnasium team, 1913, and won his Blue. From the R.M.C. he received his commission in the West Kent Regiment in August, 1914, after the outbreak of the war. After spending two weeks at the depot he joined his battalion in France on the 11th September, and was killed in action on the 26th October, 1914, at the Battle of Ypres, while gallantly encouraging his men to hold a trench which was under a heavy continuous fire of high-explosive shells.

LIEUTENANT ROBERT DENIS STEWART HARDING, 4th (attd. 1st) BATTN. BEDFORDSHIRE REGIMENT,

who was killed in action near Ypres on the 7th November, 1914, aged twenty-eight, was the only son of Mr. and Mrs. S. G. Harding, of 15, Lowndes Square, S.W.

He was educated at Harrow (Rendall's, 1889 - 1903) and Christ Church, and

joined the 4th Battalion Bedfordshire Regiment in 1912, becoming Lieutenant in March, 1913 ; on war breaking out he offered his services and was attached for duty to the 1st Battalion. The following account of the circumstances attending his death was published in the " Harrovian War Supplement " for December, 1914 :—
" His Captain writes : ' The enemy had broken through the line of trenches held by a battalion on our left, and its break caused a part of our trenches to be vacated also. Our company was in reserve, and we formed up, and brought off an entirely successful counter-attack, driving the enemy back, killing many, and capturing twenty-five prisoners. It was in this counter-attack that Harding fell, leading his men up a lightly wooded hill. I did not see him fall, but missed him when we got to the ridge, and on going back found him quite dead. Death had evidently been instantaneous. I had formed a very high opinion of his gallantry and coolness. I could rely on him always, and he had gained the confidence of his men, though he had only been with his company about a month. He was always bright and cheery, and it was a real pleasure to have his company on the line of march or in the trenches.' "
He was a member of the Bath Club.

LIEUTENANT the Honble. EDWARD CHARLES HARDINGE, D.S.O., 15th (THE KING'S) HUSSARS,

was the elder son of Charles Baron Hardinge of Penshurst, P.C., G.C.B., G.C.S.I., G.C.M.G., G.C.I.E., G.C.V.O., I.S.O., Viceroy and Governor - General of India, and was born at Constantinople on the 3rd May, 1892. He was a nephew of Viscount Hardinge, A.D.C., and of Lord Alington

Lieutenant Hardinge was educated at Wellington College, and while there was a Page of Honour of His late Majesty King Edward VII, and afterwards went to the R.M.C., Sandhurst, receiving his commission in the 15th Hussars in September, 1911, in December of which year he was Honorary A.D.C. to the Viceroy during the Durbar. He joined his regiment in South Africa in January, 1912, and became Lieutenant in August, 1914.

Lieutenant Hardinge rode with distinction in the International Horse Show at Olympia, 1914, winning full marks in the London to Aldershot ride. He was a member of the Cavalry Club, a very keen rider to hounds, and won the Subalterns' Point-to-Point Race at the regimental races in January, 1914.

He served with his regiment in the Great War, and died on the 18th December, 1914, from blood-poisoning caused by a very severe wound in the right arm, received on the 27th August, near Le Cateau, eight bullets from a machine gun fracturing the bone. He had already done good work before being wounded, for which he was awarded the D.S.O., His Majesty the King-Emperor graciously notifying the award to Lord Hardinge in the following telegram :— " I have had great pleasure in conferring the Distinguished Service Order on your son for ability and gallantry in reconnaissance under great difficulty and machine-gun fire on three successive days, when he was severely wounded. Glad to say he is progressing satisfactorily."

The following details of two conspicuous acts of great bravery and gallantry by Lieutenant the Hon. E.C. Hardinge have been recorded, the latter being the occasion on which he received his wound.

(1) On August 23rd, about 9.30 p.m., Lieutenant Hardinge was sent out from Rouveroy on a most difficult and dangerous night reconnaissance towards Binche, to ascertain movements of the Germans, of which information was very urgently needed. He succeeded in reaching the village of Estinne Hud-Mont. Having avoided Uhlan patrols, and having hidden his small patrol in a stone electric machinery building, he climbed the church tower with a sergeant, and waited for dawn to break. Whilst waiting a Uhlan patrol entered the village, and others came round it. He remained quietly in observation, and they failed to discover him or his patrol. In the early morning he was able to locate German batteries in position south-west of Binche, a brigade of cavalry moving due west from that place, and their infantry massing near a wood south of it. His difficulty was then to get away, being surrounded, but fortunately another patrol, under Lieutenant Nicolson, 15th Hussars, seeing his predicament, came to his assistance by firing on the Uhlans, and then by withdrawing drew them off and so enabled Lieutenant Hardinge to get through with his most valuable information. He was very highly complimented and noted for reward.

(2) On August 27th two troops (Lieutenant Hardinge's being one) were sent out at 4 a.m. from Oisy on rearguard work, his troop reconnoitring and observing on the right front, and right of the rearguard position being held. German columns were reported advancing, and about 10.30 a.m. the patrols were driven in by German infantry. The attack gradually developed, and shortly before 1 p.m. became very heavy, and the flanking company of the Royal Munster Fusiliers, near Bergues, was in difficulties. Lieutenant Hardinge, with his troop, was sent to their assistance, and came into action on their left, opposite three machine guns, which he located and tried to silence. A

fourth then came into action, outflanking him, and, causing some casualities, forced him to retire. Realising that the position of the Munsters was untenable (who had to hold on to prevent the rest of the battalion being cut off) unless this machine gun was put out of action, he led a few men up again most gallantly to try and capture it. Whilst trying to locate it exactly he had to stand up and use his glasses, and so became exposed to its fire. He was very severely wounded, his arm being badly shattered. After having it temporarily bound up, he told his men to hold on as long as they could, and to help the Munsters out, and then quite calmly walked back to where his horses were, and was then taken into the ambulance.

For these actions he was awarded the D.S.O.

The above details were confirmed by Major Pilkington, of the 15th Hussars, who was Lieutenant Hardinge's squadron leader, and endorsed by Major Courage, second in command of the squadron at the time.

2nd LIEUTENANT FREDERICK McMAHON HARDMAN, SPECIAL RESERVE, attd. 4th BATTN. THE ROYAL FUSILIERS (CITY OF LONDON REGIMENT), who was killed in action between the 25th and 27th October, 1914, at the age of twenty-four, was the only son of the late Captain Hardman, the Royal Dragoons, who died for his country in the South African War, and of  Mrs. Hardman, Castleton, Sherborne, Dorset. He was a grandson of the late General Sir Thomas McMahon, Bart., C.B.

He had only joined the Special Reserve of his regiment in July, 1912.

LIEUTENANT VICTOR HARRIOTT HARDY, 1st BATTN. YORK AND LANCASTER REGIMENT, attd. 1st BATTN. LINCOLNSHIRE REGT., who was killed in action on the 27th October, 1914, at Neuve Chapelle, was the youngest son of the late Captain Harmer Hardy, who served with the 97th Regiment in the Crimea, and was afterwards in the 18th Hussars, and of Mrs. Arthur

Nightingale, of West Hill, Sandown, Isle of Wight. Lieutenant Hardy belonged to a family of which many members have done, and are doing, memorable service for their country. His grandfather was one of a small body of Englishmen who held the Fort of Roseau, Dominica, West Indies, in 1804, when the French landed, until relieved by the British fleet, under Nelson. His uncle, General Fred. Hardy, C.B., is Colonel of the York and Lancaster Regiment, and has several sons and sons-in-law serving in the King's forces. Great-uncles of his served in the Afghan wars at Bhurtpoor and in the Mutiny, all of whom have descendants now serving.

Lieutenant Hardy was born on the 26th June, 1887, and was educated at Farnborough Park, and at Eastman's Royal Naval Academy. He was gazetted to the York and Lancaster Regiment from the Special Reserve in March, 1909, and was at Blackdown with the 2nd Battalion of the regiment until September of the same year, when he sailed for India to join the 1st Battalion at Quetta. After three years he came home on leave, having become Lieutenant in October, 1911. He returned to India in September, 1912, and after serving another year there he was invalided home, his health having been affected by the climate. He passed his examination for promotion to Captain in 1914.

Having recovered his health he was about to rejoin his regiment in India when the war broke out, and he at once rejoined at home, being first sent to the regimental depot at Pontefract, afterwards being posted for duty to the 6th Battalion York and Lancaster Regiment at Belton Park, near Grantham. Later he was sent to the front with a draft of the 1st Lincolnshire Regiment.

It is believed he was killed in an attack on a strong German position across a tract of open country under heavy fire, the attack being entirely successful, the Lincolnshires driving the Germans out of their trenches at the point of the bayonet. Lieutenant Hardy was reported to have been buried at Neuve Chapelle, but owing to another officer's effects having been sent home in mistake for his, there was for a time some doubt as to his death, it being hoped he might have been a prisoner of war. It is now feared the report received from the Adjutant of the battalion that he was killed on the 27th October must be accepted as correct.

While a boy Lieutenant Hardy won the first prize at Sandown in a demonstration to celebrate King Edward's Coronation in 1902. He was keen on sport of all kinds, especially riding, and was very fond of animals. While in the Reserve he secured the Regimental Cup in the officers' races, and when a 2nd Lieutenant carried the King's colours on the occasion of the visit of King George and Queen Mary to India for the Coronation Durbar.

CAPTAIN HARRY VIVIAN HARE, 2nd BATTN. DURHAM LIGHT INFANTRY,

born at Folkestone on the 10th June, 1881, was the son of Admiral the Hon. Richard Hare and grandson of the second Earl of Listowel, being thus a nephew of the present Earl of Listowel.

He was educated at Harrow, and after passing through the R.M.C., Sandhurst, received his commission in the Durham Light Infantry in August, 1900, becoming Lieutenant in February, 1902, and obtaining his company in March, 1912. From 1911 to 1913 he was Adjutant of his battalion.

Captain Hare was killed on the 20th September, 1914, while leading his company in an attack just above Troyon.

He was a keen all-round sportsman, a good tennis player, and in the hockey team of his regiment when they won the Army Cup in 1911. His favourite sport, however, was hunting, and he was a very fine point-to-point rider, winning several races on his own and other people's horses.

Captain Hare married Ellen L. M., daughter of the late Sir Edward Hudson-Kinahan, Bart., and left two children : Richard George Windham, born July, 1910 ; and Emily Lavender, born April, 1912.

LIEUT. HERBERT ANDRZEJ BIERNACKI HARINGTON, 3rd (attd. 1st) BATTN. HAMPSHIRE REGIMENT, was the only son of the late Herbert Septimus Harington, Director-General of Railway Construction in India, and a grandson of the late Colonel Thomas Lowth Harington, 5th Light Cavalry, who had the medals for Cabul, Sobraon, Gujerat, and Chillianwallah, where he was wounded.

Lieutenant Harington was born at Doonga Gali, Murree Hills, Punjab, India, on the 3rd August, 1888. He inherited his father's ability as a mathematician. He also, even as a boy, showed great mechanical and scientific talent, and studied practical chemistry and electricity. After completing his education, which was carried out privately, because he was rather delicate—though eventually attaining over six feet in height, and being broad in proportion —he served on the Indian State Railways with his father for three years, and also surveyed the Shan States Railway in Burma and the Kyber Pass.

He joined the 3rd Battalion Hampshire Regiment in September, 1911, being promoted

Lieutenant in June, 1913. He was attached to the 1st Battalion for active service, and went to the front in the autumn of 1914. He was in several small engagements, and was finally wounded at St. Yves, between Ypres and Armentières, on the 31st October. Writing home, he made light of his wound, but he died on the 9th November, 1914, at Alexandra Hospital, Cosham, Portsmouth.

He was wounded in the left hip in the morning, and having been taken out of the trench it is reported that he struggled back to rally his men, and even after being put on the stretcher tried to get back, saying his duty was with his men.

Lieutenant Harington was a good rider and polo player, and keen on all sports, and when with the 1st Battalion of his regiment at Aldershot helped to train it for the cross-country race, which it won. He was a great favourite in Simla when he was in India.

CAPTAIN REGINALD WICKHAM HARLAND, attd. 1st BATTN. HAMPSHIRE REGIMENT,

who was killed in action on the 30th October, 1914, was the seventh son of the Rev. Albert A. and Mrs. Harland, Harefield Vicarage, Middlesex.

He was born on the 10th November, 1883, and was educated at Wellington, being the youngest of three brothers who were at the same school, the second of whom was killed in the South African War. He left in 1902, and entered the R.M.C., Sandhurst, where he won the prize for battalion drill. He was gazetted to the Hampshire Regiment in October, 1903, becoming Lieutenant in December, 1905, and Captain in August, 1911.

CAPTAIN EDWARD CHARLES STAF-FORD-KING-HARMAN, IRISH GUARDS,

of Rockingham Ireland who was killed in action on the 6th November, 1914, was the eldest son of Sir Thomas and Lady Stafford, and grandson of the late Colonel the Right Honble. Edward King-Harman, M.P. He was born on the 13th April, 1881, and

was educated at Stone House, Broadstairs, and subsequently at Eton and the R.M.C., Sandhurst. At Eton he was for two years a member of the Shooting VIII. He was gazetted to the Irish Guards in September, 1911, and was promoted Lieutenant in June, 1912. He was a keen sportsman, hunted his own pack of harriers in Ireland, and played polo for his regiment, and was a good shot with both rifle and gun.

He went to Flanders in September, 1914, and was reported missing after the fighting at Klein Zillebeke on the 6th November, 1914, when his company, under the command of Lord John Hamilton, was holding the forward trench, and it was surrounded and cut off from the main body. It is reported that he and Lord John Hamilton were killed while defending this trench against an overwhelming force of the enemy.

Captain Stafford-King-Harman was promoted to the temporary rank of Captain, dating from the 15th November, there having been some doubt as to his death.

He married, in July, 1914, Olive, only daughter of Captain Henry Pakenham Mahon, of Strokestown Park, Ireland, and 33, Pont Street, London, S.W., and left one daughter, Lettice Mary, born April, 1915.

Captain Stafford-King-Harman was a member of the Carlton, the Guards', and Boodle's Clubs; and of the Kildare Street Club, Dublin.

MAJOR GEORGE MALCOLM NIXON HARMAN, D.S.O., 2nd BATTN. RIFLE BRIGADE,

who was killed in action on 27th November, 1914, was the eldest son of the late Lieutenant-General Sir George Harman, K.C.B.

He was born in London on the 14th November, 1872; was educated at Marlborough College from 1886–90; and joined the Rifle Brigade in November, 1891. He became Lieutenant in October, 1893, and Captain in January, 1898. From 1900–04 he was employed in the Uganda Protectorate and with the King's African Rifles. He took part in 1901 in the expedition into the Lango country, being for his services mentioned in Despatches ("London Gazette," 12th September, 1902), and awarded the D.S.O. and the medal with clasp.

From 1902–04 he was employed on the Anglo-German Boundary Commission, west of Victoria Nyanza. After East Africa he served in

Malta and Alexandria with the 4th Battalion ; and, having obtained his Majority in June, 1907, he joined the 2nd Battalion in Calcutta. When war was declared the battalion was in Rawal Pindi, and was then ordered to France. Major Harman was killed by a shell at Levantie. He married, in 1913, May, eldest daughter of E. D. Jones, Esq., of Addison Road, W., and Pentower, Fishguard. He was a member of the Naval and Military Club, Piccadilly.

2nd LIEUTENANT JOHN BOWER HARMAN, 29th BATTERY, 42nd BRIGADE, ROYAL FIELD ARTILLERY,

was included in the monthly official casualty list published in October, 1914, as having been killed in action, no date being given.

He was the only son of the late Colonel J. F. Harman, R.A., of 22, Egerton Terrace, London, and was twenty-one years of age when he was killed.

He joined the R.F.A. in July, 1912.

CAPTAIN ERNEST DALE CARR-HARRIS, ROYAL ENGINEERS,

killed in action on the 3rd November, 1914, in East Africa, was born on the 14th February, 1878, and joining the Royal Engineers in June, 1899, became Lieutenant in December, 1901.

He saw active service in China, 1900, for which he received the medal with clasp, and was promoted Captain in June, 1908. When war broke out he was at the Staff College, Quetta, for which he had been specially nominated.

2nd LIEUTENANT LESLIE GEORGE HAMLYN HARRIS, 2nd BATTN. THE SHERWOOD FORESTERS (NOTTING-HAMSHIRE AND DERBYSHIRE REGT.),

of whom an obituary notice appeared in "The Times," saying that he was killed in action at Ypres on the 2nd November, 1914, at the age of nineteen, but whose name has not been included in the monthly official casualty lists, was the son of the late Major-General Noel Harris and Mrs. Noel Harris, of 13, Brechin Place, South Kensington.

He was educated at Wellington, where he was in the Picton, and was gazetted 2nd Lieutenant in the Sherwood Foresters in August, 1914.

LIEUTENANT CYRIL CAZALET HARRISON, 3rd BATTN. THE WORCESTERSHIRE REGT.,

was born in Colombo, Ceylon, on the 13th July, 1891, the son of the late Harry Cazalet and Hilda B. Harrison, and grandson of Lieutenant - General M. W. Willoughby, C.S.I., Indian Army. Educated at Dunchurch Hall, near Rugby, Uppingham, and the R.M.C., Sandhurst, he obtained his commission from the latter in the Worcestershire Regiment on the 4th March, 1911, becoming Lieutenant in August, 1914.

In the Great War, during the Battle of the Aisne, he had, with his platoon, reinforced the Irish Rifles, and, while observing and directing his men's fire from a trench, was shot through the head on the 20th September, 1914.

CAPTAIN LAURENCE GEORGE HART, 61st KING GEORGE'S OWN PIONEERS, INDIAN ARMY,

son of the late Col. Horatio Holt Hart, Royal Engineers, who lived in Kashmir, was born on the 16th August, 1877, at Sialkot. He was the nephew of Major-General Fitzroy Hart - Synnot, C.B., C.M.G., and General Sir Reginald Clare Hart, V.C., K.C.B., K.C.V.O. Captain Hart was educated at Wellington College, where he got his cap, and proved himself a good all-round athlete ; he joined the East Yorkshire Regiment from the Militia in August, 1899, becoming Lieutenant in July, 1900. He was transferred to the Indian Army in December, 1901, and took part in the Thibet Expedition, 1903–04, for which he received the medal. He was killed at the attack on Tanga, East Africa, on the 3rd November, 1914, the Lieut.-Colonel commanding the regiment giving the following account of the circumstances : " At daybreak on the 3rd November, 1914, the 13th Rajputs and three companies of the 61st K.G.O. Pioneers made an attack on Tanga. We were met by a very superior force of the enemy, and were driven back with heavy losses towards our landing place. At about 8.30 a.m. Captain Hart landed with No. 1 Double Company of the 61st K.G.O. Pioneers, and he immediately pushed forward to our assistance. This he did in a most gallant manner, leading his men to where the fight was thickest, and where help was sorely needed. In my opinion, it was his timely help in coming in where he did that prevented many of the enemy from following us up, and this saved us many more casualties. It was about 9 a.m. that he met his death at the head of his men, while holding the enemy back, and giving what remained of those under me time to collect and re-form."

Many of Captain Hart's other brother officers wrote saying that, in their opinion, Captain Hart had saved the situation and their lives.

He married Winifried Beatrice Florence Breithaupt, whose great-grandfather was wounded at the Battle of Waterloo.

CAPTAIN HUGH IRVING ST. JOHN HARTFORD, 1st BATTN. CHESHIRE REGIMENT, is believed to have been killed in action at Violaines, near La Bassée, on the 22nd October, 1914, but his name had not appeared in the monthly official casualty lists up to June, 1915. He was the only son of the late Major Irving St. John Hartford, 22nd Regiment, and grandson of the late Captain Augustus Hartford, 59th Regiment, of Portarlington, Queen's County, Ireland.

He was born on the 11th January, 1883, and joined the Cheshire Regiment in December, 1904, becoming Lieutenant in January, 1906, and being promoted Captain in September, 1914.

Captain Hartford proceeded to the Continent shortly after the outbreak of the Great War and was present with his battalion during some of the severe fighting which occurred in the earlier stages of the Campaign.

LIEUTENANT HUGH PETER HARTNOLL, 1st BATTN. WORCESTERSHIRE

REGIMENT, who was killed in action on the 12th December, 1914, near Neuve Chapelle, was the third son of Sir Henry Hartnoll, of Rangoon.

He was born on the 16th September, 1893, and joined the Worcestershire Regiment from the R.M.C., Sandhurst, in September, 1913, and was promoted Lieutenant on the 15th November, 1914.

CAPTAIN HARRY HARTWELL, 2nd BATTN. 8th GURKHA RIFLES,

born at Lucknow on the 2nd December, 1880, was the son of the late Charles Elphinstone Hartwell and grandson of the late Sir Brodrick Hartwell, Bart. His immediate ancestors achieved fame in the annals of British India. His great-grandfather, General Frederick Young, H.E.I.C.S., whose name is associated with the raising of the Sirmoor Battalion of the Gurkha Rifles, served with distinction under Lord Lake in the early part of the nineteenth century, being mentioned in Thornton's "History of the British Empire in India" in connection with the Nepaulese War. Subsequently he imported at his own expense a pack of hounds from England, planted the first potatoes grown in the Himalayas, and started the first tea plantation in India, which he surrendered to the Government on being given the choice of keeping his appointment as Political Resident *or* his plantation.

Captain Hartwell's maternal grandfather, Colonel J. Hadow Jenkins, Madras Staff Corps, served in the 44th Native Infantry, a gallant Sepoy regiment that remained loyal to England during the great Indian Mutiny of 1857. He also saw active service, and held high civil appointments in India.

Captain Hartwell was educated at Haileybury, and entered the Army from the Militia, being gazetted to the Welsh Regiment in April, 1900, and transferred to the Indian Army in 1903. He served in the Thibet Expedition, 1903, for which he received the Army medal, and also that conferred by the Chapter General of the Order of the Hospital of St. John of Jerusalem, for distinguished acts of gallantry in saving life at imminent personal risk on the occasion of the disastrous earthquake at Dhurmsala, in the Punjab.

Captain Hartwell, who had only arrived at the front on the 29th October, 1914, was killed next day near Festubert.

He was a member of the United Service Club. Captain Hartwell married Emily Maybell, second daughter of Joseph Dobbs, Coolbawn House, Castleconner, and left one daughter, Evelyn Patricia, born March, 1913.

LIEUTENANT CHARLES MILNE HARVEY, 2nd BATTN. THE DUKE OF CAMBRIDGE'S OWN (MIDDLESEX REGIMENT), born at Spanish Town, Jamaica,

West Indies, on the 19th October, 1892, was the son of Thomas Lloyd Harvey, of Kingston,

Jamaica, and a grandson of Charles Harvey, of Campbell-town, Argyllshire.

He was educated at Merchiston Castle School, Edinburgh, and entered the Sandhurst Company at Woolwich in September, 1910, being gazetted to the Middlesex Regiment in September, 1911, and serving with it at Bordon and Warley Camps, 1912; at Malta in 1913, and proceeding with his battalion as part of the Expeditionary Force to France in the Great War. Lieutenant Harvey was killed on the 23rd November, 1914, in action near Estaires. An officer, writing from the trenches, gave the following account of the occurrence: " Harvey went out about 4 p.m. on the 23rd November with about a dozen men to round up a party of snipers who had stolen round behind our trenches, and were taking pot-shots at us in our backs as we went about our various jobs. He rounded them up all right, but he was hit just as he was leading his men in a final charge on the house in which the enemy were located." The doctor said death must have been instantaneous. He was buried next evening, the Chaplain holding a brief service while the enemy's bullets were actually humming round— a fitting burial for a soldier.

Lieutenant Harvey's Colonel wrote of him: " We are all terribly cut up at this sad loss, as he had endeared himself to all ranks in the regiment, and was such a promising young officer. May I convey to you the sympathy of the whole regiment in your sad loss ? "

One of the Majors of the Middlesex Regiment, describing earlier events, said: " Only this day month I saw him in action at a place not many miles from here, and as I remarked then, and also officially reported, nothing could have surpassed the cool and admirable way in which he commanded his men. He was one of whom every regiment might well have been proud, and indeed a loss."

2nd LIEUTENANT DOUGLAS LENNOX HARVEY, 9th (QUEEN'S ROYAL) LANCERS, who was killed by a shell in the trenches on the 3rd November, 1914, was the second son of the Rev. E. D. L. Harvey, Beedingwood, Horsham, Sussex.

He was born on the 22nd October, 1892, and took a scholarship at Eton, but entered Mr. Byrne's House as an Oppidan. He won the

Tomlin prize for mathematics, and became an Exhibitioner of Trinity College, Cambridge,

taking a first class in the history tripos in 1914.

He held a commission in the Cambridge O.T.C. Cavalry, and was attached to the 9th Lancers, with a view to passing into the Reserve of Officers, when the war broke out. In May, 1914, he was appointed 2nd Lieutenant in the Reserve and went to the front with the regiment in August, 1914, being present in all their engagements up to the time of his death.

Mr. Harvey was a member of the Conservative Club, and his recreations were polo, shooting, and hunting.

MAJOR PERCY HASTINGS, 1st BATTN. THE QUEEN'S OWN (ROYAL WEST KENT REGIMENT), who is believed to

have died from wounds on the battle-field in France on the 1st September, 1914, was the eldest son of W. S. Hastings, of 2, The Grange, Wimbledon, and was born on the 5th October, 1872.

He joined the R.W.K. Regiment in March, 1894, becoming Lieutenant in March, 1898, and Captain in July, 1902. He served on the north-western frontier of India, at Malakand, and the action of Landakai; also at operations in Bajaur and in the Mamund Country: Buner, and the attack and capture of the Tanga Pass, receiving the medal with clasp. Major Hastings had served as an Adjutant of Volunteers and the Territorial Force for five years from August, 1906, and obtained his rank in March, 1912.

He left a widow.

2nd LIEUTENANT FREDERICK CHARLES HATTON, ACTING ADJUTANT 2nd BATTN. ALEXANDRA PRINCESS OF WALES'S OWN (YORKSHIRE REGIMENT), born at Parkhurst, Isle of Wight, on the 9th April, 1878, was the son of Alfred Charles Hatton, part founder and at one time editor of the "Yokohama Press," Japan, and Canteen Steward of the 2nd Yorkshire Regiment. He was also

related to Dr. W. A. Hatton and to Sir Westby Brook Percival, K.C.M.G., late Agent-General for New Zealand.

He was educated privately, and obtained his commission from the ranks in October, 1914, having previously filled several regimental positions, including that of GymnasticInstructor, Depot Drill Instructor, Pay Sergeant, Orderly Room Sergeant, Canteen Accountant, Regimental Quartermaster-Sergeant, and Regimental Sergeant-Major, finally being appointed Acting Adjutant after receiving his commission. He served in the South African War, being seriously wounded at the Battle of Driefontein while Section Leader. He received the Queen's medal with three clasps, and had also been awarded the medal for long service and good conduct.

He was killed on the 30th October, 1914, at the Battle of Ypres, while acting as Adjutant, by the side of his Commanding Officer, Colonel C. A. C. King, who was also killed.

For some time he was Secretary of the " Green Howards " Old Comrades' Association, and a contributor to the " 'Green Howards' Gazette." He was also Sergeant-Major of the same regiment's " Old-time Firing and Hand-grenade Display."

2nd Lieutenant Hatton married Elsie, daughter of the late Quartermaster-Sergeant Thewlis, a brother of Alderman Thewlis, late Lord Mayor of Manchester, and left one son, Frederick Arthur, age twelve years.

LIEUTENANT VISCOUNT HAWARDEN (SIR ROBERT CORNWALLIS MAUDE), 1st BATTN. COLDSTREAM GUARDS,

Baron de Montalt, in Ireland, and a Baronet, of Hawarden, County Tipperary, son of Robert Henry, fifth Viscount Hawarden, Baron de Montalt, and a Baronet, was born in London on the 6th September, 1890. He succeeded his father as sixth Viscount in 1908. The present Lord Dunalley (through his grandmother, the Hon. Martha Prittie) was Viscount Hawarden's first cousin once removed.

He was educated at Winchester and Christ Church, Oxford, where he took his degree. He joined the Coldstream Guards as 2nd Lieutenant in the spring of 1912, becoming Lieutenant in September, 1913. He accompanied his battalion to France, as part of the Expeditionary Force, on the 12th August, and was killed by shell at Landrecies on the night of the 25th–26th August, 1914.

CAPTAIN ROBERT FRANK HAWES, 1st BATTN. LEICESTERSHIRE REGT.,

who was killed in action on the 23rd September, 1914, was the younger son of Mr. G. C. and Mrs. Hawes, of Lindfield, Sussex. He was born on the 18th April, 1883, and joined the Leicestershire Regiment in October, 1902, becoming Lieutenant in September, 1905, and Captain in May, 1910.

In September, 1911, he was appointed an Adjutant of the Territorial Force.

Captain Hawes married, in 1913, a daughter of Mr. and Mrs. Hyden, of Awbrook, Scaynes Hill.

LIEUTENANT LIONEL HOPE HAWKINS, 1st (KING'S) DRAGOON GUARDS,

was born at Chichester on the 28th July, 1886, and was the son of Isaac Thomas Hawkins, late Colonial Civil Service, and Mrs. Mary Hope Hawkins. He was related by the marriage of a great-aunt to the Berkley family, and was thus a cousin of the late Captain H. Berkley, R.N., and of the late Francis Berkley, Esq., Secretary, War Office.

Lieutenant Hawkins was educated at Waynflete, Winchester College, and the R.M.C., Sandhurst. Early in his school days he showed an aptitude for athletics, as a runner and cricketer. At Winchester he won the steeplechase for his House, and distinguished himself as a footballer and Fives player.

While at Sandhurst he was asked to join the King's Dragoon Guards, owing to his excelling in games and sports, and was gazetted to that regiment in February, 1907, becoming Lieutenant in February, 1908. He had passed for his Captaincy two years previously, and would soon have been promoted.

With his regiment he served in India, and received the Delhi Durbar medal. He competed with his troop for the shield in the regimental polo team, and was a regular polo player, being considered by some the best No. 1 there had been in the regiment for years, and helped it to win the Patiala Cup and many others.

For two years Lieutenant Hawkins was Signalling

Officer of the Ambala Cavalry Brigade, and the remarks of the General Commanding on the report of the inspection were : " An excellent report, which reflects great credit on Lieutenant Hawkins, the Signalling Officer."

On the outbreak of the war he was at home on leave from India, and was attached for active service to the 6th Dragoon Guards (Carabiniers), and was killed in an attack by the Germans on a line between Messines and Wytschaete, Belgium, on the night of the 31st October–1st November, 1914.

The Adjutant of the Carabiniers, writing on the 13th November, gave the following account of the circumstances : " It appears that after the enemy had penetrated our line a party was observed by your son approaching the trench which he held with his troop. He ordered fire to be opened on them, but they shouted, ' Don't fire ! We are the Scottish ! ' and he ordered his men to cease fire, and himself bravely, but incautiously, got out of the trench and went towards them. He had gone about thirty yards when the Germans—for it was the Germans, and not the London Scottish—opened fire, and your son was seen to fall. Two men at once went out and brought him back to the trench. He was seen to be badly wounded in the right side, and he was carried back by our men and the London Scottish towards Kemmel. On reaching a place of comparative safety two of the men went off to try and find a stretcher, and two remained with your son, who died very shortly afterwards. He had been unconscious from a few minutes after he had been hit, and passed quietly away. The men were unable to bury him then, and were obliged to leave him covered with a blanket at the edge of a wood, where I have no doubt he has since been buried. But as, unfortunately, the Germans now hold that piece of ground it has not been possible to do what otherwise would have been done. You have lost a gallant son, and we a brave and well-loved comrade who showed military qualities of a high order."

The General commanding the 4th Cavalry Brigade.wrote of him : " During the retirement and subsequently he had several difficult patrols to carry out, and he always did his part with conspicuous success. He was a very brave man, and was careful of the lives of his men."

The Carabiniers were in such fierce fighting that at one place after a night attack, on 31st October–1st November, the French, when advancing, counted three thousand five hundred dead in front of the trenches of the London Scottish and Carabiniers only.

Mrs. Hawkins received a telegram and letters of sympathy from the whole of her son's regiment. At school Lieutenant Hawkins had received many nicknames indicative of his fleetness of foot and athletic prowess, such as

" Agag " and " Diabolo." In the Army he was very popular with his men, and the officers of his regiment wrote saying : " He is a great loss to us."

He was a member of the Junior Army and Navy and the Junior Naval and Military Clubs, and of Hurlingham and Ranelagh.

CAPTAIN CYRIL FRANCIS HAWLEY, KING'S ROYAL RIFLE CORPS,

who was killed in action on the 2nd November, 1914, was the second son of the late Sir Henry Hawley, Bart., and Frances Lady Hawley, of Leybourne Grange, Kent, and brother of the present Baronet. He was born on the 24th June, 1878, and was educated at Malvern College (No. 5, 1892–94), Army Side.

He joined the K.R.R.C. from the Militia in February, 1899, and became Lieutenant a year later. He took part in the South African War, being present at operations in Natal in 1899, including actions at Elandslaagte, Rietfontein, and Lombard's Kop ; at the defence of Ladysmith, including the action of the 6th January, 1900 ; in Natal, in the Transvaal, east of Pretoria, including actions at Belfast and Lydenberg; in the Transvaal between November, 1900, and May, 1902 ; in the Orange River Colony and Cape Colony, 1901 and 1902. For his services he was mentioned in Despatches (" London Gazette," 10th September, 1910), and received the Queen's medal with five clasps and the King's medal with two clasps.

He was promoted Captain in November, 1905, and in the Great War was acting as a General Staff Officer, 3rd grade, which appointment he received on the 5th August, 1914.

CAPTAIN LORD ARTHUR VINCENT HAY, IRISH GUARDS,

was born on the 16th March, 1886, and was the second son of the tenth Marquess of Tweeddale, K.T.

He was educated at Eton, and joined the Cameron Highlanders from the Militia as 2nd Lieutenant in June, 1905, being transferred to the Irish Guards in December, 1905.

He retired from the regiment with the rank of Captain, and on the outbreak of the war rejoined the regiment on the 15th August. He was killed on the 14th September, 1914, while forcing the passage of the river Aisne at Chavonne.

Lord Arthur Hay married Menda, daughter of the Hon. Mrs. Edward Stonor and the late A. J. Ralli, Esq., and left one daughter, Jean, born August, 1911.

2nd LIEUTENANT PAUL OTREN HEANEY, 1st BATTN. KING'S OWN (ROYAL LANCASTER REGIMENT),

son of Patrick and Elizabeth Heaney, and grandson of Richard Morris, of "New Town," Waterford, was born at Waterford on the 27th October, 1876. He was educated at St. Francis Xavier's School, Liverpool, and enlisted in the King's Own in 1894. He served through the South African War, during which he gained the Distinguished Conduct Medal. Prior to the outbreak of the Great War he was on the Army Gymnastic Staff as Company Sergeant-Major, and was Instructor to the Middlesex Regiment at Mill Hill.

As a Company Sergeant-Major he had been in the firing line since the first shot of this war was fired. He was a capable and clever soldier, thoughtful for the needs and trials of those under him, with whom he was very popular. His battalion and others were holding an advanced line, and were subjected to ceaseless artillery fire, which rendered the ground immediately behind them too dangerous to be crossed. The battalions were thus isolated, and before long realised that they were out of reach of the delivery of supplies. The situation was desperate, and Sergeant Heaney, going to the Major of the A.S.C., offered to go across the zone of danger and bring back food. "Sheer madness!" declared the officer, but Sergeant Heaney did not waver. He collected wagons, drivers, and men, and went. They traversed four miles under continuous shell and rifle fire, and at last reached the camp, loaded up, and started on their return journey. They got through and reached their position, and brought food, not only to their own battalion, but to the whole brigade, thus saving the advanced line and the situation.

Many of the above details are taken from "T.P.'s Journal of Great Deeds of the Great War" of December 26th, 1914.

For his gallantry Sergeant Heaney was, in

September, 1914, given a commission, an honour he was not to enjoy long, for on the 21st October he was killed in action. It has not been possible to ascertain the exact circumstances attending his death.

LIEUTENANT VOLTELIN PERCY HEATH, ROYAL HORSE GUARDS,

was the son of Sir James Heath, Bart., of Oxendon Hall, Market Harborough, and was born at Clayton Hall, Staffordshire, on the 10th January, 1889. He was educated at Eton and Magdalen College, Oxford. At the University he had a brilliant career, having been prominent in literature, politics, and sport. He was President of the Bullingdon Club, Master of the Drag Hounds, and Captain of the Polo Team (afterwards playing in the polo team of his regiment), and finished his Oxford career by taking a good second in the final History Schools.

He received his commission in the Royal Horse Guards in October, 1911, becoming Lieutenant in April, 1912.

Serving with his regiment at the front, he was wounded in the retirement from Mons, and died from the effects at the Château Baron, France, on the 4th September, 1914.

Lieutenant Heath was a member of the Marlborough and Bachelors' Clubs, and also of Hurlingham and Ranelagh.

He was unmarried.

CAPTAIN HAROLD LUTWYCHE HELME, 1st BATTN. LOYAL NORTH LANCASHIRE REGIMENT,

born at Trewyn, Herefordshire, on the 3rd August, 1878, was the son of Harold and Mary H. Helme, of King's Thorne, Herefordshire, and a nephew of John W. Helme, of Broadfield Court, Herefordshire. Educated at Haileybury College, he first joined the Worcestershire Militia, and from it obtained his 2nd Lieutenancy in the Loyal North Lancashire Regiment in 1899, becoming Lieutenant in February, 1901, and obtaining his Company in December, 1909. He served in the South African War in 1901, in which he was wounded, having been present with Mounted Infantry at operations in the Orange Free State and Cape Colonies, receiving the Queen's medal with three clasps. He also took part in the operation of the Irua Patrol in the west of the Niger with the Onitsha Hinterland Expedition; in West Africa (South Nigeria), 1905–06; and with the Bende-Onitsha and Hinterland Expedition, receiving the medal with clasp.

In the Great War he was killed at the Battle of the Aisne on the 14th September, 1914, under the following circumstances: His battalion (mentioned in Sir John French's Despatch of the 8th October, 1914) had been ordered to take a factory north of Troyon to support the Sussex, who were being hard pressed, and during the action Captain Helme was killed, and nearly all the officers of the battalion were killed, wounded, or reported missing, including the Colonel and senior Major, both of whom were killed.

MAJOR ARTHUR FRANCIS HENDERSON, p.s.c., 27th LIGHT CAVALRY, INDIAN ARMY,

who was killed in action near Soissons, France, on the 12th September, 1914, was the third son of Mrs. Henderson, 51, Lexham Gardens, London, W., and the late Dr. Henderson, of Shanghai, and was born at Shanghai on the 21st November, 1874. He was educated at Haileybury and the R.M.C., Sandhurst.

He received an unattached 2nd Lieutenancy in June, 1895, and joined the Indian Staff Corps in March, 1896. He became Lieutenant in the Indian Army in 1897, and Captain in January, 1904.

Keenest of sportsmen, he was beloved in the regiment by all ranks for his zeal with horse and hound and spear. He whipped for the Poona Hunt for two seasons, and could have hunted the pack the following year had he been able to take it on. He was best man-at-arms at Bangalore in 1911, and again at Lucknow in 1913.

Major Henderson, who had passed through the Staff College, was appointed a Brigade-Major in India in February, 1909, and was promoted Major and Squadron Commander in the 27th Light Cavalry in January, 1913, when, in the absence of the Colonel and the Second in Command, he commanded the regiment for eight months, coming home on leave in March, 1914. He was to have acted as an umpire in the autumn manœuvres of that year, and was working on the Staff at Aldershot, when war broke out. He was appointed extra Cypher Officer at 1st Army headquarters, left England on August 12th, and was afterwards transferred to General Headquarters.

On September 12th, 1914, Major Henderson was appointed General Staff Officer, 2nd Grade, to General John Gough, and left that morning for Cavalry Headquarters, near Soissons. There he received definite information that General Gough had crossed the Aisne, by Condé Bridge, and, joining Colonel Danby Christopher, A.A. and Q.M.G., they proceeded by motor towards Condé, but were held up by the enemy near the bridge, Colonel Christopher being badly wounded and thrown out of the car. Major Henderson and Colonel Christopher's servant put up a very gallant fight, one with revolver and the other with rifle; and it was when he returned to the car to try and rescue Colonel Christopher (presumably when they had exhausted their ammunition) that Major Henderson was shot at about eighty yards range. The servant was also killed, and Colonel Christopher was taken prisoner. His grave is where he fell, by the roadside on the way to Condé Bridge, south of the Aisne.

In 1910 Major Henderson married Muriel, daughter of the late Capel Hanbury and Mrs. Hanbury, of " The Knoll," Penn, Bucks.

LIEUTENANT NORMAN WILLIAM ARTHUR HENDERSON, 1st BATTN. ROYAL SCOTS FUSILIERS,

who was killed in action on the 10th November, 1914, was the eldest son of Arthur Henderson and his wife, Gareth, late of Fairmile Court, Cobham, Surrey.

He was born at Rosary Gardens, South Kensington, on the 23rd October, 1891, and was educated at Rugby (S.H.), to which he went in 1906. Proceeding to the R.M.C., Sandhurst, in 1911, he entered the Army in February, 1912, and joined his regiment in South Africa, being promoted Lieutenant in June, 1913. He left South Africa in February, 1914, and went to the front on the 12th August.

He was in the retirement from Mons, and took part in the Battle of Cambrai, le Cateau, and also in the Battles of the Marne and the Aisne. He was killed in the wood of Herenthals Château, at Ypres, whilst leading his platoon. An attack was made by the Prussian Guard;

some of the trenches had to be retaken by a counter-attack, and it was during this attack that Lieutenant Henderson was killed.

Several of the few remaining officers of his regiment have testified in letters to his bravery and splendid qualities as an officer.

LIEUTENANT RAYMOND MONT-GOMERIE HUME HENDERSON, 2nd BATTN. CONNAUGHT RANGERS, was born at Fort Belgaum, India, on the 13th August, 1884, the son of Colonel Hume Henderson, I.M.S., retired, and grandson of the late Dr. Gordon, Hume Street, Dublin.

Lieutenant Henderson was educated at King's School, Canterbury, and obtained his commission in the Connaught Rangers from the Militia in 1907, being promoted Lieutenant in February, 1910. From December, 1909, to March, 1914, he was employed with the Gold Coast Regiment.

Returning to England he accompanied his battalion to the front in the great war, and was killed in action on the 21st September, 1914, at the Battle of the Aisne, Tilleul Hill.

His recreations were shooting, football, and tennis.

Lieutenant Henderson married Zillah Edith, eldest daughter of Vere D. U. Hunt, Esq., of Carnahalla, Doon, County Limerick.

CAPTAIN WILLIAM ALEXANDER HENDERSON, 2nd BATTN. PRINCESS LOUISE'S (ARGYLL AND SUTHERLAND HIGHLANDERS),

was born at Edinburgh on the 20th December, 1876, the son of the late Alexander Edward Henderson, Advocate, Sheriff - Substitute of the Lothians, and of Mrs. Henderson, Manor Place, Edinburgh.

He was educated at St. Salvator's Preparatory School, St. Andrews, Loretto School, and Oriel College, Oxford, where he took his B.A. degree, and played golf for the University. He entered the 1st Battalion Argyll and Sutherland Highlanders in February, 1900, and served in the South African War, being a Station Staff Officer from July, 1901. He was present at operations in the Transvaal, east and west of Pretoria, from July to November, 1900, including the action at Zilikat's Nek; at further operations in the Transvaal, April, 1901, to May, 1902; and in Cape Colony in the latter month. He received the Queen's medal with three clasps and the King's medal with two clasps.

Captain Henderson was Adjutant of the 5th Seaforth Highlanders from 1910–13, when he returned to the 2nd Battalion of his regiment. He was at first reported wounded and missing after a night attack on a German trench at Ploegsteert Wood, near Armentières, early in the morning of the 10th November, 1914. He was in command of the attack which has been described as a very gallant one. Over one hundred and thirty men of his command were killed, wounded, or missing after the attack. On the 26th December, 1914, during the unofficial armistice at Christmas, his body, with fifteen bodies of his men, was found by the British and identified by the name in the coat, the identity disc and other articles having been taken by the Germans.

He was a keen cricketer and a well-known golfer, being a member of the Royal and Ancient Golf Club, St. Andrews. In 1909 he defeated J. O. Travers, the American champion, in the first round at Muirfield in the Amateur Golf Championship. He was a member of the Royal Automobile Club.

Captain Henderson married Constance May Chambers and left one son, Alexander Edward William, born June, 1912.

LIEUTENANT RONALD LUCAS QUIXANO HENRIQUES, 2nd BATTN. THE QUEEN'S (ROYAL WEST SURREY REGIMENT),

who was killed in action in France on the 14th September, 1914, was the second son of the late David Quixano Henriques and of Mrs. Henriques, 17, Sussex Square, Hyde Park, W., and was born on the 8th June, 1884.

He was educated at Harrow (Mr. Stogdon's House) from 1898 to 1901, and obtained his commission in the R.W.S. Regiment in October, 1903, becoming Lieutenant on the 4th December, 1907.

The following account of his death, derived from a letter from a private of his regiment, was published in the " Harrovian War Supplement " of November, 1914 :—

" It was on September 14th. We had just come through—I think it was the village of Paisy—on to some very high ground. We halted, and we were told that the enemy were entrenched on the hills in front of us, and we were to drive them out. We started the advance, my platoon about thirty yards behind, Mr. Henriques in support. We had just come out of a valley when the Germans opened fire on us. However, we kept on advancing until we were about thirty yards from the enemy. We were all up in line, and I was the third man from Mr. Henriques. He just raised his head and shoulders and said, ' Advance ! ' when he was shot through the centre of the forehead, killing him instantly."

LIEUTENANT CLAUDE HENRY, 3rd BATTN. THE WORCESTERSHIRE REGIMENT,

was born at Brighton in July, 1881, being the son of James and Evelyn Henry, of Lingmell, Putney Heath, grandson of the late Sir J. H. Pelly, Bart., formerly of Warnham Court, Sussex, and of the late Captain J. Henry, formerly of Blackdown House, Sussex. He was educated at Bradfield College and Exeter College, Oxford. He joined the 3rd Battalion Worcestershire Regiment as 2nd Lieutenant in January, 1903, becoming Lieutenant in December, 1906, and served for three years in the West African Field Force on the Gold Coast, rejoining his battalion in June, 1914, accompanied it to the front, and fell on the 20th September, 1914, near Vailly-sur-Aisne.

He was a member of the Wellington Club and was unmarried.

2nd LIEUTENANT STANLEY BENSKIN HENSON, SPECIAL RESERVE, attd. 1st BATTN. PRINCE ALBERT'S (SOMERSET LIGHT INFANTRY),

who was killed in action at the end of the year 1914, aged twenty-seven years, was the only son of Dr. and Mrs. Henson, of 2, Derby Street, Mayfair, and of Elmsett Hall, Wedmore.

He was educated at King's School, Bruton, and Pembroke College, Oxford, and obtained an appointment in the Colonial Police some six years before his death, being stationed in Singapore and Penang.

Soon after the declaration of war he resigned his appointment and returned to England. He had joined the Special Reserve of his regiment as 2nd Lieutenant on probation in September, 1913, and in November, 1914, was attached to the 1st Battalion of his regiment on going to the front.

The officer commanding the battalion gave the following details : " As to the manner of your son's death, I can only tell you that he died as a very brave man. He was leading his men in the attack on the German trenches, and had outstripped the rest of his company by about twenty yards, when he was shot through the heart and killed instantly. Those of his company who were fortunate enough to come out of the action alive speak in the highest terms of your son's courage. He is a great loss to the regiment."

LIEUTENANT KENNETH PARNELL HENSTOCK, 4th BATTN. THE DUKE OF CAMBRIDGE'S OWN (MIDDLESEX REGIMENT),

was born at Up Park Camp, Jamaica, West Indies, on the 19th July, 1893, the son of Colonel F. T. Henstock, late West India and West African Regiments. He was educated at Bradfield College, Berks, where he was in the First Cricket XI, and at the R.M.C., Sandhurst, from which he received his commission in the Middlesex Regiment in August, 1912, becoming Lieutenant on the 11th August, 1914.

His amusements were hunting and shooting.

He fell leading his platoon on Sunday, the 23rd August, 1914, at the Battle of Mons, when it was said to have been completely annihilated.

2nd LIEUTENANT MALCOLM ARNOLD HEPBURN, 2nd BATTN. SEAFORTH HIGHLANDERS (ROSS-SHIRE BUFFS THE DUKE OF ALBANY'S),

was born at Hampstead, London, on the 8th January, 1892, and was the son of the late Mr. and Mrs. Hepburn, of 13, Well Walk, Hampstead. His elder brother, Captain W. D. Hepburn, now Adjutant 5th Battalion Royal Scots (Queen's

Edinburgh Rifles), is also in the Seaforth Highlanders.

2nd Lieutenant Hepburn was educated at Heddon Court Preparatory School, Hampstead, whence he obtained a scholarship at Malvern College in 1905. Subsequently he obtained a Classical Exhibition at Magdalene College, Cambridge, where he rowed in the College Lent boat in 1911; was in the College Tennis VI; and won his colours for Association football.

He joined the Reserve of Officers in the spring of 1913, and did his special training with the 2nd Battalion Seaforth Highlanders, to which he was afterwards gazetted, and with which he was serving in France when killed. He was shot while superintending sapping operations in trenches near Messines on the 30th November, 1914, and was buried in Ploegsteert Wood.

CAPTAIN HORACE FALKLAND HERD, 3rd (RESERVE) BATTN. THE WELSH REGIMENT,

youngest son of Major W. G. R. Herd, late 95th (now Nottinghamshire and Derbyshire) Regiment, was born at Hanwell, Middlesex, on the 13th July, 1883.

He was educated at Monmouth Grammar School, and after joining the Army in March, 1901, served in the South African War, being present at operations in the Transvaal and Orange River Colony in 1901, and in Cape Colony from June, 1901, to February, 1902, receiving the Queen's medal with five clasps. He was promoted Lieutenant in February, 1902, Captain in May, 1904, and had qualified at a school of musketry, as well as having obtained a first-class certificate in gymnastics, and in supply duties at the A.S.C. Training Establishment at Aldershot.

Captain Herd was a good Rugby football player, and made a reputation at school as a three-quarter back, but had little time for the game afterwards, as he went practically from the playing field to South Africa for the Boer War at the age of eighteen.

In December, 1914, he went to France with a draft of reinforcements for the 2nd Battalion Welsh Regiment, and almost immediately was engaged in fighting with that battalion, having been put in command of a company.

He was killed in the very heavy fighting in front of Festubert on the 27th December, 1914, by a bomb from a trench mortar, and was buried in a little cemetery to the west of Festubert.

LIEUTENANT ARTHUR WIDDRINGTON HERDMAN, 1st BATTN. KING'S OWN (SHROPSHIRE LIGHT INFANTRY),

late of Ewhurst Place, East Sussex, only son of the late Rev. R. M. Herdman, Vicar of Holy Trinity, North Shields, and of Mrs. Herdman, Sunny Holme, Ripon, was born on the 31st January, 1886, at Holy Trinity Vicarage, North Shields.

He was educated at Trent College, and was a graduate of Corpus Christi College, Oxford. Lieutenant Herdman first joined the Royal Sussex Regiment (Militia), and passed into the Regular Army in September, 1909, becoming Lieutenant in October, 1913.

On the outbreak of the Great War his battalion went first to Queenstown in August, and two or three weeks later embarked at Southampton for the Continent, landing at St. Nazaire, in the Bay of Biscay. Thence they proceeded by train to Paris and marched to Crecy. During the Battle of the Aisne the battalion was in the trenches at Vailly for nearly a month.

Lieutenant Herdman was killed near Lille on the 25th October, 1914. His body was found by his orderly—Griffiths—who was himself wounded in the arm when looking for his late master.

Major Luard, of his battalion, wrote: " He is indeed a great loss to the regiment, and was very popular. The men of his platoon would have done anything he asked of them."

By his will Lieutenant Herdman, who was very popular with all who knew him, left three acres of land for a recreation ground for the village of Ewhurst, and in addition the Parish Council received a sum of £300 for fencing and laying out the land, and to provide for the upkeep, and gifts to the school children at Christmastime.

CAPTAIN GEOFFREY WILMOT HERRINGHAM, p.s.c., 6th (INNISKILLING) DRAGOONS,

was the son of Sir Wilmot Herringham, M.D., and Christiana Jane, daughter of T. W. Powell, Esq. He was born in London on the 7th August, 1883.

Captain Herringham was educated at Eton and the R.M.A., Woolwich. He joined the Royal Artillery as 2nd Lieutenant in 1900, became Lieutenant in 1903, and was transferred to the 6th Dragoons in November 1906, becoming Captain in March, 1910. He passed the Staff College in 1912.

Captain Herringham was shot at Messines on the 31st October, 1914, while in command of the machine-gun section of the 5th Dragoon Guards, to which regiment he was attached at the time.

CAPTAIN ANTHONY MORRIS COATS HEWAT, 2nd BATTN. THE ROYAL SCOTS (LOTHIAN REGIMENT),

who was killed on the 8th September, 1914, at the battle of the Marne, was the son of Lieutenant-Colonel Henry Roper-Curzon Hewat, late Royal Scots Fusiliers, and of Mrs. Jessie Mc-Kenzie Hewat. He was born at Secunderabad, India, on the 27th October, 1884, and was educated at Victoria College, Jersey, and the R.M.C., Sandhurst. He entered the Army in May, 1903, becoming Lieutenant in March, 1905, and Captain in July, 1913.

Captain Hewat married Stella Eleanora, daughter of the Rev. Rhys Bishop, and left a daughter, Diana Geraldine Eleanora, born August, 1913.

He was keen on all kinds of sport, both at home and in India, especially hunting, polo, shooting (large and small game), and fishing.

LIEUTENANT GORDON HUGHES HEWITT, 2nd BATTN. THE PRINCE OF WALES'S VOLUNTEERS (SOUTH LANCASHIRE REGT.)

was born at 25, Argyll Road, Kensington, W., on the 26th January, 1892, being the son of the late Captain Percy Hughes Hewitt, 6th Dragoon Guards (Carabiniers). He was a relative of the late General Gordon. The late Captain Hewitt had raised at his own expense the first Cyclist Corps in the Army (the 26th Middlesex Cyclist Corps), for which he received the honorary title of Major.

Lieutenant Hewitt was educated at Victoria College, Jersey, from 1901-05 ; then at Haileybury till 1909, subsequently, after private tuition and coaching, entering the Royal Military Academy at Woolwich as a Sandhurst cadet in 1911, and going to Sandhurst itself in

1912. He received his commission in the South Lancashire Regiment in January, 1913.

At the Battle of the Aisne, on the 19th September, the South Lancashires, when in reserve, were informed that the Germans had broken through our line, about half a mile away, and were in a wood to the right of the battalion. Two companies were ordered to dislodge the enemy from this wood, which they did at the point of the bayonet. It was during this operation that Lieutenant Hewitt was hit by shrapnel in four places, one bullet injuring the spine. He was taken to the dressing station at Vailly, and thence at night to the Field Hospital at Braine. It was there found that he was very seriously injured, being completely paralysed from the waist down. On the 21st he seemed better, and at his own special desire was sent down to the Base Hospital at Versailles, where he died on the 24th September, 1914, of septic pneumonia. He was buried with full military honours in the Cimetière des Gouards, Versailles, the guard being furnished by a detachment of French cavalry, and many French officers being present, including a representative of the General commanding the district.

Lieutenant Hewitt had been awarded the decoration of the Legion of Honour (Croix de Chevalier) at the end of August, but it has not been possible to ascertain from the British or the French Government for what particular act of gallantry in the retirement from Mons the award was made. He was promoted Lieutenant on the 11th September, 1914.

Lieutenant Hewitt was a member of the Primrose Club, St. James's, S.W. His recreations were hockey, tennis, and billiards. He was unmarried.

LIEUTENANT JAMES FRANCIS HEWITT, 1st BATTN. THE CAMERONIANS (SCOTTISH RIFLES),

son of the Hon. W. J. Hewitt, of St. Colme House, Aberdour, Fife, was born at Gatehouse of Fleet, Galloway, on the 23rd January, 1888, and was educated at Winton House, Winchester ; Haileybury College ; and the R.M.C., Sandhurst.

In February, 1908, he was gazetted and attached to the 2nd Battalion Scottish Rifles until the trooping season, when he joined his own battalion at Cawnpore, becoming Lieutenant in March, 1910. He proceeded to South Africa in December, 1909, and was with the

Mounted Infantry till March, 1912, when he returned with his battalion to Glasgow.

Lieutenant Hewitt joined his regiment at the front at the end of August, and after being slightly wounded on the 20th October, 1914, was killed on the 26th of that month near La Boutillerie in the first Battle of Ypres.

Lieutenant J. F. Hewitt's brother—2nd Lieutenant W. G. Hewitt, Royal Scots—was killed on the 14th October, near Vieille Chapelle, in the first Battle of Ypres.

2nd LIEUTENANT WILLIAM GEORGE HEWITT, 3rd BATTN. ROYAL SCOTS (LOTHIAN REGIMENT),

second son of the Hon. William James Hewitt, was born at Gatehouse of Fleet, Galloway, on the 7th June, 1892. He was educated at Edinburgh Academy and Christ Church, Oxford. On the outbreak of the war he joined the Royal Scots from the University, where he had been in the Officers' Training Corps, proceeding to the front in September, and was killed on the 14th October, 1914, in the first Battle of Ypres.

2nd Lieutenant Hewitt's elder brother—Lieutenant J. F. Hewitt, the Cameronians (1st Scottish Rifles)—was killed on the 26th of the same month near La Boutillerie, also in the first Battle of Ypres.

LIEUTENANT EDWARD ROBERT EYRE HICKLING, 3rd BATTN. GLOUCESTERSHIRE REGIMENT, attd. 1st BATTN. LOYAL NORTH LANCASHIRE REGIMENT,

who died of wounds about the 2nd November, 1914, in hospital at Poperinghe, was the son of John Birde and Clara Hickling, and was born at Lymington on the 17th August, 1895. His maternal grandfather, Robert Eyre Applegate Eyres, was a noted mathematician. He was educated at Langharne School (John Murray, Esq.) till ten years old, and then at Bournemouth School (Dr. Fenwick). He went to the latter school in 1907, where he joined the School O.T.C. in January, 1908. He was a very keen member, and after passing through the various ranks up to Sergeant he obtained his " A " certificate by sheer hard work in November, 1912.

He was a good runner, both in long and short distances, and was fond of fishing. He had always looked forward to an Army career, and was therefore very pleased when, in October, 1913, he was gazetted 2nd Lieutenant to the 3rd Battalion Gloucestershire Regiment.

In France he was attached to the Loyal North Lancashire Regiment, and was promoted Lieutenant in the field. The following account of his death was given by an officer of his company : " It appears that we captured a lot of German prisoners, and he was detailed to bring a party of them back. He had a guard on them, with fixed bayonets, and, of course, all the Germans were disarmed ; but it appears that the German officer who was with them had a revolver which had not been taken from him ; and, while poor young Hickling took his eyes off him for a moment, this swine turned round and deliberately shot him. In the space of two or three seconds that German officer had been simply hacked to pieces by our men's bayonets, but, alas ! that didn't save poor Hickling. It was altogether a most tragic affair."

2nd LIEUTENANT SAMUEL VERNON EINEM-HICKSON, 2nd BATTN. LOYAL NORTH LANCASHIRE REGIMENT,

who was killed in action in East Africa towards the end of 1914, the actual date and place of death not having been reported, was the eldest son of Colonel S. A. E. Hickson, D.S.O., R.E., of Queen's Road, Richmond, Surrey, and was born in 1893.

He was educated at Wellington, where he was in the Hopetoun from 1908–09. He was gazetted to the Loyal North Lancashire Regiment as Second Lieutenant in September, 1912.

LIEUTENANT WALTER EDWARD HILL, 3rd BATTN. NORTH STAFFORDSHIRE REGT.,

was the only son of the late Canon Rowland Hill, Rector of Holy Trinity, Dorchester, and was born on the 6th September, 1892.

He was educated at Durnford House, Langton Matravers, Dorsetshire, and Winchester College.

He was for three years in the North Stafford-shire 3rd Battn. (Special Reserve), being promoted Lieutenant in April, 1913, and was attached to the 1st Battalion of the regiment on the outbreak of the war, proceeding with it to the Continent.

He was killed at the Battle of the Aisne on the 25th September, 1914.

Lieutenant Hill was a member of the Cavendish Club and of two automobile clubs.

2nd LIEUTENANT HENRY DENNE HILTON, 5th (attd. 4th) BATTN. THE DUKE OF CAMBRIDGE'S OWN (MIDDLESEX REGIMENT),

who was killed in action on the 19th December, 1914, was the son of the late Rev. H. M. Hilton, sometime Rector of Orlingbury, Northants.

He was educated at Haileybury and Trinity College, Cambridge.

At the outbreak of the war Lieutenant Hilton was a master at University College School, Hampstead, where he was an officer in the O.T.C. Contingent, from which he was gazetted to the Middlesex Regiment, in September, 1914.

CAPTAIN FRANK HIND, 1st BATTN. EAST YORKSHIRE REGIMENT,

who died in the Würtemberg Field Hospital, Haubourdin, near Lille, as a prisoner of war, on the 29th October, 1914, from wounds received on the 20th of the same month, was the fourth son of the late William Everatt Hind.

He was born at Howden, Yorkshire, on the 24th September, 1879, and after being attached to the Regulars for nearly a year received his commission from the 1st V.B. King's Own Yorkshire Light Infantry in the East Yorkshire Regiment in January, 1901. He served in the South African War, in which he was five times severely wounded, and was present at operations in the Orange Free State, the Transvaal (west of Pretoria), and the Orange River Colony, including actions at Lindley, Bethlehem, and Wittebergen in 1900, and again in the Orange River Colony from July, 1901, to May, 1902. He received the Queen's medal with four clasps and the King's medal with two clasps, and was one of the very few volunteer officers who earned six clasps. From August, 1903, to April, 1908—having been promoted Lieutenant in March, 1904—he served with the West African Regiment at Sierra Leone.

He returned to England in 1908, and was promoted Captain in September, 1910. Captain Hind was wounded three times, but continued to lead his men in a charge on the 20th October, 1914, dying from his wounds as above stated.

He married, in 1911, Constance Evelyn, younger daughter of Edmund Harrison, Lampton, Heston.

2nd LIEUTENANT HAROLD EDWIN HIPPISLEY, SPECIAL RESERVE (attd. 1st BATTN.) GLOUCESTERSHIRE REGIMENT,

was born at Wells, Somerset, on the 3rd September, 1890, and was the son of Mr. W. J. and Mrs. Hippisley, of Northam House, Wells, Somerset. He was educated at King's School, Bruton, Somerset, and matriculated at London University. He was also a member of the Royal Agricultural College, Cirencester, where he was gold medallist (Estate Management and Forestry), and gained the National Diploma of Agriculture. He was also a Professional Associate of the Surveyors' Institution. At Cirencester he was in the O.T.C., and subsequently joined the Special Reserve of Officers. On the despatch of the Expeditionary Force he left for France with the 3rd Brigade, 1st Division, as a 2nd Lieutenant in the Gloucestershire Regiment.

He was killed on the 23rd October, 1914, at Langemarck, Belgium, where he was in command of one of the two platoons which successfully held an exposed trench against a large force, despite the loss of all the officers and sixty per cent. of the men.

At King's School Mr. Hippisley was Captain of the cricket and football teams, and at Cirencester of the cricket and hockey teams. He played cricket and hockey for his county, and cricket for the United Services.

2nd Lieutenant Hippisley married Ivy Gwendoline, daughter of the late Mr. J. Hussey Cooper and Mrs. Hussey Cooper, of " The Lodge," Wheatley, Oxford.

LIEUTENANT CHARLES MORGAN HOARE, 15th (THE KING'S) HUSSARS,

who was killed at the age of twenty-one, was the son of Charles Twysden Hoare, of Bignell Park, Bicester, and the Hon. Blanche Frances Hoare, daughter of the first Baron Tredegar.

He was educated at Osborne and Dartmouth,

it having been intended that he should go into the Royal Navy. He, however, decided to

enter the Army, and was gazetted to the 15th Hussars in December, 1913. He was fond of polo, hunting, and point - to - point racing.

He was killed on the 25th August, 1914, during the retirement from Mons, while covering the infantry near Blaugies.

2nd LIEUTENANT SYDNEY HOWARD HODGES, RESERVE OF OFFICERS, attd. 4th BATTN. ROYAL FUSILIERS (CITY OF LONDON REGIMENT),

who was killed in action on the 17th October, 1914, was the son of W. D. and Mary Hodges, Alexander Square, South Kensington, and was born in London on the 6th July, 1891. He was educated at Rokeby School, Wimbledon, and at Monkton Combe School, Bath. On leaving school he studied for the medical profession at King's College, London, where he gained the Warnford Scholarship in 1910, and took the degree of B.Sc. with first-class honours in 1913.

The following are selected from a large number of letters received from those who knew him:—

From his C.O., Lieutenant-Colonel McMahon, who was killed in action on the 11th November, 1914:

" You will have received or read the official report of your son's death in action, which took place the day before yesterday in a successful attack on a village.

" He was leading his platoon forward at the time in splendid fashion, came under machine fire, and was shot through the heart.

" He was buried in a farm enclosure about one mile north of the village.

" Your son's loss will be deeply felt by myself and all the battalion, for he was most keen and energetic, and had a high sense of duty.

" He has done valuable work since he arrived, and was in all respects brave and efficient.

" Please accept my deepest sympathy and convey same to his relations."

From the Dean of Medical Science, King's College, University of London:

" I would ask you to accept this expression of the very deep and real sympathy which is felt for you by the members of the Staff of this College in the loss of your son.

" He was, I think, the best student of medicine I have ever had here. It was to me a real and great pleasure to help him in any way I could in his work, and his influence among the other students was the very best. The memory of his brilliant work and of his character will last a long time here, and will be an example for good to many of his fellow-students.

" I feel I have lost a very dear friend and pupil, and I realise something of what his parents must feel."

Professor Halliburton, of King's College, wrote of him to his family: " No news has grieved me more than the death of your gallant son. I got to know him so well during his work in my laboratory, and learnt, not only to value his high endeavours, but to regard him as a friend."

CAPTAIN JOHN FRANCIS HODGKINSON, 3rd (PRINCE OF WALES'S) DRAGOON GUARDS (SPECIAL RESERVE),

was born on the 25th July, 1879, at Baslow, Derbyshire, the son of the late John Grundy Hodgkinson, of Baslow. He was also related to the late Edmund Hodgkinson, J.P., of Baslow, and to Lieutenant S. C. L. Hodgkinson, of the Royal Australian Navy.

He was educated at Mount St. Mary's College, Chesterfield, from 1890–95, earning the admiration and affection of his companions. On leaving school he took to farming, but while so occupied lost no opportunity to educate himself in every way, becoming eventually an accomplished scholar, with a knowledge of the Russian, Spanish, and French languages, and a working knowledge of Kaffir and Hindustani. Nor did he neglect the physical side of life, for he was a keen fisherman, a good game shot, a good bat at cricket, and an excellent polo player.

Captain Hodgkinson commenced his military career in the ranks of the 2nd Volunteer Battalion Sherwood Foresters for one year; in March, 1902, he was gazetted 2nd Lieutenant in that battalion, and in 1905 Captain. In the following year he was transferred to the 4th Battalion Royal Dublin Fusiliers. He devoted himself seriously to his military duties, and obtained nearly all the special certificates possible, including his qualification for promotion to Captain in the Regular Army; certificates for attendance at the Infantry School at Chelsea (1903) and Dublin (1907), from which he passed first with " special " certificate; the School of Musketry, Hythe (1904 and 1909); Signalling, Aldershot (1905), with Instructor's Certificate; Military Engineering, Chatham (1906); Veterinary School, Aldershot (1908); Equitation, Dublin (1907); and a machine-gun course at Vickers, Sons & Maxim's (1909). He also passed the preliminary examination for Army Interpreter in Russian. He had hoped to serve in the South African War, but was not then thought sufficiently experienced, having only joined the Army in 1901.

In March, 1906, Captain Hodgkinson was transferred, at his own request, to the 4th Royal Dublin Fusiliers (Militia) as a Captain, and did much useful work in the training of men and horses at Woolwich while detached from his regiment. In 1910 he was transferred to the 3rd Dragoon Guards, and served with that regiment in Egypt.

On the outbreak of the war with Germany the regiment was recalled to serve in France, and, after a short period of preparation in England, left for the front. A few days after arrival there Captain Hodgkinson, while in charge of the regimental machine guns, was severely wounded in the head by a bullet at Zillebeke, and died at Boulogne on the 10th November, 1914, from the effects.

Captain Hodgkinson was a splendid type of man, standing 6 ft. 4½ in. in height. Once, when on duty as a Guard of Honour, he was specially noticed by King Edward VII. He was modest and rather reserved in manner.

After his death a solemn Requiem Mass was celebrated at the Roman Catholic Chapel at Hassop, which Captain Hodgkinson used to attend when living at Baslow, the Rector of his old college—Mount St. Mary's—being the celebrant.

CAPTAIN CHRISTOPHER ANTONY ROWLANDSON HODGSON, 3rd BATTN. THE ROYAL WARWICKSHIRE REGT.,

was the son of Arthur Pemberton Hodgson, I.C.S., and was born in 1873. He was educated at Worcester College, Oxford.

He joined the 3rd Battalion (then the 5th) Warwickshire Regiment in December, 1899, being promoted Lieutenant in July, 1900, and becoming Captain in March, 1901. During his service he qualified

at the School of Musketry, obtained a certificate in A.S.C. duties, and was attached to the Regular Forces, obtaining a satisfactory report for the rank of Field Officer.

In the South African War Captain Hodgson served with the Remount Department before 1901. After being invalided home he returned there in the same year with the Royal Warwickshire Regiment, remaining till 1902. For his services he received the Queen's medal with four clasps. In the Great War he was with a Regular battalion when killed on the 18th December, 1914, near Fleurbaix (district of Armentières).

The following account of his death was given by an officer who was near him at the time: " He went out in front of everyone, with a wire-cutter in each hand, and cut away through that zone of hell that lies between the two lines of trenches. He was not killed until he had got right up to the German trench, but his work was done, and the way was clear. So far as I can hear, he never said anything—he just went and did it, though he knew full well that nothing could save him, and that he would be dead in ten minutes. His name deserves to be written for ever on the Roll of Heroes."

Captain Hodgson married, in 1913, Miss " Alec " Hely, daughter of C. Wisdom Hely, Esq., of Dublin. He left no family.

LIEUTENANT GEORGE WILLIAM HOUGHTON HODGSON, 2nd BATTN. THE BORDER REGIMENT,

who died on the 6th November, 1914, of wounds received a day or two previously, was born on the 21st October, 1888, at The Rectory, Distington, Cumberland, the son of the late Rev. W. G. C. Hodgson, J.P., M.A., of Houghton House,

Cumberland, and of Mrs. Hodgson, only daughter of the late William Harrison, barrister-at-law, of Bishop Yards, Penrith. He was a nephew of the Bishop of Edmundsbury and of Courtenay Hodgson, Esq., Clerk of the Peace for the County of Cumberland.

Lieutenant Hodgson was educated at Westminster School and Trinity College, Cambridge, where he took his degree in 1912, and where he was in the Artillery O.T.C. He joined the Border Regiment as 2nd Lieutenant in September, 1911, and became Lieutenant in October, 1914, during the war.

Lieutenant Hodgson died in the Boulogne Hospital on Friday, the 6th November, 1914, of wounds received on the 2nd of that month. During the fighting immediately preceding that date his battalion had lost heavily, and had repeatedly earned the admiration of the Brigadier and other senior officers in the brigade. He was mentioned in Sir John French's Despatch of the 14th January, 1915.

Captain Askew, of the Battalion, himself subsequently killed in action, wrote the following account of the death of Lieutenant Hodgson : " We were holding a section of an entrenched position on the 2nd, and your son's company, ' D,' was on the right of our line . . . . and the Germans (took) an opportunity to make a very strong attack upon our right. So well were our men kept in hand by your son and the late Captain Gerrard (killed the same day) that they hung on for several hours unsupported, and even after both officers were hit they fought splendidly. The result was the German attack failed, and there is no doubt that this was due to the splendid example set by your son. He was directing the fire of his men when he was hit in the neck by a bullet."

Lieutenant Hodgson was a keen soldier and sportsman, and when at Cambridge was coxswain of the third Trinity boat.

CAPTAIN GEORGE BERTRAM POLLOCK-HODSOLL, 3rd BATTN. SUFFOLK

REGIMENT, born on the 18th June, 1875, at Loose Court, Loose, near Maidstone, Kent, was descended from the old Kent family of " Hodsoll " —Mandy Hodsoll, of Holywell, and the Hodsolls, men of Kent, were of considerable note in the Army of Edward the Black Prince—and was the second son of Charles Maxfield and Georgiana Mary Hodsoll. His mother was the elder daughter of George Kennet Pollock, granddaughter of Sir David Pollock, Chief Justice of Bombay, and grand-niece of Sir Frederick Pollock, Chief Baron of the Exchequer, and of Field-Marshal Sir George Pollock, " of the Khyber Pass."

He was educated at Maidstone School and University College, Oxford, and was an energetic speaker for the Unionist Party and for universal military service.

Captain Pollock-Hodsoll received his commission in the 4th Battalion Suffolk Regiment (Cambridgeshire Militia) in December, 1902, being subsequently transferred to the 3rd Battalion (Special Reserve), in which he was promoted Captain in August, 1914. He was

attached for active service to the 1st Battalion Cheshire Regiment, with which he was serving when he was killed in action on the 7th November, 1914, while gallantly leading a counterattack on the enemy near Ypres.

Captain Pollock-Hodsoll was a member of the Junior Naval and Military Club, and was well known as an Association football player, having for many years played for the Casuals and the Corinthians, and having captained the Army team on several occasions.

He married, in June, 1914, Olive Margaret, eldest daughter of the Rev. Dr. Milne Rae, of Edinburgh.

CAPTAIN IVAN DAYRELL MEREDITH HOGG, 101st GRENADIERS, INDIAN ARMY,

who was killed in action on the 4th November, 1914, during the attack on Tanga, East Africa, was the third and youngest son of the late General George Forbes Hogg, C.B., and of Mrs. Hogg, Cromer House, Brentwood.

He was born on the 2nd April, 1884, at 92, Oxford Gardens, London, W., and was educated at the United Services College, Westward Ho ! After passing for the Indian Army, he received an unattached 2nd Lieutenancy in January, 1903, and carried out his probationary period with the 2nd Oxford Light Infantry, and then with the 2nd Argyll and Sutherland Highlanders, joining the Indian Army on the 8th April, 1904. He became Lieutenant in April, 1905, and was promoted Captain in January,1912. Captain Hogg married, in December, 1911, Bridget Eyre, youngest daughter of the late William H. Lloyd, of Barham House, Droitwich.

LIEUTENANT-COLONEL IAN GRAHAM HOGG, D.S.O., 4th (QUEEN'S OWN) HUSSARS,

was the son of Quintin Hogg, Esq., the founder of the Polytechnic, Regent Street, London, an institution known throughout the English-speaking world. He was born on the 2nd February, 1875, at Richmond Terrace, Whitehall, and was educated at Eton and the Royal Military College, Sandhurst, and subsequently passed through the Staff College. He entered the Army in 1896, and had a long record of war services.

From 1900–05 he was employed with the West African Frontier Force, during which period he was in command of several punitive expeditions, and for his services received the distinction of the D.S.O., the rank of Brevet-Major, and the West African war medal. In the Boer War he served on the Staff of General Sir Bruce Hamilton, and was present at engagements in the Cape Colony, Transvaal, and Orange River Colony, He received the Queen's medal with four clasps.

After leaving the Staff College he held a temporary Staff appointment at the War Office, and was promoted to the command of his regiment in 1913, which he took to the Continent on the outbreak of the Great War. He was engaged in wood fighting just north of the village of Haramont, north-west of Villers Cotteret, on the 1st September, 1914, when he was shot, and succumbed to his wounds twenty-four hours later.

In the retirement from Compiègne he had commanded the rearguard, and insisted on being the last man to leave. When actually shot he was standing in an open clearing, signalling with his cap for some men to retire.

He was a good polo player, and had won several cups, and was a member of the Cavalry and Ranalagh Clubs.

He was not married.

LIEUTENANT WILLIAM HUGH HOLBECH, 2nd BATTN. SCOTS GUARDS, RESERVE OF OFFICERS,

who died in hospital at Woolwich on the 1st November, 1914, of wounds received in action on the 25th October near Ypres, was born in August, 1882, and was appointed 2nd Lieutenant to the Scots Guards in January, 1902, being promoted Lieutenant in March, 1904. He joined the Reserve of Officers in February, 1907.

MAJOR CHARLES STEWART HOLLAND, ROYAL FIELD ARTILLERY,

the son of Charles and Mrs. Holland, of 7, The Grange, Wimbledon, was born on the 28th December, 1875. He entered the Royal Artillery in November, 1895, becoming Lieutenant in November, 1898, and Captain in November, 1901.

Major Holland served in the South African War in 1902, being present at operations in the Orange River Colony, for which he received the Queen's medal with four clasps.

From February, 1905, till January, 1907, and again from July, 1909, till June, 1911, he was an Adjutant in his regiment. He obtained his Majority in May, 1912.

Major Holland's name appeared in the first list issued by the War Office on the 1st September, 1914, of British losses as killed in action in the Great War.

LIEUTENANT JOHN HOLMAN, 4th (ROYAL IRISH) DRAGOON GUARDS,

was the second son of the late John H. Holman, of Tregenna, Camborne, Cornwall, senior partner of the well-known engineering firm of Holman Bros., and was born at Camborne on the 5th December, 1894. Lieutenant Holman was educated at

Blundell's School from 1904–12, after which he entered the R.M.C., Sandhurst. After a year's training there he obtained his commission in the 4th Dragoon Guards in September, 1913, becoming Lieutenant in July, 1914, subsequently leaving for France on the 15th August. He was wounded on the 29th October, 1914, in action near Armentières while helping a wounded brother officer, and died next day at the Base Hospital, Boulogne.

Many letters were received by his mother from brother officers speaking highly of Lieutenant Holman's devotion to duty, and bearing testimony to the great affection and esteem which was felt for him, and specially mentioning his constant care and thought for others, animals as well as men.

LIEUTENANT ALEXANDER CHARLES HOLME, 1st BATTN. GLOUCESTERSHIRE REGT.,

son of Charles H. Holme, of Rawburn, Duns, Scotland, was born at Mussoorie, North West Provinces, India, on the 26th September, 1888.

He was educated at Charterhouse and the R.M.C., Sandhurst. He joined

the Gloucestershire Regiment in March, 1909, becoming Lieutenant in July, 1911 ; and served in India with his battalion. He then volunteered for service in Southern Nigeria, and was killed in action against the Germans at Nsanakang, Cameroons, on the 6th September, 1914. Lieutenant A. C. Holme's brother—Lieutenant R. H. P. Holme, 2nd King's Own Scottish Borderers—died on the 9th November, 1914, of wounds received on the 31st October.

LIEUTENANT RONALD HENRY PAULL HOLME, 2nd BATTN. THE KING'S OWN SCOTTISH BORDERERS,

son of Charles H Holme, of Rathburne, Duns, Scotland, was born on the 1st January, 1890, at Rurki, North West Provinces, India.

He was educated at Haileybury College and the R.M.C., Sandhurst, obtaining his commission in the K.O.S.B. in October, 1910, and becoming Lieutenant in February, 1914.

He was stationed with his battalion at Belfast and Dublin, and while serving with it on the Continent in the Great War was present at the Battles of Mons, the Aisne, and the Marne. He was wounded by a fragment of shell at Messines on the 31st October, and died from the effects in London on the 9th November, 1914.

Lieutenant R. H. P. Holme's brother—Lieutenant A. C. Holme, 1st Gloucestershire Regiment—was killed in action against the Germans in the Cameroons on the 6th September, 1914.

LIEUTENANT (temp. CAPTAIN) CECIL CRAMPTON HOLMES, 1st BATTN. LINCOLNSHIRE REGIMENT,

was shown in the monthly official casualty list published in May, 1915, as having been "unofficially reported killed or died of wounds," no place or date being given, but he is believed to have died about the 26th August, 1914, from wounds received in action at Frameries, near Mons.

He was the second surviving son of Captain

H. W. Holmes, of Rockwood, Galway, and Anna Holmes, daughter of the late Edmond Concanon, of Waterloo, County Galway. He was born on the 21st January, 1888, and was educated at Bedford Grammar School, where he distinguished himself as an athlete, getting his colours for rowing, water polo, and Rugby football. He passed into the R.M.C., Sandhurst, and was a Sandhurst cadet at Woolwich, where he played in the Rugby team, and came second of his year in the boxing team. On passing out of Sandhurst, he was specially commended for riding, and got his commission in the 1st Battalion Lincolnshire Regiment in October, 1907. He spent five years in India, becoming Lieutenant in November, 1911, and was given the temporary rank of Captain in November, 1914, before his death was confirmed.

He left for the front on the 13th August, 1914, as Machine Gun Officer, and took part in the Battle of Mons. The following day, at Frameries, he was wounded while working his guns with such coolness and bravery that he was mentioned in Sir John French's Despatch of the 8th October, 1914.

The news of his death was not received till the 17th February, 1915. In a letter from Captain Rose, of his regiment—a prisoner in Germany—to his wife, he said : "Poor old Holmes was in my hospital, but not in the same ward. He died two days after he was admitted, and was buried in the cemetery at Frameries, near Mons."

He was a great favourite with officers and men in his regiment. His late Colonel, now Brigadier-General R. Maxwell, wrote when his fate was uncertain : "I fear there is no hope. It gives me the greatest grief to have to write this. He was such a good fellow, a fine officer, and a great personal friend, and I cannot tell you how grieved I am, and all the regiment who are left (alas ! they are very few, I fear) will be. He was a gallant officer and beloved by all."

LIEUTENANT FRANCIS LENNOX HOLMES, 1st BATTN. SOUTH STAFFORDSHIRE REGIMENT,

who was killed in action at the first Battle of Ypres on the 23rd October, 1914, was the younger son of the late Major-General P. R. Holmes, R.M.L.I., and of Mrs. B. G. Harrison, Evesham House, Cheltenham. He was born at Stoke, Devonport,

the 11th October, 1887, and was educated Cheltenham College. He passed through e R.M.C., Sandhurst, and was gazetted to e 1st South Staffordshire Regiment in Sep- mber, 1908, becoming Lieutenant in July, 09. He was a member of the Public Schools' ub.

₃ joined the battalion at Devonport, and ₃nt with it to Gibraltar, and afterwards to etermaritzburg, Natal. On the outbreak of ₃ war with Germany he was ordered home for tive service and went with his battalion to the ₃nt.

₃e following entry relating to his death was ₃nd in his Colonel's diary : " Lieutenant ₃lmes was killed this day. He was taking servation and instructing the men where and ₃en to aim. He was in command of a half of ₃ ' Company, and had been doing excellent ₃rk the whole day. He had been looking ₃er and superintending a machine gun, which ₃ very good service. He also had done a lot very dangerous work in scouting through the ₃od in front of his section of trenches, and had ₃wn much pluck and coolness."

Lance-Corporal gave the following details : ₃n the 22nd October, 1914, I was working ₃ machine gun when Mr. Holmes came up to ₃, and acted as my number two, and also as ₃ observer, as the Germans were only five ndred yards from us, and he was quite excited, I was mowing them down in hundreds, and got over that day all right. On the 23rd tober he visited me again, and I shifted my ₃ition close to where Mr. Holmes was killed ₃ut three o'clock. He was in a trench ₃t in front of some cottages—four of them I ieve. He was at the back of his trench, ₃ing cover at the back of a bag of potatoes, ₃daging up Private Mills, who had his three ₃ers blown off. After that he was taking aim the Germans, and he was just going to pull ₃ trigger when a bullet hit him straight ₃ween the two eyes. . . . He never spoke at ₃ ; he died instantly. He was carried into ₃e cottages at the back. . . . I wish he had ₃d. I shall never forget him as long as I live. ₃was a hero."

₃utenant Holmes came of a fighting family. ₃ father—Major-General Ponsonby Ross ₃lmes, R.M.L.I.—fought in the Baltic ; his ₃le—Captain F. Holmes, of the 20th Regi- ₃nt—was wounded at the Redan, and served ₃the Indian Mutiny ; and his grandfather— ₃utenant-Colonel Stephen Holmes—was at Battles of Fuentes d'Onor and Salamanca, ₃ was particularly mentioned in Despatches the Duke of Wellington for having led a small ₃ty into the enemy's works at the Siege of ₃gos. He was also present at the Battle of ₃terloo as Major of Brigade to General ₃kenzie.

2nd LIEUTENANT THOMAS SYMONDS HOLMES, THE QUEEN'S (ROYAL WEST SURREY REGIMENT), who was killed in action on the 11th November, 1914, in France, aged twenty-two, was the only son of Commander Thomas Holmes, R.N., Chief Inspector of Lifeboats, and of Mrs. Thomas Holmes. He was a grandson of the late Admiral of the Fleet Sir Thomas M. Symonds, G.C.B., and of Dame Prestwood Mary, his wife. 2nd Lieutenant Holmes joined the Special Reserve of his regiment, on probation, in July, 1914, and, for active service was attached to the 1st Battalion East Kent Regiment.

2nd LIEUTENANT H. WILFRED HOLT, 56th COMPANY, ROYAL ENGINEERS (SPECIAL RESERVE), was killed in action at Mons on the 24th August, 1914. He was the youngest son of Mr. and Mrs. H. P. Holt, of 15, Kensington Court, London, W., and joined the Special Reserve (Supplementary Officers) Royal Engineers on the 25th June, 1910.

MAJOR WALTER GABRIEL HOME, 6th DRAGOON GUARDS (THE CARABINIERS), is believed to have died on the 13th November, 1914, of wounds received in action near Messines, France, on the 31st October, 1914.

He was born on the 25th October, 1872, and received his commission in the Carabiniers from the Militia in October, 1892, becoming Lieu- tenant in May, 1897, and Captain in July, 1900. He served in the South African War, in which he was on the Staff as Brigade Signalling Officer from December, 1899, to November, 1900 ; Divisional Signalling Officer from December, 1901, to August, 1902 ; and also served as A.D.C. to the Officer Commanding Cavalry Brigade. He took part in the relief of Kimberley, and was present at operations in the Orange Free State ; at Paardeberg, in the Transvaal ; east and west of Pretoria ; and in Cape Colony, including actions at Poplar Grove, Driefontein, Karee Siding, Zand River (near Johannesburg), Pretoria, Diamond Hill, Riet Vlei, and Belfast. He was twice mentioned in Despatches (" Lon- don Gazette," 10th September, 1901, and 29th July, 1902) ; was promoted Brevet-Major (22nd August, 1902) ; and received the Queen's medal with six clasps and the King's medal with two clasps.

He obtained his substantive Majority in Novem- ber, 1905.

Very soon after the outbreak of the Great War Major Home proceeded to the Continent for active service, and was present at much of the fighting during the early stages of the Cam- paign, including the Battle of the Aisne. He was mentioned in Sir John French's Despatch of 8th October, 1914.

LIEUTENANT JOHN RICHARDS HOMFRAY, 1st BATTN. SOUTH WALES BORDERERS,

who was killed by shell at Zillebeke, Belgium, on the 11th November, 1914, was the second son of Colonel and Mrs. Herbert Homfray, of Penllyn Castle, Cowbridge, South Wales, and was born there on the 18th October, 1893; he was a nephew of Captain J. G. R. Homfray.

He was educated at Haileybury College, Herts, and the R.M.C. Sandhurst, from which he was gazetted to the South Wales Borderers in September, 1912, getting his step in September, 1914.

LIEUTENANT WILLIAM EDWARD HOPE, 1st BATTN. IRISH GUARDS,

son of the late William Hope, M.D., and Mrs. William Hope, 18, Carlisle Mansions, London, S.W., was born on the 28th February, 1887, at 56, Curzon Street, Mayfair, W. Educated for a short time at Beaumont, Windsor, and subsequently by Army tutors, he, at the age of seventeen, joined the 3rd Battalion Duke of Cornwall's Light Infantry, being transferred to the Irish Guards in January, 1910. He remained in the battalion for three years, when he left it to go on the Special Reserve of the battalion, and was appointed A.D.C. to the Lord-Lieutenant of Ireland, in December, 1912.

On the outbreak of war he rejoined the Irish Guards, and proceeded with the Expeditionary Force to France in August, 1914. He was present at every battle from Mons up to the action at Klein Zillebeke, where he fell on the 6th November, 1914.

The Major commanding the battalion said that Lieutenant Hope made many valuable sketches of the enemy's position under fire.

He went in for sports generally, was a member of the Guards' Club, and was unmarried.

LIEUTENANT CHARLES RANDOLPH INNES HOPKINS, 2nd BATTN. THE CAMERONIANS (SCOTTISH RIFLES),

who was killed in action on the 18th December, 1914, aged twenty-one years, was the third son of Lieutenant-Colonel C. H. Innes Hopkins (late 2nd Scottish Rifles), commanding 1st Tyneside Scottish, and Mrs. Hopkins, "The Towers," Ryton-on-Tyne.

He was a cadet at the R.M.C., Sandhurst, where he was a member of the hockey team and Cricket XI. He joined the Army in September, 1912, becoming Lieutenant in October, 1913.

LIEUT. HERBERT LESLIE HOPKINS, M.D., ROYAL ARMY MEDICAL CORPS,

who was killed in action on the 19th September, 1914, was only gazetted to the R.A.M.C. with the temporary rank of Lieutenant on the 15th August, 1914.

He carried out his medical studies at Guy's Hospital, and took his degrees at the London University about 1911. After qualifying he was for some time House Physician at the Derby Royal Infirmary.

CAPTAIN CHARLES REGINALD THOMPSON HOPKINSON, EAST SURREY REGIMENT AND 1st BATTN. NIGERIA REGIMENT,

who was killed in action in the Cameroons on the 6th September, 1914, was the son of the late C. R. Hopkinson, Acomb Lodge, and Mrs. E. Hamilton Hurst, Hurst Grove, Bedford, and a grandson of the late C. N. Hopkinson, Clifton, York.

He was born at York on the 30th January, 1880, and was educated at Bedford Grammar School. He joined the Lancashire Fusiliers as 2nd Lieutenant in February, 1900; became Lieutenant in June of the same year, and Captain in November, 1907. In May, 1908, he was transferred to the East Surrey Regiment.

He took part in the South African War, being present at operations in the Transvaal in 1900; in Natal, including the action at Laing's Nek; in the Orange River Colony; and at further operations in the Transvaal from January, 1901, to May, 1902. He received the Queen's medal with three clasps and the King's medal with two clasps.

From July, 1904, to October, 1908, he was employed with the West African Frontier Force in Southern Nigeria, being mentioned for his services in Despatches ("London Gazette," 13th March, 1908), and receiving the medal with clasp. In May, 1910, he was again detached for service with the West African Frontier Force, and was serving with it when he was killed at Nsanakan. After that place had been taken two companies of British troops were left there, and early in the morning of the 6th September, 1914, were suddenly attacked by the enemy, who had raised strong reinforcements. This attack was repulsed, but a second one was made at 5 a.m., and the place surrounded by some seventy white German officers and about seven hundred men. Though overwhelmed, our men continued firing till their ammunition was exhausted, when they fixed bayonets and charged the enemy. Two officers—Captain Hopkinson and Lieutenant Holmes, Gloucester Regiment—were killed, while three others were wounded and taken prisoners.

Captain Hopkinson's relations received from the late officer's servant a letter giving some personal details of his death.

Captain Hopkinson was fond of polo, cricket, football, and shooting, and was a member of the Junior Naval and Military Club.

He married, in 1909, Beryl, daughter of the late David Stewart, of Edinburgh, and left one son.

CAPTAIN ALEXANDER HORNE, 1st BATTN. THE QUEEN'S OWN CAMERON HIGHLANDERS,

was the fourth son of the late Thomas Elliot Ogilvie Horne, Writer to the Signet, of Edinburgh, and was born there on the 30th September, 1875. He was first cousin of Major-General H. S. Horne, R.H.A., and of Lieutenant-Colonel E. W. Horne, 3rd Battalion Seaforth Highlanders.

Captain Horne was educated at St. Ninian's Preparatory School, Moffat, and at Charterhouse.

He first served in the Seaforth Highlanders (Militia), and obtained his commission in the 1st Battalion Cameron Highlanders in 1897. With it he served in Egypt in 1898, being present at the Battle of the Atbara and Omdurman, for which he received the Egyptian medal with two clasps and the Khedive's medal, and proceeded to Fashoda with his company as escort to Lord Kitchener.

With his battalion he served in the South African War, 1901-02, being present at operations in the Transvaal, Orange River Colony, Cape Colony and on the Zululand frontier of Natal, being awarded at its conclusion the Queen's medal with three clasps and the King's medal with two clasps.

While serving in France in the Great War he was severely wounded on the 14th September, 1914, near Vendresse, in the advance on the Troyon Ridge, and while lying in the fire zone was shot dead by the enemy at close quarters, as was also Private Finnie, of his company, who was attending him.

Captain Horne was a keen rider to hounds; he won the Irish Army Point-to-Point race for heavyweights in 1906, and ran third for lightweights.

He was a member of the Automobile and Caledonian Clubs, London, and was unmarried.

LIEUTENANT R. HORRIDGE, 4th (attd. 2nd) BATTN. MANCHESTER REGIMENT,

was killed in action on the 17th November, 1914. He joined his regiment as 2nd Lieutenant in October, 1911, and was promoted Lieutenant in July, 1914, proceeding to the seat of war soon after the outbreak of hostilities.

LIEUTENANT CYRIL GORDON HOSKING, ROYAL ARTILLERY,

who was killed in an aeroplane accident, was the son of Edward Hosking, I.C.S.

He was born at Karachi, Sind, India, on the 30th July, 1890, and was educated at Durham School and the R.M.A., Woolwich. He entered the Royal Artillery in July, 1910, becoming Lieutenant in July, 1913, and in the latter year he joined the R.F.C., Military Wing, as Flying Officer. While at Durham he was Captain of the School Boats, and was also Honorary Secretary of the Military Sports, R.F.C., Netheravon.

During a reconnaissance on the German lines at Gheluvelt on the 26th October, 1914, he was piloting a machine with Captain Crean, Northumberland Fusiliers as observer, when the aeroplane was fired at and shot down. It fell in our own lines, both officers being killed. They were buried together where they fell by two brother officers while under shell fire.

LIEUTENANT EDWIN CECIL LEIGH HOSKYNS, 1st BATTN. ROYAL WELSH FUSILIERS,

who was killed in action on the 20th October, 1914, was the only son and heir of Sir Leigh Hoskyns, Bart., Barrister - at - Law, J.P. for Oxford and High Sheriff, 1907, formerly Crown Prosecutor of Griqualand West, who succeeded his brother as eleventh Bart. in July, 1914.

He was born at Iffley, Oxfordshire, on the 22nd September, 1890, and was educated at Eton and the R.M.C., Sandhurst, joining the R.W.F. in September, 1911, and becoming Lieutenant in April, 1913. He was fond of hunting and polo. Lieutenant Hoskyns was killed near Ypres when the gallant VIIth Division, of which his battalion formed part, without any reserves, held in check nearly one hundred thousand Germans.

2nd LIEUTENANT WILLIAM GILBERT HOULDSWORTH, 1st BATTN. SCOTS GUARDS,

was the only surviving son of the Rev. W. T. and Mrs. Houldsworth, of 44, Lennox Gardens, London, and Cranston, North Berwick. He was born on the 17th May, 1891, and was educated at Wellington House, Westgate-on-Sea (Rev. Herbert Bull); at Eton (The Dame's, and on her death Mr. Hill's House); and Magdalen College, Oxford. There he took his B.A. degree in March, 1914. He held the rank of 2nd Lieutenant on the unattached list of candidates of the University O.T.C., and in May, 1914, he went to Aldershot and served with the 1st Battalion Scots Guards till July. On the 4th August he received his commission in the Scots Guards as 2nd Lieutenant, with the prescribed eighteen months' seniority as a University candidate, and left with his battalion for France on the 13th of the month.

He fought at Mons; was in the retirement from there, and in the subsequent advance, taking part in the engagements on the Marne and the Grand and Petit Morin. On the 13th September, at the commencement of the Battle of the Aisne, he was wounded at the village of Vendresse, and died in the American Hospital at Neuilly, Paris, on the 23rd September, 1914.

His C.O. paid a warm tribute to his leading of his platoon, and expressed his deep regret at the loss the regiment had sustained in the death of so promising a young officer.

Mr. Houldsworth was a member of the Bachelors' and Conservative Clubs, London, and of the New and Tantallon Clubs, North Berwick. He was a keen sportsman, a powerful golfer, a good horseman, and very popular with both officers and men.

2nd LIEUTENANT HAROLD HOUSECROFT, 4th (attd. 1st) BATTN. EAST SURREY REGIMENT,

born on the 22nd September, 1893, at Mayflower Road, Clapham, S.W., was the son of Harry and Emia Housecroft, and a relative of the Rev. T. Housecroft, Limpenhoe Rectory, Reedham, Norfolk. He was educated at the City of London School, and gained

a first class at the College of Preceptors. He was a Sergeant in the Cadet Corps.

He joined the Army immediately war was declared, his commission in the 4th Battalion, to which he was appointed on probation, being dated the 15th August, 1914, and joined the battalion at Plymouth. For active service he was attached to the 1st Battalion, and left Devonport for France to join it at La Bassée. Early in the morning of the 19th November, 1914, he left the front firing trench to visit a support trench in order to arrange a better distribution of rations. Sniped at all the way, he reached the trench, and was shot in the mouth while giving instructions to a sergeant.

2nd LIEUTENANT PERCY EDGAR NAPIER HOWARD, 2nd BATTN. ROYAL IRISH REGIMENT,

son of William Ivine Howard, Customs Service, Chittagong, India, was born at Darjeeling, India, on the 23rd November, 1894.

2nd Lieutenant Howard, who was a relative of Mrs. Broucke, of Earlham, Parkstone, Dorset, was educated at Taunton and Elizabeth College, Guernsey, joining the latter school in order to study for the Army. While there he made a reputation as an athlete, being a keen footballer and excellent cricketer. After leaving

Guernsey he entered the R.M.C., Sandhurst, from which he received his commission in the Royal Irish Regiment in August, 1914.

He died on the night of the 19th–20th October, 1914, having been mortally wounded by bursting shell when his battalion, on the 19th, stormed and took German trenches at Le Pilly. He was carried to the rear and died some hours later. It has not been possible to obtain any authentic details, for it is believed that only one man of 2nd Lieutenant Howard's party escaped; but it was reported that officer was commanding the leading platoon when he was badly hit in both legs.

LIEUT. AUBREY WELLS HUDSON, 5th BATTN. WORCESTERSHIRE REGT.,

who was killed at the Battle of the Aisne on the 26th September, 1914, aged thirty-one, was the youngest son of Lieutenant - Colonel A. H. Hudson, of Wick House, Pershore. His rank of Lieutenant in his regiment dated from August, 1909.

LIEUTENANT JAMES LAIDLAW HUGGAN, ROYAL ARMY MEDICAL CORPS, attd. to the 3rd BATTN. COLDSTREAM GUARDS,

was the son of the late Mr. Robert Huggan, and was born at Jedburgh on the 11th October, 1888.

He was educated at Darlington Grammar School, where he was Captain of the "Soccer" team, before going to Edinburgh University to study medicine, where he obtained first-class honours in surgery. He was a noted Scottish International Rugby football player. Before joining the University he used to play

for the Jed Forest Rugby Club, and afterwards played twice for the Army v. Navy, and eventually got his Scottish cap in March, 1914.

After qualifying he was gazetted to the R.A.M.C. in July, 1912.

He was killed in action on the River Aisne on the 16th September, 1914. The Colonel of the Coldstream Guards wrote of him as follows: "If I ever met a brave man, he was. At Landrecies, when we were under a heavy fire for some hours during the night, he remained up in the front the whole night, helping and dressing the wounded as coolly as if he were in a hospital in time of peace. At Villers Cotterets he was conspicuous for his bravery. This was a rearguard action, and the line was being pushed back; but he was always in the rear, and sometimes even nearer to the enemy, dressing the wounded and helping them back. At the Battle of the Aisne he was most conspicuous everywhere. On the day on which he was killed he again did a very brave action. There were in a barn about sixty wounded Germans. They were all cases that could not move without help. The Germans shelled this barn and set it on fire. Your brother, in spite of shot and shell raining about him, called for volunteers to help him to save these wounded men from the burning building, and I am glad to say that it was greatly in consequence of his bravery that they were all saved. After he had run this great danger successfully he moved many of his wounded men to a quarry in rear when a big shell came into it and killed him and many others. He was buried, near where he fell, in the garden of La Cour de Soupir Farm. The whole battalion regretted his loss, as we had all got very fond of him, and admired him as a really brave man, always ready to sacrifice himself for the good of those who should happen to come under him for treatment."

The Town Council of Jedburgh, his birthplace, have given permission for the erection of a memorial stone near the Abbey, close to the High Rampart.

LIEUTENANT FREDERICK DEETON HUGHES, EAST LANCASHIRE REGT.,

who was killed in action on the 21st October, 1914, by being shot through the head while leading his platoon in Flanders, was the seventh and youngest son of the late R. D. Hughes, Solicitor, Royston, and a grandson of Captain Samuel Hughes, 50th Madras Native Infantry

He was born on the 10th January, 1888, at Royston, Herts, and after his education at Mercers' School, Holborn, and the R.M.C., Sandhurst, he entered the West India Regiment in February, 1909, becoming Lieutenant in February, 1911. In August of the latter year he was transferred to the East Lancashire Regiment, and in June, 1913, was appointed to the Nigeria Regiment, West African Frontier Force. Mr. Hughes was a member of the Junior Army and Navy Club, and his recreations were tennis and cricket.

2nd LIEUTENANT GUY WILEY HUGHES, RESERVE OF OFFICERS, attd. 4th BATTN. THE DUKE OF CAMBRIDGE'S OWN (MIDDLESEX REGIMENT),

was the son of George Hughes, Esq., and was born at Bushey Heath on the 26th February, 1892.

He was educated at Charterhouse, where he was Monitor of Gownboys, and leaving there in 1911 he proceeded to the South Eastern Agricultural College, Wye, as his taste lay in the direction of agriculture, and he intended to take to it as a profession. Here he became Head Student, and gained great popularity among all with whom he came in contact there. He regularly represented the College at Association football, having been Captain of the team in his last year, and also in lawn tennis. As proof of the general confidence reposed in him he was elected Secretary of the Union Society of the College in his final year. He obtained his diploma in 1914.

Having taken his " A " certificate at Charterhouse, he joined the Reserve of Officers, and on the outbreak of the war he was called up for service and attached to the 4th Battalion Middlesex Regiment, proceeding with it to the Continent on the 15th October, 1914.

He was killed when looking for a missing private outside his trench on the 31st December, 1914, and was buried in a churchyard at Bailleul. His father received many appreciative letters from those with whom 2nd Lieutenant Hughes had been associated, including his House Master at Charterhouse, the Principal and other authorities of Wye College, and the Vicar of Wye. His Colonel wrote : " He was very popular with us all, and as an officer most reliable and keen, and one in whom I had the most perfect confidence." His Major, the Captain of his company (himself wounded), and his Company Sergeant-Major also sent letters of sympathy and regard.

2nd LIEUTENANT LIONEL HOLFORD HUGHES, 3rd (attd. 1st) BATTN. THE PRINCE OF WALES'S (NORTH STAFFORDSHIRE REGIMENT),

who was killed in action on the 29th October, 1914, aged nineteen years, in the trenches south of Armentières, was the only son of Allan Edward and Evelyn Emma Hughes, of Cintra, Budleigh Salterton.
He joined the North Staffordshire Regiment in April, 1913.

LIEUTENANT ROBERT PEYTON HUGHES, ADJUTANT 101st GRENADIERS, INDIAN ARMY,

who was killed in action on the 2nd November, 1914, was the son of Dr. and Mrs. Hughes, Down House, Whitchurch, Tavistock. He was born on the 5th March, 1882, and was educated at Marlborough (Mitre) from 1901 to 1906.

After passing for the Indian Army, he received an unattached 2nd Lieutenancy on the 17th August, 1907, and joined the Indian Army in December, 1908, becoming Lieutenant in November, 1909.

CAPTAIN THOMAS HECTOR HUGHES, 3rd BATTN. WORCESTERSHIRE REGT.,

was the son of Frederick and Alice Ellen Hughes, and was born at Reigate on the 16th July, 1881. He was educated at Repton School from 1895 to 1900, where he was in both the Cricket and Football XI's, and joined the 3rd Worcestershire Regiment at Aldershot in 1901, becoming Lieutenant in May, 1903, and Captain in June, 1911. From 1910 to 1913 he was Adjutant of his battalion.

He was shot on the 15th October, 1914, while leading a company outside the village of Richebourg St. Vaast. For his services he was mentioned in Sir John French's Despatch of the 14th January, 1915.

Captain Hughes was a member of the Army and Navy and Incogniti Clubs. He was fond of all winter sports, which he enjoyed in Switzerland. He married Gertrude Mary, daughter of C. F. Dobson, Esq., of Nottingham, and left a daughter, Joan, born in June, 1912, and a son, born in March, 1914.

2nd LIEUTENANT WILLIAM SLADEN HUGHES, 2nd BATTN. ROYAL SUSSEX REGIMENT,

who was born at Blackrock, County Dublin, on the 17th September, 1889, was the son of A. F. Hughes, Esq., Hillbrook, Birr, King's County, formerly of Cappy, Enniskillen. He was a nephew of Colonel E. A. Hughes, 2nd Queen's; Colonel P. J. Hughes, Cameronians; and Colonel G. A. Hughes, R.A.M.C.

2nd Lieutenant Hughes was educated at Aravon, Bray, and Sedbergh, Yorkshire, and was prepared for the Service examination by Army tutors. He completed two trainings with the Inniskilling Fusiliers, afterwards being attached on probation for one year to the 2nd Royal Sussex Regiment, in which he received his commission as 2nd Lieutenant on the 22nd May, 1912.

He was killed at Vendresse in the Battle of the Aisne on the 14th September, 1914.

2nd Lieutenant Hughes was a member of the Wanderers' Football Club, Dublin, and of several golf and cricket clubs.

LIEUTENANT CHARLES GEOFFREY HUME, 1st BATTN. SOUTH STAFFORDSHIRE REGT.,

who was killed on the 26th October, 1914, was born on the 5th July, 1890, at Oatlands, near Weybridge, Surrey, the son of Edward Hume, Barrister-at-Law, and Agnes Mary Hume.

He was educated at St. Aubyn's, Rottingdean; at Malvern College (the Rev. H. Foster's House); and the R.M.C., Sandhurst. He obtained his commission in the South Staffordshire Regiment in 1910, and was promoted Lieutenant in January, 1913. He was fond of polo and sailing.

When he was killed in action near Ypres, his battalion formed part of the VIIth Division, and as the senior officers had been killed he was leading his company.

2nd LIEUTENANT WILLIAM KNOX HUMFREY, 2nd BATTN. LANCASHIRE FUSILIERS,

born at Narborough, Leicestershire, on the 14th May, 1891, was the son of Colonel B. G. Humfrey, Leicestershire Regiment, who retired after twenty years' service, and then commanded the 3rd Battalion in the South African War. Colonel Humfrey's father, Captain John Keys Humfrey, served for many years in the 56th Regiment; and his grandfather was in the 45th Regiment, in which he served all through the Peninsular War, receiving a medal with nine clasps, so the young officer who gave his life in this Great War was one of a long direct line of soldiers.

He was educated at Bedford Grammar School and the R.M.C., Sandhurst, representing his School as a middleweight boxer, and getting into the finals in the Public School Boxing Competition at Aldershot in 1909. He also won the cup for the officers' middleweights at the Southern Command Boxing Tournament in 1912. 2nd Lieutenant Humfrey was gazetted to the 2nd Battalion Lancashire Fusiliers in October, 1910, and was serving with them when killed in action at Le Cateau on the 26th August, 1914, while in command of a machine-gun section.

He was a member of the Cavendish Club, London.

MAJOR GEORGE GEOFFREY PRENDERGAST HUMPHREYS, 127th QUEEN MARY'S OWN BALUCH LIGHT INFANTRY, INDIAN ARMY,

who died of wounds received in action at Hollebeke, Belgium, on the 31st October, 1914, and was buried in Kemmel Cemetery, was the youngest son of the late T. W. D. Humphreys, Esq., J.P., Donoughmore House, Castlefinn, County Donegal, Ireland, and a nephew of the late William Alexander, Primate of Ireland. His grandfather, the late Major J. Humphreys, served under Nelson at the Battle of Copenhagen.

He was born at Miltown House, Strabane, County Tyrone, on the 17th February, 1873, and was educated at Allhallows School, Honiton, Devon, where he was Captain of the Football XV, and in the Cricket XI. He then went to the R.M.C., Sandhurst, from which he was gazetted to the Welsh Regiment in July, 1892, and in June, 1895, was transferred to the 127th Q.M.O. Baluch Light Infantry with the rank of Lieutenant.

In 1897–98 he was on active service in the Uganda Campaign, East Africa, and with the China Field Force in 1901, in July of which year he was promoted Captain. He received the Uganda medal. From December, 1911, to January, 1912, he acted as extra A.D.C. to His Majesty the King-Emperor in India, and received the Coronation Durbar medal, 1911.

For his services in the Great War he was mentioned in Sir John French's Despatch of the 14th January, 1915.

Major Humphreys married, in November, 1903, Olive Muriel, only daughter of Major-General Sir James Bell, K.C.V.O., and left three children : Patrick William, born May, 1905 ; Olive Phyllis, born July, 1909 ; and Lorna Isabel, born May, 1913.

CAPTAIN FREDERICK WILLIAM HUNT, 19th LANCERS (FANE'S HORSE), LATE 19th BENGAL LANCERS,

who was killed in action on the 31st October, 1914, was the second son of the late Rev. William Cornish Hunt, of Odell Rectory, Bedfordshire, and of Mrs. Hunt, of The Warrens, Ferring, Essex.

He was born on the 22nd December, 1880, and was educated at Marlborough College (Star) from 1894 to 1897.

He joined the Leicester Regiment from the Militia in April, 1900, becoming Lieutenant in June, 1901. In July, 1903, he was transferred, with the same rank, to the Indian Army. In April, 1907, he was seconded for employment with the King's African Rifles, and was promoted Captain in April, 1909.

LIEUTENANT JOCELIN NIGEL SEAR-ANCKE HUNTINGTON, 2nd BATTN. LINCOLNSHIRE REGIMENT,

born on the 12th June, 1892, at The Rangers, Dursley, Gloucestershire, was the son of Major Herbert Huntington, Rifle Brigade, and Alice Elizabeth Huntington, daughter of F. J. Searancke, Esq., of The Rangers, Dursley. He was educated at Lady Cross, Bournemouth, and Beaumont College, Windsor, and was gazetted to the 6th Battalion Rifle Brigade (Special Reserve), and attached for duty to the 3rd Battalion at Tipperary. In December, 1912, he was gazetted to the Lincolnshire Regiment, in which he became Lieutenant in July, 1914. He served with his battalion at Gibraltar and Bermuda, acting as Adjutant at Boaz Island. As Officer Commanding a detachment of the 6th Battalion Rifle Brigade, he received the Coronation medal. His recreations were hunting, fencing, tennis, and amateur theatricals.

Lieutenant Huntington went to France in November, 1914, and was killed in action on the 17th of that month, his battalion forming part of the VIIIth Division commanded by General Lowry Cole, C.B. His Colonel and senior officers wrote saying they considered him a most promising young officer ; and the Adjutant, writing of him to his father, said : " Directly your son joined the regiment he became a great favourite with officers and men. His keenness for his work and his cheeriness at all times seemed to infect us all, and we shall in every way feel his loss most deeply. We can ill afford to lose such a promising young officer. He was one of those who had that great gift of at once getting hold of his men, and they would do anything for him."

CAPTAIN SEYMOUR FREDERIC AUCKLAND ALBERT HURT, 1st BATTN. ROYAL SCOTS FUSILIERS,

was the second son of the late Albert Frederick Hurt, J.P., D.L., of Alderwasley, Derbyshire, and Alice his wife, daughter of F. P. Delmé - Radcliffe, Esq., of Hitchin Priory, Herts. Mr. A. F. Hurt served as a Lieutenant R.N. in the Baltic and Crimea, 1854–55, commanding a gunboat in the Sea of Azov, for which he received the Order of the Medjidieh.

Captain Hurt was born at The Outwoods, Duffield, Derbyshire, on the 18th October, 1879. Two of his paternal uncles were killed in the Crimea : Francis Hurt, at Sebastopol, and Henry Hurt, of the same regiment as himself (the old 21st), was mortally wounded at Inkerman. A maternal uncle—F. P. R. Delmé-Radcliffe, of the 23rd Foot—was killed at the Alma ; another—H. Delmé-Radcliffe, of the same regiment—received bayonet wounds in both thighs when at the top of a scaling ladder at the

Redan, and afterwards served through the Indian Mutiny. A third—S. Delmé-Radcliffe, R.N.—served in the Black Sea and the Baltic, and afterwards in the Indian Mutiny, landing with the Naval Brigade from H.M.S. " Pearl," and was promoted Commander for his services, receiving all the four medals. He died on his return from the effects of sunstroke contracted on active service.

Captain Hurt was educated at Hazelwood, Limpsfield, Surrey, from 1889–93, when he went to Harrow (J. Stogdon's House) till 1898. There he was in the Cricket and Football XI's in 1897 and 1898. He received his commission in the Militia in October, 1899, and passed into the Royal Scots Fusiliers in May, 1900. From that year till 1908 he served in India, and then in Burmah till 1910, subsequently in South Africa, and at the depot, Ayr, till 1914. When in India he was selected to be Brigade Signalling Officer for service on the frontier.

He was a keen sportsman, enjoying big-game shooting, pig-sticking, and polo in India; while, when at home, he acted as Field Master to his brother's (Mr. Hurt's) foxhounds in Derbyshire.

He was promoted Captain in January, 1911, and in September, 1914, took a draft from the depot to his battalion in France, being mentioned for his services there in Sir John French's Despatch of the 14th January, 1915.

Captain Hurt, who was unmarried, was killed in action near La Bassée on the 18th October, 1914, his thirty-fifth birthday, while leading his company in an attack.

LIEUTENANT GEORGE ADOLPH HUTTON, ROYAL ENGINEERS,

was the younger son of William H. Hutton and Lucy Fiennes Hutton, of 8, The Ropewalk, Nottingham.

He was born on the 10th May, 1891, and joined the Royal Engineers in December, 1910, becoming Lieutenant in December, 1912.

Lieutenant Hutton was drowned while attempting to swim across the River Aisne with a signal cable on the 20th September, 1914.

2nd LIEUTENANT RICHARD HUTTON, 3rd BATTN. LEICESTERSHIRE REGIMENT, attd. 2nd BATTN. ROYAL WARWICKSHIRE REGIMENT,

who was reported wounded and missing, and is believed to have been killed on the 7th November, 1914, aged twenty-three, was the youngest son of the late Rev. J. H. Hutton, of West Heslerton, Yorkshire.

He was educated at Chigwell and Marlborough College. From the latter he won a scholarship at Merton College, Oxford.

He was appointed 2nd Lieutenant on probation on the 15th August, 1914, and for active service was attached to the Royal Warwickshire Regiment.

CAPTAIN J. F. I'ANSON, 3rd BATTN. THE PRINCE OF WALES'S OWN (WEST YORKSHIRE REGIMENT),

was the eldest son of Colonel J. I'Anson, of Howe, near Thirsk, Yorkshire, and was born there on the 1st June, 1883. Captain I'Anson's family have been connected with the West Yorkshire Regiment since the Crimean War, when a cousin—Major Baron Grant de Vaux—served with the old 2nd West York Militia (now the 3rd West Yorkshire Regiment) on its embodiment for garrison duty at Gibraltar. Colonel J. I'Anson was himself for twenty-three years in the West Yorkshire Regiment, having been Second in Command on his retirement from the Service. His second son—Captain I'anson's younger brother—is now serving with the 2nd Loyal North Lancashire Regiment in British East Africa.

Captain I'Anson was educated at Ripon Grammar School, and joined the 3rd Battalion West Yorkshire Regiment as 2nd Lieutenant in March, 1904. He became a Captain in the Special Reserve in January, 1907. On the outbreak of the war Captain I'Anson volunteered, on the 5th August, 1914, for active service, and joined the 1st Battalion of his regiment the next day at Lichfield, and, after accompanying it to Dunfermline and Cambridge, left for the front on the 7th September, 1914, and was killed at the Battle of the Aisne on the 20th of that month.

The following account of the circumstances was given by three privates of the battalion: " The battalion had taken up a position in the trenches, relieving the Coldstream Guards, on the evening of the 19th September, and held it till dawn. Then an order was given for a section to advance across a field to draw the enemy's fire. As a result only three out of a section of a sergeant and thirteen men got back to their trenches. Soon after one a.m. on the 20th the Germans got through on the right flank, and came up with a white flag. Thinking that the men had surrendered, a young officer gave the order ' Cease fire ! ' When the enemy were about twenty yards from the British position they opened fire with Maxim guns, and mowed the West Yorks men down, when fortunately the Sherwood Foresters came to their aid, and as the West Yorks had lost all their officers one of the Sherwood officers took command, and they fought until the position had been made secure."

Captain I'Anson, who was familiarly known to his friends in the Thirsk district as Captain " Jack." was very popular for his frank, open-hearted character and his love for children. He was an enthusiastic soldier and a keen supporter of the cause of the National Service League. He was a very keen sportsman, an excellent shot, and good across-country, hunting with the Bedale hounds.

He was a member of the Junior Naval and Military Club, and was unmarried.

LIEUTENANT CHARLES COCHRANE ILES, M.D., D.P.H., D.T.M., F.C.S., ROYAL ARMY MEDICAL CORPS (SPECIAL RESERVE), attd. to the 2nd BATTN. EAST LANCASHIRE REGIMENT,

was born at Wellington, New Zealand, on the 12th March 1886, the second son of Walter Iles, of Ngatapa, Gisborne, N.Z.

Educated at Otago University, Dunedin, N.Z., and Edinburgh University, he took his medical degrees as follows : M.B., Ch.B. Edinburgh, December, 1910 ; Diploma for Tropical Medicine (D.T.M.), Liverpool, 1911 ; M.D., Edinburgh, December, 1912 ; acted as Assistant Tuberculosis Officer at the Dispensary for Prevention of Consumption, Bermondsey, London, S.E., from August, 1912, to September, 1913 ; obtained the D.P.H. at Dublin in November, 1913, afterwards acting as Assistant Pathologist to the Royal Sussex County Hospital, Brighton, from November, 1913, till he joined the R.A.M.C. On the 6th December, 1914, he was elected a Fellow of the Chemical Society, Burlington House, London.

He volunteered for active service at the beginning of the war, receiving his commission as Lieutenant in September, 1914, in the R.A.M.C., and was sent to France on the 23rd November, proceeding at once to the trenches in the firing line. In the early morning of the 19th December, 1914, he was struck by a bullet while walking on a road near Estaires, which was thought quite safe, and for some little time was able to speak. Unfortunately he died on the afternoon of the same day in the 25th Field Ambulance of the VIIIth Division, and was buried next day in the Cemetery at Estaires, France,

his funeral being attended by the whole of the three Field Ambulances at that place, numbering some four or five hundred men, the remains being taken to the cemetery in an ambulance wagon.

The Lieutenant-Colonel commanding the 2nd Battalion East Lancashire Regiment, writing to his widow to express on behalf of his brother officers and himself their deep sympathy, spoke of Lieutenant Iles' care of the men in his charge having been unremitting. He was hit in the abdomen while going in rear of the battalion to their new trenches at about 1.30 a.m. on the morning of the 19th December. He evidently knew he was seriously wounded. There happened to be a motor ambulance near, into which he was put and taken straight back to the nearest Field Hospital. The bullet that struck him must have been fired from some distance and unaimed, for the battalion was not really under fire at the time, though occasional bullets fired at troops on the right were coming over.

Lieutenant Iles married Margaret Ross at St. Mary's Cathedral, Edinburgh, on the 24th May, 1907, and left one child, Howard Vernon D'Arcy, born 8th March, 1908.

MAJOR ALEXANDER WIGHTON INGLES, 1st BATTN. PRINCE OF WALES'S OWN (WEST YORKSHIRE REGIMENT),

was killed in action at the Battle of the Aisne on the 24th September, 1914. The Germans treacherously advanced under cover of the white flag, and with stretchers under which machine guns were hidden, and opened fire. Major Ingles called out, " All who will not surrender, follow me ! " and was shot while leading those who responded.

He was the only son of the Reverend Canon D. Ingles, Vicar of Whitham, and Canon of St. Alban's, and was born on the 20th May, 1869. He was educated at Haileybury ; then entered the Louth Rifles Militia, from which he joined the West Yorkshire Regiment in March, 1892, becoming Lieutenant in February, 1894, and obtaining his Majority in March, 1914.

Major Ingles served in the South African War, being present at operations in the Transvaal from October, 1900, to December, 1901, and received the Queen's medal with clasp.

He married Eugenia Ellen, third daughter of

Major-General C. H. Owen, late Royal Artillery, of Hanley, Camberley, Surrey.
He was a keen shot, a good rider, and a member of the Yorkshire Gentlemen's Cricket Club.

CAPTAIN DAVID INGLIS, ADJUTANT 1/4th GURKHA RIFLES,

who was killed in action on the 21st December, 1914, at Givenchy, France, was the youngest son of Mr. and Mrs. Robert Inglis, of Lovestone, Girvan, Ayrshire, and was born there on the 21st April, 1884. An ancestor, Colonel Inglis, fell at the Battle of Waterloo. Captain Inglis was educated at Bedford and the R.M.C., Sandhurst, and on passing out of the latter he received an unattached 2nd Lieutenancy in August, 1903, joining the Indian Army in December of the following year, having served his probationary period in India with the Northamptonshire Regiment.

He was promoted Lieutenant in November, 1905, and Captain in August, 1912.

His Commanding Officer gave the following account of his death : " A portion of the battalion was detailed for a night attack on the German trenches ; and, though it was not his duty to be there, he begged me to allow him to go with them. I gave him permission, and he led the charge, which captured the German trenches. I cannot express to you what a loss he is to me personally and to the battalion generally. Apart from our great personal friendship, he has always been my right-hand man in all regimental matters : keen and thoroughly up in all his work, with a knowledge of, and influence with, the men that no other officer possessed. His was one of those gallant natures that would have won the Victoria Cross sooner or later if he 'had lived, for he would always have volunteered for the most dangerous tasks ; and there are few indeed like him, and his loss is irreparable. All his brother officers ask me to send their sincere sympathy."

For his services in the war he was mentioned in Sir John French's Despatch of the 31st May, 1915. An elder brother of Captain Inglis was killed in the South African War.

He was a keen golfer and fisher, and a member of the Turnberry Golf Course.

LIEUTENANT GERALD SCLATER INGRAM, 2nd BATTN. THE QUEEN'S (ROYAL WEST SURREY REGIMENT),

who was killed in action near Ypres on the 21st October, 1914, was the only child of the late William and Mrs. William Ingram, 77, Eccleston Square, London, S.W.

He was born in July, 1890, and was educated at Winchester and Christ Church, Oxford. He was gazetted to the Queen's as 2nd Lieutenant on the 3rd September, 1912, and was promoted Lieutenant in September, 1914.

LIEUTENANT IAN CHARLES INNES, 2/2nd KING EDWARD'S OWN GURKHA RIFLES (THE SIRMOOR RIFLES),

who was killed in action on the 2nd November, 1914, was the only surviving son of the late Charles and Mrs. Innes, Bishopsthorpe, Inverness.

He was born on the 23rd October, 1885, and joined the East Kent Regiment from the Militia in January, becoming Lieutenant in June, 1910. He became a Double Company Officer in the 2nd Gurkha Rifles in November, 1912.

2nd LIEUTENANT DAVID IVE, 2nd BATTN. THE QUEEN'S (ROYAL WEST SURREY REGT.),

born on the 27th May, 1894, at Kensington, was the son of Ernest Ive, Assoc. M. Inst. C. E., of " The Hermitage," Meadvale, Redhill, Surrey, and a nephew of Rowland Ive, " The Wallands," Bedford Grove, Eastbourne.

He was educated at Reigate Grammar School, and joined the O.T.C. from its inauguration, obtaining the " A " certificate in May, 1912. Subsequently he received private tuition by tutors in Eastbourne and London.

He was gazetted 2nd Lieutenant in the 3rd Battalion of the Queen's in October, 1913, and passed the Army entrance examination in the following month, receiving his probationary training with the 1st Battalion at Bordon, and being transferred to the 2nd Battalion as 2nd Lieutenant in September, 1914.

He left England for the front with his battalion, which formed part of the VIIth Division, on the 4th October, and landed at Zeebrugge. He was fatally wounded by a shot in the abdomen in the fighting before Ypres on the 23rd October, 1914.

LIEUTENANT VICTOR MAYNARD GORDON GORDON-IVES, 3rd BATTN. COLDSTREAM GUARDS,

died on the 16th September, 1914, of wounds received in the engagement near Soupir on the 14th of that month, when the 3rd Coldstream Guards lost heavily, six officers being killed or wounded. He was born on the 24th June, 1890, and entered the Coldstream Guards from the Special Reserve in December, 1910, being promoted Lieutenant in June, 1913.

CAPT. FREDERIC HOWARD JACKSON, 2nd BATTN. CONNAUGHT RANGERS,

who was killed on the 29th October, 1914, was born at Woburn Sands, near Bedford, the only son of Percy Jackson, Esq., and a nephew of Colonel Spenser Jackson, Loyal North Lancashire Regiment. He was educated at Haileybury.

In the Great War on the 29th October, 1914, Captain Jackson was leading his company up to the German trenches and was killed in the attack, but the trenches were taken.

Captain Jackson was a member of the Junior Army and Navy Club.

CAPTAIN GEORGE MILLAIS JAMES, p.s.c., THE BUFFS, (EAST KENT REGIMENT),

was born in London in 1880, the son of Major W. James, Scots Greys, and a grandson of Sir John Millais, Bart., the great painter.

Captain James was educated at Cheltenham College and the R.M.C., Sandhurst. He joined the Northumberland Fusiliers in December, 1899, and served with them during the Boer War, having been present at operations in the Orange Free State, the Transvaal, including actions at Venterskroon (slightly wounded) and Rhenoster River. He was mentioned in Despatches ("London Gazette," 9th July and 10th September, 1901), and received the Queen's medal with three clasps and the King's medal with two clasps.

He obtained his promotion to Lieutenant in February, 1900, and to Captain in May, 1904,

and was transferred to the Buffs in May, 1908. In 1910 he entered the Staff College, Camberley, and after passing out was appointed Brigade-Major of the Pretoria district in 1912.

He accompanied the Expeditionary Force to France as Brigade-Major of the 22nd Infantry Brigade, VIIth Division, and was sniped while on duty, being killed instantaneously on the 3rd November, 1914.

Captain James married, in 1908, Hilda, daughter of Sir James Heath, Bart., and left two daughters: Aileen, born 1910; and Daphne, born 1912.

2nd LIEUT. ARNOLD SEPTIMUS GUY JARVIS, 1st BATTN. NORTHAMPTONSHIRE REGT.,

was the son of the late Lewis Page Jarvis, of Bedford and Sharnbrook, and was born on the 28th January, 1895, at The Toft, Sharnbrook, Bedfordshire. He was educated at Bedford and the Royal Military College, Sandhurst, receiving his commission on the 24th January, 1914.

He was wounded in the head in action near Ypres on the 31st October, and died in hospital on the 9th November, 1914, at Douai, where he was buried.

CAPTAIN CLAUD GIFFARD JEFFERY, 2nd BATTN. ALEXANDRA PRINCESS OF WALES'S OWN (YORKSHIRE REGIMENT),

son of Herbert James Jeffery, Solicitor, and Bertha Greenwood, his wife, was born at Manningham, Bradford, on the 13th April, 1880.

Captain Jeffery was educated at Bradford Grammar School and the Royal Agricultural College, Cirencester. In 1899 he joined the 1st Volunteer Battalion of the Yorkshire Regiment as a Private, and in the Service Company served through the Boer War, 1899–1901, taking part in operations in the Orange Free State, the Transvaal, and Cape Colony. He was present at the actions of Houtnek, Vet River, Zand River, Johannesburg, Pretoria, Diamond Hill, and Belfast, for which he received the Queen's South African medal with six clasps. Returning to England in July, 1901, he was, on Lord Kitchener's nomination, gazetted to a 2nd Lieutenancy in his regiment in September, 1901, becoming Lieutenant in May, 1904, and obtaining his company in August, 1909. In 1910–11 he acted as Adjutant of his battalion, having served with it in India and South Africa from 1902–08. In 1911 he was posted to the Egyptian Army, and served in it, and in the Arab Battalion, till January, 1914, when he rejoined his own battalion at Guernsey, proceeding with it to France as part of the VIIth Division in October, 1914.

On the 22nd October, while leading a party of volunteers to repel an attack by a large force of the enemy near Becelaere, he was wounded in the groin, and died from the effects in hospital near Ypres on the 24th October, 1914, being buried at the latter place. He was mentioned in Sir John French's Despatch of the 14th January, 1915.

Captain Jeffery was fond of hunting, pig-sticking, and polo, and rode in the regimental steeplechases.

He married, at Barbon, Westmorland, on the 10th February, 1914, Nellie (née Wilding), widow of Spencer Anketell-Jones.

LIEUT. GEORGE PIERSE CREAGH JENINGS, 1st BATTN. THE KING'S (SHROPSHIRE LIGHT INFANTRY),

the third son of Lieutenant-Colonel Ulick Albert Jenings, J.P., late Army Medical Staff, of Ironpool, County Galway, and Mervue, Monkstown, County Dublin, was born in Dublin on the 4th January, 1885.

He was educated at the R.M.C., Sandhurst, and was gazetted 2nd Lieutenant in the Shropshire Light Infantry in August, 1905, becoming Lieutenant in June, 1907. At the outbreak of the war he was Assistant Adjutant and Machine Gun Officer of his battalion. He was a good sportsman and rider to hounds, and had won many of his regimental point-to-point races.

Lieutenant Jenings was killed in action on the 6th November, 1914, at Rue de Bois, near Armentières. Writing of the circumstances, his Commanding Officer said: "He was Machine Gun Officer, and was using his glasses at the barrier to find a target for his guns when suddenly a volley was fired by the enemy, and he was shot dead. He was a very promising officer, and is a great loss, not only to the regiment, but to the Army. He was very popular

with both officers and men, and had done real good work throughout the war."

"He had been most dashing and gallant before that, and is a terrible loss," the A.D.C. to the General Officer Commanding the VIth Division wrote.

2nd LIEUTENANT RICHARD DOUGLAS PRYCE-JENKIN, 1st BATTN. SOUTH WALES BORDERERS,

was the eldest son of Richard John Pryce-Jenkin, J.P., Monmouthshire, and was born on the 29th July, 1894, at Willsbrook, Raglan, Monmouth. He was educated at Blundell's School and the Royal Military College, Sandhurst, and was ga-

zetted to the 1st Battalion South Wales Borderers on the 1st October, 1914. He was killed at Festubert on the 31st December, 1914.

CAPTAIN JOHN BANKS JENKINSON, p.s.c., RIFLE BRIGADE,

was serving on the General Staff when he met his death on the 14th September, 1914. He was the son and heir of Sir George B. Jenkinson, Bart., of Eastwood, Gloucestershire, and was born in London in 1881.

He was educated at Harrow, and was

gazetted to the Rifle Brigade in 1900, being promoted Lieutenant in March, 1901, and Captain in May, 1908. In the Boer War he served with the Mounted Infantry, and for his services received the Queen's medal with five clasps. Subsequently he served as Adjutant of Mounted Infantry in Egypt, and was seconded for service on the General Staff as Brigade-Major in 1912. In April, 1913, he was appointed Brigade-Major of the 3rd Infantry Brigade, 1st Division, and was serving in that capacity when he was killed in the Battle of the Aisne, on the above-mentioned date, at Vendresse, where his body was buried.

He was mentioned in Sir John French's Despatch of the 8th October, 1914.

Captain Jenkinson was a good horseman, very keen on shooting, securing many good heads in Asia Minor, South Africa, and other places, and was a member of the Army and Navy Club.

He married, in 1907, Joan, the daughter of Colonel Hill, C.B., of Wollaston Hall, Northants, and left two children : a daughter, Deborah Isabella, born 1908; and a son, Anthony Banks, born 1912.

LIEUTENANT MERVYN TAYLOR JOHNSON, 2nd BATTN. SOUTH WALES BORDERERS,

who died on the 14th September, 1914, of wounds received in action at the Battle of the Aisne, was the younger son of Mrs. Johnson, of Oddington, Moreton-in-Marsh, and of the late Captain William Johnson, Inniskilling Dragoons, and a grandson of Sir John Arnott, Bart.

He was born on the 13th March, 1886, and was educated at Bradfield College, being one of six brothers—all in the Army and Navy—who were educated there. He went to the school in 1898 and left in 1904.

He joined the S.W.B. from the Militia in April, 1907, and was promoted Lieutenant in May, 1909. When the war broke out he was home on leave from Tientsin, and joined the 1st Battalion for active service. He was wounded on the 14th September, 1914, in the Battle of the Aisne, and died the same day at Vendresse, where he was buried. Letters from his Commanding Officer spoke highly of his soldierly qualities and charming personality. ("Bradfield College Year Book.")

MAJOR JAMES HENRY WALLER JOHNSTONE, 115th BATTERY, ROYAL FIELD ARTILLERY,

was born at Thekhbredin, Punjab, on the 25th September, 1872, the son of Colonel J. W. H. Johnstone, late Bengal Staff Corps, who was wounded in the Indian Mutiny, for which he received the medal.

Major Johnstone was educated at Wellington College and the R.M.A., Woolwich, being gazetted to the Royal Artillery in March, 1892, becoming Lieutenant in March, 1895, and Captain in March, 1900. He served in the South African War, being present at the advance on Kimberley, including actions at Modder River and Magersfontein ; in the Orange Free State and at Paardeberg ; actions at Poplar Grove, Karee Siding, Vet and Zand Rivers ; in the Transvaal, with actions near Johannesburg and Pretoria ; and in the Orange River Colony. He was twice mentioned in Despatches ("London Gazette," 10th September, 1901, and 29th

July, 1902); received a brevet Majority on the 22nd August, 1902, and the Queen's medal with three clasps and King's medal with two clasps. From July, 1902, to September, 1903, he was Adjutant in his regiment, and from the latter date to August, 1905, he was employed in North Nigeria. He received his substantive Majority in September, 1909.

Major Johnstone was killed on the 15th September, 1914, at the Battle of the Aisne.

He married, in April, 1911, Elaine, daughter of Mr. W. J. Menzies, Empshott Grange, Hants, and left two children : Ronald James, born July, 1912 ; and Grace Elaine, born February, 1914. His recreations were hunting, golf, tennis, and gardening.

LIEUTENANT REGINALD FITZROY LEWIS JOHNSTONE, 1st BATTN. THE QUEEN'S OWN CAMERON HIGHLANDERS,

was shown in the monthly official casualty list, published in October, 1914, as having been killed in action, no date being given. He was born on the 4th June, 1884, and joined the Cameron Highlanders in May, 1904, becoming Lieutenant in December, 1909.

LIEUTENANT WILLIAM GORDON TOLLEMACHE HOPE JOHNSTONE, attd. 4th BATTN. ROYAL FUSILIERS (CITY OF LONDON REGIMENT),

was born at The Park, Catford Bridge, Kent, in 1887, the youngest son of W. J. Hope Johnstone and great-grandson of the late Mr. Hope Johnstone, of Radhills, Dumfriesshire.

He was educated by Mr. E. F. John at Winchester; subsequently at Cheltenham and the R.M.C., Sandhurst. Lieutenant Hope Johnstone first joined the 6th Dragoon Guards (Carabiniers), in February, 1907, afterwards entering the Indian Cavalry, from which he exchanged into the Royal Berkshire Regiment in October, 1913, and retired from the Army in March, 1914. On the outbreak of the war he volunteered for service, and was given a commission as Lieutenant in the Special Reserve of the Royal Fusiliers, and was attached to the 4th Battalion for active service.

He was killed on the 25th October, 1914, near Neuve Chapelle, while driving the Germans out of a village.

CAPTAIN ERNEST RAE JONES, 1st BATTN. CHESHIRE REGIMENT, who was killed in action at Mons in August, 1914, was the son of Simeon Jones, Esq., Caverhill Hall, St. John, New Brunswick. He was born on the 17th November, 1877, and entered the Cheshire Regiment as 2nd Lieutenant from the Local Military Forces, Canada, in November, 1898. He became Lieutenant in June, 1900, and from 1904 to 1907 was Adjutant of his battalion : while from April, 1910 to 1913, he was Adjutant, Special Reserve.

Captain Jones, who left a widow, attained his rank in February, 1906.

LIEUT. HENRY RICHMOND INIGO JONES, 1st BATTN. SCOTS GUARDS,

born at South Audley Street, London, W., on the 17th December, 1891, was the son of Major-General Inigo Jones, C.V.O., C.B., and a grandson of Lieutenant-Colonel the Hon. Richard and Lady Margaret Charteris.

He was educated at Eton and Magdalen College, Oxford, and joined the 2nd Battalion Scots Guards in February, 1912, becoming Lieutenant in May, 1913. In the Great War he was serving with the 1st Battalion when he was killed at the Battle of the Aisne, France, on the 14th September, 1914.

Lieutenant Inigo Jones was a member of Pratt's, the Guards', and the Conservative Clubs.

2nd LIEUTENANT JESSE JONES, OXFORDSHIRE AND BUCKING-HAMSHIRE LIGHT INFANTRY,

was born at Horton Cum Studly, near Oxford, in July, 1883, and was the son of Mr. Thomas Jones.

2nd Lieutenant Jones served in the South African War in the ranks of the 1st Oxford. and Bucks. Light Infantry, receiving the Queen's medal with two clasps.

On the 9th November, 1914, he received his commission in the Oxford. and Bucks. Light Infantry while on active service at West Hock, Belgium, and was killed in action on the 11th November, 1914.

He married Beatrice Lily, daughter of Mr. and Mrs. Johnson, and left three girls and one boy : Ivy May, age ten years ; Evelyn Beatrice, six years ; Ena Victoria, four years ; and Albert Edward, three years, at the time of their father's death.

While in the ranks 2nd Lieutenant Jones obtained a first Army School certificate. He was also a gymnastic instructor, and was distinguished for musketry.

LIEUTENANT MORYS WYNNE-JONES, ROYAL ENGINEERS,
of Treiorwerth, Anglesey, who was killed in action near Zandvoorde on the 29th October, 1914, was the son of the Rev. J. W. Wynne-Jones, Vicar of Carnarvon, and the Hon. Jessie F. Wynne-Jones, daughter of the late Lord Aberdare.

He was born at Carnarvon on the 13th May, 1887, and was educated at Fonthill, Charterhouse, and Trinity College, Cambridge, where he took his degree of B.A., becoming later a member of the Institute of Civil Engineers. He was subsequently on the staff of the Mexican Eagle Oil Co., Tampico.

Originally in the Special Reserve, R.E. (Supplementary Officers), which he joined in June, 1912, as 2nd Lieutenant, he returned unsummoned from abroad on the declaration of war, and in September, 1914, was gazetted Lieutenant in his corps. ("London Gazette," 20th May, 1915).

CAPTAIN ROBERT ARTHUR JONES, ROYAL FIELD ARTILLERY, was the eldest son of the late William Arthur Jones and Mrs. W. A. Jones, of Meonstoke, Hants.

He was born on the 27th August, 1881, and entered the Royal Artillery in May, 1900, becoming Lieutenant in April, 1901, and Captain in October, 1909.

His name appeared in the first list of British losses in the Great War, issued by the War Office on the 1st September, 1914, and published in the daily press on the 3rd of that month.

LIEUTENANT STUART KIRBY JONES, ARMY VETERINARY CORPS,

son of William and Alexandrina Jones, was born at Wavertree, Liverpool, on the 14th November, 1888.

He was educated at the Liverpool Institute and the Liverpool University, where he took his diploma of M.R.C.V.S. with honours. He was a medallist in materia medica, and won several prizes for athletics at the University.

He was gazetted to the A.V.C. (Special Reserve) in November, 1911, and was originally attached to the 2nd Dragoon Guards (Queen's Bays), and on the outbreak of the war was appointed Veterinary Officer in charge of the 25th Brigade R.F.A.

He was struck by a shell, which shattered his thigh, on the 14th September on the Aisne, and died on the 17th September, 1914, in No. 2 General Hospital, Versailles. He was buried in No. 1 grave, No. 1 row, Cimetière des Gouards, Versailles.

CAPTAIN CYRIL OSWALD DENMAN-JUBB, ADJUTANT 2nd BATTN. THE DUKE OF WELLINGTON'S (WEST RIDING REGT.),

who was unofficially reported killed in action, was born on the 9th August, 1876. He was the son of the Rev. Henry and Mrs. Denman-Jubb, and was educated at Uppingham and Oriel College, Oxford, where he took his B.A. degree.

Captain Denman-Jubb received his commission in the West Riding Regiment in January, 1900, becoming Lieutenant in February, 1901. He took part in the South African War, acting as Railway Staff Officer from February, 1902, and was present at operations in the Transvaal, east of Pretoria, including action at Rhenoster Kop, west of Pretoria in 1900, and again in the Transvaal in 1901–02. He received the Queen's medal with three clasps and the King's medal with two clasps.

In September, 1906, he was promoted Captain, and from March, 1908, to September, 1911, was an Adjutant of Volunteers and of the Territorial Force. He was a member of the Army and Navy Club, and was fond of hunting. Captain Denman-Jubb married, in 1906, Marjorie, daughter of S. Osborne, Esq., Borough Court, Winchfield.

It has been ascertained that he was killed by shrapnel at Wasmes, near Mons, on the 24th August, 1914.

LIEUTENANT GEORGE CRITCHETT JULER, 5th (ROYAL IRISH) LANCERS,

born in London in June, 1887, was the son of Mr. and Mrs. Henry Juler, Harcourt House, Cavendish Square, London, W.

Educated at St. Paul's School and the R.M.C., Sandhurst, he joined the 5th Lancers at York in 1908, becoming Lieutenant in March, 1909. He afterwards served at the Eastern Cavalry Depot, Woolwich, and at the Cavalry School in 1913. He was an exceptionally fine rider. His sports were chiefly point-to-point steeplechasing, hunting, show jumping, and all forms of horsemanship.

On the outbreak of the war with Germany, being stationed in Dublin, he left there for France with the 5th Lancers on the 15th August.

Lieutenant Juler was killed on the 31st August, 1914, his troop being attacked by Uhlans at the village of Morsain while on outpost duty covering the retirement of the British force.

He married, in 1910, Valerie, youngest daughter of Mr. and Mrs. Claude Johnson.

CAPTAIN GUY FRANCIS HEADLAM KEENLYSIDE, 1st BATTN. THE QUEEN'S OWN (ROYAL WEST KENT REGIMENT),

was born on the 9th of January, 1880, the son of the late Francis Headlam Keenlyside, Barrister-at-Law, of Gally Law, Weybridge, Surrey. He was educated at Charterhouse (Saunderites) and the R.M.C., Sand-

hurst. He received his commission in the Royal West Kent in August, 1899, becoming Lieutenant in June, 1901, and Captain in September, 1904. He served with his battalion at Aden, Malta, Shorncliffe, and Dublin. From 1906 to 1910 Captain Keenlyside was Adjutant at Blackheath, of the 2nd Volunteer Battalion of the regiment, which during his Adjutancy became part of the 20th Battalion of the County of London Territorial Force.

He accompanied his battalion to the Continent, was wounded at Neuve Chapelle on the 26th October, and died in hospital at Boulogne on the 29th October, 1914.

Captain Keenlyside married Rose Margaret, daughter of S. H. Knyvett, Esq., I.S.O., and left two sons : Richard, born May, 1909 ; and Christopher, born May, 1915.

CAPTAIN GEORGE HARVEY HUME-KELLY, 1st BATTN. THE PRINCE OF WALES'S (NORTH STAFFORDSHIRE REGIMENT),

who was killed in action on the 21st October, 1914, was the youngest son of Major and Mrs. Hume-Kelly, Glencara, Mullingar, Ireland.

He was born at Glencara, County Westmeath, Ireland, on the 13th November, 1879, and was educated at Clifton College. He joined the North Staffordshire Regiment from the Militia in May, 1899, becoming Lieutenant in June, 1900.

He took part in the South African War, during which he was employed with the Mounted Infantry. He was present at operations in the Orange Free State, Paardeberg, and the action at Driefontein ; at operations in the Transvaal, including actions near Johannesburg and Pretoria ; at operations in the Orange River Colony and Cape Colony, receiving the Queen's medal with four clasps and the King's medal with two clasps. He became Captain in February, 1906, and was appointed an Adjutant, Special Reserve, in August, 1908.

He was a keen sportsman, fond of polo, hunting, fishing, etc., and in March, 1913, won the Brigade Cup in Cork district, owner up.

Captain Hume-Kelly was shot dead when in command of his company repulsing an attack on our trenches near Armentières on October 21st, 1914. He exposed himself endeavouring to control useless firing in one of his trenches, and was shot through the head before he could get back to his observation post.

LIEUTENANT-COLONEL GEORGE HENRY FITZMAURICE KELLY, COMMANDING THE 34th SIKH PIONEERS,

born the 29th May, 1869, at Meerut, India, was the son of the late Colonel T. J. Kelly, Bey, of Boulak, Cairo, Egypt, and of 46, St. Charles Square, London.

After passing through the R.M.C., Sandhurst, he joined the Prince of Wales's Leinster Regiment (Royal Canadians) as 2nd Lieutenant in March, 1890, becoming Lieutenant in January, 1892. In June of the latter year he joined the Indian Army, receiving his Captaincy in March, 1901, and his Majority in March, 1908. In October, 1912, he became Major and Second in Command of the 34th Sikh Pioneers.

Lieutenant-Colonel Kelly had seen much war service, the present having been his sixth campaign. When a young subaltern he was with the column that went to relieve Captain Campbell, who was shut up in Chitral. He then took part in the Tirah Campaign of 1897–98, including operations in the Bara Valley, and later in Waziristan. He was with the force that went to Thibet under General Macdonald, and was in the action near the village of Naini preceding the entry to Gyangtse, and in subsequent actions round the town. He was last on service on the frontier in the campaign under Sir James Willcocks, at one time in command of the Indian forces in Flanders, against the Zakka Khel tribes, who were routed. For the above services he received the Chitral medal with clasp, the Tirah medal with two clasps, the clasp for the Waziristan Expedition, medal with clasp for Thibet (1903–04), and the Zakka Khel medal with clasp.

Lieutenant-Colonel Kelly was distinguished in musketry and machine-gun practice, and always took great interest in his men's shooting. He spoke Pushtu, Persian, and Punjabi very well, and knew several other dialects.

He succeeded to the command of his regiment on the 8th October, 1914, and accompanied it to France for the Great War. On the 23rd November, 1914, he was ordered to take a German trench " at all costs," and, leading his regiment, was one of the first to jump down into the trench among the enemy. Turning round to cheer on his men, he was shot through the lungs by a German in the trench, and died in twenty minutes. His men carried him five miles to bury him in the cemetery of Beuvry the next day. His funeral was attended by both French and English Generals. In the action in which he fell no fewer than seventeen of the officers of Lieutenant-Colonel Kelly's regiment were killed or wounded.

CAPTAIN HARRY HOLDSWORTH KELLY, F.R.G.S., ROYAL ENGINEERS,

who was shot by a sniper on the 24th October, 1914, while laying wire entanglements, was the youngest son of Lieutenant - Colonel H. H. Kelly, R.M.A. (retired), and Elizabeth Eleanor, daughter of the late Mr. John Collum, of Bellevue, County Fermanagh. He was born at the Staff Officer's house, Eastney Barracks, Portsmouth, on the 24th April, 1880, and was educated at Rugby (Stallard), which he entered in 1894. He joined the Royal Engineers in March, 1899, and became Lieutenant in July, 1901, and Captain in March, 1908. In 1901 he was the Army and Navy heavyweight champion. He was employed with the Egyptian Army for ten years from November, 1903, during which he was Resident Engineer for the construction of the town and harbour of Port Soudan, receiving for his services the fourth-class Order of the Osmanieh. From 1908 to 1913 he was Director of Roads and Communications for the Soudan, and was present at operations in the Atwot region in 1910, receiving the Egyptian medal with clasp. In the latter year he served as a member of the Lado Enclave Commission, and in 1912 in the expeditions against the Beir and Anuak tribes as Intelligence Officer, for which he received a clasp to his Soudan medal and the third-class Order of the Medjidieh. He was Chief Commissioner of the Soudan-Uganda Boundary Commission, and was responsible for the reconnaissance to the Boma Plateau in 1913, for which he received the third-class Order of the Osmanieh, for which his local rank of Lieutenant-Colonel qualified him. In 1907, 1911, and 1913 he carried out explorations in Abyssinia. Captain Kelly, who was not married, was a member of the United Service and of the Royal Automobile Clubs, London, and of the Turf Club, Cairo, and was a man of splendid physique, standing 6 ft. 5½ in. in height, and being immensely popular in the service. On one occasion during this war he walked a long distance down the trenches under heavy fire to visit his subaltern, who had been lying severely wounded all night, and took him to the dressing station, returning to his own men, who said he paid no regard to shrapnel.

CAPTAIN ARCHIBALD EDWARD KENNEDY, 2nd BATTN. ARGYLL AND SUTHERLAND HIGHLANDERS,

who was killed in the trenches at Le Cateau on the 26th August, 1914, was the eldest son of the late Sir John G. Kennedy, of His Majesty's Diplomatic Service, and of Lady Kennedy. He was born on the 7th September, 1878, and was educated at Eton and Oriel College, Oxford. He joined the Argyll and Sutherland Highlanders in May, 1900, and became Lieutenant in September, 1904. He served with his regiment in India and South Africa, and was gazetted Captain in July, 1912.

Captain Kennedy was reported missing after the Battle of Cambrai Le Cateau, but information was since received that he had been killed in the last burst of firing before the few survivors of his company were surrounded by the enemy on the evening of the 26th August.

CAPTAIN HERBERT ALEXANDER KENNEDY, 2nd BATTN. ROYAL IRISH RIFLES,

who was a member of a naval and military family, was born at Bellary, India, and was the son of Major-General H. F. Kennedy, 60th Rifles, of Bath, and grandson of Captain Kennedy, R.N.

He was educated at Bath, and after passing through the R.M.C., Sandhurst, received his commission in the 2nd Battalion Royal Irish Rifles in 1891. He served with his battalion in the South African War, his services there gaining him the Queen's and King's medals, each with two clasps. He was promoted Captain in 1900, and in 1906 joined the Reserve of Officers.

On the 5th August, 1914, on war being declared, he rejoined his regiment, which was among the first to go to France. After the retirement from Mons he went through the Battles of the Marne and the Aisne, and was in the fierce fighting round Lille. Letters from his brother officers and men tell of his great gallantry and devotion to duty. At the time of his death he was acting Second in Command. He was mortally wounded at Neuve Chapelle when leading his men in action on the 24th October, and died of his wounds at the Military Hospital, Bethune, on the 28th October, 1914.

He married, in 1912, Dorothy, only child of the late Mrs. Charles Collins, and cousin of Lieutenant-General Sir Aylmer Hunter Weston, K.C.B., D.S.O.

LIEUTENANT NIGEL KENNEDY, 2nd BATTN. ROYAL SCOTS FUSILIERS,

who was killed in action near Ypres on the 25th October, 1914, was the younger son of John

Kennedy, J.P., D.L., and Mrs. Kennedy, Bacombe Warren, Wendover, Bucks, and of

Underwood, Ayrshire. He was born on the 30th April, 1888, and was educated at Wellington College, being the younger of two brothers who entered Bevir's in 1900. In 1907 he went to the R.M.C., Sandhurst, and joined the Royal Scots Fusiliers in October, 1908, becoming Lieutenant in September, 1911. He was a keen motorist and polo player, and a good game shot.

Lieutenant Kennedy was at first reported wounded and missing on the 25th October, 1914, but in December his death was certified as having taken place at Gheluvelt, near Ypres. In Sir John French's Despatch of the 31st May, 1915, he was mentioned " for gallant and distinguished service in the field."

2nd LIEUTENANT AUBREY HAMPDEN BARRINGTON-KENNETT, 2nd BATTN. OXFORDSHIRE AND BUCKINGHAMSHIRE LIGHT INFANTRY,

who died on the 19th September, 1914, of of wounds caused by shell, during the Battle of the Aisne, was the fourth and youngest son of Lieutenant-Colonel B. H. Barrington-Kennett, His Majesty's Bodyguard, J.P. for Sussex, B.A. Trinity College, Cambridge.

All 2nd Lieutenant Barrington-Kennett's brothers have served, or are serving, in the Army: one—a Major—in the Grenadier Guards (since killed in action in this war), one in the East African Mounted Rifles, and the other —a Captain and Flight-Commander—in the Royal Flying Corps in France.

He was born on the 8th September, 1890, and was educated at Ludgrove School, Radley College, and University College, Oxford, and was appointed to his battalion in April, 1913.

LIEUTENANT EDWARD MONTAGUE SWAYNE KENT, 1st BATTN. HAMPSHIRE REGT., was the elder son of Colonel G. E. Kent, V.D., J.P., formerly commanding the 6th (Duke of Connaught's Own) Battalion of the Hampshire Regiment, and Mrs. G. E. Kent,

of " Normanhurst," Cavendish Road, Southsea. He was born on the 7th July, 1887; educated

at Boxgrove School, Guildford, and Clifton College, passing from the latter into Sandhurst, September, 1906; he received his commission in the Hampshire Regiment on the 9th October, 1907, and was promoted Lieutenant in 1911. He was Scout Officer of the battalion, and was selected by his Commanding Officer to attend the class held in North Wales by an officer of the Indian Army to instruct officers in the art of mountain warfare and scouting. He was keen on all sports.

In November, 1911, he was seconded for service under the Colonial Office with the West African Frontier Force. He had served two tours, and being home on leave on mobilisation he applied to be permitted to rejoin his regiment, which formed part of the IVth Division.

He was killed in action on the 26th August, 1914, near Cambrai.

He had recently become engaged to Sylvia, daughter of the late Mr. Arthur Gilbertson, of " Glanrhyd," Pontadawe, Glamorgan.

CAPTAIN ARTHUR MILFORD KER, 2nd (attd. 1st) BATTN. GORDON HIGHLANDERS,

was born at Simla on the 7th September, 1882, the son of Sir Arthur Milford Ker, C.I.E., M.V.O., and grandson of the late General T. D. Ker, Indian Army.

He was educated at Cheltenham College, and joined the Gordon Highlanders (from the Militia) in October, 1901, being promoted Lieutenant in February, 1906, and Captain in May, 1911. Captain Ker served in the South African War from 1900–02, being present at operations in the Transvaal and Orange River Colony, for which he received the Queen's medal with five clasps.

When he met his death Captain Ker was serving with the 1st Battalion of his regiment. The battalion first went to St. Nazaire, subsequently reaching the headquarters of the Expeditionary Force on the 19th September, 1914. After fifteen days on the lines of communication they reached the fighting line on the 28th September, and for the next two weeks were engaged in various actions. On Wednesday, the 14th October, the battalion set out as usual, and was kept rapidly advancing, in accordance with the General's orders. They were in an exposed position, near Huit Maisons, when Captain Ker saw good natural cover in front of the field they were in. He turned to his company and said : " Come on, men ! Follow me ! " About twenty who heard the order—for they were in extended formation—ran after him to cover, and after reaching it a German Maxim gun began firing over them. On the German fire slackening Captain Ker, wishing to survey the situation, looked over their cover. As he did so the fire recommenced, and he was struck on the head by a bullet. With a moan he fell back dead. The men, left without any officer to command, rejoined the main body safely, except two or three, who fell in the hail of bullets. Captain Ker's body was recovered next day, and buried in a cemetery.

The above account is based on statements by Private Harkin and several men of Captain Ker's Company, published in " The Scotsman " of 19th and 20th October, 1914.

Colour-Sergeant Borthwick, of the same battalion, spoke of Captain Ker as a brave and popular officer, who died in action as a hero.

CAPTAIN CECIL HOWARD KER, 1st BATTN. BEDFORDSHIRE REGIMENT,

was the only son of G. D. Ker, Esq., of Moorland House, Whitchurch, Tavistock.

He was born at Madras on the 4th November, 1883, and joined the Bedfordshire Regiment from the Militia in July, 1903. He served in the South African War in 1902, being present at operations in the Orange River and Cape Colonies, receiving the Queen's medal with three clasps. He was promoted Lieutenant in March, 1905, and obtained his company in November, 1912.

At the outbreak of the war he went to France with the Expeditionary Force, and was present throughout the retirement from Mons and at the Battle of the Marne. He was killed by a rifle bullet at the Battle of the Aisne on the 15th September, 1914, and was buried at Missy-sur-Aisne.

Captain Ker was educated at Cheltenham College, and played cricket and Association football for the School. He was a first-class rifle shot and a good all-round sportsman.

On several occasions he played racquets for his regiment at Prince's Club. In 1910, with Captain Leader, of the same regiment, the couple were runners-up for the (Military Doubles) Championship. In 1909 the Bedfords won the Army Hockey Championship, on which occasion Captain Ker captained the regimental team.

He married, in 1912, Dorothy, youngest daughter of Lieutenant-Colonel Hill-Climo, Army Medical Staff (retired), of Fir Glen, Yateley, Hants, and left a son, born on the 4th June, 1914.

2nd LIEUTENANT DAVID ANSELM KERR, 3rd (attd. 2nd) BATTN. THE ROYAL SCOTS (LOTHIAN REGT.),

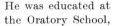

who was born at the Curragh Camp, Ireland, on the 21st April, 1893, was the younger son of Major-General Lord Ralph Kerr, K.C.B., uncle and heir-presumptive of the Marquess of Lothian.

He was educated at the Oratory School, Edgbaston, and at New College, Oxford. While an undergraduate at Oxford he volunteered for active service on the 7th August, 1914, and was appointed to the 3rd Battalion Royal Scots at Glencorse, but in September he was attached to the 2nd Battalion and joined it at the front, near Bethune, on the 10th October.

He was killed in action, only three days after joining, on the 13th October, 1914, while leading his platoon into action. He was buried at Croix Barbée.

COLONEL FREDERIC WALTER KERR, D.S.O., p.s.c., GENERAL STAFF OFFICER, 1st GRADE,

was the son of the late Admiral Lord Frederic H. Kerr and Emily, daughter of the late General Sir Peregrine Maitland, G.C.B.

He was born on the 20th May, 1867, educated at Charterhouse, and was appointed a Page of Honour to Queen Victoria at the age of twelve years, which post he held until he left that school. He proceeded to the R.M.C., Sandhurst, and after entering the Gordon Highlanders as

Lieutenant in August, 1886, had a long and varied career on the Staff and on active service. From January, 1892, to January, 1896, he was Adjutant of his battalion. In 1895 he took part in operations in Chitral, being with the Relief Force, and being present at the storming of the Malakand Pass. He was mentioned in Despatches ("London Gazette," 15th November, 1895), was awarded the D.S.O., and received the medal with clasp.

Becoming Captain in 1896 he was again on service in 1897–98 on the north-western frontier of India, with the Tirah Expeditionary Force, and took part in the action at Dargai, receiving two additional clasps to his medal.

After serving for some time with his battalion in the South African War he was appointed a Brigade-Major in April, 1900, holding that appointment till December, 1901. He took part in the advance on Kimberley, including the action at Magersfontein; was present at operations in the Orange Free State, at Paardeberg, and the actions at Poplar Grove and Driefontein; in Cape Colony, 1899–1900; and at operations in the Orange River Colony in 1900 and 1901. He was mentioned in Despatches ("London Gazette," 16th April, 1901), was promoted Brevet-Major on the 29th November, 1900, and received the Queen's medal with four clasps.

From February, 1904, to November, 1905, having received his substantive Majority in December of the former year, he was D.A.Q.M.G. of the Ist Division at Aldershot; and from November, 1905, to October, 1908, D.A.A.G. and General Staff Officer, Second Grade, in the same command. In October, 1908, he was appointed Deputy Assistant Director of Movements at the headquarters of the Army, and did valuable work in connection with the new mobilisation scheme, which has stood so successfully the test imposed on it by the war.

In the spring of 1913 he was appointed General Staff Officer, First Grade, in the Scottish Command, and in the Great War he went out as General Staff Officer, First Grade, on the lines of communication, his appointment dating from the 5th August, 1914. On the 21st September he was appointed General Staff Officer, First Grade, with the Ist Division.

He was killed by a bursting shell at the headquarters of the Ist and IInd Divisions at Château Hooge, near Ypres, on the 31st October, 1914.

For his services in the Great War he was mentioned in Sir John French's Despatch of the 8th October, 1914.

Colonel Kerr was a member of the Naval and Military Club. He married Lady Helen Kerr, daughter of the ninth Marquess of Lothian, and left two sons: Schomberg David Frederic, born 1903; and Ronald William, born 1906.

LIEUTENANT HUBERT RAINSFORD GORDON KERR, 1st BATTN. THE HIGHLAND LIGHT INFANTRY,

who was killed in action on the 21st December, 1914, at the age of twenty-two, was the only son of Mr. and Mrs. Frederick Kerr. He was educated at Cheltenham and the R.M.C., Sandhurst, joining his regiment in March, 1912, and becoming Lieutenant in September, 1914. He was killed while leading his men to attack a machine gun.

CAPTAIN WILLIAM CHARLES RAIT KERR, D.S.O., ROYAL FIELD ARTILLERY,

was the eldest son of Sylvester Rait Kerr, of Rathmoyle, Edenderry, Ireland, and was born there on the 6th August, 1886. Captain Rait Kerr belonged to a military family. His grandfather was the late Major - General Hutchinson, C.B. He had two uncles, one brother, and several relations in the Royal Artillery, and two brothers in the Royal Engineers.

Captain Rait Kerr was educated at Rugby and the Royal Military Academy, Woolwich. He received his commission as 2nd Lieutenant in July, 1907, becoming Lieutenant in July, 1910, and Captain in November, 1914.

For his earlier services in the Great War he was mentioned in Despatches, and received the D.S.O. The official account, as recorded in the "London Gazette" of the 1st December, was as follows:—

"D.S.O. Lieutenant William Charles Rait Kerr, R.F.A.

"Gallant conduct in bringing up a gun to within two hundred and fifty yards of the enemy in a wood, and blowing down a house in which the enemy were working a machine gun. (Since killed in action.)"

A more detailed account of the whole occurrence was given in the report of "Eyewitness," which appeared on the 16th November, 1914, explaining how one of our Howitzer batteries demolished three sets of buildings which were being used by the enemy as machine-gun positions for snipers and as a shelter for men.

On the 10th November, 1914, while on his way from his observation post to his gun, Captain Rait Kerr was shot through the head by a sniper. His body was recovered next day and buried beside the advanced gun near Veldhoek, four miles east of Ypres.

MAJOR JOHN HERBERT KERRICH, 2nd BATTN. THE WELSH REGIMENT,

son of General Walter D'Oyly Kerrich, Colonel Commandant Royal (late Madras) Artillery, was born at Cheltenham on the 14th March, 1874, and was educated at St. Paul's School and the R.M.C., Sandhurst.

He joined the Welsh Regiment in 1894, becoming Lieutenant in 1896 and Captain in December, 1900. He served in the South African War, 1899–1902, acting as Intelligence Officer in April and May, 1901, being present at actions at Belfast, Diamond Hill, Johannesburg, and taking part in operations in the Orange Free State, including actions at Vet River and Zand River, and in Cape Colony. For his services he was awarded the Queen's medal with five clasps and the King's medal with two clasps.

Major Kerrich, who had attained that rank in March, 1914, was killed in action at the Battle of the Aisne, courageously exposing himself to heavy fire in the open while directing his men. The Officer Commanding the brigade of which his battalion formed part wrote as follows to his widow : " He was loved and honoured by all who knew him. His loss is one which will be felt by the whole Army, as well as by his regiment and all those who knew and loved him."

Major Kerrich was an excellent polo player and a good cricketer, and was noticed by King Edward VII at an Aldershot review as a particularly good rider. He was a member of the Army and Navy Club.

He married, in 1908, Gwendolen Katherine, second daughter of Mr. John Elger, of Clayton Court, East Liss, and left two children : Geoffrey John, born August, 1909 ; and Rosemary Katherine Gwyn, born May, 1914.

COLONEL CHARLES ARTHUR CECIL KING, commanding 2nd BATTN. ALEXANDRA PRINCESS OF WALES'S OWN (YORKSHIRE REGIMENT),

was born at the Cape on the 6th February, 1863, the third son of the late James King, Esq.;

and, having passed through the Royal Military College at Sandhurst, he was gazetted to the Yorkshire Regiment on the 9th September, 1882, and joined the 1st Battalion in Halifax, Nova Scotia. In 1885 and 1886 he first saw service with that battalion on the Nile, and was present at the Battle of Ginnis, for which he received the Frontier Field Force medal

and the Khedive's bronze star. He remained with the 1st Battalion till the close of 1889, when he was transferred to the 2nd Battalion to complete the establishment, and went out to India with it in January, 1890.

He next was on active service in Burma in 1893, and took part in the only two expeditions in that country in which the Yorkshire Regiment had a share, being in command of the small party of Mounted Infantry which accompanied the Namkhan Expedition against the Kachins, under Major Hammans, D.C.L.I., and serving also in the expedition in the neighbourhood of Sima, in the Kachin Hills. For these services he received the medal and clasp. After nearly eleven years' service as Subaltern he was promoted Captain in February, 1893 ; and in November, 1896, became Adjutant to the 3rd Battalion. He accompanied the 3rd Battalion to South Africa in 1900, and served with it there till the conclusion of the war. From December, 1900, till March of the following year he was Garrison Adjutant at Rhenoster, and took part with his battalion in the operations in the Orange River Colony in 1900, and also those in Cape Colony, south of the Orange River, in the same year. From the end of 1900 to January, 1902, he served in the operations in the Orange River Colony, and from that date till the end of the war he again served in Cape Colony. For these services he was twice mentioned in Despatches, was rewarded with the Brevet of Major, and received the Queen's and King's medals each with two clasps. Colonel King was also in possession of the Coronation medal of His present Majesty. In February, 1905, he was promoted Major; in September, 1910, Lieutenant-Colonel, to command the 2nd Battalion ; and in September, 1914, Colonel, on completion of four years in command, which was continued in consequence of the war.

He went to Belgium on the 4th October, 1914, at the head of his regiment, which formed part of the VIIth Division. He shared in the desperate fighting which fell to the lot of this Division, in which the British were outnumbered eight to one. He was killed on the 30th (the official

215

casualty list says " 23rd ") October, 1914, at Ypres whilst holding on to his trenches with the remnant of his battalion. He was twice mentioned in Despatches for his services with the Expeditionary Force, 14th January and the 31st May, 1915.

He was an exceptionally good linguist, a first-rate French and German scholar, and had passed the Higher Standard in Hindustani and Persian. Fond of sport, he rode and shot well, and was a remarkably fine swimmer.

MAJOR REGINALD GARRET COOPER-KING, PRINCE OF WALES'S OWN (WEST YORKSHIRE REGIMENT),

who died in France of wounds received in action, on the 21st December, 1914, was the eldest son of the late Lieutenant-Colonel C. Cooper-King, R.M.A., of Kingsclear, Camberley, and of Mrs. Cooper-King, " The Chestnuts," Farnham, Surrey.

He was born on the 25th March, 1873, and joined the West Yorkshire Regiment in January, 1893, becoming Lieutenant in December, 1894, and Captain in November, 1900. He served in the South African War, 1900–02, receiving the Queen's medal with three clasps and the King's medal with two clasps.

From February, 1899, to February, 1904, he was employed with the Army Pay Department, and obtained his Majority in September, 1914.

CAPTAIN ROBERT NEAL KING, RESERVE OF OFFICERS, attd. 1st BATTN. THE LINCOLNSHIRE REGT.,

was killed in action on the 1st November, 1914.

He was born on the 14th September, 1874, the only son of the late Robert King, Esq.,F.R.C.P., of Moulton, Lincolnshire, and was educated at Rugby (Donkin), which he entered in 1890. He joined the Regular Army in June, 1896, becoming Captain in November, 1904. He served with the Nile Expedition of 1898, being present at the Battle of Atbara, for which he received the British medal, and also the Egyptian medal with clasp.

He took part in the South African War in 1902, where he was employed with the Mounted Infantry, being present at operations in the Transvaal, Cape Colony, and Orange River Colony, receiving the Queen's medal with four clasps.

In June, 1911, he retired from the active list of the Lincolnshire Regiment, and joined the Reserve of Officers, being called up on the 7th August, 1914, to serve with his old regiment in the war.

Captain King married Miss Kynock-Shand, second daughter of the late Robert Shand Kynock-Shand, of Hillside, Kincardineshire, and The Linn, Keith, Banffshire, and left two sons.

2nd LIEUTENANT GERALD CECIL KINGSLEY, 2nd BATTN. LOYAL NORTH LANCASHIRE REGIMENT,

who was born at Muttrapore, Assam, was the only child of Gerald Norris and Alys Kingsley, and a grandson of the late H. Walling and T. Kingsley, the latter of whom fought in the Indian Mutiny of 1857, receiving the medal.

He was educated at the Grammar School, Bedford, and the R.M.C., Sandhurst. He played Rugby football for the Bedford Town Club, being considered their fastest three-quarter. He won his colours at Sandhurst for sprinting, being chosen to run against Woolwich on two occasions.

2nd Lieutenant Kingsley was gazetted to the Army in June, 1914, and was killed on the 23rd October, 1914, after going through the war from the beginning. In the words of a Major of the battalion, himself since killed, " he had acted in a most gallant manner when we had captured the German trenches. He was getting his platoon together again for a further advance, and was shot, death being instantaneous." He added that he was a most popular young officer, who would be much missed in the battalion.

Captain Crane, commanding the company, said : " I can only tell you that he died like a soldier and the gentleman he was, leading his platoon in a charge which was the culminating effort of our attack. His death was absolutely instantaneous—he could have suffered no pain. His loss is a terrible blow to us all. He was immensely popular. I personally saw him laid to rest in a spot which I chose not far from where he fell."

CAPTAIN WILLIAM MILES KINGTON, D.S.O., 1st BATTN. ROYAL WELSH FUSILIERS,

who was killed in action on the 21st October, 1914, was the eldest son of the late Colonel Kington, formerly of the 4th Hussars, and was born at Cheltenham on the 25th April, 1876.

He was educated at Glenalmond College, and joined the Royal Welsh Fusiliers in September, 1896, becoming Lieutenant in January, 1899. He took part in the South African War, in which he was on the Staff as Brigade Signalling Officer from November, 1899, to December, 1900. He was present at the relief of Ladysmith and the Battle of Colenso; operations and action at Vaal Krans; on the Tugela Heights and action at Pieter's Hill; in the Transvaal at the beginning and end of 1900, including the action at Frederickstad; and in the Cape Colony, including the action at Ruidam. He was again in the Transvaal in 1901 and 1902, and in the Orange River Colony. He was four times mentioned in Despatches ("London Gazette," 8th February, 9th July, and 10th September, 1901; and 29th July, 1902); was awarded the D.S.O., and received the Queen's medal with five clasps and the King's medal with four clasps. From February, 1902, to May, 1904, he was employed with the South African Constabulary, and from April, 1906, in which year he received his company, to September, 1910, he was an Adjutant of Volunteers and of the Territorial Force.

He was a well-known cricketer, member of the M.C.C., the I Zingari, and the Free Foresters, and was an excellent shot. He was also very artistic and a musical genius.

He was killed by a shell in the first Battle of Ypres, where his battalion was in the VIIth Division, near Zonnebeke, Belgium, and was buried on the field in a trench. Many of the officers of his battalion were killed or wounded in the same battle.

Captain Kington was a very popular officer, and a man in the battalion who was present said in an account of the engagement: " For three days we remained in the trenches firing and being fired at without food or water. Lieutenant Hoskyns, who commanded my platoon, was killed by a sniper, and about three hours later Captain Kington, D.S.O., was killed. He was a fine officer, and would crack a joke in the trenches, which would set us all laughing our sides out. It made us all mad to avenge his death."

Captain Kington married the only daughter of Mr. F. Soames, Bryn-Estyn, Wrexham, and left one son.

CAPTAIN RICHARD CROFTON GEORGE MOORE KINKEAD, M.B., ROYAL ARMY MEDICAL CORPS,

only son of Professor and Mrs. Kinkead, was born at Galway on the 12th June, 1883, and was educated at Galway Grammar School and Protora Royal School.

He studied medicine at Queen's College, Galway, and took his degree of M.B., B.Ch. in 1908, after which he was for a short time House Surgeon in the County of Warwickshire Hospital. He was a good all-round athlete. He joined the R.A.M.C. in July, 1909, and was promoted Captain in January, 1913. Before entering the R.A.M.C. he served for four trainings in the South of Ireland Imperial Yeomanry. When the war broke out Captain Kinkead was serving in South Africa. He returned with the Xth Hussars, and at the special request of the C.O. was attached to that regiment for active service.

He was killed on the 31st October, 1914, by a high-explosive shell while attending the wounded between Zandvoorde and Klein Zillebeke, and was buried in the cemetery at Ypres.

A Deputy Director Medical Service wrote of him: " He was regarded as a daring and fearless officer, with strikingly attractive qualities, and was immensely popular with the men of the regiment. Over and over again he had risked his life in the discharge of his duties in the field."

CAPTAIN the Honble. DOUGLAS ARTHUR KINNAIRD, MASTER OF KINNAIRD, 2nd BATTN. SCOTS GUARDS,

who was killed in action on the 24th October, 1914, near Ypres, was the eldest son of the eleventh Baron Kinnaird and the Baroness Kinnaird, of Rossie Priory, Inchture, Perthshire, and was born there on the 20th August, 1879. He was related to the Duke of Leinster, the Earl of Gainsborough, and Sir Andrew Agnew. Captain Kinnaird was educated at Eton and

Trinity College, Cambridge, as Lord Kinnaird had been, taking his degree of M.A. at the University. He was a Lieutenant in the Eton College Volunteer Corps, and also in the Cambridge University Volunteer Corps. He subsequently joined the Forfar and Kincardine Artillery Militia, afterwards entering the Scots Guards in May, 1901, becoming Lieutenant in February, 1904.

The 2nd Battalion Scots Guards formed part of the VIIth Division, which left England for Belgium early in October, and in the severe fighting near Kruiseik, in which Captain Kinnaird was killed, the battalion lost many officers. The Master of Kinnaird, who obtained his company in February, 1912, was not married, and his next brother, the Hon. K. F. Kinnaird, becomes heir to the barony.

He was a member of the Guards' and Bachelors' Clubs, and among his recreations were polo and cricket.

LIEUTENANT ODBER AUGUSTUS KNAPTON, 1st BATTN. ROYAL WARWICKSHIRE REGIMENT,

who was killed in action at the Battle of the Aisne on the 18th September, 1914, was the eldest son of Captain Knapton, R.N., and Mrs. Knapton, of Rope Hill, Boldre, Hampshire, and was born on the 1st November, 1893.

He was educated at Wellington, where he was in Mr. Upcott's House from 1907–11, and at the R.M.C., Sandhurst, where he got his hockey blue. He joined the Royal Warwickshire Regiment in January, 1912, becoming Lieutenant in October, 1913.

While in the Army he played cricket and hockey for his regiment, and also for the garrison where he was stationed.

LIEUTENANT-COLONEL GUY CUNNINGHAME KNIGHT, p.s.c., COMMANDING 1st BATTN. LOYAL NORTH LANCASHIRE REGIMENT,

who died on the 11th September, 1914, of wounds received in action at Prietz, France, was born at Ajaccio, Corsica, on the 12th December, 1866, the youngest son of the late Captain Lewis Knight.

He was educated at Wellington and the R.M.C., Sandhurst, and became 2nd Lieutenant in the North Lancashire Regiment in February, 1887. He was promoted Lieutenant in September, 1888, and Captain in July, 1894, and was Adjutant of his battalion from October of that year to February, 1898.

He was employed with the Colonial Forces, New South Wales, from February, 1898, where he raised the 1st New South Wales Mounted Infantry Regiment, and commanded it in the South African War. He was present at operations in the Orange Free State, including actions at Poplar Grove, Driefontein, and Karee Siding; also the actions at Vet and Zand Rivers; operations in the Transvaal, including action near Johannesburg; in the Orange River Colony, including actions at Wittebergen and Bothaville; and operations in Cape Colony, where he was slightly wounded. For his services he was mentioned in Despatches ("London Gazette," 10th September, 1901), was promoted Brevet-Major, and received the Queen's medal with five clasps. Subsequently, being a Staff College graduate, he served on the Staff as D.A.A. and Q.M.G. in Malta and Egypt from November, 1905, to September, 1908, and in South Africa from 1909 to 1911, in February of which year he succeeded to the command of the 1st Battalion of his regiment.

Lieutenant-Colonel Knight, who was a member of the Naval and Military Club, was a good all-round sportsman. He played football (Rugby) in the Sandhurst team, was a splendid horseman, and keen on hunting and polo. All his leave in India was spent in big-game shooting, and he had many tigers to his credit. He married Menie Ethel, younger daughter of Walter Cross-Buchanan.

2nd LIEUTENANT THOMAS ALBERT KNOTT, 1st BATTN. PRINCESS CHARLOTTE OF WALES'S (ROYAL BERKSHIRE REGT.),

son of Frank and Alice Knott, was born at 5, Wynne Street, Ashton Old Road, Lower Openshaw, Manchester, on the 10th November, 1879.

He enlisted in the 4th Manchester Regiment in February, 1901. For two years from 1902 he was an Instructor in Mounted Infantry duties, and in June, 1906, was transferred to the 1st Battalion Royal Berkshire Regiment. He received his commission on the 3rd October, 1914.

He was wounded by shrapnel on the 13th November, 1914, and died in No. 11 General

Hospital, Boulogne. It has not been possible to obtain authenticated particulars, but the following details were gathered from a non-commissioned officer of the battalion, and are believed to be accurate :—

The battalion left Aldershot for France on the 4th August, 1914, and landing at Boulogne marched out the same night for Mons, thirty-five miles distant. They had hardly arrived when they came under heavy fire, and lost nearly all their transport; but 2nd Lieutenant Knott, who was in charge of it, managed to save some, though the battalion did not see it again for three weeks. During the ensuing retirement they had to march and fight night and day until they reached the outskirts of Paris. During the three weeks so occupied 2nd Lieutenant Knott was promoted to that rank for his work in saving the transport. On the 8th November the battalion was ordered to Gheluvelt, four miles east of Ypres, where it was in very heavy fighting until at one point 2nd Lieutenant Knott was the only officer left. By going out of the trench under heavy fire he succeeded in bringing in, first one, and then the other machine gun from either flank, both guns having been temporarily abandoned, and put them in position, having so far carried out his perilous action without being touched. He then attempted to get back to his post in the observation station about eight hundred yards away, and had nearly reached it when he was badly hit in the thigh, and fell at once seriously wounded. It was seven hours before the ambulances could get out to bring him in. The battalion was warmly commended by the Commander-in-Chief personally for their behaviour, informing them they had saved the position.

The non-commissioned officer furnishing these details was awarded the D.C.M.; and, had he not unfortunately died, no doubt 2nd Lieutenant Knott would have received due recognition for his gallantry.

2nd Lieutenant Knott, who was a Freemason, was a member of the Military Jubilee Lodge, Dover.

CAPTAIN JONATHAN EDWARD KNOWLES, 4th BATTN. DUKE OF CAMBRIDGE'S OWN (MIDDLESEX REGIMENT),

born on the 21st May, 1882, at Sandgate, Queensland, Australia, was the son of the late Edward Sugden Knowles and Mrs. Knowles, Rawdon, near Leeds, and grandson of the late Jonathan Knowles, Underwood, Rawdon, Leeds.

Captain Knowles was educated at Sedbergh and Bradford Grammar School, Yorkshire. He originally held a commission in the 2nd West Yorkshire Volunteer Battalion, and served with the 4th Durham Light Infantry (Militia) in the South African War, in 1902. He was present at operations in the Orange River and Cape Colonies, receiving the Queen's medal with three clasps.

In 1903 he obtained a commission in the 1st Middlesex Regiment (long known as the "Die Hards"), becoming Lieutenant in January, 1906, and being promoted into the 4th Battalion as Captain in February, 1914.

He embarked for active service with his battalion on the 13th August, 1914, and fell at Mons on Sunday, the 23rd August, 1914, while cheering and encouraging his men with great bravery. On this occasion Major Abell and Lieutenant Henstock of this battalion were also killed.

Captain Knowles was a very keen sportsman, a very good shot with the rifle, obtaining many good heads in India and Burmah, and was also keen on regimental sports.

He married Viva Brabazon Bagot, granddaughter of the late Colonel Charles Oldfield, and left three children : Nina Mary, born 1910; Viva Joan, born 1912; and Jonathan Maynard, born 1913.

CAPTAIN CAMERON LAMB, D.S.O., 2nd BATTN. BORDER REGIMENT,

son of the late Sir John Cameron Lamb, C.B., C.M.G., and of Lady Lamb, was born at Old Charlton, Kent, on the 25th May, 1879. One of his brothers is Captain B. Lamb, R.G.A., late of the Egyptian Army and A.D.C. to the Governor of Barbados.

He was educated at Blackheath School, Exeter College, Oxford, and Guy's Hospital Medical School. He was gazetted to the 4th Battalion Durham Light Infantry in August, 1900, and joined Lovat's Scouts (Imperial Yeomanry) in June, 1901, taking part in operations in Cape Colony and the Orange River Colony during the South African War, for which he received the Queen's medal with four clasps. He was gazetted to the Border Regiment in January, 1903, and served with it in South Africa, India, and Burma.

He was fond of rowing, boxing, and hockey; and in a big-game expedition in Central Africa secured many trophies. He also travelled across Canada, from east to west, on foot for a great part of the way.

Before the war with Germany broke out he spent a considerable time studying the Franco-Belgian frontier in the belief that the British would be called upon to operate there in his lifetime. He was promoted Captain in October, 1914, during the war, and was awarded the D.S.O., the decoration of which he received personally from His Majesty the King while in Belgium. The official record of the award stated it was for "repeated gallantry and exceptionally good work, scouting daily in and amongst the enemy's lines" ("London Gazette," 1st December, 1914). The following record of his work has been received: "Lieutenant Lamb went out on an average every morning and night, searching the farms for snipers, trying to discover the enemy's positions, and rounding up the enemy's patrols. He went out one morning with two men, and put four of the enemy out of action. He went to the place to see the result, and discovered an officer wounded. He insisted on bringing the officer away, and, under German fire, carried the wounded officer three-quarters of a mile. The firing, however, became too hot for him, and he left the man at a farm, and at night sent the stretcher-bearers to bring him in."

An account of another incident said: "When the front trenches were taken all that remained to hold the position were the headquarters and scouts. Lieutenant Lamb stood on the top of the trench and shouted, 'Now come on, boys, and give it to them! Show them what the Scouts are made of!' Our fire proved very effective, and some of the enemy had to retire, but they found that we were numerically weak, and came on again. We had made such a bold show that Mr. Lamb remarked that 'he could die smiling because he knew that the Scouts had done their work.'"

Of his actual death an officer of the Artists' Rifles wrote: "I have just heard that my old friend, Lamb, of the Borderers, has died of wounds. He was one of the best people I have ever met. He died a magnificent death. When they carried him out of the trenches, horribly wounded, he was whistling the whole time, and refused to pay any attention to his wounds. He died in hospital before they could get him back to England." The Colonel of the battalion wrote of him in November: "I must just write you a line to say how well your son—my Scout officer—has done during the war. He is one of the bravest young officers I know, and absolutely fearless. He has been invaluable to me, and you will, I know, be proud of him. . . . He did so well on that Monday, October 26th, when my old regiment lost so many officers and men, and he was the last to come away with me when we withdrew at dusk. . . . I only hope, when I return, I may have him with me again." And after his death he wrote: "The old battalion has lost, by his death, a very gallant officer, and we shall all deeply mourn his loss. He was so brave and full of spirit all the time, even when things looked blackest, and, as you know, he was beloved by all—officers, N.C.O.'s, and men—and on the field admired by all."

He was hit in the left arm and left leg while leading "A" Company of the 2nd Border Regiment in an attack on the German trenches near Fromelles, five or six miles west of Lille, on the night of the 19th December, 1914, and died on the 29th of that month at Wimereux, near Boulogne. His body lies in the cemetery there.

CAPTAIN EVERARD JOSEPH LAMB, 3rd BATTN. NORTHUMBERLAND FUSILIERS, attd. 2nd BATTALION THE KING'S OWN (YORKSHIRE LIGHT INFANTRY),
who was killed on the 1st November, 1914, was the only son of Mrs. R. O. Lamb, of Hayton House, near Carlisle.

Captain Lamb, who left a widow, was twenty-nine years of age when killed, and entered the 3rd Battalion Northumberland Fusiliers in October, 1905, becoming Lieutenant in June, 1910, and Captain in August, 1914.

CAPTAIN JOHN MOUNSEY LAMBERT, 3rd BATTN. NORTHUMBERLAND FUSILIERS,
born at Breamish House, Aln-wick, Northumber-land, on the 21st December, 1883, was the only son of the late Major-General G. C. Lambert, late Colonel 101st Royal Bengal (now Mun-ster) Fusiliers, and Isabella Lambert.

He was a grandson of the late Major Browne, of Doxford Hall, Chathill, Northumberland, and of the late John Lambert, Esq., of Alnwick. Captain Lambert was educated at Mr. Moore's School, Alnmouth, and Wellington College, joining the Northumberland Militia in 1903, becoming Lieutenant in November, 1906, and being promoted to Captain in August, 1914. In civil life he was Land Agent to Mr. Hope Barton, of Stapleton, Yorkshire.
Captain Lambert was a keen sportsman and a very good shot, winning the Officers' Regimental Cup several times. He was a regular follower of the Badsworth Hounds.

In the Great War Captain Lambert was attached to the 1st Battalion of his regiment, and went to the front at the end of August. He was killed in action at Neuve Chapelle, France, on the 27th October, 1914.

2nd LIEUTENANT the Honble. FRANCIS LAMBTON, ROYAL HORSE GUARDS,

who was killed in action between the 25th and the 31st October, 1914, was the ninth son of the second Earl of Durham.

He was born on the 18th January, 1871, and joined the Reserve of Officers, Royal Horse Guards, in September, 1914. The Hon. Francis Lambton was a member of the Turf Club.

LIEUTENANT GEOFFREY LAMBTON, 2nd BATTN. COLDSTREAM GUARDS,

who was born on the 13th September, 1887, was the second son of Colonel the Hon. Frederick William Lambton, 4th Battalion Northumberland Fusiliers, formerly Lieutenant in the Coldstream Guards, of Fenton, Northumberland, twin brother and heir-presumptive of the Earl of Durham, and the Hon. Mrs. Lambton, second daughter of John Bulteel, of Pamflete, Devon.

Lieutenant Lambton joined the Coldstream Guards as 2nd Lieutenant from the Special Reserve in February, 1909, becoming Lieutenant in May, 1910. He was reported as killed in action on the 3rd September, 1914.

LIEUTENANT DOUGLAS BLACKWOOD LANDALE, 3rd BATTN. RIFLE BRIGADE (THE PRINCE CONSORT'S OWN),

was killed in action on the 23rd October, 1914. He joined the Army in September, 1911, and was promoted Lieutenant in April, 1913. He served on the Continent in the Great War.

LIEUTENANT CHARLES KEITH LATTA, 2nd BATTALION GORDON HIGHLANDERS,

born at Edinburgh on the 2nd December, 1889, was the third son of the late John Latta, Esq., of 17, Royal Circus, Edinburgh, and of his wife, Margaret, daughter of the late John Jopp, Writer to the Signet, Edinburgh.

He was educated at Edinburgh Academy and the R.M.C., Sandhurst, receiving his commission as 2nd Lieutenant in the 2nd Battalion Gordon Highlanders in November, 1909, and getting his step in August, 1911. He served with the 2nd Battalion of his regiment in India till 1912, then proceeding with it to Egypt, where it was stationed when the war with Germany broke out, and accompanied it to the front, where it formed part of the VIIth Division.

He was killed on the 29th October, 1914, in the neighbourhood of Ypres. The Colonel of his battalion, intimating his death to his relatives, said : " He gave his life for his country in a gallant fight, which was necessary for the safety, not only of his own regiment, but of a large force. . . . He has always proved himself a fine example, and you may well be proud of him, as we are, and also all those of his own command. He is a great loss to us and the Army."

CAPTAIN BERTRAM LAWRENCE, 1st BATTN. EAST YORKSHIRE REGT.,

who was killed on the 28th October, 1914, was the second son of Dr. and Mrs. H. Cripps Lawrence, of " Rahere," Babbacombe, Devonshire. He was a grandson of the late General Henry Lawrence, His Majesty's Indian Army.

He was born at 158 Queen's Road, Bayswater, on the 24th December, 1876, and was educated at Tideswell Endowed Grammar School and Malvern College (Army side). At the latter he was a School Prefect, in the Shooting VIII, and in his House Football XI. He then went to the R.M.C., Sandhurst, and was gazetted to the East Yorkshire Regiment in February, 1898, becoming Lieutenant in 1899.

In the South African War he was employed with the Mounted Infantry, and was present at operations in the Orange River and Cape Colonies between January and May, 1902. He received the Queen's medal with three clasps. From July, 1903, to July, 1906, he was Adjutant of his battalion, and was promoted Captain in September, 1907. From 1909 to 1913 he was Adjutant of the discharge depot at Fort Brockhurst. He was killed between Lille and Armentières, and buried, with brother officers who fell in the same engagement, in the village of Rue du Bois, west of Lille. He was shot by a sniper while cheering and leading his men to retake a lost trench. He was mentioned in Sir John French's Despatch of the 14th January, 1915.

Captain Lawrence married Marie, daughter of the late Major-General and Mrs. Smyth, formerly of Alverstoke, Hants, and left no family.

2nd LIEUTENANT CHRISTOPHER HAL LAWRENCE, 2nd. BATTN. KING'S ROYAL RIFLE CORPS,

was born on the 11th November, 1893, at 6, Harrington Gardens, South Kensington. He was the youngest son of the Hon. Henry Arnold Lawrence, and grandson of the first Baron Lawrence, of the Punjaub and Grately, and great-nephew of Sir Henry Lawrence, killed at Lucknow.

2nd Lieutenant Lawrence was educated at Stonehouse, Broadstairs, Eton, and Cambridge. He was a good athlete and cricketer.

On the outbreak of the war he applied for and obtained a commission in the K.R.R.C., and was sent to the front at the beginning of October, 1914. On the 13th of that month he was shot in the trenches by a German sniper.

He belonged to the Pitt Club, Cambridge, to the Eton Ramblers, and the " Butterflies."

A brother of 2nd Lieutenant Lawrence's, in the same battalion, was killed on the 10th January, 1915.

MAJOR WILLIAM LYTTLETON LAWRENCE, D.S.O., 1st BATTN. SOUTH WALES BORDERERS,

who was killed in action on the 31st October, 1914, was the youngest son of Dr. and Mrs. Lawrence, " The Cedars," Chepstow. He was born on the 4th September, 1873, and was gazetted to the S.W.B. in July, 1893, becoming Lieutenant

in January, 1896, and Captain in September, 1904. From the latter date to September, 1907, he was Adjutant of his battalion, and in December of the latter year was appointed A.D.C. to a Divisional Commander in India.

Major Lawrence was mentioned in Sir John French's Despatch of the 8th October, 1914, and was awarded the D.S.O.

2nd LIEUTENANT ALFRED VICTOR LAWS, 1st BATTN. NORTHUMBERLAND FUSILIERS,

son of the late Mr. John Laws, and a relative of Mrs. Turner, of Newcastle, was born at Gateshead, Newcastle-on-Tyne, on the 9th August, 1884.

He was educated at St. John's School. Gateshead, and enlisted in 1901, reaching the rank of Sergeant in 1904. In 1908, while in the ranks, he served on the north-western frontier of India, and also in Africa, receiving the medal. He was given his commission during the Great War on the 1st October, 1914, and was mentioned in Sir John French's Despatch of the 8th October, 1914.

He married Julia, daughter of the late John Davies, of Dublin, related to Henry Carroll, Esq., of Dublin, and left two sons : Alfred George, born February, 1910 ; and John, born December, 1913.

2nd LIEUTENANT ALEXANDER SUTHERLAND LAWSON, 1st BATTN. THE BLACK WATCH (ROYAL HIGHLANDERS).

who was killed in action on the 11th November, 1914, was the eldest son of Police Judge Lawson, of Hawick. He had served for several years in the ranks of his regiment, and received his commission as 2nd Lieutenant in October, 1914.

LIEUTENANT WILLIAM BERNARD WEBSTER LAWSON, 1st BATTN, SCOTS GUARDS,

who was born in London on the 22nd August, 1893, was the younger son of Colonel the Hon. William Webster Lawson, D.S.O., and a grandson of the first Baron Burnham.

He was educated at Eton and the

R.M.C., Sandhurst, and was appointed to the Scots Guards in September, 1912, being gazetted Lieutenant on the 15th September, 1914. He was a good rider to hounds and a promising polo player. He was a member of the Royal Automobile Club.

Lieutenant Lawson was killed at Boesinghe on the 22nd October, 1914, while showing a French Territorial officer the direction for the advance of his men.

CAPTAIN GERALD ERNEST LEA, p.s.c., 2nd BATTN. WORCESTERSHIRE REGIMENT,

the son of his Honour Judge George Harris Lea, was born in Hampstead, London, on the 30th June, 1877, and was educated at Locker's Park and Charterhouse. He received his first commission from the Militia in 1897 ; was appointed Adjutant of his battalion in November, 1900, while in South Africa, and promoted Captain in December of the same year, after a little more then three years' service. He remained in South Africa for three years, serving chiefly in the Orange River Colony, and was awarded the King's and Queen's medals, each with two clasps, for the Boer War. In 1912 he passed the final examination of the Staff College, thus obtaining the right to the coveted letters p.s.c. after his name.

At the commencement of the Great War he proceeded to the Continent with the 1st Army Corps of the Expeditionary Force ; was present at the Battle of Mons, all through the retirement from Mons to the Marne ; and then in the advance from the Marne to the Aisne. At the Battle of the Aisne, on the 14th September, 1914, near the village of Verneuil, he was struck on the head by a piece of shrapnel and died three hours afterwards.

He married on the 7th August, 1912, Brenda, the only child of H. A. Wadworth, Esq., of Breinton Court, Herefordshire, and left one child, Marigold Geraldine, born on the 28th October, 1914.

Captain Lea was a member of the Army and Navy Club.

CAPTAIN FRANCIS WILLIAM MOWBRAY LEADER, 2nd BATTN. CONNAUGHT RANGERS,

born at Plymouth on the 6th November, 1881, was the son of F. H. M. Leader, Esq., late of the Royal Artillery, J.P. for Co. Cork, of Classas, Coachford, Co. Cork, and a nephew of W. N. Leader, D.L., J.P., late Scots Greys, of Dromagh, Banteer, Co. Cork.

He was educated at Eastman's Naval Academy, and in France and Germany. He served with the embodied Militia in the South African War, being present at operations in Cape Colony and Orange River Colony from 1901–02, for which he received the Queen's medal with four clasps. He also had the South Nigeria medal with clasp. Being specially recommended he was given a commission in the Connaught Rangers in January, 1903, becoming Lieutenant in December, 1905, and Captain in August, 1914.

Captain Leader was a good football player and all-round sportsman, and a member of the Empire Club.

Captain Leader was reported missing on the 29th August, 1914. He was left in charge of a rearguard at Le Cateau when the battalion was ordered to retire. Lieutenant Turner and fifty men who were with him were all killed or taken prisoners, and it must unfortunately be assumed that Captain Leader was among the killed.

LIEUTENANT EDWARD HUBERT LEATHAM, 12th (PRINCE OF WALES'S ROYAL) LANCERS,

who was killed in action near Ypres on the 31st October, 1914, was the second and only surviving son of the late Mr. E. E. Leatham, of Wentbridge House, Pontefract.

He was born at Wentbridge, Yorkshire, on the 20th July, 1886, and was

educated at Eton and the R.M.C., Sandhurst. He joined the 12th Lancers in October, 1906, becoming Lieutenant in August, 1908.

He played in his regimental polo team when it won the Inter-regimental Cup in 1914 and the Coronation Cup. He was also a successful gentleman jockey and point-to-point rider.

He was killed while helping to get a wounded man back into a trench into which he had safely got the rest of his men. While returning he was struck by a shell.

LIEUTENANT CHRISTOPHER LEATHER, 3rd (attd. 1st) BATTN. NORTHUMBERLAND FUSILIERS,

who was killed in action near Neuve Chapelle on the 26th October, 1914, aged thirty-two, was the youngest son of the late F. F. Leather, of Middleloi Hall, and of Mrs. Leather, "The Friary," Tickhill, Yorkshire. He was the youngest of six soldier brothers.

Mr. Leather was educated first at Mr. Bailey's Preparatory School at Limpsfield, afterwards privately, and in November, 1899, he joined the 3rd (Militia) Battalion Durham Light Infantry, and proceeded to South Africa in January, 1900, where he served with distinction in the Mounted Infantry. In 1901 he received a commission in the Northumberland Fusiliers, with whom he remained until the conclusion of the campaign, receiving the Queen's medal with three clasps and the King's medal with two clasps.

Lieutenant Leather left the Army in 1904, but rejoined at the outbreak of hostilities in August, 1914, when he was appointed to the Reserve Battalion of his old regiment. For active service in the war he was attached to the 1st Battalion. His Commanding Officer wrote of him after he was killed : " A good officer and a cheery friend."

He was an expert motorist, a keen amateur sailor, and a fisherman. He was unmarried.

CAPTAIN MALCOLM LECKIE, D.S.O., ROYAL ARMY MEDICAL CORPS,

younger surviving son of James Blyth Leckie, of Crowborough, Sussex, was born at Eltham, Kent, on the 18th April, 1880. He was a descendant of the Leckies of the Barony of Leckie (Stirlingshire, 1352). One of his ancestors, Sir Walter Leckie, of King Charles VII of France's Bodyguard, commanded the Scottish troops at the Battle of Lagny on the 10th August, 1432—the last exploit of the Maid of Orleans—when these troops were instrumental in the utter defeat of the English under the Duke of Bedford. Sir John French, in his first Despatch, said that for the advance from the Marne his left wing rested on Lagny.

Captain Leckie was educated at Blackheath Proprietary School, and privately abroad, and carried out his medical studies at Guy's Hospital, London. He was a member of the Blackheath Hockey Club, and used to play for the Army; he was Captain of Guy's Hockey Club when there. He had also represented England against France, and played for the Kent Hockey Club.

After having obtained his medical qualifications he entered the R.A.M.C. in February, 1908. For four years, from 1910, he was attached to the Egyptian Army, serving in the Soudan, up the Blue Nile, and in Upper Egypt. For the Great War he was attached for duty to the 1st Northumberland Fusiliers. He was awarded the D.S.O. " for gallant conduct and exceptional devotion to duty in attending to wounded at Frameries, when he was himself wounded." From the effects of these wounds, which were caused by shrapnel on the 24th August, he died at Frameries on the 28th August, 1914.

LIEUTENANT AVERELL LECKY, PRINCE OF WALES'S LEINSTER REGIMENT (ROYAL CANADIANS),

was born in Guernsey in 1885, and was the son of Lieutenant-Colonel John Gage Lecky (retired), late of the Gordon Highlanders, and a grandson of Hugh Lecky, Beardiville, County Antrim.

Lieutenant Lecky was educated at Elizabeth College, Guernsey, and received his commission in the Leinster Regiment from the Royal Guernsey Militia in 1908, becoming Lieutenant in October, 1910. He served with his battalion in India and with the West African Field Force in Sierra Leone for two years in the suppression of savage customs, services for which he was highly commended by his Commanding Officer, and in the course of which he was wounded by a poisoned arrow. In the Great War he was shot through the head while leading his men in an attack on the enemy's trenches near Armentières, and died on the 19th October, 1914.

LIEUTENANT FRANK COOPER LEDGARD, 2nd BATTN. ALEXANDRA PRINCESS OF WALES'S OWN (YORKSHIRE REGIMENT), who was killed at

Ypres on the 22nd October, 1914, was the son

of Armitage Ledgard and Helen Ledgard, of the Manor House, Thorner, Yorks, and

was born at Ashfield, Scarcroft, near Leeds, on the 15th October, 1891. He was educated at Eagle House, Berks.; at Harrow; and at the Royal Military College, Sandhurst, whence he obtained his commission as 2nd Lieutenant in the 2nd Battalion of the regiment in 1911, becoming Lieutenant in 1913. He proceeded with his battalion to the Continent, and was serving with it when he met his death. The Adjutant of the battalion sent his father the following appreciation of the young officer : " The regiment has lost in him a fine and most gallant officer, and one that we shall not be able to replace. Up to the time of his death he had done most excellent work in every way, and was here, there, and everywhere, doing damage with his machine gun. I was next to him when he was hit, and am glad to say that he was killed instantaneously and suffered no pain. Your son was carrying his gun to a more advanced position when he was hit. The M.G. section had done great slaughter in this business before your son was killed. He died a splendid death, and we all feel proud of him."

He was buried side by side with an officer of the Grenadier Guards.

A Private of his regiment gave the following account of his death : " Another very brave man was Lieutenant Ledgard. On the day of a big German attack in October he was in command of the two machine guns and some artillery, and every few minutes he had to change the position of the guns. Backwards and forwards along the trenches, from one position to another, he was running with the heavy machine gun over his shoulder and perspiration streaming down his face. Man after man in his section was hit as they mowed down the German Infantry, and eventually they were all out of action except Lieutenant Ledgard and Private Norfolk. Almost at nightfall the officer was hit by a shell, and he died—a great hero in the eyes of every ' Green Howard.' "

Another account by Private Brown, of his battalion, who was himself wounded, said : " The Germans had got round the flank of ' D ' Company at Ypres, where the position was seen to be dangerous by Lieutenant Ledgard. With a shout of ' Come on, lads ! Death or glory now ! ' the brave Lieutenant took up a Maxim gun on his shoulder, advanced to the open field, placed it in position, and for a few minutes directed a fierce and telling fire into the enemy, holding them at bay. Then he fell dead, with a bullet wound in the heart. Every man in the regiment is proud of him."

He was mentioned in Field-Marshal Sir John French's Despatch of the 14th January, 1915.

CAPTAIN HARRY NORMAN LEE, 59th SCINDE RIFLES, FRONTIER FORCE, INDIAN ARMY, was the second son of the late Mr. Harry Lee, I.C.S., and a grandson of George Nelson Barlow, I.C.S. He was born at Chupra, Behar, India, on the 15th April, 1885.

Educated at Cheltenham College and the R.M.A., Woolwich, he joined the 1st Battery, Royal Field Artillery, at Trimulgherry, India, in 1903, and was transferred to the Western Command for service with the 59th Scinde Rifles in 1906. In 1908 he took part in the Zakka Khel and Mohmand Campaigns under Sir James Willcocks, being in action at Karkha when two thousand Uknan Khels were dispersed. He received the medal and clasp for the campaigns, and was promoted Captain in 1912.

When at Woolwich he was Captain of the Hockey XI, and also played for Kent. In India he was well known as an excellent cricketer and all-round athlete, and frequently won prizes as best man at assault-at-arms in various parts of India.

Captain Lee was killed in action near La Bassée, France, on the 19th December, 1914, while leading his company to retake trenches that had been captured and were occupied by the Germans.

He married, in April, 1911, Maude Clere, elder daughter of Mr. W. B. Carter, M.I.C.E., D.P.W. India, and left no family.

LIEUTENANT COLIN BARCLAY LEECHMAN, 3rd (KING'S OWN) HUSSARS, who was included in the official monthly casualty list published in May, 1915, as having been " unofficially reported killed or died of wounds " on the 26th September, 1914, is believed to have been killed, on the night of the

23rd or 24th September, while on patrol duty at the Battle of the Aisne, near the French trenches, opposite Paissy.

He was the younger son of George Barclay and Mary Leechman, of 50, Campden House

Court, Kensington, late of Colombo, Ceylon, and was born there on the 8th May, 1888. Educated at Rugby and Exeter College, Oxford, he was gazetted to the 3rd Hussars on the 3rd February, 1911, and promoted Lieutenant in September of the same year. On the outbreak of the war he was at the Cavalry School, and was recalled to his regiment.

On the 23rd September, 1914, Lieutenant Leechman had left the men and horses of his patrol in a safe place and went forward alone. As he did not return it was thought he must have been captured, and a search was made in every possible way, but it was not till April that his family heard from friendly Germans that he was found dead near the French trenches.

His recreations were hunting, polo, and golf.

CAPTAIN EDMUND HASTINGS HARCOURT LEES, 2nd BATTN. THE BORDER REGT.,

was the son of Thomas Orde Hastings Lees, of Guilsborough, Northamptonshire, and a grandson of the Rev. John and Lady Louisa Lees, of Annaghdown, County Galway, Ireland, and was born at Northampton in December, 1875.

He was educated at Marlborough and at the Royal Academy, Gosport, and joined the Border Regiment in 1896, becoming Lieutenant in February, 1900, and Captain in June, 1906. He served with his regiment during the South African War, having been present at the actions of Spion Kop, the Tugela Heights, the relief of Ladysmith, including action at Colenso. He was wounded, and for his services was mentioned in Despatches (" London Gazette," 10th September, 1901) and received the Queen's medal with six clasps.

From 1910–13 he was Adjutant of the Artists' Rifles (Territorial), London.

He was killed on the 26th October, 1914, near Ypres, while defending a trench in the struggle against the enemy's attempt to reach Calais. An officer of the regiment, describing the fight, said : " Our men fought magnificently against odds of certainly over eleven to one. They fought desperately from nine o'clock till six, when the Germans withdrew, and our little remnant was ordered to retire. We have only about four hundred men left out of one thousand, and hardly any N.C.O.'s." No fewer than eight officers of the battalion were killed.

A non-commissioned officer of the battalion gave the following account of Captain Lees's death :

"The regiment was holding an important position for eight days, during which time we were subject to the heaviest shell fire. Captain Lees was killed by a piece of shrapnel on the 26th October, and was last seen by another man and myself in the open. We were then retiring with the enemy on top of us. The enemy gained about six hundred yards of ground, but were pushed back by the 1st Army Corps. Your brother was no doubt buried by the reinforcement that came up to our aid. Captain Lees was an officer, both brave and daring, who would always trust his men, and beloved and respected in return. Confidence in him was all that made us stick the shell fire as we did. No man can speak too highly of him."

The following extract is from a report by General Capper : " The devoted and firm conduct of this battalion repeatedly called forth the admiration of the Brigadier and of officers in other battalions in the same brigade, and I myself can testify to its fortitude and determination to maintain its position at all costs—a spirit which saved a difficult and critical situation. It is impossible to praise the battalion too highly."

The Commanding Officer of the Artists' Rifles (London) wrote : " His memory will always live in the hearts of the Artists' Rifles, and his old friends amongst us here desire me to convey to you both their sincerest sympathy."

Captain Lees was a member of the United Service Club and of the Alpine Sports Club, and had won many prizes for Swiss sports, toboganning, ski-ing, etc.

CAPTAIN GEORGE BRUCE LEGARD, ADJUTANT 1st BATTN. THE QUEEN'S OWN (ROYAL WEST KENT REGIMENT),

was born at Tealby, in the County of Lincoln, the eldest son of D. C. and Mrs. Legard, of Heighington Hall, Lincoln. Educated at Cheltenham College, he joined the Royal West Kent Regiment from the Militia in June, 1904,

becoming Lieutenant in October, 1907, and Captain in September, 1914. In January, 1912, he was appointed Adjutant of his battalion, and in that capacity accompanied it to France. Captain Legard was killed near Neuve Chapelle on the 27th October, 1914. He was twice mentioned in Sir John French's Despatches : in that of the 8th October, 1914, and that of the 14th January, 1915.

LIEUTENANT ALAN RANDALL AUFRÈRE LEGGETT, 1st BATTN. NORTH STAFFORDSHIRE REGIMENT,

born at Delce Grange, Rochester, Kent, on the 31st May, 1893, was the fifth and youngest son of Lieutenant-Colonel Fredk. O. and Mrs. Leggett, of Underhill House, Cheriton, Kent. Two of his brothers are in the service : Major W. N. Leggett, R.G.A., and Major E. H. G. Leggett, R.F.A. Lieutenant Leggett was educated at Oxford Preparatory School, C. C. Lynam's, and Tonbridge School from 1907–11. From the latter he became Hon. King's Cadet at the R.M.C., Sandhurst. Joining the North Staffordshire Regiment early in September, 1912, he served with it at Buttevant, Ireland, till proceeding on active service to France in September, 1914. He was promoted Lieutenant on the 18th September, 1914. He was mentioned in Sir John French's Despatch of 14th January, 1915, for service in an action on the 20th October, 1914, when, by his steadiness, good leadership, and well-considered action, he held up an attack of the enemy and enabled the offensive to be resumed. He was killed by a shell in the trenches near Armentières on the 31st October, 1914, his body being brought to England and buried in St. Martin's Churchyard, Cheriton, on the 2nd December, 1914.

MAJOR CHANDOS LEIGH, D.S.O., 2nd BATTN. KING'S OWN SCOTTISH BORDERERS,

born on the 29th August, 1873, was the elder son of the Hon. Sir E. Chandos Leigh, K.C.B., K.C., of 45, Upper Grosvenor Street, London, W., and a cousin of Lord Leigh, of Stoneleigh. He was educated at Harrow and Cambridge, and joined the K.O.S.B. from the Warwickshire Militia in May, 1895, becoming Lieutenant in September, 1897. He served in the South African War, being employed with the Mounted Infantry. He was present at the relief of Kimberley ; at operations in the Orange Free State and Paardeberg, with actions at Poplar Grove, Houtnek (Thoba Mountain), Vet and Zand Rivers ; in the Transvaal, May and June, 1900, with actions near Johannesburg and at Diamond Hill ; operations in the Orange River Colony, with actions at Wittebergen and Bothaville ; and at operations in the Transvaal, Orange River and Cape Colonies from November, 1900, to July, 1901. He was mentioned in Despatches (" London Gazette," 10th September, 1901), was awarded the D.S.O., and received the Queen's medal with five clasps. He was promoted Captain in April, 1901, and in April, 1902, was detached from his regiment for employment with the Egyptian Army. While with it he saw active service in the Soudan in 1905, taking part in the operations against the Nyam Nyam tribes in the Bahr-el-Ghazal Province. For his services he received the Egyptian medal with clasp, and was awarded the Orders of the Osmanieh and Medjidieh.

He was a fine horseman and polo player, and was well known on the Cairo turf, where he more than once headed the winning list of steeplechase riders, both amateur and professional. He had hunted from his boyhood in Warwickshire and Northamptonshire, and more recently with the Meath and Ward Union packs, when he was quartered with his regiment in Ireland. He also took honours in the open jumping at the horse show in Dublin.

He was with his battalion at Belfast during the troubled time of the riots at Harland and Wolff's shipyards in 1912, and through the many succeeding labour troubles in Dublin from the strikes in August, 1913.

He gave his life at Mons on or about the 24th August, 1914, where, although severely wounded and in the open, he ordered his men to leave him and retire across the Canal, so that there should be no delay in blowing up the bridge in the face of the advancing Germans.

After having been returned as " missing " for seven months, news was received in March, 1915, from a returned disabled prisoner of the K.O.S.B. that Major Leigh died and was buried at Boussu shortly after the action in which he was wounded. He married, in June, 1913, Winifred, daughter of the late Right Hon. A. F. Jeffreys, M.P., of Burkham House, Hampshire.

LIEUTENANT-COLONEL LOUIS ST. GRATIEN LE MARCHANT, D.S.O., COMMANDING 1st BATTN. EAST LANCASHIRE REGIMENT,

who was killed in action on the 9th September, 1914, was the sixth son of the Rev. Robert Le Marchant, Rector of Little Risington, Gloucestershire, and was born on the 2nd December, 1866.

He entered the East Lancashire

Regiment from the Militia in November, 1886, becoming Captain in December, 1895. From October, 1898, till 1902 he was Adjutant of his battalion. Lieutenant-Colonel Le Marchant took part in operations with the relief force in Chitral in 1895, for which he received the medal and clasp. He also served in the South African War, 1900–02, while he was Adjutant of his battalion, and was present at operations in the Orange River Colony, including actions at Karee Siding, Vet and Zand Rivers, and at operations in the Transvaal, including action near Johannesburg. He was mentioned in Despatches ("London Gazette," 10th September, 1901, and 29th July, 1902), and was awarded the D.S.O., the Queen's medal with three clasps, and the King's medal with two clasps. He succeeded to the command of the 1st Battalion of his regiment on the 23rd September, 1913.

Lieutenant-Colonel Le Marchant was killed at La Ferté-sous-Jouarre during the Battle of the Marne, and was mentioned in Sir John French's Despatch of the 8th October, 1914.

LIEUTENANT-COLONEL HENRY ANDERSON LEMPRIERE, D.S.O., p.s.c., 7th (PRINCESS ROYAL'S) DRAGOON GUARDS,

who was killed in action on the 23rd December, 1914, was the son of the late Captain George Reid Lempriere, R.E.

He was born on the 30th January, 1867, and entered the 7th Dragoon Guards in March, 1888, becoming Lieutenant in December, 1891. From April, 1896, to November, 1899, he was Adjutant of his regiment.

In the South African War he served as Adjutant of his regiment, and later on the Staff as D.A.A.G. He was present in 1900 at operations in the Orange Free State, with actions at Zand River; in the Transvaal, with actions near Johannesburg, Pretoria, and Diamond Hill; and east of Pretoria, with actions at Belfast; also at operations in the Cape Colony. In 1901 and 1902 he was present at operations in the Orange River and Cape Colonies, and on the Zululand frontier of Natal. For his services he was twice mentioned in despatches ("London Gazette," 10th September, 1901, and 29th July, 1902); given the rank of Brevet-Major, August, 1902; was awarded the D.S.O.; and received the Queen's medal with five clasps and the King's medal with two clasps. He was also placed on the list of officers qualified for Staff employ-

ment in consequence of services on the Staff in the field, and was a graduate of the Staff College, passing out in December, 1904.

From May, 1903, to January, 1904, he was Brigade-Major of the 3rd Cavalry Brigade, 3rd Army Corps.

He was promoted Substantive Major in April, 1903, and for a short time, in 1903, was Adjutant of the Cavalry Depot. He succeeded to the command of his regiment in March, 1912. For his services in the Great War he was mentioned in Sir John French's Despatch of the 31st May, 1915.

CAPTAIN PENRY BRUCE LENDON, M.V.O., 3rd (attd. 1st) BATTN. KING'S OWN (ROYAL LANCASTER REGIMENT),

was the son of R. W. P. Lendon, and grandson of the Rev. W. P. Lendon, and was born at Wandsworth on the 31st December, 1882.

He was educated at Sandroyd, Cobham, Surrey, and at Tonbridge (Manor

House). He joined the 4th (Militia) Battalion of the regiment in 1901, and on the Militia being abolished passed to the Special Reserve, from which he joined the 3rd Battalion King's Own.

He was granted the M.V.O. (fifth class) for carrying the Colours, in 1905, on the occasion of King' Edward's presentation of Colours to the battalion at Knowsley.

He had left the Special Reserve in February, 1914, and was farming at Court Lodge, Chipstead, Surrey, but on the war breaking out he immediately rejoined, and was attached to the 1st Battalion, which he accompanied to the front.

He was shot at Le Touquet, Frelinghein, on the 21st October, 1914. In an attempt to retake some trenches Captain Lendon was advised to take shelter in a loop-holed house near. He had nearly reached it when a wounded man, under fire in a ditch, called out for help. He went on to the road, and on reaching the ditch was shot through the lungs. The regiment was complimented by the General Officer Commanding for its good services, to which Captain Lendon had by his bravery and hard work on all occasions largely contributed.

Captain Lendon married Emmeline Gertrude, youngest daughter of the late Rev. Canon Richardson, Vicar of Northop, Flints, and left three daughters: Priscilla, Eira, and Sheila, age four, three, and two years respectively.

MAJOR LORD BERNARD CHARLES GORDON-LENNOX, 2nd BATTN. GRENADIER GUARDS,

who was killed in action at Zillebeke on the 10th November, 1914, was the third son of the seventh Duke of Richmond and Gordon, K.G.

Born in London on the 1st May, 1878, he was educated at Eton College and Sandhurst, from which he joined the Grenadier Guards in February, 1898, becoming Lieutenant in October, 1899.

He took part in the South African War, being present at the operations in the Orange Free State, including the actions at Poplar Grove and Driefontein, for which he received the Queen's medal with two clasps. From 1904-06 he was seconded for service with the Chinese Regiment at Wei-hai-Wei. He was promoted Captain in 1909, and was A.D.C. from November, 1907, to July, 1909, and Assistant Military Secretary, from August, 1909, to November, 1911, to the General Officer Commanding-in-Chief, Northern Command.

For his services in the war he was mentioned in the Supplement to Sir John French's Despatch of 14th January, 1915, published by the War Office in April, 1915.

In 1907 Lord Bernard Gordon-Lennox married Evelyn, second daughter of the first Lord Loch, and left two sons : George Charles, born May, 1908 ; and Alexander Henry Charles, born April, 1911.

He was a member of the Guards' and Turf Clubs, and was a thorough all-round sportsman, his principal recreations being shooting, fishing, cricket, and polo. By his death the Army has lost a keen and brilliant officer, and the world of sport an exponent of whom there were very few equals.

2nd LIEUTENANT VICTOR ALOISIUS LENTAIGNE, 2nd BATTALION CONNAUGHT RANGERS,

who was killed at the Battle of the Aisne on the 14th September, 1914, aged twenty-one years, was the youngest son of Sir John Lentaigne, F.R.C.S.I., of 42 Merrion Square, Dublin.

2nd Lieutenant Lentaigne's commission in the Connaught Rangers dated from January, 1914.

CAPTAIN NORMAN JEROME BEAUCHAMP LESLIE, 3rd BATTN. RIFLE BRIGADE,

who was killed by a sniper while on reconnaissance duty near Armentières on the 17th October, 1914, was born in London

on the 20th November, 1886, the son of Colonel Sir John Leslie, Bart., late of the Grenadier Guards, now commanding the 12th Battalion Royal Inniskilling Fusiliers. He was a grandson of Sir John Leslie, firstBart.,Glaslough, County Monaghan.

He was educated at Eton, and the R.M.C., Sandhurst, receiving his commission in the Rifle Brigade in September, 1905, becoming Lieutenant in October, 1909, and obtaining his company in May, 1914. From September, 1908, to April, 1910, he was A.D.C. to Sir John Maxwell in Egypt, and subsequently to Lord Carmichael in Bengal.

Captain Leslie, who had received the Indian Durbar medal, was fond of big-game shooting and fencing. He was unmarried.

LIEUT. SIR RICHARD WILLIAM LEVINGE, 10th BART., D.L., 1st LIFE GUARDS,

of Knockdrin Castle, Westmeath, was the son of the late Sir William Henry Levinge and his wife, Emily J. (Lady Levinge) née Sutton, and was born at Ryde, Isle of Wight, on the 12th July, 1878.

He was educated at Eton, and was first in the 8th Hussars, with which he served in the South African War, taking part in operations in Cape Colony in 1900, and in the Transvaal in 1900–01, for which he received the Queen's medal with two clasps.

On September 1st, 1914, he joined the 1st Life Guards from the Reserve of Officers, and was serving with them when killed in the trenches near Ypres on the 24th October, 1914.

His recreations were hunting, polo, golf, and fishing. He was a member of the Cavalry Club ; the Kildare Street Club, Dublin ; and St. George's Yacht Club, Kingstown.

Sir Richard Levinge married Irene Marguerite, elder daughter of the late J. W. C. Pix, Esq., of Bradford, and left one son, Richard Henry Vere, born on the 30th April, 1911, who succeeds him in the baronetcy.

LIEUTENANT FRANCIS ELLISON LEVITA, 4th (QUEEN'S OWN) HUSSARS,

who was killed in action on the 12th October, 1914, was the only child of Colonel Harry Levita (who served in the Soudan Expedition of 1885).

He was born on the 29th November, 1889, and was educated at Eton and the R.M.C., Sandhurst, joining the 4th Hussars in February, 1910, and becoming Lieutenant in March, 1911. He was fond of hunting and polo, being one of the polo team of his regiment.

Lieutenant Levita was killed in an attempt to save Captain Kirwan Gatacre, of the 11th Bengal Lancers (attached to the 4th Hussars). The incident was described by the Officer Commanding the regiment, in a letter dated the 25th October, 1914, published in " The Times " of the 30th October, 1914 :

" As Commanding Officer I would have written before had I known your address to tell you how grieved we all were to lose your boy and to express to you our deepest sympathy. He, with Captain Gatacre, had been sent out on a dangerous reconnaissance, and they rode together straight up to a big monastery on the top of a hill, having had direct orders from the General to ascertain whether it was or was not held by the German troops. The Germans let them get up quite close, and then suddenly opened a hot fire at short range. The officers and the whole troop with them (about ten men) turned to gallop back under cover when Gatacre was shot. Your boy pulled up at once, and rode back to see if he could help him, but had only got a few yards when he, too, was shot. It was a gallant intention, and, had he survived, I should have recommended him for a decoration. A few hours later the monastery was captured, and the bodies of both Captain Gatacre and your boy were found where they had been shot. Both must have fallen dead. The Germans had stripped them of everything except their actual clothes. I posted you the other day your boy's sword, which we happened to recover. We buried him with Gatacre in the monastery, and the Rev. Mr. Guinness, our brigade Chaplain, has a record of the exact spot. The monastery is on the Mountain des Cats, near Godewaersvelde, about five miles northeast of Hazebrouck."

2nd LIEUTENANT MAURICE ADEN LEY, 3rd BATTN. THE BUFFS (EAST KENT REGIMENT), was the third son of Sir

Francis Ley, Bart., of Epperstone Manor, Notts, and was born there on the 5th August, 1895.

He was educated at Malvern College, where he was a great athlete, and was within one point of winning the championship of the College (five hundred boys) in each of two years. He subsequently entered the Royal Military College, Sandhurst, and received his commission on the 1st October, 1914. He was killed at Wytschaete, near Ypres, on the 1st November, 1914, while endeavouring to assist his wounded men in a retirement.

LIEUTENANT GEORGE VYVYAN NAYLOR-LEYLAND, ROYAL HORSE GUARDS,

who died on the 21st September, 1914, of wounds received in action, was the second son of the late Sir Herbert Scarisbrick Naylor-Leyland, first Baronet, sometime Captain 2nd Life Guards, of Nantclwyd Hall, Ruthin, North Wales, and heir-presumptive to his brother, the second Baronet.

He was born on the 11th March, 1892, and was gazetted to the 16th Lancers in February, 1912. In February, 1914, he was transferred to the Royal Horse Guards, in which regiment he was promoted Lieutenant in April, 1914.

CAPTAIN FREDERICK ALEXANDER CHARLES LIEBERT, NORTH SOMERSET YEOMANRY, formerly 2nd LIEUTENANT 3rd DRAGOON GUARDS,

born at Bruges on the 9th March, 1882, was the son of John Frederick Liebert and Lena Henrietta, daughter of Jean Sprut de Bay, of Bruges, and a grandson of Edmund Liebert, Swinton Hall, Lancashire.

He was educated at Bruges and Beaumont College, and in March, 1902, obtained a commission from the Guernsey Militia in the

3rd (Prince of Wales's) Dragoon Guards, from which regiment he retired on his marriage, and joined the North Somerset Yeomanry as a Lieutenant. He got his troop on the 5th August, 1914, shortly before the regiment went out to Flanders, and being keen and capable was soon given a squadron.

Captain Liebert married Frances Elizabeth, younger daughter of A. Chamberlayne Chichester, Esq., J.P., of Gipsy Hill, Pinhoe, Devon, and on his marriage settled first at Sutton Montis, on the Somerset side of the Blackmore Vale Hunt, moving later to " The Elms," Wincanton. He was Assistant Secretary to the Blackmore Vale Hunt, and Secretary to the Wincanton Race Committee. He was devoted to hunting, a keen golfer and cricketer, and always ready to help in any good work connected with the town, where his loss is keenly felt.

Captain Liebert was killed on the 17th November, 1914. The first action in which the North Somerset Yeomanry took a prominent part was over a piece of ground only five hundred yards square, and " B " Squadron, led by Captain Liebert, held the first of a series of trenches upon which a vigorous shell fire of great intensity was directed. In the charge in which he lost his life the Germans got to within fifteen yards of our trenches, but the attack was repulsed with very heavy loss to the enemy.

LIEUTENANT ERIC CARR LIPTROTT, 6th JAT LIGHT INFANTRY,

was born at Plymouth in 1887, the son of the Rev. Boulton B. Liptrott, Vicar of West Teignmouth, Devon, and Mrs. Liptrott. He was a grandson of Lieutenant - General John Liptrott, who raised the 7th Bengal Cavalry, known as " Liptrott's Horse."

Lieutenant Liptrott was educated at Sutton Valence, where he was head boy for two years, and won the mathematical leaving scholarship ; and at the R.M.C., Sandhurst, where he was the best revolver shot of his year, 1906–07. He joined the West Yorkshire Regiment at Rawal Pindi in October, 1907, and served in the Mohmand Expedition of 1908, receiving the medal. He joined the 6th Jats in 1909, being promoted Lieutenant in 1910.

Lieutenant Liptrott was mortally wounded in the trenches at Festubert on the 21st November, 1914. He died five days later at Boulogne, where he is buried. For gallant and distin-

guished service in the field he was mentioned in Sir John French's Despatch of the 14th January, 1915. In a night attack on the 16th November it was very largely due to his cool leading of the left half of the company that the affair was brought off successfully. During this attack he saved his wounded Subadar's life by carrying him, under heavy fire, to safety.

He belonged to the Junior Army and Navy Club ; was good at all games, especially tennis, golf, and hockey. He was captain of the West Yorks Rugby team, and won his cap at Sutton Valence.

CAPTAIN EDWARD RAYMOND LLOYD, 2nd BATTN. ROYAL INNISKILLING FUSILIERS,

born at Camberley, Surrey, on the 13th November, 1882, was the son of Lieutenant-Colonel Edward Lloyd, late 5th Punjab Cavalry.

He was educated at Bedford Grammar School and the R.M.C., Sandhurst. He was a good all-round sportsman,

and represented his school in the Public Schools' Boxing Competition held at Aldershot in 1899. He was also a keen follower of the hounds, a frequent rider in point-to-point hunt steeplechases, and a good shot with both gun and rifle. He was gazetted to the 1st Battalion Royal Inniskilling Fusiliers in October, 1902, becoming Lieutenant in January, 1905. Subsequently he was transferred to the 2nd Battalion in Egypt, of which he was Assistant Adjutant and afterwards Adjutant (appointed August, 1911). For his services in the Great War he was mentioned in Sir John French's Despatch of the 8th October, 1914.

He was shot on the 26th August, 1914, while in the firing line with his men during the retirement from Mons, and died on the 3rd December in a German hospital at Cambrai.

CAPTAIN MEYRICKE ENTWISTLE LLOYD, 1st BATTN. ROYAL WELSH FUSILIERS,

killed in action on the 20th October, 1914, was the eldest son of the late Mr. Henry Lloyd, of Dolobran, Isaf, Montgomery, whom he succeeded in 1902. He was born on the 31st May, 1880, and, after serving for some months with the embodied Militia, joined the R.W.F. in June, 1900, obtaining his Lieutenancy in September, 1907, and his company in April, 1911. He was a good horseman and a keen follower of hounds. He embarked on the 4th October, 1914, for Belgium, with his battalion which formed part of the VIIth Division, and was killed near Becelaere in the severe fighting which took place at the commencement of the first Battle of Ypres.

LIEUTENANT - COLONEL WALTER REGINALD LLOYD, 1st BATTN. LOYAL NORTH LANCASHIRE REGIMENT,

born on the 18th August, 1868, was the youngest son of the late Sampson Lloyd, formerly Chairman of Lloyd's Bank, and M. P. for Plymouth and for South Warwickshire, and of Mrs. Lloyd, of Danesrood, Guildford, Surrey.

He was educated at Eton, where he rowed in the Eight and at the R.M.C., Sandhurst. He joined the 2nd Battalion of his regiment in 1888, becoming Captain in 1896. From 1897 to 1901 he was Adjutant of his battalion, and was promoted Major in June, 1906. He served in South Africa during the last eighteen months of the Boer War, and was present at operations in the Transvaal and Cape Colony, receiving the Queen's medal with four clasps.

Lieutenant-Colonel Lloyd was at first reported as missing at the end of September, 1914, but it was subsequently ascertained that he had been killed at the Battle of the Aisne on the 14th of that month. His battalion had been ordered to attack a sugar factory in the Chemin des Dames near Troyon, held by the enemy. It transpired that Lieutenant-Colonel Lloyd had continued to lead his men, though wounded in the head, and fell later in the day, shot through the heart.

Lieutenant-Colonel Lloyd was gazetted to the command of his battalion on the 12th September, 1914, only two days before his death.

CAPTAIN MICHAEL JOSEPH LOCHRIN, ROYAL ARMY MEDICAL CORPS,

who was killed in action on the 23rd October, 1914, was born on the 27th May, 1883, and took his diploma of L.R.C.P. and S., Ireland, in 1904. He joined the R.A.M.C. in July, 1906, becoming Captain in January, 1910.

2nd LIEUTENANT RICHARD WILLIAM MARK LOCKWOOD, 2nd BATTN. COLDSTREAM GUARDS,

was born in London on the 28th March, 1891, the only son of William Robert Percival Lockwood, and a grandson of the late General Mark Wood.

He was educated at Mr. Lock's School, Eversleigh, Berks, and at Eton, where he was in Mr. Brenton's House. He joined the 2nd Battalion Coldstream Guards on probation in 1910, and was gazetted 2nd Lieutenant on the 1st February, 1913.

2nd Lieutenant Lockwood was serving with his battalion when he was killed on the 14th September, 1914, at Soupir, after having carried his wounded Captain out of danger, with the help of Drummer Harris.

He was a member of the Guards' Club and of Pratt's.

MAJOR LIONEL STUART LOGAN, SUPPLY AND TRANSPORT CORPS, INDIAN ARMY,

was the son of the late Major-General Archibald George Douglas Logan, Madras Staff Corps, and was born at Mercara, India, on the 4th January, 1874.

He was educated first at Dover College, afterwards at the Royal Military College, Sandhurst, and having passed for the Indian Army was gazetted to an unattached 2nd Lieutenancy in October, 1894. In December of the following year he was appointed to the Indian Staff Corps, becoming Lieutenant in the 20th Madras Infantry in January, 1897, and Captain in the 80th Carnatic Infantry in October, 1903. In October, 1912, he was transferred to the Supply and Transport Corps, Indian Army, with promotion to the rank of Major.

Major Logan was accidentally killed on the 2nd November, 1914, while on active service in Northern France with the 3rd Lahore Divisional Supply Train, Indian Expeditionary Force.

He was a member of the East India United Service Club, and his recreations were tennis and golf.

LIEUTENANT FREDERICK LONGMAN, 4th BATTN. THE ROYAL FUSILIERS (CITY OF LONDON REGIMENT)·

was the second son of C. J. Longman, Esq., of Upp Hall, Braughing, Ware, and Mrs. Longman, daughter of the late Sir John Evans, F.R.S., K.C.B. He was born at 27, Norfolk Square, London, W., on the 9th May, 1890, and was educated at Harrow and Pembroke College, Cambridge.

He was an enthusiast for military training, having been at Harrow an active member of the School Corps, and at Cambridge of the University O.T.C. He left the latter in 1910, on receiving a commission in the Hertfordshire Territorial Regiment. At that time it was desired to raise a section of twenty-five men in Braughing, the village in which he lived, and he set himself so energetically to work that he recruited no fewer than forty-one men. He was a member of the local Rifle Club, and spent much time in training lads from the village school at the miniature range.

He was gazetted to the Royal Fusiliers as 2nd Lieutenant in February, 1912, becoming Lieutenant on the 24th August, 1914. He was wounded at the Battle of the Marne, where four bullets passed through his clothes, besides one that struck him in the arm. He was sent back to the base, where he quickly recovered and rejoined his battalion at the front, to be killed in action on the 18th October, 1914.

Lieutenant Longman's cheerful manners and sterling character gained him many friends, and caused him to be universally loved. He was unmarried.

LIEUTENANT JAMES RAYMOND McCLINTOCK LONSDALE 4th (THE QUEEN'S OWN) HUSSARS,

born on the 16th March, 1894, was the eldest son of Mr. and Mrs. Thomas Lonsdale, of Hooton, Cheshire, and grandson of the late Lieutenant-Colonel G. A. J. McClintock, of Fellows Hall, County Armagh, and Catherine Caroline Brownlow, youngest daughter of Sir James Mathew Stronge, second

Bart., of Tynan Abbey. He was also a nephew of Sir John B. Lonsdale, Bart., M.P.

He was educated at Wixenford, Wokingham, and at Eton (Mr. Marten's House). He left Eton in January, 1912, passed into the R.M.C., Sandhurst, in September of the same year, and received his commission in September, 1913, becoming Lieutenant in August, 1914.

He was a keen sportsman, played polo for his regiment on several occasions in and around Dublin in 1914, was a good rider to hounds, and did a little steeplechase riding. He won the Sandhurst heavyweight point-to-point in 1912, and rode in one or two hunt meetings in 1914. He also won the Ladies' Cup in Wirral Hunt point-to-point on his sister's horse in 1914.

On the 13th October Lieutenant Lonsdale was sent out with a party of twenty-five men to make a reconnaissance. He successfully accomplished the duty assigned him, and after reporting he bravely returned under fire to search for some men of his party who were missing. He brought the men back, but was himself severely wounded, and died in the Base Hospital at Boulogne on the 29th October, 1914.

His remains were brought to England and interred in the family grave at Hooton, Cheshire. The body, met by detachments of the Liverpool and Cheshire Regiments, was conveyed to the cemetery on a gun carriage, and the funeral was carried out with full military honours.

LIEUTENANT HERBERT REUBEN LOOMES, 1st BATTN. LOYAL NORTH LANCASHIRE REGIMENT,

who is believed to have been killed on the 14th September, 1914, aged twenty-five, at Vendresse, near Bourg, on the Aisne, but whose name has not appeared in the official casualty lists, was the eldest son of Mr. and Mrs. R. Loomes. 83, Carleton Road, Tufnell Park, N., now of "Tregenna." Prideaux Road, Eastbourne.

He was born on the 9th February, 1889, and was educated at Highgate School, and by private tuition under Lieutenant-Colonel James, Bushmead Hall, Bedford. He joined the Loyal North Lancashire Regiment from the Special Reserve in May, 1909, becoming Lieutenant in April, 1912. For two years he had been Assistant Adjutant of his battalion.

He won several prizes for shooting, and competed in the annual Military Tournament in jumping and tent-pegging. His recreations included hunting, polo, and shooting.

In the early part of the war he was invalided after the Battle of the Marne, but rejoined his battalion on the 13th September, 1914. Early on the 14th the battalion was called out to storm a factory across the Aisne. He led his men in an open charge, and was reported by them to have been shot in the neck. He continued to call out the range at which they were to fire, and whilst one of his men was bandaging his wound they were both shot through again fatally.

He was reported missing a few days later, and never heard of since. As the Germans later in the day came past our lines of dead and wounded his body was never recovered.

MAJOR CHARLES BUXTON LORING, 37th LANCERS (BALUCH HORSE), attd. POONA HORSE,

who was killed on the 21st December, 1914, was the eighth son of the late Rev. E. H. Loring, Rector of Gillingham, Norfolk, and a nephew of General Sir John Watson, V.C.

He was born at Gillingham on the 16th October, 1871, and was educated at Marlborough (Star), of which he was a Foundation scholar, from 1885–9, and the R.M.C., Sandhurst, out of which he passed with honours. He joined the Durham Light Infantry as 2nd Lieutenant in November, 1891, and was transferred to the 27th Lancers (Baluch Horse) in May, 1893, with the rank of Lieutenant. He was promoted Captain in the Indian Army in July, 1901, and Major in November, 1909. He was for a time Second in Command of the Zhob Militia, and afterwards commanded it from 1908–11.

When the war broke out he was on leave in England, and on rejoining trained recruits at York Barracks till September, 1914. He at first served with the 2nd Dragoons (Scots Greys), but at the end of November was attached to the 34th Poona Horse, and was serving with that regiment when he was shot by a concealed machine gun, after having got into German trenches at Givenchy on the 21st December, 1914, while attempting to carry a wounded native officer to the rear.

Major Loring married May, daughter of the late Major-General W. R. Alexander, Indian Army, and left three children.

He was a member of the Cavalry Club, and was keen on all games and sports, being a particularly good polo player. He was known as the finest No. 4 in North India.

LIEUTENANT - COLONEL WALTER LATHAM LORING, COMMANDING THE 2nd BATTN. ROYAL WARWICKSHIRE REGIMENT,

was the sixth son of the Rev. E. H. Loring, Rector of Gillingham, Suffolk, and was born at the Rectory there on the 3rd April, 1868. He was educated at the Fauconberge School, Beccles, and Marlborough College, where he gained a scholarship, and at Trinity Hall, Cambridge. As a boy he had lived with his mother at Ewshot, where all the members of the family were held in high esteem. He had the misfortune to lose his mother and sister by the foundering of the steamer in which they were going to Australia to visit a brother of the Colonel.

Joining the Royal Warwickshire Regiment in 1889, he served with it in India, Malta, and, with the Mounted Infantry, in the Transvaal. He obtained his steps as follows : Lieutenant in 1890 ; Captain, 1898 ; Major, 3rd November, 1904, succeeding to the command of the 2nd Battalion in 1914, and was antedated in his rank two years.

The history of the 2nd Warwicks, led by their gallant Colonel, forms one of the many stirring episodes in the earlier part of the Great War. The battalion returned from Malta in September, 1914, and after a few weeks at home landed at Zeebrugge early in October. From the 19th of that month they were almost continually engaged with the enemy, near Ypres and Menin. On the 23rd October the Warwicks and Welsh Fusiliers were on the left of the line. A large force of the enemy unexpectedly appeared on the flank, and it was with difficulty, after severe fighting, that the Warwicks were liberated from a dangerous position. During this action Lieutenant-Colonel Loring was struck on the foot by shrapnel, and, though urged to go back to the hospital to have his wound attended to, refused to do so, and continued in his command, with his foot bound up in a puttee, as he could no longer get a boot on. After the action the General commanding the Division came to see the battalion, and highly complimented their Colonel for his skill, and the battalion generally for its bravery and endurance. Next day, the 24th October, 1914, the battalion was again hotly engaged, near Becelaere, and the fighting was thus described by a General Officer : "October 24th. Again an attack on the line, and at 8 a.m. news that the line was broken. The Warwicks were sent up. They behaved splendidly : drove back the Germans, cleared a wood, and saved the situation. They lost one hundred and nine men and several officers, including the Colonel. Such a good sort, his death is a terrible loss to us." In this action, being no longer able to walk, Lieutenant-Colonel Loring insisted on leading his battalion on horseback, thus, of course, exposing himself to far greater risk. Two of his chargers were shot under him, and he himself was killed instantaneously.

A Staff Officer, who subsequently returned to England, and who was present during the fighting, described the general admiration among officers and men of Lieutenant-Colonel Loring's courage and example, and the devotion of both officers and men of the Warwicks to their Colonel.

A wounded N.C.O., who was in the action, wrote of him : " I am sorry to say our gallant Colonel was killed the same day, and, my word ! he was a brave man. He was always in front of his regiment. I have only written what I have seen with my own eyes, and it is enough to make anyone's heart bleed."

While in England Lieutenant-Colonel Loring had been, from 1908–12, Staff Officer of the Officers' Training Corps for the Birmingham and Bristol Universities and the Royal Agricultural College at Cirencester. He was known as one of the best types of Englishmen, a gallant soldier, a fine gentleman, and a Churchman who took his faith with him into everyday life. He was particularly interested in lads, and did much valuable work in connection with the C.E.M.S.

For his services in the Great War he was mentioned in Sir John French's Despatch of the 14th January, 1915.

Lieutenant-Colonel Loring married the youngest daughter of the Rev. R. M. Marshall, lately Rector of Hedenham, Norfolk, and left ten children : Constance and Grace (twins), born 1899 ; Henry, born 1900 ; Edward Christopher, born 1901 ; Patience, born 1904 ; Madeline, born 1905 ; Faith, born 1910 ; Marion, born 1912 ; and David and Joan (twins), born 1914.

LIEUTENANT EDWARD ARTHUR LOUSADA, 2nd BATTN. ROYAL SUSSEX REGIMENT,

who was shown in the monthly casualty list published in December, 1914, as killed in action, no date or place being given, was born on the 19th November, 1888. He joined the Royal Sussex Regiment in February, 1909, and became Lieutenant in October, 1910.

CAPTAIN (temp.) ARTHUR REGINALD LOVEBAND, 1st BATTN. WEST YORKSHIRE REGT.,

was born at Warkleigh Rectory, North Devon, on the 7th November, 1888. He was the eldest son of the late Rev. M. T. Loveband, Vicar of Burrington, North Devon, and Mrs. T. Loveband, of Exeter. He was a nephew of Lieutenant-Colonel Arthur Loveband, C.M.G., 1st Royal Dublin Fusiliers.

Captain Loveband was educated at Eastbourne College, and joined the West Yorkshire Regiment in India from the Special Reserve in December, 1909, becoming Lieutenant in January, 1912, and Temporary Captain in November, 1914, while engaged in this war.

He was killed in the trenches near Armentières on the 6th December, 1914.

LIEUTENANT HENRY STANLEY LOWE, 2nd BATTN. WORCESTERSHIRE REGIMENT,

who died on the 21st October, 1914, in Paris, of wounds received in action at the Battle of the Aisne on the 20th September, 1914, was the youngest son of the late Rev. E. J. Lowe, of Stallingborough, Lincolnshire, and of Mrs. Lowe, of Wetherby Mansions, London, S.W. He was born on the 7th February, 1890, at Stallingborough Vicarage, and was educated at Rugby (Michell), which he entered in 1904. He was gazetted to the Worcester. Regt. in Nov., 1909, and promoted Lieutenant in March, 1913.

LIEUTENANT GEOFFREY ARCHIBALD LOYD, 2nd BATTN. SCOTS GUARDS,

who was killed in action at Zonnebeke, near Ypres, on the 13th November, 1914, was the third son of Mr. A. K. Loyd, K.C., formerly M.P. for North Berks, and Mrs. Loyd, 21 Cadogan Square, London, S.W., and East Hendred, Berks.

He was born in London in 1890, and was educated at Eton and Magdalen College, Oxford. He was gazetted 2nd Lieutenant in the Scots Guards in Feburary, 1913, and was promoted Lieutenant on the 24th September, 1914.

In the Great War he was attached, with a cyclist company, to the Mounted Troops of the IInd Division. In recognition of his services during the rearguard actions in the retirement from Mons he was awarded the Croix de Chevalier de la Légion d'Honneur, and was also mentioned in Sir John French's Despatch of the 31st January, 1915.

He was killed by shrapnel while engaged with the cyclist company in holding an entrenched position as escort to guns, which were being fiercely shelled by the enemy (" The Times," 25th November, 1914).

He was a member of the Guards', Junior Army and Navy, and Pratt's Clubs, and was fond of rowing and hunting.

2nd LIEUTENANT RICHARD JOHN LUMLEY, 11th (PRINCE ALBERT'S OWN) HUSSARS,

who was killed in action near Ploegsteert on the 17th October, 1914, was the eldest son of Brigadier - General the Hon. Osbert Lumley, youngest son of the ninth Earl of Scarborough, and was born on the 30th June, 1894, at Sandbeck Park, Rotherham.

He was educated at Ludgrove (Mr. G. O. Smith), Eton (C. M. Wells), and the R.M.C., Sandhurst, receiving his commission in the 11th Hussars in February, 1914.

2nd Lieutenant Lumley, whose recreations were cricket, football, polo, and hunting, was a member of the Cavendish Club.

CAPTAIN CHARLES RAMSAY LUMSDEN, 1st BATTN. GORDON HIGHLANDERS,

who was killed on the 25th August, 1914, in action at Mons, was the second son of the late Mr. W. H. Lumsden, of Balmedie, Aberdeenshire, and of Mrs. Lumsden.

He was born in June, 1880, at Balmedie, Aberdeenshire, and was educated at Cheam and Eton. He was one of five brothers serving in the

Army, and joined the Gordon Highlanders from the Militia in July, 1899, becoming Lieutenant in December of the same year. He was a keen sportsman and golfer.

He served in the South African War, taking part in the advance on Kimberley, with actions at Magersfontein; operations in 1900 in the Orange Free State and Paardeberg, including actions at Poplar Grove, Driefontein, Houtnek (Thoba Mountain), Vet and Zand Rivers; in the Transvaal, east of Pretoria, and near Johannesburg, at Belfast and Lydenberg; in the Transvaal, west of Pretoria, and in Cape Colony north and south of the Orange River; also at further operations in the Transvaal between 1900 and 1902. He was mentioned in Despatches ("London Gazette," 10th September, 1901), and received the Queen's medal with five clasps and the King's medal with two clasps.

He was promoted Captain in February, 1904.

CAPTAIN CHARLES GEORGE LYALL, RESERVE OF OFFICERS, attd. LINCOLNSHIRE REGIMENT,

who was killed in action on the 18th October, 1914, was the son of Dr. David Lyall, R.N., Deputy Inspector-General of Hospitals, F.L.S.

He was born at West Hartlepool on the 28th February, 1871, was educated at Cheltenham College, and received his first commission in July, 1892, becoming Captain in November, 1901.

He served in the Nile Expedition of 1898, being present at the Battle of Khartoum, for which he received the British medal and the Egyptian medal with clasp.

Taking part in the South African War, he was present, in 1900, at operations in the Orange Free State and at Paardeberg; actions at Poplar Grove, Karee Siding, Vet and Zand Rivers; operations in the Transvaal, with actions near Johannesburg and Pretoria; also at later operations in the Transvaal in 1901, receiving the Queen's medal with four clasps. He took a keen interest in all farming and agricultural matters, and was fond of motoring and shooting. In 1907 he retired from the Lincolnshire Regiment, entering the Reserve of Officers, from which he was called up for duty on active service, with his own regiment. He was killed during night movements on the 18th October, 1914, and was buried by his regiment at La Cliqueterie Farm, Herties, France.

Captain Lyall married Marjorie, third daughter of the late Alfred B. Burton, of Lincoln, and left two children : Marjorie Joyce, born September, 1903 ; and John David, born November, 1904.

LIEUTENANT ALEXANDER PATRICK FRANCIS LYON, 1st BATTN. GORDON HIGHLANDERS,

born in London on the 5th August, 1888, was the fourth son of the late Mr. Walter F. K. Lyon and of Mrs. Lyon, Tantallon Lodge, North Berwick. He was educated at Haileybury College, where he was in the XXX (2nd XV) football team, and at the R.M.C., Sandhurst, into which he passed second. He was gazetted to the Gordon Highlanders in May, 1907, and got his step in March, 1909. He was a qualified 1st Class Interpreter in German, French, and Russian. In 1912 he was specially employed at the War Office, and in 1914 entered for the Staff College, but the result has not been published.

Lieutenant A. P. F. Lyon was killed at Bertry on the 27th August, 1914. His younger brother —Lieutenant C. J. Lyon, 1st Battalion Royal Scots Fusiliers—was killed near Ypres on the 14th November, 1914.

He was a member of the Junior Army and Navy Club.

LIEUTENANT CHARLES JAMES LYON, ACTING ADJUTANT 1st BATTN. ROYAL SCOTS FUSILIERS,

born in London on the 28th March, 1890, was the fifth son of the late Walter F. K. Lyon. He was educated at Stubbington School ; at Haileybury College, where he was in the XXX (2nd XV) ; and at the R.M.C., Sandhurst, into which he passed first. He was gazetted 2nd Lieutenant in 1909. Next year he served with the Mounted Infantry at Harrismith, South Africa. He was promoted Lieutenant in October, 1911, and was mentioned in Sir John French's Despatch of 8th October, 1914. He was killed near Ypres on the 14th November, 1914. His elder brother, Lieutenant A. P. F. Lyon, 1st Battalion Gordon Highlanders, was killed on the 27th August, 1914.

Lieutenant C. J. Lyon was a member of the Junior Army and Navy Club, and of the New Club, North Berwick. He played polo and golf.

LIEUTENANT CHARLES LINDSAY CLAUDE BOWES LYON, 3rd. (attd. 1st) BATTN. THE BLACK WATCH (ROYAL HIGHLANDERS),

who was born on the 15th September, 1885, was the eldest son of the Hon. Francis and Lady Anne Bowes Lyon, of Ridley Hall, Northumberland, and grandson of Claude, thirteenth Earl of Strathmore, and of Alexander, twenty-sixth Earl of Crawford.

He was educated at Eton, and subsequently finishing an engineering training at the Armstrong College of Science, Newcastle-on-Tyne, he became a member of the Institute of Civil Engineers. For three years he was in the Forfar and Kincardine Royal Garrison Artillery (Militia), and on this being disbanded he joined the 3rd (Special Reserve) Battalion Black Watch in 1910. He completed an engineering appointment in India with Messrs. Turner, Hoare & Co., of Bombay, and on his way home, via Japan and Canada, was one of the few survivors of the s.s. " Empress of Ireland," which was sunk in the St. Lawrence on the 28th May, 1914.

Early in September, 1914, Lieutenant Bowes Lyon was attached to the 1st Battalion of his regiment in France, where it formed part of the 1st Army Corps.

During the fighting on the Aisne he was slightly wounded, but remained on duty, and was wounded a second time in Flanders. He was killed in action on the 23rd October, 1914, near Boesinghe. Lieutenant Bowes Lyon was a keen sportsman and an enthusiastic lover of shooting, cricket, polo, and golf.

MAJOR NIGEL LUCIUS SAMUEL LYSONS, 2nd BATTN. THE KING'S OWN (ROYAL LANCASTER REGIMENT),

who was killed in action on the 21st October, 1914, was the son of the late Canon Samuel Lysons.

He was born on the 21st May, 1876, and joined the Royal Lancashire Regiment from the Militia in May, 1907, becoming Lieutenant in May, 1898, and Captain in September, 1901. He served in the South African War, taking part in the relief of Ladysmith, with the action at Spion Kop ; the operations and actions at Vaal Krans, on the Tugela Heights, and Pieter's Hill ; in the Transvaal and Natal in 1900, including actions at Laing's Nek ; also at operations in the Transvaal in 1901. He received the Queen's medal with five clasps and the King's medal with two clasps.

From July, 1902, to July, 1905, he was Adjutant of his battalion, and he obtained his Majority in August, 1913.

2nd LIEUT. ALISTER McANDREW, 1st BATTN. THE BLACK WATCH (ROYAL HIGHLANDERS),

was the son of the late Roderick McAndrew, and was born at Fodderdy, Dingwall, Ross-shire, in October, 1875.

He was educated at Fodderdy Public School and Dingwall Academy, and, having joined the BlackWatch in 1894, served in the ranks of that regiment for seventeen years, many of which were spent in India. He took part with it in several engagements in the South African War, for which he received the Queen's and the King's medals with clasps, and was afterwards awarded the Good Conduct medal. On the outbreak of the Great War he accompanied his battalion to the Continent, and in recognition of his enthusiasm and aptitude for military duties was given a commission in his own regiment in November, 1914.

He was shot through the heart by a German sniper at Givenchy on the 24th December, 1914, while leading a section of his men in a charge. 2nd Lieutenant McAndrew, who was unmarried, was well known in Edinburgh, where he had been in one of the officers' messes at the Castle for some years. He was much liked by the officers and exceedingly popular with all who happened to meet him on visits to the fortress.

LIEUTENANT IAN MACLEAN MAC-ANDREW, 1st BATTN. SEAFORTH HIGHLANDERS,

born at East Haugh, Perthshire, on the 30th October, 1891, was the only son of Major and Mrs. J. M. Macandrew, of Delnies Muir, Nairn, Scotland. He was a grandson of the late Major-General W. LambertYonge,R.A.,

of Caynton Hall, Salop, and a great-grandson of the late Lieutenant-General W. Jervois, K.H.

He was educated at Winchester (1905–10), where he was an exhibitioner and King's silver medallist for Latin Speech, being also in the football XV and winning numerous cups for running, one hundred yards, quarter-mile, and other races. He went to New College, Oxford, from 1910–13, where he took his degree of B.A. in history, with second-class honours, in June, 1913. He was gazetted to the Seaforth Highlanders with the rank of 2nd Lieutenant, antedated to September, 1911, and posted to the 1st Battalion at Agra, India.

He went to France with his regiment as part of the Indian Expeditionary Force, being promoted Lieutenant in September, 1914. On the 6th November he was wounded, but at once returned to duty. He was killed in action on the 23rd December, 1914, at Festubert, Flanders, while gallantly rallying the men around him of his own and other regiments, and holding, against enormous odds, a position which had been exposed by the abandonment of the trenches on his left, thus averting a flank attack on his regiment. During the earlier part of the war Lieutenant Macandrew had attracted attention by his ability, courage, and resource, and was mentioned in Sir John French's Despatch of the 14th January, 1915, for gallant and distinguished service in the field.

He was a member of the Junior United Service Club, and was fond of shooting and all outdoor games.

2nd LIEUTENANT GEORGE HENRY McAULIFFE, 1st BATTN. QUEEN'S OWN CAMERON HIGHLANDERS,

was killed in action on the 29th October, 1914, at Zillebeke, near Ypres.

He was born in London on the 26th October, 1874, and in November, 1897, enlisted in the 2nd Gordon Highlanders. Having risen to the rank of Company Sergeant-Major, he was, on the 10th October, 1914, granted a commission as 2nd Lieutenant in the 2nd Battalion Queen's Own Cameron Highlanders. He had previously served in the South African War, for services in which he was mentioned in Lord Roberts's Despatches, and received the King's and Queen's medals. He also had the Delhi Durbar medal of 1911.

2nd Lieutenant McAuliffe married Lily Caroline, daughter of the late Mr. and Mrs. Biddis, and left one daughter, Lily Mary, born on the 9th November, 1913.

2nd LIEUTENANT ALFRED McBRIDE, 2nd BATTN. THE HIGHLAND LIGHT INFANTRY, who died on the 1st November, 1914, of wounds received in action, was only gazetted to the Army on the 10th October, 1914. He had previously served in the Gordon Highlanders in which he reached the rank of Sergeant.

CAPTAIN ROBERT JIM McCLEVERTY, 47th SIKHS,

born on the 27th February, 1882, at Newark, Nottinghamshire, was the third son of Colonel J. McCleverty, late Sherwood Foresters. His grandfathers were General W. A. McCleverty and Surgeon-General H. H. Massy, C.B.

He was educated at Malvern College, and received his commission in the Duke of Wellington's (West Riding Regiment) on the 8th May, 1901. With it he served in the South African War, 1901–02, taking part in operations in the Transvaal, for which he received the Queen's medal with five clasps.

Captain McCleverty was transferred to the 36th Sikhs, Indian Army, as Lieutenant, in December, 1903, and subsequently to the 47th Sikhs in February, 1904. He became Captain in May, 1910, and was personal Assistant to the Chief Commissioner, Central Provinces, from May, 1913, to May, 1914.

He was killed while leading his company in an attack on Neuve Chapelle on the 28th October, 1914. After his death he was mentioned in Sir John French's Despatch of the 14th January, 1915, for his gallantry.

Captain McCleverty was a member of the Junior Army and Navy Club. He was a well-known hockey player, and won the Indian Army officers' two hundred and twenty yards race in record time.

CAPT. ROBERT JAMES McCLOUGHIN, 1st BATTN. BEDFORDSHIRE REGT.,

born in Bombay, Southern India, on the 9th June, 1881, was the son of Thomas J. McCloughin, Post Trust, Calcutta. He was educated at Bishop Cotton School, Bangalore, India, and later by tutors. He joined the Bedfordshire Regi-

ment from the 3rd Battalion K.O.S.B.'s in 1905, and was promoted Captain in January, 1913.

From 1909–11 he served with the West African Frontier Force on the Gold Coast, and subsequently was A.D.C. to the Governor of the Gold Coast and to the Governor of British East Africa. He was fond of games, always found a place in any first-class side at polo, and won numerous prizes for racing and tennis.

Captain McCloughin was serving with his battalion when he was killed at Missy-sur-Aisne on the 14th September, 1914. A wood was being attacked when he ventured into the open to select a fresh firing position for his men. He was hit twice, and subsequently died of his wounds. He was mentioned in Sir John French's Despatch of the 8th October, 1914, " for gallantry under fire and soldierly qualities displayed on every occasion since the beginning of the war." His C.O. and brother officers, writing of him, said the battalion had lost a very brave and gallant officer, and a kind-hearted and unselfish friend, and it was largely due to him that his men did so well in every action. Captain McCloughin married Flora E., daughter of Thomas P. Savage, Educational Department, India, and left one child, Flora Eileen Mary, born August, 1914.

MAJOR CHARLES RUSSELL McCLURE, 19th (QUEEN ALEXANDRA'S OWN ROYAL) HUSSARS,

born on the 16th May, 1875, at Cliff House, Wemyss Bay, Renfrewshire, was the son of the late James Howe McClure, Solicitor, Glasgow, and Charlotte his wife, daughter of the late James Russell, Q.C. He was educated at Kelvinside

Academy, Glasgow, and for two years at the Glasgow University. He then, in October 1894, entered Magdalen College, Oxford, as a commoner, and took honours in the Final School of Lit.Hum. in 1898. During 1899 he read as a pupil in the chambers of Mr. E. M. Pollock (now K.C., M.P.). He received a University commission in the 19th Hussars in 1900, and in November of that year went out to join his regiment in South Africa. He served there till the end of the war, being present at operations in Cape Colony, the Transvaal, and Orange River Colony, receiving the Queen's medal with five clasps, and remained in South Africa till January, 1904. He became Lieutenant in 1901, Captain in February, 1907, and Major in March, 1914.

On the outbreak of the Great War Major McClure

went to France with the IVth Division of the Expeditionary Force, leaving England on the 22nd August in command of " B " Squadron of his regiment. He went straight into action at Le Cateau, taking an active part in the retirement, and thereafter in the Battles of the Marne and the Aisne. Early in October the British troops moved to Belgium, and there his last active operations were carried out. Under his command, his squadron was the first of the Allied forces to enter Bailleul on the 14th October. Major McClure was killed in action at Le Gheer, near Ploegsteert, Belgium, on the 21st October, 1914, and was buried on the battlefield near where he fell. He was mentioned in Sir John French's Despatch of the 14th January, 1915. He was a member of the Cavalry and Bath Clubs, and was unmarried.

CAPTAIN JOHN HUGH GARDINER McCORMICK, 4th (attd. 2nd) BATTN. ROYAL WARWICKSHIRE REGIMENT,

was the eldest son of S. S. McCormick, J.P., S h a n d o n, M o n k s t o w n, County Dublin, and was born there on the 3rd March, 1886. He was educated at South Eastern College, Ramsgate, and joined the 6th Battalion Royal Warwickshire Regiment as 2nd Lieutenant in 1906. The 6th afterwards became the 4th Battalion, in which he became Lieutenant in 1909, and Captain in September, 1914. He was attached to the 2nd Battalion for active service, and left with it for the front in October, 1914. He was wounded in action on the 19th Oct., 1914, and having been taken prisoner died at a convent hospital at Menin the same day. He had resided for some years at Williamstown House, Kells, where he entered keenly into country life.

2nd LIEUT. PATRICK McDONAGH, SPECIAL RESERVE, QUEEN'S OWN (ROYAL WEST KENT REGIMENT),

was born at Cong, County Mayo, Ireland, on the 1st December, 1893, and was the son of Mrs. M c D o n a g h, of Loughgall, Co. Armagh, Ireland. He was a nephew of the three Messrs. Fenning, of Waterford, Edinburgh, and New York respectively.

2nd Lieutenant McDonagh was educated at St. Patrick's College, Armagh ; at St. Malachy's College ; and at Queen's University, Belfast. At the latter he was in the University contingent of the Officers' Training Corps from October, 1912, to May, 1914.

On the 2nd May, 1914, he was gazetted to a commission in the Queen's Own Royal West Kent Regiment. In the Great War he was with the 2nd Battalion Suffolk Regiment, to which he was attached for service, and was killed in action on the 18th November, 1914.

2nd LIEUTENANT EVAN RONALD HORATIO KEITH MACDONALD, 2nd BATTN. HIGHLAND LIGHT INFANTRY,

was born in the Isle of Skye on the 10th April, 1893, and was the only surviving son of the late Dr. Keith Norman Macdonald, M.D., F.R.C.P.E., the well - known collector of, and authority on, Highland music, and of Mrs. Macdonald, 21, Clarendon Crescent, Edinburgh. He was educated at the Edinburgh Academy, at Harrogate, Southport, and the Edinburgh Institution. While at school he was captain of the first XV for three years, and afterwards played in the Old Boys' team. At the School Sports in 1911 he won the cup for the mile race, and before leaving for the front was one of the secretaries of the Institution's Athletic Sports. Mr. Macdonald was also keenly interested in everything Highland, and loved to play the slower music of the piobmhor.

He joined the 3rd Battalion on the 3rd July, 1912, and was gazetted to the 2nd Battalion on the 10th June, 1914. Mr. Macdonald kept a most interesting diary of his war experiences right up to the day on which he was killed, which was published in extenso in the " Highland Light Infantry Chronicle " for October, 1914, from which also many of the details in this memoir are taken.

During the Battle of the Aisne he was hit in the temple by a bullet, on the 20th September, 1914, and instantaneously killed, while he was directing the fire of his men in the trenches; he was buried in a quiet spot close to where he fell, near Verneuil, Vailly, on the Aisne, France. His death was much regretted by his brother officers.

He was predeceased by his elder brother some

years ago—the late Lieutenant R. F. N. Keith Macdonald, 4th Battalion H.L.I.—who was on active service in the South African War.

LIEUTENANT the Honble. GODFREY EVAN HUGH MACDONALD, 1st BATTN. SCOTS GUARDS,

second and eldest surviving son of Lord Macdonald of Armadale Castle, Isle of Skye, and a relative of Ross of Cromarty and the Earl of Listowel, was shot on the 31st October, 1914, and died of his wounds. He was born at 20, Chesham Place, London, S.W., on the 6th March, 1879, and was educated at Brussels and afterwards at Fettes College, Edinburgh.

Having served in the embodied Militia for nearly five months, he joined the Scots Guards in April, 1900, serving with them in the South African War, for which he received the Queen's medal. After having reached the rank of Lieutenant in March, 1902, he retired from the active list in December of the same year, and joined the Special Reserve of his regiment in February, 1906.

On the outbreak of the war he rejoined for active service, and was posted to the 1st Scots Guards for duty.

Lieutenant Macdonald, who was a J.P. for the County of Inverness, married, in April, 1908, Helen Holm, eldest daughter of Meyricke Bankes, of Winstay, Lincolnshire, and left two sons : Alexander Godfrey, born June, 1909 ; and James Archibald, born December, 1911.

LIEUTENANT RONALD MOSSE MACDONALD, 1st BATTN. THE QUEEN'S OWN CAMERON HIGHLANDERS,

was born at Bombay on the 9th December, 1890, and was the elder son of William Mosse Macdonald of Glenmore, Isle of Skye, late Captain 3rd Battalion Cameron Highlanders, and Mrs. Macdonald, of Glenmore Cottage, East Avenue, Bournemouth.

He was educated at Horris Hill, Newbury, Winchester College, and the Royal Military College, Sandhurst, from which he obtained his commission in the Cameron Highlanders in

November, 1910. In 1913 he was Signalling Officer of the battalion, and was promoted Lieutenant in August, 1914. He left Edinburgh Castle with his battalion on the 12th of that month, with twenty-five officers, of whom, when he fell, he was the last one left. He was wounded at the Battle of the Aisne on the 14th September, 1914, recovered and rejoined on the 8th October ; and fell in action at Veldhoek, near Ypres, on the 2nd November, 1914.

Lieutenant Macdonald was an accomplished violinist. He was a member of the Aldershot Cricket XI, 1911 and 1912, and belonged to the Caledonian Club, London.

CAPTAIN IAIN MacDOUGALL, 2nd BATTN. GRENADIER GUARDS,

was born at Lunga, County Argyll, on the 31st May, 1887, the only son of Colonel MacDougall, of Lunga, Commanding the 10th (Service) Battalion Gordon Highlanders, J.P. and D.L. for County Argyll, and Gentleman-at-Arms in His Majesty's Household. He was educated at Eton and the R.M.C., Sandhurst, where he took a high place both as a student and an athlete. Joining the Grenadier Guards in 1906, he became Lieutenant in 1907 ; from 1910–12 he was A.D.C. to his Excellency Lord Islington, Governor-General and Commander-in-Chief of New Zealand ; he obtained his company in August, 1914, in which year he was appointed Adjutant of his battalion.

On the 1st September, 1914, at Villers Cotterets, while recalling some companies of the battalion which were threatened to be cut off, Captain MacDougall was shot when returning after delivering his message, his horse being killed at the same time. He was buried by the French peasants in the wood of Villers Cotteret where he fell, and at a later period his body was exhumed and laid in the family vault in the old churchyard of Kilvoree, Argyllshire.

Captain MacDougall was a member of Pratt's and the Guards' Clubs. He was a good shot, a very fine horseman, winning the Grenadier Cup at Hawthorne Hill in April, 1914, and an all-round sportsman. He was not married, and his father—Colonel MacDougall, of Lunga—now remains the last male representative of the MacDougalls of Raray and Lunga, a family of great antiquity, settled in Argyllshire since the twelfth century.

LIEUTENANT RONALD McDOUGALL, 1st BATTALION THE BUFFS (EAST KENT REGT.),

was killed in action on the 20th October, 1914. He was born on the 7th December, 1889, and joined the Army in February, 1912, his commission however, being antedated to March, 1911, because of his being a University candidate. He got his step in August, 1912.

CAPTAIN JOHN ALOYSIUS McENERY, ROYAL ENGINEERS,

was accidentally killed on the 26th October, 1914.

He was born on the 23rd December, 1877, and entered the Royal Engineers in December, 1896, becoming Lieutenant in December, 1899. He took part in the Tibet Expedition of 1903–04, in which he was Assistant Field Engineer, being mentioned in Despatches (" London Gazette," 13th December, 1904), and receiving the medal. He was promoted Captain in December, 1905.

CAPTAIN JAMES STEWART McEUEN, 20th DECCAN HORSE,

born in Hong Kong, China, on the 13th September, 1876, was the son of the late Captain J. P. McEuen, R.N., sometime Captain Superintendent of the Municipal Police, Shanghai. He was related to the late General W. Dickinson, R.E., and the late Colonel J. Clubley, Madras Infantry.

Captain McEuen was educated at Felsted School, Essex, and the R.M.C., Sandhurst. He played football for the latter v. Woolwich; and also in other important football, cricket, and polo tournaments; he was always keen on sports and games, and was an excellent shot. He received his first commission in February, 1897, in the Cameronians (Scottish Rifles). He served with the Nottinghamshire and Derbyshire Regiment in the Tochi and Tirah Expedition of 1897–98, receiving the medal and two clasps. Joining the Indian Army in September, 1901, he became Captain in February, 1906.

In the Great War he accompanied the Indian contingent of the Expeditionary Force, and was hit at Festubert on the 21st December, 1914, during a counter-attack at early dawn, within fifteen yards of the German trenches, while leading the remnants of his squadron, who followed him to the end. Captain McEuen was at first reported as " missing, believed killed," but has since been officially reported killed. His body was discovered at Festubert eight months later.

He married Enid Fraser, fourth daughter of the late Lieutenant-Colonel W. Moir, I.M.S., and niece of Sir Thomas Fraser, K.C., M.D., F.R.S., leaving two children : Heather Margaret, born 1907 ; and David Alastair Stewart, born 1910.

He was a member of the Bangalore and Secunderabad Clubs, and of Hurlingham.

LIEUTENANT NOEL GEORGE SCOTT McGRATH, 2nd DRAGOON GUARDS (QUEEN'S BAYS),

eldest son of the Hon. George McGrath, Custos Rotulorum, of St. Catherine, Jamaica, was born at Charlemont, Jamaica, on the 12th December, 1885. Educated at Beaumont College, he first obtained a commission in the Royal

lnniskilling Fusiliers in 1907, becoming Lieutenant in February, 1912, and in the following year being transferred to the Queen's Bays.

He accompanied his regiment to France for the Great War, and was wounded at Messines on the 31st October, dying from the effects in hospital at Boulogne on the 5th November, 1914. Lieutenant McGrath was a member of the Junior Naval and Military Club. His chief recreations were polo and hunting.

2nd LIEUTENANT JAMES NEIL GRANT McGRIGOR, 1st BATTN, GORDON HIGHLANDERS.

who died on the 7th November, 1914, at 59, Cadogan Square, London, of wounds received in action on the 24th October, was the younger son of Captain Sir James and Lady McGrigor.

He was born in London on the 16th November, 1894, and was educated at Evelyn's, Hillingdon ; at Eton ; and the R.M.C., Sandhurst, being gazetted to the Gordon Highlanders in August, 1914.

He was shot through the lung and shoulder near Fauquissart, Northern France, while repelling a German attack.

Mr. McGrigor was a member of the Junior

United Service Club. At Eton he was ninth man of the Eton Eight in 1913, and winner of the Junior Sculling race in 1912.

2nd LIEUTENANT BRIAN McGUIRE, 2nd BATTN. ROYAL DUBLIN FUSILIERS,

born at Clifton, York, on the 24th April, 1904, was the younger son of the late George McGuire, Town Clerk of York and Bradford, and Florence, his wife. His brother— George Patrick—was a 2nd Lieutenant in the 4th Battalion Duke of Wellington's (West Riding Regiment). After his education at St. Peter's School, York, and Sedbergh School, Yorkshire, and one year with John Sanger, Esq., The Little Hermitage, Rochester, he spent a year at the R.M.C., Sandhurst, and obtained his commission in the Royal Dublin Fusiliers in February, 1914, joining his battalion in the following month.

2nd Lieutenant McGuire was instantaneously killed in action by a fragment of shell on the 14th September, 1914, near Boucy le Long, France. A brother officer who was with him at the time said that after the Battle of Le Cateau, when large numbers of the battalion were lost, he and 2nd Lieutenant McGuire were the only two who were able to keep their platoons together during the retirement and marched to within fifteen miles of Paris. He then spoke of his comrade's glorious bravery, and what a favourite he was with officers and men. His C.O. and Captain also wrote in similar terms to 2nd Lieutenant McGuire's mother.

Mr. McGuire played for the Blackheath Second Football XV and for Sedbergh School Second XV. At the latter he organised the School O.T.C. band.

CAPTAIN JAMES FERGUS MACKAIN, 34th SIKH PIONEERS,

was born on the 28th October, 1885, the elder son of the Rev. W. James Mackain, of Ardnamurchan, Vicar of Poslingford, Suffolk, and formerly Rector of Parham, Sussex. He had many distinguished relatives of former generations in the Royal Navy,

being the eldest grandson of the late William Fergus Mackain, of the Admiralty, who was at one time Deputy Store Officer of His Majesty's Victualling Yard, Deptford; and a great-grandson of James Mackain, R.N., formerly Naval Storekeeper of His Majesty's Dockyards of Pembroke, Sheerness, and Woolwich, who, as a midshipman, was present at the Battle of Copenhagen in 1801, and—a fact of interest at this time—was at the forcing of the Dardanelles in 1807, under Admiral Sir J. J. Duckworth. A great-great-grandfather was Commander William Dobbin, R.N., who commanded His Majesty's Cutter " Diligence " at Milford Haven at the time of the French invasion of 1797, and was subsequently presented with a sword of honour by the Commissioners of His Majesty's Customs.

Captain Mackain was educated at Warden House School, Upper Deal, at Clifton College, and the R.M.C., Sandhurst, into which he passed thirtieth out of one hundred and sixty-seven successful candidates. He was posted to the Indian Army in 1904, being attached for a year to the Gordon Highlanders, and joining the 34th Sikh Pioneers in 1905. During the great earthquake in the Punjab in that year he commanded a relief column from Lahore to Kulu, and did excellent work there and in the Kangra Valley. He served in the Mohmand Expedition of 1908, receiving the medal and clasp. In 1910 he was seconded from his regiment, and served for three years as Second in Command of the 31st Signal Company of the Queen's Own Sappers and Miners. He became a Captain in 1913.

On the outbreak of the war with Germany he was on leave and joined his regiment in Egypt, proceeding with it to Northern France. He fell in action at Festubert, France, on the 24th November, 1914, while gallantly defending his trench against a determined and powerful assault by the enemy, who had sapped to within five yards and were throwing bombs and hand grenades. When Captain Mackain saw that some of them had finally succeeded in entering the extreme portion of the trench he heroically led some of his men in a charge against them, although previously wounded in the face from a splinter of a bomb. While shooting down their grenadiers with his revolver from a traverse of the trench he was himself finally shot in the forehead at close range, and died almost immediately. His name appeared in Sir John French's Despatch of the 14th January " for gallant and distinguished service in the field." The Rev. W. J. Mackain received numerous sympathetic letters on his son's death from all quarters; among others from a former Head Master of Clifton College, the Archbishop of York, and the C.O. of his son's regiment.

A brother officer wrote : " He died, as he lived,

a gallant and fearless Christian gentleman. He was shot through the head in a very gallant attempt to stem an attack in great force through breaches blown in our trenches. Your son went gallantly forward through a shower of hand grenades, and either shot or attempted to shoot the grenadiers. He was such a fine stamp of Christian soldier, and we looked on him as one likely to go a very long way."

The Macdonald Society, at their annual meeting in Glasgow on the 29th March, 1915, passed a resolution that the deep loss sustained by Captain Mackain's death be recorded in the Society's minutes. The Church of England Men's Society and the Cavendish Association passed similar resolutions of sympathy.

Captain Mackain, who was known throughout Northern India as a keen Churchman and one of the mainstays of the Church of England Men's Society, was a member of the Cavendish Club, Piccadilly, and of the Scottish Pipers' Society. His recreations were tennis, hockey, and shooting. He was unmarried.

In the Grosvenor Chapel, where Captain Mackain used to worship when residing in London, a handsome memorial has been erected to his memory by his parents.

CAPTAIN HENRY MARSHALL McKAY, ROYAL ENGINEERS,

son of Colonel H. K. McKay, C.B., C.I.E., I.M.S. (retired), was born on the 6th December, 1888, at Seoni Chapparah, Central Provinces, India.

He was educated at Shirley House, Old Charlton, Kent, and Cheltenham College, where he was in the College Cricket XI and won the Silver Dragon for bowling. He was also a keen motorist and good all-round sportsman.

After the usual period at the R.M.A., Woolwich, he entered the Royal Engineers in July, 1908, and was appointed to the Survey of India in December of that year. He was promoted Lieutenant in August, 1910, and Captain in November, 1914.

While serving at the front he took an order from one trench to another, and was killed while returning on the 13th November, 1914. He was buried at Sailly-sur-Lys.

LIEUTENANT CORTLANDT GRAHAM GORDON MACKENZIE, 2nd BATTN. ROYAL SCOTS FUSILIERS,

who was killed at Gheluvelt on the 29th October, 1914, having been thrice wounded a week or ten days previously, was the son of

H. Gordon Mackenzie, Barrister, Toronto, and Inner Temple, London, and Beatrix Kathleen, daughter of the late Alexander Donovan, of Framfield Place, Sussex.

Lieutenant Mackenzie was born in Toronto, Canada, on the 3rd November, 1889, and was educated for seven years at the Upper Canada College, Toronto, and subsequently at the Royal Military College, Kingston, Canada. From the latter he received his commission in the Royal Scots Fusiliers in June, 1911, and was stationed at various places in Ireland and England, and in Gibraltar, before he proceeded on active service in the Great War.

LIEUT. COLIN LANDSEER MACKENZIE, 2nd BATTN. HIGHLAND LIGHT INFANTRY,

was born at Malvern on the 4th May, 1892, the son of Landseer and Laura Louise (née Dobell) Mackenzie. He was a grand-nephew of Sir Edwin Landseer, the great animal painter, and a cousin of Colonel Harry Melville,

I.M.S., and of Major-General Douglas Scott, R.E.

Lieutenant Mackenzie was educated at the Naval School, Stubbington, and at Cheltenham College, joining the O.T.C. at so early an age as to be unable to carry his rifle on a march. He gained the school prize for German and his "Leaving Certificate," which entitled him to enter the Army, and he joined the 3rd (Reserve) Battalion Seaforth Highlanders on probation. After passing the Army Competitive examination he was gazetted to the Highland Light Infantry as 2nd Lieutenant in May, 1913. The young officer had a family right to his position in the Clan Connaich regiments, in both of which he served, uniformed in his own clan tartan, in the Seaforths, wearing on his bonnet the "Cabar-Feidh," this being also the cognisance of "Redcastle," of which house he was a cadet.

Lieutenant Mackenzie was a member of the

Public Schools' Club, and enjoyed polo, golf, tennis, yachting, cross-country running, and gardening.

In the Great War he was killed on the 20th September, 1914, shot in the head by a German sniper in an advanced trench near Verneuil, north of the River Aisne. The following account of his death is from the pen of Captain Guy Chichester, of Lieutenant Mackenzie's Company (since fallen) :—

" He was in the trenches at the time, defending a position, and was watching a charge of our men on his left front, and had turned round to tell his men to cease fire, in case they hit any of their own side, when he was shot in the head, death being instantaneous. He commanded a platoon in my company. He was a gallant fellow and a good officer. His death is much deplored."

He, his friend and fellow-officer—Lieutenant J. A. H. Fergusson—and Lieutenant O'Connel, R.A.M.C., were buried that night in the same grave on the ridge above the village.

CAPTAIN KEITH BETHUNE MACKENZIE, 2nd BATTN. SEAFORTH HIGHLANDERS (ROSS-SHIRE BUFFS, THE DUKE OF ALBANY'S),

who was instantaneously killed by shell near Ypres on the 12th November, 1914, was the elder son of James Mackenzie, of Daresbury, Malvern, Worcestershire, and Jane, only daughter of the Rev. Neil Bethune, of Thamesford, Ontario.

He was born on the 1st December, 1879, and was educated at Malvern (1892–96). He joined the Seaforth Highlanders from the Militia in January, 1901, becoming Lieutenant in April, 1904.

He took part in the South African War, being present at operations in the Transvaal, Orange River Colony, and Cape Colony, and received the Queen's medal with five clasps. The Order of La Maison Ernestine was conferred upon him by H.R.H. the Duke of Albany, Duke of Saxe-Coburg and Gotha, in May, 1907.

Captain Mackenzie, who reached his rank in June, 1911, married Louise, daughter of J. L. Scott, of Craigholme, Merchiston, Edinburgh. He was a member of the Junior United Service Club. His recreations were golf and football, and he belonged to the Worcestershire Golf Club and to the Nairn Golf Club.

At the time of his death he was attached to the 1st Battn. Gordon Highlanders.

CAPTAIN ANDREW DE VERE MACLEAN, EAST SURREY REGIMENT, SPECIAL RESERVE,

who was killed in action on the 19th September, 1914, was the only surviving son of Kaid Sir Harry Maclean, and was born on the 17th October, 1882.

After serving with the embodied Militia for nearly a year he joined the East Surrey Regiment in April, 1902. He took part in the South African War, being present at operations in the Transvaal, Orange River Colony, and Cape Colony, receiving the Queen's medal with five clasps. He was promoted Lieutenant in April, 1904, and Captain in April, 1910.

He retired from the active list in April, 1913, joining the Special Reserve, from which he was called up for active service in the Great War. Captain Maclean married Dulce, daughter of the late Major-General Maclachlan, R.H.A.

MAJOR ALEXANDER HARVIE MACLEAN, 2nd BATTN. PRINCESS LOUISE'S (ARGYLL AND SUTHERLAND HIGHLANDERS),

is mentioned as " believed dead " in the monthly casualty list issued on the 9th October, 1914, among the casualties which " are believed to have occurred," and is said to have been killed in the retirement from Mons on the 26th August, 1914.

He was born on the 16th October, 1868. His father, who was in business in Glasgow, died some years ago, but his mother survives him. He was educated at Kelvinside Academy, Glasgow, and joined the Argyll and Sutherland Highlanders from the Militia in January, 1891, becoming Lieutenant in December, 1895.

He was on active service on the north-western frontier of India in 1897–98, being Brigade Provost Marshal with the Tochi Field Force, and received the medal with clasp. He also took part in the South African War, being present at operations in Natal, the defence of Ladysmith, in the Orange Free State, the Transvaal, Orange River Colony and Cape Colony, and at the actions at Lombard's Kop and Zilikat's Nek. From July, 1901, he was Commandant at Van der Merwe. For his services he was mentioned in Despatches (" London Gazette," 10th September, 1901), received the Queen's medal with four clasps and the King's medal with two clasps.

Major Maclean, who was unmarried, was

promoted Captain in December, 1899, and received his Majority in May, 1912. He was a member of the Naval and Military Club, and his recreations were hunting and wild-game shooting.

LIEUTENANT ARTHUR KIRK-PATRICK MacLEAN, 2nd BATTN. PRINCESS LOUISE'S (ARGYLL AND SUTHERLAND HIGHLANDERS),

who was killed in action at Le Cateau on the 26th August, 1914, was the youngest son of the Rev. G. G. MacLean, of Jervis Lodge, Swanmore, Hants, and was born on the 25th January, 1887.

He was educated at Radley and the R.M.C., Sandhurst, and was gazetted to the Argyll and Sutherland Highlanders in May, 1907, being promoted Lieutenant in April, 1909.

Though no details of his death were obtained, his identity disc has been received through the American Embassy and our Foreign Office, and the German Government has officially reported him as " dead, burial-place unknown." Captain MacLean, of Aidgour, in a letter from Torgau, said he feared there was no doubt that Lieutenant MacLean was killed at Le Cateau, as he heard from his men later in the day that he was hit more than once leading his men to the trenches under heavy shell fire.

He married, in 1912, Enid E. Mackintosh, and leaves one daughter.

LIEUTENANT-COLONEL (Temporary), PERCY MACLEAR, p.s.c., ROYAL DUBLIN FUSILIERS,

was killed in action on the 30th August, 1914, at Garua, in the Cameroons. The third son of the late Major H. W. Maclear, the Buffs, and Mrs. Maclear, he was born on the 22nd October, 1875, and was educated at Bedford and the R.M.C., Sandhurst. He joined the Royal Dublin Fusiliers in September, 1895, becoming Lieutenant in March, 1897. From December, 1898, to December, 1902, he was Adjutant of his battalion, and was promoted Captain in February, 1900. While Adjutant he served with the 1st Battalion in the South African War, being present at the relief of Ladysmith and at operations in the Transvaal, in Natal, and in the Orange River Colony in 1900, and again at operations in the Transvaal in 1901 and 1902. For his services he was three times mentioned in Despatches (" London Gazette," 8th

February and 10th September, 1901, and 29th July, 1902), was promoted Brevet-Major in September, 1901, and received the Queen's medal with five clasps and the King's medal with two clasps.

He was employed with the West African Frontier Force from April, 1903, to March, 1908, during which time he took part in operations (1905–06) in the Kwale-Ishan district, South Nigeria, West Africa, being in command of his regiment. He was mentioned in Despatches (" London Gazette," 18th September, 1906).

He was at the Staff College, 1911 and 1912. In 1908 he was awarded the Royal Humane Society's medal for saving life in the River Nile at Khartoum.

In April, 1914, he was again detached for employment with the West African Frontier Force, with the temporary rank of Lieutenant-Colonel, and was serving with the Colonial Forces when he was killed at Garua. His brother—Captain Basil Maclear, Royal Dublin Fusiliers—was killed in action near Ypres in May, 1915.

He was fond of football, and played Rugby for the London Irish and for Sandhurst.

CAPTAIN ARCHIBALD ALASTAIR McLEOD, 1st BATTN. GLOUCESTER-SHIRE REGT.,

born at Singapore on the 3rd June, 1877, was the younger son of the late Lieutenant-General W. K. McLeod, Colonel of the Highland Light Infantry, and a grandson of the late Colonel Alexander McLeod, C.B., 61st Regiment, and a nephew of the late Lieutenant-General Sir John McLeod, G.C.B., Colonel of the Black Watch. Captain McLeod was the third generation of his family in the Gloucestershire Regiment, his grandfather and great-grandfather having served in it as far back as the Peninsular War, the former having commanded it at the Battle of Goojerat and Chillianwallah in 1849, in which year he died.

Captain McLeod received his education at Wimbledon School and the Oxford Military College, and after passing through the R.M.C., Sandhurst, was gazetted to the Gloucestershire Regiment in 1897, becoming Lieutenant in February, 1900. With his battalion he served all through the South African War, having been present at the relief of Kimberley ; actions at Paardeberg, Poplar Grove, Driefontein, Houtnek (Thoba Mountain), Vet River, Zand River ; and at actions near Johannesburg,

Pretoria, Diamond Hill, Wittebergen, Botha-ville, and Caledon River. For his services he was mentioned in Despatches, and received the Queen's medal with six clasps and the King's medal with two clasps. He had the "Special Certificate for Signalling" granted to him at Pretoria in January, 1904. He obtained his company in October, 1905.

At the commencement of the Great War Captain McLeod went to the Continent with the Ist Division in August, 1914, was all through the Battles of the Rivers (Aisne and Marne), and was killed on the 2nd November, 1914, in Belgium while gallantly leading his company to attack a farm held by the Germans.

Captain McLeod was extremely popular in his regiment, and was a brilliant officer, "distinguished" in musketry. His company were winners of the Douglas Shield (a regimental trophy) in 1912.

He was a member of the Caledonian Club, and his recreations were hunting, polo, and shooting. In June, 1914, he married, at the Chapel Royal, Savoy, Marie Jeannette Amelia, young-est daughter of Lord Henry Fitzwarrine Chichester, grand-daughter of the fourth Marquess of Donegall, niece of the fifth Marquess, and cousin to the present peer, who holds besides the title of Donegall those of Earl of Belfast, Viscount Chichester, Baron Chichester of Belfast, and Baron Fisherwick, and is Here-ditary High Admiral of Lough Neagh and Governor of Carrickfergus Castle. Mrs. A. A. McLeod's father is heir-presumptive to the marquisate.

LIEUTENANT-COLONEL NORMAN REGINALD McMAHON, D.S.O., p.s.c., COMMANDING 4th BATTN. ROYAL FUSILIERS (CITY OF LONDON REGT.),

who was killed in action at the first Battle of Ypres on the 11th November, 1914, was the young-est son of the late General Sir Thomas W. McMahon, Bart., C.B.

He was born in London on the 24th January, 1866, educated at Eton, and joined the Royal Fusiliers as Lieutenant in May, 1885. From February, 1890, to February, 1894, he was Adjutant of his battalion, and became Captain in November, 1896, Major in November, 1901, Lieutenant-Colonel in May, 1911; and before his death had been appointed to the command of

a brigade, with the temporary rank of Brigadier-General, which command he was to have taken up on the day following that on which he was killed.

He accompanied the Burmese Expedition of 1886–87, for which he received the medal with clasp, and took part in the South African War, during which he was on the Staff as A.D.C. to a Major-General commanding an infantry brigade from October, 1899, to April, 1900; as Brigade-Major from April to August, 1900; and as D.A.A.G. from February to June, 1902. He was present at the relief of Ladysmith, including the action at Colenso; at operations on the Tugela Heights, in Natal, Cape Colony (severely wounded), Transvaal, and Orange River Colony; and at the actions at Pieter's Hill. He was mentioned in Despatches ("London Gazette," 8th February, 1901); was awarded the D.S.O.; and received the Queen's medal with five clasps and the King's medal with two clasps. He passed the final examination at the Staff College in December, 1910. From June, 1905, to June, 1909, he was Chief In-structor and Staff Officer at the School of Musketry, and from June, 1909, to January, 1910, was specially employed at the headquarters of the Army.

For his services in the Great War he was mentioned in Sir John French's Despatches of the 8th October, 1914, and the 14th January, 1915.

CAPTAIN ANGUS MACNAB, M.B., F.R.C.S., R.A.M.C. (T.F.), attd. to the 14th (COUNTY OF LONDON) BATTN. THE LONDON REGIMENT (LONDON SCOTTISH),

was killed in action on the 31st October, 1914, in the first engagement of the London Scottish.

He was born in Sep-tember, 1875, at Southland, New Zealand, the son of Alexander Macnab, of Argyllshire, N.B. Captain Macnab was educated at Dunedin and Edinburgh University, where he graduated. He served in the South African War, and joined the R.A.M.C. (T.F.) in March, 1911, being attached to the London Scottish from that date.

He was fond of rifle shooting and golf, and was a member of the Royal and Ancient, and of Sandy Lodge, Herts.

Captain Macnab married Miss Evelyn Calder, who survives him.

2nd LIEUTENANT WILLIAM MAC-KINNON MACNEILL, 16th (THE QUEEN'S) LANCERS, SPECIAL RESERVE,

who was killed in action on the 12th October, 1914, was the second son of the late Mr. and Mrs. Duncan Macneill, of Park House, Kingswood Road, Tunbridge Wells.

He was gazetted to the Special Reserve of his regiment in December, 1909.

LIEUTENANT DUNCAN STUART ROSS MACPHERSON, 7th GURKHA RIFLES,

was born on the 23rd August, 1899, and was the only child of Surgeon-General W. G. Macpherson, C.B., C.M.G., K.H.P.

He was educated at Westminster, Fettes College, and the R.M.C., Sandhurst. After leaving the last he was gazetted 2nd Lieutenant on the unattached list, Indian Army, on the 20th January, 1909, and was attached to the 2nd Battalion the Black Watch until March, 1910. He was then posted to the 1st Battalion 7th Gurkha Rifles, with whom he served in Quetta and Robat, on the Persian frontier, until May, 1913, passing the examination for promotion to Captain with distinction.

He became Lieutenant in April, 1911, and was at home on leave when the war broke out. He was then gazetted to the 8th (Service) Battalion the Black Watch, and appointed Assistant Adjutant. Early in November, 1914, he was attached to the 8th Gurkha Rifles in France, and was killed in action at Festubert on the 23rd November, 1914, when commanding the advanced company in a successful counter-attack for the recovery of trenches which had been lost.

Lieutenant Macpherson was a keen polo player and golfer. He was a member of the Junior United Service Club.

MAJOR NEIL MACPHERSON, SECOND IN COMMAND OF THE 2nd KING EDWARD'S OWN GURKHAS (THE SIRMOOR RIFLES), who was killed in action at Neuve Chapelle on the 31st October, 1914, was born at Inverness on the 8th August, 1869,

the youngest son of the late Sir Herbert Macpherson, V.C., K.C.B., K.C.S.I.

He was educated at Inverness College, and, joining the East Kent Regiment as 2nd Lieutenant in June, 1890, had a remarkable military career, having been through five campaigns before the Great War.

He was transferred to the 2nd Gurkha Rifles
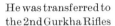
(Indian Army) as Lieutenant in September, 1891, joining his regiment in Manipur, and in the following year saw his first active service at Isazai, on the north-western frontier. In 1897–98 he again took part in operations on the frontier, at Samana, the relief of Gulistan, for which he received the medal and two clasps, and the Tirah Campaign of 1897–98, including actions of Chagru Kotal, Dargai, and of the Sampagha and Arangha Passes ; operations in the Warran Valley at and around Dwatoi against the Khani Khel Chamkannis, and in the Bara Valley, including various actions, for which a clasp was added to his medal.

His next service was in the South African War, 1900–02, when he was present at operations in the Transvaal and Orange River Colony, receiving the Queen's medal with four clasps. In December, 1901, he was on special Staff duty, and from December, 1902, till June, 1904, was Station Staff Officer at Agra.

In 1911–12 he was again on active service in the Abor Country, receiving the medal with clasp. Major Macpherson, who was a member of the Junior Naval and Military Club, married Mary M. J., daughter of Colonel Robert Home, C.B., R.E., and had four children, only two of whom —Barbara Isobel, born 1904 ; and Nancy Clare, born 1910—survive him. Major Macpherson's maternal grandfather was Lieutenant-General Eckford, C.B.

2nd LIEUTENANT IVOR A. MacRAE, 3rd (attd. 2nd) BATTN. THE KING'S OWN SCOTTISH BORDERERS,

who died in France on the 14th October, 1914, aged nineteen and a half years, of wounds received the previous day, was the only son of Mr. D. M. MacRae, of Stenhouse, Dumfriesshire.

He was educated at Harrow (The

Grove, 1909–13) and was gazetted to the King's Own Scottish Borderers on probation in January, 1914.

LIEUTENANT JAMES JULIAN GORDON MacWILLIAM, 1st BATTN. GORDON HIGHLANDERS,

who was kil'ed on the 14th December, 1914, was the son of James MacWilliam, Solicitor Supreme Courts of Scotland, of 22, Forbes Road, Edinburgh, and was born on the 16th August, 1895.

He was educated at Edinburgh Academy, where he entered the O.T.C., and was one of the first to win Certificate "A." He became Lance-Sergeant, and was a member of the Shooting VIII, making the good score of 62 at Bisley, where he shot for the Ashburton Shield. After leaving school he went to the R.M.C., Sandhurst, which he left at the end of the summer term, 1914, and was appointed Galloper to Major Oakeley, the Commanding Officer of the O.T.C. Camp at Barry. He was gazetted to the Gordon Highlanders on the 15th August, 1914, and attached to the 3rd Battalion in December, 1914. He was temporarily promoted Lieutenant in November, 1914, and confirmed in his rank in December.

He joined his regiment at the front in September, 1914, and on the 12th October was wounded in the hand by shrapnel at La Bassée. After recovering in Le Grand Séminaire Hospital, Rouen, he rejoined his battalion in the latter part of November.

The following account of his death, gathered from letters and documents, was published in the "Edinburgh Academy Chronicle" of January, 1915 :—

" On Monday, the 14th December, three companies of the Gordon Highlanders were ordered to attack a portion of the German trenches over very open ground. The German position had been previously subjected to a heavy bombardment by our artillery, and it was hoped that it had been made untenable. So far, however, from this being the case, the advancing Gordons were met by a terrific machine-gun and rifle fire, through which, in spite of severe losses, they pushed forward to well within fifty yards of the enemy's lines. It was when MacWilliam was rising to lead his men for a final rush from this forward position that he was shot through the head and instantly killed. His men hung on all day until dusk, and then had to be withdrawn. Though the attack failed of its purpose, it is described as having been as

fine an exhibition of self-sacrifice and determination as any in the annals of the regiment, and the high admiration and appreciation of the gallant effort entertained by the Brigade, Divisional, and Corps Commanders (the two latter being General Haldane and Sir Horace Smith-Dorrien) were duly conveyed to the battalion in an order of the day. In the words of his Commanding Officer, MacWilliam by his death in that action ' covered himself with glory.' ' I cannot sufficiently express,' he writes to MacWilliam's father, ' the deep sorrow which I and all of us feel at the loss of a brother officer who, though but so recently joined, had already on more than one occasion shown his sterling value. I have felt it my duty to bring to official notice the gallant manner in which your son was leading his men when he met his death.' "

Some of the rank and file, writing to his father, said : " On the morning of the 14th December the Gordon Highlanders made a glorious charge, two platoons of ' C ' Company leading, the other two to support. Your son was in charge of Nos. 9 and 11 Platoons, which led, and when the order came to advance he was the first out of the trenches. Smiling and waving his stick, he encouraged his men on. When he had got to within fifty yards of the German trenches we had to lie down for a minute to get our breath before making the final assault. It was when he raised his head to give the order to advance that he was killed."

He was a good swimmer, long-distance runner, and horseman. He distinguished himself as a rifle and revolver shot, and was a keen motorcyclist. Just before his death the Commanding Officer detailed him to take a course of instruction in machine gunnery that he might qualify as Machine Gun Officer to the battalion.

MAJOR FRANCIS JULIAN AUDLEY MACKWORTH, p.s.c., ROYAL FIELD ARTILLERY,

who was killed in action on the 1st November, 1914, was the second surviving son of the late Colonel Sir Arthur Mackworth, Bart, C.B., and of Lady Mackworth, " The Priory," Caerleon.

He was born on the 15th September, 1876, and was educated at Malvern, No. 4 (1891–95) Shell, Army side, where he was a House Scholar, a School Prefect, and won the Chance Prize. He was afterwards a scholar of Selwyn College, Cambridge, where he took his degree of B.A. (Jun. Opt.) in 1898.

He was a boy of considerable ability, and took a high place in the examination for the R.M.A., Woolwich, but was rejected on the ground of insufficient height. However, he grew into a tall man at Cambridge, and passed into the Army as a University candidate, being gazetted to the R.A. in June, 1898 (" The Malvernian," December, 1914). He became Lieutenant in February, 1901, and Captain in April, 1906. From April, 1904, to June, 1908, he was employed with the West African Frontier Force, and from February, 1912, to September, 1913, was an Adjutant of his regiment. In October, 1913, he was appointed Brigade-Major R.A., IIIrd Division, Southern Command, and was serving on the Staff when he was killed, his promotion to Major, to date from the 30th October, 1914, being subsequently gazetted.

For his services in the Great War he was mentioned in Sir John French's Despatch of the 8th October, 1914, and was promoted Major on the 30th October. Two days later he was killed by a splinter from a shell.

Major Mackworth married, in 1910, Dorothy Conran, only daughter of the late Mr. Arthur Hastings Lascelles, and left one daughter, born in August, 1911.

Major Mackworth's elder brother—Captain Digby Mackworth—was killed in action at Ladysmith, Natal, in January, 1900.

CAPT. HENRY TELFORD MAFFETT, 2nd BATTN. THE PRINCE OF WALES'S LEINSTER REGIMENT (ROYAL CANADIANS),

son of the late William Hamilton Maffett, barrister-at-law, of St. Helena, Finglas, County Dublin, was born at that address on the 24th March, 1872, and was educated at Royal School, Armagh, Ireland.

Captain Maffett joined the Leinster Regiment from the Militia in June, 1894, becoming Lieutenant in July, 1895, and Captain in August, 1900. From 1898–99 he was Garrison Adjutant at St. Lucia, West Indies, and for nearly two years from November, 1900, served with the West African Frontier Force in Northern Nigeria, during part of which time he acted as Adjutant of the 1st Northern Nigeria Regiment and Brigade-Major of the West African Frontier Force. He was present at the operations against the Emirs at Bida and Kontagora, 1901, for which he received the African medal with clasp. In 1908 he acted as Provost Marshal attached to the Staff of the 2nd Brigade Mohmand Field

Force, north-western frontier of India, receiving afterwards the medal with clasp.

Captain Maffett was killed in action in the Great War, after being thrice wounded, on the 20th October, 1914, at Armentières, France, while in temporary command of the battalion. He was a very keen sportsman and rode to hounds. He was unmarried.

2nd LIEUTENANT RICHARD HENRY COLE MAGENIS, 3rd BATTN. ROYAL IRISH RIFLES,

son of Edward Cole Magenis, of Drumdoe, Boyle, County Roscommon, and nephew of the late General Magenis, of Finvoy Lodge, Ballymoney, was born at Drumdoe on the 20th April, 1887. He was educated at Radley College, and was appointed 2nd Lieutenant in his battalion in February, 1908.

2nd Lieutenant Magenis was shot in advancing on the enemy's trenches at the Battle of the Aisne. His name was included in the monthly casualty list published in October, 1914, as having been killed in action, but no date was mentioned.

Mr. Magenis was a cricket and football player, while hunting, shooting, tennis, and fishing were also amongst his recreations.

CAPT. ARTHUR CURGENVEN MAGOR (CAPTAIN RET. PAY) 3rd BATTN. THE DUKE OF EDINBURGH'S (WILTSHIRE REGIMENT),

who was killed in action during a night attack near Ypres on the 17th October, 1914, while attached to the 2nd Battalion of his regiment, was the youngest son of the late Edward Auriol Magor, of Lamellen, St. Tudy, Cornwall, J.P., and of Mrs. Magor, Middlecot, Weybridge, Surrey.

He was born on the 3rd March, 1879, and was educated at Blundell's School, Tiverton, and Exeter College, Oxford.

He joined the 2nd Battalion Wiltshire Regiment in February, 1900, becoming Lieutenant in August of the same year. He served in the South African War, being present at operations in the Orange River Colony, including actions at Bethlehem and Wittebergen, and at operations in the Transvaal, receiving the Queen's medal with two clasps. He was promoted Captain in September, 1908, retiring from the active list in September, 1912, when he entered the 3rd Battalion of his regiment.

Captain Magor, who was fond of hunting and shooting, married, in October, 1912, Dora, eldest daughter of the late Albert Bulteel Fisher, and Mrs. Fisher, of Court Hill, near Devizes, Wilts, and left one son, Arthur Frank Tregarthen, born in July, 1914.

CAPTAIN FREDERIC HENRY MAHONY, 1st BATTN. CHESHIRE REGIMENT,

was born at Aden in 1874, the son of Captain F. H. Mahony, late York and Lancaster Regiment, and the late Mrs. Cahill Mahony, both of County Cork, Ireland.

He was educated at Dover College, and having failed in the entrance examination for the R.M.C., Sandhurst, was so determined on a military career that he enlisted, in spite of good offers of employment in civil life. He obtained his commission from the ranks in the Cheshire Regiment in 1898, and was promoted to a Captaincy in that regiment in 1906. He obtained a special certificate for Mounted Infantry, and had passed his examination for the rank of Major. He was employed with the West African Frontier Force from November, 1900, to July, 1904, and was an Adjutant of Volunteers, Durham Light Infantry, from 1906–08. For his West African services he received the medal with two clasps for the Aro Expedition. He had served in the South African War from February to May, 1900, receiving the Queen's medal with five clasps.

When the Great War broke out he was serving with the depot of his regiment at Chester, and, as was to be expected in so keen a soldier, at once volunteered for the front. While in temporary command of his battalion near La Bassée, he led a successful bayonet charge under heavy artillery fire, for which he was congratulated by Brigadier-General Count Gleichen.

Soon after that he was shot in the left shoulder by a German sniper from a cottage window one thousand yards away, and was rescued from the fighting line, under heavy fire, by Sergeant Shubotham, of his battalion, who earned the V.C. for his courageous act. Captain Mahony died some hours later at the hospital at Bethune on the 22nd September, 1914.

He was a good shot, played golf and tennis, and was a member of the Junior United Service Club. He married Ethel, youngest daughter of John Paterson, Esq., 42, Holland Park, London, W., and left a daughter, Cynthia, and a son, Patrick, age five and three years respectively, at the time of their father's death.

This gallant Irishman, apart from his soldierly qualities, was, like so many of his countrymen, brilliantly witty, and was extremely popular with both officers and men. When he left England for the front he kept all the young officers entertained and in the highest spirits by his quaint humour. Such a temperament is of enormous value in maintaining the morale of men in such trying times as fall to the lot of all taking part in this momentous campaign.

MAJOR JOHN SOUTHERN MAIDLOW, COMMANDING 49th BATTERY, ROYAL FIELD ARTILLERY,

was born in London on the 26th June, 1875, the son of Mr. John Mott Maidlow, Barrister-at-law, who took his double first at Oxford.

Major Maidlow was educated at St. Paul's School and Woolwich, where he did very well both in literary work and sports, especially riding. He joined the Royal Artillery as 2nd Lieutenant in June, 1895, and served in Egypt and India, where he was on the Staff of the Lieutenant-Governor of Bengal as A.D.C. from November, 1903, to October, 1906, and afterwards as Military Secretary, being a great favourite with all. Subsequently spending three years, from September, 1911, in New Zealand, in the organisation and training of the Artillery, he was conspicuous for his good work, and was very popular there. He had just returned from that colony when the war broke out, at once offered himself for what was his first experience of active service, and, being accepted, took his battery to France, and was in the first battle of the campaign at Mons.

On the first day he was there, the 23rd August, 1914, he was riding forward to take up a new position for his guns when he was shot in the head, and without recovering consciousness was carried to a hospital near Mons, where he died. The hospital was afterwards set on fire by shell, but his remains were recovered, and he was buried in the grounds of Mr. C. Gendebien, near Mons. Major Maidlow was a fine sportsman, and did much big-game shooting in India, securing some record heads of bison and sambur. He was also keen on pig-sticking, was a very good polo player and a first-rate swimmer, was a successful rider, and, being a lightweight, rode in many races.

Major Maidlow married, in November, 1897, Amy C. A., daughter of Colonel Lugard, Madras Staff Corps, and niece of Sir Edward and of Sir

Frederick Lugard, K.C.S.I. He left one son, John Lugard, age thirteen at the time of his father's death.

MAJOR the Honble. ALFRED HENRY MAITLAND, 1st BATTN. THE QUEEN'S OWN (CAMERON HIGHLANDERS),

whose name was included in the monthly casualty list published on the 9th October, 1914, as having been killed in action, no place or date being mentioned, was the third son of the Earl of Lauderdale, and was born on the 9th December, 1872.
He joined the Cameron Highlanders from the Militia in June, 1894, becoming Lieutenant in April, 1898. He took part in the Nile Expedition of 1898, being present at the Battles of Atbara and Khartoum, for which he received the British medal and the Egyptian medal with two clasps. He was promoted Captain in November, 1899, and took part in the South African War, being present at operations in the Orange Free State, the Transvaal, the Orange River Colony, and Cape Colony, including actions at Zand River, near Johannesburg, at Pretoria, Diamond Hill, Wittebergen, and Ladybrand. He received the Queen's medal with five clasps.
From November, 1901, to November, 1904, he was Adjutant of his battalion; from February, 1905, to August, 1909, Officer of a Company of Gentlemen Cadets, Royal Military College; and from October, 1909, to October, 1913, an Adjutant of the Territorial Force, and obtained his Majority in March, 1914.
Major Maitland, who was a member of the Caledonian Club, married, in January, 1905, Edith, youngest daughter of S. G. T. Scobell, of Redmarley, Gloucester, and left two daughters: Edith Charlotte, born November, 1905; and Nora Beatrice, born 1907.

CAPTAIN WILLIAM ALAN FULLER-MAITLAND, 1st BATTN. COLDSTREAM GUARDS,

was born on the 13th April, 1882, at 8, Hertford Street, Mayfair, London, and was the son of William Fuller-Maitland, of Standsted Hall, Essex, and the late Hon. Mrs. Fuller-Maitland, daughter of the third Lord Gardner.
Captain Fuller-Maitland was educated at Harrow, and the R.M.C., Sandhurst, and joined the Coldstream Guards as 2nd Lieutenant in 1901, becoming Lieutenant in 1903.
With his battalion he served in the South

African War, having been present at operations in Cape Colony from February to May, 1902, for which he received the Queen's medal with two clasps. He became Captain in June, 1911. In the Great War Captain Fuller-Maitland was killed instantaneously by a shell at the Battle of the Aisne on the 19th September, 1914.
Captain Fuller-Maitland was devoted to hunting, and was also a good shot and fisherman. He hunted regularly with the Puckeridge and Essex Hounds, and won the Puckeridge lightweight point-to-point run in 1914.

2nd LIEUT. WILLIAM E. MAITLAND, 3rd BATTN. SEAFORTH HIGHLANDERS, attd. 2nd BATTN. THE BLACK WATCH,

was born in Glasgow on the 1st August, 1889, the son of George Maitland, Esq., Duncrag, Kilmacolm, and a nephew of Sir Joseph P. Maclay, Bart.

He was educated at Glasgow High School and Glasgow University, where he took the degrees of M.B., Ch.B., in March, 1913. He was Captain of the University Rugby team, and was in the University O.T.C. as a Private, then a Corporal, being finally offered a commission, which he accepted, in 1913.
On the outbreak of the Great War he volunteered for active service, and was given a commission as 2nd Lieutenant in the 3rd Seaforth Highlanders on the 26th August, 1914. While attending to a wounded man on the 21st December, 1914, at Richebourg l'Avoué, he was himself wounded, and died at Lillers, France, on the 24th of the same month.
2nd Lieutenant Maitland was a member of the University Athletic and Rugby Football Clubs and of the Glasgow Rowing Club. A very appreciative article from a fellow-officer appeared in the "Kilmacolm Advertiser," giving the following account of the circumstances of his death :—
"We, No. 4 Company, were ordered into the trenches to assist the Seaforths. I sent my other subaltern and two platoons to the support trench, and Maitland and the other two to the reserve trench. I went with him along the reserve trench, and found it ended in a very wide communication trench. As the Germans were on that flank, and I didn't know how far forward, I told him to build up a parapet to prevent the trench being enfiladed. I then went off to attend to my other two platoons. I returned in about twenty minutes to find poor

Maitland was hit. One of his party (since dead) had been hit, and Maitland, finding himself unable to tie him up in the narrow trench, had lifted him on to the ground behind when he himself was hit. He was fully conscious, and told me he thought his wound was fatal." The officer went on to say how stoically young Maitland bore his sufferings, apologising to those attending him for the trouble he was causing, and finally ended : " Had he been one of their own regiment, with several years' service, I do not think the company could have mourned him more. As for myself, I can only tell you how sorry I am to have lost such a good comrade and promising soldier."

The " Glasgow University Magazine " also published a notice, in which it spoke of 2nd Lieutenant Maitland as one of the kindest-hearted and most genuine of men. He was known to all his College friends as " Teddy."

2nd LIEUT. CLAUDE JOSEPH O'CONOR MALLINS, 2nd BATTN. CONNAUGHT RANGERS,

was born at 23, Raglan Road, Dublin, on the 3rd October, 1894. He was the son of Captain Frederic W. Mallins, 3rd Battalion East Lancashire Regiment, and Eliza O'Conor, youngest daughter of Roderic Joseph O'Conor, Esq., J.P., of Milton, County Roscommon, and was a nephew of Lieutenant-Colonel J. R. Mallins, R.A.M.C., of Tigh-na-mara, Alverstoke, Hants.

2nd Lieutenant Mallins was educated at Stonyhurst College, Wimbledon Army College, and the R.M.C., Sandhurst, whence he was gazetted to the Connaught Rangers in August, 1914. He proceeded on active service in September, 1914, and for a short time was Acting Adjutant of his battalion, which shows the losses in officers suffered by our regiments in this war.

He was killed at Molenaarshoek, not far from Ypres, between Beceleare and Passchendaele, on the 2nd November, 1914, when it was said of him : " He was the soul of the defence of his part of the line, and had just succeeded in beating off a German attack (a remarkable commendation for so young an officer), when he fell by a sniper's bullet," being shot through the forehead. He was buried, with another officer, in a small garden in the village of Molenaarshoek, where he was killed.

His Commanding Officer wrote of him : " Your brave son was as promising a young officer as I have ever met."

MAJOR D'ARCY WENTWORTH MANDER, 2nd BATTALION DURHAM LIGHT INFANTRY,

was the son of Charles John Mander, Esq., of 9, New Square, Lincoln's Inn, and Carlton Road, Putney. He was related to Colonel A. T. Mander, R.E., and General F. D. Mander. Major Mander was born in London in October, 1870, and was educated at Charterhouse and Trinity College, Cambridge.

He was first gazetted in 1892, promoted Lieutenant 1896, Captain in 1900, and Major in 1912. He played polo for his regiment in India, and assisted in winning several cups. He also played cricket and football in the regimental team, was a keen golfer, and hunted when opportunity offered.

He was killed while serving with his battalion at the Battle of the Aisne on the 20th September, 1914. The following account of the circumstances attending his death was given by a brother officer: " I was with Major Mander just before he was killed. We went up and relieved a regiment in the trenches just after dark on Saturday, the 19th. As soon as it was daylight the enemy's snipers started bothering us. At about 10 a.m. on Sunday, the 20th, the Germans started an attack, chiefly against the West Yorks, on our right. We could not do anything to help, as the enemy were hidden from us by the ground, and we were expecting all the time to be attacked ourselves. At lunch time I walked along the trenches and joined Major Mander and another officer. Whilst we were eating a party of perhaps one hundred Germans walked in towards the West Yorks trenches, holding their hands above their heads, but still in possession of their rifles. We stood up to watch them, and saw that when they got in among the West Yorks they appeared to bayonet some of them. This was all happening about four hundred yards to our right. We all three jumped up and shouted to the company to stand to, and went to our places in the trenches. The Germans almost immediately faced down our line and opened fire. I was looking along the trenches, and saw Major Mander standing about fifty yards in front of me, also in the trenches. We were all shouting to some men from our trenches (not D.L.I.), who were running back, telling them to stop. This they did, and opened fire on the Germans. Just at that moment I was hit, and did not see any more. It was a very low trick the Germans played on us."

Major Mander was a member of the Sports Club.

55555

He married Esmé Mary, daughter of the late Samuel Sealey-Allin, Esq., of The College, Youghal, Co. Cork, Ireland, and left two children: a son, age five, and a daughter, age three years.

2nd LIEUTENANT JOHN DUNDAS MANLEY, 26th FIELD COMPANY ROYAL ENGINEERS,

born on the 24th January, 1892, at New Street, West Bromwich, Staffordshire, was the elder son of the late J. H. H. Manley, M.D., Barrister-at-law, and of Alice Manley (née Dundas). He was a grandson of Captain R. T. Dundas, R.N.R., and a great-grandson of Major R. T. Dundas, who died at Vittoria, Spain, while serving with the 7th Foot, British Legion. 2nd Lieutenant Manley was a scholar of Cheltenham (1906), and later proceeded to Emmanuel College, Cambridge, where he was Prizeman, took Honours B.A. Mechanical Science Tripos, 1913, and was in the O.T.C. (R.E.). In June, 1913, he received a commission in the Special Reserve of Officers, Royal Engineers; a year later he was given an appointment in the Indian Public Works Department, and was to have sailed for Bombay in September; but the war broke out, so he rejoined the 26th Field Company, and left with it for France on the 14th August in charge of No. 4 Section.

He was in charge of his section, detached from his company, when he was killed while at work in the front line of the defences at Vendresse on the 26th September, 1914, and was buried in the graveyard of Vendresse Church.

The following is an extract from a letter of Colonel Schreiber, R.E.:—

"I feel I must write and tell you of my sympathy and of the high opinion that had been formed of your boy. He had been in charge of a section of his company detached with the front line of the 3rd Brigade, and the General and his Staff Officer both expressed to me their great sorrow at his loss, and their appreciation of the excellent work he had done for them. I had personally come specially in contact with him several times since he was detached, and was much impressed with the excellent spirit in which he was carrying on his independent duties. There must be this consolation, that his death must have been instantaneous, as he was apparently killed by the burst of the shell without actually being hit, and also there is the feeling, of which you should be proud, that he was killed actually on the field of battle while in the execution of his duty. He had borne his share of the great hardships the company had gone through, and was very much appreciated by his brother officers."

Major Pritchard wrote: "I cannot tell you how much all the officers of the 26th Company sympathise with you in your bereavement, and how we mourn the loss of your son, while to me, his Commanding Officer, it is a serious handicap to lose such a keen and valuable officer. It will also, I hope, be some consolation to you to know that the General under whose orders he was working (having been detached from me) had several times on days just prior to his death told me how much your son was helping him, and what a good fellow he was. In fact, the General appreciated his services as much as I did. Your son has died for his country in the very front line, and has done his part nobly to serve his country at a time of great crisis."

A Sapper of his section said: "We could not bring your son down from the trenches until that night when myself and two more Sappers carried him down to the hospital until the grave had been dug. We buried him that night with full military honours, our section turning out in respect for poor Lieutenant Manley, who was thought the world of by his section, and highly respected by everyone. In a country graveyard in Vendresse there is a stone, just a plain graveyard stone, marking the burial-place of an officer and a gentleman."

A tablet to Lieutenant Manley's memory was erected in St. Philip's Church, West Bromwich, the ceremony of unveiling on the 10th January, 1915, being attended by a large contingent of the 5th South Staffordshire Battalion, a Red Cross contingent, and representatives of the Boy Scouts. The service was conducted by the Rev. W. Solly, Vicar, and the tablet unveiled by Mr. J. E. Mitchell, J.P.

2nd Lieutenant Manley was a life-member of the Union Club, Cambridge, and coxed the Emmanuel boats, first and second. He was also a member of the Sports Club at Chatham.

LIEUTENANT the Honble. JOHN NEVILLE MANNERS, 2nd BATTN. GRENADIER GUARDS,

eldest son of the third Baron Manners, of Avon Tyrell, Christchurch, Hants, was born on the 6th January, 1892. He joined the Grenadier Guards in 1912, becoming Lieutenant in September, 1913, and was killed in action on the 1st September, 1914, near Villers Cotterets, France.

CAPTAIN WILMSDORFF GEORGE MANSERGH, 2nd BATTN. THE MANCHESTER REGT.

born on the 9th December, 1881, was the eldest son of the late Major W. G. Mansergh and Mrs. Mansergh, of Castletownroche, County Cork, Ireland.

He was educated at Shrewsbury and Cowley College, Oxford, and joined the Militia in February, 1899, being gazetted to the Manchester Regiment in September, 1901, in which he became Lieutenant in November, 1902. He took part in the South African War, being present, in 1900, at operations in the Transvaal, east of Pretoria, and in the Orange River Colony, including the action at Wittebergen; again in the Transvaal in 1901 and in the Orange River Colony up to 1902. He received the Queen's medal with three clasps and the King's medal with two clasps.

In October, 1903, he was seconded in his regiment for employment with the West African Frontier Force, in which he was given the local rank of Captain in April, 1911. In 1913 he was attached to the Royal Flying Corps, and passed the test examination. On the outbreak of the war with Germany he joined his old regiment as Senior Lieutenant, and was promoted Captain in December, 1914.

Captain Mansergh was officially reported as missing on the 5th September, 1914; unofficially he was reported as killed while endeavouring to save his servant at Le Cateau on the 26th August, 1914, during the retirement from Mons.

The following account of the circumstances by a wounded prisoner at Würzburg, Germany, was published in "The Times" of the 7th December, 1914 :—

"I am sorry to have to record the death of W. G. Mansergh. . . . I am able to tell you how it happened. He was advancing quite near me when he got hit in the leg and could not get further. He had chanced to fall near an empty trench, and managed to crawl into this, where he was comparatively safe. But shortly after a soldier also in the regiment crawled up to the same trench, whereupon Mansergh pulled him in and got the fellow underneath him (it was a short 'two-man trench' for kneeling). Mansergh was now exposed to shrapnel, though still protected by the trench parapet from rifle fire. You can guess what happened. A shell did burst just in front of the trench quite low down. Mansergh was killed on the spot. You may have had the news that he had been killed, but it's worth knowing how it happened. The incident took place at Le Cateau on August 26th."

CAPTAIN BRUCE EDWARD ALEXANDER MANSON, 61st KING GEORGE'S OWN PIONEERS,

who was killed in action on the 2nd November, 1914, in East Africa, was born on the 7th December, 1878.

On passing for the Indian Army he was gazetted to an unattached 2nd Lieutenancy in July, 1898, being appointed to the Indian Staff Corps in October, 1899.

In 1900 he saw service in China, for which he received the medal. In October of that year he was promoted Lieutenant in the Indian Army, and obtained his company in July, 1907.

2nd LIEUTENANT FREDERICK CHARLES JENNENS MARILLIER, 2nd BATTN. ROYAL SUSSEX REGIMENT,

who was killed in action on the 30th October, 1914, while leading his men in an attack on a wood near Ypres, was the only son of Ernest F. Marillier, Artist, Richmond, Malvern Link, and a grandson of W. Marillier, at one time Captain

of the Harrow XI, son of J. F. Marillier, for fifty years a Master in Harrow School.

He was born at Fairlight, Hastings, on the 30th August, 1888, and was educated privately. He served in the ranks of the Army, went to the front as a Sergeant, and was mentioned in Despatches for having, on the 1st October, 1914, led a night attack on a German trench, which was captured and filled in. For this service he was awarded the D.C.M. ("London Gazette," 10th November, 1914).

After being for four and a half years in the ranks he was given his commission in the Sussex Regiment in September, 1914.

2nd Lieutenant Marillier was a great favourite in his regiment, and was good at all sports, playing in the regimental cricket and football elevens.

COLONEL RAYMOND JOHN MARKER, D.S.O., p.s.c., LATE COLDSTREAM GUARDS, A.A., AND Q.M.G.,

was the son of Richard Marker, Esq., J.P., of Combe, Honiton, and the Hon. Mrs. Marker, daughter of the ninth Lord Digby, and was born on the 18th April, 1867, at Upcerne Manor, Dorset. He was educated at Evelyns, Eton, and the R.M.C., Sandhurst, joining the Coldstream

Guards in 1888, becoming Captain in 1898, and obtaining his substantive Majority in 1903.

From 1892 to 1896 he was Adjutant of the 1st Battalion Coldstream Guards, and 1896–97 A.D.C. to Sir W. Ridgeway, Governor and Commander-in-Chief in Ceylon; and from 1899 to 1900 A.D.C. to Lord Curzon, Viceroy of India. In the latter year he went to South Africa on special service for the Boer War, and in 1901 became A.D.C. to Lord Kitchener, Commander-in-Chief of the Forces in South Africa, and accompanied him to India in a similar position, retaining it until 1904. In the South African War Colonel Marker was present at the actions at Vet River, Zand River, Johannesburg, near Pretoria, Diamond Hill, and Belfast. He was mentioned three times in Despatches, and with the then Colonel Hubert Hamilton brought home peace despatches to the King at Windsor; for these services he was given the Brevet-rank of Major, June, 1902, the D.S.O. for taking De Wet's guns, the Queen's medal with five clasps, and the King's medal with two clasps. He was also placed on the list of officers qualified for the Staff through Staff service in the field. In 1904 Colonel Marker proceeded to the Staff College, qualifying in the following year, for part of which he was Private Secretary to the Secretary of State for War, and was later appointed A.D.C. to the Commander-in-Chief in India, where he remained until 1906. From 1907 to 1910 he was General Staff Officer, Home Counties, and in 1912 he succeeded to the command of the 1st Battalion Coldstream Guards, being in November, 1913, appointed A.Q.M.G. on the headquarters of the Aldershot Command. He accompanied the British Expeditionary Force to France as A.A. and Q.M.G. of the 1st Army Corps.

For his services in the Great War Colonel Marker was mentioned in Sir John French's Despatches of the 8th October, 1914, and the 14th January, 1915; and was made an Officer of the Legion of Honour for his services during the retirement from Mons. He was hit by a shell on the 4th November, 1914, outside the reporting centre of the 1st Army Corps at Ypres, and died of his wounds on the 13th of that month.

Colonel Marker was a member of the Guards', Travellers', Carlton, Turf, and Pratt's Clubs. He married, in 1906, Beatrice Minnie Shrieve, third daughter of Sir Thomas Jackson, Bart., and Lady Jackson, and left a son, Richard Raymond Kitchener, born on the 18th June, 1908.

MAJOR RONALD ANTHONY MARKHAM, 2nd BATTALION COLDSTREAM GUARDS,

was the only surviving son of the late Colonel W. T. Markham, of Becca Hall, Yorkshire, who served in the Crimean War in the Rifle Brigade and Coldstream Guards, and grandson of Sir Francis Grant, P.R.A.

He was born on the 15th October, 1870; educated at Charterhouse; and joined the Coldstream Guards from the Militia in December, 1890, becoming Lieutenant in August, 1896, and Captain in December, 1899.

He served with the first advance against the Khalifa in the Nile Expedition of 1899, for which he received the Egyptian medal and clasp. From August, 1899, to August, 1903, he was employed with the Egyptian Army, acting as A.D.C. to the Sirdar from April, 1900, to December, 1902, for which he received the Insignia of the 4th Class of the Imperial Order of the Medjidieh. He was promoted Major in 1907.

He was shot through the head at St. Julien, France, on the 25th October, 1914, and, at the time of his death was Second in Command of his battalion. He was mentioned in Sir John French's Despatches of the 8th October, 1914, and the 14th January, 1915.

He was a member of the Guards', Nulli Secundus, and the Turf Clubs; also of the M.C.C. and I Zingari. He was fond of cricket and shooting, and was a very keen and hard rider to hounds. He was born at Melton Mowbray, from which place he had hunted all his life, and where his interment took place.

CAPTAIN GILBERT HOWE MAXWELL MARSH, 41st DOGRAS, INDIAN ARMY,

who was killed by shrapnel in the trenches in Belgium on the 1st November, 1914, was the youngest son of Colonel Jeremy-Taylor Marsh, R.E. (retired), of 49, Bedford Gardens, Campden Hill, London, W.

He was born on the 30th July, 1882, and educated at St. Paul's School; and after serving with the embodied Militia for nearly fourteen months he passed into the Army by competition, and was gazetted to the Dorset Regiment in January, 1902. In September, 1904, he was transferred to the Indian Army as Lieutenant, receiving his promotion to Captain in January, 1911.

CAPTAIN FRANCIS MARSHALL, 1st BATTALION THE KING'S (LIVERPOOL REGIMENT).
died of wounds received at the Battle of the Aisne on the 30th September, 1914, and was buried at Versailles on the 2nd October. He was the son of the late R. A. Marshall, Barnes, and was born on the 12th February, 1877.
He joined the Liverpool Regiment in May, 1900, became Lieutenant in July, 1906, and Captain in 1910.

LIEUTENANT GEORGE GARTH MAR-SHALL, 11th (PRINCE ALBERT'S OWN, HUSSARS)

born at South Kensington on the 6th December, 1884, was the second son of Mr. and Mrs. Victor Marshall, of Monk Coniston, Lancashire, a grandson of the late General the Hon. Sir Alexander Hamilton Gordon, K.C.B., and a nephew of Major-General A. Hamilton Gordon, C.B.
He was educated at Marlborough College, where he was in the Cricket XI. He was gazetted to the 11th Hussars in December, 1907. For the Great War he was appointed A.D.C. to Lieutenant-General Allenby, Commanding a Cavalry Division of the British Expeditionary Force, and was killed at Ypres on the 6th November, 1914, while carrying a despatch to General Sir Douglas Haig.
Lieutenant Marshall was a member of the Cavalry and the Bath Clubs.

2nd LIEUTENANT JENNER STEP-HENS CHANCE MARSHALL, 2nd BATTN. OXFORDSHIRE AND BUCK-INGHAMSHIRE LIGHT INFANTRY,
who died on the 21st October, 1914, from wounds received in action on the same day, aged nineteen, was the only son of the late Jenner Gerst Marshall, of Westcott, Barton Manor, Oxon, and Mrs. George Miller, of Teffont, Ewyas Rectory, Salisbury.
2nd Lieutenant Marshall was gazetted to the Oxfordshire and Buckinghamshire Light Infantry in September, 1913.

2nd LIEUTENANT ROGER MARSHALL, 2nd BATTALION DURHAM LIGHT INFANTRY,
son of Anthony Marshall, of Annstead, Northumberland, formerly Lieutenant - Colonel 3rd Battalion Northumberland Fusiliers, was born at Annstead on the 25th January, 1891.

He was educated for a short time at Merchiston Castle School, where he won the half-mile handicap; then privately; and entered the Special Reserve, R.F.A., in 1910. In April, 1913, he gained the Aviator's Certificate, and Pilot's Certificate of the Royal Aero Club. In July, 1914, he was gazetted to the 2nd Durham Light Infantry as 2nd Lieutenant. On the 20th September, 1914, he was killed when fighting while the Durhams were enfiladed, but held firm. His last words were : " Surrender be hanged ! Stand up and fight ! " as stated by Corporal Bell who was beside him. 2nd Lieutenant Marshall belonged to the Aero Club. He was a very good shot, both with gun and rifle, and a particularly cool and fearless rider in the hunting field.

LIEUTENANT WILLIAM M. BURT-MARSHALL, 2nd BATTN. ARGYLL AND SUTHERLAND HIGHLANDERS,
youngest son of the late James Burt-Marshall, of Luncarty, was born at Luncarty, Perthshire, on the 14th July, 1887.
He was educated at Ardvreck Crieff, Rugby, and Sandhurst, and had a distinguished athletic career.

At Rugby he was in the XI and XV (playing half-back). In 1905 his House School Field was " Cockhouse " in both cricket and football, due in great measure to him and his brother. He was Steward of athletics, middleweight boxer, and winner of the School mile.
He passed into Sandhurst in September, 1906, and while there he became Senior Sergeant of his company. He was in the XI of 1908 and the XV of 1906 and 1907, captaining the XV of 1907 when they beat Woolwich by a score, which was a record up to that period. In September, 1908, he was gazetted to the 2nd Argyll and Sutherland Highlanders (the old 93rd), and

joined the battalion at Bloemfontein, South Africa. In January, 1910, the battalion returned to Scotland, and was stationed in Glasgow. During that summer they formed the Guard of Honour to the King during his visit to Edinburgh. Lieutenant Burt-Marshall led the regimental Minto Cup team in the Scottish command rifle meeting of August, 1911. In March, 1912, the battalion moved to Fort George, Inverness-shire, where they remained until the outbreak of the war with Germany.

On the 9th August the Argyll and Sutherland Highlanders left Scotland for France, and joined the 19th Infantry Brigade. From then onwards they were in the thick of all the fighting, and were personally complimented by Sir John French on their performance in the Battle of Le Cateau.

Lieutenant Burt-Marshall was now in command of " A " Company, which command he held, save for one short period, until he fell.

Captain Clark, Argyll and Sutherland Highlanders, writing of him, said : " All through the retirement he was strong of heart and untiring in his devotion to duty. All the way back towards Paris and right up again to the Aisne he was with his men, encouraging and influencing them, and gradually the company grew to its original strength again. On November 8th a special duty in Ploegsteert Wood was detailed to us. The capture of an advanced German trench, which had proved a veritable thorn in the British side, was imperative, and the 93rd were asked to do what others had already tried to do and failed. All through the 9th the battalion lay in the wood, shelled at intervals. The attack was ordered for that night. Three companies were to advance from different points against the enemy's trench ; and, while our guns were paving the way for the assault, we silently moved forward to our allotted positions. When the shelling stopped the attack crept closer, but the German flare lights showed up our line, and we rose and dashed for the trench. He was at the head of his men, and led the charge. He ran right up to the German barbed wire, was hit, and fell, but rose again, and dashed on to the parapet of the trench, where he fell again. No one could get up to him, and those who were able crawled back to re-form with the remnant of the companies."

On the 8th February the War Office reported that news had been received that Lieutenant Burt-Marshall had died of his wounds in a German Field Hospital at Quesnoy on the 17th November, 1914, and this news has now been verified beyond all doubt.

A brother officer wrote of him : " Beloved and respected by his men, a true and fearless soldier. We are proud of him. He has fallen a hero, and our memories of him are great."

His Commanding Officer wrote : " To my great sorrow, I hear there is now no hope of him. He was such a good soldier, and is a great loss to the regiment."

MAJOR ROBERT MASEFIELD, 1st BATTALION THE KING'S (SHROPSHIRE LIGHT INFANTRY),

who was killed in action on the 24th October, 1914, was the son of Valentine Vickers Masefield, Akaroa, New Zealand, and was brought up by his uncle, Colonel Robert Taylor Masefield, C.B., late of Ellerton Hall, Newport, Salop, and now of Woodbury, Devonshire, to whom he was as a dearly loved only son.

Born at Gough's Bay, New Zealand, on the 24th May, 1872, he was educated at Marlborough (Crescent) from 1884–90, and the R.M.C., Sandhurst, 1891–92. From the latter he was gazetted to the King's Shropshire Light Infantry in June, 1892, being posted first to the 2nd Battalion in Ireland, and then to the 1st Battalion at Hong Kong, going with it later to India. He became Lieutenant in August, 1895, and Captain in June, 1901, joining the 2nd Battalion in South Africa. With that battalion he was present at operations in the Transvaal from March to May, 1902, receiving the Queen's medal with two clasps.

He returned to India with the 2nd Battalion, and was promoted Major in September, 1912, when at Secunderabad. When the war with Germany broke out he was home on leave, and was ordered to join the 1st Battalion at Tipperary, with which he proceeded to France in September, and was in the trenches on the Aisne till the 12th October. The battalion was then moved up into the firing line between Lille and Armentières, and helped to repel the Germans' first great rush for Calais.

On the 24th October, 1914, Major Masefield was left Second in Command of his battalion, as well as in command of his own company ; and his Captain wrote of his death on that day : " It was in the trenches of ' A ' Company. We had been fighting hard for five days, and ' D ' Company had lost all their officers except one, so at 12 o'clock I was taken from ' A ' to go to ' D ' Company trenches. I said good-bye, and he took my seat. It was there at about 4.30 p.m. that he was killed instantaneously by shrapnel shell in the back."

A Sergeant of his battalion wrote : " It was a critical time, as another strong attack was expected from the enemy. . . . He himself was watching the front . . . cheering his men and preventing any unnecessary risk at a most nerve-trying time. . . . He died, as he had lived, a gallant gentleman. Still under heavy fire he was buried at dawn next morning—Sunday, October 25th—between two haystacks in a little farm just behind the trenches, Le Quesne, near Bois Grenier. There are worse resting-places for one who had spent most of his life in the open air."

A Private of his (" A ") company wrote : " He was such a fine officer, always with his men. We all would have gone with him anywhere. He came right along our trenches to see how all his company were not half an hour before the Germans started to attack again (on the afternoon of the 24th October). . . . ' It is the best that go first.' "

Another Private wrote : " His last thoughts were for his men, his last words telling us to keep our heads down as much as possible."

His former Colour-Sergeant, writing on behalf of his old company in the 2nd Battalion, on hearing of his death, said : " Every one of us would have given our lives gladly for the sake of our Major." One of his brother officers wrote : " You know we all loved him, from the Colonel down to the latest recruit " ; and " we always said the regiment would be all right as long as Masefield was with it."

Someone else who knew Major " Bob " wrote : "A fine soldier and keen sportsman, his loss will be felt by both battalions, by officers and men." He, indeed, loved all outdoor pursuits—fishing, shooting (both big and small game), pig-sticking, etc.—and many a youngster in the regiment owes to him his first sporting experiences. Excelling in all games, he was chiefly interested in those in which the men could share, and had played for his regiment in most. Always cheery and ready for work under all conditions, absolutely unselfish and thoughtful for others, and thoroughly efficient, he was just one of that fine type—the British regimental officer. Adored by his men, looked up to by them in work and play and sport, his feelings for them may best be expressed in his own words, in almost his last letter : " The men are splendid, always cheery, full of thrust, and ready for anything. We cannot do enough for them."

He married, in 1908, Esmé, daughter of Colonel Henry Spencer Wheatley, C.B., late 2 /3rd Gurkhas, of The Rush, Farnham, Surrey.

LIEUTENANT ROWLAND CHARLES MASON, THE LOYAL NORTH LANCASHIRE REGIMENT,

was the only son of the late Rowland Mason, J.P., of Edgbaston, Birmingham, a well-known citizen, for many years closely identified with the social and public life of that city. He was born at Chesleigh, Edgbaston on the 23rd December, 1882.

Lieutenant Mason was educated at Edgbaston Preparatory School and at Malvern College (Lyon, 1897–99), where he was a House Prefect. At School he was a keen member of the Artillery Corps, and upon leaving it to join his father's business he took a commission in the Warwickshire Artillery Volunteers. After becoming an efficient officer in

that corps he gave up business, and left the Corps for the Special Reserve, as it was his ambition to belong to the Regular Army. He joined the 3rd Battalion Loyal North Lancashire Regiment as 2nd Lieutenant in February, 1911, being promoted Lieutenant in January, 1912, and went abroad with the 1st Battalion of the regiment, with the 1st Division of the Expeditionary Force. He was present at the Battle of Mons, was wounded at the Battle of the Aisne on the 14th September, 1914, and was brought home to Netley, where he died on the 30th of the same month. It was found that the force of the piece of shrapnel which wounded him had driven a portion of his identity disc into his lung. (The above particulars were published in " The Malvernian," his College magazine).

His Commanding Officer in France, writing to express to Lieutenant Mason's parents the sympathy of the surviving officers, said : " Your son received his mortal wound at the head of his men in the thickest of the fighting on the 14th September. More can be said of no one. We honour him."

For some years Lieutenant Mason had been Military Critic of the " Birmingham Daily Post," and was the author of a handbook entitled " Hints on Battery Drill." He was a member of the Public Schools' Alpine Club, the Auxiliary Forces, the Red Rose, and the Junior Army and Navy Club.

MAJOR JOHN HAMON MASSIE, D.S.O., ROYAL GARRISON ARTILLERY,

who was the son of Edward R. Massie, late 78th Highlanders, of Coddington, Cheshire, and a grandson of the late Admiral Thos. Leche Massie, R.N., was born on the 10th June, 1872, at Eaux Chaudes, Basses-Pyrénées, France.

He was educated at the School of Mr. Montagu Foster, Stubbington, Fareham, and at the R.M.A., Woolwich, being gazetted to the Royal Artillery as 2nd Lieutenant in May, 1892, becoming Lieutenant in May, 1895, Captain in January, 1900, and Major in February, 1913.

Major Massie served in the Chitral Relief Force, 1895, and received the medal and clasp. He passed the long course at Shoeburyness in 1898 with first-class honours. From 1900–02 he served in the South African War, in which, after landing at Cape Town in January, 1900, he acted as Transport Officer with the 30th Remount Company, Army Service Corps, being graded as Deputy Assistant Adjutant-General. He was present at several actions and operations: near De Wet's Dorp; the march to Pretoria; action at Zand River in May, 1900; entered Pretoria with Lord Roberts on the 5th June, 1900; actions at Diamond Hill and Heidelberg; in pursuit of De Wet from Bethlehem to the Transvaal; actions at Vredefort; and operations at Hekpoort Valley. He was then temporarily in command of a pom-pom section. In November, 1900, was in action near Schwartz Kopje. In January, 1902, he was appointed Staff Officer for Transport, a position he held under various Generals Commanding, and returned to England in November of the latter year.

For his services he was mentioned in Lord Kitchener's Despatches of the 17th June, 1902; was awarded the D.S.O.; and received the Queen's medal with four clasps (Cape Colony, Johannesburg, Wittebergen, and Diamond Hill) and the King's medal with two clasps.

In the Great War he proceeded on the 24th August, 1914, for a week to Havre on special duty as Staff Officer to Brigadier-General Nicolls, R.A. On the 1st September, 1914, he was gazetted as Staff Captain, Administrative Staff, and again went to Havre for duty with Heavy Artillery on the 9th November. He was kept at the base, St. Nazaire, till the 1st November, and left there to take command, on the 5th November, of the 26th Heavy Battery (sixty-pounders) at Ypres.

On the 13th November, 1914, he was mortally wounded at Ypres by a fragment of high-explosive shell while in command of the 26th Battery, and died in the Field Hospital on the 15th of that month.

Major Massie was fond of all games and good at most. On several occasions he represented his regiment against the R.E. at billiards. He was for over three years Secretary and Treasurer of the R.A. Games Fund.

He married, in September, 1903, Maria Margaret, eldest daughter of Major-General E. A. Berger, late 10th Regiment.

CAPTAIN CHARLES LIONEL MASTER, 2nd BATTN. ROYAL IRISH RIFLES,

who was killed in action on the 12th October, 1914, was the son of the late William Edward Master, of Kotmalie, Ceylon, and nephew of Harcourt Master, Rotherhurst, Liss, Hampshire. He was born on the 24th March, 1881, and, after serving with the embodied Militia for about six months, joined the Royal Irish Rifles as 2nd Lieutenant in January, 1901, becoming Lieutenant in 1905. He served in the South African War, being present at operations in the Orange River Colony from August, 1901, to May, 1902, receiving the Queen's medal with four clasps.

In January, 1908, he was appointed Adjutant of his battalion, and became Captain in June of the same year.

CAPTAIN ALEXANDER MASTERS, ADJUTANT 34th SIKH PIONEERS,

was born at Burdwan, India, on the 1st March, 1885, son of the late Mr. John Masters, Inspector-General of Police, Bengal, and was a nephew of Colonel Alexander Masters, C.B., of St. Erne, Cheltenham.

He was educated at Bedford Grammar School and the R.M.C., Sandhurst, whence he obtained his commission in the Lincolnshire Regiment in October, 1903, at the age of eighteen. He joined the Indian Army in 1905, becoming Lieutenant in 1906, and Captain in 1912, in which year he was appointed Adjutant of his regiment. He served in the Mohmand Campaign on the north-western frontier of India in 1908, receiving the medal and clasp.

Captain Masters was killed on the 23rd November, 1914, at Festubert, the following account of the circumstance being given by a brother officer:—

"We were driven out of our trenches on the morning of the 23rd, and the General gave orders for a counter-attack in the evening, with instructions to retake the trenches at all costs. Captain Masters was with a company leading the attack over about six hundred yards of open ground. He was very much liked by the men, who would follow him anywhere, which they did here in spite of the truly dreadful fire from five German Maxims. Very splendidly he led the men on till they reached the trench, and drove the Germans out. The last that was seen of him was his shooting four Germans with his revolver, with two Sepoys fighting beside him. They were all found there just as they had fallen, Captain Masters' body lying between the retaken trench and the Germans. It was brought in the third night and buried by two men of the Black Watch."

He died, as he would have wished to die, knowing that his regiment had carried the position.

LIEUT. THOMAS HUGH MATHEWS, 1st BATTN. EAST LANCASHIRE REGT.,

who was killed in action on the 2nd November, 1914, was the eldest son of John Herbert and Lydia Edith Mathews, and was born at The Rectory, Great Warley, Essex, on the 16th November, 1894.

Lieutenant Mathews was educated at Rottingdean School, Brighton, and at Repton, afterwards going to the R.M.C., Sandhurst, whence he was gazetted to his regiment in September, 1913.

In the "London Gazette" of the 27th April, 1915, his promotion to Lieutenant was notified, to take effect from September, 1914.

LIEUTENANT KENNETH RONALD MATHIESON, SPECIAL RESERVE, attd. 1st BATTALION IRISH GUARDS,

who was killed in action near Ypres on the 1st November, 1914, aged twenty-eight, was the elder son of Mr. and Mrs. Kenneth Mathieson, of 50, Princes Gate, London, S.W.

He was appointed Lieutenant in the Special Reserve of the Irish Guards on the 18th August, 1914.

CAPTAIN JOHN HUBERT MATTHEWS, 1st BATTN. NORTHUMBERLAND FUSILIERS,

son of John and Jessie Matthews, was born on the 19th September, 1878, at Walmer, Kent, and educated at Charterhouse.

He first joined a Militia Battalion of the Border Regiment, from which he was gazetted to

the Northumberland Fusiliers in January, 1899, becoming Lieutenant in February, 1900, and obtaining his company in October, 1901, at the age of twenty-three.

With his battalion he served in the South African War, being employed with the Mounted Infantry, and was present at operations in the Orange River Colony and Cape Colony. He received the Queen's medal and King's medal, each with two clasps.

He was with his battalion when, on the 15th September, 1914, he was killed in the Great War, being hit in the head by a piece of shrapnel from a gun which enfiladed the trench in which he was on duty, just north of the town of Vailly.

CAPTAIN CHARLES CARUS MAUD, D.S.O., 1st BATTN. PRINCE ALBERT'S (SOMERSET LIGHT INFANTRY),

who was killed in action on the 19th December, 1914, was the youngest son of the late Colonel William Sherer Maud, R.E., and of Mrs. Maud, of Milton House, Bournemouth.

He was born on the 15th January, 1875, and joined the Somerset Light Infantry from the Militia in January, 1896, becoming Lieutenant in 1899. He took part in the South African War, being present at operations in the Transvaal in March and April, 1902, receiving the Queen's medal with two clasps.

From December, 1902, to September, 1904, he was employed with the West African Frontier Force, and in 1903 took part in the Kano-Sokoto Campaign, for which he received the medal with clasp ; and also in operations in the district east of Zaria. He was promoted Captain in February, 1904, and in that year took part in the Sokoto-Burmi operations, for which he was mentioned in Despatches ("London Gazette," 24th January, 1905), and was awarded the D.S.O.

In 1908 he was in the Soudan, and was present at operations in the Jebel Nyima district of Southern Kordofan, for which he received the Egyptian medal with clasp, and was awarded the Medjidieh, 4th class.

LIEUT.-COLONEL AYMER EDWARD MAXWELL, CAPTAIN 1st LOVAT'S SCOUTS YEOMANRY, LATE CAPTAIN GRENADIER GUARDS (CAPTAIN RESERVE OF OFFICERS),

was the only surviving son of the Right Hon.

Sir Herbert Eustace Maxwell, P.C., seventh Baronet, and was born on the 26th October, 1877.

He was educated at Eton and the R.M.C., Sandhurst, from which he entered the Grenadier Guards in September, 1897, being promoted Lieutenant in 1899 and Captain in June, 1904. He served in the South African War, taking part in the advance on Kimberley, including actions at Belmont and Enslin, for which he received the Queen's medal with clasp. He retired from the active list, entered the Reserve of Officers, Grenadier Guards, in September, 1907, and was appointed Captain in Lovat's Scouts Yeomanry in November, 1910.

He received a temporary commission as Lieutenant-Colonel in the Royal Marines ("London Gazette," 10th November, 1914), in September, 1914, with command of the "Collingwood" Battalion of the Royal Naval Division. He was mortally wounded in the trenches at Antwerp on the 8th October, and died in the Military Hospital there on the following day.

Lieutenant-Colonel Maxwell married, in 1909, Lady Mary Percy, fifth daughter of the seventh Duke of Northumberland, and left four children : Christian, born July, 1910 ; Aymer, born December, 1911 ; Eustace, born February, 1913 ; and Gavin, born July, 1914.

LIEUTENANT CHARLES WILLIAM MAXWELL, 2/8th GURKHA RIFLES,

who was killed in action in France on the 24th November, 1914, was the only son of Lieutenant-Colonel H. St. P. Maxwell, C.S.I., Indian Army, of Ealing.

He was born on the 12th February, 1889, and was educated at Wellington (at which School his father was also educated), in the Hardinge from 1903–07, where he was a Prefect and in the XV. He then went to the R.M.C., Sandhurst, where he became a Sergeant.

Having passed for the Indian Army he was gazetted to an unattached 2nd Lieutenancy in January, 1909 ; and after being attached for a year to the Essex Regiment in India was posted to the Gurkha Rifles in April, 1910, becoming Lieutenant in April, 1911.

Lieutenant Maxwell married, in 1913, Ida, daughter of Colonel H. Clarke, late R.A., and of Mrs. Clarke, of Wimbledon, and left a son.

CAPTAIN IAN BOUVERIE MAXWELL, 3rd (attd. 1st) BATTN. SOUTH WALES BORDERERS,

was born in London on the 11th October, 1890, the son of Everard Ellison Maxwell, late Commander R.N., and a nephew of Lieutenant-General Sir Ronald Maxwell, K.C.B.

He was educated at Radley and Hertford College, Oxford, where he took his B.A. degree. After serving eighteen months in the Army he resigned, and was employed on the staff of the "Burlington Magazine." Four months later, on the outbreak of the war, he joined the 3rd Battalion of his regiment, and in September was promoted Captain being attached to the 1st Battalion on the Continent in October.

He was killed in action at the Battle of Ypres on the 31st October, 1914.

CAPTAIN PETER ("PAT") BENSON MAXWELL, p.s.c., 1st BATTN. THE EAST YORKSHIRE REGIMENT,

who was wounded at the Battle of the Aisne on the 20th September, 1914, his first day in action, died on the 23rd, and was buried at Braisne on the 24th of the month. He was the son of William Edward Maxwell, Assistant Resident, Perak,

Federated Malay States, and Lillias Grant Maxwell, and was born in Guernsey, Channel Islands, on the 10th October, 1880. His grandfathers were Sir Peter Benson Maxwell, Chief Justice of the Straits Settlements, and the Rev. James Aberigh-Mackay, D.D., Chieftain of Clan Abrach.

Captain Maxwell was educated at Bedford Grammar School, which he entered in 1888, and passed twelfth into the R.M.C., Sandhurst, in 1898, direct from the School. In 1900 he passed first out of Sandhurst, being awarded the Queen Victoria gold medal, the Sword of Honour, and field glasses for proficiency in tactics. In the same year he was appointed to the Queen's (Royal West Surrey Regiment). In April, 1901, he joined the 35th Sikhs (Indian Army), in which regiment nearly all his service was passed. In 1901 and 1902 he served with the Waziristan Expedition, for which he received the medal and clasp, and was serving with the East Yorkshire Regiment (into which he exchanged in 1912), when he was killed in the Great War.

He obtained his company in January, 1909, and entered the Staff College in 1912, passing out the following year.

Captain Maxwell married, in December, 1912, Eileen Muriel, only daughter of Major-General and Mrs. Hamilton Gordon, and left one daughter, Joan, born September, 1913.

2nd LIEUTENANT JOSEPH FREDERICK MEAD, 4th BATTN. THE ROYAL FUSILIERS, (CITY OF LONDON REGT.),

who was killed in action during the retirement from Mons on the 23rd August, 1914, was the eldest son of the late Frederick Mead, Esq., and of Mrs. Mead, of The Moorings, St. Albans.

He was born at Pietermaritzburg, Natal, in February, 1892, and was educated at The Wick, Hove, at Winchester College, and at the R.M.C., Sandhurst. At Winchester he was President of the Boat Club, Vice-Captain of " Sixes " (the Winchester game) and of " Fifteens," and gained the gold medal for athletics two years in succession. He passed into Sandhurst third, and passed out first of his year for the British Army, the two cadets above him being candidates for the Indian Army.

He joined the Royal Fusiliers in February, 1912, passed the flying tests at Brooklands, in 1913, and was to have had a further course in 1914 with a view to joining the Flying Corps Reserve, but the outbreak of war prevented this being done.

The following account of his death was received from an officer of his battalion : " It was on the 23rd August at Mons. He was in reserve at the railway station with the rest of his company. Captain Ashburner was very hard pressed and sent back for reinforcements. He was defending the bridge over the canal. It was a hopeless position, as the enemy could get within one hundred yards of the bridge and then fire from houses, gardens, etc., and never be seen. Also I believe five different battalions were recognised in front of this one company. Your son was soon ordered to reinforce the firing line, which he did in the face of a fearful fire. Directly he got into the trench he was wounded in the head by a bullet. He went to

the rear (just a few yards) to get it dressed, and was quietly whistling all the time. Directly the dressing was finished he went back to the trench, and the second he got there he got a bullet straight through the forehead."

He was fond of all outdoor sports, especially hunting and beagling. After joining the Army he always played cricket and football for his company, and was a splendid runner. He was a member of the Junior Army and Navy and of the Royal Aero Clubs.

LIEUTENANT SIDNEY ARTHUR MEAKIN 4th (attd. 1st) BATTN. THE PRINCE OF WALES'S (NORTH STAFFORDSHIRE REGIMENT),

who was killed in action in France, on the 17th December, 1914, aged twenty, was the sixth son of Mr. and Mrs. Meakin. He was born at Needwood Manor, Rangemore, Burton-on-Trent, and was educated at Uppingham Lower School and Oakham.

He was gazetted 2nd Lieutenant in 1911, and was promoted Lieutenant in his regiment in March, 1913.

He was buried at Chapelle d'Armentières.

2nd LIEUTENANT JAMES WILLIAM MEARS, 2nd BATTN. HIGHLAND LIGHT INFANTRY, was killed in action between the 12th and the 14th November, 1914. He was gazetted 2nd Lieutenant, from the rank of Company Sergeant-Major, for service on the field, on the 30th October, 1914.

LIEUTENANT THOMAS GILLIAT MEAUTYS, 1st BATTN. PRINCE OF WALES'S OWN (WEST YORKSHIRE REGIMENT),

who died on the 22nd September, 1914, of wounds received in action on the 20th at the Battle of the Aisne, was the eldest son of Thomas Arrowsmith Meautys, J.P., of Hammond's Place, Burgess Hill, Sussex.

He was born at Wimbledon, Surrey, on the 13th June, 1889, and was educated at Marlborough, where he was Captain of the Upper School, was in the School Football XV, and won the boxing challenge cup. After leaving Marlborough he was for a year at Wyllies', Cuckfield, Sussex; and in 1908 went to the R.M.C., Sandhurst, where he was a Sergeant. He joined the 2nd West Yorkshire Regiment in September, 1909, getting his step in July, 1910. He served with the 1st Battalion of his regiment in India from January, 1910, to December, 1911, and was Machine Gun Officer when the war broke out. He was mortally wounded while in the front line at the Battle of the Aisne, looking for a convenient place for his guns.

Mr. Meautys, who was a member of the Junior Army and Navy Club, married, in June, 1914, Norah Nell, only daughter of the late H. S. Hotblack, of Brighton, and Mrs. Hotblack, of Fairfield, Hambledon, Hampshire, and left one son, Thomas Gilliat, born April, 1915. His recreations were football, racquets, and shooting.

2nd LIEUT. FRANCIS LESTER HASTINGS-MEDHURST, 3rd BATTN. WORCESTERSHIRE REGIMENT,

was born at 7, Campden Hill Square, Kensington, W., on the 28th July, 1895, the only son of Mrs. F. Hastings-Medhurst, of 11, St. Dunstan's Road, Baron's Court, W., grandson of the late F. W. Hastings-Medhurst, R.A., and nephew of A. Hastings-Medhurst, His Majesty's Consul, Corunna.

He was educated at Stanmore Park Preparatory School (Rev. V. Royle) and Malvern College, where he was in No. 6 House.

He passed seventeenth into the Royal Military College, Sandhurst, where he was a Prize Cadet, joined the 3rd Battalion Worcestershire Regiment as 2nd Lieutenant on the 25th August, 1914, and left with the VIth Division on the 6th September. On the 14th October he was wounded in the head while taking his company across open ground to reinforce a trench. Two-thirds of his men were killed by German Maxim fire opening on their flank, the rest saved themselves by crawling back on their hands and knees.

On the 17th October, during very fierce fighting, a battalion on the right retired without the Worcesters receiving warning, leaving the flank of the latter exposed to the enemy. 2nd Lieutenant Medhurst volunteered to carry a message over open ground for help and orders. He had almost reached cover when he was caught by Maxim fire and killed instantaneously. His body

was recovered later, and was buried at night by his comrades.

The above particulars were given by a wounded officer and men of his battalion.

LIEUTENANT AND ADJUTANT KENNETH FORBES MEIKLEJOHN, 1st BATTN. QUEEN'S OWN CAMERON HIGHLANDERS,

was born at Woolwich on the 18th June, 1885, the son of Lieutenant-Colonel J. F. Meiklejohn, late R.H.A. He was related to the late General Sir John Forbes, G.C.B., and the late Major-General Sir William Meiklejohn, K.C.B. His brother—Major R. F. Meiklejohn, D.S.O.—was wounded at the Battle of Mons, and was taken a prisoner of war.

Lieutenant Meiklejohn was educated at Rugby and the R.M.C., Sandhurst, gaining many prizes at both. He joined the Cameron Highlanders in February, 1904; became Lieutenant in September, 1909; and was appointed Adjutant of his battalion in March, 1913. He was qualified as an Interpreter in Russian and French and passed the examination in German. He also passed successfully through several Army courses.

He was killed in the trenches at the Battle of the Aisne, France, on the 25th September, 1914. Lieutenant Meiklejohn was recommended for the Legion of Honour by his Commanding Officer.

He married Sybil Stewart, of Kinlochmoidart, Inverness-shire, and left a son, Kenneth Matthew, born January, 1915, after his father's death.

CAPTAIN WALTON MELLOR, 2nd BATTN. ROYAL IRISH REGIMENT,

elder son of John Edward Mellor, of Tan-y-Bryn, Abergele, Denbighshire, was born on the 27th June, 1878, and was educated at Rossall School. He joined the Lancashire Fusiliers from the Militia in December, 1899, becoming Lieutenant in May, 1900, and Captain in June, 1905. In 1908 he was transferred to the Royal Irish Regiment.

Captain Mellor served in the South African War, 1899–1902, being present at operations in the Transvaal, Natal, including the action at Laing's Nek; and in the Orange River Colony. For a short time, in 1901, he acted as Railway Staff Officer. For his services he received the Queen's medal with four clasps and the King's medal with two clasps. From 1910–14 he was an Instructor at the R.M.C., Sandhurst.

Captain Mellor was killed in action during the retirement from Mons on the 23rd August, 1914, being one of the earliest of British officers to fall in the Great War.

He married, on the 31st March, 1910, Kathleen Geraldine Helen, only daughter of Lieutenant-Colonel Gerald V. Wellesley, and left a daughter, Kathleen Florence Walton, born 1911.

MAJOR ARCHIBALD ARIEL MERCER, 2nd BATTN. DORSETSHIRE REGT.,

who fell on the 17th November, 1914, in the engagement on the River Shat-el-Arab, which resulted in the capture of Basra, Turkey in Asia, near the head of the Persian Gulf, was the second son of the late Mr. Charles Mercer and of Mrs. Mercer, of Lansdowne Lodge, Weymouth. He was born on the 24th February, 1875, and was educated at Marlborough and the R.M.C., Sandhurst, receiving his commission in the Dorsetshire Regiment in March, 1895, becoming Lieutenant in July, 1897, and Captain in November, 1901. Major Mercer served in the Tirah Campaign of 1897–98, taking part in the actions of Chagru and Dargai, in the capture of Sampagha and Arhange Passes, and in the reconnaissance of the Saran Sar, where he was severely wounded. He received the Tirah medal with two clasps. He was a qualified Musketry Instructor and a first-class Interpreter in Hindustani. He was fond of all games, especially polo and tennis. After the South African War, from 1902–03, he was employed in the Repatriation Department. For three and a half years from 1903 he served with the Transvaal Volunteers, and from May, 1909, to December, 1910, with the Ceylon Volunteers.

The following description of the operations in which the Dorsetshire Regiment was employed in the Persian Gulf is taken from accounts of officers who were present :—

" The force on the River Shat-el-Arab consisted of the Dorsets, the Norfolks, the 104th (Indian Army), and a Mountain Battery. The first position held by the enemy was along the edge of the date palm plantations, which border the river bank in a belt in places two miles wide. Inland is flat desert. On the 17th the whole force attacked Sahil, a place ten miles north of Sanizah, on the River Shat-el-Arab, which is about thirty-five miles from Basra. It was very heavy work advancing across the desert, as, just as the action started, a heavy rain and hail storm of half an hour came down. The enemy put up a very heavy gun and rifle fire, and advancing against it in the open it was pretty bad. The Dorsets were simply wonderful. As they neared the large fort they were enfiladed by the picked Turks who had been placed in the trenches, and suffered very heavily.

" The country over which our men advanced was as flat as a table, and would not have given cover to a mouse. It was just grand to watch them move forward — it might have been a field day in the Maidan."

Sir Arthur Barrett, in his despatch, said :
" The conduct of the troops throughout this engagement excited my warmest admiration. The behaviour of the Dorset Regiment when exposed to both frontal and enfiladed fire is especially to be commended."

Major Mercer was popular with his regiment, and a Private who was with him when killed said his last word was "Advance!" himself leading. He married Margaret Edith, daughter of Mr. and Mrs. W. A. Tennant, of Oxford House, Ugley, Essex, in August, 1913, and left a daughter, born on the 30th November, 1914.

2nd LIEUTENANT ERIC CAMERON MERCER, attd. 4th ROYAL DUBLIN FUSILIERS,

who was killed in action on the 13th October, 1914, was gazetted to the unattached list for the Indian Army in August, 1914, from the R.M.C., Sandhurst.

CAPTAIN CAMERON O'BRYEN HARFORD METHUEN, 2nd BATTN. ROYAL WARWICKSHIRE REGIMENT,

was the son of the late Colonel C. L. Methuen, Commanding 1st City of Bristol Volunteers, late of the Cameron Highlanders (the old 79th), and the late Mrs. Methuen. Captain Methuen, who was a relation of Field-Marshal Lord Methuen, G.C.B., a very distinguished soldier, and was born at Heidelberg, Germany, on the 7th May, 1876.

He was educated at a private school at Clifton, afterwards at Harrow, and subsequently with military tutors, and joined the Warwick-shire Militia in February, 1895, becoming Lieutenant in March, 1897. He was gazetted to the 1st (Regular) Battalion in January, 1898, becoming Lieutenant in August of the same year, and Captain in February, 1901. On the outbreak of the South African War he volunteered for active service, and was attached to the Royal Irish Fusiliers, with whom he sailed to South Africa. He was present at the Relief of Ladysmith, including action at Colenso ; at operations in the Orange Free State, including actions at Vet River and Zand River ; in the Transvaal, including actions near Johannesburg, Pretoria, and Diamond Hill ; also in the Transvaal, east of Pretoria, including action at Belfast. He received the Queen's medal with five clasps and the King's medal with two clasps. After Colenso he rejoined his own regiment, when that was sent out, and served with the Mounted Infantry through the remainder of the war.

His battalion was stationed at Malta when the Great War broke out, and was brought to England in September, 1914, leaving for the front on the 4th October as part of the VIIth Division, disembarking at Zeebrugge. Captain Methuen was shot on the 21st October, 1914, in the trenches, before Ypres, while looking through his field-glasses, and was killed instantaneously. He was a member of the Army and Navy Club.

CAPTAIN DAVID GEORGE METH-VEN, 2nd BATTN. SEAFORTH HIGH-LANDERS (ROSS-SHIRE BUFFS, THE DUKE OF ALBANY'S),

who was killed in action on the 20th October, 1914, was the only son of the late James Methven and Mrs. Methven, Wemyss Park, Kirk-caldy. He was born on the 2nd January, 1879, and after serv-ing with the em-bodied Militia for nearly three months was gazetted 2nd Lieutenant in the Seaforth Highlanders in March, 1900, getting his Lieu-tenancy in July, 1901.

He served in the South African War with the Mounted Infantry, and was present at oper-ations in the Transvaal, east of Pretoria, and in the Orange River Colony in 1900. Again, in 1901–02, he took part in operations in the Transvaal and Orange River Colony and in Cape Colony, receiving the Queen's medal with three clasps and the King's medal with two clasps.

He was promoted Captain in April, 1908.

CAPTAIN JOHN COLLOYRAN MICHELL, 12th (PRINCE OF WALES'S ROYAL) LANCERS,

eldest son of John Michell, I.S.O., Con-sul-General at Petro-grad, was born in Petrograd on the 22nd Sept., 1871.
He was educated at Rugby, and joined the Duke of Corn-wall's Light Infantry (Militia) in 1889. He served in the Matabele Cam-paign in 1896, and took part in the South African War during 1899–02, being employed with the Commander-in-Chief's Bodyguard, and afterwards under the Chief Staff Officer, Lines of Communication, having received his commis-sion in the Worcestershire Regiment in May, 1900. He was present at the relief of Mafeking, and at operations in Rhodesia, 1899–1900 ; operations in the Transvaal, west of Pretoria, including actions at Elands River ; and oper-ations in the Orange River Colony. For his services he received the Queen's medal with four clasps and the King's medal with two clasps. He was promoted Lieutenant in February, 1901, and Captain in the Royal Garrison Regi-ment in November, 1902, being transferred to the 12th Lancers in September, 1905.

He also received the Coronation Durbar medal. He was killed on the 28th August, 1914, while gallantly leading his squadron in what proved to be a most successful charge against the German Cavalry at Moy (Aisne) during the re-tirement from Mons. The General Commanding the Cavalry Brigade said in his despatch : " The Lancers charged through the enemy like going through brown paper."
Captain Michell, who was a member of the Cavalry and Sports Clubs, married Ella, eldest daughter of Mr. and Mrs. Alfred Hill Macnaghten, of 51, Hans Road, London.

CAPTAIN FRANK MIDDLETON, 2nd BATTN. DORSETSHIRE REGIMENT,

eldest surviving son of Hastings Burton and Charlotte Lucia Middleton, was born at Brad-ford, Peverell, Dor-chester, on the 11th February, 1877.
He was educated at the Rev. C. R. Carr's School Exmouth ; and at Eton (H.W. Mozley's

House). He joined the Dorsetshire Regiment from the Militia in June, 1898, becoming Lieutenant in November, 1900.

In the South African War he was employed with the Mounted Infantry, and was present at the relief of Ladysmith and the action at Spion Kop ; the action at Vaal Kranz ; operations on Tugela Heights, when he was wounded on the 21st February, 1900, and action at Pieter's Hill ; operations in Natal, action at Laing's Nek, and operations in Orange River Colony. He was mentioned in despatches (" London Gazette," 10th February, 1901), and received the Queen's medal with five clasps and the King's medal with two clasps. He became Captain in February, 1906.

Captain Middleton was killed on the 17th November, 1914, at Sahil, while serving in the Persian Gulf Expedition.

He married, in 1908, Emily Florence, daughter of the late Major George Bannister, of The Warrens, Feering, Kelvedon, and left one son, Hastings Frank, born October, 1910.

CAPTAIN DOUGLAS NATHANIEL CARLETON CAPEL MIERS, 1st BATTN. THE QUEEN'S OWN CAMERON

HIGHLANDERS, born at Perth, Scotland, on the 20th February, 1875, was the eldest son of the late Lieutenant-Colonel Capel H. Miers, 79th Cameron Highlanders, of Crinant, Glamorganshire, and a grandson of the late Captain Robert Douglas Macdonald, 42nd Highlanders (the Black Watch), of Inchkenneth and Gribune.

Captain Miers was a descendant of the "Mier" of whom it is recorded that at the famous victory of Odeza, on the 30th November, 1227, the King of Spain, calling on his army to advance, shouted, " Adel ante el de Mier por mas valeo! " which may be translated, " Advance, Mier ! the best able to lead." The family came to England in 1616.

Captain Miers was educated at The Oratory School, Edgbaston ; and at Downside. He was gazetted to the Cameron Highlanders from the 2nd (then Militia) Battalion in September, 1896, and obtained his company in March, 1901. He served with the Nile Expedition of 1898, being present at the Battle of Atbara, for which he received the British medal with clasp and the Egyptian medal. He also served in the South African War, being present at the actions of Vet River, Zand River, Wittebergen, and Ladysmith, being twice mentioned in Despatches.

For saving the life of an officer in the Zand River he was recommended by General Rimington for, and was awarded, the Royal Humane Society's bronze medal. During that war he served with Rimington's Guides, and was also with General Bruce Hamilton's column. He received the Queen's medal with four clasps.

From 1905-10 he was Adjutant of the 3rd Battalion of his regiment at the depot, Inverness, where he took great interest in recruiting, raising the strength of the Battalion from four hundred when he took it on to one thousand one hundred when he left. In the course of his recruiting tours he went through the Hebrides, and was very successful in enlisting the West Coast men.

He left for France on the 13th August, 1914, and went straight up to Landrecies with two hundred and fifty men to act as bodyguard to Lieutenant-General Sir J. M. Grierson, who died suddenly in the train on his way to the front. General Grierson was succeeded by General Sir H. Smith-Dorrien, and with him Captain Miers served during the whole of the retirement from Mons, being complimented by the General for his work. He was present at the battle of the Marne, and on September 14th, in the Battle of the Aisne, he brought the remnant of his battalion out of action, reduced to four officers, including himself, and about eighty rank and file.

Captain Miers was killed on the 25th September, 1914, the same day and month as that on which his brother—Captain Ronald Hill Miers, Somersetshire Light Infantry—had been killed in 1901 in South Africa. Captain Ronald Miers had been the champion middleweight boxer of the Army and Navy.

Captain Brodie, Adjutant of the 1st Battalion Cameron Highlanders, gave the following account of Captain Miers' death : " He was with the headquarters in command of the Battalion in support of two companies, holding somewhat advanced positions in a wood and on a ridge near Verneuil, on the River Aisne. With him were the Headquarters Staff and the Signallers. On the 24th September our men had been subjected to very heavy shell fire, and Captain Miers gave orders that one of these advanced trenches was not to be held on the 25th. On that day our troops were again very heavily shelled. At 7 a.m. Captain Miers received a flesh wound in the arm, and decided to go to Verneuil to have it dressed in hospital, saying he would return in the afternoon. Before he could get away the shelling recommenced, and he delayed going, having in the meantime sent a message to Captain Cameron, the next senior officer, to say he was going. Captain Cameron came up to headquarters, and just as he arrived a high-explosive shell burst on the top of the trench and blew it in. Headquarters were in a cave, the trenches having been in some underground slate quarries. The shell burst on top of the cave, and another burst at its mouth, bringing down tons of heavy stones, burying the inmates, who must all have been instantaneously killed. It took three days to dig out the cave, as the work could only be done at night, and the bodies of the killed— thirty-one in all—were recovered, including those of five officers who were in the party. The officers and sergeant-major were buried at Bourg." The Adjutant concluded : " We as a regiment deeply delore their loss, and I have lost a most kind and able Captain and Commanding Officer."

Captain Miers married, in November, 1901, Margaret Anne, youngest daughter of the late Mr. John Elliot Christie, and left three children : Ronald Douglas Martin, born November, 1902 ; Anthony Cecil Gerard, born November, 1906 ; and Rosemary Ann, born February, 1910.

CAPTAIN ROBERT PATRICK MILES, 2nd BATTN. THE KING'S (SHROP-SHIRE LIGHT INFANTRY),

was born at The Lawn, Shirehampton, Gloucestershire, on the 11th December, 1879, the son of Robert Fenton Miles, of The Old Bank (Union of London and Smith's), Bristol. He was related to Sir H. R. Miles, Bart., of Leigh Court, and was a godson of the late General Sir Patrick Macdougall, at one time Commander-in-Chief in Canada.

Captain Miles was educated at Marlborough, where he gained some athletic distinction, and joined the Yorkshire Light Infantry in August, 1899, becoming Lieutenant in January, 1901. He served in the South African War, being present at operations in the Orange Free State and at Paardeberg ; actions at Poplar Grove, Driefontein, Houtnek (Thoba Mountain). Vet and Zand Rivers ; in the Orange River Colony, Cape Colony, and the Transvaal. He received the Queen's medal with four clasps and the King's medal with two clasps. He also had the medal for King George's Durbar in India. In October, 1907, he was appointed Superintendent of Gymnasia for the Southern Army, India, in which country he served for ten years.

He was a good all-round athlete, and very interested in Army boxing, he was also fond of big-game shooting, in which he was indulging while on leave in British East Africa when the war broke out.

On his return he was attached to the 1st Battalion Royal Irish Rifles, as the 1st Battalion (to which he had been transferred) of his own regiment had already gone to the front. He was shot in the trenches on the 30th December, 1914, and was buried at Estaires.

LIEUTENANT CYRIL ROLAND EYRE MILLER, 4th BATTN. THE CAMERON-IANS (SCOTTISH RIFLES),

son of the late Captain J. Blair Miller, late 8th Hussars and Forfar Light Horse, and Mrs. Goodwin Newton, The Manor House, Upton, Andover, was born on the 17th January, 1882, at Eyre Court Castle, Ireland, and was educated at Christ's Hospital.

Lieutenant Miller served with the Transvaal Horse near Potchefstroom, in South Africa, and for two years with the Royal Scots at Glencorse. He became Lieutenant in the Cameronians in May, 1908, and in the Great War was attached to the King's Own Scottish Borderers ; he was wounded in the trenches near Ypres on the 14th November, 1914, and died in No. 7 Stationary Hospital at Boulogne on the 23rd November, being buried at the Cemetery d'Est on the 24th.

The circumstances of his death were described thus by a brother officer : " An aeroplane dropped a bomb in the trench held by the battalion. It did not explode when it fell, and Lieutenant C. R. E. Miller ran forward and lifted it up to throw it clear of the trench. But he was too late. The bomb burst, and the gallant officer was so terribly mutilated that he afterwards died of his wounds."

CAPTAIN ERNEST CYRIL MILLER (SPECIAL RESERVE), 3rd (attd. 1st) BATTN. LOYAL NORTH LANCASHIRE REGIMENT,

was the third son of the late William Pitt Miller and Mrs. W. Pitt Miller, of Merlewood, Grange-over-Sands, Lancashire, and Thistleton, Lancashire.

He was born on the 13th June, 1878, at Merlewood, Grange-over-Sands, and was

educated at Harrow (Small Houses and Druries), 1893–96; and Trinity College, Cambridge, where he took his B.A. degree in 1901.

Captain Miller had obtained a satisfactory report for the rank of Field Officer, and had qualified at a school of musketry. He obtained his Captaincy in June, 1906.

He was killed instantaneously while leading his men during the successful attack on the enemy's position near Bixschoote on the 23rd October, 1914.

He was a member of the Union Club, Trafalgar Square, London.

In November, 1913, he married Dulcie Katherine, daughter of Mr. and Mrs. A. M. Bernard, of Copdock, Ipswich.

LIEUTENANT FREDERIC WILLIAM JOSEPH MACDONALD MILLER, 1st BATTN. GRENADIER GUARDS,

who was killed in action on the 23rd October, 1914, was the elder son of Sir William Miller, Bart., of Glenlee. Lieutenant Miller's mother was the youngest daughter of Mr. Chas. Manning, brother of Cardinal Manning. His great-uncle— Lieutenant-Colonel William Miller, of the Grenadier Guards—was mortally wounded at Quatre Bras, and died the following day in Brussels.

After the usual period at the R.M.C., Sandhurst, Lieutenant Miller was gazetted to the Grenadier Guards in February, 1912, and was given his Lieutenancy in August, to date from the 30th June, 1914.

Sir William Miller's second son—2nd Lieutenant A. G. L. J. Miller, 2nd Battalion Irish Guards—becomes the heir to the baronetcy.

2nd LIEUTENANT GODFREY LYALL MILLER, ROYAL ENGINEERS,

who was included as killed in action in the casualty list issued by the War Office on the 9th October, 1914, was the son of Sir John Ontario Miller, K.C.S.I., of Rowley Lodge, Arkley, Herts.

He was born in 1893, and was educated at Rugby and the R.M.A., Woolwich, from which he passed first into the R.E., receiving his commission in December, 1912.

2nd LIEUTENANT INGLIS FRANCIS RAWLEY MILLER, 2nd BATTN. ROYAL INNISKILLING FUSILIERS,

born on the 19th January, 1893, at Millbank, Omagh, County Tyrone, was the only surviving son of the late Major Rawley Miller, of Millbank, Omagh, and a grandson of the late Rev. Alexander Rawley Miller, of Moneymore, County Tyrone. 2nd Lieutenant Miller's elder brother —Lieutenant Alexander Rawley Miller, 1st Battalion Royal Inniskilling Fusiliers—gave his life for his country in the South African War.

He was educated at Berkhampsted, and had been for four years in the Special Reserve, 3rd Battalion, and after the outbreak of the war he was attached to the 2nd Battalion of his regiment, and later was gazetted to the Regular Army.

He was wounded during the retirement from Mons on the 26th August, 1914, and died from the effects, a prisoner of war, in a hospital at Cambrai on the 13th September, 1914.

2nd Lieutenant Miller was mentioned in Sir John French's Despatch of the 8th October, 1914.

2nd LIEUT. ROY DENZIL PASHLEY MILNER, 2nd BATTN. SHERWOOD FORESTERS, (NOTTINGHAMSHIRE AND DERBYSHIRE REGIMENT),

was born on the 1st December, 1892, at Totley Hall, Derbyshire, the son of William Aldam Milner, Esq., who is descended from an old branch of the family which migrated from Notts to Yorkshire in the sixteenth century, and lived for many generations at Monk Bretton Abbey.

Lieutenant Milner was educated at Repton and the Royal Military College, Sandhurst, from which he received his commission in January, 1913, and accompanied his battalion to the Continent, leaving Southampton on the 8th September, 1914, reaching the front on the 18th of the same month.

On the morning of the 20th September the Sherwood Foresters were held in reserve at the foot of a hill on the north bank of the Aisne, near Troyon, another battalion being entrenched in the firing line on the hill above. A sudden alarm came that the Germans had penetrated our line, and had taken the trenches. The Foresters were not in formation, but sprang to arms, and, led by their officers, rushed up the hill in groups to where the Germans were entrenched in our lines. In spite of a heavy cross and frontal fire, they drove out the enemy and re-occupied our trenches. There were fourteen casualties among the officers, and 2nd Lieutenant Milner, who was with one of the leading companies, fell in storming the trenches. His Commanding Officer—Colonel Crofton-Atkins—gave to his relatives the following account of this brave young officer's gallant conduct :—

" It will be some consolation to you to know that his end was worthy of the brave young soldier he was. He died when leading his little command in the most dashing manner during our first fight on the 20th, a notable regimental anniversary—Alma Day. His action, together with that of others, secured the successful issue of a fight which was of vital importance to the safety of the whole line. It is hardly necessary for me to tell you how much we all loved and appreciated him. He was one of my most promising young officers, and his loss is a personal grief to me."

2nd Lieutenant Milner played polo for his regiment at Plymouth, and was one of the winning team that competed for the Cory Cup in 1914.

2nd LIEUTENANT ERIC ARTHUR MITCHELL, 2nd BATTN. THE PRINCE OF WALES'S VOLUNTEERS (SOUTH LANCASHIRE REGIMENT),

was the elder surviving son of the Rev. W. M. and Mrs. Mitchell, of Elson Vicarage, Gosport, Hants, and a grandson of the late G. J. Newbery, Esq., of Stafford House, Broxbourne, Herts. He was born at St. Mary's Vicarage, Leicester, on the 21st March, 1895, and was educated at Oakham School, where he excelled in sports, and obtained his colours for both cricket and football, and was one of the first to join the O.T.C.

In February, 1913, he entered the R.M.C., Sandhurst, and passed through his course with distinction. On several occasions he played for the College Rugby XV, and was a member of the champion company at arms. His recreations were cricket, football, golf, and music.

On the 7th August, 1914, he was gazetted to the South Lancashire Regiment, and left for the front on the 8th September, taking a gallant part in the Battles of the Aisne and Ypres, when his battalion fought against great odds. He was killed in action at Neuve Chapelle on the 27th October, 1914.

CAPTAIN JULIAN ALAN SPENCER MITCHELL, 3rd BATTN. THE KING'S (SHROPSHIRE LIGHT INFANTRY),

who died at Braisne on the 28th September, 1914, of wounds received at the Battle of the Aisne, aged twenty-eight years, was the second son of Captain Spencer Mitchell, formerly of the Border Regiment (temporary Lieutenant - Colonel, Commanding 20th [Service] Battalion Manchester Regiment).

He was born at Dublin on the 15th January, 1886, and was educated at Charterhouse. He joined the 3rd Battalion King's (Shropshire Light Infantry) in 1910, became Lieutenant in October, 1912, and was promoted Captain shortly before his death.

He was married, and his only child was born on the 27th September, 1914.

LIEUTENANT ALEXANDER LOGAN N. MAXWELL MOFFAT, 2nd BATTN. DORSETSHIRE REGIMENT,

was born at 11 Dean Street, Blackpool, Lancashire, on the 24th November, 1889. He was the third son of the late R. Maxwell Moffat, M.D., of St. Heliers, Jersey, and Sidmount, Dumfriesshire, and grandson of the late Alexander Maxwell Moffat, J.P., Laird of Sundaywell, Dumfriesshire.

He was educated at Victoria College, Jersey, and joined the Prince of Wales's Own (West Yorkshire Regiment) from the Militia in May, 1910, being subsequently transferred to the 2nd Battalion Dorsetshire Regiment—then in India—in which he was promoted Lieutenant in February, 1914. He was Brigade Signalling

Officer at Poona, and accompanied his battalion to the Persian Gulf.

At the taking of Basra he was severely wounded, and died three days later on the 21st November, 1914, and was buried in the desert.

Colonel Rosher, Commanding Officer, wrote : " We deplore the loss of one of our most promising young officers, a favourite in all ranks. He was severely wounded whilst gallantly leading up the machine guns, of which he had charge, to help his sorely pressed comrades."

A brother officer wrote : " He died a credit to his regiment and country."

MAJOR ERNEST KERR MOLESWORTH, ROYAL ENGINEERS,

was the son of Lieutenant - Colonel A. O. Molesworth, R.A. (retired), of Cruicksfield, Duns, N.B., and was born at Montrose, Scotland, in 1878.

He was educated privately and at the Royal Military Academy, Woolwich, from which he obtained his commission in March, 1898, and became Captain in March, 1907, being promoted to the rank of Major on the 30th October, 1914, two months before he met his death.

He served in India, was in the Tibet Expedition of 1903–04, for which he received the medal, and commanded the 2nd Field Troop of R.E. of the Indian Expeditionary Force on service in France (1914) till his death. He was killed at St. Hilaire, France, on the 31st December, 1914.

He married Hilda Rosalie, daughter of the late Lieutenant-General H. A. Brownlow, R.E., and left two children, Mollie Rosalie and David Brownlow, age seven and two years respectively.

CAPTAIN BRIAN C. B. MOLLOY, OXFORDSHIRE YEOMANRY, (QUEEN'S OWN OXFORDSHIRE HUSSARS),

T.F., Honorary Lieutenant in the Army, May, 1910, was killed in action on the 1st November, 1914.

The son of James Molloy of Cornolare, King's County, he was born on the 1st June, 1875, and was educated at The Oratory School, Bir-

mingham. He entered the Yeomanry in May, 1901, and served in the South African War, in which he was severely wounded, taking part in operations in the Orange River Colony and in the Transvaal in 1900–01, including actions at Lindley, Rhenoster River, and Venterskroon. He received the Queen's medal with four clasps. He retired from the Oxfordshire Yeomanry in February, 1905, and joined the reserve of that regiment in the same year, when he was also promoted Captain. He was a King's Foreign Service Messenger from 1901–13.

Captain Molloy, who was a member of the St. James's and the Cavalry Clubs, married May, widow of Major Harry Pakenham, 60th Rifles, and daughter of Colonel Markham, of Becca Hall, Yorks, and left one daughter, Mary Elizabeth, born January, 1912.

CAPTAIN the Honble. CHARLES HENRY STANLEY MONCK, 3rd BATTN. COLDSTREAM GUARDS,

was the eldest son of H. P. C. S., fifth Viscount Monck, and Viscountess Monck, daughter of the third Earl of Clonmel. He was born at 78, Belgrave Road, London, S.W., on the 9th November, 1876, and was educated at Eton.

He joined the Coldstream Guards as 2nd Lieutenant from the Militia in May, 1897, becoming Lieutenant in November, 1898, and Captain in November, 1903. He served with the 2nd Battalion through the South African War from 1899 to 1902, and was present at the advance on Kimberley, including actions at Belmont, Enslin, Modder River, and Magersfontein ; and also at operations in the Orange Free State in November, 1900. At the conclusion of that war he received the Queen's medal with seven clasps and the King's medal with two clasps.

In the Great War he was shot through the heart at St. Julien, France, on the 21st October, 1914, and at the time of his death he was the Senior Captain of his battalion.

Captain Monck married Mary Florence, daughter of Sir W. W. Portal, second Bart., and left three children : Henry W. S., born the 11th December, 1905 ; Elizabeth Noel, born in 1908 ; and Mary Patricia, born in 1911.

He was a member of the Guards' Club, the Kildare Street Club, Dublin ; and the M.C.C. His recreations were polo, cricket, hunting, and shooting.

LIEUTENANT FRANCIS ALGERNON MONCKTON, 1st BATTALION SCOTS GUARDS,

was the son of Francis Monckton, of Stretton Hall, Stafford, and Mrs. Monckton, daughter of Algernon Charles Heber-Percy, of Hodnet Hall, Shropshire.

He was born in London on the 6th May, 1890, and was educated at a private school at Wixenford; at Eton; and at Christchurch, Oxford, where he took his B.A. degree. He received his commission in the Scots Guards in February, 1912, becoming Lieutenant in April, 1913.

Lieutenant Monckton was killed by shell in the trenches near Ypres on the 8th November, 1914. The Germans broke through the Allied line on the flank of the Scots Guards, who remained firm, and so repulsed the attack and saved the situation.

He was a member of the Guards' and the Royal Automobile Clubs.

CAPTAIN HENRY IRONSIDE MONEY, 1st BATTN. K.G.O. GURKHA RIFLES,

killed in action on the 20th December, 1914, at Givenchy, was the youngest son of the late Lieutenant-Colonel Ernle Edmund Money, Commandant 9th Bengal Lancers, who, like his two sons, was educated at Marlborough College. Captain Money was born on the 21st September, 1883, at Kasauli, Punjab, India. His paternal grandfather was the late Rev. William Money, of Walthamstow, and his maternal grandfather the late Major-General Henry Drummond, R.E., of Strageath. Colonel Money's career was brought to a tragic end by assassination in 1894. His eldest son—Captain Ernle Francis Drummond Money, Special Service Officer to 3rd Kashmir Rifles—was at the time fighting in East Africa.

After his education at Marlborough Captain Money entered the R.M.C., Sandhurst, as King's India Cadet in 1901, and obtained his commission in August, 1903, serving in India with Prince Albert's Somerset Light Infantry till January, 1904, when he joined the 1st Gurkha Rifles, of which he became Quartermaster. He was promoted Captain in 1911. Besides being an "Old Marlburian," Captain Money was a member of the Junior Naval and Military Club and of the United Service Institution. His recreations were hockey, golf, and tennis.

An officer of his regiment gave the following details of Captain Money's last fight: "Henry was last seen fighting most valiantly and with the greatest coolness when he was shot in the head. A Mr. Cowan, in the Highland Light Infantry, who saw him fall, told me that he must have been killed instantly. His name has, I know, gone in for the D.S.O., and richly he deserved it. Each day in the trenches he had done magnificent work with the bombers, of whom he had charge."

Another officer wrote: "Since we've been in France Henry has been in charge of our bomb-throwers, and has done magnificent work. Always cheery, never sparing himself, he was like a ray of light in the trenches, and an example any one of his brother officers and men might be proud to copy. Had he lived, as you have no doubt heard, he would have been recommended for the D.S.O., and we all hope even now that he may be granted the posthumous award of the same."

His Colonel wrote: "I think, without any exaggeration, I can say he was my right hand, and any difficult and troublesome work I was sure he would carry out ably and satisfactorily; in fact, he was quite invaluable. He was always gay and cheerful, and looked on the bright side of things. His presence was like a ray of sunshine in the regiment. . . . I cannot speak too highly of him, and I have already several times mentioned him in my reports, and he must have got a Brevet or a D.S.O. had he lived. The Indian Army has lost one of its most promising officers, and the 1st Gurkhas will never get another Henry Money."

Captain Money wrote a short history of his battalion from its formation in 1815 to the year 1910, which was published regimentally in Gurkhali and in English.

An appreciative notice appeared in "The Marlburian" (his College magazine), in the course of which was quoted the tribute of the Vicar of St. Philip's, Kensington, himself an Old Marlburian: "I, who was privileged to know him, and now mourn the loss of a most loyal and true-hearted friend, can only say that I believe he served and loved his Master Christ as faithfully as he served his King."

He had a shattered arm, the result of a shooting accident which happened in Chitral, and he lost his left eye accidentally in India, but neither loss interfered with his keenness for work or play. Captain Money was mentioned in Sir John French's Despatch of the 31st May, 1915.

2nd LIEUTENANT GEORGE BERTRAM F. MONK, 2nd BATTALION ROYAL WARWICKSHIRE REGIMENT,

was the son of Dr. Charles J. Monk, of 142 Harley Street, London, W., and was born in Wiesbaden, Germany, on the 15th September, 1891.

He was educated at St. George's School, Harpenden, Herts; graduated at the Michigan State University, U.S.A.; and was finally a student at Guy's Hospital, London, where he was in the football team. He belonged to the 28th (County of London) Battalion, (Artists' Rifles), from which he was gazetted to the Royal Warwickshire Regiment in November, 1914.

2nd Lieutenant Monk was killed in action while storming German trenches on the 18th December, 1914. Canon Rawnsley wrote a poem on his heroic death. A reredos is being placed in the Chapel of St. George's School as an abiding memorial of one whose life at school, not less than his death on the field of battle, was an inspiration to his comrades.

CAPTAIN WILLIAM GRAHAM MONTGOMERIE, 2nd BATTN. LEINSTER REGIMENT,

born at Madras in 1877, was the son of Lieutenant - Colonel Patrick Montgomerie, R.E., and a grandson of Dr. William Montgomerie, the discoverer of gutta percha, and of General William Anson McCleverty, 48th Regiment, at one time Commander-in-Chief, Madras.

Educated at Sherborne, where he won the Longmuir Prize for drawing, and at the R.M.C., Sandhurst, he received his commission in 1897, his Lieutenancy in April, 1900, and obtained his company in 1903. In 1900 he was appointed A.D.C. to Sir Courtenay Knollys, Governor of Trinidad.

He went to the Continent in September, 1914, was wounded at Prenesque, Armentières, and died thirty-six hours later on the 20th October, 1914.

Captain Montgomerie, who was an excellent shot, rider, and boxer, was a member of the Junior Naval and Military Club. He married

Kate Elizabeth, only daughter of Mr. Henry Hartland, and left one daughter, Elizabeth, age eight years.

2nd LIEUTENANT ARNULF MONTGOMERY, 3rd (attd. 2nd) BATTN. THE CONNAUGHT RANGERS,

who was killed in action on the 22nd December, 1914, was gazetted to the 3rd Battalion of his regiment as 2nd Lieutenant on probation on the 4th August, 1914.

LIEUT.-COLONEL ERNEST HENRY MONTRÉSOR, COMMANDING THE 2nd BATTN. THE ROYAL SUSSEX REGT.,

who was born on the 20th November, 1863, at Burdwan, Bengal, India, was the son of the late Charles Francis Montrésor, Bengal Civil Service, and grandson of the late General Sir Henry Tucker Montrésor, K.C.B., G.C.H., of Denne Hill, near Canterbury, Colonel of the 11th Regiment of Foot.

He was educated at Haileybury College and the R.M.C., Sandhurst, and joined the Royal Sussex Regiment as Lieutenant in February, 1884, becoming Captain in August, 1894. He served in the Soudan Expedition, the Nile (1884–5), receiving the medal with clasp and the Khedive's bronze star; in the Hazara Expedition, 1888, receiving the medal with clasp. From December, 1895, to December, 1900, he was Adjutant of the 1st Volunteer Battalion Royal Sussex Regiment. Lieutenant-Colonel Montrésor also served in the South African War, being present at operations in the Orange River and Cape Colonies from March, 1901, to January, 1902, and in the Transvaal from March to May, 1902. He was mentioned in despatches ("London Gazette," 29th July, 1902); promoted Brevet-Major in August, 1902; and received the Queen's medal with five clasps. He was promoted Substantive Major in October, 1902, and succeeded to the command of the 2nd Battalion of his regiment in February, 1911.

He was killed in action on the 14th September, 1914, when in command of his battalion at the Battle of the Aisne.

Lieutenant-Colonel Montrésor married Sarah Wilhelmina, youngest daughter of the late John Killick, of Kirby Hall, Melton Mowbray, Leicestershire, and left two children: Millicent, born 1889, who married, in 1912, Lieutenant

Geoffrey Russell Fenton, 2nd Battalion Connaught Rangers, killed in action at the Battle of the Aisne on the 20th September, 1914 ; and Joan, born 1891, who married, in 1914, 2nd Lieutenant Read, 3rd Battalion Royal Sussex Regiment.

CAPTAIN ROWLAND HARRY MAIN-WARING MOODY, 2nd BATTN. LANCASHIRE FUSILIERS,

who was reported wounded and missing after the Battle of Cambrai, has since been reported as killed in that engagement on the 26th August, 1914. He was born on the 1st May, 1875, and was educated at Charterhouse. In December, 1896, he joined the Royal Fusiliers from the Militia, becoming Lieutenant in May, 1898, and being transferred in August of the latter year to the Lancashire Fusiliers, in which regiment he was promoted Captain in October, 1900.

He took part in the South African War, being present at the relief of Ladysmith, including operations on the Tugela Heights and action at Pieter's Hill ; at operations in Natal and in the Transvaal, and received the Queen's medal with three clasps. From February, 1904, to July, 1907, he was Adjutant of the 5th Battalion (Militia) Rifle Brigade.

Captain Moody, who was a keen cricketer and frequently played in the M.C.C., married, in 1910, Sybil Marie, daughter of Lieutenant-Colonel and Mrs. Conway Bishop, of Rutland Gate, London, S.W., and left one son.

2nd LIEUTENANT GILLACHRIST MOORE, 2nd BATTN. ROYAL SUSSEX REGIMENT,

younger son of Norman Moore, M.D., F.R.C.P., was born in London on the 22nd March, 1894.

He was educated at The Oratory School, Birmingham, and St. Catherine's College, Cambridge, receiving his commission in August, 1914. He went to France in September of that year, and was killed at the edge of a wood near Klein Zillebeke, a few yards from the Germans, on the afternoon of the 7th November, 1914.

MAJOR JOHN O'HARA MOORE, ROYAL ENGINEERS,

was the younger son of the late Henry O'Hara Moore, Barrister-at-Law, and was born on the 25th June, 1877. He was educated at Cheltenham College, whence he passed direct into the R.M.A., Woolwich, at the head of the list. At Woolwich he became Senior Under Officer, and was presented with the Sword of Honour. He entered the Royal Engineers in September, 1896, becoming Lieutenant in September, 1899, and Captain in September, 1905. He was Adjutant for Musketry at the School of Military Engineering, Chatham, for some time between 1905-08.

At the outbreak of war he was serving in South Africa, whence he returned with his company and proceeded to Flanders with the VIIth Division. He was wounded when taking part in an attack on the enemy's trenches on the 18th December, 1914, and died of his wounds on the 28th of that month at Wimereux, France, where he is buried. He was very keen on all kinds of sport, especially shooting—including big game in Africa—hunting, boxing, and football, and was exceedingly popular with all those who knew him, both officers and men.

Major Moore was not married. He was a member of the Royal Zoological Society and of the Junior Naval and Military Club. He was promoted Major in October, 1914, though the announcement did not appear in the " London Gazette " till the 12th January, 1915, that is, after his death.

LIEUTENANT ROGER LUDOVIC MOORE, attd. 1st BATTN. PRINCE ALBERT'S (SOMERSET LIGHT INFANTRY),

was the third son of Dr. G. E. Moore, of Redcroft, Maidenhead.

He was born on the 12th May, 1890 ; educated at Uppingham and the R.M.C., Sandhurst ; and received a commission in the Somerset Light Infantry in March, 1911, becoming Lieutenant in April, 1914. In 1913 he qualified as Interpreter in Colloquial Pekingese. He was a good shot, horseman, and polo player.

Mr. Moore was shot in the spine while visiting his sentries in Flanders, early on the morning of the 20th December, 1914, and died the same day.

He was mentioned in Sir John French's Despatch of the 14th January, 1915, for bravery in the field.

CAPTAIN WALDO ALINGTON GWENNAP MOORE, 2nd BATTN. THE WELSH REGIMENT,

born on the 14th July, 1876, at Launceston, Cornwall, was the second son of Gwennap and Mary Moore, of Garlenick, Grampound, Cornwall.

After his education at Kelly College he proceeded to the R.M.C., Sandhurst, receiving his commission in the Welsh Regiment in 1896, and being promoted Lieutenant in 1898. He took part in the South African War, being present at the actions of Driefontein, the Vet and Zand Rivers, Diamond Hill, Belfast, and Colesberg, receiving the Queen's medal with five clasps and the King's medal with two clasps. He became Captain in 1904.

He went to France for the war on the 12th August, 1914, with his battalion, which formed part of the Ist Division of the Expeditionary Force, and took part in the retirement from Mons, the Battles of the Marne and the Aisne, and the fighting at Ypres till he was killed in action at the latter place on the 31st October, 1914.

He married, in 1907, Hilda Charlotte Phillips, and left one son, Charles Anthony Gwennap, born December, 1912.

CAPTAIN CLIVE GUISE MOORES, ROYAL ENGINEERS,

who died of wounds received in action on the 1st December, 1914, was the youngest son of Lieutenant-Colonel S. Moore, late Devonshire Regiment, who fought in the Mutiny and in the Egyptian War, 1882.

He was born on the 9th May, 1887, and entered the Royal Engineers from the R.M.A., Woolwich (passing out head of the list), in

December, 1906, becoming Lieutenant in November, 1908, and Captain in October, 1914. From January, 1911, to January, 1914, he was employed on the Boundary Delimitation Commission, Peru.

LIEUTENANT-COLONEL CHARLES BERNARD MORLAND, 2nd BATTN. WELSH REGIMENT,

who died in hospital at Ypres on the 31st October, 1914, of wounds received the previous day, was born on the 12th November, 1866.

He was gazetted to the Welsh Regiment in February, 1887, becoming Lieutenant in February, 1889, and Captain in April, 1898. He was Adjutant of his battalion from March, 1900, to March, 1904, during which period he took part in the South African War, being present at the relief of Kimberley ; at operations in the Orange Free State ; at Paardeberg ; in the Transvaal, Cape Colony, and Orange River Colony, including actions at Poplar Grove, Driefontein, Vet and Zand Rivers, near Johannesburg ; at Pretoria, Diamond Hill, Belfast, and Colebrook. For his services he was twice mentioned in Despatches (" London Gazette," 8th February and 10th September, 1901), receiving the Brevet of Major in November, 1900, the Queen's medal with six clasps, and the King's medal with two clasps.

He was promoted Substantive Major in December, 1904 ; from September, 1909, to June, 1910, was on half-pay ; and succeeded to the command of the 2nd Battalion of his regiment in March, 1914.

Lieutenant-Colonel Morland was mentioned in Sir John French's Despatches of the 8th October, 1914, and the 14th January, 1915, for his services in the Great War.

MAJOR JOHN HENRY MORRAH, 1st BATTN. THE KING'S OWN (ROYAL LANCASTER REGIMENT),

who was killed by a German sniper on the 18th October, 1914, was the youngest son of the late Colonel Morrah, formerly 60th Rifles, of Winchester.

Major Morrah was born on the 20th July, 1875, and was educated at Eastbourne College and the R.M.C., Sandhurst. He was gazetted to the Royal Lancashire Regiment in March, 1896, becoming Lieutenant in November, 1897, and Captain in May, 1901. He took part in the South African War, in which he was severely wounded, being present at operations in the Transvaal, Orange River Colony, and Cape Colony in 1901 and 1902, receiving the Queen's medal with four clasps.

From December, 1908, to October, 1910, he was an Adjutant of Indian Volunteers, and in December, 1912, was promoted Major in his regiment. For his services he was mentioned in Sir John French's Despatch of 14th January, 1915.

He married Maud Florence, youngest daughter of the late Major Cortlandt Macgregor, R.E., and left three children.

LIEUTENANT ANTHONY GEORGE ATTWOOD MORRIS, 2nd (attd. 1st) BATTN. THE KING'S OWN (ROYAL LANCASTER REGIMENT),

was the younger son of Mr. and Mrs. F. A. Morris, of Pailton House, Rugby.

He was born on the 19th May, 1887, and was educated at Stubbington and Winchester. He joined the King's Own Regiment from the Militia in December, 1907, becoming Lieutenant in April, 1911.

He was killed on tne 13th October, 1914, in an attack on the village of Meteren when in charge of a machine-gun section.

Mr. Morris was a member of the Atherstone Hunt Club, and, whilst his regiment was quartered in the island, was Whip to the Jersey Drag Hunt.

LIEUT.-COLONEL the Honble. GEORGE HENRY MORRIS, p.s.c., 1st BATTN. IRISH GUARDS,

son of the late Baron Morris and Killanin, and brother of the present peer, was born at Spiddal, County Galway, on the 16th July, 1872. Educated at The Oratory School, Birmingham, he joined the Rifle Brigade in India as 2nd Lieutenant in 1892, after having passed from the R.M.C., Sandhurst.

In 1897 he was appointed Adjutant of the 3rd Battalion Rifle Brigade, which position he held for four years, and saw active service with the Tochi Valley Expeditionary Force in 1897–98, afterwards receiving the medal with clasp. In the South African War he served with Damant's Horse in 1901–02, being present at operations in the Transvaal and Orange River Colony. He was mentioned in Despatches ("London Gazette," 18th July, 1902), and received the Queen's medal with four clasps. On the conclusion of the war he rejoined the Staff College, which he had entered in 1901, and passed out in 1903. His first Staff appointment was that of D.A.A.G. at Belfast, to which he was appointed in 1904, being transferred in the same year to the War Office as Staff Captain on the Headquarters Staff. Obtaining his Majority on transfer to the Irish Guards in March, 1906, he was next General Staff Officer at the Staff College from 1908–11, succeeding to the command of the 1st Battalion Irish Guards in July, 1913.

He took the battalion to France on the 12th August, 1914, and for his services in the Great War was mentioned in Sir John French's first Despatch of the 8th October, 1914.

On the 1st September, during the retirement from Mons, the 4th Guards Brigade formed the rearguard, and got into a very hot place in a thick wood near Villers-Cotterets. Most of the 1st Battalion Irish Guards, under Colonel Morris, got clear, but he missed half a company, and leaving the main body went back alone to look for the missing men. He succeeded in finding them, but in trying to get them out of a tight place he was killed as he stood up urging the men to charge.

Colonel Morris was recognised as one of the most brilliant lecturers in the Army, and as an authority on strategy, tactics, and military history. He was a member of the Guards' Club, the Garrick Club, and the County Galway Club.

On the 29th April, 1913, Colonel Morris married Dora Maryan, second daughter of J. Wesley Hall, of Melbourne, and left one son, Michael, born 30th July, 1914.

2nd LIEUTENANT GURTH STEPHEN MORSE, ROYAL FIELD ARTILLERY,

who died on the 9th December, 1914, of wounds received in action on the 4th of the month, was the third and youngest son of Amyas and Rose Morse, of The Bourne, Bourne End, Bucks.

He was born on the 20th March, 1894, and was educated at

Ashampstead, Eastbourne, at Clifton College, and the R.M.A., Woolwich. He was gazetted to the R.F.A. in July, 1913.

2nd LIEUTENANT GORDON THOMAS HARCOURT MORSE, 4th BATTN. THE DUKE OF CAMBRIDGE'S OWN (MIDDLESEX REGIMENT),

who was killed in action between the 12th-14th October, 1914, in his twenty-first year, was the second son of Lieutenant-Colonel R. E. Ricketts Morse, R.A.M.C., and Kathleen, his wife, of Chargrove House, near Cheltenham, and was a grandson of the late Colonel Neville Hill Shute, 64th (North Staffordshire) Regiment, formerly of Clayfield, Southampton.

He was gazetted to the Middlesex Regiment on the 8th August, 1914.

CAPTAIN GERALD HENRY WALTER MORTIMER, 10th JATS, INDIAN ARMY, attd. 9th BHOPAL INFANTRY,

was killed in action on the 23rd November, 1914, at Festubert while leading his men to capture a second trench from the enemy, one trench having been taken.

He was the son of the Rev. C. Mortimer, Canon Residentiary of Lichfield Cathedral, and was born at Pitchford, near Shrewsbury, on the 24th December, 1882. He was educated at Rossall and the R.M.C., Sandhurst, from which he passed for the Indian Army in August, 1902, and was attached for a year to the King's Own Scottish Borderers in India, being gazetted to the Indian Army in January, 1904, becoming Lieutenant in November, 1904, when he joined the 10th Jats.

He obtained the certificate of the School of Musketry, and was proficient in native dialects, speaking Hindi and Baluchi well. For some time he was Cantonment Magistrate at Hyderabad, Scinde. While with his regiment he managed the regimental hockey team, and made it very successful. At Sandhurst he won the hurdles and kept goal and played cricket. He also played cricket for the Gentlemen of Staffordshire and for the Incogniti. He was, in addition, a polo player and a good shot.

When war broke out he was at home on sick leave, and having applied for employment was sent to Tidworth to train recruits, and was also Company Officer and Instructor.

CAPTAIN PERCY LIONEL MOUBRAY, 3rd (attd. 1st) BATTN. THE BLACK WATCH (ROYAL HIGHLANDERS),

born at Otterston, Aberdour, Fife, on the 3rd August, 1872, was the son of Captain W. H. Moubray, R.N., of Otterston and Cockairnie, Fife, a grandson of Sir Robert Moubray, Kt., and a nephew of the late Colonel Babington, Brooklands, Sarisbury Green, Hants. He was educated at Loretto School, Musselburgh, and entered the Royal Highlanders in 1899, becoming Captain in May, 1904.

He served in the South African War, taking part in operations in the Orange Free State and the Orange River Colony, for which he received the Queen's medal with three clasps and the King's medal with two clasps.

In the Great War Captain Moubray was reported "missing" on the 29th October, 1914, and subsequently was unofficially reported killed.

He was a member of the Caledonian Club, London, and of the Scottish Conservative Club, Edinburgh.

CAPTAIN the Honble. ANDREW EDWARD SOMERSET MULHOLLAND, 1st BATTN. IRISH GUARDS,

born on the 20th September, 1882, at Drayton Lodge, Monkstown, County Dublin, was the eldest son of the second Baron Dunleath, of Ballywalter, County Down, J.P., High Sheriff, 1884, M.P. for North Londonderry, 1885–95, some time in the Royal Engineers and in the 5th Battalion Royal Irish Rifles.

Captain Mulholland was educated at Eton, where he was in the XI, and at Christ Church, Oxford. He joined the Irish Guards in 1906, becoming Lieutenant in January, 1909, and Captain in July, 1913. He went to France with the Expeditionary Force on the 12th August, 1914, and was present at the Battles of Mons, the Aisne, and Ypres. On the 1st November, at about 2 p.m., he was hit by a bullet while rallying his men in the trenches near Ypres, and died at 9 p.m. He was buried in the cemetery at Ypres.

Captain Mulholland was a member of the Bachelors' and Guards' Clubs. He played cricket and golf for the Army and the Household Brigade. In June, 1913, he married Lady Hester Joan Byng, youngest daughter of the fifth Earl of Strafford, and left one daughter, born March, 1915.

LIEUTENANT LIONEL FRANK HASTINGS MUNDY, "L" BATTERY, ROYAL HORSE ARTILLERY,

was the son of Lionel and Ella Tisdall Mundy, of Althrop House, Barnes, S.W., and was born at Hastings in April, 1886. He was educated at Bedale's School, and entered the Royal Military Academy, Woolwich, in 1904, becoming 2nd Lieutenant in the Royal Artillery in 1906, and Lieutenant in the R.H.A. in 1912.

This young officer was one of the heroes engaged in the most glorious incident of the early part of the war, an account of which is to be found in the biography of Captain Bradbury, V.C. (page 43–44).

The action referred to took place on the 1st September, 1914, when Lieutenant Mundy was killed.

LIEUTENANT CHRISTOPHER FOWLER MURPHY, OXFORDSHIRE AND BUCKINGHAMSHIRE LIGHT INFANTRY,

born in Dublin on the 17th May, 1889, was the son of the Rev. Richard William Murphy, M.A., T.C.D., Canon of Tuam, and Incumbent of Omey, Clifden, County Galway, and was educated at The Abbey, Tipperary, and Trinity College, Dublin.

Lieutenant Murphy was gazetted to the Royal Field Artillery (Special Reserve) in 1908, and in the following year was attached to the 35th Battery at Clonmel. In 1910 he obtained a commission as 2nd Lieutenant in the Oxfordshire and Buckinghamshire Light Infantry, joining the 1st Battalion at Wellington, Madras. He was promoted to his Lieutenancy in January, 1914. While on leave, in 1913–14, he was seconded for service, under the Colonial Office,

in West Africa, but on the declaration of war he at once volunteered for active service, and was attached to the 2nd Battalion, his own battalion being at the time in India.

He was killed on the 21st October, 1914, at the beginning of the Battle of Ypres. His C.O. wrote : " He died gallantly doing his duty in leading his men on to the attack."

An officer gave the following account of the action to his parents : " The regiment was told to attack some German infantry in position as part of the 5th Brigade on the right of its front line. Your son's company was one of the two which went forward in our front line, and our casualties occurred during the first quarter-mile of the advance, after which we were stopped in order that other troops might come up on our left. Just as this happened your son got a bullet in his shoulder—not a bad wound— and was at once dressed and made comfortable close by a haystack till a stretcher arrived, when another bullet hit him in the head, and I believe he died immediately."

Another officer wrote : " He died bravely, a brave man's death, and his last moments made me very proud of him as a brother officer, . . . even urging on some men who were coming up, and showing the greatest pluck and keenness."

HON. CAPTAIN AND QUARTERMASTER ARCHIBALD MURRAY, 2nd BATTN. THE KING'S OWN SCOTTISH BORDERERS, who was shown in the monthly casualty list published in October, 1914, as killed in action, no place or date being mentioned, was born in January, 1863.

After serving in the ranks for more than fifteen years, and as a Warrant Officer for over six years, he received his commission as Quartermaster in the King's Own Scottish Borderers in September, 1903. He served in the Chin-Lushai Expedition of 1889–90, for which he received the medal with clasp, and was promoted Honorary Captain in September, 1913.

LIEUTENANT CHARLES JOHN MURRAY, 4th (RESERVE) BATTN. COLDSTREAM GUARDS, born on the 1st December, 1881, at Taymount, Stanley, Perthshire, was the son of Charles Archibald Murray, of Taymount, and a relative of the Earl of Mansfield and of Sir Robert D. Moncrieffe.

He was educated at Haileybury, and

joined the 3rd (Militia) Battalion of the Black Watch (Royal Highlanders) in 1899, being transferred to the Coldstream Guards in 1901, and serving with them till 1912. He took part in the South African War, for which he received the King's medal. He was A.D.C. to Sir Percy Girouard, Governor of Northern Nigeria, from 1907–09, and was again with him when Governor of British East Africa from 1909–11. In 1912 he settled as a breeder of horses at Invershura Njoro, British East Africa.

On the outbreak of the war with Germany he rejoined the Coldstream Guards, and was serving with them when he was killed on the 26th October, 1914, near Ypres, when leading an attack on Poezelhoek.

Lieutenant Murray was a member of the Guards', Bachelors', and Caledonian Clubs.

2nd LIEUTENANT ERIC DENNYS MURRAY, 19th (QUEEN ALEXANDRA'S OWN ROYAL) HUSSARS,

was killed in action on the 16th October, 1914, near Le Bizet and the River Lys, in France, while on patrol duty.

He was born on the 9th March, 1893, the younger son of Sir George Sheppard Murray and Lady Murray, of Cleveland House, St. James's Square, and entered the 19th Hussars from the R.M.C., Sandhurst, in September, 1913.

CAPTAIN FANE WRIGHT STAPLETON MURRAY, 12th (PRINCE OF WALES'S ROYAL) LANCERS,

of The Moat, Charing, Kent, who was shot through the heart in the trenches near Ypres, in Belgium, on the 30th October, 1914, was the eldest son of the late Colonel and of Mrs. Gostling-Murray, of Whitton Park, Hounslow.

He was born on the 16th October, 1879 ; educated at Eton ; and was gazetted to the 12th Lancers from the Militia in December, 1899, becoming Lieutenant in October, 1900. He served in the South African War, being present at operations in the Transvaal and Cape Colony between April, 1901, and May, 1902, receiving the Queen's medal with four clasps.

Captain Murray was promoted to that rank in November, 1907. He was a member of the Cavalry Club, and his recreations were polo, hunting, and big-game shooting.

LIEUTENANT PATRICK MAXWELL MURRAY, 2nd BATTN. SHERWOOD FORESTERS (NOTTINGHAMSHIRE AND DERBYSHIRE REGIMENT),

born in London on the 24th April, 1890, was the son of Arthur Turnour Murray, Esq., of Lincoln's Inn, Barrister-at-Law, and Nora Alice, daughter of the late Hugh Maxwell, Esq. He was related to Colonel Sir Wyndham Murray, C.B., Gentleman Usher of the Scarlet Rod in the Order of the Bath, and to Keith William Murray, F.S.A., Portcullis Pursuivant at Arms.

He was educated at the Rev. W. H. Wright's Preparatory School, Gisburne House, Watford, and at Repton School, from which he went to the Royal Military Academy, Woolwich, where he was in the Sandhurst Company. He shot in his School Shooting VIII at Repton in 1906, 1907, and 1908 (in 1906 Repton won the Rapid Firing Prize), and his House (the Priory, H. Vassall, Esq.) won the House Challenge Shield for shooting in 1908 and for drill in 1907 and 1908. He joined the Sherwood Foresters as 2nd Lieutenant on the 18th September, 1909, when he was posted to the 2nd Battalion, was appointed Assistant Adjutant in April, 1911, and promoted Lieutenant on the 16th August, 1911. In this year he obtained the musketry certificate at Hythe, and qualified in Maxim-gun drill. While he was Assistant Adjutant his company won the Seymour Challenge Cup for team snap shooting at the Western Rifle Meeting in 1911, several prizes for team shooting, and, in 1912, the Evelyn Wood Cup for a time march, ending with ball firing at unknown ranges. On this occasion Lieutenant Murray commanded the winning team, and was specially commended for the manner in which he led it.

On the 20th September, 1914, near Soissons, at the Battle of the Aisne, he was killed when directing the fire of his men after they had recaptured a trench lost to the enemy. All accounts of the action agree that the 2nd Sherwoods, by their gallantry on this occasion, saved a dangerous situation.

CAPTAIN WILLIAM EDWARD MURRAY, 3rd (late 1st) BATTN. THE GORDON HIGHLANDERS,

was the son of Lieutenant-Colonel John Murray, and was born in Hong Kong, China, on the 22nd December, 1880. He was educated at

Wellington College, where he was in the First Football XI, and subsequently went to the

Royal Military College, Sandhurst.

Captain Murray was gazetted to the Gordon Highlanders, joining the 1st Battalion in March, 1900, was promoted Lieutenant in May, 1904, and passed to the Special Reserve in 1913. With the 1st battalion he served through the South African War, for which he received the Queen's medal with four clasps, and afterwards, in 1904, was employed on the West Coast of Africa. He became Captain in 1914.

When the Great War broke out Captain Murray rejoined his battalion at Aberdeen, where for some weeks he helped to guard the Wireless Station. He was sent with a draft of one hundred men to join the Gordons, who were then in the firing line at the front. On his arrival, however, he found the battalion had been so badly cut up at the Battle of Mons that they had been sent back to the base, so he and his draft were temporarily attached to the Seaforth Highlanders, and with them went forward to take part in the memorable advance from the Marne to the Aisne.

He was killed on the 14th September, about two and a half miles from the Aisne River, in some trenches which had been temporarily vacated, and which it was imperative should be not only occupied, but held, to save the Seaforths and a party of Gordons from annihilation. Addressing his men, " Come on, Gordons ! There is only a handful of us, but we will do it ! " Captain Murray with his men gained the trenches. A bullet from a shrapnel shell hit him in the head, but he lived long enough to say, " You must hold on here at all costs," and then fell dead.

When the Seaforths and their comrades were relieved, after holding the trenches for a day and a half, only seven of Captain Murray's draft were in fighting condition.

A Private, in whose arms he died, said : " Our Captain was as brave an officer as I ever saw in the firing line. . . . We would have done anything for him." Thus did this officer by his heroic conduct uphold the reputation of the famous regiment with which he was so proud to be connected.

Captain Murray married, in 1906, Lilias Caroline, only daughter of Edward Drummond, Esq., late E.I.C.S., and had three children : Edward John, born 1907 ; Sybil Lilias, born 1909 ; and Mary Katherine, born 1910.

LIEUTENANT EDWARD GEOFFREY MYDDELTON, 3rd BATTN. THE SUFFOLK REGT.,

born at Boston on the 22nd August, 1893, was the son of Mr. and Mrs. Edward Brackenbury Myddelton, of Wellingborough. He was related to the Myddeltons of Denbighshire.

He was educated at Lancing, Wellingborough, and at Jesus College, Cambridge, where he took first-class honours in the first part of the Mathematical Tripos, and was to have taken the second part in Easter term, 1915. His favourite sport was rowing. He was in the O.T.C., and on leaving the University received his commission in the Special Reserve of Officers in June, 1913, being gazetted Lieutenant after his death. He was attached to the 2nd Battalion for active service, and took part in the retirement from Mons.

He was reported to have been killed at Le Cateau on the 26th August, 1914, but no details have been ascertained, as all the surviving men who were near him are prisoners of war in Germany.

2nd LIEUTENANT JAMES ROBERTSON JACK MYLLES, M.A., 3rd (RESERVE) BATTN. HIGHLAND LIGHT INFANTRY,

who was killed in action in Flanders on the 30th December, 1914, was the younger son of Charles and Mary Loudon Mylles, 86, Stevenson Drive, Shawlands, Glasgow. He was born on the 4th March, 1893, at Glasgow, and was educated at Allan Glen's School, Glasgow, afterwards becoming a graduate in Arts and a student of Medicine at Glasgow University. He was in his University O.T.C., and on the outbreak of war in August, 1914, was gazetted 2nd Lieutenant on probation in the 3rd Battalion Highland Light Infantry. At the end of December, 1914, he took a draft for the Devonshire Regiment to the front, and was himself attached for active service to the 1st Battalion Gordon Highlanders.

He was fond of golf, and was a member of University and Cowglen Golf Clubs.

MAJOR LORD CHARLES GEORGE FRANCIS MERCER-NAIRNE, M.V.O., 1st (ROYAL) DRAGOONS (EQUERRY TO THE KING),

killed in action in Flanders on the 30th October, 1914, was the second son of the fifth Marquess of Lansdowne and the Marchioness of Lansdowne, daughter of the Duke of Abercorn, K.G. Lord Charles derived his surname of Mercer-Nairne, which he assumed in January, 1914, in lieu of his patronymic of Fitzmaurice, from his maternal grandmother, Emily Jane Mercer, Baroness Nairne.

He was born on the 12th February, 1874, and joined the 1st Dragoons from the Militia in May, 1895, becoming Lieutenant in February, 1898, and Captain in 1901. He acted as A.D.C. to the General Officer Commanding the Forces in Ireland from May to October, 1899, and then took part in the South African War, being present at the relief of Ladysmith, including the action at Colenso, at operations on the Tugela Heights, in the Orange Free State and in Natal, and at actions at Spion Kop, Vaal Krans, and Pieter's Hill. He received the Queen's medal with four clasps. In October, 1898, he had qualified as an Interpreter in French. From January, 1901, to February, 1904, he was A.D.C. to the Commander-in-Chief ; and from April, 1909, to May, 1910, he was Equerry to H.R.H. the Prince of Wales. In June, 1910, he was appointed Equerry to His Majesty the King, and was promoted Major in June of the latter year.

Lord Charles married, in January, 1909, Lady Violet Mary Elliot-Murray-Kynynmound, youngest daughter of the fourth Earl of Minto, and left two children : Mary Margaret Elizabeth (for whom Queen Mary was sponsor), born in February, 1910 ; and George Charles Mercer (for whom King George V was sponsor), born in November, 1912.

CAPTAIN NORMAN NEILL, 13th HUSSARS, BRIGADE-MAJOR, 6th CAVALRY BRIGADE, 3rd CAVALRY DIVISION,

youngest son of the late Robert Neill and Mrs. Neill, was born near Manchester on the 22nd December, 1880.

He was educated at Harrow, and was gazetted to the 19th Hussars from the Militia in 1902 during the South African War, in which he took part, being present at operations in the Transvaal, Orange River Colony and Cape Colony,

receiving the Queen's medal with four clasps. He was Adjutant of his regiment for five

months in 1910, and was promoted into the 13th Hussars as Captain in July, 1910. In 1912 he passed into the Staff College, and he was also qualified as an Interpreter in French. In September, 1914, he was appointed Brigade-Major of the Household Cavalry Brigade, and was killed on the 6th November, 1914, near Klein Zillebeke, when the French gave way under overwhelming numbers of the enemy. The Cavalry Brigade advanced and held their ground. Captain Neill was hit when taking a message to his Brigade to advance, and leading them on.

The General Commanding the Brigade wrote : " The French on our right had suddenly given way, and we were sent to stop the retreat, which we were successfully doing when he was killed. I had just sent him on a message to order a further advance, and it was when returning from this that he was hit."

Sir John French, in his Despatch of the 20th November, 1914, particularly commended the work of the Cavalry Brigade under Brigadier-General Kavanagh, and Captain Neill was himself subsequently mentioned in the Despatch of the 14th January, 1915.

He married Eleanor de Courcy, daughter of the late Major-General Sir Gerald de Courcy Morton, K.C.I.E., C.B., and left one daughter, Audrey, age three years.

Captain Neill was a member of the Cavalry Club.

CAPT. ARNOLD STEARNS NESBITT, 3rd BATTN. WORCESTERSHIRE REGT.,

was the eldest son of the late William Henry and Mrs. Nesbitt, of Oatlands Drive, Weybridge, and was born at Walton-on-Thames on the 16th November, 1878. He was educated at Bradfield College, Berkshire. Captain Nesbitt

joined the Worcestershire Regiment from the Militia in 1900, becoming Lieutenant in that year and Captain in November, 1904. When

Adjutant of the 6th Battalion at the depot at Norton Barracks, Worcester, he organised a Military Tournament at the Skating Rink, which owing to his energies and foresight, as well as his tact and courtesy, was a great success.

He was employed with the Egyptian Army in 1907–08.

He was killed in action on the 7th November, 1914, at Ploegsteert, Belgium. An officer who had known him throughout his military career said he was one of the best officers the regiment had ever had. He was mentioned in Sir John French's Despatch of the 14th January, 1915. Captain Nesbitt was a good cricketer, having been a member of the Incognito, the Worcestershire County, and the Gentlemen of Worcester's Cricket Clubs. In 1914 he played for Worcestershire against Middlesex at Lord's. He was also well known in the hunting field. The news of his death was received with the greatest regret by his numerous military and civilian friends. He was unmarried.

LIEUT. GORDON STUART NESS, 3rd (attd. 1st) BATTN. ROYAL SCOTS FUSILIERS,

late of Lloyd's, who was killed in action in Northern France on the 10th - 11th November, 1914, was the youngest and only surviving son of the late Patrick Ness, of Braco Castle, Perthshire.

He joined the 3rd Battalion in April, 1906, and was promoted Lieutenant in December, 1909.

2nd LIEUTENANT JOHN HENRY GAY-THORNE NEVILL, SPECIAL RESERVE, (attd. 3rd BATTN.) GRENADIER GUARDS,

who was killed on the 24th December, 1914, was the son of the late Mr. Henry M. Nevill, of Mettingham, Suffolk, and of Mrs. Henry Nevill.

2nd Lieutenant Nevill, who was married, was attached to the 3rd Battalion Grenadier Guards, on probation, on the 15th August, 1914.

MAJOR LIONEL JOHN NEVILLE NEVILLE, ROYAL ENGINEERS,

who died on the 17th December, 1914, at the Casino Hospital, Boulogne, from wounds received near Bailleul on the 30th November, 1914, was the younger son of the late James Sewell Neville, late Judge of the High Court, Calcutta, of Sloley Hall, Norfolk, and Mrs. Neville, of 7, Mulberry Walk, Chelsea. He was a brother of R. J. N. Neville, M.P.

He was born at Calcutta on the 5th March, 1878, and was educated at Charterhouse, where he obtained prizes and senior scholarships; and passed into the R.M.A., Woolwich, in 1895, from which he received his commission in the Royal Engineers in September, 1897. He was promoted Lieutenant in September, 1900, and took part in the South African War, 1900-02, being present at operations in the Orange River Colony, including actions at Biddulphsberg and Wittebergen, and in the Transvaal. For his services in that campaign he received the Queen's medal with three clasps and the King's medal with two clasps. He was promoted Captain in September, 1906, and to his Majority in October, 1914, but his promotion was not gazetted until January, 1915, after his death.

In October, 1914, he went to Boulogne with other Royal Engineers and Royal Army Medical Corps officers to organise base hospitals, and was largely responsible for the organisation, adaptation, and equipment of the Maritime Hospital on the Quay, the Casino Hospital, and other hospitals in Boulogne and Wimereux. In November he was sent to the front to join the 5th Field Company, R.E., and on the last day of the month was transferred to the 56th Company. Within an hour of his arrival on duty in the firing zone at Kemmel he was wounded by a chance bullet, which after passing through his chest lodged in the heart of his brother officer, Captain Moores, R.E. He himself chose to be nursed in the Casino Hospital, where he died, that he might himself, as he said, test whether his work there was well done. He was buried at Sloley, Norfolk, with military honours on the 22nd December, 1914.

Major Neville, who was a most popular officer, married Agnes Lillian Fife, youngest daughter of the late Major-General Blewitt, and left two young daughters.

He was a member of the Army and Navy Club, and was a good lawn tennis player.

2nd LIEUTENANT JOHN WILLIAM HARFORD NICHOLL, 3rd (attd. 2nd) BATTN. WELSH REGIMENT,

born at Hendrefoilan, Swansea, on the 24th October, 1892, was the elder son of Lieutenant-Colonel John I. D. Nicholl, of Merthyr Mawr, Bridgend, Glamorgan, and a great-nephew of Major-General C. R. H. Nicholl, Colonel Commanding 1st Battalion Rifle Brigade.

He was educated at Eton and the R.M.C., Sandhurst, which he represented against the Royal Military Academy, Woolwich, in the sports of 1912. He was gazetted to the Rifle Brigade in 1913, and resigned his commission in June, 1914. In August he was gazetted to the 3rd Battalion Welsh Regiment, and was on active service with the 2nd Battalion when he was killed at Gheluvelt, five miles east of Ypres, on the 29th October, 1914, while retaking trenches which had been captured by the Germans.

2nd Lieutenant Nicholl was fond of hunting, shooting, and winter sports.

2nd LIEUTENANT ARTHUR KNIGHT NICHOLSON, 18th (QUEEN MARY'S OWN) HUSSARS,

was the only son of Herbert and Stella Nicholson, of Bidborough Hall, Tunbridge Wells, and was born at Helena, Montana, U.S.A., on the 6th October, 1893.

He was educated at St. Andrew's, Southborough, at Harrow, and the R.M.C., Sandhurst; and was gazetted to his regiment in January, 1913. After joining the Army he showed promise of becoming a good polo player.

He was killed by a sniper at 6 a.m. on the 31st October, 1914, while holding a very advanced trench near St. Eloi, Belgium.

CAPTAIN HUNTLY WARWICK NICHOLSON, 1st (attd. 3rd) BATTN. THE CHESHIRE REGIMENT,

who was killed in action on the 14th November, 1914, was the eldest son of Fleet-Surgeon and Mrs. Howard Nicholson, of Aulay, Kidbrook Grove, Blackheath, and a grandson of the late Captain Huntly Nicholson, The Grenadier

Guards. His maternal grandfather, Captain Pringle Green, was promoted from Midshipman to Lieutenant for gallantry at Trafalgar.

Capt. H. W. Nicholson was born on the 22nd January, 1889, and was educated at St. Helen's College, Southsea, and the R.M.C., Sandhurst. He was gazetted to the Cheshire Regiment on the 10th February, 1909, becoming Lieutenant in October, 1912, and was promoted Captain on the 15th November, 1914—two days before his death—and subsequently antedated to August, 1914.

Captain Nicholson had been Brigade Machine Gun Officer, and was killed whilst firing—on the last day of the first Battle of Ypres—by a "Jack Johnson" at Wulverghem, West Flanders. His devoted servant, Walter Deeks, who had been nearly six years in his service, and not allowed to go out with his master, was heartbroken on hearing of his death, and immediately volunteered for the front, found his beloved master's grave, and erected a beautiful cross to his memory. He has since been promoted to Corporal in the Cheshire Regiment.

Captain Nicholson was beloved by officers and men alike. He was absolutely thorough, and it was said of him in the Cheshire Regiment: "Nicholson could always be depended upon in everything."

He was a good all-round sportsman and a splendid shot, his name being on two silver shields at the R.M.C., Sandhurst. He won three silver cups for shooting in one year in the Cheshire Regiment, viz., the Regimental Challenge Cup, the Officers' Cup, and the Subalterns' Cup.

LIEUT. LAURANCE CAIL NICHOLSON, D.S.O., LATE LIEUT. 14th (KING'S) HUSSARS, 3rd (attd. 1st) BATTN. PRINCESS CHARLOTTE OF WALES'S (ROYAL BERKSHIRE REGIMENT),

who died in France on the 2nd November, 1914, of wounds received in action near Ypres on the 23rd October, was the fourth son of Frederick W. Nicholson, of Shiplake, late of Maidenhead.

He was born on the 30th August, 1882,

and educated at Uppingham. He joined the 14th Hussars in March, 1902, and served in the Boer War. He was promoted Lieutenant in January, 1905, and, having retired from the active list in 1907, was appointed Lieutenant in the 3rd Battalion Royal Berkshire Regiment in July, 1910. His recreations were polo, golf, and point-to-point racing.

For his services in the Great War he was awarded the D.S.O., the official record in the " London Gazette " of the 1st December, 1914, being as follows :—

" Led and commanded his platoon admirably during an attack on German position, Passchendaele-Becelaere Road, which resulted in the taking of the enemy's trenches and seventy prisoners. (Has since died of his wounds.)"

CAPTAIN FRANK SCOBELL NISBET, ADJUTANT 2nd BATTN. MANCHESTER REGT.,

was born at St. Luke's Vicarage, Gloucester, on the 22nd November, 1878, the son of Canon Nisbet, of Ickham Rectory, Canterbury, and nephew of the Venerable E. C. Scobell, Archdeacon of Gloucester.

He was educated at The Grange, Folkestone, at Winchester College, and at the R.M.C., Sandhurst, where he was Captain of the Association football team, and was also in the Cricket XI. He was a member of the M.C.C., the Free Foresters, and B.B. Clubs. He played for the Aldershot Command XI, United Services XI at Portsmouth, and Channel Islands XI while quartered at these places. In 1896 he won the Singles Tournament of the Royal Cinque Ports Golf Club, Deal.

Captain Nisbet joined the Manchester Regiment in 1898, becoming Lieutenant in July, 1899, and Captain in July, 1901. He served in the South African War in charge of the Ammunition Column of the 17th Brigade, and took part in the operations resulting in the surrender of the Boer forces in the Caledon Valley on the 1st August, 1900. He was with the 2nd Battalion of his regiment in the subsequent operations in the north-east of the Orange River Colony. On the conclusion of the war he was awarded the Queen's medal with three clasps and the King's medal with two clasps.

He was appointed Adjutant of his battalion in December, 1912, and in that capacity accompanied it to the front. He was killed on the 26th August, 1914, at Le Cateau, while leading a company whose Captain had been put out of action. He was mentioned in Field-Marshal Sir John French's Despatch of the 8th October, 1914.

Captain Nisbet was a member of the Junior United Service Club.

LIEUTENANT GERARD FERRERS NIXON, ROYAL FIELD ARTILLERY,

who was killed in action on the 24th October, 1914, was the youngest son of Major-General Nixon, D.L., late R.A., and Mrs. Nixon, of Clone, Ballyragget, County Kilkenny.

He was born on the 25th January, 1891, and educated at Cheltenham College and the R.M.A., Woolwich, from which he entered the R.A. in December, 1910, becoming Lieutenant in December, 1913. He was a good all-round sportsman, and rode very well. He went out with the first Expeditionary Force to France for the Great War, and was acting as Observation Officer in an advanced position when he was killed in a sudden night attack by the enemy in France. He was mentioned in Sir John French's Despatch of the 14th January, 1915.

CAPTAIN RUPERT HENRY NOLAN, ROYAL ARMY MEDICAL CORPS,

who was killed in action on the 21st October, 1914, was born on the 22nd November, 1881, and joined the Royal Army Medical Corps in January, 1909, becoming Captain in July, 1912.

LIEUTENANT RAYMOND PHILIP DRUMMOND NOLAN, 3rd (attd. 1st) BATTN. THE BLACK WATCH (ROYAL HIGHLANDERS),

of Ballinderry, Tuam, County Galway, who was killed near Veldhoek by machine gun fire while leading an attack on the 3rd November, 1914, was the eldest son of the late Philip Nolan, I.C.S., and Mrs. Philip Nolan.

He was born on the 1st July, 1883, in India, and was educated at Beaumont, Stonyhurst, and New College, Oxford, where he got his double half-blue, and was called to the Bar, Inner Temple, in 1908. He joined the Black Watch in May, 1907, becoming Lieutenant in April, 1910.

He was an International at hockey, and champion of Connaught and Galway at tennis.

Lieutenant Nolan succeeded his uncle—Lieutenant-Colonel J. P. Nolan, M.P.—in the Ballinderry Estate in 1912, and in the following year married the eldest daughter of Mr. C. A. O'Connor, Master of the Rolls in Ireland, and left one son, Anthony, born 7th September, 1914. He was a member of the Travellers' and Isthmian Clubs, and of the United Service Club, Dublin.

2nd LIEUTENANT MERVYN NOOTT, 1st BATTN. THE BUFFS (EAST KENT REGIMENT),

was the son of W. M. Noott, Esq., M.R.C.S., L.R.C.P., L.S.A., and Louisa Noott, daughter of the late Sir Alfred Hickman, Bart., and was born in London on the 17th May, 1890.

He was educated at a private school at Llandudno and at Fauconberg School, Beccles. 2nd Lieutenant Noott had hoped to enter the Army in the usual way, but an attack of illness soon after boyhood left him too delicate to enter Sandhurst under the age rules, so he joined the Special Reserve in 1911, from which he was gazetted to the Buffs (Regular Army) as 2nd Lieutenant in May, 1913.

He had taken up aviation, had gained flying certificates for both monoplane and biplane, and had hoped to join the Royal Flying Corps when the war broke out, but he was required to accompany his battalion to the front.

He was killed in action on the 20th October, 1914, at Radinghem Wood, near Lille, in France.

2nd Lieutenant Noott was a member of the United Sports Club, Whitehall, and of the Kingsgate Golf Club.

MAJOR HAROLD HENRY NORMAN, 1st BATTN. NORTHAMPTONSHIRE REGIMENT,

who was killed on the 11th November, 1914, near Ypres, while in temporary command of his battalion, resisting the advance of the Prussian Guard, was the eldest son of the late Henry John Norman and of Mrs. Norman, of 55, Eccleston Square, London. He was born on the 23rd December, 1867, and was educated at Aldin House, Slough, at Eton, and the R.M.C., Sandhurst, from which he was gazetted to the Northamptonshire Regiment in September, 1887, becoming Lieutenant in August, 1890.

He took part in the reconnaissance of the Saran Sar in the Tirah Expedition of 1897–98, in the action of the 9th November, 1897, and in the operations in the Bara Valley in December, 1897 ; while in March and April, 1898, he was Adjutant and Quartermaster of native troops at the Base Depot. For his services in the expedition he received the medal with two clasps.

He was promoted Captain in January, 1899, from September, 1905, to March, 1908, was a Brigade-Major in India, and during February and March of the latter year was D.A.Q.M.G. of the Bazar Valley Field Force during the operations in the Zakka Khel country, north-western frontier of India. For his services he received the medal with clasp. From March, 1908, to September, 1909, he was a D.A.A.G. in India, having received his Majority in June of the latter year. Major Norman returned to England in 1911, and served at the depot of his regiment for three years.

In the early part of the Great War he had been slightly wounded, but the injury was not severe enough to cause him to relinquish his duties.

He married, in September, 1899, Beatrice Charlotte, daughter of the Rev. Henry Wood, at Folkestone. She died suddenly in April, 1914.

Major Norman, who was a member of the Windham Club, made many friends during his tour of service at the depot of his regiment at Northampton, where he won the respect of all by his soldierly qualities and charming personality.

LIEUTENANT STUART SHERIDAN NORMAN, 1st BATTN. THE MANCHESTER REGIMENT,

who was killed in action on the 20th-21st December, 1914, was the only son of Colonel W. W. Norman, late 22nd Cavalry, Indian Army, and grandson of the late Lieutenant-General Sir Francis Norman, and of Major-General Sir Oliver Newmarch.

He was born on the 10th November, 1889, and was educated at Cheltenham and the R.M.C., Sandhurst, obtaining his commission in the Manchester Regiment in September, 1909, and being promoted Lieutenant in August, 1913. He was posted to the 1st Battalion with which he served in the Great War.

MAJOR CHARLES NAPIER NORTH, ROYAL ENGINEERS,

was born at Bristol on the 16th August, 1873, the eldest son of the late Colonel Roger North, R.A., and Mrs. North, of Briarwood, Camberley. His great-grandfather—Captain Roger North, 50th Regiment—fought in the Peninsula, and died, after his retirement, from the effect of wounds received in that campaign. His grandfather—Colonel Charles Napier North (godson of Sir Charles Napier)—was in the 60th Regiment (King's Royal Rifle Corps), which he commanded for some time, and was mentioned in Despatches for services in the Mutiny. He was also present at the taking of the Taku Forts, China.

Major North was educated at Radley, where he held a scholarship ; and at the R.M.A., Woolwich, from which he joined the Royal Engineers in 1893, becoming Lieutenant in February, 1896, and Captain in 1904. He served in the South African War, being present at operations in the Orange Free State, the Transvaal, Orange River Colony, and Cape Colony, afterwards being employed on the Staff under the Director of Military Intelligence, South Africa, from May to August, 1902. For his services in this campaign he received the Queen's medal with three clasps and the King's medal with two clasps.

Major North, who was promoted to that rank in July, 1913, was a member of the Army and Navy Club, Pall Mall. He was a good cricketer, and as a young officer played for the R.E. XI at Chatham.

When the war with Germany broke out he was in command of the 5th Company Royal Engineers stationed at Aldershot, and went to France with the rest of the IInd Division early in August. He was shot by a sniper on the 1st November, 1914, while superintending the erection of wire entanglements at Zonnebeke during the first Battle of Ypres. His company suffered terribly, and between August and December lost four officers killed, and two severely wounded, while the casualties among the men were very heavy. A high percentage of the latter have received the D.C.M.

Major North was mentioned in Sir John French's Despatch of the 14th January, 1915, for conspicuous gallantry. He married, in December, 1913, Norah, daughter of the late Colonel Gribbon. A daughter was born, after his death, in March, 1915.

LIEUT. KENNETH CROFT NORTH, 4th (QUEEN'S OWN) HUSSARS,

who was killed on the 31st October, 1914, was born at Headingley, Leeds, Yorkshire, on the 31st March, 1887, the son of Arthur North, Solicitor, Leeds, and his wife, Mary Fearnley North. He was a grandson of William North, Solicitor, Leeds, and of Samuel Croft, Gledhow Hall, Leeds.

He was educated at Rugby and the R.M.C., Sandhurst, from which he joined his regiment in South Africa in September, 1907, remaining in the Colony for two years. He became Lieutenant in January, 1910.

From the commencement of the Great War till he was killed on the 31st October, Lieutenant North had commanded the machine guns of the 4th Hussars. The following incidents of good service on his part were reported :—

(a) On the 25th August he remained behind his brigade to right a gun wagon, which had been overturned. Under heavy shell fire he succeeded in bringing it and his guns away.

(b) On the 1st September, during a rearguard action, Lieutenant-Colonel Hogg, D.S.O. (subsequently killed in action), was wounded in a wood in the rear fighting line. Lieutenant North took back his wagon when the Germans were at short range, and brought Lieutenant-Colonel Hogg into Huramont Village.

(c) On his own initiative on October 17th, the day after the 4th Hussars had driven the Germans out of Baswarneton, Lieutenant North returned to Baswarneton, climbed the church tower, and made a sketch of the German trenches south of Warneton, and this sketch was forwarded, per 2nd Cavalry Division, for use of the Artillery.

(d) At Hollebeke on the 30th October, after the 5th Lancers had retired, the right of the Company 129th Baluchis was attacked, and this company retired also. Lieutenant North was left isolated with his Maxim-gun detachment. He procured a wheelbarrow, and got both his guns and the men of his detachment away, covering the retirement for over a mile.

(e) On the 31st October at the Canal Bridge, north of Hollebeke, our squad, 4th Hussars, and the M.G. detachment were shelled by sixteen guns and attacked by infantry. The enemy were unable to reach the bridge largely owing to Lieutenant North's handling of his machine guns. One of these was knocked to bits, and Lieutenant North was killed in his gun trench while covering a change of position of his fellow-officer and men. The bridge remained in our possession till the 4th Hussars were relieved.

Lieutenant North was mentioned for his conspicuous bravery in Sir John French's Despatch of the 14th January, 1915.

Lieutenant North, who was a member of the Cavalry Club, married Frances Evelyn, daughter of Henry Berry, of Moor Allerton, Leeds, and left no family.

LIEUTENANT ALFRED NORTHEY, 4th BATTN. WORCESTERSHIRE REGT.,

was the younger son of the late Rev. Alfred Northey and of Mrs. Northey, of Lisworney, Torquay. He was a grandson of Colonel W. B. Northey, Coldstream Guards, and cousin of Colonel Northey, 60th Rifles, recently appointed extra A.D.C. to the King, and of Major W. Northey, D.S,O., p.s.c., Durham Light Infantry, who died at Boulogne on the 21st October, 1914, of wounds received in the present war. Lieutenant Northey's elder brother, Captain W. B. Northey, is in the 1st Gurkhas.

The subject of this memoir was born at the Vicarage, Rickmansworth, Herts, on the 10th September, 1886, and was educated at Rottingdean, Sherborne College, at Hanover, and the R.M.C., Sandhurst; later he passed as an Interpreter in German.

He joined his regiment on the 14th March, 1906, and became Lieutenant in October, 1908. For two years he was stationed with his battalion in Malta, and went with it to Bareilly, India, in 1908. He returned to England in 1911, and spent three years at the depot, Worcester.

After the war broke out he was sent as Machine Gun Officer to train Reservists at Tregantle, Cornwall, and was there until the end of August, when he took a draft of Reservists to St. Nazaire, the base, where he remained until the 17th September, when he joined his battalion at the front. He was killed with a brother officer on the 12th October, 1914, by Maxim-gun fire during desperate fighting, when the British were quite outnumbered by Bavarians. This took place at Richebourg St. Vaast, close to Bethune. He was buried there next day.

Lieutenant Northey was mentioned in Field-Marshal Sir John French's Despatch of the 14th January, 1915.

The following memoir of this officer appeared in the "Worcester Journal" of the 24th October, 1914 :—

" Lieutenant Northey was well known in military and sporting circles in the city and country, and was well liked for his social qualities and accomplishments. He was an excellent musician, and played the violin at the concerts of the Worcester Orchestral Society. He was also a good linguist, and was a capable hockey player at one time, playing for the county at centreback. In India he played in the 'All-India Tournament,' and was an all-round sportsman, hunting as regularly as possible, and taking an active interest in all sport. He was a well-known figure in local cricket, and was seen in the depot team and in the Worcester Gentlemen's team."

Lieutenant Northey was not married.

MAJOR WILLIAM NORTHEY, D.S.O., p.s.c., 2nd BATTN. DURHAM LIGHT INFANTRY,

who died on the 22nd October, 1914, of wounds received in action, leaving a widow, was the son of the late Rev. E. W. Northey and Mrs. Northey, of Woodcote House, Epsom. An uncle of Major Northey — Lieutenant-Colonel F. W. Northey—was killed in the Zulu War while in command of the 3rd Battalion King's Royal Rifle Corps ; while a brother—Lieutenant-Colonel E. Northey, 1st Battalion King's Royal Rifle Corps—was wounded in the Battle of the Aisne in the Great War.

Major Northey was born on the 29th January, 1876, and joined the Durham Light Infantry in September, 1895, becoming Lieutenant in December, 1896.

He served in the South African War, during which he was Brigade Signalling Officer (graded Staff Captain) from November, 1899, to April, 1900, and Division Signalling Officer (graded Staff Captain) from April, 1900, to November, 1900. He was present at the relief of Ladysmith and Battle of Colenso ; at operations and actions at Vaal Krans ; at operations on the Tugela Heights, Natal; and in the Transvaal in 1900, including actions at Pieter's Hill and Laing's Nek. He served as Adjutant, 13th Battalion Mounted Infantry, from November, 1900, to March, 1902, and was present at further operations in the Transvaal, in the Orange River Colony, and on the Zululand frontiers of Natal. For his services he was twice mentioned in Despatches ("London Gazette," 8th February, 1901, and 29th July, 1902); was awarded the D.S.O., and received the Queen's medal with five clasps and the King's medal with two clasps.

He was promoted Major from the 21st October, 1914, the promotion being gazetted after his death.

CAPTAIN JOHN NORWOOD, V.C., (RESERVE OF OFFICERS), 2nd COUNTY OF LONDON YEOMANRY, attd. 5th DRAGOON GUARDS,

was killed in action on the 8th September, 1914.

The son of Mr. and Mrs. John Norwood, he was born on the 8th September, 1876, at Beckenham, Kent, and educated at The Abbey, Beckenham; at Rugby; and at Exeter College, Oxford. He entered the Army as a University candidate in 1899, joined the 5th Dragoon Guards in India, and went with them to South Africa in the autumn of that year. He served through the South African War, being present at operations in Natal, including actions at Elandslaagte and Lombard's Kop; the defence of Ladysmith, including the sortie of the 7th December, 1899; and the action of the 6th January, 1900. He also took part in operations in the Transvaal in 1900, 1901, and 1902; in the Orange River Colony; and on the Zululand frontier of Natal. He was awarded the V.C. for rescuing a Trooper under heavy fire near Ladysmith on the 30th October, 1899; received the Queen's medal with four clasps and the King's medal with two clasps.

He was Adjutant of the Calcutta Light Horse, 1904–06, and retired from the active list, joining the 2nd County of London Yeomanry (Westminster Dragoons) in February, 1911. When the war broke out he rejoined his regiment, the 5th D.G.'s., on mobilisation. He was in the retirement from Mons, and fell in the Battle of the Marne at Sablonnières whilst trying to help a wounded Sergeant.

Captain Norwood married, in 1904, Lilian, daughter of Major-General Sir Edwin Collen, K.C.I.E., C.B., and left two sons and a daughter. He was a member of the Cavalry Club, and his recreations were hunting, shooting, and tennis.

LIEUTENANT RICHARD FRANCIS ROBERT NUGENT, RESERVE OF OFFICERS, 2nd BATTN. SCOTS GUARDS,

of Ballymacoll, Dunboyne, County Meath, was, it is believed, killed in France on the 18th December, 1914.

He was the only surviving son of the late Hon. Richard Anthony Nugent, who died in 1912 (the youngest son of the ninth Earl of Westmeath), of Stacumny, Celbridge, County Kildare. Lieutenant Nugent was thus a grandson of the ninth Earl, and his mother was Theresa, eldest daughter of the late Richard Gradwell, Esq., of Dowth Hall, Drogheda.

Born on the 3rd October, 1884, he was educated at The Oratory, Edgbaston. He had always intended to serve in the Army, but while preparing for the examination for the Royal Military College, Sandhurst, he contracted a severe attack of typhoid fever, which prevented his competing. He was, however, permitted, after recovering, to join the Scots Guards on probation in 1906, and, after two years, was gazetted a 2nd Lieutenant in August, 1908.

After nearly five years' service on the active list, Lieutenant Nugent retired from the Army in March, 1911, and voluntarily went into the Special Reserve of the Scots Guards and into the Reserve of Officers. On the Great War breaking out he offered his services, which were accepted, and after a short training at Warley and Sandown he embarked for France early in November, 1914, to join his old battalion. During the night of the 18th-19th December, 1914, there was a severe attack by us on the enemy, and Lieutenant Nugent when last seen was encouraging his men, and standing on the top of a German trench between Fleurbaix and Fromelles, to which place he had penetrated. He is believed to have fallen while gallantly leading some of his platoon forward to attack the enemy. Every enquiry has been made concerning him, but no trace can be found in any of the prisoners' camps in Germany.

Lieutenant Nugent, who was a member of the Guards' Club, also of the Bachelors', London, and the Kildare Street Club, Dublin, was very fond of hunting and racing; he was first whip to the Household Brigade Drag, hunted with many packs of foxhounds in England and Ireland, and also rode in the Brigade Point-to-point races.

He was not married.

LIEUTENANT CHARLES FRANCIS NUNNELEY, 3rd (attd. 1st) BATTN. NORTHUMBERLAND FUSILIERS,

was the youngest surviving son of the Rev. F. B. Nunneley, M.D., and was born on the 31st December, 1883, at Rennington Vicarage, Alnwick, Northumberland. Educated at Malvern College, he joined the 3rd Battalion Royal West Kent Regiment (Militia) as 2nd Lieutenant in May, 1903, being transferred to the 2nd Battalion Northumberland Fusiliers (Regulars) in May, 1905. In March, 1907, he retired from the Army, and at the outbreak of war was working with the Agricultural Organisation Society, becoming the first Secretary of the North Eastern Branch, where his services were much valued.

He rejoined the Army in the 3rd Battalion Northumberland Fusiliers in August, 1914; for a short time was attached to the 2nd Battalion King's Own Yorkshire Light Infantry; and finally attached to the 1st Battalion Northumberland Fusiliers in October, 1914.

The following particulars of his death were received by telegram from the Officer Commanding Northumberland Fusiliers: "Lieutenant Nunneley met his death as follows at Neuve Chapelle on the 26th October, 1914. The enemy had captured a trench in which was a gun. He attempted to recapture the trench by crawling through a wire fence, which was about thirty yards from the enemy. His men got hung up in the wire, and Lieutenant Nunneley calmly stood up, encouraging and directing them regardless of all personal risks, and was shot at close quarters by the enemy."

For his services he was mentioned in Sir John French's Despatch of the 14th January, 1915. Lieutenant Nunneley was a Fellow of the Royal Geographical Society, and held the Society's diploma for geographical surveying. He was also interested in church architecture, and took hundreds of photographs in many churches, minsters, cathedrals, and abbeys in England, some of which have been published in various books by Mr. Francis Bond. He was a member of the St. Andrews Golf Club, the "Royal and Ancient," before joining that of Sheringham.

Lieutenant Nunneley married Margery, daughter of the Hon. John Mansfield, and niece of Lord Sandhurst, and left one son, Robin Michael Charles, born at Sheringham, Norfolk, 11th October, 1911.

CAPTAIN AUBREY ULICK MARSHALL O'BRIEN, ROYAL FIELD ARTILLERY,

who was killed in action on the 1st November, 1914, was the son of the late Edward O'Brien, of Cahirmoyle, Ardagh, County Limerick, and Julia (*née* Marshall), his wife, and was born on the 7th June, 1882.

He was educated at Marlborough (Mitre, 1895–99), and was gazetted to the R.F.A. from the Militia in December, 1903, becoming Lieutenant in December, 1906.

He passed out of the R.M.A., Woolwich, in 1900, for the Royal Engineers, but ill-health prevented his accepting his commission. After recovering he joined the Militia, so as to enter the Army as he had intended. He was one of a large number of officers of the Royal Field Artillery promoted to be Captains on the 30th October, 1914. His brother, Mr. Dermod O'Brien, is President of the Royal Hibernian Academy, and an hon. member of the Royal Academy. ("The Times," 19th November, 1914.)

CAPTAIN HUGH CONOR HENRY O'BRIEN, 1st (attd. 2nd) BATTN. ROYAL MUNSTER FUSILIERS,

who was killed in action near La Bassée, France, on the 22nd December, 1914, was the son of Lieutenant-Colonel A. O'Brien, Royal Army Medical Corps, and was born on the 19th November, 1880.

He was educated at Stonyhurst, and joined the Royal Munster Fusiliers in August, 1900. He was almost immediately on active service in South Africa, being present at operations in the Transvaal from January to July, 1901, and subsequently in the Orange River and Cape Colonies. He received the Queen's medal with four clasps.

He was promoted Lieutenant in March, 1903, and was again on active service on the north-western frontier of India in 1908, when he was Brigade Signalling Officer, attached to the 3rd Brigade in operations in the Mohmand country, for which he received the medal with clasp. He was promoted Captain in April, 1910.

Some details of his last fight and death were received from an Army Chaplain in a letter to his father, which was published in the "Stonyhurst Magazine" of February, 1915. From this it appears that after having marched all the night of the 20th December, after a brief rest on the morning of the 21st, the battalion was ordered to charge an important position.

Some trenches had been evacuated by our troops, and the order was to retake them at all costs. During the charge Captain O'Brien was seen continually urging on his men, repeating, " Now, Munsters ! this is your time to get back a bit of your own." He was wounded first in the left side, while advancing over practically open ground. Captain O'Brien was always to the front cheering on his men, and it was as he knelt for a temporary protection that he was hit in the left side. There he lay down, and called for someone to dress his wound. He was still full of dash and spirit, and kept calling out : " Go on, Munsters ! Now is your time ! Get back your own ! " Another officer now came and began to dress his wound. While this was being done Captain O'Brien and the officer who was attending to him were both killed instantaneously by a shrapnel shell, which burst right over them. Both were buried near the spot where they fell. Captain O'Brien's death was deeply felt by his brother officers and men.

LIEUTENANT JAMES FRANCIS O'BRIEN, 1st (attd. 2nd) BATTN. ROYAL MUNSTER FUSILIERS,

who was killed in action on the 22nd December, 1914, was the eldest son of Mr. and Mrs. O'Brien, Ardfort, 21, Parkside, Wimbledon, and Ardfort, Thurles, Tipperary, Ireland. He was born on the 31st January, 1890, and was educated at St. Augustine, Ramsgate : Wimbledon College (Army Department), and the R.M.C., Sandhurst, where he won the two hundred and twenty yards in the sports, and was in the hockey team. He joined the Royal Munster Fusiliers in April, 1910, becoming Lieutenant in September, 1913. He played hockey for his regiment when stationed at Rangoon, in India, where he also rode in races and won a cup for the " Club Fours " in the Rangoon Boat Club Monsoon Regatta.

At La Bassée on the morning of the 22nd December, after coming over to relieve the Indian Corps, the division had to make a frontal attack and lost heavily. He was with his company when he was shot in the head.

Major Ryan wrote : " a Corporal and all the men said that nothing could have been more gallant than the way he had led them ; also I feel I must tell you how bravely he died, actually with his men during the attack, and how much I regret him. I had got to trust him with everything I wanted well done."

LIEUT. JOHN FORBES O'CONNELL, M.B., ROYAL ARMY MEDICAL CORPS,

who was killed in action on the 2nd September, 1914, was born on the 18th February, 1889, and joined the Royal Army Medical Corps in January, 1913.

CAPTAIN RICHARD DOMINIC O'CONNOR, ROYAL ARMY MEDICAL CORPS,

was born in Limerick on the 1st August, 1885, son of the late F. W. O'Connor, F.R.C.S.I., of that town.

He was educated at Clongowes Woods College, and did his medical training at St. Bartholomew's Hospital, London, obtaining his diplomas M.R.C.S., L.R.C.P. (Lond.). He entered the R.A.M.C. in 1906, and was promoted Captain in 1910, serving in India from 1909–14. He was fond of shooting, cricket, and swimming. In the Great War he was recommended for the Order of the Legion of Honour for bravery in the trenches and attending to civilians under heavy fire. He was killed in action on the 25th October, 1914, while serving with the 2nd Battalion Sherwood Foresters.

Captain O'Connor married Philippa Durane Sandilands, and left two children : Doreen Rosemary, born February, 1911 ; and Cyril Rene Richard, born May, 1913.

LIEUTENANT SIR GILCHRIST NEVILL OGILVY, BART., OF INVERQUHARITY, 1st BATTN. SCOTS GUARDS,

who was killed in action at Gheluvelt, near Ypres, on the 27th October, 1914, was the only son of the late Major A. H. R. Ogilvy, 13th Hussars, D.S.O., who died in 1906 ; he succeeded his grandfather, Sir Reginald H. A. Ogilvy, as eleventh Baronet in 1910.

He was born on the 6th September, 1892, and was educated at Eton and the R.M.C., Sandhurst. He joined the Scots Guards in January, 1913, and was promoted Lieutenant from September, 1914, the notification in the " London Gazette " appearing after his death.

He was a member of the Guards' and Bath Clubs. His favourite recreations were hunting and shooting.

LIEUTENANT GUY CHRISTOPHER OTTLEY OLDFIELD, THE QUEEN'S (ROYAL WEST SURREY REGIMENT), AND 4th (UGANDA) BATTN. THE KING'S AFRICAN RIFLES,

was killed in action on the 6th September, 1914, at Tsavo, while with the force defending the Mombasa - Nairobi Railway. He was the only son of Colonel C. G. Oldfield, late R.A., and a grandson of Sir Richard Oldfield.

He was born at Poona, India, on the 17th September, 1888, and was educated at Clifton College and the R.M.C., Sandhurst. At the former he obtained his caps in the Football XV and in the Second Cricket XI. He was always keen on cricket and football, and later on riding and shooting. From Sandhurst he was gazetted to the Queen's in September, 1908, becoming Lieutenant in April, 1911. He served with the 2nd Battalion of his regiment in Colchester, Gibraltar, and Bermuda, and in December, 1913, was seconded for employment with the 4th Battalion King's African Rifles, with whom he served in the Jubaland Expedition in the spring of 1914.

CAPTAIN ROBERT JOHN BLATCH-FORD OLDREY, ADJUTANT 4th (ROYAL IRISH) DRAGOON GUARDS,

who was killed in action on the 29th October, 1914, was the eldest son of the late Robert B. Oldrey, of Harpole Hall, Northants, and of Mrs. H. P. Sharpin, of Turvey, Beds.

He was born on the 18th June, 1883, educated at Uppingham, and joined the 4th (Royal Irish) Dragoon Guards from the Militia in March, 1902, being gazetted towards the end of the South African War, when he joined his regiment in India, afterwards being stationed in South Africa. He became Lieutenant in February, 1905, and Captain in January, 1911, and was appointed Adjutant of his regiment in January, 1914.

Captain Oldrey was a member of the Cavalry Club and of Ranelagh and Roehampton. He was a keen polo player, and played for his regiment in the Inter-regimental Tournaments. He was an ardent supporter of fox hunting, and rode in a number of point-to-point races. He was chosen to represent England in the jumping at Olympia, in 1908, before King Edward and Queen Alexandra, being presented by the King with a gold cigarette case as a memento of the occasion.

Captain Oldrey left for France with the Expeditionary Force, and was in the retirement from Mons. He was killed at Neuve Chapelle while leading his squadron to relieve the Indians.

CAPTAIN ROBERT HAROLD OLIVIER, 1st BATTN. DUKE OF CORNWALL'S LIGHT INFANTRY,

killed in action at the Battle of the Aisne, in September, 1914, was the youngest son of Canon Olivier, The Close, Salisbury, and was born on the 20th June, 1879.

He joined the Duke of Cornwall's Light Infantry from the Militia on the 15th November, 1899, and became Lieutenant in 1901. He served in the South African War, being a Station Staff Officer from March, 1901, to January, 1902. He was present at operations in the Orange Free State, including Paardeberg ; and at actions at Poplar Grove and Driefontein ; also at operations in the Transvaal. He received the Queen's medal with four and the King's medal with two clasps. Captain Olivier also saw service at Nandi in 1905-06, receiving the medal with clasp. He became Captain on the 20th March, 1909, and in 1910 was appointed Adjutant of the Territorial Force.

MAJOR RUPERT OMMANNEY, p.s.c., ROYAL ENGINEERS,

who was killed in action on the 31st October, 1914, was born on the 27th April, 1878, and joined the Royal Engineers in January, 1896, becoming Lieutenant in January, 1899.

He served in the South African War, being present at the relief of Ladysmith, including the action at Colenso ; at operations and actions at Spion Kop, Vaal Krans, Tugela Heights, and Pieter's Hill. He was mentioned in Despatches ("London Gazette," 8th February, 1901), and received the Queen's medal with three clasps

From October, 1903, to March, 1904, he was

specially employed in the Intelligence Branch at headquarters of the Army, and from April, 1904, to January, 1908, as Staff Captain, and General Staff Officer 3rd Grade at headquarters. In December, 1909, he passed the final examination, Staff College, and, from March, 1910, to June, 1914, he was again at the War Office on special employment, and as General Staff Officer (3rd Grade).

He was promoted Captain in January, 1905, and Major from the 30th October, 1914, the latter promotion having been gazetted after his death. He was mentioned in Sir John French's Despatch of the 14th January, 1915.

CAPTAIN the Honble. ARTHUR EDWARD BRUCE O'NEILL, 2nd LIFE GUARDS,

who was killed in action on the 6th November, 1914, was born on the 19th September, 1876, the eldest surviving son of the second Baron O'Neill, of Shane's Castle, County Antrim, and of Lady O'Neill, daughter of the eleventh Earl of Dundonald.

He was formerly in a Militia Battalion of the Argyll and Sutherland Highlanders, from which he joined the 2nd Life Guards in May, 1897, becoming Lieutenant in June, 1898. He served in the South African War, 1899–1900, being present at the relief of Kimberley, and at operations in the Orange Free State, at Paardeberg, and in Cape Colony, including the actions at Driefontein and Colesberg. He received the Queen's medal with three clasps. He was promoted Captain on the 3rd January, 1902, and from that date to January, 1903, was Adjutant of his regiment. In January, 1910, he was seconded, having been elected M.P. for Mid-Antrim, but rejoined his regiment when war was declared.

Captain O'Neill, who was a J.P. and D.L. for County Antrim, was educated at Eton, and was a member of the Carlton, Ulster, and Bachelors' Clubs. He was musical, a good shot, and fond of all sports.

He fell while leading his men in a most gallant attempt to save a situation. He was shot on the Klein Zillebeke Ridge, near Ypres, and shouting to his men to line the ridge was being carried out when he received another wound, and then begged his bearers to leave him and save themselves. He did not know what fear was. He saw his task accomplished.

Captain O'Neill married, in 1902, Lady Annabel Hungerford Crewe-Milnes, eldest daughter of the first Marquess of Crewe, and left five children : Shane Edward Robert, born February, 1907 ; Brian Arthur, born March, 1911 ; Sibyl, born December, 1902 ; Mary Louisa Hermione, born August, 1905 ; and Terence Marne, born 10th September, 1914.

CAPTAIN ARTHUR WILLIAM MacARTHUR ONSLOW, 16th (THE QUEEN'S) LANCERS,

who was killed near Ypres on the 5th November, 1914, was the son of the late Captain and Mrs. MacArthur Onslow, of Camden Park, New South Wales.

He was born on the 27th May, 1877, and joined the 16th Lancers in February, 1900, becoming Lieutenant in October of the same year. He served in the South African War, being present at operations in the Transvaal, including actions at Belfast and in the Orange River Colony and Cape Colony, for which he received the Queen's medal with three clasps and the King's medal with two clasps.

He was promoted Captain in September, 1904, and in September, 1911, he was seconded for employment with the New Zealand Military Forces, being appointed Instructor in Mounted Duties in the Canterbury district.

General Hubert Gough, C.B., wrote : " During the time he was out here, he had done very well, and commanded his squadron so well that Vaughan (now commanding the 3rd Brigade), has especially mentioned him for the way he handled it in the attack on Warneton."

Captain MacArthur Onslow was mentioned for his services in the Great War in Sir John French's Despatch of the 14th January, 1915. He married in 1911, Christabel, elder daughter of Colonel R. J. Beech, of Brandon Hall, Coventry.

LIEUT. HAROLD MICHAEL OPENSHAW, 1st BATTN. NORFOLK REGT.,

who died on the 28th August, 1914, at Thulin, of wounds received at Mons on the 24th of that month, was the second son of Lieutenant-Colonel Openshaw, of Winchester.

He was born on the 9th November, 1889 ; joined the Norfolk Regiment in November, 1909 ; and became Lieutenant in July, 1912.

CAPTAIN JOHN ARTHUR ORR, THE QUEEN'S OWN CAMERON HIGH-LANDERS,

was officially reported to have been missing on the 22nd October, 1914, and has since been reported to have been killed on that day near Langemarck.

He was the son of the late John Orr and the late Frances B. Orr, of St. Margaret's, North Berwick, and was born on the 15th January, 1879. He was educated at St. Ninian's, Moffat, and Loretto, received his commission in the Manchester Regiment in February, 1899, and was transferred to the Cameron Highlanders in April of the same year, becoming Lieutenant in June, 1900.

He took part in the South African War, being present at operations in the Orange Free State, the Transvaal in 1900, 1901, and 1902, the Orange River Colony, and on the Zululand frontier of Natal, including actions at Vet and Zand Rivers, near Johannesburg, at Pretoria, Diamond Hill, Wittebergen, and Ladybrand. For his services he was mentioned in Despatches (" London Gazette," 10th September, 1901), and received the Queen's medal with four clasps and the King's medal with two clasps.

From December, 1904, to December, 1907, he was Adjutant of his battalion, and was promoted Captain in October, 1905. He qualified for the Staff College in 1913, and was selected for nomination in September, 1913. When war was declared he was made Assistant Embarkation Officer at Southampton, and left to join his regiment on the 26th September.

Captain Orr, who was a member of the Caledonian Club, was good at all games, especially cricket, hockey, and golf. He was not married.

MAJOR JOHN BOYD ORR, D.S.O., 1st BATTN. NORFOLK REGIMENT,

who died, while a prisoner of war, of wounds received in action on the 24th August, 1914, at the Battle of Mons, and was buried at Thulin, was born on the 16th August, 1871. The second son of the late Colonel Spencer Edward Orr and of Mrs. S. E. Orr, of Belfield, Camberley, he was educated at Dover College, and was gazetted to

the Norfolk Regiment from the Militia in October, 1893, becoming Lieutenant in August, 1896, and Captain in December, 1901.

He took part in the South African War, in which he was employed on the Staff as A.D.C. (at first extra A.D.C.) to the Brigadier-General Commanding the Mounted Infantry Brigade, from November, 1900, to October, 1901. He took part in the relief of Kimberley, and was present at operations in the Orange Free State, at Paardeberg, and in the Transvaal, including actions at Poplar Grove, Driefontein, Vet River, Zand River, near Johannesburg, at Pretoria and Diamond Hill. He was mentioned in Despatches (" London Gazette," 10th September, 1901), was awarded the D.S.O., and received the Queen's medal with five clasps and the King's medal with two clasps.

From December, 1906, to September, 1908, he was employed with the Transvaal Volunteers, and with the West African Frontier Force from May, 1910, to December, 1913, in January of which latter year he received his Majority.

Major Orr was a member of the Caledonian Club.

CAPT. ROBERT CLIFFORD ORR, 3rd (attd. 1st) BATTN. PRINCE ALBERT'S (SOMERSET LIGHT INFANTRY),

was the son of the late Robert Harrison Orr, Solicitor, of Belfast and Ballymena, County Antrim, and Cassandra Marchaise Orr, now residing at Rockside, Newcastle, Co. Down. He was a nephew of his Honour Judge Orr, County Court Judge for Co. Down.

Captain Orr was born on the 17th September, 1880, at Belfast, and was educated at Sunningdale (Berks) Preparatory School and at Rugby. He adopted the legal profession, and was admitted a Solicitor in 1903, practising with his brother in Belfast and at Ballymena.

In 1910 he was gazetted 2nd Lieutenant in the 3rd Battalion (Reserve) Somerset Light Infantry, being promoted Lieutenant in December, 1911, and Captain in October, 1914. Soon after the war broke out he was attached to the 1st Battalion of his regiment, and served with it at the front for about two months prior to his death.

Captain Orr was a member of the Ulster and the Ballymena Clubs, and of the Golf Club at the latter place. He was an active member of the Mid-Antrim Hunt Club, frequently acting as Master. He was also Captain of the local contingent of the Church Lads' Brigade.

He was killed on the 19th December, 1914, while leading his men in an attack on the German trenches outside Ploegsteert Wood, in Flanders. The following account of the circumstances was given to his brother by the Adjutant of his battalion :—

" The company, in which your brother was, was ordered to lead the attack on the German trenches on the 19th December, 1914. After a heavy artillery bombardment all the morning the assault was made at 2.30 p.m. All the officers and men of this company, and the one which supported it, behaved with the utmost gallantry, but they were not successful in actually taking the German trenches, though several isolated parties, including one in which your brother was included, succeeded in breaking through the enemy's wire entanglement and into a house held by the enemy. Nothing was known of your brother's fate until Christmas Day. On this day an informal truce was arranged, and the Germans brought out from within their lines and handed over to us the body of your brother, amongst others, and we buried him in the little cemetery in Ploegsteert Wood near our headquarters. I feel sure it will be a great comfort to his mother and yourself, as it was to us, to know that it had been possible to recover his body and bury him properly. There is no doubt that he must have very gallantly led his men practically into the German trenches, but we could not establish ourselves there, although we were able to advance our lines some distance as the result of the attack."

LIEUTENANT BRIAN OSBORNE, 15th (THE KING'S) HUSSARS,

son of Captain Frank Osborne, late 13th Hussars, and Mrs. Osborne, Harbury Hall, Leamington, was born in Sydney, N.S.W., on the 18th November, 1888.

He was educated at Harrow, where he was in the Cricket and Football XI's, was 1st String at Racquets in 1906, and won the Ebrington Cup two years in succession. From Harrow he went direct to the R.M.C., Sandhurst, where his first promotion was to Colour-Sergeant, and on passing out was awarded the Sword of Honour. He was gazetted to the 15th Hussars in February, 1908, and joined them at Muttra, India. While there he had the record number of " first spears " for pig-sticking. He also played polo for his regiment, and formed one of the regimental team that won the Inter-regimental Tournament in South Africa in 1911.

In 1912 he was at the Cavalry School, Netheravon, and played Number 1 in the 15th Hussars polo team that won the Inter-regimental at Hurlingham in 1913, the year the regiment returned to England. He also played in the Cavalry Club team that won the Ranelagh Open Cup in 1914, being handicapped at seven points. He was a very fine horseman, and a well-known rider to hounds, especially in Warwickshire, where his home was ; and was a member of the Cavalry Club, the M.C.C., and Ranelagh.

Lieutenant Osborne was reported missing from the 11th November, 1914, when he was supporting the Duke of Wellington's Regiment with his machine gun in trenches near Herenthage Château, east of Ypres. One of the men of his machine-gun section, taken prisoner that day when the Prussian Guard made their last big attack, wrote in March, 1915, saying that Lieutenant Osborne was shot through the head about 7.30 on the morning of the 11th November.

LIEUT. GEOFFREY CLAUDE LANG-DALE OTTLEY, D.S.O., 2nd BATTN. SCOTS GUARDS,

was the son of Rear-Admiral Sir Charles Ottley, K.C.M.G., C.B., M.V.O., and Lady Ottley, daughter of Colonel Alexander Stewart, R.A., and was born at Southsea on the 20th January, 1896. He was educated at Harrow from 1910–13, and passed into Sandhurst direct from Harrow in February, 1914, being the first of his batch of Guards Cadets, gaining a Prize Cadetship. He was gazetted 2nd Lieutenant on the 1st October, 1914, and promoted Lieutenant on the 10th December, antedated to the 9th November, 1914.

After five weeks in London, serving with the 3rd Battalion, he joined the 2nd Battalion on the Continent, and fell mortally wounded when leading an attack on the German trenches on the 18th December, dying in the Australian Hospital, Wimereux, Boulogne, on the 21st December, 1914.

He was mentioned in Sir John French's Despatch of the 14th January, 1915, and was awarded the D.S.O. for conspicuous gallantry, but unfortunately did not live to personally receive the decoration.

LIEUT. JOHN ROBERTS OVENS, 1st BATTN. CONNAUGHT RANGERS, who was killed in action in France on the 5th November, 1914, according to the official casualty list (there being reason for accepting the 7th November as the correct date), was the youngest son of the late John R. Ovens, Eglinton Crescent, Edinburgh, and grandson of the late Alexander Rutherford, Hoebridge, Melrose.

He was born on the 11th February, 1889, and was educated at Edinburgh, Heidelberg, and the R.M.C., Sandhurst. ("The Times," 17th November, 1914.) He joined the Connaught Rangers from the Special Reserve in December, 1909, and was promoted Lieutenant in June, 1911.

LIEUT. ERNEST HADDON OWEN, 3rd BATTN. LINCOLNSHIRE REGT.,

born at Louth on the 4th February, 1886, was the son of William Haddon Owen, of Louth, Lincolnshire. He was educated at Llandaff and Stancliffe Preparatory School, and subsequently at Haileybury College from 1901 to 1904.

Lieutenant Owen was gazetted to the 4th Lincolns (South Lincolnshire Militia) in 1904. Later he became Lieutenant and Musketry Instructor. Upon the disbandment of the battalion in 1908 he was transferred to the 3rd (Special Reserve) Battalion, retiring in 1912 on entering into partnership with his father in the firm of Haddon Owen & Son, Solicitors, of Louth. On the outbreak of the war Lieutenant Owen applied for and obtained a commission in his old regiment, becoming 2nd Lieutenant in the 3rd Battalion on the 15th August, 1914. He left for the front with a draft for the 1st Battalion on the 11th November, and on arriving was attached temporarily to the 1st Battalion South Wales Borderers, which had lost many officers, and was serving with that regiment when he fell on the 21st December, 1914, in the severe struggle near Givenchy. He was gazetted Lieutenant on the 23rd December after his death. Major Reddie, of the 1st South Wales Borderers, gave the following account of him and of the circumstances of his death : " During the short time he was with us he became very popular both with officers and men, and besides was a good soldier. He was killed in action on the 21st instant, leading his men into the trenches, and was shot in the head when only three or four yards off them. He was slightly wounded in the neck a short time before, but gallantly led his men on."

A brother Subaltern furnished the following details : " We were attacking the Germans on December 21st. Your son was in the leading company. We had to drive the Germans from the trenches which the Indians had lost the day previously. You will be glad to hear we got those trenches. We were under artillery fire and heavy rifle fire since we started, your son and I leading our two platoons. We had not gone far with the advance before he got a bullet in his neck. He bandaged it up, and then brought his men on ! We got to the trenches, and he was rounding up his men, when he got a bullet right through his forehead. He was only a few minutes dying, and could not speak. . . . He was most brave in the advance, and those of us who saw him could not help but note his coolness and unconcern. . . . The way he led his men was splendid. He got them up to the trench when he was shot. We were all very fond of ' dear old Owen.' He was such a good fellow. Nothing disturbed him. His only fault was he exposed himself too much in the attack, and that is how he was killed, I am afraid, as they are always on the look-out for officers."

2nd LIEUTENANT NORMAN MOORE OWEN, 49th BATTERY, XLth BRIGADE, ROYAL FIELD ARTILLERY,

who was killed at the Battle of the Aisne, in September, 1914, actual date unknown, was the younger son of the Rev. O. E. and Mrs. Owen, Over Wallop Rectory, Hants.

2nd Lieutenant Owen, who was born in 1893, was gazetted to the Royal Field Artillery in July, 1913.

CAPTAIN WILLIAM HAMILTON PADDAY, 36th attd. 47th SIKHS,

born at Stoke, Devonport, on the 21st September, 1881, was the younger son of the late Colonel A. C. Padday, Royal (late Bengal) Engineers, and a grandson of Thomas Campbell Foster, Q.C., a Bencher of the Middle Temple, and Recorder of Warwick.

He was educated at Bath College, and the R.M.C., Sandhurst. He was a prominent member of the Bath College Football XV in 1898 ; and at Sandhurst in 1900 ran with his company when it won the cross-country race. He entered the R.M.C. in 1900, and from there in the following year obtained his commission in the Indian Army, and was attached to the Queen's (Royal West Surrey Regiment), then serving in the Punjab. After a year's service with this regiment he was gazetted to the 36th Sikhs. Some years later, for a short time, he joined the Military Police in Assam, rejoining his regiment in 1910.

He was a keen sportsman, fond of shooting, fishing, and yachting. For a time he was the Honorary Secretary of the Lucknow and also of the Naini Tal Yacht Clubs; and while racing with the latter club won several cups. He was also a member of the Junior Army and Navy Club, London.

On the outbreak of the war with Germany he was at home on leave, and was attached for a short time to the 8th (Service) Battalion of the Duke of Wellington's (West Riding Regiment). Early in November he joined the 47th Sikhs in France, and with them he was serving when killed in action on the 21st December, 1914, near Givenchy.

The circumstances of his death were thus related by an officer of the regiment: " On the night of the 20th and 21st December the regiment had been ordered to take a trench, which was found to be occupied at both ends by Germans with machine guns. Previous experience had shown that the best way to dislodge the enemy from such positions was by parties of bomb-throwers creeping up and throwing bombs among them. Captain Padday was in charge of a regimental party of bomb-throwers whom he had himself trained, and went off with the party to dislodge the Germans. A Sepoy who was with him said he had thrown two bombs, and was preparing to throw a third when he was shot through the head at close range. It was impossible to recover the body at the time, and a retirement being just then ordered the party had to make their way back. As a subsequent counter-attack, in which the 47th Sikhs did not participate, did not reach that particular trench, it was never possible to recover the bodies of those who died there."

His C.O. wrote that " he died a most gallant death, gallantly performing a difficult task." Another officer wrote: " His coolness and great personal bravery alone commanded admiration, and his never-failing cheerfulness under any circumstances."

LIEUTENANT GEORGE GODFREY BRANDRETH PAGET, 1st BATTALION NORTHAMPTONSHIRE REGIMENT,

was the only child of Mr. and Mrs. C. E. Paget, of Great Houghton House, near Northampton, his grandfathers being the late Sir George Edward Paget, K.C.B., M.D., F.R.S., of Cambridge, and Canon William Harper Brandreth,

M.A., Rector of Standish, Lancashire. He was a great-nephew of Sir James Paget, Bart. On his mother's side he was a nephew of Major-General Sir Alexander B. Tulloch, K.C.B., C.M.G., and Major-General F. W. Hemming, C.B., and a cousin of Admiral Sir Thomas Brandreth, K.C.B.

Lieutenant Paget was born on the 6th April, 1891, and was educated at a Preparatory School, St. Andrew's, Eastbourne, from 1901–05, and then at Charterhouse till 1908. His father and both his grandfathers were also educated at Charterhouse.

He entered the Northamptonshire Militia as 2nd Lieutenant in April, 1908, passing into the Special Reserve in July of that year. He was promoted Lieutenant in July, 1910, and in 1913 passed the Army Qualifying Examination, being gazetted as 2nd Lieutenant in the Northamptonshire Regiment (Regulars), to date from the 14th August, 1914.

He served with the 1st Battalion of his regiment, forming part of the 2nd Infantry Brigade, 1st Division of the British Expeditionary Force, from the 7th August till he was killed on the 14th September, 1914, going through the Battles of Mons, the Marne, and the Aisne.

The C.O. of his battalion wrote as follows to his father about Lieutenant Paget :—

" On the 14th September he was detached with his company ' B ' from the rest of the battalion to occupy a certain position. The company was under the command of Captain White. There was a lot of very hard fighting that day, and ' B ' Company joined with the Queen's Regiment in a flanking attack on the enemy's position. In this both the Queen's and our company had many casualties. It was in this flank attack that Godfrey was hit. 1 heard that night that he was missing, and from the evidence of men in his company we knew that he was wounded. His Captain (White) was also missing (we have reason to believe he was also killed), and most of the N.C.O.'s were killed or wounded. Two or three days later—I think on the 17th—when we had more hard fighting, an officer of the Coldstream Guards brought in letters addressed to your son, which he said had been taken from the pocket of an officer in the Northamptonshire, who was some distance in front of our trenches, and who was dead. These letters were put aside by an officer to be sent to you, but I fear in the confusion due to the fighting they have been mislaid. (This officer was wounded later, but subsequently sent the letters, which fully established the identity of G. G. B. Paget.) The fact of these letters being brought in forced us reluctantly to come to the conclusion that your boy was killed. His body has not been found, nor has his identity disc been brought in. The position where White and Godfrey got with their company is some distance ahead of the trenches we now occupy, and midway between ourselves and the Germans, so that it is impossible to get out to search the ground for those who are missing—the German fire will not allow us to do so. (Unfortunately the Northamptons were moved from the trenches along the Chemin des Dames, some four or five miles north-east of Paissy, on the 16th October, 1914, to go to Northern France. The French forces took their place. It is pretty certain that the German trench where G. G. B. Paget was killed has not yet been taken [7th June, 1915]. There is no knowledge of his having even been buried.) You should have had notice from the War Office that it was practically certain that your son was killed. The report we first sent was that he was missing and wounded. This we followed up with a second report to War Office saying that ' Lieutenant Paget, previously reported missing, was killed.' . . . May I offer you and your wife my deepest sympathy? I know what a blow the loss of your son will be to both of you. He was a most gallant chap, and when we were doing some of our long marches he stuck to it so well, even when he was not feeling very fit. We were all very fond of him."

A Captain of the 3rd Battalion, himself since killed, gave the following account: " Poor Godfrey was killed in action on the 14th September. His company were attacking under a very heavy shell fire and rifle fire also. They had just halted in a bit of a dip, where they were out of rifle fire. He moved forward to see if they could go on when he was hit. The men of his platoon say he didn't seem to mind the lead that was flying round, and was urging them on all the time."

The Adjutant wrote to his mother: " There are some consolations for you. You know he died doing his duty, and that his name will be handed down to posterity, amongst the others of the regiment, as being one who assisted to uphold the glorious traditions of our regiment, and who emulated the deeds of times gone by." He was hit twice before being killed. His men had followed him, and were fighting hand to hand with the Germans before the retirement was ordered. The loss of the company was most severe, very few returning.

MAJOR GEORGE PALEY, p.s.c., 1st BATTALION. THE RIFLE BRIGADE (THE PRINCE CONSORT'S OWN), who was killed in action on the 31st October, 1914, was the only son of Mr. William Victor Paley, of Freckenham House, Soham, by his marriage with the daughter of Canon Nepean, Chaplain-in-Ordinary to her late Majesty Queen Victoria.

He was born on the 27th January, 1872, and joined the Rifle Brigade in March, 1892, becoming Lieutenant in April, 1894, and Captain in December, 1898. He took part in the Nile Expedition, 1898, being present at the Battle of Khartoum, for which he received the British medal and the Egyptian medal with clasp. He also served in  the South African War, taking part in the defence of Ladysmith, including the sortie of the 10th December, 1899, in which he was dangerously wounded. He was twice mentioned in despatches (" London Gazette," 8th February and 10th September, 1901), and received the Queen's medal with clasp.

From February to September, 1902, he was A.D.C. (temporary) to the General Officer Commanding, Woolwich District, in 1903 qualified as an Interpreter in French, and, in December, 1914, passed the final examination of the Staff College. From February, 1905, to September, 1906, he was Staff Captain and General Staff Officer (3rd Grade) at the headquarters of the Army, and from September, 1908, to February, 1909, D.A.Q.M.G. and General Staff Officer (2nd Grade), headquarters ; while he was also specially employed there in February and March, 1909.

From October, 1909, to October, 1913, he was Director of Operations and Staff Duties (General Staff Officer, 2nd Grade), Canadian Militia ; while on the 5th August, 1914, he was appointed General Staff Officer (2nd Grade), and was serving in that capacity when killed. He was mentioned for his services in Sir John French's Despatch of the 8th October, 1914.

LIEUT. WALTER EVELYN PARKE, 2nd BATTN. DURHAM LIGHT INFANTRY, who was killed when in command of the machine-gun section of his battalion on the 13th October, 1914, was the second son of Lieutenant-Colonel Lawrence Parke, of Moreton Heath, Dorset.

He was born on the 27th July, 1891, and was educated at Winchester, where he was Captain of the XI, and was gazetted to the Durham Light Infantry in August, 1911, as 2nd Lieutenant, being posted to the 2nd Battalion, becoming Lieutenant in August, 1914. He was a first-class cricketer.

For his services in the Great War Lieutenant Parke was mentioned in Sir John French's Despatch of the 14th January, 1915.

CAPTAIN ALFRED ERNEST PARKER, 3rd BATTN. THE BLACK WATCH (ROYAL HIGHLANDERS), attd. 2nd BATTN. SEAFORTH HIGHLANDERS (ROSS-SHIRE BUFFS, THE DUKE OF ALBANY'S)

was the youngest son of the late Alfred Traill Parker, of Beechwood, Aigburth, Liverpool, and Fairlie, Ayrshire.

He was born on the 13th December, 1880, and educated at Eton. On leaving Eton in December, 1899, he was gazetted to the 3rd Battalion the Black Watch as 2nd Lieutenant, and in March, 1900, he joined the 2nd Battalion with a draft in South Africa, receiving his commission in the regular battalion in January, 1901. He served through the Boer War, being present at operations in the Orange Free State, Orange River Colony, the Transvaal, and the Zululand frontier of Natal, including the actions at Rhenoster River, Wittebergen, and Witpoort. He received the Queen's medal with three clasps and the King's medal with two clasps.

In 1906 he was transferred to the Xth Hussars, retiring with the rank of Captain in May, 1911, and in January, 1912, rejoined the 3rd (Reserve) Battalion the Black Watch as a Lieutenant. He was serving with the Seaforth Highlanders when killed on the 7th November, 1914, near Ploegsteert, leading his platoon through the wood against the German trenches.

Captain Parker married, in 1909, Miss Joan Bowes-Lyon, and leaves one daughter.

MAJOR GEORGE HASTINGS PARKER, 1st BATTN. THE HAMPSHIRE REGT.,

who was killed in action on the 19th December, 1914, was born on the 4th July, 1870.

He joined the Hampshire Regiment from the Militia in October, 1892, becoming Lieutenant in October, 1894, and Captain in July, 1900. He took part in the South African War, having been Station Commandant in April and May, 1901, and afterwards in charge of Station Transport, Barberton, from October, 1901, to May, 1902. He was present at operations in the Transvaal and Orange River Colony in 1901

and 1902. He received the Queen's medal with four clasps.

From November, 1903, to November, 1907, he was Superintendent of Gymnasia, Malta, and was promoted Major in February, 1910. In August, 1914, he was promoted temporary Lieutenant-Colonel for duty with the 10th (Service) Battalion of his Regiment, but subsequently rejoined the 1st Battalion, with which he was serving when he was killed.

For his services in the Great War Major Parker was mentioned in Sir John French's Despatch of the 14th January, 1915.

CAPTAIN ROBERT BURTON PARKER, 1st BATTN. NORTHAMPTONSHIRE REGIMENT,

born at Cressington, near Liverpool, on the 3rd July, 1879, was the son of the late Robert Parker, of Liverpool, and of Mrs. Parker, Bulbridge House, Salisbury.

He was educated at St. Edward's School, Oxford, and Wellington College, intended to proceed to the R.M.C., Sandhurst. Before he did so, however, the Boer War broke out, and he enlisted as a Trooper in the Montgomeryshire Yeomanry, with which he served in the South African War, 1900-02. He received the Queen's medal with three clasps and the King's medal with two clasps, was mentioned in despatches, and given a commission in the Army Service Corps, being subsequently transferred to the 2nd Battalion Northamptonshire Regiment in July, 1901. He became Lieutenant in August, 1903, and Captain in February, 1910. In November of the same year he was appointed Adjutant of the Territorial Force, which appointment he held until November, 1913. When the war with Germany broke out Captain Parker was at home on leave from the 2nd Battalion of his regiment, then stationed in Egypt, and was transferred for active service to the 1st Battalion with which, as part of the 1st Division, he proceeded to France on the 14th August, 1914. He was killed at the Battle of the Aisne on the 17th September, 1914, while leading a charge against German trenches.

The following is an extract from letters of sympathy received from officers and men of the regiment: " He is a great loss. We who have hunted with him know his fine qualities. No better man or more delightful sportsman ever rode over the Pytchley country. His place will be hard indeed to fill. A more gallant gentleman never lived."

In a memoir published in a Northampton paper

the following words occur : " The Battalion admired and esteemed him. He was a brave British soldier ; not a man of many words, but of much military ability, strong in will and determination, and of fine disciplinary feeling and practice. He was a fine horseman— few better in or out of the Army. He has given his all for his country, and the roll of the Northamptonshire Regiment is enriched by the further addition of, alas ! a name, but a living name of a fine example of the maintenance of our country's best traditions of duty and courage." Captain Parker was a good rider, well known with the Pytchley and Grafton Hunts when he was stationed at Northampton, and played polo. He was a member of the Junior Army and Navy Club.

LIEUTENANT RONALD ELPHIN- STONE PARKER, "D" BATTERY ROYAL HORSE ARTILLERY,

was the third son of Robert Gabbett and Louisa Parker, of Bally Valley, Killaloe, County Clare, Ireland, and was born there on the 5th January, 1886. His brother, Major R. G. Parker, D.S.O., is serving in the King's Own (Royal Lancaster Regiment). Lieutenant Parker was educated at The Abbey, Tipperary ; and at Clifton College. He joined the Clare Artillery Militia, and, taking first place in the Militia Competitive Examination, was gazetted to the Royal Artillery in May, 1907, being posted to the 87th Howitzer Battery, Royal Field Artillery. He was promoted Lieutenant in 1910, and served on the Staff of the Brigadier-General Commanding Artillery, 1st Division, Aldershot, in 1912–13. In June, 1914, he was posted to "D" Battery, Royal Horse Artillery, with which he was serving in France when he was killed in the Battle of the Marne on the 8th September, 1914.

At the time his battery was closely supporting the 3rd Cavalry Brigade in the advance to the Marne when the Germans brought back twelve guns against them. "D" Battery stood its ground, and eventually the Germans drew off, but "D" Battery lost its Major wounded and both its Subalterns killed.

The Officer Commanding his Royal Horse Artillery Brigade wrote : " He died like a hero, fighting his gun at great odds to the last."

Lieutenant Parker excelled in all field sports, was a fine horseman, keen rider to hounds, and an excellent whip. He also was a first-rate shot and a good fisherman.

LIEUT. JOE ANTHONY FRANCIS PAR- KINSON, 1st BATTN. DORSETSHIRE REGIMENT,

was struck by shrapnel and killed instantaneously on the 13th October, 1914, near Béthune. He was the son of Thomas Parkinson, Esq., J.P. for Carmarthenshire, and was born on the 28th February, 1888, and educated at Rossall, 1901–05. He joined the Dorsetshire Regiment from the Special Reserve in December, 1910, becoming Lieutenant in March, 1912.

He was a keen sportsman, being especially fond of hunting, fishing, and shooting.

LIEUTENANT GEORGE ROWORTH PARR, 1st BATTN. (PRINCE ALBERT'S) SOMERSET LIGHT INFANTRY,

was the only surviving son of the late Major - General Sir Hallam Parr, K.C.B., C.M.G. (Colonel of Prince Albert's Somerset Light Infantry), of Chaffey Moor Bourton, near Wincanton, Somerset, and was born in London on the 29th November, 1891. Lieutenant Parr's elder brother, who was a 2nd Lieutenant in the same regiment, died at Malta, aged twenty, in February, 1910.

Lieutenant Parr was educated at Wellington College, Berks, where he gained first prizes in German and English literature in 1909 and 1910. He shot at Bisley for his school in 1908 and 1909. He passed into the R.M.C., Sandhurst, where he gained prizes for Military Law and German ; and represented Sandhurst in the Foil Competition at Olympia in 1911. He received his commission in February, 1912, being promoted Lieutenant in December, 1914. He became a 1st Class Interpreter in German in January, and the same in French in June, 1914.

During the retirement to the Marne he was employed as Interpreter and as Reconnaissance Officer on the Aisne. He was personally thanked by his Brigadier, and it is believed that his name was sent up for mention in Despatches, but was " crowded out."

He was killed on the 19th December, 1914, while

leading his men under a terribly heavy fire, near Ploegsteert Wood, Belgium, and his grave adjoins the graves of five other officers of the Somerset Light Infantry who fell on the same day.

Lady Parr received a letter from his Brigadier, General Hunter Weston, in which he said : " I used him as my ' *liaison* officer ' to keep in close communication with the French Brigadier-General on our immediate left at Bucy. His knowledge of French was thus of great value to the brigade. He was a thoroughly good regimental officer—one of the best in a very good battalion. If he had been spared he would undoubtedly have followed in his father's footsteps, and would have risen to high distinction in the Army. . . . He was a good officer and a gallant gentleman, and he died a hero's death, leading his platoon in the attack on the 19th December."

General Sir Horace Smith-Dorrien wrote : " None of our brave soldiers have died a more glorious death, gallantly leading his men forward against the enemy."

CAPTAIN ROBERT CHARLES PART-RIDGE, 5th (PRINCESS CHARLOTTE OF WALES'S) DRAGOON GUARDS,

who was killed in action on the 8th September, 1914, at Le Petit Morin River, and was buried in the churchyard of Sablonnières, was the son of the late Anthony William Partridge, of Lavenham, Suffolk, and a grandson of the late Lieutenant-Colonel Tyrwhitt Drake, of Little Shardeloes, Amersham, Bucks.

He was born on the 24th July, 1882, and was educated at Haileybury and the R.M.C., Sandhurst, from which he joined the 5th Dragoon Guards in May, 1901. He took part in the South African War, being present at operations in the Transvaal and Orange River Colony from October, 1901, to May, 1902. For his services he received the Queen's medal with three clasps.

Captain Partridge was a member of the Army and Navy Club. He rode in the Officers' Ride at Olympia in June, 1914, the ride being from London to Aldershot, a distance of thirty-three miles. He was promoted Lieutenant in April, 1904, and Captain in January, 1911. In the Great War he was in command of a squadron of his regiment.

CAPTAIN LOGAN DEARE PASSY, 1st BATTN. THE DUKE OF CORNWALL'S LIGHT INFANTRY,

who was killed in action on the 21st October, 1914, was the younger son of the late Captain De Lacy Dayrell Passy, Ivy Bank, Bishopstoke, Hants.

He was born on the 20th August, 1881, and was educated at Bedford Grammar School. He served in the South African War with the Imperial Yeomanry, receiving the Queen's medal with four clasps, and joined the Duke of Cornwall's Light Infantry in December, 1901, being promoted Lieutenant in January, 1905. From February of that year to December, 1907, he was employed with the West African Frontier Force, and from January, 1910, to December, 1912, was an Adjutant of the Territorial Force. He obtained his company in January, 1912.

He fell while leading his men in a charge against the Germans, who had broken through our lines near the village of Lorgies, north of La Bassée.

Captain Passy, who was a member of the Junior Naval and Military Club, married Ethel Mary, daughter of the late General Strutt, I.A., and left two daughters.

2nd LIEUTENANT JAMES THOMAS ROBINSON-PASTFIELD, 5th BATTN. THE DUKE OF CAMBRIDGE'S OWN (MIDDLESEX REGIMENT) attd. 1st BATTN. NORTHAMPTONSHIRE REGT.,

was the second son of Mr. and Mrs. John Robinson-Pastfield, of Exeter, and was born on the 18th December, 1891, at Olivedale, St. Thomas, Exeter. A younger brother—2nd Lieutenant J. V. R. Pastfield—was, at the age of seventeen, gazetted to the 5th Middlesex Regiment. The subject of this memoir was educated at Exeter School from 1903 to 1909, when he left with a "Whale" Scholarship for Keble College, Oxford, where he graduated B.A., with honours in Modern History, in 1912. On leaving Keble he became a master at Bloxham School.

At Exeter he had his full colours for football (1909–10), and was captain of the hockey team in 1909. At Oxford he was Sergeant-Major in the O.T.C., and in the Signalling Unit. Most of his vacations were spent at Bulford Camp, and for two years in succession (1911 and 1912) he was attached to the Headquarters Staff on grand manœuvres.

Mr. Robinson-Pastfield was gazetted to the Middlesex Regiment on probation in August, 1914, and was confirmed in his rank in December, 1914, the notification being gazetted after his death.

He fell in a night attack on the 21st December, 1914, near La Quinque Rue, his Commanding Officer stating that he was shot and killed instantaneously while leading his platoon close to the German trenches.

CAPT. CHARLES JAMES PATERSON, 1st BATTN. SOUTH WALES BORDERERS,

of Hook Cottage, Horndean, Hants, who died at Ypres on the 1st November, 1914, from wounds received at Gheluvelt in the evening of the 29th October, was born on the 28th December, 1887, at Whitelee, Roxburghshire. He was the son of James Paterson, Esq., of that place, and of Ettrick Hall, Selkirkshire.

He was educated at Haileybury and the R.M.C., Sandhurst, joining the Borderers at Karachi in December, 1907. He became Lieutenant in September, 1909, Assistant Adjutant in December, 1910, and Adjutant in September, 1913, and was promoted Captain from the 1st November, the day of his death.

For his services in the Great War Captain Paterson was mentioned in Sir John French's Despatch of the 8th October, 1914.

2nd LIEUT. JOHN AGAR PATERSON, 2nd BATTN. BEDFORDSHIRE REGT.,

son of W. M. Paterson, was born at Glasgow on the 19th November, 1893, and was educated at Dulwich College, where he was in the 1st Cricket XI and the 1st Football XV. and as a boxer represented Dulwich at Aldershot in the Featherweight competition.

After passing through the Royal Military College, Sandhurst, he received his commission in September, 1913, joining his battalion in South Africa in November of that year. With it he returned to Europe for the Great War, and was killed on the 31st October, 1914, near Klein Zillebeke, south-east of Ypres.

2nd LIEUT. JOHN EDWARD PATON, 2nd BATTALION MONMOUTHSHIRE REGIMENT, T.F.,

was the eldest son of John and Susan Paton, Waun Wern, Pontypool, and was born in that town on the 6th September, 1895.

He was educated at Copthorne School, Sussex, and at Winchester College. In the spring of 1914 he passed the entrance examination for Pembroke College, Cambridge, where he was to have taken up his residence in October, 1914, had it not been for the war. At Winchester he was in the O.T.C., in which he had attained the rank of Sergeant, and was one of the eight selected to represent the school at Bisley in 1913 and 1914. He obtained Certificate "A" in 1912, thus qualifying for a commission, which he obtained in October, 1914.

2nd Lieutenant Paton was killed in action at Le Bizet on the 31st December, 1914, and was buried in the cemetery of the Essex Regiment at Calvaire, near Le Touquet. He was mentioned in Sir John French's Despatch of 14th January, 1915, for gallant and distinguished service in the field.

2nd LIEUTENANT JOHN DOSSIE PATTESON, SPECIAL RESERVE 5th (PRINCESS CHARLOTTE OF WALES'S) DRAGOON GUARDS,

in which he became 2nd Lieutenant in April, 1910, was killed in action on the 13th October, 1914, at the age of twenty-five years. He was the eldest son of Colonel H. T. S. Patteson, of Beeston, St. Andrew, Norwich, and was educated at Harrow (Small Houses and Headmaster's), 1904–07, and at Trinity College, Cambridge, where he took his degree of B.A. in 1910.

2nd LIEUTENANT GAVIN PAUL, 2nd DRAGOON GUARDS (QUEEN'S BAYS), who was killed in action on the 31st October, 1914, aged twenty-one, was the elder son of the late Gavin Paul, Coalmaster, and of Mrs. Paul, Dunstane, Edinburgh, and St. Margaret's, Gullane.

He was gazetted to the Queen's Bays in September, 1914.

LIEUTENANT GEORGE HERBERT PAYNE, 2nd BATTN. SUFFOLK REGT., was shown in the monthly casualty list published in June, 1915, under the heading " unofficially reported killed or died of wounds," no place or date being mentioned, but it is now understood he died, a prisoner of war, on the 26th August, 1914.

He was gazetted to the Army in September, 1913, and was promoted Lieutenant to date from 11th December, 1914.

2nd LIEUTENANT JOHN SYDNEY PAULSON, 2nd BATTN. LANCASHIRE FUSILIERS,  who was killed in action on the 14th September, 1914, was the son of Henry John and Charlotte Paulson and a nephew of Captain John Paulson, R.A. (retired). He was born at Kirton, Lincolnshire, on the 31st October 1889, and educated at Kirton Grammar School, De Aston School, Market Rasen, and at London University, where he took the degree of B.Sc., with honours in chemistry. He was in the University O.T.C. for four years, and was gazetted to the Special Reserve of the Lancashire Fusiliers as 2nd Lieutenant in July, 1911. Mr. Paulson was a member of Harmony Lodge of Freemasons, 272 Boston. He was in 1912 appointed Chemistry Master at Orme School, where he gained the respect and regard of the whole school by his straightforward character and unassuming manners, and by his enthusiasm in the schoolroom and playing grounds.

At the time of his death 2nd Lieutenant Paulson was serving with the 2nd Battalion of his regiment. He had passed through the Battle of, and retirement from, Mons and the Battle of the Marne. During the Battle of the Aisne his battalion was ordered, on September 13th, to take the village of Bucy-le-Long. They crossed the river on a single plank, under heavy shrapnel fire, and it was then that Mr. Paulson was hit.

The Chaplain of the Field Ambulance reported : " Lieutenant Paulson was wounded by shrapnel all down one side of his body, and died three hours later. Three attempts were made by the men of his regiment to rescue him when hit. Two men were killed and two wounded in the attempts. The body of Lieutenant Paulson lies in the churchyard of St. Marguerite, west of Bucy-le-Long, immediately inside the gate of the cemetery on the right side."

LIEUTENANT HUBERT KIRKBY PEACE, 3rd BATTN. YORK AND LANCASTER REGIMENT, was the third son of Hugh Kirkby Peace, of Sandygate, Sheffield, and was born at Sheffield on 16th October, 1881.
He was educated at Rugby, and was gazetted to the 3rd Battalion York and Lancaster Regiment in September, 1914, having previously served for ten years in the 4th (Hallamshire) Battalion of the Regiment, his commission as 2nd Lieutenant having been dated November, 1905.

He died on the 17th October, 1914, of wounds received the previous day, when going under very heavy fire to take reserves into the firing line.

Lieutenant Peace married Grace Mary, eldest daughter of Charles H. Weller, Esq., M.A., of St. Leonards-on-Sea, and left one son, George Hugh Kirkby, born December 15th, 1909.

2nd LIEUTENANT GEOFFREY VINCENT PEARCE, 2nd BATTN. ROYAL WARWICKSHIRE REGIMENT, was born at Brentwood, Essex, 19th June, 1889, and was the son of William Pearce, Esq., M.P. for Limehouse, of Shepway Lodge, Walmer, Kent, and 14, Park Crescent, Portland Place, London, W.

He was educated at Uppingham School, and was a good footballer and runner.

He afterwards joined the Artists' Rifles, and was one of their team for bayonet fighting, etc., at the Royal Military Tournament, 1914, subsequently receiving his commission in the 2nd Royal Warwickshire Regiment in October, 1914.

He was killed in action on the 18th December, 1914, while leading his men in an attack on the German trenches.

2nd LIEUTENANT MARK ROBINSON PEASE, SPECIAL RESERVE (attd. 1st BATTN.) THE EAST YORKSHIRE REGT.,

was the eldest son of Lieutenant-Colonel Harold Robinson Pease, J.P., D.L., East Yorkshire Regiment, and of Mrs. Pease, Westwood House, Beverley, East Yorkshire.

2nd Lieutenant Pease was born at Tranby House, Hessle, East Yorkshire, on the 14th October, 1892, and was educated at Haileybury College and at the R.M.C., Sandhurst, from which he received his commission as 2nd Lieutenant in the East Yorkshire Regiment in July, 1912. He served for two years at York, and in January, 1914, resigned his commission in order to take his degree. He passed the examination for Jesus College, Cambridge, in March, 1914, expecting to enter in October of that year.

In July, 1914, Mr. Pease joined the Special Reserve of Officers, and on the declaration of war against Germany he was called up to rejoin his old regiment, and for active service was attached to the 1st Battalion, with which he went to France in September, 1914. 2nd Lieutenant Pease was officially reported "missing" after the fighting on the 20th October, 1914, near Prémesques, four miles from Lille, and has since been unofficially reported killed on that date.

CAPTAIN ALAN RALPH PEEL, SOUTH WALES BORDERERS, employed with 2nd BATTN. NIGERIA REGIMENT,

who was killed in action on the 17th November, 1914, in the Cameroons, West Africa, was the eldest son of Herbert Peel, Taliaris, Carmarthenshire.

He was born on the 7th July, 1886, joined the South Wales Borderers in January, 1906, and became Lieutenant in December, 1909. In January, 1913, he was seconded for service with the 2nd Battalion Nigeria Regiment, West African Frontier Force, with which he was serving when he was killed in action, and was promoted Captain in September, 1914.

CAPTAIN WILLIAM GABRIEL KING-PEIRCE, 3rd (attd. 2nd) BATTN. MANCHESTER REGIMENT,

who was killed in action on the 26th October, 1914, at Festubert, France, was the son of the late Richard King-Peirce, M.R.C.S., England. He was born on the 5th July, 1875, and was educated at Bradfield College from 1887–94.

There he was a prefect, and was in the Football XI, being captain in 1893, and in the Cricket XI, 1893–94. From Bradfield he went to Merton College, Oxford, where he was captain of the rowing eight, and took his degree in 1898. He joined the Manchester Regiment in May, 1899, and took part in the South African War, being present at operations in the Orange Free State, Transvaal, Orange River Colony, and Cape Colony, including the actions at Biddulphsberg and Wittebergen. He received the Queen's medal with four clasps.

In December, 1901, he reached the rank of Captain, and, leaving the Regular Army in November, 1911, he joined the 3rd Battalion of his regiment in May, 1912. He had qualified at a School of Musketry, and as an Instructor in Army Signalling. After joining the 3rd battalion he assisted for some time at the O.T.C. School, Shrewsbury.

Captain King-Peirce married Mary Agnes, third daughter of Thomas B. Fisher, Esq., of Sutton, Surrey, and was living near Wimborne when he rejoined for active service.

LIEUTENANT AND ADJUTANT the Honble. HERBERT LYTTELTON PELHAM, 2nd BATTN. ROYAL SUSSEX REGIMENT,

was the fourth son of Francis Godolphin, 5th Earl of Chichester, and was born on the 3rd April, 1884, at Lambeth Rectory, London, S.E., his father, then the Hon. and Rev. Francis Godolphin Pelham, being at that time Rector of Lambeth.

Lieutenant Pelham was a grandson, on the maternal side, of the 1st Lord Wolverton; he was a great-nephew of the Earl of Lucan and the Earl of Cardigan, of Crimean fame, and was descended from Oliver Cromwell and the great Duke of Marlborough. He was also a lineal descendant of Sir John Pelham, a gallant knight of King Edward III, Constable of Pevensey Castle in 1415, and Chamberlain of the Household to King Henry V. Sir John Pelham was in the thick of the fight at Poictiers, and played a prominent part in the capture of King John of France, who gave him his sword-belt and buckles, emblematic badges of honour to-day to be seen in the Pelham arms.

Lieutenant Pelham was educated by A. Tabor, Esq., of Cheam, and at Charterhouse. He obtained his first commission in the Duke of Connaught's Own Hampshire and Isle of Wight Royal Garrison Artillery in April, 1902, being transferred to the 2nd Battalion Royal Sussex Regiment in June, 1904, joining the battalion at Malta in August of that year. He went with it to Crete in 1905, at the time of the Cretan insurrection, and served on the International Tribunal. Returning home after his Cretan services, he passed through the School of Musketry at Hythe, where he came out first in the list, and passed the Maxim-gun course with distinction ; and also went through a course of aviation, gaining the pilot's certificate of the Royal Aero Club in November, 1913.

He was at Belfast during the riots in 1908, in September of which year he became Lieutenant, and subsequently was employed during the labour strikes in Wales. He was appointed Adjutant of his battalion in December, 1911, which appointment he held at the time of his death.

Lieutenant Pelham left Woking on 12th August, 1914, with his battalion, which formed part of the Ist Division of the Expeditionary Force. The battalion was held in reserve at Mons, and formed the rearguard during the memorable retirement to the Marne. For his services during this time Lieutenant Pelham was awarded the Croix de Chevalier of the Legion of Honour by the President of the French Republic for " conspicuous gallantry " between August 21st and 30th, though the award was not actually made till after his death. His name was sent in for mention in despatches by Major-General Bulfin on September 10th.

At the Battle of the Aisne, on the 14th September, 1914, Lieutenant the Hon. Pelham was working the machine guns in a farm, " in the forefront of the battle," between Vendresse and Cerney, on the Chemin des Dames. The farmhouse in which the guns were located was struck by a shell, and Lieutenant Pelham was instantaneously killed.

Many appreciative notices were published of Lieutenant Pelham, including one from a previous Commanding Officer, in the " Sussex Daily News," the " Brighton Season," the " Brighton Standard," and other papers.

LIEUTENANT-COLONEL BEAUCHAMP TYNDALL PELL, D.S.O., p.s.c., 1st BATTN. THE QUEEN'S (ROYAL WEST SURREY REGIMENT),

younger son of the late Rev. Beauchamp Pell, Rector of Ickenham, Middlesex, was born on the 6th July, 1866, and was educated at Wellington College, where he was conspicuous for his love of natural history and his feats of daring ; and at the R.M.C., Sandhurst, where he won distinction as an athlete.

He was gazetted 2nd Lieutenant in the Queen's in September, 1887, becoming Lieutenant in May, 1890. From December of that year to November, 1894, he was Adjutant of his battalion, and was promoted Captain in September, 1896. In 1897–98 he took part in operations on the north-western frontier of India, serving with the Malakand Field, Mohmand Field, and Tirah Field Expeditionary Forces ; he was mentioned in despatches (" London Gazette," 18th March, 1898), and received the medal with two clasps. In 1900 he was again on active service, serving on the Staff as A.D.C. to General Sir Alfred Gaselee, commanding the Chinese Expedition, being present at the relief of Pekin and the actions of Peitsang and Yangstun. He was again mentioned in despatches (" London Gazette," 14th May, 1901), was awarded the D.S.O., and received the medal with clasp.

Subsequently, he had an almost continuous career of Staff service. In 1901 he was on service in South Africa on the Staff, and as Assistant Provost Marshal in the early part of 1902 ; he received the Queen's medal with five clasps. From November, 1902, to April, 1905, he was A.D.C. to different General Officers in India, and from April, 1905 to June, 1908, he was D.A.A.G. of one of the brigades of the Meerut Division, and Assistant Military Secretary to the General Officer commanding the Northern Army there.

In November, 1912, he was appointed General Staff Officer (3rd Grade) at the War Office, being advanced to the 2nd Grade in April, 1913. He was promoted Major in September, 1906, and succeeded to the command of the 1st Battalion the Queen's in September, 1914. He had only held the command for a month when he was reported wounded and missing. It was subsequently ascertained that he was badly wounded at Gheluvelt in the first Battle of Ypres on the morning of the 31st October, 1914 ; that, owing to heavy shell fire, it was impossible to move him during daylight; and that in the afternoon he, with other wounded, was captured by the Germans. Some weeks later news was received that he had been taken to the Field Hospital of the 15th German Army Corps at Werwick, Belgium, and that an operation had been found necessary, which, unhappily, did not save his life. He died on the 4th November, 1914. In his book "The First Seven Divisions," Lord E. Hamilton, in his account of the action at Gheluvelt, records that the two Regular Battalions met on the battlefield and fought alongside each other, the Commanding Officers of both being wounded.

Lieutenant-Colonel Pell married, in 1903, Alice Mary, third daughter of Mr. John Stuart Beresford, C.I.E., and left one son.

CAPTAIN FRANCIS PERCY CAMPBELL PEMBERTON, 2nd LIFE GUARDS,

was the son of Canon T. Percy Pemberton, Prebendary of York Minster, and of Mrs. Pemberton, Trumpington Hall, Cambridge. He was born at Gilling East Rectory, Yorks, on the 4th April, 1885. He was educated at St. Faith's, Cambridge, Mr. Arthur Dunn's, Ludgrove, Malvern (one term), by private tuition, and at Trinity College, Cambridge.

Captain Pemberton joined the 2nd Life Guards on probation in February, 1907, being gazetted 2nd Lieutenant on the 20th February, and Lieutenant on the 21st February, 1909. In 1912 he was seconded as Cavalry Instructor to the Officers' Training Corps of Oxford and Cambridge Universities. He rejoined his regiment on the outbreak of the war, being promoted Captain on the 5th August, 1914.

He was serving in "C" Squadron when he was killed on the 19th October, 1914, at Moorslede, near Roulers, Belgium.

He was a member of the Marlborough, Bachelors', White's, the M.C.C., Pitt Club and County Club, Cambridge, etc. His recreations included music, hunting, polo, golf, cricket, lawn tennis, and billiards.

Captain Pemberton married Winifred Mary, daughter of Sir William Worsley, Bart., and Lady Worsley, of Hovingham Hall, Yorks.

CAPTAIN OSWALD PEMBERTON, ROYAL MUNSTER FUSILIERS,

who was killed in action on the 21st December, 1914, was up to December, 1914, shown in the monthly Army List as attached to the 2nd Battalion Royal Irish Regiment, but is shown in the casualty list issued in February as having been attached at the time of his death to the Royal Dublin Fusiliers.

He was the eldest son of G. T. and Mrs. Pemberton, and was born on the 11th March, 1889; was educated at Cheltenham and joined the Royal Munster Fusiliers from the Special Reserve in December, 1909, becoming Lieutenant in July, 1910.

He was promoted temporary Captain (Supernumary) on the 15th November, 1914 ("London Gazette," 9th December, 1914), this promotion being subsequently confirmed, to date from 30th November, 1914. ("London Gazette," 13th March, 1915).

LIEUT. the Honble. ALAN GEORGE SHOLTO DOUGLAS-PENNANT, 1st BATTN. GRENADIER GUARDS,

who was officially reported as wounded and missing in November, 1914, has since been unofficially reported as killed. He was the eldest son and heir of the third Baron Penrhyn of Llandegai, Co. Carnarvon, formerly in the 1st Life Guards, Major and Hon. Lieutenant-Colonel Buckinghamshire Imperial Yeomanry, J.P. and D.L. for Carnarvonshire, and of the Hon. Blanche Fitzroy, daughter of the third Lord Southampton. Lieutenant Douglas-Pennant was born on the 11th June, 1890, and was educated at Eton. He joined the Grenadier Guards in February, 1910, becoming Lieutenant in May, 1911.

In April, 1914, he was appointed extra A.D.C. to Lord Carmichael, G.C.I.E., K.C.M.G., Governor of Bengal, but rejoined his regiment for active service, on war being declared.

His brother, 2nd-Lieutenant the Hon. H. N. Douglas-Pennant, became heir to the barony.

LIEUTENANT the Honble. CHARLES DOUGLAS-PENNANT, J.P., RESERVE OF OFFICERS, 1st BATTN. COLDSTREAM GUARDS,

who was killed in action at Gheluvelt on the 29th October, 1914, was the third son of the second Lord Penrhyn, and was born on the 7th October, 1877.

He was educated at Eton and the R.M.C., Sandhurst, and in 1899 he joined the

Coldstream Guards, with which regiment he served in the South African War. He took part in the advance on Kimberley, including actions at Belmont, Enslin, Modder River, and Magersfontein, and was present at operations in the Orange Free State, in the Transvaal, and in Cape Colony, including actions at Poplar Grove, Driefontein Vet and Zand Rivers, near Johannesburg, at Pretoria, Diamond Hill, and Belfast. He was twice mentioned in despatches ("London Gazette," 26th January, 1900, and 10th September, 1901), and received the Queen's medal with six clasps and the King's medal with two clasps.

He was promoted Lieutenant in 1905, and in May, 1911, joined the Reserve of Officers, being again gazetted to his old regiment in August, 1914, for service in the Great War, proceeding to the front in September, 1914.

Lieutenant Douglas-Pennant had been reported missing, and afterwards, unofficially, as killed, and it was some time before the fact of his death was officially confirmed.

He married, in 1905, Lady Edith Anne Dawson, elder daughter of the 2nd Earl of Dartry.

2nd LIEUTENANT FRANCIS PEPYS, D.S.O., 2nd BATTN. OXFORDSHIRE AND BUCKINGHAMSHIRE LIGHT INFANTRY,

son of Captain Arthur Pepys, late 60th Rifles, was born at Budleigh Salterton, Devonshire, on the 2nd April, 1891.

He was educated at Charterhouse, where he was in the Cricket XI, subsequently joining the Special Reserve, attached to the Devonshire Regiment. He was gazetted to the 2nd Oxford and Bucks Light Infantry as 2nd Lieutenant in May, 1913.

For his services in the Great War he was awarded the D.S.O., the following being the official record of the occasion :—

" For conspicuous good work on November 3rd in advancing from his trench and assisting in driving away a party of the enemy who were commencing to dig a new trench within thirty yards of his own. Thirty Germans were shot."

His Commanding Officer wrote of him as follows : " He most thoroughly earned it for the splendid way he, with three others, turned thirty or forty Germans out of a trench, and for his splendid leading on other occasions."

He was killed on the 12th November, 1914, while stepping out of his trench, the morning after his battalion had materially helped in the

rout of the Prussian Guard. He was mentioned in Sir John French's Despatch of the 14th January, 1915.

2nd Lieutenant Pepys was fond of hunting, steeple-chasing, cricket, rackets, golf, shooting, fishing, and ski-ing.

2nd LIEUTENANT JOHN PEPYS, 2nd BATTN. THE KING'S OWN (YORKSHIRE LIGHT INFANTRY),

elder brother of the foregoing officer, was the son of Captain Arthur Pepys, late 60th Rifles, and was born in May, 1890, at Budleigh Salterton, Devon.

He was educated at Charterhouse and the R.M.C., Sandhurst, obtaining his commission in November, 1910. He joined the 2nd Battalion at Cork ; was posted to the 1st Battalion seven months later, which he joined at Hong Kong in November, 1911 ; and exchanged into the 2nd Battalion in November, 1912. He passed the Musketry Course at Hythe in 1914, and proceeded to the front in August, 1914, in charge of the machine guns of his battalion.

On the 23rd August, while " fighting his guns splendidly " at Mons, he was shot by German snipers three hours after going into action.

He was a member of the Cavendish Club, and his recreations were hunting, steeple-chasing, shooting, fishing, ski-ing, cricket, and golf.

CAPTAIN REGINALD WHITMORE PEPYS, 2nd BATTN. WORCESTERSHIRE REGIMENT,

was the son of the Rev. Canon H. G. Pepys and Mrs. Pepys, of Lynwood, Church Crookham, Hants, and was born at Hallow Vicarage, Worcester, on the 3rd January, 1883.

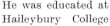

He was educated at Haileybury College and the R.M.C., Sandhurst, where he was in the running team. He joined the Worcestershire Regiment in 1902, and served in Bermuda, Barbados, and Malta from 1902 to 1908, having become Lieutenant in July, 1904. He served with the West African Regiment from 1908 to 1912, and became Captain in the 2nd

Battalion of the Worcestershire Regiment in May, 1913. In August, 1914, he proceeded to the Continent, two days in advance of the Battalion, as Billeting Officer for the 5th Infantry Brigade. He was mortally wounded on Sunday, the 20th September, 1914, at the Battle of the Aisne, while leading "A" Company, of which he was the Captain, in a very exposed position.

Captain Pepys was a member of the Junior Army and Navy Club. He married, on the 27th July, 1914, Maud Mael, youngest daughter of Mr. and Mrs. William Foster, of Beechwood, Iffley, Oxford.

MAJOR (temp. LIEUTENANT-COLONEL) ARTHUR JEX-BLAKE PERCIVAL, D.S.O., p.s.c., NORTHUMBERLAND FUSILIERS,

who was killed in action on the 31st October, 1914, was the fourth and youngest son of the Bishop of Hereford. He was born on the 1st December, 1870, was educated at Marlborough (Mitre) 1885–1887, and joined the Northumberland Fusiliers in February, 1892, becoming Lieutenant in October, 1894, and Captain in 1900. He served with the Nile Expedition of 1898, being present at the Battle of Khartoum, for which he received the British medal and the Egyptian medal with clasp. In 1899–1902 he served in the South African War, taking part in the advance on Kimberley, including the actions at Belmont and Modder River. Afterwards, from April, 1901, to June, 1902, he served on the Staff, and for his services was thrice mentioned in despatches ("London Gazette," 26th January, 1900, 10th September, 1901, and 18th July, 1902); was awarded the D.S.O.; was placed on the list of officers qualified for Staff employment in consequence of service on the Staff in the field; and received the Queen's medal with four clasps and the King's medal with two clasps. Lieutenant-Colonel Percival passed the final Staff College examination in 1909.

From January, 1903, to January, 1908, he was employed with the Egyptian Army, and took part in operations against the Nyam Nyam tribes in the Bahr-el-Ghazal Province. He was mentioned in despatches ("London Gazette," 18th May, 1906); given a clasp to his Egyptian Medal; and awarded the 4th Class Order of the Medjidieh. In 1906 he took part in operations at Talodi, in Southern Kordofan, for which he

received an additional clasp to his Egyptian medal.

He was promoted Major in August, 1908, and from April, 1909, to August, 1911, was Brigade-Major, Northern Command; and from October, 1911, to March, 1913, was a General Staff Officer, 3rd Grade, at the War Office. In January, 1914, he was appointed to be General Staff Officer, 2nd Grade, at the Staff College, with the temporary rank of Lieutenant-Colonel while so employed.

In the Great War he was appointed to the Staff of the IInd Division, and was mentioned in Sir John French's Despatch of 8th October, 1914, for his services; he also received the Croix d'Officier of the Legion of Honour.

Lieutenant-Colonel Percival married, in 1907, Cecil, daughter of the late Mr. C. Henland.

MAJOR CLAUD VICTOR NOBLE PERCIVAL, 2nd BATTN. RIFLE BRIGADE (THE PRINCE CONSORT'S OWN),

who was killed in action on the 14th December, 1914, was the elder son of the late Major-General Lewis Percival, Rifle Brigade, and of Mrs. Percival, Daglingworth, Gloucestershire.

He was born on the 1st August, 1872; educated at Harrow; and gazetted to the Rifle Brigade in October, 1892, becoming Lieutenant in March, 1895. From July, 1898, to November, 1903, he was employed with the Central African Regiment and the King's African Rifles, and in 1899, took part in the expedition against Kwamba receiving the medal with clasp.

He was promoted Captain in January, 1900, and in 1901–02 was with the Aro Expedition, for which he received the medal and clasp. During his service in the Central African Protectorate he brought home a number of different native troops to be present at the Coronation of His Majesty King Edward VII, and with them received from the King at Buckingham Palace the Coronation medal.

From February, 1905, to February, 1912, he was employed with the Egyptian Army in the Soudan, and was for some years in the Bahr-el-Ghazal and the Lado Enclave. On leaving to rejoin his regiment he received the Order of the Osmanieh as a recognition of the excellent work he had done, and also a letter of thanks from the Sirdar. He was promoted Major in October, 1909.

Major Percival, who was unmarried, was a Fellow of the Royal Geographical Society and a member of the Naval and Military and of the Sports Clubs.

LIEUTENANT CYRIL S. STEELE-PERKINS, 1st BATTN. THE KING'S OWN (ROYAL LANCASTER REGIMENT),

was the son of George C. Steele-Perkins, M.D., of 30, Weymouth Street, Portland Place,

London, W., and Kingsdown, near Deal, Kent, and was born in London in 1887. He was

a grandson of the late Samuel Steele-Perkins, M.D., of Exeter, Devon. Lieutenant Steele-Perkins was educated at St. Paul's School and at Sandhurst. He received his commission in February, 1907, after leaving the Royal Military College, being promoted Lieutenant in September, 1911. He was killed in action at Haucourt (between Cambrai and Le Cateau) on the 26th August, 1914. The circumstances are thus described in " The Times " of the 8th September, 1914, by a Sergeant of the King's Own, who returned home wounded : " Then there was Lieutenant Steele-Perkins, who died one of the grandest deaths a British officer could wish for. He was lifted out of the trenches wounded four times, but, protesting, he crawled back again, and remained there till he was mortally wounded."

Lieutenant Steele-Perkins was a member of the Cinque Ports Golf Club and the Northwood Golf Club, London, and was keen on all sports, including polo.

For several generations many members of the family have served with distinction in the Army, Navy, and Royal Marines.

2nd LIEUTENANT REGINALD GABRIEL BEALE PERKINS, 1st BATTN. PRINCESS CHARLOTTE OF WALES'S (ROYAL BERKSHIRE REGIMENT),

was born at Aldershot on the 20th May, 1892, the son of Captain and Mrs. Gabriel Perkins, and grandson of the late Thomas Selsey Beale, Esq., of Hopton Castle, Shropshire. 2nd Lieutenant Perkins' descent from the Beales can be traced back to the fifteenth century.

He was educated at Bath College and the R.M.C., Sandhurst, from 1910–11, obtaining his commission in the Royal Berkshire Regiment, and joining them at Dover in September, 1911. He left for the front on the 21st August, 1914, with the first draft of reinforcements.

He was killed while leading his men at the Battle of the Aisne on the 14th September, 1914, and was buried in the French lines.

2nd Lieutenant Perkins was a member of the Berkshire Wanderers and of the Rugby Football Club of the Aldershot Command.

LIEUTENANT ARTHUR HENNIS PERROTT, ADJUTANT 1st BATTN. PRINCESS CHARLOTTE OF WALES'S (ROYAL BERKSHIRE REGIMENT),

was the son of Major-General Sir T. Perrott, K.C.B., and was born on the 13th June, 1885. He was educated at Windlesham House and Wellington, where he was in the Hill from 1899 to 1903, in which latter year he got his cap. After a year at the R.M.C., Sand-

hurst, he was gazetted to the Royal Berkshire Regiment in August, 1905, becoming Lieutenant in July, 1909.

From April, 1909, to June, 1910, he was A.D.C. to the General Officer Commanding the Straits Settlements, and was appointed Adjutant of his battalion in February, 1913.

Lieutenant Perrott accompanied his battalion to France in August, and was killed in action on the 10th September, 1914, near Gengoulph, when the battalion was acting as vanguard to the IInd Division after crossing the Marne. He was buried in the churchyard at Hautesvesnes, prov. Aisne.

He was a member of the Junior United Service Club, and was a good sportsman.

2nd LIEUTENANT EVELYN WALTER COPLAND PERRY, ROYAL FLYING CORPS (MILITARY WING),

was the only son of the late Walter Copland Perry, M.A., Ph.D., Barrister-at-Law, and of Evelyn Emma, daughter of Robert Stopford ; he was a nephew of Lieutenant - Colonel Horace Stopford, Coldstream Guards, who was killed in command of his bat-

talion at Modder River, in the South African War.

2nd Lieutenant Perry was born on the 4th December, 1890, at 5, Manchester Square, W., and was educated at Mr. Joyce's School, Reigate ; at Repton ; and at Trinity College, Cambridge. On leaving Cambridge he worked at the Royal Aircraft Factory from February, 1911, to August, 1912; and obtained his aviation certificate, No. 130, on a Valkyrie monoplane at Hendon in 1911. In response to Lord Roberts' appeals for the increase of the Army, in January, 1913, he offered his services to the Royal Flying Corps, and joined the Reserve of that Corps in which his commission is dated August, 1914.

On the 1st August, 1914, on the mobilisation of the Army, he received orders to join the Royal Flying Corps at Netheravon, which he did on the 5th August, and was attached to the 3rd Squadron. He flew with it to Dover on the 12th August, and the next day forty-two aeroplanes flew to Amiens.

2nd Lieutenant Perry is believed to have been the first British officer to lose his life while on active duty in this war. He was killed on Sunday, the 16th August, 1914, while leaving Amiens on a B.E. 8 machine. It seems there were four of these machines, and a sadly curious feature is that in each one the pilots and observers were either killed or maimed within a very short period, the machines themselves being wrecked. Death was instantaneous, both for him and for the mechanic—H. Parfitt. The aeroplane caught fire after reaching the ground. He was buried on Monday, the 17th August, 1914, at Le Cimitière de St. Acheiul.

Sir Frederick Kenyon, on the Censor's Staff, wrote: "I attended his funeral. It was a most touching and impressive sight. The streets were lined with French people from the hospital to the cemetery, about two miles outside the town. There was an escort of Welsh Fusiliers and French troops, and behind the carriages, covered with the British flag, walked the Commandant of the Advance Base, the Chief Staff Officer, and the Principal Officer on the Staff of the Inspector-General of Communications, as well as the second French Commandant of the district and a large number of British and French officers and civil officials, besides all the members of the Flying Corps. The service was shared by the English and French Protestant ministers, and every effort was made to do honour to the first British officer to die for his country in this war, and this may, I hope, be of some comfort to you in your great sorrow. The mechanic—Parfitt—was buried at the same time."

A letter from a Flight-Commander said: "I knew your son both at Eastchurch and at Upavon, and we have lost from the Flying Corps a most gallant officer."

Another letter said: "Everyone liked him immensely, and he is a real loss to the country. So few young men have the sense to do the useful work he did. His knowledge and skill would have been most valuable to the development of aviation. Personally I miss him terribly, and he was so amusing. . . . . He was indeed, a born airman, with all the high qualifications of temperament so imperative to aviators, not only of marvellous strength of nerve, but of sound judgment, clear brain, and quick observation, and also a wonderful, calm reserve and quiet self-possession."

An account of 2nd Lieutenant Perry's career as an airman was contained in the "Aeroplane" of the 20th August, 1914, and from that the following extracts are taken: "Evelyn Walter Copland Perry did a considerable amount of flying while on the Staff of the Royal Aircraft Factory on their early experimental machines, including testing a hydroplane on Fleet Pond. On leaving the Royal Aircraft Factory he joined Mr. Sopwith, and flew very well on his old 'Burgess-Wright.' He left Mr. Sopwith to take an 'Avro' biplane to Portugal, where he put the machine through its tests for the Portuguese Army. In the course of these tests he flew over Lisbon, and eventually (owing to engine failure) made a wonderfully skilful forced landing in the Tagus without any injury to the machine, or himself or his passenger—a Portuguese—even wetting their feet. On his return to England Mr. Perry, in conjunction with Mr. Beadle, started building aeroplanes on their own account. Mr. Perry next started Aviation Works at Twickenham, and produced the interesting and beautifully made flying boat which was one of the features of the last Olympia Show (1914)."

2nd Lieutenant Perry was a member of the Public Schools' and Royal Aero Clubs.

2nd LIEUTENANT WILLIAM SINCLAIR PETERSEN, 2nd LIFE GUARDS,

who was killed on the 6th November, 1914, was the only son of Mr. and Mrs. William Petersen, of 32, Inverness Terrace, Hyde Park, London, W., and Cherkley Court, Leatherhead, Surrey.

He was born at Newcastle-on-Tyne on the 10th July, 1892, and received his earlier education at Cargilfield and Glenalmond. Even as a boy he had travelled a great deal, having crossed the continent of North America to the Pacific coast when only nine years of age; and later he crossed the Atlantic Ocean several times. After leaving the public school he studied for a time in France, and then entered Trinity College, Cambridge, where he took his B.A. degree in June, 1913. Afterwards he continued his studies in Germany, acquiring a fluent knowledge of the French and German languages—an attainment of much value in such a war as the present.

After serving in the O.T.C. at Cambridge, 2nd Lieutenant Petersen joined the Essex Royal Horse Artillery in May, 1914 ; but, understanding that his battery was not likely to go on active service at once, he volunteered at the commencement of hostilities, and was given a commission in the 2nd Life Guards, and was entrusted by the Colonel of that regiment with the training of fifty men and horses at Ludgershall Camp on Salisbury Plain. On the 19th October, 1914, he received orders to take his party to the front as a reinforcement, and left Ludgershall the same evening. Travelling to Havre through Southampton, he took his draft across France to the fighting line in Flanders, which he reached on the 29th October, 1914, after successful marches. At the front his party was posted to the 7th Cavalry Brigade, 3rd Cavalry Division, and 2nd Lieutenant Petersen received the commendations of his superior officers on the accomplishment of his duty.

On the 6th November the 2nd Life Guards were ordered to recapture a village from which the French had been driven. The regiment dismounted, and charged the village with the bayonet, cleared it of the enemy, of whom they killed thirty and captured twenty. A Major of the 2nd Life Guards thus described the part played by Lieutenant Petersen in this action : " I saw him arrive with the draft at the time the regiment was doing such arduous work in actually keeping back a very strong attack of the enemy. Your brother died with two other officers of the regiment in driving the Germans back. They accomplished the work, and in so doing actually saved, most likely, a great defeat of our arms. The fact is recognised by the General. I heard—I do not vouch for the truth of it—your brother killed sixteen Germans before he was killed. Your brother died a hero's death, giving his life for his country."

That he was a keen and enthusiastic young officer, of charming manners, and great personal courage is amply testified to by letters subsequently received from his senior and brother officers at the front.

Thus a Major of the Essex Royal Horse Artillery, who had been invalided home from the front, wrote : " During the last month I have had dozens of friends killed beside me, but I knew none of them intimately as I did your son. We became the greatest friends from the time we met. He was a very keen officer, and had all the makings of a good soldier ; and, having lived a good deal abroad, he was in addition a cultivated and interesting person to talk to. I met Colonel Ferguson a few days ago near

Ypres, and he told me how much he liked your son. He added that he was getting on so well with his brother officers. It will be some consolation to you and Mrs. Petersen to know that he died as a soldier and a gallant gentleman would wish to do."

A Captain of the 2nd Life Guards wrote of him as follows : " As the senior officer, left with the regiment, and as I was also his Squadron Leader, I write to let you know that he died leading his troop most gallantly as we advanced under a heavy fire. I had only known him a week, but in that short time I could not help realising his splendid characteristics, which endeared him to us all. He was one indeed to be proud of."

Lieutenant-General the Earl of Dundonald, K.C.B., Colonel of the 2nd Life Guards, wrote : " I hear your son was very gallant " ; and in a later letter : " I feel very much for you in your great sorrow, but the gallantry of your son of which I heard from more than one source must be a great consolation and pride to you all. His name will always be identified with the glorious records of my old regiment."

Another General, speaking of the whole action, said it was the best advance he had ever seen troops make, and added : " This was surely the more remarkable from its being done by dismounted cavalry, and it may be said that even in this campaign, distinguished by so many gallant charges and heroic stands, the fight of the 6th November and the advance of the Household Cavalry Brigade will have a record of its own."

2nd Lieutenant Petersen lies buried in the churchyard at Zillebeke, a small village about two and a half miles south-east of Ypres. His grave is alongside those of Colonel Gordon Wilson, Royal Horse Guards (Blue), and Captain the Hon. Arthur O'Neill, 2nd Life Guards, who both fell in action the same day. A simple cross marks the resting-place of a gallant young soldier and a very perfect gentleman. The Rev. A. E. Boyd, Chaplain, attached to the Cavalry Division, who officiated at his funeral, wrote : " Everything was done to carry out the burial as reverently as possible. The Germans were attacking Klein Zillebeke not far away. Two of our batteries were in action quite close to the village. It was not unfitting that so brave an officer should be laid to rest under these circumstances."

Mr. Petersen received the following telegram from their Majesties : " The King and Queen deeply regret the loss you and the Army have sustained by the death of your son in the service of his country. Their Majesties truly sympathise with you in your sorrow."

2nd Lieutenant Petersen was not the only member of his family to greatly distinguish himself in this war, for his brother-in-law—

Major Douglas Reynolds, V.C., Royal Field Artillery, who married Miss Doris Petersen early in 1914—had the almost unique distinction of earning the Victoria Cross on two separate occasions, as well as the Cross of the Legion of Honour conferred on him by the President of the French Republic.

CAPT. CLEMENT HENRY PETO, Xth (PRINCE OF WALES'S OWN ROYAL) HUSSARS,

who was killed in action near Ypres on the 17th November, 1914, was the youngest son of Mr. and Mrs. W. H. Peto, of Dunkinty, Elgin.

He was born at 169 Cromwell Road, London, S.W., on the 8th July, 1884, and was educated at Harrow (Small Houses and Mr. Davidson's), 1898–1901 ; and the R.M.C., Sandhurst, from which he received his commission in February, 1904. He was promoted Lieutenant in October, 1905, and Captain in September, 1910. He passed the musketry course, Changli Galli, in 1910 ; also telephony and Hindustani, Lower Standard.

He was a member of the Cavalry Club, and was a great explorer and big-game shot. He travelled from India through Cashmir and Turkestan to Siberia, accompanied by natives only, and shot splendid specimens of Ovis ammon, Ovis poli (51½ inches), markhor, ibex, barasingh, etc. In Northern Rhodesia and British East Africa he shot lions and much other game. He rode many winners in regimental races at Rawal Pindi and Mhow, and was a polo player.

Captain Peto was commanding " C " Squadron of his regiment near Ypres when the enemy made a strong attack on the 17th November, 1914. He allowed them to come within five yards of his trench before he gave the order to fire. He then led his squadron in pursuit of the retreating enemy. An officer present wrote that he had personally accounted for six Germans when he was shot through the head by a sniper.

The Colonel of the regiment wrote : " There was no better soldier in the Army or better fellow than your son. Personally I was very fond of him, and so was everyone in the regiment, whether officers or men. All the time he was under me I have never known him cavil or grumble at any order, however unpleasant."

The Officer Commanding the regiment on the 17th November wrote that he " met his death commanding his own squadron, which he had trained so well in South Africa, whilst repelling a fierce attack of the Germans, which his squadron successfully repulsed with heavy loss."

Private Sparks, 14th Hussars, wrote to the " Kent Messenger " on the 26th December, 1914 : " We came under a very heavy shell and rifle fire from a very short distance in front. Lord Alastair Innes Ker carried me a long way, and must have been almost exhausted when I saw two officers jump out of the trench and run towards us. They dragged me to the trench by the arms. Private Sainsbury, 13th Hussars, caught me as they pushed me into the trench. One of them bound me up as well as he was able in the dark, and gave me a drink from his flask. The officers were two brothers —Captain C. and Lieutenant R. Peto, 10th Royal Hussars. Captain C. Peto, I am sorry to say, has since been killed. He was a very brave officer."

Captain Peto was mentioned in Sir John French's Despatch of the 14th January, 1915, for gallant and distinguished service in the field.

LIEUTENANT CHARLES FREDERICK PHAYRE, 2nd BATTALION ROYAL MUNSTER FUSILIERS,

who was born on the 26th May, 1891, at Bangalore, India, was the second son of Lieutenant-Colonel Richard Phayre, J.P., D.L., and Mrs. Phayre, of " Belgaum," Woking, and a grandson of the late General Sir Robert Phayre, G.C.B.

He was educated at Repton and the R.M.A., Woolwich (Sandhurst Company), being in the Hockey XI at the latter. He joined the Royal Munster Fusiliers in October, 1910, and obtained the Hythe certificate for musketry, machine gun, and range finding. He was promoted Lieutenant in April, 1914, and left for France with the 1st Brigade, Ist Division, on the 13th August, 1914.

Lieutenant Phayre was at first reported officially as missing, but some time subsequently it was announced that he had been killed on the 27th August, 1914, during the retirement from Mons, when the battalion was acting as rearguard to the 1st Brigade, Ist Division. The battalion retired fighting for nearly four hours, during which Lieutenant Phayre met his death. His elder brother—Lieutenant R. H. Phayre—was killed on the 26th October, 1914.

LIEUTENANT RICHARD HERBERT PHAYRE, 2nd BATTN. ALEXANDRA PRINCESS OF WALES'S OWN (YORKSHIRE REGT.),

brother of the foregoing officer, was the eldest son of Lieutenant - Colonel Richard Phayre, J.P., D.L., late of the Yorkshire Regiment, and Mrs. Phayre "Belgaum," Woking; and a grandson of the late General Sir Robert Phayre, G.C.B.

He was born at Farnborough, Hants, on the 31st March, 1890, and was educated at Repton and the R.M.C., Sandhurst, joining the Yorkshire Regiment in 1909, and becoming Lieutenant in April, 1911. He was appointed Signalling Instructor to the battalion in 1912, and Assistant Adjutant in 1914.

He was killed on the 26th October, 1914, during the Battle of Ypres, and was gazetted temporary Captain, dated 14th November, 1914, shortly after his death.

MAJOR WILLIAM GRIFFITH BAYNES PHIBBS, 1st BATTN. PRINCESS VICTORIA'S (ROYAL IRISH FUSILIERS),

who died in London on the 8th November, 1914, of acute pneumonia contracted in the trenches, was the son of Major George Phibbs, Royal Irish Fusiliers, Corradoo, Sligo, Ireland, and was born at Malta on the 12th January, 1872.

He was educated at Cheltenham (Garth Garmon, 1885), where he won cups for high jumping and for short-distance foot races.

In October, 1892, he joined the Royal Irish Fusiliers from the Militia, becoming Lieutenant in August, 1895, and Captain in February, 1900.

He took part in the Nile Expedition in 1889, for which he received the Egyptian medal with clasp; and in the South African War, being present at operations in Natal in 1899, including the actions at Talana and at Lombard's Kop. He was also present at operations in the Orange River Colony, the Transvaal, and on the Zululand frontier of Natal between July, 1900, and May, 1902.

In September, 1900, he was appointed Commandant, Springs; and in May, 1901, Adjutant of his battalion. For his services he was mentioned in despatches (" London Gazette," 29th July, 1902); was promoted Brevet-Major on the 22nd August, 1902; and received the Queen's medal with four clasps and the King's medal with two clasps.

He held his Adjutancy till March, 1904, and from September, 1908, to January, 1911, he was an Adjutant of the 18th (County of London) Battalion the London Regiment, obtaining his substantive Majority in January, 1911.

Major Phibbs was a good rider, winning the regimental point-to-point race in 1914. He also played polo both in England and in India, was a first-rate tennis player and an all-round sportsman.

He married Ellie, daughter of J. Roche Hamley, Esq., Landed Proprietor, Lanespark, Thurles, County Tipperary, Ireland. He left no family.

LIEUT. DENIS DUNCAN PHILBY, 1st BATTN. ROYAL DUBLIN FUSILIERS, attd. ROYAL MUNSTER FUSILIERS,

who was killed in action on the 12th November, 1914, near Ypres, was born on the 17th August, 1889, and was gazetted to the Royal Dublin Fusiliers from the Special Reserve in June, 1910, becoming Lieutenant in March, 1912.

LIEUTENANT JOSEPH DOUGLAS PHILIPS, 1st BATTN. THE BUFFS (EAST KENT REGIMENT),

who was killed in action on the 20th October, 1914, was the younger son of Lieutenant - Colonel and Mrs. J. J. Philips, of Rosecourt, Gladstone Road, Broadstairs.

He was born at Woolwich on the 3rd March, 1886; educated at a private school and with an Army coach; and joined the East Kent Regiment from the Middlesex Militia in March, 1907. In March, 1910, he was detached for service with the West African Frontier Force, with the local rank of Lieutenant, and was permanently promoted to that rank in September, 1910. In October, 1914, he was serving with the 1st Battalion of his own regiment, and was killed instantly whilst leading his platoon through a wood at Bois Grenier to attack advancing German infantry. The previous day he had carried out several wounded from the trenches under fire.

Mr. Philips, who was a member of the Junior Army and Navy Club, was a keen Rugby footballer, and fond of cricket, tennis, and golf.

MAJOR EDWARD HAWTIN PHILLIPS, D.S.O., ROYAL FIELD ARTILLERY,

who died on the 6th November, 1914, of wounds received in action the previous day, was the eldest son of the late John Hawtin Phillips and of Mrs. P h i l l i p s , o f Hurstcroft, Ascot, Berkshire.

He was born on the 22nd February, 1878, and was educated at Wellington College (Benson, 1890–93), joining the Royal Artillery from the Militia in January, 1897, and becoming Lieutenant in January, 1900. In 1898–99 he was on active service with the Protectorate Expedition, Sierra Leone, receiving the medal and clasp. From April, 1899, to October, 1900, he was employed with the West African Frontier Force, and in 1900 with the Kaduna Expedition, West Africa (Northern Nigeria), in which he was twice wounded. For this expedition he was mentioned in despatches (" London Gazette," 10th April, 1901), and received a clasp to his medal. Again, in 1900, he took part in operations in Ashanti, West Africa, being present at the relief of Kumassi, where he was severely wounded. For his services he was mentioned in despatches (" London Gazette," 4th December, 1900), was awarded the D.S.O., and received the medal with clasp.

In 1901–02 he was on active service in the South African War, in which he was wounded, being present at operations in the Orange River Colony, Cape Colony, and the Transvaal. He was mentioned in despatches (" London Gazette," 18th July, 1902), and received the Queen's medal with five clasps. He was promoted Captain in March, 1902, and from November, 1904, was again employed with the West African Frontier Force till November, 1905, during which period he was once more on active service in Northern Nigeria in operations against the people of Semolika (1904). For this he received the medal with clasp.

From August, 1908, to August, 1911, he was an Adjutant of his regiment, and in March, 1914, was promoted from the Royal Horse Artillery into the Royal Field Artillery, and was appointed to command the 28th Battery, coming from India with the Meerut Division of the Indian Army Corps to take part in the Great War, and was only three days at the front before he was wounded.

The Inspector-General of Artillery wrote of him in the following terms : " There was no man in all the Artillery under my control belonging to this force whom I would have selected before him for any duty which called for all the highest personal qualifications of a soldier. It was the same in India. If I wanted anything done or tried I always knew it could be in no better hands than his. As a most gallant soldier and gentleman, a thorough sportsman, and a true friend, he will be very deeply regretted by the regiment." (" Wellington Year Book," 1914.)

His younger brother—Captain R. N. Phillips, Royal Welsh Fusiliers—died on the 27th December, 1914, of wounds received in action in this war. Major Phillips was a man of unbounded vigour, cheerfulness, and resource, a keen sportsman, and particularly fond of hunting, pig-sticking, and big-game shooting. He was badly mauled by a tiger in India, but in spite of a stiff arm and hand took his pilot's certificate at Brooklands in May, 1914. He was the hero of the rescue at a dangerous fire explosion. (" Royal Artillery Institution Leaflet," December, 1914.)

He was unmarried, and was a member of the Army and Navy Club.

CAPTAIN RALPH NOEL PHILLIPS, 2nd BATTN. ROYAL WELSH FUSILIERS,

who died on the 27th December, 1914, of wounds received in action on the 3rd November, was the second son of the late John Hawtin Phillips and Mrs. Phillips, of Hurstcroft, Ascot, and was born on the 26th December, 1877.

He was educated at Wellington College and at Trinity College, Cambridge, and joined the Royal Welsh Fusiliers in 1900. He saw service in South Africa with the 1st Battalion, and while attached to the A.S.C.; he was present at operations in the Transvaal and Orange River Colony, receiving the Queen's medal with three clasps and the King's medal with two clasps. He served in the Chinese Regiment for two years, was Adjutant of the 7th Cheshire Territorials from 1911–14, and had been serving with the 2nd Battalion Royal Welsh Fusiliers, 19th Brigade, Expeditionary Force, since the 12th August, 1914. For his services he was mentioned in Sir John French's Despatch of the 14th January, 1915.

His elder brother—Major E. Hawtin Phillips, D.S.O., R.F.A.—died on the 6th November, 1914, of wounds received in action in France.

Captain Phillips, who was a member of the Naval and Military Club, married, in 1911, Margaret Farmer, only daughter of H. R. Farmer, Esq., Gatacre Park, Bridgnorth.

CAPTAIN THOMAS McCANN PHILLIPS, ROYAL ARMY MEDICAL CORPS,

born on the 1st March, 1880, at Damascus, Syria, was the second son of the Rev. John Gillis Phillips, Missionary of the Irish Presbyterian Church in Damascus, and Mrs. Phillips, of Mount Charles, Belfast.

He received his early education, first at the Royal Academical Institution, Belfast, then at Trent College, Notts, and afterwards at Campbell College, Belfast, playing in the " Schools' Cup " team of 1897–98. Subsequently he was a distinguished student of Queen's College, Belfast, and graduated M.B., B.Ch., B.A.O., in the Royal University of Ireland in 1906.

After qualifying he made a voyage to India as ship's surgeon, and subsequently held a resident appointment at the Royal Victoria Hospital, Belfast, where his professional and social qualities were recognised by his colleagues. Having obtained the first place in the open examination in London, he joined the R.A.M.C. in 1907, and was attached to the 8th Hussars, accompanying that regiment to India, where he served five years. He became a Captain in 1911.

On the outbreak of the Great War he was at home on leave. He volunteered for service, and after some weeks of duty at home passing recruits for the New Army, he was sent to the front, as he wished, with the 21st Field Ambulance VIIth Division. He died on the 4th November, 1914, from wounds received by a shell, which also killed Lieutenant Richardson, R.A.M.C. He was taken to a hospital at Ypres, which that night was shelled by the Germans, and he had to be removed to No. 4 Clearing Hospital, arriving there unconscious and expiring soon after.

Captain Phillips was mentioned in Sir John French's Despatch of the 14th January, 1915, for gallantry and distinguished service in the field.

CAPT. WILLIAM CHARLES OWEN PHILLIPS, 1st BATTN. THE QUEEN'S OWN (ROYAL WEST KENT REGIMENT),

was born on the 25th December, 1882, and joined the Royal West Kent Regiment from the Militia in May, 1902, becoming Lieutenant in April, 1904, and Captain in March, 1913. In January, 1910, he was appointed an Adjutant of the Territorial Force.

Captain Phillips, whose name appeared as killed in action in the first list of British losses issued by the War Office in September, 1914, no date or place being given, was married, and was the only brother of Charles E. S. Phillips, of Castle House, Shooter's Hill, Kent.

CAPTAIN CHARLES FREDERICK LEONARD PIERSON, ROYAL GARRISON ARTILLERY,

who was killed in action on the 2nd November, 1914, was the only son of Colonel and Mrs. Pierson, of 26, The Avenue, Eastbourne. He was born on the 26th February, 1883; educated at Eastbourne College; and joined the Royal Artillery from the Militia in December, 1902. He was promoted Lieutenant in December, 1905, and was gazetted Captain after his death, the promotion to date from the 30th October, 1914.

Writing of his death the Commanding Officer of his battery (No. 114, Heavy Battery, R.G.A.), said : " He was seeing the order for taking cover being carried out by all the men before going down himself when the first shell that fell on the battery burst at his feet, killing him and the Sergeant-Major." His Commanding Officer adds : " He took hold of his work, and spared no effort to promote the efficiency of the battery, and had he been spared he would have gone far. We shall never forget him in the battery." Captain Pierson married, in 1912, Constance Sybil, daughter of Colonel Ireland, C.B., C.M.G., and Mrs. Ireland, of Southsea.

LIEUT.-COLONEL HENRY CHARLES PILLEAU, D.S.O., 1st BATTN. THE QUEEN'S (ROYAL WEST SURREY REGIMENT),

born at Bermuda on the 17th February, 1866, was the only child of Colonel H. G. Pilleau, R.E., and a great-nephew of the late General Thomas Addison, C.B., Colonel Commanding the Queen's Regiment.

He was educated at Wellington College, and the R.M.C., Sandhurst, where he was Senior Under Officer and passed out with honours, taking the prize for military topography. He received his commission in the Royal West Surrey Regiment in February, 1887, becoming Lieutenant in July, 1889, and Captain in March, 1896. He served in the South African War from 1899–1902, being present at the relief of Ladysmith, and the actions at Colenso, Spion Kop, Vaal Krans, Pieter's Hill, and operations on Tugela Heights; also in Natal, including Laing's Nek. He was twice mentioned in despatches ("London Gazette," 8th February and 10th September, 1901); was awarded the D.S.O.; and received the Queen's medal with five clasps and the King's medal with two clasps.

In the Great War Lieutenant-Colonel Pilleau, who was promoted to that rank on the 18th September, 1914, was mortally wounded in the Battle of the Aisne, but continued for four hours to direct his men. It was not known till dark, when retiring, that he had been wounded. He died a week afterwards on the 21st September, 1914, in the American Ambulance of Neuilly.

Lieutenant-Colonel Pilleau married, in July, 1904, Edith Maud, daughter of the late Lieutenant-Colonel W. E. Mockler, 4th Battalion, West India Regiment. He was a member of the M.C.C. and the Queen's Club, West Kensington, being a good cricketer and lawn tennis player.

2nd LIEUTENANT RUPERT COLERICK LAYBOURNE PILLINER, 127th BATTERY, ROYAL FIELD ARTILLERY,

was born at Llantarnam Grange, Monmouthshire, on the 5th February, 1891, the son of A. M. Pilliner, J.P., of Llanyravon, Monmouthshire, and grandson of the late Richard Laybourne, J.P., D.L.

He was educated at St. Peter's, Weston-super-Mare; and Blundell's School, Tiverton, Devon; and joined the Royal Field Artillery in December, 1912, from the Territorial Force.

2nd Lieutenant Pilliner's battery formed part of the IVth Division, with which he left for the front on the 23rd August, 1914; and he received his baptism of fire three days afterwards at Le Cateau on the 26th of that month. He was in the retirement from Mons, was present at the Battles of the Marne and the Aisne, and fell on the 4th November, 1914, at Armentières during the first Battle of Ypres.

He was a fine horseman, and well known with all the Monmouthshire packs; also the H.H. and East Kent Hounds.

2nd LIEUTENANT ALEXANDER PIRIE, 1st BATTN. GORDON HIGHLANDERS,

was the son of Mr. Alexander Pirie, Woodside, Aberdeen, and was born there on the 22nd May, 1884. He was educated at Belhelvie, Aberdeenshire.

He joined the Army on the 24th May, 1903, having been promoted to Corporal in 1906, Sergeant in 1911, and Quartermaster-Sergeant on arrival in France in October, 1914. For distinguished service in the field he was mentioned in Field-Marshal Sir John French's Despatch of the 14th January, 1915, and was given his commission in the Gordon Highlanders in November, 1914.

At Bailleul on the 13th December, 1914, while glancing over a parapet a bullet struck him in the head, and he never recovered consciousness, dying in the Clearing Hospital there. 2nd Lieutenant Pirie was a great athlete, having been a member of the Aberdeen Harriers Club. He was trainer of "A" Company, 1st Gordons, the winners of the Inter-Company Football League and Battalion Cup in 1910–11, and himself ran second in the twelve-mile Marathon race.

He married Beatrice, youngest daughter of Mr. James Cromar, of Jackson Terrace, Aberdeen, on the 21st October, 1914, just before leaving for the front.

LIEUT. JAMES MAXWELL PITT, ADJUTANT 1st BATTN. DORSETSHIRE REGIMENT,

who was killed in action on the 13th October, 1914, was the youngest son of Colonel William Pitt, Royal Engineers, and Mrs. Pitt, of Fairseat House, Wrotham, Kent. He was born on the 27th August, 1888, and joined the Dorsetshire Regiment in February, 1908, becoming Lieutenant in October, 1909. He was gazetted Adjutant of his battalion on the 1st October, 1914.

LIEUTENANT GEOFFREY BLEMELL POLLARD, 119th BATTERY ROYAL FIELD ARTILLERY,

born at Kensington on the 5th April, 1888, was the son of Alfred William Pollard, Assistant-Keeper of Printed Books, British Museum, and of Alice Pollard, sometime President of the Women's Institute.

He was educated at King's College School, Wimbledon, where he won the Rothschild Scholarship for French; and St. Paul's School, Hammersmith, where he was a Cadet Lieutenant and Captain of the Shooting Eight, and won the School Scholarship to the R.M.A., Woolwich. Gazetted 2nd Lieutenant in the R.F.A. in July, 1908, he became Lieutenant in July, 1911, having in January, 1910, qualified as 1st Class Interpreter in French. During the early part of the war he had, on the 24th August, helped to man-haul the guns of his battery at Elouges, and was mentioned in Sir John French's Despatch of the 14th January, 1915. Lieutenant Pollard was killed on the 24th October, 1914, while crossing an open space on observation duty for his battery.

LIEUTENANT FREDERICK ROBERT POLLOCK, 1st BATTN. COLDSTREAM GUARDS,

born on the 24th October, 1885, was the son of the late Erskine Pollock, Esq., K.C., of Avening Court, Avening, Gloucestershire.

He was educated at Eton and the R.M.C., Sandhurst, joining the Coldstream Guards in August, 1904, and becoming Lieutenant in June, 1907. From December, 1909, to February, 1914, he was seconded for service with the West African Frontier Force. After taking part in the retirement from Mons and the Battle of the Marne, his battalion was sent to Belgium, and he was killed in action near Ypres on the 23rd October, 1914.

LIEUT. GEOFFREY WILLIAM POLSON, 1st BATTN. THE BLACK WATCH (ROYAL HIGHLANDERS),

was born at Paisley on the 16th September, 1890, and was the son of Mrs. D. Polson, North Berwick, and the late D. M. Polson, Esq., of Paisley. He was educated at St. Ninian's, Moffat; at Charterhouse; and at New College, Oxford.

At Charterhouse Lieutenant Polson was head of the school in his last year, and was presented by Earl Roberts with a copy of his book "Forty Years in India," for being the best all-round boy of the school both in work and in sport. At Oxford he took second-class honours in history.

Lieutenant Polson was gazetted to the Black Watch in August, 1913, with twenty-three months' seniority, being an University Candidate, and was promoted Lieutenant in August, 1914. He was killed in action at the Battle of the Aisne on the 15th September, 1914, leading his men while temporarily in command of his company.

He was a very keen golfer, and played for his college at Oxford. He was a member of the Junior United Service Club, London, and of the New Club, North Berwick.

CAPTAIN GERALD MAURICE PONSONBY, 2nd BATTN. ROYAL INNISKILLING FUSILIERS,

who was wounded in the retirement from Mons, and died on the 31st August, 1914, was the eldest son of the Rev. the Hon. Maurice and Mrs. Ponsonby, Wantage. He was born at St. George's Square, S.W., on the 6th October, 1876, and

was educated at Charterhouse.

He entered the Royal Warwickshire Regiment from the Militia in May, 1898, becoming Lieutenant in March, 1899. He served in the South African War, being employed with the Mounted Infantry, and was present at operations in Cape Colony, Orange River Colony, and the Transvaal, having been slightly wounded. He received the Queen's medal with clasp.

Captain Ponsonby, who was qualified as an Interpreter in Cape Dutch, reached his rank in the Royal Warwickshire Regiment in February, 1902, and was transferred to the Royal Inniskilling Fusiliers in January, 1908. He was mentioned in Sir John French's Despatch of the 8th October, 1914.

He was a member of the Travellers' and Junior Naval and Military Clubs.

LIEUTENANT CYRIL MONTAGU POPE, B.A., B.C.L., 2nd BATTN. WORCESTERSHIRE REGIMENT,

was born at Brighton on the 6th August, 1888, and was the son of the late Reginald Barrett Pope, Solicitor, and Mary Richardson Pope, late of Sussex Square, Brighton.

He was a scholar of Winchester, and held successively a Hulme Exhibition and a Senior Hulme Scholarship at Brasenose College, Oxford. At the University he took honours in Moderations, with a second class; also a second-class in Greats, in jurisprudence, and in the B.C.L. examination. After leaving College he was articled to his father's firm, and was in the second year of his articles.

Lieutenant Pope was gazetted 2nd Lieutenant in the 5th Oxford. and Bucks. Light Infantry in 1910, and became Lieutenant in the 5th Battalion, Worcestershire Regiment (Special Reserve), in December, 1913. On the outbreak of the war he went to the front with the 2nd Battalion of the latter regiment, and was killed on the 24th October, 1914, in the woods to the east of Ypres " while leading on his men most gallantly against a strong position of the enemy."

At the University he stroked for his college the 2nd Torpid and the 2nd Eight in 1911, and the 1st Torpid in 1912, in which year he again rowed in the 2nd Eight. He also played Association football for his college.

LIEUTENANT REGINALD EDWARD PORTER, ROYAL ARMY MEDICAL CORPS,

was the younger son of Dr. G. C. Porter and Mrs. Porter, of Castleacre, Norfolk, where he was born on the 5th April, 1888.

He was educated at Banham Grammar School, where, under the headship of Mr. Fred Cole, M.A., he achieved many successes, including the gaining of the Royal Geographical Society's medal, and entered the London Hospital, taking his M.R.C.S., L.R.C.P. (Eng.), M.B., B.S. (Lond.), in 1911, being subsequently appointed House Surgeon to the Royal Free Hospital. He played golf and was fond of motor-cycling.

He was gazetted to the Royal Army Medical Corps in July, 1912. Some months previous to the outbreak of the war he was attached to the 3rd Battalion Rifle Brigade. He had been wounded on the 18th October, 1914, and was killed in action on the 26th of that month. He was buried at Bois Grenier, Northern France. For his gallant and distinguished service in the field Lieutenant Porter was mentioned in Sir John French's Despatch of the 14th January, 1915.

2nd LIEUTENANT MURRAY STUART POUND, SPECIAL RESERVE, attd. 1st BATTN. THE QUEEN'S (ROYAL WEST SURREY REGIMENT),

died on the 7th November, 1914, at Guy's Hospital, London, from wounds received in action on the 21st October at Poelcapelle, near Ypres.

He was twenty-three years of age, and was the youngest son of Sir Lulham and Lady Pound, of Shenley, Shepherds Hill, Highgate, N., and a grandson of the late Sir John Pound, Bart., who was Lord Mayor of London, 1904–05.

He was educated at Highgate School and at Pembroke College, Cambridge. He was Senior Mathematical Scholar, Head Boy, and Colour-Sergeant of the O.T.C. at Highgate School, where the Leathersellers' Company have established an annual prize in memory of him. At Cambridge he was a scholar of Pembroke College, and graduated with second-class honours. He rowed for his college in the Mays.

He was gazetted to the Special Reserve Royal West Surrey Regiment in January, 1913.

CAPTAIN HENRY MITCHELL POWELL, SOUTH STAFFORDSHIRE REGIMENT, employed with THE WEST AFRICAN REGIMENT,

who was killed in action on the 9th December, 1914, was the eldest son of the late Rev. Henry Powell, Stanningfield, Suffolk, and nephew and adopted son of the late Sir David Gill, K.C.B.

He was born on the 21st May, 1883, and

joined the South Staffordshire Regiment in April, 1903, becoming Lieutenant in July, 1907. He was promoted Captain in April, 1910, and joined the West African Regiment with seniority as Captain in November, 1911.

2nd LIEUTENANT HAROLD OSBORNE POWELL, SPECIAL RESERVE, 4th DRAGOON GUARDS,

who was killed in action at Messines in the first Battle of Ypres on the 31st October, 1914, was the only son of Hubert John and Mabel Powell, of Hill Lodge, Lewes, Sussex, and was born there on the 20th August, 1888.

He was educated at Winchester, where he was Captain of the Commoner Football VI 1905–06. He was a Trooper in the Sussex Yeomanry from 1908–11, and served in the Inns of Court O.T.C. from 1912–14 ; and joined the Reserve of the 4th Dragoon Guards in August, 1914.

2nd LIEUTENANT RHYS CAMPBELL FFOLLIOTT POWELL, 2nd BATTN. HIGHLAND LIGHT INFANTRY,

was born at Dharmsala, Punjab, India, on the 24th July, 1892, and was the son of Major-General C. H. Powell, C.B., Indian Army. He was a grandson of Captain Wellington Powell, 9th Regiment, and, on the maternal side, of James Mackenzie, Esq., of Auchenheglish, Dumbartonshire.

2nd Lieutenant Powell was educated at St. Clare, Walmer ; at Winchester College ; and at Trinity College, Cambridge. Entering the Army as a University candidate on the 23rd September, 1913, he left Aldershot with his battalion for the front in August, 1914, forming part of the 5th Infantry Brigade, IInd Division 1st Army Corps of the British Expeditionary Force.

He was killed in action on the 14th September, 1914, at Verneuil, during the Battle of the Aisne, while leading his platoon to capture a German machine gun. The gun was captured later in the day by Private Wilson of his platoon, who was accorded the V.C. for the action. 2nd Lieutenant Powell was a member of the Scotch Pipers' Club, Edinburgh, and was unmarried.

LIEUTENANT THEODORE PRAIN 1st BATTN. LEICESTERSHIRE REGT.,

who was killed in action on the 21st October, 1914, was the son of Lieutenant-Colonel Sir David Prain, C.M.G., F.R.S., Director of the Royal Botanic Gardens, Kew. He was born on the 6th November, 1887, and was gazetted to the Leicestershire Regiment in April, 1911, his commission being antedated to October, 1910. Lieutenant Prain, who reached his rank in October, 1912, was qualified as a 1st Class Interpreter in French.

For his services in the Great War he was mentioned in Sir John French's Despatch of the 14th January, 1915.

CAPT. THOMAS HAWORTH PRESTON, 3rd BATTN. EAST LANCASHIRE REGIMENT (LIEUTENANT RESERVE OF OFFICERS),

who was killed in action in Flanders on the 17th November, 1914, aged thirty-three, was the only surviving son of the late John Preston and Mrs. Preston, of Mearbeck, Long Preston, Yorkshire, his only brother— 2nd Lieutenant J. S. Preston, 1st Royal Scots—having died of enteric fever at Dewetsdorp, Orange River Colony, on the 27th June, 1900.

He was educated at Haileybury College, and was employed in the South African War with the Mounted Infantry, being present at operations in the Orange Free State, 1900 ; and in the Orange River Colony from November, 1900, to December, 1901. He was mentioned in despatches (" London Gazette," 29th July, 1902), and received the Queen's medal with three clasps. He joined the 2nd Battalion East Lancashire Regiment in 1902 in India, where he served between two and three years. After being invalided home he was transferred to the 1st Battalion, and was with them at the Curragh and Woking. He was promoted Lieutenant in November, 1904, and afterwards joined the Special Reserve.

He became Captain in the 3rd East Lancashire Regiment in November, 1911, and in 1914 was awarded the Royal Geographical Society's diploma. He was a member of the Junior Army and Navy Club; was an excellent all-round sportsman; a splendid game shot, either with rifle or gun; a good fisherman; and a daring rider. He was unmarried.

Captain Preston went to France in August, 1914, in charge of the first draft to reinforce the 1st Battalion, East Lancashire Regiment, which he joined at Le Cateau, and fought with at the Marne and the Aisne. Captain Preston also took part in the severe fighting in Flanders round Ploegsteert, surviving many narrow escapes until the 17th November, when he was fatally hit by a piece of shrapnel.

CAPTAIN CHARLES LEMPRIERE PRICE, D.S.O., 2nd BATTN. THE ROYAL SCOTS (LOTHIAN REGIMENT),

was the only child of Colonel T h o m a s Charles Price, R.A. (retired), and Mrs. Price, of 8 Inverness Gardens, Kensington, London, W., and was born on the 17th September, 1877, in Alderney, Channel Islands. He was educated at St. Paul's School and the Royal Military College, Sandhurst, receiving his commission in the Royal Scots in 1897, and becoming Lieutenant in June, 1899, and Captain in November, 1903.

He served with much distinction in the South African War from 1899–1902, being present in actions at Belfast and Lydenburg, seeing service also in Orange River Colony and Cape Colony on two occasions during operations in the Transvaal. Later on he was appointed Acting Provost-Marshal at Komati Poort, and subsequently Station Staff Officer.

The following account of Lieutenant (as he then was) Price's gallant behaviour was given by Colonel Douglas, his Commanding Officer, at an annual dinner of the Royal Scots Edinburgh Association : " Our men attacked the Boers in a very strong position at Bermondsey, their flanks being protected by precipices, the position thus being a very difficult one to turn. The Boers were, however, driven back with the aid of gun fire, and took up a rearguard position. The Commanding Officer now sent Lieutenant Price with a message to the firing line. When he reached it he found Corporal Paul in command. One officer (Lieutenant Dalmahoy) and two men had been wounded, and Lieutenant Price ran out of the very little cover the men had been able to raise with their entrenching tools, picked up the wounded officer (Lieutenant Dalmahoy) by himself, and carried him in. The work was heavy, and he called for three volun-

teers to help him. Three young Lance-Corporals responded ; and, to indicate their humane intentions, he made them discard their coats and equipment, doing the same himself, and then, unarmed and in their shirt-sleeves, they ran out to try and save the other wounded men. The Boers, however, turned a heavy fire on the small party, and in bringing the wounded back one of the bearers was hit. For his gallantry Captain Price was twice mentioned in Lord Kitchener's despatches, (" London Gazette," 20th August and 10th September, 1901) and was recommended for the V.C. Corporal Paul was promoted to Sergeant, and the three young Corporals awarded the D.C.M."

Captain Price was also mentioned in Lord Roberts's Despatches of the 29th November, 1900. He was awarded the distinction of the D.S.O., and on the conclusion of the Boer War received the Queen's medal with three clasps and the King's medal with two clasps. He was also given the Coronation medal of 1911.

At the manœuvres of 1914 Captain Price was employed as Staff Captain with Brigadier-General Doran's 8th Brigade, and was serving in the IIIrd Division under the same officer when killed at Vailly, France, on the 16th September, 1914, at the Battle of the Aisne while saving a wounded Corporal being in command of the battalion. He had been previously twice wounded, first in the hand, and afterwards in the leg, but did not go into hospital, and on one occasion his horse was shot under him.

Captain Price was mentioned in Field-Marshal Sir John French's Despatch of the 8th October, 1914. While in England, Captain Price had gained a pilot's certificate in aviation. He was an all-round sportsman, excelling in hunting, polo, motoring, golf, fishing, and was good at all games. He was a member of the Naval and Military Club, and the Royal Automobile Club, and was also past Grand Sword Bearer of England.

CAPTAIN THOMAS LEWIS PRICHARD, 3rd BATTN. ROYAL WELSH FUSILIERS,

born at Penmachno, Carnarvonshire, on the 1st October, 1881, was the second son of the Rev. Thomas Prichard, Vicar of Amlwch, Anglesey. He was educated at Friar's School, Bangor, and Trent College. He joined the 4th Battalion Royal Welsh Fusiliers in August, 1900, of which he was for some time Instructor of Musketry, and left to join the 1st Battalion in South Africa for the Boer War, being present at operations in the Transvaal and Orange River Colony from 1901–02, for which he received the Queen's medal with four clasps. He became an honorary Lieutenant in the Army in October, 1900, and Lieutenant in the 3rd Battalion of his regiment in February, 1901. In 1907 he entered the Reserve of Officers, and took up an appointment under the Board of Agriculture, which he held till he joined the 2nd Battalion of his regiment at Portsmouth on the 5th August, 1914, proceeding at once with the Expeditionary Force to France. Captain Prichard, who was promoted to that rank in September, 1914, was wounded on the 27th October, and died in the Allied Forces' Base Hospital at Boulogne on the 9th November, 1914. He was buried in Boulogne Cemetery.

He married, in August, 1908, Dorothy, daughter of Mr. and Mrs. Leopold McKenna, and niece of the Right Hon. Reginald McKenna, Chancellor of the Exchequer, and left two children : Cicely Gwladys, born May, 1909 ; and Leopold Owen, born July, 1912.

His recreations were fishing, shooting, and motoring.

CAPTAIN ARCHIBALD BERTRAM PRIESTLEY, DORSETSHIRE REGIMENT, employed with 1st BATTN. NIGERIA REGIMENT, WEST AFRICAN FRONTIER FORCE,

died on the 12th September, 1914, of wounds received at the Battle of the Marne on the 9th of that month.

He was born on the 21st June, 1882, and was educated at St. Paul's School (1896–1900) and at the R.M.C., Sandhurst, receiving his commission in the West India Regiment in November, 1903. He was promoted Lieutenant in December, 1904, and in February, 1907, exchanged into the Dorsetshire Regiment, in which he became Captain in June, 1912.

In December, 1911, he was seconded for employment with the West African Frontier Force, and was on leave in England when war broke out, so rejoined the 1st Battalion Dorsetshire Regiment. Captain Priestly married Bertha, second daughter of the late John Daker, J.P., of Caerleon, Monmouthshire.

CAPTAIN ALICK LANCELOT PRINCE, 1st BATTN. THE LOYAL NORTH LANCASHIRE REGIMENT,

was officially reported "killed" in action on 8th November, 1914; but a subsequent Casualty List shows him as having been officially reported "not killed but missing," and a still later Casualty List, of 7th June, 1915, shows him as having

been "unofficially reported killed." He was the sixth son of the late T. T. Prince, of Laurel Lodge, Barnet, and of Mrs. Prince, 44, Grange Road, Ealing, was born on the 12th September, 1878 and was educated at Malvern College, and Emanuel College, Cambridge, where he took his degree of B.A. in 1899. He received his commission in the Manchester Regiment in May 1901, becoming Lieutenant in the following December. He took part in the South African War, in which he was slightly wounded, being present at operations in the Transvaal, in 1901-02, receiving the Queen's medal with three clasps. In February 1908 he was transferred to the Loyal North Lancashire Regiment and from April 1910 to May 1913 was employed with the Malay States Guides, being promoted Captain in September 1912. He rejoined the 1st Battalion of his Regiment shortly before war broke out, and for his services was mentioned in Sir John French's Despatch of the 30th November, 1915.

As regards the Officer's death, enquiries through the Red Cross showed that Private Mulholland of the Battalion informed a R.C. representative that he saw Captain Prince shot in the head some time in the first or second week in November, and the Private, who was in Captain Prince's Company, is certain the Officer is dead, and thinks he was buried at a place he called Linden Forest near Ypres, which may be Lindenhoek, close to Kemmel. A Corporal of the Battalion also wrote most circumstantially that he was next to the Captain and saw him shot in the head, and that he saw him lying dead twenty hours after, but too near the German lines to be reached. A Major of his Battalion writing in December 1914, said that from enquiries he had made he feared it was true that Captain Prince was killed. Captain Prince married Emma Caroline, daughter of William Beadell Bacon, Tunbridge Wells, and left two sons, Harold, born in November, 1911, and Ralph Bacon, born in February, 1914.

CAPTAIN LEONEL GRAHAM PRINGLE, M.V.O., 1st BATTN. THE HIGHLAND LIGHT INFANTRY,

son of the late James Thomas Pringle, Commander R.N., of Torwoodlee, D.L. for Selkirkshire, J.P. for Roxburghshire and Selkirkshire ; and grandson of the late Vice-Admiral James Pringle, of Torwoodlee, was born on the 27th April, 1880, at Ilkley, Yorkshire.

He was educated at Vitzthum Gymnasium, Dresden ; at Sunningdale School ; at Radley College ; and at the R.M.C., Sandhurst. He subsequently qualified as an Army Interpreter in German. He joined the Highland Light Infantry in August, 1899, becoming Lieutenant in August, 1900, and Captain in June, 1908. He was awarded the M.V.O. for carrying the Colours on their presentation to the 2nd Highland Light Infantry by H.M. Queen Alexandra, on behalf of H.M. King Edward VII, at Aldershot in 1903. On the 19th December, 1914, he was dangerously wounded in the trenches, and taken prisoner of war by the Germans when they recaptured the position. He died on the 29th December, 1914, at Lille, and was buried there with military honours.

LIEUTENANT ROBERT SCOTT PRINGLE, 1st BATTN. THE QUEEN'S OWN (ROYAL WEST KENT REGT.),

who died on the 15th September, 1914, of wounds received on the previous day at the Battle of the Aisne, was the only son of Mr. and Mrs. R. B. Pringle, of Ardmore, Guildford, and Badulipar, Assam.

He was born on the 30th November, 1885, and received his commission in the Royal West Surrey Regiment from the Militia in March, 1907, getting his step in January, 1911.

CAPTAIN WALTER PENROSE PRITCHETT, 1st BATTN. GLOUCESTERSHIRE REGT.,

died on the 26th December, 1914, of wounds received on the 21st December at Festubert.

The only son of George Pritchett, Esq., of Oakleigh, Melbourne, he was born on the 21st December, 1879, and was educated at the Military Academy, Australia, receiving his commission from the Local Military Forces, Victoria, in the Gloucestershire Regiment in March, 1900, and becoming Lieutenant in July of the same year. Captain Pritchett took part in the South African War, being present at operations in Natal and in the Orange River Colony, for which he received the Queen's medal with two clasps. He obtained his company in October, 1908.

For his services in the Great War Captain Pritchett was mentioned in Sir John French's Despatch of the 31st May, 1915.

He married, in November, 1909, Norma, daughter of the late Colonel G. Forbes, Argyll and Sutherland Highlanders, of Cheltenham. He was a member of the Sports Club ; his recreations were cricket, football, hockey, and tennis.

CAPTAIN the Honble. FRANCIS REGINALD DENIS PRITTIE, 5th (RESERVE) attd. 1st BATTN. RIFLE BRIGADE, (THE PRINCE CONSORT'S OWN),

killed in action on the 19th December, 1914, was the second son of the 4th Baron Dunalley, of Kilboy, County Tipperary, late of the Rifle Brigade, and was born on the 15th October, 1880. He received his commission from the Militia in the Rifle Brigade in June, 1900, becoming Lieutenant in May, 1901. From January, 1907, to November, 1908, he was employed on the Uganda-Congo Boundary Commission, and from December, 1910, to April, 1913, was Assist. Commr. in the Anglo-Belgian and Anglo-German Boundary Commission, Uganda ; from September, 1913, to April, 1914, he was employed on special duty in Egypt. Captain Prittie, who was promoted to that rank in May, 1908, was a qualified Interpreter in French. For his services in the Great War he was mentioned in Sir John French's Despatches of the 8th October, 1914, and 14th January, 1915, and was awarded the decoration of the Legion of Honour on the 15th October, 1914, for being " the last man to leave a trench under very hot fire ; and it was his action that saved the lives of many French soldiers."

CAPTAIN THOMAS NORMAN PUCKLE, LEICESTERSHIRE REGT., employed with the WEST AFRICAN FRONTIER FORCE,

born at Mercara, Mysore, India, on the 16th February, 1875, was the son of Colonel H. G. Puckle, late of the Madras Staff Corps, and a relative of Richard Kaye Puckle, Esq., I.C.S., and of the late George Hale Puckle, Esq., M.A., J.P., D.L. for Westmorland,

and formerly Principal of the Old College at Windermere.

He was educated at the Old College, Windermere, and at Wellington College. He joined the Leicestershire Regiment from the Militia in December, 1897, becoming Lieutenant in January, 1900, and served through the South African War, being present at the first action at the Battle of Talana, went through the siege of Ladysmith, and took part in the actions at Lombard's Kop, Laing's Nek, Belfast, and Lydenberg, also in the operations on the Zululand frontier in September and October, 1901. He was twice mentioned in despatches (" London Gazette," 8th February and 10th September, 1901), and received the Queen's medal with four clasps and the King's medal with two clasps.

He was promoted Captain in February, 1908, and in October, 1912, was seconded from his regiment for service in the Nigeria Regiment, West African Frontier Force, in which he was given the temporary rank of Major from March, 1913. In this corps he trained the Hausa troops —Mounted Infantry—and fell in action at Garua in German West Africa (Cameroons) on the night of the 30th August, 1914.

Captain Puckle's chief hobby was big-game shooting, and he had many trophies, secured in India and Africa ; he was also fond of polo and golf, and all forms of sport. He was a member of the United Service and the Junior Naval and Military Clubs, and of the Windermere Golf Club. He was unmarried.

LIEUT. EDMUND ELGOOD PUNCHARD, 2nd BATTN. BEDFORDSHIRE REGT.,

son of the Rev. Elgood George Punchard, D.D. Oxon, Hon. Canon of Ely, and Vicar of Ely St. Mary's, was born at Christ Church Vicarage, Luton, Beds, on the 21st October, 1890.

He was educated at Haileybury from 1902 to 1908, and at the R.M.C., Sandhurst, from 1909 to 1910, where he was in the Gymnastic VI and gained the bronze medal.

Lieutenant Punchard obtained his commission in the Bedfordshire Regiment in October, 1910, becoming Lieutenant in June, 1912. He served with his battalion in Bermuda (1910–11) and in South Africa (1912–14), being Brigade Signaller at Pretoria (1913–14).

He was killed in the Battle of Ypres on the 31st October, 1914, when at the head of his platoon, under the woods of Zandvoorde, near Gheluvelt,

Belgium. His name appeared in Sir John French's Despatch of the 14th January, 1915, for gallant and distinguished service in the field.

CAPTAIN ARTHUR KENNETH PUZEY, 4th BATTN. ROYAL FUSILIERS (CITY OF LONDON REGIMENT),

was the only son of the late Major Arthur Robert Puzey, R.E., and was born at Boaz Island, Bermuda, on the 11th March, 1880.

He was educated at Eastman's School, Stubbington, and joined the Militia, from which he was transferred in August, 1900, to the 1st Royal Fusiliers as 2nd Lieutenant ; he was promoted Lieutenant in February, 1904, and obtained his company in November, 1909. From July, 1902, to August, 1903, he was Station Staff Officer at Mandalay ; and from November, 1903, to February, 1904, held a similar appointment at Dum Dum. From February, 1910, to February, 1913, he was Adjutant of the 8th (Territorial) Battalion, the Hampshire Regiment (Isle of Wight Rifles, Princess Beatrice's).

Captain Puzey was killed in action near Ypres on the 11th November, 1914.

He married Olive Hunter, younger daughter of the late Mr. W. Pearce, of " Standen Elms," Isle of Wight, and left two children, Eric, born September, 1911, and Olga Desirée, born posthumously in July, 1915.

CAPTAIN JAMES PYMAN, 3rd BATTN. BORDER REGIMENT, attd. 2nd BATTN. MANCHESTER REGIMENT,

who was killed in action on the 18th November, 1914, was the younger son of the late James Pyman, of Newcastle-on-Tyne.

He was promoted Lieutenant in May, 1903, and became Captain in the 3rd Battalion of his regiment in May, 1906.

CAPTAIN EDWARD OWEN St. CYRES GODOLPHIN QUICKE, 3rd (attd. 1st) BATTN. THE DEVONSHIRE REGT.,

of Newton St. Cyres, who was killed in action on the 25th October, 1914, was the eldest son of Mr. and Mrs. Quicke, of Newton St. Cyres.

He was appointed 2nd Lieutenant in May, 1904, and became Lieutenant in his battalion in September, 1908. He had been attached to the Regular Forces, and obtained a satisfactory report for the rank of field officer, having qualified at a School of Musketry.

The notification of his promotion to the rank of Captain, from 14th September, 1914, appeared in the " London Gazette" of the 19th November, 1914.

He was mentioned in Sir John French's Despatch of the 14th January, 1915.

CAPTAIN MILES RADCLIFFE, 2nd BATTN. BORDER REGIMENT,

born at Werneth Park, Oldham, on the 13th October, 1883, was the son of Henry Miles and Emily Bertha Radcliffe (*née* Platt), of Werneth Park, Oldham, and Summerlands, Kendal, and a grandson of the late John Platt, M.P., of Oldham.

He was educated at Cheam School and Harrow, joining the Border Regiment after passing through the R.M.C., Sandhurst, in January, 1904, becoming Lieutenant in August, 1906, and Captain in November, 1914. He served for three years in South Africa after the Boer War, for most of the time with the Mounted Infantry. While there he played polo, and he was also fond of hunting, and rode in point-to-point races.

Captain Radcliffe, who at the time of his death was attached to the 1st Royal Scots Fusiliers as Machine Gun Officer, was shot through the heart on the night of the 12th December, 1914, it is thought, by a sniper, near Ypres, while returning to a dug-out, and was buried in Kemmel Churchyard. He was spoken of by his comrades as a gallant and brave officer, greatly beloved by his men, who all deeply regretted his loss.

Captain Radcliffe, married Dorothy Kathleen, *née* Duffin, and left one son, Miles Claude, age eleven months when his father died.

LIEUTENANT LESLIE CLAUDE MOOR-RADFORD, 1st BATTN. SOUTH STAFFORDSHIRE REGIMENT,

born at 34, Cadogan Terrace, London, S.W., on the 10th January, 1890, was the son of Alfred Moor-Radford, Barrister-at-Law, and Mrs. Blanche Moor-Radford ; his grandfather on the paternal side was Francis Radford, Esq., of Holland Park, Kensington, and Kentisbeare, Devonshire, and on the maternal side Robert Dawson Tewart, Esq., of Chiswick, and Coupland Castle, Northumberland.

Lieutenant Moor-Radford was educated at Eastman's Naval Academy, Winchester, and the R.M.C., Sandhurst.

He was gazetted 2nd Lieutenant in April, 1910, and Lieutenant in January, 1913, serving at Devonport, Gibraltar, and in South Africa.

On war being declared, Lieutenant Moor-Radford's battalion was stationed at Pietermaritzburg, and was brought home to form part of the VIIth Division which landed in Belgium on the 7th October, 1914. He was killed on the 26th of that month at Kruiseik, near Ypres, being shot outside a trench, which he defended under fire for fifteen minutes, although mortally wounded, shouting to his men before he succumbed to " charge and stick to it."

Lieutenant Moor-Radford was founder and editor of the Regimental Gazette, the " Staffordshire Knot." His recreations were shooting, cricket, motoring, riding, and golf, and he also wrote for magazines and other publications, and was interested in photography. He was a member of the Conservative Club, St. James's Street.

LIEUTENANT SPENCER JULIAN WILFRED RAILSTON, 18th KING GEORGE'S OWN LANCERS, INDIAN ARMY,

born at Hamilton, Scotland, in January, 1889, was the younger son of Colonel H. R. Railston and his wife, Magdalen, daughter of the Rev. C. E. and Lady Georgina Oakley, and grand-daughter of the second Earl of Ducie. He was edu-

cated at Radley, whence he passed direct into the R.M.C., Sandhurst, at the age of seventeen, and passed out in 1907, taking the tenth place. He won the Champion Cup for gymnastics at his public school, and represented it in the boxing competition at Aldershot. Both at his public school and at Sandhurst he was in the Cricket XI. After getting his commission he was attached for a year to his father's regiment : the Cameronians. Soon after joining, while in India, he entered without any training for the Lightweight Boxing Championship of India, and won it. At the expiration of a year he was appointed to the 18th K.G.O. Lancers, and played in their polo team. He was a good big-game shot and a good steeplechase rider. When riding a steeplechase at Jubblepore a few months before his death his girths broke after the first fence. He managed to pull the saddle and weight cloth from under him, and rode the remaining two and a quarter miles bareback, carrying them on his arm, and, notwithstanding the horse falling once, he managed to finish the course. On completing the cavalry course at Saugor he came home on a year's leave in 1914, and played polo through the London season in Count de Madre's team (" the Tigers "). He was to have become Adjutant of his regiment on the expiration of his leave, but the Great War broke out, and he at once volunteered for active service, and was attached to the 4th Dragoon Guards, with whom he went to the front, and with whom he served from the Battle of Mons and in all subsequent actions till he was killed at Messines, Belgium, on the 1st November, 1914. The Major-General Commanding the Ist Cavalry Division sent the following account of Lieutenant Railston's death to his father : " I am deeply grieved at the death of your gallant boy, who on every occasion of this war has so distinguished himself. He is a great loss to his regiment. He lost his life by a gallant act. His regiment was holding one-half of the village of Messines, south of Ypres, and the Germans the other half for twenty-four hours. In front of his troop a poor woman was lying wounded, and your boy left his cover to bring her in. He was struck by many bullets and killed. Had he lived he would certainly have been mentioned in despatches."

Another officer wrote as follows : " His loss will be felt by the whole Cavalry Brigade, as he has been simply splendid through all these trying times—always cheery and full of go, and ready to take on anything. Surely, when the war is over, there will be no more gallant act than that to write of, and we are all so proud of him."

A memorial tablet has been put up to his memory in Tortworth Parish Church, Gloucestershire.

LIEUTENANT DUNCAN GAVIN RAMSAY, ROYAL SUSSEX REGIMENT, attd. 2nd BATTN. THE QUEEN'S (ROYAL WEST SURREY REGIMENT),

who was killed in action on the 18th December, 1914, was the only son of the late Alexander and Mrs. Ramsay of Hillcote, Eastbourne.

He was born at Worthing, in January, 1893, and was educated at Bradfield College and the R.M.C., Sandhurst, joining the Royal Sussex Regiment as 2nd Lieutenant in January, 1913, being promoted Lieutenant in November, 1914. He was a member of the Junior United Service Club, and was fond of Alpine sports.

The officer who took command of his regiment gave the following account of the young officer : " Your son has been attached to the 2nd Queen's for the past month. We made an attack on the enemy's trenches on the night of the 18th, and lost heavily. He was one of the eight officers who went forward, all of whom were wounded. Your son, I regret to say, is missing. On the morning of the 19th we had a local armistice to bury the dead and bring in the wounded. As his body was not found, he must have. been wounded near the German trenches, and taken in by them. Some of the German officers told us they had a wounded officer prisoner, and as your son was so popular, two of our officers were allowed into the German trenches to see him, and never came out again ; they were also taken prisoners.

" Your son went forward with a part of his company on the night in question to support the attack of another battalion. The fire was terrific, several machine guns and a continuous roar of musketry. He came back to the trenches shortly after to look, I think, for the remainder of his company. He was seen to go back again towards the enemy, and nobody saw him after that. I might mention that your son had shown himself to be a very brave and gallant fellow, absolutely fearless under heavy fire, and always ready to risk his life at any time. Before the attack took place he reconnoitred at night the German lines, and several times got within twenty yards of the enemy's main trenches. He was fired on by the enemy at that distance many times, but seemed to bear a charmed life. However, his reconnaissance work was so good that on the night of the 14th December he was entrusted with an attack on the enemy's picket. He took twenty-three men with him. He successfully surprised the picket, killing two and wounding two out of seven. He got in one wounded German, and also brought back our two casualties. This little affair took place four hundred yards from our lines, and only fifty yards from the enemy's. The capture of a German, dead or alive, was most needed, and this he managed to do, greatly to the joy of the Staff, who obtained valuable information.

" I cannot tell you how much I regret losing his services. I thought possibly you would like a line from me, his Commanding Officer. I have commanded this battalion since your son joined it. After the affair of the 14th, I forwarded to headquarters a report of the excellent work of your son, and I know that his name has gone forward for honours which he thoroughly deserved. I think it is a good sign, not finding his body; he is probably wounded and a prisoner, and I hope it may be only a slight wound."

Unfortunately this hope was not realized as it was afterwards discovered that Lieutenant Ramsay was killed on the above-mentioned date. He was mentioned in Sir John French's Despatch of the 14th January, 1915, for his gallant conduct.

LIEUTENANT NORMAN RAMSAY, RESERVE OF OFFICERS, attd. 4th (ROYAL IRISH) DRAGOON GUARDS,

who was killed in action in France on the 4th November, 1914, was the second son of the late Captain John Ramsay, Royal Engineers, and of Mrs. Ramsay, Cams Hall, Fareham.

He was born on the 20th April, 1880; received a commission in the Royal Artillery in January, 1900, being promoted Lieutenant in April, 1901, and served in the South African War, for his services in which he was mentioned in despatches. He retired from the service in 1903, and rejoined for the Great War, proceeding to France in October, 1914. (" The Times," 11th November, 1914.)

CAPTAIN HARRY SHERWOOD RANKEN, V.C., ROYAL ARMY MEDICAL CORPS,

was born at Glasgow on the 3rd September, 1883. He was the son of the Rev. Henry Ranken, Minister of Irvine, Ayrshire, and his wife, Helen Morton. He was educated at Irvine Royal Academy, where he was Dux boy in 1899, and at Glasgow University, where he obtained the degrees of M.B., Ch.B., with commendation. He entered the R.A.M.C., passing first in the entrance exam., on the 30th January, 1909, and obtained many distinctions in the early part of his military career, receiving medals for Pathology, Tropical Medicine, and Military Medicine, with the prizes for Hygiene, and for the highest aggregate of marks in the course open to R.A.M.C. and I.M.S.

He passed his examination for Captain in 1911 with " special certificate," and was promoted to that rank on the 30th July, 1912. He had become a member of the Royal College of Physicians, London, in 1910, was a member of the Soudan Sleeping Sickness Commission, and in charge of the Sleeping Sickness camp at Yei, in the Lado Enclave, Western Mongalla, Soudan, from 1911–14.

He was at home on leave when the war broke out, and, having volunteered for active service, went to the Continent with the first part of the British Expeditionary Force. He soon distinguished himself by an act of bravery, for which he received the V.C., the following being the official record :—

" For tending wounded in the trenches under rifle and shrapnel fire at Hautvesnes on September 19th, and, on September 20th, continuing to attend to wounded after his thigh and leg had been shattered."

He was also awarded the Cross of Chevalier of the Legion of Honour " for gallant conduct from the 21st–28th August, 1914."

Captain Ranken, V.C., died at Braisne, France, on the 25th September, 1914, from wounds received at Soupir.

He was a big-game hunter—elephant, buffalo, etc.—a member of the Royal Automobile Club, and a scratch golfer.

CAPTAIN CLEMENT GASCOYEN RANSFORD, 1st BATTN. SOUTH STAFFORDSHIRE REGIMENT,

youngest son of the late Colonel and Mrs. Ransford, was unofficially reported to have been killed on the 26th October, 1914.

He was born on the 19th April, 1882, and was educated at Bedford School from 1895 to 1900; in September of the latter year he received a commission in the Militia, and after being attached to the Regulars for a year and two months, was appointed 2nd Lieutenant in the Devonshire Regiment in December, 1901. He took part in the South African War, being present at operations in the Transvaal, the Orange River and Cape Colonies, for which he received the Queen's medal with five clasps. He was promoted Lieutenant in May, 1904, and in April, 1906, was transferred to the Bhopal Infantry, Indian Army, in which he became Captain in June, 1911. In November, 1912, he was transferred to the South Staffordshire Regiment.

LIEUTENANT URPETH RASTRICK, 2nd BATTN. NORTHAMPTONSHIRE REGIMENT,

who was killed in action at La Bassée, in France, on the 14th December, 1914, was the only son of Mrs. Rastrick and of the late George Rastrick, Esq., of Woking Lodge, Woking, Surrey.

He was born on the 10th February, 1889 was educated at Eton, and joined the Northamptonshire Regiment from the Special Reserve Battalion of the Royal Fusiliers in December, 1910, being promoted Lieutenant in January, 1912.

LIEUTENANT JOHN EDWARD RATCLIFF, 2nd BATTN. ROYAL WARWICKSHIRE REGIMENT,

who was killed in action near Becelaere on the 19th October, 1914, was the son of J. F. Ratcliff, Widney Cottage, Knowle, Warwickshire.

He was born on the 27th September, 1891, entered the Royal Warwickshire Regiment from the Special Reserve in May, 1912, and became Lieutenant in August, 1913. He accompanied his battalion to Belgium early in October, 1914, where it formed part of the 22nd Brigade, VIIth Division.

LIEUTENANT VIVIAN TREVOR TIGHE REA, 2nd BATTN. ROYAL IRISH RIFLES,

son of Henry Tighe Rea, of Glandore Park, Belfast, Vice-Consul of the Netherlands and of the Argentine Republic, and grandson of the late Hugh Rea, of Clifton Lodge, Belfast, was born at Mendoza, Argentina, on the 17th August, 1891.

He was educated at Campbell College ; at Queen's University, Belfast, where he took an Honours degree ; and at Trinity College, Dublin, where he gained several important distinctions in the Theological School, including the Downes prize for Oratory in 1914.

Lieutenant Rea had been Scoutmaster of the Bangor (Co. Down) Troop of Boy Scouts, for several years the first troop in Ireland, and was Honorary Secretary of the Ulster Scout Council and an earnest worker among young men. Many of his old boys served in the Great War and in the new Armies.

Lieutenant Rea joined the 4th Battalion Royal Irish Rifles (Special Reserve) in 1911, being promoted Lieutenant in February, 1913, and went to the front to join the 2nd Battalion in September, 1914. He took part in some of the fiercest fighting on the left of the Allies at, and near Neuve Chapelle. Two of his Captains

were lost within ten days, and he had held his trench gallantly while in command of his company. He was fatally wounded while crossing from the reserve trench on the 25th October, 1914.

His Scouts and fellow students at Trinity College are erecting a memorial window at Bangor (Co. Down) Parish Church to perpetuate his name.

He was the first student of Trinity College to fall in the war.

2nd LIEUT. ARTHUR BEDDOME READ, 1st BATTN. PRINCE ALBERT'S (SOMERSET LIGHT INFANTRY),

was born at Surbiton, Surrey, on the 20th January, 1891, having been the son of the late Robert Arthur Read, Esq., and grandson of the late Colonel R. H. Beddome, Madras Staff Corps, and of the late Robert Arthur Read.

He was educated at Sherborne School, Dorset, where he was a Colour-Sergeant in the Officers' Training Corps. He was gazetted to the Special Reserve in April, 1912, and was commissioned 2nd Lieutenant in the Somerset Light Infantry in December, 1913, joining the 1st Battalion at Colchester the following month.

2nd Lieutenant Read was killed by shrapnel in the Battle of the Aisne, France, on the 16th September, 1914.

He was a member of the M.C.C. and was also a fine Rugby forward, most of his work being done for the Richmond Club until the 1913-14 season, when he played for the Army against Sandhurst and Woolwich at Queen's Club.

LIEUT. JOHN HENRY LOFTUS READE, 1st BATTN. THE MANCHESTER REGIMENT,

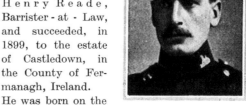

who was killed in action on the 29th October, 1914, was the son of John Henry Reade, Barrister-at-Law, and succeeded, in 1899, to the estate of Castledown, in the County of Fermanagh, Ireland.

He was born on the 21st February, 1881, and was educated at St. Columba's College, Rathfarnham, County Dublin. Having served with the 5th (Militia)

Battalion Royal Irish Rifles, when embodied, for a year and two months he received his commission in the Manchester Regiment in January, 1902. He took part in the South African War, being present in the Orange River Colony from August, 1901, to February, 1902. He was promoted Lieutenant in October, 1903, and from December, 1909, to November, 1912, was Adjutant of his battalion.

He went out to the front with the 2nd Battalion, Manchester Regiment, from the Curragh with the Vth Division of the Expeditionary Force, and was mentioned in Sir John French's Despatch of the 8th October, 1914, for his good work at Le Cateau. He was Acting Adjutant of the battalion from the time of this action at Le Cateau until the 29th October, when he was killed at Festubert.

CAPTAIN ERIC BRUCE REID, 1st BATTN. THE PRINCE OF WALES'S (NORTH STAFFORDSHIRE REGT.),

was the youngest son of the late Major-General A. T. Reid, Bombay Staff Corps, of Derby House, Victoria Road, Upper Norwood.

He was born on the 2nd September, 1880, and was educated at Dulwich College and the R.M.C., Sandhurst. He joined the North Staffordshire Regiment in January, 1900, becoming Lieutenant in November, 1900, and Captain in August, 1908.

He was killed in action on the 21st October, 1914, being shot dead near Armentières, and lies buried at Chapelle d'Armentières, together with two other officers of his regiment, who fell in the same action.

Captain Reid was unmarried.

CAPTAIN EDWARD HARINGTON REID, 2nd BATTN. SUFFOLK REGT.,

was the son of G. Boileau Reid, I.C.S. (retired), and Mrs. Reid, of Fair Hill, Camberley, and was born at Mount Abu, India, on the 7th July, 1882.

He was educated at Mr. Lee's School, Forest Row, The Park, Harrow; and

the R.M.C., Sandhurst. He was gazetted to an unattached 2nd Lieutenancy in January, 1901, and to the Suffolk Regiment in March of the same year, and immediately proceeded on active service in South Africa, being present at operations in the Transvaal from May, 1901, to May, 1902, receiving the Queen's medal with three clasps. From 1907–12 he served with the King's African Rifles in Uganda, and took part in the operations in Somaliland, 1908–10, for which he received the medal. In 1911 he was appointed Political Officer in Uganda, a position he held for nearly a year. On his leaving Uganda the Governor made the following report to the Colonial Office : " Before proceeding on tour the Governor desires to take the opportunity of bringing to your notice the excellent work performed by Captain Reid, and the able assistance that this officer has rendered to the Protectorate Government during the period he has acted in the capacity of Political Officer of the Kigezi district, viz., from the 7th July, 1911, to the 15th March, 1912. Captain Reid had to contend with exceptional difficulties in administering this new and unsettled district, which he has done without assistance under trying circumstances. He has shown marked administrative ability, and maintained good order in a district where the native population has been brought under control for the first time. He has also furnished the Government with valuable reports and maps of a country practically unknown. Under the circumstances I recommend that this officer's name may be noted for special service, and that his service as Political Officer in this protectorate may be brought to the notice of the Secretary of State for War."

Captain Reid was a member of the Sports Club ; and, having had special opportunities for big-game shooting, had a very fine collection of trophies.

He was serving with his regiment in the Great War when at Le Cateau, on the 26th August, 1914, he was seriously wounded in the head, and had been unconscious for some time when his battalion, which was covering the British retirement, suffered severe losses. Captain Reid, according to a German report, died on the field. He married Elsie Vivian, daughter of the late Ernest C. Grant and Mrs. Grant, Fosse Bank, East Camberley. A daughter was born after her father's death on the 9th May, 1915.

LIEUTENANT JAMES LESTOCK IRONSIDE REID, 2nd BATTN. 2nd KING EDWARD'S OWN GURKHA RIFLES,

was born at Eastbourne on the 4th January, 1887, the only son of Colonel James Henry Erskine Reid, late of the King's Own Scottish Borderers. On his mother's side Lieutenant Reid was first cousin (two removed) of the late Brigadier-General John Nicholson, the hero of Delhi.

Lieutenant Reid was educated at Wellington College and at the R.M.C., Sandhurst. He joined the Scottish Rifles in October, 1907; was transferred to the 10th Gurkhas in September, 1909, and to the 2nd Gurkhas in January, 1913.

He was killed in the trenches at Neuve Chapelle on the 2nd November, 1914, with all his brother officers.

Lieutenant Reid was fond of polo, football, and hockey, and was good at all games. He was not married.

LIEUTENANT RALPH ALEC REILLY, 31st PUNJABIS, attd. 58th VAUGHAN'S

RIFLES, youngest son of Colonel B. L. P. Reilly, Indian Army (retired), was born at Jubbulpore, India, on the 7th January, 1889.

He was educated at Cheltenham College, where he was Captain of his house boat; and the R.M.C., Sandhurst, obtaining his commission in September, 1908. He was attached for a year to the Sherwood Foresters (Nottinghamshire and Derbyshire Regiment), and was then posted to the 31st Punjabis, of which he became Quartermaster.

For active service in the Great War he was attached to the 58th Vaughan's Rifles, Frontier Force, and was killed near La Bassée on the 23rd November, 1914, while attempting with only six Sepoys to stop the onrush of the 112th German Infantry Regiment. He was buried in Bethune Cemetery.

His father received the following letter from Major Houston, commanding the 58th Rifles: " His loss will be very keenly felt by us all, for I have seldom seen a young officer so thoroughly keen and efficient, and so dependable. . . . Early on the 23rd I heard rumours of the line away to our left being very hard pressed, so I sent up your son to the trenches with extra ammunition, and to bring back any reports he could from our officers of the exact situation. He arrived there safely, but, unfortunately, the crisis developed very rapidly, and as he was

returning along the covered way a mass of Germans swept over the regiment on our left and reached the covered way. The last seen of your son alive was leading the half-dozen men he had with him against an overwhelming number of Germans—as honourable a death as is possible for a soldier. We subsequently drove back the Germans, and recovered all the ground lost and a good many prisoners. We recovered your son's body, and, from the wound in his head, his death must have been instantaneous."

Colonel Reilly also received a telegram expressing the sympathy of Their Majesties the King and Queen, and a letter of sympathy from the Commander-in-Chief in India, on the loss of his son.

2nd LIEUTENANT GERALD LYONS RELTON, 1st BATTN. EAST SURREY

REGIMENT, who was killed in action on the 14th September, 1914, was the third son of Mr. and Mrs. A. J. Relton, 179, Oakwood Court, Kensington, W., and was born on the 15th April, 1891.

He was educated at Rugby, and obtained his commission in the 3rd Battalion (Special Reserve) of the East Surrey Regiment in February, 1913. In the " London Gazette " of the 13th October, 1914 (that is, after his death), it was notified that Lieutenant Relton was transferred to the East Surrey Regiment (Regular Army) as 2nd Lieutenant with seniority from the 14th August, 1914.

The following details of his death were communicated to his father by the Officer Commanding the 1st Battalion, East Surrey Regiment: " Your son's death was much felt by us all. He was a fine type of a man, and promised to turn out an excellent officer. . . . Your son received three bullet wounds on the evening of the 14th September on the Chivres spur above Missy. He became unconscious at once, and died almost directly he was carried back. I was speaking to him just before he was hit. He with others on the right of our line were making a gallant stand against the Germans who were in strength just ahead of us. . . . We are glad to think that his name will be borne on the roll of officers of the regiment, for he was gazetted to us, though too late for him to know."

He was a member of the Junior Army and Navy Club.

2nd LIEUTENANT LEONARD WYNDHAM RENDELL, 1st BATTN. BEDFORDSHIRE REGT.,

who was killed in action on the 17th October, 1914, in France, was the only son of Mr. and Mrs. Wyndham H. Rendell, of Shoreditch House, Taunton, Somerset. He was born on the 26th October, 1890, and was educated at King's College, Taunton. He was gazetted 2nd Lieutenant in the 3rd Battalion Bedfordshire Regiment in September, 1910, and received his commission in the 1st (Regular) Battalion in November, 1912.

He was shot and mortally wounded on the 16th October, 1914, by three Uhlans concealed in a house, while scouting in advance of his regiment, and died the following day. His name was mentioned in Sir John French's Despatch of the 14th January, 1915, for gallant and distinguished conduct in the field.

He was very keen on all sports, a good shot and a successful fisherman.

2nd LIEUTENANT DONALD WILLIAMSON RENNIE, 5th BATTN. ROYAL FUSILIERS (CITY OF LONDON REGIMENT),

born in Glasgow in January, 1885, was the son of John Rennie, Esq., M.I.E.E., Electrical Engineer, Civil Service, of 28, Oxford Road, Putney, S.W. He was educated at St. Mark's Schools; City of London School; and St. John's College, Cambridge. In 1900 he gained an Intermediate County Council Scholarship; while at the City of London School he gained, in 1903, the Alston Special Prize for Physics and Chemistry, and in 1904 the Beaufoy Scholarship. He was also given an open Exhibition, St. John's College, Cambridge, the Senior County Exhibition, and the Price Prize and Medal for Chemistry. At Cambridge, in 1905, and again in 1906, he took the Wright Prize for Engineering Science ; and in 1906 a Foundation Scholarship of the College ; also a premium for a paper on " Electrification of Railways," obtaining his degree of B.A. Engineering, and Class Honours in 1907. In the latter year he graduated as B.Sc. (London University).

In 1908 2nd Lieutenant Rennie entered the works of Messrs. Yarrow & Co., Engineers and Shipbuilders, Glasgow, remaining there till on the 6th August, 1914, when he joined the Royal Fusiliers, having previously belonged to the O.T.C. and the Special Reserve of Officers.

For active service he was attached to the 1st Battalion Royal Warwickshire Regiment, and arrived in France on the 12th October, 1914. From his correspondence while on service several very interesting letters to his parents have been thought worthy of incorporation in a little booklet which was highly reviewed in " Great Deeds of the Great War " for February, 1915. 2nd Lieutenant Rennie was killed on the 11th November, 1914, during a night attack on the trenches near Armentières. He was buried where he fell.

Major A. J. Poole, Commanding 1st Royal Warwicks, wrote that " he died doing his job as well as, if not better than, any professional soldier of my acquaintance."

The Officer Commanding his company gave the following account of his fall : " He was killed about 8.30 p.m. last night (11th November) by the burst of a shrapnel shell during a night attack on our trenches. From what the men tell me, he was walking along the trench he was in charge of, directing their fire and encouraging them, and doing his duty when he met his death. It was, I believe, instantaneous. . . . During his short time with us he was liked and trusted by officers and men."

Another comrade, an old schoolfellow, wrote : " He was a good comrade, quiet, shrewd, k̇ndly, and with a fund of humour. Anything like bravado was foreign to him, but I remember him saying quietly, only about ten days ago, that he was prepared to die, and that if one did, one was joining a company of gallant gentlemen."

In the " Eagle " for March, 1915, a magazine of St. John's College, Cambridge, appeared an appreciative memoir.

So died a gallant young officer who had, only a few months before, in answer to the call of his country, abandoned what gave every promise of being a most prosperous civil career.

MAJOR HENRY BINGHAM WHISTLER SMITH-REWSE, p.s.c., ROYAL FIELD ARTILLERY,

who died on the 22nd November, 1914, of wounds received in action near Ypres, was the eldest son of Colonel and Mrs. Smith-Rewse, The Lodge, Alphington, Exeter. He was born on the 22nd August, 1876, and educated at

Dover College, King's School, Rochester, and the R.M.A., Woolwich. He joined the Royal Artillery in 1897, becoming Lieutenant three years later. From June, 1901, to July, 1904, he was employed with the West African Frontier Force. He was promoted Captain in March, 1902, and from September, 1904, to October, 1905, he was Instructor and Officer of a company of Gentlemen Cadets (Class " B ") at the Royal Military Academy, Woolwich. He was a graduate of the Staff College at Quetta and a 1st Class Interpreter in French, and obtained his Majority in April, 1914.

When in command of the 51st Field Battery at the front, and under heavy shell fire, he left his dug-out to attend men reported wounded, and was hit in the head by a splinter of shell. He was buried at Poperinghe.

Major Smith-Rewse married, on the 16th September, 1911, Olive, eldest daughter of the late Sir Oliver St. John, K.C.S.I., Resident at Mysore, India.

CAPTAIN HENRY CLENDON COLLIS REYNOLDS, 3rd BATTN. THE DUKE OF EDINBURGH'S (WILTSHIRE REGT.),

who was killed in action on the 19th September, 1914, in France, aged thirty years, was the only son of T. C. and Mrs. Reynolds, of 92, Cambridge Gardens, North Kensington, London, W.

Captain Reynolds served during the South African War, 1901, in St. Helena, receiving the Queen's medal. He was appointed 2nd Lieutenant in his battalion in June, 1901, and became Captain in May, 1906. He had qualified at a School of Musketry, and had obtained, after being attached to the Regular Forces, a satisfactory report for the rank of Field Officer.

CAPT. THOMAS JAMES REYNOLDS, 3rd (attd. 2nd) BATTN. ROYAL IRISH RIFLES,

who was shot by a sniper at Neuve Chapelle on the 25th October, 1914, was the second son of the late Thomas James Reynolds, C.E., Ceylon, and of his first wife, Margaret, eldest daughter of the late Dr. Slevin, Longford, Ireland, and nephew of the late Deputy Surgeon-General Reynolds.

He was born in Ceylon on the 19th January, 1871, and educated at Terenure College, County Dublin ; and Belvidere College, Dublin, joining the Royal Irish Fusiliers from the Militia in April, 1900. He was employed with the Gold Coast Constabulary and the King's African

Rifles from April, 1900, to October, 1902, during which time he took part in operations in Ashanti, for which he received the medal. He was promoted Lieutenant in February, 1902, and Captain in the Royal Irish Rifles in May, 1909. From March, 1910, to January, 1911, he was an Adjutant of the Territorial Force, and in May, 1914, was appointed Adjutant of the 3rd (Reserve) Battalion of his regiment.

Captain Reynolds, who was a member of the United Service Club, Dublin, and the Junior United Service Club, London, was a keen and enthusiastic cricketer, and was a member of the Leinster Cricket Club, Dublin. He was unmarried.

CAPTAIN WILLIAM SUTTOR RICH, 1st BATTN. CHESHIRE REGIMENT,

who died on the 9th November, 1914, of a wound in the head, was the son of William Morton Rich, of Mount Victoria, New South Wales, both his parents being Australians.

On his mother's side he was a grandson of the first Bathurst Suttor, and on his father's side a grandson of the naturalist in Sir Thomas Mitchell's Expedition.

He was born in Geneva, Switzerland, on the 3rd August, 1879, and was educated at " The School," Mount Victoria, New South Wales.

He went to South Africa to take part in the Boer War with the second contingent, and was appointed Galloper to Colonel Knight. For some months while he was with the Australians he was Orderly to two General Officers ; and in May, 1900, was given his commission in the Cheshire Regiment. He served in the Cheshire Mounted Infantry in that war, in the course of which he was wounded, taking part in operations in the Orange Free State, including actions at Driefontein, Poplar Grove, Karee Siding, the Vet and Zand Rivers ; also in the Transvaal, including actions near Johannesburg, Pretoria, and Diamond Hill ; again in the Transvaal, east of Pretoria, including operations at Riet Vlei and Belfast ; and was present at later operations in the Transvaal, Orange River Colony, and Cape Colony. He received the Queen's medal with five clasps and the King's medal with two clasps.

He was promoted Lieutenant in February, 1902, and from Africa went to India, being stationed at Quetta with the 1st Battalion of his regiment for six months. He was then appointed Sectional Officer at Mount Abu, in the Punjab, and afterwards came to England with his battalion. From 1905 to 1909, having been promoted Captain in November, 1907, he was employed with the West African Frontier Force, and was for a time Commandant at Katsena, and later served at Sierra Leone.

On the outbreak of the Great War he proceeded to the Continent with the Vth Division of the Expeditionary Force, and fought at Mons, and in the retirement therefrom, during which his battalion lost half its officers.

All that remained of the 1st Cheshires during the action at Le Cateau on the 26th August, were in reserve, but found themselves called upon to help in covering the retirement of other troops. Captain Rich, with a Subaltern, a Sergeant, and seven men, held a shallow trench on the left; and with another small party posted on a ridge to the right succeeded in holding up some hundreds of the enemy, and so secured the retirement of the troops, who passed between the parties. It was for this fine piece of work that Captain Rich was first mentioned in despatches. The men of the battalion used to speak of Captain Rich as a fatalist, for when spoken to about exposing himself he laughingly said, " I know I was never born to be shot," and he appeared, for a time, to have such a charmed life that the men of his company began to believe there was something in his confidence in his future.

But it was destined otherwise, for after several escapes he received a wound in the jaw on the 20th October. Although his wound prevented him from eating for three days he was still as cheerful as ever, and the life and soul of his battalion.

Two days later, while acting as Second in Command of his battalion and defending his trenches at Violaines, near La Bassée, he received his fatal wound during a sudden onslaught by the enemy. With several other wounded officers he was taken prisoner, and removed to a hospital at Namur, and later to the Military Hospital, 4th Army Corps, Douai, France, where he died on the above mentioned date.

Captain Rich was twice mentioned for his gallantry in Sir John French's Despatches of the 8th October, 1914, and of the 14th January, 1915.

CAPTAIN SIR EDWARD AUSTIN STEWART-RICHARDSON, 14th BARONET, 3rd (attd. 1st) BATTN. THE BLACK WATCH (ROYAL HIGHLANDERS),

died on the 28th November, 1914, from the effects of wounds received at Ypres on the 27th October. He was the eldest son of Sir James Stewart-Richardson, thirteenth Bart., Pencaitland, Pitfour Castle, Perth, N.B., and was born at Edinburgh on the 24th July, 1872.

He was educated at Rugby and Trinity College, Glenalmond, Perthshire. In September, 1890,

he joined the 3rd Battalion Royal Highlanders, being promoted Lieutenant in March, 1892, and Captain in February, 1900; from 1899–1902 he was A.D.C. to the Governor of Queensland. In the South African War he served with the 2nd Battalion of the Black Watch and with the Queensland Mounted Infantry, taking part in the operations in the Orange Free State, including the action at Vet River, and in the Orange River Colony, including the actions at Rhenoster River, Wittebergen, and Witpoort, receiving the Queen's medal with two clasps.

On volunteering for service in the Great War he was attached to the 1st Battalion of his old regiment, and was serving with it when killed. He was a member of the Caledonian and the Royal Automobile Clubs, London, and of the New Club, Edinburgh. He married Lady Constance Mackenzie, younger daughter of the second Earl of Cromartie, and left two sons: Ian Rory Hay, who succeeds him in the title at ten years of age; and Torquil Cathel Hugh, aged six years at the time of his father's death.

LIEUTENANT MARTIN JAMES RICHARDSON, M.B., ROYAL ARMY MEDICAL CORPS, "C" SECTION, 21st FIELD AMBULANCE,

who was killed in action on the 3rd November, 1914, before Ypres, and was buried in the cemetery there, was the youngest son of Martin Richardson, Esq., Solicitor, Roseville, Bridlington, Yorkshire, where he was born. His uncle was Major-General George B. Heastey, R.M.L.I.

He was educated at Durham School and Edinburgh University, where he took his medical degree, and on the outbreak of the war volunteered for temporary service, receiving his commission as temporary Lieutenant in August, 1914. He proceeded to Belgium with the VIIth Division in October, 1914.

For his services in the war he was mentioned in Sir John French's Despatch of the 14th

January, 1915, " for gallant and distinguished service in the field," and was confirmed in his rank of Lieutenant " in recognition of his good service and ability."

Lieutenant Richardson married Maud, youngest daughter of Dr. Eagland, Burleywood, Harrogate, and left three children : Norman Martin Heastey, born November, 1893, who was gazetted to the Royal Marine Artillery as 2nd Lieutenant (temporary) in September, 1914, and promoted Lieutenant in January, 1915 ; Dorothy Jennie Heastey, born February, 1896 ; and Evelyn Joan Victoria Heastey, born January, 1901.

LIEUTENANT LESLIE RICHMOND, 1st BATTN. GORDON HIGHLANDERS,

who was reported as killed in action in the official list of casualties issued by the War Office on the 11th September, 1914, was the son of Mr. and Mrs. James Richmond, of Kippenross, Dunblane, and Hadden Rig, New South Wales. He was born on the 13th June, 1888, entered the Gordon Highlanders as 2nd Lieutenant in August, 1906, and became Lieutenant in February, 1909.

Lieutenant Richmond married, four months before his death, Ruth Margaret, elder daughter of Captain Greenwood, of Swarcliffe, Birstwith.

CAPTAIN T. H. RICHMOND, 3rd (attd. 2nd) BATTN. THE KING'S OWN (YORKSHIRE LIGHT INFANTRY),

died on the 1st November, 1914, of wounds received in action.

He was appointed 2nd Lieutenant in the 2nd (Volunteer) Battalion of the Border Regiment in December, 1902, and became Lieutenant in August, 1904, from which he was promoted into the 3rd Battalion King's Own Yorkshire Light Infantry on the 4th September, and obtained his company in September, 1914.

MAJOR STUART HAMILTON RICKMAN, 2nd BATTN. THE RIFLE BRIGADE (THE PRINCE CONSORT'S OWN),

was the eldest surviving son of the late Lieutenant-Colonel Albert Divett Rickman, the Rifle Brigade, and of Mrs. Edward Dunn, of Childrey Manor, Wantage, Berkshire.

He was born on the 11th May, 1872, at Chatham; was educated at Eton ; and passed second on the

list in the Militia competitive examination for the Army. He was gazetted to the 3rd Battalion the Rifle Brigade in 1893, and joined at Rawal Pindi in November, becoming Lieutenant in March, 1896, and Captain in 1900.

From 1897–98 he was on active service in the Tochi Valley, north-western frontier of India, receiving the medal with clasp. In 1899, being at home on leave, he applied for active service in the South African campaign, and joined the 1st Battalion Rifle Brigade as their Transport Officer. He was in the actions of Colenso, Spion Kop, Tugela Heights, Vaal Krans, Pieter's Hill, and relief of Ladysmith ; and was mentioned in Sir Redvers Buller's Despatch of the 30th March, 1900, for gallant and meritorious service, and again in Lord Roberts' Despatch of the 4th September, 1901. He received the Queen's medal with three clasps.

He saw service in the West African Field Force from May, 1907, to November, 1908, and received his Majority in December, 1911.

In March, 1914, he came home on leave from India, and when war with Germany broke out placed his services at the disposal of the War Office. He was attached again to the 1st Battalion the Rifle Brigade, and with them went out from Colchester on the 22nd August, 1914, and was mortally wounded while commanding them in their retirement on the 26th of that month in the Cambrai-Le Cateau action, dying of his wounds the following morning (27th August, 1914), in the temporary hospital, Fontaine au Pire, Cambrai.

It was written of him, in connection with his work on the 26th August : " He was a man— the best man in that battle. His conduct was magnificent. He died gloriously—a loss, not only to the Rifle Brigade, but to the Army and the nation. All loved him. A splendid soldier and man, always cheery, he was just the bravest of the brave."

Another officer wrote of him : " He was the best, the cheeriest, always the same, always helping people along with a cheery word and act, and that is priceless in really hard times. His death is a great sorrow to his brother officers and a great loss to the Rifle Brigade."

His Eton Master wrote : " He was a boy of whom I always felt sure that he would grow up as he did—a high-minded, straightforward man, with a great power of affection and of inspiring affection, fearless in life, fearless in death, the kind of man that makes England, and that England mourns and is proud of in life or in death."

He was officially reported wounded and missing in September, 1914, but through the Army Surgeon of the 1st Battalion the Rifle Brigade, who was a prisoner of war in Germany, definite details of his death were received later. Major Rickman was mentioned in Sir John French's

Despatches of the 8th October, 1914, and the 14th January, 1915, for gallant and distinguished service in the field.

He was a keen soldier, fond of sport, hunting, polo, and shooting, and had some good trophies of big game from the Himalayas, Baltistan, and Nigeria. He was a member of the Army and Navy Club, and was unmarried.

LIEUT. DAVID WYLIE RINTOUL, ROYAL ARMY MEDICAL CORPS,

born on the 23rd May, 1889, at Clifton, Bristol, was the son of David Rintoul, M.A., House Master at Clifton College.

He received his education at Clifton College and St. Andrews University, where he graduated M.B., Ch.B., passing into the R.A.M.C. in January, 1914. On mobilisation for the war he was posted to No. 5 Field Ambulance, IInd Division, being afterwards appointed Medical Officer in Charge of the 2nd Battalion Coldstream Guards on the 2nd September, and transferred on the 19th September to the 3rd Battalion of that regiment. Lieutenant Rintoul was killed not far from St. Julien, near Ypres, on the 21st October, 1914, while advancing with the leading company.

The Officer Commanding 3rd Battalion Coldstream Guards wrote of him: " He was brave and fearless, and most gallant. He had no idea what fear was, his one idea being to assist the wounded."

LIEUTENANT CHARLES ROGER RIPLEY 3rd (attd. 2nd) BATTN. YORK AND LANCASTER REGIMENT,

who was killed in action near Lille on the 22nd October, 1914, was the son of the late Sir Frederick Ripley, Bart., and Katherine Lady Ripley, of Earl's Avenue, Folkestone, and a grandson of Sir Henry Ripley, Bedstone Court, Shropshire. He was born at Scarborough on the 13th November, 1888.

Educated at Farnborough School and Cheltenham College, he entered the Army as 2nd Lieutenant in the 3rd Battalion York and Lancaster Regiment, in June, 1910, becoming Lieutenant in June, 1913, and joined the 2nd Battalion for active service at the commencement of the war.

Lieutenant Ripley was mentioned for his services in the Great War in Sir John French's Despatch of the 14th January, 1915, for gallant and distinguished service in the field.

MAJOR ROBERT EDWARD RISING, D.S.O., 1st BATTN. GLOUCESTERSHIRE REGIMENT,

was born on the 23rd May, 1871, the son of Thomas and Kate Rising, of The Manor House, Ormesby, Great Yarmouth, Norfolk.

He was educated at Charterhouse, where he was in the Football XV and in the Cadet Corps; and at Trinity College, Cambridge. He passed into the R.M.C., Sandhurst, sixth on the list, and passed out twelfth with honours, receiving his commission in the Gloucestershire Regiment in November, 1892. He obtained his Company in February, 1900.

Major Rising took part in the South African War, being present at the relief of Kimberley, and at operations in the Orange Free State, including actions at Paardeberg, Poplar Grove, and Driefontein, and also in Natal. He received the Queen's medal with four clasps. He obtained the " extra " certificate in musketry in 1898, and in November, 1902, passed the examination for promotion, attaining the higher standard of proficiency, carrying a special certificate. In April, 1906, he passed the signalling course, also with the special certificate.

In the earlier part of the Great War Major Rising was awarded the D.S.O. for gallant action at the defence of Langemarck on the 23rd October, 1914, when he went up with supports, and conspicuously controlled the defence of the battalion's trenches against a determined attack by the enemy. But for this stout defence the line would have been penetrated. He received his Majority in November, 1914, the promotion not being gazetted till after his death.

Major Rising, who had been wounded at Klein Zillebeke, was killed in action at the first Battle of Ypres on the 7th November, 1914.

He was twice married: in 1896 to Amy Worship, who died the following year; and in 1901 to Constance Elizabeth, youngest daughter of Colonel R. W. Edis, C.B., of The Old Hall, Ormesby, Great Yarmouth; and left two children : Robert Edis, born August, 1905 ; and Elsie Mary Elizabeth, born July, 1909.

Major Rising was mentioned in Sir John French's Despatch of the 14th January, 1915.

2nd LIEUTENANT ARCHIBALD FREDERICK RITCHIE, 1st BATTN. THE KING'S OWN (YORKSHIRE LIGHT INFANTRY),

who was killed at Le Cateau on the 26th August, 1914, was the son of the late Major John Robert Ritchie, Royal Garrison Artillery, and a grandson of Major-General J. Ritchie, Montagu House, Southsea. He was born at Queenstown, Co. Cork, on the 6th October, 1894, and was educated at Brightlands, Newnham, Gloucestershire, where he was the best all-round boy in games and athletic sports. In 1909 he went to Haileybury College (Trevelyan), where he won the bronze medal for swimming, 1910 ; House badge, 1910 ; and football stars, 1911. From Haileybury 2nd Lieutenant Ritchie passed into the R.M.C., Sandhurst, and received his commission in the King's Own in February, 1914.

CAPTAIN ARTHUR GERALD RITCHIE, 1st BATTN. THE CAMERONIANS (SCOTTISH RIFLES),

was the second son of the late William Irvine Ritchie, of the Board of Education. He was born on the 30th October, 1879, and was educated at St. Paul's School, 1893–97. He made his mark in school life, being a Foundation Scholar, winner of the John Watson and Landscape prizes three years in succession, and winner of the Shepard Cup for athletics in 1897. He also played for the First XV. He joined the 1st Battalion Scottish Rifles in February, 1899, becoming Lieutenant in January, 1900, and Captain in October, 1906. In November, 1909, he was appointed Adjutant of the East Indian Railway Volunteer Rifles. He still held that post in the summer of 1914, up to which time his military service had been wholly in India.

He was in England at the outbreak of the war ; and, after some service with reserves of his regiment, he rejoined his original battalion at the front on the 11th October, 1914. On the 23rd he was given the command of " C " Company, holding an advanced trench and farmhouse near La Boutillerie, west of Lille. Here an eventful week culminated in an attack by the enemy during the night of the 29th-30th October, which was successfully repulsed. It was during a lull in this attack that Captain Ritchie fell severely wounded by a sniper. He died at Boulogne on the 22nd November following, and was buried in the cemetery there. He was mentioned in Sir John French's Despatch of the 14th January, 1915.

Captain Ritchie was a keen sportsman and big-game shikari. He was a clever draftsman, and from childhood onwards used to illustrate his letters and diaries with amusing sketches. He was not married.

MAJOR ALEXANDER KIRKLAND ROBB, 2nd BATTN. DURHAM LIGHT INFANTRY,

was the eldest son of Lieutenant-Colonel Robb, I.M.S., M.D., of Aberdeen, and was born at Poona, India, on the 26th August, 1872.

He was educated at Aberdeen Grammar School, and afterwards at Aberdeen University, proceeding to the R.M.C., Sandhurst. On leaving the college he passed out first with honours, and was awarded the Anson Memorial sword.

Major Robb was gazetted to the 2nd Durham Light Infantry as 2nd Lieutenant on the 20th May, 1893, becoming Lieutenant on the 21st May, 1896 ; Captain, 19th February, 1900 ; and Major, 23rd August, 1913. He was on active service, attached to the Yorks. Light Infantry, in the Tirah campaign of the north-western frontier in 1897 and 1898. Here he greatly distinguished himself, volunteering with only one non-commissioned officer and one private to keep the enemy off a peak on the flank, which, had it been captured, would have exposed the British force to a heavy flanking fire. Major Robb fought with his revolver only, using up all his cartridges. To the surprise of all, he and his comrades returned safely when the order to retire was given. For his gallantry Major Robb was twice mentioned in despatches and received the Tirah medal with two clasps. Colonel Seppings, Commanding the Yorkshire Light Infantry, wrote to Major Robb's own

Commanding Officer a most appreciative report of his conduct in this campaign; and Major Robb's Commanding Officer, writing to the Brigadier-General, said: "The Yorks. Light Infantry are speaking in the highest terms of young Robb at the fight in the Shin Kamar." Later Major Robb was attached to the Burma Intelligence Branch in connection with the Chinese Boundary Commission for reconnaissance duty during the cold season of 1899–1900. He was Adjutant of the Rangoon Volunteer Rifle Corps, 1902–07. Returning to England, he served at the depot of his regiment, Newcastle-on-Tyne, from 1910–12. In September, 1912, he was appointed Adjutant of the Durham University Officers' Training Corps and Lecturer in Military Education. The University recognised his services by granting him the honorary degree of M.A. in June, 1913. On mobilisation for the Great War he was recalled to his regiment in August, 1914, and early in September proceeded to the front with his battalion. At the Battle of the Aisne, in his battalion's first engagement on the 20th September, 1914, having reached the trenches the night before, Major Robb was severely wounded, but continued to lead his men, falling at last within forty yards of the enemy's trenches. He was carried to the rear, and died of his wounds the same night. Major Robb played Rugby football and hockey for his regiment. He married, in 1904, Ethel Violet (Queenie), daughter of the late Edward Rule, Comptroller Indian Treasuries, I.C.S. (uncovenanted), and left two children: Sheila Kirkland, born in 1905; and Betty Kirkland, born 1907.

2nd LIEUTENANT ANTHONY GERALD MALPAS ROBERTS, SPECIAL RESERVE, (attd. 2nd BATTALION), ROYAL INNISKILLING FUSILIERS,

was born in London on the 29th July, 1895, the son of Mr. and Mrs. J. H. Malpas Roberts, 16, Dumbarton Road, Brixton Hill, and of Chester.

He was educated at Ardingly College, Sussex, where he was Victor Ludorum for three years in succession, 1911–13 (Public Schools record). He joined the O.T.C. in 1911, was awarded Certificate "A" in 1913, and in May of the same year joined the Special Reserve of the Royal Inniskilling Fusiliers. On mobilisation he was gazetted to the regiment as 2nd Lieutenant, and attached to the 2nd Battalion.

In 1914 he became a member of the London Athletic Club, and at the Jubilee Meeting in July won the members' two hundred and twenty yards. He also won many other events in different parts of England, and was looked upon as one of the most promising young sprinters of the year.

He was killed in action on the 21st October, 1914, while saving a desperate situation at Le Gheer, one and a half miles east of Ploegsteert, Flanders.

CAPTAIN KENNETH FORBES-ROBERTSON, 2nd BATTN. SEAFORTH HIGHLANDERS (ROSS-SHIRE BUFFS, THE DUKE OF ALBANY'S),

born at Slead Hall, Brighouse, Yorkshire, on the 17th April, 1882, was the elder son of the late Farquhar Forbes-Robertson and Mrs. Forbes-Robertson, of Keynsham Bank, Cheltenham, grandson of the late William Forbes-Robertson, of Hazlehead, Aberdeen, and great-grandson of William  Forbes of Echt, of the family of Watertoune.

He was educated at Cheltenham College and the R.M.C., Sandhurst. In August, 1900, he received his commission, and was posted to the 1st Battalion of the Seaforth Highlanders, becoming Lieutenant in May, 1902.

He saw active service in East Africa in 1904, taking part in the operations in Somaliland and the action at Jidballi, for which he received the medal with two clasps. He was also on active service on the north-western frontier of India in 1908, receiving the medal with clasp. In the spring of 1914 he left the 1st Battalion in India to take up duty at the depot, Fort George, and on the 5th October went out to join the 2nd Battalion in France.

He was killed on the 7th November, 1914, while leading a reconnoitring party in Ploegsteert Wood. A correspondent wrote in "The Times" of the 24th November, 1914: "The loss to the Seaforth Highlanders of Captain Kenneth Forbes-Robertson, whose death was announced in 'The Times,' will be very deeply felt. His death is a heavy blow to his comrades, who valued his good-fellowship to the point of love. It is their desire to record a personal sorrow, which cannot find a place in the annals of the regiment, and to pay a tribute to the memory of a man who was a brave soldier to his country, and to them a very genial, constant friend." Captain Forbes-Robertson, who was promoted to that rank in April, 1911, was a member of the Caledonian Club, St. James's Square, London, and was unmarried.

CAPTAIN LEWIS ROBERTSON, 1st BATTN. THE QUEEN'S OWN CAMERON HIGHLANDERS,

who died at Ypres from wounds received in action on the 2nd November, 1914, was the third son of the late James Robertson, 7, Eglinton Crescent, Edinburgh.

He was born on the 4th August, 1883, and educated at Cargilfield, Fettes ; and the R.M.C., Sandhurst, from which he passed out with honours. He joined the Cameron Highlanders in April, 1903, becoming Lieutenant in March, 1909. In June, 1911, he was appointed Assistant Superintendent of Gymnasia, Eastern Command ; and he was gazetted Captain on the 16th January, 1915, to date from the 30th September, 1914.

Captain Robertson was a member of the United Service Club. He was an enthusiastic football player, and belonged to the following football clubs : Fettesian-Lorettonian, London Scottish, Monkstown, Edinburgh Wanderers, United Services. He was captain in 1914 of the Army Officers' Rugby team, and had played for the team in every match. An extract from the "Windsor Magazine" of April, 1915, said : "Captain Lewis Robertson, Cameron Highlanders, Fettes, United Services, and Scotland, who fell at the Battle of Ypres, was one of the most honest forwards we have had of recent years. A charming instance of self-effacement occurred in what this popular player did when he offered voluntarily to give up the captaincy of the Army XV v. the Navy at Queen's, and with it the honour of presenting his team to his Majesty. This he did because he thought he was out of form, and not good enough to play for the Army." This match was won by the Army after several defeats in previous years.

The day before his gallant death at Ypres, Captain Robertson was met by an old King's School, Canterbury, Woolwich half-back—Henry Gardener, R.F.A.—to whom he expressed himself as being thankful he had put his back into his job as Bayonet-fighting Instructor to the South East Command for the last two years.

An extract from "Sporting Life" said : "Captain L. Robertson, Cameron Highlanders, one of the best known Rugby players in the Service, played for the London Scottish for ten seasons, and had nine Scottish Rugby cups, and played for Army v. Navy for six successive years, 1909–14. He represented the R.M.C. v. R.M.A. in 1902 ; was also a fine athlete ; and as Superintendent of Gymnasia in the Eastern Command took a leading part in the organisation of Army sport."

He was in the trenches at Ypres on the 2nd November, 1914, and was wounded early in the afternoon in the arm. His wound was dressed, but he returned to his company, and was afterwards wounded a second time seriously, and died the following day.

LIEUTENANT EDWIN WINWOOD ROBINSON, 5th (ROYAL IRISH) LANCERS,

who was killed in action near Ypres on the 26th October, 1914, was the fifth son of the late Herbert J. Robinson and of Mrs. Robinson, of Moor Wood, Cirencester.

He was born on the 25th November, 1887, and was educated at Malvern College, Upper IV A (Lower Shell) ; and Hertford College, Oxford. He joined the 5th Lancers from the Special Reserve in December, 1911, becoming Lieutenant in August, 1914. He was fond of hunting, polo, and steeplechasing.

He went to France with his regiment on the outbreak of war, and was killed in action whilst the regiment was being used as infantry.

LIEUTENANT FRANCIS EDWARD ROBINSON, 3rd (attd. 2nd) BATTN. SOUTH STAFFORDSHIRE REGIMENT,

was born at Sligo on the 30th January, 1895, the youngest son of the late Mr. St. George C. W. and Mrs. Robinson, of Woodville, Sligo, and a nephew of Sir Edward Carson.

He was educated at The Link, Stubbington, and at Malvern College, where he proved to be a good all-round athlete, and promised to become a good shot. Joining the 3rd Battalion South Staffordshire Regiment as 2nd Lieutenant in April, 1912, he was promoted Lieutenant in July, 1913, and, on the outbreak of the war, was attached to the 2nd Battalion, which, forming part of the IInd Division, was among the first regiments to be landed in France. He was killed on the 27th October, 1914, while leading his platoon in an attack across the Becelaere-Passchendaele Road.

Lieutenant Robinson's parents received after his death many sympathetic letters saying he was an excellent officer, greatly regretted by both officers and men of his battalion.

CAPTAIN EDGAR ROBSON, 1st (attd. 2nd) BATTN. PRINCE OF WALES'S VOLUNTEERS (SOUTH LANCASHIRE REGT.),

son of John Stephenson Robson and Mary, his wife, was born in the parish of Jesmond, Newcastle-on-Tyne, on the 21st November, 1878, and was educated at Bedford Modern School under Dr. Poole. Captain Robson was descended from the old border clan of the Robsons of North Tyne, whose record is to be found in the annals of Northumberland, and from the McLeans of Mull. His brother—Captain Richard Robson, of the South African Constabulary—assisted in raising that corps, and commanded a division of it during the South African War, being afterwards appointed Commandant at Standerton, a position he held for some years.

For the South African War, 1900–02, Captain Edgar Robson received the Queen's medal with four clasps and the King's medal with two clasps, having been present at operations in the Transvaal and on the Zululand frontier. After the South African War he served with his battalion in India, returning to England early in 1913. During the Great War he was appointed to the 2nd Battalion of his regiment, and proceeded to France in November, 1914. He was mortally wounded in the trenches at Wyschaete by the accidental explosion of a hand grenade, and died in the base hospital on the 3rd December, 1914. He belonged to several clubs in India, where he was a polo player, and was a good sportsman as well as a lover of his profession.

CAPTAIN RALPH GEORGE GRIFFITHS CUMINE-ROBSON, ROYAL ENGINEERS,

son of S. Robson, M.A., Indian Educational Service (retired), Principal, Prince of Wales College, Jammu, Kashmir State, and Mrs. Robson (née Cumine), was born at Chinsura, in Bengal, in the house which was formerly the residence of the

Dutch Governors, on the 13th August, 1888. His only brother is Captain H. W. Cumine-Robson, 7th Gurkha Rifles, Adjutant, Makrán Levy Corps.

Captain R. Cumine-Robson went to England in 1905, and was educated at Pretoria House, Folkestone, and at Eton, where he was a King's scholar. At Eton he distinguished himself in the wall game, and acquired a reputation for absolute fearlessness, which was one of his most prominent characteristics, and which made a deep impression on his brother officers during his brief but distinguished service at the front. After leaving Eton he passed into the R.M.A., Woolwich, out of which he passed sixth, and obtained a commission in the Royal Engineers, dated the 18th December, 1908, being promoted Lieutenant in December, 1910. After two years at Chatham he went to India in 1911, and was posted to Military Works, Rawal Pindi, but was very soon transferred to the Imperial Durbar Works, Delhi. After the Durbar, at which Delhi was made the capital of India, he continued to serve under the Imperial Delhi Committee, and was employed on works connected with the building of the new capital. There he won golden opinions from the officers under whom he served, gained the reputation of a zealous and efficient officer, and had charge of works not usually entrusted to one so young.

Captain (then Lieutenant) Robson played polo, but his favourite sport was pig-sticking, at which he showed himself absolutely fearless ; and he took many first spears on his favourite pig-sticker, "The Subaltern," which he took with him to the front.

When war broke out between England and Germany Captain Robson at once volunteered for active service, and his services being accepted he was posted to the 3rd Company, 1st King George's Own Sappers and Miners, attached to the Meerut Division of the Indian Expeditionary Force, which sailed from Bombay.

The Corps of Indian Sappers and Miners were specially mentioned for their skill and resource in Sir John French's Despatch of the 20th November, 1914, and Captain Robson was mentioned by name in the Despatch dated the 14th January, 1915. He was promoted Captain, to date from the 18th December, 1914.

He was killed in action at the junction of the Rue du Bois with the Estaires La Bassée Road, near Neuve Chapelle, on the 23rd December, 1914, and is buried in Grave No. 218 in the English portion of the Estaires Cemetery.

The following has been communicated by the Secretary of State to the Viceroy : " In fighting from the 23rd November to the 24th November it fell to the 39th Garhwali Rifles to make the final assault, which owing to its well-considered and gallant character was entirely successful.

" With dashing courage and initiative two young British officers of the Royal Engineers and a well-known Frontier Force regiment—Captain R. Cumine-Robson and Captain D. H. Acworth respectively—preceded the Garhwalis against the first section, and by throwing bombs across the traverses cleared the way for the head of the 39th Garhwalis."

Captain Acworth wrote of him : " About 2 p.m. your son came and told me that he had been down the communication trench to reconnoitre *by himself*, and had found the Germans hard at work, improving the position they had taken. To appreciate his pluck in making this trip down the communication trench *alone*, you must understand that it was only about three feet deep, and so winding that one could never see more than five yards ahead, and one never knew that the next turning would not bring one on to a German with his finger on the trigger. About an hour later he went down the trench again alone, and threw six bombs into the German working party with excellent effect. When I remonstrated with him afterwards, he said that anyone with him would have only been in the way ! I consider that one of the most gallant individual acts I have ever heard of. It is hard to find words to describe what I feel about your son's work on that occasion. All the credit for the success of the operations on the enemy's right is undoubtedly his. The attack was completely successful, and the entire conception and practically the whole execution was due to him."

The following issued by the Press Bureau appeared in the " Daily Telegraph " of the 27th January, 1915 : " The operation was a difficult one, and complicated by the intense darkness of the night. It would have been well-nigh impossible had it not been for the dashing courage and initiative of two young British officers, one a Royal Engineer, and a handful of Afridis. By throwing bombs they cleared the way for the 39th, who were thirsting to be let go at the enemy."

A Captain of the 130th Baluchis wrote of him : " Our people had tried three counter-attacks, but they all failed. It was there that he did such magnificent work. It was his plan, and he carried it out. It was a truly splendid and marvellously brave performance."

Regarding the service in which he fell, the General Commanding the Meerut Division wrote : " He was a most gallant and capable officer, who gave up his life in a daring effort to carry out an extremely dangerous duty for the good of the cause. No man could do more, and none could show greater personal bravery than he did on this and other occasions. At all times and in all ways he showed himself to be as brave and capable an officer as ever wore the King's uniform."

MAJOR THOMAS ROCHE, p.s.c., 1st BATTN. THE DUKE OF EDINBURGH'S (WILTSHIRE REGIMENT),
born on the 16th June, 1874, at Annakissa House, Killavullen, County Cork, was the son of the late Thomas Roche, J.P., of Annakissa House. His brother—Major B. R. Roche—is in the Bedfordshire Regiment, and their aunt is Miss Mayne, of Richmond House, Cork.

Major Roche, who was educated at Eastman's Academy, Southsea, and Fawcett's School, Cork, joined the Wiltshire Regiment from the Militia in 1895, becoming Lieutenant in November, 1896, and Captain in 1900. He served in the South African War, being present at operations in the Transvaal and Cape Colony, for which he was mentioned in Despatches (" London Gazette," 10th September, 1911), and received the Queen's medal with four clasps. From 1902–06 he was Adjutant of his battalion, and then, after passing through the Staff College, was Brigade-Major in India from 1909 to 1913. In April of the latter year he obtained his Majority. Major Roche, who was mentioned in Sir John French's Despatch of the 14th Jan., 1915, was killed on the 17th November,1914, by a shell during the bombardment of our trenches. He was a member of the Junior United Service Club, and his recreations were hunting, polo, and shooting.

CAPTAIN ARTHUR ROBERT MONTGOMERY ROE, p.s.c., 1st BATTN. DORSETSHIRE REGIMENT,
was the son of Sir Charles Roe, Knight, of 1, Holywell, Oxford. He was born on the 6th September, 1882, and was educated at Rugby (Steel), which he entered in 1906, and at the R.M.C., Sandhurst, from which he was gazetted to the Dorsetshire Regiment in August, 1900.

He was promoted Lieutenant in January, 1902, and from April, 1908, to September, 1911, was Adjutant of his battalion. He obtained his company in April, 1909. Captain Roe was at the Staff College from January, 1912, and in February, 1914, rejoined his battalion in Ireland. While there he was well known in Belfast on account of the keen interest he took in the football and general sports of the battalion. When war broke out he left Ireland for the front, attached to the General Staff of the IIIrd Division, but rejoined his regiment during the retirement from Mons on account of the shortage of officers.

He was wounded first in the arm whilst leading an attack on the 9th September, 1914, but refused to have his wound attended to then, and was shot through the head later in the day. He died of his wounds on the 16th—a week later—in the hospital at Le Mans, and is buried in the cemetery there. He was mentioned in Sir John French's Despatch of the 14th January, 1915. Captain Roe married, in 1911, Joan Hilda Marian, youngest daughter of the late Captain Sir William Wiseman, Bart., R.N., and left one daughter, Alison Margaret.

CAPTAIN SAMUEL GEORGE ROE, 2nd BATTALION ROYAL INNISKILLING FUSILIERS,

who was killed at Le Gheer on the 21st October, 1914, was the eldest son of Lieut.-Colonel Roe, of Sion House, Glenageary, Co. Dublin, and a nephew of Surgeon-General S. B. Roe, C.B., Ballyconnell House, Ballyconnell, Co. Cavan. He was born in India on the 23rd August, 1875, and was educated at Bedford College and Trinity College, Dublin. At school he was a hockey player, and then and afterwards a Rugby footballer. He joined the Inniskilling Fusiliers in January, 1899, became Lieutenant in April, 1900, and Captain in July, 1904. From October, 1907, to October, 1911, he was an Adjutant of the 3rd Battalion of his regiment (Militia and Reserve).

Captain Roe married Irene Eveline, daughter of J. W. Cross, Esq., who survives him.

2nd LIEUTENANT CHARLES HUNTER ROGERS, 135th BATTERY, ROYAL FIELD ARTILLERY,

who died in Guy's Hospital, London, on the 9th November, 1914, of wounds received in action on the 2nd of that month, was the eldest son of Mr. Charles J. Rogers, formerly of 85, Caversham Road, London, N.W., afterwards of 17, Park Avenue North, Hornsey, N.

He was born on the 25th April, 1890, and joined the Royal Artillery from the Territorial Force in June, 1914. He was buried at Highgate.

LIEUTENANT LEONARD CASTEL CAMPBELL ROGERS, 1st BATTN. 7th GURKHA RIFLES,

born at Cuttack, Orissa, India, on the 29th January, 1886, was the son of Archibald Colin Campbell Rogers, ex-engineer Public Works Department, India, and a grandson of the late Rev. R. H. Gatty, the Manor House, Buckden, Huntingdon.

He was educated at Blundell's School, Tiverton, where he was in the Cricket and Football XI's; and proceeded to the R.M.C., Sandhurst, whence he received his commission in the Bedfordshire Regiment in 1906. A month after his promotion to Lieutenant, which occurred in November, 1908, he joined the Indian Army, being gazetted to the 7th Gurkha Rifles, of which he was made Quartermaster in 1913.

He died on Christmas Day, 1914, from wounds received the previous day while rescuing a wounded man under heavy fire. For this act he was awarded the Military Cross, "London Gazette," February, 1915, the official record being: "For conspicuous gallantry at Festubert on 24th December, 1914, in assisting in the rescue of a severely wounded man who had been lying in front of the enemy's trenches for forty-eight hours."

The following account of the circumstances was given by a brother officer: "We had one poor fellow killed called Rogers. He joined us from the 7th Gurkhas not long ago. I must say he died a magnificent death. The Loyal North Lancashires had done a counter-attack two nights before, and a number of their dead were lying out in the open between our lines and the Germans. Rogers noticed that one of them was wounded. He ran into the open towards the man, picked him up, and started back towards the trenches. The wounded man was, however, too heavy, and he was obliged to stop and lie down. Another man in our battalion ran out to help him, and between them they put him on to his back and started again. Poor Rogers was hit through the back, the bullet coming out where his ribs curved away. The man, however, carried on, and got back to a shallow ditch. The poor wounded fellow was again hit in the leg, and the other man of ours who carried him in had a bullet through his coat. Poor Rogers managed to crawl back to the ditch, where our men pulled him in. He was very badly hit, and died the next morning. It was a rash but very gallant act, and I hope both will be rewarded as they deserve."

Lieutenant Rogers was a good all-round man at sport, and an enthusiastic polo player. He was known for his great personal courage, and had given every promise of succeeding in his profession.

MAJOR (temp.) HUBERT CHARLTON ROME, 20th DUKE OF CAMBRIDGE'S OWN INFANTRY (BROWNLOW'S

PUNJABIS), was killed in action on the 18th December, 1914.

He was the son of Mr. Thomas Rome, J.P., and Mrs. Rome, Charlton House, Charlton Kings, Cheltenham, Gloucestershire, and was born on the 2nd October, 1883. He was educated at Cheltenham College and the R.M.C., Sandhurst, on passing out of which for the Indian Army he was gazetted 2nd Lieutenant, unattached, on the 21st January, 1903. He passed out of Sandhurst with honours and as Under Officer.

He went to India in March, 1903, and was attached to the 2nd Battalion King's Royal Rifle Corps at Rawal Pindi until April, 1904, when he was posted to the Duke of Cambridge's Own Infantry, then stationed at Mian Mir. He was promoted Lieutenant in April, 1905.

In March, 1909, he was seconded for service with the Khyber Rifles (Militia), with whom he served for five years. He received his promotion to Captain in January, 1912. In March, 1914, he rejoined his regiment at Poona, and came to England the following month on leave. At the outbreak of war he was one of some two hundred and forty Indian Army officers detained at home for the New Army, and was appointed to the 9th (Service) Battalion Essex Regiment at Shorncliffe, and whilst with that regiment was gazetted temporary Major in October, 1914.

Major Rome was ordered to France to replace casualties in the 129th Baluchis, with whom he was serving when killed in action near Givenchy. He was married on the 24th June, 1914, to Doris, only child of the late W. S. Dykes, Writer to the Signet, and Mrs. Dykes, of Darnaconnar, Barrhill, Ayrshire.

CAPTAIN ARTHUR HOVELL ROMILLY, 1st BATTN. THE DUKE OF CORN-WALL'S LIGHT INFANTRY, who was killed in action on the 21st October,

1914, was the elder son of the late Captain Francis J. Romilly, R.E. (who lost his life in

action in the Soudan at "Trofek" in March, 1885), and of Mrs. Romilly. He was of Huguenot descent, belonging to the family of which Etienne Romilly, who was born at Montpellier, in France, 1678, was the first member to settle in England in 1701 after the revocation of the Edict of Nantes in 1685.

He was a great-grandson of Lieutenant-Colonel Samuel Romilly, R.E., of Dulwich, in the County of Surrey ; also a collateral descendant of Sir Samuel Romilly, Solicitor-General and law reformer, who died in 1818.

Captain A. H. Romilly was born on the 3rd February, 1877, and was educated at Wellington, where he was in the Lynedoch, 1889–93, in which year he got his cap. In 1895 he went to the R.M.C., Sandhurst, from which he was gazetted to the Duke of Cornwall's Light Infantry in September, 1896, becoming Lieutenant in November, 1898.

He took part in the South African War, being employed with the Mounted Infantry, and was present at the relief of Kimberley ; at operations in the Orange Free State, Paardeberg, and the Transvaal, including actions at Driefontein ; near Johannesburg, Diamond Hill, and Belfast. He was twice mentioned in Despatches ("London Gazette," 10th September, 1901, and 29th July, 1902), and received the Queen's medal with six clasps and the King's medal with two clasps. He was promoted Captain in January, 1904, and from January, 1905, to January, 1910, was Adjutant of the 5th Battalion Manchester Regiment (T.F.).

He landed in France with his regiment, of which he commanded a company, on the 15th August, 1914. He took part in the action on the Mons Canal, on the 23rd August, and in the Battle of Le Cateau on the 26th August, and was present during the great retirement from the 23rd August to the 5th September. He led his company through the Battles of the Marne, the 8th and 9th September, and of the Aisne, the 13th–25th September. After the movement of the British Army from the Aisne to Flanders he took part in the severe fighting about Festubert and La Bassée, 11th–21st October, on which latter date he was wounded twice and fell gallantly leading a portion of his company in a local counter-attack near the village of Lorgies. This last period of fighting in which he took part formed part of the great battle now known as the first Battle of Ypres. His body was never recovered.

He was mentioned in Sir John French's Despatch of the 14th January, 1915.

Captain Romilly married, in February, 1905, Annie Palmer MacCall, elder daughter of the late Colonel George MacCall, 8th Bengal Cavalry, and of Mrs. MacCall, and left a widow and four daughters : Monica Blanchflower, born December, 1905 ; Nancy Hermione, born February, 1907 ; Daphne Patricia, born November, 1911 ; and Cynthia Josephine, born March, 1914. His recreations were hockey, polo, and hunting.

MAJOR REGINALD TREVOR ROPER, p.s.c., 1st BATTN. DORSETSHIRE

REGIMENT, was born on the 16th February, 1872, the son of the late William and Mrs. Roper, of Beechfield, Sutton, County Dublin. After passing through the R.M.C., Sandhurst, he joined the Dorsetshire Regiment as 2nd Lieutenant in January, 1892, becoming Lieutenant in March, 1894. From 1897–1901 he was Adjutant of his battalion, obtaining his Company in June, 1900, and his Majority in February, 1910. He served in the Tirah Campaign, 1897–98, being present at the actions of Chagru Kotal and Dargai, and the capture of the Sampagha Pass, for which he received the medal with two clasps. In 1903 he passed through the Staff College, and held an appointment as 3rd Grade General Staff Officer at the War Office from 1904-08. In 1909-10 he was Brigade-Major of the 8th Brigade South Command, and from 1910–13 on the Directing Staff of the Staff College, with the temporary rank of Lieutenant-Colonel from January, 1911.

Major Roper was killed on the 12th October, 1914, at Pontefixe, near Bethune ; he was mentioned in Sir John French's Despatch of the 14th January, 1915.

He married, in April, 1906, Florence Alice, daughter of J. Staples Hawkins, of St. Fenton's, Baily, Co. Dublin, and left two sons : Denis Reginald, born 1907 ; and Kenneth Trevor, born 1908.

CAPTAIN ARTHUR HUGH PERCY ROSE, 3rd. (attd. 2nd.) BATTN. ESSEX

REGIMENT, who was killed in action, near Armentières, France, on the 23rd November, 1914, was the only surviving son of the late Major-General J. Rose, A.D.C. to the late Queen Victoria, at one time commanding the Queen's Royal West Surrey Regiment, and of Mrs. Rose, of Fryerning, Ingatestone, Essex. Major-General Rose served in the Crimean

War, being wounded in the Battle of the Alma. Captain Rose was born in India on the 13th

December, 1871, and joined the 1st Battalion Essex Regiment from the Militia in April, 1900. He served in the South African War, taking part in operations in the Orange Free State, including the actions on the Vet and Zand Rivers ; operations in Cape Colony and the Transvaal, including actions near Johannesburg, at Pretoria and Diamond Hill, and east of Pretoria, including the action at Frederickstad. He received the Queen's medal with five clasps and the King's medal with two clasps.

After the Boer War he served with his battalion in India, returning to England in 1906 to take up the Adjutancy of the 4th Battalion, being transferred, on its disbandment, to the 5th Battalion. In 1912 he retired from the active list, and joined the 3rd Battalion (Special Reserve), from which he went to the 2nd Battalion, with which he was serving when he was killed.

Captain Rose, who was a member of the Junior Naval and Military Club, Ranelagh, and Hurlingham, married Lilian, daughter of Robert Gordon, Esq., and widow of Lieutenant-Colonel John Trevor Spencer, Essex Regiment. He left no family.

CAPTAIN SIR FRANK STANLEY ROSE, BART., Xth (PRINCE OF WALES'S OWN ROYAL) HUSSARS,

was born on the 27th April, 1877. He succeeded his father—Sir Charles Day Rose—as second Baronet in 1913, and he was a grandson of the Right Hon. Sir John Rose, P.C., G.C.M.G. Sir Frank Rose was educated at Eton and Trinity College,

Cambridge, joining the 10th Hussars in May, 1900, becoming Lieutenant in June, 1904.

He served with his regiment in the South African War, being present at operations in the Transvaal and Cape Colony. For his services he was mentioned in Despatches ("London Gazette," 17th January, 1902), and received the Queen's medal with four clasps.

One of the characteristics of the Great War has

been the liability of the cavalry to be employed on dismounted duties, and Sir Frank Rose was so employed when he was killed, on the 26th October, 1914, while fighting with his regiment in the trenches, near Zandvoorde, where he is buried. These trenches were under heavy shell fire all day and the casualties were very severe, Lieutenant Turner also being killed. Sir F. Rose married Daphne, daughter of the late Captain Henry Brooks Gaskell, of Kiddington Hall, Oxfordshire, and left three children: Charles Henry, who succeeds him in the Baronetcy, born October, 1912 ; Amy, born May, 1911 ; and Helen Briar, born June, 1915.

He was a member of the Army and Navy Club, Boodle's, and the Royal Automobile Club, while his chief recreations were music and hunting.

LIEUTENANT JOHN CHARLES REGINALD ROSE, 2nd BATTN. PRINCESS LOUISE'S (ARGYLL & SUTHERLAND HIGHLANDERS),

was born on the 18th June, 1891, the son of Lieutenant - Colonel J. S. Rose.

He was educated at Rugby and the R.M.C., Sandhurst, from which he joined the Argyll and Sutherland Highlanders in March, 1911, becoming Lieutenant in April, 1914. He was a member of the Junior United Service Club.

Lieutenant Rose was accidentally shot in the trenches on the 8th November, 1914, towards the closing stages of the first Battle of Ypres ; the attack by the Prussian Guard on the 11th being regarded as the final attempt of the enemy to break through the British line.

MAJOR LAUNCELOT ST. VINCENT ROSE, ROYAL ENGINEERS,

who was killed in action on the 27th November, 1914, was the son of Frederick William Rose, and grandson of Major Hugh Monro St. Vincent Rose, 12th Lancers, of Glastulloch, and of Tarlogie, Rossshire. Major Rose's brother — Captain R. H. W. Rose, The Cameronians—was killed in action on the 22nd October, 1914. They were descendants of William Rose of Clava, a junior branch of the Roses of Kilmarnoch.

He was born on the 4th August, 1875, at 4,

Cromwell Crescent, London, S.W., and was educated at St. Paul's School (1887–92), for which he had gained a scholarship, followed by another. He then went to the R.M.A., Woolwich, from which he was gazetted to the Royal Engineers in March, 1895, being promoted Lieutenant in March, 1898, and Captain in April, 1904. At St. Paul's he was in the rowing four, being captain for some time, and at the R.M.A. he was in the Gymnasium Eight in 1894, which is thought as much of by Cadets as is their " blue " by University men. He was also in the running team, winning many prizes. At the School of Military Engineering at Chatham, where he went after being gazetted to the Army, he represented the officers at Rugby football ; also rowed for the two-seaters ; and later was stroke of the R.E. Four when they defeated the R.A. In 1897 he went to Gibraltar, where he was for a time Adjutant of his corps, and where he made a reputation as a polo player, being one of the garrison team. While there he ran his ponies in several races, winning, amongst others, the steeplechase for the Subalterns' Cup, open to the garrison, on his own pony, and many prizes at Gymkhanas. He also started a boxing club for the N.C.O.'s, which he left in a flourishing condition. He went to South Africa in 1910, where he did some big-game shooting. He returned to England in September, 1914, and, after being for a fortnight with the VIIth Division on mobilisation at Lyndhurst Camp, Hants, he embarked for France in command of the 55th Field Company, and went through the fighting at and near Ypres. He could have obtained short leave in November, but refused it ; for, he thought, as he could not spare any of his officers, he ought not to go himself. He was mentioned for his services in Sir John French's Despatch of the 14th January, 1915.

Major Rose married Agneta Wendela Elizabeth, daughter of the Jonkheer van Citters, of Zeeland, Holland, and left one daughter, Noreen Leonie Ross, born at Pretoria in October, 1913. He was a member of the Naval and Military Club.

CAPTAIN RONALD HUGH WALROND ROSE, 1st BATTN. THE CAMERONIANS (SCOTTISH RIFLES),

who was killed in action on the 22nd October, 1914, was the son of Frederick William Rose, and grandson of the late Major Hugh Rose, of the 12th Lancers, of Tarlogie, Rossshire, N.B.

He was born in London on the 11th July, 1880 ; was

educated at St. Paul's School ; and joined the Royal Warwickshire Regiment from the Militia in January, 1899, becoming Lieutenant in March, 1900. In May, 1905, he obtained his company in the Royal Warwickshire Regiment, and in May, 1908, was transferred to the Scottish Rifles. From October, 1906, to January, 1910, he was Adjutant of the 5th Battalion The King's (Liverpool Regiment),(Volunteers and Territorial Force). After giving up his Territorial Adjutancy he joined the 1st Battalion of his regiment at Bloemfontein, and later was appointed Commandant of the School of Signalling at Pretoria. His battalion returned to Glasgow in 1912, and on the outbreak of the war with Germany formed part of the British Expeditionary Force. He was present at Mons, Le Cateau, the Marne, the Aisne, and the first Battle of Ypres.

When he was killed Captain Rose was in command of a covering party, and was hit in the ankle, but went on leading his men till, being hit twice again, he was killed. He was mentioned in Sir John French's Despatch of the 14th January, 1915, for gallantry.

He married Hetty, youngest daughter of the late George Fletcher, of Liverpool, and left two children : Audrey, born April, 1912 ; and Jean Diana, born May, 1914.

2nd LIEUTENANT HAROLD WILLIAM ROSEVEARE, SPECIAL RESERVE, THE DUKE OF EDINBURGH'S (WILTSHIRE REGIMENT),

was the eldest son of the Rev. R. P. Roseveare, Rector of St. Paul's, Deptford, and Rural Dean of Greenwich, formerly Rector of Great Snoring in Norfolk, and Vicar of the Church of the Ascension, Blackheath.

He was born on the 18th February, 1895, and educated at Little Appley, near Ryde, and at Marlborough, where he held scholarships, was Senior Prefect 1913–14, Cadet Captain in the O.T.C., and was a member of the Rugby XV. He was a Scholar Elect of St. John's College, Cambridge, having won an open Classical Scholarship there in December, 1913. He was appointed to the Special Reserve on probation in April, 1914.

For the Great War he was attached to the 1st Battalion of his regiment, and when the Germans forced part of our lines at the Aisne he was sent with his platoon to locate and seize their machine gun, and fell leading his men, wounded in the head and lungs, on the 20th September, 1914, dying from his wounds the same evening.

MAJOR FLEETWOOD GEORGE CAMPBELL ROSS, 2nd KING EDWARD'S OWN GURKHA RIFLES (THE SIRMOOR RIFLES),

who was killed in action at Neuve Chapelle on the 2nd November, 1914, was the eldest son of Colonel George Campbell Ross, late 16th Bengal Cavalry, of "Bayfields," Headley.

He was born on the 18th March, 1869, and was educated at Victoria College, Jersey. He was gazetted to the Wiltshire Regiment from the Militia in July, 1890, becoming Lieutenant in March, 1892. In April of the latter year he was transferred to the Indian Staff Corps, and in 1900 took part in the relief of Pekin, receiving the medal with clasp. He was promoted Captain in July, 1901, and took part in the Tibet Expedition in 1903–04, being present at the action at Niani ; at operations at and around Gyangtse ; and in the march to Lhassa. He was mentioned in Despatches ("London Gazette," 13th December, 1904), and received the medal with clasp.

Major Ross obtained his Majority in July, 1908. He was a member of the Junior Naval and Military Club, and took great interest in polo. He was unmarried.

LIEUTENANT AURIOL FRANCIS HAY ROUND, 2nd BATTN. ESSEX REGT.,

fourth son of Francis R. Round, C.M.G., of Witham, Essex, was born on the 11th November, 1891.

He was educated at Felsted School, Essex, and the R.M.C., Sandhurst, and joined the Essex Regiment in March, 1911,

becoming Lieutenant in January, 1912. In 1913 he was appointed Assistant Adjutant of his battalion.

Lieutenant Round was a good cricketer and athlete, representing his regiment in long-distance races ; but hockey was the game in which he most distinguished himself, having been captain of the Felsted XI in 1909 and of the Sandhurst XI in 1910, playing regularly for the County of Essex in the last two seasons of his life, and for the Army against the Navy. He was also a member of the team sent from

England, so lately as Whitsuntide, 1914, to play several teams of Germans at Munich.

His battalion, which formed part of the 12th Brigade, IVth Division, only landed in France on the 23rd August, 1914, and thus was not present at the Battle of Mons, but on arrival was at once pushed into the firing line and was engaged in covering the retirement when Lieutenant Round was wounded near Le Cateau by a bullet from a shrapnel shell in the afternoon of the 26th August, described by Sir John French as " the most critical day of all." Tetanus supervened, and Lieutenant Round died from it on the 5th September, 1914, in King Edward VII Hospital for Officers, Grosvenor Gardens, S.W.

CAPTAIN KENNETH JAMES ROY, 4th BATTN. THE DUKE OF CAMBRIDGE'S OWN (MIDDLESEX REGIMENT),

who is believed to have been killed on the 23rd August, 1914, was the son of the late Rev. James Roy, Rector of Stockton-on-Forest, Yorkshire, and of Mrs. Roy, York Lodge, Beaconsfield, Bucks. Three of his brothers are in the Navy : Commander R. S. Roy, Staff Paymaster N. F. Roy, and Surgeon D. W. Roy, F.R.C.S., R.N.V.R.

He was born at Appleton Vicarage, Bolton Percy, Yorkshire, on the 21st January, 1877, and was educated at St. Peter's School, York, where he was in the First XV ; and at The Oaks, Upper Deal. He received his commission in the 3rd Battalion West Yorkshire Regiment in February, 1896. In 1898 he was attached to the depot, Manchester Regiment, Ashton-under-Lyne, and from 1899-1904 was seconded for employment with the 2nd Gold Coast Regiment, West African Frontier Force. In the meantime he had in June, 1901, been gazetted to the Middlesex Regiment as 2nd Lieutenant, and had been promoted Lieutenant in March, 1903. In 1905-06 he served with the 4th Battalion of his own regiment at Londonderry ; and in May, 1907, was seconded for service with the South Nigerian Regiment, West African Frontier Force, remaining with it till May, 1908. He was pro-romoted Captain in the Middlesex Regiment in November, 1910, having served with it in the Channel Islands, 1909-10 ; and from February, 1911, to September, 1912, again served on the African Coast with the West African Regiment. He took part in the Ashanti Campaign of 1900, for which he received the medal.

Referring to his death an officer, since a prisoner

of war, said : " I saw Captain Roy killed in a hand-to-hand fight on the Mons Road. He fought splendidly, but we had no chance. There were about two hundred and fifty Germans against forty of us, the remnant of my company who defended Obourg Station on the canal. I was lying on the ground helpless. We managed to keep the Germans in check for a bit, but were eventually overpowered. Only a few, I fear, escaped to tell the tale. It was a great day for our boys, but the odds against us were overwhelming."

Captain Roy was an enthusiastic Freemason, and was a member of the Albert Victor Lodge in York.

LIEUTENANT ARTHUR CLEGG FANSHAWE ROYLE, 1st BATTN. THE PRINCE OF WALES'S (NORTH STAFFORDSHIRE REGIMENT),

was the eldest son of Arthur F. W. and Harriette Royle, of Lympsham Manor, Somerset, and was born at Oakfield, Hale, Cheshire, on the 2nd January, 1883. He was a nephew of the late Rear-Admiral H. L. Fanshawe Royle,

D.S.O., and of the Rev. Vernon Royle, Stanmore Park, Middlesex.

Lieutenant Royle was educated at Wellington College, Berkshire, from 1897-1901, and joined the 1st North Staffordshire Regiment from the Militia in 1903, becoming Lieutenant in February, 1907, and served with that battalion at Lichfield, Shorncliffe, Aldershot, and Buttevant.

Accompanying his battalion to the front on the outbreak of the war, he was mortally wounded on the 22nd September, 1914, on his first night in the trenches, at the Battle of the Aisne, dying in hospital on the 29th September. He was buried in Braisne Cemetery, near Soissons.

His recreations were cricket, football, golf, hunting, and shooting.

2nd LIEUTENANT KENNETH STANES RUEGG, 2nd BATTN. THE SHERWOOD FORESTERS, (NOTTINGHAMSHIRE AND DERBYSHIRE REGIMENT),

was killed in action on the 20th September, 1914.

Mr. Ruegg only received his commission from the rank of Lance-Sergeant on the 15th September, 1914.

CAPTAIN ARTHUR MONTAGU RUNDALL, 1st BATTN. 4th GURKHA RIFLES,

who was born on the 20th October, 1878, at Kherwara, Rajputana, India, was the eldest surviving son of Colonel F. M. Rundall, C.B., D.S.O., late Commanding 1st Battalion 4th Gurkha Rifles. He was a grandson of the late General F. H. Rundall, R.E., C.S.I., and of the late Right Rev. E. H. Bickersteth, Bishop of Exeter.

He was educated at Marlborough College, where he was in Gould's House from 1891–94. He joined the 1st Bedfordshire Regiment from the 4th (Militia) Battalion Devonshire Regiment in February, 1899, becoming Lieutenant in February, 1900. In January, 1901, he joined the 27th Punjabis, late 27th (Punjab) Bengal Infantry, and was subsequently transferred to the 4th Gurkha Rifles. He obtained an extra first-class Hythe Musketry Certificate, was Instructor in Signalling, and had been Adjutant of his battalion.

Captain Rundall, who was a member of the Junior United Service Club, was a good shot with both gun and rifle.

He was with his battalion in Egypt till the beginning of December, 1914, and on coming to Europe proceeded with it to Northern France, where they went into the trenches at Festubert. In manning these trenches, which were in very bad repair, Captain Rundall had shortly before risked his life to extract a Gurkha who had become literally engulfed in the mud, and this Captain Rundall succeeded in doing under heavy fire. He was voluntarily in command of the bomb-throwing section—a most dangerous task. On the morning of the 20th December, 1914, a large portion of the 4th Gurkha trenches was blown up by German mines, and the enemy at once advanced in great numbers. Captain Rundall was at the far end of the trench, so escaped being blown up, but was left with only three Gurkhas armed with hand grenades. The little party stood up, undaunted, to the mass of Germans, and Captain Rundall killed three of the enemy with his revolver before being himself shot dead. Two of the men escaped to tell the story. His body was never recovered.

Captain Rundall's younger brother—Lieutenant L. B. Rundall, 1st King George's Own Gurkha Rifles—was killed very near the same place on the previous day.

Captain Rundall married, in 1913, Margaret Frances, daughter of the late Frank Marshall, Esq., of Cullercoats, Northumberland. There is one son of the marriage, born posthumously in April, 1915.

LIEUTENANT LIONEL BICKERSTETH RUNDALL, 1st BATTN. 1st KING GEORGE'S OWN GURKHA RIFLES (THE MALAUN REGIMENT),

who was born at Bakloh, Punjab, India, on the 9th April, 1890, was the youngest son of Colonel F. M. Rundall, C.B., D.S.O., late Commanding the 1st Battalion 4th Gurkha Rifles, and a grandson of the late General F. H. Rundall, R.E., C.S.I., and of the late Right Rev. E. H. Bickersteth, Bishop of Exeter.

He was educated at Charterhouse (Sanderites) and the R.M.C., Sandhurst, where he gained the prize for topography. He was in the 4th (Militia) Battalion Scottish Rifles for a year from April, 1907, but resigned his commission on passing into the R.M.C. After serving his probationary period with the 1st Battalion North Staffordshire Regiment he joined the 1/1st King George's Own Gurkha Rifles in December, 1910. While with them he was promoted Lieutenant in December, 1911, passed as a Transport Officer, and was Instructor in Signalling.

Lieutenant Rundall was a sportsman who enjoyed both big and small game shooting. He was the author of a book, "The Ibex of Sha Ping and other Himalayan Studies," published in 1915. He was a member of the Junior Army and Navy Club.

He was killed on the 19th December, 1914. His double Company Commander was ordered to charge a German sap-head with twenty-four Gurkhas. It was not intended that Lieutenant Rundall should accompany the party, but he preferred not to let his Captain go alone on what seemed a most dangerous exploit. All the party were killed except five men.

Lieutenant Rundall's elder brother—Captain A. M. Rundall, 1st/4th Gurkha Rifles—was killed on the 20th December, 1914, in this same action at Festubert.

LIEUTENANT FREDERIC HORNBY LEVER RUSHTON, 2nd BATTN. THE ROYAL IRISH REGIMENT,

was the elder son of the late Frederic Lever Rushton and his wife, Frances Alice Birley, and was born at Gresford, Denbighshire, N.W., on the 29th August, 1888.

He was educated at Charterhouse, where he was captain of football and sports. He first joined  the Liverpool Regiment in 1907, and obtained his commission in the Royal Irish Regiment, from the Special Reserve in December, 1909, becoming Lieutenant in October, 1911. He went to the front with his battalion on the outbreak of the war.

At the Battle of Mons Lieutenant Rushton, with another officer, took their C.O., when wounded, out of the firing line, and so saved his life. Subsequently he saved also the life of the Adjutant. Lieutenant-Colonel Cox, his Commanding Officer, whose life he saved, wrote to Lieutenant Rushton's sister: " You have every reason to be very, very proud of your brother. I was wounded in the leg, and could not get along, . . . so he and others carried me out of action under an extremely heavy fire."

At Vailly, on the 15th September, 1914, he was killed while leading a party to take a machine gun which was on an eminence, and was inflicting severe losses on his section.

For these services Lieutenant Rushton was mentioned in Sir John French's Despatch of the 8th October, 1914, and was subsequently awarded the Military Cross, but his death at an earlier date prevented his personally receiving the decoration.

A brother officer wrote of him to a friend: " He was absolutely splendid in the field, and in addition to other deeds of gallantry he undoubtedly saved Dick Phillips' (the Adjutant) life at Mons. Rushton was killed in an advance action in which he had been previously wounded and dressed by Laing, who implored him not to advance any more, as he was wounded right through the shoulder; but he insisted on going on, and was killed shortly afterwards."

Lieutenant Rushton was a keen fisherman and motorist, and was Captain of the regimental football team. He was generally known to his acquaintances as "Hornby," an old family name.

LIEUTENANT LAWRENCE EDWARD RUSSELL, 2nd BATTN. THE DUKE OF WELLINGTON'S (WEST RIDING REGIMENT),

who was included in the War Office monthly casualty list, published on the 9th October, 1914, as unofficially reported killed in action, was the son of Mrs. Russell, Bryn, Digswell, Welwyn, Herts. He was born on the 10th June, 1892, joined the West Riding Regiment in September, 1911, and became Lieutenant in April, 1914.

CAPTAIN WALTER RUSSELL RUSSELL, 2nd BATTN. (attd. 1st) NORTHAMPTONSHIRE REGIMENT,

who was killed in action at Pilkem, near Ypres, on the 23rd October, 1914, was the son of the late Captain Sir William Russell Russell, formerly Minister for Defence and Colonial Secretary of New Zealand, and late of the 58th Regiment of Foot.

He was born at Flaxmere, Hastings, N.Z., on the 8th September, 1880; educated at Wanganin College, New Zealand; and received his commission in the Northamptonshire Regiment from the local military forces, New Zealand, in April, 1900, becoming Lieutenant in December, 1902.

He took part in the South African War attached to the Mounted Infantry, and was present at operations in the Transvaal in the early part of 1902, for which he received the Queen's medal with two clasps.

From November, 1905, to November, 1908, he was Adjutant of his battalion, and was promoted Captain in December, 1908. He was a member of the Naval and Military Club.

LIEUT. EDWIN JOHN BERKELEY HAYES SADLER, ROYAL ENGINEERS,

who was killed in action in the village of Neuve Chapelle on the 28th October, 1914, was the third son of Lieutenant-Colonel Sir James Hayes Sadler, K.C.M.G., C.B., late Governor of the Windward Islands, and was born on the 1st October, 1887.

He was educated at Wellington College, to which he went as a scholar, and where he was from 1901 to 1904. He then passed into the R.M.A., Woolwich, from which he was gazetted 2nd Lieutenant in the Royal Engineers in December, 1906, and became Lieutenant in January, 1909. From December, 1909, to October, 1911, he was A.D.C. to the General Officer Commanding at Mauritius.

Latterly Lieutenant Hayes Sadler had been employed in the Military Work in India, from which at the outbreak of the war he was posted to the 21st Company, 3rd Sappers and Miners. His elder brother, Captain E. R. Hayes Sadler, Indian Army, was killed on the 30th October, 1914.

CAPTAIN ERNEST REGINALD HAYES SADLER, p.s.c., 2/8th GURKHA RIFLES,

who was killed in action on the 30th October, 1914, in the German attack on our position at Festubert, was the second son of Lieutenant - Colonel Sir James Hayes Sadler, K.C.M.G., C.B., late Governor of the Windward Islands.

He was born on the 4th September, 1878, and was educated at the United Services College, Westward Ho ! whence he passed direct into the R.M.C., Sandhurst. He passed out for the Indian Army, receiving an unattached 2nd Lieutenancy in July, 1899. He was promoted Lieutenant in the Indian Army in October, 1900, and was on active service in Nandi, 1905–06, receiving the medal with clasp. He became Captain in July, 1907, and in 1908–10 was on active service in Somaliland, East Africa, on Brigadier-General Gough's Staff, for which he had a clasp added to his medal. From 1906 to 1909 he was A.D.C. and Private Secretary to his father when Governor and Commander-in-Chief, East Africa Protectorate.

In 1913 he passed out of the Staff College, and was the author of articles on military and topographical subjects in East Africa, and on military administration in India. He was proficient in Eastern languages.

His younger brother, Lieutenant E. J. B. Hayes Sadler, R.E., was killed in the Great War on the 28th October, 1914.

Captain Hayes Sadler married, early in 1914, Eleanor, elder daughter of Mr. A. F. C. Tollemache, The Red House, Westgate-on-Sea.

CAPTAIN GERARD GLOAG SADLER, 3rd (PRINCE OF WALES'S) DRAGOON GUARDS,

son of the late Sir Samuel A. Sadler, was born at Eaglescliffe, County Durham, on the 12th January, 1881.

He was educated at Durham School, and joined the Durham Light Infantry (Militia) in 1899, from which he was transferred to the 3rd Dragoon Guards in September of the following year.

Captain Sadler served in the South African War, taking part in the several operations in the Transvaal, Orange River Colony, and Cape Colony from February, 1901, to May, 1902. He received the Queen's medal with five clasps. He was promoted Captain in April, 1910, and in February, 1911, retired from the active list, and joined the Special Reserve of his regiment.

On going to the front he was attached to the 6th Dragoon Guards (Carabiniers), and was present at the Battles of Mons, the Marne, the Aisne, and Ypres.

He was reported missing after a night attack on the 1st November, 1914, near Ypres. Fifteen weeks later he was reported to have died of wounds on that day, and to have been buried at Wytschaete, near Messines, Belgium.

Captain Sadler married Phœbe, daughter of the late W. M. Roche, Esq., of Sunderland, County Durham, and left one daughter—Elizabeth— born August, 1914.

He was a member of the Junior Naval and Military Club.

2nd LIEUTENANT the Honble. PIERS STEWART ST. AUBYN, 6th (RESERVE), attd. 2nd BATTN. THE KING'S ROYAL RIFLE CORPS,

was wounded on the 31st October, 1914, on which date he was seen by a brother officer lying on the ground. The latter officer said 2nd Lieutenant St. Aubyn had been hit in the shoulder, but it was not possible to go to his assistance then. The Germans afterwards advanced over the ground, and the wounded officer has not since been heard of. The High Court subsequently allowed it to be presumed that his death occurred on or since the 31st October, 1914.

2nd Lieutenant St. Aubyn was the fifth son of the first Baron St. Lovan and his wife, Lady Elizabeth Clementina Townshend, daughter of the fourth Marquess Townshend, and was born on the 11th April, 1871. He served in South Africa in 1900 as a Lieutenant in Thornycroft's Mounted Infantry.

On the outbreak of war 2nd Lieutenant St. Aubyn was gazetted to the 6th Battalion K.R.R.C. in September, 1914, and went to France almost at once, where he was attached to the 2nd Battalion.

He was a J.P., for the County of Cornwall, and a member of Brooks', the Travellers', and Bachelors' Clubs. He was a well-known owner of greyhounds.

CAPTAIN the Honble. CHARLES HENRY MURRAY ST. CLAIR, 1st BATTN. SEAFORTH HIGHLANDERS (ROSS-SHIRE BUFFS, THE DUKE OF ALBANY'S),

younger son of the Right Hon. Charles William St. Clair, fifteenth Baron Sinclair, was born on the 19th December, 1878, and was educated at Eton and the R.M.C., Sandhurst. He was gazetted to the 2nd Battalion Seaforth

Highlanders in May, 1898, becoming Lieutenant in December, 1899.

He served with his battalion in the South African War of 1899–1902, being present in the advance on Kimberley, including the engagements of Magersfontein, Paardeberg, Poplar Grove, and Driefontein. During the operations in the Orange River Colony and the Transvaal in 1900–01 he was attached to Brigadier-General Sir Henry Rawlinson's column as Signalling Officer, and was present at the action at Wittebergen. For his services he was mentioned in Despatches (" London Gazette," 10th September, 1901, and received the Queen's medal with five clasps and the King's medal with two clasps.

From 1903 to 1906, having obtained his company in April, 1902, he was Adjutant of the 2nd Battalion of his regiment, and in 1906–07 was A.D.C. to General Sir Bruce Hamilton, Commanding the IInd Division at Aldershot; whilst from 1908 to 1912 he was Staff Captain on the Headquarters Staff of the Scottish Command. In the latter year he was posted to the 1st Battalion of his regiment at Agra, India. Captain St. Clair landed in France with the Indian (Meerut) Expeditionary Force on the 13th October, 1914, and served in the North of France until the 20th December, 1914, when he was killed in action in the trenches near La Bassée. He was mentioned in Sir John French's Despatch of the 31st May, 1915.

Captain St. Clair, who was a member of the King's Bodyguard for Scotland (Royal Company of Archers) and a Knight of the Order of St. Ernestine, of Saxe-Coburg and Gotha, belonged to the United Service and Bath Clubs, London, and to the New Club, Edinburgh.

2nd LIEUTENANT HOWARD AVENEL BLIGH ST. GEORGE, 1st LIFE GUARDS,

who was killed in action at Zillebeke on the 15th November, 1914, in his twentieth year, was the second son of Mr. and Mrs. St. George, of Ashorne Hill, Leamington.

He was gazetted to the 1st Life Guards on probation in January, 1914.

CAPT. FRANK HARRISON SAKER, 4th BATTN. CONNAUGHT RANGERS,

who was killed in action in Flanders on the 30th October, 1914, leaving a widow, was the youngest son of the late Edward Saker, of Liverpool.

He was thirty-four years of age at the time of his death, and entered the fifth (afterwards the 4th) Battalion Connaught Rangers as 2nd Lieutenant in February, 1904, and became Lieutenant in June, 1906. He had passed through a School of Instruction, and was qualified for appointment as Instructor of Musketry; he was promoted Captain in September, 1914.

2nd LIEUTENANT ARTHUR MOLESWORTH SAMUELS, SPECIAL RESERVE, attd. 1st BATTN. PRINCESS VICTORIA'S (ROYAL IRISH FUSILIERS),

born on the 11th June, 1889, at Birr, King's County, Ireland, was the son of the late Lieutenant - Colonel W. F. Samuels, A.M.S., who served in the Ashanti Campaign of 1873–74; his grandfather, the late George McCulloch, Staff Surgeon, 2nd Life Guards, died when on his way home from the Crimea.

2nd Lieutenant Samuels, who was educated at Corrig School, Kingstown, and Mountjoy School, Dublin, joined the Royal Guernsey Light Infantry (Militia) in 1909. The following year he was attached to the 2nd Battalion Royal Inniskilling Fusiliers for training; and in 1913 joined the 3rd Battalion (Special Reserve) of the Royal Irish Fusiliers, being attached to the 1st (Regular) Battalion in August, 1914. With the latter corps he was serving at the front when he was killed in action near Ypres on the 13th October, 1914.

It was learnt from one of the men of the regiment that 2nd Lieutenant Samuels was twice wounded, and fell whilst leading his men to attack a German trench, which they eventually captured. 2nd Lieutenant Samuels belonged to the First XI of the Dundrum (County Dublin) Hockey Club.

LIEUTENANT WILLIAM ALASTAIR FRASER SANDEMAN, 1st BATTN. GORDON HIGHLANDERS,

who was wounded and taken prisoner on the 13th October, 1914, died from the effects of his wounds at Laventie, in France, on the 19th October, 1914.

He was the only son of Captain W. W. Sandeman, late Seaforth Highlanders, and

Mrs. Sandeman, 8, Queen's Gardens, Hove, Sussex, and was born on the 27th March, 1889. He was educated at Harrow (Mr. Davidson's, 1902–05), and joined the Gordon Highlanders in July, 1909, becoming Lieutenant in March, 1911. From December, 1911, to January, 1913, he was A.D.C. (extra) to the Governor and Commander-in-Chief, Ceylon.

CAPTAIN MERVYN KEATS SANDYS, 2nd BATTN. YORK AND LANCASTER REGIMENT,

who was born at 73, Sheep Street, Northampton, on the 17th July, 1884, was the younger twin son of Lieutenant - Colonel Edwin Del Sandys, 2nd Battalion Northamptonshire Regiment (the old 58th), and of Clarissa Marion, his wife, who was the only child of Lieutenant-Colonel George Edward Owen Jackson, R.M.L.I. He was also a grandson of Lieutenant-General George Sandys, 6th Madras Cavalry and Governor of the Northern Division of the Madras Presidency, and great-grandson of Myles Sandys, Esq., J.P., D.L., of Graythwaite Hall, North Lancashire. His twin brother is Captain G. O. Sandys, J.P., Westmorland and Cumberland Yeomanry, of Graythwaite Hall.

Captain M. K. Sandys was educated at Bedford Grammar School and the R.M.C., Sandhurst. He joined the 2nd Battalion York and Lancaster Regiment in October, 1903, becoming Lieutenant in November, 1907, and Captain in April, 1913. He was killed at Touquet, near Fleurbaix, France, in an attempt to recover a lost trench. His body was never recovered. Captain Sandys was at first reported as having been wounded on the 22nd October, 1914. A little later he was stated to have been wounded and missing on the 25th October, but finally his Commanding Officer notified his death on the 28th November, 1914. This latter report was ultimately confirmed by a brother officer and by wounded soldiers of his battalion who have since returned to England.

Captain Sandys belonged to the Conservative Club, St. James's, and was a member of the Limerick Hunt.

2nd LIEUTENANT (temp.) ALFRED SANG, INTELLIGENCE CORPS,

was born in Paris on the 6th September, 1876, the son of Frederic J. Sang, Marine Artist, and Johanna Garth. After an elementary education in France he was at Ratcliffe College, England, and subsequently at the Conservatoire National

des Arts et Métiers in Paris. He was possessed of considerable mathematical and mechanical

ability, and in 1900 he invented a calculating machine. In that year he went to the United States, and at Pittsburg specialised in the corrosion of metals and means for its prevention, publishing a book on the subject. He also contributed to many scientific publications. Returning to Paris in 1909, he founded the company of Sang & Rafinesque, metallurgical engineers, and later still the firm of Sang & Russell in London. He was elected a member of the Royal Society of Arts in 1911, from whose journal of the 27th November, 1914, many of the details of this biography have been taken.

Prior to the war 2nd Lieutenant Sang had no military experience, but on its outbreak he at once volunteered for the Intelligence Corps, for which he was specially fitted, as he spoke English and French equally well, and also had a thorough knowledge of German. Moreover, the roads of Northern France were familiar to him, as he was an ardent cyclist. His services were accepted and he was given a temporary commission as 2nd Lieutenant in August, 1914. He was severely wounded in the head on or about the 9th September, 1914, by shrapnel, and died in No. 8 Hospital, Rouen, France, on the 2nd October, 1914.

2nd Lieutenant Sang married Sara Alice Spang, of Pittsburg, Pa., U.S.A., and left three children : Frederick, aged fifteen ; Elizabeth Ewing, aged ten ; and Henry, aged eight years.

MAJOR WILLIAM STOPFORD SARSFIELD, 2nd BATTN. CONNAUGHT RANGERS,

born at Doughcloyne, County Cork, on the 23rd February, 1868, was the son of Dominick Ronayne Patrick Sarsfield, of that place, and was related to General Patrick Sarsfield.

He was educated at Cheltenham College, and was gazetted to the 1st Battalion Connaught Rangers in September, 1888, becoming Lieutenant in February, 1890, and Captain in May, 1897. He served all through the Boer War with his regiment and on the Staff, being present at the relief of Ladysmith, including action at Colenso, operations and actions at Spion Kop and Vaal Krans ; operations on the Tugela Heights, in Natal, and in Cape Colony, north and south of Orange River. He received the Queen's medal with three clasps and the King's medal with two clasps. He held the appointment of Assistant Press Censor and Deputy Assistant Adjutant-General from July, 1900, to February, 1903. Subsequently he was from December, 1906, to December, 1908, Adjutant of the 5th (Militia) Battalion (Special Reserve) at Boyle ; and receiving his Majority in December of the latter year was appointed to the command of the depot at Galway, which post he held for four years.

He accompanied his battalion to France for the Great War, and died on the 20th September, 1914, of wounds received at the Battle of the Aisne when in temporary command of the battalion, after the Commanding Officer had been wounded.

Major Sarsfield married Beatrice Lalagé Powell, daughter of Percy Maynard, D.L., Ratoath, County Meath, and left one son, Patrick, born April, 1899.

CAPTAIN JOHN ARDKEEN SAVAGE, 1st BATTN. NORTHAMPTON-SHIRE REGT.,

was the son of the Rev. Francis Forbes Savage and Ethel Margaret Savage, of Flushing Vicarage, Falmouth, Cornwall, and of The Ards, County Down, and was born at Chatham on the 16th September, 1883. He was a grandson of Captain John Morris Savage, R.A., who fell in the Crimea, and great-grandson of General Sir John Boscawen Savage K.C.B., K.H., who fought at Copenhagen and the Nile. Captain Savage was educated at Kelly College, Tavistock, and joined the 3rd West Riding Regiment in October, 1900. With it he served in the South African War, 1899–1901, and was present at operations in Cape Colony, December, 1900, to June, 1901. He received the Queen's medal with four clasps.

He afterwards joined the Royal Garrison Regiment, and on its disbandment in July, 1905, he was transferred to the 1st Battalion Northamptonshire Regiment in India, in which he became a Captain in March, 1912. He was seconded for service with the West African Frontier Force in Gambia and South Nigeria from 1911–13.

He was shot in the trenches at the Battle of the Aisne on the 17th September, 1914. The following is an account of the circumstances : " On Monday, the 15th September, the English advance trench on the Aisne was occupied by one hundred and sixty men of ' B ' Company, 1st Northamptonshire Regiment, who had fought their way back from Mons. On Tuesday, all the officers except a Subaltern having been killed, Captain Savage was sent from his own (' D ') Company to take command. At about 2.30 on the following day (Wednesday) word came down the line that the Germans were showing the white flag. This was unconfirmed, but about an hour later it was reported that they were laying down their arms, and had actually hoisted the white flag over the trench. On this Captain Savage got out of the trench, and laying down his sword and revolver advanced unarmed towards the German position, which was about eight yards distant. He was followed by his Subaltern—Lieutenant Dimmer, K.R.R.C.—who afterwards received the Victoria Cross. The German officer in command met Captain Savage in the middle of the intervening ground, and both officers were seen to salute. After about five minutes' conversation they again saluted, and each turned to return to his trench. Just as Captain Savage reached his own, Mr. Dimmer, who looked round, saw that the Germans were in the act of firing, and called out to warn Captain Savage, at the same time throwing himself on the ground. As Captain Savage did so the scabbard of his sword caught in the ground, causing a moment's delay, and he fell dead riddled by the bullets of a treacherous enemy. Captain Savage was buried on the same day. Of him it was written that he was an officer dearly loved by his men, and a man who seemed utterly without a knowledge of fear. It is said that when ' B ' Company came out of their trench on Friday their strength was eight sound men and four wounded."

LIEUTENANT RICHARD CHARLES GRAVES-SAWLE, 2nd BATTALION COLDSTREAM GUARDS,

was the only son of Rear-Admiral Sir Charles Graves-Sawle, Bart., M.V.O., and Lady Graves-Sawle, of Penrice, Cornwall, and Barley, Exeter. He was a nephew of Colonel Sir Francis Graves-Sawle, Bart., M.V.O., who at one time commanded the Coldstream Guards.

Lieutenant Graves-Sawle was educated at

Harrow and the R.M.C., Sandhurst, receiving his commission in the Coldstream Guards in 1908, getting his promotion in 1910. From 1913 to the outbreak of the war with Germany he was Assistant Adjutant of his battalion. He left for France on the 12th August, and fought all through the retirement from Mons, and was in every action up to the day he was killed at Ypres on the 2nd November, 1914.

Lieutenant Graves-Sawle, who was a member of the Guards' Club, was a keen yachtsman and big-game hunter. His marriage with Muriel, eldest daughter of Lieutenant-Colonel Heaton-Ellis, J.P., D.L., of Wyddiall Hall, Hertfordshire, which had been arranged to take place in October, took place, owing to the outbreak of war, on the 6th August, 1914.

CAPTAIN GEORGE HENRY VAUGHAN-SAWYER, 34th SIKH PIONEERS,

who was killed in action on the 27th October, 1914, was the only son of Colonel G. W. Sawyer, and was born on the 6th July, 1875. After passing for the Indian Army from the R.M.C., Sandhurst, he was gazetted 2nd Lieutenant unattached, in August, 1895, and joined the Indian Staff Corps in December, 1896, becoming Lieutenant in November, 1897. He was on service on the north-western frontier of India in 1897–98, being present at the engagement near Shabkadr in August, 1897, and at operations on the Samana and in the Kurram Valley in August and September, 1897. He received the medal with two clasps. He also served in the Bazar Valley, Tirah Campaign, 1897–98, receiving an additional clasp to his medal, and in the Tibet Campaign 1903–04 for which he received the medal.

He was promoted Captain in August, 1904, went on half-pay in May, 1909, returning to duty in December of the same year.

Captain Vaughan-Sawyer, who was married to Dr. Ethel Vaughan-Sawyer, retired from the active list in April, 1914, but rejoined the Army for the war.

2nd LIEUTENANT ROBERT SAYERS, 4th BATTN. DUKE OF CAMBRIDGE'S OWN (MIDDLESEX REGT.),

son of George Sayers, was born in London on the 16th July, 1879.

He served for eighteen years in the ranks, taking part in the South African War, for which he received the Queen's medal with six clasps and the King's medal with two clasps, having been present at operations and fighting at Laings Nek, in the Transvaal; the relief of Ladysmith, in the Orange Free State; and the Tugela Heights, in Cape Colony.

He was the best shot in his company for nine years in succession, was a splendid athlete, captain of his regimental hockey team, and played football, cricket, tennis, and bowls.

He was given his commission in the Middlesex Regiment during the Great War for saving his company during the retirement from Mons in August, 1914, and was mentioned in Sir John French's Despatch of the 8th October, 1914. He died between the 16th–22nd October, 1914. A farm at Le Rietz, near Lille, occupied by our men, had been heavily shelled, and 2nd Lieutenant Sayers gave the order for the wounded to be brought out, going himself to help in the work. When he was inside the building it collapsed and he never came out.

CAPTAIN THOMAS SCATCHARD, ROYAL ARMY MEDICAL CORPS,

who was killed in action on the 8th September, 1914, was the youngest son of Dr. and Mrs. Scatchard, of Boston Spa, Yorkshire.

He was born on the 6th July, 1878, and entered the Royal Army Medical Corps in July, 1905, being promoted Captain on the 31st January, 1909. Immediately preceding the war he was stationed at Aldershot.

He married, in 1907, Ada Mary, daughter of Colonel de la Motte Hervey, 13th Bengal Lancers, and a granddaughter of General Hervey, C.B., and left one child—Phyllis May Lindsay.

LIEUTENANT HERBERT HUGO SCHNEIDER, ROYAL ENGINEERS,

was born in East Dulwich, London, on the 5th January, 1888. He was educated at the Bedales School, Petersfield, Hants. and received his technical education at the Crystal Palace School of Practical Engineering, after which he served an apprenticeship of fifteen months in the shops, specialising in electric motors and generators. He was an assistant to Messrs. Barry, Leslie

& Egerton for three years (1907–10), when he joined the Special Reserve for one year as 2nd Lieutenant, Royal Engineers.

In 1911 he went to West Africa, where he served as Assistant Engineer on the Lagos Railway, Northern Extension, Northern Nigeria. After his leave of absence he returned to West Africa in 1912 as Assistant Engineer on the Sierra Leone Government Railway. In 1914 he was appointed Surveyor to the Survey of Northern Nigeria, and was still there on the outbreak of the war, when he left to take part in the operations in West Africa. He was killed in action in the Cameroons on the 5th December, 1914.

His promotion to Lieutenant, to date from 1st September, 1914, was notified in the " London Gazette " of the 20th May, 1915.

He was elected a Graduate of the Institution of Mechanical Engineers in 1909, and an Associate Member in 1914.

2nd LIEUTENANT ROGER HENRY SCHUNCK, 1st BATTN. THE QUEEN'S (ROYAL WEST SURREY REGIMENT),

was born on the 2nd October, 1884, at Falkenham, Suffolk. He was the only son of Hubert Schunck, Esq., of Harrogate, Leeds, and Manchester, and a grandson of Dr. Edward Schunck, Ph.D., F.R.S.

He was educated at Radley College, Oxford, at Düsseldorf, and at Bordeaux. After serving as 2nd Lieutenant in the Special Reserve of the 3rd Battalion of the regiment he obtained his commission in the 1st Battalion on the outbreak of the war, and proceeded with his battalion to the front. He was in heavy fighting at the battles on the Aisne, where he got a bullet through his cap.

At the first Battle of Ypres, he was killed on the 30th-31st October, 1914, near Gheluvelt, by a piece of shell while holding an advanced post, when only three officers of the battalion were left. He was buried in Ypres Cemetery.

Lieutenant Schunck was a member of the Public Schools' Club, Berkeley Street, London.

LIEUTENANT ALFRED F. SCHUSTER, SPECIAL RESERVE, 4th (QUEEN'S OWN) HUSSARS,

was born in Hampstead on the 30th July, 1883, and was the son of Ernest J. Schuster, Barrister-at-Law.

He was educated first at Stoke House, Stoke Poges, and then at Charterhouse, where he held junior and senior scholarships ; and finally he was an Exhibitioner of New College, Oxford, where he took a second class in Moderations and a second class in Lit. Human.

Lieutenant Schuster joined the Kerry Militia in July, 1905, as 2nd Lieutenant, being promoted Lieutenant in August, 1908, and when the Militia was disbanded was transferred to the 4th Hussars Special Reserve in July, 1910. He was serving with the 4th Hussars when he was killed on the 20th November, 1914, in the most advanced trench at Hooge, near Ypres.

Lieutenant Schuster was called to the Bar in 1906, and joined the publishing firm of Sidgwick and Jackson in 1913. He was a member of the New University Club, the Cavendish Club, and the Garrick. He hunted with the Quorn, V.W.H. Devon and Somerset Staghounds, and won the Bar Point-to-point Lightweight Race in 1908.

2nd LIEUTENANT BASIL JOHN HARRISON SCOTT, 2nd BATTN. SOUTH STAFFORDSHIRE REGIMENT,

who was shot in the first Battle of Ypres, near Pilkem (Belgium) on the 23rd October, 1914, was born in Fitzwilliam Square, Dublin, on the 10th May, 1894, the elder son of the late John Harrison Scott, F.R.C.S., Ireland,

and of Mrs. Scott, of Wimbledon.

He was educated at Winchester and the R.M.C., Sandhurst, joining the South Staffordshire Regiment at Aldershot in October, 1913. He accompanied his battalion to France in the second week of August, and took part in the great retirement from Mons to the Marne, and in subsequent actions.

For his services he was mentioned in Sir John French's Despatch of the 14th January, 1915.

2nd LIEUTENANT EDWARD CLAUD SCOTT, ROYAL GARRISON ARTILLERY,

who was killed in action near Armentières on the 21st November, 1914, was the son of General Hugh A. Scott, R.A., of The Garth, Winchester. He was born on the 15th May, 1892, educated at Repton and the R.M.A., Woolwich, and joined the Royal Artillery in December, 1911.

CAPTAIN JOHN KEARSLEY DAWSON-SCOTT, ROYAL ENGINEERS,

son of General Dawson-Scott, Colonel Commandant Royal Engineers, and grandson of Colonel Robert Kearsley Dawson, C.B., R.E., was born in London on the 18th May, 1883.

He was educated at Tonbridge School, from which he went direct to the R.M.A., Woolwich, and passed out fourth on the list, joining the School of Military Engineering, Chatham, in July, 1902. He was next stationed at Aldershot in a Field Company, and subsequently served for five years in Egypt. After returning to England he was appointed Assistant Instructor in Fortifications at the School of Military Engineering, Chatham.

He was good at all games, won many cups for rifle shooting, and at the R.M.A. had his colours for hockey. He was a good polo player, and won cups at the Turf Club, Cairo, and prizes for cricket, tennis, and croquet. He was also very musical, playing the 'cello; and sketched well.

On the outbreak of the war with Germany he joined the 5th Field Company, R.E., and left England on the 15th August, 1914. He was killed on the 29th October by high-explosive shell while making a reconnaissance in connection with trench fighting at the Battle of Ypres. For his services earlier in the war he had been awarded the Order of Chevalier of the Legion of Honour " for special gallantry " between the dates 21st–30th August, 1914.

CAPTAIN WALTER FALCONER SCOTT, 59th SCINDE RIFLES, (FRONTIER FORCE),

who was killed in action between the 24th and the 26th October, 1914, was the fourth son of Walter Scott, of Tan-y-gyrt, Denbigh.

He was born on the 20th December, 1879, and entered the 6th Battalion King's Liverpool Regiment in September, 1900, and, after serving with this battalion during embodiment for about a month, and being attached to the Shropshire Light Infantry for a year, he was gazetted to the Border Regiment as 2nd Lieutenant in December, 1901. In November, 1903, he was transferred to the Indian Army, in which he became Lieutenant in March, 1904, and Captain in December, 1910. In 1908 he was on active service on the north-western frontier of India, taking part in operations in the Zakka Khel country, and in the Mohmand country with the engagements of Matta and Kargha. He received the medal with clasp for these campaigns.

TEMPORARY 2nd LIEUTENANT JAMES HERBERT SEABROOK, INTELLIGENCE CORPS, 5th SIGNAL TROOP, ROYAL ENGINEERS,

was the youngest son of Mr. and Mrs. William Seabrook, of The Bungalow, Springfield, Chelmsford, and was born at Brent Hall, Boreham, Chelmsford, on the 20th October, 1883. He was the descendant, on his mother's side, of an old Huguenot family—Pertwee (Pertuis)—who settled near Langenhoe on being expelled from their native country on the revocation of the Edict of Nantes.

2nd Lieutenant Seabrook was educated at Chelmsford College, and volunteered for active service on the outbreak of the war with Germany, being gazetted to the Army in August, 1914. Previous to joining the Army 2nd Lieutenant Seabrook had been a partner in Messrs. W. Seabrook & Sons, Nurserymen, Chelmsford, and was a member of the Chelmsford Club, and of the Golf and Tennis Clubs of that town.

At the time of his death he was acting as despatch rider, attached to the 5th Cavalry Brigade, and was killed at the Battle of the Marne, near Gandelu, on the 10th September, 1914, while returning after the delivery of a despatch.

He was buried in the village churchyard at Gandelu.

The late Officer's Troop Commander gave the following account to his parents : " He was sent to me some weeks ago as a motor-cyclist despatch rider, and he had done splendid work for me, and was immensely popular with all. The circumstances of his death are these. We were in touch with the Germans early in the morning, and moved to turn their flank. I sent your son to headquarters of Second Army with a message before this, and when he returned to the point of despatch we had gone. He was told by another of my motor-cyclists where we had gone, and which road to take, but he appears to have missed his way, coming into contact with the enemy. The end must have come very quickly and painlessly, as he was shot in the head. Two other bullets also found their mark. All this we found later in the day, as we were in action all the forenoon, and I was not informed of his death till late in the evening, when, I am glad to say, we had gained a decisive success. . . . Your son died a glorious death, which we must all be prepared for, doing his duty in the service of his country."

CAPTAIN LOUIS EDMUND HARINGTON MOLYNEUX-SEEL, 2nd BATTN. BORDER REGIMENT, was killed in action on the 29th October, 1914, though his name did not appear in the monthly official casualty list up to June, 1915.

He was the second son of the late Henry Harrington Molyneux-Seel, and was born on the 8th October, 1872, receiving his commission in the Border Regiment from the Militia in December, 1894. He became Lieutenant in September, 1896, and Captain in August, 1902. From April, 1910, to August, 1913, Captain Molyneux-Seel, who was qualified as a 1st Class Interpreter in Turkish, was Vice-Consul at Van.

CAPTAIN BEAUCHAMP HENRY SELBY, 1st BATTN. THE NORTHUMBERLAND FUSILIERS,

son of Beauchamp Prideux Selby, Esq., of Pawston, Northumberland, was born in London on the 4th June, 1882, and was educated at Harrow and the R.M.C., Sandhurst. His whole service was spent in the Northumberland Fusiliers, which he joined in March, 1901, becoming Lieutenant in May, 1902, and Captain in October, 1912. For six years, from 1906 to 1912, he was with his battalion in India. He served on the north-western frontier of India, taking part in operations in the Mohmand country, including the engagement of Matta. He received the medal with clasp.

Captain Selby was shot in the trenches near Vailly on the 19th September, 1914, and never recovered consciousness after being hit.

LIEUTENANT DOUGAL CLIFFORD CAMPBELL SEWELL, 3rd (att'd. 1st) BATTN. QUEEN'S OWN (ROYAL WEST KENT REGIMENT),

was the fourth son of the late William Sewell, J.P., of Tillingham, Essex, and was born at Tillingham Hall. He was wounded at Mons on the 23rd August, 1914, and died in Colliery Hospital at Wasmes a few days later at the age of twenty years.

He was educated at Wellingborough School, where he made a reputation as an athlete. He was in the Shooting VIII and the Football XI, and for three seasons was captain of the Cricket XI. In cricket he had an aggregate of 617 runs in thirteen innings, and during his captaincy his XI was accepted as being one of the strongest Public School teams in the field. He also made a school record in athletics in his last term by winning no fewer than six events : the one hundred yards, one hundred and twenty yards, quarter-mile, long jump, high jump, and throwing the cricket ball. He was known to all his friends as " Dougal," and at school was beloved by both masters and boys. He joined the Army in September, 1912, becoming Lieutenant in the 3rd Royal West Kent Regiment in July, 1913. In the Army, no less than at school, he was very popular with all ranks, officers and men.

CAPTAIN ARTHUR DUNCOMBE SHAFTO, D.S.O., 2nd BATTN. THE ROYAL SCOTS (LOTHIAN REGT.),

was the only surviving son of the late Charles Ottiwell and Mrs. C. Duncombe Shafto, of 9, South Bailey, Durham, and was born in London on the 8th April, 1880.

He was educated at Durham School and the R.M.C., Sandhurst, obtaining his commission in the Northumberland Fusiliers in October, 1899, and becoming Captain in December, 1903.

He served in the South African War, being present at operations in the Orange Free State and the Transvaal. He was twice mentioned in despatches ("London Gazette," 16th March, 1900, and 10th September, 1901), and received the Queen's medal with three clasps, the King's medal with two clasps, and the D.S.O. From 1905 to 1908 he was Staff Captain of the Border Grouped Regimental District, and from 1908 to 1910 of No. 5 District. In May, 1908, he was transferred to the Royal Scots.

He was serving with his battalion when he was killed in action at Audincourt on the 26th August, 1914.

Captain Duncombe Shafto, who was a member of the Naval and Military Club, married Marguerite Cécile Catherine, daughter of the late Lieutenant-Colonel Stapleton, 19th Hussars, and left two children: Mark, born August, 1905; and Betty, born November, 1906.

LIEUTENANT BERNARD HENRY GILBERT SHAW, 2nd BATTN. PRINCE OF WALES'S OWN (WEST YORKSHIRE REGIMENT),

was the son of the Right Rev. E. D. Shaw, Bishop of Buckingham, and Mrs. Agnes Shaw, and was born on the 11th October, 1893.

He was educated at Marlborough College, where he was in the Cricket XI in 1911, and scored ninety-four at Lord's v. Rugby; and at the R.M.C., Sandhurst. He was captain of the Sandhurst Hockey Team in 1912, and captain of the Cricket Team in 1913. He was also in the Bucks County XI in 1911–13. He was gazetted 2nd Lieutenant in the West Yorkshire Regiment in 1913, becoming Lieutenant in May, 1914.

He was killed on the 19th December, 1914, near Neuve Chapelle. The Captain of his company furnished the following account of the circumstances: "He [Lieutenant Shaw] was sent up to support me with his platoon in the German trench we had taken. He had just retaken the traverse, and on returning to his post he was shot through the head and died instantaneously."

The Commanding Officer of his battalion, writing to his father, said: "Your boy died most gallantly fighting in a German trench which had been taken during the night."

2nd LIEUTENANT CUTHBERT FRANK SHAW, SPECIAL RESERVE (attd. 2nd BATTN.) ROYAL SUSSEX REGIMENT,

who was killed in action on the 31st October, 1914, near Ypres, at the age of twenty-two, was the son of Frank H. Shaw, of The Gables, St. Leonards-on-Sea. He was a student of King's College, London, where he was a very active figure in the social life of the college during his three years in the Engineering Department. During his last year he was Secretary of the Rifle Club, Editor of the Engineering Faculty's section in the "College Review," and General Sub-editor of the publication. On entering the College he joined the O.T.C., and eventually rose to the rank of Sergeant. Having obtained his "A" certificate while in the junior O.T.C. at Gresham School, he soon qualified for his "B" Certificate.

He was gazetted to the Special Reserve of his regiment in January, 1914.

CAPTAIN HUGH JAMES SHAW, 5th (attd. 1st) BATTN. ROYAL FUSILIERS (CITY OF LONDON REGIMENT),

who was born in Madras, India, on the 16th May, 1886, was the eldest son of Mrs. R. F. de Winton, The Grange, Folkestone, by her first husband, Mr. W. S. Shaw (partner of Messrs. Parry & Co., Madras). He was a relative of the painter, Byam Shaw.

Captain Shaw was educated at Warren Hill, Eastbourne; and at Harrow, where he was a monitor in 1904, in the Football XI in 1903–04, and in the Gymnasium VIII in 1903.

When the war with Germany broke out he was in the 5th Battalion (Special Reserve) of the Royal Fusiliers, in which he had ranked as Lieutenant from October, 1910. For active service in the war he was attached to the 2nd Battalion of his regiment, and in September, 1914, he was promoted Captain. He was killed early in the morning of the 12th November, 1914, by his trench or dug-out, which was only one hundred and fifty yards from the German lines, falling in on him and suffocating him in his sleep.

2nd LIEUTENANT MAURICE ARTHUR PRITCHARD SHAWYER, 5th (attd. 1st) BATTN. THE DUKE OF CAMBRIDGE'S OWN (MIDDLESEX REGT.),

who was killed in action probably in November, 1914, no date being given in the monthly casualty list, was the second son of Mr. and Mrs. A. W. Shawyer, Cardridge, St. Margaret's Road, Manor Park, Essex.

He was educated at East Ham Technical College and London University, where he graduated with honours in science in November, 1913. He was for four years a member of the University O.T.C., and on the outbreak of war, resigning an appointment abroad under the Ordnance Survey Department, was gazetted to the 5th Battalion Middlesex Regiment, on probation, in August, 1914.

For active service he was attached to the 1st Battalion, and was killed at Croix Barbée. (" The Times," November, 1914.)

CAPTAIN GRAHAM PERCIVAL SHEDDEN, 35th HEAVY BATTERY ROYAL GARRISON ARTILLERY,

who was killed in action on the 31st October, 1914, near Ypres, was the third son of George Shedden, Esq., J.P., and Alice, his wife, of Spring Hill, East Cowes, Isle of Wight. He was born at that address on the 27th July, 1886

Educated at Burney's Royal Academy, Gosport, he passed into the Royal Military Academy, Woolwich, at the age of sixteen. He joined the Royal Artillery in December, 1904, becoming Lieutenant in December, 1907, and was promoted Captain on the 30th October, 1914, the day before he was killed. For three years he served in Hong Kong, and while there he qualified in Colloquial Cantonese, and was sent for a year to the Legation Guard at Pekin. Afterwards, at the time of the Canton rebellion, he was sent there in command of a detachment for the protection of the British colony.

In the Great War he was one of the officers who died of wounds received at the Château of Hooge, near Ypres, when a shell struck the

British headquarters, killing Colonel Percival, Colonel Kerr, and four other officers, and wounding Lieutenant - General Lomax so severely that he afterwards died of his wounds. (See Vol. II.)

LIEUTENANT GEORGE ARCHER-SHEE, 3rd (attd. 1st) BATTN. SOUTH STAFFORDSHIRE REGIMENT,

who was killed in action near Ypres on the 31st October, 1914, aged nineteen, was the younger son of the late Martin Archer-Shee, and the only son of Mrs. Archer-Shee, Woodchester, Gloucestershire.

He was educated at Stonyhurst and joined the 3rd Battalion of his regiment in May, 1913, becoming Lieutenant in February, 1914, and on the outbreak of the war was attached to the 1st Battalion for active service.

CAPTAIN GERALD ALEXANDER GASELEE SHEPHERD, 57th WILDE'S RIFLES, (FRONTIER FORCE), INDIAN ARMY, who was shot in the trenches at La Bassée on the 20th December, 1914, was born at Kasauli, India, on the 14th July, 1882, eldest son of the late Major Alexander Innes Shepherd, of the same regiment (then known as the 4th Punjaub Infantry), and was a nephew of General Sir A. Gaselee, G.C.B., G.C.I.E.

He was educated at Bedford and at Dover College, being gazetted to the Suffolk Regiment in 1901. In the following year he was transferred to the Indian Army, in which he was promoted Lieutenant in August, 1903, and obtained his Captaincy in 1910. Captain Shepherd was on active service in 1902 on the north-west frontier in the operations against the Darwesh Khel Waziris, and subsequently, in 1903–04, in Tibet, when he was present at the action at Niani, the operations at and around Gyantse, and the march to Lhassa. For these services he received the medal and clasp.

Captain Shepherd was a member of the Junior Naval and Military Club, and was unmarried.

CAPTAIN GERARD LOURDES EDWARD SHERLOCK, 3rd (KING'S OWN) HUSSARS, who was killed in action on the 25th August, 1914, was appointed to the Nigeria Regiment, West African Frontier Force, in May, 1912.

He was born on the 13th December, 1883, and

joined the Royal Garrison Artillery Militia as 2nd Lieutenant in February, 1901, being pro-

moted Lieutenant in June, 1902. He was gazetted 2nd Lieutenant in the 3rd Hussars, in July, 1906, becoming Lieutenant in December, 1908, and Captain on the 10th August, 1914. He served in the South African War with the embodied Militia, being present at operations in the Transvaal from December, 1901, to May, 1902, receiving the Queen's medal.

2nd LIEUTENANT ALEXANDER NIMMO SHERRIFF, 1st BATTN. NORTHAMPTONSHIRE REGIMENT,

who was killed in action near Ypres on the 1st November, 1914, was the second son of the late Mr. George Sherriff of Stenhouse, Kersie, and Carronvale, Stirlingshire.

He was born on the 13th August, 1894, and was educated at Sedbergh School, Yorkshire, and the R.M.C., Sandhurst, from which he was gazetted to the Northamptonshire Regiment in February, 1914.

On the outbreak of war he accompanied his battalion to France, and took part in the retirement from Mons, and in the Battles of the Aisne and Marne.

He inherited the estates of Kersie and Carronvale from his father, and he was unmarried.

LIEUTENANT HUGH JOHN SLADEN SHIELDS, ROYAL ARMY MEDICAL CORPS,

was killed in action near Ypres on the 26th October, 1914, while attending to a wounded man in the firing line, and was buried at Huize Berkershorst, Zillebeke.

He was the son of the Rev. Arthur John Shields, Rector of Thornford, Dorset, and was born at Calcutta on the 16th June, 1887. He was educated at Loretto School and at Jesus College, Cambridge,

where he graduated with honours B.A. and M.B. in 1910. He rowed in the Jesus College head of the river crew, and gained his blue in 1910, when he stroked the Light Blues against Oxford. The same year, with Eric Fairbairn, he won the Lowe Double Sculls. He also rowed at Henley in the Jesus Grand Challenge Cup crew, which three years in succession were runners-up for that trophy, and won the Ladies' Plate in 1908. He rowed No. 2 in the Jesus crew, composed of past and present members, which was the first English crew to beat the Belgians, winning the International Race at Ghent in 1911.

At Jesus College he was captain of the Rugby Football Club, and when at Middlesex Hospital, where he was a scholar and prizeman, was captain of their XV. In 1912 he played for the United Hospitals against the Army at Queen's Club. In that year he competed for the Army and Navy Boxing Championship, winning in the semi-finals of the middleweights, and being runner-up in the light heavyweights in 1913.

He was keenly and self-denyingly interested in religious work and social work at Cambridge and in London, giving his evenings and Sundays largely to work among lads at the Magdalen College Union Club in Camberwell. He received his commission in the R.A.M.C. in July, 1912. On the outbreak of the war he was placed in medical charge of the Irish Guards, and for his services in the field was mentioned in Sir John French's Despatch of the 8th October, 1914.

2nd LIEUTENANT JOHN DENYS SHINE, 1st BATTN. ROYAL IRISH REGIMENT,

who died on the 25th August, 1914, from wounds received at Mons, was born on the 11th September, 1894, at Corradino House, Malta, the son of Colonel J. M. F. Shine, A.M.S. 2nd Lieutenant Shine had two brothers serving in the Army: Captain J. O. W. Shine, in the Royal Dublin Fusiliers; and 2nd Lieutenant H. P. Shine, who was in the Royal Irish Fusiliers, and was killed in action in 1915. (See Vol. II.)

2nd Lieutenant J. D. Shine was educated at Downside School, near Bath, where he was captain of the Cricket XI; and at the R.M.C., Sandhurst, for whom he played in the Association football team, and won the "putting the weight" event in the R.M.C. v. R.M.A. Sports. He was a good all-round sportsman, playing cricket, hockey, football, and tennis.

He was posted to the 1st Battalion Royal Irish Regiment, and was attached to the 2nd Battalion at Devonport pending embarkation for India, where his own battalion was stationed, when the war with Germany broke out, and he accompanied the 2nd Battalion to the front, and was serving with it when he died.

LIEUTENANT JAMES REGINALD SHIPPEY, LATE 2nd LIEUTENANT ROYAL WEST KENT REGIMENT, 3rd (attd. 1st) BATTN. BEDFORDSHIRE REGIMENT,

was the son of the late Frederic Shippey, Esq., and Mrs. Shippey, of Pietermaritzburg, Natal, and was born there in March, 1891.

He was educated at Bedford Grammar School, and was gazetted 2nd Lieutenant in the 3rd Battalion Bedfordshire Regiment in September, 1911, and joined the 1st Battalion Royal West Kent Regiment with the same rank in January, 1914. He shortly afterwards left the Army but, on war breaking out, was brought back as a Lieutenant in the 3rd Battalion Bedfordshire Regiment in August, 1914.

He was wounded at Givenchy on the 12th October, 1914, and died from the effects on the 14th of that month.

Lieutenant Shippey was a keen football player, and successful in shooting.

CAPTAIN GUY MAXWELL SHIPWAY, p.s.c., 1st BATTN. GLOUCESTERSHIRE REGIMENT,

was the son of Lieutenant - Colonel R. W. Shipway, V.D., J.P., and was born in London on the 21st June, 1877. He was educated at Clifton College and at the R.M.C., Sandhurst. He received his commission in the Gloucestershire Regiment in February, 1897, becoming Lieutenant in December, 1898, and Captain in October, 1905, passing through the Staff College. Captain Shipway served in the South African War, 1900–02; was present at the relief of Kimberley (severely wounded); took part in the operations in the Orange Free State from February to May, 1900; in Orange River Colony, May to November, 1900; Cape Colony, south of Orange River, 1900; Cape Colony, north of Orange River; in the Transvaal, July, 1901, to May, 1902; and again in the Orange River and Cape Colonies from November, 1900, to July, 1901. For a time he was attached to the Army Service Corps, graded as Staff Captain, and received the Queen's medal with three clasps and the King's medal with two clasps. He also served in West Africa (South Nigeria), in 1905–06, with the Bende-Onitsha Hinterland Expedition, for which he received the medal with clasp.

In the Great War he was seriously wounded on the 25th August, while in command of his double company, covering his battalion while it was entrenching in some fields in the rear at Favril, France. He was taken to Etreux, where he died on the morning of the 26th August, 1914.

Captain Shipway married Gladys Blanche Katherine, second daughter of Mr. and Mrs. Frank Cooper, late of Lisle Court, Wootton, Isle of Wight, and left one daughter, Priscilla Mary, born 10th October, 1910.

CAPTAIN HENRY HAMMOND SHOTT, D.S.O., 1st BATTN. PRINCESS CHARLOTTE OF WALES'S (ROYAL BERKSHIRE REGIMENT),

was shown in the monthly casualty list published in October, 1914, under the heading of "casualties believed to have occurred," as "believed to have been killed in action," no place or date being mentioned. It has since been ascertained that he was killed on the 25th August, 1914. He was the son of the late N. Schjott, Esq., of Dover, and was born there on the 13th October, 1877. He was educated at Dulwich College, and served in the ranks of Bethune's Mounted Infantry for one year and thirty-six days, and with a commission in the same corps for one year and forty-nine days. As a Trooper he was in operations in South Africa in 1896, for which he received a medal. He next served in the South African War with Bethune's Mounted Infantry, being present at operations in the Transvaal and Orange River Colony, and at the actions of Spion Kop, Vaal Krans, on the Tugela Heights, and at Laing's Nek. He was three times mentioned in despatches ("London Gazette," 8th February and 16th April, 1901, and 17th June, 1902), was awarded the D.S.O., and received the Queen's medal with six clasps and the King's medal with two clasps.

In February, 1902, he was given his commission as 2nd Lieutenant in the Royal Berkshire Regiment, becoming Lieutenant in February, 1905. From October, 1904, to July, 1909, and again from July, 1910, to July, 1913, he was employed with the West African Frontier Force. During that time he was on active service in North Nigeria, 1906, for which he was again mentioned in despatches ("London Gazette," 2nd July, 1907), and received the medal with clasp. He was promoted Captain in June, 1911.

A Sergeant of his battalion, describing the fight at Mons, said : " Captain Shott, D.S.O., of our regiment, was, I think, the bravest man I ever met. On August 23rd, when we were near and were lying in our trenches with shell fire constantly around us, he walked out into the open, and, with his cheery words, gave us good heart. He was puffing a cigarette, and he said, ' Lads, we will smoke ! ' He was an officer and a gentleman in every sense of the word, and when he was killed two days later it was a great blow to us."

This incident was mentioned by a French writer (R.P.) in " Le Temps " of the 15th September, 1914, as evidence of " *le sang froid britannique.*"

Captain Shott, who was a member of the Naval and Military Club, married Hazel Morris Brown, of Jonkers, New York.

CAPTAIN ROBERT YARDLEY SIDEBOTTOM, 2nd BATTN. THE LANCASHIRE FUSILIERS,

who was born at Alderley Edge, Cheshire, on the 13th August, 1881, was the son of Ralph Sidebottom and grandson of Ralph and Mary Sidebottom, of Millbrook, Hollingworth, Cheshire.

He was educated at Bilton Grange, Cheltenham College, and the R.M.C., Sandhurst.

After receiving an unattached 2nd Lieutenancy in January, 1901, he joined the Lancashire Fusiliers in March of the same year, becoming Lieutenant in February, 1904. He served for eighteen months with the Mounted Infantry in South Africa, and was promoted Captain into the 2nd Battalion of his regiment in July, 1914.

He was a well-known big-game hunter in South Africa and India.

He was reported to have been shot in the head and killed instantly on or about the 26th August, 1914, near Le Cateau, during the retirement from Mons.

2nd LIEUTENANT CHARLES CALDWELL SILLS, 1st BATTN. SOUTH WALES BORDERERS,

was born in London on the 24th December, 1893, the son of George Turner Sills, Barrister-at-Law, H.B.M.'s Magistrate at Zanzibar from 1909–14; the grandson of George Sills, Recorder of Lincoln, and great-nephew of Colonel J. F. Caldwell, of the 24th Regiment.

He was educated at Oakham from 1905–12, and entered the Royal Military College, Sandhurst, in 1912, being gazetted thence to a 2nd Lieutenancy in the South Wales Borderers in September, 1913. He proceeded to France with the 1st Division of the Expeditionary Force, and was present at the Battles of Mons, the Marne, and the Aisne. In the latter he was killed on the 26th September, 1914, near Vendresse, while his battalion was engaged in repelling a German attack in force on the trenches.

At school he was captain of the cricket XI in 1911 and 1912, and was also in the Rugby XV. He was a successful athlete, having been a Double Blue at Sandhurst in 1913 for the high-jump and cricket, having scored in the same year 103 for Sandhurst v. Woolwich. When at Aldershot he played regularly at cricket and football for the Aldershot Command. He was a member of the M.C.C.

2nd LIEUTENANT ANSON LLOYD SILVESTER, SPECIAL RESERVE, attd. 2nd BATTN. ROYAL SUSSEX REGIMENT,

was born on the 11th December, 1888, at 6, Belgrave Terrace, Bath. His father — the Rev. James Silvester, M.A.—was at that time Senior Curate of Walcot, Bath, and subsequently became Vicar of Great Clacton and Little Holland, Essex. Mrs. Constance Ellen Silvester (*née* Lloyd), his mother, was formerly an

Army Nursing Sister at Netley and Devonport. 2nd Lieutenant Silvester's great-grandfather— Edward Bell Lloyd—served under the Duke of Wellington in the Peninsula, and at Waterloo was A.D.C. to his uncle, General Anson.

Through his mother's line, Lieutenant Silvester's descent could be traced back to the ancient independent Princes of Wales, and he was of the twenty-first generation from King Edward III (see the Plantagenet Roll of the Blood Royal, Part I, compiled by the Marquis de Ruvigny).

He passed through Trent College, Derbyshire, with distinction, obtaining an exhibition at Jesus College, Oxford. In Moderations he obtained third-class mathematical honours, and in the Final School of Modern History was placed in the second-class honour list in 1912. He was 6 feet 3 inches in height, and developed into a fine athlete. He obtained the first place for Oxford University in a cross-country running contest for the Southern Counties Association Championship, and a gold medal was awarded him by the President.

At Oxford he belonged to the Officers' Training Corps, and obtained the certificate qualifying him for the Special Reserve, in which he joined the Royal Sussex Regiment in 1913, training at Woking, and taking part in the Army Manœuvres that year. In the spring of 1914 he studied German in Berlin with a view to appointment to H.M. Consular Service, for which he had received a nomination, and he would have returned to the Continent to complete his studies but for the war.

For several years he took part in the camp work of the Y.M.C.A., and was actually engaged in it, in August, 1914, when the war broke out. On mobilisation he was stationed at Dover for some time before joining the Expeditionary Force. With five other officers he landed at Havre towards the end of September. During his war service his parents received many most interesting and touching letters. In the last one, written on Christmas Day just before returning to the trenches, he said : " Well, dear parents, I mustn't say more now. I think of you and the brother and all my friends, and know that I am out here for your sakes, and that is a comfort to me ; and God has been very good to me lately, and seems to be always near me, so I keep very cheery and thankful in spite of all."

On the 31st December, 1914, the Germans gained possession of one of the trenches at Guinchy, near La Bassée at 4 p.m., and an attack was made on the enemy at 10 p.m. that night. While gallantly leading his men in this attack 2nd Lieutenant Silvester was killed.

2nd Lieutenant Silvester was one of the O.T.C. Guards of Honour at the funeral of King Edward VII and at the Coronation of King George.

CAPTAIN GEORGE NORMAN SIMMS, M.V.O., 2nd BATTN. ROYAL MUNSTER FUSILIERS,

who was unofficially reported to have been killed on the 27th August, 1914, at Noyon, was the youngest son of the late George Simms, of Summer Grange, Sunningdale, and of Mrs. Simms, of Gilderdale House, Gerrards Cross.

He was born on the 21st October, 1875, and joined the Royal Munster Fusiliers from the Militia in December, 1897, becoming Lieutenant in March, 1899.

He served in the South African War, being present at operations in the Orange River Colony in the early part of 1902, receiving for his services the Queen's medal with two clasps. The senior surviving officer of the battalion gave the following account of Captain Simms' death : " On August 27th his company was on outpost duty with mine in front of the battalion, which was to cover the withdrawal of our brigade. The latter got away safely, but to achieve this the battalion had to sacrifice itself. The enemy was coming from the north, and began working round to eastward of us. Your son's company was sent to the post of danger to prevent this. It was a most difficult undertaking, involving his complete isolation from the rest of us, but he carried it through, fought a smart little action ' on his own,' and returned with the loss of but three men. We then continued the withdrawal, and it was discovered that the enemy had surrounded and cut us off. Again George Simms was sent to the post of danger, this time in front. He went off at the head of his men, and having located the enemy in an entrenched position straight across our line of retreat he proceeded to attack at once. A murderous fire was opened on him and his men, and a destructive cross-fire was brought to bear on them from a loop-holed house. While gallantly exposing himself, as an example to his men, he was shot in the body and fell dead. The whole five officers of his company were killed, a magnificent example to the remainder of the battalion. The next day the Germans sent out a party of our men, whom they had taken prisoners, to bury our dead, and your son was placed in a grave with eight of his brother officers who fell in the same action. His personal effects were buried with him, nothing being touched. His kit was on our transport wagons, which may have escaped. When I came to this battalion four months ago

I was attached to your son's company, so that I might see how the new system was run, and it really was a lesson in the art of managing men. The Brigadier, after inspecting his company, said : ' I should like to serve under Captain Simms myself.' No higher praise is needed. The whole battalion was devoted to him, and his company was far the best of the battalion. In the mess we shall miss him more than any-where : his invariable good temper, tact, and sense of humour made him an ideal senior member of a mess."

Captain Simms, who was promoted to his rank in June, 1906, was a member of the Army and Navy Club, a keen polo player, and fond of steeplechasing. He was not married.

LIEUT. GEORGE PRESCOTT BLACK-ALL-SIMONDS, RESERVE OF OFFI-CERS, SOUTH WALES BORDERERS,

was the only son of Mr. and Mrs. George Blackall-Simonds, of Bradfield, Berkshire, and was born in 1881. He was educated at Bradfield College, near Reading. He served in the South African War as a Railway Staff Officer, and received the Queen's medal with three clasps. His rank as Lieutenant dated from April, 1910.

He was attached for active service to the 1st Battalion of his regiment and was killed at Vendresse on the 27th September, 1914, while leading his men to attack the Germans in a stone quarry. He was shot through the head, death ensuing in a few minutes.

CAPTAIN JOHN EDMUND SIMPSON, 2nd BATTN. KING'S OWN YORKSHIRE LIGHT INFANTRY),

born on the 9th July, 1873, at Bayswater, London, was the son of the Rev. John Curwen Simpson, formerly of Thurscoe, Yorkshire, and a nephew of Judge Edmund Sheppard, of Brisbane. A brother — Captain L. Simpson, M.V.O., of the same regiment—was wounded and taken prisoner at Le Cateau.

After his education at St. Paul's School, Stony

Stratford, Captain J. E. Simpson received a commission from the 2nd (Volunteer) Battalion Yorkshire Regiment, in the 1st Battalion, K.O.Y.L.I., in May, 1900, being promoted Lieutenant in 1901, and obtaining his company in the 2nd Battalion in January, 1907. He was Adjutant of the 3rd Reserve Battalion of his regiment from October, 1910, till September, 1913. He served at Gibraltar, South Africa, and in Ireland, being at Carrickfergus when war broke out. He left with the first contin-gent of the Expeditionary Force on the 10th August, 1914.

During the war he was mentioned in Sir John French's Despatch of the 8th October, 1914. Captain Simpson was killed at Messines, Flanders, on the 31st October, 1914, while leading his men. His death was almost instantaneous.

LIEUTENANT W. H. M. SIMPSON, 3rd (attd. 1st) BATTN. EAST SURREY REGT.,

who died of wounds on the 19th December, 1914, at No. 7 Stationary Hospital, Boulogne, was the eldest son of William F. J. Simpson, of Mitcham, Surrey.

He joined the East Surrey Regiment as 2nd Lieutenant on probation in February, 1912, and was promoted Lieutenant in September, 1914.

LIEUTENANT RONALD FRANCIS SIMSON, ROYAL FIELD ARTILLERY,

was the son of the late D. J. Simson, Esq., Advocate, and Mrs. Simson, of Balmanno, Mary-kirk, N.B., and was born at Edinburgh on the 6th Septem-ber, 1890.

He was educated at Edinburgh Academy and at the R.M.A., Woolwich. Both at school and at the Royal Military Academy Lieutenant Simson achieved many distinctions, academic and athletic. At the former he proved a good mathematician, and also gained the First Prize for Modern Languages, having a good knowledge of written and conversational German. He was popular with both boys and masters. Proficiency in athletics has never been found other than an advantage in a military career, and here Lieutenant Simson was a leader. A good bat at cricket, he was pre-eminent at football and at the games. He was a brilliant centre three-quarter back, and at the games in his last year he took the first place in five open events winning the Burma

Cup and the Bradbury Shield in 1909, thus stamping himself as the best all-round athlete of the year.

At the Royal Military Academy he was in the Woolwich XV of 1909–10, and scored twice in the match against Sandhurst when his side won by 49—9. After Christmas, 1909, he became captain of the team. He was also to the front as a runner, winning three open events in 1910 and the Silver Bugle. At Woolwich he was also an under-officer, and very much liked by cadets and officers. He joined the Royal Artillery as 2nd Lieutenant in July, 1911, in which year he played for the Army and Navy in football, and in the same year was selected to play for Scotland v. England.

He became Lieutenant n July, 1914, in the 116th Battery, 26th Brigade, and was said to be the most popular man in his battery. He was killed on the 15th September, 1914. When riding back to bring his battery into action a shell fell under his horse, killing instantaneously both horse and rider. His Major, who had a high opinion of him, had recommended him for recognition.

Lieutenant Simson was a member of the London Scottish Football Club.

CAPTAIN KANWAR INDARJIT SINGH, M.B., M.R.C.P., INDIAN MEDICAL SERVICE, MEDICAL OFFICER OF THE 57th WILDE'S RIFLES (FRONTIER FORCE),

was the son of Rajah Sir Harman Singh, Ahluwalia, K.C.I.E., of Kapurthala, Punjab, a grandson of his late Highness the Maharaja Sir Randhir Singh, G.C.S.I., of Kapurthala, and a first-cousin of H.H. Maharaja Sir Jagatjit Singh, G.C.S.I., of Kapurthala.

He was born at Lucknow, Oudh, on the 27th December, 1883, and was educated at Forman Christian College, Lahore, and at the Punjab University (1901), where he took the degree of B.A. He was also a B.Sc. (1905) and M.B. (1910) of Cambridge (Pembroke College), and passed third on the list of successful candidates for the Indian Medical Service, in which he received his commission in January, 1911. In the same year he became (by examination) M.R.C.P., London.

While in India he served as Medical Officer to three regiments, and was promoted Captain in April, 1914. He was a keen horseman, and a member of the Rawal Pindi and Ferozepore Clubs.

He accompanied the 57th Wilde's Rifles to Europe for active service in August, 1914; was twice mentioned in despatches; and awarded the Military Cross for distinguished service and conspicuous gallantry (" London Gazette," 1st January, 1915). Captain Indarjit Singh was killed at Festubert on the 23rd November, 1914, while attending to the wounded in a house which was completely destroyed by the enemy's shells.

His father received a letter from Colonel C. C. Manifold, I.M.S., saying: " It has just been my lot to meet an officer who was attached to the 57th Wilde's Rifles, who . . . was giving me an account of the desperate fighting the 57th had had, and the vicissitudes they had, losing nearly all their officers. I asked him, ' Who was your Medical Officer ? ' He said, ' A most splendid fellow. Nothing I could say would be too great praise for him. Ten Victoria Crosses would not have been too much for what he did. There could not be found a braver man. I am filled with admiration, which will always last, for him.' I need not say it was your son he was talking of."

The Adjutant of his regiment wrote : " During the whole of the hard-worked and frequently trying time we have had since receiving our mobilisation orders, Captain Indarjit Singh has worked whole-heartedly and ungrudgingly, and at a time when we had only three combatant officers left with the regiment, and most of our companies were very deficient of Indian officers, he gave me the very utmost assistance in the routine part of the work of the regiment, frequently looking after the duties of Quartermaster and Transport Officer in addition to his own duties. As a doctor he worked untiringly for the good of the men, and will be missed by them almost as much as by us who had come to know him very well during the last few months."

Captain Singh was the first scion of the family of an Indian ruling chief to lay down his life for the King-Emperor and the Empire.

CAPTAIN ARTHUR FREDERIC SKAIFE, 1st BATTALION THE DUKE OF CAMBRIDGE'S OWN (MIDDLESEX REGIMENT),

who was killed in action at La Boutillerie on the 1st November, 1914, was the elder son of Frederic Skaife, of North Street House, Chichester.

He was born on the 24th August, 1883, and was educated at Winchester, from which he passed direct into the R.M.C. Sandhurst. On leaving Sandhurst he was gazetted to the Middlesex Regiment in October,1914,and joined the 1st Battalion, then in India. He was promoted Lieutenant in July 1904, and Captain in March,1912. His battalion left Woolwich for the front on the 9th August, 1914, and took part in the battle of Mons, the retirement therefrom, and the battles of the Marne and the Aisne. Captain Skaife was buried at La Boutillerie, which is five miles from Armentières, in a field near the trenches, which were only 400 yards from the German lines.

MAJOR CHARLES GODFRAY MITFORD SLADE, 4th BATTN. PRINCE OF WALES'S OWN (YORKSHIRE REGT.),

was the son of Bertram Mitford Slade, and a relative of Colonel Cargill and Captain Bamber, and was born at Teddington on the 2nd July, 1878.

He was educated at Colchester and the R.M.C., Sandhurst, and joined the Prince of Wales's Own Regiment in May, 1901. Retiring from the Regular Battalion, he joined the 4th Battalion as Captain in April, 1907.

He served with the 1st Battalion through the whole of the Boer War, having been present at the relief of Kimberley, and at Paardeberg, and took part in the operations to the east of Pretoria from July to the end of November, 1900. In the fighting he was severely wounded. On the conclusion of the war he received the Queen's medal with three clasps and the King's medal with two clasps. He obtained his Majority in September, 1914.

In the Great War Major Slade was attached to the Loyal North Lancashire Regiment, and was killed on Tuesday, the 8th November, 1914. After taking a German trench, he was ordering the prisoners to be removed when he was shot. Major Slade was a Freemason, belonging to the Abbey Lodge, Abingdon. He was a very keen sportsman and a member of the Firfield Golf Club, Abingdon, and of the Cricket and Football Club. He married Adelaide Luduvina, daughter of Daniel Turner, of Cardiff, and granddaughter of Dr. Bennett, of Sydney, New South Wales, and left two children : Godfray Bertram, born 25th August, 1906 ; and Gladys May, born 24th May, 1908.

CAPTAIN LEONARD SLATER, 2nd BATTN. ROYAL SUSSEX REGIMENT,

was the son of the Rev. Francis Slater, Sherards,

Godalming, and was born at Instow, North Devon, on the 11th October, 1875. He was educated at Marlborough College and the R.M.C., Sandhurst.

In August, 1895, he was gazetted to an unattached 2nd Lieutenancy and joined the Indian Staff Corps in October, 1896, being promoted Lieutenant in the Indian Army in November, 1897, and Captain in August, 1904. He served in the 22nd Cavalry, Punjab Frontier Force for eight years, and in December, 1904, he exchanged into the Royal Sussex Regiment. He was Adjutant of the Cinque Ports Battalion for four years, from March, 1909.

Captain Slater served in the Waziristan (northwestern frontier of India) Campaign, for which he received the medal with clasp.

He was killed on the 14th September, 1914, during the early part of the Battle of the Aisne, when no fewer than six officers of his battalion were killed and several wounded. This action the Commander-in-Chief described as of so skilful, bold, and decisive a character as to gain positions which alone enabled him to maintain his ground for more than three weeks of very severe fighting on the north bank of the river. His Commanding Officer had a very high opinion of Captain Slater's capacity as a Company Commander and leader of men.

Captain Slater was full of energy and fond of games and sport of all kinds. He was a very keen cricketer, and played for the M.C.C., the Gentlemen of Sussex, and other good teams.

He married, in 1901, Constance Dorothy, daughter of Colonel F. Pridham, of Instow, Devon, and left three children : Leonard Francis, born 1902 ; Helen Elizabeth Constance, born 1903 ; and John Frederick, born 1908.

LIEUTENANT RONALD MORTIMER SLATER, 1st BATTN. WORCESTERSHIRE REGIMENT,

who died of wounds on the 21st November, 1914, in France, was the son of the late Major M. J. Slater, R.E., an old Wellingtonian, and of Mrs. Slater, Lionel Road, Bexhill, and grandson of the late Colonel J. M. Slater, N.L.I.

He was born on the

2nd October, 1891, and was educated at Wellington (The Hill), 1905–09, proceeding to the R.M.C., Sandhurst, in the latter year. He was gazetted to the Worcestershire Regiment in March, 1911, and was promoted Lieutenant in September, 1914.

The following account of the circumstances under which he was wounded has been received : " One of his men was lying seriously wounded. Slater went out and brought him in, and was hit on the top of the head by a bullet. For the moment he was dazed, but for the rest of the day he was cheery and bright. When taken to hospital at night his case was declared hopeless. He was well spoken of in the regiment as a soldier and as a promising polo player." (" Wellington Year Book," 1914.)

2nd LIEUTENANT WILLIAM MILES SMALLEY, SPECIAL RESERVE, attd. 1st BATTN. THE SHERWOOD FORESTERS (NOTTINGHAMSHIRE AND DERBYSHIRE REGIMENT),

son of William Arthur Smalley, of Chapel Bar, Nottingham, and a relative of H. Dallard, Esq., Merry Hill, Wolverhampton, and of C. W. Wiggin, Walsall, was born on the 18th January, 1891. Two of his brothers were serving in the Army as 2nd Lieutenants.

Mr. Smalley was educated at Shenley Road Secondary School, Nottingham, and University College, Nottingham, where he was a Demonstrator in the College Theatre, and after four years' apprenticeship with Alderman Cook obtained the position of Lecture Assistant in the Chemical Department. He entered the College O.T.C. at its inception, and quickly gained the estimation of his superiors, obtaining the " A " and " B " certificates. The Captain of the Corps spoke of him as one of his right-hand men.

He received his commission in February, 1914, on the supplementary list Special Reserve.

He was killed on the 9th December, 1914, by a sniper, while carrying out and supervising in the daytime needful work in " Port Arthur " trench, near Neuve Chapelle.

A man of tireless energy and marked ability, 2nd Lieutenant Smalley threw himself wholeheartedly into any work he was called upon to undertake.

Brigadier-General Marshall wrote of him : " We miss him, for he possessed valuable first aid and medical knowledge rarely met with outside the profession. He had been served out with a medical pack, and was first-aid officer to our battalion (1st Sherwood Foresters)."

A Company Commander wrote : " One of the best-equipped and most brilliant young officers I ever met," and his men referred to him as one of the best officers they had ever had.

He was fond of boating, swimming, and tennis, and was a clever debater and lecturer.

At the time of his death he was engaged to be married to Miss F. Hartshorn, daughter of Captain Hartshorn, Indian Army. The lady was serving as a Red Cross Nurse, and is a qualified dispenser.

CAPTAIN GEORGE HENRY SMART, 4th (EXTRA RESERVE) BATTN. THE PRINCE OF WALES'S OWN (WEST YORKSHIRE REGIMENT)

was born at Bombay on the 29th April, 1883, and was the only son of the late Major-General G. J. Smart, R.A., who served in the Mutiny and was twice mentioned in despatches.

Captain Smart was educated at Dover College and at the R.M.C., Sandhurst. He received his commission in the West Yorkshire Regiment in 1901, becoming Lieutenant in 1904. He served in the South African War, taking part in the operations in the Transvaal from November, 1901, to May, 1902, receiving afterwards the Queen's medal with three clasps.

At the time of the Great War, having retired from the Regular Army in 1909, he was in the 4th Battalion of the regiment, in which he had been Captain from May, 1909, and was attached for active service to the 1st Battalion, Loyal North Lancashire Regiment. He was killed at Le Touret, France, on the 22nd December, 1914, in a counter-attack made by the Germans after the retaking by us of a trench which had been lost by our men the day before.

LIEUTENANT CECIL SMEATHMAN, 1st BATTN. LEICESTERSHIRE REGT.,

who died on the 24th October, 1914, of wounds received in action, was born on the 20th May, 1889, and was educated at Rugby (Steel), which he entered in 1903, and where he won his football cap in 1907. From Rugby he went to University College, Oxford, and joined the

Leicestershire Regiment as 2nd Lieutenant, with antedate as a University candidate to September, 1911.

He was promoted Lieutenant in May, 1913. His elder brother—Lieutenant J. M. Smeatham, R.E.—was killed on the 24th-25th October, 1914, practically on the same day as himself.

LIEUTENANT JULIAN MISSENDEN SMEATHMAN, ROYAL ENGINEERS,

who was killed in action on the 24th-25th October, 1914, was born on the 24th December, 1887, and was educated at Rugby (Steel), which he entered in 1900, and from which he went to the R.M.A., Woolwich.

He obtained his commission in July, 1907, and was promoted Lieutenant in April, 1910.

Lieutenant Smeathman married, only a few months before his death, on returning home from foreign service.

His younger brother—Lieutenant C. Smeathman, Leicestershire Regiment—died of wounds received in action on the 24th October, 1914.

LIEUTENANT ARTHUR GILLIAT SMITH, 26th FIELD COMPANY, ROYAL ENGINEERS,

was born at Blackheath on the 3rd July, 1888, the son of Mr. and Mrs. H. Gilliat Smith, and great-grandson of the late Joseph Smith, formerly of The Oaks, Woodmansterne, Surrey. He was also related to the late Sir Edmund Bainbridge, K.C.B.

He was educated at St. Paul's House, St. Leonards-on-Sea ; Hillside, Goldalming ; and subsequently at Rugby and the R.M.A., Woolwich. He was gazetted to the R.E. in December, 1908, and after leaving Chatham joined the 26th Field Company at Bordon Camp, Hampshire, where he served all the time he was in England. He became Lieutenant in February, 1911.

He was a cross-country rider, and won several point-to-point races in 1913-14. He was also expert on ski, and always spent part of his winter leave in Switzerland or Norway.

In the Great War he was killed on the 1st November, 1914, near Ypres, when leading his section to reinforce some infantry under a very hot fire. His Commanding Officer wrote of him : " I have lost a loyal friend and a most keen and efficient officer."

LIEUTENANT ARTHUR GEORGE MURRAY SMITH, 2nd LIFE GUARDS,

died in a German Military Hospital on the 2nd November, 1914, of wounds received in action on the 20th October, and was buried in Lille. He was the eldest son of George and Ellen Murray Smith, of Gumley Hall, Market Harborough, and was born on the 27th September, 1886. Educated at Eton and Trinity College, Cambridge, he entered the 2nd Life Guards in August, 1911, becoming Lieutenant in July, 1912.

He was a member of the Bachelors' Club, and his recreations were hunting and big-game shooting.

Lieutenant Murray Smith married Margaret, youngest daughter of J. S. Ainsworth, M.P., of Ardanaiseig, and left one son.

LIEUTENANT ARCHIBALD JOHN DENROCHE-SMITH, 18th (QUEEN MARY'S OWN) HUSSARS,

elder son of T. Denroche-Smith, late B.C.S., and a grandson of the late General John Bayly, C.B., Colonel Commandant R.E., was born at Balhary, Meigle, Perthshire, on the 30th September, 1890.

He was educated at Cheltenham College and the R.M.C., Sandhurst, and joined the 18th Hussars in February, 1910, becoming Lieutenant in April, 1912.

He was a member of the Cavalry Club, was fond of hunting and shooting, and was captain of his regimental polo team.

Lieutenant Denroche-Smith was killed in action on the 13th September, 1914, near Vendresse, while leading his troop during the Battle of the Aisne.

CAPTAIN ARTHUR KYRKE-SMITH, 1st BATTN. THE KING'S (LIVERPOOL REGIMENT),

the eldest son of H. Kyrke-Smith, Esq., of Liverpool, was born on the 19th April, 1878, and was educated at the Merchant Taylors' School, Crosby, near Liverpool. He was a keen Volunteer officer, and obtained his Captaincy in the 4th Volunteer Battalion the King's, in February, 1899, before reaching his twenty-first birthday, being one of the

youngest Captains in the Army. On the outbreak of the Boer War he volunteered for active service, and went out to South Africa as 2nd Lieutenant, and after being attached to the Regulars for over three months he adopted the military profession, and joined the King's (Liverpool Regiment) in May, 1900. He was present at the operations in Natal, was at the action of Laing's Nek, and was with the forces that marched thence to Machadodorp, afterwards taking part in the operations to the east of Pretoria in 1900, including actions at Belfast and the subsequent operations in the Transvaal in 1901 and 1902. For part of the time he acted as Intelligence Officer. He received the Queen's medal with three clasps and the King's medal with two clasps.

He was promoted Lieutenant in January, 1901, and Captain in July, 1910. In June of the latter year he was appointed Adjutant to the 9th Battalion, the King's (Liverpool) Territorial Regiment, in which capacity he continued to act for three and a half years.

He rejoined the 1st Battalion of his regiment in January, 1914, at Aldershot, leaving for the front with the first Expeditionary Force at the outbreak of the war in August, 1914. He was fatally wounded on the 20th September, 1914, at the Battle of the Aisne, and died on the 23rd, of that month, being buried in the cemetery of Braisne, in France.

Captain Kyrke-Smith married Catherine Mabel, only daughter of C. Buchanan Spittall, Esq., and Mrs. Spittall, and granddaughter of Dr. Andrew Spittall, M.D., Staff-Surgeon, Coldstream Guards.

CAPTAIN BERNARD RIDLEY WINTHROP SMITH, 1st BATTN. SCOTS GUARDS,

who died on the 15th November, 1914, at the Base Hospital, Boulogne, of wounds received in action near Ypres on the 8th of the same month, was the only son of Mr. Francis Nicholas Smith and Mrs. Smith,

of Wingfield Park, Ambergate, Derbyshire. He was born on the 19th December, 1882, and was educated at Eton and Trinity College, Cambridge, where he took his degree of B.A., got his "blue," and rowed for Cambridge v. Oxford in 1905. He joined the Scots Guards on the 1st August, 1907, becoming Lieutenant in May, 1910. On the 13th August, 1913, he was appointed A.D.C. to the Governor and Commander-in-Chief, East African Protectorate. He was promoted Captain in November, 1914, subalterns immediately senior and junior to him in his regiment having been promoted Captains to date from the 15th of that month. He tried hard to get back to his regiment from East Africa, and succeeded with great difficulty. While with his regiment at the front he was ordered to take his platoon and turn out some Germans from a trench which had been vacated by some Zouaves on the flank of his trench. On his way over the open ground he was struck by a bullet from shrapnel shell and wounded at the base of the skull, a compound fracture. He was taken that afternoon (8th November) to Poperinghe Field Hospital, arriving on the 11th at the Hôtel Christol Hospital, Boulogne, where he died on the 15th November, having never regained consciousness or recognised his parents, who were by his side. He was buried at the private cemetery at his home, Wingfield Park, Derbyshire.

Captain Smith was an exceptionally fine man, 6 feet 5 inches in height, and broad in proportion. He was much liked by his men of the right flank company of the 1st Battalion, Scots Guards, and by his brother officers. He was unmarried.

MAJOR FREDERICK MANNERS-SMITH, 3rd BATTN. QUEEN ALEXANDRA'S OWN GURKHA RIFLES,

who died on the 3rd November, 1914, from wounds received on the same day near La Bassée, was the youngest son of the late Surgeon-General Charles Manners Smith, of Kempsey, Worcestershire.

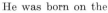

He was born on the 15th November, 1871, and was educated at Norwich and the R.M.C., Sandhurst. He joined the Gloucestershire Regiment in May, 1891, becoming Lieutenant in October, 1892. In June, 1893, he was transferred to the Indian Army, and in 1895 was with the relief force in operations in Chitral, for which he received the medal with clasp. He was Adjutant of his battalion from 1901 to 1905, and was promoted Captain in July, 1901, receiving his Majority in May, 1909.

Major Manners-Smith married, in 1902, Hilda, youngest daughter of the late Mr. Henry Carnsew, formerly of Somers Place, Billingshurst, Sussex.

LIEUTENANT GRANVILLE KEITH-FALCONER SMITH, 1st BATTN. COLDSTREAM GUARDS,

who was reported as missing in October, and again in November, 1914, has since been unofficially reported to have been killed near Gheluvelt on the 29th October, 1914, during the first Battle of Ypres.

He was the eldest son of Colonel Granville R. F. Smith, C.B., C.V.O., and Lady Blanche Smith, of Daffield, Derbyshire, and a nephew of the Earl of Kintore, and was born on the 26th February, 1886.

He was educated at Eton, and joined the Coldstream Guards in August, 1907, becoming Lieutenant in December, 1909. He was killed while in command of the battalion machine-gun section. He went forward with a party of volunteers, and succeeded in retaking a trench, but was shot through the head, dying at once. Lieutenant Granville Keith-Falconer Smith married, in March, 1910, Lady Kathleen Clements, youngest daughter of the fourth Earl of Leitrim, and left two daughters, age three years and fifteen months respectively.

2nd LIEUTENANT HENRY LEONARD CHAPPELL SMITH, SPECIAL RESERVE, attd. 2nd BATTN. THE SHERWOOD FORESTERS (NOTTINGHAMSHIRE AND DERBYSHIRE REGIMENT),

who was killed in action on the 18th October, 1914, was the eldest son of Henry and Annie Smith, The Grove, Cropwell-Butler, Nottingham, and was born on the 11th January, 1891. He was a scholar of Felsted School, Essex, and afterwards went to Queen's College, Cambridge, where he graduated B.A. with honours in 1913. He was gazetted to the Special Reserve of his regiment in April, 1913, having previously been a Lieutenant in the O.T.C., King's School, Worcester, and, on war being declared, joined the 2nd Battalion Sherwood Foresters, at Sheffield in August, 1914; he fought at the Battle of the Aisne on the 20th September, and again at Ennetières, near Lille, on or about the 18th

October, 1914, where he was said to have been killed in hand-to-hand fighting. He was never heard of again. For his services he was mentioned in Sir John French's Despatch of he 14th January, 1915.

He was fond of rowing and shooting.

2nd LIEUTENANT JOHN HERBERT MICHAEL SMITH, 2nd BATTN. MANCHESTER REGIMENT,

who was killed on the 9th September, 1914, in the Battle of the Marne, was the son of J. H. Smith, of Cobthorne, Cundle.

He was born on the 30th September, 1889; educated at Eton and Trinity College, Cambridge; and joined the Manchester Regiment from the Special Reserve in September, 1913. He was fond of all field sports and games, and was a good cricketer and golfer.

2nd LIEUTENANT (temp.) JULIAN HORACE MARTIN SMITH, INTELLIGENCE CORPS, attd. 9th (QUEEN'S ROYAL) LANCERS,

was wounded during the retirement from Mons on the 5th September, 1914, and died of his wounds at Nangis, near Paris, on the 7th of that month. He was the son of Martin Ridley Smith, of Warren House, Hayes, Kent, a collateral of the family of the Marquess of Lincolnshire.

He was born in London in 1887, and was educated at Eton and at Trinity College, Cambridge. At Eton he was Keeper of the Field, and won the school racquets. In civil life he was a partner in the firm of Messrs. Rowe & Pitman, Stockbrokers. At Cambridge he played golf for the University, and in after life he was one of the most prominent golfers at Sandwich, North Berwick.

He joined the Army on the outbreak of war, and is believed to have been the first officer who volunteered for service, to fall in the Great War.

2nd Lieutenant Smith, who was unmarried, was a member of White's, Brook's, and Pratt's Clubs.

LIEUTENANT JOHN LAWSON-SMITH, 1st BATTN. THE PRINCE OF WALES'S OWN (WEST YORKSHIRE REGIMENT),

son of E. M. Lawson-Smith, was born at Colton Lodge, Tadcaster, Yorkshire, in March, 1892. His elder brother — Lieutenant T. E. Lawson-Smith, 13th Hussars —was killed on the 30th October, 1914, in the Great War.

After his education at Repton, Osborne, and the R.M.C, Sandhurst, he joined the West Yorkshire Regiment in September, 1913, becoming Lieutenant in September, 1914.

He was killed near Boisgrenier on the 20th October, 1914, and for his services in the war he was mentioned in Sir John French's Despatch of the 14th January, 1915.

LIEUTENANT THOMAS EDWARD LAWSON-SMITH, 13th HUSSARS,

son of Mr. E. M. Lawson - Smith, of Colton Lodge, Tadcaster, Yorkshire, was born there on the 14th March, 1889. His younger brother — Lieutenant J. Lawson-Smith, 1st Battalion West York-shire Regiment— was killed in the Great War on the 20th October, 1914.

Educated at Harrow and the R.M.C., Sandhurst, he joined the 13th Hussars in India in September, 1909, becoming Lieutenant in December, 1913. He was killed in the trenches on the 30th October, 1914, while attached to the 11th Hussars, his own regiment being in India.

2nd LIEUTENANT THOMAS SYDNEY SMITH, 1st BATTN. DORSETSHIRE REGIMENT,

son of the Rev. Sydney E. Smith, Sprotbrough Rectory, Doncaster, was born at Womersley Vicarage, Yorkshire, on the 31st March, 1895.

Educated at Hill House, St. Leonards-on-Sea, and at Radley,

where he held a Mathematical Scholarship, he obtained a Prize Cadetship at the R.M.C., Sandhurst, out of which he passed in July, 1914, being gazetted to the 1st Battalion Dorsetshire Regiment in August, 1914. He joined his battalion at the front in September, and was killed near La Bassée on the 13th October, 1914.

CAPTAIN WALTER ADRIAN CARNEGIE BOWDEN-SMITH, 4th BATTN. ROYAL FUSILIERS (CITY OF LONDON REGIMENT),

was born at Guernsey on the 25th September, 1881. He was the son of Walter Baird Bowden-Smith, Esq., of Vernalls, Lyndhurst, Hants. His great-great - grandfather was William, seventh Earl of Northesk, who was third in command at Trafalgar.

Captain Bowden-Smith was educated at Rugby, where he was in the Shooting and Gymnastic Eights ; and at the R.M.C., Sandhurst. He was gazetted 2nd Lieutenant in August, 1900 ; Lieutenant in February, 1904 ; and Captain in November, 1909. He served in the Tibet Expedition, 1903–04, being wounded at Gyantse. He received the medal and clasp. Captain Bowden-Smith was dangerously wounded at Mons while bringing up reinforcements under a fierce fire on the 23rd August, and died on the 27th or 28th of the same month in the Convent of St. Joseph, Maissières, Belgium.

He was a member of the Junior Army and Navy Club.

2nd LIEUTENANT DONALD STUART STIRLING-SMURTHWAITE, 1st BATTN. THE BLACK WATCH (ROYAL HIGHLANDERS),

was killed at Ypres on the 26th October, 1914, while leading his platoon, his last words being: " Come on, men ! Follow me ! "

He was born on the 12th June, 1894, so was only twenty years old at the time of his death, and was the only son of Mrs. Smurthwaite, 25, Emperor's Gate. London. S.W.

2nd Lieutenant Smurthwaite was a grandson of the late Mr. Richard Stirling, of Craig Wallace, Bridge of Allan, the last surviving son of William Stirling, of Cordale and Dalquharran, Dumbartonshire, whose family trace their unbroken descent from the twelfth century, and are believed by many to be the oldest branch of the Stirling family, " Honest and True " John Stirling, Lord Provost of Glasgow in 1600, being an ancestor.

He was educated at Westminster, and passed from his crammer's into the R.M.C., Sandhurst, as a Prize Cadet. He passed out of Sandhurst at the top of the list, being the only Cadet who obtained honours in the examination, and was gazetted to the Black Watch on the 12th August, 1914.

Mr. Smurthwaite was qualified as an Interpreter in French.

CAPTAIN ALGERNON BERESFORD SMYTH, 2nd BATTN. THE KING'S OWN[(YORKSHIRE LIGHT INFANTRY),

was the younger son of the late Mr. Devaynes Smyth, D.L., of Bray Head, County Wicklow, where he was born on the 11th January, 1884. He was a grandson of the late Charles Putland, of Bray Head. His only brother— Captain C. D. Smyth, Royal Irish Rifles—was wounded in action in October, 1914.

Captain Smyth was educated at Gisburne House, Watford ; and at Haileybury College. He entered the R.M.C., Sandhurst, in 1901, and received his first appointment in the Army in May, 1903, when he was gazetted 2nd Lieutenant in the Manchester Regiment. In April, 1907, he was transferred with the rank of Lieutenant to the Yorkshire Light Infantry, and was promoted Captain in September, 1914. He was killed on the night of the 15th November, 1914, after being specially selected to lead an attack on a farm building about five miles east of Ypres. For his services on that night he was mentioned in Sir John French's Despatch of the 14th January, 1915.

Captain Smyth, who was a very good all-round sportsman, was a member of the Free Foresters, Yorkshire Gentlemen's Cricket Club. He played cricket for the Aldershot Command when stationed there with his battalion, and he was also a keen rider to hounds, a good golfer and tennis player, in which two games he had won several cups.

2nd LIEUTENANT JOHN ROSS SMYTH, 3rd (attd. 2nd) BATTN. THE ROYAL IRISH REGIMENT,

was the son of Ross Acheson Smyth, of Ardmore, Londonderry (Lieutenant - Colonel 10th [Service] Battalion Royal Inniskilling Fusiliers, late Major in the Royal Irish Regiment), and was born at Clonmell on the 11th June, 1896.

He was educated at Portora Royal School, Enniskillen, and joined the 3rd Battalion Royal Irish Regiment as a 2nd Lieutenant in March, 1914. Shortly after the outbreak of the Great War he was attached to the 2nd Battalion for active service.

He was killed on the night of the 19th-20th October, 1914, at Le Pilly.

CAPTAIN RICHARD ALEXANDER NOEL SMYTH, ROYAL GARRISON ARTILLERY,

who died on the 7th November, 1914, of wounds received in action at Armentières, France, was born on the 18th December, 1883, and was the son of Lieutenant-Colonel F. A. Smyth, late I. M. S. and Queen Alexandra's Own Gurkha Rifles, who served in four campaigns, and was mentioned in despatches. His deceased mother was the daughter of the late Rev. J. Cole, Vicar of Ilebrewers, near Taunton, Somerset, and formerly Principal and Chaplain of the Lawrence Military Asylum, Sanawar, India.

He was educated at Weymouth College, from which school he passed into the R.M.A., Woolwich, in 1900, joining the Royal Artillery in July, 1902, and becoming Lieutenant three years later. He served on garrison duty at the Nothe, Weymouth, for four years, and then for six years in Colombo, Ceylon. He was celebrated as a hockey player, and was excellent at lawn tennis and short-distance foot races. When the war broke out, he was at Portsmouth, and on the 23rd September, 1914, he left for France with the 5th Siege Battery.

The following extracts were received by his father from different officers, giving details of his son's death :—

From the Commanding Officer 2nd Siege Brigade, 8th November: "At about 4 p.m. yesterday he was testing a telephone wire behind our trenches. A gunner with him directed his attention to a man signalling for assistance and lying on the ground. He at once went to the spot, and saw a wounded infantryman, whom he proceeded to assist to a place of safety. Whilst doing this he was hit in the abdomen by a bullet. The gunner with him put him for safety in a dyke, and then went back for assistance to the trenches. Two infantrymen came out—one of these two was dangerously wounded as well—and the party then remained in the dyke until dark, when they all returned to the infantry lines. A doctor and two stretcher-bearers were immediately available. I may say the above-mentioned gunner bandaged the wounds as well as he could at the outset. As soon as our own doctor heard of it, which was late in the evening, he at once went off and spent the night with your son, but he expired this morning, and the Adjutant, myself, and our doctor buried him in a little village called Erquinghem, between Armentières and Lille, to-day at 1.30 p.m., the Rev. Webb Peploe, Army Chaplain, reading the service.

"I can truthfully say ever since we have been in action (a fortnight) your son had been doing most excellent work cheerfully — keen and always ready for anything—and for some days past I had fully made up my mind to forward his name to higher authority for the manner in which he carried out his work. I miss the best of officers—the very best. . . . He was buried at the back of the hospital where he was attended to. . . . We all feel his loss very much indeed, and in the battery his loss is irreparable."

From the Officer Commanding VIth Division : " The Siege Battery to which your son belonged only came under my command about a week ago, and ever since he had been doing perfectly invaluable work as forward Observing Officer, most of the time in the trenches with the infantry. . . . I have had continued testimony from the Middlesex Regiment, with which he was chiefly associated in the trenches, of the great assistance he had been to them in directing the fire of his guns, and thus helping to beat off the enemy's attacks, and his loss will be greatly felt by all."

Captain Smyth was mentioned in Sir John French's Despatch of the 14th January, 1915, for gallant and distinguished conduct in the field.

He had been recommended for the Military Cross, but unfortunately, through delay in gazetting the award, the gallant officer died before the announcement could be published, and it was decided that no posthumous rewards, save only the Victoria Cross, can be granted.

2nd LIEUTENANT FREDERICK FLEMING SMYTHE, 2nd BATTN. WORCESTERSHIRE REGIMENT,

who was killed in action on the 18th September, 1914, at the Battle of the Aisne, was born on the 2nd December, 1893, and was educated at Tonbridge, School (Judde House 1905-06). It was intended that he should go into the Navy, but instead he continued his education at Sutton Velence School and eventually joined the Worcestershire Regiment in September, 1912.

He was buried in the grounds of the Château Verneuil with other officers.

LIEUTENANT CLAUDE DAVIS SNEATH, attd. 4th BATTN. MIDDLESEX REGIMENT,

the son of George Sneath, Esq., J.P., and Mrs. Marian E. H. Sneath, was born on the 18th January, 1889, at Greta House, Church End, Finchley, N.W.

He was educated at the private school of Miss Batsford; College Villas School, Finchley Road ; at Christ's College, Finchley ; and at London University. At the latter he was in the Officers' Training Corps, and was appointed to the 6th Middlesex Regiment as 2nd Lieutenant in February, 1911, becoming Lieutenant in December, 1912. On the outbreak of the war he was attached to the 4th Battalion Middlesex Regiment, and accompanied it to the Continent. He was killed in action at Croix Barbée, France, on the 14th October, 1914.

His Commanding Officer wrote of him that " he died doing his duty, and therefore deserved well of his country."

He was a member of several Hendon and Middlesex hockey, football, and cricket clubs, including those of University College. He was not married.

CAPTAIN THOMAS HUMPHREY SNEYD, 4th (attd. 2nd) BATTN. LANCASHIRE FUSILIERS,

who was killed in action at Ploegsteert on the 2nd November, 1914, was the only son of Major-General Sneyd, of Ashcombe Park, near Leek,

Staffordshire, who commanded the Queen's Bays from 1877 to 1882. Captain Sneyd was

born at Lightoaks, near Cheadle, Staffordshire, on the 20th October, 1883, and was educated at Sandroyd, Wellington College, and the R.M.C., Sandhurst. He was gazetted to the Queen's Bays in April, 1903, joining his regiment in South Africa, where he was A.D.C. at Pretoria to the Commander-in-Chief, General Sir Henry Hildyard; he was promoted Lieutenant in May, 1904.

While in Africa he had some successful big game shooting, going as far as Lake Benguelo with a brother officer. In 1910 he retired from the Army and went to the Argentine, South America, for a year and a half, joining the Special Reserve of the Lancashire Fusiliers as Captain in October, 1912, on his return to England. On the outbreak of the war with Germany he was called up to join the 2nd Battalion of his regiment, with which he went to the front.

Captain Sneyd, who was a member of the Cavalry Club, married, in June, 1914, Phœbe Marianne, younger daughter of John Sharp Callender Brodie, of Idvies, Forfar. There was one daughter of the marriage, Averil Marion Anne, born, after her father's death, in April, 1915.

LIEUTENANT HAROLD MARTIN SOAMES, 20th HUSSARS,

son of W. A. Soames, Esq., of Moor Park, Farnham, Surrey, was born on the 13th September, 1886. He was educated at Eton, and was gazetted to the 20th Hussars in June, 1908, becoming Lieutenant in July, 1911.

Lieutenant Soames' name appeared in the first list of British losses in the Great War, issued by the War Office on the 1st September, 1914. He was killed on Sunday, the 23rd August, 1914, while on reconnaissance duty near Binche, in Belgium, his patrol suddenly coming upon the enemy, who were concealed in a wood. He was shot through the chest, and died a few hours later at the Couvent de Bonne Espérance at Vellereille les Bayeux, where he was laid to rest in the convent grounds.

Lieutenant Soames was a polo player of exceptional promise, and represented his regiment in the inter-regimental tournaments in 1912–13. He was a keen rider to hounds and a good shot. He married, in October, 1913, Colleen Ruth, younger daughter of A. W. Addinsell, Esq., M.B., of 10, Curzon Street, Mayfair, and Derryquin, Sunningdale, and left one daughter, born on the 6th August, 1914, a few days before her father left for France.

2nd LIEUTENANT NORMAN ARTHUR HENRY SOMERSET, 1st BATTN. GRENADIER GUARDS,

who was killed in action on the 23rd October, 1914, was the only son of Captain the Hon. Arthur Charles Edward Somerset, late Rifle Brigade (Prince Consort's Own), and a grandson of the second Baron Raglan. He was born on the 8th September, 1894, and was educated at Mr. E. Hawtrey's School at Westgate-on-Sea and at Eton, from which he passed direct into the R.M.C., Sandhurst, and was gazetted to the Grenadier Guards in September, 1913. He was a very promising young soldier and a fine horseman.

He was killed near Kruiseik when taking a message during the earlier part of the first Battle of Ypres whilst serving with his battalion, which formed part of the heroic VIIth Division.

CAPTAIN HANS ROBERT SPARENBORG, 1st BATTN. THE KING'S OWN (ROYAL LANCASTER REGIMENT),

who was first reported to have been wounded in September, 1914, and in October as wounded and missing, was included in the monthly official casualty list published in April, 1915, under the heading "unofficially reported killed or died of wounds." It was subsequently ascertained that he was killed in action on the 26th August, 1914, at Harcourt, near Le Cateau, a Corporal of his Battalion stating that the bursting of a shell caused his death.

He was the eldest son of J. Sparenborg, of

Forest Lodge, Kingswood, Surrey, and was born in Calcutta on the 2nd November, 1876. He was educated at Dulwich College, where he got his colours for football ; and at Caius College, Cambridge ; and joined the Royal Lancaster Regiment in May, 1900, becoming Lieutenant in January, 1902. From May, 1902, to October, 1904, he was employed with the West African Frontier Force, and while so employed took part in the Kano-Sokoto Campaign, West Africa (North Nigeria), in 1903, receiving the medal with clasps. He was also in command during operations in the Kabba Province. He was promoted Captain in January, 1910, and from January, 1911, to December, 1913, was an Adjutant of the 4th Territorial Battalion of his Regiment. He was a first-class interpreter in German.

Captain Sparenborg married Flora Alexandra Vigers, who survives him, and left one son, Colin, age eleven years at the time of his father's death. He was at one time a member of the Junior United Service Club, and played cricket and football.

LIEUTENANT LEWIS GEORGE SPARROW, 3rd BATTN. SOUTH WALES BORDERERS, attd. 2nd BATTN. KING'S OWN SCOTTISH BORDERERS,

was born at Ivybridge, Devon, on the 11th February, 1882, the only son of the late Lewis Sparrow, Strode, Ivybridge, and only brother of Irene Bainbridge, wife of Lieutenant-Commander J. H. Bainbridge, R.N.

He was educated at Eastman's Naval Academy, and afterwards at a military tutor's. He joined the 4th Battalion South Wales Borderers, as 2nd Lieutenant in April, 1900, and was attached to the 2nd Battalion for service in the South African War; he also served with the Mounted Infantry being subsequently invalided home on account of enteric fever. He received the Queen's medal. He became Lieutenant in the 4th Battalion in May, 1902, and in 1904 he left the Army, and was engaged in tobacco and sugar growing in Argentina and Central Africa. On the outbreak of the Great War he rejoined the service as Lieutenant in the 3rd Battalion in September, 1914, and shortly afterwards proceeded to the Continent with the 2nd Battalion King's Own Scottish Borderers.

He was wounded in the neck and throat on the 20th December, and died on the 23rd December, 1914, being buried at Bailleul.

CAPTAIN CHARLES JAMES SPENCER, 2nd BATTN. DEVONSHIRE REGIMENT,

son of C. A. Spencer, was born at Leicester on the 10th January, 1879. He was educated by the Rev. Bode, Yarlet Hall, Stafford, and afterwards at Charterhouse.

Captain Spencer was gazetted to the 2nd Battalion Devonshire Regiment as 2nd Lieutenant from the Cardigan Artillery Militia in 1899, became Lieutenant in May, 1901, and obtained his company in July, 1908. He was Adjutant of the 7th Cyclist Battalion Devonshire Regiment from 1908–12. He served with distinction in the South African War, in which he was severely wounded, and was present at the relief of Ladysmith ; operations in the Transvaal, the Orange Free State, and on the Tugela Heights ; and action at Laing's Nek. He was employed with the Mounted Infantry. For these services he received the Queen's medal with five clasps and the King's medal with two clasps.

Captain Spencer was killed on the 18th December, 1914, while leading his company in an attack on the German trenches.

He was a member of the Junior United Service Club, and his recreations were hunting, polo, and shooting.

He married, in 1909, Katherine Margaret, youngest daughter of the late Robert Bayly, of Torr, Plymouth, and left one son, Charles Richard, born 5th December, 1910.

LIEUTENANT EDMUND SPENCER, 2nd BATTN. THE DUKE OF EDINBURGH'S (WILTSHIRE REGIMENT),

was the son of the Rev. W. E. and Mrs. Spencer, and was born on the 12th November, 1889, at South Benfleet, Essex.

He was educated at Mowden Hall, Essex ; at Forest School, where he was head of the school and captain of the cricket and football teams ; and at the R.M.C., Sandhurst, where he played in the " Soccer " team.

He joined the Wiltshire Regiment as 2nd Lieutenant in April, 1910, becoming Lieutenant in May, 1913, and served with his battalion at

Dublin, Gosport, and Gibraltar. Lieutenant Spencer accompanied his battalion to Belgium in October, 1914, and was killed on the 20th of the same month in an advanced guard action between Ypres and Becelaere.

Lieutenant Spencer obtained a first-class certificate in the Army Gymnasium Course at Aldershot, and was captain of the battalion " Soccer " team, and was also in the Cricket XI.

2nd LIEUTENANT GERVASE THORPE SPENDLOVE, 2nd BATTN. THE PRINCE OF WALES'S VOLUNTEERS (SOUTH LANCASHIRE REGIMENT),

was the son of J. G. Spendlove, of The Willows, Beeston, and was born on the 29th December, 1896.

He was educated at Oundle School, and before the war belonged to the motor section of Frontiersmen. With three others he rode through France with a letter to Sir John French, and they were attached by the Commander-in-Chief at General Headquarters to the R.E. as Despatch Riders, with the rank of Corporal. Mr. Spendlove was given a commission in the South Lancashire Regiment, and was killed on the 17th November, 1914, a month before attaining his eighteenth year, by a shell exploding in his dug-out, two days after joining his battalion.

2nd Lieutenant Spendlove must have been one of the youngest officers, if not the youngest, to fall in the Great War.

CAPTAIN JOHN SPOTTISWOODE, 6th (attd. 2nd) BATTN. KING'S ROYAL RIFLE CORPS,

was born in London on the 18th April, 1874, the son of George Andrew Spottiswoode and his wife, Grace Frances, eldest daughter of the Rev. Sir St. Vincent Love Hammick. He was a nephew of William Spottiswoode (President of the Royal Society, 1876–83, President of the London Mathematical Society, 1870–72, and of the British Association, 1878).

Captain Spottiswoode was educated at Winchester College and the R.M.C., Sandhurst.

He obtained the highest marks ever made in Physics, viz., 1,764 (88·4 per cent. of the maximum) in the entrance examination for the R.M.C. in 1892.

He joined the 2nd Battalion K.R.R.C. as 2nd Lieutenant in October, 1894, being promoted Lieutenant in January, 1898. In May, 1899, he became Captain in the 7th Battalion and was with the Mounted Infantry in the South African War, where he was twice wounded.

He was granted the honorary rank of Captain in the Army in October, 1900, but retired in 1901. On the Great War breaking out he joined the 6th Battalion in August, 1914, and the 2nd Battalion in September, 1914, with which he was serving when he was killed at the head of his company on the 31st October, 1914, at Gheluvelt, in the Battle of Ypres.

Captain Spottiswoode, who was distinguished in radio-telegraphy, married Sybil Gwendolen, daughter of Dr. Christian David Ginsburg, LL.D., J.P., and left two sons : Raymond John, born 1913 ; and Nigel Lawrence, born 1915, after his father's death.

LIEUTENANT (temp.) RALPH LESINGHAM SPRECKLEY, 2nd BATTN. CONNAUGHT RANGERS,

was born at Worcester on the 29th May, 1893, and was the son of H. W. Spreckley, of that place.

He was educated at Bromsgrove School, where he was head monitor and Colour-Sergeant in the Officers' Training Corps, and had his colours for the Cricket XI and the Football XV. After the usual term at the R.M.C., Sandhurst, he was gazetted to the Connaught Rangers as 2nd Lieutenant in February, 1913, and became temp. Lieutenant in September, 1914.

He was killed on the 14th September, 1914, was mentioned in Sir John French's Despatch of the 8th October, 1914, and had been awarded the Military Cross.

The following account of his death was given by a Staff Officer : " One fellow—Spreckley—who comes from north of Worcester, earned the V.C. twice over before he was killed. He was hit in the leg at a critical moment, went back and got dressed, and hobbled up to the firing line in the woods, cheering his men on. He was hit again, and did ditto, getting back just as his fellows were breaking. He rallied them, and drove the Germans on, only to be shot when the situation was saved."

CAPTAIN GEORGE PATRICK OSBORN SPRINGFIELD, 2nd DRAGOON GUARDS (QUEEN'S BAYS),

son of Thomas Osborn and Rose Maria Springfield, was born at Old Charlton, Kent, on the 2nd January, 1873.

He was educated at Uppingham School and Trinity Hall, Cambridge; and entering the Army served in the ranks of Lumsden's Horse in the South African War, being present at operations in the Orange Free State, in the Transvaal, Orange River Colony, Cape Colony, and on the Zululand frontier of Natal, including actions at Vet and Zand Rivers, near Johannesburg, and at Pretoria. He received the Queen's medal with two clasps. From Lumsden's Corps he was given his commission in the 3rd Dragoon Guards in August, 1900, becoming Lieutenant in February, 1901. In September, 1904, he got his troop in the 2nd Dragoon Guards, of which he was Adjutant from June, 1910, to June, 1913. From April, 1908, to May, 1910, he was A.D.C. to Sir Hamilton Goold-Adams at Bloemfontein, Governor and Commander-in-Chief, Orange River Colony.

In the Great War he was shot dead at Braine, in France, while reconnoitring in the town, dismounted, looking for snipers, on the 12th September, 1914.

Captain Springfield, who was a member of the Norfolk Club and of the Army and Navy Club, was a fine steeplechase rider, very fond of hunting, and a well-known gentleman rider and owner. He was unmarried.

LIEUTENANT IVAN BOYD SPROT, 1st BATTN. THE QUEEN'S OWN CAMERON HIGHLANDERS,

who was killed in action on the 22nd October, 1914, near Langemarck, in Belgium, was the youngest son of the late Mr. Edward W. Sprot and of Mrs. Sprot, of Dry-grange, Roxburgh-shire.

He was born on the 14th September, 1889, and was educated at Stanmore Park,

Middlesex; and Eton, for which school he played cricket. He was also a member of the Middlesex Cricket Club, and was a fine athlete. He received his commission in the Cameron Highlanders from the Special Reserve in May, 1911, becoming Lieutenant in September, 1914.

He was shot in the temple by a sniper while leading his men on. His last words were, "Come on, boys, come on! Let's at them!" A brother of Lieutenant Sprot's is in the Black Watch, and another in the Gordon Highlanders. The former has been "missing" since November, 1914, and the latter has been wounded in the war.

Lieutenant Sprot married, in March, 1914, Agnes Mary Gordon (Nancy), youngest daughter of Mr. and Mrs. Berry, 31, Drumsheugh Gardens, Edinburgh, and a granddaughter of the late Sir William Muir, of Dean Park House, Edinburgh.

CAPTAIN LOSCOMBE LAW STABLE, 2nd BATTN. ROYAL WELSH FUSILIERS,

born on the 21st March, 1886, at Wanstead Lodge, Wanstead, Essex, was the son of Daniel Wintringham Stable, LL.B., J.P., Barrister-at-Law, and his wife, Gertrude Mary (née Law), of Plas Llwynowen, Llan-brynmair, Montgomeryshire, and a great-nephew of Sir Frederick Halliday, K.C.B., Lieutenant-Governor of Bengal.

He was educated at The Wells House, Malvern Wells; and Winchester College. After passing through the R.M.C., Sandhurst, he was gazetted to the Royal Welsh Fusiliers in February, 1907, becoming Lieutenant in April, 1911. His promotion to Captain dated from the 21st October, 1914, only a few days before his death.

He was killed near Armentières, France, on the 26th October, 1914, having left his trench to bring in Private Ellis, of the battalion, who was lying wounded outside the trench, and exposed to heavy fire. The circumstances were described by another Private as follows: "Private Ellis, lying wounded some distance away from the trenches, was rescued under a hail of bullets. I drew Lieutenant Stable's notice to Private Ellis, and asked whether he was one of our men. Looking through his glasses he found that Ellis belonged to our company. The Lieutenant would not allow me to go to him, but rushed out of the trench to our wounded comrade's assistance. Then Private Taylor rushed to help, and they were returning to the trenches when the Lieutenant was struck in the side with a bullet, but managed to get back. ' What's the matter, sir ? ' I asked. ' I am hit,' was the reply. ' Hit where ? ' ' In the side.' At this the officer fainted, and shortly afterwards succumbed to his wound. Had Lieutenant Stable lived he would no doubt have been recommended for the V.C. Private Taylor has since been awarded the D.C.M. Private Ellis managed to scramble into the trench, and we found his knee had been smashed."

Captain Stable was a fine polo player, and played for his battalion at several tournaments, finally being one of the team that won the Infantry Polo Tournament at Delhi on the 27th February, 1913, before the Viceroy of India and Lady Hardinge.

2nd LIEUTENANT HAROLD ROLLESTON STABLES, 5th (RESERVE) BATTN. THE ROYAL FUSILIERS (CITY OF LONDON REGIMENT),

who was born on the 1st July, 1886, at Horsforth, Yorkshire, was the son of Henry and Mary Stables.

He was educated at Cheltenham College and New College, Oxford, where he rowed in the College VIII in 1906, 1907, and 1908. He took his degree of B.A. in 1909. Subsequently he studied for the Bar, and while so engaged joined the Inns of Court O.T.C. in 1911. He was called to the Bar at the Inner Temple in 1912.

He was a member of the Public Schools' and Leander Clubs, and of the Hardwicke Debating Society. He frequently spoke on eugenics and woman suffrage. He was made a Freemason in the Apollo Lodge at Oxford, and in 1908 held the office of Assistant Grand Pursuivant in the Provincial Grand Lodge of Oxfordshire.

After the outbreak of war with Germany he obtained a commission in the Royal Fusiliers in August, 1914. Very soon afterwards, owing to the training he had received while a member of the Inns of Court O.T.C., 2nd Lieutenant Stables was ordered to proceed to France for active service. At the time of his death he was serving at the front with the 1st Battalion Cheshire Regiment. He was shot through the head on the 15th November, 1914, while helping to defend trenches three miles south of Ypres.

CAPTAIN EDWARD HUGH BAGOT STACK, 2nd BATTN. 8th GURKHA RIFLES,

son of the late Edward Stack, Esq., Bengal Civil Service, and of Mrs. Luttman - Johnson, of Redhill House, Petworth, Sussex, was born at Shillong, Assam, India, on the 14th September, 1885. He was a great-nephew of the late Right Rev. Charles Maurice Stack, Bishop of Clogher, Clones, Ireland.

Captain Stack was educated at Temple Grove Preparatory School and Winchester College. He went to India in August, 1905, and was attached to the K.R.R.C. (late 60th Rifles) at Bareilly, receiving his commission in his Indian regiment at Lansdowne in 1906. He was gazetted Captain on the 5th August, 1914.

He fell in action on the 31st October, 1914, near Festubert, while leading his men. He was shot first in the face and later in the arm, but continued fighting all day, and when the enemy came on with a rush he fell shot through the chest by a third bullet, firing his revolver as he was killed.

Captain Stack married, in 1912, Mary Meta, daughter of the late Theodore Stack, Esq., of Dublin, and left one daughter, born July, 1914.

2nd LIEUTENANT C. C. STAFFORD, RESERVE OF OFFICERS, attd. 2nd BATTN. BEDFORDSHIRE REGIMENT,

was killed in action on the 13th October, 1914. He joined the Reserve of Officers in September, 1913.

LIEUTENANT RICHARD TERRICK STAINFORTH, 2nd BATTN. ROYAL WARWICKSHIRE REGIMENT,

was born at Chester on the 23rd December, 1893, the younger son of Colonel R. T. Stainforth, Army Ordnance Department (retired), and of Mrs. Stainforth.

He was educated at Mr. Gurney's School, Brandon

House, Cheltenham, from which he entered Cheltenham College in 1908 ; thence he passed into the R.M.C., Sandhurst, in 1912. He was a good athlete, a fine cricketer, very active in the field, a good bowler, and a promising bat. Only an attack of illness prevented his getting into the Cheltenham XI in 1911. In 1912 he won the cup in the Fives Competition, and when at Sandhurst was in the hockey team. He joined the Royal Warwickshire Regiment in April, 1914, at Malta. His cricket soon attracted attention, for he kept on making long scores for the battalion, as well as succeeding as a bowler, so he was asked to join a United XI of the station to represent the Army v. the Navy.

On the outbreak of the war with Germany his battalion came home, and after three weeks at Lyndhurst sailed with the VIIth Division on the 4th October, 1914, and landed at Zeebrugge on the 7th of that month. The battalion formed part of the 22nd Brigade under Brigadier-General Lawford. Lieutenant Stainforth, who got his step in September, was killed at the Battle of Ypres on the 19th October, 1914. He was ordered forward with his platoon in the advance line of attack in skirmishing order at Kezelberg, on the Roulers-Menin Road, when a shell burst, wounding him in five places. He would not allow the Sergeant to bandage his wounds, but said, " I'm done ! Advance platoon to cover." Later on he was picked up, and his wounds dressed, but he died in the ambulance wagon on the way to Ypres Hospital. He was buried in a plot near the prison, the town being so constantly and violently shelled at that time that it was impossible to bury him in the cemetery.

2nd LIEUTENANT BENJAMIN ARTHUR STANDRING, 2nd BATTN. ROYAL WARWICKSHIRE REGIMENT,

son of Arthur Hamilton and Ellen Standring, was born at Oporto, Portugal, on the 26th December, 1886, and was educated at the Oporto British School and Charterhouse (Bodeites).

He joined the 28th City of London Regiment (Artists' Rifles) in 1909, becoming successively Corporal and Sergeant, and with this corps he proceeded to join the Expeditionary Force in France in October, 1914. Shortly after the Artists' Rifles arrived in France they became an Officers' Training Corps, and in November, 1914, 2nd Lieutenant Standring received his commission in the Royal Warwickshire Regiment, which he joined at the front.

He died on the 19th December, 1914, of wounds received the same day in action at Rouges Bancs, and was buried in the churchyard at Sailly-sur-Lys.

2nd LIEUTENANT GEORGE HOPKINS STANLEY, 1st BATTN. EAST LANCASHIRE REGIMENT,

was the son of Willaim Stanley, and was born at Pontypool, Monmouthshire, on the 9th November, 1875.

He served through the South African War, for which he held the Queen's and the King's medals with clasps ; and he was also awarded the Long Service and Good Conduct medal.

He went to the front at the commencement of the war, and received his commission for services in the field on the 16th September, 1914. He was killed on the 31st October, and his C.O. sent the following account in a letter of sympathy to his widow : " Your husband was killed in the trenches on Saturday, the 31st October, by a portion of shell that struck him in the back. I had, as you know, a great regard for your husband. I had known him many years in the regiment and at the depot, and had always a very high opinion of him ; consequently I was delighted when he was given a commission in the 30th, and now he has passed away from us. He had done excellent service out here, and I had intended, if he had lived, to have sent his name in for mention in despatches at the first opportunity. He was killed outright, and we buried him the same night in a grave close to three of his brother officers and several men who have all been killed during the shelling of the last five days. He lies one mile east of Ploegsteert (which is three miles north of Armentières), along the Ploegsteert-le-Gheer Road."

2nd Lieutenant Stanley was married, and left three children, two girls and a boy.

2nd LIEUTENANT CHARLES MARTIN STANUELL, 2nd BATTN. DURHAM LIGHT INFANTRY,

born at Muree, Punjab, India, on the 29th July, 1894, was the only son of Lieutenant-Colonel H. S. Stanuell, late Royal Scots Fusiliers. Many relatives on both sides of the family have won distinction in the services.

He was educated at

Eagle House School, Sandhurst, from 1903–08, where he was in the XV and the XI, and made a record long jump of 16 feet 7 inches in May, 1908. From September of the latter year until 1912 he was at Cheltenham College, where he was in the XV, a brilliant three-quarter back. In 1910 he won the Troughton medal and cup for most events under sixteen, and in 1911 and 1912 the Ladies' Challenge Cup and Gold Medal for most events.

He then went to the R.M.C., Sandhurst, where he was again distinguished as a three-quarter back at football, and played for the college for two seasons, 1912 and 1913, and represented it in the Sandhurst v. Woolwich Sports in the hurdles, long jump, and one hundred yards, winning the latter and the silver medal in 1913. After joining the service he played for the Army in the Rugby XV, and also in the combined Sandhurst and Woolwich team v. the Services. He received his commission in the Durham Light Infantry in January, 1914, and was killed in action at the Battle of the Aisne, while gallantly leading his platoon, on the 20th September, 1914.

MAJOR GRANVILLE JOSEPH CHETWYND STAPYLTON, ROYAL FIELD ARTILLERY,

born on the 17th September, 1 8 7 1, was the elder son of Lieutenant - General and Lady Barbara Emily Maria Stapylton, daughter of the fourth Earl of Milltown.

Major Stapylton joined the Royal Artillery in February, 1891, becoming Lieutenant in February, 1894, and Captain in February, 1900. He served in the South African War, 1899–1902, being present at the relief of Kimberley ; at operations in the Orange Free State, including actions at Paardeberg, Poplar Grove, Karee Siding, Houtnek (Thoba Mountain), and Zand River ; operations in the Transvaal, including actions near Johannesburg and Diamond Hill ; also the later operations in the Transvaal and Cape Colony, including the action at Colesberg. He received the Queen's medal with five clasps and the King's medal with two clasps.

Major Stapylton, who obtained his Majority in September, 1908, was reported as killed in action on the 3rd September, 1914.

MAJOR ROBERT PERCY STARES, 2nd BATTN. BEDFORDSHIRE REGIMENT,

who was killed in action on the 30th October,

1914, was the second son of John Twynam Stares, Manor House, Upham, Hants.

He was born on the 22nd November, 1866, and was educated at Weymouth College and abroad. He was gazetted to the Bedfordshire Regiment from the Militia in November, 1888, becoming Lieutenant in 1890. He took part in the Isaazi Expedition, 1892, and in operations in Chitral in 1895, being present at the storming of the Malakand Pass, and the action near Khar at the descent into Swat Valley. For these operations he received the medal with clasp.

From May, 1892, to April, 1896, he was Adjutant of his battalion, and was promoted Captain in October, 1896. From August of that year to May, 1900, he was an Adjutant of Indian Volunteers, and during that period took part in operations on the north-western frontier of India with the Tirah Expeditionary Force, being Brigade Transport Officer to a column from November, 1897, to April, 1898. For these operations two clasps were added to the medal previously received.

He was promoted Major in October, 1908 ; and from January, 1907, to January, 1911, was first a Brigade Major, then D.A.A.G. in India.

He went out to Belgium with the 21st Brigade, VIIth Division, and was killed near Ypres while gallantly leading his men, being shot at close range by some Germans who had crept up. For his services he was mentioned in Sir John French's Despatch of the 14th January, 1915. Major Stares was a great polo player, and very fond of hunting and shooting He was unmarried.

CAPTAIN WILLIAM HENRY JOSEPH BARBER-STARKEY, 52nd BATTERY ROYAL FIELD ARTILLERY,

was born on the 4th March, 1880, at The Hall, Huttons-Ambo, Yorkshire, the eldest son of W. J. S. Barber-Starkey, Esq.

He was educated at Harrow and Trinity College, Cambridge, joining the Royal Artillery from the Militia in October, 1900. He became Lieutenant in October, 1903, and Captain in May, 1912.

Captain Barber-Starkey was officially reported missing on the 2nd September, 1914, and twice afterwards unofficially reported a prisoner of war, unwounded, at Torgau. Unfortunately these reports proved unfounded, and his parents finally received information through the Red Cross International Agency of Prisoners of War, Geneva, that their son had died in a German Field Hospital at Le Cateau on the 10th September, 1914, from wounds received in the Battle of Le Cateau on the 26th August, 1914.

MAJOR EDWIN BEDFORD STEEL, B.A., M.B., B.Ch. Dub., ROYAL ARMY MEDICAL CORPS,

son of the late Charles Steel, A.V.C., attached to 12th Lancers, was born at Aldershot on the 16th September, 1871.

Major Steel was educated at Rugby, where he won the "Crick," and was in the Football XV; and at Trinity College, Dublin, where, as also at Dr. Steevens' Hospital, he distinguished himself as a footballer. He graduated M.B., B.Ch. in the University of Dublin in 1893, joining the R.A.M.C. in January, 1895, being promoted Captain in 1898, and Major in 1906. Between 1897 and 1912 he served twice in India, and in the latter year was made an Associate of the Order of St. John of Jerusalem, in recognition of his services in connection with plague duty. Major Steel held the Indian Durbar medal, 1911.

In the Great War he went abroad in command of Field Ambulance No. 20, and was mentioned for his services in Sir John French's despatch of the 8th October, 1914. At the beginning of October he was appointed Assistant Director of Medical Services attached to the 1st Cavalry Division. He was wounded by a shell at La Clytte on the morning of the 23rd November, 1914, and died on the afternoon of the same day in Bailleul Clearing Hospital. He was buried in the cemetery at Bailleul.

Major Steel married, in 1899, Ethel Mary Robinson, and left a daughter, Rachel Mary, aged eleven, and two sons, Anthony Bedford and Christopher Bedford, aged fifteen and eight respectively.

CAPTAIN FREDERICK WILBERFORCE ALEXANDER STEELE, 4th BATTN. ROYAL FUSILIERS,

who was killed in action on the 26th or 27th October, 1914, was the eldest son of Mr. and Mrs. Philip J. Steele, of Normanhurst, Kew,

Melbourne, Australia. He had at first been reported, in December, as "wounded and miss-

ing," and had been present at the Battle of Mons.

He was born on the 12th September, 1885, and was educated at the Church of England Grammar School, Melbourne, and at Messrs. Carlyle and Gregson's, London. He received his commission in the Royal Fusiliers from the Commonwealth Military Forces in July, 1907, becoming Lieutenant in April, 1910. His promotion to Captain, to date from the 13th December, 1914, was gazetted on the 1st March, 1915.

The following is an extract from a letter written by Captain Steele's Commanding Officer: "He was leading a night attack through a village when he was shot, and death appears to have been instantaneous. Sergeant Woodcock was close by when your son was hit, and, though he got to him at once, he says he was undoubtedly dead. I cannot say how highly we all thought of your son. He was equal to the best officer I have ever met, and I had undoubted confidence in him. I had already recommended him for special distinction, and hope that some mark of appreciation in the shape of a posthumous honour may yet be conferred on him. I also brought him personally to the notice of Sir John French, who congratulated him on his distinguished service." And the Adjutant of his battalion wrote: "Your son was one of the very best officers I have ever seen, always cheery and energetic, and most capable. The Colonel, I know, had the very highest opinion of him." For his services in the war Captain Steele was mentioned in Sir John French's Despatches of the 8th October, 1914, and 14th January, 1915.

Captain Steele, who was unmarried, was a member of the Junior Army and Navy Club. His three brothers were all serving in the war.

CAPTAIN OLIVER STEELE, 1st BATTN. PRINCESS CHARLOTTE OF WALES'S (ROYAL BERKSHIRE REGIMENT),

was born at Wairoa, Hawkes Bay, New Zealand, on the 7th April, 1882, the son of Mr. and Mrs. Thomas James Steele, of Remuera, Auckland, New Zealand, and a nephew of A. R. Steele, Loddington Hall, Northants. He was educated at Auckland Grammar School, where he made a record in the school sports in 1895 for the one hundred yards under fourteen, which he did in eleven seconds, the record being still unbroken in 1915. He obtained his commission in May, 1900,

during the South African War, from the ranks of the 5th New Zealand Contingent, being present at operations in Rhodesia, in the Transvaal, including actions at Eland's River, from May, 1900, to July, 1901, and Cape Colony, July, 1901, to May, 1902. He received the Queen's medal with four clasps and the King's medal with two clasps. He became Lieutenant in March, 1902, and Captain in July, 1910. He also held the Coronation Durbar medal, 1911.

He was killed at Zonnebeke on the 25th October, 1914, by a bursting shell while reforming his company after a charge, and was mentioned in Sir John French's Despatch of the 14th January, 1915, for his bravery.

Captain Steele, who was not married, was a member of the Junior Naval and Military Club.

LIEUTENANT JOHN HENRY GORDON LEE STEERE, 3rd BATTN. GRENADIER GUARDS,

who was killed in action on the 17th November, 1914, was the only son of H. C. Lee Steere, of Jayes Park, Ockley, Surrey. He was born on the 14th June, 1895, and joined the Grenadier Guards in February, 1914, being promoted Lieutenant on the 15th November, 1914.

CAPTAIN ALBERT ALEXANDER LESLIE STEPHEN, D.S.O., ADJUTANT 1st BATTN. SCOTS GUARDS,

was killed in action on the 31st October, 1914. He was born on the 3rd February, 1879, and joined the Scots Guards from the Militia in January, 1899, becoming Lieutenant in April, 1900. He served in the South African War, where he was present at a large number of engagements. He took part in the advance on Kimberley with action at Belmont, Enslin, Modder River, and Magersfontein ; and was present at operations in the Orange Free State, Transvaal, Orange River Colony, and Cape Colony, including actions at Poplar Grove, Driefontein, Vet and Zand Rivers, near Johannesburg, at Pretoria, Diamond Hill, and Belfast. From January, 1901, he was Assistant Provost-Marshal. He was twice mentioned in Despatches ("London Gazette," 10th September, 1901, and 29th July, 1902); was awarded the D.S.O.; and received the Queen's medal with six clasps and the King's medal with two clasps.

He was promoted Captain in April, 1904, and from April, 1906, to March, 1909, was employed with the Macedonian Gendarmerie ; and from the latter date to January, 1911, with the Turkish Gendarmerie. He was awarded the order of the Medjidieh, 3rd Class. From September, 1910, to September, 1913, he was an Adjutant of the Territorial Force ; and in April, 1914, was appointed Adjutant of the 1st Battalion of his own regiment.

CAPTAIN DOUGLAS CLINTON LESLIE STEPHEN, 2nd BATTN. GRENADIER GUARDS,

died of wounds received in action on the 10th September, 1914.

He was born on the 7th February, 1877, and in May, 1900. received his commission from the Militia, with which he had served during embodiment for four months. He took part in the South African War, being present at operations in the Orange River Colony, Cape Colony. and Transvaal, including the actions at Wittebergen. He received the Queen's medal with three clasps and the King's medal with two clasps.

He was promoted Lieutenant in November, 1903, and Captain in June, 1908. From April, 1906, to March, 1909, he was employed with the Macedonian Gendarmerie, and from December, 1909, to January, 1914, was A.D.C. to the General Officer Commanding London District.

MAJOR HERBERT ARTHUR HERBERT-STEPNEY, 1st BATTN. IRISH GUARDS,

was the son of Mr. George Herbert - Stepney, and was born on the 10th January, 1879. His grandfather—Colonel Arthur St. George Herbert - Stepney— commanded the 2nd Battn. Coldstream Guards.

Major Herbert-

Stepney was educated at Rugby and the R.M.C., Sandhurst, from which he passed out first. He joined the Coldstream Guards in 1898, became Lieutenant in 1899, and was transferred to the Irish Guards in 1901, soon after their formation : he was Adjutant of his battalion from January till December, 1902, and was promoted Captain in September, 1904.

He served in the South African War during 1900 and 1901, being present at operations in the Transvaal, including the action of Belfast, where he was slightly wounded. He afterwards received the Queen's medal with three clasps. Major Herbert-Stepney left Wellington Barracks with his battalion for France, on the 12th August, as Senior Company Commander. He was in command of the battalion, from the 1st to the 17th September, till after the Battle of the Aisne, and again for the first days of November during the great struggle at Ypres. For his services he was mentioned in Field-Marshal Sir John French's Despatch of the 14th January, 1915. He was killed at Klein Zillebeke, near Ypres, on the 7th November, 1914.

Major Herbert-Stepney was an Irishman, whose home had always been in that country. He was a good shot, keen fisherman, and fond of all games.

CAPTAIN REGINALD WALTER MORTON STEVENS, p.s.c., ROYAL IRISH RIFLES, BRIGADE MAJOR 9th INFANTRY BRIGADE,

who died on the 28th August, 1914, of wounds received on the 26th of that month at Le Cateau, was the second son of Colonel George Morton Stevens, late Royal Artillery.

He was born on the 18th December, 1876, and was educated at Mr. Thomas Eastman's, at Stubbington, at Mr. Hanson's, Appledurcombe College, Isle of Wight ; and at the R.M.C., Sandhurst. He joined the Royal Irish Rifles in September, 1896, becoming Lieutenant in August, 1898. He served in the South African War, in which he was severely wounded at Stormberg, and afterwards acted as Assistant Staff Officer to the Assistant Inspector-General, Western Section, Lines of Communication, from December, 1900. He was present at operations in Cape Colony and Orange River Colony, and received the Queen's medal and King's medal each with two clasps. In 1903–04 he was on the Staff as Special Service

Officer with the Somaliland Field Force, and was present at the action at Jidballi, receiving the medal with two clasps. In 1904 he was promoted Captain ; and from January, 1905, to January, 1908, was Adjutant of his battalion. From January, 1908, to January, 1910, he was an officer of a company of Gentlemen Cadets at the Royal Military College. From 1910 to December, 1911, he was at the Staff College, afterwards being attached to the Naval War College, Portsmouth ; and in November, 1912, was appointed Brigade-Major of the 9th Infantry Brigade, Southern Command. He also did a great deal of examination work for the War Office for the O.T.C.

He embarked with his Brigade in August, 1914, and on the day of the Battle of Le Cateau he had been told to telephone the order to retire through to the trenches. He must have found something wrong with the telephone, for shortly after he was seen riding straight to the trenches in full view of the enemy and in the face of a heavy fire. He succeeded in giving the order before he was shot. No news was received of him for two and a half months, when word came from Germany that he had died two days later in a farmhouse at Troisvilles.

Captain Stevens, who was a member of the United Service Club, married, in 1912, Elizabeth, daughter of the late Rev. J. C. Mace, and left a daughter, who was born a fortnight after her father was killed.

LIEUTENANT ADRIAN HARRY STEWART, THE GLOUCESTERSHIRE REGIMENT,

was the youngest son of Colonel Harry Hutchinson Augustus Stewart (brother of Sir Augustus Stewart, ninth Baronet, of Fort Stewart, County Donegal), and of the late Mrs. Stewart, of Hopton Hall, near Lowestoft.

He was born on the 25th February, 1888, at Morningthorpe Manor, Norfolk, and finished his education at the R.M.C., Sandhurst, on passing out of which he was appointed to the Gloucestershire Regiment (in which corps his father had served for several years as Adjutant and Captain) in May, 1907, being promoted Lieutenant in December, 1909. In March, 1914, he was seconded for service under the Colonial Office, and joined the 3rd Battalion Nigeria Regiment, West African Frontier Force, and fell on the 30th August, 1914, at the unsuccessful assault of Garua, Cameroons, German West Africa.

He was a keen all-round sportsman, an expert rifle shot and swimmer, and of remarkably fine physique.

The house of Fort Stewart has sent many representatives to the Army uninterruptedly since its foundation two or three centuries ago, several of whom gained high rank and distinction. It is believed he was the first Army officer of his name to fall in this war, waged on three continents.

Lieutenant Stewart was a member of the Junior United Service Club.

CAPTAIN BERTRAND STEWART, WEST KENT (QUEEN'S OWN) YEOMANRY, attd. INTELLIGENCE CORPS,

was killed at the Battle of the Aisne on the 12th September, 1914. He was the only son of Charles Stewart, Esq., of Achara, Appin, Argyllshire, and of 38, Eaton Place, London, one of the " Stewarts of Appin," and owner of Castle Stalcaire, a well-preserved ruin with historic connections, it having been the hunting seat of James IV of Scotland, who was slain on Flodden Field. In this castle, which is open to the public, has been placed a marble tablet to Captain Stewart's memory.

Captain Stewart was born in London in December, 1872. He was educated at Eton (Durnford's House) and Christ Church, Oxford, where he remained until 1892. In 1897 he was admitted a solicitor, and became a member of the firm of Markby, Stewart & Co., of Coleman Street, London.

When the Boer War broke out Captain Stewart enlisted in the Imperial Yeomanry, and took part in operations in the Cape Colony, Orange River Colony, and the Transvaal. He was awarded the Queen's medal with two clasps.

In April, 1906, he received a commission in the West Kent Yeomanry, and became a Captain in 1913.

On the outbreak of the Great War Captain Stewart was appointed to the Intelligence Department on the Staff of Major-General Allenby, C.B., commanding the Cavalry Division of the Expeditionary Force. He was serving in this position when he met his death. The following account of his fall was furnished by one who was with him in a letter dated Rheims, 16th September :—

" I was with him at the time, and must tell you that I am certain it was the death he would have chosen—painless, sudden, and doing his duty. . . . A patrol of ours was attacked entering the village of Braisne, and the supporting party . . . retired. Captain Stewart at once jumped up, and, putting himself at their head, rallied them and took them to the assistance of those cut off. I was sent back for reinforcements, and on my return . . . had got to within a few yards of his side when the end came. . . . Those who, like myself, worked with him had become very fond of him, and his memory as an English officer will remain with us."

He was buried in the cemetery in the village of Braisne, near where he fell. The officers and men of the West Kent Yeomanry have presented his widow with a handsome bronze tablet, commemorating his services.

He was the author of a useful manual, entitled " The Active Service Pocket Book," which ran through several editions, and an article of his, entitled " Germany and Ourselves," in the " National Review " for June, 1914, attracted much attention. He was for some time co-editor of the " Cavalry Journal."

His chief recreations were hunting, shooting, and deer-stalking, but he always made his work, civil and military, his first consideration. His life and death show that it was the " great game of war " that had the supremest attraction for him.

The most momentous occurrence in Captain Stewart's life remains to be recorded. When travelling in Germany it was his misfortune to fall under the suspicion of the German Government, and he was arrested at Bremen in August, 1911, on a charge of espionage. His trial by the Supreme Court of Germany opened at Leipzig on the 31st January, 1912, and, after the preliminaries, was conducted *in camera*. The charges brought against him related mainly to naval defences at many places he had never seen. The only specific evidence against him was that of a penniless ex-criminal in the employment of the prosecutors. After a trial lasting four days, Captain Stewart was found guilty, and sentenced to detention in a fortress for three and a half years. Before leaving the Court Captain Stewart proudly told his judges that if their distinguished nation was ever at war with Britain, he hoped he would be in the field against them in defence of his country. His hope was soon to be fulfilled. He was imprisoned under rigorous conditions in the fortress of Glatz, and was released, as an act of clemency, on the visit to Berlin of his Majesty King George V in May, 1913. After his release he prepared a memorandum completely vindicating himself from the charges brought against him, and his countrymen may well be content to place their reliance on the honour of a brave soldier.

Captain Stewart married, on the 1st August, 1905, Daphne, daughter of Colonel Osmond Priaulx, of The Mount, Guernsey. He left no issue.

He was a member of the Athenæum and Carlton Clubs.

CAPTAIN GEOFFREY STEWART, 1st BATTN. COLDSTREAM GUARDS, RESERVE OF OFFICERS,

son of Major-General Sir Herbert Stewart, K.C.B., was born at Binfield, Berkshire, on the 28th October, 1878, and was educated at Eton.

He joined the Coldstream Guards in 1898, and served with them throughout the South African War, 1899–1902, taking part in the advance on Kimberley, including actions at Belmont, Enslin, Modder River, and Magersfontein ; he was also present at operations in the Orange Free State, including actions at Vet and Zand Rivers, at operations in the Transvaal, including actions near Johannesburg, Pretoria, and Diamond Hill ; and at operations in the Transvaal, East and West of Pretoria, including the action at Belfast (1900). He was present at further operations in the Transvaal and in Cape Colony in 1901–02, and at the conclusion of the war received the Queen's medal with six clasps and the King's medal with two clasps. From 1905–07 he served in the Egyptian Army and retired in 1910, joining the Reserve of Officers. He also served with the Leicestershire Yeomanry, having been promoted Major in February, 1914, and when war broke out was given an appointment as Staff Captain to the North Midland Mounted Brigade. At the front he was serving with the 1st Battalion of his old regiment when he was killed while retiring from a reconnaissance he made, alone, to the enemy's trenches at Givenchy, in Flanders, on the 22nd December, 1914. He was mentioned in Sir John French's Despatch of the 31st May, 1915.

Captain Stewart, who had been a Page of Honour to her Majesty Queen Victoria, was a member of the Guards' Club. He married Violet, daughter of W. Clarence Watson, Esq., and left two children : Jean, born 1909 ; and Malise, born 1911.

2nd LIEUTENANT HUBERT REGINALD STOCK, 1st BATTN. THE BUFFS (EAST KENT REGIMENT),

who was killed in the trenches on the 25th October, 1914, only gained his commission in the beginning of that month for service in the field. He was the son of Edwin Stock (at

one time Sergeant in the 57th Foot, now the 1st Middlesex Regiment), and of Zellah Stock. He was born on the 3rd September, 1888.

He had obtained, while serving in the ranks, a first-class Certificate of Education, and an Auxiliary Schoolmaster's Certificate. 2nd Lieutenant Stock was Signalling Instructor in his battalion. He was a good mounted infantryman, and gained a "distinguished" Musketry Certificate at Hythe. He was a keen all-round sportsman, a good shot and scoutmaster, and was a strict teetotaller.

LIEUTENANT MICHAEL GEORGE STOCKS, 2nd BATTN. GRENADIER GUARDS,

was the elder son of Michael Stocks, of Wood Hall, Downham Market, Norfolk, and Upper Shibden Hall, Yorkshire. He was a grandson, on his mother's side, of the late Colonel Sir Richard Ellison, of Boultham, and his paternal grandfather—Major Stocks—took part in the charge at Balaclava, and, as a thank-offering for his safe return, the family built the Church of St. Mary, Halifax.

Lieutenant Stocks was born on the 24th November, 1892 ; educated at Eton and the R.M.C., Sandhurst ; and entered the Guards in February, 1912, becoming Lieutenant in October, 1913. His recreations were polo, hunting, and shooting.

He was killed in the trenches near Ypres, on the 10th November, 1914, and is buried at Zillebeke.

MAJOR CHARLES INGLIS STOCKWELL, 2nd BATTN. SEAFORTH HIGHLANDERS (ROSS-SHIRE BUFFS, THE DUKE OF ALBANY'S),

died at Armentières on the 23rd October, 1914 (the official date being given as the 21st October), of wounds received in action on the 20th October during street fighting after the successful storming of the village of Frelinghien, three miles North-East of Armentières.

He was the son of the late Major-General C. M. Stockwell, C.B., Seaforth Highlanders, and was born on the 7th October, 1875, joining the Seaforth Highlanders in September, 1895, becoming Lieutenant in February, 1898. He took part in the Nile Expedition of 1898, being present at the Battles of the Atbara and Khartoum. He received the British medal and the Egyptian medal with two clasps. From December, 1899, to December, 1909, he was employed with the Egyptian Army, during which period he was on service in the Soudan in 1900–02, on the reoccupation of the Bahr-el-Ghazal Province, receiving a clasp to his Egyptian medal.

He was promoted Captain in March, 1901, and from April, 1911, to April, 1914, was an Adjutant of the Territorial Force, obtaining his Majority in September, 1914.

For his services in the Great War Major Stockwell was mentioned in Sir John French's Despatch of the 14th January, 1915.

CAPTAIN FREDERICK WILLIAM STODDART, 1st BATTN. THE DUKE OF EDINBURGH'S (WILTSHIRE REGT.),

born at Stowe Hill, Hartest, Suffolk, was the son of Colonel Stoddart, Madras Staff Corps.

He was born on the 1st July, 1871, was educated at Bedford Grammar School, and after serving five years in the ranks of the Royal Inniskilling Fusiliers received his commission in the Wiltshire Regiment in 1895, becoming Lieutenant in 1897, and spending several years in India with the 1st Battalion.

He served for five years from January, 1900, to January, 1905, in the Chinese Regiment at Wei-Hai-Wei, and took part in the relief of Pekin, 1900, for which he received the medal with clasp. From September, 1908, to October, 1912, he was Adjutant of the 4th (Territorial) Battalion Welsh Regiment.

In England he was stationed with the 2nd Battalion of his regiment at Pembroke Dock, afterwards rejoining the 1st Battalion at Tidworth.

He was killed on the 27th October, 1914, at Neuve Chapelle, his battalion forming part of the 7th Infantry Brigade (IIIrd Division) of the Expeditionary Force, which left England on the 13th August, 1914, for the front.

Captain Stoddart's company became sur-

rounded, but he would not surrender, and was shot down by the enemy.

He had been awarded the Legion of Honour for special gallantry during the operations between the 21st and 30th August.

He married Marguerite Fanny, youngest daughter of the late Major Arthur Wellesley Williams, late 10th Hussars and 12th Lancers, and a granddaughter of Sir Robert Williams, Bart., of Friars, Anglesea, North Wales. Two children survive him: Rose Marguerite Lena, nine years old, born while her father was at Pembroke Dock; and Nigel, two years old, born at Tidworth. His elder son—Frederick Norman Llewellyn, born the 18th February, 1908—died the 3rd October, 1909, at Haverfordwest, South Wales.

2nd LIEUTENANT ELLIS ROBERT CUNLIFFE STONE, 2nd BATTN. ROYAL WELSH FUSILIERS,

who was killed in the trenches on the 25th October, 1914, was the son of Mr. H. J. Stone, of Bedfords, Havering-atte-Bower, Essex, and Mrs. Stone, second daughter of Mr. Ellis Brooke Cunliffe, of Petton Park, Shropshire.

He was born in 1893, and was educated at Malvern College (1907–12), Lower Shell (Army I). There he was a School Prefect, and in his House Cricket XI. From Malvern he went to the R.M.C., Sandhurst, from which he was gazetted to the Royal Welsh Fusiliers in August, 1914.

His C.O. described him as "one of the finest young officers I have ever had under my command," and added: "He was absolutely fearless and dashing to a degree. He behaved with exceptional gallantry, and handled his men with great skill on the Marne. I had every intention of sending in a special report on him on account of the excellent work he did on several occasions." ("The Malvernian," December, 1914.)

2nd LIEUTENANT HARRY HILTON STOREY, 2nd BATTN. DURHAM LIGHT INFANTRY,

son of the late Mr. Thomas Storey, of Shildon, County Durham, was born at that place on the 12th January, 1875.

He joined the Army in the ranks in September, 1894, and served eighteen years in India, returning home in January, 1914. He proceeded to France with his battalion in September, and was given his commission as 2nd Lieutenant in September, 1914. On the 13th October, 1914, he was killed by a bullet passing through the head while he was leading his platoon at Merris, near Hazebrouck, France.

MAJOR PERCY BELCHER STRAFFORD, 2nd BATTN. THE DUKE OF WELLING-TON'S (WEST RIDING REGIMENT),

son of the late Robert James Strafford and his wife, Louisa Mary (*née* Belcher), was born at St. Michael's Hamlet, Liverpool, on the 10th October, 1872. He was educated at Malvern College, where he was a brilliant football back in the XI, and was also in the Cricket XXII.

Passing out of the R.M.C., Sandhurst, which he entered in 1890, he was gazetted to the 1st Battalion the Duke of Wellington's Regiment (the old 33rd) in July, 1892, becoming Lieutenant in November, 1895, and Captain in February, 1900. He served with his battalion all through the Boer War from 1899–1902, being present at the relief of Kimberley ; in the Orange Free State he took part in the actions of Paardeberg, Poplar Grove, and Driefontein, and subsequently in operations in the Transvaal. He was twice mentioned in despatches (September, 1901, and July, 1902), and was awarded the Queen's medal with four clasps and the King's medal with two clasps.

Major Strafford, who attained that rank in November, 1909, and was posted to the 2nd Battalion on promotion, was killed instantaneously at the Battle of Mons on the 24th August, 1914, by a bullet, which pierced his temple, while he was leading and inspiring his men to the last. He was mentioned in Sir John French's Despatch of the 8th October, 1914.

In his younger days, and at Sandhurst, Major Strafford was a brilliant footballer ; while latterly he was very keen on cricket, being captain of the regimental team, and taking a prominent place in all garrison and regimental matches. He also played for the Yorkshire Gentlemen when stationed in that county, being a first-rate bat and wicket-keeper.

He married Edith Mabel, younger daughter of Major-General Hamilton Chapman, late 8th Cavalry, and left two children : Jennie Constance, born June, 1907 ; and Orrell Hamilton, born July, 1910.

CAPTAIN CHARLES ERIC STRAHAN, 2nd BATTN. THE BLACK WATCH (ROYAL HIGHLANDERS),

born in Mussoorie, India, on the 1st April, 1883, was the son of Lieutenant-General Charles Strahan, Colonel-Commandant Royal (late Bengal) Engineers, late Surveyor-General of India, and a grandson of the late General A. Dick, of the Indian Army. Through his mother he was also related to the late Sir Robert Dick, who was killed at Sobraon while in command of the 42nd Highlanders (Black Watch).

He was educated at Harrow and the R.M.C., Sandhurst, from which he received his commission in the Black Watch in January, 1902, being posted to the 1st Battalion, which he joined in South Africa during the Boer War. He was present at operations in the Orange River and Cape Colonies, for which he received the Queen's medal with two clasps. At the end of the South African War he returned to England and was promoted Lieutenant in May, 1906, and in September, 1909, was appointed Staff Officer to the local forces in the Windward Islands, an appointment he held till October, 1912, when he returned to England. For some months he was at the depot of his regiment at Perth, and in January, 1913, joined the 2nd Battalion in India. He was promoted Captain in May, 1914.

When the war with Germany broke out he was sent on in advance as billeting officer, his work, however, being principally to arrange for taking on lease houses for hospitals and permanent quarters. Colonel Fasken, under whose orders he was then serving, expressed himself as being thoroughly satisfied with the way in which he did his work, and sent in his name to Sir J. Willcocks for mention. After the arrival of the troops from India he rejoined his battalion at the front, and was shot on the 28th November, 1914, while on duty in the trenches a few miles from Bethune, where he was buried. He had been made a Staff Officer a few days before his death.

He was a good rider, a very keen golf player, and a good shot.

LIEUTENANT HOWARD BERTIE STRONG, 1st BATTN. THE QUEEN'S (ROYAL WEST SURREY REGIMENT),

who was killed in action north of Gheluvelt, near Ypres, on the 30th October, 1914, was the only son of Mr. and Mrs. E. Howard Strong, and was born at Sutton, Surrey, on the

15th August, 1892. He was educated at The College, Epsom, Surrey, where he was in the first Football XV, the Fives team, and the O.T.C. For two years he served in the Special Reserve of the Queen's, becoming 2nd Lieutenant in the 1st Battalion in December, 1912. He was interested in flying, and took his certificate at Brooklands in August, 1913. He was a member of the Junior Army and Navy Club.

While at the front in the Great War he was promoted to his Lieutenancy in September, 1914. He was present at the Battles of Mons, the Aisne, and the Marne, and when he was killed he was acting as Captain of "C" Company.

LIEUTENANT CECIL EDGAR STUART, 2nd BATTN. LANCASHIRE FUSILIERS,

son of Francis Stuart, Civil Engineer, was born in London in 1887.

He was educated at Ealing, afterwards in Australia, Tasmania, and in Argentina, and was a Spanish scholar. He joined the Lancashire Fusiliers as 2nd Lieutenant in May, 1910, and served as Lieutenant in the Southern Nigerian Regiment from 1911–14. In August of the latter year he rejoined his regiment in which he was promoted Lieutenant to date from July, 1914, receiving his commission in the Lancashire Fusiliers.

He was killed in September, 1914, during the Battle of the Aisne.

LIEUTENANT JAMES STIRLING STUART, 1st BATTN. SCOTS GUARDS,

who was once wounded in the Battle of the Aisne on the 14th September, but rejoined after recovery, and who died on the 9th November, 1914, of wounds received in action that same day at Ypres, aged twenty-three, was the elder son of William Stirling Stuart, of Castlemilk, Lanarkshire.

He was born in 1891, and after being at Eton and Christ Church, Oxford, where he took his degree, was gazetted to the Territorial Force in July, 1912. On the outbreak of war he was gazetted 2nd Lieutenant in the Scots Guards, with antedate, as a University Candidate, to January, 1913, and was promoted Lieutenant on the 17th September, 1914, the notification appearing in the "London Gazette" of the 26th November, 1914, after his death.

MAJOR HUMPHREY ST. LEGER STUCLEY, 1st BATTN. GRENADIER GUARDS,

was the youngest son of the late Sir George Stucley, first Bart., of Moreton, and of Lady Stucley, Bideford, and was born on the 7th June, 1877.

He was educated at Eton and the R.M.C., Sandhurst. He joined the 1st Battalion Grenadier Guards in July, 1897, and served with it in the Egyptian Campaign of 1898, being present at the Battle of Khartoum, and receiving the Egyptian medal with clasp. He became Lieutenant in December, 1898; Captain in May, 1904; and Major in February, 1912.

With the 2nd Battalion he served throughout the Boer War, 1900–02, having been present at operations in the Orange Free State; in Orange River Colony, including actions at Biddulphsberg and Wittebergen; and in the Transvaal. He received the Queen's medal with three clasps and the King's medal with two clasps.

From September, 1902, to February, 1905, he was Adjutant of his battalion, and from February, 1906, to February, 1907, was Commandant of the School for Volunteer officers at Chelsea Barracks.

He proceeded to Belgium with the VIIth Division on the 4th October, 1914, as Second in Command of the 1st Battalion, and fell at the head of the King's Company in action against the Germans at Kruiseik in the Battle of Ypres on the 29th October, 1914. For his services in the Great War Major Stucley was mentioned in Sir John French's Despatch of the 14th January, 1915.

Major Stucley married Rose, daughter of the late Francis Carew, of Collipriest, Tiverton. He left two sons: Peter Francis Carew, born 10th August, 1909; and Lewis Robert Carew, born 14th December, 1910.

2nd LIEUTENANT LOGAN STUDLEY, 1st BATTN. EAST YORKSHIRE REGT., who was killed in action on the 25th October, 1914, was gazetted to the East Yorkshire Regiment in October, 1914, from the ranks of the Yorkshire Regiment, in which he was a Lance-Corporal.

LIEUTENANT FREDERICK ERNEST STYLES, SPECIAL RESERVE, ROYAL MUNSTER FUSILIERS,

who was killed in action on the 27th August, 1914, at Etreux, France, was the eldest son of the late Mr. Frederick Styles and of Mrs. Styles, of Blackmoor, Four Elms.

He was born in 1884, and was educated at Harrow and the R.M.C., Sandhurst, obtaining his first commission in 1903, and receiving his promotion to Lieutenant in 1906. He retired from the active list in April, 1914, going into the Special Reserve, but rejoined the 2nd Battalion of his regiment on the outbreak of the war.

The Adjutant of the regiment, who was taken a prisoner of war on the day of Lieutenant Styles's death, wrote to Mrs. Styles, under date the 31st August, 1914, as follows : " You will already have heard that poor Fred was shot on Thursday, the 27th inst. At the time he was gallantly leading his men under a heavy fire, and had he survived would certainly have been mentioned in despatches. I was not actually present when he was hit, but I have been told by those who were on the spot that his death was painless and instantaneous. When I saw him a few minutes later he was lying peacefully as though asleep. As this letter will be censored by the German authorities I am unable to give you any details as to the action or the situation of the battlefield. All the officers who fell were buried in one grave, and a service was conducted by a German clergyman. Fred's loss is infinitely regretted by all of us who survive, and I wish to convey to you, on behalf of the regiment, the utmost sympathy of all ranks with Miss Styles and yourself."

2nd LIEUTENANT PHILIP HAMILTON SULIVAN, 1st BATTN. ROYAL MUNSTER FUSILIERS, was born at Mayfield Hall, Ashbourne, Derbyshire, on the 27th August, 1894, the son of Colonel and Mrs. E. F. Sulivan, of Wilmington, Woking.

He was educated at Malvern College and the R.M.C., Sandhurst, from which he was

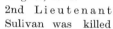

gazetted to the Royal Munster Fusiliers in February, 1914. He was attached to the 2nd Battalion at Aldershot, and proceeded with it to Belgium for active service on the 13th August, 1914.

2nd Lieutenant Sulivan was killed near Etreux, France, on the 27th August, 1914, during the retirement from Mons.

2nd LIEUTENANT CHARLES GORDON VILLIERS SURTEES, 2nd BATTN. THE BORDER REGIMENT, who was unofficially reported to have been killed in action on the 26th October, 1914, was born on the 13th February, 1892, and was gazetted to the Army in January, 1913.

2nd LIEUTENANT HENRY POYNTZ SWAINE, 2nd BATTN. ROYAL IRISH RIFLES, whose name was included as killed in action in the official list of casualties published by the War Office on the 9th October, 1914, was the elder son of Colonel A. T. Swaine, late Royal Irish Rifles, and Mrs. Swaine, Morris

Lodge, Farnham, and was born on the 31st March, 1890.

He joined the Royal Irish Rifles as 2nd Lieutenant on the 5th October, 1910.

LIEUTENANT-COLONEL CHARLES OLIVER SWANSTON, D.S.O., p.s.c., q.s., COMMANDANT 34th PRINCE ALBERT VICTOR'S OWN POONA HORSE, born at Cuddalore, Southern India, on the 8th April, 1865, was the son of the late Major-General William Oliver Swanston, Madras Staff Corps who served as a Trooper in Havelock's Volunteer Cavalry in the

Indian Mutiny. His grandfather was the late Captain Charles Swanston, who raised one thousand men for the Poona Auxiliary Horse ; and he was a great-grandnephew of Horatio Lord Nelson, his mother being a granddaughter of Mrs. Kitty Matcham.

Educated privately and at the R.M.C., Sandhurst, he was gazetted to the Royal Irish Fusiliers in May, 1885. Promoted Lieutenant in 1887, he was transferred to the Indian Army. He served on the Staff in the Tirah Campaign of 1897–98, for which he was mentioned in despatches ("London Gazette," 5th April, 1898), and received the medal with two clasps. He was appointed D.A.Q.M.G. with the Waziristan Expedition, 1901–02, for which he was awarded the D.S.O., received an additional clasp to his former medal, and was mentioned in despatches ("London Gazette," 8th August, 1902).

In 1902 he took part in the operations against the Darwesh Khel Waziris, acting as Staff Officer to the General Officer Commanding, and was again mentioned in despatches ("London Gazette," 5th June, 1903).

He was on the Headquarters Staff as D.A.Q.M.G. in the Somaliland Campaign of 1903–04, for which he received the medal with two clasps, and was mentioned in despatches ("London Gazette," 2nd September, 1904). In 1905 Lieutenant-Colonel Swanston passed the final examination of the Staff College and in 1910 was placed on the list of officers considered qualified for staff employment for service in the field.

He was promoted Major in May, 1906, and reached the rank of Lieutenant-Colonel in May, 1911, being appointed Second in Command of the 34th Poona Horse from the Bengal Lancers in 1914, and while serving on the General Staff succeeded to the command of his regiment in April of the same year.

He was killed on the 2nd November, 1914, near Neuve Chapelle, while at the head of his regiment, which had been ordered up to the support of some of our trenches.

Lieutenant-Colonel Swanston, who was a member of the Cavalry Club, was a fine horseman, and won many flat races in India. He married Miss Kathleen Bruce Johnston, daughter of the late Bruce Johnston, Esq., Writer to the Signet, of Edinburgh. His wife, however, predeceased him, and he left no family.

LIEUTENANT RUSSELL KEN-NETH SWANWICK, 3rd (attd. 1st) BATTN. GLOUCESTERSHIRE REGT., born on the 27th September, 1884, was the son of Russell Swanwick, of Cirencester.

He was educated at Uppingham and Trinity College, Cambridge. While at the University he joined the Cambridge University Mounted

Infantry, and later the Officers' Training Corps of the Royal Agricultural College, Cirencester, from which he obtained his commission in the 3rd Battalion Gloucestershire Regiment (Special Reserve of Officers), being gazetted Lieutenant in August, 1913.

On the outbreak of the war he was attached to the 1st Battalion, which left England with the 1st Expeditionary Force on the 14th August, 1914. He was killed on the 14th September, 1914, near Troyon, on the Aisne, while leading his platoon to the help of his hard-pressed comrades under heavy fire, and died cheering on his men.

He was a keen sportsman, and was well known in the hunting field as a plucky rider.

LIEUTENANT EDMUND SWETENHAM, 2nd BATTN. THE DURHAM LIGHT INFANTRY, only son of Clement William Swetenham, Lieutenant, R. N. (retired), of Somerford Booths, Congleton, Cheshire, was born there on the 30th April, 1890. He entered the R.M.C., Sandhurst, from Eastman's R.N. Academy and

Army School, Stratford - on - Avon, and was gazetted to the Durham Light Infantry on leaving Sandhurst in April, 1910, becoming Lieutenant in January, 1914.

While serving with his battalion in France, he was shot by a sniper in the trenches at Rue de Bois, near Armentières, on the 27th October, 1914.

Lieutenant Swetenham was a member of the Junior United Service Club.

MAJOR FOSTER SWETENHAM, 2nd DRAGOONS (ROYAL SCOTS GREYS), born on the 21st June, 1876, at Cam-yr-Alyn, Rossett, Denbighshire, was the son of the late Edmund Swetenham, Q.C., M.P. for Carnarvon Burghs, of Cam-yr-Alyn, Rossett, and a grandson of the late Clement Swetenham, of Somerford Booths, Congleton, Cheshire.

After leaving Eton, where he was educated, he joined the Militia, and from it was appointed to the Scots Greys as 2nd Lieutenant in December, 1896, becoming Lieutenant in April, 1899,

and obtaining his troop in November, 1901. He took part in the South African War, being present at the relief of Kimberley, and actions at Paardeberg, Poplar Grove, Driefontein, and Karee Siding, for which he received the Queen's medal with three clasps. From 1906–11 he was Adjutant of the Ayrshire Yeomanry, and obtained his Majority in December of the latter year.

In the Great War, while directing the fire of his men in dismounted action near St. Quentin on the 28th August, 1914, during the retirement from Mons, he was shot through the heart.

Major Swetenham was an accomplished horseman and fine rider to hounds ; a keen polo player, being in the regimental team in South Africa ; rode in steeplechases and point-to-point races, in which he was very successful, establishing a record by winning for four years in succession the " Grey Horse Race " (a regimental point-to-point) on the same horse, his charger " Robert."

Major Swetenham married, in 1908, Muriel Gladys, daughter of Colonel J. W. Chaplin, V.C., C.B., of Kibworth Hall, Leicester, and left three children : John Edmund, born 1909 ; Anthony Clement, born 1911 ; and Vanda Gertrude Isabel, born 1912.

He was a member of the Carlton, Ranelagh, and Cavalry Clubs.

LIEUTENANT JAMES HUBERT SWORD, 4th (QUEEN'S OWN) HUSSARS,

son of F. Sword, "Teneriffe," Eastbourne, was born in the Argentine Republic on the 20th December, 1892.

He was educated at The Grange, Eastbourne; and at Osborne College and Dartmouth, at both of which latter places he was made Cadet Captain. He went afterwards as a Midshipman on H.M.S. " Vanguard " and H.M.S. " Defence." He left the Navy in November, 1911, and in September, 1912, went to the R.M.C., Sandhurst, where he

got a Prize Cadetship and passed out third in July, 1913. He obtained his commission in the 4th Hussars n September, 1913, joining the following month. He was promoted Lieutenant in August, 1914.

Lieutenant Sword embarked with his regiment for the Continent in August and was killed on the 10th September, 1914, when out reconnoitring in command of a small patrol at the Battle of the Marne. He discovered a large body of the enemy, and sent in a report, which enabled them to be surrounded and destroyed the same afternoon.

MAJOR JOHN FREDERICK LODER-SYMONDS, 1st BATTN. SOUTH STAFFORDSHIRE REGIMENT,

who was killed in action on the 31st October, 1914, was the eldest son of Captain F. C. Loder-Symonds, J.P., of Hinton Manor, Berks, late Royal Artillery.

He was born on the 23rd December, 1873, at Dharwar, India ; educated at Eton ; and joined the South Staffordshire Regiment from the Militia in June, 1894, becoming Lieutenant in 1896. From July, 1899, to August, 1900, he was employed with the West African Frontier Force, being on active service in 1900 in Northern Nigeria, where he was dangerously wounded. He was mentioned in despatches (" London Gazette," 16th April, 1901), and was promoted Captain in June of that year.

From August, 1903, to August, 1906, he was Adjutant of the 4th (Volunteer) Battalion the King's Liverpool Regiment, and obtained his Majority in September, 1911.

The 1st Battalion South Staffordshire Regiment was brought home to England from Natal to take part in the Great War, leaving for Belgium on the 4th October. During the first Battle of Ypres Major Loder-Symonds was killed instantly with several brother officers on the 31st October, 1914, while in command of the battalion.

He married, in 1907, Mary Josephine, daughter of Sir William Vavasour, Bart., and left no issue.

LIEUTENANT HAROLD ARTHUR TAGG, 4th BATTN. THE DUKE OF CAMBRIDGE'S OWN (MIDDLESEX REGIMENT), was the son of Captain

James Tagg, A.V.C. (attached at the front to the 1st Life Guards) and Mrs. Alice Tagg, and

was born at High Wycombe on the 6th December, 1893. Lieutenant Tagg was educated at Victoria College, Jersey ; and Bedford Grammar School, whence he won a Prize Cadetship at the R.M.C., Sandhurst, at the end of 1911. Entering the R.M.C. in 1912, he obtained his commission in the 4th Middlesex Regiment on the 5th February, 1913.

He served with the Expeditionary Force through the St. Quentin and Mons engagements, the retirement, and subsequent advance to the Aisne and the Marne.

On the 14th October, 1914, while marching with his men through a village towards the line of the Yser, then occupied, he was shot by a sniper from a window, between Lille and Béthune.

Lieutenant Tagg was an enthusiastic egg-collector, and had a very good collection of British birds' eggs collected from nests by himself. At Bedford College he played half in the second Rugby team, and had his colours for that team.

2nd LIEUTENANT HENRY FREDERICK THORNTON RENNY-TAILYOUR, ROYAL ENGINEERS,

was the son of Colonel H. W. Renny - Tailyour (late R.E.), of Newmanswalls, Montrose, Forfarshire, Scotland, and was born at Homebush, Sydney, New South Wales, Australia, on the 31st July, 1893. He was educated at Arnold House, Llanddulas, North Wales, and Rugby, whence he proceeded to the Royal Military Academy, Woolwich. While there he was successful in athletics, winning the mile race, and running second in the two-mile.

He joined the R.E. in December, 1912, and went to France from the School of Military Engineering, Chatham, having been posted to the 5th Field Company, R.E., forming part of the IInd Division, 1st Army Corps. He went through the retirement from Mons, the advance to the Marne, the Battle of the Aisne, and the Battle of Ypres.

He was mentioned in Sir John French's Despatch of the 14th January, 1915, for gallant conduct in the field.

On the 14th September he was wounded during the Battle of the Aisne, but remained on duty. He was killed near Ypres on the 11th November, 1914, while leading his section in a successful counter attack on a German trench held by the Prussian Guard.

LIEUTENANT ERIC LAWRENCE TALBOT, ROYAL HORSE ARTILLERY,

who died in the ambulance between Klein Zillebeke and Ypres on the 24th October, 1914, from wounds received the previous day at Zandvoorde, was the son of the late John Arthur and Alice Buckley Talbot, and was born on the 15th December, 1883, at Milford Hall, Newtown, Montgomeryshire.

After having been educated at Marlborough College he proceeded to the R.M.A., Woolwich, whence he received a commission in the R.F.A. in July, 1902, being posted to the 50th Battery, then stationed at Woolwich, and subsequently served in Ireland. He became Lieutenant in 1905, and in 1908 exchanged to the 58th Battery R.F.A., quartered at Neemuch, India. In July, 1910, he was transferred to " T " Battery R.H.A. at Ambala, moving with it to Abbassiyeh, Egypt. After being for a time at the depot at Woolwich he was posted to " P " Battery.

At the beginning of the war he volunteered for active service, and was appointed to " C " Battery, with which he was serving when he was killed.

Lieutenant Talbot was Master of the R.A. Draghounds, Woolwich, from 1912 to 1914.

LIEUTENANT HUMFREY RICHARD TALBOT, 3rd (PRINCE OF WALES'S) DRAGOON GUARDS,

who was killed in action on the 14th November, 1914, was the youngest son of Gustavus and Susan Talbot, of Marchmont House, Hemel Hempstead.

He was born on the 11th September, 1889, and was educated at Wellington (Anglesey, 1903–06).

He was gazetted to the Liverpool Regiment from the Special Reserve in December, 1909, and was promoted Lieutenant in September, 1912. In February, 1913, he was transferred to the 3rd Dragoon Guards.

LIEUTENANT ARCHDALE MAURICE STRATFORD TANDY, 2nd BATTN. ROYAL IRISH REGIMENT, who was killed in action on the 20th October, 1914, at Le Pilly, France, was the younger son of Colonel H. Stratford Tandy, Indian Army, and was born on the 17th December, 1890.

He was educated at Cheltenham College, which he entered at Easter, 1905, was gazetted to the Royal Irish Rifles in March, 1911, and was promoted Lieutenant in February, 1914.

CAPTAIN RALPH EYRE TANNER, 1st BATTN. THE KING'S (LIVERPOOL REGIMENT),

was the elder son of Ralph Tanner, M.A., Senior Assistant Master of Westminster School, of 2, Little Dean's Yard, Westminster Abbey, S.W., and Lucy Lawrence Le Grice, daughter, of George Lewis Phipps Eyre, and was born at 18, Cumberland Terrace, Regent's Park, on the 16th July, 1885. Captain Tanner was a great-nephew of the late Major-General Edward Tanner, C.B., formerly commanding the King's (Liverpool Regiment). He was educated at Westminster, where he was in Grant's House from 1898–1903 ; and at the Royal Military College, Sandhurst, from 1904–05, receiving his commission as 2nd Lieutenant in the King's in August, 1905. He became Lieutenant in 1908, and from that year till 1910 served in India. He obtained his company in September, 1912.

On the 14th September, while leading his men through a wood during the Battle of the Aisne in this war, he was wounded, and died at Versailles from the effects on the 23rd September, 1914.

His Commanding Officer—Lieutenant-Colonel Bannatyne—himself afterwards killed in action, wrote of Captain Tanner : " We in the regiment are sustained by the knowledge that he met his death while leading the van in a magnificent attack on the enemy, who were holding an enormously strong position. The regiment was advanced guard to the whole division, and he . . . most gallantly sustained the honour of the King's. Our great sorrow at his loss will consequently be mingled with pride at his most gallant conduct."

Captain Tanner married, in Westminster Abbey in June, 1913, Edith Vere Marjorie, daughter of John Henry Brodie, formerly of Chart's Edge, Westerham, Kent, and left one son— Peter Ralph Eyre—born 13th September, 1914.

MAJOR HAROLD TATUM, 101st GRENADIERS, INDIAN ARMY,

was the eldest son of the late Commissary-General Henry Tatum, C.B., and a grandson of Captain William Tatum, Royal Inniskilling Fusiliers, Military Secretary at Barbados. He was born on the 24th May, 1874, at 52, Westbourne Park Road, London, W.

He was educated at Bedford Grammar School, where he was in the Shooting Eight, shot for the School at Bisley, and won the cup for the Crescent House Steeplechase in 1892 ; and subsequently went to the R.M.C., Sandhurst, out of which he passed in the ninth place.

Major Tatum was gazetted to the K.O. Yorkshire Light Infantry in 1894, and became Lieutenant in 1897. In 1899 he joined the Indian Army, in which he became Captain in 1903, and Major in 1912. He served on the north-western frontier of India, with the Tirah Expeditionary Force in 1897–98, and again at Waziristan in 1901. For his services he obtained the medal with three clasps.

In the Great War Major Tatum was serving with his regiment in German East Africa. The Indian troops sailed from Bombay in October, 1914, and arrived off Tanga, where they were to land on the 2nd November. The German Governor refused to surrender when called upon to do so, Tanga having been believed to be an undefended town, and the British troops were landed by 9 a.m. on the 4th November. The advance began at 2.30 p.m., and the troops came under heavy rifle and machine-gun fire. Owing to the surrounding bush it was not possible to secure support from our artillery on shore, so the guns were left on board and fired from the deck of a transport in the outer harbour. The 101st Grenadiers, making an effort to fill a gap in the firing line, due to the difficulty of an even advance through the bush, came under a heavy cross-fire, and darkness coming on it was deemed advisable to withdraw our forces to an entrenched position, and later to re-embark them.

No details of Major Tatum's actual death were procurable. A former Commanding Officer considered him a man of marked ability, and said he had seldom met a better soldier or one who knew his profession better. He was a splendid regimental officer, and though recommended for it he would not accept Staff employ. Major Tatum was not married.

CAPTAIN HUGH TAYLOR, 2nd BATTN. SCOTS GUARDS,

was the elder son of Mr. and Mrs. Taylor, of Chipchase Castle, Northumberland, and was born on the 24th December, 1880.

He was educated at Harrow and at Balliol College, Oxford, where he graduated with honours. He joined the Scots Guards in June, 1904, becoming Lieutenant in May, 1905, and Captain in November, 1914. Previous to the war he was Machine Gun Officer of his battalion, and on going to the front he became Brigade Machine Gun Officer.

He led his company in an attack near Rouges Bancs on the night of the 18th–19th December, 1914, and succeeded in reaching and occupying part of the German trenches. He returned alone to the British trenches to report, and while going back to rejoin his men was caught by machine-gun fire and killed instantaneously. During the informal Christmas truce his body, which was lying near the German trenches, was brought over to the British lines by the Saxon soldiers with their heads bared, and was buried in the little military graveyard at La Cardonière Farm.

He was mentioned in Field-Marshal Sir John French's Despatch of the 14th January, 1915, for gallant and distinguished conduct.

It is interesting to note that on Christmas Day, when the Saxons and British soldiers met during their " truce," each side collected and brought the dead to the centre of the space between their respective lines. Two trenches were dug, and the British and Saxon soldiers were buried, the English Chaplain reading the service, which was translated into German as he read. The soldiers afterwards fraternised for some hours.

Captain Taylor married, in 1907, Mary, daughter of Mr. Henry Villiers Stuart, of Dromana, and left a son and a daughter.

CAPTAIN GEORGE RYEFIELD TAYLOUR, 2nd BATTN. ROYAL WARWICKSHIRE REGIMENT,

about whose fate there was for many months much uncertainty, was the son of the late Major-General Lord John Taylour and Lady John Taylour, 39, Argyll Road, Kensington, W., and a grandson of the second Marquess of Headfort, K.P.

He was born at the Curragh Camp, Ireland, on the 13th February, 1875, and was educated at Summerfields, Oxford, and Wellington College. He joined the 3rd Battalion Bedfordshire Militia

from which he was gazetted to the Royal Warwickshire Regiment in May, 1897, becoming Lieutenant in June, 1898, and Captain in February, 1901.

He took part in the South African War, being present at operations in the Orange Free State and the Transvaal, including actions at Vet and Zand Rivers, near Johannesburg, at Pretoria, Diamond Hill, and Belfast. He was twice mentioned in despatches (" London Gazette," 7th May and 10th September, 1901), and received the Queen's medal with six clasps. In that war he was slightly wounded in an attack on a hospital train near Pan, and was captured after a gallant defence.

In November, 1912, he proceeded with his battalion to Malta, when he was sent to Albania in command of the British Detachment of the International Force at Scutari.

A letter giving the following information, derived from a German source, was received by Captain Taylour's relatives : " We are told that Captain Taylour was killed about the 22nd October of last year (1914) by three bullets of a shrapnel shell, when charging in front of his men near Menin, in Belgium, not far from Ypres. He died as a very brave soldier."

Captain Taylour, who was a member of the United Service Club, was well known in the Army as a keen amateur heavyweight boxer.

LIEUTENANT AMBROSE MARY ANTHONY ITURDIDE DE LONE TEELING, 3rd BATTN. NORFOLK REGIMENT,

who was killed in action on the 24th September, 1914, at the Battle of the Aisne, aged twenty-two years, was the youngest son of Captain Bartholomew Teeling, Private Chamberlain to the Pope and Pontifical Zouave.

He was born in Bordighera in 1892, and was educated by the Benedictines in England and the Jesuits in France. He was gazetted 2nd Lieutenant in January, 1910, becoming Lieutenant in his battalion in July, 1912.

CAPTAIN ARTHUR HILLIARD WILLIAMS TEMPLE, RESERVE OF OFFICERS, attd. 2nd BATTN. SUFFOLK REGIMENT,

was killed in action at Kemmel on the 14th December, 1914.

The second son of the Rev. C. Temple, Rector of Thorpe Morieux, Suffolk, he was born on the 12th January, 1875 ; was educated at King's School, Canterbury ; and received his first commission in the Suffolk Regiment in December, 1897, being promoted Lieutenant in January, 1900. He took part in the South African War, in which he was employed with the Mounted Infantry, and was present at operations in the Transvaal, Orange River Colony, and Cape Colony, including action at Colesberg. He received the Queen's medal with three clasps and the King's medal with two clasps. After the Boer War he was seconded for service in Somaliland with the King's African Rifles.

He was promoted Captain in April, 1905, and retired from the active list with that rank, joining the Reserve of Officers in February, 1913. On the outbreak of war he rejoined his old regiment, and was attached to the 2nd Battalion which formed part of the 14th Infantry Brigade, Vth Division.

A Private in the battalion, writing to his sister, said of Captain Temple : " It was in the trenches that we lost our beloved Captain—Captain Temple. He was loved and respected by all— those who served with him in South Africa, also in this campaign. The kindness he showed to our company when they came from the trenches, sodden wet through, giving us new socks and other articles of clothing which his wife had sent out to him for his company, we shall never forget. I have seen him when meeting refugees put his hand in his pocket and assist them. No one knew what he gave. He did not believe in show. A shell burst in the trenches in which I was lying, and the Captain came up and enquired if anyone was hurt. His cheery remarks always gave us inspiration, and when the word was passed round that he was wounded, and subsequently that he had died, there was grief among all — officers and men. He was fearless, brave, and self-sacrificing under all conditions, and was never satisfied until he had done his very best for all. He will be missed by all who came in contact with him."

He was mentioned in Sir John French's Despatch of the 14th January, 1915.

Captain Temple married, in October, 1909, Enid Adela Powys, daughter of Percy G. Stone, of Merstone, Isle of Wight, and left a son and a daughter. He was a fine big-game shot, and collected many trophies from India and Africa.

CAPTAIN WILLIAM ARTHUR MOULD TEMPLE, 1st BATTN. GLOUCESTERSHIRE REGIMENT,

born at the officers' quarters, Woolwich Arsenal, on the 14th June, 1872, was the eldest son of Lieutenant - Colonel W. Temple, V.C., late A.M.S., and a grandson of the late Major - General Mould, C.B., R.E.

He was educated at Portsmouth Grammar School ; at Brussels ; and at the R.M.C., Sandhurst, winning medals for running while at school, and being a good football player.

He was gazetted on the 19th July, 1893, joining his regiment at Aldershot the following month, and serving in Malta, Egypt, India, Ceylon, and South Africa, where he took part in the Boer War, being present at the actions of Rietfontein and Lombard's Kop, and at operations in the Transvaal and Orange River Colony, for which he received the Queen's medal with three clasps. He was promoted Lieutenant in March, 1897, and Captain in May, 1903.

During the Great War he was wounded in the right lung at Koekuit, near Langemarck, Belgium, on the 21st October, 1914, and died the next day at Poperinghe in No. 4 Clearing Hospital.

Captain Temple married Rhoda Mary Hebe, daughter of J. P. L. Hazledine, Esq., Barrister-at-Law, Inner Temple, of Bragborough Hall, Northamptonshire, at one time J.P. for the County of Carnarvon. He left one daughter, Hazel Rhoda, born at Kasauli, India, in May, 1908.

CAPTAIN FREDERICK GEORGE THEOBALD, 1st BATTN. KING'S OWN (ROYAL LANCASTER REGIMENT),

who was killed in action on the 26th August near Le Cateau during the retirement from Mons, was the son of the Rev. Frederick Theobald, and was born at Drayton, Berkshire, on the 19th December, 1875.

He was educated at Haseley Manor, Oxford-shire, and at Harrow, joining the King's Own as 2nd Lieutenant from the Militia in April, 1900, becoming Lieutenant in 1901. He served in the South African War, 1899–1902, being present at operations in the Transvaal, for which he received the Queen's and the King's medals, each with two clasps. It was during this war that Captain Theobald distinguished himself by gallantly holding a dangerous post under heavy fire for twelve hours with only ten men, an incident which is referred to in Sir Conan Doyle's book, "The Great Boer War."

From July, 1905, to July, 1908, having in the meantime become Captain in July, 1907, he was Adjutant of the 2nd Battalion of his regiment, and from 1908 to 1913 was A.D.C. to the Governor and Commander-in-Chief, Ceylon. Captain Theobald was fond of motoring, hunting, and polo.

LIEUTENANT ALMA CYRIL THOMAS, 2nd BATTN. THE QUEEN'S (ROYAL WEST SURREY REGIMENT),

who died on the 8th November, 1914, of wounds received in action at Ypres, was the eldest son of Mrs. Bloor, Naval and Military Hotel, Harrington Road, London, S.W. He was born on the 9th August, 1891, and was educated at Clifton College and the R.M.C., Sandhurst, from which he was gazetted to the Royal West Surrey Regiment in March, 1911, becoming Lieutenant in February, 1913.

At the time of his death he was acting as Brigade-Major to the 22nd Brigade. The Staff were billeted in a house opposite Ypres Cathedral, and during the night the building over which shells had been passing for some time, was struck, and Lieutenant Thomas was wounded, and afterwards died in hospital at Poperinghe. These particulars were received from a soldier, and other accounts appear to confirm them.

Lieutenant Thomas was a member of the Junior Army and Navy Club.

CAPTAIN CHARLES HERBERT THOMAS, 2nd BATTN. SOUTH STAFFORDSHIRE REGIMENT,

who died in the Allies' Hospital at Boulogne on the 5th November, 1914, from wounds received

near Ypres on the 27th October, was the only son of Mr. and Mrs. Howard Thomas, of 10,

Westminster Palace Gardens, S.W., and was born at Charlton, near Bristol, in April, 1880. He was a grandson of Charles Thomas, of Pitch and Pay, Stone Bishop, Bristol.

Educated at Clifton, Abbotsholme, and Edinburgh University, he joined the 2nd Battalion of his regiment from the Militia in 1900, and was promoted Lieutenant in 1901. He took part in the South African War, being present at operations in the Cape Colony, south of the Orange River, for which he received the Queen's medal with clasp. Having obtained his Captaincy in 1909, he accompanied his battalion to France for the Great War, and for his services was mentioned in Sir John French's Despatch of the 14th January, 1915, after his death.

Captain Thomas married Dorothy Catherine, only daughter of Philip Everard, Miltons, Dulverton, and left one son, Charles Richard, born 15th June, 1913.

CAPTAIN DUNCAN COLLISSON WILLEY THOMAS, 4th BATTN. PRINCESS LOUISE'S (ARGYLL AND SUTHERLAND HIGHLANDERS), attd. 1st BATTN. GORDON HIGHLANDERS,

who was killed at the first Battle of Ypres on the 12th November, 1914, was the only son of Lieutenant-Colonel and Mrs. W. F. Thomas, the younger and junior branch of Ap Thomas, first Bart., of Wenvoe Castle,

Glamorganshire, Wales, and was born at Quilon, India, on the 19th November, 1890.

Captain Thomas was educated at Holm Leigh, Buxton; at Uppingham School; and at Caius College, Cambridge, proceeding subsequently to the R.M.C., Sandhurst. During his school and college career he won many prizes for athletics and sports. In February, 1911, he received a commission as 2nd Lieutenant in the Army Service Corps, and in April, 1914, he resigned from that corps, and joined the Special Reserve of the Argyll and Sutherland

Highlanders, becoming Lieutenant in August of that year.

On the outbreak of the Great War Captain Thomas was attached for active service to the 1st Battalion Gordon Highlanders, and was serving with them when he met his death. The battalion formed part of the 8th Brigade, IIIrd Division, and was present at the Battle of Mons and the subsequent fighting. He had been recommended for promotion in his own battalion in the hope that it would go out as a complete unit, but, before his promotion was gazetted, a draft of junior officers was called for, and Captain (then Lieutenant) Thomas was one of the four Subalterns selected to go. He became Captain on the 15th September, 1914.

An account of the circumstances attending his death was given by Captain Paterson, of the Gordon Highlanders : " Duncan (Captain Thomas) was back that day in some trenches in reserve to our position, which was at the time in the woods near Ypres. These reserve trenches were a line of small dug-outs roofed in with straw, and were very rarely shelled. Duncan, Captain K. B. McKenzie in the Seaforths, and 2nd Lieutenant Cook in the 3rd Black Watch were in the same dug-out. A shell burst right on the top, one of these big 60-lb. high-explosives. The trench was completely buried. Their Company Sergeant-Major and their cook— Private Huggins—dug them out at once, but found that Duncan had been struck on the head by a piece of shell, and McKenzie was dead too, either from shock or suffocation. Cook was untouched, but had concussion of the brain. I believe he may recover. They were buried together in a place quite close."

Though Captain Thomas had been such a short time with the Gordon Highlanders he had already made many friends, for, as one of his young brother officers said, " it would have been difficult for anyone *not* to get on well with him." From his old masters, too, Lieutenant-Colonel Thomas received sympathetic and appreciatory letters.

A letter of the officer promoted to the command of the Gordon Highlanders indicated the appalling losses in officers we are suffering in this war. Writing in March, 1915, he said : " Since I took command on the 1st November no less than fifty-two officers have served under me at various times, and of these thirty-two have come and gone, and yet I have never at one time had more than eighteen officers present. Of the seventeen officers now serving I am the only one that has been here continuously for over four months."

Captain Thomas was a good rider, a first-class football player (centre-forward), good cricketer, excellent at tennis, and fond of sports of all kinds. He was unmarried.

2nd LIEUTENANT the Honble. GERARD FREDERICK ¦ FREEMAN-THOMAS, 1st BATTN. COLDSTREAM GUARDS,

is believed to have been killed on or since the 14th September, 1914, in France ; but his name had not been included in the monthly official casualty lists up to November, 1915, although it is omitted from the Army List of that month.

He was the elder son and heir of the first Baron Willingdon and the Baroness Willingdon, daughter of Earl Brassey, and was born on the 3rd May, 1893. He was gazetted to the Coldstream Guards in September, 1913, and when killed was serving with the 1st Battalion, which formed part of the Ist Division.

2nd LIEUTENANT JAMES GRANT BRANDON THOMAS, 2nd BATTN. ROYAL INNISKILLING FUSILIERS,

was born at Chelsea on the 1st November, 1894, the son of the late Brandon Thomas, the well-known actor and playwright, author of probably the most popular play ever produced in this country, " Charley's Aunt."

He was a nephew of Captain H. A. Leverson, late of the 27th Regiment (now the Royal Inniskilling Fusiliers) and employed as a Staff Officer during the Great War.

2nd Lieutenant Brandon Thomas was a scholar of Winchester College, where he was captain of the shooting team, and was also an undergraduate of University College, Oxford. For two years he was in the Special Reserve of the Inniskilling Fusiliers, and was gazetted to the Regular Battalion as 2nd Lieutenant shortly after going to the front.

He died on the 17th November, 1914, of wounds received near Armentières, after the taking of a trench full of Germans, who surrendered to him. For his services he was mentioned in Field-Marshal Sir John French's Despatch of the 14th January, 1915.

2nd Lieutenant Brandon Thomas was a good shot. He was fond of writing parodies, essays, verses, etc., and was a frequent contributor to the " Isis " and " 'Varsity," Oxford.

LIEUTENANT RHYS IVOR THOMAS, 1st BATTN. CONNAUGHT RANGERS,

who was killed in action at the Battle of the Aisne on the 14th September, 1914, was the only son of Lieutenant-Colonel G. T. and Mrs. Thomas. He was born on the 2nd November, 1890, and was educated at Rugby (Donkin), 1904–07. He entered the Army from the R.M.C., Sandhurst, in April, 1910, becoming Lieutenant in October, 1912.

CAPTAIN CHOLMELEY SYMES-THOMPSON, 1st BATTN. GRENADIER GUARDS,

was the son of the late Professor Edmund Symes-Thompson, M.D., F.R.C.P., (Physician to the Hospital for Consumption, Brompton, and Provost for nine years of the Guild of St. Luke), and of Mrs. Symes-Thompson. Captain Symes-Thompson was born at 33, Cavendish Square, London, W., on the 16th April, 1881. Of his brothers H. E. Symes-Thompson, M.D., M.R.C.P., is Physician to the Royal Hospital for Diseases of the Chest and to the Great Northern Hospital; a second—the Rev. Francis— is Vicar of Stanton Harcourt, Oxon; while the third is Captain A. H. Symes-Thompson, R.F.A.

The subject of this memoir was educated at Harrow. He was a good cricketer, being a member of the Household Brigade Officers' Cricket Club, and was also a polo player.

Captain Symes-Thompson joined the 3rd (Militia) Battalion Yorkshire Light Infantry as 2nd Lieutenant in September, 1899, becoming Lieutenant in July, 1900.

During the South African War he served with his battalion at Malta, subsequently receiving the South African medal. In May, 1901, he was appointed 2nd Lieutenant in the Grenadier Guards, and was promoted Lieutenant in January, 1905, obtaining his Company in July, 1910. At the beginning of the Great War he was transferred to the 2nd Battalion of the Grenadier Guards and sent to the front. His Major wrote of him: "He was never a single day off duty from the first day till his death." He was killed on the 17th November, 1914, in

the Battle of Ypres, and was carried to the churchyard of Zillebeke, and buried there side by side with six other Grenadier officers, who had fallen about the same time. Strong wooden crosses with their names have been erected over each grave, and a memorial tablet has been placed in the church at Firmere, Oxfordshire, where Mrs. Symes-Thompson resides.

Captain Symes-Thompson married, on the 18th January, 1912, Grace Edith Gordon, elder daughter of Charles Churchill, Esq., of 1, Egerton Gardens, S.W., and left a daughter, Sibill Laura, born January, 1913.

2nd LIEUTENANT EDWARD JAMES VIBART COLLINGWOOD-THOMPSON, 2nd BATTN. ROYAL WELSH FUSILIERS,

born at Taunton on the 8th December, 1893, was the only son of the late Edward Collingwood-Thompson and Mrs. Andrew Wylie (née Collingwood), of 120, Harley Street, W., and a grandson of Frederick Collingwood, of Rhyl.

2nd Lieutenant Collingwood-Thompson was educated at Cheltenham and The Oratory School, Edgbaston. He gained a Prize Cadetship for Sandhurst which he did not take up but passed into Woolwich. He obtained his commission in the 3rd Battalion Royal Welsh Fusiliers on probation in September, 1913, and, having been attached to the 2nd Battalion, accompanied it to the front at the commencement of the war, being subsequently gazetted to the Regular Army, to date from the 1st September, 1914.

He was shot at the Battle of the Marne on the 9th September, and died from his wounds, on the 10th September, 1914, at La Ferté-sous-Jouarre, being the first officer of his battalion to fall.

LIEUTENANT GEORGE MASTERMAN THOMPSON, 1st BATTN. THE ROYAL SCOTS (LOTHIAN REGIMENT),

to whom a particular interest attaches as being the first British Officer killed in action in the Great War while fighting against the Germans, was born at Eshowe, Zululand, on the 21st February, 1890, the son of Colonel G. W. Thompson, the

Royal Scots, and Mrs. George Thompson, of Beechwood, Burley, Hants. At the time of his death Lieutenant Thompson was serving with the Gold Coast Regiment, West African Frontier Force.

He was educated at Mr. Stanford's Preparatory School, St. Aubyn's, Rottingdean; and Wellington College (Hopetoun Dormitory), where his name is the first inserted in the " Roll of Honour " for the Great War, and whence he passed direct into the R.M.C., Sandhurst. After a successful career there, during which he represented the College in fencing at the Naval and Military Tournament, he was gazetted to the Royal Scots, in which regiment his father's name is still held in regard, joining the 2nd Battalion in Edinburgh in October, 1909. In the following year he was transferred to the 1st Battalion, and served with it in India till 1913, when he was seconded for service with the W.A.F.F., and joined the Gold Coast Regiment in November.

When in India he passed the Higher Standards in Hindustani and in Persian, and also qualified in signalling.

Having become Lieutenant in February, 1913, he went with his company to the coast, and after the declaration of war was for some days Military Commandant of the border town of Quittah, where his influence on the natives and his acquisition of their language were noticed as very remarkable. On the 10th August he crossed over the border into the enemy territory of Togoland, and, leaving Lome on the 11th with the allied troops, marched, skirmishing in the rear, one hundred miles to Chra, where the Germans had concentrated their forces, and were strongly entrenched, with four Maxims and four hundred or five hundred rifles. Lieutenant Thompson was with the advance column, and did well in a sharp fight on the evening of the 21st, sleeping that night, with other white men, under a gun. On account of his knowledge of the language he was placed with the French, and in the morning of the 22nd led a mixed party in a flank attack; and, having got through a most difficult position, forced the enemy to evacuate their trenches that night, but he himself was unfortunately mortally wounded in the attack. The whole allied force was under the command of Captain Castaing, a French officer of the Dahomey Brigade, and the small force was composed of twenty-two British troops, which the French Captain reinforced by a Sergeant, two Corporals, and fourteen Tirailleurs.

The following brief account was given by a correspondent of " the story of how at Chra, in German Togoland, an English Lieutenant and a little band of Senegalese died together."

" Lieutenant Thompson, of the Gold Coast Regiment, with twenty-two British native troops, was placed on August 22nd at the disposition of Captain Castaing, of the Dahomey Brigade. To reinforce the little troop, of which the moral had been shaken by a preceding engagement, Captain Castaing added to it a Sergeant, two Corporals, and fourteen Tirailleurs.

" At the very beginning of the fight the mixed section thus constituted found itself assailed by a sharp fusillade from strongly entrenched troops of the enemy, who had further the help of machine guns. It maintained an undaunted front, and four hours later, about half-past three in the afternoon, after the artillery had entered into action, Lieutenant Thompson, thinking the way sufficiently prepared, led his troop forward to push the attack to a finish.

" All the Castaing unit lent a vigorous support to him in this. But under the deadly hail of bullets the attack could not be carried beyond a point some fifty yards from the line of the enemy's trenches.

" Lieutenant Thompson, mortally wounded, fell to the ground, and the British native troops wavered. But the Senegalese Tirailleurs, faithful to a long tradition of gallantry and faithfulness, refused to abandon the body of the unknown leader their Captain had given them, and they succeeded in holding the ground they had won.

" When the enemy withdrew it was seen at what cost this ground had been kept. Side by side round the body of Lieutenant Thompson and an English native Sergeant lay the Sergeant, the two Corporals, and thirteen out of fourteen of the Tirailleurs. The Sergeant, the Corporals, and nine of the Tirailleurs were dead; four Tirailleurs were wounded, three severely, the dead body of one of the Corporals having been eight times pierced.

" One Tirailleur alone remained unhurt. Only after he had seen all his comrades fall did he retire and join another section of the little force."

Lieutenant Thompson and his brave little band of Senegalese were buried together where they fell.

General of Brigade Pineau, commanding the allied troops in this region, issued the following:
" Ordre Général."
Le Général Commandant Supérieur
cite à l'Ordre des Troupes de l'A.O.F.
Le Lieutenant Anglais THOMPSON,
du Régiment de la Gold Coast.

Placé le 22 août avant le combat de Chra sous les ordres du Capitaine Castaing, de la Brigade de Dahomey, a fait preuve d'un très grand courage et de belles qualités de commandement en enlevant ses tirailleurs à l'attaque des tranchées allemandes vigoureusement défendues. Est tombé mortellement, frappé à cinquante mètres de l'ennemi. A mérité par son bel exemple que la presque totalité des Tirailleurs français temporairement placés sous ses ordres se fassent tuer en défendant son corps.

The Governor-General of French West Africa wrote to His Britannic Majesty's Consul-General, informing him that the General Officer in Command of the troops of French West Africa had decided that the splendid behaviour on the 22nd August, 1914, in the affair of Chra, of Lieutenant Thompson, of His Britannic Majesty's Army, and of the detachment of French native troops commanded by that officer, deserved to be recorded among the great deeds of military history, and should be commemorated in a special General Order, so that their conduct should be made known as an example to all the troops in the Colony, adding : " I have arranged that this splendid display of valour should be brought to the knowledge of all French West Africa by the insertion of this General Order in the official Journal of the Colony."

The Lieutenant-Colonel commanding the Togoland Field Force wrote as follows of the gallant young officer : " His conduct during the action was particularly gallant. He was killed while attempting to storm the German trenches on the enemy's left. He was an officer who was genuinely popular with all ranks, and one whom we could ill afford to lose. I wish to convey to you, not only my own profound sympathy at your loss, which is also mine, but also that of all ranks of the Togoland Field Force. He is buried at Chra village, close to the railway station where he fell, and a concrete cross inscribed with his name marks his grave."

He was a member of the Royal Institution and of the United Service Club, and a good fencer and polo player.

2nd LIEUTENANT GEORGE SAMUEL RODIE THOMPSON, 2nd BATTN. KING'S ROYAL RIFLE CORPS,

who was killed in action at the Battle of the Aisne on the 14th September, 1914, at the age of twenty, was the only son of G. Rodie and Elizabeth Thompson, of Lynwood, Ascot, Berks. He was born on the 2nd October, 1893, was educated at Harrow (Druries 1907-11) and received his commission as 2nd Lieutenant in the K.R.R.C. in September, 1912, from the R.M.C., Sandhurst. His battalion formed part of the 20th Brigade, 1st Division. It was recorded in his College

Magazine that he successfully led his men in an attack, with severe losses among the officers. As he too fell, mortally stricken, he cried : " Go on boys, never mind me ! "

LIEUTENANT JOHN HENRY LUIS THOMPSON, 2nd BATTN. THE DUKE OF WELLINGTON'S (WEST RIDING REGIMENT), was born on the 21st June, 1882, the eldest son of J. H. Thompson, of Leicester.

He joined the 3rd (Militia) Battalion Duke of Wellington's Regiment in January, 1901, being promoted Lieutenant in February, 1902, and served with that battalion in the South African War, 1900–02, being present at operations in the Cape Colony, for which he received the Queen's medal with three clasps.

In January, 1903, he was given a commission as 2nd Lieutenant in the West Riding Regiment, joining the 2nd Battalion, in which he became Lieutenant in October, 1905.

From June, 1907, he was for some time employed with the West African Frontier Force, becoming in February, 1912, Adjutant of the 3rd Battalion of his regiment.

Lieutenant Thompson appeared as killed in action in the first list of British officers lost in the Great War, issued by the War Office on the 1st September, 1914, but subsequently a correction was made to the effect that he died on the 17th September of wounds received on the 24th August, 1914. He was mentioned in Sir John French's Despatch of the 14th January, 1915.

2nd LIEUTENANT M. N. THOMPSON, THE QUEEN'S OWN (ROYAL WEST KENT REGIMENT), who died on the 29th November, 1914, of wounds received in action, was gazetted to his regiment from the ranks, in November, 1914, for service in the field.

LIEUTENANT OFFLEY CHARLES WYCLIFFE THOMPSON, 1st BATTN. THE PRINCE OF WALES'S OWN (WEST YORKSHIRE REGIMENT), who was included in the monthly casualty list of November, 1914, as " reported killed in action " on the 20th September, 1914, was the elder son of Major-General C. W. Thompson, C.B., D.S.O., Commanding Cape of Good Hope District, South Africa.

He was born at Charminster, Dorset, on the 21st January, 1891 ; was educated at Haileybury College ; and joined the West Yorkshire Regiment in March, 1911, being promoted Lieutenant in December, 1912.

It has been ascertained that Lieutenant Thompson fell at the Battle of the Aisne on the 20th September, 1914. He was buried north-east of Troyon close to the Chemin des Dames.

MAJOR EDMUND PEEL THOMSON, 2nd BATTN. ROYAL MUNSTER FUSILIERS,

son of William Thomson, of Manchester, was born on the 22nd April, 1874. He was educated at the Rev. E. W. Hobson's private school in Southport, Fettes College (Carrington House), and the R.M.C., Sandhurst.

He joined the Royal Munster Fusiliers in October, 1893, becoming Lieutenant in February, 1896 ; from May, 1899, to May, 1903, he was Adjutant of his battalion; and was promoted Captain in July, 1901.

He took part in the South African War, being present at operations in the Transvaal in 1902. He was mentioned in despatches (" London Gazette," 29th July, 1902), and received the Queen's medal with two clasps. From March, 1906, to June, 1909, he was Staff Captain, Pretoria Sub-district, South Africa, and he was promoted Major in February, 1912.

He was appointed Brigade-Major, Middlesex Infantry Brigade, Eastern Command, in April, 1912, which appointment he held till October, 1914, when he rejoined the 2nd Royal Munsters in France.

Major Thomson was killed on the 22nd December, 1914, at Festubert, when as Senior Major of his battalion he was gallantly leading an attack on the German trenches.

He excelled in all sports and games, having learnt cricket at Southport and at Fettes College, Edinburgh, where he was captain of the XI for two years. Later he played for his corps in the Inter-regimental Racquet's Tournament in 1913, and became prominent among soldier cricketers. He was a member of the Army and Navy Club, the Free Foresters, and the M.C.C.

LIEUTENANT KENNETH CLARKE THOMSON, 2nd BATTN. ROYAL SCOTS FUSILIERS, was the son of the late Samuel Marshall Thomson, Colliery Proprietor, and was born at Glasgow in June, 1891.

He was educated at Uppingham, and passed into the R.M.C., Sandhurst, in January, 1911,

obtaining his commission in the Royal Scots Fusiliers in January, 1912, and becoming Lieutenant in February, 1913. He served with his battalion in Ireland and Gosport, and was stationed at Gibraltar when the Great War broke out.

At the time he met his death he was assisting the Artillery Observation Officer, when he was shot in the spine on the 31st December, 1914, and was taken to Merville Hospital, France, where he died, and was buried in the same place. After the other officers were killed, wounded, or missing, he had led the remnant of his battalion into action. He was subsequently mentioned in Sir John French's Despatch of the 18th February, 1915.

LIEUTENANT RICHARD ANTHONY COMPTON-THORNHILL, 1st BATTN. SCOTS GUARDS, who was killed in action in 1914 on an unknown date, was the only son of Sir Anthony John Compton-Thornhill, Bart., of Riddlesworth Hall, Norfolk, and Pakenham Lodge, Suffolk, J.P. for Suffolk and Oxon.

Lieutenant Compton-Thornhill was born on the 29th June, 1892, and was educated at Eton and the R.M.C., Sandhurst, obtaining his commission in the Scots Guards in September, 1912, being gazetted after his death to the rank of Lieutenant, dating from September, 1914.

LIEUTENANT EDWARD GERALD MYTTON THORNYCROFT, KING'S OWN (ROYAL LANCASTER REGT.),

who was killed in action about the 12th September, 1914, near Kisumu, British East Africa, was the younger son of the late Rev. J. Mytton Thornycroft, of Mrs. M. Morris Glenmore, Queenstown, Ireland.

He was born on the 7th July, 1886, and joined the Royal Lancaster Regiment in August, 1905, becoming Lieutenant in November, 1907.

From December, 1909, Lieutenant Thornycroft had been employed with the 4th Uganda Battalion, King's African Rifles, with the local rank of Captain from May, 1912, and was serving with that regiment when he was killed.

MAJOR FRANCIS GORDON GRANT THOYTS, 1st BATTN. PRINCE ALBERT'S (SOMERSET LIGHT INFANTRY),

was born at Cheltenham on the 12th June, 1870, the younger son of Colonel N. B. Thoyts, of Mythe House, Tewkesbury, late of Sulhamstead, near Reading.

He was educated at Marlborough and the R.M.C., Sandhurst, joining the Somerset Light Infantry in October, 1890. Three years later he was promoted Lieutenant, and became Captain in March, 1900. He took part in the Tirah Campaign, 1897–98, being present at the capture of the Sampagha and Arhanga Passes, and at the operations in the Waran and Bara Valleys. For his services he received the medal with two clasps.

From 1906–08 he was Adjutant of the 2nd (Volunteer) Battalion, Bedfordshire Regiment. He was killed in action on the 26th August, 1914, at Fondant le Pire, North France, and was buried at Beauvois.

Major Thoyts, who obtained his Majority in April, 1910, married, in 1904, Irene Margaret, daughter of the late Mr. W. M. Rae, of Berkeley House, Cheltenham, and left no family.

CAPTAIN ARTHUR GEORGE TILLARD, 3rd (attd. 2nd) BATTN. THE MANCHESTER REGIMENT,

was born at Hastings on the 10th November, 1874, the son of the Rev. James Tillard. He was educated at Marlborough College and the R.M.C., Sandhurst. Joining the regiment in February, 1895, he became Lieutenant in August, 1896, and Captain in September, 1899. He served with the 1st Battalion in the South African War, 1899–1902, taking part in the action at Lombard's Kop and Siege of Ladysmith, and being present at operations in the Transvaal, including the action at Belfast. He received the Queen's medal and the King's medal, each with two clasps. After the war he served on the Staff in the Transvaal, July–September, 1902. In January, 1908, he went on half pay and in January, 1913, retired from the active list, becoming Captain in the 3rd (Reserve) Battalion of his regiment.

He was attached for active service in the Great War to the 2nd Battalion and was killed on the 20th October, 1914, in the fighting near La Bassée.

Mrs. Tillard's brother, who had received a commission in the same regiment, wrote as follows, 19th March, 1915 : " I had quite a long talk in the trenches with a Private who was with Arthur all the time. Like everyone else, he says Arthur was a most popular officer, and they all thought the world of him. The Adjutant of the battalion says that apparently Arthur's company had advanced further than those on his right and left, and he held up the whole German force for about thirty hours by repeated bayonet charges, and undoubtedly not only saved the whole line from defeat, but also kept the Germans from pushing right through."

His widow also received two or three letters from Captain E. von Selasinsky, A.D.C. of the 25th Brigade of Infantry, Prussian Army, written in remarkably good English, from which it is an unexpected gratification to be able to make the following extracts : " Enclosed I send you the money found in the pockets of your husband, killed near Les Trois Maisons, near La Bassée. He was killed in the morning of the 20th October as Prussian Jäger took the village defended by him as a hero. Enclosed you receive too a picture of yourself and the picture of your children. You can be sure, dear Madam, that your husband was honoured by us like we are accustomed to honour our enemies."

In another letter the Prussian officer sent a small sketch map showing the position of Captain Tillard's grave, or, as he expressed it, " where I have marked his place of rest. He has his own place, not amidst other soldiers. As I know he was killed at once, I am sure that he had not to suffer a long time. When our soldiers took the place, which he defended, he had a single fight with the German Captain, whose Browning didn't work, and whom he wounded with his Browning. After this happened he got several shots of the German soldiers, who were naturally excited about the accident, because they saw that their German Captain was shooten. But your husband was not disfigured, and easily to recognise. His face showed peace. . . . I hope you think we have done for your husband all we could do for him as honest enemies. My General, too, sends to the widow of the brave officer expressions of his estimation."

Captain Tillard married Emily Katherine (*née* Close-Brooks), and left five children : Katherine Lilian, born 1905 ; Arthur James, born 1906 ; Hilda Joyce, born 1908 ; Hermione Emily Margaret, born 1911 ; and David George, born 1915, after his father's death.

2nd LIEUTENANT ERIC VICKERS TINDALL, 2nd BATTN. KING'S ROYAL RIFLE CORPS,

was the son of the late Walter S. Tindall and Mrs. Stanley Williams, and was born at Scarborough on the 13th September, 1892.

He was educated at Cheltenham College, and first served in the Leicestershire Militia, which he entered in September, 1911, being promoted Lieutenant in May, 1912, and from which he was transferred to the King's Royal Rifle Corps, which he had joined as 2nd Lieutenant on the 10th June, 1914, just before the war broke out.

He was mortally wounded by shrapnel in the Battle of the Marne, while leading his platoon on the 11th September, 1914, and died the following day.

2nd Lieutenant Tindall was a member of the Junior Naval and Military Club.

MAJOR CHARLES ARTHUR TISDALL, 1st BATTN. IRISH GUARDS,

of Charlesfort, County Meath, Ireland, was born on the 22nd April, 1875, in Mauritius. He was the eldest son of the late Captain John Know Tisdall, R.E., and Jane Elizabeth, daughter of Robert Adams, Esq.

Major Tisdall joined the 2nd Royal Irish Rifles from the Militia in April, 1900, and was transferred to the Irish Guards in July, 1901, becoming Lieutenant in February, 1902, Captain in September, 1909, and Major in September, 1914. He served in the South African War, 1899–1901, taking part in the operations in Orange River Colony, for which he received the Queen's medal with two clasps.

Major Tisdall was killed in the forest of Villers Cotterets on the 1st September, 1914. The Irish Guards with the 2nd Coldstreams were holding the northern edge of the forest in a rearguard action at a spot called Rond de la Reine. Two other officers of the regiment— Lieutenant-Colonel the Honble. G. H. Morris and Major Crichton—were killed at the same time.

Major Tisdall was a remarkably fine violin player. Outside his profession his chief interests were dry fly fishing and motoring, in which he was one of the pioneers.

He married, in 1904, Gwynneth May, only child of Charles Adshead, Esq., and left two daughters.

CAPTAIN THOMAS TODRICK, 8th BATTN. (TERRITORIAL) ROYAL SCOTS (LOTHIAN REGIMENT),

who was killed in action in France on the 15th December, 1914, was born at Haddington on the 26th December, 1879, the elder son of Mr. Robert Todrick, Hon. Sheriff - Substitute and Agent for the Haddington branch of the Bank of Scotland.

He was educated at the Knox Institute, Haddington, and Leys School, Cambridge. He took his law course at Edinburgh University, and in 1904 was admitted as a Writer to the Signet. In 1900 he received a commission in the (then) 7th (late Haddingtonshire) Volunteer Battalion of the Royal Scots, and in 1908 was appointed to command the Headquarters Company at Haddington, a position he held for some years. He was then, on his own initiative, transferred to the Territorial Force Reserve, and early in 1914 was given the command of the Dalkeith Company. After mobilisation for the war, officers and men of the Territorials were asked to volunteer for service abroad, and Captain Todrick at once answered the call, and left for the front with the 8th Royal Scots on the 2nd November, 1914, reaching France in a day or two, and being in the firing line by the 15th of the month.

Captain Todrick was the first member of the Incorporation of Writers to the Signet to fall in the war. He was mentioned in Sir John French's Despatch of 31st May, 1915.

Captain Todrick, who was well known and respected in civil as in military life, practised as a lawyer in Edinburgh. He married Brenda, daughter of Mr. John List, head of the engineering department of the Union Castle Line, and is survived by his wife and two young children—a son and a daughter.

2nd LIEUTENANT BEVIL DOUGLAS TOLLEMACHE, SPECIAL RESERVE, attd. 1st BATTN., COLDSTREAM GUARDS,

was born at Melton, Suffolk, in April, 1889, the son of the Hon. Douglas Tollemache, and grandson of the first Lord Tollemache.

He was educated at Eton (Mr. Somerville's House) 1902–1906, where he was remarkable for intelligence, vigour, and thoroughness in work and games, especially football. After leaving Eton he had a business training in London. He became interested in the subject of small holdings, and was the author of a book entitled " The Occupying Ownership of Land." He was appointed Secretary to the Central Land Association in January, 1913, which appointment he was holding on the outbreak of the war, when the Committee gave him leave of absence and kept his appointment open so that he might serve his country abroad.

In August, 1914, he joined the Special Reserve of the Coldstream Guards, and was attached to the 1st Battalion for active service, which formed part of the 1st Brigade, 1st Division. They went to Belgium at the commencement of the war, taking part in the Battle of Mons, the subsequent retirement and the action at Le Cateau.

Mr. Tollemache was killed in action at Givenchy on the 22nd December, 1914, while his battalion was attacking German trenches. The following account of the action was published in the "East Anglian Daily Times" of 26th February, 1915:—
" This attack, which had to be made over open ground, and in face of a heavy rifle and machine-gun fire, was unfortunately attended by considerable loss of British lives. In this attack Lieutenant Tollemache, whose platoon was the first ordered to leave the trenches on the morning of December 22nd, kept saying to his men: ' Come on, men ! Keep your spirits up. We will shift them out of it.' He, however, fell, having been shot down within a few yards of the German trenches. The Coldstreams held the trenches for one hour, when they had to retire, owing to support not coming up on their left. Sergt. Briggs, 1st Battalion Coldstream Guards, has reported that he went to Lieutenant Tollemache during the retirement, and though wounded himself tried to help him, but could not get him away ; that Lieutenant Tollemache then said : ' You must leave me, Sergeant Briggs, or you will be captured.' These must have been his last words."

LIEUTENANT FREDERICK ROGER JOHN TOMLINSON, 1st BATTN. SOUTH STAFFORDSHIRE REGIMENT,

born at St. Michael Penkevil Rectory, Cornwall, on the 22nd October, 1891, was the son of the Rev. Arthur Roger Tomlinson, M.A.(formerly Rector of St. Michael Penkevil, afterwards Vicar of Bolton-le-Sands, Carnforth Lancashire) and,

Theresa Juliana Marie, his wife. 2nd Lieutenant Tomlinson was a nephew of the late Sir W. E. M. Tomlinson, Bart., and a great-grandson of Rear-Admiral Sir W. Symonds, K.C.B.

He was educated at Westminster School, and Trinity College, Cambridge, where he took his degree of B.A. He was studying Marine Engineering at the North Eastern Marine Engineering College when he received a commission, in August, 1914, in the South Staffordshire Regiment.

He had fought through the night of the 25th October, and captured six German snipers, when he was wounded in the arm, and while being taken to the base hospital he was killed on the way by a shell on the 26th October, 1914, near Ypres. He was gazetted Lieutenant after his death, which was not known for some months after it occurred, and which was only recorded in the monthly casualty list of June, 1915.

LIEUTENANT ARTHUR WOODLAND TOMS, 3rd BATTN. DEVONSHIRE REGIMENT, attd. 2nd BATTN. THE CAMERONIANS (SCOTTISH RIFLES),

who was accidentally killed on the 27th November, 1914, while serving with the British Expeditionary Force in Flanders, aged twenty-three, was the second son of Mr. and Mrs. Woodland Toms, of Jersey, and a grandson of the late Mr.

Frederick Toms, formerly Editor of " The Field."

He was educated at Victoria College, Jersey, and was gazetted to the 3rd Battalion (Reserve) Devonshire Regiment in February, 1912, being promoted Lieutenant in February, 1914.

Mr. Toms was a keen football and hockey player and a very promising golfer. He was a good shot, and on six occasions represented his school at Bisley in the Ashburton and the Public Schools' Veterans competitions. In 1913 and 1914 he was captain of the Young Soldiers shooting team of his battalion.

For some time he had been preparing for service under the Colonial Office, and had been offered an appointment in West Africa a few days before the declaration of war.

The Commanding Officer of the 3rd Devons described him as " a great favourite in the regiment and a most promising officer." He is buried in the cemetery at Estaires, North France.

CAPTAIN SELWYN LUCAS LUCAS-TOOTH, 3rd (attd. 2nd) BATTN. LANCASHIRE FUSILIERS,

who was killed in action on the 20th October, 1914, was the eldest son of the late Sir Robert Lucas Lucas-Tooth, Bart., and Lady Lucas-Tooth, of Holme Lacy, Herefordshire, and was born on the 19th March, 1879.

He entered the 5th (Militia) Battalion Lancashire Fusiliers in April, 1904, becoming Lieutenant in May, 1905, and Captain in the 3rd Battalion in May, 1907.

Captain Lucas-Tooth married, in June, 1908, Everild Blanche Marion, second daughter of Sir Edward Law Durand, Bart., C.B., and left one daughter — Everild Vera Undine — born March, 1909.

His younger brother, Captain D. K. L. Lucas-Tooth, in the 9th Lancers, was killed in action on the 13th September, 1914.

CAPTAIN DOUGLAS KEITH LUCAS LUCAS-TOOTH, D.S.O., 9th (QUEEN'S ROYAL) LANCERS,

killed in action at the Battle of the Aisne on the 13th September, 1914, was the second son of the late Sir Robert Lucas Lucas-Tooth, Bart., and Lady Lucas-Tooth, of Holme Lacy, Herefordshire. He was born on the 10th October, 1880, and joined the 9th Lancers in August, 1900,

becoming Lieutenant a year later. He served in the South African War, 1889–1902, with the New South Wales Mounted Infantry, and was slightly wounded. He was present at the relief of Kimberley ; operations in the Orange Free State and at Paardeberg, including the action at Driefontein ; operations in the Transvaal, including actions near Johannesburg, Pretoria, and Diamond Hill ; operations in the Orange River Colony, including actions at Bethlehem and Wittebergen ; further operations in the Orange River Colony and in Cape Colony. He was mentioned in despatches (" London Gazette," 16th April, 1901), and received the Queen's medal with six clasps and the King's medal with two clasps.

Captain Lucas-Tooth obtained his troop in January, 1910. In the Great War the 9th Lancers formed part of the 2nd Cavalry Brigade, and, embarking with the Expeditionary Force, were, it is believed, the first British forces to come into contact with the enemy on the Continent on August 22nd. For his services in the Great War he was mentioned in Sir John French's Despatch of the 8th October, 1914, and was awarded the D.S.O. (" London Gazette," 9th November, 1914).

His elder brother—Captain S. L. Lucas-Tooth, 3rd Battalion Lancashire Fusiliers—was killed in action on the 20th October, 1914.

CAPTAIN HARRY STANLEY TOPPIN, 1st BATTN. NORTHUMBERLAND FUSILIERS,

killed in action at the Battle of the Aisne on the 14th September, 1914, was the eldest son of General and Mrs. Toppin, of Westminster Cottage, Branksome Park, Bournemouth, and Blacklands Park, Calne, Wilts. He was born on the 27th July, 1874, and was educated at Wellington (Lynedoch, 1887–89), and the R.M.C., Sandhurst. He joined the Northumberland Fusiliers in February, 1895, becoming Lieutenant in October, 1896, and Captain in May, 1900.

Captain Toppin, who was a qualified Interpreter in French, served in the Nile Expedition of 1898, being present at the Battle of Khartoum, receiving the British medal and the Egyptian medal with clasp.

He also served in the South African War, during which he was employed with the Mounted Infantry, and as Acting Assistant Provost Marshal, Lines of Communication, from June,

1900. He was present at operations in the Transvaal and Cape Colony. For his services he was mentioned in despatches (" London Gazette," 10th September, 1901), and received the Queen's medal with seven clasps.

For his services in the Great War he was mentioned in Sir John French's Despatch of the 8th October, 1914, and was awarded the Croix de Chevalier of the Legion of Honour. (" London Gazette," 3rd November, 1914.)

2nd LIEUTENANT ERIC HAROLD TOTTIE, 1st BATTN. NORTHUMBERLAND FUSILIERS,

who died on the 22nd September, 1914, at Braisne, from wounds received in the Battle of the Aisne on the 19th September, aged nineteen years, was the son of Mr. and Mrs. W. H. Tottie, of Sherlocks, Ascot. He only received his commission from the R.M.C., Sandhurst, on the 15th August, 1914, and was posted to the 1st Battalion of his regiment.

CAPTAIN GEOFFREY PERCY ROBERT TOYNBEE, 1st BATTN. THE RIFLE BRIGADE (THE PRINCE CONSORT'S OWN),

who was killed in action near Armentières on the 15th November, 1914, was the only son of the late Percy Toynbee, 92, Westbourne Terrace, and of Mrs. Francis Raitt, Brockfield Hall, York.

He was born on the 18th May, 1885, and was educated at Winchester and the R.M.C., Sandhurst. At Winchester he was in the XI in 1903, and also in the Football XV and in Sixes. At Sandhurst he was captain of the cricket, and represented the R.M.C. at golf. He joined the Rifle Brigade in August, 1905, becoming Lieutenant in May, 1909, and captain in February, 1914.

Captain Toynbee was a member of the United Service Club, Pall Mall, and of I Zingari and the M.C.C. His recreations were hunting, shooting, fishing, cricket, and golf. He played cricket for Hampshire in 1912. He was unmarried.

LIEUTENANT the Hon. FELIX CHARLES HUBERT HANBURY-TRACY, 2nd BATTN. SCOTS GUARDS,

was the son of Charles Douglas Richard, fourth Baron Sudeley, and Lady Sudeley, daughter of the Hon. Frederick Tollemache, niece of the seventh Earl Dysart, and was born on the 27th July, 1882.

He was educated at Harrow, where he reached the 6th Form (Modern Side), and passed direct into Sandhurst, taking the second place in the examination.

In 1903 Lieutenant Hanbury-Tracy was gazetted to the 3rd Battalion Scots Guards, retiring from the active list and voluntarily joining the Reserve of Officers in 1907. On the outbreak of the war he joined the 2nd Battalion, with which he proceeded to the front.

On the 18th December, 1914, he was wounded during an attack on German trenches at Fromelles. He refused to be carried back out of the firing line on account of the great risk to the bearers, and unhappily died from his wounds within two days.

Lieutenant Hanbury-Tracy was a member of the Guards' and Bachelors' Clubs. He married Madeleine Llewellen, only daughter of George Llewellen Palmer, Esq., of Lackham, Wilts, and left two sons : Michael David Charles, born March, 1909 ; and Ninian John Frederick, born December, 1910.

MAJOR JOHN MURRAY TRAILL, 2nd BATTN. BEDFORDSHIRE REGIMENT,

who was killed in action on his birthday, the 30th October, 1914, was the son of the late Mr. James Christie Traill, of Hobbister, Orkney, and Rattar, Caithness.

He was born on the 30th October, 1865, and was educated latterly at Trinity Hall, Cambridge. He joined the Bedfordshire Regiment from the Militia in November, 1887, and was promoted Lieutenant in July, 1889. He served with the Isazai Expedition in 1892, and was promoted Captain in February, 1896. From July, 1899, to August, 1904, he was Adjutant of the 1st (Volunteer) Battalion Essex Regiment, and obtained his Majority in December, 1906.

During the strikes in South Africa, in 1914, he was specially commended by the Commander-in-Chief for his prompt assistance in suppressing a native rising. (" The Times," 28th November, 1914.)

He was mentioned in Sir John French's Despatch of the 14th January, 1915, for his services while in temporary command of his battalion in the Great War.

CAPTAIN HUGH MORTIMER TRAVERS, D.S.O., 5th (attd. 2nd) BATTN. ROYAL MUNSTER FUSILIERS,

born at Calcutta on the 2nd September, 1873, was the son of Lieutenant - Colonel Joseph Oates Travers, Leicestershire Regiment, Chevalier of the Legion of Honour, a distinction he received for the Crimean Campaign. Captain Travers was descended from most distinguished military ancestors, his grandfathers having been General Sir Robert Travers, of the Rifle Brigade, and Major-General Sir Henry Marion Durand, R.E., K.C.S.I., C.B. Sir Robert Travers was one of six brothers, four of whom were in the Rifle Brigade, and two in the Navy, and the six brothers had between them twenty-four sons, all of whom went into the Army. At the time Sir Robert and three of his brothers were in the Rifle Brigade there were also two first cousins in it, making no fewer than six officers of the name of Travers in the regiment at one time. It is doubtful if any other family has produced so many soldiers, and they well deserved their nickname of " the fighting Travers." In their crest is a cockle shell, indicating that their ancestors took part in the Crusades. Their name is carved at Battle Abbey, and is on the Battle Abbey roll. They trace their descent from Baron Robert de Travers, who in 1067 married the heiress of Nateby, in Lancashire.

Another ancestor—Admiral Sir Eaton Travers —was engaged with the enemy over one hundred times, and was eight times mentioned for gallant conduct.

Captain Travers, who was educated at Wellington College, was appointed to the 1st Leicestershire Regiment from the Militia, in December, 1896, joining the battalion at the Cape in 1897, where he remained till 1902, taking part in the South African War. He had been promoted Lieutenant in October, 1899, and was present with his battalion at Talana Hill, in the retreat from Dundee, at the action of Lombard's Kop, in the siege of Ladysmith, and in Sir Redvers Buller's advance on Lydenberg, and under Field-Marshal (then General) Sir John French in the Eastern Transvaal. In the last thirteen

months of the war he was on an armoured train, and received the thanks of Lord Kitchener. For his services he received the Queen's medal with five clasps and the King's medal with two clasps. He also had the Coronation medal.

In April, 1902, he became Captain, and was selected for the Egyptian Army, but retired in 1907, having contracted blackwater fever. He joined the 5th Battalion Royal Munster Fusiliers in November of that year.

At the outbreak of the Great War he was attached to a battalion of the Regular Army and was present at the Battle of the Aisne, at La Bassée, and Givenchy, at all of which he did exceedingly well. He fell finally on the 8th November, 1914, in a bayonet charge, in which he gallantly led his men, shot through the head, near Hooge, a small village near Ypres. For his conduct in this action he was awarded the D.S.O., the official record stating it was bestowed for " conspicuous gallantry and ability on November 8th near Ypres in organising an attack and recapturing a trench from the enemy, and subsequently for leading a second attack and capturing another position fifty yards farther to the front. Captain Travers was killed while maintaining his post on this occasion."

Several officers of his regiment wrote to the effect that it was entirely owing to his skill and gallantry that the operation was successful, and that his death had cast a gloom over them all. The Adjutant of his battalion, in a letter, said that he " died the death of a soldier and a very gallant gentleman " ; and a Sergeant described his behaviour as " the coolest deed I have ever seen. It was gloriously brave."

Captain Travers, at the time of his death, was engaged to be married to Wiliemina Annette, daughter of Surgeon-General Sir William Taylor, M.D., K.C.B., and Lady Taylor, and the marriage had been postponed owing to Captain Travers having had to leave for the front at twenty-four hours' notice.

MAJOR FRANCIS MAXWELL CHENEVIX-TRENCH, p.s.c., ROYAL FIELD ARTILLERY,

who was killed in action on the 31st October, 1914, was the son of Colonel C. Chenevix-Trench, of Bromfield, Camberley. He was born on the 23rd September, 1879, and was educated at Loretto School, Edinburgh, and the R.M.A., Woolwich, from which he was gazetted to the Royal Artillery on the 23rd December, 1898, becoming Lieutenant in February, 1901.

He took part in the South African War, during which he was A.D.C. to the Lieutenant-General Commanding an Infantry Division, and afterwards the 1st Army Corps, from March, 1901, to January, 1902. He was present at operations in Natal in 1899, including actions at Talana Hill and Lombard's Kop; took part in the defence of Ladysmith, including the action on the 6th January, 1900; operations in Natal in 1900, including action at Laing's Nek. He was twice mentioned in despatches ("London Gazette," 8th February and 10th September, 1901), and received the Queen's medal with six clasps.

He was promoted Captain in May, 1907, and from November of that year to December, 1910, was employed with the Egyptian Army. In 1908 he took part in operations in the Blue Nile Province, Soudan, receiving the Egyptian medal. Major Chenevix-Trench, who was qualified as a 1st Class Interpreter in Arabic, and was a graduate of the Staff College, obtained his Majority on the 30th October, 1914, the day preceding his death. In August, 1913, he had been appointed Brigade-Major, R.A., of the IInd Division, Aldershot, and was employed in the same capacity in the Great War. For his services he was mentioned in Sir John French's Despatch of the 14th January, 1915.

He was killed by the explosion of a shell from the German lines on the plateau of Hooge, near Ypres. On the same occasion five officers of the Divisional Headquarters Staff lost their lives, and were buried in the cemetery near Ypres.

Major Chenevix-Trench married, in March, 1914, Sibyl, daughter of E. Lyon, Esq.

LIEUTENANT HILLYAR GEORGE EDWIN HILL-TREVOR, 1st BATTN. SCOTS GUARDS,

who was killed while gallantly leading his men at Givenchy, near La Bassée, France, on the 21st December, 1914, was the son of the Hon. George Edwyn Hill-Trevor, and grandson of the first Baron Trevor, of Brynkinalt, Chirk, North Wales. His ancestress was Anne Trevor, of that place, who was the mother of Arthur, Duke of Wellington. She was a daughter of Viscount Dungannon, afterwards created Viscountess Mornington.

Lieutenant Hill-Trevor was born on the 31st December, 1895, at the Hotel Paoli, Florence, Italy. Educated at Wellington College and the R.M.C., Sandhurst, he joined the Scots Guards in August, 1914, and was promoted Lieutenant in November, 1914, while on active service with his battalion.

He was fond of Alpine sports and of shooting, motoring, golf, and fencing, for which last he held a silver shield, won at Wellington College.

LIEUTENANT ATHOL BENEDICT TREWMAN, 1st BATTN. THE DUKE OF CAMBRIDGE'S OWN (MIDDLESEX REGIMENT),

who died of wounds on the 22nd October, 1914, in Field Hospital No. 2 at Haubourdin, near Lille, was the only son of Lieutenant-Colonel G. T. Trewman, late R.A.M.C. Lieutenant Trewman was born at Cape Town on the 26th August, 1892, and was educated at Reading and Wimborne Schools. He was gazetted to the Middlesex Regiment in June, 1914, from the Special Reserve of the Dorsetshire Regiment, and went to the front with the first part of the Expeditionary Force. He had been reported missing since the 21st October, and the report of his death was subsequently received through the American Embassy in Berlin.

He received his promotion to Lieutenant, dated 14th October, 1914, which was not gazetted till 15th April, 1915. The following accounts of his death were received some months later. A Sergeant in the regiment wrote: " 2nd Lieutenant Trewman was wounded at a place called Le Mesnil on October 21st. He was leading his platoon when he was hit in the arm. He continued to go forward, and was again wounded, this time being hit in the leg and high up in the groin. A Private—since killed—and myself tried to get him away, but he told us to leave him on account of the awful fire we were drawing. We had to retire from the village about half an hour after."

An officer in the regiment wrote: " Poor Trewman was hit in the sword arm and changed his sword into the other hand, and pluckily pushed on. However, soon after, he was hit in the leg, and his head was grazed. Of course he fell, but even under such conditions his thought was for others instead of himself, ordering back to safety the men who were trying to save him. He died as that other ' very gallant gentleman,' true to the traditions of an officer and a gentleman."

His Company Commander said of him : " He

was always very quiet, but very reliable, and one always knew if he was given an order it would be executed properly without any fuss." A letter was also received from a Sergeant of the same platoon, wounded at the same time, and afterwards a prisoner in Germany. He said : " Mr. Trewman was a great favourite with his men. He joined us just before the war, and from the first day he made his presence felt. . . . The men called him brave, generous, and kind. ' A ' Company of the A. and S. Highlanders were hard pressed by the enemy. ' B ' Company of my regiment, who were on the other side of the village, were ordered to reinforce them. The Captain ordered Mr. Trewman, No. 6 Platoon, to advance half his platoon. Mr. Trewman went first with two sections, and I followed later with the other two sections. That was the last I saw of Mr. Trewman until the night of October 21st. In the meantime I went forward with my two sections, hoping to join Mr. Trewman, but before we could leave the village we were surrounded by the enemy. I was severely wounded, and eventually found myself in the enemy field hospital, and to my surprise saw Mr. Trewman lying on a stretcher. He was full of praise of the treatment he had received from the Germans. . . . The German doctor, who was very kind, said to me, ' What a pity, and such a young fellow ! ' I questioned him, and he said Mr. Trewman was severely wounded, but might pull through with good nursing. The last words I heard my officer say were, ' Aren't they kind ! ' "

LIEUTENANT WILLIAM DOUGLAS MACLEAN TRIMMER, 1st BATTN. HAMPSHIRE REGIMENT,

born at Surbiton on the 29th December, 1891, was the son of Mr. and Mrs. E. D. Trimmer, of Oakrigg, Walton-on-Thames, and was related to Commander P. H. Trimmer, R.N., Lieutenant-Colonel F. F. Weedon, R.E., and Lieutenant - Colonel McDouall, D.S.O., The Buffs (East Kent Regiment).

He was educated at Aldenham School, Herts, where he made school records for the mile and half-mile in the school sports in 1910. He proceeded to the R.M.C., Sandhurst, where he was fourth in the cross-country race in 1911. From the R.M.C. he obtained his commission in the 1st Hampshire Regiment in September, 1911,

and was promoted Lieutenant in March, 1914. He and his whole platoon (with one exception) were killed on the 30th October 1914, in defending an advanced isolated trench near Ploegsteert Wood during the first Battle of Ypres. The following account of his death was given by the Medical Officer attached to the battalion : " He died like a hero. He *was* a hero, and the way he and his men fought to the last is one of the finest acts I have heard of in the whole war. He was found in his trench, wounded fatally in the head, grasping unexpended cartridges in his hand— game to the last. He must have died immediately on receiving the fatal shot." He was buried in Ploegsteert Churchyard, next to Captain R. W. Harland, who was in command of his company, and was killed on the same day.

Another officer, speaking of earlier incidents, said : " On the Aisne he did his work excellently, and I myself was particularly struck with the quiet courage he showed when on real dangerous patrol work. . . . When poor Connellan (a brother officer) was killed, he dashed out and brought him in to cover. . . . He was extraordinarily popular with his men."

The following further account of his death was received indirectly from an officer at the front : " About October 28th he was holding an advanced trench with his platoon in front of Ploegsteert Wood. He was very heavily shelled, and attacked by infantry all day, losing most of his platoon. He sent back for reinforcements, but apparently there were none to be had ; anyhow none were sent. He held his men together, and stuck to his trench all day, being finally killed by a shell towards the evening. The remains of his platoon—nine men out of about forty—stuck on, and were finally all killed by German Infantry except, I believe, one man, who is now wounded and prisoner. The only survivor of his platoon—the messenger he sent back—was killed about two months later. Young Trimmer certainly held his trench very gallantly."

The officer who commanded Lieutenant Trimmer's company at Aldershot before the war, spoke in the very highest terms of him. It is understood he was recommended for mention in despatches, and senior officers on the Staff of the Division of which Lieutenant Trimmer's battalion formed part, had specially referred to the gallant way in which his platoon " stuck it to the last man."

Lieutenant Trimmer was a good cross-country and long-distance runner, and ran in the battalion team in 1912, 1913, and 1914, when the 1st Hants won the cross-country races of the Aldershot Command (twice) and of the Eastern Command. He was, moreover, a good swimmer, and a useful player at Rugby football and hockey.

CAPTAIN LANCELOT BARRINGTON CROFTS TRISTRAM, 2nd BATTN. THE LEICESTERSHIRE REGIMENT,

who was killed in action on the 31st October, 1914, was the eldest son of Samuel Barrington and Blanch Ellen Tristram, of Sompting Abbotts, Worthing.

He was born on the 17th March, 1882, and joined the Leicestershire Regiment in February, 1903, becoming Lieutenant in September, 1905, and being promoted Captain in October, 1912.

CAPTAIN ALAN GEORGE TRITTON, 3rd BATTN. COLDSTREAM GUARDS,

who was killed in action in France on the 26th December, 1914, was the youngest son of Mr. and Mrs. J. Herbert Tritton, Lyon's Hall, Great Leighs, Essex, and 4, Lowndes Square, London, S.W. Captain Tritton was born on the 28th January, 1882, and was educated at Winchester, from which he passed direct into the R.M.C., Sandhurst. He received his commission in the Coldstream Guards in August, 1900, proceeded almost at once to South Africa on active service, and was present at operations in Cape Colony from December, 1901, to May, 1902.

Becoming Lieutenant in October, 1903, he was from November, 1906, to March, 1907, Adjutant at the Guards' depot, and from April, 1907, to April, 1910, Adjutant of his battalion.

In May, 1910, he obtained his company, and in October of the same year was appointed A.D.C. to the General Officer Commanding-in-Chief, Western Command, Chester.

For his services in the Great War he was mentioned in Sir John French's Despatch of the 8th October, 1914.

LIEUTENANT ARCHIBALD TROTTER, 3rd BATTN. COLDSTREAM GUARDS,

who was killed in action on the 31st December, 1914, was the only surviving son of Colonel Trotter, South Notts. Hussars, and the Hon. Mrs. Trotter, of Barton Hartshorne Manor, Buckingham.

He was born on the 29th April, 1892, and after his education at Eton and the R.M.C., Sand-

hurst, joined the Coldstream Guards in September, 1911, becoming Lieutenant in September, 1914. Lieutenant Trotter was slightly wounded at Landrecies in August, 1914, and again at the Battle of the Marne in September, 1914.

He was a member of the Guards' and Bachelors' Clubs. He was a very promising polo player, a straight rider to hounds, and well known with the Bicester and Grafton Hunts and on London polo grounds.

LIEUTENANT ALEXANDER NIGEL TROTTER, 3rd (attd. 2nd) BATTN. THE ROYAL SCOTS (LOTHIAN REGIMENT),

was the son of Alexander Pelham Trotter, and was born in London on the 17th September, 1894.

He was educated at Packwood Haugh, Warwickshire, and Clifton College. Lieutenant Trotter joined the 3rd Battalion Royal Scots in the Special Reserve of Officers in December, 1912, and received his promotion in July, 1914, on rejoining for his yearly training.

During the forced passage of the canal near Vieille Chapelle on the 14th October, 1914, he was wounded three times, and was carried into a house near, where he died the same night.

LIEUTENANT JAMES KEITH TROTTER, 1st BATTN. THE GORDON HIGHLANDERS,

who was killed in action on the 26th August, 1914, was the only son of Major - General Sir J. K. Trotter, K.C.B., C.M.G., and Lady Trotter, of Aislaby Lodge, Sleights, Yorkshire. Lieutenant Trotter had been

reported wounded and missing, but up to June, 1915, his death had not been officially reported, and he had not therefore been included in the official monthly casualty lists up to that date. Major-General Trotter received the intimation of his son's death from the officer in command of the battalion, who was a prisoner of war at Torgau.

Lieutenant Trotter was born on the 19th December, 1888, and was educated at Wellington, where he was in the Combermere, a prefect, and a very efficient head of the Rifle Corps. He joined the Gordon Highlanders in January, 1909, becoming Lieutenant in October, 1910. From November of the latter year to July, 1911, he was A.D.C. to the General Officer Commanding the South Coast Defences, Southern Command.

CAPTAIN CHARLES FITZGERALD HAMILTON TRUEMAN, 2nd BATTN. MANCHESTER REGIMENT,

the son of Lieutenant - Colonel Charles Hamilton and Mrs. Dorothea Magdalena Trueman was born on the 22nd March, 1877, in the parish of Stoke Damerel, Devonport.

He was educated at King's School, Canterbury, and the R.M.C., Sandhurst, joining the Manchester Regiment as 2nd Lieutenant in September, 1897. He was promoted Lieutenant in August, 1898, and Captain in January, 1901.

Captain Trueman took part in the South African War, being present at operations in the Transvaal and Orange River Colony, receiving the Queen's medal with four clasps. From April, 1908, to August, 1909, he was Superintendent, and from the latter date to April, 1912, Assistant Inspector of Gymnasia at Aldershot.

He was fond of all sports and athletics, especially cricket and shooting, and was a member of the Army and Navy Club.

Captain Trueman was reported " missing " after Le Cateau on the 26th August, 1914, and as nothing has been heard from or of him since it must unfortunately be assumed that he was killed on that day.

2nd LIEUTENANT ALAN ROBERT LLOYD TUCKER, unattd. list for INDIAN ARMY, attd. 4th BATTN. ROYAL WARWICKSHIRE REGIMENT,

who was killed in action between the 18th and 20th December, 1914, was gazetted to the Army in August, 1914.

LIEUTENANT CECIL MORTIMER PITTS TUCKER, 1st BATTN. HIGHLAND LIGHT INFANTRY,

who was killed near Festubert, France, on the 20th December, 1914, was the second son of William Edwin and Violet Emily Pitts Tucker, of Crosslands, near Barnstaple.

He was born at Barnstaple on the 12th April, 1890, and was educated at Ellerslie, Fremington, North Devon, Charterhouse (House Lockites), 1903–08, which he entered with a Junior Scholarship, and the R.M.C., Sandhurst. From the latter he was gazetted to the Highland Light Infantry in April, 1910, becoming Lieutenant in December, 1912. From October of the latter year to March, 1913, he was extra A.D.C. to Colonel the Hon. Sir James S. Meston, K.C.S.I., Lieutenant-Governor of the United Provinces, India.

He was in his regimental polo team, and in December, 1913, played in the final of the Amateur Golf Championship of India at Calcutta. He was beaten, but got the cup for the best stranger's score.

His C.O. wrote of his death : " Your son was killed on the 20th December after making a gallant charge to go to the aid of a brother officer with a few men he had gathered round him. All were shot down. He was as fine a soldier as one could wish to see, and a true and affectionate comrade ; and he met his soldier's death just in the manner all who knew him knew he would." He was buried near Festubert, France.

2nd LIEUTENANT JOHN AYRE TUCKER, ROYAL FIELD ARTILLERY,

who was killed in action on the 2nd November, 1914, was the only son of the late Wallace Tucker, and of Mrs. Wallace Tucker, of 8, Hurst Road, Eastbourne, and 75, St. Mary's Mansions, London, W.

He was born on the 22nd April, 1894, and was gazetted to the Royal Artillery in July, 1913.

LIEUTENANT HERVEY ROBERT CHARLES TUDWAY, 2nd BATTN. GRENADIER GUARDS,

died in hospital at Boulogne on the 18th November, 1914, from wounds received in action at Ypres on the 9th of that month. He was the eldest son of Charles Clement Tudway, of Wells, by his second marriage with Alice, daughter of the late Sir Frederick Hervey Bathurst, third

Bart., whose ancestor, the Hon. Felton Hervey, eighth son of the first Earl of Bristol, fought at

Waterloo and lost one arm there. Lieutenant Tudway's grandfather, uncle, and cousin on the maternal side all served in the Grenadier Guards.

Lieutenant Tudway was born on the 23rd September, 1888, at 17, Lower Berkeley Street, W., and was educated at Evelyns and Eton, where he won the School Fives in 1907, was captain of his house, in the Sixth Form, and a member of the Eton Society.

He received his commission in the Grenadier Guards in February, 1910, becoming Lieutenant in September of the same year, and served with his regiment till the summer of 1914, when he was appointed A.D.C. to Viscount Buxton, Governor-General of South Africa, and arrived there to find that war had broken out. He at once resigned his appointment and returned to England, and had hardly arrived when he received orders to rejoin his regiment at the front.

Lieutenant Tudway was a member of the Guards' and Pratt's Clubs, and of I Zingari and the M.C.C. At Eton he was noted for his cheery and charming manners. He was a good cricketer and an excellent shot, and became very popular with his brother officers and in society. At the Wells County Petty Sessions after his death the Chairman (Colonel Alfred Thrale Perkins, C.B.) paid a touching tribute to the young officer, and a brass tablet has been fixed in the wall of the north choir aisle in Wells Cathedral to his memory.

The Officer Commanding at the Grenadier Guards Headquarters at home wrote to his father extolling his late son's soldierly qualities and charming personality.

LIEUTENANT CARLETON WYNDHAM TUFNELL, 2nd BATTN. GRENADIER GUARDS,

third son of Carleton Fowell Tufnell, of Watendone Manor, Kenley, and nephew of Rear-Admiral Lionel Grant Tufnell, C.M.G., was born at Sydenham, Kent, on the 5th August, 1892.

He was educated at Eton, where he was captain of the Cricket XI, and for two years captain of the Football XI ; was the winner of the Victor Ludorum Cup, President of the Eton Society, and winner of the King's medal in the O.T.C. Passing through the R.M.C., Sandhurst, he joined the Grenadier Guards in September, 1912, becoming Lieutenant in September, 1914, and being for some time in the King's Company in the 1st Battalion.

Lieutenant Tufnell was killed on the 6th November, 1914, while proceeding in command of his machine-gun section to defend a wood near Ypres, and was buried in Zillebeke Churchyard. He was a member of the M.C.C. and I Zingari. While at school he played for two years in the Eton v. Harrow and Eton v. Winchester matches. He represented the Army in Association Football v. the Dutch Army on two occasions, and was a prominent member of the Household Brigade Cricket Club.

CAPTAIN JOHN DRYSDALE TULLIS, 1st BATTN. ROYAL SCOTS FUSILIERS,

who died of wounds on the 18th November, 1914, in the British Hospital, Hôtel Bellevue, Wimereux, France, was the second son of Mr. and Mrs. Tullis, of Strathenry, Leslie, Scotland.

He was born on the 11th April, 1881, and was educated at Cargilfield and Fettes College, Edinburgh, joining the Royal Scots Fusiliers in January, 1901, and becoming Lieutenant in April, 1904. He served in the South African War, being present at operations in the Transvaal, 1901–02, for which he received the Queen's medal with four clasps.

Captain Tullis, who was promoted to that rank in November, 1911, was fatally wounded whilst leading his company in a counter-attack against a portion of the Prussian Guard near the Château of Hooge at Ypres on the 11th November, 1914. He was mentioned in Sir John French's Despatch of the 8th October, 1914.

He married, at Stirling on the 7th April, 1914, Mary Rachel, daughter of Thomas Franklin Pedley, Doctor of Medicine, Rangoon. His recreations were hunting, polo, shooting, and football.

CAPTAIN GRAHAM DE MONTMORENCY ARMSTRONG - LUSHINGTON- TULLOCH, 1st BATTN. CONNAUGHT RANGERS, was born in London

on the 27th November, 1885, son of William Cairns Armstrong-Lushington-Tulloch and Kate

France - Lushington-Tulloch, of Shanbolard, Moyard, County Galway. He was a great-nephew and godson of the late General de Montmorency, and a nephew of the late Captain Armstrong, Argyll and Sutherland Highlanders.

He was educated at Summerfields, Oxford ; and at Rugby, from which he passed into the R.M.C., Sandhurst, in 1903, and joined the Connaught Rangers in January, 1905, becoming Lieutenant in April, 1906. He gained a special certificate in Signalling in 1906.

Captain Tulloch, who was gazetted to that rank in March, 1915, but dated from September, 1914, was killed in action while retaking a trench on the 5th November, 1914. All the officers with him at the time were killed, but the following account of the circumstances was obtained from a wounded man who was present : " It was necessary to vacate the trench occupied by ' A ' Company, owing to its being enfiladed by German fire, and to make a new trench behind it. There was no time to fill in the vacated trench, which was occupied by the enemy, and this made a parallel trench held by ' B ' Company untenable. On the night of the 4th November two platoons of ' A' Company were ordered to retake the trench vacated earlier by them, and to fill it in. They charged under Captain Hack and Lieutenant Tulloch and retook the trench, Lieutenant Tulloch being slightly wounded, but continuing to lead and encourage the men till he was shot through the head, having previously said that the position must be held. The rifles, however, jammed, and the men of ' A ' Company were thus unable to retain the position. The bodies of Captain Tulloch and of Lieutenant George (also killed) were subsequently recovered at great risk, and, as they had been great friends, were buried side by side in the orchard of a farm near Neuve Chapelle."

The Commanding Officer of his battalion, writing to Captain Tulloch's mother, said : " He died a soldier's death, and I am sure no one in the regiment is more mourned by his brother officers and his company than he was. He was loved by both officers and men."

Captain Payne, of the battalion, described the event as follows : " It was on the night of the 4th that ' A ' Company made a gallant attack on a forward German trench. They were ordered to take the trench and fill it in. Half the com-

pany attacked and took the trench under Captain Hack, Graham (Mr. Tulloch), and Mr. George, who were all killed. They all died, as soldiers would wish to die, bravely at the head of their men, and especially Graham. He was wounded, but went on fighting, and then was killed. Some of his company brought him back to where I was. His face was so peaceful and calm that one almost thought there was a smile on it. I was present at the funeral. He was beloved by officers and men, who would do anything for him."

Captain Tulloch had just been elected to the Junior United Service Club at the time of his death. He was a keen sportsman, a first-rate shot with gun and rifle, winning several shooting competitions in his regiment. When in India he kept racing ponies, and won the Merchants' Stakes at the Karachi Autumn Meeting, 1912, with his pony " Young Lomond."

CAPTAIN CECIL FALCONER TULLOH, 3rd BATTN. THE DUKE OF CAMBRIDGE'S OWN (MIDDLESEX REGT.),
born at St. Leonards-on-Sea on the 3rd June, 1882, was the son of the late Major-General John Stewart Tulloh, C.B., R.H.A., and a cousin of Lieutenant - Colonel G. S. Tulloh) who commanded the 2nd Battalion Gloucestershire Regiment, and who was killed on Hill 60), and a relative of Colonel Hendley Paul Kirkwood, R.E. (retired), of Bath.

After fifteen months' service in the 3rd Battalion King's Own (Yorkshire Light Infantry), while embodied, he was gazetted to the 4th Middlesex Regiment, in January, 1903, becoming Lieutenant in August, 1905. During the South African War he served in Malta for six months, in 1900, with the 3rd Battalion K.O. Yorkshire Light Infantry, receiving the Queen's medal.

He was shot in the head on the 13th October, 1914, close to Croix Barbes (near La Bassée) while instructing his men how to make straw socks as a protection against frost-bite.

Captain Tulloh, who was a member of the Public Schools' Club, was promoted Captain in January, 1914. He was unmarried.

LIEUTENANT GLADWYN MAURICE REVELL TURBUTT, 3rd (attd. 2nd) BATTN. OXFORDSHIRE AND BUCKINGHAMSHIRE LIGHT INFANTRY (SPECIAL RESERVE),
was the elder son of William Gladwyn Turbutt

and Mrs. Turbutt (*née* Edith S. Hall), of Ogston Hall, Derbyshire, and was born there

on the 17th May, 1883. He was a great-grandson of General Henry Glad-wyn, of Stubbin Court, Derbyshire, the famous defender of Fort Detroit, Canada, in the war of 1763, against the Indians.

"The Guardian" gave the following account of his career :—

" Lieutenant Turbutt was educated at Harrow and Magdalen College, Oxford, where he took his degree in 1904. A love of all that was ancient and beautiful marked his undergraduate days, and was the cause of an episode which will perpetuate his name in that venerable building which of all in Oxford was, after his own college, dearest to him, the Bodleian Library. For among other volumes which he brought up from time to time from the old and most interesting library of his home to compare with books in Oxford was the ' Turbutt Shakespeare,' a fine folio, which was quickly identified as the original copy of Shakespeare presented by Stationers' Hall to the Bodleian, and afterwards sold. In consequence of this discovery the book was subsequently purchased and restored to the library.

" Mr. Turbutt, after taking his degree, studied architecture for some years in London under the direction of Mr. E. P. Warren. Among his Magdalen friends was the present Principal of Wells, who in 1906 was one of the little band of graduate students whom Dr. Armitage Robinson used to gather together to live with him in the Deanery at Westminster. Mr. Turbutt was in this year invited to join the group, and quickly became an intimate sharer of the Dean's architectural and archæological interests. He was one of his companions on several excursions into France, made about this time, with a view to studying the origins and early growth of Norman architecture, with special reference to Edward the Confessor's Church at Westminster ; and when in 1911 the Dean removed to Wells it was to him that he entrusted the task of restoring the Deanery there to something of its original form and beauty. The work was done with characteristic care and good sense, its most notable result being the opening out of that noble chamber in Gunthorpe's building which now serves as a private chapel.

" For the past seven years Mr. Turbutt has lived mostly at home in Derbyshire, busying himself, not only as an architect, but as a justice of the peace, an officer in the Special Reserve, a

Commissioner of Boy Scouts, and as a supporter of many useful causes. He was a loyal and religious son of the Church, of which his family for generations have been benefactors. A gentleness, gaiety, and goodness all his own won for him everywhere affectionate regard. For his friends the early loss of a life of such fair promise will prove not the least precious of the sacrifices they are called to share in offering on the altar of their country's duty in its day of need."

He became Lieutenant in his battalion in March, 1910, and during the retirement from Mons joined the 2nd Battalion of his regiment. He was killed on the 21st October, 1914, during the early part of the Battle of Ypres, together with many other officers of the battalion which suffered severely both in killed and wounded.

CAPTAIN HUGH VINCENT CORBETT TURNBULL, 2nd BATTN. KING'S OWN SCOTTISH BORDERERS,

who was killed in action on the 13th November, 1914, was the only son of the late Charles Cubitt Turnbull, of Mur-vagh, Cheltenham, and Upper Colletts, Cleeve Hill, Glouces-tershire.

He was born on the 20th July, 1877, and was gazetted to the

King's Own Scottish Borderers, from the Militia, in May, 1898, becoming Lieutenant in May, 1900, and Captain in June, 1908. From January, 1911, to August, 1912, he was Adjutant of his battalion, and on the 8th August, 1912, was detached from his regiment for employment with the Egyptian Army. When war was declared he returned to England and was posted to the 2nd Battalion of his regiment.

CAPT. BINGHAM ALEXANDER TUR-NER, D.S.O., 6th (RESERVE) BATTN. RIFLE BRIGADE, attd. 2nd BATTN. KING'S ROYAL RIFLE CORPS,

was killed in action on the 2nd Novem-ber, 1914.

He was the son of the late Gen-eral Bingham Turner, R.A., and was born on the 30th May, 1877.

He received his com-mission in the Rifle Brigade in January, 1898, becoming

Lieutenant in December, 1899, and Captain in 1902. Captain Turner served with the Nile Expedition of 1898, and was present at the Battle of Khartoum, receiving the Egyptian medal with clasp. He also served in the South African War, 1899–1902, being for part of the time employed with the Mounted Infantry, and taking part in operations in Natal, including the action at Lombard's Kop ; was present at the defence of Ladysmith, including the sortie of the 10th December, 1899, and action of 6th January, 1900 ; in Natal, 1900, including action at Laing's Nek ; in the Transvaal, east of Pretoria, including actions at Belfast (where he was slightly wounded) and Lydenberg. He was mentioned in Despatches (" London Gazette," 25th April, 1902), was awarded the D.S.O., and received the Queen's medal with three clasps and the King's medal with two clasps.

In July, 1909, Captain Turner retired from the Regular Army, and joined the 6th (Reserve) Battalion of his regiment, being attached to the 2nd Battalion K.R.R.C. for active service.

LIEUTENANT JOHN REGINALD TURNER, 3rd (attd. 1st) BATTN. DORSETSHIRE REGIMENT (SPECIAL RESERVE),

the son of Mr. and Mrs. J. M. B. Turner, of " Hartshill," Wimborne Road, Bournemouth, was born at Stoke-on-Trent, Staffordshire, on the 20th November, 1892.

He joined the Special Reserve of Officers, Dorsetshire Regiment from the O.T.C. in December, 1911, becoming Lieutenant in May, 1913. For the war he was attached to the 1st Battalion of his regiment, and was killed near Festubert on the 13th October, 1914. Sir John French, in his next Despatch after that date, referred to " the gallant fighting of the Dorsets " on this occasion, and at the place where Lieutenant Turner fell.

Lieutenant Turner had been articled with his father as a solicitor in Bournemouth, and was Hon. Secretary of the Bournemouth and District Law Students' Society.

LIEUTENANT CHRISTOPHER RANDOLPH TURNOR, Xth (PRINCE OF WALES'S OWN ROYAL) HUSSARS,

born on the 16th August, 1886, at 37, Pont Street, London, S.W., was the second son of Algernon Turnor, C.B., formerly Financial Secretary of H.M. Post Office, and Lady Henrietta Turnor, daughter of Randolph, ninth Earl of Galloway, and Lady H. Blanche Somerset, daughter of Henry, sixth Duke of Beaufort :

he was a grandson of Christopher Turnor, of Stoke Rochford, Lincolnshire.

Educated at the Rev. the Marquess of Normanby's private school at Mulgrave Castle, at Eton, and at Christ Church, Oxford, he took his degree in 1908. In December of that year he received his commission in the Xth Royal Hussars, and became Lieutenant in September, 1910.

He joined the regiment at Rawal Pindi, India, and served with it there and in South Africa, returning with it to England in September, 1914, to take part in the Great War. The regiment embarked at Southampton on the 6th, and landed at Ostend on the 8th October, and was soon engaged in the fierce struggle near Ypres, which stemmed the advance of the Germans to the coast.

He was killed in action in the trenches at Zandvoorde on the 26th October, 1914, while trying to locate an enemy's field gun with his glasses, and was buried in the churchyard at Zandvoorde, a cross marking his grave.

A soldier of much promise, he was devoted to his profession, and was a great student of military history, as well as a lover of books and music.

The " Eton Chronicle," recording his death, said : " He was a boy of strong character and considerable ability, a fine football player, and only a passing heart weakness prevented him winning his field colours."

His C.O. wrote of him : " He was a universal favourite, a very good officer, and a great loss to the regiment and his country."

His Major also wrote : " He is a very great loss to us as an educated and thoroughly grounded soldier and officer, and also from his personal charm which endeared him to all ranks."

Lieutenant Turnor was a member of the Bachelors' Club. He was a keen all-round sportsman, a good rider to hounds, and fond of shooting, especially big-game shooting, which latter pursuit he followed successfully in Kashmir, Central India, and British East Africa.

CAPTAIN ARTHUR TWENTYMAN, 10th (SCOTTISH) BATTN. THE KING'S (LIVERPOOL REGIMENT), T.F.,

who was killed in action near Ypres on the 29th November, 1914, received his first commission in March, 1909, was promoted Lieutenant in December, 1910, and Captain in September, 1912.

CAPTAIN ARTHUR MONTAGUE TWISS, ROYAL ENGINEERS, commanding 2 COMPANY 3rd SAPPERS AND MINERS, INDIAN ARMY,

who was killed in action at the Persian Gulf on the 17th November, 1914, was the third and youngest son of the late Mr. E. C. Twiss, Stipendiary Magistrate of Hull, and of Mrs. Twiss, of Beverley, Yorkshire. He was born on the 17th March, 1881, and was gazetted to the Royal Engineers in May, 1900, becoming Lieutenant in May, 1903, and being promoted Captain in May, 1910.

LIEUTENANT JERVIS MOORE TYLEE, 15th (THE KING'S) HUSSARS,

who was killed in action while on reconnaissance duty near Mons on the 23rd August, 1914, was the only son of the late Moore Tylee, formerly of Avenue d'Jéna, Paris, and Ashley Place, Westminster. He was born on the 16th September, 1887, was educated at Wellington (Hardinge), and joined the 3rd Battalion the Buffs in 1907, being gazetted in December, 1908, to the 15th Hussars from the Special Reserve. He received his promotion to Lieutenant in November, 1913, and served with his regiment in India and South Africa.

His recreations were hunting, polo, and golf.

LIEUTENANT ALBERT TYLER, ROYAL ENGINEERS,

was the only child of Colonel H. E. Tyler, R.E., and Mrs. Tyler, grandson of Captain Sir H. W. Tyler, R.E., and great-grandson of General Sir C. W. Pasley, K.C.B., R.E. He was born on the 1st February, 1893, and educated at Mr. Parry's School, Stoke House; and at Charterhouse, where he took Junior and Senior Scholarships, and passed fourth for the R.M.A.,

Woolwich. He passed out third into the Royal Engineers in July, 1912, and was promoted Lieutenant in July, 1914.

Being posted to the 11th Field Company R.E., at Aldershot on leaving Chatham, he went to France in August, 1914, and fought at Mons, through the retirement at the Aisne, and again at Ypres. The 5th and 11th Field Companies R.E. were improving defences by night, and supporting infantry by day throughout the attack by the German Guards, and on the 12th November, 1914, Lieutenant Tyler with two sections of his company, by his prompt action, saved the situation when the flank of the Staffordshires had become exposed, before he was killed by a bullet through his heart. His uncle—Major A. H. Tyler, R.E.—had been killed on similar duty in command of the 5th Field Company R.E. the day before.

The Brigadier-General in command reported that had Lieutenant Tyler lived he would have been recommended for the D.S.O. He was mentioned in Field-Marshal Sir John French's Despatch of the 14th January, 1915, for gallant and distinguished service in the field.

MAJOR ALFRED HERBERT TYLER, ROYAL ENGINEERS,

who was killed in action on the 11th November, 1914, was the son of the late Sir H. W. Tyler, R.E., M.P., and grandson of the late General Sir C. W. Pasley, K.C.B., R.E.

He was born at Hampton Court on the 27th December, 1870, and was educated at Cheltenham College, where he held a scholarship; and at the Royal Military Academy, Woolwich. From the latter he was commissioned to the Royal Engineers in July, 1890, becoming Lieutenant in July, 1893. From December, 1895, to May, 1896, he was employed on the Sierra Leone Boundary Commission, and in 1898–99 took part in operations in Sierra Leone with the Karene Expedition, where he was wounded, and for which he received the medal with clasp.

He took part in the South African War, where he was on special service with the Rhodesian Field Force from March, 1900, to January, 1901, and, from January to May, 1901, was employed as a Staff Officer (graded Staff Captain). He was present at operations in the Transvaal and Cape Colony, receiving the Queen's medal with four clasps and the King's medal with two clasps. From January, 1907, to April, 1912, he was First Assistant Superintendent Building Works, Royal Arsenal, Woolwich. In the Great War he was at first employed on the lines of communication, but afterwards commanded No. 5 Field Company, R.E., in the IInd Division.

Major Tyler left a widow and three young boys. His nephew—Lieutenant A. Tyler, R.E.—was killed in action at the same place next day.

CAPTAIN WILLIAM ANNESLEY UNDERHILL, 3rd BATTN. WORCESTERSHIRE REGT.,

son of William Henry Underhill, was born at Tettenhall, near Wolverhampton, on the 20th October, 1882, and was educated at Repton. He served with the 3rd (Militia) Battalion North Staffordshire Regiment in March, 1902, from which he was gazetted to the 1st Worcestershire Regiment in July, 1904, serving with it at Templemore and Dublin, being promoted Lieutenant in November, 1907. He afterwards served for four years from August, 1909, with the West African Frontier Force. Early in 1914 Captain Underhill learnt flying at Brooklands, and took his pilot's certificate. He then went to the Royal Flying Corps at Upavon, but shortly before the outbreak of the war he rejoined his regiment at Tidworth, and accompanied the 3rd Battalion to France in August, 1914.

At Mons, on the 26th August, he was wounded, a bullet passing through his left shoulder, but he refused to go into hospital, and continued on duty with his arm strapped to his side. He was killed in action at Illies, near La Bassée, on the 21st October, 1914, having continued to act as dispatch rider to his C.O. until his death. Captain Underhill, who was promoted to his Captaincy on the 13th October, 1914, only eight days before he was killed, was mentioned after his death in Sir John French's Despatch of the 14th January, 1915.

He was a finished horseman, fond of hunting, and was well known with the Albrighton hounds. A few years before the war he rode Mr. Hanly's " Teddie," who ran second to " Famous " for the Conyngham Cup at Punchestown.

2nd LIEUTENANT JOHN ALFRED UNDERY, 4th BATTN. ROYAL FUSILIERS (CITY OF LONDON REGIMENT),

was born on the 11th October, 1881, at Monmouth, Wales, and was the son of First Port Officer William Charles Undery, Port Department, Gibraltar.

After receiving his education in Wales and in Gibraltar, he joined the Royal Fusiliers in 1901, becoming Sergeant three years later. He was promoted Company Sergeant-Major in 1913, and was granted his commission for services in the field, during the Great War, on the 1st October, 1914.

He was killed in action near Herlies on the 26th October, 1914. The following account of the circumstances was furnished to his widow by a comrade : " We had been fighting in the trenches hard all day, your husband being the only officer there during the greater part of the day. Early in the afternoon the enemy made a vigorous attempt to take our trench. During the heaviest of the fire, whilst using a rifle, he was shot in the head and passed away a few minutes later. His last words, as far as I can remember, were, ' Good-bye, boy ! ' He was buried a short time afterwards by four men of my company, who are all, I am sorry to say, either killed or prisoners. A small wooden cross was placed at the head of his grave, showing his regimental rank and name. I have no hesitation in saying that he was admired and respected by all, both as a C.S.M. and officer. I was with him to the end. His death was without a doubt caused by his doing so much. If he had not been so keen on using a rifle and exposing himself unnecessarily it is quite possible he would have been alive and well to-day."

2nd Lieutenant Undery played football for his company in the season 1913–14, was also in the regimental running team, and won several prizes for shooting.

He married Susannah, daughter of Sergeant-Major W. Overell, at one time serving with H.M. Forces at Windsor, and left two boys : William Alfred, age six ; and Edwin Maurice, age five years.

CAPTAIN EDWARD FREDERICK MALTBY URQUHART, 1st BATTN. THE BLACK WATCH (ROYAL HIGHLANDERS),

was the only son of the Rev. Edward William Urquhart, M.A., formerly Vicar of King's Sutton, Northants, and was born in Edinburgh on the 26th January, 1877.

He was educated at Cheltenham College, where he won the Mathematical medal, 1895 ; and at the R.M.C., Sandhurst, gaining there a medal as one of the Athletic Eight against the R.M.A., Woolwich, in 1896.

He was gazetted to the Black Watch in February, 1897, becoming Lieutenant in May two years later, and Captain in April, 1902. He served through the Boer War, 1901–02, being present at operations in the Transvaal and Orange River Colony, for which he received the Queen's medal with four clasps. In 1906–07 he was Assistant Superintendent of Gymnasia, Irish Command, and Superintendent from the latter year until 1910. He then went to India, where he was, in 1913, Inspector of Physical Training, Northern Army. Both in India and Ireland reports from his superior officers bore testimony to his devotion to duty and great ability in training men, and to his keen interest in all the men's athletics and sports. His brightness of disposition and perfect good temper endeared him to all his brother officers, and his family have received numerous letters showing that he was highly esteemed by the men who served under him.

He was a member of the Caledonian Club, St. James's, and president of various athletic and sporting associations in Ireland.

On the outbreak of war with Germany Captain Urquhart was at home on sick leave, but immediately asked to be sent out with the 1st Battalion of his regiment under Lieutenant-Colonel Grant Duff. His application was refused on the ground that he held an important Staff appointment in India, and was bound to return when pronounced medically fit. The Marquess of Tullibardine then applied for, and obtained his services to train the Scottish Horse in Perthshire, and he was engaged in this work at Scone when he received orders to embark immediately at Southampton for the front. This he did on the 22nd September, 1914. Letters from the Marquess of Tullibardine and Captain Urquhart's successor showed how greatly his services at Scone were appreciated, and how much he was missed.

He was killed instantaneously on the 23rd October, 1914, at Pilkem, on his return from inspecting a trench which the company under his command had recovered from the Germans the previous night. He was buried with Lieutenant Bowes-Lyon, of the same regiment, in Boesinghe Churchyard, the service being conducted by the Rev. H. W. Blackburne, Church of England Chaplain to the Forces.

CAPTAIN STEPHEN USSHER, 129th DUKE OF CONNAUGHT'S OWN BALUCHIS,

born at 52, Eaton Place, London, S.W., on the 4th October, 1882, was the third son of the Rev. Richard Ussher, Vicar of Westbury, Bucks. His two brothers were also in the Service, viz., Captain Beverly Ussher, Prince of Wales's Leinster Regiment (Royal Canadians); and Lieutenant Richard Ussher, R.N., H.M.S. "Hyacinth."

Captain Ussher was educated at St. Edward's, Oxford, and the R.M.C., Sandhurst. He was the fifth of the old St. Edward's boys to fall on the field of honour. Passing high out of the R.M.C., he was gazetted to an unattached 2nd Lieutenancy in August, 1902, and after serving for a time with a battalion of the East Kent Regiment, was posted to the Indian Army in June, 1904, becoming Lieutenant in December, 1904, and Captain in the 129th Baluchis in August, 1911. For two years he was Adjutant of his battalion, serving at Poona, Karachi, Hong Kong, and Ferozepore. He had also travelled in Japan.

Before proceeding to the fighting line Captain Ussher had been acting as Railway Staff Officer at Cairo. With his regiment he landed, in September, 1914, at Marseilles, where he was for a time in hospital. He rejoined his regiment at the front on the 1st November, and from that date was continually engaged in the advanced trenches, and wrote home very interesting letters, some of which were published in the "St. Edward's, Oxford, School Chronicle" for December, 1914. Captain Ussher was killed in action on the 16th December, 1914, while in charge of machine guns in the trenches at Givenchy. He was buried in Beuvry Cemetery. The Rev. R. Ussher received a letter of sympathy on his son's death from the Commander-in-Chief in India.

Captain Ussher, who was a member of the Junior Naval and Military Club, was well known in the cricket field, and frequently played for the Buckingham Cricket Club.

2nd LIEUTENANT GEORGE HERBERT VACHER, 4th (attd. 2nd) BATTN. ROYAL WARWICKSHIRE REGIMENT,

who was killed in action about the 30th October, 1914, was the eldest son of H. P. Vacher, A.M.I.C.E., and Mrs. Vacher, and was born in Winchester in February, 1894.

He was educated at Sherborne School, and at Worcester College, Oxford, and was a keen athlete, boxing and running being the sports in which he excelled. He represented his school at Aldershot in 1913 as a welterweight, and reached the finals in the Oxford University trials in 1914.

On the outbreak of the war he applied for a commission through his College O.T.C and was gazetted to his regiment in August, 1914. On being attached to the 2nd Battalion he left Lyndhurst for the front with the VIIth Division in October, 1914, and was killed near Zandvoorde on or about the date given above.

CAPTAIN JOHN FRANKS VALLENTIN, V.C., 1st BATTN. SOUTH STAFFORD-SHIRE REGT.,

born on the 14th May, 1882, was the son of the late Grimble Vallentin and Mrs. Grimble Vallentin. He was a grandson of Colonel Finnis, the first victim of the Indian Mutiny, and a nephew of Major Vallentin, killed in the Boer War.

Captain Vallentin was educated at Wellington College, and joined the 6th (Militia) Battalion, Rifle Brigade in August, 1899, becoming Lieutenant in July, 1900. That battalion was embodied at the Curragh Camp, Kildare, from the commencement of the Boer War for nearly a year, and on its disembodiment he was attached to the 3rd Royal Sussex Regiment. In July, 1903, he received his commission in the Royal Garrison Regiment (formed during the Boer War) in July, 1903, being transferred to the South Staffordshire Regiment as 2nd Lieutenant in June, 1905. He became Lieutenant in September, 1907, and Captain in June, 1909. He served in the Boer War with the 3rd (Militia) Battalion Royal Sussex Regiment, taking part in operations in the Orange River Colony from April to December, 1901, and in the Transvaal from the latter date till May, 1902. For his services he received the Queen's medal with five clasps.

In the Great War the 1st South Staffordshire Regiment formed part of the VIIth Division which landed at Zeebrugge on October 7th, and was through all the fighting in the first Battle of Ypres. So severe were its losses that the day before Captain Vallentin was killed, his battalion and the 2nd Royal Warwicks were formed into one small battalion under the command of Captain Vallentin. There were no officers of higher rank in either battalion, and so well did he lead his command on the 7th November, that he was awarded the V.C., the official account being as follows : " For conspicuous bravery on the 7th November at Zillebeke. When leading the attack against the Germans under a very heavy fire he was struck down, and on rising to continue the attack was immediately killed.

" The capture of the enemy's trenches which followed was in a great measure due to the confidence which the men had in their Captain, arising from his many previous acts of great bravery and ability."

He was mentioned in Sir John French's Despatch of the 14th January, 1915.

Captain Vallentin was a keen polo player and captain of the regimental Polo Club. He was specially qualified in musketry. He was not married.

LIEUTENANT JAMES VANCE, 2nd BATTN. ESSEX REGIMENT,

who was killed in action on the 21st October, 1914, was the eldest son of the late W. J. Vance, Surgeon, Bexleyheath, Kent, and of Mrs. Vance, 3, Vanbrugh Fields, Blackheath. He was born on the 2nd January, 1886, and was educated at Dover College (St. Martin's House), where he was in the Cricket XI, 1903–04 ; and at the R.M.C., Sandhurst. He received his commission in February, 1906, becoming Lieutenant in January, 1911.

He had been slightly wounded on the 20th September, 1914, but did not leave the trenches. His servant gave the following account of his death : " ' D ' Company had just relieved the Rifle Brigade, at Le Gert, when they were immediately attacked by an enfilade fire from the enemy. Lieutenant Vance, who was in charge of two platoons, directed the men to leave the trenches, and then gave the command to charge. His words were, ' Come on, men ! Charge the bounders ! ' Taking the lead, he was shot through the abdomen. The action had a victorious result."

Lieutenant Vance played hockey and football for his regiment.

LIEUTENANT JOHN BEAUCLERK VANDELEUR, 3rd BATTN. LEICESTERSHIRE REGT.,

was born at Winchester in 1887, and was the son of Colonel John Ormsby Vandeleur, C.B., of Ballinacourty, Castle Connell, County Limerick. He was educated at Wellington College from 1901 to 1904.

Lieutenant Vandeleur was gazetted to the Durham Light Infantry in April, 1910. He retired from the Regular Army in 1912, and joined the 3rd Battalion Leicestershire Regiment as Lieutenant in October, 1913.

For the Great War he was attached to the 3rd Battalion Worcestershire Regiment, and was killed on the 7th November, 1914, at Ploegsteert Wood, north of Armentières.

CAPTAIN WILLIAM MOUNTCHARLES CROFTON VANDELEUR, 2nd BATTN. THE ESSEX REGIMENT,

was killed in action in September, 1914, no place or date being given in the monthly official casualty list in which the notification appeared.

The son of Colonel William Vandeleur, of 18, Salisbury Road, Hove, Brighton, he was born on the 29th May, 1870, and was educated at Wellington (Anglesey, 1883–87). He joined the Royal Fusiliers from the Militia in December, 1889, being transferred to the Essex Regiment in October, 1890, receiving his promotion to Lieutenant in October, 1894.

In 1897–98 he took part in the Mohmand Campaign, north-western frontier of India, being for a time Assistant to the Division Transport Officer, and was also with the Tirah Expedition Force. He received the medal with three clasps.

He was promoted Captain in May, 1900, and was employed during the South African War as a Special Service Officer from October, 1899, to February, 1902, including employment as Orderly Officer, Base, at the end of 1899, with the South African Light Horse, and as Assistant to Staff Officer, Colonial Forces; with Roberts's Horse from January, 1900, to February, 1902 (Adjutant from November, 1900), and Acting Intelligence Officer; afterwards on the Staff as Assistant Provost Marshal from February to June, 1902. He took part in the advance on and relief of Kimberley, operations in the Orange Free State, at Paardeberg, in the Transvaal, east and west of Pretoria, Orange River Colony and Cape Colony, including actions at Poplar Grove, Driefontein, Houtnek (Thoba Mountain), Vet River, and Zand River. He received the Queen's medal with four clasps and the King's medal with two clasps.

From July, 1902, to March, 1903, he was employed under the Civil Government, Transvaal. In April, 1904, he was placed on half-pay, but

was restored to the establishment of his regiment in September of the same year.

On war being declared Captain Vandeleur was serving at Chatham with the 2nd Battalion, which belonged to the IVth Division, arriving in France in time to take part in the action at Le Cateau, the retirement to the Marne, and the subsequent advance to the Aisne. It is probable that Captain Vandeleur fell in the fighting at the latter battle.

LIEUTENANT HENRY IVANHOE VANDELL, RESERVE OF OFFICERS, attd. 1st BATTN. NORTHAMPTONSHIRE REGT.,

only son of Henry Arnold and Sara A. Vandell, of Gillingham, Kent, was born at New Brompton, Kent, on the 8th December, 1890.

He was educated at His Majesty's Royal Dockyard School (Engineering Branch), Chatham, and at East London College (University of London), becoming later a graduate of the Institute of Mechanical Engineers. He was for two years in the University O.T.C., and received a commission in the Reserve of Officers of that Corps in December, 1912.

In August, 1914, he trained with the Royal West Kent Regiment, and proceeding to the front in September was attached to the Northamptonshire Regiment. He was in the trenches at the Aisne, and took part in the fighting near Ypres, where he was killed on the 11th November, 1914, while leading his platoon to intercept an attack made by the Prussian Guard.

The following is an extract from the letter of a N.C.O., dated the 19th December, 1914, describing the event: " The Prussian Guard, through sheer weight of numbers, broke through our line. We were called upon to intercept them. After a terrific hand-to-hand encounter the enemy turned and fled. Away we went after them in a mad, headlong rush. We caught and killed heaps of them, but some of them succeeded in occupying some old ruined farmhouses, and poured a murderous fire into us. A lot of our fellows went down, but the remainder of us went straight at the houses. Lieutenant Vandell was at the very head of us. When actually outside the door of the house a bullet struck poor Mr. Vandell in the head, killing him instantly. We eventually drove the enemy out, and occupied a position close by. In the dead of night we crept out and buried poor Mr. Vandell as decently as circumstances would allow."

LIEUTENANT CHARLES HYLTON VAN NECK, 3rd (attd. 1st) BATTN. NORTHUMBERLAND FUSILIERS, who was killed in action on the 20th October, 1914, aged twenty-one years, was the youngest son of the late Mr. Charles Van Neck, of Lily Hill, Bracknell, and of Mrs. Van Neck, of 32, Pont Street, London, S.W.

He was educated at Harrow (The Headmaster's, 1907-11) and joined the Northumberland Fusiliers in October, 1913, and got his step in September, 1914. His eldest brother—Lieutenant P. Van Neck, Grenadier Guards—was killed on the 26th October, 1914.

LIEUTENANT PHILIP VAN NECK, 1st BATTN. GRENADIER GUARDS,

who had been reported missing since the 26th October, 1914, was afterwards stated to have been killed in action on that date at Kruiseik, near Ypres.

He was the eldest son of the late Mr. Charles and Mrs.Van Neck, of 32, Pont Street, London, and was born in March, 1887. He was educated at Eton, and joined the Grenadier Guards in August, 1910, becoming Lieutenant in June, 1912, and went on active service with his battalion in October, 1914. He was a member of the Guards' and Pratt's Clubs, and his chief recreations were hunting, shooting, and cricket.

His youngest brother—2nd Lieutenant Charles Hylton Van Neck, Northumberland Fusiliers —was killed in action on the 20th October, 1914.

CAPTAIN EVAN NANNEY JONES-VAUGHAN, 2nd BATTN. ROYAL WELSH FUSILIERS,

who was killed on the 26th October, 1914, was the younger son of Major - General Jones-Vaughan, C.B., Colonel of the Loyal North Lancashire Regiment, and Mrs. Jones - Vaughan, of Llwydyn Rhydyclafdy, Carnarvonshire, and a cousin of Sir Hugh Nanney. He was born on the 5th September, 1885, and was educated at Wellington and the R.M.C., Sandhurst. He received his commission in the Royal Welsh Fusiliers in February, 1905, becoming Lieutenant in December, 1909, and Captain in April, 1913.

He was fond of big-game shooting, and collected some very fine heads in Tibet, Kashmir, and other countries.

He was killed by shell near Armentières in a very violent attack on the trenches. His C.O. wrote of him : " I have lost a very gallant and capable officer and a very dear companion."

2nd LIEUTENANT HARRY ROBERT VAUGHAN, 2nd BATTN. CONNAUGHT RANGERS, who was killed in action in Flanders on the 27th October, 1914, was the son of Charles Vaughan, late Colour-Sergeant in the Durham Light Infantry, and was born at Dagshai, India, on the 1st May, 1885. His relative—Lieutenant William Charles Taylor—is in the Army Pay Corps.

2nd Lieutenant Vaughan joined the Durham Light Infantry as a boy in December, 1899, and having reached the rank of Colour-Sergeant in that corps was granted a commission as 2nd Lieutenant in the Connaught Rangers, and was posted to the 2nd Battalion of that regiment in September, 1914. When killed he was attached to the Durham Light Infantry.

LIEUTENANT-COLONEL WALTER EDWIN VENOUR, 58th VAUGHAN'S RIFLES (FRONTIER FORCE), who was killed in action on the 31st October, 1914, was the son of the late General Edwin Venour, Indian Army.

He was born on the 17th May, 1864, was educated at Weymouth College, and was gazetted to the West India Regiment as Lieutenant in September, 1885. In January, 1889, he was transferred to the Indian Staff Corps, and became Captain in the Indian Army in September, 1896.

He took part in the Chin-Lushai Expedition of 1889-90, for which he received the medal with clasp ; in the first Miranzai Expedition, 1891 ; and in operations on the Samana and in the Kurram Valley, north-western frontier of India, 1897-98. For the latter he received the medal with two clasps. He was also on active service in the Tirah Expedition at and around Divatoi, and the action of the 24th November, 1897, in which he was slightly wounded, and for which he received a clasp to his medal.

In 1900 he was appointed Second in Command of the Khyber Rifles, and during the time he held that appointment he officiated as Commandant of that corps and as Political Officer, Khyber. In 1906 he was appointed Staff Officer to Sir Harold Deane, Chief Commissioner North West Frontier Provinces, and on his return to his regiment (58th Rifles) he was thanked by him in a letter saying: " Sir Harold Deane wishes to place on record the appreciation of your work under him both as an officer of the Khyber Rifles and latterly as his Staff Officer for Militia and Border Military Police. He is assured that the high state of efficiency attained by the Khyber Rifles is due in a great measure to your zeal and capacity as Second in Command of that corps. As Staff Officer he has to thank you for the great interest you evinced in all matters relating to the Militia and Border Military Police, and for the pains you took to carry out the administration of these corps on the lines indicated by him. The Chief Commissioner trusts that the good work which you have done while under his orders in this Province may be reckoned to your credit in your future career."

He obtained his Majority in September, 1903, and was promoted Lieutenant-Colonel in May, 1911. His regiment came from India with the Expeditionary Force, for the Great War, and, on the occasion of his death had been ordered to recapture some trenches which the Germans had occupied. We attacked in the dark, and drove out the enemy, some of whom fell back into a trench some thirty yards or so behind. The enemy were dressed in Gurkha uniforms taken from the dead, and the Colonel, who had just come to this part of our position, as it was getting light, thought they were Gurkhas and was shot as he was looking over the parapet. Death was instantaneous, the bullet passing through the brain.

Lieutenant-Colonel Venour married Annie Lilian, daughter of Robert Barton, Esq., Deputy Master Royal Mint, Melbourne, Australia, and left four children: three daughters and one son. He was a Freemason, a Knight Templar, and Chaplain of his Lodge.

2nd LIEUTENANT ROBERT HUM. PHREY MEDLICOTT VEREKER, 2nd BATTN. GRENADIER GUARDS,

killed in action near Landrecies, on the night of the 25th August, 1914, was the son of Mr. and Mrs. George Medlicott Vereker, of Sharpitor, near Salcombe, South Devon. He was born on the 15th October, 1892, and was educated at Cheam, at Osborne, and at the R.M.C., Sandhurst, from which he was gazetted to the Grenadier Guards in September, 1913.

The Rev. B. G. O'Rorke, Chaplain to the Forces, who was taken prisoner of war and sent to Torgau, writing on the 30th August, 1914, gave the following particulars: " Your brave son met his death on the 25th inst. while trying to draw Corporal Bacchus, of his regiment, who was wounded, out of the range of the German fire. The Corporal is now convalescent. Your son was buried in the next grave to some of his brother officers and eight men of the Coldstream Guards. We erected a rough cross giving their names. The following day the wife of the Garde Cimetière brought me a wooden cross of a more substantial kind, and I left instructions for their names to be painted on it. It was her own thought and her own tribute."

In Mr. Vereker's memory his parents have lent their house, near Salcombe, for use as a Red Cross Hospital for the duration of the war.

His recreations were hunting, riding, and golf, and he was also fond of music. He was a member of the Guards' Club.

LIEUTENANT FREDERICK CHARLES VERNER 1st BATTN. THE KING'S (SHROPSHIRE LIGHT INFANTRY),

born on the 30th November, 1891, at Kenley, Surrey, was the son of the late William Henry Verner, I.C.S., and was related to Major-General Thomas Edward Verner, C.B., and Colonel Willoughby Verner, late of the Rifle Brigade.

He was educated at Harrow and at Brasenose College, Oxford. He was a good athlete and ran for his college. At Harrow he received his cap and fez for football in 1909. He had taken a third class in the Honour School of Jurisprudence in July, 1914, having gone to Brasenose College, from Harrow, in the Michaelmas term of 1911, and was soon seen to be a man of independence and character, chivalrous, and determined to succeed. At Oxford he was a member of the Phœnix Club, Brasenose.

He was gazetted, as a University candidate, to the O.T.C. in March, 1914, being transferred to his regiment with antedate to January, 1913, being promoted Lieutenant in August, 1914. He soon went to the front, and was killed on the 25th October, 1914, by the bursting of a shell. The following account of the occurrence was given by the Captain of his company to his mother: " Your son had charge of his platoon on a little knoll, which had a little tope of trees on it, which was a mark to the German guns. . . . On Sunday, October 25th, some Germans broke our line on the left of your son's knoll, and he, by a message he sent to me, realised the possible danger of it, and thence during the whole day his platoon was subjected to a very heavy shell fire. He had some casualties amongst his men all day, and about 5.30 p.m. a shell from the big gun struck close in front of his own trench, and he was hit straight on the head and killed, A message came down to me to that effect. The men had to leave the trench shortly after, owing to shell fire. I may say that your son during the whole time behaved in the most gallant manner. All his men speak in the most extraordinary terms of his conduct, and say they would have gone anywhere with him, and are unanimous in saying that he stuck to a practically untenable position with extraordinary pluck. I may also say that I have recommended him to my Commanding Officer for some award, which I trust he may get, as I know he fully deserved it. Had he lived another two hours he would have been out of it. The men of his platoon came and asked me for even pennies from his money as souvenirs, which they thought I had, as ' he was the bravest man they ever saw.' "

Another account said that after sending many of his men back to a safer trench, he insisted on remaining where he was to keep a look-out ; and after the shelling had finished, as he did not answer when called, was found to have been killed.

His C.O., writing of him, said : " He must have died a splendid death. One of his officers said, ' His name will always be remembered that he made a gallant fight for eight hours against an overwhelming force.' "

His mother received also very appreciative letters of her son's character and ability from heads of the college and from college friends.

LIEUTENANT CHRISTOPHER FRANCIS VERRALL, 2nd BATTN. ROYAL SUSSEX REGIMENT,

born at Brighton on the 5th February, 1889, was the son of Thomas Jenner Verrall, M.R.C.S., L.R.C.P., Hon. LL.D., Aberdeen.

He was educated at the school of the Rev. C. E. Williams, D.D., Summer Fields, Oxford, at Wellington College, and Trinity College, Cambridge. He represented the University in swimming.

He joined the Army as a University candidate in October, 1911, his commission being ante-

dated to October, 1910, and became Lieutenant in November, 1912.

Lieutenant Verrall was killed in the trenches at Epinette, near La Bassée, on the 22nd December, 1914. He was mentioned in Sir John French's Despatch of the 14th January, 1915.

LIEUTENANT HORATIO JOHN VICAT, 1st BATTN. THE QUEEN'S OWN (ROYAL WEST KENT REGT.),

was the son of the late Horatio Nelson Vicat and Mrs. Vicat, of East Lodge, Sevenoaks, and was born on the 24th June, 1885, in the Province of Quebec, Canada.

He was educated at Cheltenham College, and passed thence into the Royal Military College, Sandhurst. He was first gazetted to the Royal West Kent Regiment in January, 1905, joining the 1st Battalion in Malta, and became Lieutenant in May, 1908. He was attached to the Gold Coast Regiment for fourteen months in 1910–11, and took part in actions against native tribes at Zonagara.

He was killed during the Battle of the Aisne on the 13th September, 1914, near Missy, while in command of his company when they formed the advance guard to their Brigade, and was leading his men down to capture a bridge-head held by the enemy. Lieutenant Vicat having been wounded, four of his men volunteered to bring him back. No sooner had they lifted him, however, than the enemy fired, killing the officer and two of the men and wounding the other two. Lieutenant Vicat was a member of the Junior Naval and Military Club.

CAPTAIN PERCIVAL CAMPBELL HAMPE-VINCENT, 129th DUKE OF CONNAUGHT'S OWN BALUCHIS,

was born at Hyderabad on the 27th August, 1881, the son of the late Mr. Robert W. E. Hampe-Vincent, C.I.E., Comsioner of Police (retired), Bombay.

Educated at Bedales and Northwood Park School, he received an unattached 2nd

Lieutenancy in May, 1901, and joined the Indian Army in November, 1902, becoming Lieutenant in August, 1903. He proceeded on special service with the Somaliland Field Force in January, 1901, and took part in the operations in that country in 1903–04, receiving the medal with clasp. In September, 1905, he joined the King's African Rifles, with whom he served for several years in East Africa, and for two years commanded a contingent of Sikhs in Zomba, Nyassaland, and, having been promoted Captain in May, 1910, subsequently commanded a double company of his own regiment at Ferozepore, Punjab. He accompanied the Indian contingent to France, and was killed in action on the 26th October, 1914, near Ypres—one of the first Indian officers to fall—leading his men to attack Prussian cavalry.

Captain Hampe-Vincent married Blanche Robinson, daughter of Mr. Foster Robinson, who died at Kasauli, India, in May, 1914, leaving no children.

CAPTAIN PHILIP ERNEST VINEY, 1st BATTN. LEICESTERSHIRE REGIMENT,

was the second son of Dr. and Mrs. Viney, Cintra, Swanage.

He was born on the 23rd April, 1888, and educated at Summerfields, Oxford, and at Aldenham School, Elstree, joining the Leicestershire Regiment from the R.M.C., Sandhurst, in 1908. He became Lieutenant in May, 1910. On the 5th October, 1911, he was seconded for employment with the West African Frontier Force, and in 1914 was A.D.C. to Sir Hugh Clifford. On the outbreak of the war he rejoined the 1st Battalion Leicestershire Regiment as Captain, to which rank he had been promoted in August, and was sent to the front in September, 1914. His Battalion formed part of the 16th Brigade, VIth Division, which took part in the advance to the Aisne, the battle at that river, and the subsequent fighting.

He was mortally wounded by a high-explosive shell on the afternoon of the 14th December while in the trenches. He was removed to the Field Hospital, Bailleul, and died on the evening of the 17th, deeply regretted by his brother officers and the men who served under him, to whom he had endeared himself by his cheerful unselfishness and thought for others.

Captain Viney was a member of the Junior Army and Navy Club, and was unmarried.

CAPTAIN WILLIAM GEOFFREY VYVYAN, 1st BATTN. ROYAL WELSH FUSILIERS,

who died at Droogenbroodhoek on the 24th October, 1914, of wounds received near Zonnebeke on the 21st of the same month, leaving a widow, was the youngest son of the late Rev. A. F. Vyvyan and Mrs. Vyvyan.

He was born on the 21st January, 1876, and joined the Royal Welsh Fusiliers from the Militia in June, 1899. He took part in the relief of Pekin, China, 1900, for which he received the medal with clasp.

He was promoted Lieutenant in May, 1902, and Captain in April, 1909. From October, 1910, to October, 1913, he was an Adjutant of the 5th (Territorial) Battalion of his Regiment. Captain Vyvyan was reported missing after the action at Zonnebeke on the 21st October. For some time his fate was uncertain, but in March, 1915, information was received from the Foreign Office that Captain Vyvyan had died, as stated above, while in the hands of the Germans.

2nd LIEUTENANT SAMUEL SHORTER ARTHUR WADE, 2nd BATTN. LINCOLNSHIRE REGIMENT,

was born on the 15th January, 1876, at Great Yarmouth, and was the son of James and Maria Wade, of that town. His brother was Colour-Sergeant James Wade (Distinguished Conduct Medal for South African War), of the same regiment. He was educated at the Hospital Boys' School, Great Yarmouth.

2nd Lieutenant Wade enlisted in May, 1895, when he joined at Woolwich, afterwards serving at the depot, where he was for four years Acting Schoolmaster in charge. He then joined his battalion in South Africa for the Boer War, receiving on its conclusion the war medals. After returning from South Africa, he served with his battalion at various stations at home and abroad, including Salisbury Plain, Aldershot, Gibraltar, and Bermuda. He left the latter for Halifax, Nova Scotia, arriving on the 16th September, 1914, where the battalion awaited the arrival of the Canadian Contingent, and sailed for Europe, reaching Plymouth in October.

In the meantime he had received several steps in promotion : Corporal, 1896 ; Sergeant, 1899 ; Colour-Sergeant, 1903 ; Regimental Quartermaster-Sergeant, January, 1914. He received the Long Service medal in 1913. He was highly commended by the Commandant of the School of Mounted Infantry at Longmoor, where from 1908–10 he acted as Sergeant-Major of the Mounted Infantry Battalions.

He received his commission on the 1st November, 1914, during the Great War. Subsequently he was reported " missing," and is believed to have been killed on the 8th December, 1914. Mrs. Ward received an appreciative letter of sympathy from a Major of the battalion in which he said : " I am afraid I can hold out no hope that your husband is alive. You know what a brave man he was, and when he heard there was an attack he stayed and took part in it. He charged with his company and did not return, but his cap was picked up with a bullet through it. (*Mrs. Wade afterwards received the cap from the front.*) He had only joined this battalion the night before in the trenches. He was a brave officer, and died doing more than his duty, and is a great loss to the regiment."

A Private of his battalion wrote : " On the night of the 8th December we made an attack in the front of a wood at Kemmel. Mr. Wade said to me, ' Come on, my lad ; it only wants one to lead,' and Mr. Wade and I set off, getting well in front of the company. We got to a German dummy trench, and I jumped in, and lying down turned round looking for the officer. I heard he was wounded, and asking if he was attended to they said, ' No,' and I got up and retired to the officer, and got him out of the trench and dressed him, seeing that he was hit in the head, and in my idea the officer was dead when I left him."

The British and German lines were so close together that it was impossible to go out and collect the dead and wounded.

2nd Lieutenant Wade was a good shot, having taken part in all the regimental cup shoots since 1904. He was also a certificated referee for Association football.

He married, in September, 1899, Rosina Frances, daughter of Alice and Walter Rainer Pitt, of Great Yarmouth, and left two daughters : Rose Alice, born July, 1900 ; and Vera Edna, born September, 1905.

2nd LIEUTENANT LEONARD PENGELLY WAGHORN, 3rd BATTN. THE QUEEN'S OWN (ROYAL WEST KENT REGIMENT), who was killed at Ypres on the 6th November, 1914, was born at 8,

Glenluce Road, Blackheath, on the 24th January, 1891, the second son of Engineer-Captain J. W. Waghorn, R.N., D.Sc., formerly Professor of Physics at the Royal Naval College, Greenwich. He was educated at the Preparatory School, Scaitcliffe, Englefield (Messrs. Morton and Vickers) ; and at Marlborough College. He was a Lance-

Corporal in the O.T.C. (Cavalry). Intending to enter the medical profession, he was in his fourth year at Guy's Hospital when, on the outbreak of the war, he volunteered for active service, was given a commission in the 3rd Battalion Royal West Kent Regiment, in August, 1914, and was stationed at Chatham for about six weeks, leaving for the front on the 3rd October. At the time of his death 2nd Lieutenant Waghorn was serving with the 1st Battalion Princess Charlotte of Wales's (Royal Berkshire Regiment).

2nd LIEUTENANT GEOFFREY CHAUNER WAINWRIGHT, 3rd (attd. 1st) BATTN. NORTHAMPTONSHIRE REGT.,

second son of Charles Henry Wainwright, J.P., Edgware, Middlesex, and Mrs. Wainwright, was born in London on the 27th January, 1895. He was educated at Stanmore Park and Wellington College, Berks, where he was in the Cricket XI

in 1911, 1912, and 1913 ; in the Football XV in 1912 ; and in the Running VIII in 1912 and 1913. He then went to Clare College, Cambridge, where he had just finished his first year, and had been elected Secretary to the Clare College Cricket Club for 1915, when the war with Germany broke out, and he was gazetted to the 3rd Battalion Northamptonshire Regiment in September, 1914. He trained at Weymouth, proceeded to France in November, 1914, and was attached to the 1st Battalion of his regiment.

He was wounded in a night attack to regain some lost trenches on the 21st December, 1914, near Givenchy, Rue de l'Epinette, leading on his men after his Captain had been wounded, and died the next evening in hospital.

He married Ada Delamere Doveton Deane, daughter of William John Deane and Mrs. Deane, of Bath, and left two children : John Leonard Grey Dudley, born March, 1915, posthumously ; and Monica Vivian Grey Dudley, born March, 1913.

MAJOR HUGH ST. AUBYN WAKE, M.V.O., 8th GURKHA RIFLES,

who was killed in action on the 1st November, 1914, was the fourth son of the late Admiral Charles Wake, R.N., and of Mrs. Wake, Helens, Sidmouth. He was born on the 27th March, 1870, and was gazetted to the Northumberland Fusiliers from the R.M.C., in May, 1891, becoming Lieutenant in February, 1893. In May, 1895, he was transferred to the Indian Staff Corps, and was promoted Captain in the Indian Army in July, 1901.

In 1897–98 he was on active service on the north-western frontier of India, in the Tirah Expedition, for which he received the medal with clasp.

Major Wake, who obtained his Majority in May, 1909, married, in 1899, Kathleen Mary, second daughter of Lieutenant-Colonel Edward Evans Grigg, of Cuselea, Bedford, and left a son and a daughter.

LIEUTENANT ROGER OWEN BIRK-BECK WAKEFIELD, 1st BATTN. PRINCESS VICTORIA'S (ROYAL IRISH FUSILIERS),

was the only son of Mr. and Mrs. Edward Wakefield, of Farnagh, Moate, County Westmeath, and was born there on the 20th July, 1892. He was educated at Moorland House, Heswall and Repton School. He shot in his school team for the Ashburton Shield at Bisley, 1908, and also won the Fry prize in the same year. He went to the R.M.C., Sandhurst, in February, 1911, and was gazetted to the Royal Irish Fusiliers in February, 1912, joining his battalion at Shorncliffe. He was promoted Lieutenant in January, 1914.

He left for France with his battalion, which formed part of the 10th Brigade, IVth Division, on the 21st August, 1914, and was seriously wounded on the 26th of that month at Coudry, dying the next day in the temporary hospital there.

Lieutenant Wakefield was a good all-round sportsman, was well placed in many cross-country and hurdle races, and won seven point-to-point races in 1913–14. He was also a keen follower of hounds.

2nd LIEUTENANT JOHN HENRY LYONS WALCOTT, 2/2nd KING EDWARD'S OWN GURKHA RIFLES (THE SIRMOOR RIFLES),

who was killed in action on the 2nd November,1914,was the only child of Mr. and Mrs. Robert C. S.Walcott, Tenby Lodge, Cavendish Road, Southsea. He was born on the 2nd May, 1894, and was educated at Christ's Hospital, where he got his cricket colours; and at the R.M.C., Sandhurst, where he also was in the cricket XI. After passing out with honours for the Indian Army, he was gazetted 2nd Lieutenant in January, 1913, and attached to the 2nd Battalion Leicestershire Regiment for the usual probationary period. He was transferred to the Indian Army in the early part of 1914.

2nd LIEUTENANT CUTHBERT TEMPLE WALDY, 2nd BATTN. THE PRINCE OF WALES'S VOLUNTEERS (SOUTH LANCASHIRE REGIMENT),

was born at Horsley, Woodhouse, Derby, on the 31st August, 1891, the son of the late Rev. Arthur G. Waldy, M.A., Priest, Rector of Yarm, and of Mrs. Waldy. He was educated at Marlborough College, and was gazetted to the Special Reserve of Officers in August, 1912. In August, 1914, he was attached to the 3rd Battalion York and Lancaster Regiment, and in October joined the 2nd South Lancashire Regiment.

He was killed in action at Lorgies, near La Bassée, on the 20th October, 1914. Before the war he had been employed in Messrs. Huntley and Palmer's Biscuit Factory, Reading. He was a Lieutenant in the Church Lads' Brigade.

CAPTAIN EDGAR WILMER WALKER, 3rd (attd. 1st) BATTN. EAST YORK-SHIRE REGT.,

was born at Scarborough on the 3rd August, 1875, the elder son of Admiral C. F. Walker, of The Hall, Beverley, East York-shire, and a grand-son of the late Sir James Walker, Bart., of Sand Hut-ton, York.

He was educated at Eton and Balliol College, Oxford, where he took a fourth class B.A., Lit. Hum., in 1898. At Eton he was in the Fives Choices, and represented the University at billiards. He subsequently entered the legal profession, and was called to the Bar, Inner Temple, in 1901, practising in the North Eastern Circuit. He was in the Inns of Court Volunteers, and entered the 1st Cadet Battalion of the Queen's Royal West Surrey Regiment as 2nd Lieutenant, in March, 1903, joining the Special Reserve (3rd Battalion East Yorkshire Regiment) as a Captain in 1905. He had been Instructor of Musketry to his battalion.

He was killed in action on the 28th October, 1914, by shrapnel, near Armentières, while serving with the 1st Battalion of his regiment.

He married Charlotte Rankin, second daughter of Sir Robert Maule, of Ashbrook, Edinburgh, and left one son, Francis Robert, born February, 1910.

Captain Walker, who belonged to the Con-servative Club, London, and the Yorkshire Club, York, was fond of sport, shooting, fishing, golf, and motoring.

CAPTAIN OSWALD BETHELL WALKER, 15th (THE KING'S) HUSSARS,

born on the 28th May, 1875, was the eldest son of Captain and Mrs. Edwyn Wal-ker, of Mill Mount House, York, and a grandson of Sir James Walker, Bart., of Sand Hutton.

He was educated at Eton, and was gazet-ted to the 15th Hus-sars from the Militia

in September, 1896, becoming Lieutenant in July, 1897, and Captain in October, 1903. After serving in India for ten years, he was Adjutant of the Territorial Force (Yorkshire Hussars) from October, 1908, to January, 1912,

having been ordered home to take up that ap-pointment. Prior to the War breaking out he had rejoined his regiment, and was in command of a squadron when he left England with the Expeditionary Force in August, 1914.

Captain Walker was reported missing in the very early part of the war, and was afterwards found to have been killed on the 23rd August, 1914, when the retirement from Mons com-menced. Major W. B. Walker, Yorkshire Regiment, a brother of Captain O. B. Walker, was killed near Ypres in October, 1914, and the last surviving brother was serving with the Yorkshire Hussars.

He was a keen polo player and pig-sticker in India, a fine rider, and an active follower to hounds. He won his regimental race at Alder-shot a few days after joining his regiment, and hunted with the York and Ainsty, the Boreham Moor, and, for two seasons before his death, with the Blackmore Vale Hounds.

Captain Walker married, in 1910, Marcia Eugenia, daughter of Colonel and Mrs. Mansel, of Smedmore, Dorset, and left two children : Lois Adeline, born in February, 1912 ; and Consarde Elizabeth, born in August, 1913.

2nd LIEUTENANT REGINALD FYDELL WALKER, 2nd BATTN. MANCHESTER REGIMENT,

who died on the 21st October, 1914, of wounds received in action, was the son of the Rev. David Walker, Vicar of Darlington, and nephew of the late General J. T. Walker, R.E., C.B., F.R.S., Surveyor-General of India.

He was educated at Shrewsbury, where he was head of Mr. Ingram's House for over two years, and played for the Football XI. Thence he went to the R.M.C., Sandhurst, from which he was gazetted to his regiment in August, 1914, and at the end of that month took a draft of reservists to the front. He took part in the charge on Les Trois Maisons, and his Company Commander wrote of him that he " did most excellent work—so good, indeed, that I had intended to bring his name before the Commanding Officer. . . . Led several bayonet charges, and inflicted very heavy losses on the enemy." He fell mortally wounded on the 20th October, 1914, and died on the following day, aged twenty. (" The Times," 17th November, 1914.)

2nd LIEUTENANT WALTER ARTHUR BEAUMONT WALKER, ARMY SERVICE CORPS, attd. 2nd BATTN. THE BEDFORDSHIRE REGIMENT,

son of Richard Beaumont Walker, Ranchi, Chota Nagpur, India, was born at Dilrugahm, Upper Assam, on the 24th March, 1892.

He was educated at Bedford Grammar School,

where he got his colours for the 2nd Rugby XV, and also played in many matches for the

First XV. He was keen on all outdoor sports, and latterly belonged to the Rosslyn Park Football Club.

He joined the 3rd Battalion Bedfordshire Regiment as 2nd Lieutenant in 1912, obtaining his step in May, 1914, and on the outbreak of war was attached for active service to the 2nd Battalion, taking part with it in the retirement from Mons and the subsequent battles of the Marne, the Aisne, and La Basseé. While defending a trench at the latter place on the 25th October, 1914, he was struck in the abdomen by a rifle bullet, and died from his wound on the 30th at Havre.

2nd Lieutenant Walker used to say his motto was " Blood and Iron," which he appeared to live up to. He was never known to grumble at hardships or pain. When he was lying wounded on a stretcher in a communication trench for several hours during the fighting he constantly spoke cheerfully to the supports and reserves who had to pass him on their way to the fire trench.

In the " London Gazette " of the 13th October, 1914, Lieutenant Walker was appointed 2nd Lieutenant in the A.S.C. to date from 14th August, 1914, but continued to serve with his original regiment until his death.

MAJOR WILFRED BECKETT WALKER, 2nd BATTN. ALEXANDRA, PRINCESS OF WALES'S OWN (YORKSHIRE REGT.),

who was killed in action near Ypres, on the 29th October, 1914, was the second son of Captain and Mrs. Edwyn Walker, of Mill Mount House, York, and was born on the 5th August, 1876.

He joined the Yorkshire Regiment in February, 1897, and became Lieutenant in October, 1899. He took part in the South African War, during which he was employed with the Mounted Infantry, and acted as Supply Officer for two months, being present at operations in the Orange Free State and the Transvaal from 1900–02. He was mentioned in Despatches

(" London Gazette," 17th January, 1902), and received the Queen's medal with four clasps and the King's medal with two clasps.

He was promoted Captain in June, 1904, and Major in December, 1913.

His brother, Captain O. B. Walker, 15th Hussars, was killed in action on the 23rd August, 1914.

2nd LIEUTENANT DAVID STEPHENSON WALLACE, RESERVE OF OFFICERS, attd. 2nd BATTN. PRINCE OF WALES'S VOLUNTEERS (SOUTH LANCASHIRE REGIMENT),

born at North Shields, Northumberland, on the 22nd June, 1890, was the son of the late William Wallace, of that place, and a grandson of the late Captain John Wilkinson, of Tynemouth. He was educated at Tynemouth High School, and at Armstrong College, Durham University, where he was a member of the Students' Representative Council, and won his 'Varsity colours for football in 1909–10. He was also a member of the University Officers' Training Corps from 1908–10, becoming a Sergeant in the latter year, and received a commission in the Special Reserve, O.T.C., in 1912.

On mobilisation for the Great War he was called up on the 7th August, 1914, and a few days later sailed from Southampton with the first part of the Expeditionary Force, landing at Rouen. He was at the Battle of Mons, and took part in the retirement thence, fighting at Solesmes, Le Cateau, St. Quentin, and the Marne, being killed on the 20th September, 1914, while attacking a hill at Vailly-sur-Aisne. He was buried with two comrades at that place. The Captain of his company gave the following particulars to his sister : " He was a splendid fellow, absolutely fearless, . . . and took part in the awful retirement, marching nearly three hundred miles. Always cheerful and well liked by his men. . . . His regiment, which was in support, had to retake a hill where the Germans had got through. He went forward with his men, and was shot through the head in his attempt to get some men into a good fighting position. We regained the hill, but lost nine officers, killed and wounded."

His sister received many letters of sympathy from several of the University professors and societies.

2nd Lieutenant Wallace played football for

several seasons for the Percy Park Football Club, North Shields, and was captain of the club in the final for the Northumberland Cup, 1913–14.

2nd LIEUTENANT HAROLD BRUCE WALLACE, 3rd (attd. 1st) BATTN. THE KING'S (LIVERPOOL REGIMENT),

son of the late Dr. James R. Wallace, of Calcutta, India, was born there on the 24th September, 1893. He was educated at Dulwich College, where he was in the Second XV, and joined the 3rd Battalion of his regiment in December, 1913, who was attached to the 1st Battalion as 2nd Lieutenant in August, 1914.

In the Great War, while leading the men of his platoon in an attack upon the village of Noord Westhoek, Belgium, a few miles from Ypres, he was killed on the 26th October, 1914.

The Major of his battalion, writing to his relatives, said : " He had only been with us a short time, but had done well, showed great promise, and took such an interest in his work."

CAPTAIN SIR FRANCIS ERNEST WALLER, BART., 6th (attd. 4th) BATTN. THE ROYAL FUSILIERS (CITY OF LONDON REGIMENT),

who was killed in action on the 25th October, 1914, succeeded his father, Major-General Sir G. H. Waller, sometime Colonel of the 7th Fusiliers, as fourth Baronet in 1892.

He was born on the 11th June, 1880, and was educated at Harrow (Head Master's House, 1894–98). He joined the Army in August, 1899, and served in the South African War, in which he was severely wounded. He took part in the relief of Ladysmith, including the action at Colenso, was present at operations on the Tugela Heights and actions at Pieter's Hill, and at operations in Natal, the Transvaal, and Cape Colony, receiving the Queen's medal with five clasps and the King's medal with two clasps.

He retired from the Regular Army in January, 1908, when he joined the 6th Battalion of his regiment, and rejoining for the war was posted to the 4th Battalion.

In 1913 he was High Sheriff, and was Deputy-Lieutenant for the County of Warwick. He is succeeded in the title by his brother, Wathen Arthur Waller, born October, 1881.

CAPTAIN RICHARD HOPE WALLER, p.s.c., 38th DOGRAS,

was the eldest son of Mr. R. M. Waller (late I.C.S.) and Mrs. Waller, Rathmore, Bray, Ireland. His family is a branch of the Wallers, of Castletown Manor, County Limerick.

He was born on the 4th July, 1877, and was educated at Mr. Strangway's School in Dublin and Dr. Crawley's in the same city. He then went to the R.M.C., Sandhurst, from which he passed with honours, and was gazetted to the Royal Inniskilling Fusiliers in February, 1898, becoming Lieutenant in October, 1899. In September, 1900, he was transferred to the Indian Army, in which he became Captain in February, 1907. He served with the Waziristan Expedition, N.W. frontier of India, 1901–02, for which he received the medal with clasp. He officiated as Adjutant at the Delhi Durbar, in August, 1903, receiving the medal, and he also served as Adjutant of his Regiment.

In August, 1914, he was appointed D.A.A.G. of the VIIth Division I.E.F., and afterwards became Staff Captain to Brigadier-General Tighe, Commanding the Force attacking German East Africa. At the attack on Tanga, in German East Africa, on the 3rd November, 1914, being Staff Captain, he was sent by the General Officer Commanding to give the order to retire, when he was hit twice, but went on and gave the order, and was then shot dead.

Captain Waller married Ethel May, daughter of Captain J. Liddell, R.N., of Rodlease, Boldre, Hants, and left a son, John Patrick, born December, 1909.

LIEUTENANT HENRY DIGBY WALLIS, SPECIAL RESERVE, attd. 3rd BATTN. COLDSTREAM GUARDS,

who was killed in action at St. Julien on the 21st October, 1914, was the only son of Aubrey Wallis, of Drisham Castle, Millstreet, County Cork, Ireland, and was born at Auckland, New Zealand, on the 3rd June, 1885.

He was educated at Wellington College, and joined the Royal Scots on probation, but resigned and travelled abroad for some time, afterwards becoming a 2nd Lieutenant in the Special Reserve Coldstream Guards in March, 1912, and was promoted Lieutenant in September, 1914. For the Great War he was attached to the 3rd Battalion, which went to France with the IInd Division, British Expeditionary Force.

Lieutenant Wallis was a fine horseman, a good

four-in-hand whip, played polo, rode in many point-to-point races, and whipped in to the Duhallow Hounds, and also the Four Burrno.

LIEUTENANT RICHARD WALMESLEY, 3rd (attd. 2nd) BATTN. ALEXANDRA, PRINCESS OF WALES'S OWN (YORK-

SHIRE REGT.), was born on the 21st November, 1890, in London. He was the son of John Walmesley, Esq., of The Hall of Ince, Lancashire, and of Lucknam, Chippenham, Wilts, and the grandson of the late Colonel B. B. Haworth-Booth of Haworth Hall, Hull, and, Rolston Hall, Hornsea, Yorks.

Lieutenant Walmesley was educated at Eton and Magdalene College, Cambridge. He was gazetted to the 3rd (Special Reserve) Battalion of the Yorkshire Regiment on the 13th August, 1910, being promoted Lieutenant in May, 1912; in August, 1914, he was attached to the 2nd Battalion, and proceeded with it early in October to Belgium, landing at Zeebrugge, thence marching to the defence of Ypres.

He was killed instantaneously by a sniper (being one of the first of the regiment to fall) in a trench on the 21st October, and was buried next day close to where he fell, about six or eight miles from Ypres. He had shown much courage in action, and was much beloved by his men, of whom he had proved a great leader. He was devoted to horses and hunting. In the winter of 1912–13 he had been Master of the Cambridgeshire Harriers, and hunted with the Quorn, Belvoir, and the Cottesmore, 1913-14, where he was one of the hardest and most fearless riders. He was unmarried.

LIEUTENANT EDWARD J. CORMAC-WALSHE, 2nd BATTN. PRINCE OF WALES'S LEINSTER REGI-MENT (ROYAL CANADIANS),

who died on the 5th November, 1914, of wounds received in action, was a younger son of Edward Cormac - Walshe, J.P., D.L., of Castle Hill, Crossmolina, County Mayo, and was born in 1892. He was educated at Stonyhurst,

where he was captain of the Cadet Corps, and was in the Cricket XI. He then went to Trinity College, Dublin, and took his B.A. degree there. He was gazetted 2nd Lieutenant in August, 1913, to date from January, 1912, becoming Lieutenant in May, 1913, three months after joining.

The following account of the circumstances attending his death was published in the " Stonyhurst Magazine " of December, 1914: " Lieutenant Cormac-Walshe was badly wounded at Premesques, about three miles from Lille. He had previously been for two weeks in the fighting line on the Aisne. In the action in which he was wounded his regiment was directed to hold some trenches against superior numbers at all costs. On the 21st October a strong force of the enemy developed a surprise attack on the British line, with the result that the Leinsters suffered heavily, two Captains being killed, and Lieutenant Cormac-Walshe being mortally wounded in the head." He is buried at Boulogne.

2nd LIEUTENANT SYDNEY WALTER, 1st BATTN. GRENADIER GUARDS,

who was killed in action near Kruiseik on the 25th October, 1914, was the only son of Mr. Godfrey Walter, of Malshanger, Hants, by his marriage with Edith Elizabeth. fifth daughter of the late Mr. Robert Abel Smith, of Goldings, Herts.

He was born on the 16th March, 1893, and was educated at Eton and the R.M.C., Sandhurst, from which he was gazetted to the Grenadier Guards in February, 1913. His battalion, which formed part of the 20th Brigade, VIIth Division, mobilized at Lyndhurst, and, having embarked on the 4th October, landed at Zeebrugge on the 7th of that month.

2nd LIEUTENANT EDWARD CHARLES WALTERS, 3rd (RESERVE) attd. 1st BATTN. GLOUCESTERSHIRE REGT.,

who was killed in action on the 22nd December, 1914, was the youngest son of the late Rev. Frank Bridgman Walters, M.A., Fellow of Queens' College, Cambridge, and Principal of King William's College, Isle of Man, and of the late Mrs. Walters, of Broadstone, Dorset.

He was educated at Cheltenham College, and was a scholar of Keble College, Oxford. 2nd Lieutenant Walters, who was twenty-four years of age, was gazetted to the 3rd Battalion Gloucestershire Regiment on probation in August, 1914.

LIEUTENANT RICHARD CRAWHALL WALTON, 1st BATTN. 9th GURKHA RIFLES,

was the elder son of Mr. Richard Walton, of Croxteth Grove, Liverpool, and was born at Clifton on the 1st March, 1886. He was educated at Liverpool College, passing therefrom in 1905 to Sandhurst, where he was third on the list in that half-year's entrance examinations. A year later Lieutenant Walton passed out second in order of merit, with honours, and was placed first of the Cadets for the Indian Army, winning the coveted Norman medal, then presented for the first time. Upon this Lieutenant Walton received the personal congratulations of Field-Marshal Lord Roberts. He was attached to the 1st Battalion Prince of Wales's Own West Yorkshire Regiment, then in India, and a year later was posted to the 9th Gurkhas.

During his service in India he continued to achieve success in all his examinations, attaining distinction in Musketry and Machine Gun courses, and a special certificate as Instructor in Army Signalling. He was a highly qualified surveyor, and as such acted as Staff Officer during the survey of the Yassin Valley, and on one occasion as Compensation Officer during cavalry manœuvres.

Whilst at Sandhurst Lieutenant Walton obtained a shooting prize, and later was bracketed first in the regimental shooting competition of the Prince of Wales's Own West Yorkshire Regiment. He was an all-round sportsman, and when in garrison at Chitral engaged in big-game shooting, fine specimens of markhor, oorial, tahr, black and red bear, deer, and leopard being amongst his trophies. He was also an expert horseman and polo player, and was considered one of the best judges of ponies on his station. He rode Mr. Lee's "Ringette," the winner of the Murree Cup, at Gharial Races in 1907.

Lieutenant Walton came to Europe with the Indian Expeditionary Force for the Great War, and saw much of the fighting. He was killed in action on the 7th November, 1914, and was buried near Neuve Chapelle.

Referring to Lieutenant Walton, his Commanding Officer, wrote : " He was universally beloved by men and officers." A more appropriate and soldierly tribute to the character of a fallen officer could scarcely be made than that with which his Commanding Officer concludes his account of the death of Lieutenant Walton : " He fell beside the Maxim gun he was working."

2nd LIEUTENANT ARTHUR WARD, 1st BATTN. THE KING'S (LIVERPOOL REGIMENT),

was killed in action on the 17th October, 1914. This junior officer, who received his commission from the ranks of the Royal Welsh Fusiliers, in which he was a Lance-Sergeant, had the unique but sad experience of giving his life for his country on the very day on which he became an officer, for the " London Gazette " of the 16th October, 1914, notified his appointment as 2nd Lieutenant, to date from the 17th October, 1914.

CAPTAIN ARTHUR CLAUD WARD, D.S.O., 2nd BATTN. LANCASHIRE FUSILIERS,

who was born at Roslyn Hall, Jamaica, West Indies, on the 15th April, 1878, was the third son of Colonel the Hon. C. J. Ward, C.M.G. His great-great-grandfather on the maternal side was J. Z. Holwell, Governor of Fort

William, Calcutta, famous for his bravery and leadership of the gallant defence of the old Fort of Calcutta in June, 1756. He survived the horrors of the Black Hole, and erected a monument to those who perished. He died in London in 1798 at the age of eighty-seven.

Captain Ward was educated at Beaumont College, Old Windsor, and joined the 6th (Militia) Battalion of the Lancashire Fusiliers in 1899. He served in the South African War in 1900, being present at operations in Cape Colony, for which he received the Queen's medal with two clasps and a commission in the Lancashire Fusiliers (Regulars), as 2nd Lieutenant in April, 1900 ; he was promoted Lieutenant in February, 1901, and Captain in March, 1910.

In 1901 and 1903 he was seconded for service under the Colonial Office, taking part in the Aro and Igarra Expeditions with the 3rd South Nigerian Frontier Force. For his services he was mentioned in Despatches (" London Gazette," 28th October, 1904), received the D.S.O. and the African General Service medal with three clasps.

In the Great War there was a sudden attack on the 12th Infantry Brigade, of which his battalion formed part, near Cambrai at dawn on the 26th August, 1914, forty-eight hours after landing in France, by an overwhelmingly superior force of the enemy, and it was smothered by machine-gun fire. The battalion held on most gallantly, but had scarcely any artillery to assist them, and had not time to dig themselves in. Captain Ward was killed instantaneously while trying to assist two wounded Subalterns.

Captain Ward, who was a member of the Naval and Military Club, married Ruby, daughter of R. W. Mansbridge, Esq., of Staines, and left two children : Daphne, age six ; and Audrey, age three years.

LIEUTENANT - COLONEL BERTRAM EDMUND WARD, COMMANDING 1st BATTN. THE DUKE OF CAMBRIDGE'S OWN (MIDDLESEX REGIMENT),

who was born at Fermoy, County Cork, Ireland, on the 7th December, 1863, was the son of the late Major Edmund Ward, 107th Regiment, and Mrs. Ward (née Ogle), granddaughter of the late Rev. John Savile Ogle, of Kirkby, Northumberland. He was educated at Brighton College and the R.M.C., Sandhurst, where he was a Queen's Cadet. He joined the Middlesex Regiment as Lieutenant in May, 1882, and became Captain in 1890. From 1887 to 1896 he was Superintendent of Gymnasia for the Scottish District. From May, 1892, to May, 1897, he was Adjutant of the 3rd (Volunteer) Battalion Surrey Volunteers ; and from September, 1898, to September, 1901, was Superintendent of Gymnasia, Cork District.

In 1894, 1895, and 1896 he had the entire charge of arranging and carrying out the combined display at the Royal Military Tournament at Islington, and in January, 1912, organised and managed the Military Tournament and the Torchlight Tattoo at Calcutta on the occasion of the visit of Their Majesties the King and Queen, for which he was personally complimented by His Majesty, and received the Durbar medal.

He obtained his Majority in 1901, and succeeded to the command of his battalion on the 1st September, 1910. His normal period of command being about to expire, he had been appointed Commandant of the Army School of Music, Kneller Hall, but because of the war he was retained in the command of his battalion. He was mentioned in Sir John French's Despatches of the 8th October, 1914, and the 14th January, 1915, and had been recommended for further promotion. He was wounded on the 21st October, 1914, at La Boutillerie, and died

on the following day in an ambulance train on the way to Boulogne, where he was buried.

The Brigadier-General, the Hon. F. Gordon, on hearing of Lieutenant-Colonel Ward's death, wrote to the Officer Commanding 1st Battalion as follows : " His was a very lovable, bright, and brave spirit. Just such a man to command with credit a battalion which long ago earned the name of ' Die-hards.' I respected and liked Colonel Ward as a loyal-hearted, modest soldier and good friend. For such a man death, as we know it, can have no terror."

Lieutenant-Colonel Ward was a member of the Duhallow and United Hunt Clubs when stationed in Ireland, and was a keen fisherman and yachtsman.

He married, in 1891, Florence Isabelle, daughter of the late A. Fitz-Gibbon, Esq., M.I.C.E., and left two children : Randall Murray Bertram, born 1894, afterwards 2nd Lieutenant in the Army Service Corps ; and Kathleen Hazel, born 1897.

2nd LIEUTENANT JACK BOUVERIE MALLAM WARD, 2nd BATTN. OXFORDSHIRE AND BUCKINGHAMSHIRE LIGHT INFANTRY,

who was killed in action on the 4th November, 1914, aged nineteen, was the second son of Frank Ward, " Wallasey," Caterham, Surrey. He was educated at Marlborough College (Littlefield, 1909–10), and at the R.M.C., Sandhurst, from which he was gazetted to his regiment in August, 1914, joining the 2nd Battalion at the front.

2nd LIEUTENANT NEVILLE LASCELLES WARD, 1st BATTN. EAST SURREY REGIMENT,

was born at Bassein, Burmah, on the 17th December, 1893, the son of Henry Branson and Nora Grace Ward. He owed his names to the fact that he was descended from the Nevilles of the north, who intermarried with the Wards mentioned in " Via Crucis." His grandmother was a Lascelles, who was a granddaughter of General Lascelles, of the Court of George IV. Lieutenant Ward's paternal grandfather was a Judge in India, having belonged to the Madras Civil Service, and his maternal great-grandfather was in the Ceylon Civil Service.

He was educated at Blundell's School, Tiverton, Devonshire, where he was in the cricket and football teams, having been captain of the latter in 1911 ; and at the R.M.C., Sandhurst. He obtained his commission as 2nd Lieutenant in the 1st East Surrey Regiment in January, 1914.

After holding a bridge-head with small numbers of other troops for a whole day against very superior numbers of the enemy, he was killed while charging with a few men of his platoon in a little village called Boussy, near Mons, on the 23rd August, 1914, and was thus one of the officers killed very early in the war.

2nd LIEUTENANT EDWARD ROBERT WARING, 1st BATTN. KING'S ROYAL RIFLE CORPS,

who was killed in action on the 28th October, 1914, aged twenty, was the younger son of Captain and Mrs. Waring, of Beenham House, Berkshire.

He was educated at Wellington (Stanley, 1908–10), and was gazetted to the 5th Battalion King's Royal Rifle Corps in October, 1913, being promoted Lieutenant in June, 1914. He was granted a commission as 2nd Lieutenant in the 1st Battalion in September, 1914.

CAPTAIN WILFRID PICTON-WARLOW, WELSH REGIMENT, AND FLIGHT COMMANDER ROYAL FLYING CORPS, MILITARY WING,

was born at Laleston, Bridgend, Glamorganshire, on the 6th April, 1884, the younger son of Colonel John Picton Turbervill, Ewenny Priory, Bridgend, and a great-grandnephew of General Sir Thomas Picton, G.C.B., who was killed at Waterloo.

Captain Picton-Warlow was educated at Clifton College, and joined the Welsh Regiment from the Guernsey Militia in January, 1903, becoming Lieutenant in November, 1906, Captain in his regiment in June, 1913, and serving with his battalion in India and South Africa.

He joined the Royal Flying Corps in August, 1913. On the 20th December, 1914, he left St. Omer, France, to fly to Dover, was seen passing over Calais, but after that was never seen or heard of again.

CAPTAIN HERBERT MOLINE WARNER, 1st BATTN. EAST LANCASHIRE REGIMENT,

was the son of Herbert Warner, and was born at Sheffield on the 13th January, 1889.

He was educated at Wellington College, and joined the East Lancashire Regiment as 2nd Lieutenant in November, 1909, becoming Lieutenant in December, 1911. He was promoted Captain in November, 1914.

On the 14th November his lung was pierced by a piece of shrapnel in a trench, near Le Gheer, and he died in No. 2 Clearing Hospital at Bailleul, on the 16th November, 1914.

Captain Warner married Marjorie V., daughter of Lieutenant-Colonel Ravenhill, R.F.A. He left no family.

LIEUT.-COLONEL DAWSON WARREN, Commanding 1st BATTN. THE QUEEN'S (ROYAL WEST SURREY REGIMENT),

was killed in action on the 17th September, 1914.

The only son of the late Major-General Dawson Stockley Warren, C.B., Prince of Wales's Own (West Yorkshire Regiment), he was born on the 8th June, 1865, and educated at Cheltenham College and the R.M.C., Sandhurst, which he entered as an Honorary Queen's Cadet. He joined the Queen's Regiment in August, 1885, as Lieutenant, and became Captain in April, 1895. He took part in the Burmese Expedition of 1885-87, for which he received the medal with clasp.

While in India Lieut.-Colonel Warren held some

Staff appointments, acting as Assistant to the D.A.A.G. at Kasauli for nearly a year, and as Officiating Deputy Assistant Adjutant-General of the Southern Army in India, being at the School of Musketry, Pachmarhi, for several months, while holding that appointment. Lieutenant-Colonel Warren compiled the Musketry Scoring Book, now in general use in the Army. He was promoted Major in March, 1903, and, having succeeded to the command of his battalion in March, 1913, left England in August, 1914, with the Ist Division of the British Expeditionary Force.

LIEUTENANT JAMES BOOKER BROUGH WARREN, 1st (attd.2nd)BATTN.

BORDER REGT., son of J. Brough Warren, Esq., was born on the 3rd April, 1889. He was educated at Oundle School and Trinity College, Dublin, where he took his degree of B.A. in 1909, with honours in French.

He received his commission in the Border Regiment as a University candidate in September, antedated to March, 1910, and was promoted Lieutenant in October, 1912. When serving with his battalion in Burma he was for some time in command of the Mounted Infantry at Maymyo.

He was an enthusiastic sportsman, and was distinguished as a first-class hurdler. He created a school record, and while at Dublin University won the Inter-'Varsity race, and was second in the International. He was also a fine polo player.

He had been home on leave from Burma for three weeks when the war broke out, and was posted for active service to the 2nd Battalion, leaving for the front early in October, 1914, with the VIIth Division. A brother officer gave the following account of the circumstances attending his death : " Your son was killed in action on the afternoon of Sunday, October 25th, 1914, at 5 o'clock, when holding an entrenched position at Kruiseik, east of Ypres. He had been reconnoitring out to the front of his trenches, and had just returned when a shell burst in the trench immediately beside him, and killed him instantaneously."

Mrs. Warren received a very sympathetic letter from the Officer Commanding the young officer's late battalion in Burma, expressing the regret of all his brother officers at their loss, and his own appreciation of his professional qualifications and character.

2nd LIEUTENANT V. WATERFALL, 3rd BATTN. EAST YORKSHIRE REGT., AND ROYAL FLYING CORPS (M.W.),

was shown in the monthly official casualty list published in October, 1914, as having been " reported (unofficially) killed in action," no place or date being given.

He was gazetted to the 3rd Battalion East Yorkshire Regiment in January, 1912, and was appointed to the Military Wing of the Royal Flying Corps in August, 1914.

2nd LIEUTENANT ARVED WATERHOUSE, 3rd (RESERVE) attd. 1st BATTN. THE KING'S OWN (ROYAL LANCASTER REGT.),

who was born at Vienna on the 4th October, 1891, was the son of the late Dr. C. H. Waterhouse, of Liverpool. He lost his parents when he was still very young, and was brought up by his uncle and aunt, the late Rev. Canon and Mrs. Herbert Woodward of Liverpool, and after their death by his aunt, Miss S. M. Waterhouse, who then resided at Shenstone, Kendal.

He was educated privately and at Oriel College, Oxford, where he took his degree of B.A., History Honours in 1913, Diploma in Economics in 1914, and in the latter year won the challenge cup for Sculling. At the University he joined the O.T.C., was connected with the Oxford and Bermondsey Mission, and was a member of the Christian Union, Oxford. He was a life member of the Oxford Union. He belonged to the Conservative Club, Kendal, and to the Windermere, Kendal, and Radley (Oxford) Golf Clubs. He also played tennis and enjoyed all outdoor pursuits.

The Provost of Oriel wrote of him : " He had won the respect and affection of us all. He was a steady influence for good among his fellows. He set himself to realise a high standard in conduct, so that he was an example and an encouragement." The Dean of Oriel wrote of him in the same strain. The influence of his home life, and especially of his uncle, Canon Herbert Woodward, had great effect in the formation of his strong character, an influence he always gratefully recognised.

On the outbreak of the war with Germany he was in camp with the Oxford and Bermondsey Mission near Lowestoft. Being anxious to serve his country, he at once hastened home and applied for a commission, as he was entitled to do, having obtained his certificates " A " and " B " while in the O.T.C. He was gazetted to the 3rd Battalion Royal Lancaster Regiment on the 21st August, and went to Saltash for training. On the 26th September he sailed for France, and was at St. Nazaire till the 8th October, when he left for the fighting line. He was killed in the first engagement on the 13th October, 1914, while leading and directing his men in the taking of Meteren, near Hazebrouck, France.

The following details are extracted from a letter of Captain Hodgson, his Company Commander : " The battalion, with two others, was ordered to attack the village of Meteren, a few miles west of Bailleul, and my company was advancing in four lines, one behind the other, with about two hundred yards interval, well extended. Waterhouse was in charge of the last line. The attack succeeded by nightfall, and the three first lines got more or less collected, but the fourth (Waterhouse's) platoon was missing. At first it was hoped he was safe, as it appeared the Colonel had sent his platoon to reinforce the Warwickshire Regiment on the left of the line. Later it was discovered that he had got his platoon right up to the front line when he was killed by a fragment of shell while leading and directing his men." He concluded by saying what a great loss his death was to himself and the regiment.

Another officer wrote : " Waterhouse was thought very much of by the officers of the regiment, although he was only with them for a short time;" and an officer on the Headquarters Staff of the 3rd Army Corps, who sent his aunt photographs of his grave, said : " I heard from my friends in the regiment at the time how gallantly he behaved that day, and how much they regretted his loss."

Writing a farewell letter to his aunt from Southampton on his way out, 2nd Lieutenant Waterhouse said : " I sat on the quay and thought about the future, and wondered what it would bring forth. What a comfort our faith is at a time like this. . . . Let us remember that, whether we live or whether we die, we are the Lord's. He suffered much more for us than we can ever be called upon to suffer, either for Him or for our country. . . . I look upon this war as a holy one. . . . A war for righteousness, for liberty, and for peace, and one that it is a great privilege to be able to take part in."

This officer's career affords another instance of a man giving up his natural bent to assist in his country's cause.

LIEUTENANT EDGAR LEAKE WATERIDGE, 2nd BATTN. LEICESTERSHIRE REGIMENT,

born at Shrewsbury on the 18th July, 1892, was the second son of Mr. Frederick William Wateridge, of Marche Manor, Shropshire, late head of the firm of Wm. Hall Wateridge and Owen, Shrewsbury.

His education was commenced at Mr. Deedes's School, Millmead, from which he went to Rossall, where he remained till he was eighteen, and on leaving, studied for the Army. He was gazetted to the Antrim Royal Garrison Artillery in October, 1912, and was stationed at Londonderry and various forts in the R.G.A. North Irish Coast Defences, where he continued his studies, being finally gazetted from the Special Reserve to the Leicestershire Regiment as 2nd Lieutenant in May, 1913. After serving a few months with his battalion at Fermoy, he proceeded with it to India, and was with it at Rhaniket when the war with Germany broke out. The battalion left for France early in October, and soon after arrival at Marseilles, was ordered to the front, and arrived in the trenches by the end of October.

Lieutenant Wateridge was killed on the 21st November, 1914, at Richebourg l'Avoué, near Bethune, France. He was shot at close range, having fearlessly volunteered to locate a formidable sap-head at midnight with a N.C.O. and two men. He had accomplished his self-imposed duty, and was returning, when a volley was fired from the enemy's trench, and he was the first to fall.

It was assumed the body was taken by the enemy, for in spite of an immediate attempt to find it, in a search during the whole night, it was never recovered.

Lieutenant Wateridge, who only got his step a week before he was killed, was a keen sportsman, a bold and straight rider across country, and an excellent shot. He had endeared himself to all ranks of his regiment.

2nd LIEUTENANT HORACE HOLMES WATKINS, 3rd (attd. 1st) BATTN. SOUTH WALES BORDERERS,

who was killed in action on the 21st October, 1914, was the sixth son of Thomas Watkins, Solicitor, of The Wern, Pontypool, Monmouthshire, and Fanny Maria, his wife.

He was born on the 31st January, 1891, at Castle Parade House, Usk, Monmouthshire, and was educated at West Monmouth School, Pontypool, and afterwards at Monmouth

Grammar School, where he won and held school scholarships during his stay. Thence he proceeded to Hertford College, Oxford, where he won an Exhibition and took a leaving one from Monmouth. He took second-class honours in Moderations and Greats at Oxford (double second).

At Monmouth Grammar School he was a 2nd Lieutenant in the Cadet Corps, and a Colour-Sergeant in the O.T.C. at Oxford. He obtained Certificates " A " and " B," qualifying him for a commission, and also a qualification in Musketry at a course which he attended on his own initiative one summer. As a Recruiting Sergeant he had no equal, and, entering the O.T.C. as a real preparation for the crisis, his arguments, explained to everyone in the College at personal interviews, doubled the size of the Hertford Detachment during the two years he worked in it.

He was one of the first to appear before the Nominating Board at Oxford in August, 1914, and received his commission as 2nd Lieutenant on probation in the 3rd Battalion South Wales Borderers in that month, being attached to the 1st Battalion for active service.

He was an athlete of some repute. At Monmouth he represented his school at cricket, Rugby football, and hockey, and rowed in the school boat. At Oxford he played hockey for the University, obtaining his half blue, and playing for the winners in the Inter-'Varsity match the season before his death. He also represented his college at Rugby and Association football, hockey, tennis, and in the Torpid.

When killed he was leading his platoon, No. 4, from Langemarck village to a frontal attack over some open ground, the only cover being that afforded by the beet and turnip leaves. He was hit by two bullets, both entering the abdomen, and the back of his neck was also blown away by a shell, but it is said this occurred after death.

2nd Lieutenant Watkins had no fewer than seven brothers serving or preparing to serve in His Majesty's forces, one of whom, Captain Vivian Holmes Watkins, 1/2nd Battalion Monmouthshire Regiment (T.F.), was wounded in January, 1915, and died from his wound the following February; a second, Captain H. Holmes Watkins, 2/2nd Battalion Monmouthshire Regiment (T.F.), was stationed at Bedford; a third was a Private in the Canadian

Horse; two others applied for commissions, one in the Royal Engineers, and the other in the Royal Artillery; while the sixth was at Hertford College, Oxford, in the O.T.C., and also applied for a commission; a seventh was attested under Lord Derby's scheme; and an eighth was rejected on medical grounds.

2nd LIEUTENANT ERNEST GUTHRIE WATSON, RESERVE OF OFFICERS, attd. 2nd BATTN. THE PRINCE OF WALES'S VOLUNTEERS, (SOUTH LANCA-SHIRE REGT.), was born at Gateshead, Durham, on the 6th June, 1890, and was the son of John Watson, Chief Engineer, M.F.A., of Blacktoft, and Eliza Emily Watson. He was a grandson of the late William Timms, an old tradesman, of

Barnard Castle and Darlington.

2nd Lieutenant Watson was educated at Armstrong College, Newcastle-on-Tyne, and was for four years in the Officers' Training Corps.

He was first appointed to the Reserve of Officers, O.T.C., in August, 1912, and, being called up on the 3rd August, 1914, was attached as 2nd Lieutenant to the 2nd Battalion South Lancashire Regiment, accompanying it to France with the Expeditionary Force, in which it formed part of the 7th Brigade, IIIrd Division. He was killed in action at the Battle of the Aisne on the 19th September, 1914. Mr. and Mrs. Watson received many appreciative letters of sympathy from the authorities of Armstrong College and others regarding their son.

Professor Wright, of the Department of Education, Armstrong College, wrote : " He left a favourable and interesting impression on our minds for his steadiness and for his loyalty. We are proud of the sacrifice he made for England in her time of need."

The Durham University Officers' Training Corps heard with deep regret of the sad death of an old member.

The Honorary Secretary of the Old Students' Union of the University of Durham, said : " The college is honoured in having so gallant a son."

The Director of Education wrote : " He will still live in the memory of the community as an efficient servant and as a self-sacrificing citizen of the State."

A Private of his battalion (Clugston), wounded in the same bayonet charge, said : " While we were reinforcing the Worcester and Wiltshire Regiments, when ordered to charge the German trenches, Lieutenant Watson got killed."

2nd Lieutenant Watson was an artist, and at the time of his death had four of his pictures hung in the Laing Art Gallery of Water Colours.

MAJOR WILLIAM ERNEST WATSON, D.S.O., 6th DRAGOON GUARDS (CARABINIERS),

was shown among the casualties included in the Army List for March, 1915, as " missing, believed killed," on the 31st October, 1914.

He was born on the 3rd September, 1876, and joined the 6th Dragoon Guards from the Militia in May, 1897, becoming Lieutenant in January, 1899.

He served in the South African War as Adjutant of the 1st Imperial Light Horse from January, 1901, to May, 1902. He took part in the relief of Kimberley, and was present at operations in the Orange Free State, at Paardeberg, in the Transvaal (May–November, 1900), and Cape Colony, including actions at Poplar Grove, Driefontein, Karee Siding, Zand River, near Johannesburg, at Pretoria, Diamond Hill, Riet Vlei, Belfast and Colesberg. He was mentioned in Despatches ("London Gazette,"10th September, 1901), was awarded the D.S.O., and received the Queen's medal with six clasps and the King's medal with two clasps.

He was promoted Captain in December, 1901, and was Adjutant of his regiment from July, 1907, to April, 1910, in which latter year he obtained his Majority.

CAPTAIN CHARLES HAROLD REYNELL WATTS, 2nd BATTN. NORTHAMPTONSHIRE REGIMENT,

who was killed in action on the 19th December, 1914, was born on the 7th November, 1882, and received his commission in the Northamptonshire Regiment from the New Zealand Local Military Forces in January, 1906, becoming Lieutenant in November, 1908, and Captain in June, 1913.

LIEUTENANT LIONEL DOUGLAS WAUD, 1st BATTN. EAST LANCASHIRE REGIMENT,

was born at Cranleigh Court, Guildford, on the 5th June, 1895. He was the second son of Major W. H. and Mrs. Denise

C. Waud, and a nephew of Baron et Baronne de la Borie de la Batut, and great-nephew of the late Count and Countess Maire.

He was educated at the Army School, Holyport, and passed into the R.M.C., Sandhurst, in 1913. He held the record score for revolver shooting, and won the first prize in the bayonet competition at the R.M.C., and represented Sandhurst in the bayonet competition at the Royal Military Tournament at Olympia in May, 1914, obtaining third prize. He passed first out of Sandhurst for the English Army, was gazetted to the 1st Battalion East Lancashire Regiment on the 8th August, 1914, and proceeded to the front on the 27th of that month, being promoted Lieutenant on the 2nd November. He was killed in action near Armentières on the 8th November, his name subsequently appearing in Sir John French's Despatch of the 14th January, 1915, in connection with his gallantry at Le Gheer. The Officer Commanding Lieutenant Waud's company wrote of him as follows : " Short as was the time your son has been with us, he had quickly gained the respect and affection of all ranks in the battalion. . . . I grieve for the loss of a splendid officer. He was absolutely fearless, and I had the pleasure of officially bringing his excellent work to the notice of our Commanding Officer on the occasion on which the battalion obtained much credit for an attack on the Germans on the 21st October. During the following day, under a heavy shell and rifle fire, he continued to encourage his men very much by his personal example and gallantry and cheerfulness."

A Captain of the battalion wrote : " His only fault was he would take risks. He was too tall for the trenches, and wouldn't trouble to stoop. He was very brave, and his action—which I remember well—of running along, knocking down the rifles of his men to make them fire low, was one of the finest things I have seen out here."

Some corroborative particulars of the occasion were received from a wounded German officer, who, describing the German assault, said : " Our whole front was stricken down by a volley from a point much nearer than the trench we had been shelling." This was at Le Gheer, and it seems that when the mitrailleuse fire from the German attack began, and there was a momentary loss of fire-control of his own company, Lieutenant Waud, to regain control, sprang from the trenches, and, running in front of them, with the flat of his sword struck down the men's rifles, and so prevented the Germans finding out where the trenches really were.

2nd LIEUTENANT JOSEPH FRAIN WEBSTER, 3rd (RESERVE) BATTN. THE BLACK WATCH (ROYAL HIGHLANDERS), attd. 1st BATTN. GORDON HIGHLANDERS, was the second son of Sir Francis and Lady Webster, of Ashbrook, Arbroath, Forfarshire, and was born there on the 2nd December, 1892. He was educated at Seafield House, Broughty Ferry; then at Clifton College, where he was the champion boxer, in the XV, and in the Officers' Training Corps; and subsequently at Trinity College, Cambridge, where he was the champion middleweight boxer in 1914.

2nd Lieutenant Webster was one of the many members of distinguished families to set an example in the Great War by enlisting which he did in the King's Royal Rifle Corps, being afterwards given his commission in the 3rd Battalion Black Watch in October, 1914.

For the Great War he was attached to the 1st Battalion Gordon Highlanders, and was killed in a charge near Gheluvelt on the 30th October, 1914. His C.O. and Company Commander wrote in high terms of 2nd Lieutenant Webster's conduct. The latter, describing a previous incident, said that on the 26th October men holding a trench on their flank were driven out and forced to withdraw. 2nd Lieutenant Webster jumped out of his own trench, and rallied the men under severe fire, retook the trench, and held it for the rest of the day, saving the flank, which, but for his action, would have been compelled to retire.

On the 30th October he volunteered for the charge in which he was killed. A Sergeant of his company also recounted many gallant deeds of 2nd Lieutenant Webster, among them the bringing in of a wounded man under fire after he had sent his own men back to the trench.

2nd LIEUTENANT JOHN RICHARD BAGGALLAY WEEDING, 2nd BATTN. WELSH REGIMENT, who was killed in action on the 22nd December, 1914, aged thirty-two, was the son of T. W. Weeding, Esq., of Addlestone, Surrey.

He was educated at Marlborough (as was his father) from 1894–1900 (Maltese Cross), where he was in the XV of 1899 and the Hockey XI of 1900. After leaving Marlborough he was an active member of the Nomads until the amalgamation with Rosslyn Park.

Mr. Weeding was a Solicitor by profession. On the outbreak of war he first joined the Royal Flying Corps, and was gazetted to the Welsh Regiment in October, 1914. ("The Marlburian," 11th February, 1915.)

MAJOR GLYNNE EVERARD EARLE WELBY, 1st BATTN. SOUTH WALES BORDERERS,  was the son of Edward M. E. Welby, M.A., Barrister-at-Law, Norton House, near Sheffield, Stipendiary Magistrate for Sheffield since 1874, and of the late Mrs. Sarah Elizabeth Welby, daughter of Robert Everard, Esq., of Fulney House, near Spalding. He was born at Norton House on the 24th November, 1872, and was educated at Eton (Mr. Everard's House), and afterwards joined Colonel Roberts's Army Class, at Freiburg, in Baden. He was gazetted to the South Wales Borderers from the Militia in December, 1893, joining the 1st Battalion in Egypt, and was promoted Lieutenant in November, 1896. With the 2nd Battalion of his regiment he took part in the South African War, being present at operations in the Orange Free State, including action at Karee Siding, Vet River, and Zand River; in the Transvaal, including action near Johannesburg; and in the Orange River Colony. He received the Queen's medal with four clasps. He became Captain in December, 1905, and obtained his Majority in March, 1914. He accompanied the 1st Battalion to the Continent with the first part of the Expeditionary Force, embarking at Southampton on the 17th August, 1914, reaching France the next day. From his letters written at the front his relatives were able to compile a very interesting record of the part he took in the Great War, from which it appears he was in the fighting line on the 29th August. He referred to his diary as giving more precise details than the strict censorship permitted him to do in his letters, but unfortunately this dairy was never recovered. During the Battle of the Aisne one of his horses was shot under him, but he managed to secure the horse of a wounded German officer. Officers and men who were interviewed later, in speaking of these days, " wondered the Major had not been killed before he was, considering the fearless way he went about his work under fire." Other wounded men of his company said: " The Major was very good to us, and always had tea with us." He was noticed to have a strong dislike to putting risks on others with any appearance of being unready to face them himself. From September 14th to 21st, his company, with another company of the battalion, alternately occupied trenches, which seemed to those in them to be " exposed to shells all day and attacks every night." " Many a time," it was said, " when we had been almost buried by the dirt from a shell or subjected to a particularly close explosion, it was invariably his cheery laugh which brought matters round again."

He was killed on the 26th September, 1914, near Vendresse, and was buried in the trenches, close to a stone quarry he had defended. The following particulars were received from an officer who was himself killed in action, from another officer who was wounded on the 26th September, and from privates, one of whom, recounting events, ended by remarking: " That's the sort of officer to have." It seemed that on the night of the 25th Major Welby's company took over a position which had been frequently attacked, and the night was spent in trench-digging, and " for a wonder it was a perfectly peaceful night." Just before dawn, when the Major and others had gone to lie down in the main trench, the crash came. The enemy appeared to number one thousand five hundred to two thousand, and a terribly heavy fire began. Major Welby sent to ask for reinforcements, and a further German attack developed on the flank of the position. While awaiting reinforcements Major Welby made arrangements in the quarry forming part of the position, and then ran out of it across into the front trench to encourage the sorely pressed men in it. The last words he was heard to say were: " Keep calm and shoot straight." He was then shot, his death being instantaneous. At night he was buried, with two other officers and the men who fell, in the communication trench of the position he and his men had defended so gallantly.

The following is extracted from a letter published in the " Morning Post ":—" Fight for a quarry. An Officer in the South Wales Borderers, writing to a friend at Newport, says: ' We had a very hard time altogether right up to the 26th, when we had a desperate fight for a quarry, with a happy result. Early that morning Major Welby and the "D" Company were attacked by a force of about two thousand five hundred Germans. Major Welby sent Captain Pritchard down for support from the " C " Company: we at once went up and found Major Welby and his company in a difficult situation. The " D " Company were in a trench about thirty yards from the quarry, and nearer on the left flank. They were being hotly attacked by the Germans who were in a wood in front. Right on the left side the Germans had swarmed into a quarry and had occupied a large part of it. Our leading platoon under Lieutenant Simmonds immediately advanced into the quarry, on the right side, and the remainder of the company followed. Poor Simmonds was killed and a number of our men were killed and wounded. Meanwhile, poor Welby and his company were

having a bad time of it in the trench, but they bravely stuck to it until we were able to take up a position on the edge of the quarry, when those who were left retired on to us. Poor Welby, three other officers and about sixty men of the " D " Company were killed. After about four hours more fighting the Germans retired through the wood. At dusk we reoccupied the trenches and collected our dead and wounded. Poor Welby and those who perished with him were most gallant, and fought heriocally against overwhelming odds, but alas, they did not survive to witness the successful result of their work.' "

The General Officer Commanding the Brigade and Major Welby's Commanding Officer sent his father most feeling letters, giving him the satisfaction of knowing that his son was most gallantly doing all that was possible to repel the German attack.

Major Welby, who was a member of the Army and Navy Club, enjoyed playing polo when stationed abroad and was also fond of hunting and shooting.

LIEUTENANT RICHARD WILLIAM GREGORY WELBY, 2nd BATTN. GREN-ADIER GUARDS, the elder son of Sir Charles G. E. Welby, Bart., C.B., by his wife, Lady Maria, sister of the fourth Marquess of Bristol, was born at Denton Manor, Grantham, on the 16th October, 1888. Educated at Eton and Christ Church,  Oxford, he received his commission in the Grenadier Guards in February, 1910, becoming Lieutenant in 1911. Lieutenant Welby, in the Great War, went with his battalion which belonged to the IInd Division to the neighbourhood of Mons, and took part in the retirement, including the Battles of Landrecies and Villers-Cotterets and the Marne, and subsequently in the advance to the Aisne. After crossing the latter river on the 14th September he was wounded on the heights above the village of Soupir. All the officers of his company (No. 3) were killed or wounded on that day, Captain Gosselin (who received the D.S.O. for the action, and was subsequently killed) and Lieutenant Welby remaining on duty. On the 15th September a bullet was extracted from Lieutenant Welby's shoulder, but he returned to duty, and on the next day (16th September, 1914), was killed. He was buried in the churchyard at Soupir. A brother officer gave the following account of the circumstances to his relatives: " We had a very severe action on Tuesday when Dick Welby was wounded in the shoulder. . . . We were very short of officers, owing to our heavy casualties. He very pluckily insisted on remaining at duty (instead of going into hospital) to help us through the difficulty, and remained at duty during the day. On the third day we got a terrible shelling, and poor Dick was killed. His death was absolutely instantaneous —he was hit in the head by a shrapnel bullet —so that he had no pain or suffering, and he was cheerful and happy up to the minute before his death. . . . I can't tell you how we all deplore Dick's loss, nor how gallantly he did his duty to the end, and I hope his people will accept the most deep and hearty sympathy of all his brother officers."

Lieutenant Welby was mentioned in Sir John French's Despatch of the 8th October, 1914.

LIEUTENANT WALTER GEORGE FREDERIC WELCH, 117th BATTERY, ROYAL FIELD ARTILLERY,

only son of Reginald Courtenay Welch, Principal of the Army College, Farnham, near Aldershot, was born on the 7th March, 1890, at 6,Southwick Place, London, W. He was educated at Charterhouse and the Army College, and in November, 1908, passed twenty-fifth into the R.M.A., Woolwich. After three terms he was gazetted, in July, 1910, 2nd Lieutenant in the Royal Field Artillery, and was posted to the 127th Battery, then at Bordon. He was promoted Lieutenant three years later.

In January, 1913, he went to the depot at Preston, where he soon became a great favourite, and remained there till mobilisation, when he joined the 44th Ammunition Column. Shortly afterwards he was posted to the 117th Battery with which he served both on the Aisne and in Flanders. It was on the evening of the 30th October, 1914, during the first Battle of Ypres, that this gallant young officer met his death. His guns were posted in a wood about twelve hundred yards south of Veldhoek, east-south-east of Ypres. The position was rapidly becoming untenable, and just before the order to retire was given Lieutenant Welch was struck down by a shell, and buried "alongside the guns he had fought." A high-spirited lad with a keen sense of humour, Lieutenant Welch was, in the words of his Commanding Officer, "the life and soul of our little mess, a keen and good soldier." One of those who served under him wrote: "Mr.

Welch was always very popular with the men, but especially so in action."

LIEUTENANT ERIC LLEWELYN WELCHMAN, 1st BATTN. THE LINCOLNSHIRE REGIMENT,

who was one of the earliest officers to be killed in France in the Great War, was the son of the Rev. Canon and Mrs. W. Welchman, of The Temple (or Holy Cross) Vicarage, Berkeley Square, Clifton, Bristol, and was born at Colombo, Ceylon, on the 21st July, 1893. He was educated at a Preparatory School (Mr. Black) at Colwall, near Malvern, and at Clifton College from 1906–11. There he won the "house run," under sixteen, and came in third in Short Pen, won his cap for football, and played for the college as "scrum half," won the Budworth cup for Fives in 1909, and in 1911 was in the college Shooting Eight at Bisley. In the latter year he went to the R.M.C., Sandhurst, joining the Lincolnshire Regiment in September, 1912, and being promoted Lieutenant in January, 1914, in which year he boxed for the regiment at Aldershot. He passed successfully a transport course in December, 1913, and a machine-gun course at Hythe in July, 1914. He was a member of the United Services Club, Portsmouth, played football and hockey for it, and acted as Secretary for regimental games. In 1914 he was entered for the swordsmanship competition at Olympia, which was abandoned on account of the war.

Lieutenant Welchman died on the 24th August, 1914, from wounds caused by a shell at Frameries during the retirement from Mons, while directing the fire of his platoon.

CAPTAIN EDWARD THEODORE WELCHMAN, D.S.O., 2nd BATTN. THE PRINCE OF WALES'S OWN (WEST YORKSHIRE REGIMENT),

was the son of Dr. Edward Welchman, and was born at Southea, Cambs., in 1881. He was educated at Sleaford School, Lincolnshire; and the R.M.C.,Sandhurst. He also passed into the Staff College, Camberley, for which he had been specially selected.

He joined the West Yorkshire Regiment in August, 1900, being promoted Lieutenant in March, 1902. He saw service in the South African War, 1901–02, being present at operations in the Transvaal, for which he was mentioned in Despatches (" London Gazette," 17th January, 1902), was awarded the D.S.O., and received the Queen's medal with three clasps. In 1908 he served in operations in the Mohmand Country, N.W. Frontier of India, for which he received the medal with clasp.

Captain Welchman, who was promoted to that rank in March, 1910, joined his battalion in France on the 2nd October, 1914, and was wounded in action near Lille on the 20th of the same month, dying of his wounds in the Boulogne Base Hospital on the 26th October, 1914. He was buried at Boulogne.

He was a member formerly of the Army and Navy Club, and of the York and Ainsty Hunt. His recreations were polo and golf.

CAPTAIN LORD RICHARD WELLESLEY, 1st BATTN. GRENADIER GUARDS,

second son of the fourth Duke and the Duchess of Wellington, who was killed in action near Ypres on the 29th October, 1914, was born in London on the 30th September, 1879.

He was educated at Eton, and was gazetted to the Grenadier Guards from the Militia in 1900, becoming Lieutenant in January, 1904. From October, 1906, to September, 1908, he was Adjutant of his battalion. He was promoted Captain in June of the latter year.

He served in the South African War, in which he was slightly wounded during the operations at Paardeberg. He was present also in the action at Poplar Grove, Karee Siding, Houtnek, Thoba Mountain, Vet and Zand Rivers, and at those near Belfast, Johannesburg, and Pretoria. At the conclusion of this war he received the Queen's medal with four clasps and the King's medal with two clasps.

For his services in the Great War he was mentioned in Sir John French's Despatch of the 14th January, 1915, published after his death.

Lord Richard Wellesley married Louise Nesta Pamela, only daughter of Sir Maurice Fitzgerald, Bart., Knight of Kerry, and left two daughters : Pamela, born May, 1912 ; and Mary, born after her father's death in January, 1915.

CAPTAIN WALTER NEAVE WELLS, 3rd BATTN. THE BUFFS (EAST KENT REGIMENT),

was the son of Admiral Sir Richard Wells, K.C.B., and was educated at Girdlestone School, Sunningdale. He joined his battalion as 2nd Lieutenant in November, 1900, becoming Lieutenant in 1904, and Captain in March, 1906. He served in the South African War, taking part in operations in Orange River Colony, and also in Cape Colony, receiving the Queen's medal with five clasps.

In the Great War Captain Wells was attached to the 1st Battalion King's Royal Rifle Corps when he was shot in the head and killed while leading his company on the 27th October, 1914. Captain Wells was a member of the Junior Naval and Military Club, Piccadilly.

CAPTAIN ERNEST BROCKLESBY WESCHÉ, THE PRINCE OF WALES'S VOLUNTEERS (SOUTH LANCASHIRE REGIMENT),

born in Stoke Newington on the 24th April, 1886, was the son of Ernest John Dunbar and Lizzie Matilda Wesché (*née* Brocklesby).

He was educated at St. Paul's School (1899–1901), and joined the South Lancashire Regiment in August, 1905, becoming Lieutenant in November, 1907. From October, 1911, he was employed with the Nigeria Regiment, West African Frontier Force, with which he was serving when he was killed in action in the Cameroons on the 19th October, 1914. Captain Wesché was promoted to that rank in September, 1914, only a few weeks before he was killed.

CAPTAIN JOHN PERCY WHELAN, 2nd BATTN. ROYAL IRISH RIFLES,

who was killed in action on the 11th December, 1914, no details being procurable, was born in May, 1879, the son of Mr. Joseph Whelan, Barna, Osbourne Park, Belfast.

He was educated at Loretto College, near Edinburgh,

and obtained a commission in the Royal Garrison Regiment (raised during the Boer War) from the Militia in August, 1902, being promoted Lieutenant in March, 1903. On its disbandment he was transferred as Lieutenant in July, 1905, to the Royal Irish Rifles, in which he obtained his Company in March, 1910. For over two years, from March, 1910, to November, 1912, he was Adjutant of the 10th Battalion London Regiment. Subsequently he was posted to the 1st Battalion of his regiment at Aden, whence he was invalided home shortly after the declaration of war with Germany, and was attached to the 2nd Battalion Royal Irish Regiment for active service.

Captain Whelan married Gladys Lily, youngest daughter of the late Captain John Wray Mitchell, of Aroughty Grange, County Roscommon, and left one daughter, Sheila Maureen, born July, 1907.

CAPTAIN CECIL BODDAM-WHETHAM, 3rd. BATTN. (RESERVE) THE BLACK WATCH (ROYAL HIGHLANDERS), attd. 1st. BATTN. THE GORDON HIGHLANDERS,

born on the 11th February, 1879, was the second son of the late Colonel A. T. Boddam - Whetham, late Royal Welsh Fusiliers, and of Mrs. Boddam - Whetham, of Folkestone.

He was educated at Wrexham and at Bedford Schools; also in France and in Germany, afterwards going to " Wrens," and he passed through the R.M.A., Woolwich, into the Royal Artillery in September, 1898, becoming Lieutenant in February, 1901. In 1902 he was on active service in South Nigeria, West Africa, for which he received the medal with clasp. He attained the rank of Captain in 1906, and two years later retired from the Royal Field Artillery, being appointed Captain in the Reserve Battalion Black Watch in September of the same year.

In October, 1914, Captain Boddam-Whetham was attached to the 1st Battalion Gordon Highlanders, and went to the front. He was prominently mentioned in the body of Sir John French's Despatch of the 2nd February, 1915, for his " splendid dash " in the attack on the Maedelsteed Spur. The last seen of him was jumping into the enemy trench on the 14th December, 1914, followed by Lieutenant Dobie and a few men, and it is believed he was killed on that date. Captain Boddam-

Whetham's body was not found until October, 1915, when it was buried by the 24th Canadian Infantry Battalion at Bois de Wytschaete.

His Commanding Officer wrote of him : " Captain Boddam-Whetham has been one of our greatest helps, and his loss to me and the regiment at this time cannot be measured. . . . In my opinion, no one has ever shown greater gallantry."

Captain Boddam-Whetham was a member of the Naval and Military Club, and his favourite recreations were shooting, cricket, and golf. He married, in 1906, Gyda, youngest daughter of the late Mr. Henry Rawcliffe, of Gillibrand Hall, Lancashire, and left three sons.

CAPTAIN HERBERT CONNELL WHIPPLE, 1st BATTN. DEVONSHIRE REGIMENT,

born at St. Andrew's Lodge, Plymouth, South Devon, on the 6th September, 1879, was the sor of Mr. Connell Whipple, for many years Surgeon of the South Devon Militia, and of the South Devon and East Cornwall Hos-

pital, and a nephew of Colonel Batson, C.B., who commanded the 2nd Battalion of the Devons which formed part of the force that relieved Ladysmith in the Boer War.

Captain Whipple was educated at Mr. Bradshaw's School, near Birmingham ; and at Rossall. He joined the Devonshire Regiment from the old South Devon Militia in October, 1899, just at the commencement of the Boer War, in which he served, having been present at the relief of Ladysmith, including the action at Colenso, action at Spion Kop, and operations in Natal, including the action at Laings Nek ; also at operations in the Transvaal, receiving the Queen's medal with four clasps and the King's medal with two clasps.

He afterwards served in South Nigeria for three years, for which he received the King's West African medal with one clasp. He obtained his Captaincy in November, 1911.

During the early days of the Great War the exposure and long periods of duty without relief told somewhat on Captain Whipple's health, and brought on a return of African fever, but his cheery spirits were never affected. After being laid up for a few days he returned to the trenches, and was shot in the head on the 19th November, 1914, dying, without regaining consciousness, on the 24th of that month.

In his home circle, as with his regiment, he was

a general favourite, much appreciated also by his men. He had a great love for music, and was a very good pianist with a perfect touch, which made him in great demand among his friends. He was a member of the Junior United Service Club.

Captain Whipple married, on the 2nd July, 1913, Joan, daughter of Gerald Stapylton-Smith, of Hutton, Essex.

CAPTAIN JOHN KENNETH TULLOCH WHISH, 1st EAST SURREY REGIMENT,

was born at Fort William, Calcutta, on the 23rd November, 1876, the only son of the late Colonel J. T. Whish, Bengal Staff Corps, grandson of the late General G. P. Whish, Indian Army, and great-grandson of the late General Sir William Sampson Whish, Bengal Artillery. On his mother's side he was great-great-grandson of Major Fletcher, who fought at Waterloo.

Captain Whish was educated at Brighton College and the Army College, Farnham, under Colonel Wilkinson, and passed into the service through the Militia from the tutorship of Captain James, Lexham Gardens, London. A month after entering the Army, in September, 1899, Captain Whish proceeded on active service; as, joining the 2nd Battalion East Surrey Regiment, he accompanied it to South Africa in October of the same year. With it he was present at the relief of Ladysmith; at the actions of Colenso, Spion Kop, Vaal Krans, Tugela Heights, Pieter's Hill, and Laing's Nek, besides other actions in the Transvaal. At Pieter's Hill, his Captain having been wounded, the command of his company devolved on Captain Whish, a position in which he showed marked coolness and presence of mind. For this war he received the Queen's medal with six clasps, the King's medal with two clasps, and was twice recommended for mention in Despatches.

Captain Whish was soon to have further war experience, for in 1905–06 he took part in the Somaliland and Nandi Expeditions in East Africa while serving with the King's African Rifles, for which he received a medal with one clasp. He became a Captain in the 1st East Surrey Regiment in March, 1907, in which year he rejoined his own regiment. He trained the first reinforcements for his regiment, and leaving Dublin on the 21st August, 1914, for the front he was mortally wounded at the Battle of the Marne,

France, on the 8th September, 1914, dying in the field ambulance the same evening.

He was a very keen soldier and sportsman, being an excellent shot, having had much big-game shooting in East Africa, and was also a good cricketer and swimmer.

Colonel Pearse, who commanded the 2nd Battn. East Surrey Regiment in the South African War, wrote of him that " Captain Whish's untimely death in action, while fighting with our Allies in France, was universally regretted in his regiment, in which his memory will long be cherished. He was always a most keen and satisfactory officer; his character was a charming one, and everyone who knew him was his friend." In short, he was a very true gentleman and soldier, whose greatest happiness lay in helping others.

Captain Whish married, on the 14th October, 1911, Evelyn Anne, daughter of Fleet-Surgeon J. Wood, R.N., and granddaughter of Captain Moneypenny-Wood and of Captain Sir Alfred Balliston, R.N., H.M.S. " Alberta." It will thus be seen that both Captain Whish and his wife had a very distinguished naval and military ancestry.

Mrs. Whish died on the 27th June, 1914, and left no surviving children.

CAPTAIN HAROLD WHITAKER, 2nd BATTN. THE RIFLE BRIGADE, (THE PRINCE CONSORT'S OWN),

was the eldest son of Arthur and Emily Whitaker, of 52, Cadogan Square, W., and was born in London on the 22nd September, 1885.

He was educated at Westgate - on - Sea (Mr. E. M. Hawtrey); at Eton (Mr. E. Impey); and the R.M.C., Sandhurst, out of which, in 1904, he passed first of the infantry candidates of his term. He was gazetted to the Rifle Brigade in 1904, and served with the 2nd Battalion in Egypt, the Soudan, and India. He received the Durbar Coronation medal, 1911, having acted as Assistant Provost Marshal at Delhi. He was promoted Captain in September, 1913.

Captain Whitaker passed the Higher Standard examination in Hindustani, compiled a small grammar dictionary of the Turke language, and wrote an article on travel and exploration. He was a Fellow of the Royal Geographical Society, an ardent explorer, and keen big-game shot. Besides expeditions on the White Nile, in Kashmir and Mesopotamia, he returned to

India in 1908 through Russia, Central Asia, and Turkestan. The latter part of his journey he made with a native following only, which no English traveller had done before, crossing twenty-three passes over ten thousand feet high, the highest being the Karakoram, 18,137 feet above sea level.

He was killed on the night of the 1st December, 1914, when, after visiting his sentries, he went forward alone, at about 1.30 a.m., to reconnoitre, it having been rumoured that fresh German troops had taken up positions in front of our trenches.

Captain Whitaker married, in April, 1910, Madeleine Eléonore de Pury, and left two children : John de Pury, born October, 1911 ; and Lorraine Marie de Pury, born July, 1914.

mined attack. He held on, though the enemy were in force only a few yards from him.

Another officer, who was quite near him when he was killed, says he blazed away at the Germans, and really started the movement which caused them to retreat. " His was a very gallant act, and it gave us all great help in driving off the enemy. I shall never forget him that last morning. He was full of enthusiasm, and his men would have followed him anywhere."

Letters from India also expressed great admiration for him, not only by British officers, but by the native officers and rank and file, especially the men of his own squadron, who all felt they had lost a most gallant officer.

CAPTAIN LESLIE SEDGWICK WHITCHURCH, 21st PRINCE ALBERT VICTOR'S OWN CAVALRY (FRONTIER FORCE),

son of the late Rev. W. B. Gurney Whitchurch, Rector of Spixworth, Norfolk, was born at Lockeridge House, Wiltshire, on the 6th April, 1880. He was educated at Marlborough College, where he excelled in all games, and passed direct into the R.M.C., Sandhurst, where he took the Queen's gold medal, the Sword of Honour, and six other prizes. On passing out with this excellent record, he was appointed to an unattached 2nd Lieutenancy in July, 1899, and was posted to the Indian Staff Corps in October, 1900, becoming Lieutenant in the Indian Army in October, 1901. He saw much active service on the Indian frontier, including operations in Waziristan in 1901–02, for which he received the medal and clasp. He also took part in the operations against the Darwesh Khel Waziris, on the N.W. frontier of India, in 1902, and was promoted Captain in 1908.

Captain Whitchurch went to France on the 8th September, 1914, attached to the 5th Dragoon Guards, and was killed at dawn on the 31st October, 1914, at Messines.

An officer of the 1st Cavalry Brigade spoke of him as a gallant and most capable officer, whom he was fortunate to have had with him. He was killed when most bravely holding on to an advanced post, which he had occupied with a few men on the edge of the town of Messines when the enemy made a very deter-

CAPTAIN EDWARD ERSKINE WHITE, 1st BATTN. NORTHAMPTONSHIRE REGIMENT,

who was killed in action on or about the 14th September, 1914, at the Battle of the Aisne, was born on the 3rd April, 1877.

He was educated at Stonyhurst and joined the West India Regiment from the Imperial Yeomanry in February, 1902. With the Imperial Yeomanry he served in the South African War, in which he was severely wounded. He took part in the relief of Mafeking and in operations in Rhodesia and the Transvaal, receiving the Queen's medal with five clasps.

He was promoted Lieutenant in January, 1904, and in July, 1907, was transferred to the Bedfordshire Regiment. From March, 1906, to March, 1911, he was employed with the West African Frontier Force, having been transferred to the Northamptonshire Regiment in January, 1908.

He was promoted Captain in May, 1910, and in April, 1913, was again seconded in his regiment for employment with the West African Frontier Force.

The following short account of the circumstances attending his death was published in the " Stonyhurst Magazine " for December, 1914 : " ' He was shot through the head, and died immediately,' is all that could be gleaned from a soldier of his regiment lying wounded in hospital, who spoke very highly of him."

His Commanding Officer, writing to his relatives, said : " We have lost a very capable and gallant officer."

LIEUTENANT LYNTON WOOLMER WHITE, 1st (KING'S) DRAGOON GUARDS,

who died on the 4th September, 1914, at Château Baron, Senlis, from shrapnel wounds received in action on the 1st September at the fighting at Néry, was the elder son of Mr. and Mrs. Woolmer White, of Southleigh, Hants, and Salle, Norfolk.

He was born on the 5th May, 1886, at Southsea, Hants, and was educated at Cheltenham and Trinity College, Cambridge. He joined the 1st Dragoon Guards in October, 1907, and became Lieutenant on the 25th March, 1910.

Lieutenant White was a member of the Cavalry Club, and was fond of big-game shooting. He married Dorothea, daughter of Mr. W. K. Haughton, of Calcutta.

2nd LIEUTENANT GEORGE EDWARD TAYLOR-WHITEHEAD, 9th (QUEEN'S ROYAL) LANCERS,

was the son of the late George Henry Taylor - Whitehead, Esq., Barrister - at - Law, formerly of Burton Closes, Bakewell, and was born at 18 Marloes Road, Kensington, on the 28th May, 1893.

He was educated at Eton College and the R.M.C., Sandhurst, and obtained his commission in the 9th (Queen's Royal) Lancers on the 28th August, 1913.

He was killed by a shell fired from the north-east side of the Aisne on the 29th September, 1914, in the yard of a farmhouse at Longueval, Soissons, where he and his troop were billeted. A Corporal of the regiment gave the following account of the incident : " We had some bad luck on the 29th ult., being shelled out of our billets. It was about midday, and we were just going to feed our horses, when a shell dropped in the centre of the yard, killing one officer and twelve men, and wounding twelve, besides killing twelve horses. I was only about ten yards from the shell when it burst." 2nd Lieutenant Taylor-Whitehead was a keen sportsman, good polo player, and a follower of the Blackmore Vale Hunt.

He was a member of the Wellington Club.

2nd LIEUTENANT PERCY JOHN WHITEHOUSE, 3rd BATTN. THE QUEEN'S OWN (ROYAL WEST KENT REGIMENT), attd. 1st BATTN. NORTHAMPTONSHIRE REGIMENT,

who was killed in action at Hooge on the 2nd November, 1914, in his twenty-first year, was the only son of John and Florence Whitehouse, 1 St. Augustine's Road, Belvedere, Kent.

He was educated at the Erith County School, and matriculated at London University in 1911, taking the Intermediate in the B.Sc. examination in 1913 from the East London College, where he was an Honours student in Chemistry.

He played football, cricket, and tennis, and was also a runner and jumper. 2nd Lieutenant Whitehouse, who was a member of the O.T.C. at the East London College, received his commission in August, 1914.

LIEUT. ARTHUR NOEL WHITFELD 2nd BATTN. ROYAL IRISH RIFLES,

was the son of the Rev. Arthur L. Whitfeld, M.A., Vicar of Hughenden, Bucks, and was born at Bradenham, Rectory, High Wycombe, on the 20th December, 1890. He was educated at Kent House, Eastbourne, at Malvern College, and the R.M.C., Sandhurst, from which he received his commission as 2nd Lieutenant in October, 1910, was promoted Lieutenant in March, 1914, and embarked for the seat of war with the IIIrd Division in August, 1914.

For his services in the war he was mentioned in Field-Marshal Sir John French's Despatch of the 8th October, 1914.

Lieutenant Whitfeld was killed in action at Croix Barbée, near Bethune, on the 14th October, 1914.

LIEUTENANT CYRIL HERBERT SPENCE WHITTLE, 15th (THE KING'S) HUSSARS, son of Herbert John Whittle, was born at Tilworth, Sutton, Yorkshire, on the 17th August, 1883. He was educated at Hurst Court, Hastings, at Charterhouse, where he was in the XI in 1900, and at the R.M.C., Sandhurst.

He received a commission in the King's Own (Yorkshire Light Infantry) in October, 1902, and

served with his battalion in Aldershot, Gibraltar, and South Africa, where he was attached to the Mounted Infantry. In December, 1908, he exchanged into the 15th Hussars at Muttra, and later accompanied the regiment to Potchefstroom. He formed one of the escort to H.R.H. the Duke of Connaught on his visit to South Africa in 1910 to open the first Parliament of the Union. In 1911 he was seconded and attached to the Egyptian Cavalry, with which he served in the expedition to the Bahr-el-Gazel in 1913, receiving the fourth class of the Order of the Medjidieh. He was killed on the 24th August, 1914, and the following account of the circumstances has been given by a non-commissioned officer of his regiment, who was wounded, taken prisoner, and later exchanged : " On Monday, August 24th, the senior officers being either killed or missing, the squadron, under Lieutenants Whittle and Hoare, were ordered to reconnoitre as far as Blaugies, near Mons, until 5.30 p.m., and then retire south to Bavai, the last of the whole line. Just before retiring they came to a village, which they galloped through with drawn swords. They came to a lane with high banks each side, when a terrible rifle fire was opened upon them, and Mr. Whittle and Mr. Hoare were both killed leading their men."

Lieutenant Whittle was a member of the Cavalry and Army and Navy Clubs. In 1906 he was well known as the rider of many winners in Gibraltar Races, and he was one of the winning team of the 15th Hussars polo team in the regimental championship competition in 1911 at Potchefstroom.

LIEUTENANT ANTHONY THEODORE CLEPHANE WICKHAM, 4th (attd. 2nd.) BATTN. THE CONNAUGHT RANGERS,

was killed in action near Ypres on the 2nd November, 1914, aged twenty-seven.

He was the only son of the Rev. J. D. C. Wickham, J.P., and Mrs. Wickham, of Holcombe Manor, Somerset. He joined the 4th Battalion Somerset

Light Infantry in 1904, and was transferred to the 4th Connaught Rangers in October, 1907. He was Musketry Instructor and Machine Gun Officer to his battalion for three or four years.

He was killed by a German sniper whilst trying to effect the rescue of a wounded officer, who was lying outside the trenches.

The officer in command of his battalion wrote of him that he was a most promising officer, beloved by all ranks, and would have been promoted Captain in December, 1914, had he lived.

He was a member of the Hibernian United Service Club, Dublin, and of the Kilkenny County Club He was a keen follower to hounds, and hunted with the Royal Meath for three years. He was also a clever amateur actor.

CAPTAIN (local) THOMAS STRANGE WICKHAM, D.S.O., NIGERIA REGT., M.I., LIEUTENANT MANCHESTER REGIMENT,

was born at Bideford on the 2nd June, 1878, the son of the late T. T. Wickham, J.P., of that town. He was educated at the Imperial Service College, Westward Ho ! and joined the 4th (Volunteer) Battalion Devonshire Regiment, being promoted Lieutenant in June, 1899, and Captain in May, 1900. He then served in the South African Light Horse and was granted a commission as 2nd Lieutenant in the Manchester Regiment in September, 1901, becoming Lieutenant in November, 1902.

Captain Wickham had seen much service. He took part in the Jameson Raid in South Africa. As a Trooper in the Mounted Police he served in the Matabeleland Campaign in 1896, for which he received the medal. He was in the South African War, where he became a Captain in the South African Light Horse, and was present at the relief of Ladysmith, including operations and actions on the Tugela Heights, Colenso, Spion Kop, Vaal Krans, Pieter's Hill, Laing's Nek, Belfast, Lydenberg ; and also at operations in the Orange River and Cape Colonies. For his services he was mentioned four times in Despatches, "London Gazette," 4th February, 16th April, and 20th August, 1901, and 29th July, 1902; was awarded the D.S.O., and received the Queen's medal with six clasps and the King's medal with two clasps.

In 1906 he took part in operations in West

Africa, for which he received the West African medal. He also received the Coronation medal, 1911.

Captain Wickham was killed at Tepe in the Cameroons on the 25th August, 1914, while serving with the Mounted Infantry of the Nigeria Regiment. The Mounted Infantry were ordered to take Tepe, which they did, against superior numbers of the enemy. Later on the place was retaken by the Germans, who had discovered what a small British force had expelled them.

Captain Wickham married Bertha W. Grieveson, and left one daughter, Katherine Mary Strange, born December, 1909.

CAPTAIN WILLIAM JOSEPH WICKHAM, 1st BATTN. SCOTS

GUARDS, was killed in action on the 31st October, 1914, at the Battle of Ypres, and is buried at Château Gheluvelt.

He was the eldest son of Captain Henry Lamplugh Wickham, late Rifle Brigade, late of Wootton Hall, Warwickshire, by his marriage with the Hon. Teresa Mary Josephine, daughter of the eleventh Baron Arundell, of Wardour, and widow of Sir Alfred Joseph Doughty Tichborne, Bart.

He was born on the 5th November, 1874, was educated at The Oratory, Edgbaston, and at Trinity Hall, Cambridge, joining the Scots Guards in August, 1900. He served in the South African War, being present at operations in Orange River and Cape Colonies, receiving the Queen's medal with three clasps. He was promoted Lieutenant in January, 1903, and Captain in June, 1906. He also received the Coronation medal.

Captain Wickham was a member of the Guards', Bachelors', Boodle's, Pratt's, and the Army and Navy Clubs. His recreations were shooting, golf, and boating.

2nd LIEUTENANT A. J. H. R. WIDDOWSON, SPECIAL RESERVE, PRINCE OF WALES'S VOLUNTEERS, (SOUTH LANCASHIRE REGIMENT),

was killed in action probably in September, 1914, no place or date being given in the monthly casualty list (October, 1914) containing the notification of his death.

He was gazetted to the Special Reserve in July, 1913.

2nd. LIEUTENANT (temp. LIEUT.) DOUGLAS HOLME WIGGIN, 1st BATTN. GLOUCESTERSHIRE REGT.,

who died on the 23rd December, 1914, in Flanders, of wounds received in action, was the youngest son of the late Francis Holme Wiggin, of Norwood, Ceylon, and a nephew of Miss Wiggin, Langton Lodge, Charlton Kings.

He was born in Ceylon on the 4th December, 1895, and was educated at Marlborough, 1910–13, and at the R.M.C., Sandhurst, from which he received his commission in August, 1914. For a time he was attached to the 3rd (Reserve) Battalion of his regiment, but later returned to the 1st Battalion with the temporary rank of Lieutenant from November, 1914.

He was mortally wounded during the great counter-attack between Le Touret and La Bassée on the 21st December, in which the line captured by the Germans was recaptured by the 1st Division. Lieutenant Wiggin was in command of a platoon in the firing line, and was shot through the chest, near the road leading south from Festubert, just as darkness fell, when within three hundred yards of the enemy's position. Picked up on the following day, he was taken to Lillers, still conscious, and speaking cheerfully; but he had suffered much from exposure, and died, twelve hours after admission to hospital, early in the morning of the 23rd. He was buried in the cemetery at Lillers side by side with others of his battalion who had fallen in the same engagement.

2nd LIEUTENANT REGINALD CONNOR PHILLIPS WILDER, 3rd (RESERVE) attd. 2nd BATTN. SUFFOLK REGIMENT,

was shot by a sniper on the 18th November, 1914, while doing trench duty, and killed instantaneously, the bullet severing the jugular vein.

He was the son of the Rev. W. B. C. Wilder and Mrs. Wilder, daughter of the late Dr. Grove, of St. Ives, Hunts, a great-grandson of the late Lieutenant-General Sir Francis Wilder and of Admiral Sir John

Marshall, and a grandson of the late Rev. John McMahon Wilder.

He was born at Great Bradley Rectory, near Newmarket, on the 25th February, 1896, and was educated at Forest School, Walthamstow. He was one of the Shooting VIII of his school at Bisley in 1913, and was very fond of athletics, especially boxing.

In January, 1914, he joined the 3rd Battalion of his regiment, and trained at the Curragh until war broke out. He was then sent with a draft to Felixstowe, from which he proceeded to the front at the end of August, 1914.

His C.O. wrote of him: " I thought him a charming, bright, lad, who did his hard work cheerily and willingly, and his death is a truly sad loss to me and all the battalion, which cannot spare good officers as your son was." His Captain wrote: " He was shot through the neck at about seven in the morning, and I am glad to say death was instantaneous. He commanded a platoon in my company, and I cannot speak too highly of the way in which he carried out his duties on all occasions. He was buried the following night beside one of his brother officers, killed within a few hours of each other."

LIEUTENANT and QUARTERMASTER EDMUND WILKINSON, 1st BATTN. LOYAL NORTH LANCASHIRE REGIMENT,

was the son of Mr. and Mrs. Wilkinson, of 22, Queen Street, Colne, and was forty-three years of age at the time of his death.

He served twenty-six years with the Colours, and had a distinguished career, having risen from the ranks through his ability, courage, and good conduct. He served through the Boer War, having been besieged in Kimberley for four months, and was presented with the Kimberley Star. He was awarded the South African medals and the Distinguished Conduct medal for distinguished gallantry at Hartebeestfontein, leading the company in a charge when the officers were out of action, which gallant act probably saved the whole column. He received his commission in June, 1912.

He was killed in action on the 31st October, 1914, and the news of his death was conveyed in a letter written by Lieutenant-Colonel Carter, D.S.O., of his battalion, himself soon afterwards killed in action, who wrote: " We have lost officers and men, but the greatest loss to me personally is caused by poor Wilkinson's death. He was the whitest man that ever breathed, with the heart of a lion. He fell fighting at the head of a number of men of various corps on the road near Ypres. He attempted to stem the onflood of the German advance down the road—and apparently did so with the men he collected. It has been said he should be given the Victoria Cross. His duty did not lie with the battalion in the fighting line, but he was ever present where the fighting took place. The regimental Sergeant-Major of the 1st K.R.R.C. witnessed his last heroic action, and the words he used to me were, ' If ever soldier earned a V.C. your Q.M. did the night of the 31st October, 1914.' "

Lieutenant Wilkinson was mentioned in Sir John French's Despatch of the 14th January, 1915.

He was a great sportsman, a fine athlete, probably the best in the regiment for several years, and as a cyclist he had few equals. He was generous to a fault, a staunch friend, and beloved by everyone who had dealings with him.

Lieutenant Wilkinson married Eliza Harriet, daughter of William Parkhouse, of Parkham, and left three daughters : Irene Ethel, born November, 1907 ; Audrey Dora, born December, 1911 ; and Edwina Mary, born, after her gallant father's death, in January, 1915.

LIEUTENANT JOHN ROTHES MARLOW WILKINSON, 4th BATTN. THE DUKE OF CAMBRIDGE'S OWN) MIDDLESEX REGIMENT),

was the eldest of three brothers, all members of Worcester College, Oxford, sons of the late Rev. H. M. Wilkinson, M.A., formerly Vicar of Milford - on - Sea, himself also a member of Worcester College, of which his brother, Lieutenant Wilkinson's uncle, had been a Fellow.

Lieutenant Wilkinson was born at the Vicarage, Milford, near Lymington, Hampshire, on the 17th October, 1887, and was educated at Winchester College, from which he proceeded to Worcester College, Oxford, in 1907, where he took his degree of B.A. in 1911.

He joined the Middlesex Regiment as a University Candidate in February, 1912, being given antedate to March, 1911, becoming Lieutenant in October, 1913, and served with the 4th Battalion at the front. He was killed about the 23rd August, 1914, at the Battle of Mons.

He was of a frank, genial character, of high animal spirits, readily stirred to adventure or escapades, but checked by a chivalrous sense of honour. Well and strongly made and with indomitable energy, he early found his way into the College Eight and became captain of the Boat Club. His buoyant, manly qualities secured him many friends in the college and outside, and made natural his selection of the Army as a profession.

A Private of the battalion gave the following account of Lieutenant Wilkinson's death : " I had the honour to be under Lieutenant Wilkinson's command at Mons. On Sunday, August 23rd, we were entrenched in front of a convent when Captain . . . gave him, Lieutenant Wilkinson, an order to take half his platoon (two sections) to reinforce ' A ' Company. This company was at the left of our position, and was being hard pressed. I started off with Lieutenant Wilkinson along the rear of the fighting line. We were being fired on all the time. We came to a house, which was blown up immediately we left it. Lieutenant Wilkinson still led on to the left, eventually coming to a group of houses. It was here that we took up position. Your son went into one of the houses, and was heard directing the fire of his two sections through the skylight in the roof. He directed his fire so well that he forced the Germans to retire from his front. Noticing this, he laughingly remarked, ' Oh. they don't like it ; they have retired ! ' It was from this house that he saw overwhelming numbers of Germans coming through the wood to his front. The Germans came on again until they were within two hundred yards. Lieutenant Wilkinson then came out of the house into the trench. It was here that he got the order to retire. He got the order twice, but would not take it, as he thought it was not an official order. Eventually he got his order from the General Officer Commanding to retire. He then started to retire his sections by groups. It was then I noticed he was limping. To retire we had to go through barbed wire. Here we got separated owing to the heavy shelling and rifle fire. I was the only man of those two sections to get away from that place. No officers could give me any information of Lieutenant Wilkinson. I reported to the Commanding Officer what had happened, and told him that Lieutenant Wilkinson was a very brave man. He replied, ' Yes, I know that, and I am very sorry to lose him.' "

LIEUTENANT ROBERT ST. JOHN WILLANS, 3rd (attd. 1st) BATTN. NORTHUMBERLAND FUSILIERS, who died on the 9th November, 1914, near Ypres, was the only son of the late Colonel St. John Willans, and grandson of the late Robert

Courage, of Snowdenham, Bramley, Surrey. He was born on the 8th September, 1877, and after serving with the embodied Militia for four months, was gazetted to the Northumberland Fusiliers as 2nd Lieutenant in April, 1900, being promoted Lieutenant in June, 1901. He served in the South African War, 1899–1901, being present at operations in the Transvaal and Orange River Colony, receiving the Queen's medal with three clasps. He retired from the Army in 1905, and on the outbreak of the Great War was re-gazetted to the 3rd Battalion of his old regiment, with the rank he held on retirement.

2nd LIEUTENANT ALMERICUS (ERIC) JOHN FALKINER DE COURCY WILLIAMS, THE WEST INDIA REGT., attd. 4th BATTN. MIDDLESEX REGT., son of Dr. J. A. de Courcy Williams, of St. Etchens, Killucan, County Westmeath, and first-cousin of Lord Kingsale, was born on the 4th May, 1895, at Green Hills, Killucan, Ireland. He was educated at Abingdon School and  the R.M.C., Sandhurst, and received his commission in the West India Regiment in August, 1914. Subsequently he was attached to the 1st, and later to the 5th Middlesex Regiment, from which he volunteered for active service and was then sent to the 4th Battalion, with which he was serving when he was killed on the 20th October, 1914.

He was shot through the body while standing on the traverse of a trench to take aim at the enemy, and was buried in Bethune Cemetery. Bandsman Imeson, of the battalion, who was with him in the trench when he met his death, wrote : " If ever there was a hero it was Lieutenant de Courcy Williams. He frequently exposed himself to danger, giving directions to his men to take careful aim and exhorting them to make every shot tell, . . . and even when lying wounded at the bottom of the trench he continued giving orders, and his last words were, ' Give it them ! ' "

His C.O. afterwards Brigadier-General Hull, said of him : " He was a most promising boy. We were proud of him, and shall miss him much."

Lord Kitchener, telegraphing from the Clearing Hospital, where he died, said : " He was a loss to the Army." 2nd Lieutenant Williams was the only officer with the 4th Middlesex who was unwounded at the Battle of Vieille Chapelle.

2nd LIEUTENANT ALEXANDER JOHN NEEVE WILLIAMSON, SPECIAL RESERVE, attd. 2nd BATTN. SEAFORTH HIGHLANDERS (ROSS-SHIRE BUFFS, THE DUKE OF ALBANY'S),

who was killed in action, during the Battle of the Aisne, at Bucy-le-long, near Soissons, on the 14th September, 1914, was the son of the late Mr. Robert A. Williamson, of Calcutta, and Mrs. Williamson, of 21, St. Stephen's Square, Bayswater, London, W.

He was born on the 22nd December, 1887, and was educated at Highgate School. There he made a record for the half-mile, not only for his school, but also for the Public Schools, and held the cup three years running. He was a member of the School Cadet Corps, which he entered in 1903, and left as a Colour-Sergeant, in 1907, on proceeding to Pembroke College, Cambridge. At Cambridge he threw himself wholeheartedly into the work of the O.T.C., becoming proficient in musketry, signalling, and topography, as well as in the ordinary routine of drill and manœuvre. After leaving the University he became a Master at Blundell's, was gazetted to the School Corps, and in July, 1911, joined the Special Reserve. He was a Master of his old school at Highgate from 1912, and was Second in Command of Highgate School Corps.

Having returned from camp on the 3rd August, 1914, he reported himself on the outbreak of war at Shorncliffe on the 5th August. After serving at different places at home he arrived in France on the 23rd August, and on the 24th received orders to go to the front with the 2nd Battalion of his regiment, which formed part of the 10th Brigade, IVth Division, British Expeditionary Force, afterwards taking part in the Battle of the Marne and the fighting at the Ourcq.

A brother officer, giving an account of the circumstances of his death, said : " At the time we had just taken up a position on high ground to the north of the River Aisne, near Soissons. It was at a critical moment, and your son went up with his platoon in support of the two companies in the firing line. Apparently he was hit and killed instantaneously by a shell. His body has been recovered and buried by the side of the Colonel, Sir Evelyn Bradford. He was extremely popular in the battalion, and a great loss to the company and to us all. He was recognised as being a most efficient officer."

LIEUTENANT GEORGE WILLIAMSON, 3rd (attd. 2nd) BATTN. THE DUKE OF WELLINGTON'S (WEST RIDING REGIMENT), who died on the 12th November, 1914, aged thirty-one, of wounds received in action on the 8th November, was the son of the late Mr. C. J. Williamson, of New York, and of Lady Skinner, of Pont Street, London, S.W., and The Gables, Worthing. He entered the 3rd Battalion of his regiment as 2nd Lieutenant in November, 1905, being promoted Lieutenant in September, 1907 ; in the Great War he served with the 2nd Battalion.

2nd LIEUTENANT ROBERT HAMILTON WILLIAMSON, 118th HEAVY BATTERY, ROYAL GARRISON ARTILLERY,

who died at Boulogne on the 27th December, 1914, of wounds received in action, was the only son of Dr. George Williamson, 256, Union Street, Aberdeen.

He was born on the 27th September, 1893, at Stonehaven, N.B., and was educated at Glenalmond. In June, 1911, he was gazetted 2nd Lieutenant in the 1st Highland Brigade, Royal Field Artillery (T.F.), and in June, 1913, was promoted Lieutenant. After being attached to a regular battery of Field Artillery for a year he gained a commission in the Royal Garrison Artillery (Regular) at the military competitive examination in April, 1914, and joined on the 10th June, 1914.

At the front he was wounded in the head whilst making observations for his battery in an advanced observation post in a ruined church tower and died of his wounds as stated above.

2nd LIEUTENANT RUSSELL WILLIS, SPECIAL RESERVE, YORK AND LANCASTER REGIMENT, attd. 1st BATTN. LINCOLNSHIRE REGIMENT, was born at Denton, near Manchester, on the 9th November, 1894, the son of William Willis, Head Master of Russell Scott Memorial Schools, Denton, Lancashire.

He was awarded a scholarship from Russell Scott School by the Lancashire

County Council. He attended the Manchester Municipal Secondary School; gained the £180 Scholarship awarded by the Manchester Education Committee, tenable at Manchester University, and finally obtained the degree of B.Sc. (Tech.) 1st Class Honours at Manchester University in July, 1914, the first prize in Chemistry, and was awarded a Research Scholarship. He also gained the Chess Championship at the Municipal Secondary School, Manchester. At the University he was a Cadet in the O.T.C., and although his academic record and attainments seemed rather to point to a scientific or scholastic career, he preferred to enter the Army, and received his commission in the Special Reserve, York and Lancaster Regiment, in March, 1914, after passing the qualifying examinations, and being presented with a Sword of Honour by the University.

Having been attached to the 1st Battalion Lincolnshire Regiment for active service he was killed in action on the 25th October, 1914, three and a half miles north-east of Neuve Chapelle, after recapturing a trench and two guns from Germans who had taken them from our troops. A Corporal of the battalion gave the following account of the young officer's death: "Lieutenant Willis had not long joined us when we were engaged in action in a small village some three and a half miles from Neuve Chapelle (in a north-easterly direction, I think), but the name of the village I cannot remember. . . . On the morning of the 25th October Nos. 16 and 13 (platoons) retired for a short spell in the reserve trenches some four hundred yards away behind the firing line. Lieutenant Willis was in charge of 16 Platoon, and about noon an order came from headquarters (regimental) that a platoon was required on the right. . . . No. 13 was sent, and almost immediately No. 16 had to go also. We had some very dangerous ground to cover before we could get in a position to retake the trenches or guns, and a house occupied by some thirty snipers had to be taken first, which was soon dealt with; then a small wood was the next place of attack, and we were not long in driving the Germans out of this. . . . After a few minutes we were led by Lieutenant Willis in the charge for the trench and guns, which we managed to take, and also hold, but I am sorry to say that Lieutenant Willis, on the very edge of the trench, was hit when half turning to encourage the men on, and he fell into the trench. I soon saw he was badly hit, and sat him in a corner, but there was nothing I could do for him. His last words were, ' Have we retaken the guns, Corporal ? ' I then left him for a few moments, . . . and when I returned Lieutenant Willis had passed away quite peacefully. . . . He was buried by the Royal Irish Rifles."

CAPTAIN ARTHUR HENRY WILSON, 1st BATTN. THE EAST YORKSHIRE REGIMENT, who was killed in action on the 18th October, 1914, was the only surviving son of Colonel and Mrs. W. H. Wilson, of Broadview, Petersfield, and was born on the 15th July, 1875. He entered the East Yorkshire Regiment  from the Militia in December, 1896, becoming Lieutenant in June, 1898. From December, 1899, to May, 1900, he acted as Adjutant of his battalion.

He served in the South African War, taking part in the operations in the Orange Free State, including the action at Houtnek (Thoba Mountain), in the Orange River Colony, including actions at Biddulphsberg, Wittebergen, and Caledon River; and was employed with the Mounted Infantry. He also served in Cape Colony, and again in the Orange River Colony in 1901–02, and received for his services the Queen's medal with three clasps and the King's medal with two clasps.

Captain Wilson obtained his company in January, 1903.

CAPTAIN CHARLES EDWARD WILSON, 1st BATTN. THE QUEEN'S (ROYAL WEST SURREY REGIMENT), born at Fermoy, Ireland, on the 2nd June, 1871, was the son of the late Major-General F. E. G. Wilson, C.B., York and Lancaster Regiment, and Mrs. Wilson, of 15, Spencer Road, Southsea.

He was educated at Dover College and the R.M.C., Sandhurst, and joined the Army in July, 1892, becoming Lieutenant in July, 1896, and Captain in August, 1901.

Captain Wilson served in the Boer War on the Staff, as Railway Staff Officer and Assistant Provost Marshall, and was present at the relief of Ladysmith, including action at Colenso, operations at Spion Kop and Vaal Krans, operations on Tugela Heights; and action at Pieter's Hill; and operations in Natal (March to June, 1900). For his services he was mentioned in Despatches (" London Gazette," 29th July,

1902), and received the Queen's medal with two clasps and the King's medal with two clasps.

He served as Adjutant of the 3rd (Volunteer) Battalion of the Queen's from January, 1903, to December, 1907, and in October, 1913, was appointed Adjutant of his battalion, and in this position accompanied it to the Continent with the Expeditionary Force. He was killed in action at the Battle of the Aisne on the 17th of September, 1914. After his death the War Office forwarded to his relatives the decoration of the " Légion d'Honneur," which had been awarded him.

Captain Wilson married Mabel, daughter of the late Colonel Carr, but was a widower at the time of his death. He left two sons, aged seventeen and ten years respectively.

LIEUTENANT DAVID REX WILSON, 2nd BATTN. THE QUEEN'S (ROYAL WEST SURREY REGIMENT),

son of George David Wilson, C.C., of Darlington, and a grandson of Alderman Jonathan Angus, of Newcastle-on-Tyne, was born at Pensbury, Darlington, on the 5th February, 1891. He was educated at Aysgarth Preparatory School, at Clifton College, and at Jesus College, Cambridge. At Clifton he was captain of the Shooting VIII and of the football team ; while at Cambridge he was captain of the O.T.C., and was thirty-eighth in the King's hundred at Bisley.

He joined the Queen's in December, 1912, and went to Bermuda in March, 1913, being promoted Lieutenant in that month, and thence to South Africa in February, 1914. In August of the latter year the battalion returned to England and went to Flanders with the 22nd Brigade, VIIth Division, early in October. Lieutenant Wilson was killed on the 30th October, 1914, in action near Ypres, after having retaken with his platoon some trenches from the enemy.

Lieutenant Wilson's gallantry on the day he was killed is mentioned in "The First Seven Divisions" by Lord E. Hamilton. The order to retire did not reach him as he was in an advanced position with his platoon ; being a marksman he laid himself out to pick off the Germans right and left, and appears by his audacity to have rendered splendid service until he was eventually shot through the head and killed.

LIEUTENANT EWEN HOLMES HUMPHREY JAMES WILSON, 1st BATTN. THE BLACK WATCH (ROYAL HIGHLANDERS),

only son of the late James Humphrey Wilson, was born at Ayr, Scotland, on the 18th January, 1892.

He was educated at Harrow and the R.M.C., Sandhurst. At the former he played cricket and football for his house, and at the latter he was a Colour-Sergeant.

He joined the Black Watch in February, 1912, becoming Lieutenant in May, 1914.

He fell, mortally wounded, on the 8th September 1914, at Sablonnières, France. His Company Commander had been badly wounded, and he had to lead his men against the German Guard. A Corporal of his platoon wrote : " He died leading the men who adored him."

2nd LIEUTENANT ERIC WESTERN WILSON, SPECIAL RESERVE, attd. 1st BATTN. THE PRINCE OF WALES'S OWN (WEST YORKSHIRE REGIMENT),

born at Thornton-le-Moor, Yorkshire, on the 12th July, 1893, was the only son of the late John Western Wilson, Dufton, Appleby, and of Mrs. Wilson, The Corse, Laugharne, Carmarthen, South Wales. He was a nephew of Engineer Lieutenant-Commander T. M. David, R.N., H.M.S. " Hawke." 2nd Lieutenant Wilson was educated at the Grammar School, Carmarthen; at Kelly College, Tavistock, and at Leeds University. Passing from the University O.T.C., he was gazetted 2nd Lieutenant in the Special Reserve, West Yorkshire Regiment in July, 1913, and joined the 1st Battalion of his regiment on the outbreak of the Great War to proceed with it on active service.

He fell on the 20th September, 1914, in the Battle of the Aisne while leading his platoon to recapture a trench near Troyon, which had been taken by the enemy earlier in the day.

LIEUTENANT-COLONEL GORDON CHESNEY WILSON, M.V.O., COMMANDING THE ROYAL HORSE GUARDS, who was killed in action on the

6th November, 1914, was the eldest son of Sir Samuel Wilson, M.P., and was born on the

3rd August, 1865. He joined the Royal Horse Guards from the Militia in May, 1887, becoming Lieutenant in December, 1888, and Captain in November, 1894. He took part in the South African War, during which he was on the Staff as A.D.C. to Major-General Baden-Powell, Commanding the Mafeking Frontier Forces from August, 1899, to May, 1900, and A.D.C. to the same officer after appointment as Major-General, South Africa, from May to July, 1900. He was present at the defence of Mafeking, including actions of the 26th December, 1899, and 12th May, 1900. He was twice mentioned in Despatches ("London Gazette," 8th February and 10th September, 1901), and received the Queen's medal with three clasps.

He was promoted Major in January, 1903; Brevet Lieutenant-Colonel in October, 1907; and succeeded to the command of his regiment as Lieutenant-Colonel in October, 1911.

Lieutenant-Colonel Wilson married, in 1891, Lady Sarah Isabella Augusta, sixth daughter of the seventh Duke of Marlborough, and left no issue.

CAPTAIN ROBERT SYM WILSON, 1st BATTN. THE SEAFORTH HIGHLANDERS (ROSS-SHIRE BUFFS, THE DUKE

OF ALBANY'S), was the son of the late Andrew Hay Wilson, and was born at Leith, Scotland, on the 17th November, 1876.

He was educated at the Edinburgh Academy and at Trinity College, Glenalmond, where he was captain of the XV (Rugby football) and of the VIII (shooting), and was also in the Cricket XI.

Captain Wilson joined the Army in 1897, becoming Lieutenant in 1899 and Captain in 1902. He served with his battalion in the South African War, taking part in the advance on Kimberley, including action at Magersfontein, where he was wounded, and operations in Orange River Colony, May to November, 1900, also at operations in the Transvaal, and

again in the Orange River and Cape Colonies, 1901–02. He received the Queen's medal with three clasps and the King's medal with two clasps.

In the Great War he was instantaneously killed by rifle shot on the 8th November, 1914, while acting as Observer in a trench near Lille.

CAPTAIN ARTHUR WINN, 3rd (attd. 2nd) BATTN. THE SUFFOLK REGT.,

killed in action near Soissons on the 9th September, 1914, was the only son of Arthur Thomas Winn, Barrister-at-Law, Middle Temple, and Constance Winn, of Aldeburgh, Suffolk.

He was born on the 13th April, 1884, at Ewell, Surrey, and was educated at Eton. He joined the Suffolk Regiment in March, 1902, becoming Lieutenant in February, 1904, and Captain in August, 1913.

2nd LIEUTENANT ARTHUR WINSPEAR, 2nd BATTN. THE CONNAUGHT RANGERS,

was killed in action on the 5th–6th November, 1914. He had served in the Irish Guards, in which he became Company Sergeant-Major, and was gazetted 2nd Lieutenant in October, 1914. While a drill Sergeant in the Irish Guards he was mentioned in Sir John French's Despatch of the 8th October, 1914.

LIEUTENANT JOHN RUDOLF WISSMANN, 22nd BATTERY, ROYAL FIELD ARTILLERY,

only son of Rudolf Wissmann, Great Duryard, Exeter, was born at Dulwich on the 23rd October, 1890, and educated at Dulwich College, whence he passed direct into the R.M.A., Woolwich, in September, 1909.

He received his commission in the R.F.A. in December, 1910, joined the 22nd Battery at Bulford Camp in 1911, moved with his brigade (34th) to Aldershot in 1913, and became Lieutenant in December, 1913. He was qualified as an Interpreter in German. He went to the seat of war with the IInd Division and was killed in action on the 15th September, 1914, on the heights of the Aisne, near Verneuil.

He married, in 1914, Gladys, daughter of the Rev. Worthington Jukes, Rector of Shobrooke, near Crediton, and left a daughter, Joan Rosemary, born on the 9th January, 1915 (posthumous).

He was a member of the Junior United Service Club. His recreations were riding and hunting.

CAPTAIN CECIL STRACHAN WOOD, RESERVE OF OFFICERS, 3rd (attd. 1st) BATTN. EAST YORKSHIRE

REGIMENT, who was accidentally killed at Havre on the 2nd December, 1914, and was buried in the cemetery of St. Marie at that place (the official list stating that he died on the 31st December, of wounds received in action), was the third son of Canon Wood, D.D., M.V.O., late Headmaster of Harrow School, and of Mrs. Wood, Prebendal House, Rochester. He was a younger brother of the Hon. J. B. Wood, I.C.S., Political Secretary to the Government of India.

He was born on the 3rd December, 1872, at Leamington, and was educated at Leamington College ; Tonbridge School ; and at the R.M.C., Sandhurst, from which he joined the Army in March, 1894. At both Tonbridge and Sandhurst he was in the Cricket XI, and at the former in the Football XV. Later he proved himself a keen sportsman.

He was gazetted to the East Yorkshire Regiment in 1894, and joined the 1st Battalion in Alexandria, afterwards going with it—in the following year—to India. He was promoted Lieutenant in November, 1896, Captain in December, 1899, and from 1903 to 1908 he was Adjutant of the North Staffordshire Volunteers, rejoining the 1st Battalion at Bordon in the latter year. In 1910 he retired from the active list, settling at Aldeburgh, Suffolk, where he became Secretary of the local Golf Club in 1911. On the outbreak of war, having been on the Reserve, he joined the 3rd Battalion of his old regiment in August, 1914, and was attached to the 1st Battalion for active service.

Captain Wood married, in 1900, Gladys Katharine, daughter of Charles E. Salmon, of Bury St. Edmunds, and left two children : John Garrett, born in Madras in December, 1901 ; and Mark, born at Barlaston in September, 1904.

LIEUTENANT LIONEL STREATFEILD WOODGATE, 1st BATTN. THE KING'S OWN (ROYAL LANCASTER REGIMENT),

was the youngest son of the late Alderman Ernest Woodgate, J.P., and Mrs. Woodgate, and was born on the 11th June, 1888, at Star Hill, Rochester, Kent.

He was related to the late Major-General Sir Edward R. P. Woodgate, K.C.M.G., C.B., and to Colonel Henry Streatfeild, C.B., M.V.O. Equerry to Her Majesty Queen Alexandra. Lieutenant Woodgate's brother — Lieutenant William Ernest Streatfeild Woodgate, of the same regiment and battalion—died of wounds received at Vryheid, South Africa, in 1900.

The subject of this memoir was educated at Bradfield College, Reading, Berks, and passed thence direct into the Royal Military College, Sandhurst. He was gazetted 2nd Lieutenant in his regiment in February, 1908, and promoted Lieutenant in October, 1911. In 1913 he passed through the School of Musketry, Hythe, and qualified " with distinction."

He was killed while leading his company at La Ferté, France, on the 8th September, 1914, and was buried in the garden of the Château at La Ferté.

Lieutenant Woodgate was mentioned in Sir John French's Despatch of the 8th October, 1914, for his gallantry.

He was an all-round sportsman.

CAPTAIN ALFRED JAMES WOODHOUSE, ROYAL FIELD ARTILLERY,

who was killed in action on the 30th October, 1914, was the second surviving son of the late Mr. Robert H. Woodhouse, 1, Hanover Square, London, W., and of Mrs. Woodhouse of Ralsbury, Ealing Common, W.

He was born on the 1st August, 1886, and was educated at Cheltenham, where he was head prefect of the school and captain of the Rifle Corps and of the Shooting VIII ; and at the R.M.A., Woolwich, where he became Senior Under Officer, and was awarded the Sword of Honour. He was gazetted to the Royal Artillery in July, 1907, and served two years at Ewshott, whence he went to India, becoming Lieutenant in 1910. His promotion to Captain was dated the 30th October, 1914, the day of his death.

During the whole of his time in India, whenever he was free from his military duties, he was on shooting expeditions in the jungle, and brought home many specimens which sportsmen of longer experience would envy and prize.

An elder brother—Lieutenant R. W. Woodhouse—was killed in the South African War, and two other brothers were killed in the Great War in 1915 : one a 2nd Lieutenant in the R.F.A., who fell in France in October, 1915 ; and the other a Private in the H.A.C., killed in February, 1915.

Captain Woodhouse married, in August, 1914, Esther Margaret, daughter of the Rev. A. C. Woodhouse, Rector of Winterborn, Monckton, Dorset.

LIEUTENANT NEVILLE LESLIE WOODROFFE, 1st BATTN. IRISH GUARDS,

who was killed in action at Klein Zillebeke, near Ypres, in an attack on the German trenches, on the 6th November, 1914, aged twenty-one, was the son of Allen and Beatrice Woodroffe, of 21, Cornwall Gardens, London, S.W.

He was educated at Eton and Trinity College, Cambridge, and joined the Irish Guards as 2nd Lieutenant on probation in February, 1913, being confirmed in his rank some months later, and was gazetted Lieutenant after his death, the rank to date from the 2nd November, 1914. He was mentioned in Sir John French's Despatch of the 14th January, 1915.

2nd LIEUTENANT BASIL HAMILTON WOODS, 1st FIELD CO., EAST LANCASHIRE DIVISION, ROYAL ENGINEERS (T.F.),

son of Mr. and Mrs. W. H. Woods, Ravenstone, Hale, Cheshire, was born at Chorlton-cum-Hardy, near Manchester, on the 18th August, 1891.

He was educated at Repton, where he was Sergeant in the Officers' Training Corps, and at Oriel College, Oxford. He first joined the Reserve of Officers, in May, 1912, but resigned from it in April, 1914, to take a commission in the East Lancashire Territorial Engineers, as an officer of which he was on active service in the Great War.

He was drowned on the 17th November, 1914, together with six N.C.O.'s and men, in the Suez Canal through an explosion on a launch which his company was using in connection with their work on the defences of the Canal, and he was buried with full military honours at Suez on the 24th December, Major-General Mellis, V.C., C.B., and the whole of his Staff attending. General Douglas made special reference to the accident in orders, and in connection with the casualties the following telegram was sent to General Douglas by the Commander of the Canal Defences: " All ranks of the Indian Expeditionary Force desire to express their sincere sympathy and regret at the lamentable accident which has resulted in the death of Lieutenant Woods and six N.C.O.'s and men. They were doing excellent work, and their skill and soldierly 'conduct were highly appreciated."

In his reply General Douglas said : " All ranks appreciate kind sympathy of Indian Expeditionary Force. Lieutenant Woods, the N.C.O.'s and men who have lost their lives serving their country were much respected, and we all value the knowledge that their good work and soldierly conduct has been appreciated by you and your troops."

2nd LIEUTENANT CHARLES STEPHENSON WOOLLCOMBE, 2nd BATTN. THE KING'S OWN SCOTTISH BORDERERS,

born at Newton Abbot, Devonshire, on the 12th December, 1895, was the younger son of Lieutenant-General Charles Louis Woollcombe, C.B., Colonel of the King's Own Scottish Borderers, and Mrs. Woollcombe, daughter of the late General Sir John Irvine Murray, K.C.B., Indian Army. He was a cousin to Major John Morth Woollcombe, of Ashbury, Devon.

He was educated at Marlborough, from which he entered the R.M.C., Sandhurst, in September, 1913, and was gazetted to the K.O.S.B. in August, 1914, joining the 2nd Battalion, which belonged to the Vth Division, in France the following month.

He was killed in action at Cuinchy on the 12th October, 1914. The 13th Brigade, of which his regiment formed part was ordered to clear the enemy out of a position, and almost as soon as it advanced three officers—of whom 2nd Lieutenant Woollcombe was one—and several men were killed.

CAPTAIN ALEXANDER GERALD WORDSWORTH, 2nd BATTN. THE DUKE OF CAMBRIDGE'S OWN (MIDDLESEX REGIMENT),

was the son of the Rev. John Wordsworth, Vicar of Allhallows, Cumberland, and Rose Geraldine Wordsworth, and was born at Gosforth Rectory, Cumberland, on the 28th October, 1880. He was a great-grandson of the poet Wordsworth.

He was educated at Charney Hall, Grange-over-Sands and at Loretto School, Musselburgh; and joined the 3rd (Militia) Battalion Border Regiment in May, 1900. In January, 1902, he was gazetted from the Militia to the 2nd Battalion Middlesex Regiment, his father's old regiment. He served in the South African War, being present at operations in the Transvaal in 1902, receiving the Queen's medal with two clasps. He was promoted Lieutenant in May, 1904, and was appointed Adjutant of his battalion in March, 1911, a position he held till 1914, having been promoted Captain in March, 1912.

Captain Wordsworth was killed in action in the trenches near Laventie, Belgium, on the 6th December, 1914.

He was a member of the Cavendish Club.

LIEUTENANT JOHN LIONEL WORDSWORTH, 5th (ROYAL IRISH) LANCERS,

who was killed in action on the 4th November, 1914, was the son of the late Captain John Wordsworth, of Blackgates, Yorkshire.

He was born on the 21st April, 1882, was educated at Caius College, Cambridge, and entered the Yorkshire R.G.A. (Militia) in April, 1902, becoming Lieutenant in June, 1904. He joined the 5th Lancers as

2nd Lieutenant in May, 1906, becoming Lieutenant in May, 1908. From August, 1909, to November, 1911, he was A.D.C. to the General Officer Commanding-in-Chief, Northern Command.

LIEUTENANT CHARLES SACKVILLE PELHAM, LORD WORSLEY, ROYAL HORSE GUARDS,

who was killed at Zandvoorde on the 30th October, 1914, was the eldest son of the Earl and Countess of Yarborough, Brocklesby Park, Lincolnshire.

He was born on the 14th August, 1887, and joined the Royal Horse Guards in October, 1907, becoming Lieutenant a year later. From March, 1912, to April, 1913, he was A.D.C. (extra) to Lieutenant-General Sir D. Haig, K.C.I.E., K.C.V.O., C.B., Commanding-in-Chief, Aldershot Command.

Lord Worsley, who was at first reported as missing early in December, was gazetted Captain (Temporary) to date from 15th November, 1914, which promotion will apparently not now be considered as having taken effect.

Lord Worsley married, in 1911, the Hon. Alexandra Mary Freesia, youngest daughter of the third Baron Vivian.

LIEUTENANT REGINALD GEORGE WORTHINGTON, 2nd BATTN. OXFORDSHIRE AND BUCKINGHAMSHIRE LIGHT INFANTRY,

who was killed in action on the 16th September, 1914, was the second son of the late George Montagu Worthington, of Dyson's Wood, near Reading, and Mrs. Worthington, and was born on the 4th December, 1886.

He was educated at Branksome, Godalming, and Charterhouse, and was gazetted 2nd Lieutenant in the 3rd Oxfordshire Light Infantry in February, 1904. From the Militia he was gazetted to the Oxfordshire and Buckinghamshire Light Infantry in May, 1908, and was posted to the 2nd Battalion (old 52nd), he was Assistant Adjutant and Scout Officer, and became Lieutenant in April, 1911.

Lieutenant Worthington was awarded the Croix de Chevalier of the Legion of Honour.

He was a member of the Junior Army and Navy and the Junior United Service Clubs.

CAPTAIN EDWIN WRIGHT, 3rd (PRINCE OF WALES'S) DRAGOON GUARDS, was killed in action near Ypres on the 18th November, 1914. He was born on the 27th November, 1879, and joined the Royal Marine Artillery as 2nd Lieutenant in 1897, becoming Lieutenant in 1898, and Captain in December, 1904.

From August, 1905, to August, 1908, he was Adjutant of the south-east of Scotland R.G.A. (Militia) and in February, 1909, went on half-pay on appointment as A.D.C. to the Governor of South Australia, which he held till December, 1910. In January, 1911, he was transferred to the 3rd Dragoon Guards as Captain, with which regiment he was serving at Cairo, when war was declared.

2nd LIEUTENANT GEORGE DRENNAN CRON WRIGHT, 2nd BATTN. BEDFORDSHIRE REGIMENT,

son of the late George Wright, of Grahamstown, Cape Colony, and Mrs. Wright, and a grandson of the late William Drennan, C.E., was born in Kensington, London, on the 4th April, 1891.

He was educated at the Elstow School, Bedford, England, and received his commission in December, 1913, joining his battalion at Roberts's Heights, Pretoria, in the following month.

He was killed on the 23rd October, 1914, during the fighting before Ypres, while gallantly leading his platoon into action.

CAPTAIN HUGH STAFFORD NORTHCOTE WRIGHT, 2nd BATTN. 8th GURKHA RIFLES,

who was born at Akola, Berar, India, on the 14th December, 1877, was the second son of the late Frederick Wright, Esq. (for many years Senior Superintendent, and subsequently Inspector-General, of Police in Berar), and of Mrs.

Wright, afterwards residing at Kilcor Castle, Fermoy, County Cork. Captain Wright was named after his godfather, the first Lord Iddlesleigh —Sir Stafford Northcote—to whom he was related, being a member of the family of Wrights, of Longstone Hall, Derbyshire, whose ancestors have lived there before Doomsday Book was issued, and still hold their land and manor.

He was educated at Chigwell School, Essex, of which the Rev. Canon R. D. Swallow was Headmaster, and afterwards at Heidelberg University. When the South African War broke out he was on plague duty in India, and at once enlisted in Lumsden's Horse, sailing with it in February, 1900, for South Africa. In September, 1900, he was given a commission in the Army Service Corps. Captain Wright's younger brother enlisted at the same time, and both did so well that they were both given commissions. Captain Hugh Wright took part in operations both in the Transvaal and Orange River Colony, receiving the Queen's medal with three clasps and the King's medal with two clasps. He became Lieutenant in December, 1901, and returned to England in November, 1902. After a course at Aldershot he was a short time at Cork, and from there went to India for five years, arriving in Bombay in 1904, and serving mostly at Poona. In the next year he was at Rawal Pindi for manœuvres in connection with the Prince of Wales's visit. He returned to England in 1909, becoming Captain in September of that year, and served with the A.S.C. at Bulford Camp, Salisbury, till 1912, when he exchanged into the Indian Army, joining the 8th Gurkha Rifles at Lansdowne, in the Himalayas, in April of the same year. While in India he passed for his Majority, and also qualified in Kashura, the Gurkha language.

In August, 1914, he sailed from Karachi for France, his ship, the " Erinpura," being one of a convoy of forty-two transports, with H.M.S. " Dartmouth " as escort. Reaching Marseilles on the 12th October, his regiment was put in the Meerut Division, commanded by Major-General Keary. Captain Wright was one of the many brave officers to fall at the Battle of Ypres, being killed in action on the 1st November, 1914. His last message home was to say that his regiment had gone hurriedly to the front, and that he was " very fit and awfully keen." In a previous letter from India, when acquainting his family that his regiment was one of those chosen for service, he said how disappointed he and they would have been had the orders for any reason been countermanded.

The following account of Captain Wright's part in the action in which he gave his life was written by his Commanding Officer : " At 10 p.m. on the 29th October the regiment went into action, and he (Captain Wright) got his company in the advanced trench, next to that occupied by Captains Hartwell and Hayes-Sadler. During the night his trench was attacked twice to my knowledge, as I was with him during one attack, and with his Double Company Commander—Major Wake—in the supporting trench during the other. He did all that a man could do, and acted with the greatest courage and coolness. During the very trying shell fire to which these trenches were subjected from 7 a.m. to 1 p.m. on the 30th October he did all it was possible to do. During this time he was wounded, but continued to command his men. When the furious attack developed it was mainly directed to his trench and that held by Captain Sadler. He repelled line after line of the enemy, and held on till a very large proportion of his men had been killed or wounded and till he himself was killed. What more could a man do? A soldier can do no more than die at his post—game to the last!"

His Commanding Officer also gave the following tribute to him: "A more gallant officer or better comrade either in peace or war I have never met."

Another officer wrote: "To know Wright was to like him, and the better one knew him, the more one liked him. He was far and away out of the ordinary at both polo and tennis. He was the moving spirit at Lansdowne."

Captain Wright was a good shot, and very successful in big and small game shooting. He played tennis for his corps (A.S.C.) in regimental tournaments in England at Queen's Club, twice being in the finals. He won the Open Singles, Salisbury Lawn Tennis Club, in 1909. He was of a fine character and disposition, and at the same time most modest in his estimation of himself. His late Headmaster — Canon Swallow—testified that he was "honourable and pure-minded, with many charming qualities. His conduct was always on the side of good."

Captain Wright was unmarried, and was a member of the Junior Naval and Military Club.

2nd LIEUTENANT NEIL JAMES ROBERT WRIGHT, 15th BATTERY, ROYAL FIELD ARTILLERY,

was the only son of the late James Wright, of Tunbridge Wells, and of Mrs. Wright, The Leas, Westcliff - on - Sea.

He was born on the 4th February, 1894, and was educated at Brighton College and the R.M.A., Woolwich. At the latter he distinguished himself as an athlete, winning the long jump for Woolwich against Sandhurst in 1913. He received his commission in the R.F.A. in September, 1913.

He took part in the Battles of Mons, the Marne, and the Aisne, and was killed on the 15th September, 1914, at the Battle of the Aisne.

CAPTAIN THEODORE WRIGHT, V. C., ROYAL ENGINEERS,

who was killed on the 14th September, 1914, while helping wounded men into shelter, was the son of the late William Walter Wright and Mrs. Wright, of Albury, near Guildford, and was born at Brighton on the 15th May, 1883.

He was educated at Clifton College and at the R.M.A., Woolwich, where he was in the first Cricket XI and in the hockey team. He also played cricket for the Army v. Hampshire.

Passing out of the R.M.A., he obtained his commission in the Royal Engineers in October, 1902, subsequently serving at Gibraltar and Cairo. He was promoted Lieutenant in June, 1905, Captain in October, 1913, and accompanied the British Expeditionary Force to France in August, 1914.

For his gallantry in the very early part of the war he was awarded the much coveted decoration of the Victoria Cross, the following being the official record of the service for which it was given: "Gallantry at Mons on the 23rd August in attempting to connect up the lead to demolish a bridge under heavy fire. Although wounded in the head, he made a second attempt. At Vailly, on the 14th September, he assisted the passage of 5th Cavalry Brigade over the pontoon bridge, and was mortally wounded while assisting wounded men into shelter."

Colonel Wilson, of his Corps, writing to his mother, said of him: "No one has earned a V.C. better, and I am truly glad they have given it to him. I have known him so long, and have always been very fond of him. He was one of the finest officers I have ever had, and I feel his loss every day. . . . I enclose a cutting you may not have seen from a letter of one of the Scots Greys officers, and I can endorse every word of it."

The following is the account of the Cavalry officer referred to: "We got across the river at . . . the day before yesterday, a bit before our time, and had to get back over a pontoon bridge considerably quicker than was pleasant—under a very unpleasant fire, too. At the head of the bridge was a gallant Engineer officer, repairing bits blown off and putting down straw as cool as a cucumber—the finest thing I have ever seen. The poor fellow was killed just after my troop got across. No man ever earned a better V.C."

Corporal Jarvis, who was on the same duty as Captain Wright, said : " The work on the bridge was done under fire from three sides. Near the bridge I found Captain Theodore Wright, V.C., wounded in the head. I wished to bandage him, but he said, ' Go back to the bridge ! It must be done '—and so I went. The British infantry were posted behind barricades, and I had to make quite a detour to get round where I had to start operations."

A chauffeur at the front related the following incident of Captain Wright : " Poor Captain Wright got killed here the other day. He was the officer who got wounded in the head while I was driving him at Mons. When I was under fire there I took a wounded soldier to the hospital, and returned into the fire for the Captain. It was a bit risky with eight cases of dynamite on the car. But he was a brave man."

Mrs. Wright received a letter from His Majesty the King, dated the 5th October, 1915, from Buckingham Palace, which said : " It is a matter of sincere regret to me that the death of Captain Theodore Wright deprived me of the pride of personally conferring upon him the Victoria Cross, the greatest of all military distinctions.—George R.I."

Captain Wright belonged to the Free Foresters and Incogniti Clubs.

2nd LIEUTENANT MUSGRAVE CAZENOVE WROUGHTON, 12th (PRINCE OF WALES'S ROYAL) LANCERS,

who was killed in action near Ypres on the 30th October, 1914, was the only son of William Musgrave and of Edith Constance Wroughton, of 77, Chester Square, London, S.W., and of Creaton Lodge, Northamptonshire.

He was educated at Harrow and at Christ Church, Oxford, and during his school and college vacations was a keen follower of the Pytchley Hounds, of which pack his father was Master for many years.

On leaving Harrow he received a commission in the Northamptonshire Yeomanry in March, 1910, and in 1912 he accompanied Sir Robert Baden-Powell as A.D.C. on his world tour in connection with the Boy Scout movement.

After serving nearly four years in the Northamptonshire Yeomanry, he was given a commission in the Special Reserve, 12th Lancers, as 2nd Lieutenant (on probation) in October, 1913. The appointment was confirmed after his death, to date from the 29th October, 1914. In August, 1914, he accompanied his regiment to the front, and was mentioned in Sir John French's Despatch of the 14th January, 1915, for gallant and distinguished service in the field.

2nd Lieutenant Wroughton, who was twenty-three years of age when he was killed, was buried in the churc yard at Kemmel, Belgium.

CAPTAIN GEORGE RICHARD WYLD, 3rd BATTN. THE DUKE OF EDINBURGH'S (WILTSHIRE REGIMENT),

son of Canon Wyld, Vicar of Melksham, Wiltshire, was born at Woodborough, in that county.

He was educated at Marlborough College, and joining the 13th Middlesex V.R.C., as 2nd Lieutenant in December, 1898, was promoted Lieutenant in July, 1900. He served in the South African War, 1899–1902, for which he received the Queen's medal with four clasps.

He subsequently joined the Reserve of Officers, and in October, 1914, was appointed as Captain to the 3rd Battalion Wiltshire Regiment, but was attached to the 1st Battalion Berkshire Regiment for service in the Great War. He was killed by a sniper in the trenches near Givenchy on the 24th December, 1914.

LIEUTENANT PERCY LYULPH WYNDHAM, 3rd BATTN. COLDSTREAM GUARDS,

was born at Saighton Grange, Chester, on the 5th December, 1887. He was the son of the late Right Hon. George Wyndham, M.P., at one time Chief Secretary to the Lord-Lieutenant of Ireland, and Countess

Grosvenor, daughter-in-law of the first Duke

of Westminster, through whom Lieutenant Wyndham was closely related to the Countess of Shaftesbury and Countess Beauchamp (half-sisters), and to the present Duke of Westminster (half-brother).

Lieutenant Wyndham entered the Coldstream Guards in February, 1909, becoming Lieutenant in May, 1910. He was with his battalion, which belonged to the Guards' Brigade, IInd Division, when he was killed in action at the Battle of the Aisne, near Soissons, on the 14th September, 1914.

Lieutenant Wyndham, who was a member of the Guards' and Bachelors' Clubs, married, in April, 1913, the Hon. Diana Lister, daughter of Lord Ribblesdale. He left no family.

CAPTAIN the Honble. WILLIAM REGINALD WYNDHAM, LINCOLNSHIRE YEOMANRY, attd. 1st LIFE GUARDS,

killed in action on the 6th November, 1914, was the third son of the second Baron Leconfield, and was born on the 16th March, 1876, and was heir presumptive to his brother, the third Baron Leconfield.

Captain Wyndham joined the 17th Lancers as 2nd Lieutenant in March, 1896, becoming Lieutenant in May, 1897, and Captain in July, 1901. He served in the South African War, 1899–1900, receiving the Queen's medal with three clasps. He retired from the Army in 1903, owing to a riding accident, and took a farm in East Africa, going more lately to the Rocky Mountains. He afterwards returned home and became well known in Ireland on the turf as an owner of winning race horses, and as a member of the Jockey Club, to which he was elected in 1912.

On the outbreak of the war he made every effort to return to the service, and in August, 1914, was gazetted Captain in the Lincolnshire Yeomanry. Being anxious to proceed on active service he was finally successful in being attached to the 1st Life Guards, in which his father and two of his brothers had served.

2nd LIEUTENANT CHARLES WATKIN WILLIAMS-WYNN, 1st BATTN. COLDSTREAM GUARDS,

son of Arthur W. Williams-Wynn and Mary Williams-Wynn, of Coed-y-Maen, Welshpool, Montgomeryshire, was born in London on the 19th May, 1896.

He was educated at Evelyns, West Drayton and at Eton (Mr. R. S. de Havilland's House).

At the latter he was a member of the O.T.C., and when war broke out was gazetted to the Special Reserve of Officers, Coldstream Guards, on the 15th August, 1914. He was sent to join the 1st Battalion of his regiment in October, and within three days of reaching the front was reported missing. It has since been ascertained, from prisoners of war in Germany that he was killed in action at Zandvoorde, near Ypres, on the 29th October, 1914.

MAJOR HUGH TALBOT WYNTER, 22nd BATTERY, ROYAL FIELD ARTILLERY,

killed in action at the Battle of the Aisne on the 15th September,1914, was the son of Hugh Bold Wynter, of Canon's House, Taunton, and Brecon, South Wales, and was born on the 26th September, 1872.

He joined the Royal Artillery in February, 1893, becoming Lieutenant in February, 1896, and Captain in May, 1900. From April, 1906 to June, 1908, he was Adjutant to the 15th Brigade, R.F.A., and from the latter date to November, 1909, was employed as an Adjutant of the Territorial Force.

Major Wynter, who attained his rank in February, 1910, married, in 1898, Eva Mary Florence, younger daughter of the late Edward Chicester Incledon-Webber, of Buckland Ho! and St. Brannocks, Braunton, North Devon, and left one son, born in September, 1899, now serving as midshipman in the Grand Fleet, having been appointed in September, 1915.

Major Wynter fell in action on the heights of the Aisne, and was mentioned in Sir John French's Despatch of the 8th October, 1914, for his distinguished bravery.

He was a member of the Bath Club.

LIEUTENANT WILLIAM STANLEY YALLAND, 1st BATTN. GLOUCESTERSHIRE REGT.,

was born at Fishponds, Bristol, on the 27th June, 1889, the son of T. K. Yalland, Esq., of The Manor House, Fishponds, Bristol.

He was educated at a private school and at Clifton College, and in December, 1910, was  appointed to the 3rd Battalion Leicestershire Regiment (Special Reserve), from which he was given a commission as 2nd Lieutenant in the Gloucestershire Regiment in December, 1912, being promoted Lieutenant in August, 1914.

He was serving with his battalion which formed part of the 3rd Brigade, 1st Division, when he died very gallantly at Langemarke on the 23rd October, 1914. He was ordered to take his platoon to a trench to prevent the Germans making further ground. This he did, and his platoon, at considerable loss, drove the Germans back, and the trenches were reoccupied by the British. During this action he was killed.

Lieutenant Yalland was a good three-quarter back at football, and played for his regiment in the regimental cup, 1913–14. He was also a good cricketer, having played for his county (Gloucestershire).

MAJOR CHARLES ALLIX LAVINGTON YATE, V.C., p.s.c., 2nd BATTN. THE KING'S OWN (YORKSHIRE LIGHT INFANTRY),

 who was born on the 14th March, 1872, at the Vicarage, Madeley, Shropshire, was the son of the Rev. George Edward Yate, Vicar of Madeley and Prebendary of Hereford.

He was educated at Weymouth School and the R.M.C., Sandhurst. Major Yate joined the King's Own Yorkshire Light Infantry in 1892, becoming Lieutenant in February, 1894, and Captain in July, 1899. He served in the Tirah Campaign, 1897–98, and in the South African War, being present at the advance on Kimberley, including actions at Belmont and Enslin (dangerously wounded), and operations in the Transvaal. He received the Tirah medal with clasp, and for the South African War was mentioned in Despatches ("London Gazette," 10th September, 1901), and received the Queen's medal with four clasps. He was selected to go to Japan in 1903, and in 1904–05 was present at the siege of Port Arthur,

being awarded the Japanese Order of the Sacred Treasure.

He passed out of the Staff College in 1902, and was almost continuously employed on the General Staff at the War Office and elsewhere from July, 1904, until six months before the outbreak of the war with Germany. He was then, being qualified as a first-class interpreter in French and German, and a Staff Officer of experience and approved merit, appointed to the Staff of the French Commander-in-Chief. This post he asked to be allowed to decline, as he wished to serve with his regiment, which he had meanwhile rejoined from the Staff. Major Yate was also a first-class interpreter in Japanese.

The part he played in the war was brief but distinguished. He won the Victoria Cross, the official record of the award, as published in the "London Gazette" of the 25th November, 1914, being as follows: "Major Charles Allix Lavington Yate (deceased), 2nd Battalion King's Own Yorkshire Light Infantry, commanded one of the two companies that remained to the end in the trenches at Le Cateau on August 26th, and when all other officers were killed and wounded, and ammunition exhausted, led nineteen survivors against the enemy in a charge in which he was severely wounded. He was picked up by the enemy, and has subsequently died as a prisoner of war."

This heroic act of Major Yate and his gallant band of nineteen, all the sound men left of his company at the moment, is referred to in all accounts of the Battle of Le Cateau. Lord E. Hamilton mentions it as "the Thermopylae of 'B' Company K.O.Y.L.I."; and Sir A. Conan Doyle considers Major Yate "one of the heroes of the battle."

Major Yate was the author of an article, in the September (1914) issue of "Blackwood's Magazine," entitled "Moral Qualities in War," which received special notice in "The Times," of the 17th September, 1914. The reviewer described it as, "not only a striking confession of a soldier's faith, but also the military testament of one who was among the first to lay down his life for his country in the present war"; and added: "Major Yate concluded his article with some reference to the spirit of the Japanese soldier—' the spirit in which soldiers must go forth to fight—not dreaming of the home-coming, the medal, the batta. These are distant and problematical. Nearer and more probable are the enemy and the tomb. Few, few shall part, where many meet.'" Before these fine words were in type the author had proved their truth. They stand as a prophecy and an epitaph, and, if his message from the grave is as widely read as it deserves to be, a gallant soldier will not have died in vain.

Major Yate married Florence Helena, daughter of John F. Brigg, J.P., of Greenhead Hall, Huddersfield, and his wife, Martha Ann Adelaide Brigg.

CAPTAIN MARWOOD EDWARDS YEATMAN, 1st BATTN. SOUTH WALES BORDERERS,

eldest son of the late Marwood Shuttleworth Yeatman, was born on the 29th September, 1883, at Holwell Manor, near Sherborne, Dorset : he was a first cousin of the present Lord Bishop of Worcester. He was educated at a private school at Winchester and at the R.M.C., Sandhurst, from which he joined the South Wales Borderers as 2nd Lieutenant in October, 1903, proceeding at once to India. He became Lieutenant in June, 1907, and in 1909 was sent to the Depot of his regiment. In 1912 he travelled in Russia, afterwards qualifying as a 1st Class Interpreter in that language. He was gazetted Captain on the 4th August, to date from the 30th April, 1914, and accompanied his battalion to France in August, 1914, took part in the retirement from Mons, and was present at the subsequent Battle of the Aisne : while the battalion was digging itself in near the river during that battle, he was known to have shot with his revolver four Germans at a distance of 60 yards, and was himself soon afterwards shot through the heart by a German sniper on the 15th September, 1914.

Captain Yeatman, who belonged to the Cocoa Tree Club, was a well known shot, having been in the Army Rifle Eight and Revolver Eight at Bisley in 1913 and 1914. He was good at outdoor sports and games, hunted, fished, yachted, and played golf, tennis and racquets. He married in 1909, Gwladys Mary, daughter of Major General F. Koe, C.B., C.M.G., and left two sons : Marwood John Richard, born in 1910, and Benedictus Godfrey William, born in 1914.

MAJOR ARTHUR YOUNG, p.s.c., 1st GURKHA RIFLES, BRIGADE-MAJOR GURHWAL BRIGADE,

born at Dharmsala, Punjab, on the 3rd December, 1876, was the son of Colonel G. Young, late Commanding 1st Gurkha Rifles. His brother is Captain G. H. Young, 38th Dogras. Major Young, who was educated at Blairlodge School, Polmont, Stirlingshire, and the R.M.C., Sandhurst, from which he was gazetted to an unattached 2nd Lieutenancy in August, 1896, and was appointed to the Indian Army in December, 1897. He was attached to the Gordon Highlanders at Rawal Pindi, and served with them in the Tirah Campaign of 1897–98, being present at the actions of the Chagru Kotal, Dargai, and of the Sampagha and Arhanga Passes ; also at operations in the

Waran Valley, including action of the 16th November, 1897, and operations in the Bara Valley, 7th to 14th December, 1897. He was mentioned in Despatches (G.G.O. 483 of 1898), and received the medal with two clasps. He was promoted Lieutenant in January, 1899, and Captain in August, 1905.

Major Young passed out of the Staff College, in December, 1910, and was appointed Brigade-Major of the Gurhwal Brigade, in June, 1912, in which capacity he was serving in the Great War. Having reached Field Rank in August, 1914, he was killed when returning from shelter trenches on the 14th December, 1914. For his services he was mentioned in Sir John French's Despatch of the 14th January, 1915.

CAPTAIN JOHN ERSKINE YOUNG, 1st BATTN. ROYAL SCOTS FUSILIERS,

was shown in the monthly official casualty list published in October, 1914, under the heading of casualties which are believed to have occurred as " believed killed," no place or date being given.

He was born on the 24th February, 1880, and joined the Royal Scots Fusiliers from the Militia in April, 1900, becoming Lieutenant in December, 1901, and Captain in September, 1911. He embarked for France with his battalion, which formed part of the 9th Brigade, IIIrd Division, with the first part of the British Expeditionary Force.

2nd LIEUTENANT ROGER ASSHETON YOUNG, 2nd BATTN. ROYAL MUNSTER FUSILIERS,

who was born on the 20th December, 1894, at St. Leonards-on-Sea, was the son of Archibald Edward and Cicely

Young, and a nephew of the late Colonel W. A. Young, who commanded the Royal Scots Fusiliers, and of Lieutenant - Colonel C. H. Young, formerly commanding the 2nd Battalion Welsh Regiment, and afterwards in command of the 9th Battalion of that regiment. 2nd Lieutenant Young was educated at the Royal Naval College, Osborne, where he had some athletic successes, winning the junior term high jump and the four-oared race. He afterwards went to Uppingham and the R.M.C., Sandhurst. He was gazetted to the Munster Fusiliers in August, 1914, and was killed in a frontal attack on German trenches near Festubert, La Bassée district, on the 22nd December, 1914.

2nd Lieutenant Young played football for the Richmond Club. At Sandhurst he was in the champion team, " G " Company, and was one of the representatives of Sandhurst v. Woolwich in athletic sports in 1913 and 1914.

Printed and bound by Antony Rowe Ltd, Eastbourne

1487017R0

Printed in Great Britain by
Amazon.co.uk, Ltd.,
Marston Gate.